FROMMER'S

BUDGET TRAV[EL GUIDE]

HAWAII '93 ON $75 A DAY

by Faye Hammel and
Sylvan Levey

PRENTICE HALL TRAVEL

NEW YORK • LONDON • TORONTO • SYDNEY • TOKYO • SINGAPORE

FROMMER BOOKS

Published by Prentice Hall General Reference
A division of Simon & Schuster Inc.
15 Columbus Circle
New York, NY 10023

ISBN 0-13-333592-5
ISSN 1059-7603

Design by Robert Bull Design
Maps by Geografix Inc.

FROMMER'S HAWAII '93 ON $75 A DAY
Editor-in-Chief: Marilyn Wood
Senior Editors: Judith de Rubini, Alice Fellows
Editors: Thomas F. Hirsch, Paige Hughes, Sara Hinsey Raveret, Lisa Renaud, Theodore Stavrou
Assistant Editors: Margaret Bowen, Peter Katucki, Ian Wilker
Managing Editor: Leanne Coupe

Special Sales
Bulk purchases of Frommer's Travel Guides are available at special discounts. The publishers are happy to custom-make publications for corporate clients who wish to use them as premiums or sales promotions. We can excerpt the contents, provide covers with corporate imprints, or create books to meet specific needs. For more information write to Special Sales, Prentice Hall Travel, Paramount Communications Building, 15 Columbus Circle, New York, NY 10023

Manufactured in the United States of America

CONTENTS

LIST OF MAPS

INVITATION TO THE READERS

In researching this book, we have come across many wonderful establishments, the best of which we have included here. We are sure that many of you will also come across appealing hotels, inns, restaurants, guesthouses, shops, and attractions. Please don't keep them to yourself. Share your experiences, especially if you want to comment on places that have been included in this edition that have changed for the worse. You can address your letters to:

Faye Hammel and Sylvan Levey
Frommer's Hawaii '93 on $75 a Day
c/o Prentice Hall Travel
15 Columbus Circle
New York, NY 10023

A DISCLAIMER

Readers are advised that prices fluctuate in the course of time and travel information changes under the impact of the varied and volatile factors that affect the travel industry. Neither the authors nor the publisher can be held responsible for the experiences of readers while traveling. Readers are invited to write to the publisher with ideas, comments, and suggestions for future editions.

SAFETY ADVISORY

Whenever you're traveling in an unfamiliar city or country, stay alert. Be aware of your immediate surroundings. Wear a moneybelt and keep a close eye on your possessions. Be particularly careful with cameras, purses, and wallets, all favorite targets of thieves and pickpockets.

HURRICANE INIKI

The Hawaiian island of Kauai was badly damaged by Hurricane Iniki in September 1992. Though facilities on the island should be repaired quickly, it is suggested that travelers inquire about hurricane damage before visiting Kauai.

CHAPTER 1

GETTING TO KNOW HAWAII

This book is written for the express purpose of disposing of a couple of myths. The first is that a South Seas idyll—that longed-for journey to enchanted islands that everyone dreams of at one time or another—is beyond the means of the budget traveler. We're here to tell you that all that is ancient history. Less than five jet hours and less than $200 away from the West Coast lie the islands of Hawaii, a name to conjure dreams, a place to explore on a shoestring budget.

People will tell you, of course, that the 50th American state is one of the most expensive areas on earth to visit. It is—and it isn't—depending on which Hawaii you care to see. If you choose prepackaged and preconceived Hawaii, you'll undoubtedly stay at plush hotels, dine at expensive restaurants, be herded around in sightseeing limousines with people just like the folks you left back home—and pay a pretty penny for it. But if you agree with us that travel is a do-it-yourself activity, if you'd rather leave the plush and nonsense to others and strike out on your own to find out how the islanders really live, you'll find that a vacation in Hawaii is one of the best travel bargains anywhere. For, contrary to legend, Hawaii has dozens of comfortable, clean, and reasonable hotels; scores of restaurants where the food is exotic and inexpensive; and most important, an almost endless list of free and low-cost entertainment—from beaches to bon dances, from museum browsing to mountain climbing, from hiking to dancing the hula. Add to that an incredibly low airfare, and you've got the ideal place for a budget vacation—even in these costly times.

MYTHS & PARADOXES

The second myth was neatly put by a friend of ours, a sophisticated woman who travels regularly to Europe. "Why go all the way to Hawaii," she asks, "just to find yourself at a beach?" Now no one in his or her right mind would dispute the glory of Hawaii's beaches, some of the best in the world. But anyone who looks on Hawaii as merely a seaside resort is missing some of the most profound, exciting, and exotic travel experiences available anywhere.

The essence of Hawaii, its special mystery, lies in its startling and subtle paradoxes. Take its people, as fascinating a mixture of humanity as you'll find on this planet. The children and grandchildren of Stone Age warriors, New England missionaries, and

DID YOU KNOW . . . ?

- In Hawaii, pineapples are planted to stunt their growth: They must grow to a uniform size in order to fit into cans!
- Charlie Chan's real-life counterpart was Chang Apana, a flamboyant member of the Honolulu Police Department in the early years of the century.
- Hawaii has the longest life expectancy of any of the states, 77 years, for someone born in 1979–81.
- All fish in Hawaii are line-caught, so no dolphins are endangered.
- Hawaii consumes more Spam than all other states combined!
- For political and administrative purposes, Honolulu County is the largest in the United States—it goes all the way to Midway Island, encompassing over 1,000 miles.
- Hawaii is the only state with an active volcanic eruption (since 1983).
- Three of the four major Hawaii counties are governed by women mayors: Linda Crockett Linge on Maui; Lorraine Inouye on the Big Island; Joanne Yukimura on Kauai.
- There are 10,000 species of insect in the Hawaiian Islands, and of these, 98% are found nowhere else on earth.
- In 1989, the median age in Hawaii was 32.3.
- Waialeale, on the island of Kauai, is one of the wettest spots on earth: Average annual precipitation is 444 inches.
- The highest sea cliffs in the world—3,200 feet—are found on the northern coast of Molokai.

Asian plantation workers mingled and intermarried to create nothing less than a new race. Scratch an islander and you'll find a Hawaiian-Chinese-Portuguese, a Japanese-American-Tahitian, or perhaps an English-Filipino-Korean. The typical islander—if such a creature exists—long ago gave up counting the racial strains in his or her background; it got too complicated. Hawaii's people, American in ideals, optimism, and drive, still retain the serenity of Polynesia and Asia. They avidly follow the scores of baseball games played by fellow citizens 6,000 miles away in Boston or Philadelphia, yet many of them dream of going to visit "the old country"—Japan, China, the Philippines. And as if in answer to the bigots who cringe at "mongrelization," the interracial mingling has produced some of the most attractive Americans. Hawaii's children are exquisite, a mixture of the best the races can give to each other.

But the paradoxes don't stop here. They are even more astonishing on a sheer topographical level; Hawaii has the kind of scenery that all but overwhelms the senses. Steep cliffs tumbling down to coral beaches, tropical rain forests and woods that run a hundred shades of green, black-sand beaches and pounding blue surf, scores of tropical blossoms, vying for attention at every turn—this is the landscape. Even more awe-inspiring, the volcanoes that created these islands from the vast nothingness of ocean are still alive. The land is still being born. Drive mile after mile on the Big Island of Hawaii and see where the lava flows have scalded their way to the sea and how slowly life renews itself over the years. Then go to Kauai and see what the centuries and the forces of erosion have done to a much older and extinct volcano. You'll have a sense of the youth—and age—of the earth that you can get nowhere else.

The paradox of Hawaii continues on a third level as well. In less than 200 years it has gone from Stone Age to Space Age, from a primitive island kingdom ruled by stern gods of nature to the fastest-growing state in the United States, ruled by booming laws of economics. Industry is thriving, hotel and apartment construction grows apace, population and tourism increase astronomically, Space Age science and education become established, and wherever one looks, something new is being built, planned, developed. "Full speed ahead" are the words on every front. Still, despite the aggressive energy of the times, Hawaii somehow manages to retain its gentleness, its warmth, its relaxed nature. The spirit of aloha remains untouched, a calm center in the eye of the hurricane of progress. Which is perhaps why so many people who have been everywhere and back can't seem to get enough of Hawaii.

THE ALOHA SPIRIT

The warm, welcoming hospitality of the islanders is perhaps what impresses the visitor most. One celebrated visitor expressed it very well. Mrs. Jacqueline Kennedy Onassis, returning home after a visit to Hawaii with her family some years back, wrote to the editors of the *Honolulu Star Bulletin and Advertiser* (who had asked the public to give the Kennedys privacy and assigned no reporters or photographers to follow them around): "In this strange land everyone constantly goes out of his way to be kind to the other. From Governor Burns, who so kindly watched over us and asked people to help make our visit private, to the driver of a vegetable truck who went out of his way to lead us several miles, when we merely asked for directions, everyone in Hawaii has been the same. Now I know what the Aloha spirit means. I hope it is contagious—for it could change the world."

1. GEOGRAPHY, HISTORY & POLITICS

GEOGRAPHY

Most people think of Hawaii as synonymous with Honolulu and Waikiki Beach (and probably know both are on the island of Oahu), but they're a bit vague about the names of the other islands. Actually, there are 122 islands in the Hawaiian chain, a great volcanic mountain range spreading 1,500 miles across the floor of the Pacific, from Hawaii on the southeast to Midway and Kure islands in the northwest. Many of these are just jagged rocks or sand shoals, however, and the term "Hawaiian Islands" usually refers only to eight: Oahu (on which you find Honolulu), Hawaii or the Big Island, Maui, Kauai, Molokai, Lanai, Kahoolawe, and Niihau. The first five are the ones of greatest interest to the visitor, and the ones we'll describe in this book. Of the last three, Lanai, formerly a pineapple plantation island, owned almost completely by Castle & Cooke, the parent company of the Dole Pineapple Company, has just begun resort development with the opening of two new luxury Rockresorts, The Lodge at Koele and the Manele Bay Hotel. Kahoolawe, uninhabited, is a target range for American planes and ships; and Niihau, where an ancient Hawaiian community survives, is private property, not open to the general public.

HISTORY

The Hawaiian Islands were settled between 1,200 and 1,500 years ago by Polynesians who most likely came from the Marquesas and Tahitian islands, a feat of navigation undreamed of by their European contemporaries. They crossed thousands of miles of ocean in double-hulled sailing vessels, connected by long bamboo poles that supported a tiny hut between the canoes. They brought with them their animals and plants, introducing such new foods as the sweet potato.

They settled primarily on the largest islands of the Hawaiian archipelago—Hawaii, Kauai, Maui, Molokai, and Oahu. The islands were fragmented into little kingdoms, each ruled by its own chief, with its own *kapus* and particular customs. Power belonged to the strongest, and the bloody overthrow of leaders was quite common. But

DATELINE

- **A.D. 400–790** First Polynesian settlers arrive from the Marquesas and Tahitian islands.
- **1778** Capt. James Cook discovers the islands, naming them the Sandwich Islands after his patron, the Earl of Sandwich.
- **1779** Cook is slain on the island of Hawaii.

(continues)

life was stable, and very probably even comfortable. None of the settlers ever made any attempt to return to the tribes from which they had come. In the warmth of the sun, these Stone Age people remained undisturbed and untouched by outsiders until the 18th century.

In 1777 Capt. James Cook, looking for the Northwest Passage, stumbled on the island of Kauai. The natives, who had long believed that their great god Lono would one day return to them, mistook Cook and his crew for the god and a full entourage of lesser deities. At first Cook received a god's reception, but soon fighting broke out between the natives and the sailors, and eight months later, on another voyage, Cook was clubbed to death by natives and drowned off the Kona shore of the island of Hawaii. But from that time on, the Sandwich Islands, as he had named them in honor of the Earl of Sandwich when he claimed them for Great Britain, became part of the modern world. By 1790 King Kamehameha the Great, based on the island of Hawaii, conquered the other islands in the chain in a series of bloody forays (except for Kauai, which surrendered) and united them under his rule. Hawaii was already one nation when the first emissaries from the Western world—merchants, fur traders, whaling men—started their invasion of the islands.

19TH CENTURY In 1820 a band of New England missionaries arrived in Hawaii, determined to save the heathen islanders from the devil. They brought piety, industry, and Congregationalism to the natives; their arrival speeded the end of the old Hawaiian life. (Their story is eloquently told in James Michener's *Hawaii,* in both the novel and the film.) They smashed the idols and continued the destruction of the rigid *kapus* (already weakened by the king prior to their arrival), taught the people to read and write, and "civilized" the natives. And although they undoubtedly did an enormous amount of good, many of the natives here have never forgiven them, as the island saying goes, for doing so well. Some of the missionaries' children turned into businesspeople, bought up the land, and started industries; it is their descendants who are still among the ruling forces of Hawaii's great corporate empires.

The native Hawaiians never really adjusted to the *haole*'s (white man's) world, refused to work the plantations, and died from diseases in horrendous epidemics. Today, just a few thousand pure-blooded Hawaiians remain. The rest have disappeared or become intermingled with the other races—mostly Japanese and Chinese—who came to work the plantations.

The Asians began to arrive around 1852, when the whaling trade was dropping off and the sugar plantations were becoming big business. The Chinese came first to work the plantations, then the Japanese, last the Filipinos. The Hawaiian melting pot began to simmer.

DATELINE

- **1790** Kamehameha the Great controls all the islands, establishing the Kingdom of Hawaii.
- **1820** New England missionaries of the Congregational church arrive.
- **1824** Kamehameha II (Liholiho) dies; his brother, Kauikeaouli, becomes Kamehameha III and transforms a semifeudal state into a constitutional monarchy.
- **1831** Lahainaluna School, the oldest high school west of the Rockies, is opened.
- **1840** A Hawaiian constitution is proclaimed.
- **1843** Great Britain cedes the Hawaiian Kingdom, and Hawaii's independence is officially recognized.
- **1850** Kamehameha III officially declares Honolulu the capital of the Hawaiian Kingdom.
- **1852** Chinese arrive under contract to work the sugar plantations. The Japanese begin arriving in 1868; the Filipinos, Koreans, Portuguese, Puerto Ricans at a much later date.
- **1872** King Kamehameha the

(continues)

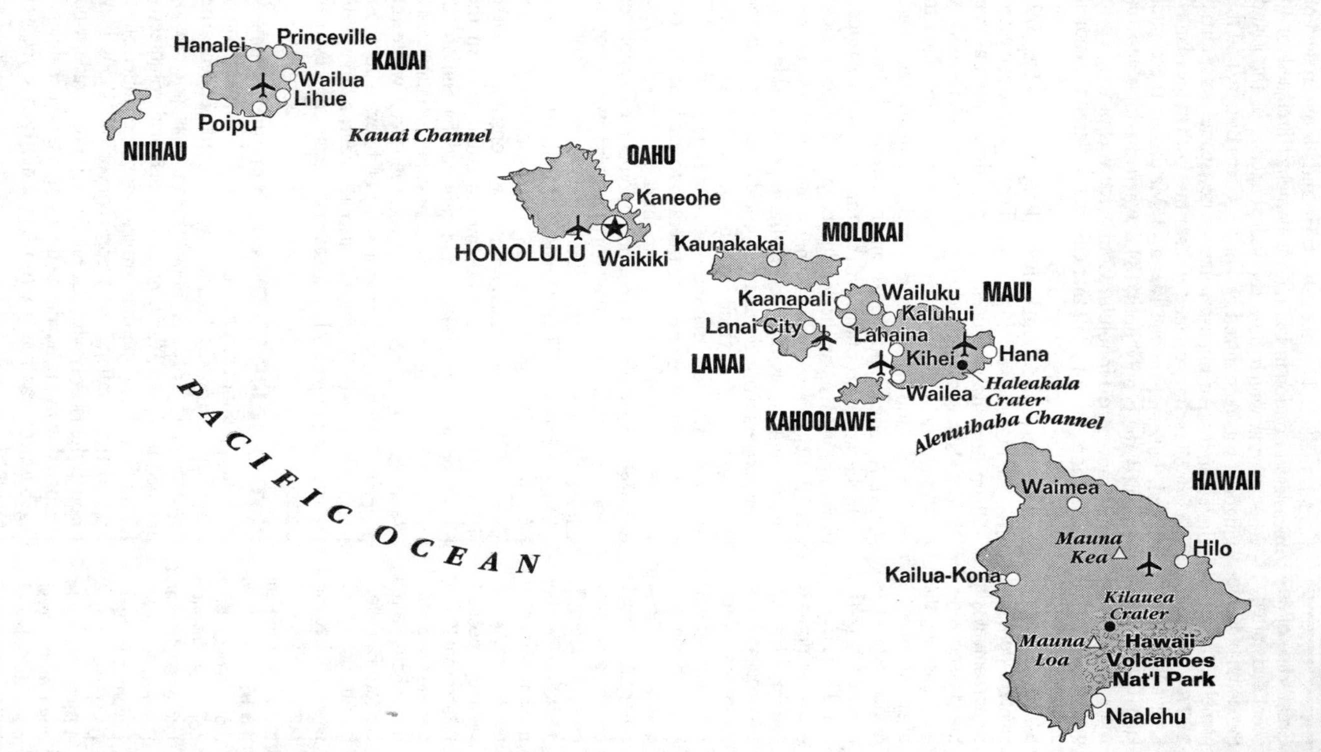
N
0
50 km
31 mi
KAUAI
Hanalei
Princeville
Wailua
Lihue
Poipu
NIIHAU
Kauai Channel
OAHU
Kaneohe
HONOLULU
Waikiki
MOLOKAI
Kaunakakai
MAUI
Kaanapali
Wailuku
Kaluhui
Lahaina
Kihei
Hana
Wailea
Haleakala Crater
LANAI
Lanai City
KAHOOLAWE
Alenuihaha Channel
HAWAII
Waimea
Mauna Kea
Hilo
Kailua-Kona
Kilauea Crater
Mauna Loa
Hawaii Volcanoes Nat'l Park
Naalehu
PACIFIC OCEAN
Airport

DATELINE

Great's line of descent ends after the death of Kamehameha V.

- **1874** David Kalakaua elected king; Queen Emma, widow of Kamehameha IV, loses her claim to the throne.
- **1875** Sugar planters work out an agreement with the U.S. government assuring them of an American market; when it is renewed in 1887, the U.S. is given exclusive rights to use Pearl Harbor as a coaling station for its ships The American Age in Hawaii begins.
- **1891** Kalakaua's sister Liliuokalani becomes queen upon his death.
- **1893** When her plans to strengthen the monarchy are violently opposed, Liliuokalani is deposed and put under house arrest; Sanford B. Dole, an American businessman, becomes head of a provisional government.
- **1894** The Provisional Government converts Hawaii into a republic, and Sanford P. Dole becomes its first president.
- **1898** Hawaii is annexed by President McKinley; Dole is appointed governor.

(continues)

Meanwhile, the reign of the second Kamehameha, Kamehemeha II, had been short. He and his queen died of measles in London in 1824. Kamehameha III reigned for 30 years, during which time the independence of the island kingdom was recognized by France, Great Britain, and the United States. An English-language newspaper was started and a public school opened at that time, both in the islands' capital, Lahaina, on the island of Maui. But the capital remained there only until 1845, when the king and his court moved to Honolulu. Commerce was picking up in the harbors, and in 1850 that city was declared the capital of the 19th-century kingdom.

The line of the Kamehameha descent ended by 1872, after Kamehameha IV and V. The legislature elected William Lunalilo as successor, but he died within a year; David Kalakaua succeeded him. Queen Emma, the widow of Kamehameha IV, appeared to have a rightful claim to the throne, and it was to this end that many riots were staged. American and British marines were called in.

In the latter part of the 19th century, industry continued to boom, with sugar the leading crop and coffee a close second. (Rice, now of small importance in the state, was once the number-two crop.) Finally, in 1875, the Hawaiian sugar planters worked out a reciprocal agreement with the U.S. government by which Hawaiian sugar companies were assured an American market; when it was renewed in 1887 the Americans were given the freedom to use Pearl Harbor as a coaling station for American ships. The American Age was beginning in Hawaii; the annexation of the Republic of Hawaii took place in 1898, but statehood would not be achieved until more than half a century later, in 1959.

King Kalakaua, "The Merry Monarch," was followed by Queen Liliuokalani, the last reigning monarch of the islands. When her plans for a new constitution were violently opposed, she was removed from office in the bloodless uprising of 1893 and replaced by Sanford B. Dole, a haole representing American commercial interests. While she was under house arrest, the queen wrote the poignant "Aloha Oe," now a song of farewell to those leaving the islands. But it was also a lament, a farewell to the days of the past when kings and queens, and even an occasional god, walked the earth.

20TH CENTURY The 20th century saw the booming of the pineapple industry in Hawaii. The U.S. Armed Forces moved into the area and made Hawaii an independent army department in 1913. Although Hawaii was not directly involved in World War I, many islanders had volunteered for the French and German armies before the United States entered the conflict. The Depression of the 1930s blew through the islands with the relative calm of a trade wind, compared with the hurricane devastation on the mainland. Big business was not yet too big, industry not yet well developed.

But Hawaii felt the impact of World War II more than

any American state. Because the United States had developed the harbors and military installations on the islands, they were a prime target area for the enemy. After the dreadful bombing attack of December 7, 1941, Hawaii entered a period of martial law. Liquor consumption was regulated, curfews were imposed, and blackouts were common. Fortunately, the islands' Japanese population was not herded off into concentration camps as it was in California. In fact, a group of Nisei volunteers became one of the great heroic regiments of the U.S. Army, fighting in southern Europe. The 442nd Regimental Combat Team has been called "probably the most decorated unit in United States military history," and one of its members, Daniel K. Inouye, is the senator of Watergate fame. This participation in the war did a great deal to break down race lines in Hawaii. Today, the Japanese are the largest single ethnic group, and one of the most powerful, in the state.

After the war, increasing lines of transportation developed between the American mainland and Hawaii. Tourism became a major industry and the already existing industries grew at phenomenal rates. Years of labor disputes in the 1940s, spearheaded by the militant ILWU, raised the standard of living for the Hawaiian worker to an all-time high. Finally, in 1959, after a 30-year struggle for statehood that began with Hawaii's first representative to Congress, Prince Jonah Kuhio Kalanianaole, delegate John A. Burns (later Hawaii's governor) affected passage of the bill that made Hawaii the 50th American state. Dancing in the streets celebrated a goal long promised and arduously won.

DATELINE

- **1903** James Dole produces the first canned pineapple.
- **1936** Pan American Airways inaugurates commercial passenger flights to Hawaii.
- **1941** Pearl Harbor bombed, December 7, by Japan. Martial law declared. Nisei volunteers in the U.S. Army in southern Europe are noted for extraordinary valor.
- **1959** Hawaii achieves statehood on August 21, 1959, now known as Admission Day.

Since statehood, Hawaii has blossomed and boomed and burst forth into a new era. Now largely Democratic in politics, with a mostly Japanese/American legislature, it is liberal in its outlook, proud of its ability to blend the races, to let the newcomer "do his own thing." Garment industries, steel mills, and cement factories are growing. Agriculture uses the most advanced techniques, and pineapple and sugar are still big business, although on the island of Lanai, pineapple is being phased out. Technology has moved in and made Hawaii the mid-Pacific outpost of America's space efforts and oceanography research. The University of Hawaii and the East-West Center for Cultural and Technical Interchange have raised the level of education in the state remarkably, bringing in scholars from all over the world. Population is up to 1.15 million; more than six million tourists are expected annually. Despite economic uncertainty here as everywhere, it looks as if Hawaii is still going strong.

POLITICS

A Republican stronghold for many years, in the days when the Big Five ruled the islands, Hawaii, with the rise of the labor unions and of the ethnic groups to positions of political and financial power, has become strongly Democratic in its politics. Up until 1954, there had never been a Democratic majority in either house of the legislature; in 1962, the Democrats captured both branches of the legislature and the governorship as well. Both of its senators in the U.S. Congress, Daniel K. Inouye and Daniel Akaka, are Democrats, as are its representatives in Congress, Patsy Mink and Neil Abercrombie. Both Inouye and Mink are of Japanese/American backgrounds; Akaka is pure Hawaiian; and Abercrombie is 100% haole.

In the state legislature, there are 51 representatives (only 3 are Republicans), and 25 senators (3 are Republicans). Most are of mixed backgrounds; 6 are Hawaiian. John

Waihee, the current governor, is about 75% Hawaiian; Lt. Gov. Benjamin Cayetano is pure Filipino.

2. FAMOUS ISLANDERS

Kamehameha I (1758–1819) Kamehameha the Great was the first to unite all the islands under one rule by a combination of generalship, gunpowder, and treachery. After he had captured Maui, Molokai, and Oahu, he won Kauai and Niihau by treaty negotiations in 1810. He defended the islands against the Russian general Georg Anton Scheffer. He learned the value of explosives when he was wounded in a battle with Capt. James Cook, the British discoverer of the islands. The dynasty he founded lasted until 1872, after which Hawaiian kings were elected by the people.

Hiram Bingham (1789–1869) The model for Abner Hale in Michener's *Hawaii*, Bingham and his wife, Sybil, were among the missionaries who arrived on the brig *Thaddeus* in 1820. Popular with the Hawaiian rulers but very unpopular with the whaling captains, Bingham helped create the written Hawaiian alphabet, which was used to translate the Bible into Hawaiian. He was the first pastor of Kawaiahao Church.

Bernice Pauahi Bishop (1831–84) Married to the American Charles Reed Bishop, this great-granddaughter of Kamehameha I declined the succession to the throne offered her by Kamehameha V in 1872. But her name lives on in modern Hawaii in the Bishop Museum and the Bishop Estate, which administers the huge portion of Kamehameha lands she inherited, almost 9% of the entire area of the Hawaiian islands. The Kamehameha School, which educates children of Hawaiian blood, was established by the terms of her will.

King David Kalakaua (1836–91) Known as the "Merry Monarch" for his fun-loving, high-living ways, he ruled over Hawaii for 17 years, from 1874 until his death in 1891. He was the elected monarch, the first to visit the United States, the first to be crowned publicly (by himself), and the first to construct a royal statue (Kamehameha's, in front of Aliiolani Hale). The ineptness and corruption of his reign gave rise to numerous antimonarchy movements.

Queen Liliuokalani (1839–1917) The last of the reigning monarchs of the kingdom of Hawaii, Liliuokalani sought to strengthen the monarchy by means both fair and foul; for her troubles, she was deposed and later confined to house arrest in a room of her former palace. It was here that Liliuokalani wrote Hawaii's most famous song: "Aloha Oe."

Father [Joseph de Veuster] Damien (1840–69) Born in Belgium and ordained in Honolulu, Damien was assigned at his own request to the dread leper colony on Molokai in 1873. He died there 16 years later after contracting the disease. He is now a candidate for canonization by the Roman Catholic church. Marisol's statue of Damien is one of the two statues in the United States Capitol (along with that of King Kamehameha the Great) representing Hawaii.

Princess Kaiulani (1875–99) The widely beloved princess, named heiress apparent to the throne on the accession of her aunt, Queen Liliuokalani, died at the age of 24. She traveled to Washington, D.C., to argue unsuccessfully for the restoration of the monarchy after it was overthrown. Her estate, Ainahau, in Waikiki, where in 1889 she entertained Robert Louis Stevenson, who was enchanted with the young princess, is now the site of the Princess Kaiulani Hotel.

Juliette May Fraser (1887–1983) The dean of island painters in her time, she studied mural and fresco painting under Jean Charlot. Her works can be seen at Bilger Hall at the University of Hawaii, among many other places on the island. She continued a busy life of working in many media, and at the time of her death, at age 96, was busy creating a ceramic mural for the District Court Building in downtown Honolulu. She has been named a "living treasure" of Hawaii.

Madge Tennent (1889–1972) An important figure in the arts in Hawaii, Madge Tennent came to the islands in the 1920s via South Africa and Paris, and broke away from the academy and its conventions to record on canvas her massive portraits of the Hawaiian people. The Tennent Art Foundation, still open, was a showplace for the work of island artists.

Duke Kahanamoku (1890–1968) Hawaii's most famous athlete, Kahanamoku won Olympic swimming medals in 1912, 1920, 1924, and 1928. He has been honored by the Swimming Hall of Fame and the Surfing Hall of Fame. The Invitational Surfing Championships of Hawaii are named in his honor. His trophies and mementos are on display at the Parker Ranch Visitor Center on the Big Island.

Jean Charlot (1898–1979) Born in Paris, he worked with the great Mexican muralists Rivera and Siqueros. His work in that medium can be seen in Hawaii, Fiji, Mexico, and mainland United States. He came to Hawaii in 1946, published plays in both English and Hawaiian, and taught at the University of Hawaii until 1967, where the Hamilton Library houses the remarkable Jean Charlot Collection.

John Anthony Burns (1909–75) Elected governor in 1962, Burns was instrumental in devising the strategy that led to Hawaiian statehood in 1959. During his three terms in office he spearheaded the movement that led the state from the Republican to the Democratic camp. The John A. Burns School of Medicine at the University of Hawaii bears his name.

Rev. Abraham Akaka (1917–) Since 1957 the pastor of Hawaii's oldest and most prestigious church, Kawaiahao in Honolulu, Akaka, whom the islanders affectionately call "Kahu," delivered the keynote address at the Statehood Service of Dedication, linking the spirit of aloha with the spirit of Christianity in a sermon that has since become a classic in the writings of Hawaii.

Daniel Inouye (1924–) Hawaii's senior senator in the U.S. Congress, Daniel Inouye won national fame in 1974 as a member of the Watergate committee, and again in 1987 as chairman of the committee to investigate the Iran-Contra affair. He continues to hold major positions among Senate Democrats. Inouye has been reelected to the Senate four times. The grandson of Japanese immigrants who came to Hawaii to work the sugar plantations, Inouye was born in Honolulu, graduated from the University of Hawaii and the George Washington University Law School. During World War II, he was a member of the distinguished 442nd Regimental Combat Team, perhaps the most decorated unit in U.S. military history.

Wally Amos (1936–) This unofficial ambassador of Hawaii is an adopted son: He has lived in the islands since 1977 and claims he'd "rather be a beggar in Hawaii than a king anywhere else." King of the designer cookie market, "Famous Amos" promotes his "Chip & Cookie" line (dolls, clothing, and books as well as cookies) when he's not busy traveling around the country as a motivational speaker. For more than a decade, he's been national spokesman for Literacy Volunteers of America. Amos and his wife and daughter live in Lanikai, on the island of Oahu.

Bette Midler (1945–) Hawaii's gift to show business was born and raised in Hawaii (and named after Bette Davis by her mother, a movie buff). Active in local community theater, she was chosen to play a missionary wife in the movie *Hawaii* when she was 18; she saved her movie money, moved to New York, got a job as understudy in *Fiddler on the Roof*, appeared on "The Tonight Show," started making records—and the rest is history.

Lt. Col. Ellison S. Onizuka, USAF (1946–86) The first Asian-American in manned space flight, astronaut Onizuka died with his six fellow crew members 74 seconds into the flight of the *Challenger* space shuttle on January 28, 1986. A Big Island boy, he was an outstanding athlete and scholar, and flew his first mission on the space shuttle *Discovery* in 1978.

3. HAWAIIAN CULTURE

Traditional Hawaiian culture centers around a worldview best summarized in the term "Aloha Aina"—love for the land. To the Hawaiian, the world and everything in it—minerals, plants, animals, humans, gods—is alive and conscious, sentient. Matter is not something mechanical, a view that dominates Western thinking. It is something that humans can communicate with directly, which nourishes and protects them, and which they, in turn, must nourish and protect. To the Hawaiians, the world is peopled with gods; they may take the forms of mountains, or trees, or the sun or the ocean; they may inhabit the taro root or the breadfruit. Nature is not only conscious, it is often divine.

Out of this understanding of the cooperative relationship between humans and nature grew a system of ethical rules designed to keep this harmony. For example, one was never to take anything from nature—even a flower or a rock—without first asking permission, lest the spirits be displeased. It was also good to leave something of value as a replacement. (It's interesting to note how this ancient prohibition still seems valid. Numerous visitors who have taken lava rocks from Kilauea Volcano on the Big Island, the domain of the volcano goddess, Pele, have sent them back to the park rangers, telling of all sorts of misfortunes that had befallen them afterward.) Because the Hawaiians took care of nature, it took care of them: Thus many plants, stones, etc., were thought to have helpful and healing powers.

Although the traditional religion went underground with the growth of Christianity in the islands, many of its ideas still bubble beneath the surface; they are still in the consciousness of the Hawaiian people. Today something extremely interesting is taking place. There is a drive afoot for a sovereign Hawaiian nation, for establishing places on each island where Hawaiians can live in harmony with nature in the old ways. Unless this happens, they fear, more and more lands will be given away for foreign investment, more and more concrete will cover the once sacred earth, and the old ways—of people and gods and nature living in community the way they did in ancient Hawaii—will be irrevocably lost.

4. HUNA — THE ANCIENT RELIGION

The ancient religion of Hawaii—Huna—remained a mystery to Westerners for many years, as the old teachings were forced underground with the coming of the Christian missionaries and the outlawing of the *kahunas,* the native priests. The tradition had been strictly an oral one, passed on from one generation of kahunas to another. It was not until Max Freedom Long, a teacher who lived and worked in Honolulu in the early years of the century, broke the code after almost 50 years of research into Huna lore and began publishing his works (especially *The Secret Science Behind Miracles* and *The Secret Science at Work*) in the late 1940s and early 50s, that this knowledge became available.

Long and writers who came after him believe that Huna religious beliefs can be traced back to ancient Egypt, and that its followers have left traces in the languages and teachings of many peoples as they brought their philosophy across the world to its last stop in the Polynesian islands.

Although Huna (which means "secret") does not include the concept of a supreme being, the kahunas ("keepers of the secrets") may have included that teaching among those that were never given out except under threat of death. The highest gods of the

Hawaiians—Kāne, Kū, Lono, Kanaloa, and Hina—each possessed enormous power, or *mana,* of different qualities, which gave each of them different abilities, such as creation, manifestation, fertility. Similar ideas have been found throughout Polynesia.

But the Hawaiians made a unique contribution to Huna—namely, the belief that lesser gods can be created by the kahunas through special ritual ceremonies in which sufficient mana is given to the bones of deceased chiefs so they take on various degrees of *akua,* or spirit consciousness. (Chiefs go to different heavens than commoners.) This is done to keep the departed spirits bound to their descendants for purposes of protection. The practice of imparting mana—*ho'omanana*—was central to the deification process.

Huna includes the belief that humankind has evolved from the animal kingdom and we are each allied to some specific animal, or totem, which can be called on for help. Unlike Westerners, the Polynesians believe that humans live communally with all forms of life, not just with other humans. This requires attention to all lesser forms of nature. Every aspect of life is made sacred, and there is constant praying for every activity in life—planting and harvesting, relating to people, sailing, swimming, etc.

All life forms operate in pairs: Each sea animal has its land counterpart, night has day, directions are paired with their opposites, the rising sun has the setting sun, male has female—such is the world of polarity.

It is claimed that "all the souls of the departed went to *pō,* place of night, and were . . . eaten by the gods there." Eventually, all human souls are reincarnated, to learn additional lessons on their evolutionary path to godhood. This is called *hou-ola* (ola = life, hou = new) or "preceding life."

In addition to this process of spiritual evolution, God is brought down to the level of humans in the form of the *aumakua* or High Self, which is the guiding spirit of each human, which also possesses a low self or animal self (the *unihipili*) and a middle self or intellect (*uhane*). There is an allowance for higher beings in the cosmos, but for the purpose of daily living, the practical Polynesians consider it sufficient to know that there is a divine soul in humans that is an intimate part of our total being and is ever ready to aid us when we call to it.

The process by which humans enlist the aid of the High Self or aumakua is known as *ho'oponopono.* This process requires the cooperation of the middle and low selves. The middle self or uhane asks the low self or unihipili to carry a message to the aumakua on the medium of desire (which is lacking to the intellect). First one charges the unihipili by a special breathing technique, and if one is on good terms with his low self the low self is perfectly willing to carry the prayer to the High Self, which responds by meeting the request. Many unanswered prayers are thus explained as a lack of a friendly relation between the intellect and one's emotional nature, or subconscious mind, as it is called in Western psychology.

When one's male and female uhanes are united after a life of living in love, the uhane graduates to the status of aumakua upon death and is eventually reincarnated as a guiding spirit for a new uhane and unihipili for a new round of incarnation.

It has been speculated that corrupt kahunas had the ability to extract mana from human sacrifices, which they absorbed into their beings for malignant uses. These dark kahunas often used departed spirits to murder their enemies. Women were considered less advanced than men and were discriminated against in many ways,

---

IMPRESSIONS

The loveliest fleet of islands that lies anchored in any ocean.
—MARK TWAIN, 1872

"See Naples and die"—They spell it differently here: See Hawaii and live.
—JACK LONDON, 1916

including the prohibition from eating many kinds of food and from participating in religious ceremonies. The tabu system was not broken until the widow of Kamehameha I, Kaahamanu, confronted the old gods and smashed their powers in the 1820s.

5. PERFORMING ARTS & EVENING ENTERTAINMENT

Hawaii has a rich artistic life, ranging from chamber music concerts to Broadway revivals, from performances of ancient hulas to nightclub Polynesian spectaculars. Visitors can go to concerts by the Honolulu Symphony and the Hawaii Opera Theater or hear Chamber Music Hawaii; they can choose from a variety of theaters including the 41-year-old Diamond Head Theater, the always-innovative Manoa Valley Theatre, the Starving Artists Theatre Company, and the John F. Kennedy Theater at the University of Hawaii, known for performances of everything from Kabuki to Shakespeare. And Waikiki at night is a continuous festival of music, dance, and entertainment. For details, see Chapter 7, "Honolulu Attractions," as well as the chapters on the individual Hawaiian islands.

6. SPORTS & RECREATION

The opportunities are endless: swimming, snorkeling, sailing, scuba diving, hiking, tennis, golf, parasailing, windsurfing—even ice skating and snow skiing! Hawaii's got them all, and more. For details, see Chapter 7, "Honolulu Attractions," as well as the chapters on the individual Hawaiian islands.

7. FOOD & DRINK

THE CUISINE

The food of Hawaii, like its people, reflects a cultural diversity—a lot of American, quite a bit of Japanese, a little less of Chinese, a smattering of Hawaiian, Korean, Filipino, and you-name-it thrown in for good measure. You quickly get used to the fact that a delicatessen can be Japanese and to the fact that saimin (a Japanese-type noodle soup with a seaweed base) is just as popular as a hamburger and is often served at the same counter.

You soon learn that the exotic-sounding *mahimahi* is Hawaiian for dolphin, a pleasant-tasting fish—not to be confused with the intelligent mammal of the same name, the porpoise. You'll be introduced to poi (crushed taro root), the staff of life of the early Hawaiians, at your very first luau—you may develop a liking for this purple-gray goo that's one of the most nutritious foods known, so high in vitamin B and calcium that it's fed to babies and invalids. Just ignore the old joke that it tastes like library paste; the Hawaiians, and quite a few malihinis, think it's delicious.

Hawaii's fruits are among the islands' special glories. Pineapple, while not exactly invented here, might just as well have been. It's well priced in the markets, served everywhere, and as good as you'd imagine. Pineapple juice is a kind of national drink, something like tea for the English. If you hit the mango season in summer, when the local trees are bursting with this succulent fruit, you're in for a great treat. Guavas, coconuts, and papayas (one of the most common breakfast foods) are all superb, as are guava juice and passion-fruit juice, which you'll often see listed under its Hawaiian name, *lilikoi* (lilikoi sherbet is wonderful). In the supermarkets, you'll see a very popular drink called POG—that's short for passion-fruit juice, orange juice, and guava juice—very popular and very good. Macadamia-nut pancakes, as well as coconut ice cream and syrup, are special treats that taste better in Hawaii than anywhere else. We should warn you coffee addicts right here and now—the kind of coffee you'll get everywhere is Kona coffee, grown on the Big Island of Hawaii, and it's so good that you may find yourself drinking innumerable cups a day.

Don't miss the chance to try Hawaii's game fish, caught fresh in local waters and served up in fish houses under "catch of the day." If you're lucky, the catch that day will be ahi (a kind of tuna and a personal favorite), aki (another tuna), marlin, ulua, opakapaka, rock cod, or a special island delicacy called ono. That word has, in fact, slipped into local parlance as meaning "delicious"—or even "great"—as in "ono ono." At this writing, "catch of the day" was selling for about $16–$20 in most restaurants.

LUAUS You'll probably first experience Hawaiian food at a luau, and then you'll find the same dishes in Hawaiian restaurants. You're already on speaking terms with poi. Other basic dishes are kalua pig (pig steamed in an underground oven, or *imu*), laulau (ti leaves stuffed with pork, salt fish, bananas, sweet potatoes, and taro shoots, and steamed), chicken luau (chicken cooked with coconut milk and taro or spinach leaves), sweet potatoes, pipikaula (jerked beef), and lomi-lomi salmon. The last is a triumph of linguistics: Lomi-lomi means massage, and this is salmon "massaged" with tomatoes and chopped onions, then marinated. Haupia (coconut pudding) and a piece of coconut cake are the usual desserts, along with fresh pineapple.

Most luaus are serve-yourself buffet affairs; food is usually eaten from paper plates, with plastic cutlery. The correct way to eat poi, by the way, is to dip one or two fingers in it (in the old days, you could actually order "one-" or "two-finger" poi, scoop it up quickly, and attack). But nobody expects that of a malihini.

LOCAL FOOD "Local food" does not really have deep roots in Hawaiian culture. What most people refer to as local food—and it's eaten in "plate lunches" popular everywhere in Hawaii—consists of dishes such as fried chicken, beef stew, teriyaki pork, breaded mahimahi, and the like; much of it is deep-fried. This is invariably accompanied by *two* carbohydrates, usually rice and a macaroni or potato-macaroni salad. A very popular local dish is called the loco moco—that's a hamburger patty over rice topped with a fried egg and brown gravy. Warning: Don't go local if you're counting calories!

PACIFIC RIM CUISINE A style called Pacific Rim or Contemporary American cuisine is served more and more in better restaurants. This cuisine marries the remarkable fresh local produce of the islands, the freshly caught fish, the locally grown beef, and the like, with the best of European and Asian cooking traditions. Prime examples: Avalon Restaurant in Maui, A Pacific Café in Kauai, and Roy's in Honolulu and Maui.

IMPRESSIONS

Midway across the North Pacific, space, time and life uniquely interlace a chain of islands named "Hawaiian." . . . These small fragments of land appear offered to the sky by water and pressed to earth by stars.

—Charles A. Lindbergh

KOREAN CUISINE The islands contain quite a few Korean restaurants, and they're good to know about for the budget traveler because of their modest price and delicious food. Although Koreans make up a small part of the population, their culinary tradition has left its mark, especially in the ubiquitous kimchee—pickled cabbage seasoned with red-hot peppers. You'll find it in grocery stores, on menus everywhere in Honolulu, and even at beach stands along Waikiki serving kimchee dogs. Korean cuisine has much more to offer, including barbecued meat and chicken, hearty noodle soups, tasty meat dumplings, fish filets sautéed in spicy sauces, and daintily shredded vegetables. Some but not all dishes are served with fiery hot sauces; if you're not accustomed to that sort of thing, check with the serving staff before you order.

SHAVE ICE A unique treat that's loved by just about all islanders is a phenomenon called shave ice. That's not "shaved" ice, or a snow cone, or a slush. It's just wonderful Hawaiian shave ice. You can have a "plain" shave ice—that's just the incredibly fine ice particles bathed in syrup—and there are all kinds of syrups. Strawberry is the most popular, but there's also vanilla, guava, lemon, cherry, orange, root beer, coconut, and combinations of the above, known as "rainbow." Or you can have ice cream or adzuki beans (a sweet Japanese bean used in desserts) on the bottom, or throw caution to the winds and order ice cream *and* beans on the bottom. Shave ice is served in a cone-shaped paper cup, with both a straw and a spoon.

DRINK

Generally, you need not worry about drinking tap water, except, alas, in some areas upcountry on the Big Island. Because of acid rain, it's best to drink bottled spring water here. Soft drinks and mineral waters are the same as you find back home. As for beer, the favorite local brew is called Primo. There's a potent local liquor called okolehao, distilled from the ti root. Wine is now produced on Maui: Tedeschi Vineyards offers a pineapple wine, two champagnes, a blush, and a red table wine in the Beaujolais Nouveau tradition. Wine and liquor are sold in supermarkets.

8. RECOMMENDED BOOKS, FILMS & RECORDINGS

BOOKS

HISTORY, POLITICS & SOCIOLOGY The definitive book on Hawaii is Gavan Daws's *A Shoal of Time* (University Press of Hawaii), a history of Hawaii from 1778 until statehood (1959). It reads like a novel. Collaborating with George Cooper, Daws has also written *Land and Power in Hawaii* (University of Hawaii Press), a controversial, much-talked-about book on politics and personal financial interests in the state.

Frederick Simpich, Jr.'s book *Anatomy of Hawaii* (Coward, McCann & Geoghegan) is considered one of the most comprehensive historical and sociological studies. Also of note is *Hawaii, an Uncommon History* by Edward Joesting (Norton). *Hawaii* by Gerrit P. Judd (Macmillan) is another worthwhile study, from the point of view of the missionaries. Kristin Zambucka's book on Princess Kaiulani is considered a classic: *Kaiulani, The Last Hope of the Monarchy* (Mana Publishing Co.).

The Real Hawaii, Its History and Present Condition, Including the True Story of the Revolution (reprint edition published by Arno Press) by Lucien Young, USN, covers the author's personal observations of the political situation in 1892 and 1893 and later years.

FICTION James Michener's *Hawaii* (Random House) is required reading before a trip to Hawaii. Michener has taken a leading figure from each of the groups who settled the islands—the Polynesians, the American missionaries, the Chinese, the Japanese—and through their stories, told the story of Hawaii. Reading it will illuminate your trip as nothing else will. Also illuminating, beautifully written, and tremendously informative are the five historical novels written by O. A. Bushnell, a kamaaina with a touch of Hawaiian blood, and a reverence for Hawaii and his heritage. They are: *Molokai,* which tells the story of the leper colony (University Press of Hawaii); *The Return of Lono* (University of Hawaii Press), dealing with Captain Cook; *Kaawa* (University Press of Hawaii), set in the Hawaii in the 1850s; and his last two, *The Stones of Kannon* (University Press of Hawaii) and *The Water of Kane* (University Press of Hawaii), both of which are about the Japanese who came to the islands to work the sugar plantations. For another fictional account of the Japanese in Hawaii, read Kazuro Miyamoto's *Hawaii, End of the Rainbow* (Tuttle).

James Jones's *From Here to Eternity* (Scribner's), set at Schofield Barracks, was a big best-seller of the 1950s and is still worth reading for its portrayal of army life in Hawaii in the early 1940s. There is also a noted film adaptation.

Several collections of short stories make for absorbing reading. Among these are *A Hawaiian Reader,* edited by A. Grove Day (Appleton), and its companion volume, *The Spell of Hawaii* (Meredith), which include, among others, stories by Jack London, Robert Louis Stevenson, W. Somerset Maugham, Mark Twain, and James Michener. Jack London's *Stories of Hawaii* (Appleton) and Gerrit P. Judd's *A Hawaiian Anthology* (Macmillan) are also engaging.

NATURE Sherwin Carlquist's *Hawaii: A Natural History* (Doubleday) is comprehensive and authoritative. George Munroe's *Birds of Hawaii* (Tuttle) is well illustrated and very helpful for birdwatchers. For a well-illustrated guide to Hawaii's seashells, with 380 full-color illustrations, read *Seashells of Hawaii* by Stephen Quirk and Charles Wolfe (W. W. Distributors). *Stars Over Hawaii,* originally written by E. H. Bryan, Jr., of the Bishop Museum and published by the Petroglyph Press, is an illustrated paperback with monthly star charts of the Hawaiian skies. Robert Decker's *Volcano Watching* (Hawaii Natural History Association and U.S. National Park Service), features colorful photos of volcanic eruptions.

PHOTOGRAPHY Scores of photographers were given one-day assignments in Hawaii and the result was a fascinating tome: *A Day in the Life of Hawaii* (Workman Publishing). Robert Wenkham has produced five superb pictorial books with magnificent full-color photographs, all published by Rand McNally. They are *Honolulu Is an Island; Hawaii; Maui: The Last Hawaiian Place; Kauai;* and *The Park Country of Hawaii.* A wonderful remembrance of the Big Island is *Hawaii: The Big Island, a Visit to a Realm of Beauty, History and Fire* (Mutual Publishing), with text by Glen Grant and breathtaking photos by principal photographers Peter French and Greg Vaughn.

IMPRESSIONS

You'll never know Hawaii 'til you've felt the foaming surf about your knees; 'til you've plunged into the breakers with a cry of pagan glee.

—DON BLANDING, 1928

FOLKLORE, LEGEND & PHILOSOPHY Martha Beckwith's *Hawaiian Mythology* (University of Hawaii Press) is a reprint of a valuable scholarly text. David Kalakaua's *The Legends and Myths of Hawaii: The Fables and Folklore of a Strange People* (Tuttle) is an early source of folklore recorded by King Kalakaua. *Man, Gods and Nature,* by Michael Keone Dudley (Na Kane Oka Malo Press), outlines traditional Hawaiian spiritual practices.

The classic books on Huna, the ancient philosophy of Hawaiians passed down by secret oral tradition, were written by Max Freedom Long, beginning with *The Secret Science Behind Miracles* (Huna Research Publications). Leilani Melville's *Children of the Rainbow* (DeVorss Publishers) is another classic on Huna. A modern-day Hawaiian shaman, Serge Kahili King, has also written books on Huna, including *Kahuna Healing, Mastering Your Hidden Self* and *Imagineering for Health* (both published by Quest) and *Urban Shaman* (Simon & Schuster). All these books are available at Kauai Village Museum, 4-831 Kuhio Hwy. in Kauai (tel. 808/822-9272).

RECREATION Craig Chisholm's *Hawaiian Hiking Trails* (Touchstone Press) is considered one of the best hiking guides. As for surfing, read Fred Hemming's *Surfing, Hawaii's Gift to the World of Sport* (Zokeisha Publications), which covers everything from history to surfboards to wave formation. Tony Rizzuto's *Modern Hawaiian Gamefishing* (University of Hawaii Press) tells all about fish, alive and cooked, including some fish stories. *Hawaii Parklands* gives the would-be camper complete information about national, state, and county parks on all six major islands, as well as 97 full-color photographs of wild and scenic places (available from Hawaii Geographic Maps & Books, 49 South Hotel Street, Suite 218, Honolulu, HI 96813; tel. 808/538-3952).

TRAVEL For an understanding of travel in Hawaii over a century ago, read Isabella Bird Bishop's *Six Months in the Sandwich Islands,* an engaging account of Hawaiian life in 1873. Robert Wallace's *Hawaii,* part of the Time-Life American Wilderness series, focuses on the wilderness areas of the state.

VIDEOS/FILMS

Our favorite Hawaiian video is called *Hawaii's Children in Dance,* a performance of the Young People's Hula Show, which is presented each Sunday morning at the Ala Moana Shopping Center. It is available there, and also at World of Music at Ala Moana. Other popular videos at World of Music include *You Can Do the Hula, The Polynesian Cultural Center, Portrait of Elegance,* and—not to be missed—*The 1990 Merrie Monarch Hula Festival,* highlights from the annual world Olympics of hula.

Hawaiian Paradise is the only video sold by the Bishop Museum. It's a breathtaking travelogue, showing volcanic eruptions, underwater scenes, and many other scenic wonders.

Tropical Visions Video (62 Halaulani Place, Hilo, HI 96720) puts out *Volcano Scapes I* and *Volcano Scapes II,* which documents the current nine-year-long eruption of Kilauea with some extraordinary footage.

Forever Hawaii (P.O. Box 26147, Honolulu, HI 96825) presents four exciting videos: *Forever Hawaii, Forever Maui, The Volcanoes of Hawaii,* and, on the unusual side, *Whalesong, Whales and Dolphins of the Pacific;* profits support cetacean research and conservation.

RECORDINGS

Here are some of Hawaii's favorite recording artists. For music of the Monarchy period, listen to anything by Palani Vaughan. Emma Veary features many lovely Monarchy songs on her albums. Aunty Edith Kankaole is known for wonderful

Hawaiian music and chants. For lyrical old Hawaiian songs, the best are recordings by Aunty Genoa Keawe and the Brothers Cazimero. For authentic, spirited Hawaiian music, it's the Makaha Sons of Niihau. And for true Hawaiians falsetto singing, nobody can beat Tony Conjugación.

For mostly contemporary Hawaiian and hapa-haole music, our favorite group is Olomana, starring a wonderful singer named Jerry Santos. Also rating way up there are two sets of brothers—the Cazimeros, Roland and Robert, and the Beamers, Keola and Kapono, who have made albums together and separately—and a delightful group of three hefty local gentlemen called the Pandanus Club. Women vocalists offering mostly contemporary music are Nohelani Cypriano, Karen Keawehawaii, and Melveen Leed. (Leed is leaning toward a sort of "country" sound these days.) For awesome slack-key guitar: the Beamer brothers again, and the late Gabby Pahiniu. Also, the Peter Moon band, featuring two of Gabby's sons, Cyril and Martin. The three brothers Pahiniu—Cyril, Martin, and rascally Bla—will have issued a new album by the time you read this.

Regarding comedy albums, we'd recommend anything by the incredibly funny Frank DeLima or by impressionist Billy Sage, who does devastating takeoffs on local and national politicos. Albums of the late, lamented Rap Reiplinger, who wrote his own material, and did all the voices, are also hysterically funny.

CHAPTER 2

PLANNING A TRIP TO HAWAII

In this chapter, the where, when, and how of your trip to Hawaii is discussed—the advance planning that gets your trip together and takes it on the road.

After deciding where to go, most people have two fundamental questions: What will it cost? and How do I get there? This chapter not only helps answer those questions, but addresses such important issues as when to travel, whether to take a tour, what kind of health precautions to take, what kind of insurance to carry, where to obtain additional information, and much more.

WHAT PART OF HAWAII SHOULD I VISIT?

Too many tourists start and end their Hawaiian holidays in Honolulu on Oahu—and think they've seen Hawaii. Yes—and no. They've seen the largest city and the principal resort area, but far more awaits: a Hawaii at once more gentle and more savage, where the old gods still have powers. To see the desolate moonscapes of the volcanoes and Hawaiian cowboys riding the range, to see beaches so remote and pristine as to make Waikiki seem like Times Square, and to visit South Seas villages just coming into the modern age, plan to venture to the three other important Hawaiian Islands: the Garden Island of Kauai, the Big Island of Hawaii, and the Valley Isle of Maui. If you have more time, you may also want to visit Molokai and Lanai.

Hawaii is made up of islands that can't be reached by driving overland at the spur of the moment. Therefore, planning ahead regarding your stay in Hawaii can help you get the most from your vacation there. Following is an overview of the individual Hawaiian islands. Much more information on each appears later in this guide.

OAHU Known as the Gathering Place, the island of Oahu contains Honolulu, Hawaii's capital and main cultural center, in the southeast, and great ocean surfing locations in the northwest and west. Among Oahu's many other attractions are the U.S.S. *Arizona* Memorial at Pearl Harbor, Waimea Falls Park, and Nuuanu Pali, scene of a bloody battle in 1795.

KAUAI Kauai is not as well known as it should be. It's refreshingly rural, small, beautiful, and easily assimilated. Waimea Canyon, a smaller version of the Grand Canyon, is its principal natural attraction. It also has a string of unforgettable beaches (you've seen them as Bali H'ai in the movie version of *South Pacific* and as Matlock Island in the television production of *The Thornbirds*).

HAWAII The Big Island of Hawaii encompasses the most varied geography of the islands, and is like a small continent in miniature. It has few beaches (except in the Kona area), but contains the islands' second-biggest city (Hilo), the volcanic wonderlands of Mauna Kea and Mauna Loa (Volcanoes National Park is a must on any itinerary), and a cattle ranch big enough for Texas.

MAUI Maui has become the most popular of the neighboring islands and appeals especially to an affluent condo crowd; it has some of the best golf courses in the state of Hawaii. Maui's great natural wonder is Haleakala, the largest dormant volcano in the world, with a moonlike crater that you can explore on foot or horseback. Also alluring are the popular, picturesque old whaling town of Lahaina, remote and lovely Hana, and a succession of golden beaches.

MOLOKAI & LANAI Next to largely unaccessible Niihau, Molokai is the most Hawaiian of the Hawaiian islands, with the largest number of native Hawaiians. A festival celebrating the birth of the hula takes place there every year. The island of Lanai, once nothing more than a gigantic pineapple plantation, has entered the world of modern tourism with two posh Rockresorts—Manele Bay and Keole Lodge. You may want to splurge about $139 on one of the sailing-ship cruises out of Lahaina, Maui, that spend the day on Lanai.

1. INFORMATION, ENTRY REQUIREMENTS & MONEY

SOURCES OF INFORMATION

For further information on traveling and living in Hawaii, you can contact the **Hawaii Visitors Bureau (HVB),** which has offices in the following cities:

On the Mainland Suite 1031, 180 N. Michigan Ave., **Chicago,** IL 60601 (tel. 312/236-0632); Room 502, Central Plaza, 3440 Wilshire Blvd., **Los Angeles,** CA 90010 (tel. 213/385-5301); Room 1407, 441 Lexington Ave., **New York,** NY 10017 (tel. 212/986-9203); and Suite 450, 50 California St., **San Francisco,** CA 94111 (tel. 415/392-8173).

In Hawaii Suite 801, Waikiki Business Plaza, 2270 Kalakaua Ave. (P.O. Box 8527), **Honolulu,** HI 96815 (tel. 808/923-1811); 75-5719 West Alii Dr., **Kailua-Kona,** HI 96740 (tel. 808/329-7787); Suite 104, Hilo Plaza, 180 Kinoole St., **Hilo,** HI 96720 (tel. 808/961-5797); Maui Visitors Bureau, 172 Alamaha St., Suite N16, **Kahului,** Maui, HI 96732 (tel. 808/871-8691); and Suite 207, Lihue Plaza Building, 3016 Umi St. (Kauai P.O. Box 507), **Lihue,** Kauai, HI 96766 (tel. 808/245-3971).

ENTRY REQUIREMENTS/MONEY

If you're a U.S. citizen or permanent resident, one of the nicest things about going to Hawaii is that you don't have to fiddle with passports or visas. Nor do you have to worry about currency exchange. Despite its exotic flavor, Hawaii is still part of the U.S.A. Entry requirements for foreigners are discussed in Chapter 3.

WHAT THINGS COST IN HAWAII	U.S. $
Taxi from Honolulu International Airport to Waikiki	$20–$25
Van from Honolulu International Airport to Waikiki	$5.00
Local telephone call	.25
Double room at the Westin Kauai (deluxe)	$195–$395
Double room at the Maui Islander (moderate)	$83.00
Double room at the Royal Grove, Honolulu (budget)	$36.00
Lunch for one at Green Garden, Kauai (moderate)	$6.00
Lunch for one at Ocean View Inn, Big Island (budget)	$5.00
Dinner for one, without wine, at the Black Orchid, Honolulu (expensive)	$25.00
Dinner for one, without wine, at the Hanamaulu Tea House, Kauai (moderate)	$15.00
Dinner for one, without wine, at the Old Spaghetti Factory, Honolulu (budget)	$4.35
Bottle of beer	$2.50
Cup of coffee	$1.50
Coca-Cola	$1.50
Roll of ASA 100 Kodacolor film, 36 exposures	$4.50
Admission to Bishop Museum, Honolulu	$5.95
Movie ticket	$5.50
Theater ticket to Manoa Valley Theater, Honolulu	$14–$20
Brothers Cazimero Show, Monarch Room, Royal Hawaiian Hotel, Honolulu	
dinner show	$59.50
cocktail show	$25–$30

2. WHEN TO GO — CLIMATE, HOLIDAYS & EVENTS

CLIMATE

The Hawaiian "season" has little to do with the weather in the islands. Rather, it's tied to the weather back home. In the islands, the weather is usually good year round. Hawaii's climate is subtropical, with springlike temperatures averaging about 75°F and seldom ranging more than 6° or 7° above or below this point. In midwinter, you can occasionally get some "raw" days in the low- to mid-60s, and in midsummer, you can experience some humid ones in the 80s. (August is probably the most humid month of the year; if your room does not have cross-ventilation to allow the trade winds to come through, air conditioning is essential at that time.) Cool waters drifting down from the Bering Sea make the islands 10° cooler than other places in the same latitude—and the trade winds provide balmy breezes. As for rain, we have experienced some dreary, rainy days here, especially in winter—anytime from November to March. But most of the time, showers are brief and seldom heavy enough to spoil the pleasures of a vacation.

HOLIDAYS

Just about all businesses and banks will be closed on the major holidays: Christmas, New Year's, Easter Sunday, and Thanksgiving Day. In addition to the legal holidays observed throughout the United States—Memorial Day, July 4th, Labor Day, Martin Luther King, Jr., Day, Election Day, and Veterans Day—there are specific Hawaiian holidays on which many businesses close: Prince Kuhio Day (March 26), Kamehameha Day (June 11), and Admission Day (the third Friday in August).

HAWAII CALENDAR OF EVENTS

JANUARY

☐ **Cherry Blossom Festival.** A Japanese cultural and trade show, complete with a queen, pageant, and a coronation ball, plus demonstrations of tea ceremonies, flower arranging, and more. Early Jan to early Apr.

✪ ***PUNAHOU SCHOOL CARNIVAL.*** *One of the most popular family events in Honolulu, this yearly carnival features 23 rides, including a Ferris wheel and a merry-go-round, and 60 booths offering plants, foods, arts and crafts, and so forth. Best of all is the White Elephant tent at the end of the carnival, when leftovers—often clothing in good condition—sell for ridiculously low prices.*

Where: *Punahou School, 1601 Punahou Street, Honolulu.* ***When:*** *January 29 and 30.* ***How:*** *Free admission. Call 808/944-5753 for information.*

FEBRUARY

☐ **Narcissus Festival.** For three weeks before and five days after the Chinese New Year (which usually falls in the first week of February), a series of lantern parades, fashion and flower shows, banquets, house-and-garden tours, the crowning of the Narcissus Queen, and dancing in the streets. For information, call the Chinese Chamber of Commerce at 808/533-3181.

MARCH

☐ **Prince Kuhio Day.** Hawaii's beloved "people's prince" and first delegate to the U.S. Congress is honored with impressive ceremonies at Prince Kuhio Federal Building. At Kuhio Beach in Waikiki, the site of his home, a memorial tablet is decorated with leis. Hawaiian societies hold special programs and events. Mar 26.

MARCH/APRIL

☐ **Easter Sunrise Service** at Punchbowl Cemetery is a moving Honolulu tradition. Apr 11 in 1993.

APRIL

✪ ***MERRIE MONARCH FESTIVAL COMPETITIONS.*** *Workshops, performances and more hula than you can shake a hip at. The state-wide olympics of hula, and one of the most popular events in the islands. Nightly television broadcasts are watched by just about everyone.*

Where: *Wailoa Center, Hilo, Hawaii.* ***When:*** *Mid-April.* ***How:*** *Around January 1, send order to Merrie Monarch Festival, Dorothy Thompson, Director, Waiakea Villas, Building 8, Room 289, 400 Hulani St., Hilo, HI 96720 (tel. 808/935-9168). Payment by cashier's check or postal money order only. (Note: If orders are received too far in advance, they will be returned with a request to resubmit closer to Jan 1.) Prices for 1993 were unavailable at press time; for 1992, they were $15 for open seating, $20 for reserved seating.*

MAY

✪ ***LEI DAY.*** *May Day is Lei Day in Hawaii. Lei competitions are held throughout the state. Everybody wears a lei, a Lei Queen is crowned, and there's a Lei Day concert at the Waikiki Shell, usually with the beloved Brothers Cazimero in the evening.*

Where: *Oahu events are held in Kapiolani Park.* ***When:*** *May 1.* ***How:*** *Tickets are on sale at Waikiki Shell after 5pm (before that at Blaisdell Center and Sears outlets). The price is around $15 for general admission. Come early, bring a picnic supper and a blanket, and join Hawaii's people for a joyous event. Some visitors plan their entire trip around this event.*

☐ **Buddha Day.** Flower festival pageants at island temples throughout the state celebrate the birth of Buddha. May 7.

JUNE

☐ **Kamehameha Day.** A state holiday (many offices closed), honoring Kamehameha the Great, Hawaii's first monarch. It's one of the biggest celebrations of all; there are parades and festivities all over the islands. In Honolulu, the annual King Kamehameha Celebrations Floral Parade includes floral floats, pageantry, Pa'u mounted riders, bands, and more, concluding with a cultural and arts festival at Kapiolani Park. June 11, with festivities starting a few days earlier.

JULY

☐ **Hale'iwa Bon Odori Festival.** This is one of the happiest and most colorful events in the islands, and includes traditional dances to welcome the arrival of departed souls in paradise. The dances are sponsored by Japanese Buddhist temples whose members practice their steps for months. Usually mid-July.

☐ **Prince Lot Hula Festival.** Local hula halaus perform ancient and modern hulas in a festival that honors King Kamehameha V. At Moanalua Gardens in Honolulu. Usually the third week in July.

AUGUST

✪ ***35TH ANNUAL HAWAIIAN INTERNATIONAL BILLFISH TOURNAMENT.*** *This is the leading international marlin fishing tournament in the world, and it draws fishers and fans from everywhere.*

Where: *Kailua-Kona, Big Island.* ***When:*** *Aug 14–29, with a parade around Aug 22.* ***How:*** *Book rooms in Kailua-Kona well in advance; the place is mobbed. Telephone 808/836-0974 for information.*

SEPTEMBER

☐ **Aloha Festivals.** Take the celebrations of all the ethnic groups, roll them into one, and you'll get some idea of Aloha Festivals, which are held on the different islands in a more-or-less progressive order. The Asian, Polynesian, and Western groups all get together for this *hoolaulea* (gathering for a celebration), each vying to demonstrate the warmth and beauty of the wonderful Hawaiian aloha. Music and dance events, demonstrations of ancient arts and crafts, a beautiful orchid show, water sports, an enormous flower parade, pageants, the crowning of both a king and a queen, are featured. Check with the Hawaii Visitors Bureau for the exact dates of the Aloha Festivals. They usually begin on Oahu in mid-September, then move to Hawaii, Molokai, and Lanai, before ending in late October on Kauai and Maui. Telephone 808/944-8857 for information.

OCTOBER

✪ ***WAIMEA FALLS PARK MAKAHIKI FESTIVAL.*** *Hawaiian games, music, and food are featured in this festival, whose highlight is the Hula Kahiko Competition, in which ancient dances of Hawaii are performed.*

Where: *Waimea Falls Park, Oahu.* ***When:*** *Usually the first week in October.* ***How:*** *Events are included in general admission to the park. For information, telephone 808/638-8511.*

✪ ***GATORADE IRONMAN WORLD TRIATHLON CHAMPIONSHIPS.*** *Only world-class athletes need apply. This internationally acclaimed event includes a 2.4 mile swim, a 112-mile bicycle ride, and a 26.2 mile run, with no resting between events.*

Where: *Kailua-Kona, Big Island.* ***When:*** *Usually the first week in October.* ***How:*** *Make reservations at least six months in advance. For information, telephone 808/329-0063.*

NOVEMBER

☐ **Kamahameha School Hoolaulea.** This old-time Hawaiian festival features continuous hula, Hawaiian and contemporary entertainment, arts and crafts, Hawaiian children's games, and food. Festivities are held on all five islands; on Oahu, at Kamehameha Schools. Usually mid-November. For information, telephone 808/832-4104.

☐ **Mission Houses Museum Christmas Fair.** This popular Honolulu event features many specialty gift items for Christmas and food. Craftspeople from all over the islands show their wares. Free admission. Thanksgiving weekend. For information, telephone 808/531-0481.

DECEMBER

☐ **Bodhi Day.** The enlightenment of Buddha is commemorated with religious observances in the Buddhist temples and with Japanese dance programs and ceremonies elsewhere. Nearest Sunday to Dec 7.

✪ ***HONOLULU MARATHON.*** *This is one of the most popular—and scenic—U.S. marathons. It draws some 15,000 entrants, about 10,000 from Japan, but many from the U.S. mainland, Europe, and Canada.*

Where: *The marathon starts at Ala Moana Beach Park and ends at Kapiolani Park.* ***When:*** *December 13.* ***How:*** *Spectators line the route; no admission fees.* For runners: *To obtain entry forms, send a stamped, self-addressed business-size envelope to Honolulu Marathon Association, 3435 Waialae Avenue, Honolulu, HI 96816.*

- ☐ **Princess Bernice Pauahi Bishop's Birthday.** Hawaiian societies and schools remember the beloved princess at the Royal Mausoleum. Dec 19.
- ☐ **Christmas.** What could be nicer than a Polynesian Christmas? There aren't any chimneys, so Santa might arrive in an outrigger canoe or on a surfboard. He might—it's not as bad as it sounds—be wearing a hula skirt. Carols are sung to ukulele accompaniment. Christmas lights are hung on everything from evergreens to bamboo. There are special programs for children at the Honolulu Academy of Arts. The stores are jammed, just as they are on the mainland, but surprisingly, a view of the bustling crowds (thronging the mall at Ala Moana Center, for example) is one of the prettiest of holiday pictures. The Christmas greeting: "Mele Kalikimaka!"
- ☐ **New Year's Eve.** "First Night," a moveable feast of theater, music and dance performances, art exhibits, and cultural demonstrations is held on sidewalks, streetcorners, and in lobbies and store windows all over town. Otherwise, celebrations are much like those on the mainland, except that the firecrackers are noisier (Asian style), costume balls are held at the leading hotels, and purification ceremonies are performed at Buddhist temples (visitors welcome). Jan 1 is open house among island Japanese families.

3. HEALTH & INSURANCE

HEALTH You don't have to worry about unsanitary food or polluted drinking water in Hawaii. Standards of sanitation are very high, and the islands have an excellent supply of pure water (except in some mountain areas where there is a problem with acid rain). As far as health goes, Hawaii is way ahead of the rest of the United States: Males have a life expectancy of 74 years compared to 66.5 on the mainland; females have a life expectancy of 78.1 years compared to 73 for women in the other 49 states.

INSURANCE It probably won't be necessary for you to take out any insurance for your trip to Hawaii if you already have adequate coverage at home. Take a look at your current insurance policies first. Many plans cover doctor and hospital visits you may need while traveling. Your homeowner's insurance policy may cover stolen luggage. Your automobile insurance may be sufficient for Hawaii. Should you not be adequately covered, you might contact the following organizations to get supplemental insurance:

Access America, 6600 West Broad St., Richmond, VA 23230 (tel. 804/285-3300, or toll free 800/424-3391), offers a comprehensive travel insurance package, including medical expenses, on-the-spot hospital payments, medical transportation, baggage insurance, trip-cancellation insurance and collision-damage insurance for a car rental. Their 24-hour hotlines connect you to coordinators who can offer advice and help on medical, legal, and travel problems.

Carefree Travel Insurance, P.O. Box 310, Mineola, NY 11501 (tel. toll free 800/645-2424), offers comprehensive plans that include trip cancellation, interruption, and delay; accident and sickness medical expense; accident insurance; emergency evacuation; and baggage loss and baggage delay. A telephone hotline offers worldwide assistance with medical, travel, and legal problems.

Travel Guard International, 1145 Clark St., Stevens Point, WI 54481 (tel. toll free 800/826-1300), has been endorsed by the American Society of Travel Agents as its preferred supplier of travel insurance. Included in its comprehensive coverage are medical and accident insurance, medical transportation, on-the-spot hospital payment, baggage insurance, trip-cancellation insurance with penalty waiver, and collision-damage insurance for a car rental. They also have a 24-hour worldwide emergency service network.

4. WHAT TO PACK

An important way to save money on your Hawaiian trip is to give careful thought to the clothes you take and the way you pack. First rule is not to go on a big shopping spree in advance—the Hawaiian stores are packed with colorful island resort clothes at prices lower than those you'll probably pay at home.

Second important rule: Try to limit yourself to one suitcase (you can also carry a small travel bag for reading matter on the plane, then use it later as a beach bag). If you can carry your own bag, you are not dependent on porters, bellhops, and expensive taxis. Having a light bag, or a bag with wheels (or at least one of those wheeled luggage carriers), is practically essential, since it's sometimes difficult to locate porters at the airports, and in small hotels and condos you are usually expected to carry your own luggage.

If you plan to shop, you may want to leave some space for bringing back the things you'll buy. It's best to buy your luggage before you go; it will generally be more expensive in Hawaii, although we've been able to purchase reasonably priced, lightweight luggage at many of the Woolworth's stores in Hawaii. If, however, despite your best intentions, you find you've got just too much to carry home, head for one of the inexpensive gift stores (like ABC in Honolulu), and buy yourself one of those soft, standup bags (usually under $25).

CLOTHING You need only spring or summer clothes of the simplest kind. There are no extremes in temperature between day and night, so you don't need the usual all-purpose travel coat or overcoat you'd take to Europe or Mexico—unless you're coming from the eastern United States and plan to spend a few days in San Francisco on the way back; then you'll have good use for it. A light raincoat is helpful, and so is a folding umbrella—and let's hope you won't need them! Women will find a stole or shawl useful at night. The only heavy garment that you will require is a warm sweater or hooded parka for exploring the volcano regions on the islands of Hawaii and Maui. Good canvas or other heavy-soled hiking shoes and socks are a must for hiking or for trekking over recent lava flows on Hawaii.

For Men Island dress is extremely casual, and many of our readers say they've never worn a suit in the islands! Some of the fancier places do require a jacket for dinner, however. The islands are dotted with quick-service launderettes (many apartment-hotels have their own), so you can have a stack of clothes washed and ready to wear in a few hours. Think about buying a colorful aloha shirt when you're in

Hawaii (it's worn outside the trousers and cut a little fuller than the usual sports shirt). You can use it back home for beach or country wear.

For Women Before you pack, you'll want to know a little bit about what women wear in Hawaii. Allow us to introduce you to the muumuu, the most comfortable garment known to woman. Try one and see. They're loose enough to provide their own inner air conditioning, require a minimum of underwear underneath (the girdle industry must be nonexistent in Hawaii), and look pretty enough to flatter almost everybody—especially large women, who look positively graceful in them. (You'll see more than a few hefty Polynesian women, by the way, a carryover from the days when the *alii,* the nobility, cultivated fat as a royal status symbol.)

The thing we love most about Hawaiian fashion is that many women wear muumuus or other long dresses outdoors, especially at night. Even though many island women are extremely fashion-conscious and favor the same kinds of spring-summer fashions that might be seen in New York or Paris or San Francisco, the muumuu is still seen, especially on "Aloha Fridays," when many women wear them to work. You'll see full-flowing muumuus (the colorful Hawaiian version of the Mother Hubbards the missionaries forced on the natives); long, slim adaptations of classic Chinese tunics; or, prettiest of all, holomuus, long muumuus, slightly fitted at the waist. We strongly urge you to buy a long dress while you're in the islands. You can use it later for an at-home gown, and you'll have a great time walking through the streets with it swishing gracefully at your ankles. Be sure that the muumuu at least touches the instep if you want to look like a kamaaina. You may also want to buy a short muumuu or island-style sundress; the selection is tremendous, and the prices suit everybody. Of course, many women visitors live in pants and shorts in Hawaii, and there's no reason why you shouldn't. It's just that muumuus are so much more a part of the island scene.

We should warn you: Matching aloha shirts and muumuus for couples are considered definitely "tourist tacky" by the local people.

So pack your bathing suit (or get a bikini in Hawaii), a sturdy pair of sandals or sneakers (maybe some hiking boots if you're going to go out on the trails), a lightweight woolen sweater, stole, or throw to wear in the evenings, a warm jacket if you're going up into the mountains. Leave your stockings at home; only businesswomen seem to wear them. You'll live in sandals or Japanese zoris, or go barefoot the way many islanders do. (Island kids, by the way, wear shoes as little as possible, usually not even to school, with resulting household crises when they need to find their shoes to go to a movie or restaurant.) The idea, in summer, is to fortify yourself against the heat by wearing open shoes and sleeveless dresses. Leave all your city cottons and little dark dresses at home. In the winter months, when Hawaiian weather can be springlike, pants and tops are practically a uniform. And T-shirts are worn everywhere, year round. Wash-and-dry clothes are helpful but not crucial, since launderettes are so handy. As for jewelry, the only kind most people wear is island craft, shell or coral necklaces, and the like, which can be picked up in any gift shop. The most beautiful jewelry of island women is the natural kind: blossoms in the hair, flower leis around the neck.

A final word on Hawaiian clothing: We don't want to give you the impression that the islanders never get dressed up. They do, especially for fancy social events. In downtown Honolulu, businesswomen wear more conservative summer clothing, and many men wear regular business suits with tuck-in shirts. But that's for work—not fun.

OTHER ITEMS It's not necessary to bring a travel iron from home: Most hotels have boards and irons for guests. Get plastic bottles for your liquid toilet articles; they won't break and they take up less space. Seal perfume bottles with wax for plane flights. Get little packets of cold-water soap and scatter them in odd corners of your suitcase. The plastic clotheslines, complete with miniature clothespins and soap, sold in most department stores, are very, very handy. Those inflatable or plastic hangers are good to have too, since you can't always count on finding wooden hangers on which to drip-dry your clothes in an inexpensive hotel. Disposable wash-up tissues are nice to carry with you, particularly on long plane or auto trips.

SOME PRECAUTIONS Let's hope your suitcase won't be stolen, lost, or misdirected onto the airlines to Australia. But it doesn't hurt to take a few sensible precautions, especially if you're flying in a huge group where bags often get shipped to the wrong hotels and you may have to go without them for several hours. Always tag your bags, inside and out, with your name and home address. Inside each bag, put a note that gives your address in Hawaii—so that, if your bag should arrive at somebody else's hotel, it can easily be sent to yours. Carry with you your valuables, medicines, prescriptions, cameras, and so on—anything that you can't easily replace if your bag is among the missing.

5. TIPS FOR THE DISABLED, SENIORS & FAMILIES

FOR THE DISABLED Disabled people are made very welcome in Hawaii: There are more than 2,000 ramped curbs on Oahu alone, hotels provide special facilities, and tour companies offer many services. In fact, the Society for the Advancement of Travel for the Handicapped considers Oahu the country's most accessible place. Helpful brochures are available for each island. Each brochure lists accessibility features of Hawaii's major hotels, shopping malls, beach parks, and sightseeing and visitor attractions. Write to the **Commission on Persons with Disabilities,** 5 Waterfront Plaza, Suite 210, 500 Ala Moana Blvd., Honolulu, HI 96813 (tel. 808/586-8121), or to **Hawaii Centers for Independent Living,** 677 Ala Moana Blvd., Suite 118, Honolulu, HI 96813 (tel. 808/537-1941; TTY/TDD, 521-4400). Enclose a check or money order for $3 payable to *Aloha Guide to Accessibility.*

Handicabs of the Pacific, P.O. Box 22428, Honolulu, HI 96823 (tel. 808/524-3866), provides special transportation facilities for the disabled: wheelchair taxi service and a variety of tours, including luaus, cruises, and sightseeing journeys.

FOR SENIORS See "Educational/Alternative Travel," below, for information on educational tours for seniors.

For information on activities for senior citizens, contact the **Hawaii State Senior Center** (tel. 808/847-1322) and be sure to check local newspapers for special events, sightseeing tours, picnics, etc.

Discounts for seniors are available at almost all major attractions in the islands, and occasionally at hotels and restaurants. When making a hotel reservation, always ask. Members of the American Association of Retired Persons (AARP), 1990 K St. NW, Washington, DC 20049 (tel. 202/872-4700), are usually eligible for discounts.

In Honolulu, seniors can ride MTL buses free at all times after obtaining a bus pass at 811 Middle St. (tel. 808/848-4444).

If you're visiting some of the national parks on the neighboring islands, like Hawaii Volcanoes National Park on the Big Island, you may get a **Golden Age Passport** free. It can be picked up at the park, and is available to anyone over age 62 who can show proof of age.

FOR FAMILIES Hawaii is a very easy place to travel with children (we did it with our own daughter for many years). Airlines provide a discount for children under 12, and most hotels allow children to stay free in their parents' rooms providing they use existing bedding (there is usually a fee for a crib or a rollaway bed). Strollers can be easily rented. Many restaurants offer special menus for the *keikis,* as they're called here. And you'll have no trouble amusing children—in addition to numerous attractions suitable for them, they have the best playground in the world right at their doorstep—the beach.

6. EDUCATIONAL/ALTERNATIVE TRAVEL

Everybody has a different idea of what travel should be like. If your ideas include some hands-on participatory tours as opposed to the "just looking" variety; or if you wish to learn something new while you're on vacation; or if you're interested in going to a spa or to a New Age center where you can cultivate body, mind, and spirit—all against a background of the natural beauty of the Hawaiian Islands—read on.

You'll see that for these tours and trips, you'll need to break our usual $75-a-day budget. But while these may be considered "Big Splurges," all of them represent excellent value.

Note: Other active adventures—snorkeling, horseback riding, helicopter trips, and the like—are listed in their appropriate chapters.

EDUCATIONAL/STUDY TRAVEL

You've had enough of sightseeing, swimming, shopping, and the usual tourist pleasures. Want to learn something new, stimulate your imagination and curiosity? The following will provide some suggestions.

FOR SENIORS If you're 60 or older, or the spouse or companion of someone of that age, you are eligible to participate in one of the splendid Elderhostel educational programs, held all over the world, and sometimes in Hawaii. Rates are reasonable. Write or call for their latest catalog: **Elderhostel,** 76 Federal St., Boston, MA 02110-1941 (tel. 617/426-7788).

FOR ALL AGES **Nature Conservancy of Hawaii,** 1116 Smith St., Honolulu, HI 96817 (tel. 808/537-4508), a local affiliate of the Nature Conservancy, a national, nonprofit conservation organization, runs week-long natural-history tours of Maui and Molokai, which include in-depth tours of nature preserves and accommodations at luxury hotels. Fees are on the high side. Weekend tours and day trips may also be offered. Write or call the Field Trip Coordinator at the above address for information or reservations.

Oceanic Society Expeditions, Fort Mason Center, Building E, San Francisco, CA 94123 (tel. 415/441-1106, or toll free 800/326-7491), is a nonprofit environmental education and research organization providing specially designed natural-history expeditions. Since 1972 Oceanic's expert naturalists have led small groups to destinations such as Hawaii, Micronesia, Indonesia, Africa, the Arctic, the Antarctic, and the Americas. Oceanic is the travel affiliate of Friends of the Earth, a global environmental advocacy organization. Planned for 1993 is a five-day Hawaii Whale Watch, including meals and accommodations aboard the vessel and naturalist leadership, for about $995. Write or call for schedules and itineraries.

University Research Expeditions Program, Desk M05, University of California, Berkeley, CA 94720 (tel. 510/642-6586), offers a number of research programs in the United States and abroad; the cost of the programs may be tax-deductible. Write for information about current offerings. Previous trips included a three-week expedition to the island of Lanai to study the social patterns and behavioral interactions of spinner dolphins; a two-week $1,395 expedition to Hawaiian petroglyph fields on the Kona coast of the Big Island to compare the ancient rock art of Hawaii with that of other Polynesian sites; and another two-week $1,395 expedition to the Big Island to study volcanic formations.

Want to take a summer course? The **University of Hawaii** enrolls more than 17,000 summer students in some 500 courses. Get into Hawaii's social and cultural mix with, perhaps, some Asian Studies courses in history, languages, literature, etc. For a physical view of the islands, try ethnobotany, geography of the islands, or oceanography. For a catalog and details, write in advance to the Summer Session office, 101 Krauss Hall, 2500 Dole St., Honolulu, HI 96822. The university's noncredit summer courses are also intriguing. How about sailing, stained-glass craft, ikebana (Japanese flower arranging), hula, ESP, and self-hypnosis—for starters?

READERS RECOMMEND

"I have a suggestion for vacationers who would like to make a very reasonable trip. My mother took two very interesting but not difficult courses at the University of Hawaii, one on the geography of Hawaii, the other on the botany of Hawaii. Both courses enhanced our trip very much. My mother is a teacher, and with these credits she moved up one notch in her income bracket, about $1,000! Also, for the time she was in school (about two months), the trip was deductible from her taxes!" —Bonny Warner, Mt. Baldy, Calif.

HOME EXCHANGES

If you'd like to exchange your own home or apartment for a place to stay in Honolulu, contact the **Vacation Exchange Club,** P.O. Box 820, Haleiwa, HI 96712 (tel. toll free 800/638-3841), a worldwide home-swapping group. You can be listed in their directory for $50 a year and find out what's available in Hawaii. (A recent listing, for example, offered a three-bedroom/two-bath house, along with two cars and two bikes, in the posh Kahala region, for a three-month exchange.) Rentals are also available. Vacation Exchange Club provides information only (it is not a travel agency); the actual arrangements are all up to you.

Another organization that provides a similar service is **Intervac US International Home Exchange,** P.O. Box 590504, San Francisco, CA 94159 (tel. 415/435-3497, or 800/756-HOME). Membership fee to be listed in one of their directories is $45 plus postage and handling; subscription to the publication only is $55 plus postage and handling. All told, they have nearly 8,500 home listings, with about 100 in the Hawaiian Islands—on Oahu, Maui, Kauai, and the Big Island.

Teachers have more time for vacations than most of us, so it was inevitable that a service like **Teacher Swap Directory of Homes** would come about. They have an excellent list of international locations, as well as quite a few in Hawaii. The price is $40 for both a listing and the directory, $45 for the directory only. Contact Teacher Swap, P.O. Box 4130, Rocky Point, NY 11778 (tel. 516/744-6403).

READERS RECOMMEND

"We spent five weeks in Oahu, having previously arranged to exchange homes with a couple who lived in a delightful home in Manoa Valley. Surprisingly, many island people do like to have excursions to the mainland, and home exchange is an ideal way of providing the basis

for a really inexpensive vacation. A government employees' bulletin circulates in Honolulu and elsewhere, and at the University of Hawaii; this provides a good place to advertise." —David Brokensha, Santa Barbara, Calif.

NEW AGE CENTERS & ACTIVITIES

Several programs and retreats in the serene Hawaiian environment are listed below.

ON OAHU The **Foundation of I, Inc.** (Freedom of the Cosmos), 2153 N. King St., Suite 321 B, Honolulu, HI 96819 (tel. 808/842-3750), presents evening lectures and classes on Ho'oponopono, an ancient Hawaiian process of problem solving that was updated for today's world by the late Morrnah Simeona, a native Hawaiian. Classes are presented in Honolulu, throughout the islands, and in many other parts of the world.

Science of Mind Center of Hawaii, 2909 Waialae Ave., Honolulu (tel. 808/735-6832), is a nondenominational organization that offers classes, workshops, and seminars. Sunday services are at 11am.

Silva Mind Control Training, P.O. Box 4466, Kaneohe, HI 96744 (tel. 808/247-5458), welcomes graduates and others seeking training to the seminars and workshops offered.

Unity Church of Hawaii, 3608 Diamond Head Circle, Honolulu, HI 96815 (tel. 808/735-4436), not far from Waikiki, warmly welcomes visitors to services held every Sunday at 7:30, 9, and 11am. Minister John Strickland is an outstanding inspirational speaker; singer Guy Merola is one of the island's best voices. After the program, meet the people and browse in the excellent New Age bookstore. Classes and workshops are held on such subjects as relationships, yoga, tai chi, nutrition, and holistic healing.

ON THE BIG ISLAND [HAWAII] The **Dragonfly Ranch,** P.O. Box 675, Honaunau, HI 96726 (tel. 808/328-2159, or toll free 800/487-2159), is a private retreat on the Kona coast, a two-minute drive from Honaunau Bay, an ancient Place of Sanctuary, with beaches and snorkeling. Hosts Barbara Moore and David Link will work out arrangements to provide guests with either total privacy or total attention: The Royal Treatment can include lomi-lomi (Hawaiian massage), health-oriented meals, fasting, flower essences, exercise program, and references to many healers. Amenities of this two-bedroom country home include private sun decks, an outdoor canopied waterbed, cable TV, fireplace, organic garden, and beautiful landscaping. Also available for B&B rentals. Rates range from $80 to $140 a day and $400 to $700 a week. For information, contact Barbara Moore and David Link at the address above.

Kalani Honua, P.O. Box 4500, Pahoa, HI 96778 (tel. 808/965-7828, or toll free 800/800-6886), is Hawaii's prime intercultural retreat and conference center and offers a varied program of workshops and seminars in everything from dance and the arts to sports, health, and personal growth. Kalani Honua itself sponsors a limited number of programs, including an African/Hawaiian Dance Festival in June, and a Merrie Monarch Festival Cultural Celebration, which coincides with the annual hula competition held on the Big Island every spring. The cost of programs varies with each group. Kalani Honua is located in a spectacularly beautiful spot on the Kalapana coast, near a black-sand beach, and consists of four two-story wood lodges, each with an ocean-view meeting room/studio space on the upper level and a shared kitchen on the ground floor. There are accommodations for individuals, couples, families, and groups (see Chapter 12, "The Big Island," for specifics). Meals are largely vegetarian, with fish or fowl option. There's a pool, a spa, a sauna, and a hot tub. Guests are welcome to attend conferences, schedule their own, or use the facilities for their own personal vacations or retreats.

ON MAUI The **Akahi Farm and Bamboo Mountain Sanctuary,** 915 Kapakalua Rd., Haiku, Maui, HI 96708 (tel. 808/572-8795 for the farm or 808/572-5106 for the sanctuary), is a unique spot, a combination retreat center and bed-and-breakfast establishment situated on 55 magnificent acres on the slopes of Haleakala, overlooking the ocean far below. The place is rented to groups for workshops and seminars—in meditation, or yoga, or aikido, or rebirthing—and New Age teachers of the caliber of Ram Dass, Brook Medicine Eagle, Paul Horn, and Robert Masters, to name a few, are frequent presenters. You can write to the farm for a brochure about forthcoming workshops, or, if you're already in Maui, simply call the owner, Rick Smith, and he may be able to find an opening for you.

Adjoining the farm is the Bamboo Mountain Sanctuary, until recently known as the Old Maui Zendo. This wonderful old plantation house, with a huge deck overlooking the ocean, really was a Zen monastery for 17 years. Now it's a B&B, but still given over to those who favor quiet pursuits; arrangements can be made for guests who wish to work with alternative health-care practitioners (Hellerwork, rebirthing, etc.), some of whom reside on the grounds. Rooms are nicely furnished with queen-size or double futons on frames, and have Japanese artwork on the walls and a lovely spare—but not monastic—aesthetic. Some of the rooms have private baths, but the shower is shared. Rates are $55 for one, $75 for two, seventh day free. Breakfast, served on the deck, features papayas from their own trees and bananas from their own banana plantation. A wonderful spot for a healing retreat, solitary or communal.

Miracles Unlimited, 81 Central Ave., Wailuku, Maui, HI 96793 (tel. 808/242-7799), is a charming store that sells jewelry, crystals, fine art, art-to-wear, books, cards, gifts, and more, and should be a first stop for anyone interested in where the classes, workshops, lectures, and other New Age happenings are taking place. On the first Wednesday of each month they have an Ohana Luncheon at which they present speakers; the cost is $15, and much networking takes place. Once a month, they publish a complete calendar of events through their Alaya Unlimited office at 56 Central Ave.; it's yours free at the bookstore, or write them before your visit to get a copy. The shop is open Monday through Saturday from 10am to 5:30pm.

Romy Leah, the founder and director of Miracles Unlimited, is also in charge at **Island Adventures,** 760 S. Kihei Rd., no. 608, Kihei, Maui, HI 96753 (tel. 808/879-0108), a service that offers "magical journeys in nature." Romy custom-tailors programs for small groups or individuals. Programs include hiking in Hana and in Haleakala Crater, a hike to birthing pools used by ancient Hawaiian women, a trip to bamboo forests and waterfalls, canyons, and ocean-fed pools, and more. Off-island trips to Lanai and Kauai are also available. Romy provides a safe, easy, and loving environment for people of all ages. Hikes are provided on a donation basis ($40–$70 per day is suggested), of which 10% will be sent to a nonprofit environmental organization. Out-of-pocket expenses (plane, boat, meals, lodging, etc.) will be charged accordingly.

Natalie and John Tyler, 3270 Kehala Dr., Kihei, HI 96753 (tel. 808/879-0097), who describe themselves as "fun-loving and spiritual psychotherapists who specialize in PAIRS" (Practical Application of Intimate Relationship Skills), have opened their lovely home in the Kihei area as a B&B accommodation for "nonsmoking, conscious people." Their house is a mile from the beach and is filled with books, artwork, and classical music. Guests can watch the sunset over the ocean with cool drinks and pupus on the deck and enjoy morning breakfast on the screened porch to the sound of birds. They offer an ocean-view room for $80 a night ($75 per night for three days or more, $60 a night for a week) and a mountainside room for $75 ($70 per night for a three-day stay, $55 a night for a week's stay). Optional extras include a daily "Course in Miracles" meditation; gourmet dinners with wine on the screened porch; and individual, couple, and family therapy. Snorkeling, scuba lessons, and special trips are also available. Contact the Tylers for reservations.

ON KAUAI Dr. Serge Kahili King, who was adopted and trained by a Hawaiian family in the ancient traditions of Polynesian Huna, is in charge of **Hawaiian Shaman Training,** c/o Aloha International, P.O. Box 665, Kilauea, HI 96754 (tel.

toll free 800/877-7277, ext. 888, from the U.S. mainland and 808/826-9097 from Hawaii and Canada), which presents frequent workshops in the islands. His organization also operates the Kauai Village Museum & Gift Shop in Kapaa (tel. 822-9272).

Pick up a copy of ***The Source,*** P.O. Box 1259, Koloa, HI 96756 (tel. 808/246-9535), a free bimonthly newspaper, for listings and notices of New Age activities on Kauai, and on the Big Island and Maui as well. You'll find information on retreats, workshops, classes—everything from crystals and channeling to rebirthing, self-transformation, and yoga.

HOLISTIC HOLIDAYS

SPA & FITNESS CENTERS At the **Plantation Spa,** 51-550 Kamehameha Hwy., Kaaawa, HI 96730 (tel. 808/237-8685 or 237-8442), 14 lucky guests at a time can be pampered in the first health spa on Oahu, housed in one of the last true Hawaiian retreats, snuggled between the ocean and mountains in Kaaawa. The seven-acre estate stretches all the way to the mountains and has its own waterfall, a nearby river, a pool on the grounds, and the ocean just across the street. Director Bodil Anderson, from Sweden, runs her retreat more like a European health spa than a fitness center, and combines exercise classes, beach walks, mountain hikes, canoeing, massages, herbal wraps, and the like with mind exercises, iridology, and classes in cooking, food combining, and how to maintain the proper alkaline/acid balance in the body. European juice fasting is available, and very popular. Don't be surprised if you see familiar television and movie faces here, as it's a popular place for celebrities—Richard Chamberlain, Margaux Hemingway, and Susan Ruttan ("L.A. Law"'s Roxanne) have been guests. The six-night program costs $1,145 per person double occupancy, $1,490 single occupancy. A two-night/two-day program is $411 per person double, $526 single.

Three of the fabulous Hyatt Resorts in Hawaii offer extraordinary spa facilities. Newest and most opulent is the beachfront Spa Grande at the $600-million **Grand Hyatt Wailea Resort & Spa,** 3850 Wailea Alaniu, Wailea, HI 96753 (tel. 808/875-1234, or toll free 800/233-1234), which combines the philosophies and practices of European, Japanese, and American spas. It offers such unique services as a soni relaxation room, a cascading waterfall massage, and green- and black-sand body treatments. Lomi-lomi massage, Hawaii ti-leaf wraps, and limu (seaweed) baths are some of the special only-in-Hawaii services.

On the Big Island of Hawaii, there's ANARA (*A New Age Restorative Approach*) Spa at the **Hyatt Regency Waikoloa,** 1 Waikoloa Beach Dr., Kohala Coast, HI 96743 (tel. 808/885-1234, or toll free 800/233-1234). Eastern and Western philosophies are blended to offer guests at the fantasy resort spa options like oceanfront tai chi, yoga and meditation classes, morning power walks, five kinds of facials, seven kinds of massage (including lomi-lomi), and body treatments utilizing products from the sea.

On Kauai, there's another ANARA Spa at the **Hyatt Regency Kauai,** 1571 Poipu Rd., Koloa, Kauai, HI 96756 (tel. 808/742-1234, or toll free 800/233-1234), a tropical sanctuary whose design alone helps guests unwind. Each massage room has its own private garden and open-air lava-rock shower. In keeping with the resort's authentic island theme, services include an ancient Hawaiian clay treatment and a ti-leaf body pack which alleviates the effects of sunburn.

All three Hyatt spas offer services to nonguests as well as guests and have facilities for both men and women. A great way to give yourself a holiday treat.

Kauai Lagoons Spa is at The Westin Kauai, Kalapaki Beach, Lihue, Kauai, HI 96766 (tel. 808/246-5062), and you needn't be a guest at this fabulous resort to enjoy the facilities and services of its plush European health spa. Visitors can sign up for a massage, facial, full-body skin treatment, or wellness screening, all of which include unlimited use of the spa facilities and exercise classes for the day. If you're feeling especially indulgent, treat yourself to one of their comprehensive day packages, like the Spa Experience, which includes a massage, in-depth facial, and full-body skin treatment of your choice for $165. Or experience the Total Wellness Package, which includes a range of wellness screenings by a qualified health professional, consultations, and a take-home fitness program for $200. A variety of pampering services are offered, including facials, massage, and skin treatments.

After your visit to the spa and/or the Wellness Center, have a lovely light lunch at the Terrace, an indoor/outdoor restaurant featuring spa cuisine and overlooking the swimming pool and the mountains beyond. Then wander and explore the other features of this fabulous seaside playground (see Chapter 11, "What to See and Do on Kauai").

7. ADVENTURE/WILDERNESS TRIPS

The spectacular beauty of the Hawaiian Islands is made to order for exciting adventure travel opportunities. Here's a sampling.

Neophyte and experienced outdoorspeople alike can enjoy the 13-day, three-island adventure trips planned by **Pacific Quest,** P.O. Box 205, Haleiwa, HI 96712 (tel. 808/638-8338, or toll free 800/776-2518), the islands' leading adventure travel company. Zane Bilgrav, the young owner, leads small groups in snorkeling, hiking, camping, and more on the islands of Kauai, Maui, and the Big Island. Two nights of camping at the beach alternate with two nights of lodging in rustic cabins in mountainous volcano areas. Most participants are in the 25–40 age group, but there are many older couples and young family groups as well. The cost, around $1,650, includes all expenses—meals (except for one dinner), group camping equipment, the services of two guides, ground and air transportation, and boat charters within the islands (the trip starts in Kauai and ends in Honolulu).

Trips that are sensitive to environmental and cultural issues are offered by the **Sierra Club,** 730 Polk St., San Francisco, CA 94109 (tel. 415/776-2211), an organization that has set the standard for wilderness travel. Most trips are of 7–10 days' duration, and are held from spring through Christmas. Most are on the Big Island, and several are on Maui, Kauai, and sometimes on Molokai. These are considered leisurely trips, with some backpacking portions. Bicycle tours are also available. There's often a choice of activities: hiking a trail or lazing on a beach. Price range is $760–$1,080 per week, including all ground costs. For the current catalog, write to the above address and enclose a $2 check made out to the Sierra Club. Profits from these trips help support the conservation efforts of the Sierra Club.

BICYCLING TOURS

We've had excellent reports on a bicycle touring service that promises fascinating adventures on the islands of Hawaii, Maui, and Kauai: **Island Bicycle Adventures,** P.O. Box 458, Volcano Village, HI 96785 (tel. 808/967-8603, or toll free 800/233-2226). Ron Reilly and his associates are all dedicated cyclists who gave up professional careers in other fields, and what they really enjoy is taking people off the beaten tourist track. Although there are reputable mainland companies that also offer bicycle tours of the islands, none has the insights, understanding, and local experience that these people have. Trips are exceptionally well planned; they do the work and the participants have the fun. Six-day/five-night cycling tours—Maui Magic, Kauai Keepsake, and Hawaii Highlights—cost approximately $885 per tour based on double occupancy, and include all accommodations, meals, maps, a support van, and the guidance of two experienced leaders. This does not include your bicycle rental or your airfare to the islands. There's a maximum of 12 on each tour.

Backroads Bicycle Touring, 1516 Fifth St., Suite Q422, Berkeley, CA 94710 (tel. toll free 800/BIKE-TRIP from U.S. and Canada), is a well-known outfit that runs bicycling tours in Europe, China, the U.S., and the Pacific. From November through April, they take a number of tours to Hawaii. Couples, singles, families, and seniors of all levels of ability are welcome. Tours, which average $140 a day, include all meals and accommodations at attractive inns. Write for their free catalog.

BACKPACKING/HIKING

Crane Tours, c/o Bill Crane, 15101 Magnolia Blvd., Suite H10, Sherman Oaks, CA 91403 (tel. 818/784-2213, or Ron Jones at 714/773-5570), offers moderate to moderately strenuous trips for experienced backpackers. Planned for 1993 are two series. A backpacking/kayak series includes backpacking in Haleakala Crater in Maui and in Waimea Canyon on Kauai ($700 each trip) and backpacking ($700) or kayaking ($875) on the Na Pali coast of Kauai. A second series explores the Big Island, Maui, and Kauai in week-long trips at similar prices. Bring your own tents and backpacks. One or two nights are spent in mountain cabins, and the last night is usually spent in a hotel. Prices include ground transportation, breakfast, and dinner; participants make their own lunches. Groups are usually 10–15 people. Day hikes are also offered. Summer only.

ON OAHU The **Hawaiian Trail and Mountain Club,** P.O. Box 2238, Honolulu, HI 96804 (tel. 808/534-5515 or 808/488-1161), welcomes visitors to join weekend and holiday hikes with an avid group of outdoor enthusiasts. Check the schedule in Thursday's "Today" section of the *Honolulu Star-Bulletin,* or, several weeks before your visit, send a stamped, self-addressed legal-size envelope for their current schedule. Add $1.25 and you will receive a packet of valuable information about hiking and camping in Hawaii.

Contact the **Sierra Club,** Hawaii Chapter, P.O. Box 2577, Honolulu, HI 96803 (tel. 808/538-6616), for hiking information. They also have groups on Maui, Kauai, and the Big Island.

ON THE BIG ISLAND Shena W. Sandler of **Wilderness Hawaii,** P.O. Box 61692, Honolulu, HI 96839 (tel. 808/737-4697), leads a unique wilderness experience. An accomplished outdoorswoman and former instructor for the Hawaii Bound School, Sandler leads backpacking trips in Hawaii Volcanoes National Park that are designed to be adventurous and challenging, to take people beyond their set limitations. Although most of her work is with Hawaii's teenagers, she will put together 4- to 15-day trips for groups of at least six people of any age. Cost of the 4-day trip is $300; the 15-day trip, $900.

On **Hawaiian Walkways,** P.O. Box 2193, Kamuela, HI 96743 (tel. 808/885-7759), psychologist Dr. Hugh Montgomery, a longtime Hawaii resident, leads day-long and half-day hikes (see Chapter 13, "What to See and Do on the Big Island," for more information). For minimum groups of four he will also lead three-day/two-night camping trips along the Ala Trail, with stops for swimming, sunning, exploring historical artifacts, and visiting petroglyph fields. At night, around the campfire, the groups learn the history and legends of old Hawaii. All camping equipment is provided; no backpacking is necessary. The trip is for those who are "reasonably fit" and can handle about six hours a day of hiking under a hot sun. No children under 12. Cost is $425 for the Thursday-to-Saturday trips.

ON MAUI Ken Schmitt is everybody's favorite naturalist and tour leader (see

Chapter 15, "What to See and Do on Maui"), and in addition to his regular day hikes, he designs special itineraries with lodging in country inns for groups of four to eight people. Prices start below $600 per person for five days of trekking and six nights of lodging, including lunches and some breakfasts. Contact **Hike Maui,** P.O. Box 330969, Kahului, HI 96733 (tel. 808/879-5270).

WATER SPORTS

Hawaii holds out myriad opportunities for snorkeling, scuba diving, underwater photography, windsurfing, and more.

KAYAKING TRIPS In addition to simple half-day kayaking trips for beginners ($48) and one-day sea-kayaking adventures along Kauai's southeast coast in the shadow of 2,000-foot cliffs ($105 for a full-day excursion), **Outfitters Kauai,** P.O. Box 1149, Koloa, HI 96756 (tel. 808/742-9667), also offers an escorted Kayak Experience along the Na Pali cliffs, either as a one-day trip from Haena to Polihale following trade winds and currents, or as a two-or-more-day expedition featuring camping at Kalalau and Miloli'i, some of the most breathtakingly beautiful spots on the islands. Two-person kayaks may also be rented for self-guided tours to jungle rivers. Each boat comes with racks/straps to secure it to your car, maps, and personal information to help you select the ideal river. The cost is $30 or $60 for one- or two-person kayaks. Their store is located at Poipu Plaza, 2827A Poipu Rd.

Kayak Kauai–Na Pali Outfitters, 1340 Kuhio Hwy., Kapaa (tel. 808/822-9179), or on the Main Street in Hanalei (P.O. Box 508, Hanalei, HI 96714; tel. 808/826-9844), offers summer (May to September) journeys along 14 miles of Kauai's dramatic Na Pali coastline that involve some of the most challenging wilderness paddling to be found in Hawaii. Five-day packages cost $782 per person. The same company offers guided one-day kayak trips around the Na Pali cliffs, including lunch on an isolated beach ($115), and a three-hour Hanalei Wildlife Refuge and Bay Snorkel and/or Kapaa Reef Paddle and Snorkel tours ($45). Their private canoe/kayak rentals, $48 and up for two persons, are very popular. From October to April, you can kayak Kipu Kai, the "little Na Pali," on Kauai's south shore; paddling, snorkeling, and whale watching are included ($90). Hiking and camping tours are also offered—guided one-day hiking tours ($75) and multiday camping expeditions ($150 a day). Winter trips are also offered on the Big Island.

SAILING CRUISES With **Honolulu Sailing Company,** 47-335 Lulani St., Kaneohe, HI 96744 (tel. 808/239-3900, or toll free 800/829-0114), you can sail away aboard a sleek, modern yacht to the islands of Oahu, Maui, Lanai, and Molokai. This company runs day, overnight, and one-week cruises out of Honolulu Harbor, combining sailing and snorkeling, at rates of about $60 for a half day, $130 overnight. Nautical weddings and whale-watching cruises are specialties. Boats sleep 4 to 10 passengers. There's hot and cold running water and private state rooms for couples. One-day sailing, snorkeling, and Zodiac trips on Oahu are also available for about $95 per person.

SAILING/HIKING ECOTOURS ON HAWAII The goal of **Eye of the Whale,** Marine/Wilderness Adventures, P.O. Box 1269, Kapaau, HI 96755 (tel. 808/889-0227, or toll free 800/657-7730), is to promote understanding of Hawaii's delicate ecosystem through firsthand experience. Beth and Mark Goodoni lead 7- to 10-day hiking/sailing adventures for groups of no more than 6–10 people. Days are spent outdoors—hiking through mountain valleys and jungles or sailing the Big Island's Kona coast—but nights are spent either on boats (for sailing trips) or in scenic inns and B&Bs. There is no backpacking or camping. Beth, a marine biologist and naturalist, introduces participants to the natural history of Hawaii and emphasizes the origin and identification of tropical flora, the development and exploration of coral-reef ecosystems, and the biology and observation of marine mammals. On the boat, she's the crew; husband Mark is the licensed USCG captain. Costs are about $125–$140 per day, including meals, accommodations, transportation, and inter-island fares. A highlight of the trip is a private luau, where guests learn to dig the imu, string their own leis, and dance the old-time hulas.

SCUBA-DIVING PACKAGES **On Oahu** At **Aaron's Dive Shop** (tel. 808/262-2333) you'll get custom-designed package tours to suit a variety of needs. Four-day certification courses are offered. They also offer some neighbor-island trips. Call for details.

On Kauai With **Aquatics Kauai** (tel. 808/822-9213, or toll-free 800/822-9422), seven nights in a beachfront condo, a Tropical Rent A Car, and three dives begin at $739 double occupancy.

On the Big Island You can get dive packages at **Jack's Diving Locker** (tel. 808/329-7585, or toll free 800/345-4807), and **Kohala Divers** (tel. 808/882-7774) charges for only four days if you take a five-day package.

Packages offered by **Kona Coast Divers** (tel. 808/329-8802, or toll free 800/KOA-DIVE) include lodging at Kona Billfish Condos and transportation to dive sites. Rates for three nights/two days and four dives are $348 single and $253 per person double. Rates for five nights and six dives are $551 single, $394 per person double.

Sea Paradise Scuba (tel. 808/329-2500, or toll free 800/322-KONA) offers lodgings at Kona Surf Resort and Keahou Beach Hotel, plus a rental car. Packages are available.

On Maui You'll get custom packages at **Dive Maui** (tel. 808/667-4363 or 667-2080), and **Lahaina Divers** (tel. 808/667-7497, or toll free 800/657-7885) offers seven nights at Plantation Inn, a Dollar Rent A Car, and three dives for $599 per person, based on double occupancy.

And **Sea Safaris Diving Center** (tel. 213/546-2464, or toll free 800/821-6670) offers a seven-night stay at Plantation Inn and three dive days, for $665–$765.

WINDSURFING PACKAGES **On Maui** **Maui Windsurfari,** P.O. Box 330254, Kahului, Maui, HI 96733 (tel. 808/871-7766, or toll free 800/736-MAUI), is the ticket for an ideal windsurfing vacation and is especially designed for the windsurfing enthusiast who can stay in Maui for a week or longer. Custom packages include choice of accommodations (ranging from quiet North Shore studios to deluxe oceanfront condos near prime sailing spots), rental cars with unlimited mileage, and high-tech sailboard equipment. Also available are windsurfing lessons using Hawaiian Sailboard Techniques (HST) by world-famous sailor Alan Cadiz. Complete seven-day land packages start at $469 per person in a double and $425 per person in a quad.

8. HAWAIIAN WEDDINGS

What could be nicer than marrying in Hawaii? You can marry and honeymoon in the same place, and the cost need not be exorbitant. The idea has become so appealing that thousands of visitors are now seeking out Hawaiian weddings in offbeat settings: on the beach, on top of a mountain, aboard a catamaran, in a helicopter—even in a church. For help in planning a Hawaiian wedding, you can contact several private organizations suggested by the Hawaii Visitors Bureau:

Aloha Wedding Planners offers a variety of picturesque locations and takes care of every detail, from the ministers to the photographers. Susan and Sheryl, the wedding coordinators in charge, are both incurably romantic and decidedly practical; they promise that their service is "always first class, even if your budget is strictly economy." Contact them at 1031 Auahi St., 2nd Floor, Honolulu, HI 96814 (tel. 808/523-1441, or toll free 800/288-8309), for a free brochure.

SOL-Hawaii (that's for "Sounds of Love") offers weddings in the great outdoors as well as in more intimate settings, and also on the neighbor islands. They can be reached at P.O. Box 8494, Honolulu, HI 96830-0494 (tel. 808/734-5441, or toll free 800/262-1995).

Rainbows are considered a good omen when they appear on the day of a wedding. **Rainbow Connection** does not guarantee one, but they do guarantee to coordinate your entire Hawaiian wedding at one of their beautiful sites—even on a yacht at sea. From standing in as witnesses to arranging video coverage, they take care of every detail. Prices run $195–$795. Contact Rev. Barry D. McLean, 45-995 Wailele Rd., Suite 73, Kaneohe, HI 96744 (tel. 808/247-0754).

Waimea Falls Park is one of Hawaii's most popular locations for weddings. The experienced staff can make all the necessary arrangements for the perfect ceremony and reception, including minister, flowers, music, limousine, champagne, and more. Custom wedding packages are available with a wide range of prices suitable for any budget. Contact the Wedding Department, Waimea Falls Park, 59-864 Kamehameha Hwy., Haleiwa, HI 96712 (tel. 808/638-8511).

Planning to marry in Maui? **Aloha! Hawaiian Weddings!** began by specializing in west Maui weddings, but it became so popular that it has expanded its services to the other major islands as well. They've been pioneers in planning romantic weddings for islanders as well as visitors for many years, offering everything from sunrise ceremonies on the slopes of Haleakala to sunset weddings at the beach, weddings on horseback in the mountains, or lavish Royal Hawaiian Wedding Luaus. Contact Kalani Kinimaka, who runs this family operation, at Aloha! Hawaiian Weddings!, Central Reservations, P.O. Box 8670, Honolulu, HI 96830-8670 (tel. 808/926-6688 or 926-6689), for wedding information on Maui, Kona, Kauai, and Waikiki.

On the Big Island, a sunset wedding at the lush **Kona Village Resort** would be pure heaven: P.O. Box 1299, Kaupulehua-Kona, HI 96745 (tel. toll free 800/367-5290). Guests of the glamorous **Kona Surf Resort** on the Big Island can be married at the hotel's Kona Royal Chapel. For information on wedding and honeymoon packages, contact Kona Surf Resort & Country Club, 78-128 Ehukai St., Kailua-Kona, HI 96740 (tel. toll free 800/367-8011).

On Kauai, the **Coco Palms Resort** has been a favorite wedding and honeymoon spot for years, with its private wedding chapel nestled amid a lush, 45-acre coconut grove. They'll do everything from selecting the minister, music, and flowers, to providing a Hawaiian conch-shell blower: P.O. Box 631, Lihue, Kauai, HI 96766 (tel. toll free 800/42-MARRY). The luxurious megaresort, the **Westin Kauai** at Kauai Lagoons, also offers some spectacular wedding ideas—like being married on a 40-acre lagoon overlooking the water at its Chapel by the Sea. The wedding couple is driven to the chapel in a horse-drawn carriage. Call the hotel's wedding consultant (tel. 808/245-5050) for information.

Kauai's restored-plantation estate of the 1930s, **Kilohana,** is also the site of numerous weddings; they can be held indoors in an elegant living room overlooking the gardens, in the gardens themselves, or even in a turn-of-the-century carriage riding through the plantation's grounds. Write to wedding coordinator Shelley Yokote at Kilohana, P.O. Box 3121, Lihue, Kauai, HI 96766.

Wedding Tips: If you're planning the details yourself, you should contact the State Health Department, 1250 Punchbowl St., Honolulu, HI 96813 (tel. 808/548-5862), for rules and regulations. You will need a permit to be married in a state park. Contact State Parks Division, P.O. Box 621, Honolulu, HI 96809 (tel. 808/548-7455). If you plan to be married in one of Hawaii's national parks, contact the Superintendent, Haleakala National Park, P.O. Box 369, Makawao, HI 96768 (tel. 808/572-9306); or the Superintendent, Hawaii Volcanoes National Park, HI 96718 (tel. 808/967-7311). Of course, if you use the services of a wedding planner, these details will be handled for you.

9. GETTING THERE

What will it cost you to travel to Hawaii? We wish we could tell you precisely, but our crystal ball is cloudy. Ever since the federal government deregulated the airline industry, competition—and massive confusion—has set in. Fares can vary from airline to airline, and even within one airline, depending on when you're going, how long you're staying, whether you make land arrangements through the airlines, and how far in advance you book your ticket. Fares can also vary depending on what new, low-cost gimmick one airline might introduce to beat the competition. But you can rely on this: The airlines want your business, and the 2,400-mile route from California to the Hawaiian Islands is a highly competitive one. A little smart shopping on your part and that of your trusted travel agent will usually turn up a good deal.

A tip: Try not to arrive in Hawaii on a weekend, when Honolulu is crowded with visitors from the outer islands. Everything is easier and less crowded on weekdays, especially checking into hotels, plus airfares are lower during the week.

BY PLANE

To get the very best deal on a ticket to Hawaii you have to do some intensive shopping. Either you or your travel agent should get on the phone to the airlines that serve Honolulu and your area (see below), and find out what the lowest possible prices are. Ask for the lowest economy-class fare. On a specific date last summer, for example, Continental Airlines offered a round-trip ticket from Los Angeles to Honolulu for only $373! Remember that you'll secure lower fares if you're willing to pay in advance, travel in the middle of the week rather than on weekends, and also in the fall or off-season rather than during holidays or peak winter vacation months.

THE AIRLINES The largest carrier with the most frequent service to Hawaii is United Airlines. Continental Airlines is the second-largest U.S. carrier serving Hawaii, with over 160 flights weekly. Its major connecting hubs are Denver, Newark, Cleveland, Los Angeles, Boston, and New Orleans; Honolulu is its main Pacific hub. Nonstop flights depart daily from Houston to Honolulu and then travel on to Tokyo nonstop, with a daily reverse flight. Continental has also recently expanded its service from Honolulu to Cairns and Brisbane, Queensland, and to Guam. As for fares, Continental frequently offers low-cost promotional fares, and you can also save a bundle by booking one of their package deals: In 1992, for example, a seven-night stay in Waikiki was available for $499, including round-trip airfare from Los Angeles! Packages to Maui, Kauai, and the Big Island are also available. Note that fares vary and restrictions apply, but, overall, this is one of the best travel bargains we know.

Airlines that fly into Honolulu include **America West Airlines** (tel. toll free 800/247-5692), **American Airlines** (tel. 808/526-0044, or toll free 800/433-7300), **Canadian Airlines International** (tel. 808/922-0533, or toll free 800/426-7000), **China Airlines** (tel. 808/536-6951, or toll free 800/227-5118), **Continental Airlines** (tel. 808/523-0000, or toll free 800/525-0280), **Delta Air Lines** (tel. toll free 800/221-1212), **Garuda Indonesian** (tel. 808/945-3791, or toll free 800/826-2829), **Hawaiian Airlines** (tel. 808/537-5100, or toll free 800/367-5320), **Japan Airlines** (tel. 808/521-1441, or toll free 800/525-3663), **Korean Air** (tel. 808/923-7302, or toll free 800/223-1155 on the East Coast, 800/421-8200 on the West

Coast), **Northwest Airlines** (tel. 808/955-2255, or toll free 800/225-2525), **Philippine Airlines** (tel. 808/536-1928, or toll free 800/435-9725), **Qantas** (tel. 808/836-2461, or toll free 800/227-0290), **Singapore Airlines** (tel. 808/524-6063, or toll free 800/742-3333), **Trans World Airlines** (tel. toll free 800/221-2000), and **United Airlines** (tel. 808/547-2211, or toll free 800/241-6523).

BEST-FOR-THE-BUDGET FARES **Super-APEX/APEX** Although it carries restrictions and cancellation penalties, this fare is decidedly the best for the budget. APEX stands for *A*dvance *P*urchase *Ex*cursion and typically you are required to reserve and pay for the ticket 14 or 21 days in advance, stay for a minimum and maximum number of days, and possibly fulfill some other requirements like flying before a specific date.

Continental's APEX fares Los Angeles to Honolulu range from $373 to $597 round-trip, depending on which days of the week you travel and how far in advance you purchase your ticket. They are invariably the cheapest way to fly. These fares are known interchangeably as economy or APEX fares.

Regular Airfares Here's a price breakdown on how economy-class tickets compare with business and first class. Continental's fares for a first-class ticket from Los Angeles to Honolulu in summer 1992 were $1,924 round-trip; business class, $1,676; full coach, $1,136; economy, $364–$664.

Special Promotional Fares You never know when an airline—or airlines—are going to offer promotional fares. Sometimes there's a price war, and then the consumer really benefits. Keep watching the newspapers for announcements of special deals. A few years ago, one airline was flying from Los Angeles to Honolulu for $99 for a very short period of time. Always ask your travel agent to inquire about promotional fares, too.

Bucket Shops These discount travel agencies purchase blocks of tickets direct from the airlines at wholesale prices, which they then discount. We found five agencies on the West Coast that offer flights to Hawaii at discounts ranging anywhere from 20% to 40%—depending on the season you fly and availability. You may do as well on your own or with your regular travel agent, but it wouldn't hurt to give these people a call and see what they might have for you. Remember that it's very difficult to return these tickets, and many restrictions apply: So once you've bought them, they're all yours.

The following agencies offer discount flights to Hawaii: **All Unique Travel,** 1030 Georgia St., Vallejo, CA 94590 (tel. 707/648-0237); **Euro-Asia, Inc.,** 4203 E. Indian School Rd., Phoenix, AZ 85018 (tel. 602/955-2742); and **Community Travel Service,** 5299 College Ave., Oakland, CA 94618 (tel. 510/653-0990).

JET LAG If you're going all the way through from the East Coast to Honolulu or the neighbor islands in one stretch—about 10 air hours—you'll be crossing at least six time zones, and your normal body rhythms are going to be thrown out of sync. Here are some tips for avoiding jet lag. First, several days before your departure, gradually accommodate your eating and sleeping times to be closer to those of your destination. You'll be heading west, so go to bed a little later each night and sleep a little later in the morning. When you come home, reverse that pattern. Second, avoid smoking, drinking, and heavy eating on the flight—another reason to bring your own picnic lunch! You may have heard of the Argonne Anti-Jet-Lag Diet, which alternates feasting and fasting for several days before departure, and is effective for many people. To get a free copy of the program (more than 200,000 cards have been sent out to date), send a stamped, self-addressed envelope to Office of Public Affairs, Argonne National Laboratory, 9700 S. Cass Ave., Argonne, IL 60439.

Our personal prescription for avoiding jet lag is to stop off at one of the airport hotels in either Los Angeles or San Francisco en route. For years we've enjoyed staying at the Los Angeles Airport Marriott, which has a pool set in a magnificent garden and a variety of restaurants, including the very reasonable Fairfield and Lobby Bistro. If you call far enough in advance (tel. toll free 800/228-9290), you may be able to get a Family Plan rate (for at least two people) during the week; weekend rates are always available, and both of these are approximately $79, about half the regular price. After a swim in the pool (or a workout in the exercise room), and a good night's sleep, we board our plane the next morning and arrive in Hawaii refreshed.

BY SHIP

Forget about it. Only luxury cruise ships now call at Honolulu Harbor.

PACKAGE TOURS

We usually prefer the do-it-yourself brand of travel, but some excellent values are available on group tours, which usually involve short periods of one or two weeks. Many package options are available: The most expensive ones park you at the luxury hotels and take you sightseeing in private limousines; the cheapest put you up in standard hotels, take you sightseeing in motor coaches, and may not provide meals. Do some careful studying and comparing before you sign up for one. Often you can find inexpensive restaurants that charge much less than what the tour companies figure on as the cost of three meals.

To help you get started, some of the major travel companies that offer tours to the outer islands are listed below. You can also consult your travel agent or airline for a variety of choices.

Akamai Tours, 2270 Kalakaua Ave., Honolulu, HI 96815 (tel. 808/922-4685, or toll free 800/922-6485).

American Express, 2222 Kalakaua Ave., Honolulu, HI 96815 (tel. 808/942-2666, or toll free 800/241-1700).

Hawaiian Holidays Tours, 2222 Kalakaua Ave., Honolulu, HI 96815 (tel. 808/926-9200).

Island Holidays Tours, 2255 Kuhio Ave., Honolulu, HI 96830-0519 (tel. 808/945-6000).

Pleasant Hawaiian Holidays, 270 Lewers St., Honolulu, HI 96815 (tel. 808/926-1833).

Trade Wind Tours of Hawaii, 150 Kauilani Ave. (P.O. Box 2198), Honolulu, HI 96815 (tel. 808/923-2071).

10. GETTING AROUND

INTERISLAND TRAVEL

BY PLANE

Hawaii's two major interisland carriers are Hawaiian Airlines and Aloha Airlines; both have been around for many years and offer similar fares, give or take a few dollars. Because fares change often, and because both offer periodic promotional fares and tie-ins with hotel and car-rental packages, it pays to do some personal shopping either by calling the airlines directly or by consulting your travel agent. Expect fares to be highest during peak winter and summer travel periods. Standby tickets are no longer offered.

Hawaiian Airlines (tel. toll free 800/367-5320) has recently put into effect one of the most exciting concepts in interisland travel in many years. Similar to a Eurail

FROMMER'S SMART TRAVELER: AIRFARES

1. Use a travel agent only if you know he or she will really put in time and effort to get you the cheapest fare; otherwise, do your own homework; it pays off!
2. Shop all the airlines that fly to your destination.
3. Always ask for the lowest fare, not just a discounted fare.
4. Keep calling: Airlines sometimes open up additional low-cost seats as departure date nears.
5. Make sure you purchase your tickets in advance to take advantage of the very cheapest APEX (advance purchase) fares.
6. Check "bucket shops."
7. Ask for air/land packages. Land arrangements are cheaper when booked with an airline ticket, although your choice of hotels is then limited.

train pass, the Hawaiian Airpass allows visitors to take an unlimited number of interisland flights for a flat fee. Considering that a regular flight costs $69.95, the bargains are substantial: A 5-day Airpass costs $129; a one-week pass, $149; a 10-day pass, $199; and a two-week pass, $239. With prices like these, you can island-hop at will, or use one island as your base and make day trips to see the others. For those with limited vacation time, it's ideal. In addition, users of the Hawaiian Airpass receive special prices on car rentals, hotels and condos, restaurants, and other visitor attractions with major companies like Alamo Rent A Car, Aston Hotels, Hyatt Resorts, Outrigger Hotels, and ITT Sheraton Hotels Hawaii. A phone call to the airline or to your travel agent can give you the details.

To save money on regular flights ($69.95), remember that the first and last flights of the day are $49.95. If you fly Hawaiian from the West Coast (Los Angeles, San Francisco, Seattle), simply add $40 to your round-trip fare for one neighbor island, or $60 if you make a stop in Honolulu. Special fares are available for senior citizens, children 2–11, and the military. Hawaiian's mileage program, known as "Gold Plus," offers many advantages, and Gold Plus members may also join Hawaiian's Premier Club and enjoy such extra niceties as free interterminal transportation, special check-in and boarding privileges, use of club lounges and free telephones, and priority baggage handling (membership is around $90 for one, $125 for a member and a spouse).

Aloha Airlines (tel. toll free 800/367-5250; TDD toll free 800/554-4833) has the only commuter partner in Hawaii. Together with its sister carrier, Aloha Island Air, it offers daily service to all 12 commercial airports in the islands, including exclusive service to Princeville, Kauai; Hana, Maui; and Kamuela, Hawaii. The regular fare is $69.95; Sunset and Sunrise flights are $49.95, the senior-citizen fare is $49.95, active-duty military pay $54.80, and children 2–11 are charged $52.95. Aloha also offers first-class service for $93.95. Aloha mileage counts toward Mileage Plus when you fly United Airlines or Canadian Airlines. Both Aloha and Aloha Island Air provide daily jet service to Lanai, scheduled to meet mainland connections. Aloha is highly regarded by frequent business travelers and rates very favorably in the area of passenger complaints, according to U.S. Department of Transportation surveys.

SAVING MONEY ON TRAVEL TO THE NEIGHBOR ISLANDS

- Take advantage of the Hawaiian Airpass if you have a limited stay.
- Note the special prices for the first and last flights of the day, as well as the senior, military, and other discounts mentioned above.

- Check the special fly/drive deals that Aloha and Hawaiian frequently make with the leading car-rental companies. If the airlines are sold out on any of these special programs, try a local travel agency; they'll often be able to help you.
- See the neighbor islands on your own. While many people do it the easy way, taking a package tour in which one flat fee, paid in advance, covers plane fares, hotels, meals, and sightseeing, we find it's usually cheaper to do it on your own, using the hotels and restaurants we suggest.
- Unless you have money to spare, don't "flightsee" the islands from the air, landing briefly for meals and hurried sightseeing and returning the same night; this is about as satisfying as those European jaunts that take you to seven countries in six days. And the one day costs about $175 to boot!

ON THE ISLANDS

Your major expense on the outer islands will be transportation. Only one city on one island—Hilo, on the island of Hawaii—has anything resembling a public transportation system, and even that is not very extensive. (Buses do cross the island of Hawaii east to west and back.) There is also bus service in the Lahaina-Kaanapali area of Maui, but none of the buses run for any great distance. So unless you want to stay put, you have only two choices: taking expensive sightseeing tours or renting your own car. The latter is not cheap either, especially on days when you must pile on a lot of mileage, driving from one end of an island to another. Plus, the high-season markup on hotels extends to car rentals and other visitors' services. The motto seems to be, alas: "Get what the traffic will bear."

BY RENTAL CAR

The quoted price for a car rental is not always what it appears to be. There have, in fact, been a great many complaints from consumer groups who are hoping to force the industry to include all mandatory charges in their basic advertised fees; many car-rental companies oppose the plan. Thus, the budget-wise car renter must be on the alert for hidden charges (delivery, drop-off, extra charges for drivers under 25, for example, and most especially, for insurance coverage).

It's a good idea to have a major credit card if you're going to rent a car in Hawaii. Otherwise, you'll have to pay cash in advance, or leave a deposit or a blank check with a personal signature.

Be sure to check your self-drive carefully before going on a long trip, and get a phone number where you can reach the agency at night in case of problems. Remember, too, to ask the agency for some good road maps indicating distances, and don't hesitate to ask questions and directions before you leave.

If you're under 21, you're out of luck here when it comes to renting a car. Hawaii state law prohibits anyone under 18 from driving with an out-of-state license (even though islanders can get licenses at 15!). There used to be one or two agencies that would rent to drivers 18–20, but at press time, there are none that we know of. There may be special stipulations for 21- to 24-year-olds, like paying a surcharge and having a major credit card. When you reach 25, you can just show your license, fill out the papers, and drive away.

A further tip: In general, it's cheaper to pick up a car at the airport than to have it delivered to your hotel and picked up when you're finished with it. And airport pickup, of course, avoids the costs of cabs or bus coming into town.

If you're going to visit several of the major islands, the easiest way to rent your cars is to make one telephone call to a company that provides service on all of them. We've had excellent cars and service from **Dollar Rent A Car** of Hawaii, one of the major companies in Hawaii, with locations on the *six* major islands—including Molokai and Lanai (it's the only major company on Lanai). There are half a dozen offices in Waikiki alone (one is at 333 Royal Hawaiian Ave.; tel. 926-4254); there are another half a dozen on Maui. Their range goes from economy cars like Geo on up to full-size sedans, Jeeps, convertibles, and Cadillac luxury sedans. For their compact cars with standard transmission, it's as low as $23 daily, $109 weekly; compact deluxe automatics go for $38 daily, $199 weekly. They will rent to drivers under 25 at an extra charge of $5 per day, with a major credit card. The local reservations number is 944-1544. For toll-free reservations from the U.S., call 800/367-7006.

Give **Alamo Rent A Car** a call and find out if they're offering one of their "Sun Sale" specials if you're traveling in the winter. They often offer a good deal on an economy two-door Metro; last year it was $20 per day, $98 per week. Regular rates are about $24 per day, $124 per week for an air-conditioned, automatic, economy car, all with unlimited free mileage. Alamo is in Honolulu, Waikiki, Maui, Hilo, Kona, and Lihue (cars at airport terminals on neighbor islands, courtesy bus in Honolulu). Call Alamo toll free at 800/327-9633, 24 hours a day. Certain restrictions apply, including age and credit-card requirements. Rates do not include gas, tax, or a nominal under-25 surcharge.

With a fleet of more than 10,000 cars, **Budget Rent A Car of Hawaii,** the well-known mainland and international car-rental agency, offers a vehicle for every taste and pocketbook. Since rates fluctuate so much, Budget does not care to quote them, but they're always competitive. Their exclusive gift program—given to all renters—includes many free admissions, meals, and gifts. There are 9 offices in Waikiki (tel. 922-3600) and 31 others throughout the state, with airport locations on Oahu, Maui, Kauai, and the Big Island. For reservations, call toll free 800/527-7000, or write Budget Rent A Car of Hawaii, Central Reservations, P.O. Box 15188, Honolulu, HI 96830-0188.

Friendly service and good deals are available at **Tropical Rent-A-Car Systems,** 765 Amana St. (tel. 957-0800), which offers flat rates only (no mileage charges). Automatic compacts with air conditioning begin at $21 daily and $119.95 weekly. Tropical features such G.M. cars as Geos and Pontiac Grand Ams and a few Geo Trackers. Convertibles are available. Tropical has offices on all the major islands and rents to drivers 21 years of age (with a major credit card) and to older drivers up to age 70. They have two offices in Waikiki (tel. 942-4293), or call toll free 800/678-6000.

National Interrent has convenient airport and downtown locations on Oahu, Hawaii, Kauai, and Maui, and offers competitive unlimited-mileage rates for all types of cars. They're known for excellent service. The toll-free number is 800/CAR-RENT.

Thrifty Car Rental has locations on Oahu, Maui, and Kauai (but not on Hawaii). They have direct-line courtesy phones at all baggage-claim areas. Usually, standard compacts rent for $29.95 daily, $169 weekly. There's no mileage charge. Call 833-0046 in Honolulu for reservations, or write to them at 3039 Ualena St., Honolulu, HI 96819.

Avis Rent A Car, Honolulu International Airport (tel. 834-5536), serves all five major islands, and offers a special for seven days of driving an automatic Dodge or similar car on a combination of two or more islands—about $147 a week. For toll-free reservations, call 800/831-8000.

Hertz Rent A Car, 233 Keawe St., Room 625, features an All-Island touring rate that covers seven days or more on any combination of the four major islands. Days do not have to be consecutive and there is no mileage charge. The seven-day rate starts at $149 for a compact car, or $32 for one day. Daily rates offer free unlimited mileage. For toll-free reservations and information, call 800/654-3131. Hertz has offices at airports and hotels on all the major islands. You are advised to reserve at least a day in advance. A major credit card is required.

AUTO INSURANCE Since Hawaii is a no-fault state, if you don't have insurance you are required to handle any damages before you leave the state. However, you may be able to avoid the cost of collision-damage waivers (anywhere from $10 to $12 per day), which the car-rental companies are eager to sell you, if your car insurance back home provides rental-car coverage. Your policy should include personal liability, property damage, fire, theft, and collision. Your insurance company should also be able to provide fast claim service in the islands. It would be a good idea to obtain the name of your company's local claim representative in Hawaii before you leave home; bring along your policy or identification card if you plan to do that. And check with your credit-card company to see if it provides rental-car coverage.

DRIVING TIPS In general, Hawaiian drivers seem more courteous than those in big cities on the mainland—and they often drive more slowly. You should be aware of some special rules:

- The state has a mandatory seat-belt law. Be sure to buckle up.
- You may make a right turn in the right lane at a stoplight after coming to a full stop, unless noted otherwise.
- You may make a left turn at the stoplight from the left lane on a one-way street onto another one-way street after coming to a full stop.
- The pedestrian is usually right.
- Remember that driving distances on the neighbor islands can be great, particularly on the Big Island, and you may have trouble finding gas stations open, especially on Sunday. Keep the tank full.
- Should you have a breakdown, call your car-rental agency for emergency service.
- Current mainland driving licenses may be used until their expiration date. After that, you'll need a Hawaiian license, obtainable from the Department of Motor Vehicles, for those 15 and older.

ROAD MAPS For most driving, the road maps printed in the various "Drive Guides" to the neighbor islands, and given free with your car rental, are excellent. Should you wish to have topographic maps, they can be ordered by mail from the Hawaii Geographic Society, P.O. Box 1698, Honolulu, HI 96808 (tel. 808/538-3952), or the Map Information Center, Federal Center, Denver, CO 80225.

SAVING MONEY ON TRANSPORTATION

- Shop around for the best car-rental deals: Be persistent.
- Inquire as to whether your hotel has a car-rental package. Outrigger Hotels in Honolulu, for example, provides free cars with every one of their thousands of hotel rooms. On the neighbor islands, car-rental packages are usually available from Sand & Seas hotels, among others. If you're staying in a small hotel or guesthouse, they may also be able to get you attractive rates; inquire when you make reservations.
- Remember that prices fluctuate according to the season; a car will always be a few dollars cheaper in the summer than in the winter, and when business is slow.

SUGGESTED ITINERARIES

Since it's easy enough to get to a neighbor island right after you land in Honolulu, you can be flexible with your itinerary. You might, for example, start in Honolulu, travel from there to Kauai, then to Maui, from there to Molokai, and on to Kona, where you pick up your plane for your return flight to Los Angeles or San Francisco. Another route that we have found very pleasant is to fly directly to Kona from the West Coast, then on to Maui, Molokai, and Kauai, making the last stop Honolulu, and departing from there for home. (Plan it this way if you want peace and quiet first, excitement later.)

IF YOU HAVE ONE WEEK Spend at least two or three days in Honolulu, then visit the neighbor island that appeals to you most.

IF YOU HAVE TWO WEEKS Spend four days in Honolulu, then five days each on two neighbor islands that appeal to you.

IF YOU HAVE THREE WEEKS Twenty-one days is enough time to see the three major neighbor islands—Maui, the Big Island, Kauai—plus Honolulu, and maybe a visit to Molokai too. We'd spend five days each in Honolulu, Maui, and the Big Island, four days on Kauai, and two on Molokai.

READERS RECOMMEND

"If you wait until you get to Hawaii to book your trips to the other islands, you can take advantage of the overnighter packages available, which include round-trip airfare for two and a room and rental car for two nights, for low fees, from Roberts of Hawaii. You have to be in the islands to make these reservations."—Kenneth Kendall, Omaha, Nebr. [Authors' Note: There are many deals like this that can only be booked from Hawaii, since the companies are usually forbidden from advertising them outside the islands; they are mainly for kamaainas. It's wise to check these out when you are in the islands.]

11. ENJOYING HAWAII ON A BUDGET

THE $75-A-DAY BUDGET

Our aim is to show you how to keep your basic living costs—*room and three meals only*—down to somewhere around $75 a day. The costs of transportation, shopping, sightseeing, and entertainment are all in addition to that figure.

By keeping room and meal expenses low, you can make a substantial dent in the overall cost of your trip. But more important, we believe you'll have more fun—and enjoy a more meaningful vacation—by relying on your brains rather than your pocketbook. Hawaii is one of the few places where you can still live comfortably on a limited budget. In fact, many people who used to travel abroad for their holidays are finding Hawaii one of the best bargain areas anywhere. And considering that this is an enormously popular resort area, $75 a day per person is very little to pay.

WHERE TO STAY

Hotel rates in Hawaii usually vary according to season and demand. The hotel industry is highly competitive, and room prices go up or down as conditions dictate. We've attempted in this book to tell you about the very best lodging values in Hawaii, whether in hostels, moderately priced hotels, or condos. If the B&B alternative appeals to you, check out the reservations services listed below. Remember that B&B accommodations are no longer necessarily the cheapest; that they are best for couples, since there is usually only one double (or queen-size) bed; and that they do not provide cooking facilities. For a family or several people traveling together, an apartment with kitchenette usually works out more economically. Also, most B&Bs are in residential areas rather than tourist areas, so a car is essential.

BED & BREAKFAST RESERVATION SERVICES Evelyn Warner and Al Davis started **Bed & Breakfast Hawaii,** P.O. Box 449, Kapaa, HI 96746 (tel. 808/822-

7771, or toll free 800/733-1632; fax 808/822-2723) years ago, "not as a big business operation, but as a low-key, intimate way for people to visit Hawaii." They offer accommodations in private homes and apartments on all the islands, for rates ranging from $35 to $50 single, $40 to $125 double, including continental breakfast. Working mostly with Dollar Rent A Car, they can often pass on substantial savings on car rentals to their guests. Write or phone for a free brochure. For $10, you receive a directory of homes and apartments with rooms for rent called *Bed & Breakfast Goes Hawaiian*.

Mary Lee, the woman who runs **Bed & Breakfast Honolulu,** 3242 Kaohinani Dr., Honolulu, HI 96817 (tel. 808/595-7533, or toll free 800/288-4666), doesn't believe directories do the trick; in almost 10 years of operating her business, she's found that almost any place a guest picks from a directory will probably be unavailable at the time the request comes in. So Mrs. Lee installed an 800 number and she, or one of her family, will engage you in a personal conversation and help you find accommodations—either a room in a home or a studio in an apartment building. She charges a $10 reservation fee for each unit she reserves. She currently offers more than 400 "homestays" and studios on all the major islands, even including Lanai! Prices range upward from about $40 single, $50 double. Mrs. Lee also handles car rentals and inter-island flights, and she can get you good discounts on each.

The lovely suburb of Kailua, not far from Waikiki, is the home of Doris Reichert, who runs **Pacific-Hawaii Bed & Breakfast,** 19 Kai Nani Place, Kailua, HI 96734 (tel. 808/263-4848, or toll free 800/999-6026; fax 808/261-6573). Most of her Oahu rentals are in that area. It's one of our favorites too, since both Kailua and Lanikai beaches are superb—and it's also one of the new meccas for windsurfers. She also has a few listings on Maui, the Big Island, and Kauai. Rates begin at $45 a day for a room for two with bed and bath, and go up to complete homes or estates that can accommodate up to 16 guests at $2,000 a week! She requests 20% of the cost of the stay for confirmation, but she promises a complete refund if the room does not meet your expectations or you do not take occupancy because of a serious emergency; she's serious when she says "satisfaction guaranteed."

Upscale B&B lodgings throughout the state are the province of **Hawaii's Best Bed & Breakfasts,** hand-picked by Barbara Campbell from her headquarters on the Big Island. Each home is selected for its distinctive personality, attention to details, and the warm hospitality of its hosts. Daily rates go from $65 to $150. For a brochure describing these hidden gems, contact Barbara Campbell, P.O. Box 563, Kamuela, HI 96743 (tel. 808/855-4550, or toll free 800/262-9912 for reservations).

Go Native . . . Hawaii, 65 Halaulani Place (P.O. Box 11418), Hilo, HI 96721 (tel. 808/935-4178, or toll free 800/662-8483), has been matching guests with Hawaiian hosts for more than a decade. Coordinator Fred Diamond has 250 locations on all islands except Lanai, ranging from oceanfront to mountain sites, from traditional B&B rooms in private homes to unhosted studios and cottages. Rates begin around $40 single, around $50 double.

My Island, P.O. Box 100, Volcano, HI 96785 (tel. 808/967-7110; fax 808/967-7119), is a Hawaii-island-only reservation service run by Gordon and Joann Morse; they have rentals all over the Big Island, and encourage people to move around to explore the different atmospheres and climates of the various districts. Prices range from $30 to $45 single, $45 to $85 double.

Focusing on Maui, but with accommodations on the Big Island and Kauai as well, **B&B Maui Style,** P.O. Box 98, Puunene, HI 96784 (tel. 808/879-7865, or toll free 800/848-5567), has charming accommodations all over the Valley Island, from oceanside to mountain slopes. They handle rooms in private houses from $45 to $60 double, and vacation rentals in condos, cottages, studios, and homes, which go for $65 to $100. They're happy to offer advice on out-of-the-way places and activities.

A CONDO & HOUSE-RENTAL SERVICE Savings of up to 50% on condo rentals can be realized by working through **HALE** (Hawaiian Apartment Leasing Enterprises), 479 Ocean Ave., Suite B, Laguna Beach, CA 92651 (tel. 714/497-4253, or toll free 800/854-8843, 800/472-8449 in California, 800/824-8968 in Canada), which handles rentals on all the major islands (including Molokai) with a wide range of prices, sizes, and locations. Most of the condos are custom-decorated and of high quality. Rates run roughly between $60 and $95 per night double. HALE also has some 200 private homes available, beginning with a two-bedroom/two-bath house in Kauai for $420 a week. Cleaning services, cooks, chauffeurs, day care, and additional custom services can be arranged.

CAMPING Camping is popular with families on all the islands, but, unfortunately, tent camping is no longer as safe as it used to be, and there is no place where one can rent a camper or RV. Should you decide to camp, note that advance permits are required. Check with the offices of the Hawaii Visitors Bureau (see "Information, Entry Requirements, and Money," above in this chapter) to find out where to obtain permits for each island.

SAVING MONEY ON ACCOMMODATIONS

- To stay within the $75-a-day budget, you should be part of a twosome, which means that you will have a total of $150 per day to spend on room and meals. Unless otherwise noted, the rates do not include Hawaii's hefty hotel tax—9.43%. Also, all rooms include baths, unless otherwise noted.
- Stay at a small apartment-hotel or condominium complex, complete with a built-in money-saving device: a kitchenette. This doesn't mean, however, that you'll spend your vacation slaving away at a hot stove. It means only that you'll fix breakfast, maybe pack a sandwich or some marvelous fresh fruit for a picnic or a light supper, and dine out once a day (preferably at lunchtime, when prices are always low and values best). We've scoured the state looking for budget apartment-hotels and have come up with a surprisingly large number of them.
- Find bed-and-breakfasts with the help of the organizations mentioned above.
- Avoid the winter season—mid-December to mid-April. That's when everybody seems to want to go to Hawaii, and many visitors—especially those from cold areas like western Canada and Alaska—often stay a few months at the budget apartment-hotels. Many hotels routinely impose a surcharge of as much as $10–$20 per room during that period. The summer months of June, July, and August are also busy, but many hotels maintain "low-season" rates in those months, and during the months of October, November, and May all kinds of choice rooms are yours for the picking. If you think you'd like to spend the Christmas–New Year's season in the islands, make reservations as far in advance as you possibly can; many hotels accept reservations as much as six months to a year in advance for this insanely popular period. The months of January and February are also extremely popular.
- Contact the **Hotel Exchange,** 1946 Ala Moana Blvd., Honolulu, HI 96815 (tel. 808/942-8544; fax 808/955-2627), which offers discounted hotel rooms. It works with 180 hotels on Oahu and all the neighbor islands and will take advance reservations over the phone with an approved credit card, or you can simply walk in and see them if you're already in town and not happy where you're staying. Savings can average $5–$10 a day at many leading hotels.

READERS RECOMMEND

"Some hotels will give a 25%–50% discount off published room rates for military personnel and their families. We stayed at three- and four-star hotels at half the normal room rate. I believe

that many of your readers are in the U.S. military and would be happy to know about this benefit!"—Joe and Robin Gruender, Wright-Patterson AFB, Ohio.

WHERE TO EAT

We'll show you how to eat inexpensively and well, figuring about $18 for dinner, about $5 or $6 for lunch, roughly $4–$5 for breakfast. Of course, whatever you save by eating in means that much more in the kitty for other pleasures.

Also, even though it's easier than it used to be to find inexpensive places to eat as you scoot around the islands because of the rise of fast-food outlets, it can be a long drive between meals. It's always a good idea to throw a few sandwiches and some fruit in your beach bag, along with the suntan lotion and the road maps.

SAVING MONEY ON MEALS

If you really want to save money, plan to eat breakfast and at least one meal a day at home; that's when your kitchenette apartment more than pays for itself. Remember that lunch is always cheaper than dinner—often for much the same meal. Early Bird specials offer excellent dinner bargains all over town.

OTHER BUDGET TIPS

SAVING MONEY ON SIGHTSEEING & ENTERTAINMENT

- Check local tourist publications for discount coupons.
- Consider renting a car from a company that gives out free coupons.
- Check numerous sources of free and low-cost entertainment in Chapter 7, "Honolulu Attractions."

SAVING MONEY ON SHOPPING

- Patronize the ABC stores for best prices on sundries and souvenirs.
- Check our listings of discount and outlet stores in Chapter 8, "Savvy Shopping in Honolulu."

SAVING MONEY ON SERVICES & OTHER TRANSACTIONS

TIPPING As in other mainland cities, standard restaurant tips are 15%. Baggage handlers and porters should receive 50¢–$1 for each large piece of luggage. To save money—carry your own. Cleaning service should get $1 per night.

TELEPHONE CALLS Check with your hotel to find out if there is a surcharge on calls. (There almost always is.) If so, use pay phones in the lobby.

MATTERS OF USAGE

It's preferable to refer to the residents of the 50th state as "islanders," rather than as natives or Hawaiians—unless they happen to be of Hawaiian descent. You are from the mainland, not the States; islanders are very sensitive about this. And don't make the dreadful mistake of calling Americans of Japanese ancestry "Japs." They're as proud of being Americans as any descendants of *Mayflower* passengers. During World War II, in fact, the Nisei volunteers so distinguished themselves in the bloody battles of southern Europe that their unit—the 442nd Regimental Combat Team—was designated probably the most decorated unit in United States military history. One of its veterans is Daniel K. Inouye (of Watergate and "Irangate" fame), chosen as

Hawaii's first representative in Congress, now its senior senator. The late Spark M. Matsunaga, formerly its junior senator, was also a veteran of the 442nd. Recent state leaders of Japanese ancestry have included the house leader, the past president of the University of Hawaii, the chairman of the Senate's powerful Ways and Means committee, and a number of judges. Remember, too, that although statehood was achieved only in 1959, residents of Hawaii have been American citizens since 1898, when, five years after the Hawaiian monarchy was overthrown in a bloodless coup with U.S. Marines standing by (a triumph for the haole sugar and other commercial interests), the Republic of Hawaii was annexed by the administration of President McKinley.

FAST FACTS HAWAII

Area Code All the Hawaiian Islands share one area code: 808.

Business Hours Most office workers in Hawaii are at their desks by 8am, sometimes even earlier, and it's *pau hana* (finish work) at 4 or 5pm, the better to get in an afternoon swim or a round of golf. Hawaii may be the only place where even executives can be reached by 8:30am! Normal bank hours Monday through Thursday are 8:30am to 3 or 3:30pm, until 6pm on Friday. Most shopping malls are open Monday through Friday from 9 or 10am to 9pm, on Saturday until 5:30pm, and for a shorter period on Sunday, usually until 4pm. Individual establishments at these malls will vary their hours, and some will close earlier than others.

Cigarettes Noncitizens over 21 are allowed to bring in 200 cigarettes or 50 cigars or two kilograms of tobacco.

Climate See "When to Go," in this chapter.

Crime See "Safety," below.

Driving Rules See "Getting Around," in this chapter.

Drug Laws Strictly enforced.

Electricity Hawaii uses standard North American current, 110 volts AC, 60 cycles.

Emergencies Dial 911 for an ambulance, a fire, or the police.

Holidays See "When to Go," in this chapter.

Information See "Information, Entry Requirements, and Money," in this chapter.

Language You don't have to learn a new language, since everyone speaks English. But the islanders do pepper their vocabulary with lots of Hawaiian words, and almost all place names are Hawaiian. So it's a good idea to bone up on a few pronunciation rules and learn a few words. The original Hawaiians spoke a Polynesian dialect, but they had no written language. Missionaries transcribed it in order to teach Hawaiians to read the Bible, and made it as easy as possible. There are only 12 letters in the Hawaiian alphabet: five vowels and seven consonants: *h, k, l, m, n, p, w*. Every syllable ends in a vowel; every vowel is pronounced, no matter how many there are in the word (these have a frightening way of piling up one after another); and the accent is almost always on the penultimate syllable (the next to the last), as it is in Spanish. Consonants receive their English sounds, but vowels get the Latin pronunciation: ***a*** as in farm, ***e*** as in they, ***i*** as in machine, ***o*** as in cold, and ***u*** as in tutor.

Lists of Hawaiian words can be obtained in most tourist offices, but check out our Appendix—"Hawaiian Vocabulary"—first. Do bear in mind that the name of the state is pronounced Ha-WYE-ee (it does not rhyme with how-are-yuh). You are a newcomer, a *malihini* (mah-lee-HEE-nee), and longtime residents of the islands are *kamaainas* (kama-EYE-nahs). The *haoles* (properly pronounced ha-O-lays, but more commonly HOW-lays) are the whites, originally foreigners.

The mysterious *lanai* (lah-*neye*) that landlords are always boasting about is nothing but a balcony or porch. *Kau kau* (*cow*-cow) means food; you'll go to a lot of luaus (*loo*-ows), Hawaiian feasts; and people will say thank you—rather, *mahalo* (mah-*hah*-low)—for your *kokua* (ko-*koo*-ah), your help. It's *kanes* (*kah*-nays) for men, *wahines* (wah-*hee*-nays) for women. You probably already know that a *lei* (lay) is a necklace of flowers. And just as you expected, everyone says *aloha* (ah-*low*-hah)—one of the most beautiful words in any language—meaning hello, good-bye, good luck, and *salud!* It also means love, as in "I send you my aloha."

Laundry Most hotels have washing machines and dryers for the use of guests; if not, self-service laundries can be found everywhere.

Legal Aid The main office of the Legal Aid Society of Hawaii is at 1108 Nuuanu Ave. (tel. 536-4302).

Liquor Laws The legal drinking age in Hawaii is 21.

Maps Island maps suitable for driving tours are supplied by car-rental companies; more detailed ones are available at most bookstores and newsstands. An excellent source is Hawaii Geographic Maps and Books, 49 S. Hotel St., Suite 218 (P.O. Box 1698), Honolulu, HI 96808 (tel. 808/538-3952). Write or call to request lists of suggested books and maps. They have USGS topographic maps of Hawaii, plus various other road maps. You can visit their small store at the above address when in Honolulu. On the Big Island of Hawaii, Basically Books, 45 Waianuenue Ave. (tel. 961-0144), in downtown Hilo, has a complete selection of maps of Hawaii, including USCG topographic maps, NOAA nautical charts, road and street maps.

Newspapers In Honolulu, it's the *Honolulu Advertiser* and the *Honolulu Star-Bulletin;* in Maui, it's the *Maui News;* in Kauai, the *Garden Island News.*

Radio/TV See "Fast Facts: Honolulu," in Chapter 4, for a comprehensive listing of Honolulu radio and TV stations. All the major islands are equipped with cable TV and get all major mainland television channels.

Rest Rooms Since this is the U.S.A., signs usually read MEN and WOMEN, although sometimes it will be KANES and WAHINES.

Safety Yes, it's true; there is crime and violence in Hawaii, as there is everywhere else in the world. And because Hawaii was indeed a trouble-free paradise for so many years, people tend to ignore basic safety precautions. Our advice is: Don't! Never carry large sums of cash; traveler's checks are much safer. Don't go hiking on deserted trails except in a group; don't go wandering on isolated beaches alone; and don't go jogging in the cane fields alone at the crack of dawn, as one crime victim did (there are many marijuana farms in secluded areas, and the owners do not take kindly to strangers). Stay in well-lighted areas at night, travel with a friend if possible, lock your car and remove valuables from your trunk, and use your common sense—just as you would at home. Follow these precautions, and you should find a visit to Hawaii no more dangerous than one to your own hometown.

It's always advisable to put your valuables into your hotel's safe or an in-room safe. If you don't want to use a safe, then at least take your valuables with you. Never leave them unprotected in a hotel room, to which any number of people—staff, service personnel, guests past or present, and others—could have access.

Taxes The hotel occupancy tax is 9.43%. Sales tax is 4%.

Telephone/Fax The cost of a local call (from any one part of an island to another) at a pay phone is 25¢. Inter-island calls cost more. Be aware that most hotels impose a surcharge on all calls.

Fax services are available at many copy centers around the islands, and at all Phone Mart locations (see separate chapters for listings).

Time There are five time zones between the East Coast of the United States and Hawaii. That means that when it's noon Hawaiian standard time, it's 5pm eastern standard time, 4pm central, 3pm mountain, and 2pm Pacific. Hawaii does not convert to daylight saving time as the rest of the nation does, so from May through October, noon in Hawaii would mean 6pm Eastern, 5pm central, and so on.

Tipping See "Enjoying Hawaii on a Budget," in this chapter.

Tourist Offices See "Information, Entry Requirements, and Money," in this chapter.

CHAPTER 3

FOR FOREIGN VISITORS

Although American fads and fashions have spread across Europe and other parts of the world so that the United States may seem like familiar territory before your arrival, there are still many peculiarities and uniquely American situations that any foreign visitor will encounter. The following text will explain some matters. It will also be wise to be alert for American customs as you explore Hawaii and other parts of the United States.

1. PREPARING FOR YOUR TRIP

ENTRY REQUIREMENTS

DOCUMENTS Canadian nationals need only proof of Canadian residence to visit the United States. Citizens of Great Britain and Japan need only a current passport. Citizens of other countries, including Australia and New Zealand, usually need two documents: a valid **passport** with an expiration date at least six months beyond the scheduled end of their visit to the United States and a **tourist visa,** available at no charge from a U.S. embassy or consulate.

To obtain a tourist or business visa to enter the United States, contact the nearest American embassy or consulate in your country; if there is none, you will have to apply in person in a country where there is a U.S. embassy or consulate. Present your passport, a passport-size photo of yourself, and a completed visa application, which is available through the embassy or consulate. You may be asked to provide information about how you plan to finance your trip or show a letter of invitation from a friend with whom you plan to stay. Those applying for a business visa may be asked to show evidence that they will not receive a salary in the United States. Be sure to check the length of stay on your visa; usually it's six months. If you want to stay longer, you may file for an extension with the U.S. Immigration and Naturalization Service once you are in the country. If permission to stay longer is granted, a new visa is not required unless you leave the United States and want to reenter.

MEDICAL REQUIREMENTS No inoculations are needed to enter the U.S. unless you are coming from, or have stopped over in, areas known to be suffering from epidemics, particularly of cholera or yellow fever.

If you have a disease requiring treatment with medications containing narcotics or drugs requiring a syringe, carry a valid signed prescription from your physician to allay any suspicions that you are smuggling illegal drugs.

CUSTOMS REQUIREMENTS Every adult visitor may bring in free of duty one liter of wine or hard liquor, 200 cigarettes or 100 cigars (but no cigars from Cuba) or three pounds of smoking tobacco, and $100 worth of gifts. These exemptions are offered to travelers who spend at least 72 hours in the U.S. and who have not claimed them within the preceding six months. It is forbidden to bring into the country most foodstuffs (particularly cheese, fruit, and cooked meats) and plants (vegetables, seeds, tropical plants, and so on). Foreign tourists may bring in or take out up to $10,000 in U.S. or equivalent foreign currency with no formalities; larger sums must be declared to Customs on entering or leaving.

INSURANCE

Unlike in most other industrialized countries, there is no national health system in the United States. Because the cost of medical care is extremely high, we strongly advise every traveler to secure health insurance coverage before setting out. You may want to purchase a comprehensive travel policy that covers sickness or injury costs (medical, surgical, and hospital); loss of, or theft of, your baggage; trip-cancellation costs; guarantee of bail in case you are arrested; and costs of accident, repatriation, or death. Such packages (for example, "Europe Assistance" in Europe) are sold by automobile clubs at attractive rates, as well as by insurance companies and travel agencies.

2. GETTING TO THE U.S.

Travelers from overseas can take advantage of **APEX (Advance Purchase Excursion) fares** offered by the major U.S., Asian, Australian, and European carriers. Aside from these, attractive values are offered by **Icelandair** on flights from Luxembourg to New York and by **Virgin Atlantic** from London to New York/Newark.

Some large American airlines (for example, TWA, American, Northwest, United, and Delta) offer travelers—on their transatlantic or transpacific flights—special discount tickets under the name **Visit USA,** allowing travel between any U.S. destinations at minimum rates. They are not on sale in the U.S., and must, therefore, be purchased before you leave your foreign point of departure. This system is the best, easiest, and fastest way to see the U.S. at low cost. You should obtain information well in advance from your travel agent or the office of the airline concerned, since the conditions attached to these discount tickets can be changed without advance notice.

The visitor arriving by air, no matter what the port of entry, should cultivate patience and resignation before setting foot on U.S. soil. Getting through immigration control may take as long as two hours on some days, especially summer weekends. Add the time it takes to clear Customs and you will see that you should make very generous allowance for delay in planning connections between international and domestic flights—an average of two to three hours at least.

In contrast, for the traveler arriving by car or by rail from Canada, the border-crossing formalities have been streamlined to the vanishing point. And for the traveler by air from Canada, Bermuda, and some places in the Caribbean, you can sometimes go through Customs and Immigration at the point of departure, which is much quicker and less painful.

For further information about travel to Hawaii, see "Getting There," in Chapter 2.

FAST FACTS FOR THE FOREIGN TRAVELER

Business Hours **Banks** are typically open Monday through Friday from 8:30am to 3pm, and there's 24-hour access to the automatic tellers (ATMs) at most banks and other outlets. Generally, **offices** are open Monday through Friday from 9am to 5pm. **Stores** are open six days a week with many open on Sunday, too; department stores usually stay open until 9pm one or more days a week.

Climate See "When to Go," in Chapter 2.

Currency The U.S. monetary system has a decimal base: one American **dollar** ($1) = 100 **cents** (100¢). Dollar bills commonly come in $1 ("a buck"), $5, $10, $20, $50, and $100 denominations (the last two are not welcome when paying for small purchases and are not accepted in taxis or by mass-transit). There are six coin denominations: 1¢ (one cent or "penny"), 5¢ (five cents or "nickel"), 10¢ (ten cents or "dime"), 25¢ (twenty-five cents or "quarter"), 50¢ (fifty cents or "half dollar"—rare), and the rare $1 pieces (both the older, large silver dollar and the newer, small Susan B. Anthony coin).

You can easily cash **traveler's checks** in *U.S. dollars* in payment for goods or services at most hotels, motels, restaurants, and large stores. The best rates, however, are given at banks; a major bank is also the only place where you can confidently cash traveler's checks in any currency other than U.S. dollars.

The most widely used method of payment by travelers in the United States is **credit cards.** In Hawaii, VISA (BarclayCard in Britain, Chargex in Canada) and MasterCard (EuroCard in Europe, Access in Britain, Diamond in Japan) are accepted almost everywhere; American Express and JCB, a Japanese card, by most establishments; Diners Club and Carte Blanche, by a large number; Discover, by an increasing number; enRoute is beginning to come into favor as well. Use of "plastic money" reduces the necessity to carry large sums of cash or traveler's checks. It is accepted almost everywhere, except in food stores selling groceries and liquor. Credit cards can be recorded as a deposit for car rental and used as proof of identity (often preferred to a passport) when cashing a check, or as a "cash card" for withdrawing money from banks that accept them.

Currency Exchange Many hotels will exchange currency if you are a registered guest. Otherwise, **Thomas Cook Currency Services** (formerly Deak International) (tel. toll free 800/582-4496) offers a wide variety of services: exchange of more than 100 currencies, commission-free traveler's checks, drafts and wire transfers, check collections, and precious metal bars and coins. Rates are competitive and service excellent.

Note: The foreign-exchange bureaus so common in Europe are rare even at airports in the U.S. and are nonexistent outside major cities. Try to avoid exchanging non–U.S. money or nondollar traveler's checks at small-town banks or even at bank branches in a big city. In fact, leave most non-U.S. currency at home—it may prove to be mostly a nuisance.

Drinking Laws See "Fast Facts: Hawaii," in Chapter 2.

Electricity The U.S. uses 110–120 volts A.C., 60 cycles, compared to 220–240 volts A.C., 50 cycles, as in much of the rest of the world. Besides a transformer (sometimes incorrectly called a converter), small appliances of non-American manufacture, such as hairdryers or shavers, require a plug adapter with two flat, parallel pins.

Embassies and Consulates All embassies are located in the national capital, Washington, D.C.; some consulates are located in major cities, and most countries have a mission to the United Nations in New York City.

Listed here are the embassies and some consulates of major English-speaking countries. Travelers from other countries can obtain telephone numbers for their embassies and consulates by calling "Information" in Washington, D.C. (tel. 202/555-1212).

The embassy of **Australia** is at 1601 Massachusetts Ave. NW, Washington, DC 20036 (tel. 202/797-3000). The Australian consulate in Hawaii is at 1000 Bishop St., Penthouse, Honolulu, HI 96813 (tel. 808/524-5050). There are consulates on the mainland West Coast at 611 N. Larchmont Blvd., Los Angeles, CA 90004 (tel. 213/469-4300), and at 360 Post St., San Francisco, CA 94108 (tel. 415/362-6160); and on the East Coast in the International Bldg., 636 Fifth Ave., Suite 420, New York, NY 10111 (tel. 212/245-4000). Other Australian consulates are in Chicago and Houston.

The embassy of **Canada** is at 501 Pennsylvania Ave. NW, Washington, DC 20001 (tel. 202/682-1740). There are Canadian consulates on the mainland West Coast at 300 S. Grand Ave., Suite 1000, Los Angeles, CA 90071 (tel. 213/687-7432); One Maritime Plaza, Golden Gateway Center, San Francisco, CA 94111 (tel. 415/981-8541); and 412 Plaza 600, Sixth and Stewart, Seattle, WA 98101 (tel. 206/443-1777). On the East Coast, there's a consulate at 1251 Ave. of the Americas, New York, NY 10020 (tel. 212/768-2400). Other Canadian consulates are in Atlanta, Buffalo (N.Y.), Chicago, Cleveland, Dallas, Detroit, and Minneapolis.

The embassy of the **Republic of Ireland** is at 2234 Massachusetts Ave. NW, Washington, DC 20008 (tel. 202/462-3939). There are Irish consulates on the mainland West Coast at 655 Montgomery St., Suite 930, San Francisco, CA 94111 (tel. 415/392-4214); and on the East Coast in the Chase Bldg., 535 Boylston St., Boston, MA 02116 (tel. 617/267-9330); and 515 Madison Ave., New York, NY 10022 (tel. 212/319-2555). There's another Irish consulate in Chicago.

The embassy of **New Zealand** is at 37 Observatory Circle NW, Washington, DC 20008 (tel. 202/328-4800). The only New Zealand consulate in the U.S. is at 10960 Wiltshire Blvd., Suite 1530, Los Angeles, CA 90024 (tel. 213/477-8241).

The embassy of the **United Kingdom** is at 3100 Massachusetts Ave. NW, Washington, DC 20008 (tel. 202/462-1340). There's a consulate on the mainland West Coast at 1766 Wiltshire Blvd., Suite 400, Los Angeles, CA 90025 (tel. 310/477-3322), and a consulate-general on the East Coast at 845 Third Ave., New York, NY 10022 (tel. 212/745-0200). Other British consulates are in Atlanta, Chicago, Houston, and Miami.

Emergencies In most areas of Hawaii, call **911** for fire, police, or an ambulance. In areas without a central 911 line, dial **0** (zero, not the letter "O") to speak with an operator.

If you encounter such travel problems as sickness, accident, or lost or stolen baggage, call **Traveler's Aid,** an organization that specializes in helping distressed travelers, whether American or foreign. Check the local telephone directory for the nearest office.

Holidays On the following legal U.S. national holidays, most banks, government offices, and post offices and many stores, restaurants, and museums are closed: January 1 (New Year's Day), third Monday in January (Martin Luther King, Jr., Day), third Monday in February (Presidents' Day), last Monday in May (Memorial Day), July 4 (Independence Day), first Monday in September (Labor Day), second Monday in October (Columbus Day), November 11 (Veterans Day/Armistice Day), fourth Thursday in November (Thanksgiving Day), and December 25 (Christmas Day).

The Tuesday following the first Monday in November, Election Day, is a legal holiday in presidential-election years (1992, 1996).

Legal Aid If you are stopped for a minor infraction (for example, of the highway code, such as speeding), never attempt to pay the fine directly to a police officer; you may be arrested on the much more serious charge of attempted bribery. Pay fines by mail, or directly into the hands of the clerk of the court. If accused of a more serious offense, it is wise to say and do nothing before consulting a lawyer. Under U.S. law, an arrested person is allowed one telephone call to a party of his or her choice. Call your embassy or consulate.

Mailboxes are blue with a red-and-white logo, and carry the inscription "U.S. MAIL." A first-class **stamp** for mail within the U.S. and to Canada costs 29¢.

Newspapers and Magazines Foreign publications may be hard to find in Hawaii. Major hotels may provide a few periodicals, but your best bet for staying abreast of foreign news is to pick up a copy of *The New York Times* or an American weekly newsmagazine.

Radio and Television There are dozens of radio stations (both AM and FM), each broadcasting talk shows, continuous news, or a particular kind of music—classical, country, jazz, pop, gospel—punctuated by frequent commercials. Television, with three coast-to-coast networks—ABC, CBS, and NBC—joined in recent years by the Fox network, the Public Broadcasting System (PBS), and a growing network of cable channels, plays a major part in American life. See also "Fast Facts: Honolulu," in Chapter 4.

Safety Whenever you're traveling in an unfamiliar city or country, stay alert. Be aware of your immediate surroundings. Wear a moneybelt and don't flash expensive jewelry and cameras in public. This will minimize the possibility of your becoming a crime victim. Be alert even in heavily touristed areas. See also "Fast Facts: Hawaii," in Chapter 2.

Taxes In the U.S. there is no VAT (Value-Added Tax) or other indirect tax at a national level. Every state, and each city in it, is allowed to levy its own local tax on all purchases, including hotel and restaurant checks, airline tickets, and so on. In Hawaii the state sales tax is 4% and the hotel occupancy tax is another 9.43%.

Telephone, Telegraph, Telex, and Fax Pay phones can be found on street corners, as well as in bars, restaurants, public buildings, stores, and service stations. Intraisland calls cost 25¢. Interisland calls cost more.

For **interisland and other long-distance calls and international calls,** stock up with a supply of quarters; the pay phone will instruct you when you should put them into the slot. For long-distance calls in the U.S., dial 1 followed by the area code and number you want. For direct overseas calls, first dial 011, followed by the country code (Australia, 61; Republic of Ireland, 353; New Zealand, 64; United Kingdom, 44; and so on), and then by the city code (for example, 71 or 81 for London, 21 for Birmingham) and the number of the person you wish to call.

Before calling from a hotel room, always ask the hotel phone operator if there are any telephone surcharges. These are best avoided by using a public phone, calling collect, or using a telephone charge card.

For **reversed-charge or collect calls,** and for **person-to-person calls,** dial 0 (zero, not the letter "O") followed by the area code and number you want; an operator will then come on the line and you should specify that you are calling collect, or person-to-person, or both. If your operator-assisted call is international, ask for the overseas operator.

For local directory assistance ("Information"), dial 411; for long-distance information, dial 1, then the appropriate area code and 555-1212.

Like the telephone system, **telegraph** and **telex** services are provided by private corporations like ITT, MCI, and above all, Western Union. You can bring your telegram to the nearest Western Union office (there are hundreds across the country), or dictate it over the phone (call toll free 800/325-6000). You can also telegraph money, or have it telegraphed to you, very quickly over the Western Union system.

Most hotels have **fax** machines available for guests (ask if there is a charge to use it). You will also see signs for public faxes in the windows of small shops.

Time The U.S. is divided into six time zones. From east to west, these are: eastern standard time (EST), central standard time (CST), mountain standard time (MST), Pacific standard time (PST), Alaska standard time (AST), and Hawaii standard time (HST). Always keep the changing time zones in mind if you are traveling (or even telephoning) long distances in the U.S. For example, noon in New York City (EST) is 11am in Chicago (CST), 10am in Denver (MST), 9am in Los Angeles (PST), 8am in Anchorage (AST), and 7am in Honolulu (HST). When it is noon in London (GMT, or Greenwich mean time), it is 7am in New York.

Although Hawaii has not adopted it, **daylight saving time** is in effect throughout most of the rest of the U.S. from 1am on the first Sunday in April until 2am on the last Sunday in October (except in Arizona, Hawaii, part of Indiana, and Puerto Rico).

Toilets Often euphemistically referred to as "rest rooms," public toilets are just about nonexistent on the streets of America. They can be found, though, in bars, restaurants, hotel lobbies, museums, department stores, and gasoline stations—and will probably be clean (although ones in the last-mentioned sometimes leave much to be desired). Note, however, that some restaurants and bars display a notice that TOILETS ARE FOR USE OF PATRONS ONLY. You can ignore this sign, or better yet, avoid arguments by paying for a cup of coffee or soft drink, which will qualify you as a patron. The cleanliness of toilets at railroad stations and bus depots may be questionable; some public places are equipped with pay toilets that require you to insert one or two dimes (10¢) or a quarter (25¢) into a slot on the door before it will open. In rest rooms with attendants, 25¢ tip is customary.

Yellow Pages There are two kinds of telephone directory. The general directory, called the "white pages," lists subscribers (business and personal residences) in alphabetical order. The inside front cover lists emergency numbers for police, fire, and ambulance, and other vital numbers (like the Coast Guard, poison-control center, crime-victims hotline, and so on). The first few pages are devoted to community-service numbers, including a guide to long-distance and international calling, complete with country codes and area codes.

The second directory, the "yellow pages," lists all local services, businesses, and industries by type, with an index at the back. The listings cover not only such obvious items as automobile repairs by make of car, or drugstores (pharmacies), often by geographical location, but also restaurants by type of cuisine and geographical location, bookstores by special subject and/or language, places of worship by religious denomination, and other information that the tourist might otherwise not readily find. The "yellow pages" also include city plans or detailed area maps, often showing postal ZIP Codes and public transportation routes.

AMERICAN SYSTEM OF MEASUREMENT

LENGTH

1 inch (in.)			=	2.54cm				
1 foot (ft.)	=	12 in.	=	30.48cm	=	.305m		
1 yard (yd.)	=	3 ft.			=	.915m		
1 mile	=	5,280 ft.					=	1.609km

To convert miles to kilometers, multiply the number of miles by 1.61. Also use to convert speeds from miles per hour (mph) to kilometers per hour.

To convert kilometers to miles, multiply the number of kilometers by 0.62. Also use to convert to mph.

CAPACITY

1 fluid ounce (fl. oz.)			=	0.03 liters		
1 pint	=	16 fl. oz.	=	0.47 liters		
1 quart	=	2 pints	=	0.94 liters		
1 gallon (gal.)	=	4 quarts	=	3.79 liters	=	0.83 Imperial gal.

To convert U.S. gallons to liters, multiply the number of gallons by 3.79.

To convert liters to U.S. gallons, multiply the number of liters by 0.26.

To convert U.S. gallons to Imperial gallons, multiply the number of U.S. gallons by 0.83.

To convert Imperial gallons to U.S. gallons, multiply the number of Imperial gallons by 1.2.

WEIGHT

1 ounce (oz.)			=	28.35g				
1 pound (lb.)	=	16 oz.	=	453.6g	=	0.45kg		
1 ton			=	2,000 lb.	=	907kg	=	0.91 metric tons

To convert pounds to kilograms, multiply the number of pounds by 0.45.

To convert kilograms to pounds, multiply the number of kilograms by 2.2.

AREA

1 acre			=	0.41ha		
1 square mile	=	640 acres	=	259ha	=	$2.6km^2$

To convert acres to hectares, multiply the number of acres by 0.41.

To convert hectares to acres, multiply the number of hectares by 2.47.

To convert square miles to square kilometers, multiply the number of square miles by 2.6.

To convert square kilometers to square miles, multiply the number of square kilometers by 0.39.

TEMPERATURE

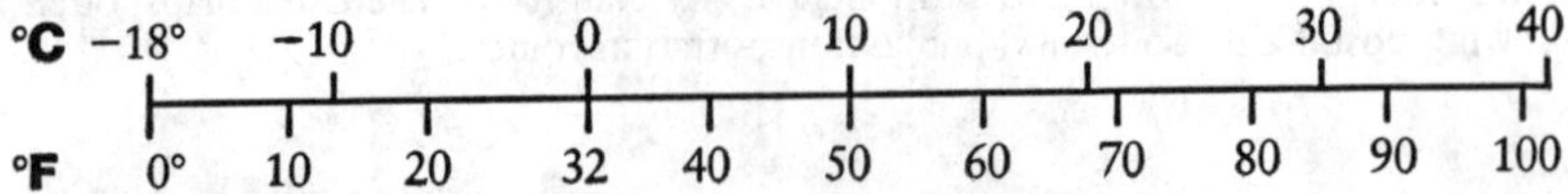

To convert degrees Fahrenheit to degrees Celsius, subtract 32 from the number of degrees Fahrenheit, multiply by 5, then divide by 9 (example: 85°F − 32 × 5/9 = 29.4°C).

To convert degrees Celsius to degrees Fahrenheit, multiply the number of degrees Celsius by 9, divide by 5, and add 32 (example: 20°C × 9/5 + 32 = 68°F).

CHAPTER 4

INTRODUCING HONOLULU

Oahu means "the gathering place" in Hawaiian, and no other name could be so apt. Although it's merely the third largest of the islands in size (40 miles long, 26 miles wide), it is the most populous (850,000, and more arriving all the time). It also has the most skyscrapers, schools, hospitals, radio and television stations—and the most tourists.

Honolulu, the bustling capital city plunked in the middle of the Pacific, is the center of island life, the metropolis youngsters from the other islands dream of. It is also a tremendous military stronghold where approximately one-tenth of the island is owned by the military; defense is a major industry.

Just 10 minutes away from downtown Honolulu is **Waikiki Beach,** a favorite resort of Hawaiian royalty long before the word "tourist" was invented. For the visitor, this is an ideal situation; it's as if Mexico City were just 10 minutes away from Acapulco, Paris a short bus ride from the Riviera. You can, with such geography, have the best of both worlds—as much beach or city, laziness or excitement, as you choose.

The island is dominated by two mountain ranges: the Waianae, along the west coast, and the Koolaus, which form the spectacular backdrop to the city of Honolulu. On the other side of the Koolaus is **Windward Oahu,** which is what islanders are referring to when they talk of going to the "country." Commuters tunnel through the mountains to pretty little suburbs that are developing here as the population booms. For the visitor, it's the closest thing you'll see—if you don't visit the neighbor islands—to rural Hawaii: tiny plantation villages, miles of red earth planted with pineapple and sugarcane, a breathtaking succession of emerald beaches, and gorgeous trails for riding and hiking.

1. FROM A BUDGET TRAVELER'S POINT OF VIEW

BUDGET BESTS & DISCOUNTS

FOR EVERYONE

- Try to travel to Hawaii during the "low season"—from April 1 through mid-December, when rates on air travel, hotel rooms, and rental cars can be significantly lower.

- Try to secure fly-drive packages from the inter-island airlines.
- Travel with someone else; savings on hotel rooms are great. If a third person is in the party, per-person rates go down even more.
- If you're making long driving tours, try teaming up with friends and splitting the costs.

FOR STUDENTS

- Investigate the hostels and inexpensive hotels mentioned in this book.
- Consider taking some courses and staying at the University of Hawaii; participate in their student activities whether or not you take courses.

FOR SENIORS

- Always inquire about senior discounts—on airlines, in hotels, some restaurants, all sightseeing attractions.
- Contact the **Hawaii State Senior Center** (tel. 847-1322) for news of many activities of interest to seniors.
- In Honolulu, ride TheBUS free at all times: For information on getting a bus pass, phone 848-4144.

WORTH THE EXTRA BUCKS

- Meals at some of Hawaii's fabulous restaurants, like Alfred's European Restaurant or Sunset Grill (see Chapter 6, "Honolulu Dining").
- An evening at the Royal Hawaiian's Monarch Room, to see Hawaii's most beloved entertainers, the Brothers Cazimero.
- Sunset cocktails to the strains of Hawaiian music at the House Without a Key, an open-to-the-sea lounge at the Halekulani Hotel—a Honolulu tradition.
- An evening at the Peacock Room of the Queen Kapiolani Hotel to see Hawaii's funniest funny man, Frank DeLima.
- A submarine dive on the *Atlantis,* to see the life of the coral reef, far below Waikiki's waters (see Chapter 7, "Honolulu Attractions").

2. ORIENTATION

ARRIVING

BY PLANE The **Honolulu International Airport,** about five miles out of town, is one of the world's largest and busiest airports. If you're traveling light, with one small bag that you can hold in your lap, you can hop right on **public bus** no. 19 (Hickam–Waikiki) or no. 20 (Pearlridge–Waikiki) that goes from the terminal to the beach area for 60¢. (The bus has no special section for luggage; your bag must not take up any extra space.) If you are traveling with luggage, then take **Waikiki Express** (call 942-2177, toll free 800/553-2388, to make arrangements for them to pick you up). The cost is $5 from the airport to Waikiki. A taxi into town will cost around $25.

If you've rented a car in advance, you can pick it up right at the airport.

BY SHIP Forget about it. Only luxury cruise ships now call at Honolulu Harbor.

TOURIST INFORMATION

The **Hawaii Visitors Bureau,** 2270 Kalakaua Ave., 7th floor (tel. 923-1811), in the heart of Waikiki, has a helpful staff. Stop in to pick up leaflets and brochures on all kinds of activities and on neighbor-island hotels. They also have a booth at the Royal Hawaiian Shopping Center.

For daily news of what's going on, consult the *Waikiki Beach Press, Guide to Oahu, This Week on Oahu, Spotlight Oahu, Paradise News,* or *Key,* **free publications** found in most hotel lobbies, on Kalakaua Avenue, and elsewhere. (These papers also carry many bargain discount coupons, which can add up to considerable savings on shopping, restaurants, car rentals, and the like.) The "Aloha" section of the *Sunday Star Bulletin & Advertiser* lists events for the coming week. *Oahu Drive Guide,* available at the offices of rental-car companies, has plenty of information, plus excellent driving maps.

CITY LAYOUT

GETTING YOUR DIRECTIONAL SIGNALS

In order to get your bearings, you should know that one seldom refers to directions in the standard north-south, east-west way out here. Since the islands sit in a kind of slanted direction on the map, those terms just wouldn't make much sense.

This is how it's done in Hawaii. Everything toward the sea is **makai** (MAH-kye); everything toward the mountains is **mauka** (MOW-kah). The other directions are **Diamond Head** (roughly eastward) and **Ewa** (roughly westward), named after two of the major landmarks of the city. Once you move out beyond Diamond Head, roughly eastward directions are referred to as **Koko Head** (Aina Haina is Koko Head of Kalani Valley, for example). Once you learn to use these simple terms, you'll be well on the way to becoming a kamaaina yourself.

NEIGHBORHOODS IN BRIEF

The Honolulu neighborhoods most tourists will be concerned with are:

Waikiki The Waikiki area runs from Ala Moana Boulevard in an Ewa direction, up to Kapahulu Avenue in a Diamond Head direction, and from the Ala Wai Canal on the mountain side to the ocean. Within Waikiki, Kalakaua Avenue is the main thoroughfare, bordering the ocean; parallel to it is Kuhio Avenue; and parallel to that is the Ala Wai Boulevard. Along these avenues and their side streets are the main hotels, restaurants, shops, and sights of the tourist area.

Kapahulu This is the area centered around Kapahulu Avenue, going one or two blocks on either side of the H1 Highway, otherwise known as the Expressway. Many stores, businesses, and restaurants are located here.

University This district runs from McCully to South King Street, until South King becomes Waialae Avenue, then mauka (toward the mountains) up into Manoa Valley. It includes the University of Hawaii.

McCully-Moiliili This area runs from Kapiolani Boulevard to South King Street. There are stores, businesses, and Asian restaurants.

Ala Moana The Ala Moana area extends mauka of Ala Moana Boulevard, between Waikiki and Restaurant Row. The Ala Moana Shopping Center is here.

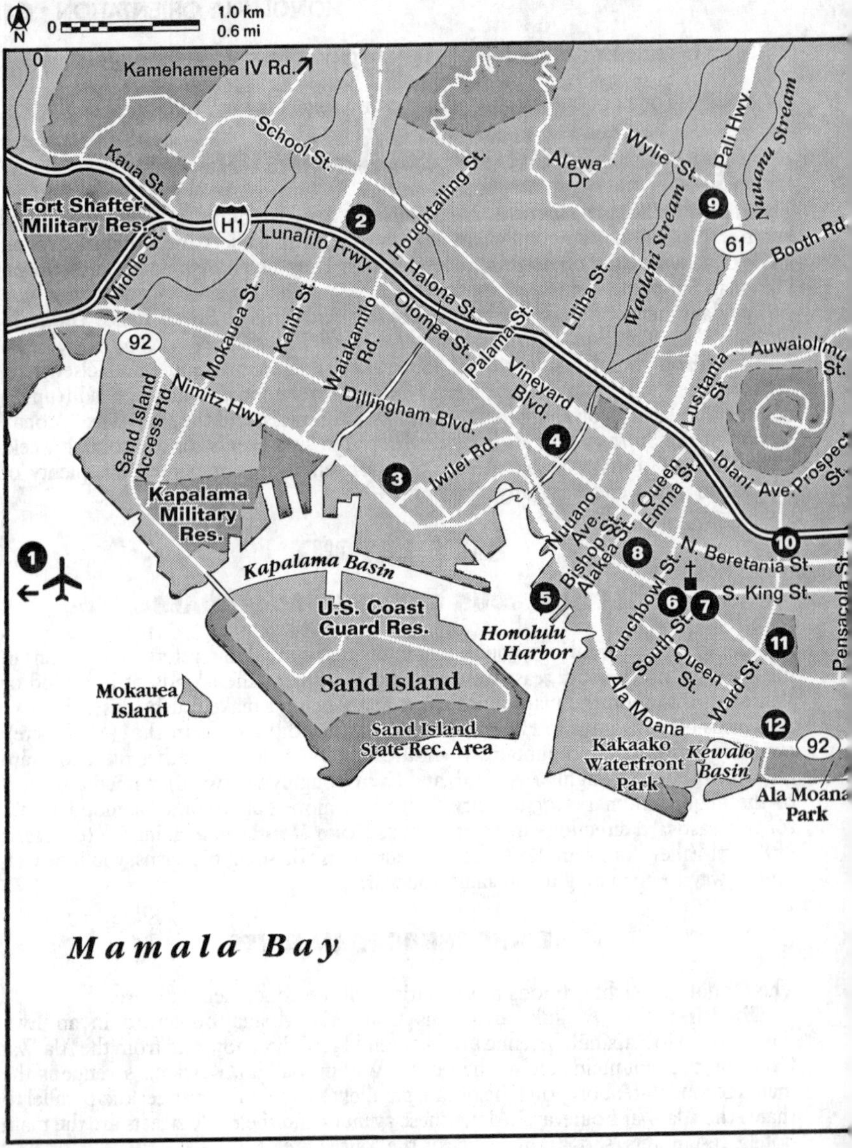

N 0 1.0 km 0.6 mi

- Ala Moana Park 13
- Ala Moana Shopping Center 14
- Bishop Museum 2
- Diamond Head State Monument 19
- Dole Cannery Square 3
- Fisherman's Wharf 12
- Foster Botanic Garden 4
- Hawaii Maritime Museum 5
- Hawaii Visitor's Bureau 16
- Honolulu Academy of Arts 10
- Honolulu International Airport 1
- Iolani Palace 8

HONOLULU ORIENTATION

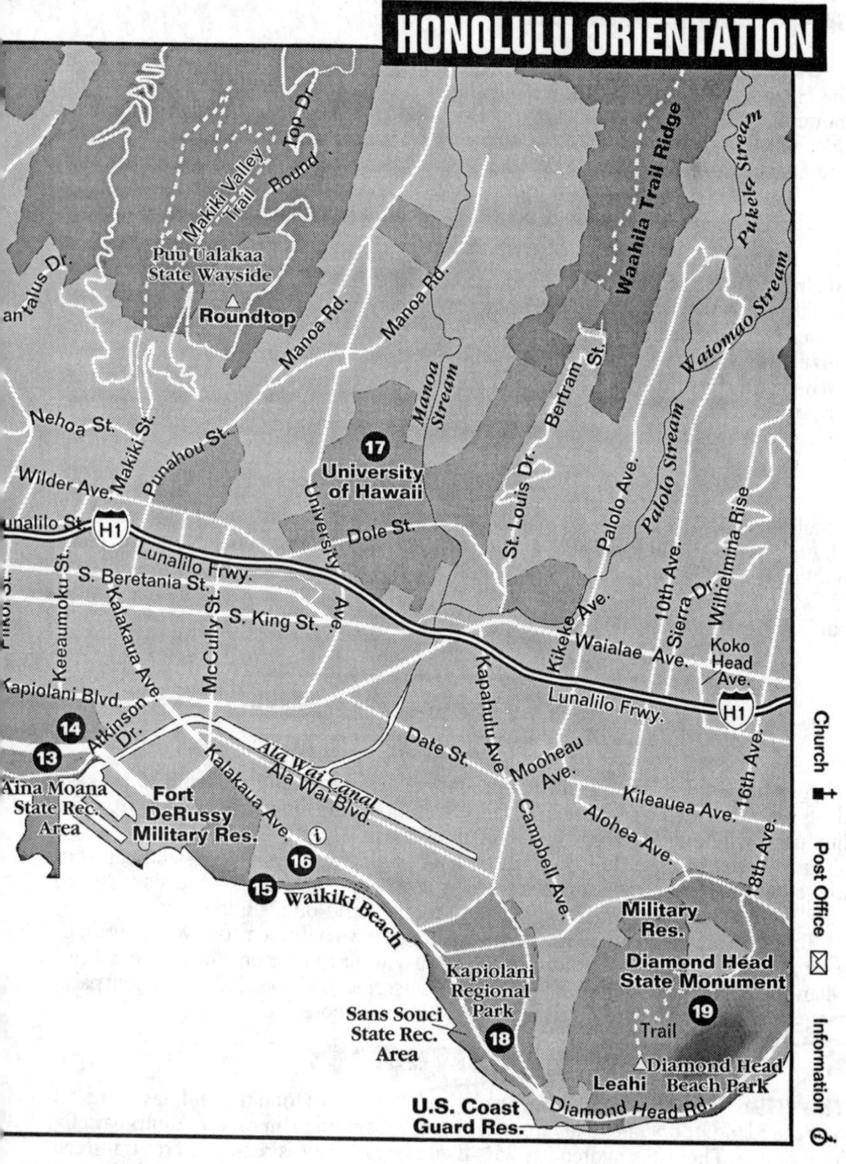

Kapiolani Park 18
Kawaiaihao Church 6
Mission Houses Museum 7
Neal S. Blaisdell Center 11
Royal Mausoleum State Monument 9
University of Hawaii 17
Waikiki Beach 15

Downtown Honolulu This includes everything from Restaurant Row to the Historical Chinatown District. The latter is bordered by Beretania Street on the mountain side, Nuuanu Avenue on the Diamond Head side, Nimitz Highway, harbor side, and River Street on the Ewa/airport side. It contains the city's major business and financial district.

MAIN STREETS & HIGHWAYS

Your first introduction to the thoroughfares of Honolulu will probably be **Nimitz Highway/Ala Moana Boulevard,** a two-way divided highway that runs between the airport and Waikiki. **King Street** goes one way from downtown Honolulu to the University of Hawaii, passing Iolani Palace and the downtown historical sights. **Beretania Street** is one way going in the opposite direction; it starts at University Avenue and runs through Chinatown. The **H1 Freeway** runs from Pearl Harbor/Airport to Kahala Mall, then continues as a divided express highway, Kalanianaole, which goes around the island.

STREET MAPS

Locals consider the best Oahu maps to be Bryan's *Sectional Maps of Oahu* and the *Oahu Reference Maps* by James A. Bier, Cartographer. Both can be obtained in many bookstores, or from Hawaii Geographic Maps and Books, 49 S. Hotel St., Suite 218, (P.O. Box 1698), Honolulu, HI 96808 (tel. 808/532-3952). Maps in free tourist publications are acceptable for most ordinary touring.

3. GETTING AROUND

Many people think it's difficult to get around the islands and succumb to package deals that wrap up the vacation in advance: transportation, hotels, sightseeing from the limousine window, all for one flat—and unnecessarily high—fee. And even if they've already discovered the do-it-yourself trick of staying at budget hotels and eating at low-cost restaurants, panic strikes when it comes to sightseeing—and how else to "do" Honolulu unless someone takes you by the hand on a guided tour?

Tours are pleasant and useful, of course, if you have only a day or two and want to pack in as many sights as you can. And you may want to take one (or else rent a car) when you circle the island of Oahu. But for sightseeing in Honolulu, at your own pace, there are options that are much cheaper, and much more fun.

BY BUS/TROLLEY

TheBUS TheBUS is owned by the city and county of Honolulu and has routes all over the island. It operates daily from 5am to 12:30am on main routes. Adults pay 60¢ for a ride on TheBUS; children pay 25¢. Exact fare in coins is required. Free transfers, which can extend your ride considerably in one direction, must be requested when you board and pay your fare. Senior citizens can use the buses free by showing a bus pass. (Call 848-4444 for information on the E & H Bus Pass program.)

Bus schedules are not, unfortunately, available on the buses themselves, but if you have any questions about how to get where, simply call **TheBUS information number** (tel. 848-5555) between 5:30am and 10pm. Keep in mind that the buses you will take from Waikiki to Ala Moana Shopping Center or to downtown Honolulu must be boarded on Kuhio Avenue.

If you're at Ala Moana Center, you can use the no-cost direct telephones to TheBUS information, located at the bus stops on the north and south sides of the center. You should also note that traffic on Kalakaua Avenue, Waikiki's main thoroughfare, goes Diamond Head most of the way. All buses running from Waikiki either uptown or downtown should be boarded on Kuhio Avenue.

THE WAIKIKI TROLLEY A way to make your sightseeing a bit more comfortable without breaking the bank: Hop aboard the Waikiki Trolley. All-day passes cost $15 for adults, $5 for children, and you can travel from 8am to 4pm between the Royal Hawaiian Shopping Center and Dole Cannery Square, making stops en route at Ala Moana Center, the Hilton Hawaiian Village, the Honolulu Academy of Arts, Ward Warehouse and Fisherman's Wharf, Ward Centre, the state capitol and Iolani Palace, the Mission Houses Museum and the King Kamehameha Statue, Chinatown, the Hawaii Maritime Center, Restaurant Row, and the Hilo Hattie Factory. You can stay on for the entire two-hour, narrated trip or hop on and off whenever you like and continue on another trolley. Recalling Honolulu's turn-of-the-century streetcars, these jaunty red motorized trolleys with an old-fashioned look (etched-glass windows, polished brass rails, hand-carved oak interiors) stop each hour at the locations listed above. As you study the trips outlined below, you'll be able to see when and where the trolley can take you to some destinations. Call 526-0112 or check local papers for exact routes and schedules. Tours operate daily between 8am and 4pm.

MONTHLY PASSES If you're staying in Honolulu and doing extensive bus riding for any length of time, it may pay to buy a monthly pass. They cost $15 for adults, $7.50 for youths up to high-school age (generally considered 19 or younger). Bus passes may be purchased anytime during the month. They are available at 811 Middle St. (tel. 848-4444). Fares are subject to change.

BY TAXI

It's easy to get a cab in Waikiki. Simply step to the edge of any major thoroughfare, lift your hand to signal, and within five minutes you'll undoubtedly be on your way. Although not cheap (the first flip of the meter is usually $1.40), taxis are useful for emergencies and for short trips, and can be practical if you are traveling in a group. If you want to call a cab in advance, your hotel desk can usually get one for you, or you can call any of the numerous companies listed in the telephone book. Here are a few: **Charley's Taxi** (tel. 531-1333), **Aloha State Cab** (tel. 847-3566), and **Sida of Hawaii** (tel. 836-0011).

BY BICYCLE

Honolulu, like big cities everywhere, has become very bicycle conscious. Bicycles used to be available for rental at a number of locations, but lately most hotels and car-rental agencies (like Hertz) have stopped renting them because of the high equipment-mortality rate. "We kept finding them in the ocean," said one supplier. But we did find *one* place where they can still be rented: **University Cyclery** at 1728 Kapiolani Blvd., but weekly only, at $50 per week.

BY RENTAL CAR

If you're going to stay mostly in Waikiki and only venture forth to downtown Honolulu, the convenience of renting a car will not justify the expense. On top of that, street parking is very difficult to find, and most lots are very expensive. Most hotels charge parking fees. If, however, you want to spend time on the windward side of Oahu, or tour the entire island, then a car is a must.

If you decide to rent, you'll have your choice of just about any type of vehicle, foreign or domestic, from the numerous car-rental agencies in town. The most inexpensive cars are usually those with manual shifts. Prices are also higher for mid-size cars. And rates are always higher—by as much as $5 or $10—in the busy winter season than in summer. As for the car-rental agencies themselves, they are very much in competition for your business, and since rates are constantly changing and new attractive deals are offered all the time, a little comparison shopping at the time of your arrival will pay big dividends. However, we'll pass on the warning they gave to us: "Rates are subject to change at any time without notice." Most companies offer flat rates with unlimited free mileage.

See "Getting Around," in Chapter 2, for details on the car-rental agencies that operate throughout Hawaii and for some general tips on renting a car.

PARKING Parking for the night can be a problem in the Waikiki area. *Tip:* Ala Wai Boulevard, along the canal, is less crowded than other main thoroughfares. In the downtown area, there are both municipal and private parking lots. Street meters charge 1¢ per minute; in some busy locations the meters allow no more than 12 to 24 minutes. Read each meter carefully.

DRIVING RULES A few words about driving in Honolulu. Many major thoroughfares are now one-way streets, which helps the flow of traffic, but often makes it seem that you are driving miles out of your way to reach a specific destination. Downtown Honolulu is an especially confusing place to drive in. You may want to keep in mind that in this area Beretania Street is Ewa, King Street is Diamond Head, Pensacola traffic now heads makai (to the sea), and Piikoi cars go in a mauka (to the mountains) direction. In Waikiki, Kalakaua traffic is Diamond Head most of the way, with a short stretch downtown running in both directions; Kuhio Avenue is two-way and the Ala Wai Boulevard is Ewa.

Those painted white arrows on the various lanes are not to be ignored. They indicate in which directions you are permitted to drive from each lane: right only, left only, left and straight ahead, or right and straight ahead. It's legal to make right turns when the light is red at most—but not all—intersections, so read the signs first. And if you come across a sign reading WE APPRECIATE YOUR KOKUA, it's not an invitation to pay a toll. *Kokua* means cooperation in Hawaiian.

HONOLULU

AAA Hawaii The local office of the American Automobile Association is at 590 Queen St. (tel. 528-2600, or 537-5544 for road service).

Animal Hospital Your pet can get 24-hour emergency care at the Care Animal Hospital, 1135 Kapahulu Ave. (tel. 737-7910), and at the Kaneohe Veterinary Clinic, 45-480 Kaneohe Bay Dr. (tel. 235-3634).

Area Code The entire state of Hawaii has one telephone area code: 808.

Babysitters Check first at your hotel desk. You can also try Aloha Babysitting Service (tel. 732-2029), Available Sitters (tel. 951-6118), and Sitters Unlimited (tel. 262-5728).

Bookstores Waldenbooks has several bookstores on Oahu, including branches at the Royal Hawaiian Shopping Center, Waikiki Shopping Plaza, Waikiki Trade Center, and Ward Warehouse. Honolulu Bookshops has five locations, including one at the Ala Moana Center and another downtown at 1001 Bishop St.

Business Hours See "Fast Facts: Hawaii," in Chapter 2.

Camping Permits For information about camping permits for city/county parks, call 523-4525; for state parks, call 548-7455.

Car Rentals Major car-rental companies, which rent automobiles on all four major islands, include Alamo Rent A Car, 2055 N. Nimitz Hwy. (tel. 808/833-4585 or 924-4444, or toll free 800/327-9633); Avis Rent A Car System, at Honolulu International Airport (tel. 808/834-5536, or toll free 800/831-8000); Budget Rent A Car, with many locations in Honolulu (tel. 808/922-3600, or toll free 800/527-0700); Dollar Rent A Car of Hawaii, 1600 Kapiolani Blvd. (tel. 808/944-1544, or toll free 800/367-7006); Hertz Rent A Car, 233 Keawe St., Room 625 (tel. toll free 800/654-3131); and Tropical Rent-A-Car Systems, 765 Amana St. (tel. 808/957-0800, or toll free 800/678-6000). See "Getting Around," in this chapter and in Chapter 2, for details.

Climate See "When to Go," in Chapter 2.

Crime See "Safety" in "Fast Facts: Hawaii," in Chapter 2.

Dentists Dental Care Centers of Hawaii offers 24-hour emergency service. It has many locations around the island; addresses can be found in the telephone book. The after-hours number is 488-5200. Hawaii Family Dental Center (tel. 944-0011) is conveniently located at Sears at the Ala Moana Shopping Center (1450 Ala Moana Blvd.), and has a number of dentists on hand who can provide speedy treatment at reasonable cost.

Doctors We hope it won't happen, but should you need medical assistance while you're in Honolulu, you have several good possibilities. The Straub Clinic and Hospital, one of Hawaii's best-known medical centers, now has a Waikiki satellite: the **Straub Walk-In Health Center,** on the third floor of the Royal Hawaiian Shopping Center (2201 Kalakaua Ave.). The clinic is open Monday through Friday from 8:30am to 5:30pm, and no appointment is necessary. Japanese and German are spoken, as well as English. For information, call 926-4777; after hours and on weekends, call 971-6000.

Prominent Queen's Medical Center also has a Waikiki affiliate: **Queen's Health Care Center,** 1778 Ala Moana Blvd. (tel. 943-1111), in the Discovery Bay Shopping Center. The clinic is open daily from 8am to 10pm, and no appointment is needed. If you are staying in Waikiki, your taxi fare to the Waikiki clinic and back to your hotel will be deducted from your bill; see any hotel desk for a taxi slip.

Should you require a house call—or hotel call—contact **Doctors on Call** (DOC). They're on duty every day, 24 hours a day, and a phone call to 926-4777 will bring them to your hotel room promptly; the charge is a hefty $96. DOC also maintains 24-hour walk-in clinics at the Hyatt Regency Hotel (Diamond Head Tower, 4th floor; tel. 926-4777), the Outrigger Reef Towers Hotel (Room 242; tel. 926-0664), and at the Hawaiian Regent Hotel (Kuhio Tower, 2nd floor; tel. 923-3666). No appointments are necessary.

Of course, in a medical emergency, you can always call 911 and ask for an ambulance, or go to the emergency department of the Queen's Medical Center, 1301 Punchbowl St. (tel. 547-4311).

Drugstores In Waikiki, try the Outrigger Pharmacy at the Outrigger Hotel, 2335 Kalakaua Ave. (tel. 923-2529), or the Kuhio Pharmacy, in the Outrigger West Hotel, 2330 Kuhio Ave. (tel. 923-4466); at Ala Moana Shopping Center, Long's Drug Store, 1450 Ala Moana Blvd. (tel. 941-4433). The Pillbox Pharmacy, 1133 11th Ave. (tel. 737-1777), is open Monday through Saturday from 9am to 11pm and on Sunday from 7 to 11pm, and provides 24-hour emergency service (for prescriptions only).

Emergencies Dial **911** for fire, ambulance, or police; if you cannot reach 911, dial 0 (zero, not the letter "O") and the operator will assist you. For **poisoning** emergencies, call the Poison Center (tel. 941-4411).

Eyeglasses Elite Eyes, 2255 Kuhio Ave. (tel. 922-4884), in the Waikiki Trade Center, and Iris Optical, in the Moana Hotel, 2371 Kalakaua Ave. (tel. 923-5217), can help with emergency repairs or provide new glasses. Lenscrafters (tel. 947-3805), on the mall level mauka at Ala Moana Center, can prepare eyeglasses in about an hour.

Hairdressers/Barbers Both J. C. Penney and Liberty House at Ala Moana Center have good hairdressing salons. There's an inexpensive barber at Hemenway Hall at the University of Hawaii.

Holidays See "When to Go," in Chapter 2.

Hospitals For emergency medical service, Queen's Medical Center, 1301 Punchbowl (tel. 547-4311), has 24-hour emergency-room service and offers outstanding trauma care. On the windward side, it's Castle Medical Center, 640 Ulukahiki in Kailua (tel. 263-5500).

Information See "Tourist Information," in this chapter.

Laundry/Dry Cleaning Should your hotel not provide washers and dryers (most do), try Waikiki Laundromats, which also provide irons, ironing boards, and hairdryers, with four central locations: 2335 Kalakaua Ave., across from the International Market Place; in the Outrigger West Hotel, 2330 Kuhio Ave.; in the Outrigger East Hotel, 150 Kaiulani Ave.; and in the Edgewater Hotel, 2168 Kalia Rd. These are open daily from 7am to 10pm. The location at the Coral Seas Hotel, 250 Lewers St. (tel. 923-2057), is open around the clock. Quick dry-cleaning service is available from Al Phillips the Cleaner in the Waikiki Market Place, 2310 Kuhio Ave. (tel. 923-1971), open Monday through Saturday from 7am to 6pm and on Sunday from 10am to 4pm.

Libraries Hawaii has an excellent public library system. Visit the Hawaii State Library at 478 S. King St. (tel. 548-4775) or the Waikiki-Kapahulu Public Library at 400 Kapahulu Ave. (tel. 732-2777).

Newspapers/Magazines There are two daily newspapers, both published by the Hawaii Newspaper Agency. The *Honolulu Advertiser* is the morning paper; the *Honolulu Star-Bulletin* is the evening paper with the bigger circulation. On Sunday, they combine forces to put out the *Honolulu Star-Bulletin and Advertiser.*

Aloha magazine and *Honolulu* magazine, published monthly, make for interesting reading.

Photographic Needs Best sources at the most reasonable prices are the ABC discount stores and Long's Drug Store at Ala Moana Shopping Center.

Police Dial 911; if that doesn't work, dial 0 for the operator.

Post Office In Waikiki, it's at 330 Saratoga Rd., next to Fort DeRussy (tel. 941-1062), open Monday through Friday from 8am to 4:30pm and on Saturday from 9am to 11:30am.

Rentals If you need to rent something while you're in Honolulu—maybe a TV set, a radio, a stroller, even wheelchairs or crutches, we have a terrific place to recommend: Dyan's Rental (tel. 531-5207). Their rates are low, and they deliver to your hotel cheerfully and promptly. Rent-A-Center (tel. 947-9933) is good for VCRs, video cameras, fax machines, typewriters, word processors, and other electronic paraphernalia.

Shoe Repair There are very few shoe-repair shops in town. Two good ones are Biltrite, 1145 S. King St., near Pensacola (tel. 533-2766), and Joe Pacific, 1680 Kapiolani Blvd., Shop 7F (tel. 946-2998).

Radio/TV For all-Hawaiian music, tune in KCNN (1420 AM); for island music, contemporary Hawaiian to reggae, it's KCCN (100.3 FM). KHPR (88.1 FM) is Hawaii Public Radio for classical music and news; KIPO (1380 AM and 89.3 FM) is Hawaii Public Radio for news and jazz, classical, and folk music. Station KTUH (90.3 FM) presents jazz, classical, rock, and Hawaiian music. Try KHVH (990 AM) for news, sports, and talk.

Most hotels have cable TV, as cable is necessary virtually everywhere on Oahu; 95% of the island is served by Oceanic Cablevision, whose major channels are: Channel 3, KHON (NBC); Channel 6, KITV (ABC); Channel 7, KGMB (CBS); Channel 10, PBS; Channel 14, CNN; Channel 24, HBO; Channel 25, Cinemax; Channel 28, A&E; Channel 29, TNT; Channel 31, MTV; Channel 32, TMC; Channel 33, Showtime; Channel 34, Disney.

Religious Services Among Honolulu's many churches and temples, the following are easily accessible by public transportation: **Buddhist:** Honpa Hongwanji Buddhist Temple, 1727 Pali Hwy. (tel. 536-7044), has an English service

Sunday morning. **Roman Catholic:** The historic Cathedral of Our Lady of Peace, 1184 Bishop St. (tel. 536-7036), with daily masses; there's a Hawaiian Mass on the beach at Fort DeRussy, Sunday morning. **Episcopalian:** St. Andrew's Cathedral, Queen Emma Sq. (tel. 524-2822), has a Sunday Hawaiian Eucharist at 8am. **Presbyterian:** First Presbyterian Church of Honolulu, 1822 Keeaumoku at Nehoa (tel. 537-3321), has Sunday services at 8 and 10am. **Methodist:** First United Methodist Church, 1020 S. Beretania St. (tel. 522-9555), begins morning worship at 10:30am. **United Church of Christ Congregational:** Kawaiaiahao Church, Punchbowl at King (tel. 522-1333), known as "The Westminster Abbey of Hawaii," offers a Hawaiian-English service at 10:30am on Sunday. **Jewish:** Temple Emanu-El, 2550 Pali Hwy. (tel. 595-7521), a Reform Congregation, holds regular services on Friday night, Saturday morning, and on all Jewish holidays. Orthodox Jewish services are held Friday night and Saturday morning at 444 Niu St., in the Hawaiian Monarch Hotel, in the sixth-floor conference room, under the auspices of Chabad of Hawaii; call Rabbi Itchel Krasnjansy (tel. 635-8161) for details.

Sundries ABC Discount Stores offer a little bit of everything one might need under one roof, from suntan lotion to sandwiches, from groceries to gifts, from liquor to laundry detergent, from postcards to photo processing and film, and much more, all at bargain prices. There are 30 ABCs in town, and most are open from 7am to midnight daily. Walk a block or two from where you are and you'll probably find one.

The 7-Eleven Food Stores now have almost 50 shops on Oahu; two convenient locations are 1901 Kalakaua Ave. and 707 Kapahulu Ave. They carry everything from grocery and toiletry items to pantyhose, hot food, soft drinks, etc. Open 24 hours daily.

Taxis See "Getting Around," in this chapter.

Telegrams/Telex/Fax Telex services are available 24 hours a day from Business Center Services (tel. 955-9555) and Western Union (tel. toll free 800/227-5099). Fax services are available at many copy centers and at all Phone Mart locations. The ones closest to Waikiki are at Ward Warehouse (tel. 521-3373; fax 538-0361) and downtown Honolulu (tel. 521-2722; fax 523-6418).

Telephone Calls Five dollars doesn't buy a great deal in Hawaii these days, but it can buy you a 10-minute phone call back to the mainland, or a series of phone calls for up to 10 minutes. Here's how it works: You go to one of Phone Line Hawaii's Waikiki telecom centers at either the International Market Place, 2330 Kalakaua Ave., or the Discovery Bay Center, 1778 Ala Moana Blvd., where the cards are on sale, every day from 8:30am to 11pm. Then you use your card from any telephone, either in a phone booth or your hotel room, and you eliminate the charges that hotels levy on operator-assisted calls. Cards for calling Canada cost $12, and cards for other countries are also available.

Transit Information For information on TheBUS, call 848-5555.

Useful Telephone Numbers For time, call 983-3211. For a surf report, call 836-1952.

Weather In the Honolulu area, call 833-2849; for the rest of Oahu, call 836-0121; for the Hawaiian waters, call 836-3921.

READERS RECOMMEND

"During a recent trip to Honolulu I located two establishments that sold newspapers from the United Kingdom (a rare item in the middle of the Pacific). The Financial Times *is available at the King Fort Magazine Store, 1122 Fort Street Mall. The store, one of my favorite magazine*

places, is just up the mall from Tay Do's Restaurant. And the London Sunday Times *can be purchased from the Honolulu Book Shop at Ala Moana Center on the following Tuesday if it catches the air transport."*—M. G. Roach, Angaston, South Australia, Australia.

4. NETWORKS & RESOURCES

FOR STUDENTS The **University of Hawaii at Manoa** sponsors a number of low-cost activities for the benefit of its students; nonstudents may also join in the fun and savings simply by paying an activity fee that covers a six-week summer session. Inquire at the Campus Center, Room 212, on the Manoa Campus of the University of Hawaii.

FOR GAY MEN & LESBIANS The gay-and-lesbian information line can be reached at 536-6000.

FOR SENIORS The **Honolulu Senior Citizens Club** welcomes newcomers to its social and recreational activities every Wednesday from 9am to 2pm at the Ala Wai Center. There's bridge, canasta, and checkers. Membership is only $5 a year, and it's certainly worth that to go on some of the club's regular outings—sightseeing tours, picnics, etc. These usually start from the Ala Wai Center (on the other side of the Ala Wai Canal) on Wednesday mornings, under the auspices of the city recreation department. For more information on other activities for senior citizens, contact the **Hawaii State Senior Center** (tel. 847-1322).

FOR THE DISABLED **Handicabs of the Pacific,** P.O. Box 22428, Honolulu, HI 96823 (tel. 524-3866), provides special transportation for the disabled: wheelchair taxi service and a variety of tours, including luaus, cruises, and sightseeing journeys.

5. MOVING ON — TRAVEL SERVICES

Akamai, 2270 Kalakaua Ave. (tel. 971-3131), offers a number of well-priced one-day and overnight tours to the neighbor islands.

Roberts Hawaii, 680 Iwilei Rd. (tel. 523-7750), is known for excellent overnight tours to the major islands.

Sears Hawaii Activity Center, Ala Moana Shopping Center, 1450 Ala Moana Blvd. (tel. 944-3222), offers a variety of neighbor-island overnighters at good prices.

CHAPTER 5

HONOLULU ACCOMMODATIONS

1. **DOUBLES FOR ABOUT $40 TO $70**
2. **DOUBLES FOR ABOUT $70 TO $100**
3. **HOSTELS, Y'S & A MILITARY HOTEL**
4. **AT THE AIRPORT**
5. **BED & BREAKFASTS**

Most planes and ships to the Hawaiian Islands land first on the island of Oahu, near the capital city of Honolulu. For those on a budget, Oahu is a good choice; it's the cheapest of all the Hawaiian Islands—and one of the most fascinating to boot.

However, inflation—as it is elsewhere—has been rampant in Hawaii. Many of the cozy little guesthouses that used to enable budget tourists to live comfortably very cheaply some years ago have been torn down and new, more expensive structures have been built. Because of the tremendous number of accommodations in Waikiki, though, it's still possible to find plenty of good rooms that are reasonably priced.

Prices Remember that prices fluctuate, so they may vary slightly from the figures quoted below. Even so, these establishments will be your best hotel buys on the island. Almost all hotels up their rates—by as much as $10–$20 per unit—during the busy winter months. In slow seasons, however, rates are often discounted, and you can do especially well on weekly rentals. The hotel may eliminate cleaning service (which is costly), but you may be able to book a decent apartment for a low price.

Unless otherwise stated by us, all rooms listed below have private bath.

Note that Hawaii's hotel tax is a hefty 9.43%. The tax is not included in rates given in this book.

Reservations If you plan to arrive in Hawaii during the summer season—June through Labor Day—advance reservations are a good idea. They are essential during the peak winter season—roughly from December 20 to April 15. During the winter, reservations up to a year in advance at some of the most desirable places are not unheard of. But last-minute reservations are always possible.

How the Listings Are Organized The hotels are listed first by price and then by geographic location. The Waikiki hotels are split into the following areas: Diamond Head Waikiki, that part of town closest to Kuhio Beach and Kapiolani Park; Central Waikiki, the area centering, roughly, around the International Market Place; and Ewa Waikiki, the section near the Hilton Hawaiian Village Hotel and Ilikai Hotel and the closest area to downtown Honolulu; Near the Ala Wai, that area closest to the Ala Wai Boulevard; and Near Ala Moana, the area close to the Ala Moana Canal. Remember that all these areas are close to each other and all are comparable in terms of comfort and convenience. And they're all near the beach. The other geographic areas we've used are Downtown Honolulu and Windward Oahu.

HOTELS IN WAIKIKI Most tourists stay in Waikiki, mecca of the malihinis. This is a relatively small area of Honolulu, but within it are concentrated most of the town's best beaches, and therefore most of the hotels and entertainment facilities. Downtown Honolulu is only a short bus ride away.

Whether you choose to spend $70 or $100 a night, you'll be living sensibly and pleasantly—and far more inexpensively than most tourists, who are led to believe that a hotel in Waikiki under $100 a day doesn't exist. It certainly does exist, particularly at that Hawaiian wonder of wonders: the **apartment-hotel with kitchenette.** Many of them are individually owned condominium units, and they're almost always cheaper than the rooms in the large seaside hotels.

They are a good choice for a number of reasons: They have excellent locations near the beach and mountains; they are fully available to transients; they permit you to reduce expenses by cooking at least one meal in (dishes and utensils are always provided); and, most important, they offer what many consider the most relaxing and enjoyable type of accommodation in Hawaii. We offer names, addresses, and descriptions of several dozen of these establishments below.

As a point of orientation, remember that most fancy hotels are located right on the beach and on Kalakaua Avenue, the main drag. Between Kalakaua and Ala Wai Boulevard (which marks most of the makai and mauka boundaries of Waikiki) are dozens of tree-lined pretty streets containing the bulk of the smaller and less expensive hotels. Waikiki itself is small enough that you can easily walk from any of these hotels to the beach; they are also near each other, so you should have no trouble in getting from one to another if you have to do some hotel hunting.

You can save money on hotels through **Hotel Exchange,** 1946 Ala Moana Blvd., Honolulu, HI 96815 (tel. 808/942-8544; fax 808/955-2627), an organization that makes deals with hotels at substantial discounts and passes on some of the savings to guests. They will take advance reservations with an approved credit card, or you can simply walk in if you're already in town and not happy where you're staying. Savings can average $5–$10 a day at many leading hotels. Hotel Exchange works with some 180 hotels on Oahu and the neighbor islands.

Note: Since most tourists spend far less than a month in Waikiki, we have not covered apartment buildings that take only monthly or seasonal rentals; if you plan to stay for at least a month, it may be worth your while to investigate them, too. And, of course, many of the apartment-hotels listed here will accept guests for several months or more.

A CONDO- & HOUSE-RENTAL SPECIALIST If you're thinking of staying in a condo or a house on any of the Hawaiian islands, you should know about **HALE** (Hawaiian Apartment Leasing Enterprises), 479 Ocean Ave., Suite B, Laguna Beach, CA 92651 (tel. 714/497-4253, or toll free 800/854-8843, 800/472-8449 in California, 800/824-8968 in Canada). Hale means "home" in Hawaiian, and this outfit aims to provide visitors with a "home away from home" either in a privately managed condominium or a private house.

Daily rates in condominiums can be up to 50% less than the regular rate, and weekly and monthly rates are even lower. Most condos are custom decorated and high quality. And they're often available when a property seems sold out, since this is a separate inventory within the property. HALE's condos offer a wide range of price, size, and location. For example a studio at the Island Colony on Oahu starts at $60 a night for two in the low season, with Foster Towers studios at $75 a night for two in the high season. On Maui, rates range from $350 a week for two in Kihei at Kihei Bay Surf in low season and $455 a week for two in high season. Just north of Kaanapali, an oceanfront studio for two at Papakea is $65 a night in low season and $95 a night in high season. Condos are also available on Kauai, the Big Island, and Molokai.

As for private houses, there are some 200 of them available on all the islands; cleaning staff, cooks, chauffeurs, day care, and additional custom services can be arranged. Possibilities include a two-bedroom/two-bath house on the Kona Coast of the Big Island at $1,110 a week for six, and a two-bedroom/two-bath house in Princeville on Kauai for $420 a week.

For information, write HALE, requesting their brochure, which describes the properties and also shows proximity to golf, tennis, restaurants, and shopping.

1. DOUBLES FOR ABOUT $40 TO $70

WAIKIKI

DIAMOND HEAD WAIKIKI

CONTINENTAL SURF, 2426 Kuhio Ave., Honolulu, HI 96815. Tel. 808/922-2755, or toll free 800/367-5004 in the continental U.S. and Canada. Fax 808/533-0472, or toll free 800/477-2329 in the continental U.S. and Canada. Telex 723-8582. 140 rms and 4 suites. A/C TV TEL

$ Rates: Apr–Dec 17, $63–$90 single or double; $150 suite. Dec 18–Mar, $73–$100 single or double; $160 suite. AE, DC, MC, V. **Parking:** $6 per day.

A tasteful Polynesian decor of earth-browns and golds prevails at this attractive, 22-story high-rise. The lobby is large and airy and rooms are comfortable, though without lanais. The one-bedroom suites with kitchenettes can accommodate up to four persons. A complimentary Budget Rent A Car is included (subject to availability) in the room rate, and parking on the premises is available. Considering all this, prices are reasonable. The Continental Surf has no pool, but the beach is just two blocks away.

HALE WAIKIKI APARTMENT HOTEL, 2410 Koa Ave., Honolulu, HI 96815. Tel. 808/923-9012. 15 apts. TV

$ Rates: Summer $38.50–$45 apt. Winter, $50–$65 apt. No credit cards.

If you think a homey management makes up for an old-but-livable building, check out this hotel. Vera Brady (the term "house mother" fits her better than manager) has been helping guests enjoy their Waikiki stay for 11 years.

Outside, an iron gate is kept locked most of the time. Inside, a long walkway lined with greenery fronts the low-rise building. Each unit accommodates two people comfortably, with a kitchenette and a bath with shower. There is no phone, but you can install your own (the room is wired for a phone). There is cleaning service twice a week and laundry facilities on the premises. You might have to scurry to find parking, but the central location, just one block from the beach and big hotels, makes up for it.

HONOLULU PRINCE, 415 Nahua St., Honolulu, HI 96815. Tel. 808/922-1616, or toll free 800/922-7866 on the mainland U.S., 800/445-6633 in Canada, 800/922-2268 inter-island. Fax 808/922-6223. 125 rms, 22 apts. A/C TV TEL

$ Rates: Apr–Dec 22, $63–$73 double; $99 one-bedroom apt; $125 two-bedroom apt. Dec. 23–Mar, $77–$87 double, $120 one-bedroom apt; $140 two-bedroom apt for four $160 for six. AE, CB, DC, JCB, MC, V. **Parking:** $7 per day.

This is one of Waikiki's older apartment hotels that has seen many years of comfortable, casual living. Our favorite units here are the spacious, nicely furnished one-bedroom apartments which have full kitchens and separate bedrooms and can accommodate four. Four to six people can be accommodated in the two-bedroom kitchen apartments, which have two double beds, a sofa bed, and plenty of room for puttering around. The studios are furnished with either two doubles or a king-size bed plus a sofa bed. Most units have lanais. Cleaning service is provided every day.

Country Life Vegetarian Restaurant serves excellent breakfast, lunch, and dinner buffets on the ground floor. No pool, no frills, but good value here.

LEALEA HALE APARTMENT HOTEL, 2423 Cleghorn St., Honolulu, HI 96815. Tel. 808/922-1726. 20 rms. A/C TV

$ Rates: Apr–Dec 20, $45–$60 twin or double. Dec 21–Mar, $85–$90 twin or double. Discounted weekly rates available. DISC, JCB, MC, V. **Parking:** $5 per day.

On a quiet, narrow, one-way road in the center of Waikiki, this three-story hotel is in well-preserved condition and boasts bedrooms with double or twin beds, full kitchen, lanai, and bath with shower. Weekly rates offer good bargains. There is no pool, and few amenities. Parking is limited. One of the better budget bets in Waikiki during the summer months.

ROYAL GROVE HOTEL, 151 Uluniu Ave., Honolulu, HI 96815. Tel. 808/923-7691. 87 rms. A/C TV TEL

$ Rates: $36–$52 single or double; $70–$75 one-bedroom suite: $90–$100 condo. Each additional person $10. AE, DC, MC, V. **Parking:** $4–$6.50 per day.

An old standby in this part of town, this is one of the prettiest of Waikiki's small hotels. The six-story pink concrete building is about three minutes from Kuhio Beach, but if you're really lazy you can dunk in the tiny pool right on the grounds. Some studios have kitchenettes while efficiencies have private lanais. The accommodations become fancier as prices go up, and all are nicely furnished and comfortable and have tub/shower facilities; the kitchens are all electric. Subject to availability, one day is free if you stay for seven consecutive nights or longer from April through November. Amenities and dining facilities include round-the-clock desk service; twice-weekly or weekly cleaning service; Ruffage Natural Foods and Sushi Bar for health-food supplies, sandwiches, and sushi; and Na's B-B-Que, with Korean plate-lunch specials. Both restaurants are open daily.

Over the years, readers have continued to write to comment on the friendliness of the owners, the Fong family, who frequently have potluck dinners and parties so that everyone can get acquainted. Lots of aloha for a small price at this one.

The Fongs also rent a number of units at the lovely **Pacific Monarch Hotel and Condominium,** just across the street. These are comfortable, spacious quarters wonderfully set up for family living. Inquire about these when you make your reservations.

WAIKIKI CIRCLE HOTEL, 2464 Kalakaua Ave., Honolulu, HI 96815. Tel. 808/923-1571. Fax 808/926-8024. 99 studios. A/C TV TEL

$ Rates: $47–$62 studio without kitchenette. AE, DC, JCB, MC, V. **Parking:** $5 per day.

This is one of the few bargain spots left in Waikiki. Yes, it's a circular hotel, and it's right across the street from Kuhio Beach. This older hotel is best suited to undemanding types—it's simple, but clean and well maintained. The studios can accommodate up to four guests. All rooms have private lanais with wide-angle views (the rooms are more or less pie-shaped) from Diamond Head to the Koolaus. A budget restaurant with a small bar is located off the lobby, and there's parking beneath the lobby.

WAIKIKI HANA, 2424 Koa Ave., Honolulu, HI 96815. Tel. 808/926-8841, or toll free 800/367-5004 in the continental U.S. and Canada. Fax toll free 800/477-2329. 73 rms. A/C TV TEL

$ Rates: Apr–Dec 17, $65–$95 double; $160 one-bedroom suite. Dec 18–Mar, $75–$105 double; $170 one-bedroom suite. AE, DC, MC, V. **Parking:** $7 per day.

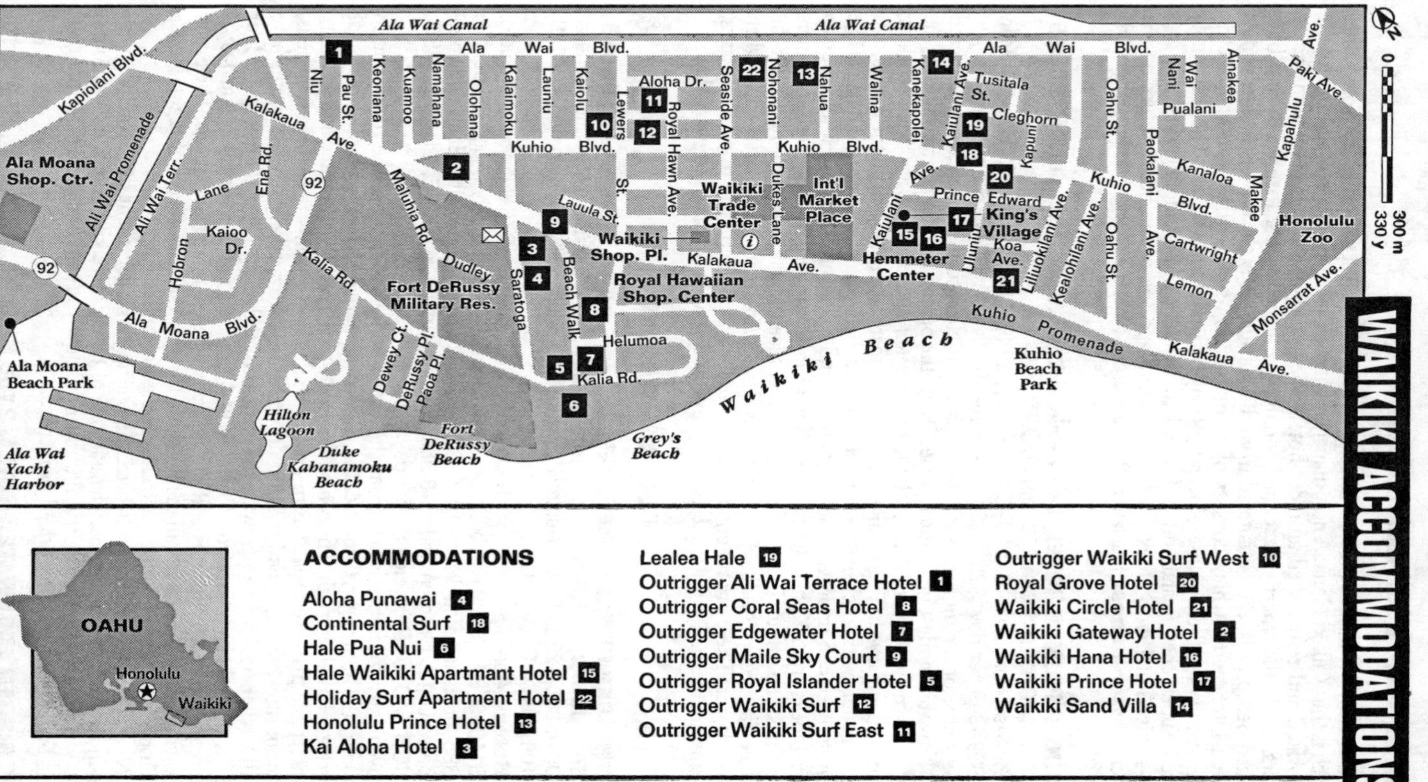
WAIKIKI ACCOMMODATIONS
0
300 m
330 y
Ala Wai Canal
Ala Wai Blvd.
Kapiolani Blvd.
Kalakaua Ave.
Kuhio Blvd.
Ali Wai Promenade
Ali Wai Terr.
Lane
Ena Rd.
Kaioo Dr.
Hobron
Kalia Rd.
Ala Moana Blvd.
Niu
Pau St.
Keoniana
Kuamoo
Namahana
Olohana
Kalaimoku
Launiu
Kaiolu
Lewers St.
Aloha Dr.
Royal Hawn Ave.
Seaside Ave.
Nohonani
Nahua
Walina
Kanekapolei
Kaiulani Ave.
Tusitala St.
Cleghorn
Kapuni
Prince Edward
Oahu St.
Paokalani Ave.
Wai Nani
Pualani
Ainakea
Paki Ave.
Kapahulu
Kanaloa
Makee
Cartwright
Lemon
Monsarrat Ave.
Liliuokalani Ave.
Kealohilani Ave.
Koa Ave.
Uluniu
Dukes Lane
Lauula St.
Maluhia Rd.
Dudley
Saratoga
Beach Walk
Helumoa
Dewey Ct.
DeRussy Pl.
Paoa Pl.
Kuhio Promenade
Ala Moana Shop. Ctr.
Ala Moana Beach Park
Ala Wai Yacht Harbor
Hilton Lagoon
Duke Kahanamoku Beach
Fort DeRussy Beach
Fort DeRussy Military Res.
Grey's Beach
Waikiki Beach
Kuhio Beach Park
Waikiki Trade Center
Waikiki Shop. Pl.
Int'l Market Place
Royal Hawaiian Shop. Center
Hemmeter Center
King's Village
Honolulu Zoo
92
OAHU
Honolulu
Waikiki
ACCOMMODATIONS
Aloha Punawai 4
Continental Surf 18
Hale Pua Nui 6
Hale Waikiki Apartmant Hotel 15
Holiday Surf Apartment Hotel 22
Honolulu Prince Hotel 13
Kai Aloha Hotel 3
Lealea Hale 19
Outrigger Ali Wai Terrace Hotel 1
Outrigger Coral Seas Hotel 8
Outrigger Edgewater Hotel 7
Outrigger Maile Sky Court 9
Outrigger Royal Islander Hotel 5
Outrigger Waikiki Surf 12
Outrigger Waikiki Surf East 11
Outrigger Waikiki Surf West 10
Royal Grove Hotel 20
Waikiki Circle Hotel 21
Waikiki Gateway Hotel 2
Waikiki Hana Hotel 16
Waikiki Prince Hotel 17
Waikiki Sand Villa 14
Post Office
Information

Tucked away behind the posh Hyatt Regency Hotel and just a short block from Kuhio Beach is the Waikiki Hana. A new management took over several years ago and totally renovated and refurbished an older hotel. The sparkling lobby is filled with wicker chairs, while the smartly decorated rooms have light woods, rose walls, and blue quilted bedspreads; each is entered from the outside. Only the top-of-the-line rooms have a kitchenette, which consists of a combination sink, refrigerator, and electric hotplate. In the other rooms, refrigerators may be rented for $3 a day. The reasonably priced Super chef Restaurant is located in the lobby. Considering that this is a full-service hotel with an excellent location, this is one of the better values on the beach. **Reservations:** Hawaiian Pacific Resorts, 1150 S. King St., Honolulu, HI 96814.

WAIKIKI PRINCE HOTEL, 2431 Prince Edward St., Honolulu, HI 96815. Tel. 808/922-1544. 30 rms. A/C TV

$ Rates: Apr–Dec 19, $36–$48 per day, $245–$320 per week. Dec 20–Mar, $39–$49 per day, $252–$335 per week. MC, V. **Parking:** $3 per day.

Some of the most reasonable prices in this close-to-the-beach area are offered by this modest little hotel. James Patey, the personable manager, took over the six-story Waikiki Prince about seven years ago, and he has been working steadily to improve it: Furnishings are adequate, there is cable TV in all the rooms, and the 20 rooms with kitchenettes have new drapes, bedspreads, and pots and pans. The location needs no improvement: It's right behind the Hyatt Regency Hotel, just two short blocks from Kuhio Beach. The Waikiki Prince is very popular with foreigners (they make up about 75% of the clientele). It received a four-star rating within the budget class from a leading Japanese tourist guide. And many students stay here when school is out. There are no phones, but a buzzer system alerts you to your messages. Rooms are cleaned every three or four days, and towels are changed every day.

CENTRAL WAIKIKI

OUTRIGGER CORAL SEAS HOTEL, 250 Lewers St., Honolulu, HI 96815. Tel. 808/923-3881, or toll free 800/733-7777 in the U.S. and Canada, 0014-800/126-985 from Australia. Fax toll free 800/456-4329. Telex MCI 634178. 108 rms. A/C TV TEL

$ Rates: Apr–June and Sept–Dec 18, $65 double; $75 kitchenette studio; $110–$130 one- or two-bedroom suite. Dec 19–Mar and July–Aug, $75 double; $85 kitchenette studio; $110–$130 one- or two-bedroom suite. Each additional person $15. Children under 18 stay free in parent's room. AE, CB, DC, DISC, JCB, MC, V. **Parking:** $7 per day.

Conveniently located a block from the beach and a block from the main drag in Waikiki, the Outrigger Coral Seas is one of the original hotels in the empire of Outrigger Hotels Hawaii. The rooms and lobby were recently renovated and are more comfortable than ever. Spacious rooms have either two queen-size or three twin beds, in-room safes, showers, and colorful decor; all have private lanais. Most rooms have small kitchenettes (with microwave oven, utensils, and refrigerator). The suites for four are a real family find. Cars from Dollar Rent A Car are free for every day of your stay if you request the "Outrigger Free Ride" package when making reservations. The beach is down the street, and right in the hotel are three restaurants: Pieces of Eight, House of Hong, and Perry's Smorgy, which offers good buffet bargains.

Note: If there are no rooms here, the Outrigger management can probably place you in an equivalent room elsewhere in one of their 21 Waikiki hotels. At last count, they were handling more than 7,500 rooms! Below you will find listings for many of their budget and medium-priced properties.

OUTRIGGER EDGEWATER HOTEL, 2168 Kalia Rd., Honolulu, HI 96815. Tel. 808/922-6424, or toll free 800/733-7777 in the U.S. and Canada,

0014-800/126-985 from Australia. Fax toll free 800/456-4329. Telex MCI 634178. 184 rms. A/C TV TEL

$ **Rates:** Apr–June and Sept–Dec 18, $65–$70 double; $80 efficiency with kitchenette; $145–$175 suite. Dec 19–Mar and July–Aug, $75–$80 double; $80–$90 efficiency with kitchenette; $145–$175 suite. Each additional person $15. AE, CB, DC, DISC, JCB, MC, V. **Parking:** $7 per day.

Situated right on the corner of Lewers, this hotel has long enjoyed one of the best locations in Waikiki. Halfway between the ocean and Kalakaua Avenue, the Outrigger Edgewater is a two-minute walk to either the peace of sun and surf or the bustle of restaurants, shops, and nightspots. Rooms are pleasantly furnished, the color TV includes in-room movies, and the bathrooms have stall showers. Your lanai will be furnished, but nothing will separate you from your neighbor's porch. This is a homey place, with lots of space to stroll around the building, plenty of lobby area and public rooms. The Trattoria Restaurant, right on the grounds, is a Waikiki favorite for northern Italian food. Chuck's Original Steakhouse is another popular old-timer, and the Pâtisserie is a favorite French bakery. Cars from Dollar Rent A Car are free for every day of your stay if you request the "Outrigger Free Ride" package when making reservations.

OUTRIGGER SURF HOTEL, 2280 Kuhio Ave., Honolulu, HI 96815. Tel. 808/922-5777, or toll free 800/733-7777 in the U.S. and Canada, 0014-800/126-985 from Australia. Fax toll free 800/456-4329. Telex MCI 634178. 251 rms. A/C TV TEL

$ **Rates:** Apr–June and Sept–Dec 18, $60–$75 kitchenette studio for up to three people; $90 junior suite for four; $125 studio suite for four. Dec 19–Mar and July–Aug, $80–$95 kitchenette studio for up to three; $110 junior suite for four; $125 studio suite for four. AE, CB, DC, DISC, JCB, MC, V. **Parking:** $7 per day.

For those watching their dollars, this hotel on the corner of Nohonani Street and a short walk from the beach is one of the most suitable. It has the greatest number of standard units, with kitchenettes throughout. Adding even greater value is the use of a Dollar Rent A Car, free for each day of your stay if you request the "Outrigger Free Ride" package when making reservations.

The tall, modern building has 16 floors of comfortable studios, each with a lanai, carpeting, in-room safe, and beds in a studio arrangement providing a living-room look. There's a stall shower in the bathroom, two closets for storage, a two-burner range, and small refrigerator. The lobby is small but comfortable, and there's a pool on the lobby level. The Waikiki Pasta Company is right at hand.

OUTRIGGER WAIKIKI SURF EAST HOTEL, 422 Royal Hawaiian Ave., Honolulu, HI 96815. Tel. 808/923-7671, or toll free 800/733-7777 in the U.S. and Canada, 0014-800/126-985 from Australia. Fax toll free 800/456-4329. Telex MCI 634178. 80 rms, 13 suites. A/C TV TEL

$ **Rates:** Apr–June and Sept–Dec 18, $65–$75 double; $90–$100 suite. Dec

MONEY-SAVING TIP

You can have the use of a compact automatic car from Dollar Rent A Car for free at almost all Outrigger Hotels *if you request the car when you make your reservation.* Certain restrictions apply, and insurance, taxes, refueling service charges, and other expenses are your responsibility, but considering the cost of car rentals, this is an extraordinary offer.

19–Mar and July–Aug, $70–$75 double; $95–$105 suite. Each additional person $15. AE, CB, DISC, JCB, MC, V. **Parking:** $6 per day.

This is one of the lower priced of the Outrigger hotels, but there's no obvious reason why. It's quiet, rooms are tastefully and newly appointed, and there are many amenities. Perhaps it's the size; there's no wasted space here—when you register at the desk, be careful not to fall into the pool! All rooms have a refrigerator, cooking top or microwave, toaster and dining ware, stall shower in the bathroom, and a sliding glass door leading to a lanai large enough for dining or sunbathing. The corner rooms have two lanais. Cars from Dollar Rent A Car are free for every day of your stay if you request the "Outrigger Free Ride" package when making reservations. It's a five-minute walk to the beach, the International Market Place, and the heart of the Waikiki action.

OUTRIGGER WAIKIKI SURF HOTEL, 2200 Kuhio Ave., Honolulu, HI 96815. Tel. 808/923-7671, or toll free 800/733-7777 in the U.S. and Canada; 0014-800/126-985 from Australia. Fax toll free 800/456-4329. Telex MCI 634178. 303 rms. A/C TV TEL

$ Rates: Apr–June and Sept–Dec 18, $65–$70 double, $70–$75 double with kitchenette; $100–$140 one-bedroom suite. Dec 19–Mar and July–Aug, double, $75–$80 double with kitchenette; $105–$115 one-bedroom suite. Each additional person $15. AE, CB, DC, DISC, JCB, MC, V. **Parking:** $7 per day.

Like all the Outrigger properties, this hotel is well set up for comfortable living. The spacious rooms usually have twin beds (a few double and queen-size beds are available) and a long, narrow lanai that is shared with the next room. Doubles with complete kitchenettes are available, and suites have kitchens. Cars from Dollar Rent A Car are free for every day of your stay if you request the "Outrigger Free Ride" package when making reservations. The comfortable chairs in the lobby afford a view of passersby on the sidewalk, while the bustle of Kalakaua is just one long block away; the Pacific, two. There's a pleasant pool for at-home swimming.

OUTRIGGER WAIKIKI SURF WEST, 412 Lewers St., Honolulu, HI 96815. Tel. 808/923-7671, or toll free 800/733-7777 in the U.S. and Canada; 0014-800/126-985 from Australia. Fax toll free 800/456-4329. Telex MCI 634178. 38 rms, 77 suites. A/C TV TEL

$ Rates: Apr–June and Sept–Dec 18, $65–$75 double; $100–$110 suite. Dec 19–Mar and July–Aug, $70–$80 double; $105–$115 suite. Each additional person $15. AE, CB, DC, DISC, JCB, MC, V. **Parking:** $7 per day.

This hotel shares the lobby and front desk with the main Waikiki Surf across the street, but it has its own large pool area. All the recently renovated rooms have kitchenettes, a bath with shower, and lanais. Suites can accommodate up to four. Cars from Dollar Rent A Car are free for every day of your stay if you request the "Outrigger Free Ride" package when making reservations.

EWA WAIKIKI

ALOHA PUNAWAI, 305 Saratoga Rd., Honolulu, HI 96815. Tel. 808/923-5211. 19 apts. A/C TV

$ Rates: $45–$50 studio; $55–$60 one-bedroom. Minimum stay 3 days; weekly and monthly discounts available. No credit cards. **Parking:** $4 per day.

The owners of this place try hard to keep a low profile, but we are revealing their secret: There are not many places in Waikiki that are this cheap. Here you get a clean, comfortable apartment with a furnished kitchen, bath with shower, and a lanai. The same unit with air conditioning is $5 more. There are no telephones, although phones can be installed for those on long stays. Stay a month and the rate goes down to $30 and $45 a day. There are also both small and large one-bedroom apartments available. Towels and linens are provided and there is chamber service twice a week. Saratoga Road is near Fort DeRussy, and the hotel is only a block from the beach.

HALE PUA NUI, 228 Beach Walk, Honolulu, HI 96815. Tel. 808/923-9693. 22 studio apts. TV TEL

$ Rates: Mar 16–June 15 and Sept 16–Dec 15, $40 single or double. June 16–Sept 15 and Dec 16–Mar 15, $55 single or double. Each additional person $5. MC, V. **Parking:** $6–$10 per day at nearby garage.

One of our favorite streets in Honolulu is Beach Walk, a tiny street running from Kalakaua smack into the ocean, and relatively—for Waikiki—quiet. Here you'll find this lovely little complex of large studio apartments, many of whose guests come back year after year. The location is tops—just half a block to the beach at the Outrigger Reef Hotel and just around the bend from Fort DeRussy, where the swimming is excellent. The studio apartments have either twin or double beds and are tastefully outfitted with new carpets, drapes, bedspreads, and artistic touches. They all have cross-ventilation, soundproofing, and ceilings. Kitchenettes are thoroughly equipped (even to ironing boards). A maximum of three people can stay in a room. An excellent value!

KAI ALOHA HOTEL, 235 Saratoga Rd., Honolulu, HI 96815. Tel. 808/923-6723. 18 apts. A/C TV TEL

$ Rates: $60–$65 studio apt with lanai; $68–$73 one-bedroom apt for two people, $80–$85 for three, $90–$95 for four. Each additional person $10. AE, DC, DISC, JCB, MC, V. **Parking:** $7 per day.

Faithful fans return year after year to this simple little hotel. They prefer the homey atmosphere, the friendliness of the management, and the feeling of intimacy, rare at the more impersonal concrete high-rise hotels. The location, very close to the beach and shopping area, is convenient, and the lush tropical plantings add an island flavor. Every unit has either a modern kitchen or kitchenette. Apartments have full-size refrigerators; the studios, half-size ones. All units have a garbage disposal, toaster, and ironing board. There are coin-operated laundry facilities available on the premises. One-bedroom apartments, also with lanais, can comfortably accommodate families of four or five; children are welcome.

OUTRIGGER MAILE SKY COURT HOTEL, 2058 Kuhio Ave., Honolulu, HI 96815. Tel. 808/947-2828, or toll-free 800/733-7777 in the U.S. and Canada, 0014-800/126-985 from Australia. Fax toll free 800/456-4329. Telex MCI 634178. 554 rms, 42 studios and suites. A/C TV TEL

$ Rates: Apr–June and Sept–Dec 18, $60–$70 double; $80–$85 double with kitchenette; $105 studio; $150–$180 suite. Dec 19–Mar and July–Aug, $75–$85 double; $95–$100 double with kitchenette; $120 studio; $150–$180 suite. Maximum two in doubles, three people in studios. Each additional person $15. AE, CB, DC, DISC, JCB, MC, V. **Parking:** $7 per day.

Designed for the easy life, this hotel is located across the road from the well-known Nick's Fishmarket Restaurant, at the "Gateway to Waikiki," within easy walking distance of the beach and all the attractions of Kalakaua Avenue. There's a very pleasant ambience here, evident as soon as you walk into the pretty open-air lobby, with its maroon-and-beige rugs and dusty-rose and rattan sofas. This 44-story resort offers a variety of accommodations. Rooms are of modest size, but most have views (some, from the higher floors, are spectacular) and all have attractive furnishings and cable TV. There are clocks, radios, and tub/showers, but no lanais. Even the hotel rooms boast small refrigerators; studios and suites add a two-burner electric range for light cooking. There's a pool and a Jacuzzi on the large, 360° sun deck. Cars are free for every day of your stay if you request the "Outrigger Free Ride" package when making reservations.

OUTRIGGER ROYAL ISLANDER HOTEL, 2164 Kalia Rd., Honolulu, HI 96815. Tel. 808/922-1961, or toll free 800/733-7777 in the U.S. and Canada. Fax toll free 800/456-4329. Telex MCI 634178. 95 rms, 6 apts. TV TEL

$ Rates: Apr–June and Sept–Dec 18, $60–$85 double; $125 penthouse apt. Dec 19–Mar and July–Aug, $70–$95 double; $125 penthouse apt. Each additional person $15. AE, CB, DC, DISC, JCB, MC, V. **Parking:** $7 per day.

Rooms here are not large, but they are tastefully decorated with tapa-print spreads and shell lamps, and Hawaiian-type pictures on the walls. Each room has a private lanai, refrigerator, and a modern bathroom with shower. Families will do well in the one-bedroom apartments and suites. This hotel has a superb location, right near the Halekulani and Outrigger Reef hotels, across the road from a very good beach. The lobby is small and open to the street. There's a McDonald's right in the hotel. Cars from Dollar Rent A Car are free for every day of your stay if you request the "Outrigger Free Ride" package when making reservations.

WAIKIKI GATEWAY HOTEL, 2070 Kalakaua Ave., Honolulu, HI 96815. Tel. 808/955-3741, or toll free 800/633-8799 in the mainland U.S. and Canada. Fax 808/955-1313. 190 rms. A/C TV TEL

$ Rates: Apr–Dec 20, $55–$115 double; $125 penthouse suite. Dec 21–Mar. $80–$125 double. AE, DC, JCB, MC, V. **Parking:** $6 per day.

This hotel is well known as the home of Nick's Fishmarket, one of Honolulu's favorite restaurants. It's also well known as a good-value hotel. Recently renovated, it offers rooms with a private lanai, cable TV, an under-the-counter refrigerator, an in-room safe, and a luxurious bath with tub and shower. There's daily cleaning service and a guest laundry. The beach is less than a 10-minute walk, but if you'd rather swim at home, try the beautiful pool backed by a volcanic rock wall and a spacious sun deck.

NEAR THE ALA WAI

HOLIDAY SURF APARTMENT HOTEL, 2303 Ala Wai Blvd., Honolulu, HI 96815. Tel. 808/923-8488. 34 rms. TV

$ Rates: Mid-Apr to Dec 14, $48–$57 studio; $51–$66 one-bedroom. Dec 15 to mid-Apr, $54–$69 studio; $60–$78 one-bedroom. Each additional person $3. AE, CB, DC, DISC, JCB, MC, V. **Parking:** Free.

A clean, white six-story building stands at the corner of Ala Wai Boulevard and Nohonani Street, anything but imposing, but well worth considering because it offers delightfully appointed accommodations at low rates. Most of the units have small lanais that accommodate two chairs. Most of the bathrooms have stall showers, but some have tub/shower combinations. There are no telephones in the rooms, but guests may make free local calls at the lobby office phone. Kitchens are fully equipped. From here to the beach it's two long blocks, about a seven-minute walk.

OUTRIGGER ALA WAI TERRACE HOTEL, 1547 Ala Wai Blvd., Honolulu, HI 96815. Tel. 808/949-7384, or toll free 800/733-7777 in the U.S. and Canada. 0014-800/126-985 from Australia. Fax toll free 800/456-4329. Telex MCI 634178. 239 units. A/C TV TEL

$ Rates: Apr–June and Sept–Dec 18, $50 studio; $60–$100 one-bedroom. Dec 19–Mar and July–Aug, $50 studio; $55–$110 one-bedroom. Each additional person $15. AE, CB, DC, DISC, JCB, MC, V. **Parking:** $2.50 per day.

Some of the lowest rates in Waikiki are being offered at this hotel, which is located at the very beginning of Ala Wai Boulevard, not far from Ala Moana. This 45-year-old apartment building was converted into a hotel a few years ago, and while there's nothing at all fancy about it (don't expect tourist amenities like a pool or restaurant), it does offer clean and comfortable units all with full kitchens and all the necessities. There are two buildings: the renovated, 16-story Tower Building; and the low-rise, walk-up Garden Building. Cars from Dollar Rent A Car are free every day of your stay if you request the "Outrigger Free Ride" package when making reservations.

WAIKIKI SAND VILLA HOTEL, 2375 Ala Wai Blvd., Honolulu, HI 96815. Tel. 808/922-4744, or toll free 800/247-1903 in the U.S. Fax 808/923-2541. 211 rms. A/C TV TEL

$ Rates: Off-season, $56–$89 double; $130 one-bedroom suite. Winter, $70–$98 double; $190 one-bedroom suite. Each additional person $10. Children under 8 stay free in parent's room using existing bedding. AE, DC, DISC, JCB, MC, V. **Parking:** $4 per day.

The Waikiki Sand Villa Hotel is looking better than ever these days, thanks to a $3-million top-to-bottom renovation. The lobby now has a Hawaiian plantation-style ambience accented with a Chinese pink slate floor. The best views are of the Ala Wai Canal, the golf course across it, and the Koolau mountains, but even the opposite views are not obscured by neighboring buildings. Rooms are adequate in size, and the decor is handsome; two tables—one inside and one out on the cozy lanai—afford a choice of breakfast spots. The rooms include a refrigerator and an in-room safe for valuables, and the bathrooms have both tub and shower.

Opening off the lobby is the also completely redecorated Noodle Shop Restaurant, an attractive place for three meals a day; it's best known as the launching pad for Hawaii's "Crown Prince" of comedy, zany Frank DeLima.

NEAR ALA MOANA

BIG SURF HOTEL, 1690 Ala Moana Blvd., Honolulu, HI 96815. Tel. 808/946-6525. 10 small rooms, 18 mountainview studios, 20 oceanview one-bedroom suites. TV.

$ Rates: $33–$37 single small rooms, $37–$42 single or double mountainview studios, $50–$65 one-bedroom oceanview suites. MC, V. **Parking:** $3 per day.

Located 1½ blocks from Ala Moana Beach and a block from the Ala Moana Shopping Center, this one has some of the lowest rates in Waikiki. There is no pool, no restaurant, and the only telephone is one for local calls only in the small lobby. The small single rooms have one bed, a hotplate, and a private bath with shower. A couple would require one of the larger studios, which come with twin beds and lanais. For parties of up to five people, there are one-bedroom suites with full kitchens. Color TV is available in the larger studios and some of the singles.

Most of the accommodations have been renovated and, though simple, are adequately furnished. Don't expect spaciousness at this price. The hotel is a few minutes' stroll around the Ilikai lagoon to the beach, and just a few minutes in the other direction to the Ala Moana Shopping Center.

DRIFTWOOD HOTEL, 1696 Ala Moana Blvd., Honolulu, HI 96815. Tel. 808/949-0061. Fax 808/949-4906. 69 rms. TV TEL

$ Rates: $45–$75 single or double. Each additional person $10. AE, CB, DC, MC, V. **Parking:** $5 per day.

This small hotel is across the road from the luxury Hawaiian Prince Hotel; it's also at the other end of the price spectrum. All rooms have been attractively renovated, and offer refrigerators, kitchenettes, and daily cleaning service. There is a swimming pool, launderette, and parking on the premises. The hotel is less than two blocks from the Ala Moana Shopping Center and Ala Moana Beach Park, an excellent swimming beach and a local family favorite.

A stay at the Driftwood Hotel also entitles you to two tickets to the Hawaii Polo Club's Sunday polo matches at Mokuleia, from March through April; off-season, you can get a 10% discount on a polo lesson or beach ride. For details, call 808/637-POLO.

OUTRIGGER HOBRON, 343 Hobron Lane, Honolulu, HI 96815. Tel. 808/942-7777, or toll free 800/733-7777 in the U.S. and Canada, 0014-800/126-985 from Australia. Fax toll free 800/456-4329. Telex MCI 634178. 550 rms, 46 suites. A/C TV TEL

$ Rates: Apr–June and Sept–Dec 18, \$60–\$65 double, \$70–\$75 double with kitchenette; \$95 studio; \$145–\$175 suite. Dec 19–Mar and July–Aug, \$70–\$75 double, \$85–\$90 double with kitchenette; \$115 studio; \$150–\$180 suite. Each additional person \$15. AE, CB, DISC, JCB, MC, V. **Parking:** \$6 per day.

A skyscraper for this area, this 44-story condominium has attractive accommodations to its credit; it's very popular with tour groups. Most rooms look similar, the major difference being in height. All rooms have attractive blond-wood furniture (desk, vanity, chair), multicolored drapes and bedspreads, and in-room safes; they are small but well appointed, and many offer very good views of ocean, city, mountains, and the nearby Ala Wai Yacht Harbor. Most rooms have twin beds; only four on each floor have queen-size beds, which must be requested in advance. There are also differences in housekeeping facilities: The hotel rooms have refrigerators only; the studios have mini-kitchenettes. There's a pool on the mezzanine level, a sun deck plus Jacuzzi whirlpool and sauna on the fifth floor. All the excitement of the Ilikai and Hilton Hawaiian Village complexes is about five minutes away. Cars from Dollar Rent A Car are free for every day of your stay if you request the "Outrigger Free Ride" package when making reservations.

DOWNTOWN HONOLULU

Tourists who prefer to stay in downtown Honolulu (an easy bus ride from Waikiki) rather than in the beach area will have somewhat tougher sledding. There are so few hotels outside Waikiki that most tourists never hear about them at all. They are primarily occupied by businesspeople. But there are a few in our budget category, and because this area is ideal for serious sightseeing, you may want to consider them.

NAKAMURA HOTEL, 1140 S. King St., Honolulu, HI 96814. Tel. 808/537-1951. 41 rms. TEL

$ Rates: \$35 single; \$40 double; \$42 twin. Each additional person \$5. No credit cards. **Parking:** Free.

Though this isn't a large hotel, you may be lucky enough to find a room on the spur of the moment since it's out of the tourist mainstream. Just off Piikoi Street, this clean and quite comfortably appointed building offers rooms with wall-to-wall carpeting, a large tiled bathroom with a tub/shower combo, good drawer and closet space, and even a telephone. We prefer the rooms facing the mountains; even though they do not have air conditioning, they do have those refreshing trade winds. In the air-conditioned rooms, the machine also drowns out the traffic on King Street (so keep those jalousied windows closed). Some of the rooms are too small for a third person. Mrs. Winifred Hakoda, the personable desk clerk and day manager, advises that no late arrivals (after 10pm Mon–Sat, after 9pm Sun and holidays) are accepted.

TOWN INN, 250 N. Beretania St., Honolulu, HI 96817. Tel. 808/536-2377. 26 rms. TEL

$ Rates: \$34.90–\$37.05 single; \$37.05–\$42.05 double. MC, V. **Parking:** Free.

This tastefully modern Japanese establishment is where you'll mingle, so the management promises, "with important personages and travelers of every race." And all this cosmopolitanism is very reasonable, too! Lower-priced singles and doubles do not have air conditioning; the higher-priced do. Don't expect to sleep on the floor Japanese style; the bedrooms are as Western as the air conditioning. There's a Japanese restaurant, Miyajima, on the premises. Nearby, you should know, is a fairly large tent city for Honolulu's homeless.

WINDWARD OAHU

Windward Oahu is on the other side of the mighty Koolau mountain range, which serves as a backdrop to Honolulu. The scenery is comparable to what you'll find on the neighboring islands. This is "the country," where many local people spend their vacations, and it's far off the usual tourist track. Although this is a good jumping-off spot from which to visit many of the attractions of the windward side, it's essentially a place where you sit on the gorgeous beach surrounded by sea, sky, and fragrant blossoms and do absolutely nothing at all.

Dreaming of a cottage right on the beach? They're not easy to come by in modern Hawaii, but Pat O'Malley of **Pat's Kailua Beach Properties,** 204 S. Kalaheo Ave., Kailua, HI 96734 (tel. 808/261-1653 or 808/262-4128; fax 808/262-8275 or 808/261-0893), may be able to help you out. Pat offers more than 40 fully furnished houses and cottages along Kailua Beach, from a million-dollar beachfront estate to "beachy" cottages on or close to the water. About half of these fall within our budget, costing $55–$80 a day. Each is different, but all are fully furnished and provide cooking and dining utensils, bedding and towels, and television. Some are duplex. The interiors of the cottages we saw were well maintained; some have been recently renovated. The exteriors of some are weather-beaten, which gives them a rustic look. Settings and views are lovely, and many have delightful yards and gardens.

A one-bedroom/one-bath beachfront cottage once owned by a prominent Hawaiian family is priced at $70 a day and can sleep two adults and two children. Overlooking Kailua Beach Park, less than 100 yards from the surf, are one-bedroom/one-bath units for $55–$75 that can sleep three to four people. Three blocks from the beach is one unit at $50, which can sleep three people.

Call Pat O'Malley for information and reservations, and ask about the deposit requirements.

BACKPACKERS, VACATION INN/PLANTATION VILLAGE, 59-788 Kamehameha Hwy., Haleiwa, HI 96712. Tel. 808/638-7838. Hostel bunks, rms, apts, cabins.

$ **Rates:** At Vacation Inn, $14 hostel bunk across from the beach, $16 hostel bunk oceanfront; $35–$45 room across from the beach; $70–$85 oceanfront studio apt. At Plantation Village, $16 hostel bunk; $95–$105 cabin for four to six, $105–$115 large cabin for six, $100–$120 deluxe ocean-view cabin for six, $135–$155 large ocean-view cabin for eight. MC, V. **Parking:** Free.

(S) There are several possibilities here for comfortable, casual country living. At Vacation Inn, one can find basic accommodations overlooking Waimea Bay. Backpackers like the inexpensive hostel facilities, which consist of several rooms furnished with four bunks each. There's a common living room with TV, a bathroom, and a kitchen. The quarters are cleaned each morning. Moving one step up, you can rent a single or double room with a common bath, kitchen, and TV room. Studio apartments can sleep up to four and are comfortably furnished, with TV and kitchenette; all have good views of surf and beach. Some of these units are right on Three Tables Beach, which is next to Waimea Bay; others are higher up in a building on the mountain side of the road and command great ocean vistas.

Plantation Village consists of nine restored plantation cabins located across from Three Tables Beach Park, on an acre of gardens; bananas, papayas, ginger, and mangos grow in the yard. Each cabin has its own kitchen and bath, cable TV, linens, and dishes; a common area offers pay telephone, picnic and barbecue areas, and laundry facilities. The Circle Island bus stops out front every half hour; all facilities are a short walk to Waimea Bay, Waimea Falls Park, and a good supermarket, so one could conceivably get by without a car here. A protected area is safe for children's swimming. Boogie boards and snorkels are part of the North Shore lifestyle, so they are supplied free to guests. Chaz Wagner and Sharlyn Foo are warm hosts, who provide inexpensive sailboat and hiking trips and island tours. Scuba-diving instruction is available in summer. They also rent many vacation homes and condos "in all shapes, sizes, and locations" (rates on request). Again, remember that Waimea Bay is perfect for summer swimming, but the water is extremely rough in winter.

2. DOUBLES FOR ABOUT $70 TO $100

WAIKIKI

DIAMOND HEAD WAIKIKI

DIAMOND HEAD VIEW HOTEL, 230 Makee Rd., Honolulu, HI 96815. Tel. 808/922-7828. Fax 808/923-0050. 10 rms. TV TEL

$ Rates: $75 and $80 kitchenette studio single or double; maximum of two. AE, MC, V. **Parking:** Free, but limited (only four spaces).

This small, newly renovated hotel offers comfortable rooms and an excellent location—across Kapahulu Avenue from the Honolulu Zoo and a block away from the beach at Waikiki. And yes, there are magnificent, unobstructed views of Diamond Head. Rooms are of a decent size, nicely furnished with twin beds and lovely quilted spreads, large bureaus, table and chairs, wall-to-wall carpeting, and a compact little kitchenette on one wall. Bathrooms have full tub and shower.

EWA (EAST-WEST ADVENTURE) HOTEL WAIKIKI, 2555 Cartwright St., Honolulu, HI 96815. Tel. 808/922-1677, or toll free 800/367-8047. Fax 808/923-8538. 90 studios, 12 suites. A/C TV TEL

$ Rates: $73, $78, $88, $98 studio; $120–$133 one-bedroom suite. AE, DC, MC, V. **Parking:** $4 per day.

Up near the Honolulu Zoo, this old hotel has a new name and look thanks to a $3-million renovation. Italian-marble floors and counters, grass cloth on the walls, sand-colored carpets, and pastel color schemes in the lobby and the rooms make this hotel very attractive. The higher-priced studios have kitchenettes; all units have in-room safes, and tub-shower combos. Most have twin beds; some have queen-size beds. Studios are for one to three people, and suites, one to four people. There is no swimming pool or dining facility, but with the ocean and restaurants two short blocks away, this is no problem.

KAIMANA VILLA CONDOMINIUMS, 2550 Kuhio Ave., Honolulu, HI 96815. Tel. 808/922-3833, or toll free 800/367-6060. Fax 808/922-8061. 113 apts. A/C TV TEL

$ Rates: Apr–Dec 19, $95–$110 one-bedroom apt; $150–$165 two-bedroom apt. Dec 20–Mar, $105–$120 one-bedroom apt; $165–$180 two-bedroom apt. Each additional person $15. AE, DC, DISC, JCB, MC, V. **Parking:** $3 per day.

Every room here has a private lanai facing Diamond Head: From the higher floors, you'll feel like you can almost touch it. Located two blocks from the beach and from shopping and nightlife, this is the place for those who like space: Each tastefully appointed unit has over 600 square feet. Amenities include your own washer and dryer, dishwasher, clock radio, a full kitchen, and daily housekeeping services. There is also 24-hour front-desk service. The two-bedroom apartments can accommodate up to six guests. A modest front lobby has lounging facilities that extend to a covered outdoor area.

Reservations: HTH Corp., 2490 Kalakaua Ave., Honolulu, HI 96815 (tel.

808/922-3833, or toll free 800/367-6060 in the U.S. and Canada; fax 808/922-8061; telex 633101).

KAULANA KAI, 2425 Kuhio Ave., Honolulu, HI 96815. Tel. 808/922-7777, or toll free 800/367-9473 in the mainland U.S. Fax 808/922-9473. 77 rms, 13 suites. A/C TV TEL

$ Rates: $85–$95 studio; $130 one-bedroom suite; $150–$200 suite for four. AE, DC, JCB, MC, V. **Parking:** $5 (limited).

Located in a great spot three minutes from Kuhio Beach, this tall pyramidlike building designed by Scandinavian architect Jo Paul Rognstad has been taken over and transformed by a new Japanese management. The hotel is a little jewel, its lobby and guest rooms all done in shades of mauve and pink, with gold fixtures. Rooms are not large but they are attractive, with twin beds, small lanais, and a tidy two-burner kitchenette with a refrigerator underneath the range. Bathrooms are marble, and the kitchen and bathroom floors are tiled, as are the lanais. The lobby is beautiful, with its marble floors, indented Japanese-style ceiling, and gorgeous flower arrangements. There's free coffee in the lobby.

KUHIO VILLAGE RESORT, 2463 Kuhio Ave., Honolulu, HI 96815. Tel. 808/926-0641, or toll free 800/367-5004 in the U.S. and Canada. Fax 808/922-2148. 125 rms, 15 suites. A/C TV TEL

$ Rates: Apr–Dec 17, $85–$100 double, $110–$115 large double with kitchenette for up to three people; $150 junior suites for up to five. Dec 18–Mar, all rates increase $10. AE, DC, JCB, MC, V. **Parking:** $4 per day.

Just 1½ blocks from the beach, this newly renovated Hawaiian Pacific Resorts hotel enjoys a convenient central location. The 21-story two-tower structure has its own restaurant, a round-the-clock minimart, a launderette, and lots of big-hotel amenities. The rooms are newly furnished in soft pastels, with white furniture, in-room safes, and a refrigerator in every room. The rooms and suites with kitchenettes have microwaves and dining areas, and cooking and dining utensils. The junior suites have a sitting room with a sofa bed, and all bedrooms have queen-size beds. The handsomely renovated lobby is paneled in natural koa wood and has sections that are open to the sky, with planter boxes filled with palms and ferns.

OCEAN RESORT HOTEL WAIKIKI, 175 Paoakalani Ave., Honolulu, HI 96815. Tel. 808/922-3861, or toll free 800/367-2317, 800/999-6640 in Canada. Fax 808/924-1982. 450 rms, 7 suites. A/C TV TEL

$ Rates: Diamond Head Tower, Apr–Dec 22, $68–$96 single or double; Dec 23–Mar, $79–$107 single or double. Pali Tower, Apr–Dec 22, $91–$125 single or double; Dec 23–Mar, $91–$125 single or double. Each additional person $15; $105–$275 suite. AE, DC, DISC, ER, JCB, MC, V. **Parking:** $4 per day.

A very welcome find in this area close to Kapiolani Park, this is a cheerful, sparkling hotel with a waterfall at the entrance, a golden lobby, and friendly people behind the desk. It has every hotel amenity, including two small swimming pools on the third floor, a tour desk, laundry room, and daily maid service. Prices are lowest in the Diamond Head Tower; rooms here do not have kitchenettes, but there are compact refrigerators, and you'll enjoy your lanai and the view. All rooms in the Pali Tower have kitchenettes. Rooms in both buildings are of standard size, and have dressing areas, and stall showers large enough and deep enough for a bath. The Mala Restaurant, adjacent to the lobby, serves three Japanese/American meals a day.

ROYAL KUHIO, 2240 Kuhio Ave., Honolulu, HI 96815. Tel. 808/538-7145 or 808/923-2502, or toll free 800/367-5205. Fax 808/533-4621. 385 apts. A/C TV TEL

$ Rates: Apr 16–Dec 15, $80 one-bedroom apt. Dec 16–Apr 15, $110 one-bedroom apt. AE, DC, DISC, MC, V. **Parking:** Free.

Apartments at this towering condominium building are quite attractive and nicely decorated, with a bedroom with twin beds that can be closed off from the sitting room or opened to make one big area. The sitting room has sofa beds, and rollaways are available for additional people. The kitchens are all-electric (with dishwashers), the closet space is ample, and every apartment has its own lanai. A pool and sun-deck area, billiard room, Ping-Pong, a shuffleboard court, and a huge laundry room and recreation area all make for easy living—not to mention that the Royal Kuhio is close to the beach. There is weekly chamber service.

Reservations: Paradise Management Corporation, Suite C-207, 50 S. Beretania St., Honolulu, HI 96813; or phone the toll-free number above.

WAIKIKI GRAND, 134 Kapahulu Ave., Honolulu, HI 96815. Tel. 808/923-1511, or toll free 800/535-0085. Fax 808/922-2421. 105 rms. A/C TV TEL

$ Rates (including continental breakfast): $70–$95 double. Each additional person $15. Children under 18 stay free in parents' room (using existing bedding). AE, MC, V. **Parking:** $5 per day.

Now a member of the Condofree Resorts group, this older hotel has recently been upgraded and remodeled, and like the other hotels in its group, offers a manager's cocktail reception daily, daily maid service, and either a free car with a weekly stay or the seventh night free. And what a pleasant location this one has, just across the street from Kapiolani Park and all its activities, and just around the bend from Kuhio Beach. From the lower-priced rooms, views are of the center of Waikiki, but go a little higher and you'll be rewarded with breathtaking views of Diamond Head. Super views or not, the rooms are pleasant if small (very little closet space), and have tub/showers. There's a pleasant swimming pool in a secluded court, and a Japanese restaurant on the premises. Many Japanese guests favor this one.

READERS RECOMMEND

Colony's Pacific Monarch Hotel, *142 Uluniu Ave., Honolulu, HI 96815 (tel. 808/923-9805). "I would like to strongly recommend Colony's Pacific Monarch Hotel, where we have vacationed for many years. It is ideally located one block from the beach and King's Village and close to many fine restaurants. The skytop pool, Jacuzzi, and sauna with weatherproofed picnic activity area add to the many pleasures available. Lanais are equipped with table and chairs so that you can have a relaxing meal while watching the beautiful views (many of them oceanfront) and the sunset. Rooms have kitchenettes and include a welcome kit of coffee, tea, etc. Rates are structured by season. The studios with kitchenettes and walk-out lanais are $105 and $115. One-bedroom apartments with full kitchens and large lanais are $140 and $150. Maid service is included."*—Dr. John Lopresti, Jr., Bricktown, N.J.

CENTRAL WAIKIKI

CORAL REEF, 2299 Kuhio Ave., Honolulu, HI 96815. Tel. 808/922-1262, or toll free 800/922-7866 in the mainland U.S., 800/445-6633 in Canada. Fax 808/922-8785. Telex 634479 ASTHUW. 242 rms, 45 suites. A/C TV TEL

$ Rates: Apr–Dec 20, $65–$75 double; $85 junior suite; $100 one-bedroom suite. Dec 21–Mar, $85–$95 double; $105 junior suite; $120 one-bedroom suite. Each additional person $10. AE, DC, MC, V. **Parking:** $5 per exit.

You get a really large room at this modern high-rise hotel directly behind the International Market Place and a short walk from Waikiki Beach. The hotel boasts every facility—swimming pool, garage, restaurants, shops—and nicely furnished rooms that have either one or two double beds (or a double and a single), private lanai, and cable TV. The hotel is managed by Aston Hotels & Resorts, 2255 Kuhio Ave., Honolulu, HI 96815.

HOTEL HONOLULU, 376 Kaiolu St., Honolulu, HI 96815. Tel. 808/926-2766, or toll free 800/426-2766. Fax 808/922-3326. 15 studios, 9 one-bedroom suites. TEL

$ Rates: $64–$76 studio; $98 one-bedroom suite. Each additional person $8. AE, DC, DISC, MC, V. **Parking:** Free, covered off-street.

A beautiful orchid collection, tropical birds, and hundreds of potted plants give a garden atmosphere to Hawaii's only gay hotel. They call it a "deco–post modern" building, but we call it a reminder of the plantation days. Whatever you call it, the Hotel Honolulu is an oasis in time and space. Located two blocks from the beach, the two buildings of the hotel compound are isolated from traffic. There's a rooftop garden sun deck, very popular for evening barbecues and drinks, and a variety of clubs, restaurants, and shops just around the corner.

Best choice for budgeteers here is the smaller, two-story building called the Bamboo Lanai, where small, nicely furnished studios go for $70. They have a small, fully equipped kitchenette, a bathroom with a tile-enclosed shower, and a closet. Larger studios and one-bedroom suites in the three-story main building, which is air-conditioned, are more elaborate and more expensive. The studios have a sitting area, queen-size bed, complete kitchen, full bathroom, ceiling fans and cross-ventilation, and a lanai. The one-bedroom suites are quite large, with king-size bed, lanai, complete kitchen, and full bath, and each one is distinctively decorated in various styles: Japanese, Chinese, bamboo, safari, Chippendale, deco, and so on. TVs (free) are available on request. There's free coffee all day in the lobby, and a laundry room as well.

ILIMA HOTEL, 445 Nohonani St., Honolulu, HI 96815. Tel. 808/923-1877, or toll free 800/876-5278 in the mainland U.S. and Canada. Fax 808/924-8371. 74 studios, 18 one-bedroom suites, 6 two-bedroom suites. A/C TV TEL

$ Rates: Apr–Dec 14, $69–$94 single; $77–$106 double; $114–$146 executive suite for three; $124–$136 large one-bedroom suite; $106–$199 two-bedroom suite; one-, two-, or three-bedroom penthouse. Dec 15–Mar, add $12 to all rates. Each additional person $8. AE, DC, DISC, JCB, MC, V. **Parking:** Free.

Still going strong after 23 years, the Ilima is eminently comfortable and offers many facilities and services, and a recent $1.2-million renovation has not upped the rates unreasonably. A walk of less than 10 minutes will take you to the beach. You can really kick off your shoes and feel at home here; floors are carpeted, rooms are condominium-size spacious, and the studios include two double beds, a fully equipped kitchen with microwave, TV, radio, full tub and shower, plenty of storage space, and a private lanai. There's a swimming pool at ground level and two sun decks on the 10th floor, as well as an exercise room and sauna. Generosities not usually found in most Waikiki hotels include free parking and free local phone calls—not to mention those fully equipped kitchens in every unit. Sergio's Italian Restaurant is right at hand.

MARINE SURF, 364 Seaside Ave., Honolulu, HI 96815. Tel. 808/923-0277, or toll free 800/367-5176 in the mainland U.S., 800/663-1118 in Canada. Fax 808/926-5915. 117 studios, 1 one-bedroom suite. A/C TV TEL

$ Rates: Apr–Dec 20, $75–$80 studio single or double; $120 one-bedroom penthouse suite. Dec 21–Mar $85–$95 studio single or double; $140 one-bedroom penthouse suite. Each additional person $14. Children under 18 stay free in parent's room. Cribs $10 a day. CB, DC, MC, V. **Parking:** $4 a day.

★ The Marine Surf has just about everything going for it. Located about 1½ blocks from the beach, this 23-story condominium hotel features smartly decorated studio apartments, each one with two extra-length double beds, lots of drawer space, a dressing room, a safe, and a bath with tub and shower. Best of all, each studio has a full electric kitchen, just in case you choose not to eat every night at Matteo's Italian Restaurant, one of the finest in town, right in the lobby. Rooms, which have been completely renovated, are serviced daily. Those too lazy to walk to the beach can swim and sun at the lovely outdoor pool on the fourth floor. Studios accommodate up to four, and penthouse suites, six. There's on-site parking.

OUTRIGGER EAST HOTEL, 150 Kaiulani Ave., Honolulu, HI 96815. Tel. 808/922-5353, or toll free 800/733-7777 in the U.S. and Canada, 0014-800/126-985 from Australia. Fax toll free 800/456-4329. Telex MCI 634178. 445 rms. A/C TV TEL

$ Rates: Apr–June and Sept–Dec 18, $85–$105 double; $105 studio; $125–$150 suite. Dec 19–Mar and July–Aug, $100–$120 double; $120 studio; $140–$250 suite. Each additional person $15. AE, CB, DC, DISC, JCB, MC, V. **Parking:** $7 per day.

Outrigger Hotels Hawaii has a number of establishments in central Waikiki, and this newly renovated (to the tune of $5 million) hotel is the top of the line in the chain's mid-priced category. The 18-floor building is a short block from Waikiki Beach and has just about everything a visitor needs, from four restaurants (Pepper's, Islander Coffee Shop, Chuck's Cellar, and Jolly Roger) to a beauty shop, travel and tour desks, and laundry facilities. Rooms have been smartly furnished, each with either two double beds, a king-size bed, or a queen-size bed; all have TVs with pay movies, in-room safes, and refrigerators; studios have kitchenettes. Studios can accommodate up to three guests and suites can accommodate up to four. Cars from Dollar Rent A Car are free for every day of your stay if you request the "Outrigger Free Ride" package when making reservations.

OUTRIGGER MALIA HOTEL, 2211 Kuhio Ave., Honolulu, HI 96815. Tel. 808/923-7621, or toll free 800/773-7777 in the U.S. and Canada, 0014-800/126-985 from Australia. Fax toll free 800/456-4329. Telex MCI 634178. 280 rms. A/C TV TEL

$ Rates: Apr–June and Sept–Dec 18, $75–$90 double; $90 suite. Dec 19–Mar and July–Aug, $85–$100 double; $100 suite. Each additional person $15. AE, CB, DC, DISC, JCB, MC, V. **Parking:** $7 per day.

This bright and beautiful place features two wings. The rooms in the Malia wing, the taller of the hotel's two sections, have two double beds with Polynesian-print bedspreads in soft, muted colors and wall-to-wall carpeting. All rooms in the hotel have a lanai, both tub and shower in the bathroom, a small refrigerator, and an ironing board. Disabled people will be glad to know that there are 16 rooms in this wing specially designed for them, with wider doorways, grab bars in the bathrooms, and twin-size rather than double beds for greater wheelchair mobility.

The Luana wing has junior suites which can accommodate four guests comfortably; all contain a sitting room with two couches and a bedroom with two beds. The lanais in the suites are much larger than those in the bedrooms of the Malia wing. Pluses for guests at both wings include a Jacuzzi whirlpool, a rooftop tennis court, and the excellent Wailana Coffeeshop, open 24 hours a day. And, of course, the beach is just three blocks away. Cars from Dollar Rent A Car are free for every day of your stay if you request the "Outrigger Free Ride" when making reservations.

OUTRIGGER VILLAGE HOTEL, 240 Lewers St., Honolulu, HI 96815. Tel. 808/923-3881, or toll free 800/733-7777 in the U.S. and Canada; 0014-800/126-985 from Australia. Fax toll free 800/456-4329. Telex MCI 634178. 399 rms. A/C TV TEL

$ Rates: Apr–June and Sept–Dec 18, $80–$95 double; $85–$100 studio; $120–$130 suite. Dec 19–Mar and July–Aug, $90–$105 double; $95–$110 studio; $120–$130 suite. Each additional person $15. AE, CB, DC, DISC, JCB, MC, V. **Parking:** $6 per day.

This is the first hotel we've ever seen with a swimming pool in the center of the lobby!

The lobby is a quadrangle built around the pool, and there's no ceiling in the center, so you can swim and sunbathe while checking out the new arrivals. The hotel is decorated from lobby to rooms in a bright blending of contemporary and Polynesian styles. Each of the units has an in-room safe, and most have lanais. Rooms are all similar, although those on the lower floors are cheaper. Studios have kitchens; family suites have half-size refrigerators and hotplates. The Village boasts its own restaurant, cocktail lounge, video dance palace, and several attractive shops—and a superb location right in the middle of everything and close to the beach. Cars from Dollar Rent A Car are free for every day of your stay if you request the "Outrigger Free Ride" when making reservations.

OUTRIGGER WAIKIKI TOWER HOTEL, 200 Lewers St., Honolulu, HI 96815. Tel. 808/922-6424, or toll free 800/733-7777 in the U.S. and Canada, 0014-800/126-985 from Australia. Fax toll free 800/456-4329. Telex MCI 634178. 419 rms. A/C TV TEL

$ Rates: Apr–June and Sept–Dec 18, $80–$95 double; $85–$100 studio; $120–$130 suite. Dec 19–Mar and July–Aug, $90–$105 double; $95–$110 studio; $120–$130 suite. Each additional person $15. AE, CB, DC, DISC, JCB, MC, V. **Parking:** $7 per day.

This recently renovated hotel is next to the Outrigger Edgewater Hotel, which means that it shares a prime, close-to-the-beach location. Access to restaurants is just as easy as to the beach; the Waikiki Broiler is downstairs, Trattoria and Original Chuck's Original Steakhouse at the Edgewater and popular Denny's are across Lewers Street. The open-air lobby is chock full of convenience desks and shops. The pleasantly decorated rooms have a lanai, an in-room safe, a shower, and a king-size or queen-size bed or two twin beds. Studios have kitchenettes, but whether or not you get a kitchenette, you will get a refrigerator, and that goes a long way to cutting costs on food. Kitchenette units include a microwave oven, refrigerator, and utensils. Cars from Dollar Rent A Car are free for every day of your stay if you request the "Outrigger Free Ride" package when making reservations.

PATRICK WINSTON'S HAWAIIAN KING RENTALS, 417 Nohonani St., Honolulu, HI 96815. Tel. 808/922-3894, or toll free 800/545-1948. Fax 808/924-3332. 26 units in 66-unit hotel/condominium. A/C TV TEL

$ Rates: Apr 15–Dec 15, $65–$75. Dec 16–Apr 14, $65–$95. Each additional person $10. Airline discounts. Minimum stay 4 days. AE, MC, V. **Parking:** $4 per day.

You could call Patrick Winston's units here a hotel-within-a-hotel—they're really something special. Winston, a delightful young man who takes a caring, personal interest in his guests, many of whom return year after year, purchased his first unit in the Hawaiian King when it became a condominium hotel back in 1981. He was the interior designer-contractor who furnished the entire project. All his units have gone through complete $20,000-and-more renovations. One unit is called the Blue Hawaiian Suite, since it is furnished with blue rattan and blue carpeting along with an accent coral color. Two large units (780 sq. ft.) are called the Corporate Suites; they contain a separate room with a complete work station including a typewriter, calculator, and other business supplies, along with a large living room with VCR, electronic safe, and a conference area. The Mount Fuji Suite has white-marble and black accents along with Oriental furniture, futons, and shoji screens. His other one-bedroom units have new carpeting and furniture, ceramic tiles, floor-to-ceiling mirrors, stereos and cable remote televisions, kitchens with microwave and convection ovens, and washer/dryers. Winston states: "I am dedicated to concepts that ring out time and again in your literature and that is quality lodging at a price, with the aloha spirit ringing in loudly."

The Hawaiian King is a five-story building built around a lovely pool and garden area, about two blocks from the beach. The delightful Swiss Café is next door. There's a laundry on the premises, a cocktail lounge, a minimart, and 24-hour front-desk and telephone switchboard service. This is a good bet even if you don't get one of the special rooms—even better if you do.

WHITE SANDS WAIKIKI RESORT, 431 Nohonani St., Honolulu, HI 96815. Tel. 808/923-7336. 80 rms. A/C, TV, TEL

$ **Rates:** $62–$79 single; $69–$85 double. AE, DC, DISC, MC, V. **Parking:** Free, but very limited, in the hotel; public lot across the street.

On pleasant Nohonani Street, about halfway between Kuhio Avenue and Ala Wai Boulevard, this low-rise garden hotel is a longtime favorite. It's a time-sharing establishment, so it's not always easy to get an opening here, and reservations cannot be confirmed until two weeks before your arrival date. However, when you consider that rooms are nicely furnished and that you get a kitchenette and a private lanai with even a standard room, it's worth a try. Each apartment is furnished differently, but nicely, in a Polynesian decor, and the beds are large and comfortable. Rooms have daily cleaning service. The deluxe swimming pool, in an inner court, is surrounded by gardens, shady nooks, and pathways for exploring this tranquil acre in the heart of Waikiki. Coffee is served free in the lobby in the morning, and rum punch at sunset.

EWA WAIKIKI

AMBASSADOR HOTEL OF WAIKIKI, 2040 Kuhio Ave., Honolulu, HI 96815. Tel. 808/941-7777. Fax 808/922-4579. 315 rms. A/C TV TEL

$ **Rates:** $72–$96 single; $80–$104 double; $140–$165 one-bedroom suite. AE, CB, DC, JCB, MC, V. **Parking:** $3 per day.

An old-timer in Waikiki, the Ambassador still gives good value for the dollar. It's a comfortable hotel with all the conveniences. No wonder you always find airline personnel staying here! All the rooms in this high-rise building are approached from outside walkways. Even the lower-priced studios, from the second through seventh floors, boast private lanais, contemporary furniture, and deep furo-type shower tubs. You can relax at the big pool and sun deck on the second floor and eat at the Café Ambassador; you're also fairly close to all the attractions of Waikiki. The deluxe one-bedroom suites are equipped with full electric kitchens. Studios with kitchens are available on request.

CONDOFREE WAIKIKI ROYAL SUITES, 255 Beach Walk, Honolulu, HI 96815. Tel. 808/926-5641, or toll free 800/535-0085. Fax 808/922-2421. 47 suites. TV TEL

$ **Rates** (including European breakfast): Apr–Dec 22, $143–$247 one-bedroom suite for up to four. Dec 23–Mar, $164–$285 one-bedroom suite. Crib or rollaway $5. AE, JCB, MC, V. **Parking:** $6 per day.

Enjoying a superb location half a block from the ocean, this is Waikiki's first all-suite hotel. You'll be able to stretch out and relax here, since the suites are all of good size, and the lanais, many of which have ocean views, are extra large. There's a queen-size sofa bed in the living room, large mirrored closets, and in-room safes, and each suite has its own fully equipped kitchen, with microwave oven, coffee makers, and fresh ground coffee. There is no pool. There's a warm feeling of hospitality here, and there's a sunset evening cocktail party daily. Laundry facilities are available.

HAWAIIANA HOTEL, 260 Beach Walk, Honolulu, HI 96815. Tel. 808/923-3811, or toll free 800/367-5122 in the mainland U.S. and Canada. Fax 808/926-5728. 94 studios, 7 one-bedroom suites. A/C TV TEL

$ **Rates:** $80–$90 single; $85–$95 double; $135–$143 one-bedroom suite; $190 Alii Studio. Each additional person $8. Packages available. AE, MC, V. **Parking:** $6 per day (limited).

A favorite old-timer in Hawaii, this place gets more mellow every year. One of the few low-rise garden hotels left in Waikiki, the Hawaiiana is wonderfully located just half a block from a good swimming beach in front of the Outrigger Reef Hotel and Fort DeRussy. Rooms are situated around a gorgeous tropical garden and two swimming pools in the two- and three-story buildings, so you can step out your door for a swim in the pool or a complimentary breakfast of juice and coffee out on the patio. Comfortable chairs at poolside are occupied most of the day by guests too content to move. All rooms have been remodeled and furnished with rattan furniture; each has an electronic safe and an electric kitchen; most have a lanai. One-bedroom suites can accommodate up to four guests. Niceties include free newspapers in the morning or afternoon, Hawaiian shows twice a week, and free use of washers and dryers.

HAWAII DYNASTY HOTEL, 1830 Ala Moana Blvd., Honolulu, HI 96815. Tel. 808/955-1111, or toll free 800/421-6662 in the U.S. and Canada. Fax 808/947-1799. 199 rms, 2 suites. A/C TV TEL

$ Rates: Apr–Dec 19, $70–$80 double; $165 suite. Dec 20–Mar, $83–$93 double; $165 suite. Each additional person $12. AE, CB, DC, MC, V. **Parking:** $3.50 per day.

A good budget choice in the Ilikai and Hilton Hawaiian Village complex of hotels, stores, and restaurants is this high-rise hotel with an inn atmosphere. The accent is on comfort, with medium-size rooms and oversize beds; twin beds are as big as most doubles, and the doubles are enormous. Suites can accommodate up to four guests. Rooms are tastefully furnished and have combination tub/showers in the bathrooms. There are no cooking facilities, but there is a 24-hour Chinese restaurant, Dynasty, on premises. A laundry room is available. The pool on the second floor is one of the largest in Waikiki. (Note: A planned refurbishment may up the rates.)

OUTRIGGER REEF LANAIS, 225 Saratoga Rd., Honolulu, HI 96815. Tel. 808/923-3881, or toll free 800/733-7777 in the U.S. and Canada, 0014-800/126-985 from Australia. Fax toll free 800/456-4329. Telex MCI 634158. 62 rms. A/C TV TEL

$ Rates: Apr–June and Sept–Dec 18, $80 double, $85 double with kitchenette; $110–$150 suite. Dec 19–Mar and July–Aug, $90 double, $95 double with kitchenette; $110–$150 suite. AE, CB, DC, DISC, JCB, MC, V. **Parking:** $7 per day.

This hotel is yet another member of the popular Outrigger hotel chain. It's tops in location, with the beach just a hop-skip-and-a-jump away; there's a public right-of-way to the ocean just across Kalia Road. Although it lacks some of the frills of the other Outrigger hotels, this spot is still a good value for the price. The lobby and rooms have all been renovated. Guest rooms are nicely decorated and have either twin or queen-size beds, an in-room safe, and a shower (no tub); some rooms have kitchenettes, which include a microwave oven, refrigerator, and utensils. There is no pool on the premises, but guests may use the one at Outrigger Village, right around the corner on Lewers Street. The ever-popular Buzz's Steak & Lobster is located on the premises. Cars from Dollar Rent A Car are free for every day of your stay if you request the "Outrigger Free Ride" when making reservations.

WAIKIKI TERRACE HOTEL, 2045 Kalakaua Ave., Honolulu, HI 96815. Tel. 808/955-6000, or toll free 800/445-8811 in the mainland U.S. and Canada. Fax 808/943-8555. 250 rms and 3 suites. A/C TV TEL

$ Rates: Apr–Dec 19, $120–$150 double; $295 suite. Dec 20–Mar, $110–$114 double; $275 suite. Each additional person $15. Children under 12 stay free in parents' room when using existing bedding. AE, CB, DC, DISC, JCB, MC, V. **Parking:** $6 per day.

"Affordably elegant" is the operative term here. A $10.5-million renovation has transformed an older hotel into a sparkling new property, with four-star service and amenities not usually found in hotels in this price category. Completely refurbished guest rooms are handsome, with light furniture and splendid marble and granite bathrooms with grooming products, and Berber carpeting. Each room has its own safe, a refrigerator, and a dry bar with an instant hot-water dispenser and a complimentary basket of coffees and teas. Views from your private lanais—of the ocean or mountains—are special. Rooms for the disabled and nonsmokers are available on request. A great stretch of Waikiki Beach (fronting Fort DeRussy and the Hilton Hawaiian Village) is about a seven-minute walk away (through Fort DeRussy Park), but there's also a sun deck with pool and spa at home, as well as a fitness center. And there's room service too, from the hotel's outstanding restaurant, the Mezzanine, which has become one of the hottest new spots in Waikiki.

NEAR THE ALA WAI

COLONY'S COCONUT PLAZA, 2171 The Ala Wai, Honolulu, HI 96815. Tel. 808/923-8828, or toll free 800/777-1700 in the mainland U.S. Fax 808/923-3473. 88 studios, 3 suites. A/C TV TEL

$ Rates (including continental breakfast): Apr–Dec 19, $70–$100 studio. Dec 20–Mar, $80–$110 studio. Suites from $150. AE, DISC, JCB, MC, V. **Parking:** $7 per day.

This genteel hotel fronting the Ala Wai Canal could easily be in Switzerland or on the Mediterranean. Sedate brass nameplates, a waterfall, and proud palms give a special ambience to the stone entry. Up front, near the waterfall, is a small, free-form pool. All studios are beautifully furnished, with tile floors, woven-fiber walls, a kitchenette with microwave oven, and a private lanai. The lovely complimentary continental breakfast includes fruits, juices, banana bread, breakfast rolls, and tea or Kona coffee. A nice way to start a Hawaiian day! Colony's Coconut Plaza is across from the Ala Wai Golf Course, and 3½ blocks from Waikiki Beach.

HAWAIIAN MONARCH, 444 Niu St., Honolulu, HI 96815. Tel. 808/949-3911, or toll free 800/535-0085 in the mainland U.S., 800/445-6623 in Canada. Fax 808/922-2421. 293 rms, 73 suites. A/C TV TEL

$ Rates: Apr–Dec 21, $65–$84 double. Dec 22–Mar, $80–$98 double. Each additional person $10. Children under 18 stay free in parent's room. Suites $84. AE, MC, V. **Parking:** $6 per day.

This skyscraper hotel is very close to the Ala Wai Canal and halfway between Ala Moana Shopping Center and the beaches of Waikiki. It's a well-run establishment with a mixed international clientele, and complete with all the amenities of tourist life: a huge sun deck and regular pool, plenty of shops in the arcade, and a coffee shop and cozy bar in the main lobby.

The Hawaiian Monarch is part hotel, part condo, and the hotel rooms, which occupy the 7th–24th floors, all have a refrigerator, a coffee bar, and bathrooms with full tubs and showers. They are done in modern tropical decor with whitewashed rattan furniture, pastel island-style pictures, and new bedspreads and chairs with color-coordinated fabric. The nicest views are those overlooking the Ala Wai Canal. Studio suites are available with kitchenette or kitchens.

NEAR ALA MOANA

INN ON THE PARK, 1920 Ala Moana Blvd., Honolulu, HI 96815. Tel. 808/946-8355, or toll free 800/922-7866 in the mainland U.S., 800/445-6633 in Canada. Fax 808/922-8785. Telex 634479 ASTHIUW. 134 units. A/C TV TEL

$ Rates: Apr–Dec 21, $67–$89 double; $89 studio. Dec 22–Mar, $82–$100 double; $104 studio. AE, CB, DC, MC, V. **Parking:** $6 per day.

Not far from the Hilton Hawaiian Village and a block from the popular Fort DeRussy Beach, this is a completely renovated hotel/condominium. The smallish but pretty rooms are decorated with floral spreads setting off the modern furnishings and decor. Very helpful for those wishing to fix breakfast or a light lunch are the refrigerators and wet bars in most of the units; kitchenette units are also available. This place would be most suitable for two, or perhaps three, people in a room, but families might find it a bit tight. There's a modern lobby with a convenience store and a nice pool and sun deck on the fifth floor, next to the Inn Beer Garden Lounge, which provides jazz entertainment.

Accommodations here are in three classes: standard (city or mountain view); superior (ocean view); and deluxe kitchenette (city view or ocean view), the latter on request only). In standard or superior accommodations, refrigerators and lanais are available on request only.

PAGODA HOTEL, 1525 Rycroft St., Honolulu, HI 96814. Tel. 808/941-6611, or toll free 800/367-6060 in the mainland U.S. and Canada. Fax 808/922-8061. Telex 633101. 361 rms. A/C TV TEL

$ Rates: Pagoda Hotel, $78–$88 studio apt single or double. Pagoda Terrace, $73 studio apt; $93 one-bedroom apt; $110 two-bedroom apt. Each additional person $15. AE, CB, DC, DISC, JCB, MC, V. **Parking:** $2 per day.

Although this hotel is about a 10-minute drive from Waikiki, you won't be isolated here: Not only are you near the Ala Moana Shopping Center, but right on the grounds is one of Honolulu's most spectacular restaurants, the Pagoda, with its colorful displays of flashing carp. Two buildings flank Rycroft Street—Pagoda Terrace and the Pagoda Hotel. All rooms at the Pagoda Hotel have recently been refurnished and are cheery and bright. Rooms at the Pagoda Terrace offer studio apartments nicely set up for housekeeping, with a full-size refrigerator, four-burner range, and all the necessary equipment. One- and two-bedroom apartments also offer plenty of comfort. There are full baths. Two swimming pools are here for dunking.

WAIKIKI PARKSIDE, 1850 Ala Moana Blvd., Honolulu, HI 96815. Tel. 808/955-1567, or toll free 800/237-9666. Fax 808/955-6010. 250 rms, 5 suites. A/C TV TEL

$ Rates: Apr–Dec 19, $85–$115 double; $175–$375 suite. Dec 20–Mar, $95–$125 double; $175–$375 suite. Children under 17 stay free in parents' room when using existing bedding. Each additional person $15. AE, CB, DC, DISC, JCB, MC, V. **Parking:** $4 per day.

Located close to Ala Moana Shopping Center and Ala Moana Beach Park, this older hotel has completed a multi-million-dollar renovation and offers cozy, comfortable lodgings at reasonable prices. Newly refurbished guest rooms have rattan furniture, double or queen-size beds, refrigerators, private safes, and tile bathrooms. Guests enjoy the outdoor pool deck with its snack bar and the convenience of having a branch of the popular Denny's chain on hand for meals or snacks 24 hours a day—and for room service too, from 7am to 9pm. Rooms for the disabled and nonsmokers are available on request.

WINDWARD OAHU

KE IKI HALE, 59-579 Ke Iki Rd., Haleiwa, HI 96712. Tel. 808/638-8229. 12 units.

$ Rates: $80–$125 one-bedroom unit; $145 one-bedroom cottage; $145–$165 two-bedroom cottage. AE, DC, DISC, MC, V. **Parking:** Free.

Here's a place for those who long to be right on the beach, or just a few steps away from it. Alice Tracy's rental cottages on the North Shore are on 1½ acres of palm-fringed land near Waimea Bay. They are nicely furnished, with full kitchens; some have large picture windows overlooking the ocean. Guests can enjoy the barbecue facilities, the picnic tables at water's edge, and a small volleyball court. There's a public telephone on the premises, but not a TV in sight. Remember that Waimea Bay is ideal for swimming in the summer months, but during the winter its sky-high waves are for experienced surfers only.

LANILOA LODGE HOTEL, 55-109 Laniloa St., Laie, HI 96762. Tel. 808/293-9282, or toll free 800/LANILOA (526-4562). 47 rms. A/C TV TEL

$ Rates: $79 single or double; $89 double with car; $89 triple or quad. Children under 8 stay free in parents' room. Weekly packages available. AE, DC, DISC, MC, V. **Parking:** Free.

Located right next door to the Polynesian Cultural Center, this modern, motel-like building offers lots of comfort and a good location not far from many of the attractions of the North Shore. Right at your feet is a sandy ocean beach and pool; a short drive away is all the swimming, surfing, windsurfing, diving, horseback riding, championship golfing, and the like available in the Sunset Beach and Haleiwa area. Waimea Bay offers some of the world's best swimming (in summer) and best surfing (in winter). Waimea Falls Park is delightful, and Haleiwa has many shops and restaurants and an artsy-craftsy atmosphere. Rooms at Laniloa Lodge overlook the pool and courtyard and have private lanais and cable TV. The lodge is within walking distance of the Brigham Young University Hawaii Campus and the Mormon Temple. Temple-patron rates are available upon request.

SCHRADER'S WINDWARD MARINE RESORT, 47-039 Lihikai Dr., Kaneohe, HI 96744. Tel. 808/239-5711, or toll free 800/735-5711. Fax 808/239-6658. 53 units. A/C TV TEL

$ Rates: $70–$125 one-bedroom; $100–$190 two-bedroom, $170–$315 two-bedroom with den. Each additional person $7.50. AE, DC, MC, V. **Parking:** Free.

On the shores of Kaneohe Bay, this older, rural hotel, about a half-hour drive from both Waikiki and downtown Honolulu, is something special for those who like a country setting. It's a world unto itself, dedicated to introducing the field of marine recreation to its guests. Its own pier services the North Bay Boat Club and Sailing School; daily boat trips are available and a variety of sailboats, windsurfers, kayaks, and jet boats are also on hand. Beginners can learn how, and experts can just take off.

Five buildings here share a compound bordered by a stream on one side and Kaneohe Bay on the other. There's a swimming pool and a therapy pool (a Jacuzzi with unheated water). Picnic tables and barbecues abound.

Each unit has a living room, bathroom, lanai, and full-size refrigerator; some have kitchen facilities as well. Furnishings are modest but comfortable in this older establishment; you might have an old-fashioned tub instead of a shower. Rooms with waterfront views are more expensive. Daily cleaning service is provided. Three-bedroom suites are also available.

3. HOSTELS, Y's & A MILITARY HOTEL

HOSTELS

HALE ALOHA, 2417 Prince Edward St., Honolulu, HI 96815. Tel. 808/926-8313. Fax 808/946-5904. 50 beds, 4 studios.

$ Rates: $12 bed; $26 studio. MC, V. **Parking:** $2 per day.

This youth hostel is just the ticket for beach buffs, since it's two short blocks from Waikiki Beach. It's for AYH or IYHF members only (you can purchase a $25 membership at the hostel in Manoa Valley—see below), and offers dormitory accommodations for 20 women and 30 men. Two common rooms provide kitchens, patios, TV, and the relaxed camaraderie for which youth hostels are famous. Dorms are closed and locked from 10am to 5pm daily in accordance with the hostel tradition of promoting outdoor life. Couples might consider renting one of the four studios here which feature private bath and shower, mini-refrigerators, private entrance, and 24-hour access to the rooms; some have TV. The staff is helpful with information on low-cost vacationing and travel. Stays are guaranteed for three days; they'll let you stay longer if they're not busy.

INTERCLUB HOSTEL WAIKIKI, 2413 Kuhio Ave., Honolulu, HI 96815. Tel. 808/924-2636. 140 beds in shared rms (three-night minimum stay), 5 private rooms.

$ **Rates:** $15 bed; $45 private room. Each additional person $10. No credit cards. **Parking:** Free but limited, mostly on street.

This hostel, just two blocks from the beach at Waikiki, is for international travelers only: You must show a passport and a ticket to a foreign destination. (Foreigners need only show tickets to the United States; Americans must be going beyond Hawaii.) According to one guest we met, it's "the looser of the hostels" in Waikiki, since it's open 24 hours and has no curfew, and there are no chores to be done. Dorm rooms, with four or seven bunks in each room, each has its own private bath and shower. Private rooms are nicely set up with a couch out front, a bed in the back, and these, too, have their own private baths. There are common rooms, kitchen and laundry facilities, and a friendly atmosphere. There are movies on Wednesday, barbecues on Saturday, and many special events.

NEAR THE UNIVERSITY OF HAWAII

HONOLULU INTERNATIONAL AMERICAN YOUTH HOSTEL [AYH], 2323A Seaview Ave., Honolulu, HI 96822. Tel. 808/946-0591. Fax 808/946-5904. 38 beds. **Parking:** Free.

$ **Rates:** $10 members, $13 nonmembers. MC, V.

In lovely Manoa Valley, this hostel facility has developed a reputation over the past 23 years as a safe, clean, friendly environment for world travelers. Nonmembers are accepted. There are beds for 18 women and 20 men. Common rooms, a kitchen, a Ping-Pong table, games, and a patio under the stars create a relaxed mood here. House parents Thelma and Susan Akau are helpful sources of information. Walking, hiking, and restaurant tours are available. Many restaurants are available within a quarter mile. Facilities are locked between 10am and 5pm daily.

Note: Hostels are for "the young at heart, regardless of age," although students—Australian, European, Canadian, Japanese, as well as American—do predominate. Simple chores are expected of all guests.

THREE Y's

WAIKIKI

CENTRAL BRANCH YMCA, 401 Atkinson Dr., Honolulu, HI 96814. Tel. 808/941-3344. Fax 808/941-8821. 115 rms. TEL

$ **Rates:** $30 single without bath, $36.50 single with bath; $42 double without bath, $50.50 double with bath. Weekly rates available. AE, MC, V.

Located across the street from Ala Moana Beach Park and the Ala Moana Shopping Center, just a five-minute bus ride to the heart of Waikiki, this is an ideal choice for the single male tourist (*no women accepted*). It's a beautiful place, complete with an outdoor swimming pool and lovely grounds. The "Y-style" rooms are small but adequate, and you can add a rollaway bed to create a double. The Y has a reasonably priced coffee shop, a large-screen TV in the residents' lounge, and no end of recreational activities; guests are welcome to use all athletic facilities, including the weight-training center and racquetball courts. Reservations are accepted and welcomed.

DOWNTOWN HONOLULU

FERNHURST YWCA, 1566 Wilder Ave., Honolulu, HI 96822. Tel. 808/941-2231. 60 rms (all with adjoining bath). TEL

$ Rates (including two meals Mon–Fri): $28 single for YWCA members, $33 for nonmembers; $20 per person double for YWCA members, $25 per person for nonmembers. No credit cards. **Parking:** Limited parking at daily, weekly, and monthly rates.

For women tourists who'd like to stay at a Y, Honolulu has a terrific answer. Women can stay for up to six months at this pleasant tropical residence about halfway between downtown Honolulu and Waikiki. The residence accepts both short- and long-term visitors, many of the latter from afar. So staying here is a good way to get to know people from many countries and backgrounds. The accommodations consist of nicely furnished double rooms, each joined to another room by a common bath. Sometimes single rooms are available. Y membership ($25) is required for stays longer than three nights. Rates include two meals a day on weekdays—surely one of the best buys in town! Linens may be rented for a nominal fee if you don't provide your own. Pluses include a swimming pool, garden, laundry room, and a lounge area. Also available for use: typewriters, piano, TV, sewing machine. Advance reservations are accepted with a one-night deposit. Fernhurst recommends that you write first to inquire about future accommodations.

NUUANU YMCA, 1441 Pali Hwy., Honolulu, HI 96813. Tel. 808/536-3556. 70 rms.

$ Rates: $27 single. Weekly rates available. AE, MC, V.

For men only, this modern, $1.3-million facility downtown, convenient to bus lines, is a good bet. Advance reservations are accepted. There's a cafeteria here, excellent athletic facilities are made available to residents, and local phone calls are free.

READERS RECOMMEND

University of Hawaii at Manoa. *"Might I suggest to your readers that they visit Hawaii as I did? I spent six weeks in Honolulu as a student at the University of Hawaii at Manoa. The cost of dorm room and board was very economical. Many tours, at special prices, were provided through the university. Our summer student-identity cards even got us "kamaaina" rates at various clubs and attractions. We were often roomed with local students and were thus able to share our different cultures. This is not just meant for single students; there were some dorm facilities for couples. The course selection is wide, ranging from golf and tennis to more academic studies. By the end of six weeks, I was referring to the dorm as 'home.'"*—Susan McEwin, Stratford, Ontario, Canada.

HOTEL FOR THE MILITARY

HALE KOA HOTEL, Armed Forces Recreation Center, Fort DeRussy, 2055 Kalia Rd., Honolulu, HI 96815-1998. Tel. 808/955-0555, or toll free 800/367-6027. 419 rms. A/C TV TEL

$ Rates (depending on rank): $39–$67 standard; $48–$79 superior; $54–$91 partial ocean view; $62–$98 ocean view; $74–$106 oceanfront. Single occupancy deduct $2; more than two persons, add $10 per person. Children under 12 stay free in parents' room using existing bedding. AE, CB, DC, MC, V. **Parking:** Free.

This hotel has a select guest list: It's available only to active-duty and retired military of all services and their families. What a deal! Fronting a superb stretch of Waikiki Beach next door to the posh Hilton Hawaiian Village, it's comparable to any first-class beachfront hotel in Waikiki, and prices, depending on one's rank, are far less than what one pays in regular hotels. Reservations are hard to come by; they can be made up to a year in advance, and are often honored within a much shorter time period. Rooms are of good size and nicely furnished, and most have two double beds. There's a pool, fitness center with sauna, volleyball and racquetball courts, and many services on the premises, including a Post Exchange, a military discount travel office, laundry facilities, and car-rental desk.

One needn't, however, be a guest at Hale Koa to use many of its facilities. Reservists, National Guard members, and military club members are also welcome to enjoy many of the dining and recreational facilities, including a Sunday Champagne Brunch at the Hale Koa Room, and four shows that include a delicious dinner or buffet: Tama's Polynesian Revue on Wednesday, Hale Koa Luau on Thursday, Paniolo (Cowboy) Night on Sunday, and a Tuesday-night Magic Show.

4. AT THE AIRPORT

HONOLULU AIRPORT MINI HOTEL, Main Terminal Central Lobby, Honolulu International Airport. Tel. 808/836-3044. Fax 808/423-2029. 17 rms.

$ Rates (per person, single occupancy only): $30 sleep and shower (8 hr.), $17.50 nap and shower (2 hr.), $7.50 for shower only, including towels and toiletries. MC, V.

Here's something every airline traveler should know about—just in case. In case your plane departure is delayed, in case you have to wait several hours to make a connecting flight, in case you arrive late at night and there's no inter-island plane service until the next morning—or in case you simply need a place to go if you've checked out of your hotel early and have a late-night flight. That's where the Honolulu Airport Mini Hotel comes in. This clean and pleasant facility offers private rooms and resting facilities and the opportunity to take a shower. "Travelers travel under stress," says owner Mona Dunn. "When they walk in this door, the stress ends." Each guest receives personal attention and a real feeling of aloha. There's a coffee pot perpetually brewing, plus a kitchen where flowers or medication can be refrigerated. The Honolulu Airport Mini Hotel is open 24 hours a day. Reservations are advised for sleeping space; they are usually booked after 10pm.

5. BED & BREAKFASTS

Windward Oahu is rural, easygoing, and just a few miles but seemingly worlds away from the hustle-bustle of Waikiki. We've picked a quartet of B&Bs in this area, where you can enjoy rural charm, but be in town in a half hour or less when you crave excitement.

In addition to the following, see "Enjoying Hawaii on a Budget" in Chapter 2 for information on several organizations that will hook you up with the perfect bed-and-breakfast.

HAWAII KAI

JOAN WEBB AND BARBARA ABE, P.O. Box 25907, Honolulu, HI 96825. Tel. 808/396-9462. 2 rms (1 with bath). TV

$ Rates (including breakfast): $50–$60 double. No credit cards. **Parking:** Free.

If you'd like a bed-and-breakfast accommodation close to Hanauma Bay and Sea Life

Park (and about a 25-minute drive from Waikiki), contact Mrs. Joan Webb, or her daughter, Barbara Abe—two Englishwomen who have a beautiful home, with garden and swimming pool, in Hawaii Kai. The larger room, with access to the pool area, has a queen-size bed, a small refrigerator, and a private bath. The smaller room, also cozy, has a double bed and shares a bath with the hosts. Joan and Barbara prepare full island breakfasts for their guests, who join them at the dining table for fresh fruits, juices, homemade breads, English muffins, cereals, and beverages. They are generous with sightseeing advice and tips and also provide beach mats and towels.

KAILUA

AKAMAI BED AND BREAKFAST, 172 Kuumele Place, Kailua, HI 96734. Tel. 808/261-2227, or toll free 800/642-5366. 2 studios. TV

$ Rates: $60 double. Each additional person $10, to a maximum of four. Minimum stay three nights. No credit cards. **Parking:** Free.

Three blocks and an eight-minute walk from the beautiful white sand beaches of Kailua is this charming home. A separate wing from the main house has two spacious studios, each with its own kitchen, including a refrigerator and microwave oven. The refrigerator is stocked with some breakfast foods, and guests are free to do light cooking. Guests enjoy the convenience of the pool and lanai in a lovely tropical setting. Diane Van Ryzin and her husband, Joe, are cordial hosts.

Kailua is about a half-hour drive from Waikiki; its beaches are what Waikiki's used to be like, before the crowds.

LANIKAI BED & BREAKFAST, 1277 Mokulua Dr., Kailua, HI 96734. Tel. 808/261-1059. 1 studio (with bath). TV TEL

$ Rates: $55 single or double. No credit cards. **Parking:** Free.

If you love being right on the beach, you can't beat this one. Mahina and Homer Maxey's large, comfortable home is just across the street from idyllic Lanikai Beach with its soft white sand and inviting, always-calm water. There's a large covered lanai in front (where you'll often find Samantha, the Maxeys' cat, taking a snooze), with banana trees, lawa'e ferns, and plenty of tables and chairs. The studio, which has a private entrance, is at the back of the house overlooking the garden with a stunning view of what many consider the most beautiful mountains in the islands—the Windward Koolaus. There's a queen-size bed, a sitting room/TV area, and a kitchen/dining area, complete with microwave, refrigerator, and coffee maker. Every few days, Mahina will bring homemade bread, juice, and coffee for your continental breakfast. There are ceiling fans, lots of beautiful plants, and, of course, that heavenly beach just across the street. There will very likely be a second unit (upstairs), with its own staircase and private entrance, next year. By the way, both Maxeys are from old kamaaina families; ask Mahina about the family photos.

SHARON'S SERENITY, 127 Kakahiaka St., Kailua, HI 96734. Tel. 808/262-5621 or 263-3634. 2 rms. TV TEL

$ Rates: $45 single; $55 double. No credit cards. **Parking:** Free.

Sharon and Bob Price's lovely home is located on a quiet, tree-shaded residential street just a short walk from Kailua Beach. The house is decorated in an elegant contemporary style, beautifully enhanced by Sharon's striking flower arrangements. The larger guest room has a sitting room with a comfortable sofa and leather chair, plus a queen-size bed and a full bath with a beautiful, private, garden view. The smaller guest room has twin beds and a similar bathroom. Each room has a color TV, but guests are welcome to join the Prices in their spacious living room with its two huge comfy couches, big TV, and plenty of books. We love the stained-glass panels in the windows and the big, L-shaped bar where breakfast is served. The gorgeous pool area overlooks Kaelepulu Stream and is landscaped with Tahitian gardenia, bougainvillea, and palm trees. A cuddly bichon frisé named Trouble (a misnomer if we've ever heard one) and two sun-worshipping cats complete the Price menage.

SHEFFIELD HOUSE BED & BREAKFAST, 131 Kuulei Rd., Kailua, HI 96734. Tel. 808/262-0721. TV TEL available. 1 rm, 1 one-bedroom suite.

$ Rates: $40 double; $60 one-bedroom suite; $95 two-bedroom suite. Minimum stay three days; monthly rates on request. No credit cards. **Parking:** Free.

Paul Sheffield is an architect and his wife, Rachel, is a landscape architect who works out of their home so as to be a full-time mother to the two bouncy little Sheffield children. Their house is in an ongoing process of renovation, but the cozy guest accommodations are all finished. Each has a private entrance, Mexican tile floors, bright tropical-print bedspread and accessories. The one-bedroom suite has a kitchen area with a refrigerator, microwave, toaster oven, and coffee maker; the room has all of these except the refrigerator. The suite has its own sitting room with lots of books, a small dining area, a queen-size bed in the bedroom, and a view of its own private garden. The room, which is wheelchair-accessible, has a double bed. The two units may be combined as a two-bedroom/two-bath suite. There's no pool, but who needs one when you're just a hop, skip and a jump from beautiful Kailua beach. *Note:* Complimentary continental breakfast is provided on the first day only.

KANEOHE

A 5-STAR BED AND BREAKFAST—BJR'S, 14-491 Kaneohe Bay Dr., Kaneohe, HI 96744. Tel. 808/235-8235. 3 rms (1 with bath).

$ Rates: $65 and $75 single or double. No credit cards. **Parking:** Free.

Next door to the posh Kaneohe Bay Yacht Club is the movie set–style home of Bonnie and Richard Green. We were entranced by the magnificent Italian tile pool nestled in a tropical garden and guarded by two stone lions. The house is decorated in an Asian motif with some extraordinary antiques and pictures. The living room has a great collection of books and magazines, which guests are invited to peruse. Two rooms share a bathroom; one has twin beds and the other has a queen-size bed. The master bedroom, which has a king-size bed, overlooks the pool area. Both bathrooms are gracefully appointed, with makeup lights and private garden views. Breakfast is served in the dining room or by the pool. The pool area is a sight to behold at night, when it's illuminated by tiki torches.

EMMA'S GUEST ROOMS, 47-6000 Hui Ulili St., Kaneohe, HI 96744. Tel. 808/239-7248. 3 rms.

$ Rates: Jan 16–Dec 14, $45 single or double, $5 more for stay of only one night. Dec 15–Jan 15, add $5. Children 2–15 pay $8. AE, DISC, MC, V. **Parking:** Free.

Emma and Stan Sargeant's white Mediterranean-style house is located in lovely Temple Valley, a peaceful rural area on the windward side, not far from the imposing Byodo-In Temple. Guests have their own private entrance, a fully equipped guest kitchen for fixing light meals, a dining area, and a lounge with color television. Three bedrooms, nicely furnished, have king-size, queen-size, or twin beds; all have their own bathrooms. The Sargeants own the Temple Valley Travel Agency, so they can also be helpful with low-cost airline fares, neighbor-island packages, car rentals, and vacation activities at good prices.

WINDWARD BED & BREAKFAST, 46-251 Ikiiki St., Kaneohe, HI 96744. Tel. 808/235-1124. 2 rms.

$ Rates: $50 Circus Room; $55 Victorian Room. No credit cards. **Parking:** Free.

Set in a lush tropical garden with a pool, this charming home is filled to the brim with Victorian antiques—toys, posters, teddy bears, ornaments—and fine paintings, reminders of the days when hosts L. De Chambs and Donald

Munro ran an art gallery in New York. Now they're here in Hawaii, in a gracious home overlooking Kaneohe Bay and very close to wonderful swimming beaches; the excitement of Waikiki is about a half-hour drive away. Their guest wing consists of the Victorian Room, with a wonderful old china doll on its double bed, and an attached private bath. The Circus Room has antique teddy bears on each of the twin beds, circus posters from all over the world on the walls, and a private bath across the corridor. The hosts are delightfully warm people who enjoy having their guests in for late-afternoon tea in the living room. In the evening they put out glasses and ice in the library. And they serve breakfast—fruits, cereal, juices, toast, and coffee—out on the pool lanai whenever guests wish. Beach mats and towels are provided. Two Maltese dogs, Buckwheat and Oatmeal, are very much in evidence.

CHAPTER 6

HONOLULU DINING

Can the average tourist still find romance, happiness, and a good, inexpensive meal in Hawaii? Well, we won't make any promises on the first two counts (that's up to you), but on the third we can be quite positive. Despite inflation everywhere, Honolulu's restaurants still do very well for the tourist. Although the price for dinner at one of the really elegant restaurants can easily zoom into the stratosphere, there are still plenty of places where you can get a terrific meal for under $20. And there are also lots of places where you can eat well for under $10. To keep on a really tight budget, plan to eat breakfast and at least one meal a day at home; that's when your kitchenette apartment more than pays for itself. Remember that lunch is always cheaper than dinner—and often it's almost the same meal. Early Bird specials offer excellent dinner bargains all over town.

1. WAIKIKI

DIAMOND HEAD WAIKIKI

MEALS FOR LESS THAN $12

MONGOLIAN BAR-B-QUE, at Kuhio Mall, 2301 Kuhio Ave. Tel. 923-2445.

Cuisine: MONGOLIAN. **Reservations:** Not accepted.

$ Prices: Appetizers $2.95–$3.95; main courses $9.95–$11.05. AE, MC, V.

Open: Daily 10am–10pm.

The culinary adventurers among you will want to experience the cuisine here, which is indeed different. Seems that a very special dish in the northern part of China is strips of beef, barbecued with vegetables and spices, and this is one of the few restaurants we know of in Honolulu that serves it. You select your own meats, sauces, vegetables, and spices and pass them on to the chefs, who then cook them in an open fire pit. Complete dinners, from $9.95 for barbecued chicken to $11.05 for New York steak, come with crisp wun tun chips or an egg roll, chicken vegetable soup and salad, fresh vegetables, rice or fries, and dessert. For $13.95, adults ($8.95 for kids under 10) can have the full barbecue with seconds. Or have a "quick meal" or "mini" meal—the chefs make the selection—at $4.95 and $5.95. Also available: lunch plates, soups, salads, beers, wines, and cocktails. The barbecue has quite an unexpected taste, but many local people are addicted to it. It's one of those things you have to experience for yourself to judge.

NA'S BAR-B-QUE, in the Royal Grove Hotel, 151 Uluniu St. Tel. 926-9717 for take-out orders.
Cuisine: KOREAN. **Reservations:** Not accepted.
$ Prices: Main courses $4.60–$6.10.
Open: Mon–Sat 10:30am–9pm, Sun 10:30am–8pm.

If you like tasty Korean barbecue dishes, you'll be thrilled to discover Na's, where it's no trick at all to have a hearty meal for around $6. Each of the dishes, like our favorite, the barbecue chicken, or the barbecued beef, or fish jun, or the hot spicy chicken wings, comes with a choice of vegetables, plus two scoops of rice. The hot noodle and soup dishes are also delicious. This is a tiny place, with a counter inside (always seemingly jammed with Koreans, by the way), and just a few tables outside. Lots of condo dwellers nearby come here for take-out and go back home to feast.

RUFFAGE NATURAL FOODS, in the Royal Grove Hotel, 2443 Kuhio Ave. Tel. 922-2042.
Cuisine: VEGETARIAN/SUSHI BAR. **Reservations:** Not accepted.
$ Prices: Main vegetarian courses $1.50–$6.75; sushi dinner $9.95.
Open: Daily 8:30am–7pm.

What a treat to find a health-food store, restaurant, and juice bar right in the heart of the busy Waikiki scene and just a block from the beach. Ruffage specializes in organic foods and those that are as free as possible of processing, all modestly priced. They serve freshly squeezed juices; good fruit and vegetable salads; lunch and dinner dishes on the order of whole-wheat spaghetti with chili-and-cheese or veggie burritos; sandwiches like zucchini-cheese or tofu-tuna, on multigrain bread, stuffed with tomatoes and sprouts and practically a meal in themselves ($2.75–$4.50); and yummy shakes and smoothies. At the front of the store is an authentic Japanese sushi bar, where you can get a complete sushi lunch or dinner or order by the piece (yes, they have vegetable sushi). Take it out and go to the beach, or dine here at one of the several open-to-the-street tables. While you're here, pick up a few organically grown papayas to take back to your hotel for breakfast. Hours for the sushi bar are 11am to 2pm and 5 to 11pm.

WAIKIKI CIRCLE HOTEL RESTAURANT, 2466 Kalakaua Ave. Tel. 923-1571.
Cuisine: AMERICAN. **Reservations:** Not accepted.
$ Prices: Main courses $5.95–$8.75. AE, CB, DC, JCB, MC, V.
Open: Breakfast daily 6:30am–2pm; lunch daily noon–2pm; dinner daily 6:30–9:30pm.

This restaurant is oriented toward the budget traveler, from its breakfast specials for $2.85 to daily dinner specials at $7.95. You enter through the open lobby of the circular building, but before you do, read the menu and specials of the day on large posters that practically scream "save money." The bargains are not at the expense of quality either, but the ambience is plain—just tables and chairs. Low prices continue all day. Lunchtime offers sandwiches for $4.75–$6.25 and salads for $1.45–$4.95. Come dinnertime there's a daily special, perhaps brisket of beef with cabbage. From baby beef liver to filet of beef with shrimp tempura, regular dinners include rolls, tossed green salad, vegetables, and rice or potatoes. There is also a bar and lounge.

WAIKIKI SIDEWALK CAFE, 2526 Kalakaua Ave. Tel. 926-5105.
Cuisine: JAPANESE. **Reservations:** Not accepted.
$ Prices: Main courses $3.50–$8. No credit cards.
Open: Daily 7am–10:30pm.

Despite its name, this is really just a tiny Japanese fast-food restaurant with only a dozen small tables and even fewer counter seats, not far from Kapahulu Avenue. It's run by the Japanese for the Japanese, but visitors from elsewhere love this place too, for both the food and the low prices. You choose your dish by looking in the window

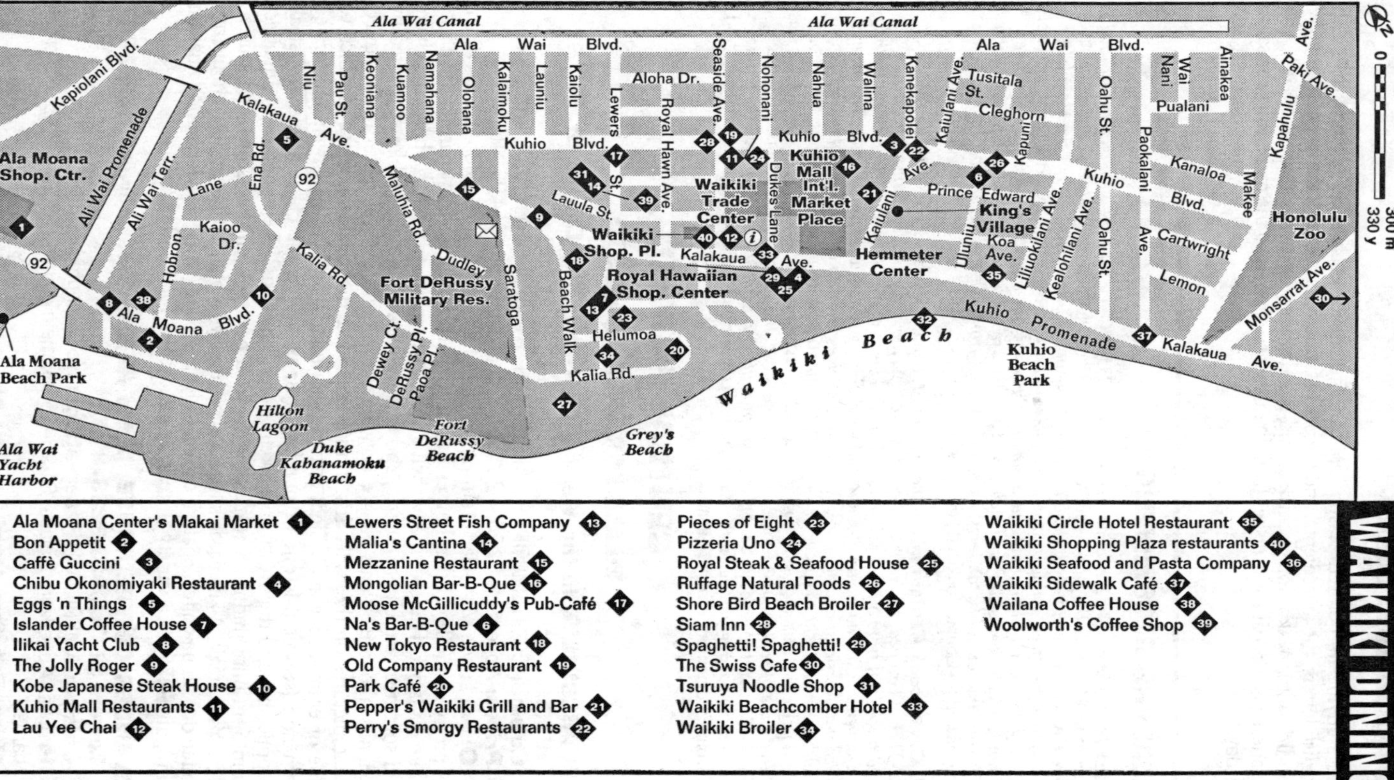
WAIKIKI DINING
0
300 m
330 y
Ala Wai Canal
Ala Wai Blvd.
Kapiolani Blvd.
Kalakaua Ave.
Ali Wai Promenade
Ali Wai Terr.
Lane
Ena Rd.
Kaioo Dr.
Hobron
Ala Moana Blvd.
Kalia Rd.
Maluhia Rd.
Dudley
Saratoga
Beach Walk
Helumoa
Dewey Ct.
DeRussy Pl.
Paoa Pl.
Niu
Pau St.
Keoniana
Kuamoo
Namahana
Olohana
Kalaimoku
Launiu
Kaiolu
Lewers St.
Royal Hawn Ave.
Aloha Dr.
Seaside Ave.
Nohonani
Nahua
Walina
Kanekapolei
Kaiulani Ave.
Tusitala St.
Cleghorn
Kapuni
Kuhio Blvd.
Lauula St.
Dukes Lane
Prince Edward
Uluniu
Koa Ave.
Liliuokilani Ave.
Kealohilani Ave.
Oahu St.
Paokalani Ave.
Wai Nani
Pualani
Ainakea
Kanaloa
Cartwright
Lemon
Makee
Kapahulu
Paki Ave.
Monsarrat Ave.
Kuhio Promenade
Ala Moana Shop. Ctr.
Ala Moana Beach Park
Ala Wai Yacht Harbor
Hilton Lagoon
Duke Kahanamoku Beach
Fort DeRussy Beach
Fort DeRussy Military Res.
Grey's Beach
Waikiki Beach
Kuhio Beach Park
Waikiki Shop. Pl.
Waikiki Trade Center
Royal Hawaiian Shop. Center
Kuhio Mall
Int'l. Market Place
Hemmeter Center
King's Village
Honolulu Zoo
Ala Moana Center's Makai Market 1
Bon Appetit 2
Caffè Guccini 3
Chibu Okonomiyaki Restaurant 4
Eggs 'n Things 5
Islander Coffee House 7
Ilikai Yacht Club 8
The Jolly Roger 9
Kobe Japanese Steak House 10
Kuhio Mall Restaurants 11
Lau Yee Chai 12
Lewers Street Fish Company 13
Malia's Cantina 14
Mezzanine Restaurant 15
Mongolian Bar-B-Que 16
Moose McGillicuddy's Pub-Café 17
Na's Bar-B-Que 6
New Tokyo Restaurant 18
Old Company Restaurant 19
Park Café 20
Pepper's Waikiki Grill and Bar 21
Perry's Smorgy Restaurants 22
Pieces of Eight 23
Pizzeria Uno 24
Royal Steak & Seafood House 25
Ruffage Natural Foods 26
Shore Bird Beach Broiler 27
Siam Inn 28
Spaghetti! Spaghetti! 29
The Swiss Cafe 30
Tsuruya Noodle Shop 31
Waikiki Beachcomber Hotel 33
Waikiki Broiler 34
Waikiki Circle Hotel Restaurant 35
Waikiki Shopping Plaza restaurants 40
Waikiki Seafood and Pasta Company 36
Waikiki Sidewalk Café 37
Wailana Coffee House 38
Woolworth's Coffee Shop 39
Post Office
Information

and studying its colored plastic replica. Underneath each is its Japanese name in English letters, the ingredients, and the price. Good bets are the kake udon (saiminlike noodle soup), oyako-don (a chicken-and-egg dish), and gyu-don (beef and rice). The Japanese visitors eat these dishes from breakfast to supper, so the menu stays the same all day.

READERS RECOMMEND

Jack-in-the Box, *134 Kapahulu Ave. (tel. 922-2235). "One of the few high-quality fast-food eateries in Waikiki is the Jack-in-the-Box restaurant next door to the Waikiki Grand Hotel. Here the customer can have his choice of window-booth dining with views of the Honolulu Zoo across the street, sitting at one of the tables in back facing a pool and courtyard, or simply ordering 'to go.' Highly recommended, among the many fine budget offerings which include hamburgers, chicken, steak sandwiches, and shrimp, are the various Breakfast Crescents stuffed with combinations of bacon, eggs, ham, and cheeses, from $1.80 to $2.50. This spot deserves recognition!"*—Connie Tonken, Hartford, Conn.

W. C. Peacock Restaurant, *in the Sheraton Moana Surfrider, 2365 Kalakaua Ave. (tel. 922-3111). "Granted, the normal prices here are heady, but they have a Sunset Special fixed-price meal from 5:30 to 6:30pm for $14.95. This is a gem! If you're celebrating a birthday or anniversary, let the maître d' know and* voila! *singing waiter, cake, and candle. The meal is served with decorum and elegance. We had two choices: teriyaki chicken or mahimahi, including an excellent salad bar and delicious soup served with fresh, warm buns. Our choice, teriyaki chicken, was succulent, served on a bed of tasty rice pilaf and veggies. The dessert was a large piece of scrumptious lemon cake with meringue and icing. Sipping a glass of house wine (red or white Mondavi, $5 a glass) was pure luxury, while we contemplated the setting sun and the passing parade on the beach from this luxurious patio restaurant . . . a must!"*—J. A. Douin, Edmonton, Alberta, Canada.

CENTRAL WAIKIKI

MEALS FOR LESS THAN $12

CAPPUCCINO'S, in the Waikiki Joy Hotel, 320 Lewers St. Tel. 924-1530.

Cuisine: CONTEMPORARY AMERICAN. **Reservations:** Recommended.
$ Prices: Appetizers $2.25–$9.75; main courses $7.50–$14.90. AE, MC, V.
Open: Lunch Mon–Sat 11am–2pm, Sun 11am–6pm; dinner Mon–Sat 5–10pm.

As pretty as the hotel that houses it, this tiny (10-table) place is charming, with its white walls and French windows with transom tops, its rosy-pink upholstered chairs and soft green tufted banquettes, and the beautiful round glass tables supported by ceramic tabourets. Plants hang everywhere, and there are soft pastel Italian street-scene pictures on the walls. It's an intimate, altogether charming place in which to dine or enjoy coffee and a light snack. Pasta tossed with codfish caviar and topped with nori (seaweed) is one of our favorites, as well as the chicken tofu and steak Cappuccino, and the breast of chicken with mushrooms. Their pupu menu, in effect from 5pm until midnight, features steak fried potatoes, chicken strips, and sautéed New York steak. As its name suggests, coffee plays a big part here: How about Irish coffee or Kahlua coffee, Spanish coffee, Calypso coffee (with Tía Maria and Jamaican rum), all $4.75, or a variety of teas, hot and cold, for $1.50–$2.50.

ISLANDER COFFEE HOUSE, in the Kaiulani Reef Towers Hotel, 247 Lewers St. Tel. 923-3233.

Cuisine: AMERICAN. **Reservations:** Not accepted.
$ Prices: Appetizers (salads) $1.95–$5.95; main courses $7.25–$9.45. No credit cards.
Open: Daily 6am–11pm.

Both locations of this coffeehouse are always dependable for excellent food at very reasonable prices, and both are impeccably clean and attractive. The original Islander is oceanfront in the Kaiulani Reef Towers Hotel; the newer, and much bigger one, at 150 Kaiulani Ave., is in the Outrigger East Hotel. Visit whichever one you happen to be closest to, and you won't go wrong. At both you can get their famous fresh-baked orange bread, served hot with dinner, as French toast, or as dessert; you can even take home a loaf for $1.45. Those who love breakfast food should note that the Islanders serve breakfast all day: the Jamboree Breakfast, a favorite, offers all the pancakes you can eat, plus bacon or sausage, and two eggs, for $4.95. The menu is largely the same at lunch and dinner. At dinner, along with your main course—perhaps mahimahi, teriyaki steak, or shrimp-fry platter—you get home-style soup or salad, potatoes or rice, plus hot orange bread. Don't miss one of their great pies from their Yum Yum Tree Bakery—maybe macadamia-nut cream, coconut cream, or the "pie of the month."

LEWERS STREET FISH COMPANY, in the Outrigger Reef Towers Hotel, 247 Lewers St. Tel. 971-1000.

Cuisine: SEAFOOD/PASTA. **Reservations:** Not required.

$ Prices: Appetizers 95¢–$3.95; main courses $5.95–$14.95. AE, MC, JCB, V.

Open: Dinner only, daily 5–11pm.

It doesn't surprise us a bit to see the lines in front of this restaurant at dinnertime. This place has just about everything a hungry tourist could want: great tasty food, an attractive ambience with sparkling tiled floors, a piano bar, a '40s decorative scheme, and prices that are downright appetizing. There are a number of main dishes under $10, such as mahimahi fish-and-chips, beer-batter mahimahi, teriyaki beef kebabs, garlic chicken, and fisherman's pasta Alfredo, a house specialty. Fresh fish from their own fishing boat is featured ("subject to season and condition of the weather and our captain"), and it is handsomely presented on an oversize, fish-shaped platter. All dinners come with a choice of rice, french fries, or fresh garlic pasta (we recommend the latter) and freshly baked bread. Start your meal with an excellent seafood chowder and end with one of their homemade cheesecakes, each only $3. There's entertainment at the piano bar nightly from 6 to 11pm.

MALIA'S CANTINA, 311 Lewers St. Tel. 922-7808.

Cuisine: MEXICAN. **Reservations:** Not accepted.

$ Prices: Appetizers $4.95–$8.95; main courses $7.50–$11.95. AE, MC, V.

Open: Daily 6:30am–2am.

If you like tasty Mexican food, good prices, and a lively, boisterous atmosphere, you'll enjoy this restaurant. Malia's award-winning chili is indeed a winner, and so are the Mexican pizza and nacho macho among the appetizers. Dinners are served with Malia's beans and Mexican rice, made fresh several times daily; the house specialty is succulent chicken fajitas. Good salads that can be a meal in themselves are priced $2.50–$8.25, and Early Bird special dinners, served from 5 to 6:30pm, are all $6.50. A large bar covers one side of the restaurant (Malia's is reputed to have the widest selection of tequilas on the islands), and there are paneled walls, wood floors, and a large photomural of Diamond Head, around 1910. There's free live music Tuesday through Saturday, and happy hour is daily from 11am to 6pm. Everything on the menu is available for take-out.

MOOSE McGILLICUDDY'S PUB-CAFE, 310 Lewers St. Tel. 923-0751.

Cuisine: AMERICAN. **Reservations:** Not accepted.

$ Prices: Appetizers $3.95–$7.95; main courses $4.95–$12.95. AE, MC, V.

Open: Daily 6:30am–1:30am.

If you can bring yourself to walk past the huge stuffed moose head with a lei around its neck—the first thing you see when you walk in—you'll love this place. It's big and airy—in fact, it's open to the street and has lots of plants and a shiny ceramic-tile floor. It's very popular among the local folks, since portions are large and prices very reasonable. Their Early Bird Breakfast Special, served from 7:30 to 9am, is one of the best buys in town: two eggs, bacon, toast or rice or potatoes, orange juice, all for $2.50. And their three-egg omelets, served with fries, rice, or Texas toast are quite a buy at $4.95. Lunch features gourmet hamburgers, several Mexican dishes, hot soups, sandwiches, and very good salads, like the chicken taco and spinach. There are Early Bird dinners from 5 to 6:30pm at $7.95. Regular dinners feature hot specials like roast prime rib of beef, teriyaki chicken breast, and a delicious mahimahi stuffed with crab and shrimp, topped with mornay sauce and grilled. Moose's serves up great margaritas and daiquiris for $4, and to go with them, some neat snacks, like deep-fried zucchini in beer batter; fried potato skins with cheese, chicken, or bacon; and yummy hot Texas chili. Rock-and-roll bands play nightly for dancing in the upstairs pub, from 9pm to 1:30am. A half-price happy hour is from 4 to 8pm.

There's another Moose at 1035 University Ave. (tel. 944-5525), where the UH kids hang out, and it's lots of fun.

PEPPER'S WAIKIKI GRILL AND BAR, 150 Kaiulani Ave. Tel. 926-4374.

Cuisine: TEX-MEX. **Reservations:** Not accepted.

$ Prices: Appetizers $3–$8; main courses $5–$15. AE, CB, DC, JCB, MC, V.

Open: Daily 11:30am–2am.

Here you are in the tropics, but you love the desert, too. What to do? Ride that lonesome trail to Pepper's, a hybrid of the islands and the Southwest, sprouting both cacti and palm trees, and serving some of the best Tex-Mex food in town. It's a casual, yet sophisticated spot in the very heart of Waikiki, dominated by a lively bar (watch out for those frosty margaritas!) but with well-spaced booths and tables conducive to good conversation. The secret ingredients here are the wood-fired smoke oven that gives a true barbecue taste to the chicken and ribs, and the mesquite grill that turns out super burgers and steaks. In addition to the Mexican dishes, you can order smoke-oven baby back ribs and excellent salads, including the Cobb and the chicken-taco salad. Nachos, sandwiches, quesadillas, and yummy potato skins offer inexpensive and tempting possibilities for grazing. For dessert, try hula pie, a specialty of Hawaii, or fried ice cream, a specialty of Mexico (no, it's not really fried, but in such a simpatico spot, it's hard to quibble).

PIZZERIA UNO, 2256 Kuhio Ave. Tel. 926-0646.

Cuisine: ITALIAN. **Reservations:** Not accepted.

$ Prices: Appetizers $2.95–$5.25; main courses $7–$10. MC, V.

Open: Daily 11am–midnight.

This one's a great favorite with the younger crowd. Although it serves all sorts of good things—burgers, chili, salads (seafood, spinach, Caesar, and antipasto)—the specialty here is definitely the Chicago-style deep-dish pizza. We're especially fond of the Sea Delico, with the flavor of shrimp and crab; the steak and cheese; and the chicken fajita pizza, sizzling strips of marinated chicken breast, with a blend of cheeses, peppers, and onions. Pizzas come in two sizes: individual, priced from $6.25; and a larger size that serves two or three, priced from $12.50. Beer is at hand, by the glass or bottle. The full-service bar also dispenses some of the best piña coladas in town.

SHORE BIRD BEACH BROILER, in the Outrigger Reef Hotel, 2169 Kalia Rd. Tel. 922-2887.

Cuisine: SEAFOOD/STEAK. **Reservations:** Not accepted.

$ Prices: Main courses $6.95–$14.95. AE, JCB, MC, V.

Open: Daily 7:30am–10pm.

It's not hard to figure out why this spot quickly became one of the most popular restaurants in Waikiki. First of all, you can't beat the location: The large, attractively decorated open dining room is right on Waikiki Beach. Second, the food is good; and third, the price is right because you're the chef, broiling your own portion of teriyaki chicken, ribs, fresh fish, seafood, New York steak, ground steak, or top sirloin. While the fire is doing its work, you can have a few drinks, then fill up on salad bar, chili, rice, and fresh pastas, all included in the price of your main course. Dessert (including their homemade cheesecake) is extra. This is the perfect place for sunset drinks and dinner; Early Bird specials are from 5 to 6:30pm. They also have an all-you-can-eat breakfast buffet at $6.95, served until 11am.

SIAM INN, 407 Seaside Ave. Tel. 926-8802.

Cuisine: THAI. **Reservations:** Recommended at dinner.
$ **Prices:** Appetizers $2.75–$5.95; main courses $5.95–$15.95. AE, MC, V.
Open: Lunch daily 11am–3pm; dinner daily 5–10:30pm.

A touch of Thai lives in Waikiki. This pretty, second-floor restaurant is the place to make, or renew, acquaintance with the subtle (and not-so-subtle) spiceries of Thai cuisine. Dine inside in a setting of white walls covered with colorful murals of Thai scenery, crisp green tablecloths, and tile floors; or outside on a little balcony under potted trees. When last we lunched here, the daily specials, $6.95, were Bangkok chicken, served with rice and the chef's special soup, and the chicken masaman curry—slices of tender chicken on a bed of avocado, peanuts, and coconut milk, served with curried rice and cucumber sauce (mild or hot). Other luncheon possibilities are also very reasonable (there are 10 dishes under $6.50) and include a variety of noodle dishes featuring chicken, beef, pork, or shrimp. Your waiter will ask if you wish your meal mild, hot, or very hot (for newcomers to Thai cooking, mild is the safest). Main dishes, which are also priced reasonably, include chicken, beef, pork, shrimp, and rice dishes, as well as fish specialties.

SPAGHETTI! SPAGHETTI!, in the Royal Hawaiian Shopping Center, 2201 Kalakaua Ave. Tel. 922-7724.

Cuisine: ITALIAN. **Reservations:** Not required.
$ **Prices:** Spaghetti buffet and salad bar, $6. AE, DC, JCB, MC, V.
Open: Daily 11am–10pm.

Everybody seems to like spaghetti, so it's good to know that you can eat your fill—from a spaghetti buffet and salad bar—for just $6. This is a large, multilevel restaurant with stylish furnishings, a huge and busy bar, and, on the buffet table, a choice of four different pastas, four freshly made sauces, and a variety of salad ingredients. Salad bar alone is $3.50; with soup, it's $4.50; and with the pastas, $6. A $2 slice of garlic bread rounds out the meal nicely. Also available are soups; hot meatloaf, mahimahi, and other sandwiches; chicken in a basket; and a giant burger. Top off a not-exactly-slimming meal here with cheesecake or a super Baskin-Robbins mud pie.

THE SWISS CAFE, 2310 Kuhio Ave., in the Waikiki Market Place. Tel. 921-9070.

Cuisine: SWISS/GERMAN/AMERICAN.
$ **Prices:** Appetizers $2.50–$3.50; main courses $4.90–$12.50. MC, V.
Open: Daily 7am–10:30pm.

European visitors as well as the rest of us who savor good Swiss-German cooking are finding their way to this cozy café, with just a few tables inside and more outside under pink umbrellas. Lily Kraft and Hedwig Burkhard, both from Switzerland, put a great deal of care into their operation, and have come up with quality cooking at very modest prices. Their $2 eggs Benedict, made with an unusual, slightly lemony hollandaise, is surely one of the wonders of Waikiki. Lunch features a different European specialty every day—perhaps chicken Hawaii, or a Swiss gourmet sandwich, or catch of the day—for all of $4.90, even including soda. At dinner, you get a chance to sample the flavorful meatloaf, the hearty sauerbraten, or geshnetzeltes—that's a sautéed julienne of turkey breast in white wine cream sauce, with mushrooms and parsley—very rich, very popular. Don't miss desserts—they bake all their own pastries, and the day's treats could include chocolate tarte Meissner or a heavenly banana cake or mango cheesecake. The emphasis here is on quality, not quantity—so coffee-lovers be advised: They serve only a six-ounce cup, and there are no refills.

TSURUYA NOODLE SHOP, 325 Lewers St. Tel. 922-3434.
Cuisine: JAPANESE. **Reservations:** Not accepted.
$ Prices: Main courses $4.75–$8.95. MC, JCB, V.
Open: Mon–Sat 11am–10pm, Sun 11am–9pm.

We're great fans of Japanese noodle houses: They're just the ticket for those times you want a simple, tasty, nutritious, and extremely low-cost meal. So we were delighted to find this sparkling, clean little place with a horseshoe-shaped counter in the middle, four tables with comfortable leather chairs, and some mirror-framed paintings on the walls. Try the hot soba broth called sansai, with vegetables and garnishes, or the teriyaki chicken teishoku—grilled, marinated chicken and salad, which comes with miso soup and pickled vegetables—two hearty meals for $5.45 and $5.95, respectively. Cold soba (buckwheat) noodles are available, as are various other Japanese dishes, and side orders of shrimp tempura, cooked in "100% vegetable oil." Your food is served promptly, on a lacquered tray in a beautiful bowl. Take-out orders are available.

WAIKIKI BROILER, in the Outrigger Waikiki Tower, 200 Lewers St. Tel. 923-8836.
Cuisine: AMERICAN. **Reservations:** Not accepted.
$ Prices: Appetizers $1.45–$6.25; main courses $5.45–$14.95. AE, CB, DC, JCB, MC, V.
Open: Daily 6am–2am.

The budget crowd is kept well in mind at this cozy place, which is brightened by shell-shaped ceiling lights and modern paintings. The dining room overlooks the pool area of the Outrigger Edgewater Hotel; in fact, two of the tables are practically in the pool! The Broiler offers low-priced dinner main courses, like fish-and-chips, teriyaki chicken breasts, and mahimahi, in addition to such higher-priced offerings as lobster tail, scampi, and prime rib, the specialty of the house. At lunch, there are special sandwiches served with soup or salad (around $6), burgers, and a chef's special salad. Breakfast is served all the way from 6am to 2pm; waffles or buttermilk pancakes are a good bet at $2.45. There's a long daytime happy hour from 6am to 9pm when exotic drinks are sold for the price of standards. There's entertainment Tuesday through Sunday from 9pm to 2am.

WAIKIKI SEAFOOD AND PASTA COMPANY, in the Outrigger Surf Hotel, 2280 Kuhio Ave. Tel. 923-5949.
Cuisine: SEAFOOD/PASTA. **Reservations:** Not accepted.
$ Prices: Appetizers 95¢–$3.95; main courses $6.95–$14.95. AE, MC, JCB, V.
Open: Dinner daily 5–11pm.

The same management responsible for Lewers Street Fish Company runs this place, and it's an equally good bet. And it's so pretty, with its dining room ceiling totally covered by plants, and a smart New York–style deli and a bar up front. The food is inexpensive and delicious; gourmet pastas are made on the premises (you can ask to visit the "Pasta Factory"), so you know they're fresh. The fresh pasta comes along with house specialties, such as garlic basil chicken, chicken parmesan, and chicken Italiano. Other popular menu items are fresh fish, seafood, mahimahi sauté, calamari steak, teriyaki beef kebab, and baby back ribs. Desserts? Just $3. Again, good food, good value, and a fun atmosphere. Piano bar from 6 to 11pm nightly.

WOOLWORTH'S COFFEE SHOP, 2224 Kalakaua Ave. Tel. 923-1713.

Cuisine: AMERICAN. **Reservations:** Not accepted.
$ Prices: Main courses $5.95–$7.50. AE, DISC, JCB, MC, V.
Open: Daily 7am–10pm.

The atmosphere is pleasant and the prices are right. Beef stew, chopped steak, and filet of fish are all $6.75 at both lunch and dinner. Sandwiches are $4.75–$6.25, served from morning on. Japanese and Chinese dishes are also served, and you can have southern fried chicken to go. Note, too, Woolworth's Far Eastern snack bar in the back of the store, where you can sample all kinds of unusual goodies.

You'll find a larger, equally bustling and cheerful Woolworth's restaurant at Ala Moana Center.

READERS RECOMMEND

Waikiki Beachcomber Hotel, *2300 Kalakaua Ave. (tel. 922-4646). "The Waikiki Beachcomber Hotel serves a very nice prime-rib buffet for only $11.95 before 6pm, in an attractive dining room. A chicken dish, mahimahi, and salad bar are also included. . . ."*

Honolulu Elks Club, *2933 Kalakaua Ave. (tel. 923-5722). "Visiting Elks may enjoy good food in a very pleasant atmosphere at the Honolulu Elks Club on the no. 2 bus line. Their buffets are excellent and prices are reasonable. The atmosphere is great. Some of the 'Magnum P.I.' TV shows were filmed here."*—both, Dr. John Lopresti, Jr., Bricktown, N.J.

MEALS FOR LESS THAN $20

CAFFÈ GUCCINNI, 2139 Kuhio Ave. Tel. 922-5287.

Cuisine: ITALIAN. **Reservations:** Recommended for more than four.
$ Prices: Appetizers $3.95–$6.50; main courses $8.95–$13.95. MC, V.
Open: Dinner only, daily 4–10:30pm.

Everyone likes Caffè Guccinni, both for the Italian meals and the delectable desserts. This is a modest place, with a counter inside, tables outside, and the menu posted beside the counter. Dinner specials include various pasta dishes on the regular menu (we're partial to the manicotti stuffed with five kinds of cheese), and two or three daily specials, such as veal, calamari, and Italian sausage. Homemade ravioli is a specialty. Main courses are accompanied by soup, salad, and homemade bread. As for desserts, we're always hard put to decide among a heavenly crème brûlée or chocolate torte, a Sicilian cannoli, or a light and lemony cheesecake. The best solution is to bring a group of friends and share. Desserts are all $3.50. (If you've eaten elsewhere, come here just for dessert.) Along with your feast, have some of the best espresso and cappuccino in the islands, or an ice cream "shake with a shot." Mango daiquiris are also special. Everything is homemade in owner Jocelyn Battista's kitchen.

CHIBU OKONOMIYAKE RESTAURANT, in the Royal Hawaiian Shopping Center, 2233 Kalakaua Ave. Tel. 922-9722.

Cuisine: JAPANESE. **Reservations:** Recommended.
$ Prices: Main courses $12–$47. AE, DC, MC, JCB, V.
Open: Lunch Mon–Sat 11am–2pm; dinner daily 5–10:30pm.

There's a feeling of space and quiet elegance about this place, and an altogether new dining experience for Hawaii. The Chibo restaurants were founded in 1973 in Osaka, the city referred to as the "gourmet kitchen of Japan." Okonomiyake originated in the Edo period as a snack made of baked flour flavored with miso. Okonomiyake itself hasn't changed radically since the Edo period, but the Chibo restaurants have made it into something unique—a sort of Japanese pizza—by heaping it with all sorts of wonderful things. The okonomiyake pizza, the house specialty ($23 at dinner), is smothered in sirloin, prawns, and squid, or prawns, squid, and scallops. On a smaller scale, you can build your own okonomiyake for $12, choosing any two of the following: bacon, sirloin, pork, octopus, chicken, prawns, or vegetables. Then there's yoshikuyaki, which looks almost like a tortilla with green noodles, vegetables, and an egg on top—definitely something different. For big splurges, there are teppanyaki dinners ($26–$47), cooked by your teppan chef at one of the teppan tables or counter. At lunch, prices go down $3–$4 for pretty much the same specialties: We like the special okonomiyake lunch served with chef's salad, at $16.50. The restaurant is decorated with black lacquer and natural-wood furniture, gray carpeting and walls, and bright-orange napkins; it has soft track ceiling lights and abundant mirrors, a gracious setting for a special experience.

THE JOLLY ROGER, 2244 Kalakaua Ave. Tel. 923-1885.

Cuisine: AMERICAN. **Reservations:** Not accepted.

$ Prices: Appetizers $3.25–$6.25; main courses $8.95–$11.45. AE, DC, JCB, MC, V.

Open: Daily 6:30am–1am.

You can't go wrong at either branch of the popular Jolly Roger restaurants. The original one, in the center of Waikiki, gives you a choice of a sidewalk table right out on the busy avenue or, more peacefully, a table inside under an umbrella. The Crow's Nest, a lounge above the restaurant, has entertainment Tuesday through Saturday nights and a popular happy hour from 4 to 8pm. The newer Jolly Roger, at the corner of Kuhio and Kaiulani Avenues, is big and bright and has its own cocktail lounge, Blue Kangaroo, with a similar entertainment and happy-hour policy. As for the food, it's American coffeehouse style, quite tasty, and at good prices. Complete dinners—served with soup or salad, potatoes or rice, and dinner roll—include chicken Polynesian, mahimahi, barbecue beef ribs platter, and a vegetable stir-fry. There are daily specials like roast beef or steak or shrimp; burgers, salads, and sandwiches are also available. Breakfast is a special treat, since that's when you can get the MacWaple, a waffle covered in sliced, spiced hot apples topped with macadamia nuts. The cocktail lounges are open until 2am.

There's a branch at 150 Kaiulani Ave. (tel. 923-2172).

NEW ORLEANS BISTRO, 2139 Kuhio Ave. Tel. 926-4444.

Cuisine: CAJUN/CREOLE. **Reservations:** Recommended.

$ Prices: Appetizers $4.95–$9.95; main courses $14.95–$24.95. AE, DC, DISC, MC, V.

Open: Dinner only, daily 5–10pm (cocktails until 2am).

Like a boîte in one of those little streets in old New Orleans, the Bistro abounds in rococo black wrought iron, streamers hanging from the ceiling, white stucco walls, pink tablecloths, and prints of riverboats and characters reminiscent of Huck and Jim on the walls. The chef is from Louisiana, where he specialized in Cajun country cooking and Créole city cooking. Don't get blown away by a New Orleans Hurricane or a Cajun martini from the bar before you have a chance to sample Louisiana red-hot prawns, the blackened prime rib, or Louisiana crayfish étouffée or the mesquite-grilled lemon chicken. Appetizers, which are served until 2am, include Cajun popcorn (beer-battered and deep-fried shrimp), oysters Bienville, and New Orleans–style jambalaya. Betty Lou Taylor plays the piano, and late in the evening there's a jazz singer over by the bar. The staff is very friendly and attentive. On the way out you could get a T-shirt that says "I Ate Alligator"—or just a New Orleans Bistro logo shirt. Good fun here.

OLD COMPANY RESTAURANT, 2256 Kuhio Ave. Tel. 923-3373.

Cuisine: AMERICAN. **Reservations:** Not accepted.

$ Prices: Appetizers $3.25–$5.75; main courses $11.45–$14.95. AE, CB, DC, JCB, MC, V.
Open: Breakfast daily 6am–4pm; lunch daily 11am–4pm; dinner daily 4pm–midnight.

When you step off Kuhio into this spot on the first level of a two-story building (there's another dining spot on the second floor) it's almost like entering someone's living room. Objets d'art fill the dividers while comfortable captain's chairs, polished wood tables, low rafters, plants, and carpeting contribute to the homey feel. Lunch is fun here, since it features an all-you-can-eat fruit, soup, and salad bar for $6.95. Sandwiches run the gamut from grilled cheese at $3.05 to chicken and avocado at $5.95. And dinner prices are modest, too: Barbecued ribs or teriyaki chicken, for example, is $11.95; the seafood combination plate is $12.95. All regular dinners include a trip to the fruit, soup, and salad bar, plus vegetables and rice or potatoes (four choices). There's a bar with three television screens for viewing sports events, and live entertainment nightly, from 9pm. Arrive before noon and you can take advantage of the Sunrise Special: pancakes, egg, and bacon, for only $2.30.

PIECES OF EIGHT, in the Outrigger Coral Seas Hotel, 250 Lewers St. Tel. 923-6646.
Cuisine: SEAFOOD/STEAK. **Reservations:** Not required.
$ Prices: Main courses $9.95–$14.95. AE, MC, V.
Open: Dinner only, daily 5–11pm.

One of Waikiki's oldest steak and seafood houses, Pieces of Eight has won many dining awards since it opened in 1967. The cannon located on the piano bar goes all the way back to the time of King Kamehameha II, and was presented to him by a Russian sea captain in 1822. This is the place for fresh fish of the day (market-priced), Pacific oysters, beer-battered shrimp, mahimahi amandine, top sirloin, and steak-and-seafood combos. Add $3 to your check if you take a turn at the salad bar; the salad bar alone is $5.95. In typical steak-house fashion, there's one major dessert: homemade cheesecake, $3. The bar is open from 4 to midnight.

ROYAL STEAK AND SEAFOOD HOUSE, 2201 Kalakaua Ave., in the Royal Hawaiian Shopping Center. Tel. 922-6688.
Cuisine: STEAK/SEAFOOD. **Reservations:** Recommended Sat–Sun.
$ Prices: Appetizers $1.95–$7.95; main courses $12.95–$25.95. AE, MC, V.
Open: Lunch daily 11:30am–2:30pm; dinner daily 5:30–10pm.

This attractive new addition to the Royal Hawaiian Shopping Center is decorated in ocean colors, peacock-blue carpeting, blue and green upholstery, and a huge marine aquarium. The restaurant is divided into several small sections, separated by potted plants or natural-wood panels. The specialty here is seafood in combination with meat: All entrées include rice or potatoes and vegetables. Among the many choices, some of our favorites are the steak and shrimp, the steak and salmon, steak and fresh oysters, and tournedos of beef and shrimp. Luncheon entrées are similar fare: chicken or beef curry, chopped Hawaiian steak ($7.95–$10.95), and a variety of salads and sandwiches. Were you wondering about that sinister, mean-looking little guy who rules the saltwater aquarium? He's a baby white-tip reef shark.

EWA WAIKIKI

MEALS FOR LESS THAN $12

EGGS 'N' THINGS, 1911B Kalakaua Ave. Tel. 949-0280.
Cuisine: AMERICAN. **Reservations:** Not accepted.
$ Prices: Main courses $4–$8. No credit cards.

Open: Daily 11pm–2pm.

This longtime Waikiki favorite is near Ala Moana Boulevard. It's a spick-and-span white tile dining room with decorative wall plaques containing amusing sayings. Note the unusual hours. Various early- and late-riser specials are available. House specialty is the three buttermilk pancakes with eggs any style and a choice of meat (from $5.25 for Vienna sausage to $7.25 for steak). Also special are the nine kinds of crêpes ($5.25–$6.50), even more varieties of omelets ($6.25–$7.75), 10 ways to enjoy pancakes ($3.50–$6.50), and eight different approaches to waffles ($3.75–$6.50). Lots of side orders and fruit juices, too. Great for those who are truly devoted to breakfast.

WAILANA COFFEE HOUSE, 1860 Ala Moana Blvd. Tel. 955-1764.

Cuisine: AMERICAN. **Reservations:** Not required.

$ Prices: Main courses $7.25–$10.75. AE, DC, MC, V.

Open: Daily 24 hours.

Although this place looks imposing and expensive, its prices will surprise you. The nicest thing about the Wailana is that lunches and dinners are the same price—the tab does not go up after 5pm as it does in so many other places. So any time of the day you can have the homemade soup and sandwich lunch for $4.50, or the delicious "broasted" chicken, juicy and tender, served with a generous helping of french fries, coleslaw or salad, roll and honey, for $6.95. Other good buys are the old-fashioned beef stew at $6.75 and the New York steak at $10.75. All these are served with soup, salad bar, or fresh-fruit cup, as well as a choice of potato or rice. The salad bar is available from 11am to 11pm. Breakfast is served around the clock, so you can come by anytime to try their delicious classic French toast or their Irish breakfast, which features a three-egg omelet stuffed with corned-beef hash and topped with Cheddar cheese, plus grilled fresh pineapple spears and hash-brown potatoes—guaranteed to put you on top of the morning at $6.50. All the pancakes you can eat, plus bacon and eggs, costs just $4.25.

There's another Wailana Coffee House in mid-Waikiki, with the same menu; it's called the **Wailana Malia** and it's located in the Outrigger Malia Hotel, 2211 Kuhio Ave. (tel. 922-4769). It's also open 24 hours a day. Another Wailana winner for Waikiki!

READERS RECOMMEND

Sizzler Steak House, *1945 Kalakaua Ave. (tel. 955-4069). "Sizzler Steak House offers senior citizens a 20% discount on meals with the exception of advertised specials on Monday nights. Senior ages start at 55. Their salad bar is bigger and better than it was last year—and the food, too."*—Barbara and Ron LePage, Port Colborne, Ontario, Canada.

Chuck's Cellar, *150 Kaiulani Ave. (tel. 923-4488). "Chuck's Cellar in the Outrigger East Hotel has $5.95 Early Bird Specials from 5:30 to 6:30pm, which include very good thick soup, all-you-can-eat salad bar, and different main courses each night. A good variety salad bar and a good bargain."*—Barbara and Ron LePage, Port Colborne, Ontario, Canada.

Kyo-Ya, *2057 Kalakaua Ave. (tel. 947-3911). "We discovered a 'Big Splurge' restaurant which is so good that we ate there three times. It is Kyo-Ya. Mostly Japanese eat there. The food is exquisite to look at and tastes wonderful. Portions are large, which is unusual for a Japanese restaurant"*—Caryl Ritter, Dillon Beach, Calif.

MEALS FOR LESS THAN $20

KOBE JAPANESE STEAK HOUSE, 1841 Ala Moana Blvd. Tel. 941-4444.

Cuisine: JAPANESE. **Reservations:** Recommended.

$ Prices: Main courses $13–$32.50. AE, DC, JCB, MC, V.

Open: Dinner only, daily 5:30–10:30pm.

A meal here is a show in itself. First, there's the beautiful Japanese-country-inn surroundings and artifacts everywhere; second, the splendid sushi bar; and third, and most important, the communal tables where you and fellow diners can chat and watch your meal being prepared teppanyaki-hibachi style, by a master chef who stands at the grill in the center of it all. Order your teriyaki chicken, sukiyaki sirloin, or teppan shrimp; or a steak-and-teriyaki combo, and you have a complete meal. First, the chef sautés some teppan shrimp and serves you a delicate soup; then he stir-fries your order with mushrooms, onions, peppers, and bean sprouts. Vegetables, rice, and tea come with the meal, and you top it all off with delicate green-tea ice cream. Japanese beers and warmed saké make a perfect accompaniment to a fun meal.

MEZZANINE RESTAURANT, in the Waikiki Terrace Hotel, 2045 Kalakaua Ave. Tel. 955-6000.

Cuisine: CONTEMPORARY AMERICAN. **Reservations:** Recommended.

$ Prices: Appetizers $4.25–$8.25; main courses $9.95–$18.95. AE, CB, DC, JCB, MC, V.

Open: Breakfast daily 6:30–10:30am; lunch Mon–Fri 11:30am–1:30pm; dinner daily 6–10pm.

The raves keep coming in for one of Honolulu's newer restaurants and it's not a bit surprising. Mezzanine is on the mezzanine level of the sparkling new Waikiki Terrace Hotel, and, like the hotel, it's handsome, with a sleek, contemporary look. Casual elegance is the keynote here. The indoor-outdoor setting showcases a kiawe-wood-burning oven and grill, from which come forth some extraordinary breads and pizza pies, with the chef concocting new and exciting combinations every evening ($6.95–$8.75); try one for a special beginning to your meal. From the kiawe-wood broiler come baked North Shore prawns and roast chicken, and there are wonderful pasta platters, fresh salads big enough to share (Caesar, spinach, chicken Oriental, butter lettuce with plum tomatoes), and such tantalizing appetizers as chilled snow crab and cucumber salad, grilled vegetables with basil vinaigrette, and smoked salmon with Maui onions and capers. The chef dreams up extraordinary specials every day, including heavenly desserts. Premium wines can be had by the glass as well as the bottle.

Breakfast features granola and fresh fruit, waffles, French toast, and local favorites like eggs with Portuguese sausage.

NEW TOKYO RESTAURANT, 286 Beach Walk. Tel. 923-5411.

Cuisine: JAPANESE. **Reservations:** Not required.

$ Prices: Appetizers $2.95–$5.25; main courses $8.25–$19. AE, DC, JCB, MC, V.

Open: Lunch Mon–Sat 11:30am–2pm; dinner daily 5:30–9:30pm.

This restaurant is getting to be an institution in Waikiki, attracting tourists and locals alike. The anteroom, with its Asian ambience and aquarium display of live seafood, is both decorative and functional, and gets you in the mood for seafood. For lunch, you might have the grilled fish marinated in soy sauce for $4.95, or the assorted tempura vegetables with tempura fish at $6.25. Combination lunches run $7.25–$8.95. At dinner, main courses range from noodle dishes to old favorites, such as sukiyaki and shabu-shabu.

2. BEYOND WAIKIKI

KAPAHULU

MEALS FOR LESS THAN $12

HEE HING, 449 Kapahulu Ave. Tel. 734-8474.

Cuisine: CHINESE. **Reservations:** Not accepted.

$ Prices: Main courses $6.95–$15.75. MC, V.
Open: Daily 10:30am–9:30pm.

One of the most popular Chinese restaurants in Honolulu since 1963, Hee Hing is still going strong. There's good reason for its popularity: It's a handsome, spacious restaurant, with good-luck murals, paintings, and collages adorning the walls, and a superb Cantonese cuisine. And the prices for these delicious, authentic Chinese treats are always reasonable. The menu is voluminous, so take a little time to study it, or ask the waiter for advice. Don't miss the dim sum; they serve over 75 Hong Kong–style dim sum every day. The house specialty is drunken prawns—live prawns, marinated in white wine, cooked tableside, and priced seasonally. There's a vast variety of other live seafood dishes too, as well as fresh fish. Or you might decide to feast on one of the sizzling specialties, such as chicken with black-bean sauce, tenderloin of beef, or pork chops with onions, for $7.95–$13.95. Earthen-pot casserole dishes ($6.95–$15.75) are another way to go. Then there are taro-nest specialties and at least 16 vegetarian offerings. Everything we've tried here has been excellent. For dessert, forgo the fortune cookies in favor of a seasonal fruit pudding or fried apple fritters. A great find!

IRIFUNE, 563 Kapahulu Ave. Tel. 737-1141.

Cuisine: JAPANESE. **Reservations:** Not accepted.
$ Prices: Appetizers $2.50–$4.50; main courses $5–$9.50. MC, V.
Open: Lunch Tues–Fri 11:30am–1:30pm; dinner Tues–Sun 5–9:30pm.

For Japanese food with a local flavor, try Irifune. Short on decor, it's long on good food, large portions, and low prices, which are the same at lunch and dinner. For example, it's only $6.50 for the kushiyaki stick meal, which consists of miso soup, pickled vegetables, three skewers of barbecued chicken and veggies, a salad of lettuce, tomatoes, and chopped cabbage with a delicious house dressing, rice, and green tea. With seafood it's $7; with mixed seafood and chicken, $8. Irifune specialties include their barbecued chicken and beef teriyaki, and a variety of garlic creations, such as garlic tofu with veggies, and chicken or seafood with vegetables. Be sure to try their breaded tofu among the appetizers. Best of all, go with their fresh spicy garlic ahi, market-priced. Unlike most Japanese restaurants, Irifune does serve dessert, and a delicious one at that: ice-cream crêpes, filled with seasonal fruit, and just $2.50.

JO-NI OF HAWAII, 1017A Kapahulu Ave. Tel. 735-8575.

Cuisine: FILIPINO. **Reservations:** Not accepted.
$ Prices: Main courses $3.95–$9.50. MC, V.
Open: Lunch Tues–Sun 11am–2pm; dinner Tues–Sun 5–9pm.

Filipino food, it is said, originated with Malay settlers, was spread by Chinese traders, stewed for 300 years of Spanish rule, and was finally hamburger-ized by the Americans. What has arrived in Honolulu is delicious, especially so at Jo-ni of Hawaii. The windowed dining room is bright with a pink-and-cream decor and cane chairs made in the Philippines. Your first decision is whether to select a festive main dish or a regional specialty: You needn't worry about prices, since both are inexpensive; festive dishes range from $4.95 to $9.50, and regional specialties, mostly from $3.95 to $5.95. Festive items include langua—tender slices of ox tongue simmered in mushroom sauce (delicious!)—and beef flank rolled and stuffed with boiled eggs and sausage. Among the regional specialties, you might try adobo Manila, a stew with pork and/or chicken in a vinegar, garlic, and soy sauce; or the more delicate hipon sa gatong bicol, shrimps simmered in coconut milk, along with squash and long beans. Choose a few side dishes like pickled vegetables, to act as dipping sauces.

There's a smaller version of Jo-ni at Makai Food Court at Ala Moana Center.

ONO HAWAIIAN FOODS, 726 Kapahulu Ave. Tel. 737-2275.

Cuisine: HAWAIIAN. **Reservations:** Not accepted.
$ **Prices:** Main courses $5–$7.25. No credit cards.
Open: Mon–Sat 11am–7:30pm.

Close to Waikiki, this very popular place offers ono Hawaiian food. It's a little place with about 10 tables and walls covered with photos of popular local entertainers who are patrons. Try the kalua pig at $5.25, or the laulau plate at $5.65, or go mad and have the combination kalua pig *and* laulau at $7.25. These and other plates come with pipikaula (Hawaiian beef jerky), lomi-lomi salmon, poi or rice, and haupia. The atmosphere here is very friendly; the place may be short on size, but it's definitely long on aloha.

McCULLY/MOILIILI

MEALS FOR LESS THAN $12

CHIANG-MAI THAI RESTAURANT, 2239 S. King St. Tel. 941-1151 or 941-3777.

Cuisine: THAI. **Reservations:** Recommended.
$ **Prices:** Appetizers $4.25–$7.25; main courses $5.25–$8.25. AE, MC, V.
Open: Lunch Mon–Fri 11am–2pm; dinner daily 5:30–10pm.

Here's a small restaurant that the locals favor. With perhaps a dozen tables and simple decor, it specializes in the food of northern Thailand, and calls itself the "home of sticky rice and exotic food." Yes, you can order the sticky rice (really mochi rice in a bamboo container), and the exotic foods might include anything from golden-fried calamari with fresh lemongrass and spices among the appetizers and a creamy tofu soup to a shrimp pineapple curry, or hot-and-spicy clams, ginger beef, or cashew chicken. Vegetarians have a full menu—almost two dozen dishes—from which to choose.

DIÊM VIETNAMESE RESTAURANT & COFFEE SHOP, in University Square, 2633 S. King St. Tel. 941-8657.

Cuisine: VIETNAMESE. **Reservations:** Recommended.
$ **Prices:** Appetizers $1.85–$4.75; main courses $4–$8.95. MC, V.
Open: Daily 10am–10pm.

To sample the exotic cuisine of Vietnam, you need only go to this little place, just a block Diamond Head of University Avenue, close to Waikiki. The small, family-run eatery is kept sparkling clean; its checkerboard floor is the dominant decorative theme. Nothing fancy here but the food. Spring rolls, roast shredded-pork roll, and beef grilled with lemongrass make good appetizers. There's a wide range of vermicelli (noodle) dishes—curry chicken vermicelli, seafood saimin, barbecued shrimp cake, chicken noodle soup—and none will set you back more than $6.50 for a filling meal. As for the house specialties, the Vietnamese shrimp crêpe, the coco-steamed chicken, and the seafood steamboat are especially good. Or try a Vietnamese fried-rice dish like ginger chicken, steamed whole fish, or fried fish with black-bean paste. Desserts are cool and soothing—yellow mung-bean pudding, black-eye bean pudding, banana pudding—and just $1.25. The friendly management invites you to call ahead "for even faster service," and take-out orders are welcome.

GRACE'S INN, 1296 S. Beretania St. Tel. 537-3302.

Cuisine: LOCAL. **Reservations:** Not accepted.
$ **Prices:** Main courses $4.25–$5.80. No credit cards.
Open: Mon–Sat 6am–10:30pm, Sun 7am–10pm.

Even before it was immortalized in song by Hawaii's favorite funny man, Frank DeLima, Grace's Inn and the staple food of Hawaii—the plate lunch—were all but synonymous. Grace caters more than her share of baby luaus—the Hawaiian tradition of celebrating the first birthday of a *keiki o ka aina* (child of the land)—weddings, office parties, and any other occasion you can think of. Her food isn't fancy or unique, but its popularity is mind-boggling. Chicken or beef katsu, teriyaki beef or pork, sweet-and-sour pork, seafood mix, and mixed beef curry, ribs, and teri pork plates, with the traditional two scoops of rice and salad, are the staples. Specialties include fried noodles, fish tempura, and big bowls of curry stew. There are a few tables inside, but the bulk of Grace's trade is take-out. The lady is definitely doing something right. Consult the telephone book for other locations around town.

HOUSE OF PARK, 2671D S. King St. Tel. 949-2679.

Cuisine: KOREAN. **Reservations:** Not accepted.

$ Prices: Main courses $4–$8.75. No credit cards.

Open: Daily 11am–9pm.

Honolulu has only a handful of Korean restaurants, and this one in Moiliili, on the way to the university, is the oldest and best. This is the kind of family-style place that gives you a real experience in nontourist dining. Small and tidy with white walls and flower arrangements, it caters to local Korean and other Asian families (lots of cute keikis mill about), and a smattering of university students. There are a few booths and tables up front (at one, a man may be rolling dumplings for the soup), from which you can see the big open kitchen in the back. We love the combination of mon doo and kuk soo—hot noodle soup with Korean dumplings stuffed with beef, pork, and vegetables. The waitress once explained to us that this is "New Year's soup, but so popular we make it every day." The house specialty is kalbi, barbecued short ribs, and it's excellent. The plate lunch—barbecued meat, na mul (Korean-style vegetables and fish fried in an egg batter), and rice is a buy at $4.40. Kimchee and hot sauce come with all orders. While you're here, try the famed Korean ginseng tea.

KING'S BAKERY AND COFFEE SHOP, 1936 S. King St. near McCully. Tel. 941-5211.

Cuisine: AMERICAN/LOCAL. **Reservations:** Not accepted.

$ Prices: Main courses $5.95–$7.50. No credit cards.

Open: Daily 24 hours.

We often wonder why Honolulu's tourists haven't caught up with this place, a popular local rendezvous for years. Even though it's open around the clock, it's always jammed, and you sometimes have to wait a few minutes for a seat at the counter, tables, or booths. Certainly it's not because of the decor, which is perfectly plain with plastic-topped tables. It's because of the good service, the good food, and the fact that breakfast, lunch, and dinner are served around the clock. This means you can always count on a plate of beef stew, Hawaiian chopped steak, crispy fried chicken, sautéed mahimahi, or breaded veal cutlet. Daily specials at $7.50 include pork pot roast, short ribs, and mushroom chicken, served with a tossed green salad, vegetable, rice or potatoes, butter, and roll. This is also a bakery, and a good one. People come from miles around to shop for King's bread, rolls, and delicious pies and cakes. After you've had your fruit pie, or cream-cheese pie, you may be tempted to join the crowd at the bakery counter and take some home with you—and don't forget the very special sweet bread, $2 and $2.45 per loaf. (Try it for French toast!) Send some home to your friends—King's has them already packaged—and they'll bless you forever.

You can also get the standard sandwiches here at low prices, plus soups, salads, and soda-fountain concoctions.

King's also has two other locations, at the Kaimuki Shopping Center, 3221 Waialae Ave., and at Eaton Square, on Hobron Lane.

KING TSIN, 1110 McCully St. Tel. 946-3273.

Cuisine: CHINESE. **Reservations:** Recommended.

$ **Prices:** Appetizers \$2.95–\$7.95; main courses \$4.75–\$7.95. AE, DC, MC, V.
Open: Lunch daily 11am–2pm; dinner daily 5–9:30pm.

There are precious few northern Chinese restaurants in the islands, so praise be for this attractive, pleasantly decorated place popular with both visitors and local folk. The food is reasonably priced, subtly flavored, and most fun to eat with a group, as we did the last time we were there. A Chinese friend had ordered for us over the phone, and our soup and appetizer were whisked to our table moments after we arrived. Our party of four began with potstickers, small dumplings stuffed with pork, and two orders of sizzling rice soup. For our main courses, we had moo shu pork; dry-fried beef—super hot; King Tsin chicken, a delicate combination of tender white meat of chicken and pea pods; braised bean curd; and sweet-and-sour fish, an entire rock cod, complete with tail and head, smothered in sauce. We all ate until we couldn't manage another bite—and still had a huge doggie bag to take home. Lunch prices are about 10% lower than dinner. With the exception of the aforementioned beef—about which the menu warns you—the food here is not overly spicy, as it can be at other northern Chinese restaurants.

KOZO SUSHI HAWAII, in the McCully Shopping Center, 2334 S. King St. Tel. 973-5666.
Cuisine: SUSHI.
$ **Prices:** Sushi rolls 95¢–\$5.30.
Open: Most locations daily 9am–7pm, Sun 9am–6pm.

These little sushi-counter take-out places are insanely popular in Hawaii, just as they are in Japan. Everybody seems to love them. Sushi is fresh and delicious, the platters are artfully presented, and prices are remarkably low. Samples are displayed in sparkling glass cases. The \$4.95 lunch box and the \$5.95 dinner box are both generous, with a plentiful selection of roll sushi, nigiri, and shrimp. California maki (a blend of avocado, crab, and cucumber), at \$3.50, is their biggest seller. Other favorites: salmon or crab sushi (\$4 per roll); cucumber, egg, or ume (red plum) roll (\$1); ahi (tuna) sashimi special (\$4.50); shrimp special (\$4.50). Almost all these places are strictly take-out, but the one at 2334 S. King St. does have two tables.

Kozo Sushi has counters at 900 Fort Street Mall (tel. 522-9517), 1150 Bishop St. (tel. 522-9515), and Kahala Mall (tel. 733-5733). For other locations around the island, consult the telephone book; new Kozo Sushis seem to be opening all the time.

MAPLE GARDEN, 909 Isenberg St. Tel. 941-6641.
Cuisine: CHINESE. **Reservations:** Recommended.
$ **Prices:** Appetizers \$1.95–\$7.75; main courses \$4.95–\$7.95. AE, MC, V.
Open: Lunch Mon–Sat 11am–2pm; dinner daily 5:30–10pm.

★ Rating high with the local Chinese community is this small, attractive dining room with Chinese decorations on the walls, wood paneling, and soft lights. *Travel Holiday* magazine has named it one of the top 10 restaurants in Honolulu. The Szechuan dishes are so tasty and authentic that a doctor friend of ours from Taiwan brings all his visiting friends and relatives here. Mr. Robert Hsu, the owner, is constantly adding new delights to the menu. The house specialty is Szechuan smoky duck, crispy on the outside and tender on the inside, served with steamed buns—you tuck the meat into the buns. A very generous order (you'll probably need a doggie bag) is \$6.95. If you really like the superhot Szechuan-style cooking, you'll love the eggplant with hot garlic sauce or the pork with hot garlic sauce; they're real eye-openers. (The eggplant recipe has received an award from the *Los Angeles Times.*) There are more than 75 main dishes on the menu priced at \$6.50 or less, including hard-to-find singing rice—actually it's more of a whistle—served either with pork and vegetables or with shrimp. There's ample parking space; and you can phone for easy bus or driving directions from Waikiki.

MEKONG RESTAURANT, 1295 S. Beretania St. Tel. 521-2025 or 523-0014.

Cuisine: THAI. **Reservations:** Not required.

$ **Prices:** Appetizers $2.25–$8.95; main courses $4.95–$8.95. AE, DC, MC, V.

Open: Lunch Mon–Fri 11am–2pm; dinner daily 5:30–9:15pm.

Every now and then one discovers a place where the food is exotic and delicious, the staff cordial and attentive, the atmosphere warm and cozy, and the prices painless. Such a find is Mekong. The small dining room is outfitted with white linen tablecloths and blue linen napkins, posters on the wall, and a pretty latticed ceiling. The voluminous menu will explain the basics of Thai cooking, but you'll do just as well to tell your waiter what you like and follow his or her suggestions. Thai cooking resembles both East Indian and Chinese, and while it can be highly spicy, almost every dish can be ordered either mild, medium, or hot. The hottest—and most popular—dishes are Thai green curry (beef, pork, or chicken sautéed in green chile and curry in fresh coconut milk) and Evil Jungle Prince (beef, pork, or chicken sautéed with hot spices with either hot or sweet basil leaves). Mild dishes include not-to-be-missed spring rolls, a memorable chicken-ginger soup in a fresh coconut-milk base, a dish of thin, crisp noodles with tiny bits of chicken, water chestnuts fried rice, and shrimp curry. Bring your own bottle if you want wine. (Mekong II serves both beer and wine.) Dessert is another unforgettable treat: tapioca pudding unlike any you've ever tasted, in a warm coconut milk; and half-ripe Thai apple-bananas, again cooked in coconut milk. Thai teas are just a little bit different, brewed with vanilla beans and served with condensed milk to make them quite sweet.

A branch called **Mekong II** is located at 1726 S. King St. (tel. 941-6184).

Owner Keo Sananikone has three more Thai restaurants: **Keo's Thai Cuisine,** 625 Kapahulu (tel. 737-8240 or 737-9250), **Keo's at Ward Centre** (tel. 533-0533), and **Keo's at King Street,** 1486 S. King St. (tel. 947-9989).

THE NATURAL DELI, 2525 S. King St. Tel. 949-8188.

Cuisine: VEGETARIAN. **Reservations:** Not accepted.

$ **Prices:** Main courses $4.50–$4.75. No credit cards.

Open: Daily 10am–9pm.

Enter Down to Earth Natural Foods, just west of University Avenue, go to the rear, and there you'll find this delightful spot where you can dine on "healthy, home-style vegetarian cooking at its best." Only natural ingredients are used (no sugar, white flour, eggs, lard, rennet, caffeine, MSG, or preservatives); there are many nondairy alternatives for vegans and those watching their cholesterol—and the food is delicious, as well! There's a changing parade of hot specials every day (you're invited to call and find out what's cooking for the day), that might include almond-vegetable tofu, chickpeas à la king, nondairy lasagne, or shepherd's pie, for $4.50–$5.75. Always on hand are tofu or tempeh burgers, a variety of veggie sandwiches, like avocado or mock tuna ($2.75 each), hearty homemade soups, and a plentiful salad or pita-pocket sandwich bar that goes for $3.20 a pound. There are plenty of cold deli items, like tabbouleh, pesto pasta, burritos, and basmati salad to take out. Nearly a score of healthful desserts await your guilt-free enjoyment, none more than $2. There's a counter, a few tables right there, and more seating upstairs.

PATAYA THAI RESTAURANT, 1614 S. King St. Tel. 942-7979.

Cuisine: THAI. **Reservations:** Recommended.

$ **Prices:** Appetizers $5.95–$7.75; main courses $5.95–$9.95. AE, MC, V.

Open: Dinner only. Sun–Thurs 5–9pm, Fri–Sat 5–10pm.

This neighborhood place is small—minuscule, in fact—but its kitchen is powerful. This is the place to experiment with some unusual Thai dishes, such as Kuruma shrimp curry (shrimp and vegetables cooked in southern Thai style) or chicken sautéed in pepper sauce and basil. Or stick to more familiar dishes such as "the original Evil Jungle Priest": It can be made with beef, chicken, or shrimp; the ingredients are sautéed in a very hot pepper sauce and coconut milk over a "hot, rocking flame"—not for the cautious! Vegetarians have a choice of about a dozen dishes.

QUINTERO'S CUISINE, 2334 S. King St. Tel. 944-3882.

Cuisine: MEXICAN. **Reservations:** Not accepted.

$ **Prices:** Appetizers $2.75–$4.50; main courses $7.75–$10.75. No credit cards.

Open: Mon–Sat 11am–10pm, Sun 4–10pm.

Authentic Mexican dishes cooked in the Aztec tradition would be baked in underground ovens. That's not quite feasible in a city like Honolulu, but Mary and Louis Quintero do the next best thing in their restaurant, which is next to the Old Stadium Square shopping area. Tasty dishes include carne al arriero, steak cooked with garlic, onions, and peppers. Pollo a la mexicana, chicken fried with ranchero sauce, is also good. Among the appetizers and soups, we like the nachos and the fideo, a tomato-based broth with sautéed noodles and Mexican spices ($2.75). This is a small and plain little restaurant, but the service is personal and homey. The same menu is available all day.

SALERNO, in the McCully Shopping Center, 1960 Kapiolani Blvd. Tel. 942-5273.

Cuisine: ITALIAN. **Reservations:** Required.

$ **Prices:** Appetizers $2.90–$5.90; main courses $6.90–$11.90 small, $8.90–$15.90 regular. AE, DC, MC, V.

Open: Lunch Mon–Sat 11am–2:30pm; dinner daily 5–10pm.

Everybody raves about the authentic Italian food at Salerno, and no wonder. Only the freshest pastas, vegetables, seafoods, and the like are used in preparing the dishes; all the wonderful breads and pastries are baked right in their own kitchens; and they are happy to satisfy special dietary needs. On top of all that, the price is right! You have your choice of excellent antipasti, soups, salads, pizza pies, and a variety of pastas, like the popular linguine pesto or fettuccine carbonara, for $8.90–$11.90 for a regular portion, $2 less for a smaller serving. Among the notable main courses are veal marsala, shrimp scampi, chicken oregano, and such house specialties as calamari vegetable, stuffed eggplant, and pollo linguine, for $10.90–$15.90 regular, $2–$4 less for smaller orders. Beer, wine, drinks, and espressos are modestly priced, as are some filling Italian pastries. The setting is pretty, with soft lighting, plants, natural woods, lamps on the tables, and partitions affording a feeling of privacy. On the way out, check out Salerno's Italian Grocery and maybe take home some homemade bread, pastas, sauces, or deli items for your hotel kitchenette.

SUEHIRO, 1914 King St. Tel. 949-4584.

Cuisine: JAPANESE. **Reservations:** Recommended.

$ **Prices:** Main courses $8–$13. MC, V.

Open: Lunch daily 11am–2pm; dinner Mon–Fri 5–9pm, Sat–Sun 5–9:30pm.

We have always liked Suehiro. Try to get one of their ozashiki or tatami rooms, where you sit on the floor and dine at a low lacquered table (take off your shoes before you enter); the setting will immediately put you in a tranquil mood, ready for a different kind of experience. You usually need a party of eight and a reservation for these rooms, but if a room happens to be open you may double up with other waiting guests. On one visit we teamed up with a big, charming family of Japanese-Americans and had a family-style dinner at $13.50 per person that included a tasty miso soup, namasu (pickled cucumber), sashimi, shrimp tempura, tenderloin filet, and mixed sushi, served with several side vegetables, sauces, rice, dessert, and plenty of tea. At the regular restaurant tables, you may order a similar dinner special for $25 for two people, or order à la carte. There is an extensive sushi menu, and half a dozen special lunches for $7.95–$9.95. *Note:* You can also get a tasty Japanese box lunch here, for picnics and trips.

SUNNY SEAFOOD, in the McCully Shopping Center, 1960 Kapiolani Blvd. Tel. 949-4559.

Cuisine: SEAFOOD.

$ Prices: Main courses $4.20–$7.50. No credit cards.

Open: Mon–Sat 9:30am–7pm, Sun noon–6:30pm.

Located in the McCully Shopping Center (a block over the McCully Bridge at the corner of McCully and Kapiolani), Sunny is a seafood market with a take-out counter and limited in-store seating. Their take-out fish and seafood plates are super-fresh (most of it comes from the daily fish auction), and so reasonably priced that people come from all over for these treats. Possibilities include the butterfish sweet miso, sashimi, ahi teriyaki, and salmon fry. We recently sampled the mahimahi plate, which came with two scoops of rice, salad including tasty crab poki with seaweed, plus the mahimahi. Arrive at least half an hour before closing.

TEMPURA HOUSE, 1419 S. King St. Tel. 941-5919.

Cuisine: JAPANESE. **Reservations:** Not required.

$ Prices: Main courses $9.50–$17. AE, MC, V.

Open: Lunch Mon–Sat 11am–2pm; dinner Mon–Sat 5–10pm.

You can sit at a tempura bar here, pretty much like a sushi bar, and watch the chef prepare tasty tidbits in this long, narrow store converted into a restaurant. Black vinyl chairs line the black vinyl bar. Tables are all for four. At lunch, prices start at $6.50 for chicken cutlet but rise quickly to $10.50 for sashimi. Most of the authentic Japanese tempura, such as the popular unagi (eel), are over $11 ($14 for the combination seafood and vegetable tempura) and all are very light and delicate tasting. Prices for the same items, in larger portions, go up about $3 at dinner. Console yourself knowing that these dishes would cost four times as much in Japan. There is limited free parking in the rear; in the evening, street parking is plentiful.

WOODLANDS POTSTICKER RESTAURANT, 1289 S. King St. Tel. 526-2239.

Cuisine: CHINESE. **Reservations:** Recommended.

$ Prices: Appetizers $5.95–$19.50; main courses $5.25–$19.50. MC, V.

Open: Lunch Wed–Mon 11am–2pm; dinner Wed–Mon 5–9pm.

Do you like potstickers? That's one good reason for coming here, but not the only one. All the food is especially good, and this place is a local favorite. The Chinese-tiled ceiling and impressive Asian statuettes and art prepare you for a special experience. You may want to start with some of those potstickers: We like the pan-fried dumplings, the chicken with chives, and the onion cake ($4.95–$5.25). Bird's-nest soup—the real thing—with chicken is another impressive starter, or try the crabmeat tofu soup. Prawns, scallops, and steamed catch-of-the-day dominate the dozen seafood dishes. Best bargains are some 30 specialty chicken and duck choices (most $5.95–$6.95), but watch out—some of these may be highly spiced. Parking is in the rear.

YUEN'S GARDEN SEAFOOD RESTAURANT, 2140 S. Beretania St. Tel. 944-9699.

Cuisine: CHINESE. **Reservations:** Not required.

$ Prices: Appetizers $4.25–$7.95; main courses $5.50–$12.50. MC, V.

Open: Daily 10:30am–10pm.

Of the many items on the menu, which includes Cantonese, Szechuan, and Mandarin dishes, it is the seafood that inspires most of the raves here. Prawns can be bought by the pound at $18; half a pound usually produces five large prawns. We like the fried prawns, served with radish and cilantro. Other good seafood choices, most in the $7.95 range, are scallops, clams with black-bean sauce, sweet-and-sour shrimp, and sea bass filet. Also great are the hot-pot courses served in casseroles. We vote for the seafood combo and the roast duck hot pot made with eggplant and plum sauce.

READERS RECOMMEND

Kamaaina Suite at the Willows, *901 Hausten St. (tel. 946-4808). "Kamaaina Suite at the Willows was superb. It charges a fixed price for each person, and wine and drinks are extra. The price is $42.50. With tax and tip, it's virtually impossible to get out for under $100—but it's worth it. In fact, this restaurant may well be worth the trip to Hawaii, all by itself. We will definitely return to Oahu if only to experience Kamaaina Suite again."*—Barbara Bazemore and Dave Butenhof, Hudson, N.M.

"We saved The Willows for our last night in the islands and what a perfect choice. It was expensive with wine, tax, tip, etc., but worth every cent. The atmosphere outside is incredible; the three-piece ensemble playing 'Hawaii City Lights' reduced me to tears. The food was superior, as was the service; all in all, a must."—Sheila Pritchett, Villanova, Pa.

NEAR WAIKIKI

MEALS FOR LESS THAN $12

HARD ROCK CAFE, 1837 Kapiolani Blvd. Tel. 955-7383.

Cuisine: AMERICAN. **Reservations:** Not accepted.
$ Prices: Appetizers $2.95–$6.95; main courses $5.95–$13.95. AE, MC, V.
Open: Sun–Thurs 11:30am–1am, Fri–Sat 11:30am–1:30am.

Honolulu is home to the world's ninth Hard Rock Café, which, like its sibling restaurants in Europe and on the mainland, is a restaurant-cum-museum of rock-music memorabilia and 1950s artifacts. Nonstop rock blares forth. The management prides itself on the fact that one can see and be seen by everyone in the place at all times, no matter where one is seated. Gold records and musical instruments—either donated by their famous owners or purchased at auctions—adorn the walls. A real '50s station wagon is suspended from the ceiling over the bar! Larger-than-life busts of Mick Jagger and Keith Richards dominate the foyer, where souvenirs such as T-shirts, lapel pins, baseball caps, and cigarette lighters bearing the HRC logo are for sale. Like all the other Hard Rock Cafés, this one will not accept reservations; lines are common but seem to be part of the fun. The menu features house specials, such as watermelon barbecued ribs and lime barbecued chicken; burgers served with home-cut fries, green salad, and your choice of made-from-scratch dressing; sandwiches, including grilled chicken breast and avocado, Swiss cheese, and tomato; and thick, cold shakes. Hard Rock Café is proud of the fact that it "uses absolutely no preservatives or additives."

ALA MOANA AREA

MEALS FOR LESS THAN $12

AUNTIE PASTO'S, 1099 S. Beretania St., at Pensacola. Tel. 523-8855.

Cuisine: ITALIAN. **Reservations:** Not accepted.
$ Prices: Appetizers $1.95–$4.50; main courses $5.95–$11.95. MC, V.

Open: Mon–Fri 11am–10:30pm, Fri 11am–11pm; Sat 4–11pm; Sun 4–10:30pm.

With its brick interior, café curtains, and checkered cloths, this place resembles a little trattoria in Florence or Rome. The food here is marvelous, and at lunchtime Auntie Pasto's attracts a lively crowd, many of whom work at the shops and medical clinics in the neighborhood. Special lunches, $3.95–$5.50, include frittata (an open-face omelet), a mortadella scramble, pan-fried sausage and vegetables, and a club sandwich served with pasta salad. Also very popular are Auntie's big sandwiches (meatball, salami, subs) for $3.95–$5.75, and her super pastas, especially those with clams and spinach, for $4.95–$6.95. At dinnertime, there are also some flavorful specialties like stuffed calamari, veal parmigiana, and osso buco.

CHICKEN ALICE'S, 1470 Kapiolani Blvd., at the corner of Keeaumoku. Tel. 946-6117.

Cuisine: FRIED CHICKEN. **Reservations:** Not accepted.

$ Prices: Plate lunches $3.95–$5.75. No credit cards.

Open: Daily 9am–10:30pm.

One of our favorite places to pick up wonderful, portable food for a picnic or the beach—or just to take back to our hotel—is this spot. The stellar attraction here is Alice Gahinhin's flavorful fried chicken. It's ever-so-delicately spiced and definitely habit-forming. And you can't beat the price—$5.25 for a small box containing 12 pieces, $10.50 for the large box of 24 pieces, $26.25 for some 60 pieces (in case you're throwing a party or have a very large family to feed). Chicken is also available by the piece. And plate lunches are king-size, to say the least. Our favorite is the combination Korean plate: kalbi (tender barbecued ribs), chicken, rice, and kimchee, for $5.75.

EMILIO'S PIZZA, 1423 Kalakaua, near the corner of King St. Tel. 946-4972.

Cuisine: ITALIAN. **Reservations:** Accepted only for parties of six or more on Fri and Sat.

$ Prices: Appetizers $1.50–$6.25; main courses $5.50–$12.50. MC, CB, DC, V.

Open: Dinner only, Mon–Thurs 5–10pm, Fri–Sat 5–11:30pm.

One of Honolulu's favorite pizza parlors, Emilio's is a cozy spot, with interesting framed pictures and glass shelving lending a homey atmosphere. This is Sicilian-style pizza with a professional touch. There is a choice of 14 toppings, which are piled abundantly on the crusts, making a 10-inch pie a filling meal for two or three. Prices run from about $7.50 for the 10-inch cheese pie up to $19.50 for the mind-blowing combo with six toppings. Emilio's makes their own tasty dough every day, and their own sausages and sauces. They also make an excellent soup of the day—it might be seafood bisque or black bean—in addition to the regular homemade minestrone. There are also pasta specials every day, unusual appetizers like fresh pesto and cream cheese, and many vegetarian and low-fat specialties, all gourmet quality. Customers are welcome to bring their own beer or wine; there is no corkage charge. And yes, they will deliver to most hotels and condos in Waikiki.

HARBOR PUB AND PIZZERIA, 1765 Ala Moana Blvd. Tel. 941-0985.

Cuisine: ITALIAN/AMERICAN. **Reservations:** Not required.

$ Prices: Appetizers $2.25–$4.95; main courses $4.75–$16.50. AE, DC, MC, V.

Open: Daily 11am–1:30am.

In the evening, a "fun" crowd usually fills this cheerful little spot just below the Chart House. It's a favorite watering hole for people employed at nearby hotels and offices. The fare is not terribly varied here, but what there is, is just fine. Good sandwiches—roast beef, breast of turkey, vegetarian delight submarine, and tuna melt—go for $4.75–$5.85. The specialty is pizza: Plain cheese pies are $7.95 small, and the Harbor combo, with everything, is $10.50 small. This is the sort of place where everyone talks with everyone else, and the atmosphere is friendly and fun.

ORIGINAL PANCAKE HOUSE, 1221 Kapiolani Blvd. Tel. 533-3005.

Cuisine: AMERICAN. **Reservations:** Not accepted.
$ Prices: Main courses $4.75–$7.25. AE, MC, V.
Open: Daily 6am–2pm.

This is a pleasant place to have breakfast or lunch on your way to or from Ala Moana Center. We like to sit out in the pretty little garden, where English sparrows, doves, Brazilian cardinals, and mynahs, all come looking for a handout. Pancakes and crêpes include blueberry pancakes at $4.50; cherry crêpes, made with liqueur, at $5.50; and the house special, apple pancakes (allow 30 minutes), at $6.75. Among the many omelets, all served with three buttermilk pancakes, my favorite is potato—made with green onions and bacon bits and served with a flavorful sour-cream sauce ($6.60). There are also hot sandwiches, such as teriyaki steak and French dip, in the $2.95–$4.70 range, and daily specials, such as mahimahi, chicken-fried steak, spaghetti, and beef stew, are all priced at $4.75.

PENNEY'S RESTAURANT, 1450 Ala Moana Blvd., at Ala Moana Center. Tel. 946-8068.

Cuisine: AMERICAN. **Reservations:** Not accepted.
$ Prices: Main courses $4.45–$7.95. AE, MC, V.
Open: Mon–Thurs 8am–7pm, Fri 8am–8pm, Sat 8am–7pm, Sun 9am–4pm.

Although J. C. Penney's, the huge department store at Ala Moana Center, is right up-to-date with its fashions, the prices they charge at Penney's Restaurant on the third floor went out of style years ago—which makes it a great place for us. It's a good deal for breakfast, lunch, or dinner. At lunch, for example, hot plates are all under $4.75. At 4pm, some dinner items are added to the menu, like grilled beef liver or choice sirloin steak. Main dishes are served with potatoes, vegetable, dessert, and beverage. Try to avoid the peak lunch hour unless you don't mind lining up for a few minutes. Early arrivals must use the special third-floor entrance.

SIAM ORCHID, 1514 Kona St. Tel. 955-6161.

Cuisine: THAI. **Reservations:** Not required.
$ Prices: Appetizers $4.95–$7.95; main courses $5.95–$10.95. AE, DC, MC, V.
Open: Lunch Mon–Sat 11am–2pm; dinner Mon–Sat 5:30–9:30pm.

Just across Kona Street from the Ala Moana Shopping Center is the Siam Orchid. The setting is charming: fans, Thai artwork on the wall, rattan chairs, pink cloths under glass, orchids on the tables, banquettes. The menu is authentic, reflecting the different styles of the various regions of the country. And prices are modest at both lunch and dinner. There's a huge array of dishes, some hotter than others (ask your waiter), but you can't go wrong with such appetizers as stuffed chicken wings or squid salad. Or begin with a white tofu or fresh cabbage clear soup and choose from such main dishes as fresh chile chicken, beef on a sizzling platter, pork with ginger-curry sauce, or Thai garlic shrimp. As in most Thai restaurants, there's a healthy list of vegetarian specialties. Lunch is always a good buy, with half a dozen noodle specials around $5. Everything is prepared to order, and no MSG is used.

VIM AND VIGOR FOODS, 1450 Ala Moana Blvd., at Ala Moana Center. Tel. 955-3600.

Cuisine: VEGETARIAN/AMERICAN. **Reservations:** Not accepted.
$ Prices: Sandwiches $3.50 and $4.35; hot main courses $3.50 and $4.50. AE, DC, JCB, MC, V.

Open: Mon–Sat 9am–9pm, Sun 9am–5pm.

Need a healthful snack while you're shopping Ala Moana? Vim and Vigor, the big health-food store on the lower level, mountain side, has a tidy little take-out bar up front, which keeps huge lunch crowds happy with luscious sandwiches like avocado, tuna, or egg combinations on whole-grain breads with sprouts. Hot dishes, such as veggie burgers, chicken adobo, and teriyaki chicken, are also available. Fruit smoothies made with fresh Hawaiian fruits are especially good. There are a few tables where you can picnic in front of the store. While you're here, check out their selection of vitamins, teas, herbs, sports nutrition products, and natural cosmetics and beauty aids. This is one of the best health-food stores in Honolulu.

There's another Vim and Vigor in Kailua, right outside the Holiday Mart.

THE WISTERIA, 1206 S. King St. Tel. 531-5276.

Cuisine: JAPANESE/AMERICAN. **Reservations:** Not required.

$ Prices: Appetizers $2.25–$5.50; main courses $5.25–$12.75. AE, MC, V.

Open: Sun–Thurs 6am–10:30pm, Fri–Sat 6am–11:15pm.

When a restaurant has been going strong for nearly 40 years, it must be doing something right. Such a place is the Wisteria, a family restaurant very popular with the local crowd. The dining room is bright and airy, the atmosphere is pleasantly businesslike, the service swift and professional, and the deep booths comfortable. The menu is mostly Japanese, but there's a little bit of everything here: Daily specials often include Hawaiian plates, and such dishes as boiled corned beef brisket with cabbage, Hungarian beef goulash with egg noodles, and roast beef sirloin au jus, as well as a huge array of various sushi dishes, donburi, tempura, and sukiyaki specials. For a real local experience, try the chef's famous bowl of oxtail soup, served steaming hot with rice and grated ginger ($7.50). For dessert, go with the Portuguese doughnut—deep-fried and filled with ice cream—or have the peach Melba or strawberry sundae and take home the souvenir glass. The cocktail lounge, which always features daily bar specials, is open from 11am to 1am. A Saturday and Sunday brunch buffet is $4.60.

ZIPPY'S, 1450 Ala Moana Blvd., at Ala Moana Center. Tel. 942-7766.

Cuisine: LOCAL.

$ Prices: Plate lunches $3.90–$6.25. No credit cards.

Open: Daily 6:30am–9pm.

The kamaainas are mad about Zippy's and it's no wonder. The food is plentiful and the prices are as reasonable as you'll find anywhere in Hawaii. There are 17 Zippy's restaurants on Oahu (they're all listed in the phone book), including this convenient one at Ala Moana Center. Two of their most popular specialties are chili and fried chicken. In fact, many local clubs and children's athletic teams sell tickets for the chili to raise funds, and they sell like . . . Zippy's chili! A "barrell" of this taste treat is $15.85; a take-out for four people is $4.85. Fried chicken is $13.50 for a 12-piece bucket. And everyone seems to love Zippy's plate lunches: big platters of beef or pork, teriyaki, breaded beef cutlet, fried chicken and the like. There's good news for the diet-conscious, too: Zippy's huge salads—we especially like the Italian chicken and chef's salads—are all $5.15 or less. Zippy's are self-service restaurants where you place your order at one window, pay, and collect it in very short order at the next windows. Eleven of them have table-service dining rooms as well, and all have a "Napoleon's Bakery," waiting to fatten you up with luscious cakes, pies, and freshly baked breads.

MEALS FOR LESS THAN $20

CAFE CAMBIO, 1680 Kapiolani Blvd. Tel. 942-0740.

Cuisine: CONTEMPORARY ITALIAN. **Reservations:** Not accepted.

$ Prices: Appetizers $3.75–$7.50; main courses $7.50–$14. MC, V.

Open: Lunch Tues–Fri 11am–2pm; dinner Tues–Sun 5:30–10:30pm.

The cooking of chef Sergio Mitrotti has created quite a stir among those who favor a highly sophisticated, contemporary Italian cuisine. The small, narrow dining room is simple, with a large bar on one side, marble slabs on plain black pedestals for tables, Italian murals and photographs on the walls, and track lighting. But the food and flavors are marvelously complex. Consider, among the huge pasta selection (35, at last count) such dishes as salmone alla fiorentina (mostaccioli with salmon in a creamy lemon-whiskey sauce); scampi alla vodka capperi (shrimp and clams in a light vodka-caper-cream sauce); linguine alla noci, a standout among the vegetarian selections, with its homemade walnut–pine nut sauce and sautéed mushrooms; or perhaps pollo Medici, a traditional Florentine favorite, with chicken breast, bacon, and peas in a white wine sauce. Although the menu is largely devoted to pasta, there are half a dozen veal dishes, plus some intriguing salads (like marinated squid on a bed of mixed greens), as well. A generous assortment of appetizers provides an opportunity to sample some regional dishes not found in too many Italian restaurants; the bagna calda, fresh vegetables with a warm anchovy garlic sauce, and the bruschetta—toasted bread, rubbed with garlic, and topped with diced fresh tomato and olive oil—are both delicious. Desserts—like the homemade canteloupe or mango sherbet—are also exemplary.

So popular has this restaurant become, that another establishment, **Sistina,** has opened under the direction of Signor Mitrotti, at 1314 S. King St. (tel. 526-0071). It's another winner.

EL CRAB CATCHER, 1765 Ala Moana Blvd. Tel. 955-4911.

Cuisine: SEAFOOD. **Reservations:** Not required.

$ Prices: Seaside Café Section, appetizers $2.95–$6.95; main courses $6.95–$13.95. Main Coral dining room, appetizers $3.50–$8.95; main courses $10.95–$21.95. AE, DC, JCB, MC, V.

Open: Daily 11:30am–midnight.

A meal at El Crab Catcher need not be expensive if you know where to sit and what to eat. Try the Seaside Café section, set off from the main Coral dining room by a beautiful aquarium of rainbow-colored fish. Pupus, light main dishes, and generous tropical drinks are featured every day from 11:30am to midnight, and they are terrific. Happy hour is from 4:30 to 6:30pm daily. The house specialty is crab-stuffed mushrooms, topped with melted Jack cheese ($6.95). Shrimp, scallops, fresh fish, oysters, and clams are presented in various ways, for $6.95–$10.95. The shredded chicken salad is heaven, and the Crab Catcher sandwich—snow crab, cheese, tomato, and sprouts baked on cheese bread—is equally delightful. In the Coral dining room, which serves dinner only, light supper selections offer Hawaiian chicken, seafood salad suprême, and mahimahi macadamia for around $13. Fresh Hawaiian fish and other specialties begin at $17.95. With all main dishes, fresh vegetables, sautéed red potatoes or rice, and fresh baked breads are served. There's entertainment on Thursday, Friday, and Saturday evenings.

HACKFELD'S, ground level of Liberty House, 1450 Ala Moana Blvd., at Ala Moana Center. Tel. 945-5243.

Cuisine: FRENCH/CONTINENTAL. **Reservations:** Not accepted.

$ Prices: Appetizers $2.75–$5.50; main courses $10.25–$14.75. AE, CB, DC, JCB, MC, V.

Open: Lunch Mon–Sat 11am–2:30pm; dinner Mon–Fri 5–8:30pm.

Call Hackfeld's an elegant bistro; the food has a French accent, and the artful presentations make continental dishes as pleasing to the eye as to the palate. Prices are the most reasonable at lunch, when main dishes run $7.95–$12.50, and include such dishes as veal piccata, Thai curry, and New England crab cakes, all served with a choice of soup of the day or salad. The dinner menu is also intriguing: Try escargots maison or fettuccine Alfredo among the appetizers and the wonderful Burnt Crème

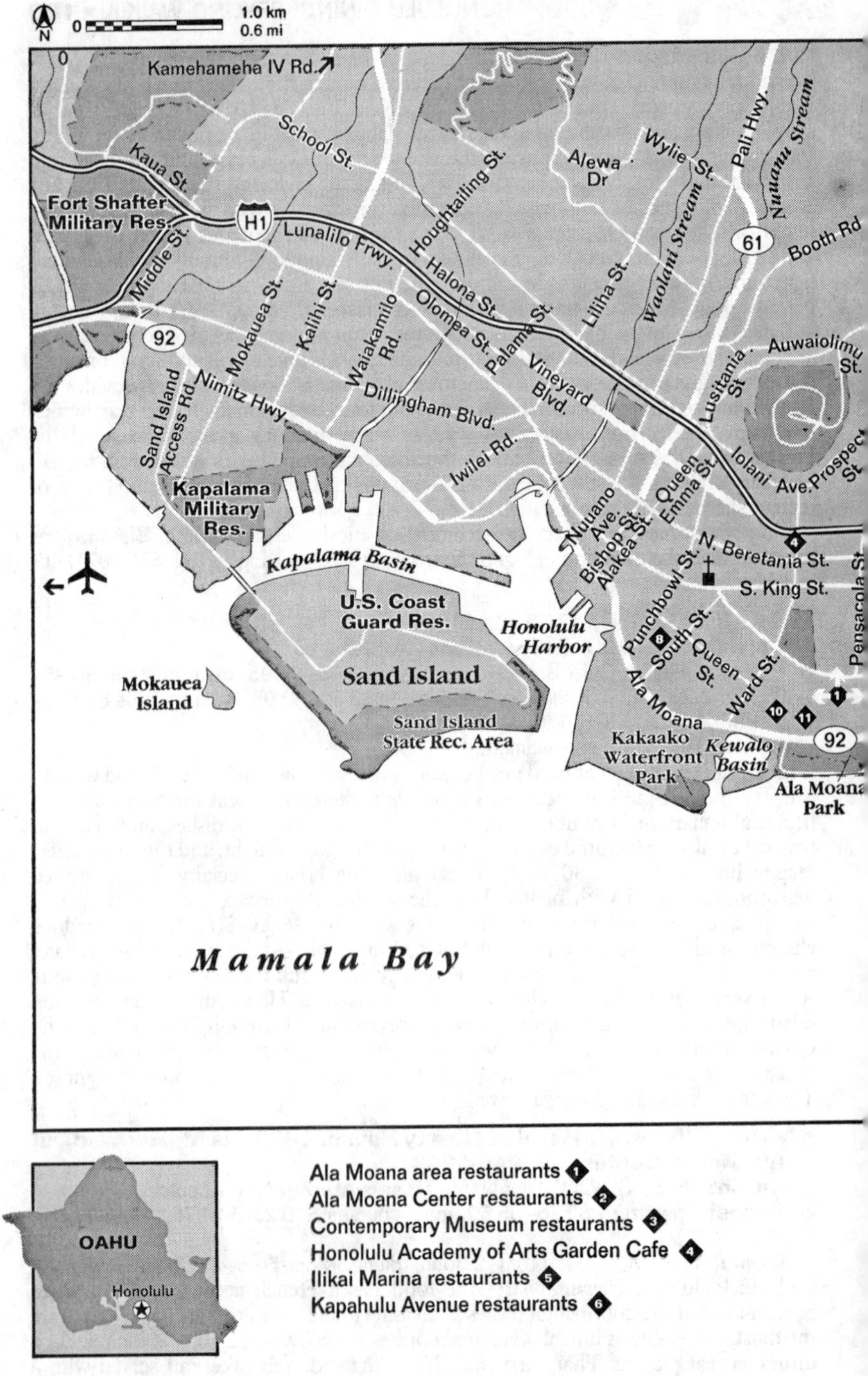

1.0 km
0.6 mi

Kamehameha IV Rd.
School St.
Kaua St.
Fort Shafter Military Res.
H1
Lunalilo Frwy.
Houghtailing St.
Alewa Dr
Wylie St.
Pali Hwy.
Nuuanu Stream
Waolani Stream
61
Booth Rd
Middle St.
Mokauea St.
Kalihi St.
Halona St.
Olomea St.
Liliha St.
Palama St.
Waiakamilo Rd.
92
Sand Island Access Rd
Nimitz Hwy.
Dillingham Blvd.
Vineyard Blvd.
Lusitania St
Auwaiolimu St.
Iwilei Rd.
Iolani Ave.
Prospect St.
Kapalama Military Res.
Nuuano Ave.
Bishop St.
Alakea St.
Queen Emma St.
N. Beretania St.
Punchbowl St.
S. King St.
Pensacola St.
Kapalama Basin
U.S. Coast Guard Res.
Honolulu Harbor
South St.
Queen St.
Ward St.
Sand Island
Mokauea Island
Ala Moana
Sand Island State Rec. Area
Kakaako Waterfront Park
Kewalo Basin
Ala Moana Park
Mamala Bay

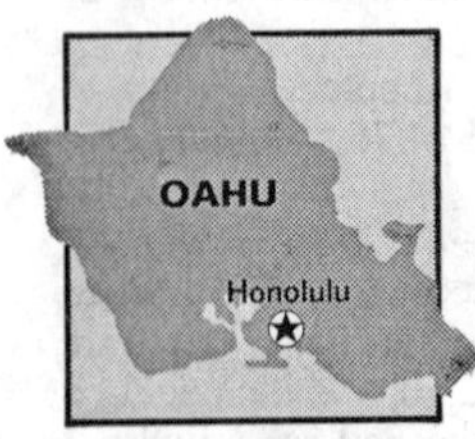

Ala Moana area restaurants 1
Ala Moana Center restaurants 2
Contemporary Museum restaurants 3
Honolulu Academy of Arts Garden Cafe 4
Ilikai Marina restaurants 5
Kapahulu Avenue restaurants 6

DINING ELSEWHERE IN HONOLULU

McCulley/Moiliili area restaurants 7
Restaurant Row establishments 8
University area restaurants 9
Ward Centre restaurants 10
Ward Warehouse restaurants 11

(or any of the French pastries and tortes) for dessert. In between are dishes such as the fresh catch of the day, teriyaki steak, chicken fettuccine, veal Oscar and lamb chops, all served with soup of the day or salad, plus garlic pasta, fresh mashed potatoes, potato pancakes, or steamed rice.

LE GUIGNOL, 1614 Kalakaua Ave. Tel. 947-5525.

Cuisine: FRENCH. **Reservations:** Recommended.
$ Prices: Appetizers $3.95–$5.95; main courses $10.95–$16.95. AE, MC, V.
Open: Dinner only, Tues–Sun 5:30–10pm.

At last, a moderately priced French restaurant par excellence in Honolulu! This tiny place, reminiscent of a small dining room in a French boîte, is owned by French chef Marcel Trigue and his wife, Madeleine. It is most pleasant, with its crisp tablecloths and paintings of French scenery. Appetizers are typically Gallic: pâté, escargots, crevettes provençal; and some a bit different, like scampi flambé in Pernod with cream and garlic. The French onion soup is also flavorful. Main courses include Cornish game hen in a mustard sauce; rack of lamb béarnaise; sliced veal in a light, creamy mushroom sauce; shrimp with fresh basil sauce; and fresh fish-of-the-day. These are served with bread and butter, vegetable, and potato. Finish your dinner with a light sherbet, caramel flan, or blueberries jubilee. Le Guignol is between King Street and Kapiolani Boulevard.

PAGODA FLOATING RESTAURANT, 1525 Rycroft St. Tel. 941-6611.

Cuisine: SEAFOOD. **Reservations:** Recommended.
$ Prices: Appetizers $3.50–$6.75; main courses $8.95–$14.95. AE, DISC, MC, V.
Open: Lunch daily 11am–2pm; dinner daily 4:30–9pm.

The Pagoda Floating Restaurant is one of those rare places where the scenery alone is worth the price of admission. The glass-enclosed Koi Room on the first floor, which specializes in seafood, and the more elegant La Salle overlook a lotus-blossom pond stocked with almost 3,000 brilliantly colored Japanese carp. Walkways lead to individual pagodas seemingly afloat in the pond. The pagodas are reserved for groups of eight or more, but don't despair! The view from the main dining rooms is also quite beautiful. The house specialty, mahimahi, is $9.50. Lunch is buffet-style, priced at $8.95 Monday through Friday and $11.95 on Saturday. There's a dinner buffet too, $13.95 from 4:30 to 5:30pm and $15.95 from 5:30 to 9:30pm. Try to plan your visit to catch the grand show at carp-feeding time—8am, noon, or 6pm. Bring the kids and the cameras.

RESTAURANT KYOTO, 1240 S. King St. Tel. 524-0511.

Cuisine: JAPANESE. **Reservations:** Not required.
$ Prices: Sushi $7.50–$11.50; main courses $6.50–$13.50. AE, MC, V.
Open: Lunch Mon–Sat 11am–2pm; dinner daily 5–9:30pm.

You'll think you're in Kyoto when you dine at this place. It's a pretty brown Japanese "house" with shojis at the windows, wood walls, a brick floor, and an attractive red-and-black color scheme. Whatever kind of Japanese food you like, it's here: a wide range of sushi, sashimi, plus many robayaki dishes, tempura, nabemone, ippinyori, donburi, and gohanmono. Kyoto's Combination (beef teriyaki, sashimi, and tempura) is a good buy at $12.95, as are the hearty udon and soba noodle dishes at $4.25–$6.95. The sushi bar stays open until 2am nightly for sushi and karaoke.

TAHITIAN LANAI RESTAURANT, in the Waikikian Hotel, 1811 Ala Moana Blvd. Tel. 946-6541.

Cuisine: AMERICAN/SEAFOOD. **Reservations:** Recommended.
$ Prices: Appetizers $2.25–$9.50; main courses $14.95–$22.50. AE, MC, V.
Open: Breakfast daily 7am–11am; lunch daily 11am–2:30pm; dinner daily 6–11pm.

Just because you're saving money, it doesn't mean that you can't dine in style. To have breakfast at one of the most glamorous tropical settings in town, at coffeehouse prices, try this favorite old-timer, nestled beside a tranquil lagoon and surrounded by tikis, native carvings, Polynesian-style huts, and tapa designs. You can dine outdoors under striped umbrella tables or in the casual, open-air dining room. Recommended for breakfast: their renowned eggs Benedict or Florentine ($5.95 for half order, $7.75 whole), served with hash browns, and a banana muffin or popover. Coconut waffles or fresh banana griddle cakes ($4 each) are other winners.

Lunch and dinner are also good bets. You can still get those eggs Benedict or Florentine at lunch, plus specialties like chicken and shrimp curries ($7.50–$9.50) and some very good salads—spinach, niçoise, and the Green Goddess Surprise: chicken or shrimp tossed with romaine lettuce ($6.95–$9.95). There are complete dinners, with choice of soup or greens, potatoes or rice, garlic roll, and beverage accompanying such main courses as teriyaki steak, baked chicken, and seafood fettuccine, for $15.95–$17.50. The new French-imported rôtisserie produces delicious roast chickens. Higher-priced house specialties include jet-fresh seafood (Maine lobster and Dungeness and Jonah crabs are flown in fresh daily and displayed in live tanks), fresh catch of the day prepared in a variety of ways, and steak from the broiler. Don't miss the lively singing around the piano in the Papeete Bar nightly.

VANDA COURT CAFE, in the Ilikai Hotel, 1777 Ala Moana Blvd. Tel. 949-3811.

Cuisine: AMERICAN. **Reservations:** Not accepted.

$ **Prices:** Appetizers $2.50–$9; main courses $7.25–$13.95. AE, CB, DC, DISC, JCB, MC, V.

Open: Daily 6am–10pm.

To dine modestly at the Ilikai Hotel, try one of the most atmospheric "coffeehouses," in town, where all the booths and tables have a view of the ocean and of the passersby on the boardwalk. A window table gives you the added advantage of a bank of beautiful vanda orchids and the marina beyond. There, an early dinner provides a front-row seat for the sunset and the Ilikai's nightly torchlighting ceremony. There are a few dinnertime bargains, like the soup and salad bar at just $6.75. Among the lower-priced dishes are the Oriental chicken salad at $7 and the chicken, Madras beef, or seafood curry for $10.50–$10.75. Sandwiches and burgers are well worth the tab as they are robust and served with all the trimmings. A stylish spot.

READERS RECOMMEND

China House Restaurant, *1349 Kapiolani Blvd. (tel. 949-6602). "This restaurant at Ala Moana (though probably not part of the center) serves outstanding dumplings as well as the usual menu. Two of us feasted for lunch, and the bill came to just over $10. There's plenty of parking outside the mall-level entrance, mauka side of Sears."*—Pearl Ann Schwartz, Ardsley, N.Y.

RESTAURANT ROW

Restaurant Row, Honolulu's newest dining-shopping address, is alive and well and flourishing mightily at 500 Ala Moana Blvd., not far from downtown Honolulu. It's a high-tech, strikingly modern, neon environment, surely not your "old Hawaii," but an enjoyable contemporary urban playground.

In addition to those listed below, popular Restaurant Row establishments include Marie Callender, a popular family-style chain; Ruth's Chris Steak House, for top-of-the-line beef; and Studebaker's, a nightclub in the style of the '50s and '60s, where "you bop 'til you drop." From Waikiki, take any no. 19 or no. 20 bus from the Kuhio Avenue bus stop; it will take you directly to Restaurant Row.

MEALS FOR LESS THAN $10

PIZZA BOB'S RESTAURANT, GAME ROOM & BAR, 500 Ala Moana Blvd., in Restaurant Row. Tel. 532-4000.

Cuisine: ITALIAN. **Reservations:** Not accepted.

$ **Prices:** Pizzas $7.95–$13.25; pastas $5.95–$7.95. AE, MC, V.

Open: Mon–Thurs 11am–11pm, Fri 11am–2am, Sat 5pm–2am, Sun 5–11pm.

Voted "Hawaii's Best Pizza," this longtime favorite from Haleiwa, on the North Shore, is now in town and packing in the crowds here as well. It's a big, bustling place with a games room in back where you can try your hand at pinball or miniature basketball, and a lanai in front where you can eat, sip an espresso, and ogle the passing parade. In between is a large, rather high-tech–looking room done in black and gray, with a big and very popular bar. Despite its name, Pizza Bob's has lots more than just pies. There are beautiful salads, like the fresh spinach, a Caesar salad to which bay shrimp and avocado are added, and a green veggie salad topped with crunchy cashew nuts, which run $2.95–$7.95. Then there are hot sandwiches like grilled mahimahi and cold ones like the Haleiwa health nut, a treat for vegetarians, at $4.95–$6.95. But to get back to those pizza pies: They are super-fresh and delicious, and range from traditional to innovative. We like the Mediterranean seafood pizza, with shrimp, scallops, and clams. Individual slices, too, at $2.50. A good place to pop into just about any time of day or night.

ROSE CITY DINER, 500 Ala Moana Blvd., in Restaurant Row. Tel. 524-ROSE.

Cuisine: AMERICAN. **Reservations:** Not accepted.

$ **Prices:** Appetizers $1.10–$6.50; main courses $4.20–$8.90. AE, DC, MC, V.

Open: Mon–Thurs 7am–midnight, Fri–Sun 8am–1am.

The best bet for stylish budget dining here is this counterpart of the popular Los Angeles restaurant of the same name. This restaurant and soda fountain is pure '50s camp (it was purportedly started by Rosie Cheeks, a local gal who went to the mainland in the '50s to make it big as a model but became the "Queen of the Diners" of New Jersey instead). It's complete with 1950s artifacts, including miniature jukeboxes at each table playing old Harry Belafonte records. There are meatloaf specials, roast turkey with gravy, chicken parmesan, malted-milk shakes, hot dogs, and nothing on the menu over $8.90. Most dinner plates range from $6.75 to $8.90, and they include sensational lumpy mashed potatoes with bits of onion and potato skin in the lumps! Rosie's "Sliders"—hamburger, tuna, or chicken salad on miniature rolls, served in a basket—are fun for lunch ($5.10–$5.90). During the daily happy hours, from 4 to 7pm, margaritas, wine, and beer are $1.

The Rose City Diner is also a great place to bring the family: There's a special menu for keikis which begins at $2.75, and includes such possibilities as a fresh roast-turkey sandwich, spaghetti with meatballs, burgers, burritos, griddle keiki cakes, and fabulous milkshakes and malts for only $1.75.

The Rose City Diner is always celebrating something, so you might wander into a game of Twister or a Hula Hoop competition. Stylish and fun.

MEALS FOR LESS THAN $20

THE BLACK ORCHID, 500 Ala Moana Blvd., in Restaurant Row. Tel. 521-3111.

Cuisine: CALIFORNIAN/ITALIAN. **Reservations:** Recommended.

$ **Prices:** Appetizers $3.50–$9.50; main courses $6.95–$14.95 at lunch, $15.95–$25.95 at dinner. AE, DC, MC, V.

Open: Lunch Mon–Fri 11am–2pm; dinner daily 6pm–closing; late-night appetizer menu daily to 3am.

This premier fine-dining gourmet restaurant is the cornerstone of Restaurant Row, a celebrity hangout, a place to see and be seen. While dinner is pricey, lunch is very affordable; some of the finest of Venetian-born chef Eugenio Martignango's California-Italian creations are available at surprisingly low prices. Favorites include the seared ahi salad with shiitake mushrooms ($8.95); the caprese of mozzarella and sliced tomato with roasted bell pepper ($7.95); the risotto with chicken, shrimp, asparagus, and mushrooms ($8.95); and a variety of lovely pastas (from $6.95). Desserts are worth a trip in themselves, especially the knockout tiramisu and the mango-enhanced crème brûlée—a great way to enjoy the friendly service and the exemplary ambience of the Black Orchard at realistic prices.

SUNSET GRILL, 500 Ala Moana Blvd., in Restaurant Row. Tel. 521-4409.

Cuisine: CONTEMPORARY AMERICAN. **Reservations:** Recommended.

$ **Prices:** Appetizers $4.95–$10.95; main courses $11.95–$24.95. AE, DC, MC, V.

Open: Mon–Thurs 11:30am–10pm, Fri–Sat 11:30am–midnight, Sun 10am–10pm.

Our favorite Restaurant Row dining place—indeed, one of our favorites in all Honolulu—is this handsome 200-seat restaurant featuring grilled, rôtisserie, wood-fire, and oven-roasted foods in a sophisticated indoor-outdoor setting. Blond woods, glass walls, and a large grill in the center of the restaurant set the mood for dining that's casual in style but elegant where it counts, in every detail of food preparation and service. Among the little touches that make a difference: parmesan cheese grated at the table for your onion soup, and wines poured tableside, even if all you order is a glass. Have a drink—they're known for terrific martinis—and doodle on the placemats (crayons are provided) while you're waiting for your meal; the best placemat art is displayed on the walls up front, along with autographs of famous visitors.

If you're watching the budget, come for just a sandwich: Their half-pound hamburger, typical of the grilled specialties here, sizzles over kiawe logs and is topped with grilled onions, peppers, and a choice of cheese, plus french fries, a meal in itself at $9.95. Or splurge a bit and try some of the appetizers and soups—the Maui onion soup is a winner, or you can have deep-fried calamari in black-bean sauce, or roasted garlic with goat cheese on sourdough bread—just to start. Make your main course a pasta, perhaps the sautéed rock shrimp fettuccine in garlic–white wine sauce ($13.95); or choose one of the excellent rôtisserie dishes, which come with grilled fresh vegetables. From the charcoal grill, the baby ribs (marinated in a secret sauce of shoyu and marmalade) are unlike any ribs you've tasted elsewhere; also tops are the fresh fish (from $12.95) and the marinated breast of chicken with salsa ($14.95). Desserts are always splendid here, especially the crème brûlée with seasonal berries.

The Sunset Grill is also a great spot for weekend brunch (Saturday from 11am to 4pm, Sunday from 10am to 3pm); brunchgoers not only get complimentary muffins, but complimentary copies of the major weekend papers as well. Remember it, too, on a Friday or Saturday night after the theater or a concert for a late-light bite or just dessert.

TRATTORIA MANZO, 500 Ala Moana Blvd., in Restaurant Row. Tel. 522-1711.

Cuisine: ITALIAN. **Reservations:** Not required.

$ **Prices:** Appetizers $4.50–$10; main courses $8–$15.75. AE, DC, DISC, MC, V.

Open: Mon–Thurs 11am–10pm, Fri–Sat 11am–11pm, Sun 5–10pm.

Open to the court at Restaurant Row, with a beautiful fountain right outside the main entrance and ornate black iron gates to enclose it at night, this little trattoria might well be in Florence or Rome. Inside are graceful bentwood chairs and tables sporting bright-red cloths. The walls are lined with modern Italian oil paintings and numerous photographs of celebrities. Personable owner Signor Manzo greets passersby with a cheery "buona sera" and directs traffic within. Signor Manzo points out that, since they have 8 kinds of pasta and 20 sauces to choose from, they offer 160 ways to eat pasta. Whichever one you choose—maybe frutti di mare (seafood), pollo (sliced chicken and vegetables), vongole (clams with white or red sauce), or just a simple aglio olio (oil and garlic), it's going to be very good. And the antipasti, soups, salads, open-face sandwiches, and a few chicken and veal dishes, like the chicken parmigiana and the veal milanese, are also fine choices. Stylish and fun.

WARD WAREHOUSE

Just opposite Kewalo Basin is the delightful Ward Warehouse shopping complex, where there are several charming restaurants that match the appeal of the shops.

MEALS FOR LESS THAN $12

CHOWDER HOUSE, 1050 Ala Moana Blvd., in Ward Warehouse. Tel. 521-5681.

Cuisine: SEAFOOD. **Reservations:** Not accepted.

$ Prices: Appetizers $1.50–$8.50; main courses $4.25–$12.75. AE, DISC, JCB, MC, V.

Open: Daily 11am–9pm.

The Chowder House is a bright, bustling, and inexpensive seafood house, where you can watch the boats of Fisherman's Wharf through the glass wall behind the bar and have a light seafood lunch or dinner for under $10. At a recent meal, we enjoyed a good-size fresh salad, French bread, and a filet of red snapper with french fries for $9.25. Prices are the same all day. Fish sandwiches, also served with fries, are also inexpensive: $4.05 for mahimahi, $4.40 for calamari. There are also salads, seafood, cocktails, and three kinds of chowder, all reasonably priced.

OLD SPAGHETTI FACTORY, 1050 Ala Moana Blvd., in Ward Warehouse. Tel. 531-1513.

Cuisine: ITALIAN. **Reservations:** Not accepted.

$ Prices: Complete dinners $4.35–$7.50; lunches $3.45–$5.65. MC, V.

Open: Lunch Mon–Sat 11:30am–2pm; dinner Mon–Thurs 5–10pm, Fri–Sat 5–11pm, Sun 4–10pm.

This is perhaps the most stunning budget restaurant in town. It's worth a visit just to see the setting, which might be described as "fabulous Victorian," the rooms brimming with authentic European antiques and Oriental rugs, ornamental lamp shades, overstuffed chairs, many mirrors, and huge chandeliers. You may dine in an authentic trolley car or, more likely, at large, comfortable tables on plush velvet seats, some with backs made from giant headboards. So popular is this place that you can always anticipate a wait for lunch and dinner, even though the main dining rooms seat 350 and the bar upstairs about 125!

The menu is modest, concentrating mostly on spaghetti, and the food is not as dazzling as the surroundings; but you'll eat heartily and well. Complete dinners include a good green salad with choice of dressing, sourdough bread with marvelous garlic butter (a whole loaf is brought to your table with a knife, and seconds are available), beverage, and spumoni ice cream in addition to the main dish. It's fun to have either the Pot Pourri, a sample of the four most popular sauces, or the Manager's Favorite, which serves up two different sauces. Our favorite sauces are the clam and the browned butter with mizithra (a Greek cheese). Oven-baked chicken is tasty, and so is the homemade lasagne and spinach tortellini. At lunch there are smaller portions, and the tab does not include beverage and dessert. Beer, wine, and cocktails are available.

ORSON'S RESTAURANT, 1050 Ala Moana Blvd., in Ward Warehouse. Tel. 521-5681.

Cuisine: SEAFOOD. **Reservations:** Recommended.

$ Prices: Appetizers $2.75–$11.25; main courses $8–$24. AE, DISC, JCB, MC, V.

Open: Daily 11am–10pm.

The people who run the Chowder House at Ward Warehouse also operate this much fancier restaurant, which is upstairs. It's a lovely dining room with spacious ocean and mountain views and a delightfully open and breezy feeling. Although there are a number of seafood specialties in the higher-priced ranges, you can get a good variety of fish and seafood sandwiches, served with salad and fries, for under $10; the smoked-salmon Reuben on sourdough bread is one of our favorites.

WARD CENTRE

The elegant Ward Centre shopping/dining complex at 1200 Ala Moana Blvd. and Auahi Street, a block from Ward Warehouse, boasts a number of first-rate restaurants. We could happily spend weeks eating here and nowhere else.

MEALS FOR LESS THAN $12

BIG ED'S RESTAURANT AND DELI, 1200 Ala Moana Blvd., in Ward Centre. Tel. 536-4591.

Cuisine: DELI. **Reservations:** Not accepted.

$ Prices: Appetizers $2.25–$6.50; main courses $7.25–$11.25. AE, MC, V.

Open: Sun–Thurs 7am–10pm, Fri–Sat 7am–11pm.

There comes a time when the wandering traveler, far from home, suddenly develops an irrepressible longing for, say, a corned beef on rye, a bowl of matzoh-ball soup, or a big plate of brisket of beef. Happily, a remedy is at hand right here in Honolulu: Big Ed's, which packs in the crowds at its counter and large table section at Ward Centre. Big Ed serves up all kinds of delicatessen delights, super sandwiches, salads, deli platters, and hot meals. You can start your meal with a wonderful borscht or a chicken matzoh-ball soup. House specialties include roast brisket of beef with potato pancakes and vegetables. Try the stuffed cabbage at $7.25, or a sandwich—corned beef, pastrami, liverwurst, beef tongue, and roast beef are priced $4.75–$7.50. Salad and delicatessen platters—our favorite is smoked salmon with Maui onions—range in price from $6.50 to $11.25. Beer, wine, and cocktails are available, and the atmosphere is cheerful.

CREPE FEVER, 1200 Ala Moana Blvd., in Ward Centre. Tel. 521-9023.

Cuisine: GOURMET VEGETARIAN. **Reservations:** Not accepted.

$ Prices: Main courses $4.75–$7.25. MC, V.

Open: Mon–Thurs 8am–10pm, Fri–Sat 8am–11pm, Sun 8am–4pm.

The quality of the food and the charm of the surroundings make this casual restaurant, on the street level and inside Le Pavillon shopping area, quite special. Red-tile floors, oak tables, pastel pennants overhead, plus tables in the pretty garden outdoors, set a sparkling background for a menu that's not limited to just crêpes. It has a lot to offer vegetarians, sophisticated "grazers," and those who just want to eat delicious, healthy food at very reasonable prices. Our favorite lunch here used to be the homemade soup served in a bowl of scooped-out cracked-wheat bread with salad; it's a satisfying meal for $4.95. But ever since owner Sandee Garcia came up with her Grain & Green salad bar (at lunch Monday through Friday only), it's been a toss-up. Here you build your own vegetarian meal from a selection of complementary protein combinations that changes every day; grains, legumes, greens, beans, and seeds are provided in a variety of ways that might have a Mexican or Italian or Indian accent. Have a medium-size bowl at $3.50 or a huge bowl for $4.80. Begin with a cup of that wonderful homemade soup and you've got a super meal. Now for those crêpes: They're filled with the likes of chicken and ham, tuna-salad melt, and lemon spinach (with cream cheese), as are croissants; either can be had with brown rice or salad or both for an under-$6 meal. Desserts are yummy, too: cheese blintzes topped with sour cream, fresh strawberries and cream, and bananas-and-cream crêpes. Since Crêpe Fever serves the same menu continuously, you can have breakfast anytime: three-egg omelets, waffles, and (especially good) their French toast—thick slices of bakery wheat bread, garnished with bananas, at $3.95.

Right next to Crêpe Fever and under the same management is **Mocha Java,** an espresso fountain bar with a variety of hot and iced gourmet coffees, cappuccino, plus real milkshakes (try the chocolate espresso), and homemade cakes and sundaes. Take anything from here as a dessert for your Crêpe Fever meal: perhaps a simple but satisfying choice like espresso over a scoop of vanilla ice cream at $2.95. Wine, beer, and a full bar menu are available.

KEO'S, 1200 Ala Moana Blvd., in Ward Centre. Tel. 533-0533.

Cuisine: THAI. **Reservations:** Recommended.

$ Prices: Appetizers $3.75–$6.95; main courses $7.95–$11.95. AE, DC, MC, V.

Open: Lunch Mon–Sat 11am–5pm; dinner daily 5–10pm.

The most picturesque restaurant at Ward's Centre must surely be Keo's, one of the latest creations of Thai restaurateur Keo Sananikone. Keo runs six restaurants in town and this one is exquisite, with lovely plantings, flowers, a fountain splashing into a languid pool, pink tablecloths, black bentwood chairs, and seating indoors and out—just beautiful! Enjoy the European-Asian café ambience at either lunch or dinner for reasonable prices. While you're here, pick up a copy of *Keo's Thai Cuisine,* so you can try your hand at creating these delicate wonders back home.

YUM YUM TREE, 1200 Ala Moana Blvd., in Ward Centre. Tel. 523-9333.

Cuisine: AMERICAN. **Reservations:** Not required.

$ Prices: Main courses $8.45–$11.95. AE, CB, DC, JCB, MC, V.

Open: Sun–Thurs 7am–midnight, Fri–Sat 7am–1am.

Fans of the delightful pie shop and restaurant at Kahala Mall (see below) are thrilled to find another branch at Ward Centre. That makes it all the easier to stop in whenever the urge for pie—maybe macadamia-nut, lemon-crunch or English-toffee—becomes overwhelming. Take home a whole pie or have a delicious slice here. All three meals are served: excellent breakfasts featuring omelets, waffles, and eggs Benedict; lunches and dinners with a wide variety of salads, sandwiches, burgers, pastas, and complete meals—all at low prices. The menu is the same as at Kahala, and the setting is charming, both inside and out, with the feel of a big country house with a large porch, shady and cool, thanks to the big blue umbrellas. Cocktails are served from 7am to 2am. As you travel around the island, you'll find Yum Yum Trees at Pali Palms, Mililani, and Pearlridge.

MEALS FOR LESS THAN $20

ANDREW'S, 1200 Ala Moana Blvd., in Ward Centre. Tel. 523-8677.

Cuisine: ITALIAN. **Reservations:** Recommended.

$ Prices: Appetizers $2.75–$12.75; main courses $10.75–$25.95. AE, CB, DC, JCB, MC, V.

Open: Lunch Mon–Sat 11am–3pm, Sun 10am–4pm; dinner Sun–Tues 4–10pm, Wed–Sat 4–11pm; brunch Sat 11am–3pm, Sun 10am–3pm.

Another star at Ward Centre is this gourmet Italian restaurant. Muted rose and brown tones from floor to ceiling produce a sedate effect, reinforced by the upholstered banquettes with dropped lamps, fabric-covered walls, and flowers on the tables. You could have a complete dinner, including antipasto, mixed green salad, minestrone, ice cream, plus a beverage along with your main courses for $17.25–$24.95. Or choose à la carte; pastas begin around $10.75, and include a tasty and filling cannelloni di mare (stuffed with seafood). There are also a few seafood and chicken dishes for under $14.

Lunch is à la carte, with a dozen pastas for $9.95–$15.95. There are choices galore of fish and fowl in the same price range; beef and veal run a little higher. Daily specials, such as spaghetti putanesca, are $10.50. Drinks are moderately priced. Skilled service contributes to a memorable experience.

COMPADRES MEXICAN BAR & GRILL, 1200 Ala Moana Blvd., in Ward Centre. Tel. 523-1307.

Cuisine: MEXICAN. **Reservations:** Not required.

$ **Prices:** Appetizers $3.95–$9.95; main courses $8.95–$16.95. AE, DC, MC, V.

Open: Sun–Fri 11:30am–11pm, Sat 11am–midnight.

Mexico is represented at Ward Centre by Compadres, which gets a resounding *olé!* from us. We're not at all surprised that it has been voted "Best Mexican Restaurant" in Hawaii by the *Honolulu* magazine poll for several years in a row. It's a big, very attractive place with comfortable rattan basket chairs and soft lights, and a young and energetic staff. It's fun to sit on the lanai outdoors. The food is *muy bueno,* and the prices won't damage your budget. The same menu and prices are in effect all day long. The sandwiches, like the chicken and avocado at $7.50, are all served with thick-cut deep-fried potatoes and Mexican salad, but you'll probably want to sample such Mexican specialties as the various combinaciones, which include refried beans, fiesta rice, and Mexican salad, $9.45–$13.95. Arroz con pollo at $12.50 and mahimahi ala Vera Cruz at $12.95 are both good, and everybody loves the house specialty of fajitas—grilled, marinated beef or chicken, sliced thin and stuffed into warm tortillas with a great salsa. Vegetarians have a number of good choices. As for the desserts, we can't resist the banana chimi—a whole banana wrapped in a flour tortilla, rolled in cinnamon, and topped with ice cream. And the new "Compadres 400" Menu features dishes of 400 or fewer calories, including the Vegetable Fiesta, Grilled Chicken Caesar Salad, and the Ceviche Topopo, to name a few. On weekends only, Compadres serves breakfasts, offering a wide assortment of omelets, plus chili rellenos, huevos dos Ricardos, and much more.

MONTEREY BAY CANNERS, 1200 Ala Moana Blvd., in Ward Centre. Tel. 536-6197.

Cuisine: SEAFOOD. **Reservations:** Not required.

$ **Prices:** Appetizers $3.75–$8.75; main courses $10.95–$34.95. AE, DC, JCB, MC, V.

Open: Lunch Mon–Fri 11am–4pm; dinner Sun–Thurs 4–11pm, Fri–Sat 4pm–midnight.

This is one of Honolulu's most popular restaurants, a big, bustling, nautical-type place which serves a tremendous variety of seafood specialties. If you're lucky enough to get a table by the window, you can overlook Kewalo Basin, where the commercial fishing charter boats are berthed. Fresh fish is the specialty of the house; in fact, several of the local radio stations carry MBC's "Fresh Catch" report several times a day. Fish is broiled over real kiawe-wood charcoal, and such main courses as mahimahi, Hawaiian ono, Alaskan halibut, catfish, salmon steak, and seafood combination ($11.45–$15.45) can be topped with either black-bean, Créole-cream, oyster, ginger, or dill sauce. San Francisco–style sourdough bread, fresh steamed vegetables, and a choice of starch are included; add another $1–$1.50 and you get chowder or salad as well. There are also pasta dishes from $10.75 (for chicken fettuccine). For dessert, try the watermelon sherbet. A similar lunch menu offers smaller portions ($7–$16). There's music and live entertainment Tuesday through Saturday nights from 9pm to 1:30am.

RYAN'S GRILL AT WARD CENTRE, 1200 Ala Moana Blvd., in Ward Centre. Tel. 523-9132.

Cuisine: AMERICAN. **Reservations:** Recommended at dinner.

$ Prices: Appetizers $4.95–$6.95; main courses $8.95–$17.95. AE, MC, V.

Open: Lunch Mon–Sat 11am–5pm; dinner daily 5–11pm.

Ryan's is a big, rambling stunner of a room with highly polished wood floors, gleaming brass, lazily rotating ceiling fans, windows all around, myriad lush plants, and a shiny kitchen open to view. Ryan's is seriously committed to "foods for all moods"—and that means quality in everything from simple fare to gourmet dishes, from "heart-healthy" recipes to sinfully rich creations for sybarites. The menu includes meat, chicken, and fish broiled with mesquite-wood charcoal from Mexico; fish fresh from Hawaiian, mainland, and Alaskan waters; pasta made fresh daily; and desserts that range from low-cal Tofutti to Chocolate Suicide Cake. Special dietary needs will be given consideration. Prices, considering the high quality, are quite reasonable. Consider, for example, dishes like mesquite-grilled chicken with apricot-cilantro glaze ($8.25 at lunch, $10.95 at dinner) or lemon-pepper fettuccine with bay shrimp and fresh mushrooms ($8.95–$10.95); or the Three-Salad Sampler, which includes Mediterranean chicken, pea salad, and pasta with pesto ($7.95 and $8.95). A good selection of California wines is available by the bottle or by the glass. There are also temperature-controlled beers and a moderately priced bar list. The bar is open until 1:15am.

DOWNTOWN HONOLULU & ENVIRONS

MEALS FOR LESS THAN $12

A LITTLE BIT OF SAIGON, 1160 Maunakea St. Tel. 528-3663.

Cuisine: VIETNAMESE. **Reservations:** Not required.

$ Prices: Appetizers $3.50–$5.95; main courses $5.95–$7.95. MC, V.

Open: Daily 11am–11pm.

Because it's just around the corner from many of the Chinatown art galleries, you'll always find artists—as well as savvy businessfolk—frequenting this place. Changing art exhibits are the main decor. The food is artistic too, simple but sophisticated, and appealing to a wide variety of tastes. There's plenty for vegetarians. Only vegetable oils and coconut water (not the fat-rich coconut milk used in many Asian restaurants) are used in the food preparations, so cholesterol-watchers can rest easy. Many of the dishes—like the chicken brochettes, the catch of the day, or the shrimp on sugarcane—can be ordered as pupus, as meals in a bowl, or as rice-paper rollups. That last preparation is especially intriguing: You're presented with a large tray containing rice-paper wrappers, vegetables, sprouts, condiments, and your main course. You dip the wrappers in a finger bowl, stuff them like a burrito, then dip it all in a peanut or pineapple/anchovy sauce. Also recommended are the curries, the hearty noodle soups, and the sweet and tender coconut chicken. Try the desserts—you may never again get a chance to taste azuki beans and tapioca strips in coconut milk. A treat!

Note: By the time you read this, the same management probably will have opened Miss Saigon at 1088 Maunakea St.

COLUMBIA INN, 645 Kapiolani Blvd. Tel. 531-3747.

Cuisine: AMERICAN. **Reservations:** Not accepted.

$ **Prices:** Appetizers $1.55–$5.95; main courses $5.75–$13. MC, V.
Open: Breakfast daily 6:30am–9am; lunch daily 11am–4pm; dinner daily 4–11:30pm.

News dominates the conversation at this favorite hangout for the staffs of Honolulu's two daily newspapers just a few doors away. The news about food is also good at this large, wood-paneled spot with its leather booths. At lunch you can choose from 26 complete lunches between $6.05 and $12.55, and that includes boiled brisket of corned beef and cabbage, oysters cooked in garlic butter, pepper steak with rice pilaf, all accompanied by fish chowder or fruit salad, dessert, and beverage. Order à la carte and the range is $5.50–$11.30. At dinner there are some two dozen choices for $10.75 and under, beginning at $7 for a complete meal (higher-priced meals go up to $16).

DONNA'S DINER, 1148 Bishop St. Tel. 531-8660.
Cuisine: AMERICAN. **Reservations:** Not accepted.
$ **Prices:** Soups $2.75–$4.95; plate lunches $3.25–$4.95. No credit cards.
Open: Mon–Fri 5:30am–2:45pm.

For a quick, inexpensive, and very good breakfast or lunch while shopping or sightseeing downtown, pop in at this tiny place. You can tell it's good because of its popularity with the office and shop workers. Breakfast begins at $2.75 and includes coffee. Soups are a specialty and a meal in themselves: Portuguese bean soup is $4.50; pig's feet or oxtail soup is $4.95; wonton min, $3.10; and saimin, $2.75. And generous plate lunches start at $3.25, burgers at $1.50.

Donna has another diner at 2227 S. Beretania St., in the McCully–Moiliili area.

FLAMINGO KAPIOLANI, 871 Kapiolani Blvd. Tel. 538-6931.
Cuisine: AMERICAN. **Reservations:** Not required.
$ **Prices:** Main courses $4.60–$18.95. AE, MC, V.
Open: Daily 6am–2am.

For years the Flamingo restaurants have been offering terrific quality for little money. Pink booths and paneled walls at this remodeled Flamingo provide a good background for the excellent food. They're well known for their oxtail soup ($6.65), roasts, and specials (brisket of beef, pot roast with noodles, and the like). Lunch offers half a dozen sandwich platters, including soup and fries, for $4.85–$5.80, as well as 10 lunch plates for $5.95–$9.50. At dinner, you get a complete meal, with a choice of soup or salad, vegetable, starch, buns, and beverage. After 10pm, the crowd gathers at the bar for karaoke.

The same management also runs the Flamingo Chuck Wagon at 1015 Kapiolani Blvd. (tel. 538-1161). In the business district downtown, the Flamingo Coffee Shop, 841 Bishop St. (tel. 521-6616), and Arthur's Restaurant, at 841 Bishop St. (tel. 521-7133), are big local favorites. Flamingos at the Windward City Shopping Center in Kaneohe (tel. 235-5566) and at Pearl City, 803 Kamehameha Hwy. (tel. 456-5946), are very popular with local families.

HAWAIIAN BAGEL, 753B Halekauwila St. Tel. 523-8638.
Cuisine: BAGELS/DELI. **Reservations:** Not accepted.
$ **Prices:** Main courses $2–$6. No credit cards.
Open: Mon–Thurs and Sat 6am–3:30pm, Fri 6am–5:30pm.

Hawaiian Bagel—how's that for a marriage of concepts? This wholesale-retail delicatessen with a few tables for those who can't make it out the door is in a new, contemporary-style building located in the run-down but picturesque Kakaako section of Honolulu. The sights and scents are surpassed only by the tastes. Needless to say, proprietor Stephen Gelson is not a full-blooded Hawaiian. Nor are the bagels, blueberry muffins, and homemade rye bread. But the little restaurant and take-out bakery-deli is a hit with the local folk. And our readers love it, too.

They carry 10 varieties of bagels, including onion, sesame seed, and poppy seed, at

40¢ each. Muffins, bearclaws, and cinnamon rolls are 95¢. The sandwiches are typical deli variety: roast beef, lox or whitefish and cream cheese, corned beef, liverwurst, turkey, pastrami, and the like, for $4.50–$5.50. In true deli tradition, they even serve celery tonic. You may want to take home a fragrant, round loaf of fresh-from-the-oven rye bread. There's parking on the premises.

HEIDI'S BISTRO, Grosvenor Center on Queen St. Tel. 536-5344.

Cuisine: GOURMET AMERICAN/ITALIAN. **Reservations:** Not required.
$ **Prices:** Main courses $7.95–$13.95; soup and sandwich $7.25; sandwich and salad $7.50; salad and soup $7.25. AE, DC, MC, V.
Open: Breakfast Mon–Fri 6:30–11am; lunch Mon–Fri 11am–2:30pm; dinner Mon–Fri 5–9pm.

A great place to break a sightseeing tour of downtown Honolulu, Heidi's is just half a block from the Aloha Tower and the Fort Street Mall. At lunch it's jammed with businessfolk, but it's pleasantly relaxed for evening dining. The spot is intimate and casual, smartly appointed, with candles on the table, lots of greenery, comfortable chairs, and white-clothed tables. Serious dieters and health-conscious eaters are given extra consideration here, with a number of special dishes, like chicken Pritikin style, chicken rosemary, pollo broil, or catch of the day. Other popular—and delicious—choices include an array of pastas and several seafood dishes, all done with gourmet flair. Heidi's generous sandwiches and salads are served from 11am to 9pm, and are also available for take-out. A separate bar and lounge area offers entertainment and karaoke singing every night.

TAY DO'S RESTAURANT, 1138 Fort St. Mall, at Pauahi St. Tel. 531-8446.

Cuisine: VIETNAMESE. **Reservations:** Not required.
$ **Prices:** Main courses $5.25–$6. No credit cards.
Open: Mon–Fri 8:30am–6pm, Sat 8:30am–4pm.

Tay Do's in the downtown area is the place for authentic Vietnamese cuisine. Most Vietnamese restaurants are small and bare bones, but this one is of moderate size, with ceiling spotlights and beige benches and tables. You can start with those lovely rice-paper rolls—spring rolls, pork rolls, or shrimp rolls—then move on to the Vietnamese plate meals which offer 10 choices. They are served not on plates but on platters, and they're huge. Our barbecued boneless chicken, on a bed of rice with lettuce, cucumber, and tomato slices, was very good. Of course, there are noodle dishes, soups, and steak choices. Almost everything is $5.25.

TGI FRIDAY'S, 950 Ward Ave., at King St. Tel. 523-5841.

Cuisine: AMERICAN. **Reservations:** Not accepted.
$ **Prices:** Appetizers $2.95–$6.25; main courses $8.35–$12.95. AE, DC, MC, V.
Open: Sun–Thurs 11am–1am, Fri–Sat 10am–2am.

Everything about this place is delightfully different—from the *big* menu with some 160 items to the art nouveau leaded-glass hanging lamps and lovely antique furniture and accessories. It's obvious that no expense was spared. The food, too, is far from run-of-the-mill. Appetizers are super, including skewered and char-broiled Thai chicken, potstickers, and "loaded potato skins"—baked potatoes, scooped and fried to a delightful crispness, and slathered with cheese and crumbled bacon, plus a sour-cream dip ($5.95). Specialties include southwestern, Oriental, American, and pasta dishes. Among the main courses, which are accompanied by a cup of soup, a salad, fresh vegetable, and a warm garlic roll, we especially like the lemon chicken and the blackened Cajun filet mignon. Save room for one of the sinful desserts, like the mocha mud pie. Friday's is insanely popular, and it's first-come, first-served. A super place to dine or have a drink.

VIETNAM CITY SEAFOOD, 100 N. Beretania St. Tel. 599-5022.

Cuisine: VIETNAMESE/CHINESE. **Reservations:** Not required.

$ Prices: Appetizers $1.25–$6.95; main courses $4.95–$7.95. MC, V.
Open: Lunch daily 11am–3pm; dinner daily 5–9pm.

This is a popular spot in the Chinese Cultural Center, featuring both Vietnamese and Cantonese cuisine, as well as a cocktail lounge and entertainment. Prices are modest, with the same menu served all day. Especially good buys are the long-rice dishes, which range from $3.75 (for shrimp and crabmeat) to $7 (for fresh prawns with shredded pork). You could have a duck curry with French bread at $4.95, but better call your shots—mild, medium, or hot—on the curries. Be sure to have an appetizer at dinner: Their sizzling barbecue taste tempters—beef satays and shrimp kebabs—are irresistible. Main-course selections include Vietnamese soups, casserole dishes, vegetable dishes, seafood choices, even some dishes which date from the French influence in Vietnam. And there are French coffees too, plus lemon drinks and a variety of Vietnamese beverages. Entertainment and cocktails from 5 to 9pm.

YONG SING, 1055 Alakea St. Tel. 531-1366.
Cuisine: CHINESE. **Reservations:** Not required.
$ Prices: Appetizers $4–$7; main courses $6–$20. MC, V.
Open: Daily 9am–9pm.

One of the most popular Chinese restaurants in town, Yong Sing is a huge place that occupies all of a downtown building, and its vast dining room is nicely, if not elaborately, decorated in red and gold. There's a huge menu from which to choose, with many well-priced goodies. The last time we were here we had a succulent almond duck and chicken with oyster sauce, the house specialty. An excellent $22 dinner for two includes egg-flower soup, almond chicken, sweet-and-sour pork, beef broccoli, and fried rice. For something unusual, ask the waiter for a dim sum lunch. This consists of many different varieties of Chinese dumplings: either steamed, baked, or fried, some filled with sweetmeats and served as main dishes; others, dainty pastries for dessert. Have five or six of these and plenty of the free-flowing tea, and you've had a lovely, inexpensive treat. But be sure to get there between the hours of 9am and 2pm for the dumplings; they sell out fast. Yong Sing also has cocktails at reasonable prices, take-out orders anytime, and plenty of public parking in the area.

READERS RECOMMEND

Central Union Church, *1660 S. Beretania St. (tel. 941-0957). "Central Union Church has a nice lunch at their Union Station for seniors on Tuesday, Wednesday, and Thursday from 11am to 2:30pm, with a suggested donation of $3, for salad bar, main course, dessert, and beverage. And the second-floor cafeteria of the Kapiolani Women's and Children's Medical Center, Punahou Street, near Wilder Street, also has good food."*—Mrs. Dorothy Astman, Northport, N.Y.

MEALS FOR LESS THAN $20

KABUKI RESTAURANT AT KAPIOLANI, 600 Kapiolani Blvd. Tel. 545-5995.
Cuisine: JAPANESE. **Reservations:** Recommended.
$ Prices: Appetizers $5.50–$10.50; dinners $10.85–$16.50. AE, DC, MC, V.
Open: Lunch daily 11am–2pm; dinner Mon–Sat 5–9:30pm (sushi bar until midnight), Sun 5–9pm (sushi bar until 10pm).

Here's a very pretty restaurant—light-wood paneling, lots of mirrors, white stoneware dishes with blue flowers, an attractive little sushi bar—that offers a chance to sample many Japanese dishes at reasonable prices. Live Maine lobsters and live Dungeness crabs are available and prepared to your liking; also popular is the lobster sashimi. Hibachi dinners, cooked at your table for two or more people, include soup, rice, tsukemono, special sauces, and tea, along with main courses, such as beef or chicken yakiniku, and are mostly $13.95; tasty teishoku dinners might include a main course of salmon, sashimi, and assorted vegetables for $12.75. For lunch, the combination teishoku meal is $9.75.

UNIVERSITY AREA

MEALS FOR LESS THAN $12

ALOHA POI BOWL, 2671 S. King St., in University Sq. Tel. 944-0798.

Cuisine: HAWAIIAN. **Reservations:** Not accepted.

$ Prices: Appetizers $3–$5; main courses $5.25–$9. No credit cards.

Open: Mon–Sat 11am–8:30pm, Sun 3–8pm.

This is a good spot for Hawaiian food and it's close to Waikiki. There are only six booths and a few big, white plastic-topped tables in a plain, storelike room, but the food is the star here. In addition to those luau staples like laulau, lomi salmon, kalua pork, tripe or beef stew, and chicken long rice, which run $3–$5, there's always a daily special; the day we were there it was fried akule fish at $7. Be sure to top off your meal with that coconut dessert called haupia.

CAMPUS CENTER, University of Hawaii. Tel. 956-7235.

Cuisine: AMERICAN/LOCAL.

$ Prices: Main courses $1.50–$3.75. No credit cards.

Open: Mon–Fri 7am–2pm.

The best place to eat at the University of Hawaii is this spot close to University Avenue in the middle of the campus. Its huge, upstairs cafeteria serves both breakfast and lunch. Depending on the day, you may get lemon chicken, tasty seafood items, veal cutlets, or barbecued ribs. They also have fresh pizza, pasta, grilled items, and a variety of salads and desserts. The lower level of the Campus Center is the Snack Bar (open 9:30am–3pm), which features "local foods," such as loco moco, bentos, chili and rice, and plate lunches, for $1.50–$3. Bakery items and gourmet salads can be purchased at Kampus Konfections, located in the convenience store called Kampus Korner (open 9am–6:30pm).

CHAN'S CHINESE RESTAURANT, 2600 S. King St. Tel. 949-1188.

Cuisine: CHINESE. **Reservations:** Not accepted.

$ Prices: Main courses $5.25–$9.25. AE, MC, V.

Open: Daily 10:30am–11:25pm.

We like everything about this restaurant, from the sparkling clean, modern decor (pale pink and gray walls, white cloths and red napkins, and Chinese art and artifacts) to the cheerful service and that delicious food—at very reasonable prices. Owner Jennifer Chan blends an array of Mandarin, Szechuan, Shanghai, Cantonese, and Peking dishes. The Mandarin menu offers slightly spicier fare, such as the spicy stir-fried shrimp. If it's in season, go for the lusty crab with black-bean sauce, market-priced. Or feast on a meal of tasty dim sum, offered from 9am to 2pm. If you'd like to try a Chinese breakfast, then join the locals who come here for their *jook*—that's rice soup, with a choice of chicken, seafood, meat, or fish; most jooks are $3–$5.50. For lunch or dinner, there are dozens of dishes under $6—like a chicken with black-mushroom casserole, moo shu pork with pancakes, or roast duck. Parking in Puck's Alley is validated.

LITTLE CAESAR'S PIZZA, 2752 Woodlawn Dr., in Manoa Marketplace. Tel. 988-4998.

Cuisine: PIZZA.

$ Prices: Pizzas $8–$19.50. No credit cards.

Open: Mon–Thurs 10am–9pm, Fri–Sat 10am–10pm.

Three cheers for the Little Caesar's chain of pizza take-out shops, of which there are almost a dozen in Honolulu (see the phone book for other addresses): one cheer for their luscious pizza, deep-dish or regular; two for their speedy preparation; and three for their money-saving concept—two pies for the price of one! This is not a now-and-then coupon promotion, but an all-year-round pricing policy. You can phone ahead for pickup in 20 minutes or so (they don't deliver) or just go into one of their cheerful locations and have a soft drink while your pies are in the oven. For something unique and yummy, get an order of their home-baked "Crazy Bread," thin dough strips with cheese on top ($1.70 an order). Salads, antipasto, and a few sandwiches are also available.

MAMA MIA, 1015 University Ave., in Puck's Alley. Tel. 947-5233.

Cuisine: ITALIAN. **Reservations:** Not accepted.

$ Prices: Pizzas $7–$13; subs $5–$6; main courses $8–$11.75. AE, DC, MC, V.

Open: Daily 11am–2am.

The longtime mecca for pizza-lovers in this area is Mama Mia's, and real "New York pizza" it is, since the owner is a transplanted New Yorker. There's a pie for every taste (even a vegetarian pizza with whole-wheat crust—$9.90), terrific spaghetti and lasagne dinners for under $10, and some really lusty and crusty hero sandwiches. They have a full liquor license. The place stays open late, so it's fun to come here—and fun to sit at the sidewalk café. Occasionally there's entertainment here, too—perhaps a grownup puppet show, or just music.

MANOA GARDEN, Hemenway Hall, University of Hawaii. Tel. 956-6468.

Cuisine: DELI/STIR-FRY. **Reservations:** Not accepted.

$ Prices: Appetizers $2.50–$6; main courses $3.25–$6.50. No credit cards.

Open: Daily 8am–8pm.

Also pleasant at UH is Manoa Garden, which features deli sandwiches to order, "Grab 'N' Go" sandwiches, and delicious stir-fry concoctions made before your eyes. The bar opens at 2:30pm daily. On most Fridays, a Manoa Garden Jam Session features live outdoor entertainment.

O-BOK, 2756 Woodlawn Dr., in Manoa Marketplace. Tel. 988-7702.

Cuisine: KOREAN. **Reservations:** Not accepted.

$ Prices: Main courses $4.20–$6.95. MC, V.

Open: Tues–Sun 10am–8pm.

Small, sparkly clean, and friendly sums up this little Korean place that serves wonderful food at very moderate prices. The menu is the same all day. All main dishes are served with na mul (vegetables), kimchee (a fiery coleslaw), and rice. The most popular Korean specialty in Hawaii seems to be kalbi, tender barbecued short ribs. They are particularly good here, and priced at $6.95. Other very good dishes are the barbecued chicken, the fish or meat jun (breaded with an egg batter), and the bi bim bap (mixed vegetables, beef, and fried egg on rice). Very tasty, too, are the mon doo (a kind of Korean wonton); try them in soup or fried, as a side dish. To explore several taste sensations, order one of the mixed plates. The special plate at $4.85 includes kalbi, barbecued chicken, mon doo, tae-ku (dried codfish) and na mul.

WAIOLI TEA ROOM, 3016 Oahu Ave. Tel. 988-2131.

Cuisine: AMERICAN. **Reservations:** Recommended.

$ Prices: Lunch $8–$9; Sun brunch $11.50–$12.50. MC, V.

Open: Lunch Tues–Fri 11am–2:30pm; brunch Sun 11am–2pm; evenings, only for private banquets and special theme events (Spanish, Chinese, '50s, Mexican, etc.). Phone for information.

★ Great news! The famous Waioli Tea Room, a Honolulu tradition for many years, and shuttered for the past few, will reopen by the time you read this. The charming restaurant, done in Victorian decor with flowers on every table, has been leased and is being operated by Tad & Pat, Hawaii's premier caterers, used by discerning folk for private parties and also by many organizations for their fund-raisers. We've sampled their food on numerous occasions, and if past performance is any indication, it should be terrific. Lunch will consist of a soup and salad bar featuring hot crab dip with toasted pita chips, plus such dishes as pastina (rice pasta), spinach and feta wrapped in phyllo pastry on pesto sauce, grilled chicken, prime rib sandwiches, and mahimahi sandwiches. The Sunday brunch menu will feature a salad bar, pastas, Waioli chicken, fresh grilled fish, fresh fruits, and homemade desserts.

The Waioli Tea Room is on the Historical Register; it is rumored that Robert Louis Stevenson courted the muse in the little grass shack now rebuilt as the Robert Louis Stevenson Memorial Grass House. The beautiful tropical grounds are yours for the strolling, and unless there's a wedding going on, you can visit the Little Chapel on the grounds, designed for the children of Waioli.

READERS RECOMMEND

Aloha Cafeteria. *"The Aloha Cafeteria at the University of Hawaii has good food. It is on the first floor of the Aloha dormitory, off Dole Street, almost opposite East/West Road. For nonstudents there's a flat rate, inexpensive, and all you can eat."*—Mrs. Dorothy Astman, Northport, N.Y.

MEALS FOR LESS THAN $20

BUZZ'S ORIGINAL STEAK HOUSE, 2535 Coyne St. Tel. 944-9781.

Cuisine: STEAK/SEAFOOD. **Reservations:** Not required.

$ **Prices:** Appetizers $2.50–$5.50; main courses $9.95–$25.95 (lobster). AE, CB, DC, MC, V.

Open: Dinner only, Sun–Thurs 5–10pm, Fri–Sat 5–10:30pm.

The Buzz's restaurants have been popular with residents and visitors alike for as long as we can remember. Our favorite of these handsome places is this one, just off University Avenue. The decor is art nouveau, with wood paneling, stained glass, and wonderful '30s light fixtures. Steak and seafood are the mainstays of Buzz's bill of fare, but they also have one of the best salad bars in town, at just $6.95. A perennial-dieter friend of ours swears by it. This is one place where we wouldn't want to pass up the appetizers: sautéed mushrooms, artichoke surprise, escargots. A good dinner choice is the kalbi platter (marinated beef ribs, Korean style) at $11.95. All main dishes come with bread, veggies, and that salad bar. And don't miss Buzz's incredible ice-cream pies, at $3.25 a serving.

CAFE BRIO, 2756 Woodlawn Dr., in Manoa Marketplace. Tel. 988-5555.

Cuisine: CONTEMPORARY AMERICAN. **Reservations:** Not required.

$ **Prices:** Appetizers $4–$7; main courses $12–$15. AE, DC, DISC, MC, V.

Open: Lunch Mon–Fri 11:30am–2pm; dinner Mon–Sat 5:30–10:30pm.

An island friend of ours says that the only thing wrong with Café Brio is that you never want to leave. It's a veritable indoor garden—plants in boxes, plants hanging from the rafters, huge tropical leaf patterns on the carpeting, and smashing hand-painted leaves and flowers on the backs of the banquettes. There are whimsical murals on the natural-wood plank walls and fresh flowers on the tables. Out on the lanai are nine small tables and still more plants.

The menu is creative with a contemporary touch: witness the poached, shredded chicken with rotelle pasta in a ginger-sesame-soy vinaigrette among the appetizers; and the seared and skewered prawns with cucumbers and capers in a cilantro vinaigrette and the grilled boneless chicken breast with fresh fruit salsa and black beans among the main courses. Lunch is similar, with dishes $1 or $2 lower, and sophisticated sandwiches—like the grilled medallions of rib-eye steak on a bun with horseradish-Dijon cream—for $7–$8. Desserts are spirited, too—there are different homemade ones, plus gelatos and sorbettos every day. And, of course, the music is sprightly—the last time we had dinner there, it was Offenbach providing the background.

CASTAGNOLA'S ITALIAN RESTAURANT, 2752 Woodlawn Dr., in Manoa Marketplace. Tel. 988-2969.

Cuisine: ITALIAN. **Reservations:** Recommended.

$ Prices: Appetizers $2.90–$7.90; main courses $7.90–$17.90. AE, MC, V.

Open: Mon 11:30am–3pm, Tues–Sat 11:30am–10pm.

Castagnola's reminds us of a little trattoria in Italy, except that, more likely than not, you will be served by a friendly Asian or Polynesian. Decor is fresh and simple, the food terrific, and the prices reasonable. Complete meals, offered all day, can be ordered in a regular portion or for the light eater; for instance, rigatoni ricotta, linguine marinara or with white clam sauce, and eggplant parmigiana are all $10.95 regular, $7.70 for the light eater. There are luncheon sandwiches under $6, and an individual pizza is just $3.40. Castagnola's is one of the few places in Honolulu where you can find cannoli. Try it, or chocolate gelato, spumoni, or zabaglione for dessert.

INDIA HOUSE, 2632 S. King St. Tel. 955-7552.

Cuisine: INDIAN. **Reservations:** Recommended.

$ Prices: Appetizers $7.50; main courses $13.50–$19.95. MC, V.

Open: Dinner only, Mon–Sat 5–9:30pm, Sun 5–9pm.

Ram Arora, formerly the specialty chef at the elegant (and super-expensive) Third Floor Restaurant at the Hawaiian Regent Hotel, owns this restaurant near Puck's Alley. His own place, besides being very much more within our budgetary reach, is attractive, cool, and relaxing. Brass lamps and lush plants abound in the small dining room that accommodates perhaps a dozen tables. A sari-clad hostess will greet you, make you welcome, and assist you in ordering. Should you wish to try tandoori (clay oven) cooking, have the boti kebab, the fish tikka, or tandoori chicken, served with pullao (rice pilaf) and a wonderful naan bread. Combination dinners are a good buy, and there are plentiful à la carte choices—curries, keema, chicken, shrimp, lamb, or vegetarian dishes. A particularly good dessert choice is the gulab jaman, a "dairy delicacy served in rosewater syrup." This is one thoroughly delightful dining experience.

DESSERTS ONLY

BUBBIES, 1010 University Ave. Tel. 949-8984.

Cuisine: ICE CREAM/DESSERTS. **Reservations:** Not accepted.

$ Prices: Desserts $1.65–$5.25. No credit cards.

Open: Mon–Thurs noon–midnight, Fri–Sat noon–1am, Sun noon–11:30pm.

A popular destination in the Varsity Center is Bubbies, a favorite after-theater spot. Keith Robbins, who hails from the East Coast and named the shop after his grandmother, serves wonderful homemade ice cream and desserts. In addition to delectable ice cream ($2.25 per scoop), you can have cheesecake or apple pie, or chocolate-chip or macadamia-nut cookies along with your coffee. Curtains at the window, fans overhead, plants, an old-fashioned pendulum time clock, and a photograph of "Bubbie" complete the scene. Bubbie's ice cream is also served at some of Honolulu's finest restaurants.

WAIALAE–KAHALA

MEALS FOR LESS THAN $12

BERNARD'S NEW YORK DELI, in Kahala Mall Shopping Center. Tel. 732-DELI.

Cuisine: DELI. **Reservations:** Not accepted.

$ Prices: Main courses $6.95–$8.95. DC, MC, V.
Open: Mon–Sat 8am–9pm, Sun 8am–8pm.

Manhattan-style delicatessens may be catching on in Hawaii—this one is certainly getting kudos. Bernard's is kosher style from chicken soup to apple strudel. New Yorkers will get homesick just reading the menu: half a broiled chicken with matzoh balls and carrots, stuffed cabbage rolls with potato pancakes and salad, two kosher-beef knockwursts with baked beans and salad are all $7.95, as is gefilte fish with borscht and matzoh. You might want to start your meal with a bowl of homemade chicken soup or cold schav or borscht with sour cream. Then perhaps on to a deli sandwich of corned beef or chopped liver, hot pastrami or kosher salami. Fancy a side dish, such as potato latkes, potato knishes, stuffed derma? They're all available. So are blueberry or cheese blintzes with sour cream, delicious old-fashioned creamy rice pudding, and homemade cheesecake, with a choice of over 90 flavors. Bernard's is a full-service restaurant with cane chairs and checkerboard floors. Deli breakfasts are served all day.

THE PATISSERIE, in the Kahala Mall Shopping Center. Tel. 735-4402.
Cuisine: SANDWICHES/DESSERTS. **Reservations:** Not accepted.
$ Prices: Sandwiches $3.40–$4.50. MC, V.
Open: Mon–Fri 7am–9pm, Sat 7am–7pm, Sun 7am–5pm.

For a bit of Mittel Europa in Kahala Mall, stop in at the Pâtisserie, a bakery that also serves sandwiches and pastries at its sparkling counter and several little booths. Sandwiches, served on home-baked breads (we like the country Swiss), with sprouts or lettuce, include Black Forest ham, head cheese, roast beef, bratwurst, and pastrami. There's hot German potato salad, quiche Lorraine, and carrot salad, too. If you don't want anything quite so heavy, Black Forest cake, dobosh, and freshly baked pies should be just right.

Look for Pâtisserie shops at the Edgewater and Outrigger West hotels in Waikiki, and, downtown, at 33 S. King St. and 700 Bishop St.

YEN KING RESTAURANT, in the Kahala Mall Shopping Center. Tel. 732-5505.
Cuisine: NORTHERN CHINESE/VEGETARIAN. **Reservations:** Recommended.
$ Prices: Appetizers $3.95–$10.50; main courses $5.95–$9.95. AE, MC, V.
Open: Lunch daily 11am–4pm; dinner Mon–Tues 4–9:30pm, Wed–Sun 4pm–2am.

Vegetarians who love Chinese food swear by this place near the Kahala Hilton. So do a lot of other folks who've discovered this attractive restaurant that specializes in the cuisines of Peking and Szechuan. There's a lot to choose from here—including at least 30 meatless dishes—but two dishes that we never miss are the famous Singing Rice Soup (it "sings" when the crispy rice is added to the hot broth), and Chinaman's Hat, which consists of very light "pancakes" that you stuff and wrap at the table with a luscious filling of pork and vegetables. From then on, choose what you like: crackling chicken, lemon beef, sautéed clams—they're all good. As for vegetarian dishes, we found the lo hon chai vegetable dish delectable. MSG is never used. Desserts at many Chinese restaurants are unimaginative, but not here. If they're not too busy, they might make you their unforgettable fried apple with honey: flaming apple cubes covered with a honey–maple syrup sauce and dipped in ice water right at your table. Everything on the regular menu is available for take-out, and take-outs during the dinner hours are charged lunchtime prices. Yen King has full bar service. There's karaoke music Wednesday through Sunday nights from 9:30pm to 2am.

YUM YUM TREE RESTAURANT AND PIE SHOP, in the Kahala Mall Shopping Center. Tel. 737-7938.
Cuisine: AMERICAN. **Reservations:** Not required.

$ Prices: Main courses $7.95–$12.95. AE, CB, DC, JCB, MC, V.
Open: Daily 7am–midnight.

Long a favorite in the lovely Kahala residential area, this pretty place has seating both on the lanai and in the wood-and-stone inside room. Service is fast and friendly, and the food is always good. We like their delectable chicken pot pie, a meal in itself for $7.95. Salads such as papaya stuffed with shrimp, and chicken salad Oriental, and sandwiches and burgers and pasta dishes are good, too. Dinners are served with soup or green salad, rice or potato, plus vegetables and fresh baked cornbread and honey butter. Selections include broiled chicken, mahimahi, shrimp fry, and broiled sirloin. Best of all are the yummy pies for dessert, baked in their own kitchens; the pie display at center stage makes it difficult to resist taking a whole one back to your hotel. It's rumored that folks who stay at the posh Kahala Hilton Hotel a few blocks away like to come here now and then for a quick and inexpensive change of pace. It's open for all three meals.

Also see the listing above for the newer Yum Yum Tree at Ward Centre. There's still another one by the beach in Kailua.

MEALS FOR LESS THAN $20

CHE PASTA, 3571 Waialae Ave. Tel. 735-1777.
Cuisine: ITALIAN. **Reservations:** Not accepted.
$ Prices: Appetizers $3–$8; main courses $8–$18. AE, DISC, MC, V.
Open: Lunch Tues–Fri 11:30am–2pm; dinner Tues–Sat 5:30–9:45pm.

The food is quite special at this charming, elegantly furnished Italian restaurant in the Kaimuki neighborhood. The ambience of the place is warm and friendly, and the service, impeccable. Dinner can be quite reasonable here if you stick with the pastas, perhaps the delicious saffron cannelloni, the spaghetti al pomodoro funghi, or the lasagne al forno ($8–$15). Other excellent house specialties include pollo al cacciatore, veal parmigiana or marsala, and the fresh catch of the day at market price. It's a great temptation to overdose on their wonderful fresh Italian bread, but be strong and save room for gelato and sherbet, or the chocolate Grand Marnier cake. *Bellissimo!*

Note: If you're in downtown Honolulu, you can enjoy similar cuisine at slightly lower prices at Che Pasta, A Bar & Grill, at 1001 Bishop St. at Bishop Square. The same fresh cuisine prevails there. It's a bustling business-lunch spot, as well as an early-evening jazz club.

HALE VIETNAM, 1140 12th Ave., Kaimuki. Tel. 735-7581.
Cuisine: VIETNAMESE. **Reservations:** Not accepted.
$ Prices: Main courses $10–$13.50. MC, V.
Open: Mon–Fri 11am–2:30pm and 5–9:30pm, Sat–Sun and hols 11am–10pm.

Only a few restaurants in Honolulu offer Vietnamese cuisine, which combines a number of Asian and sometimes European influences. Chef Mark Fu, who is well known for his catering work, specializes in the cuisine of the Mekong Delta region, served in a casual setting of Southeast Asian art and tropical plants. Your entrée is accompanied by an appetizer of imperial rolls, fried cr nonfried Southeast Asian delights wrapped in rice paper and filled with seafood, pork, and fresh herbs. The prices also include a hearty Vietnamese beef-noodle soup. We like their Vietnamese vegetable dish. The beef or spiced chicken dish is grilled at your table. Unless you're an old hand at Asian food, ask that your dishes be prepared "mild" or "medium."

KEEHI LAGOON

MEALS FOR LESS THAN $20

LA MARIANA RESTAURANT & BAR, 50 Sand Island Rd. Tel. 841-2173.

Cuisine: SEAFOOD/STEAK. **Reservations:** Not accepted.
$ Prices: Appetizers $7.75; main courses $7.95–$14.95. AE, DC, V.
Open: Lunch daily 11am–2pm; dinner daily 6–9:30pm.

Few Honolulu residents and practically no tourists know about Keehi Lagoon. This restaurant, too, is a well-kept secret, a hideaway for the boat owners of the La Mariana Sailing Club at Keehi Lagoon. The restaurant and the marina itself are owned by a feisty lady named Annette La Mariana Nahinu, who has been fighting to keep the area alive for over 40 years. The restaurant is ramshackle romantic, its furnishings—wooden tables, rattan chairs, glass balls, and fishing nets—reputedly salvaged from the old Don the Beachcomber restaurant. Dine either indoors or on the shaded lanai, in full view of the boats. Nothing formal, nothing fancy here—just the way Hawaii used to be before the big money took over. The restaurant's chef is excellent, specializing mostly in steak, seafood, and freshly caught fish. Prices are reasonable, and island favorites, including ahi, marlin, ulua, and red snapper, are all available. The price of a main course includes french fries, mashed potatoes, or rice, salad, hot rolls, and coffee or tea. Lunch is reasonable too, with the emphasis on meaty sandwiches (burgers from $3.25, a steak sizzler on a bun at $5.50). You'll need to drive here (it's not far from the airport); it's best to call for precise directions.

HAWAII KAI

MEALS FOR LESS THAN $25

PACIFIC BROILER, 7192 Kalanianaole Hwy., in the Koko Marina Shopping Center. Tel. 395-4181.

Cuisine: CONTEMPORARY AMERICAN. **Reservations:** Recommended.
$ Prices: Appetizers $4.95–$7.95; main courses $11.95–$18.50. AE, MC, V.
Open: Lunch Mon–Sat 11:30am–2pm; dinner daily 5:30–9:30pm; brunch Sun 9am–2:30pm.

You'd hardly know from looking at this little restaurant that it's considered one of the best on Oahu. It's small and attractive, with a counter overlooking the open kitchen, round tables and booths, fish prints on the wall, and a few tables overlooking the water. But nothing about the decor suggests the extent of the creativity that emerges from the kitchen. Pacific Broiler calls itself "a contemporary grill devoted to the fine art of creative barbecue," and that's just what it is. From the kiawe-hardwood broiler come such succulent creations as lime-marinated breast of island chicken with barbecued hollandaise and potato-cheese stuffed chiles, memorable smoked lamb chops with fresh rosemary-zinfandel sauce, kiawe-broiled catch of the day with a crabmeat-béarnaise sauce. Creativity extends to the appetizers, like the quesadilla with Brie and buffalo mozarella, seedless grapes and a sour cream and mango salsa, and to the salads, as well; try crackling fried chicken salad with popcorn croutons or rolled Bibb lettuce salad with crushed peanut dip, fresh basil, and tofu. Pastas are special too, and there's even one for Pritikin devotees. Desserts are also terrific. We're always hard put to choose between the bottomless bittersweet-chocolate mousse and the flourless double-chocolate cake with English crème.

Lunch features salads, sandwiches, burgers, small plates, and desserts. Sunday brunch offers omelets, waffles, and the like, among other main dishes.

Pacific Broiler is located in Hawaii Kai, about a half-hour drive from Waikiki on weekends and evenings, more at other times.

READERS RECOMMEND

John Richards Restaurant, *Koko Marina, Hawaii Kai. (tel. 396-6393). "We made one great restaurant discovery which we would like to pass along. On our way to Hanauma Bay we discovered the John Richards Restaurant at Koko Marina in Hawaii Kai. We had a* *soup-and-salad-bar buffet lunch for $6.95. Our table had a beautiful view of the harbor. The buffet lunch is served every day from 11am to 2:30pm."*—Ted and Eileen Matthew, Santa Barbara, Calif.

3. SPECIALTY DINING

BUFFETS

COUNTRY LIFE VEGETARIAN BUFFET, in the Honolulu Prince Hotel, 421 Nahua St. Tel. 922-5010.

Cuisine: VEGETARIAN. **Reservations:** Not accepted.

$ **Prices:** Average meals $3–$8. MC, V.

Open: Lunch Sun–Fri 11am–2:30pm; dinner Sun–Thurs 5–8pm.

If you've ever eaten at a Country Life restaurant in New York, Paris, London, or Osaka, you know how good these places are. And if you haven't, you're in for a treat. The Honolulu branch is a delight for vegetarians and health-conscious people. No animal products of any kind (including no eggs or dairy products) are used. Delicious desserts are made with fruit concentrates, dates, and honey.

The buffet table features such main dishes as pecan loaf with cashew gravy, baked potatoes with soy sour cream, lasagne, taco salad, and tofu and rice croquettes. There's a generous salad and fresh fruit bar; freshly baked whole-grain breads and homemade spreads; and guilt-free desserts on the order of carob brownies, pumpkin pie, and blackberry cobbler.

Country Life restaurants are a project of lay members of the Seventh-Day Adventist church: The only proselytizing they do (if you ask) is on the benefits of good nutrition, as they are anxious to help people improve their health. They can provide you with an excellent collection of vegetarian recipes for a modest price. Meals are priced by weight: $4.40 a pound at lunch, $4.90 a pound at dinner. They offer validated parking at any Outrigger Hotel. The restaurant is next to the Outrigger West, and just behind the International Market Place.

DYNASTY II, 1050 Ala Moana Blvd., in Ward Warehouse. Tel. 531-0208.

Cuisine: CHINESE. **Reservations:** Not required.

$ **Prices:** Buffet lunch $8.45; appetizers $3.75–$16.75; main courses $7.75–$9.95. AE, CB, DC, DISC, JCB, MC, V.

Open: Lunch Mon–Fri 11am–2pm; dinner daily 6–10pm.

This elegant Chinese restaurant offers a popular weekday lunch buffet; you can eat all you want for $8.45. For a splurge, you might want to come back here for dinner. Appetizers such as stuffed crab claw, and main courses like a whole Peking duck ($38), deep-fried crispy chicken, and king prawns sautéed with seasonal vegetables, have earned this restaurant many awards. Even before you dine, you will be impressed by the impeccably coutured maitre d', the Oriental carpets, and the distinctive serving ware.

KENGO'S ROYAL BUFFET, 1529 Kapiolani Blvd. Tel. 941-2241.

Cuisine: JAPANESE/AMERICAN. **Reservations:** Accepted only for groups of six or more.

$ **Prices:** Buffet lunch $9.50 Mon–Fri, $11 Sat–Sun; buffet dinner $18.50.

Open: Lunch daily 11am–2pm; dinner daily 5–9:30pm.

This spot is immensely popular with local people, who keep it packed day and night. Although the atmosphere is plain, the combination of hearty food and low prices makes it a winner. The dinner buffet is especially good, with many luscious seafood dishes, such as shrimp tempura and lobster in black-bean sauce, as well as roast beef carved to order. There are two buffet tables, one laden with Japanese specialties such as sushi and salads; the other, haole favorites such as fried fish and lamb chops. There's a modest dessert bar. Soup (we sampled a tasty Portuguese bean soup) is served at your table, as is your beverage ($1 more). There's karaoke singing in the bar and lounge from 8pm to 2am, and in the main dining room from 10pm to 2am, every night.

PARC CAFE, in the Waikiki Parc Hotel, 2233 Helumoa Rd. Tel. 921-7272.

Cuisine: AMERICAN/JAPANESE/HAWAIIAN. **Reservations:** Recommended.

$ Prices: Breakfast buffet $10.50; lunch buffet $11.50; Hawaiian lunch buffet $14.50; dinner buffet $19.50; Sun brunch $18.50. AE, CB, DC, JCB, MC.

Open: Breakfast daily 7–10am; lunch daily 11:30am–2pm; dinner daily 5:30–10pm; brunch Sun 11am–2pm.

For a buffet meal that's also a fine dining experience, the Parc Café, across from the Halekulani Hotel, is just the ticket. The garden-terrace atmosphere is charming, the service attentive, and the food of a gourmet quality not usually found on buffet tables. The dinner buffet features the likes of Peking duck salad, celery rémoulade, fresh fish of the day, pastas, and Asian favorites. The carving station offers roast beef or pork, char-broiled top sirloin, plus poultry and lamb freshly done in the rôtisserie. For dessert, you can have freshly baked pies and cakes or chocolate mousse, or make your own frozen yogurt sundaes with a lavish choice of toppings. Sunday brunch is another feast. One of our favorite things to do is to stop by on Wednesday for a spectacular Hawaiian lunch buffet; the food is better than at many a luau. Lomi-lomi salmon, kalua pig, chicken long rice, lau lau, and the traditional hapia pudding are all featured, along with such gourmet delicacies as a chilled yam-and-leek soup with a hint of champagne, wild-bamboo-shoot salad, and mashed Molokai potatoes. The rest of the week, the luncheon buffet features a create-your-own sandwich bar, a Cobb salad station, pastas, chicken from the rôtisserie, a do-it-yourself yogurt bar, and more. The breakfast buffet has a table full of goodies, including exotic fresh fruits, pastries, eggs, meats, cereals, pancakes, and delicious French toast. A great place to conduct quiet business or a morning tête-à-tête. Full à la carte service is also available.

PEACOCK ROOM AND GARDEN LANAI, in the Queen Kapiolani Hotel, 150 Kapahulu Ave. Tel. 922-1941.

Cuisine: INTERNATIONAL. **Reservations:** Recommended.

$ Prices: Buffets $11.95–$21.95. AE, CB, DC, JCB, MC.

Open: Breakfast daily 6:30–10:30am; lunch Mon–Sat 11am–2pm; dinner daily 5:30–9pm; brunch Sun 11am–2pm.

This restaurant provides a variety of intriguing buffets at lunch and dinner. On Monday and Tuesday evenings, there's an all-you-can eat poultry, beef, and seafood buffet for $11.95; on Wednesday and Thursday it's a Japanese buffet dinner at $17.95, very popular since it features all the sashimi you can eat. On Friday night it's the seafood buffet dinner at $21.95, and on Saturday and Sunday, the prime rib and international dinner buffet at $16.95. A Hawaiian luncheon luau lunch can be enjoyed every day except Thursday and Sunday for $11.95; on Thursday it's a Japanese buffet luncheon, and on Sunday a traditional brunch. Every day, there's a breakfast buffet at $7.95. Live entertainment is featured at many meals. Prices, schedules, and types of buffets may change slightly, so be sure to check in advance.

PERRY'S SMORGY RESTAURANT, 2380 Kuhio Ave., at the corner of Kanekapolei. Tel. 926-0184.

Cuisine: SMÖRGÅSBORD. **Reservations:** Not accepted.

$ Prices: Breakfast buffet $4.45; lunch buffet $5.95; dinner buffet and Sun brunch, $7.95. AE, MC, V.

Open: Breakfast Mon–Sat 7–11am; lunch daily 11:30am–2:30pm; dinner daily 5–9pm; brunch Sun 11:30am–2:30pm.

Buffets are very popular in Honolulu, and ideal for the budget-minded. Just about the best values are offered at the two Perry's restaurants, which have been serving hearty American-style buffet meals for as long as we can remember. The food is really good, there's no limit to how much you can eat, and the prices make it one of the best budget buys in Honolulu. Both restaurants are attractive, especially the one on Kuhio, with its lush indoor-outdoor garden setting. At both, lunch and dinner feature a huge fruit and salad bar; hot vegetables; rice or potatoes; homemade corn muffins and dinner rolls; and lots of hot main dishes, including mahimahi, beef and vegetable stew, southern-style chicken, Italian spaghetti and garlic bread, and baked macaroni and cheese. Dinner adds a hand-carved round of roast beef au jus, golden fried shrimp, and sliced turkey. In addition to the generous dessert table, there's also a create-your-own sundae and dessert bar. Fresh island pineapple and local Kona coffee are served at each meal. Breakfast features carved smoked ham, French toast, pancakes, blueberry muffins, fresh doughnuts and cinnamon rolls, an attractive fruit bar, and more. You can have as many refills as you like, but no doggie bags, please. There's live Hawaiian entertainment every night.

The second Perry's is at the Coral Seas Hotel, 240 Lewers St., oceanside of Kalakaua Avenue (tel. 922-8814).

PIKAKE TERRACE BUFFET & BROILER, in the Princess Kaiulani Hotel, 120 Kaiulani Ave. Tel. 922-5811.

Cuisine: SMÖRGÅSBORD. **Reservations:** Recommended for dinner.

$ **Prices:** Breakfast buffet, $12.95 adults, $5.25 children 12 and under; lunch buffet, $13.95 adults, $6.25 children 12 and under; dinner buffet, $17.95 adults, $6.95 children 12 and under. AE, CB, DC, JCB, MC, V.

Open: Breakfast daily 6–11am; lunch daily 11am–2pm; dinner daily 5:30–10pm.

It all began with a few tables around the pool at the newly expanded Princess Kaiulani Hotel. But every year the tables increased, and now this restaurant is a dominant feature of the hotel's poolside and public areas. It lives up to its name with sumptuous buffets served morning, noon, and night in an open-air fantasia. All-you-can-eat breakfast buffets offer juices, fruits, cereal, crêpes, meats, and eggs. At lunch, choose from a huge salad table, a hot table with half a dozen choices, gourmet burgers, and a dessert table that tempts you to take one of each. The salad buffet alone is $9.50; the chef's table alone, $10.95. At dinner, choose between an expanded buffet at $17.95 and an elaborate menu, featuring such dishes as herb-marinated jumbo shrimp en brochette at $19.50 and filet mignon at $21.50.

PLANTATION CAFE, in the Ramada Renaissance Ala Moana Hotel, 410 Atkinson. Tel. 955-4811.

Cuisine: INTERNATIONAL. **Reservations:** Not required.

$ **Prices:** Breakfast buffets $10.50; lunch soup-and-salad bar $8; weekend dinner buffets $14.95–$16.95. AE, DC, JCB, MC, V.

Open: Breakfast daily 6–11am; lunch daily 11:30am–2pm; dinner daily 6pm–midnight.

Although this place serves more than just buffets, it's hard to resist the luscious treats at the smörgåsbord. The restaurant looks opulent, with a huge glass wall that opens onto a richly planted area, but prices are not out of line. The sumptuous breakfast buffet includes fruits, juices, eggs, meats, and pastries galore. Lunch features a soup-and-salad bar. The regular menu includes nasi goreng, Indonesian fried rice with chicken, shrimp, veggies, and eggs, and there are also Chinese, Indian, and other exotic dishes. Come dinnertime, the chef's talents are displayed with out-of-the-ordinary soups and tantalizing appetizers, such as the fettuccine Alfredo.

At this writing, buffet dinners were being held on weekends only; Friday, a Mediterranean one at $14.95; Saturday, a southwestern barbecue spread at $14.95; and Sunday, a Pacific Rim buffet at $16.95. Call to make sure of the schedule.

RESTAURANT BENKEI, 1050 Ala Moana Blvd., in Ward Warehouse. Tel. 523-8713.

Cuisine: JAPANESE. **Reservations:** Recommended.

$ Prices: Buffet lunch $7.95; buffet dinner $15.95. AE, MC, V.

Open: Lunch daily 11am–2pm; dinner Tues–Sun 5:30–9:30pm.

Japanese food can be expensive, so it's great to know that you can go to this delightful place and feast on a bountiful buffet table of Japanese delicacies for just $7.95 at lunchtime, $15.95 at dinner. The restaurant is decorated in old-world Japanese style, and pleasant tables look out over the street. (If there are 20 people in your party, you can command the upstairs teahouse-style room for a special $35 kaiseki menu.) The buffet table always features miso soup, an array of chicken, beef, and seafood dishes, plus sashimi, noodle dishes, and a tasty array of Japanese salads. Tea comes with your meal; dessert is extra. If you opt for the à la carte menu (appetizers $4–$12, main courses $12–$20 at dinner), you can choose from a variety of seafood tempura, fried and broiled fish, sashimi, steak salad, and Japanese-style steak—all served with appetizer, rice, pickles, and soup.

READERS RECOMMEND

Maiko, *in the Ilikai Hotel, 1777 Ala Moana Blvd. (tel. 946-5151). "The lunch buffet at Maiko at the Ilikai Hotel is a steal at $9.50, considering that they offer crab, sushi, sukiyaki, salad bar, dessert, and many other things, plus validated parking. It's a relaxing place to eat, where the tea and Japanese soup are brought to your table. No view to the outside, but you can step outside and be on the beach in a few footsteps. At dinner, the price is $16.95 Monday through Wednesday and $17.95 Thursday through Sunday"*—Mark Terry, Maui, Hawaii.

Trellisses Restaurant, *in the Outrigger Prince Kuhio Hotel, 2500 Kuhio Ave. (tel. 922-0811). " . . . Trellisses Restaurant at the Outrigger Prince Kuhio Hotel charges around $18 for its Friday-night seafood buffet. It is excellent in every way, recommended for a 'Big Splurge' meal."*—Lynda Lamb, Colo, S.C.

EXOTIC SNACK FOOD

Honolulu has myriad snack bars where you can sample exotic cuisines at penny-pinching prices. Right in Waikiki, for example, is the **Hung Yun Chinese Kitchen** in Kuhio Mall, where the luscious aromas wafting from the restaurant will lead you to Chinese dishes that start at $1 for pieces of chicken, beef, and pork. Top prices on other main courses: $2.95–$3.95!

The **Oriental Snack Bars at Woolworth's,** at 2224 Kalakaua Ave. and also at Ala Moana Center, are great places to sample authentic Japanese dishes for just pennies. Both are big hits with the office workers and shoppers. Prices vary minutely at the two (sushi selections $1.80–$7.95; saimin, $4.50); the Kalakaua Avenue store also has a sushi bar. We slightly favor the Ala Moana Woolworth's, where, after filling up your paper plate, you can go out and sit in the pretty mall watching islanders mill about. Incidentally, two cone sushis (cold, marinated rice cakes) tucked in your bag make a tasty lunch-on-the-run. (Many of the ubiquitous ABC Discount Stores also carry cone sushi to go.)

Ala Moana Center has another extraordinary source for sampling Japanese food: the gourmet food department on the second floor of **Shirokiya,** the large Japanese department store. There are dozens of booths and counters where delicious food is cooked, baked, and/or sold. Booths offer freshly roasted chestnuts, tasty manapuas, and, of course, a vast array of wonderful sushi and other traditional Japanese fare. You can assemble a meal for yourself out of these offerings, and then take them home or to a little dining lanai to savor on the spot. Most days, from 3:30 to 8pm, there's an evening buffet and sushi bar, priced according to what you eat.

Rada's Piroscki, 1144-1146 Fort Street Mall (tel. 532-2388), is practically a Honolulu institution. This Russian snack bar specializes in piroshki—delicate, flaky buns stuffed with beef, cheese, cabbage, mushrooms, or whatever combination suits your fancy. We simply can't resist the chicken, mushrooms, and cheese piroshki, but the other combinations are also delicious. One big pirog is $1.40. The Russian fried squid, $1.10 a bag, are . . . uh, different. Rada's is a family operation, and the people in charge make you feel welcome. *Warning:* Piroshki may be habit-forming.

MUSEUM DINING

CONTEMPORARY CAFE, in the Contemporary Museum, 2411 Makiki Heights Dr. Tel. 523-3362.

Cuisine: INTERNATIONAL. **Reservations:** Recommended.

$ **Prices:** Appetizers $2.25–$8.25; main courses $7.25–$9.75. AE, MC, V.

Open: Lunch Wed–Sat 11am–2pm; (desserts and beverages to 3:30pm), Sun noon–2pm (desserts and beverages to 3:30pm).

If you visit the Contemporary Museum—and you should—you can also enjoy an artistic dining experience in its small and highly popular café. Done in old Hawaiian-style architecture, the Contemporary Cafe is set in a lush tropical garden. On the walls are some of Hawaii's finest contemporary art exhibits. The menu is sophisticated: You can graze on such appetizers as smoked salmon carpaccio or moules à la crème (New Zealand green-lipped mussels sautéed in a Thai curry paste); on pastas, quiches, and salads (the wilted spinach is a favorite); or on sandwiches ($7.95–$8.50) such as the vegetarian favorite, grilled tempeh with tahini. And if all you want is an espresso or cappuccino and a rich dessert, like flourless chocolate roulade or amaretto crème caramel, you've come to the right place.

GARDEN CAFE, in the Honolulu Academy of Arts, 900 S. Beretania St. Tel. 531-8865.

Cuisine: INTERNATIONAL. **Reservations:** Recommended.

$ **Prices:** Fixed-price $7.50 at lunch, $12.50 at dinner. No credit cards.

Open: Lunch Tues–Sat 11:30am–2pm; Sun 2–4pm; dinner Thurs at 6:15pm. **Closed:** Aug and two weeks at Christmas.

At the Garden Cafe of the Honolulu Academy of Arts, the dining lanai is under the trees just outside one of the world's great art collections. The serving staff, the cashier, and even the cooks are volunteers, and all profits from your meal go to further the work of the academy. Almost everything has a gourmet touch: The soups include chicken curry and crème mongole; you might have crunchy pea salad or a tuna mousse or green salad with sliced fresh mushrooms; as for sandwiches, it's turkey, ham, and roast beef. Lunch includes tea or coffee; wine and beer are available. The desserts, $1.50 extra, include ice cream, guava sherbet, and special dessert bars. Only one menu is served each day. Since there is usually a film or lecture at the academy at 7:30pm Thursday night, the volunteers also serve a Thursday supper, a light meal of international cuisine. Wine and dessert are extra.

A RESTAURANT FOR KIDS

SHOWBIZ PIZZA PLACE, 820 W. Hind Dr., in the Aina Haina Shopping Center. Tel. 373-2151.

Cuisine: PIZZA/SALAD BAR. **Reservations:** Not required.

$ **Prices:** Appetizers $2.25; pizzas $7.95–$12.50 small. DISC, MC, V.

Open: Mon–Thurs 11am–9pm, Fri 11am–11pm, Sat 10am–11pm, Sun 10am–5pm. **Closed:** Christmas.

So you're traveling with the kids? By all means, take any youngsters up to age 12 or so to this spot, which is on Kalanianaole Highway, not far from the Kahala Mall. There's a big stage at the front of the dining room, and every so often the curtains part to reveal very cleverly designed, life-size mechanical-animal musicians and singers, such as Chuck-E-Cheese, Jaspar, and Pasqually. These ingenious creations appear most lifelike, and they "sing" and "play" instruments. There are also people in animal costumes who circulate in the dining room and visit with young diners. As if that weren't enough, there are myriad video games. This is a most popular place for local kids to celebrate birthdays. And the food isn't half bad. The pizzas include Super Combo (cheese, sausage, beef, pepperoni, etc.), Aloha Delight (cheese, ham, pineapple, toasted almonds), and Vegetarian Favorite. There's a salad bar with a good variety of fixings, $4.90 for all-you-can-eat, plus minipizzas, sandwiches, beer, and wine. You can even buy the kids a Showbiz Pizza T-shirt.

DINING COMPLEXES

INTERNATIONAL MARKET PLACE & KUHIO MALL

Few tourists who set foot in Waikiki leave without at least one visit to the **International Market Place** in the heart of the beach area at 2330 Kalakaua Ave., where throngs of merchants offer everything from grass skirts to wooden idols to T-shirts and pearls-in-the-shell. Immediately adjoining it, and fronting on Kuhio Avenue, is **Kuhio Mall,** another lively bazaar. Just about in the middle of the two of them is the attractive **International Food Court** (follow the yellow-brick line), where some 30 fast-food stands offer a variety of tempting foods that you eat at central tables. You can certainly make a meal here, lunch or dinner, for $5 or under: Some of our favorites include Peking Garden, Beef & Burger, The Mad Greek, Aloha Yakitori, Beaches and Cream, Choi's Kitchen, Bautista's Filipino Kitchen, Yummy Korean BBQ, and Mario's Pizza and Pasta. Cinn-a-Yums dispenses enormous, fattening, delicious cinnamon buns with various toppings. Open daily from 8:30am to 11pm.

WAIKIKI SHOPPING PLAZA

Shopping here (2250 Kalakaua Ave., at the corner of Seaside) can be expensive, and most of the upper-level restaurants are pricey, but the below-street level is a veritable bonanza for the budget-conscious diner who wants something a little bit different. Start in the Japanese sector at **Ramen** for freshly made Japanese noodles. You can have them seated at the open tables or at the Japanese counter flanked by Japanese lanterns. Prices start at $6.25 for shoyu ramen and go to $6.75 for gyoza—Japanese dumplings—and shrimp tempura. This is one of the few plaza spots that opens early, at 10am. There are no tables at the Japanese fast-food outlet **Okazu-Ya Bento** (*bento* means take-out). Here they custom-design your take-out lunch or dinner, filling the large plate with Japanese favorites: yaki soba, meatballs, chicken cutlet, and cone sushi, for 65¢–$4.95. All items are in view in a glass showcase, Japanese style, so you can just point, or take their daily special at $5. To round off this Japanese trio, there's **Plaza Sushi,** a tidy little restaurant that serves a mostly Japanese crowd (prices run $6.50–$11.50 during the day, $8.50–$18.50 at night).

Want more variety? **Plaza Burger** is versatile, serving a quarter-pounder for $2.05, a taco dinner for $4.50, and a fried chicken dinner for $5.50. At the **Chinese Kitchen,** you get your choice of main dishes, plus noodles, chow fun, or steamed rice at the price of $4.85 for two main dishes, $5.85 for three, $6.85 for four. **Plaza Pizza** is one of the few places around town where you can get pizza by the slice ($1.95), plus daily specials. And of course there's a **Plaza Ice Cream,** with parlor chairs and tables, offering cooling cones, sodas, and sundaes.

Your best all-around choice here is the huge **Plaza Coffee Shop,** where changing lunch specials go for $5.75–$6.95 and include the likes of boneless barbecued chicken, corned beef and cabbage, and filets of mahimahi. Similar specials at dinner are $9.95–$12.95.

ALA MOANA CENTER'S MAKAI MARKET

Makai Market, occupying half an acre of space, has a score of self-service specialty kitchens where 13,000 meals a day are prepared. It employs more than 500 people—who obviously don't starve. Name your desire—Hawaiian, Italian, New York deli, seafood, Japanese, Chinese, health food—the food is here and you can put together a meal for around $4–$5 at lunch, $6–$7 at dinner. You serve yourself, then take your food to the pretty tables under the bright buntings overhead. There's karaoke singing every Saturday night from 6 to 8:30pm. You can start with a drink from the center bar with its LET'S MAKE A DAIQUIRI neon sign; daiquiris, piña coladas, and other favorites are about $3–$4, and there are smoothies and nonalcoholic cocktails as well.

Take a look around and see what you might like. **Thirst Aid Station** has "Remedies and Prescriptions" that include sodas, smoothies, yogurt, and soup (70¢–$2.20). **Tsuruya Noodle Soup** dishes up bowls of hot soba or udon, at $3.50–$5.15. At **Sbarro Pizza,** folks line up for the calzone (under $3.30), and for specials like baked ziti Sicilian style at $4.

Panda Express has Mandarin dishes on one side, Szechuan on the other. On the Mandarin side, try the spicy chicken with peanuts at $2.95, or go Szechuan with roast duck at $3.25. There's no way you can miss **Hawaiian Poi Bowl,** which dishes out food from a bright-red lunchwagon. There's a teri-chicken plate and a poi-bowl combo, for $4.25–$5.65.

Yummy Korean BBQ has full-meal combo plates at $4.95, lunch or dinner. **The Aloha Grill Bar** is a '50s theme eatery, with '50s music on the jukeboxes; it has its own bar seats on which to enjoy the super burgers, at $3–$5. At **La Cocina,** jumbo burritos served with beans and rice are $3.95, with other Mexican combo dishes up to $4.95.

Looking for light food? Try the **Kitchen Garden,** which offers croissant sandwiches and salads, plus baked potatoes, plain and fancy; both quiche and chili go for $4.50. For a cholesterol feast, however, we might suggest **Kiawe-Q-Ribs,** where you can get kiawe-wood-smoked pork, beef brisket, ham, chicken, or turkey on a hot French roll at $3.95. **La Rôtisserie** offers a fried-food buffet including seafood, beef burgundy, and mahimahi in ginger butter for $4.75–$5.25—as well as a delicious seafood salad for $7.50.

For years before Makai Market opened, **Patti's Chinese Kitchen** and **Lyn's Delicatessen** were bywords among visitors and locals alike. Now they've moved into the market and are still mighty crowd pleasers. Patti's is famous for its plate lunches; for a choice of any two items, the price is $3.50, $4.45 for three items, $5.50 for four. As for Lyn's, it has long been one of the best kosher-style delis in town, known for thick corned beef and pastrami sandwiches ($3–$4.30), lox and bagels, fragrant and garlicky hot dogs, plus plate lunches, and very special buys on steak dinners.

Want more? **Orson's Chowderette** is a small version of the popular Orson's in Ward Warehouse. Finger foods like fish nuggets and clam strips, salads, and burgers of mahimahi, shrimp, or oysters, are all low-priced, $2.50–$5.95. You can sample Thai food—plate lunches for $2.80–$5.45, spring rolls at $1.95—at **Little Cafe Siam.** No MSG here! **Wingo** is fine when you crave fried chicken; it's served on a jumbo plate for $5.

NEARBY CHOICES Not in Makai Market itself, but not far from it, on the same street level, are two restaurants we like a lot. **Hanako,** a new Japanese place, is clean, spare, done in black and white, with beautiful arrays of sushi to eat in or take out.

Most individual sushi are 60¢. Combination plates from their "hot line" run $3.45–$6.45, hearty noodle dishes are $3.95–$4.95, and a satisfying Japanese breakfast of rice, egg, fish, nori, tsukemono, and miso soup is a reasonable $5.50.

Peppermill, a few doors away, is another counter-style restaurant, open, with wicker chairs and a cozy feeling. Daily specials, like chicken tarragon, German pot roast, or chicken curry Malay, run $5.50. Sandwiches are served with 10-grain molasses or sourdough bread and run $4.25 for roast sirloin of beef or chicken mango-chutney salad. Good salads too, and everything here is inexpensive.

WORTH THE EXTRA BUCKS

ALFRED'S EUROPEAN RESTAURANT, 1750 Kalakaua Ave. Tel. 955-5353.

Cuisine: FRENCH/CONTINENTAL. **Reservations:** Recommended.
$ Prices: Appetizers $6.50–$12.50; main courses $16–$25. CB, DC, MC, V.
Open: Lunch Mon–Fri 11am–2pm; dinner Tues–Sat 6–10pm.

The dining critic of the *Honolulu Star-Bulletin* has called this "one of the top five restaurants in the city." We couldn't agree more. A visit to chef/owner Alfred Vollenweider's gracious dining room on the third floor of the Century Center, at the corner of Kapiolani Boulevard, is like visiting a fine restaurant on the continent where every detail is handled perfectly, from the china on the table to the attentive service by the waiters to the superb cuisine. Everything is prepared fresh, using only the best market ingredients. And nothing comes out of the kitchen until Alfred—who spends part of each evening walking around the restaurant in his tall chef's hat—makes sure that it's perfect. While a meal here is not inexpensive, neither is it overpriced and it offers top value for the dollar.

Dinner starts with four or five salad-relish dishes prepared according to the season, plus a basket of European-style breads. Soup du jour follows that, and then it's your choice of such dishes as a flavorful coquilles St-Jacques au beurre blanc, grilled breast of duck, filet mignon aux champignons, live Maine lobster, or fresh fish taken from local waters and sautéed, steamed, or poached in a light champagne sauce. Desserts are more than worth the price, especially for creations like the soufflé glâcé Grand Marnier or the unforgettable strawberries Romanoff, fresh strawberries marinated in liqueur and topped with ice cream. Wines are decently priced. Irish, Swiss, and other specialty coffees, English and herbal teas, plus brandies and cordials top off the meal. Lunch is also pleasant and well priced, from about $9 to $15 for egg dishes, salads, fresh fish, sandwiches, plus a daily chef's special that includes soup or salad. Validated parking.

A TOUCH OF THE EAST, JAPANESE BISTRO AND SUSHI BAR, 500 Ala Moana Blvd., in Restaurant Row. Tel. 521-5144.

Cuisine: JAPANESE. **Reservations:** Not accepted.
$ Prices: Appetizers $6.95–$8.95; main courses $13.95–$25.95. AE, MC, V.
Open: Lunch daily 11am–2pm; dinner daily 5–10pm (sushi bar, Sun–Thurs to 11pm, Fri–Sat to 1am).

One of the most striking establishments in Restaurant Row, this popular bistro and sushi bar is a study in red and black, from the dramatic red-and-black facade out front to the black lacquer tables, bar, and sushi bar and the red walls, hung with pictures of Kabuki and Noh performers, within. The food is superb, from a wide variety of sushi and sashimi (platters are $10.95–$22.95 at dinner, $5.95–$12.95 at lunch) to appetizers like braised tofu dumplings or fresh fried mozzarella, on to such main courses as chasoba (green tea pasta with Japanese eggplant, tomato sauce, and sausage), breast of chicken; sea scallops, and some very non-Japanese veal chops and hearty cioppino. Lunch features pleasant salads like the chicken salad with ginger-honey sauce ($4.60–$9.50) and such dishes as butterfish, sea scallops, teriyaki chicken, and oyako-yaki (grilled salmon topped with salmon caviar). You could have chocolate mousse or cheesecake for dessert at either meal, but green-tea ice cream better suits the mood. Stay late and join the crowd for karaoke, every night from 9:30pm.

BON APPETIT, 1778 Ala Moana Blvd. Tel. 942-3837.

Cuisine: FRENCH. **Reservations:** Recommended.

$ **Prices:** Appetizers $5.25–$12; main courses $15–$27.50; fixed-price dinner $24.50. CB, DC, DISC, JCB, MC, V.

Open: Dinner only, Mon–Sat 5:30–10pm.

Discovery Bay, a two-level shopping area topped by a huge condominium, opposite the Ilikai Hotel, houses one of Honolulu's most enjoyable French restaurants. Bon Appétit is master chef Guy Banal's contribution to the cause of fine French cooking; he does both traditional country fare and some nouvelle cuisine dishes with an island flair as well. And prices are not out of sight for food of this quality. You might want to begin with the delicate scallops and lobster mousse, served warm with cucumbers and a dollop of red caviar; or perhaps with baked escargots in puff pastry with a touch of Pernod. For main dishes, choose from among Guy's French Provincial specialties, like a thick and hearty cassoulet, moules marinières, or bouillabaisse marseillaise with fresh island fish of the day. On the lighter side (and the low side of the menu), you could have Cajun angel-hair pasta with seafood and vegetables, lobster raviolis in a lobster bisque sauce, or Kona crab cake. Desserts change daily and can be memorable. There is an excellent wine list and a popular wine and appetizer bar as well, the biggest in town.

HAU TREE LANAI, in the New Otani Kaimana Beach Hotel, 2863 Kalakaua Ave. Tel. 923-1555.

Cuisine: AMERICAN. **Reservations:** Recommended.

$ **Prices:** Appetizers $6.50–$8.95; main courses $18.50–$22.50. AE, CB, DC, JCB, MC, V.

Open: Breakfast daily 6:30–11am; lunch daily 11:30am–2pm; dinner daily 5:30–9pm.

This is one of those sparkling, over-the-water spots, where the atmosphere and food contend for the honors. It's so nice to dine here under the hau tree, watching the waves wash up to the shore at Sans Souci Beach, in the very setting that Robert Louis Stevenson once favored. Breakfast here is one of our favorite Honolulu experiences. The standard American breakfast, called the "Kamaaina," consists of two eggs and a choice of meat, potatoes or rice, and toast, for $9. Even more fun: the "Japanese Breakfast" at $15; that's a bowl of miso soup, rice, seaweed, grilled salmon, an egg, fresh fruit, pickled vegetables, and green tea—a meal big enough to last you for quite a while.

At lunch you can have many choices: refreshing salads like the Oriental chicken, the chicken seafood taco, and the crab-stuffed artichoke ($8.95–$12.50); a variety of fitness selections including pastas and curries ($10.50–$14.50); tasty sandwiches such as asparagus roll with turkey or mahi burger ($8.50–$10.50); or main courses such as roasted garlic herb chicken, Kah ku shrimp rigatone and seafood fettuccine, served with rice and vegetables ($10.50–$13.50). The dinner menu is even more extensive, including shrimp scampi, stuffed jumbo tiger prawns, veal medallion in wild-mushroom sauce, and broiled noisettes of lamb ($18.50–$22.50). Complete dinners, which include soup or salad, sautéed fresh vegetables, and a selection from the dessert tray, plus beverage, are good buys at $29.50 and $32.50.

ILIKAI YACHT CLUB, RESTAURANT AND BAR, 1777 Ala Moana Blvd. Tel. 949-3811.

Cuisine: CONTINENTAL. **Reservations:** Recommended.

$ **Prices:** Appetizers $2–$9; main courses $13–$27. AE, CB, DC, DISC, JCB, MC, V.

Open: Dinner only, daily 5:30–10pm.

Save this one for a special night and enjoy every moment of it. This is a dining spot where eloquence and sophistication dominate the decor, music, and cuisine. The restaurant affords sheltered outdoor seating with views of the Ala Wai Yacht Harbor and, inside, a feeling of being served on a yacht. Large blue-glass columns are fish-filled aquariums. Upholstered chairs with a mahogany look seat you at the ample marble-top tables. You start your dinner with a choice of hot appetizers (perhaps a kettle of clams or poached salmon with spinach and chives) or cold (the Alaskan king crab served with salmon caviar is outstanding). The regular soup is seafood chowder, hearty with big chunks of fish, at $3. The price of main dishes includes a garden salad, home-baked breads, and fresh vegetables. On the low-priced end of the menu, you might have fettuccine Alfredo or fettuccine with scallops and shrimp. One of our favorites is the breast of chicken Nantua, stuffed with crab and served on a bed of spinach with lobster sauce; it comes with a rice mixture and assorted fresh vegetables. Desserts are indescribable; the chef creates new wonders every day. Tony Chardo plays the guitar and sings nightly from 5:30 to 10pm.

TRIPTON'S AMERICAN CAFE, 449 Kapahulu Ave. Tel. 737-3819.

Cuisine: AMERICAN/CONTINENTAL. **Reservations:** Recommended.

$ Prices: Appetizers $6.50–$9.50; main courses $13.75–$22. AE, DC, MC, V.

Open: Dinner only, Mon–Fri 5:30–10pm, Sat–Sun 5:30–11pm.

A modest splurge and a modest distance from Waikiki—two blocks—is Tripton's, one flight above Hee Hing (there's parking in the basement garage). The owners, who ran restaurants in the Virgin Islands and, more recently, on Kauai, serve world-class cuisine at reasonable prices. Their liver pâté is more than just chopped liver: It is carefully blended with nutmeg, mace, parsley, and garlic ($5.50). The salmon mousse is highlighted with dillweed and cucumber and blended with sour cream. Create your own salad at your table by choosing five condiments and the dressing; your server will toss it with romaine lettuce, tomatoes, cucumbers, and croutons. It comes with soup, is large enough to be a full meal, and costs $13.75; they call it "the biggest salad you've ever seen." Main dishes include daily chicken specials, fresh catch of the day—broiled or sautéed—New York steak, and prime ribs. The decor is lovely—peach and green tones accented by tropical greenery, and there are two levels, which add privacy. A well-equipped bar adds spirit. Check Susie's Dessert Board for marvelous desserts of the day, like the apple, cherry, and blueberry crisps with ice cream, lemon meringue pie, and much more.

4. IN NEARBY KAILUA

MEALS FOR LESS THAN $10

CAFETERIA, in Castle Medical Center, 640 Ulukahiki St. Tel. 263-5500

Cuisine: VEGETARIAN. **Reservations:** Not accepted.

$ Prices: Main courses $1.40. No credit cards.

Open: Breakfast Mon–Fri 6:30–9:30am; lunch Sun–Fri 11am–1:30pm, Sat and hols 11am–1pm; dinner Sun–Fri 4:30–6pm.

The most reasonable meals in Kailua can be found here at the cafeteria of the Castle Medical Center. The hospital is run by Seventh-Day Adventists, and, in keeping with their philosophy, everything served is vegetarian. The food is delicious, and at old-fashioned prices. All the hot dishes—like stir-fry veggies with tofu, or Créole patties—are $1.40; a salad-and-sandwich bar is 20¢ an ounce, so you can easily put together a very reasonable meal. The à la carte breakfast menu features waffles, eggs, fresh fruit, and vegetables. Take the elevator or stairs down one flight as you enter the hospital.

GEE . . . A DELI!, 418-F Kuulei Rd. Tel. 261-4412.

Cuisine: DELI. **Reservations:** Not accepted.

$ Prices: Appetizers $1.50–$4; daily sandwich special $3.95. No credit cards.

Open: Mon–Thurs and Sat 10am–6pm, Fri 10am–7pm, Sun 11am–5pm.

When we first saw this place, we exclaimed, "Gee, a deli!" and that turned out to be its name. You'll know this is a New York–style deli right away: Sandwiches can be served on onion roll or rye and are inches thick. There are all the usuals, plus a terrific Italian sub at $4.95, a dozen or more clubs and subs, and bagels with cream cheese and lox. This is an extremely popular place, but service is fast and efficient. And there are five or six large tables, so you don't have to eat in the car. It's located directly behind McDonald's.

YANI'S CAFE, 30 Aulike. Tel. 263-4601.

Cuisine: GREEK. **Reservations:** Not accepted.

$ Prices: Salads $2.50–$4.95; sandwiches and burgers $3.95–$5.75. No credit cards.

Open: Mon–Fri 7am–2pm, Sat–Sun 8am–2pm.

Right in the middle of the medical section of Kailua, this tiny, delightful café is full of doctors and nurses at lunchtime (don't worry, there'll be room for you), possibly because the food is healthful as well as delicious. Favorites include the gyros (grilled seasoned lamb in a warm pita bread), the traditional platter of Greek appetizers, the Greek burger (smothered with cheese), and a variety of omelets served at any hour. For a true Greek specialty, try the yummy loukoumades, tiny round doughnuts served piping hot and topped with a cinnamon-honey syrup.

MEALS FOR LESS THAN $20

ASSAGIO ITALIAN RESTAURANT, 354 Uluniu St. Tel. 261-2772.

Cuisine: ITALIAN. **Reservations:** Recommended for Sat–Sun dinners.

$ Prices: Appetizers $2.90–$8.90; main courses $7.90–$12. AE, CB, DC, MC, V.

Open: Lunch Mon–Fri 11:30am–2:30pm; dinner daily 5–10pm.

A tiny (10-table) place that's won a big following for its wonderful food at oh-so-reasonable prices, Assagio is something special. The service is special, too. The whole staff takes care of everyone; there's always someone watching to see if you're happy. At dinner the hot antipasto—which has *everything*—is exceptional. At dinner only, one may order a small or regular portion of pasta or any other entrée. Our favorite pasta here—and one you don't see everywhere—is the baked ziti alla Sicilina. Chicken, veal, pizzas, seafood dishes—they're all good, especially the sauces. Lunch entrées are pretty much the same, and go down $1 or $2 in prices. Even if you have to get a take-out bag, don't leave Assaggio without sampling their wonderful ricotta cheesecake ($2); of course, you'd be perfectly safe with the zabaglione with imported marsala, too, at $3.50. The restaurant is pleasant enough, with the obligatory Italian street scene and still-life pictures on the walls—but it's the food that shines here.

CINNAMON'S, 315 Uluniu St. Tel. 261-8724.

Cuisine: AMERICAN. **Reservations:** Recommended for parties of more than four.

$ Prices: Appetizers $4.95–$10.95; main courses $8.95–$18.95. MC, V.

Open: Breakfast daily 7am–2pm; lunch daily 11am–2pm; dinner Thurs–Sat 5–9pm.

Named after the bear in a French children's story, Cinnamon's is an immensely popular restaurant on the ground floor of a neighborhood shopping plaza. Its aim is to provide wholesome, natural, nutritious foods with no preservatives in a smoke-free atmosphere, and this it does—with style. The restaurant is small and cozy; four of the tables are under a pretty white gazebo. And the tab will be very reasonable. For lunch, we like the chicken-cashew salad ($6.50) and the grilled three-cheese deluxe sandwich ($3.95). Country quiches with salad, the garden vegetable platter, and burgers are all very popular, too. At dinnertime, pick one of the house specials, such as chicken fantasy, with broccoli hollandaise; kebabs of chicken, beef, or mahimahi; or barbecued ribs. Meals come with soup or salad; rice, fries, or baked beans; vegetables; and hot dinner rolls. On the à la carte dinner menu, the fiesta taco grande salad and the chef's super salad ("a veritable salad bar brought to your table") are inexpensive and fun, as are the roast pork with apple dressing, chicken cutlet with country gravy and vegetables, seafood crêpes Florentine, seafood platter, and fresh fish. Breakfast has its own delights, including eggs Benedict, carrot pancakes, three-egg omelets, and freshly baked cinnamon rolls.

L'AUBERGE SWISS, 117 Hekili St., Kailua. Tel. 263-4663.

Cuisine: SWISS. **Reservations:** Recommended.

$ Prices: Appetizers $3–$8.50; main courses $9.75–$18.50. CB, DC, MC, V.

Open: Dinner only, Tues–Sun 6–10pm.

One of Honolulu's finest restaurants, L'Auberge Swiss is just a short drive across the Pali in pretty little Kailua town. The owner/chef is Alfred Mueller, formerly head chef at the Hilton Hawaiian Village. The dining room very much resembles the little country inns one sees in Switzerland, Mueller's boyhood home. The food is superb and the service friendly; the dining room is presided over by Mrs. Mueller. It's difficult to choose what to start with: There's country pâté, oysters Rockefeller, escargots bourguignon, and a French-onion soup gratiné that is sheer poetry! Then take your choice of the likes of chicken piccata albergo (boneless breast of chicken on pasta); wienerschnitzel; émincé de veau zurichoise (tender pieces of veal in a rich cream sauce with mushrooms and rösti potatoes); or scallops and shrimp sautéed in a delicate sauce, served with pasta. There's also that great Swiss favorite, cheese fondue, with dinner salad, for at least two. Light Swiss dinners, such as bratwurst with rösti potatoes, and the fresh pasta-of-the-day, are all about $8.50. Kamaainas come from all corners of the island to dine here.

CHAPTER 7

HONOLULU ATTRACTIONS

The fantastic bargain of Honolulu is the enormous number of things to see and do that are inexpensive or free. Part of the reason for this, of course, is Hawaii's need to attract tourists—for tourism is one of its largest industries. But commercial motivations aside, there's enough genuine aloha to go a long way—and to give you so much to do that it becomes hard to decide what to sample and what to pass up!

There are three vital areas where the action takes place; they surround each other like concentric circles. First, there's Waikiki, the heart of the tourist scene. Some people never leave it and feel they've had a marvelous vacation. Just beyond that is the big, exciting world of Honolulu, one of the great cities (the 12th largest in the United States, in fact). And beyond that, Windward Oahu and the joys of country life and rural beauty. We think you ought to try some of the doings in all three areas.

SUGGESTED ITINERARIES

IF YOU HAVE ONE DAY Get up early, drive, or take the bus to the U.S.S. *Arizona* Memorial at Pearl Harbor. Spend the rest of the day touring the Bishop Museum or loafing on Waikiki Beach.

IF YOU HAVE TWO DAYS Spend your first day as above. Spend the second day driving around the island of Oahu, seeing the Polynesian Cultural Center and the activities of the North Shore at Waimea and Haleiwa.

IF YOU HAVE THREE DAYS Spend your first two days as suggested above. On the third day take a walking tour of downtown Honolulu, stopping in at the Mission Houses Museum, Iolani Palace, and the Hawaii Maritime Center.

IF YOU HAVE FIVE DAYS OR MORE Follow our suggestions above for the first three days. If you have more time, visit the National Memorial Cemetery of the Pacific at Punchbowl Crater, study the masterpieces at the Honolulu Academy of Arts, tour Chinatown or the University of Hawaii, or take the kids to see the dinosaurs at Paradise Park.

1. THE TOP ATTRACTIONS

DOWNTOWN HONOLULU

HONOLULU ACADEMY OF ARTS, 900 S. Beretania St. Tel. 531-8865.

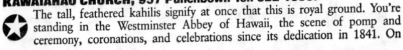

Don't leave Hawaii without a visit to the academy, one of the most beautiful small art museums in the world; it offers a look at the best of both Eastern and Western art. The physical plant is ideal for viewing art, divided as it is into a series of small galleries that open into tranquil courtyards; the Chinese garden, in particular, is exquisite. There's a superb collection of Asian art—a magnificent sculpture of Kwan Yin, the Chinese goddess of mercy; Chinese scrolls and carvings; Korean ceramics; Japanese screens—as well as a good representation of Western masters, including Picasso, Braque, Monet, and van Gogh. Note also the Kress Collection of Italian Renaissance painting. Stop in the bookshop for prints and other distinctive gift items, and perhaps have a meal at the lovely Garden Café (see "Specialty Dining" in Chapter 6).

Admission: Free.

Open: Tues–Sat 10am–4:30pm, Sun 1–5pm. **Bus:** 2; get off at the corner of Ward and Beretania, about a 15-minute ride from Waikiki. **Closed:** Major hols.

THE MISSION HOUSES, 553 S. King St. Tel. 531-0481.

Three 19th-century buildings offer tremendous insight into the lives of the missionaries in Hawaii—and the unlikely intermingling of New England and Polynesia. One of the houses, the home of missionary families, was built of ready-cut lumber that was shipped around Cape Horn from New England; a second, made of coral, houses a replica of the first printing press in the islands, which produced a Hawaiian spelling book in 1822; the third, also of coral, was the warehouse and home of the mission's first business agent.

A new orientation exhibit and video introduces the Mission, its work with Hawaiians, and the controversy that still surrounds the role it played in Hawaii's history. Monthly "Living History" programs feature historical role-playing, hearth cooking, storytelling, work demonstrations, and candlelit evenings. Contact the museum for a current schedule of monthly events.

Be sure to visit the Museum Gift Shop, with an outstanding collection of Hawaiian and Pacific handcrafts, Hawaiian quilt patterns and kits, children's games and clothing, and many books. And try to take one of their morning walking tours of historic Honolulu, held Tuesday through Friday at 9:30am. The cost is $10 for adults, $5 for children 6–15; reservations are required.

Should you happen to be in town in June for the celebration of Kamehameha Day, don't miss their Fancy Fair; or if you're here on the weekend after Thanksgiving, join the festivities at their wonderful Christmas Fair, the opening of the holiday season in Honolulu.

Admission (including 45-minute tour): $5 adults, $3 youths 6–15, free for children under 6.

Open: Tues–Sat 9am–4pm, Sun noon–4pm. **Bus:** 2 to the State Capitol; then walk one block down Punchbowl to King St., turn left, and walk half a block to the Mission Houses. The Waikiki Trolley also passes within a block.

KAWAIAHAO CHURCH, 957 Punchbowl. Tel. 522-1333.

The tall, feathered kahilis signify at once that this is royal ground. You're standing in the Westminster Abbey of Hawaii, the scene of pomp and ceremony, coronations, and celebrations since its dedication in 1841. On

March 12, 1959, the day Hawaii achieved statehood, the old coral church was filled with ecstatic islanders ringing its bell noisily, giving thanks for the fulfillment of a dream long denied. The next day, the Rev. Abraham Akaka linked the spirit of aloha with the spirit of Christianity in a sermon that has since become a classic in the writings of Hawaii. Note the vestibule memorial plaques to Hawaiian royalty and to the Rev. Hiram Bingham, the missionary who designed the church. Note, too, the outstanding collection of portraits of the Hawaiian monarchy by artist Patric. If you have time, come back on Sunday morning at 10:30am to hear a Hawaiian-English service and some beautiful Hawaiian singing.

Admission: Free.

Open: Mon–Fri 9am–3pm, Sat 9am–noon, Sun service at 10:30am. Group tours Mon–Fri by appointment. **Bus:** 2 to Punchbowl and Beretania Sts.; then walk one block to King St.

IOLANI PALACE, S. King and Richards Sts. Tel. 522-0832.

Take a good look at the only royal palace on American soil. Until 1969 the state capitol, it was built during the glittering golden era of Hawaii by King Kalakaua and his queen, Kapiolani. But it housed its royal tenants for only 11 years, from 1882 until the monarchy was overthrown in 1893 by a group of haoles linked to American sugar interests. Kalakaua's successor, his sister, Queen Liliuokalani, spent nine months in the royal bedroom under house arrest after the abortive coup to restore the monarchy. (She is known for her song of farewell, "Aloha Oe.")

Now, after nine years of work and at a total cost of $7 million, a massive restoration has been completed by the Friends of Iolani Palace, and the Hawaiian flag flies over it once again. Some of the furnishings are still being restored, but several rooms are ready for the public, and the American-Florentine building is eminently worth seeing. The crowns of King David Kalakaua and Queen Kapiolani, as well as the royal scepter and sword of state, are on display in the throne room.

Tours are conducted by extremely knowledgeable docents who will fill you in on plenty of Hawaiian history as they show you the throne room with the king's tabu stick (made of a 17-foot narwhal tusk and topped by a gold sphere), the king's quarters, the entry hall, and the dining room with its royal portraits of European monarchs. Reservations are requested, and tickets not claimed 15 minutes before the start of a tour will be sold to anyone who happens to be waiting for a cancellation. You'll have to don enormous khaki "airplane slippers" over your shoes to protect the delicate wooden floors.

Also on the grounds are the Archives of Hawaii (open Monday through Friday from 8am to 4:30pm), the largest collection of Hawaiiana in existence.

Admission: Tours, $4 adults, $1 children 5–12; children under 5 not admitted.

Open: Tours, Wed–Sat every 15 min. 9am–2:15pm. **Bus:** 2 to Punchbowl and Beretania Sts.

HAWAII MARITIME CENTER, Pier 7. Tel. 536-6373.

The Hawaii Maritime Center brings the stories of Hawaii's seas to life. The newest of the center's components—and its crowning glory—is the stunning, $6-million Kalakaua Boathouse, named after King David Kalakaua (the "Merry Monarch"). He was devoted to water sports, and his late 19th-century boathouse—of which the new structure is reminiscent in design—stood very close to this location. There's plenty to see here, so plan at least an hour to take it all in. William Conrad, the film and TV actor, narrates the museum's Sony Walkman Audio Tour.

Tastefully designed and brilliantly executed, the center traces the maritime history of Hawaii from the first Polynesian settlers of the islands, and encompasses the arrival of the first Westerners, whalers, missionaries, plantation workers, and visitors. Suspended from the ceiling are giant canoes that once voyaged across the Pacific. On the second floor, you'll want to linger at such displays as the 1850s ship chandlery, a full-scale, walk-in diorama of H. Hackfeld & Co., the all-purpose whaler's store that later became Hawaii's leading department store, Liberty House! Dioramas and exhibits of the famed Matson Line luxury ships of the 1930s and 1940s recall the langorous romanticism of early Hawaiian tourism. Audiovisual exhibits—like the one showing scenes from the 1922 silent film on whaling, *Down to the Sea in Ships*—abound.

At Pier 7 you can see the *Hokule'a*, a Hawaiian double-hulled canoe that is a replica of the one in which the islands' first settlers are believed to have sailed from the Society Islands, using no instruments or charts—only stars, planets, and ocean signs. Also here is the national historic landmark *Falls of Clyde,* the only four-masted, full-rigged sailing ship in existence. Climb the nine (short) flights to the Widow's Walk to see a glorious view of Honolulu Harbor. The gift shop has Boat Day posters, T-shirts decorated with old prints, *Falls of Clyde* aloha shirts, shark's-teeth pendants, and the like.

Kids will enjoy everything here, and especially a visit to the *Cory Sause,* where they can steer a tot-size replica of a ship.

Note: From the Hawaii Maritime Center, you're just a short walk from the **Aloha Tower** at Pier 9. Long a symbol of Honolulu, it provides a good view of the harbor and the city in all directions, and it's also a fine spot for nighttime photography of harbor lights and the downtown area. Open daily from 8am to 9pm.

Admission (including boarding *Falls of Clyde*): $7 adults, $4 children 6–17, free for children under 6.

Open: Daily 9:30am–5pm. **Bus:** 19 or 20 (Airport) to the Federal Building. There's a free shuttle via Hilo Hattie buses; the Waikiki Trolley also stops here.

PUNCHBOWL, LOWER TANTALUS & NUUANU

NATIONAL MEMORIAL CEMETERY OF THE PACIFIC, Punchbowl Crater. Tel. 541-1434.

Buried inside the crater of an extinct volcano (named, with prophetic irony, the Hill of Sacrifice by the ancient Hawaiians) are some 26,000 American service personnel who perished in the Pacific during World War II, the Korean War, and the Vietnam War. Astronaut Ellison Onizuka is also buried here. Also listed here are the names of all Pacific war service people who have been recorded as missing or lost or buried at sea (visit the administration office for information regarding grave locations).

Parents from all over the mainland and from the islands come to Punchbowl on pilgrimages. The endless rows of gravestones of young people form a sobering sight, an awesome monument to the futility of war. When you've had enough, walk for another 10 minutes to the lookout at the crater's rim for a sweeping panorama of Honolulu just below.

Admission: Free.

Open: Oct–Feb, daily 8am–5:30pm; Mar–Sept, daily 8:30am–6:30pm. *Note:* Possible federal budget cuts may necessitate closings on some days; call before coming out. **Directions:** Take bus no. 2 from Waikiki toward town (request a transfer). Get off at Alapai Street and walk half a block left and pick up bus no. 15 (Pacific Heights); this leaves every hour on the half hour, so time your trip carefully. Get off at Puowaina Drive and walk approximately 10 minutes.

QUEEN EMMA SUMMER PALACE, 2913 Pali Hwy. Tel. 595-3167.

Emma and her consort, King Kamehameha IV, called their Victorian country retreat Hanaiakamalama, and it is faithfully maintained as a museum by the

Daughters of Hawaii. Hawaiiana mingles comfortably with the 19th-century European furnishings of which Hawaiian royalty was so fond. There are conducted tours through the rooms for all visitors. Stop in at the gift shop for Hawaiian books, notepaper, postcards, and other items.

Admission: $4 adults, $1 children 12–18, 50¢ children under 12.

Open: Daily 9am–4pm. **Directions:** From Waikiki take bus no. 20 toward town (request a transfer); get off at corner of King and Bethel Sts. and change to bus no. 4 (Nuuanu/Dowsett); ask driver to let you off near the palace.

ROYAL MAUSOLEUM, 2261 Nuuanu Ave.

Here's where the last of the Kamehameha and Kalakau dynasties and others of royal blood are buried. The curator gives a short orientation in the chapel; then you're free to pay your respects.

Admission: Free.

Open: Mon–Fri 8am–4:30pm. **Closed:** Hols, except Kuhio Day (Mar 26) and Kamehameha Day (June 11). **Directions:** See Queen Emma Summer Palace, above.

FOSTER BOTANICAL GARDEN, 50 N. Vineyard Blvd. Tel. 522-7060.

This is a marvelously cool oasis on a hot day, and one of the most impressive botanical collections to be found anywhere. There are 15 acres of rare trees, flowers, plants, and unusual species of vegetation, many of them from Asia. Orchids bloom throughout the year. Here you can measure your minuteness against a tree 20 times taller than you are, and ogle such rare specimens as the cannonball tree, the bombax, and the sunshine tree. On the grounds is a C-shaped granite monument, presented in 1960 to Honolulu by its cousin city of Hiroshima, from which most of the first Japanese immigrants came to work the island plantations. A free, self-guided-tour brochure is available at the reception office.

Note: Foster Botanical Garden is one component of the Honolulu Botanical Gardens, which also has three other splendid gardens to visit: the **Wahiawa Botanical Garden** in Wahiawa, a 27-acre rain forest in central Oahu; **Hoomaluhia Botanical Gardens** in Kaneohe, 400 lush acres at the base of the Koolau mountains in Windward Oahu; and **Koko Crater Botanical Garden,** near Sandy Beach, still in the early stages of development. For information on all of these gardens, phone 522-7060.

Admission: $1, free for children under 13 with an adult; guided tours free.

Open: Daily 9am–4pm. Guided tours Mon–Wed at 1pm (reservations necessary). **Closed:** New Year's Day, Christmas Day. **Directions:** From Waikiki take bus no. 2, 19, or 20 (Airport or Airport–Hickam) toward town (request a transfer); get off at the corner of Hotel and Bethel Sts. and change to bus no. 4 (Nuuanu/Dowsett); ask the driver to let you off at the garden.

UNIVERSITY OF HAWAII

UNIVERSITY OF HAWAII, Manoa Campus. Tel. 965-8855.

Although many of Hawaii's socially prominent families still send their children off to mainland colleges (in the old days it was the Punahou–Yale route), the island's own university is the goal of thousands of others. Established in 1907 as a small agricultural and mechanical arts college, the university has grown into an important center for the study of tropical agriculture, marine biology, geophysics, astronomy, linguistics, and other fields. Its student body of more than 21,000 reflects the multiracial composition of the population of Hawaii. In addition, students come from the 49 other states and more than 60 foreign countries.

The **East-West Center** at the Manoa campus is particularly noteworthy. A meeting place of Eastern and Occidental cultures, it brings students, professionals, and research scholars here from Asia, the Pacific islands, and the United States for an

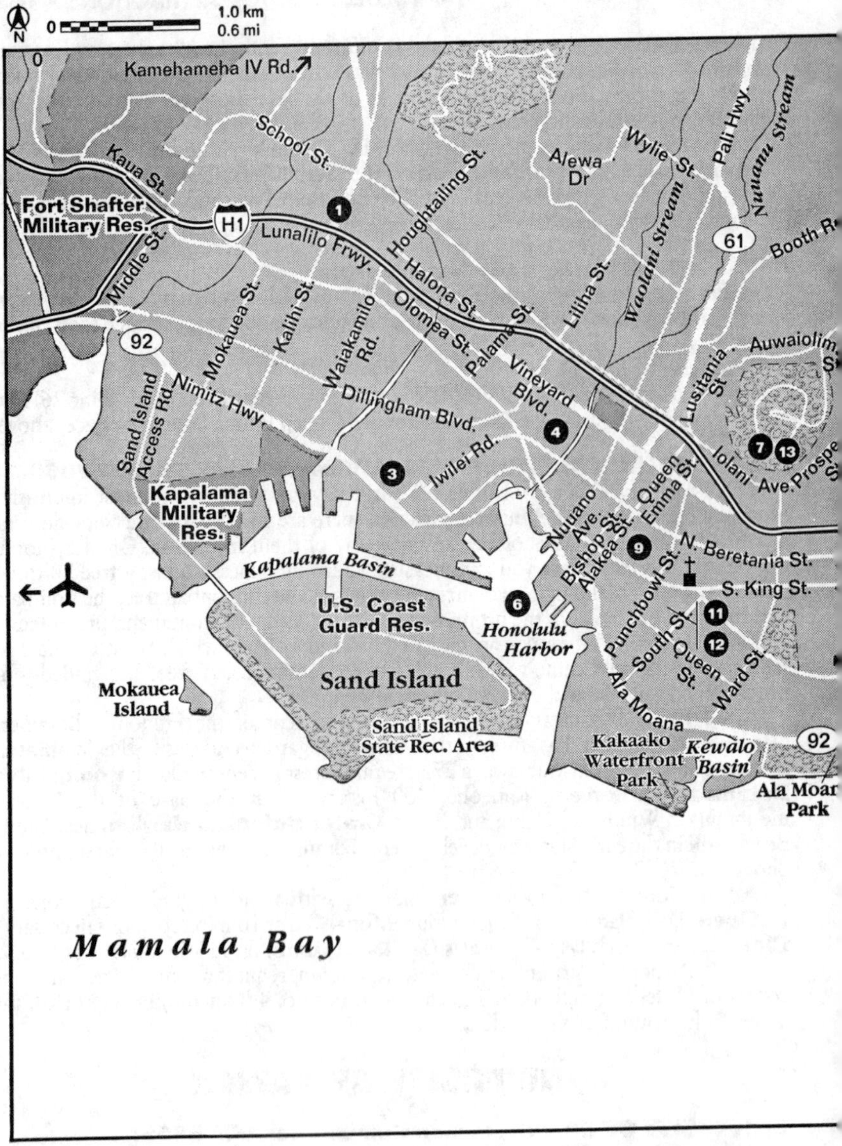

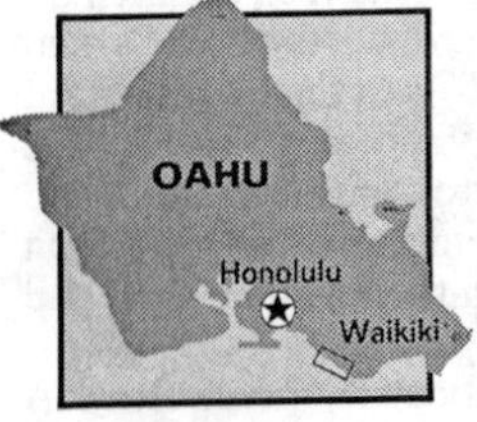

- Bishop Museum 1
- Damien Museum 2
- Dole Pineapple Cannery 3
- Foster Botanical Garden 4
- Gandhi Statue 5
- Hawaii Maritime Center 6
- Honolulu Academy of Arts 7
- Honolulu Zoo 8
- Iolani Palace 9
- Kapiolani Park 10
- Kawaiahao Church 11
- Mission House Museum

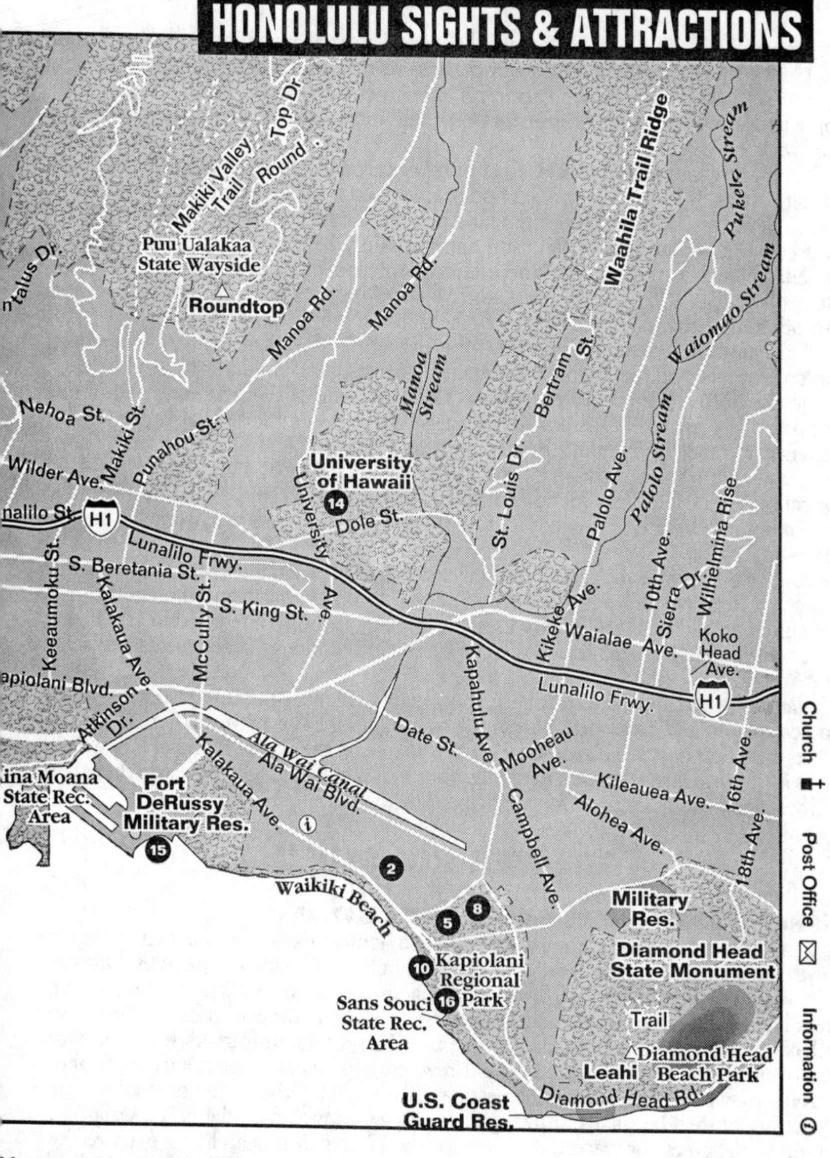

National Memorial Cemetery of the Pacific 13
University of Hawaii 14
U.S. Army Museum 15
Waikiki Aquarium 16

exciting exchange of ideas. All students have been given awards that send them first to the University of Hawaii and later out on field work—in the mainland United States for the Asians, in Asia or the Pacific for the Americans. Later, most Asians return home to teach or work in government posts, and most Americans, too, will go to live and work in Asia.

The starkly simple East-West Center buildings are a masterful blend of Eastern and Western styles. Free tours leave Wednesday at 1:30pm from the Friends Lounge on the garden level of Thomas Jefferson Hall, but it's easy enough to walk around by yourself. The lounge area of Jefferson must certainly be one of the most interesting student centers in the world. Where else might you pick up copies of *Thailand Illustrated, The Wall Street Journal,* and *Social Casework,* all from one rack? Asian and other art exhibitions are frequently held in the lounge art gallery.

Walk now to the rear of Jefferson for a peaceful moment at the lyrical Japanese garden, with its waterfalls, stone ornaments, lanterns, and flashing carp. And be sure to see the **John Fitzgerald Kennedy Theater,** one of the best equipped in the world for staging both Western and Eastern dramas. It's the official home of the university's dance and drama department, and a technological center that draws theater people from both sides of the Pacific to study, teach, and produce plays. A typical season includes productions of a Japanese Kabuki classic, Shakespeare, and a contemporary Broadway comedy. An authentic Beijing opera was recently staged here—in English.

You'll want to tour the rest of the University of Hawaii campus, too. Stop in at the University Relations office in Bachman Annex 6 to obtain maps and directions for a self-guided tour. You'll find plenty to see, especially if you're interested in art: There are two art galleries, and frescoes, sculptures, and works in other media are seen everywhere.

Nature-lovers can have a treat here, too, trying to identify the 560 or so varieties of tropical plants and trees that bloom all over campus. The university's map shows names and locations. We'll give you a start: The tree on the side of Hawaii Hall, which looks as if it has large sausages dangling from it, is a native of West Africa, where the oddly shaped fruits are used for medicinal purposes.

GREATER HONOLULU

BISHOP MUSEUM, 1525 Bernice St. Tel. 847-3511.

Inside the museum's stone walls (which look more like those of a fortress than a museum) is a world center for the study of the Pacific—its peoples, culture, history, artifacts. Most fascinating for visitors is the Hawaiian Hall, where special exhibits illustrate particular aspects of early Hawaiian culture. Note the collection of priceless feather cloaks; one uses half a million feathers from the rare mamo bird (each bird produced only a few feathers, so the kings built up feather treasuries—which were among the prime spoils of war). Other exhibits re-create the way of life of the Hawaiians, showing the outrigger canoes, a model heiau, weapons, wooden calabashes, or trace the history of the Hawaiian monarchy or explore the marine and plant life of the Pacific. A "please touch" gallery for children in the Hall of Discovery ties in with exhibits throughout the museum. All this, plus the fascinating exhibits of ethnographic art, makes for a rewarding visit, worth as much time as you can give it. You can have an inexpensive snack at the Museum Lanai Restaurant. Stop in, too, at Shop Pacifica for Hawaiian gifts, a cut above the usual, with books on Hawaiian and other Pacific cultures, handcrafted feather leis and native koa-wood boxes and bowls, reproductions of Polynesian artifacts, and rare and unique jewelry of the Pacific.

Note: If you're interested in studying **Hawaiian crafts,** you've come to the right place. Classes are held Monday through Saturday from 9am to 3pm, at a nominal charge (usually $5, plus a materials cost). It's quilting on Monday and Friday, fresh-flower lei-making on Tuesday, lauhala weaving and hula-implement making on Wednesday. Classes are held in the Atherton Halau (call 847-3511 for schedules), also the site of special events, which are usually held on weekends. Inquire, too, about field trips and special programs.

Admission (including a show at the adjacent Atherton Halau and entrance to Kilolani Planetarium): $5.95 adults, $4.95 children 6–17, active military, and senior citizens. Children under 6 free.

Open: Mon–Sat and first Sun of every month 9am–5pm. **Closed:** Christmas. **Directions:** Bus no. 2 to School and Kapalama Sts.; walk one block makai on Kapalama and then turn right on Bernice St.; the entrance is midblock.

KILOLANI PLANETARIUM. Tel. 848-4136 for recorded program information.

Sharing the grounds of the Bishop Museum is Kilolani Planetarium, a great spot for anyone interested in space exploration and astronomy. Sky shows are held every day at 11am and 2pm, and also on Friday and Saturday at 7pm. After the evening shows, there's free observatory telescope viewing, weather permitting.

Admission: $2.50; or included with museum admission.

Directions: See Bishop Museum, above.

PEARL HARBOR

U.S.S. *ARIZONA* MEMORIAL. Tel. 422-0561.

Anyone who remembers—or has heard about—December 7, 1941, should not leave the Hawaiian Islands without seeing Pearl Harbor. As many as 5,000 visitors—many from Japan—come here every day. The handsome $4.2-million visitor center provides the starting point for your boat trip to the U.S.S. *Arizona* Memorial. Its museum contains exhibits related to the events surrounding the attack on Pearl Harbor by the Empire of Japan. Step up to the information desk where you will be given a tour number, and find out approximately when your shuttle boat will leave. Expect a wait of approximately two hours. While you're waiting, you can study a detailed mural of the *Arizona* or check out the books in the bookshop. When your number is called, you enter the theater to see a 20-minute film, and then are ferried on a navy boat to the memorial.

Dedicated in 1962, the memorial is a covered white-concrete bridge rising starkly above the hull of the battleship *Arizona,* victim of a direct hit on the day that bombs fell on Hawaii, and the tomb of more than 1,000 American service personnel (some 2,403 in all were killed that day). The outlines of the ship shimmer just below the water, and oil slicks still rise from the rusting hulk. Like Punchbowl Crater, it's an eloquent witness to the fury and folly of war. A big experience.

Note: If the weather is stormy, call the *Arizona* Memorial at 422-0561 to find out if the boats will be operating. Bathing suits and bare feet are taboo.

If you have time, you can take a short walk from the *Arizona* Memorial to visit ***Bowfin* Park** (tel. 423-1341 for information), where the U.S.S. *Bowfin,* a World War II submarine launched one year after the attack on Pearl Harbor, is moored. Next to the submarine is the ***Bowfin* Museum,** with fascinating submarine memorabilia and a gift shop. You can look through periscopes at a new structure built over the submarine's conning tower. A memorial honors submariners lost during World War II. Admission is $6 for adults ($1 for military personnel with ID), $1 for children 6–12. Open daily from 8am to 4:30pm.

Admission: Free.

Open: Tours daily 8am–3pm. **Directions:** From Waikiki, bus no. 20 goes to Pearl City; from the Ala Moana Center, take bus no. 51 or 52. The trip should take about an hour. Ask the driver to let you off at the U.S.S. *Arizona* Memorial. Private bus service is $6 round-trip (tel. 926-4747).

PEARL HARBOR BY SEA

Another way to get to Pearl Harbor—and a moving and dramatic one—is by sea, aboard Paradise Cruise's sleek new luxury vessel, *Star of Honolulu.* During the roughly 45-minute cruise to Pearl, '40s music plays on the loudspeaker, and a thoughtful narration, in both English and Japanese, sets the scene for the momentous events of December 7, 1941. At the *Arizona* Memorial, the ship stops for a few moments as the captain tosses a lei upon the waters in tribute to those still entombed there. Also clearly visible is the wreckage of the battleship *Omaha* nearby. The trip takes the better part of the morning (from about an 8am pickup at Waikiki hotels to a return around noon). Cost is $20 adults, $10 for children. Highly recommended. For reservations, call 536-3641, or toll free 800/334-6191 from the continental U.S.

2. MORE ATTRACTIONS

CANNERY SQUARE

DOLE PINEAPPLE CANNERY, at Cannery Square. Tel. 523-3653.

In this worthwhile family excursion, you can tour the Dole Pineapple plant, visit the Hawaii Children's Museum of Arts, Culture, Science and Technology (see "Cool for Kids," below), and do a little shopping at the same time.

The visit to the world's largest fruit cannery begins in the Dole Theatre with a multimedia show and proceeds to the walk-through tour of the cannery itself; overhead video displays explain the operations each step of the way. The sheer size and efficiency of the operation is impressive. You'll see thousands and thousands of pineapples bobbing along on huge conveyor belts, looking oddly like lambs for the slaughter. There's an amazing machine (the Ginaca) that can peel and core 100 pineapples in 60 seconds! And there are rows of workers checking and sorting the fruit before it goes into the cans; during the height of the summer harvest season, when the cannery operates at peak capacity, many of the workers are high school and college students earning next year's tuition. That silly-looking pineapple on top of the building, by the way, is not filled with pineapple juice; it's the water tower.

When you come to the end of the tour you'll be given free juice and a taste of pineapple. After that, you may want to stop for a snack or do some shopping at Cannery Square. Of interest is the Logo Shop, featuring T-shirts, visors, and assorted paraphernalia bearing the Dole logo; the Dole Marketplace for pineapples to ship home; and Island Accents, which has some interesting jewelry and wood carvings. Good Vibrations has novelties to take home as memorabilia, Island Gems shows costume jewelry at reasonable prices, and Pearl Factory is one of the ubiquitous places where you buy an oyster and gamble on the pearl you'd like to find inside.

Note: Trips to the cannery are widely advertised for 50¢, but that covers only transportation and admission to Cannery Square, which features a shopping mall, a restaurant, and some historical displays. There is a charge (see below for the actual tour of the cannery). Our personal feeling is that the trip, in a neat little air-conditioned bus, is worth your time (it actually makes for a pleasant little sightseeing tour), but if you're watching your pennies and if there are several in your group, the admission fee is a factor to consider.

Admission: $5 for the full tour, when the cannery is in operation; $1.50 for a mini-tour, when the cannery is not; 50¢ children 5–12; free for children under 5.

Open: Daily 9am–4pm. **Transportation:** Take the "Pineapple Express" bus, which makes frequent pickups at major stops in Waikiki (50¢ one way), or bus no. 19 (Airport–Hickam).

LYON ARBORETUM, 3860 Manoa Rd. Tel. 988-7378.

Few tourists know about the arboretum, but Honolulu residents certainly do. It's prized as one of the most beautiful nature spots in Honolulu, an important research facility for the University of Hawaii, and an educational center where you can take short courses in such subjects as flower arrangement, bonsai, island cookery, orchid growing, and much more. You're welcome to visit on your own, admiring the beautiful gardens lush with orchids, camellias, gardenias, ginger, coffee, and many native plants; if you can manage to take a tour (see below), even better. Visit the gift and book store, which has high-quality items: haku leis, palm-seed and fungus jewelry, handmade cards, books on horticulture and Hawaiian history, kukui leaf T-shirts, and implements for use in Hawaiian crafts. Write for a class schedule.

Admission: $1 Donation requested.

Open: Mon–Fri 9am–3pm, Sat 9am–noon. Tours given first Fri and third Wed at 1pm, third Sat at 10am; group tours by prior arrangement. **Closed:** Public hols.

FROMMER'S FAVORITE HONOLULU/OAHU EXPERIENCES

Annual Lei Day/May Day concert at Waikiki Shell On May 1, everybody wears leis and there are contests for the most beautiful, with judging at Kapiolani Park. In the evening, the Brothers Cazimero present a fabulous show, and all Honolulu, in their aloha finery, turns out to attend. A joyous event.

Young People's Hula Show Sunday morning at 9:30, on the Centerstage at the Ala Moana Shopping Center. The performers, ranging in age from about 3 to the teens, are talented amateurs, bursting with charm and aloha. It's free, and more enjoyable than many a slick nightclub show.

Sunset cocktails at open-air House Without a Key At the Halekulani Hotel. As you watch the sun sink slowly into the Pacific, and a beautiful hula girl dances to melodious music, you know picture-postcard Hawaii still exists.

A walk through historic Chinatown Examine the open-air fish and vegetable stalls at the Oahu Market, peek in at herbalist's shops and noodle factories, stop for goodies at the Chinese bakeries, and end with a visit to some of the town's most sophisticated art galleries.

A swim at Sans Souci Beach Across from Kapiolani Park, the ocean is gentle, the water temperature perfect, and the crowds far away.

Snorkeling at Hanauma Bay This idyllic beach cove, created centuries ago when one side of Koko Head Crater was washed into the sea, is now a marine reserve, and the fish are so gentle that they eat right out of your hand.

A visit to Byodo-In Temple on Windward Oahu This exact replica of the venerable Byodo-In in Japan has a magnificent carving of Amida, the Buddha of the Western Paradise.

Directions: Take TheBUS no. 8 from Waikiki to Ala Moana; transfer to no. 5 (Paradise Park); then walk approximately 15 minutes.

WAIKIKI

U.S. ARMY MUSEUM, Fort DeRussy Park. Tel. 438-2821.

Housed in Battery Randolph, built in 1909 as a key installation in defense of Honolulu and Pearl Harbor, this museum contains military memorabilia dating from ancient Hawaiian warfare to the present. On the upper deck, the Corps of Engineers Pacific Regional Visitors Center graphically shows how the corps works with the civilian community in managing water resources in an island environment.

Admission: Free.

Open: Tues–Sun 10am–4:30pm. **Bus:** 8 (Ala Moana Center) from Kuhio Avenue, in an Ewa direction.

DAMIEN MUSEUM, 130 Ohua St. Tel. 923-2690.

In the Diamond Head area, behind St. Augustine's Catholic Church, this small museum presents a moving account of the work that Father Damien did with the victims of leprosy on the island of Molokai. The museum contains prayer books used by Father Damien in his ministry, as well as his personal items. A continuously running video, recounting Damien's story, is narrated by Terence Knapp, a local actor who has portrayed Father Damien in award-winning performances on stage and on TV. He fittingly honors one of Hawaii's heroes.

Admission: Free; donations accepted.

Open: Mon–Fri 9am–3pm, Sat 9am–noon. **Closed:** Holidays. **Directions:** Within walking distance of most major hotels, or take TheBUS no. 8, 19, or 20, running in a Diamond Head direction.

GANDHI STATUE, in front of the Honolulu Zoo.

A new addition to the Hawaii scene is an impressive statue of Mahatma Gandhi, recently unveiled by the City and County of Honolulu and the Gandhi Memorial International Foundation. Created by the artist Zlatko Paunov of New York and a gift to the people of Hawaii from the Jhamanadas Watumull Fund, the statue is accompanied by a plaque quoting from Gandhi's philosophy: "It is possible to live in peace."

Directions: See Honolulu Zoo, below.

HONOLULU ZOO, 151 Kapahulu Ave. Tel. 971-7171.

The Honolulu Zoo is noted for its collection of native Hawaiian and other tropical birds, displayed in various bird-jungle habitats. There's also an elephant given to the children of Hawaii by Indira Gandhi (try to catch the elephant show; call for schedule), a Bengal tiger, four lions, and four adorable Himalayan sun bears. Three species of lemurs (primitive monkeys) are very popular and active exhibits. With Diamond Head providing the background, plenty of trees and flowers (including a giant banyan and date palms), white doves, and keikis tumbling about, it's one of the most charming small zoos anywhere. At the moment, it's undergoing a multi-million-dollar renovation. Phase I, "The African Savannah," is now under way.

During the summer there's free entertainment on Wednesday starting at 6pm at the stage under the earpod tree, just behind the flamingos. Take a picnic supper and join the fun. Local artists hang their work on the fence outside on Tuesday, Saturday, and Sunday. Be sure to stop in at Zootique, the charming gift shop.

Admission: $3 adults, free for ages 12 and under.

Open: Daily 8:30am–4pm (June–Aug, also Wed to 7:30pm). **Closed:** New Year's Day and Christmas Day. **Directions:** You can walk from most major hotels, or take TheBUS no. 8, 19, 20, 58, or 2 (Kapiolani Park), running in a Diamond Head direction.

KAPIOLANI PARK, Kalakaua and Monsarrat Aves.

The 220 acres of the park have facilities for just about everything from tennis, soccer, and rugby to archery and picnicking. The Royal Hawaiian Band plays frequently in the bandstand, and major musical events take place in the Waikiki Shell. For a particularly beautiful view, note Diamond Head framed in the cascading waters of the splendid Louise C. Dillingham Fountain.

Bordering the ocean on the right is a stretch of wide, palm-dotted grass lawn with a fringe of sand to let you know you're still at the beach. Swimming here is excellent, since the surf is quite mild; it's a big favorite with local families. **Kapiolani Beach Park,** with locker room, rest rooms, picnic tables, and snack bar, is just ahead.

Admission: Free.

Directions: Take TheBUS no. 2 (Waikiki–Kapiolani Park) from Kuhio Ave. in a Diamond Head direction.

WAIKIKI AQUARIUM, 2777 Kalakaua Ave. Tel. 923-9741.

Here's your chance to see, among other sea creatures, such as giant clams and sharks, the *lauwiliwilinukunukuoioi;* if you can't pronounce it, just ask for the long-nosed butterfly fish. An outdoor display, **Edge of the Reef,** is a simulated living reef environment that includes hundreds of colorful fish, live coral, and a tidal surge. Stop in to see their attractive gift shop, the Natural Selection. Everything in it, from T-shirts with fish designs, books, posters, cards, linen, and home accessories—relates to the ocean and its life forms. They have a good selection of children's toys and books, too.

Admission: $3 donation requested; free for children 16 and under.

Open: Daily 9am–5pm. **Closed:** Thanksgiving and Christmas. **Directions:** Take TheBUS no. 2 (Waikiki–Kapiolani Park) from Kuhio Ave. in a Diamond Head direction.

READERS RECOMMEND

United Fishing Agency, *117 Ahui St. (tel. 536-2148). "A fish auction is held every Monday through Saturday at 5:30am at United Fishing Agency. We went about 7am and saw fish we didn't know existed, such as a 114-pound moon fish. This auction was far bigger than others we've seen and the people were more than happy to answer our questions."*—Kenneth Kendall, Omaha, Neb.

THE ART SCENE

A lot of good artists are coming out of Hawaii—young people with a mixture of backgrounds whose work shows multiple influences. Perhaps because of the natural beauty that surrounds them, their paintings tend to be more representational here than in other art centers, but ways of seeing are as modern as they are in Paris or New York. Not a few have married Eastern atmosphere with Western techniques, another example of the fortuitous cross-fertilization that goes on in every area of Hawaiian life.

GALLERIES AROUND THE ISLAND

As you drive around the island, you'll have a chance to visit several worthwhile galleries. The ✪ **Ko'olau Gallery,** located on the second level of the Windward Mall Shopping Center in Kaneohe, is a co-op gallery, staffed by the artists themselves, showing a variety of locally produced artworks in many media. Over 30 artists from around the island are represented. You can say hello to the gallery artists daily from 9:30am to 9pm. Also in Kaneohe, serious lovers of art and beauty must not miss a visit to ✪ **Hart, Tagami & Powell Gallery and Gardens,** 45-754 Lamaula Rd., where painters Hiroshi Tagami and Michael Powell open their gallery and tranquil Japanese gardens to visitors on Saturday, Sunday, and Monday from around 10am to 3:30pm. An appointment is necessary: Call 239-8146. The **Fetting Art Studios,** 61431 Kam Hwy. in Haleiwa (tel. 637-4933), specializing in Hawaiiana, has always been a good spot to see works by local artists and craftspeople. Phone for an appointment.

GALLERIES IN TOWN

Art is, in fact, everywhere in Honolulu; the builders of large public facilities are becoming more and more art-conscious, and you'll find monumental pieces of sculpture—some outstanding, such as a Henry Moore in Tamarind Park at Bishop and King Streets downtown, some less distinguished—in such places as the Ala Moana Shopping Center, Hemmeter Center, Royal Hawaiian Center, the Waikiki Shopping Plaza, the University of Hawaii, the state capitol, and at Sea Life Park in Windward Oahu. The fountain sculptures at Ala Moana are particularly worth a look.

To see some excellent works by Hawaii's talented craftspeople (and perhaps to pick up some distinctive small presents), pop into some of our favorite places. **Following Sea,** at the Kahala Mall Shopping Center, 4211 Waialae Ave. (tel. 734-4425), is a visual experience. It presents the works of many American craftspeople in ceramics, glass, jewelry, fiber, and woodwork. Each piece is more glorious than the next. Many island artists are represented. A high level of taste and artistry is evident in the works found at **Nohea** at Ward Warehouse. Quality crafts have come to the heart of Waikiki: The **Crafts Court** at Kuhio Mall is an artisans' working gallery, featuring handcrafted jewelry, pottery, weavings, ceramics, clothing, painting, and more.

A great lady of the arts in Hawaii was Madge Tennent, who came to Hawaii at the turn of the century via South Africa and Paris and broke away from the academy and its conventions to record on canvas her massive portraits of the Hawaiian people. You can visit her gallery, the **Tennent Art Foundation,** on the slopes of Punchbowl at 203 Prospect St. (tel. 531-1987), from 10am to noon Tuesday through Saturday, 2 to 4pm on Sunday, or by special appointment.

Other fine galleries are all over town. You'll want to visit **Arts of Paradise** on the second floor of the International Market Place. Artist-owned, it features work in all media of Hawaii's top professional artists. Call about free demonstrations and talks by participating artists (tel. 924-2787). Then there's **Images International of Hawaii,** with galleries at Ala Moana Shopping Center, at Palm Boulevard (tel. 926-5081), and at Otsuka Gallerie (tel. 947-5081), featuring internationally acclaimed artists: Hisashi Otsuka, Caroline Young, Tatsuo Ito, Raymond Page, Gary Hostallero, and leather sculptor Liu Miao Chan. Worth your attention at Ward Centre is **Art A La Carte** (tel. 536-3351), an artists' co-op featuring ceramics as well as paintings.

Downtown, the impressive **Honolulu Advertiser Gallery** on the first floor of the News Building at 605 Kapiolani Blvd. (tel. 526-1322) continues to be a showcase for local and mainland artists despite its new galleries at the Contemporary Museum (see below). The **Gallery at Pauahi Tower** in Bishop Square always has an outstanding show running. For the past 20 years the **Territorial Savings and Loan Association** has been presenting exhibitions by Hawaii's artists as a public service (no commission is taken) at its Downtown Office Gallery, Ground Floor, Financial Plaza of the Pacific, at the corner of Bishop and Merchant Streets (tel. 523-0211). Exhibits are open Monday through Thursday from 8am to 3:30pm, and on Friday to 6pm, January through November. The **AMFAC Plaza Exhibition Room** at

AMFAC Center, Fort Street Mall and Queen Street, has interesting group exhibitions of contemporary paintings, crafts, sculpture, and photography, as well as cultural and historical presentations. Exhibitions change monthly. It's open 9am to 5pm Monday through Friday. On Saturday and Sunday, local artists exhibit and sell their work on the zoo fence near Kapiolani Park.

In Chinatown Something of an artistic renaissance is going on in Chinatown these days. Old buildings have been refurbished, there is new construction, and a small artistic colony continues to grow. At last count, there were a dozen galleries here: Take a little time to explore them. Pen-and-ink artist **Ramsay,** who has achieved national and international fame (an exhibition of her masterful architectural drawings appeared at the Senate Rotunda in Washington, D.C., in 1988), has her own gallery at 1128 Smith St. (tel. 537-2787), where she also shows works by prominent artists in other media. Next door is her café, with a sophisticated, medium-priced menu. **Pegge Hopper,** whose images of Polynesian women are seen everywhere in the islands, also has her own gallery here, at 1164 Nuuanu Ave. (tel. 524-1164). It features Hopper's original paintings, drawings, and collages, in addition to her posters, limited-edition prints, calendars, and gift items. At the corner, at 1050 Nuuanu, is an upbeat gallery, the **Gateway Gallery** (tel. 599-1559), featuring fine arts and unique gift items. They specialize in floral and tropical theme paintings and sculpture. Accessories start at $20.

At **Bakkus Gallery,** 928 Nuuanu Ave. (tel. 528-4677), owner Shirley Kukonu shows original island artwork both lovely and witty, great artisan jewelry, handcrafted gifts, and some smashing clothing—both hand-painted and manufactured. **Robyn Buntin** of Honolulu, 999 Maunakea (tel. 599-3920), excels in Japanese art—modern printing, antiques, and jewelry. The **Waterfall Gallery,** 1600-A Nuuanu Ave. (tel. 521-6863), shows a collection of fine arts and crafts from the Pacific Rim, as well as fine art photography by founder William Waterfall.

THE CONTEMPORARY MUSEUM AT THE SPALDING ESTATE, 2411 Makiki Heights Dr. Tel. 526-1322.

★ With the opening of this museum, Honolulu has become the art center of the Pacific. The lovely old 1920s mansion in a magnificent garden setting overlooking the city and the sea has been transformed into a series of state-of-the-art galleries, housing exhibits focusing on 40 years of art in Hawaii. Local artists like Jean Charlot and Madge Tennent are represented, as are such internationally known stars as the late Andy Warhol. A permanent pavilion houses David Hockney's stage set from the Metropolitan Opera production of *L'Enfant et les Sortilèges,* complete with a stereo sound system playing the Ravel opera that inspired this major work. Docent tours are available. Galleries, art, gardens—all vie for attention. The gardens alone, a series of exquisite terraces meandering down to a stream bed, falls, and pools, are worth the trip. They were designed by a Japanese landscape artist as a place to meditate and experience harmony, so each vista has its stone seat for contemplation. There's also an attractive gift shop with artist-designed T-shirts, jewelry, cards, and the like, and the Contemporary Café, an indoor-outdoor eating spot with sophisticated cuisine and moderate prices (see Chapter 6 for details).

Admission: $4 ages 15 and over; free for children under 15; free for everyone Thurs.

Open: Tues–Sat 10am–4pm, Sun noon–4pm. **Bus:** 15 to Makiki Heights Dr.

3. COOL FOR KIDS

In addition to the attractions listed below, your kids will also enjoy several of the attractions already described. At Pearl Harbor, U.S. history comes to life for children, with a visit to the U.S.S. *Arizona* Memorial and *Bowfin* Park. At the Hawaii Maritime Center, kids can steer a child-size ship's replica. At the Kahala Hilton Hotel kids can get close to porpoises at the daily feedings.

HAWAII CHILDREN'S MUSEUM OF ARTS, CULTURE, SCIENCE & TECHNOLOGY, Cannery Square. Tel. 522-0040.

If you've brought the kids with you, don't leave Cannery Square without a visit to this delightful museum, so enthralling, in fact, that it's worth an excursion in its own right. It's a state-of-the-art learning center, where everything is designed to give the child a hands-on experience. Five main galleries all revolve around "You . . . Wonderful You." Kids unzip a seven-foot-tall doll and take out its organs or actually walk through a huge mouth. They can ride a bike next to a kid-size skeleton (suitably attired in bike helmet and athletic shoes) also riding a bike and see what bones come into play in bike-riding. They can play with gigantic soap bubbles, work with pulleys and gears, or explore a bug zoo.

Admission: $5 adults, $3 children 2–17.

Open: Tues–Fri 9am–1pm, Sat–Sun 10am–4pm.

PARADISE PARK, 3737 Manoa Rd. Tel. 988-0200.

A $5-million renovation has made this old favorite for families with children even better than before. Located on 15 acres of lush tropical rain forest atop Manoa Valley, filled with tropical plants, flowers, and exotic birds, Paradise Park now houses a crew of Dinamation's Dinosaurs, more than a dozen amazingly lifelike robotic creatures that move and roar to life around every bend. Children will be thrilled by Hale Nane (House of Fascination), which features exhibits that come to life with movement and sound, including a "ground-shaking" exhibit of volcanic activity and earthquakes. At the Discovery Center, they'll explore interactive scientific amusements that focus on rainbows, light, water, and color. Visitors may take self-guided walking tours to discover the ginger, orchids, coffee trees, bamboo forest, koloa ducks, koi ponds, and more, and visit the five ethnic "Gardens of Color."

Aviaries housing hundreds of exotic birds, ranging from bright red-and-green macaws to snow-white, plumed cockatoos are scattered throughout the grounds. Rare Hawaiian nene (geese), flamingos, peacocks, and pheasants wander the grounds, and can be persuaded to pose for photographs. The Treetops Restaurant provides an island-style buffet lunch.

Admission: $14.95 adults, $7.95 children 3–12, free for children under 3.

Open: Daily 9:30am–5pm. **Bus:** 8 from Waikiki to Ala Moana; then transfer to no. 5 to Paradise Park.

4. WALKING TOURS

Now we come to the serious center of any trip to a new place—seeing the basic sights. If you want to know what makes the 50th state tick, you must explore the city of Honolulu. And if you really want to experience the sights and sounds and feel of a city, the best way to do it is to get out and walk. Happily, it's also the cheapest way and the most fun.

Many commercial tours are expensive and touch only on the highlights. We think the city merits more attention. The local public buses, a good pair of walking shoes, and the instructions that follow will get you to all major places. And, more important, you can go at your own pace, devoting the most time to what most interests you—and you alone.

See also the walking tours described below, under "Organized Tours."

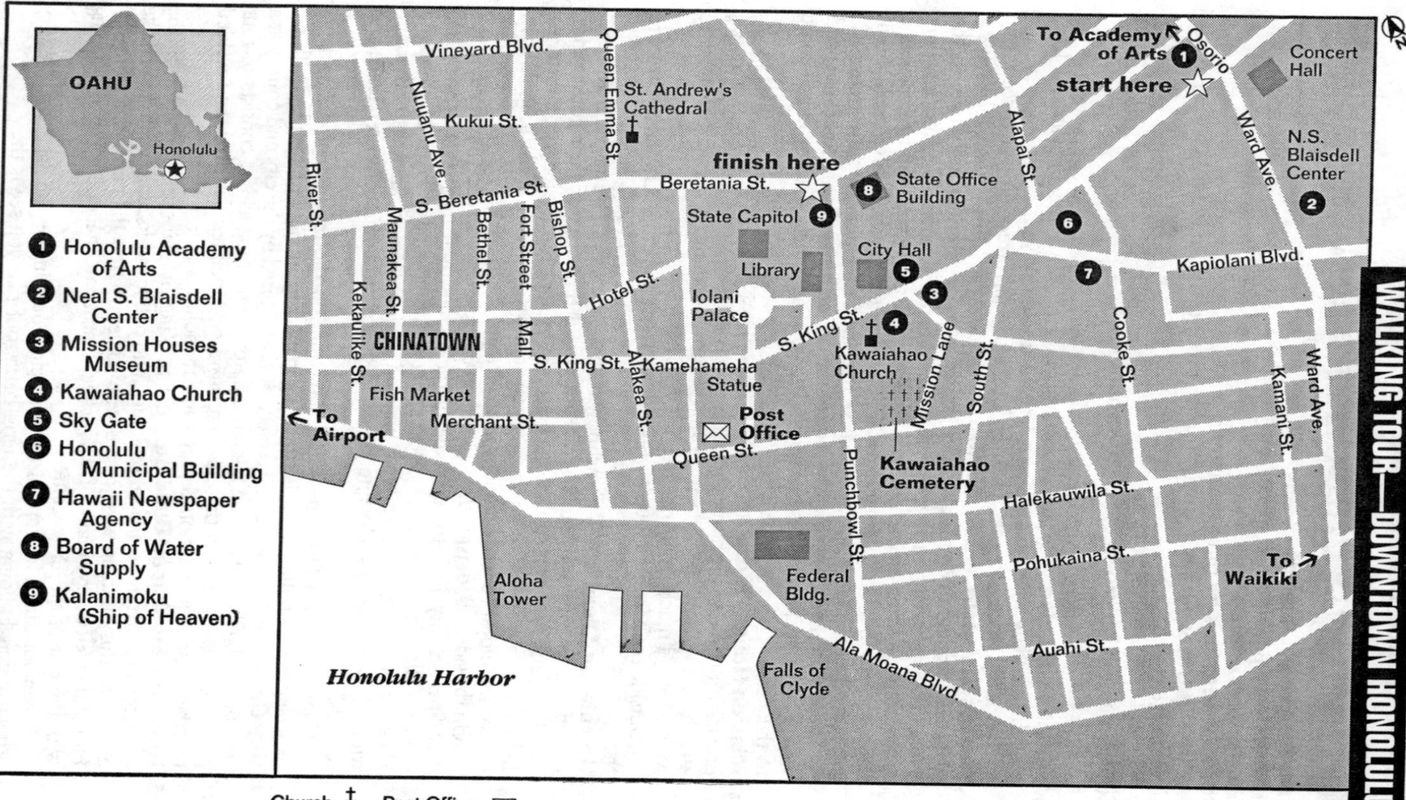

WALKING TOUR—DOWNTOWN HONOLULU
OAHU
Honolulu
1 Honolulu Academy of Arts
2 Neal S. Blaisdell Center
3 Mission Houses Museum
4 Kawaiahao Church
5 Sky Gate
6 Honolulu Municipal Building
7 Hawaii Newspaper Agency
8 Board of Water Supply
9 Kalanimoku (Ship of Heaven)
To Academy of Arts
Osorio
start here
Concert Hall
N.S. Blaisdell Center
Ward Ave.
Vineyard Blvd.
St. Andrew's Cathedral
Kukui St.
Nuuanu Ave.
Queen Emma St.
Alapai St.
finish here
Beretania St.
S. Beretania St.
State Office Building
State Capitol
River St.
Maunakea St.
Bethel St.
Fort Street Mall
Bishop St.
City Hall
Library
Kapiolani Blvd.
Hotel St.
Iolani Palace
S. King St.
Kekaulike St.
CHINATOWN
Kawaiahao Church
Mission Lane
South St.
Cooke St.
Kamani St.
Kamehameha Statue
Fish Market
Merchant St.
Alakea St.
Post Office
Queen St.
To Airport
Kawaiahao Cemetery
Punchbowl St.
Halekauwila St.
Pohukaina St.
To Waikiki
Federal Bldg.
Aloha Tower
Auahi St.
Ala Moana Blvd.
Falls of Clyde
Honolulu Harbor
Church
Post Office

WALKING TOUR 1 — DOWNTOWN HONOLULU

Start: Honolulu Academy of Arts.
Finish: Kalanimoku (Ship of Heaven).
Time: Approximately three hours.
Best Times: Tuesday through Saturday.
Worst Times: Sunday and Monday, when the Art Academy and Mission Houses Museum are closed.

TheBUS no. 2 in Waikiki will take you right to the:

1. **Honolulu Academy of Arts,** at the corner of Ward and Beretania, a low, graceful building where magnificent art treasures await you.
   Retrace your steps across Thomas Square to King Street and you'll see the:
2. **Neal S. Blaisdell Center,** 777 Ward Ave., known as "NBC" to the locals. It's a giant $1.25-million complex with an arena, a concert theater (it's home to the Honolulu Symphony), and a convention hall. There are no official tours, but apply at the administration office if you're interested in seeing it; they will have someone show you around. Don't forget to ask for a schedule of upcoming events. Kids will enjoy feeding the tame ducks and geese that live in the ponds on the grounds.
   Cross Ward Avenue on the Ewa side of the center, turn left onto King Street and walk Ewa three short blocks to King and Kawaiahao Streets. There you will come to the:
3. **Mission Houses Museum,** 553 S. King St. These three 19th-century buildings provide a glimpse of the historic encounter between the New England missionaries and the native Hawaiians in early 19th-century Honolulu. It was here that James Michener did much of his research for *Hawaii*.
   Outside the Mission Houses Museum, turn left and cross Kawaiahao Street to the:
4. **Kawaiahao Church,** 957 Punchbowl. This is Hawaii's "Westminster Abbey," the church of the royal families of Hawaii and the scene of their coronations, weddings, and funerals. Explore the graveyard looking for missionary tombstones. Behind the church, and seven or eight years older than it, is an adobe schoolhouse, one of the oldest school buildings in the state.
   On the sidewalk outside the Kawaiahao Church, walk across King Street to the Neo-Spanish City Hall to see some of the architectural highlights of the Civic Center, called Honolulu Hale, 530 S. King St. Just Diamond Head of Honolulu Hale are two very attractive New England–style red-brick buildings with white trim. These house such city and county departments as municipal reference and records.
   Continuing in a Diamond Head direction, on the expanse of rolling lawn between these buildings and the towering gray-stone monolith beyond, you'll see:
5. ***Sky Gate,*** a highly controversial piece of art acquired by the city and county at a cost of $120,000. Created by famed sculptor Isamu Noguchi, it consists of four pieces of what is apparently a gigantic stove pipe, painted flat black and welded together. The aforementioned gray-stone monolith is the:
6. **Honolulu Municipal Building,** 650 S. King St. This is the home of the departments of transportation, buildings, and public works, and much more. Like *Sky Gate*, this building was greeted with something less than unmitigated joy by Honolulu's citizenry, many of whom feel that its architecture is out of keeping with the rest of the Civic Center.
   When you stand in front of the municipal building by the flagpoles, the very attractive gray building with the terra-cotta roof that you see is the:
7. **Hawaii Newspaper Agency,** 618 Kapiolani Blvd., which houses the two daily

newspapers. Many consider it one of the loveliest Monarchy-style buildings in the city.

Walk through the municipal building and out the other side, cross the little park area, and on the other side of Beretania Street you'll see the:

8. **Board of Water Supply,** 630 S. Beretania St., a lovely pale-green building with a beautiful lawn and fountain.

Now retrace your steps in an Ewa direction, this time along Beretania Street; the beautiful new building you see across from the rear of Honolulu Hale is:

9. **Kalanimoku (Ship of Heaven),** 1151 Punchbowl, a state office building at the Civic Center. It houses the state departments of land and natural resources, fish and game, and forestry, among others. The building has a cool, wonderfully open design, and at night, softly colored lights filter through the cutout designs at its top. It's gorgeously landscaped.

WALKING TOUR 2 — HAWAII MARITIME CENTER & HAWAII'S WALL STREET

Start: Aloha Tower.
Finish: Fort Street Mall.
Time: Two or three hours.
Best Times: Any day before 5:30pm, when the Maritime Center closes.

From Waikiki take TheBUS no. 19 (Airport or Airport–Hickam) or no. 20 (Airport–Halawa Gate), and get off at the Federal Building on Ala Moana Boulevard. Then walk toward the water to the first component of the Hawaii Maritime Center:

1. **Aloha Tower,** at Pier 9, on the waterfront. Once the tallest building in Hawaii, it still provides a great view of the city in all directions. Then visit the:
2. **Kalakaua Boathouse,** an absorbing museum full of exhibits that highlight the maritime history of Hawaii. This is the centerpiece of the Hawaii Maritime Center. From Kalakaua Boathouse, you can step right onto the *Falls of Clyde,* the only four-masted, full-rigged sailing ship still in existence. If it's in port, you can also see the *Hokule'a,* an authentic replica of an ancient Hawaiian double-hulled canoe, similar to the ones that brought the first Hawaiians to these shores.

REFUELING STOP After your visit here, relax with a slightly splurgy meal or snack at lovely **Coaster's Restaurant,** behind the center and facing Honolulu Harbor. The food is sophisticated and upbeat, and the setting cannot be topped, but the service can be a mite slow at times.

Leave the Maritime Center and walk across Ala Moana Boulevard to see some of the newer buildings of the State Civic Center Mall, including the:

3. **Prince Jonah Kuhio Kalanianaole Federal Building and the U.S. Courthouse,** two unusual low-lying structures with terraced roofs in the style of Nebuchadnezzar's Hanging Gardens of Babylon. (They are situated makai of the Civic Center; the state capitol is mauka, and Iolani Palace is in the middle). Two outdoor sculptures here have also caused quite a stir. *Two Open Angles Eccentric* (and that's just what they are—two huge stainless-steel open and transparent frames that slice through the air but never collide as they frame buildings and sky) and *Barking Sands* (Peter Voulkos), composed of serpentine and geometric forms. Be your own art critic and give your verdict. Some lovely fiberworks by Ruthadell Anderson and Sharyn Amii Mills can be seen in the lobby and on the fourth floor of the courthouse.

Two blocks mauka of the federal building is Merchant Street, known as the:

4. **Wall Street of Hawaii.** The "Big Five," the great financial powers of the islands, have their offices here. You'll see the handsome offices of Dole Inc., Davies Pacific Center, Dillingham Transportation, AMFAC Center (at Merchant and Bishop), and the almost-Asian decor of the Alexander and Baldwin, Ltd., building.

On Merchant Street, turn left until you come to the:

5. **Fort Street Mall,** a lively shopping thoroughfare lined with fast-food stands and throngs of local people. You'll find Liberty House here, one of Hawaii's leading department stores, as well as a big, fascinating Woolworth's, with plenty of souvenirs.

MORE WALKING TOURS

STATE CAPITOL & IOLANI PALACE

This tour, which begins at the State Capitol and winds up at Iolani Palace, will take you two to three hours. The best time to go is Wednesday through Saturday before 2:15pm. Don't forget to make a reservation for the Iolani Palace.

Take TheBUS no. 2 from Waikiki to the corner of Punchbowl and Beretania. Across from you will be the **Hawaii State Capitol,** on Beretania Street between Punchbowl and Richards Streets. This magnificent structure, completed in 1969 at the cost of $25 million, has an open-air roof that sweeps skyward like the peak of a volcano, reflecting pools signifying an ocean environment, and Hawaiian materials and motifs throughout. If the state Senate and House of Representatives are in session, you're invited to come in and see politics in action in the 50th state. You are also invited to visit, browse, and "experience" the offices of Hawaii's governor and lieutenant-governor during regular working hours. Note, too, Marisol's controversial statue of Father Damien, and other works of art in front of the building, facing Beretania Street. Just outside the makai side of the building are two relatively new works: a replica of the Liberty Bell and a statue of Hawaii's last reigning monarch, Queen Liliuokalani.

Go back the same way you came in. Walk makai and you're at the central building of the **Hawaii State Library,** 478 King St., a Greco-Roman edifice with a delightful open-air garden court. Visit the Edna Allyn Children's Room to see Hawaiian legend murals by Juliette May Fraser, and take in the other paintings hung throughout the library. (Closed for renovation at press time, but should reopen soon.)

Directly across King Street is the **State Judiciary Building,** and right outside it, the famous statue, ***King Kamehameha,*** dressed in a royal feathered cape and a helmet that looks curiously Grecian. A symbol of Hawaii (you'll see it in countless pictures and on postcards), this larger-than-life statue of the unifier of the islands is not a great work of art, but it's appropriately heroic. On Kamehameha Day, June 11, the local citizenry decks the statue with huge leis.

Just Ewa of the library you'll see a streamlined building, the **Archives of Hawaii.** Inside are invaluable documents, journals, photographs, and other records, the largest collection of Hawaiiana in existence. The archives are on the grounds of **Iolani Palace,** which is Diamond Head of the building (at King and Richards Streets). This is the high point and the end of the tour: Plan your walking tour so that you'll arrive in time for your reservation to tour the only royal palace on American soil (tel. 522-0382 for reservations).

ASIAN NEIGHBORHOODS

Take this two- to three-hour tour during the day—the area is not considered safe at night.

From Waikiki, take TheBUS no. 2 or 19 (Airport or Airport–Hickam) or no. 20

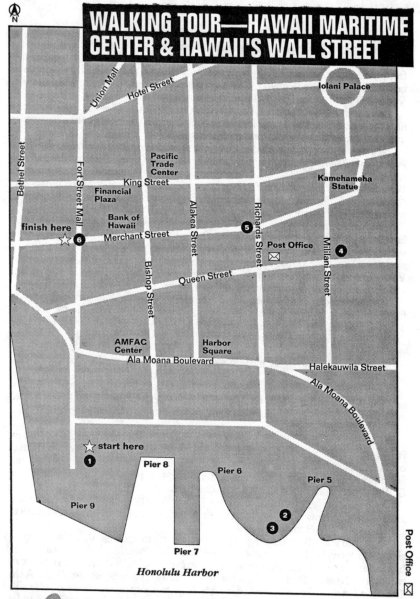

WALKING TOUR—HAWAII MARITIME CENTER & HAWAII'S WALL STREET

N

Iolani Palace
Union Mall
Hotel Street
Bethel Street
Fort Street Mall
Pacific Trade Center
King Street
Kamehameha Statue
Financial Plaza
Alakea Street
Richards Street
Bank of Hawaii
finish here
6
Merchant Street
5
Post Office
Mililani Street
4
Bishop Street
Queen Street
AMFAC Center
Harbor Square
Ala Moana Boulevard
Halekauwila Street
Ala Moana Boulevard
start here
1
Pier 8
Pier 6
Pier 5
Pier 9
2
3
Pier 7
Honolulu Harbor

Post Office

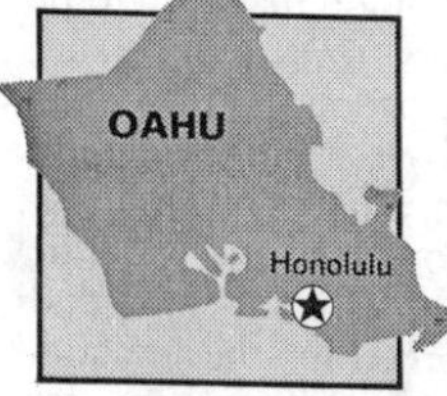

1. Aloha Tower
2. Kalakaua Boathouse
3. Coaster's Restaurant
4. Prince Jonah Kuhio Kalanianole Federal Buliding & U.S. Courthouse
5. Wall Street of Hawaii
6. Fort Street Mall

(Airport) toward downtown Honolulu. Get off at Maunakea Street and you'll find yourself in the midst of the **Historical Chinatown District.** With its jumble of shops laden with crafts, herbs, and Chinese groceries, and with many new merchants from Vietnam, Thailand, and other parts of Southeast Asia here, the area is more fascinating and exotic than ever. There are several Chinese acupuncturists and Hong Kong herb doctors here (many locals swear by them).

Begin with a look at an old Chinatown fixture, the **Oahu Market,** on King Street near the waterfront. The open-air stalls contain all variety of fish, poultry, vegetables, in a dizzying array. A look at presupermarket Hawaii!

Next, walk over to one of the area's newer landmarks, the **Chinese Cultural Plaza,** in the block bounded by Beretania, Maunakea, Kukui, and River Streets. This is not one of our favorite shopping centers, since many of the goods seem overpriced. We do, however, like the Dragon Gate Bookstore, with dragon puppets, books, and calendars (in Chinese, of course), as well as Excellent Gems and Bin Ching, both of which carry pearls and jade and do jewelry repairing.

The biggest new development in Chinatown, however, is the **Maunakea Marketplace,** in the block bounded by Hotel, Puahi, and Maunakea Streets. There's a statue of Confucius, a clock tower, and thousands of bricks engraved with personal messages. The office of the Historical Hawaii Foundation is here, as is the Chinese Visitor Center, where you can pick up self-guided tour maps and tapes of Chinatown, and see a historical presentation on old Chinatown.

The Maunakea Marketplace Food Court has a truly international array of fast-food stands, with a central courtyard for dining. You can sample the foods of Thailand, Korea, the Philippines—even Puerto Rico—as well as China, of course. Directly behind the food court is a fresh seafood market, wholesale and retail; many restaurants shop here.

As you wander through Chinatown's little streets, you'll notice that Old Chinatown is giving way to several new buildings, a park, and continued upgrading of historic older buildings such as the **Hawaii Theatre,** 1130 Bethel St., which is in the process of being restored to its original '20s art deco architecture. It has hosted everything from beauty pageants and band concerts to the Hawaii International Film Festival and even political functions.

There are now about a dozen art galleries in the neighborhood, including **Pegge Hopper,** at 1164 Nuuanu St. (her works are seen all over the islands); **Robyn Buntin of Honolulu,** 900A Maunakea St., a specialist in Asian art and jewelry; and **Ramsay,** 1128 Smith St., the renowned pen-and-ink artist, who has the charming Gallery Café adjacent, for light, sophisticated meals.

Before you leave Chinatown, be sure to check out the **lei sellers** on Maunakea Street, near Beretania. There are at least a dozen of them, and they offer the best prices and finest work in Honolulu.

You could end your tour here, or you may choose to walk another few blocks to climax your trip with an exotic sight: the Kuan Yin Buddhist Temple. Walk three blocks mauka from King Street to Beretania Street. Turn left and walk Ewa a block or two to the Nuuanu Stream, where the ambience is slightly Southeast Asian. **Aala Triangle Park** is the sad home of a fairly large tent city, where many of Hawaii's homeless have taken shelter. Much of the old Japanese neighborhood that used to be here—scrubby little saimin stands and pool halls, fish and grocery stores under quaint Asian roofs—has been torn down to make way for new construction. You'll see the **Kukui Market,** with its distinctive blue roof. Now follow River Street toward the mountains—you're likely to see local people fishing for tiliapa, a nutritious fish that breeds rapidly in such brackish water—then cross Vineyard Boulevard and you'll be at the **Kuan Yin Buddhist Temple,** 170 N. Vineyard St. Slip off your shoes and walk inside. Joss sticks and incense burn at the altar, food offerings calm the ancestral spirits, and the U.S.A. seems far, far away. (There is another statue of Kuan Yin—far more splendid, we think—in the Honolulu Academy of Arts.)

PUNCHBOWL, LOWER TANTALUS & NUUANU

This adventure begins at Honolulu's number-one visitor attraction, the National Memorial Cemetery of the Pacific, covers some historic sites, and ends at a superb botanical garden. Begin it early enough to have time to explore Foster Botanical Gardens, which closes at 4pm. Plan on spending about half a day on this tour.

Start with TheBUS no. 2 on Kuhio Avenue heading for town (request a transfer). Get off at Alapai Street and walk a quarter of a block left, where you can pick up the TheBUS no. 15 (Pacific Heights). This leaves every hour on the half hour, so time your trip carefully. Get off at Puowaina Drive and walk for 10 minutes to the **National Memorial Cemetery of the Pacific,** in Punchbowl Crater. Buried inside the crater of an extinct volcano are some 26,000 American military personnel who perished in the Pacific during World War II, the Korean War, or the Vietnam War.

Walking back to the bus stop, get TheBUS no. 15 again and continue on it for a grand ride through **Pacific Heights,** a residential district. At the end of the line, another breathtaking view of the city and the Pacific awaits. When you pay for the return trip, get a transfer and leave the bus at Pauoa Road, along which you walk right two blocks to Nuuanu Avenue and TheBUS no. 4R (Nuuanu–Dowsett). This bus will take you through **Nuuanu Valley,** damp, lush, glorious in scenery and island history (here Kamehameha won the battle that gave him control of Oahu). Unfortunately, there's no bus to the Nuuanu Pali with its magnificent view of Windward Oahu.

On the left side is the white-frame **Queen Emma Summer Palace,** 2913 Pali Hwy. Emma and her consort, King Kamehameha IV, called this Victorian country retreat of theirs Hanaiakamalama, and it is faithfully maintained as a museum by the Daughters of Hawaii.

Ride on the same bus farther down Nuuanu Avenue, past the brightly colored Chinese Consulate to the **Royal Mausoleum,** 2261 Nuuanu Ave., on the right. Here's where the last of the Hawaiian alii, the Kamehameha and Kalakaua dynasties, and others of royal blood are buried. Browse around.

Resuming your makai trip on TheBUS no. 4, ride down to the **Soto Mission of Hawaii,** at 1708 Nuuanu Ave. (between School and Kuakini Streets). This is a Zen Buddhist temple; just look for its severe central tower and eight smaller octagonal ones, which represent Buddha's Path of Life. Walk in and have a look. They'll be happy to answer any questions. Free.

Leaving the temple, walk mauka to Kuakini Street, then turn right one block to Pali Highway, and right again for half a block to the **Honpa Hongwanji Mission Temple,** on Pali Highway. This is the cathedral of the Jodo Shin Buddhist sect in Hawaii.

Now retrace your steps to Nuuanu Avenue and walk makai two blocks to Vineyard Boulevard. Turn right and about one block away you'll find the entrance to the **Foster Botanical Garden,** 180 N. Vineyard Blvd. Founded in the 1850s on royal lands, this superb botanical collection is one of Honolulu's favorite places.

For the return, walk back to Nuuanu Avenue below School Street, board TheBUS no. 4 to Hotel and Bethel Streets, where you will transfer to TheBUS no. 2 back to Waikiki.

UNIVERSITY OF HAWAII AT MANOA & MANOA VALLEY

Here's your chance to see what all those students are doing when they're not on the beach at Waikiki. Try to take this two- to three-hour tour during the week, when classes are in session.

Take TheBUS no. 4 (Nuuanu–Dowsett) from the corner of Kapahulu and Kalakaua to the **University of Hawaii at Manoa campus.** From here you can meander around the beautiful grounds of the university, one of the most relaxed institutions of higher learning we've seen anywhere. Nobody thinks it's unusual for that fellow in the library poring over the card catalog to be barefoot, so why should you?

After you've absorbed the ambience a bit, walk over to **Bachman Annex 6,** not far from the Founder's Gate. Here you can pick up maps and directions for a self-guided tour. The map will direct you to numerous examples of fine art on campus, and to some 560 varieties of tropical plants and blossoms that make the campus a garden.

Next make your way to the **East-West Center,** on East-West Road. Eastern and Western influences are reflected in the student composition and in the architecture. Visit **Thomas Jefferson Hall** and explore the student center. Tours leave every Wednesday at 1:30pm from the Friend's Lounge on the garden level. Walk to the rear of Jefferson for a peaceful moment at the lyrical **Japanese Garden,** and you'll find yourself face to face with the **John Fitzgerald Kennedy Theater,** home of the university's Department of Theater and Dance and the scene of fascinating productions, from Kabuki to Shakespeare.

If you're feeling hungry, head for the **Campus Center Cafeteria** close to University Avenue in the middle of campus, which offers excellent low-cost breakfasts and lunches. Or try **Manoa Garden** at Hemenway Hall, offering deli sandwiches and stir-fries all day.

Walk back to University Avenue, where you entered the campus, and board TheBUS no. 6. The ride up East Manoa Road to Woodlawn will take you past a **Chinese cemetery,** marked with a big Chinese gate at the intersection of Akaka Place, where there are often food offerings on the graves.

Taking the same bus back (on the opposite side of the road) toward the university, get off at the intersection of Manoa Road and Oahu Avenue. If you walk a little way to the right on Oahu Avenue, you'll discover the **Waioli Tea Room,** 3016 Oahu Ave., a charming place for lunch or Sunday brunch (See Chapter 6, "Honolulu Dining"). Even if you don't eat here, take a little time to explore the grounds, the Little Chapel, and the **Robert Louis Stevenson Memorial House** where it is said that the poet once lived.

WAIKIKI

There's more to Waikiki than just the beach. It's fun to explore the magnificent hotels, do some shopping, and stop in at a small museum or two (the Damien Museum, however, is closed on Sunday).

Take TheBUS no. 8 or walk to **Fort DeRussy Military Reservations,** a great, low-cost recreation area for the military, on a prime strip of Waikiki Beach. The beach is open to the public, and many claim it's the best in Waikiki. You may want to stop in for a quick visit to the **U.S. Army Museum in Fort DeRussy Park,** which contains military memorabilia dating from ancient Hawaiian warfare to the present.

From there it's a short walk to the **Hilton Hawaiian Village,** 2005 Kalia Rd., which has recently undergone a major, $80-million face-lift. It's a fascinating cornball beach city of its own, with 20 acres of tropical gardens, an artificial lagoon, a vast array of indoor and outdoor bars and restaurants, six pools, a beautiful beachfront (you're welcome to swim if you like), a dazzling array of shops, and even its own post office.

Leave the Hilton and walk (about 10 minutes), or take TheBUS no. 8 up Kuhio Avenue, which runs parallel to Kalakaua, to Royal Hawaiian Avenue. Walk one block toward the ocean to Kalakaua and the **Royal Hawaiian Shopping Center.** After you've browsed a bit, walk behind the shopping center to the magnificent **Royal Hawaiian Hotel,** the pink stucco Moorish-style hotel that is as much a landmark on the Waikiki skyline as Diamond Head. Explore the grounds and the magnificent interiors.

A few doors Diamond Head of the Royal Hawaiian, walk to the **Sheraton**

Moana Surfrider Hotel. The $50-million restoration of the venerable Moana Hotel, for years the classic South Seas hostelry on the beach at Waikiki, is magnificent. Enter and step back into the elegant refinement of the 19th century, updated for sophisticated living today. Now cross Kalakaua, walk to the corner of Kalakaua and Uluniu, and stop in to explore the **Hyatt Regency Waikiki,** its inner courtyard dramatically landscaped with tropical foliage, trees and plantings, huge sculptures, many-storied waterfalls, flowing lagoons, picturesque kiosks, and Polynesian objets d'art.

On a more serious note, you may wish to visit the **Damien Museum,** 130 Ohua St. (corner of Kalakaua Avenue, behind St. Augustine's Catholic Church), which presents a moving account of the work that Father Damien de Veuster did with the victims of leprosy on the island of Molokai.

On the other side of Ohua Street, reward yourself with a visit to the **Hawaiian Regent Hotel,** where you'll enjoy one of the most beautiful daytime views in Waikiki. The hotel is tastefully done, with its open-air lobby surrounding a central court aglow with a fountain and two lagoons. Walk up two flights of stairs to the pool and the Ocean Terrace, which seemingly juts out right over the beach (even though it's across the street). The glorious colors of ocean and sky surround you wherever you look. From here, cross the street to **Kuhio Beach,** where you may want to take a picture in front of the statue of Duke Kahanamoku with a surfboard, and spend the rest of the day loafing in the sun.

DIAMOND HEAD WAIKIKI — ST. LOUIS HEIGHTS

There are more than a few things to see at the Diamond Head end of Waikiki, up near Kapiolani Park. This tour takes you from Honolulu Zoo to St. Louis Heights in about two hours. Be sure to go before 5pm, when the Aquarium closes.

Past Kuhio Beach, at Kapahulu Avenue on your left is the **Honolulu Zoo,** 151 Kapahulu Ave. It's noted for its collection of native Hawaiian and other tropical birds, displayed in various bird-jungle habitats.

From here on, Kalakaua Avenue is a regal, although narrow, tree-lined drive. And a little farther on, where Kalakaua meets Monsarrat Avenue, begins **Kapiolani Park** (those are the Koolau Mountains in the background). The 220 acres of the park have facilities for just about everything from soccer to rugby to picnicking; also archery, a golf driving range, and tennis. Just ahead is **Kapiolani Beach Park,** with locker room, rest rooms, picnic tables, and snack bar. Also up here, just past the beach, is the **Waikiki Aquarium,** 2777 Kalamaua Ave. Here's your chance to see, among other sea creatures like giant clams and sharks, the *lauwiliwilinukunukuoioi,* the long-nosed butterfly fish.

Now it's time to rest your feet—and see something new—by hopping aboard TheBUS no. 14 going Diamond Head on Kalakaua Avenue. The bus will take you through the suburbs of Waialae-Kahala and Kaimuki, and up the mountain to Maunalani Heights. From there, you can look straight down into **Diamond Head Crater.** Koko Head is on the left, Waikiki slightly to your right.

For your return trip, change to TheBUS no. 2, and you'll be back in Waikiki. Or if you prefer, stay on the no. 14 and ride up to **St. Louis Heights,** for a magnificent panorama of Honolulu. A forest of beautiful Norfolk pines with picnic tables and a splendid view of Manoa Valley awaits you here at **Waahila Ridge State Recreation Area.**

Note: If you're making this little trip by car, you can actually drive right inside Diamond Head Crater—the only drive-in crater on Oahu, except for Punchbowl. Here's how you do it. Follow Kalakaua until it circles left, just past the Colony Surf Hotel; then make your first right to Diamond Head Road. Come up Diamond Head Road, past the lighthouse on the right. Take your first left before the triangular park; you are now entering the Fort Ruger area. Watch for the DIAMOND HEAD CRATER sign on the left and follow the road to the left. Go through the tunnel, and you're in Diamond Head State Monument. Hiking trails go up to the rim of the crater. The area looks quite undramatic, but where else can you drive into a volcano!

5. ORGANIZED TOURS

WALKING TOURS The people at **Kapiolani Community College** would like to take you for a walk. In the course of their popular 2½-hour walking tours, which leave from various points downtown, you can visit with "Ghosts of Old Honolulu," explore Honolulu's famous cemeteries, and follow in the footsteps of Mark Twain. Costumed historic role-players take part. Cost is $5 for adults, $2 for children and students. Highly recommended! Make reservations as far in advance as possible by calling 734-9211. Tours are usually listed in the *Waikiki Beach Press*.

The **Mission Houses Museum** presents a walking tour of "Historic Downtown Honolulu" every Monday and Friday morning at 9:30am. The cost of $10 also includes admission to the museum (tel. 531-0481 for reservations).

Aunty Malia Solomon, the well-known Hawaiiana expert, leads a free walk to places of historical interest in Waikiki, on Wednesday in summer at 10:30am, weather permitting, from Hyatt's Hawaii, a cultural and historical center on the second floor of the Hyatt Regency, behind the waterfall. Wear comfortable shoes, for it's about a two-mile, two-hour trek. For more information, call 923-1234, ext. 6410.

The **Hawaii Geographic Society** (tel. 538-3952) offers several unusual and highly worthwhile tours from April through September. One is "A Temple Tour," including Chinese, Japanese, Christian, and Jewish temples, cathedrals, and houses of worship. Another is "A Historic and Sociological Tour of Honolulu," including many out-of-the-way, unusual, historic, and colorful parts of Honolulu not often seen. Then there are three different Archeological Tours: one of Honolulu, one of Ewa/Waianae, and one of Central/North Shore Oahu. Some walking and climbing is involved, but these tours are not strenuous. Call for details, reservations, and charges on all these tours.

Three different organizations offer walking tours of Chinatown. Tours offered by the **Chinatown Historical Society,** a nonprofit organization, are free and very popular. They offer two different walking tours of Chinatown and Foster Botanical Garden. The morning tour departs Monday through Friday at 10am, and covers shops and historical buildings. The afternoon tour departs Monday through Friday at 1pm. This tour visits several Chinese and Japanese temples and the Foster Botanical Garden ($1 admission). The tours meet inside Asia Mall, 1250 Maunakea St. Reservations aren't necessary; for information, call 531-3045.

The three-hour "Walk-A-Tour" run by the Chinese Chamber of Commerce only on Tuesday mornings at 9:30am is an old favorite. It includes visits to shops, markets, and historic sites. The price is $5, and lunch can be arranged. The tour leaves from **Chinese Chamber of Commerce** headquarters at 42 N. King St. (tel. 533-3181 for reservations).

The **Hawaii Heritage Center** at 1128 Smith St. (tel. 521-2749) has a tour of Chinatown on Friday (except holidays) from 9:30am to 12:30pm. The cost is $4 per person. Call for information and reservations.

FREE & LOW-COST FACTORY TOURS Free refreshments and more than 40,000 fashions to select from at factory prices are available at **Hilo Hattie Fashion Center,** 700 Nimitz Hwy. (tel. 537-2926); call and they'll tell you where their free bus will pick you up in Waikiki. The **Hawaii Jewelry Design Center,** 1520 Liona St. (tel. 949-6729), is the home of Maui Divers of Hawaii, who were the first to mine black coral more than 30 years ago; now their creations include a variety of corals, as well as other precious stones, in 14-karat-gold settings. The half-hour tour, given daily from 9am to 3pm, includes a film and a walk through the manufacturing center where you may watch artisans at work, followed by a visit to the show room. Call for reservations and information. To see how many Hawaiian gift items—hula skirts, dolls, shell jewelry, ornaments, kitchen accessories, etc.—are made, you can take a free tour of **Lanakila Crafts** at 1809 Bachelor St., Monday through Friday (except holidays) from 8am to 3:30pm. Lanakila is a private nonprofit organization that provides vocational training and employment placement services for severely disabled adults. Their products are sold in the finest gift stores in Hawaii. They are also available in their Gift Shop. Call 531-0555 for information and to arrange tours. If you're driving around the island, you may want to take time to stop off in Waialua, not far from Haleiwa, to visit the **Hawaii Kukui Nut Co.** at 66-935 Kaukonahua Rd. (tel. 637-5620). Here you can see raw kukui nuts being processed into beautiful jewelry (kukui-nut leis were once reserved only for Hawaiian royalty), and you'll also get a chance to sample pure Kukui Nut Oil, a remarkable ancient beauty secret. Factory specials at the gift shop and free samples are available. Free tours are held daily from 9am to 5pm. And don't forget the **Dole Cannery** tour (see above).

TOURS FOR THE DISABLED **Handicabs of the Pacific** offers special tours for handicapped passengers, including luaus, cruises, and sightseeing tours in specially equipped vans that can handle six wheelchairs. Typical city tours cost $40 per person. For information, call 524-3866.

6. EDUCATIONAL/ ALTERNATIVE ACTIVITIES

HAWAIIAN PHILOSOPHY The early Hawaiians were very practical psychologists, and some of their ancient practices are gaining the attention of psychologists and educators today. If you'd like to learn some of the secrets of that ancient wisdom, updated for today's world, try to catch one of the free evening lectures on Ho'oponopono (the art of problem-solving and stress release), at the **Foundation of I (Freedom of the Cosmos),** 2153 N. King St., Suite 321B. The foundation was started by the late Morrnah Simeona, a native Hawaiian renowned throughout the islands as Kahuna Lapa'au, a healer, herbalist, and authority on the Hawaiian teachings. Among her colleagues is psychologist Stanley Hew Len, Ph.D. We attended one of these free lectures and a Ho'oponopono workshop (for which there is a fee) on a recent trip and found it fascinating. For information, call 842-3750.

CHANOYU: THE JAPANESE TEA CEREMONY As refreshing as a quick trip to Japan, the twice-weekly demonstrations of the Japanese tea ceremony held at 245 Saratoga Rd. (near Fort DeRussy) offer a fascinating look at the ancient "Way of Tea." Sponsored by the **Urasenke Foundation of Hawaii,** a nonprofit group whose goal is "to find peacefulness through a bowl of tea," the demonstrations are held every Wednesday and Friday (excluding holidays) from 10am to noon: Donations are welcomed. Seated in a formal Japanese tatami room in a garden setting, guests are introduced to the proper customs for the preparation and partaking of tea, and are served a sweet and powdered green tea from exquisite "tea bowls." You may ask questions and take pictures if you wish. A must for lovers of Asian culture. Monthly Tea Gatherings are also held. For information, call 923-3059.

MEDITATION Visitors are welcome at the **Siddha Meditation Honolulu Center,** 1925 Makiki St. (tel. 942-8887). Free evening programs of chanting and meditation are held every Wednesday and Saturday at 7:30pm. Newcomers to Siddha meditation should come at 7pm for a brief orientation. The center is up in the hills, in a beautiful residential area of Honolulu. Call for information.

7. SPORTS & RECREATION

Oahu has myriad facilities for riding, waterskiing, skin diving, plain and fancy fishing, even birdwatching. (Look for listings of Audubon Society programs in the daily papers.) The Hawaii Visitors Bureau can direct you to the right places.

Kapiolani Park is certainly one of the world's most active recreational areas. It has archery and golf driving ranges; fields for soccer, rugby, and softball; courts for tennis and volleyball; a jogger's circuit training course; and lots more. For details, call the Department of Parks and Recreation headquarters (tel. 523-4631); (they can also give you information on swimming lessons).

BEACHES The best place, of course, to get your basic training for a Hawaiian vacation is **Waikiki Beach,** that fabled stretch of sand that curves from the Ala Wai Canal to the shadow of Diamond Head. Stretched out among other bodies in various states of pose and repose, you can calmly watch the frantic traffic out in the breakers where the surfboard and outrigger-canoe crowds are busy trying to run each other down. The blue Pacific, the coconut palms, the trade winds—everything around you induces a lotusland lethargy that has caused more than one vacationer to tear up a return ticket home ($75-a-day'ers, naturally, should cash theirs in). The best part about all this is that it's absolutely free; there's no need to stay at any of the lush seaside caravansaries to use the beach. All the beach area is public property, up to the high-water mark, even though some of the big hotels do rope off special areas for their guests. Swim in front of the hotels if you like, but you'll have just as much fun at **Fort DeRussy Beach,** near the Ewa end of the beach (a good bet for families, but you can't buy anything at the snack bar unless you have a military card), and in the Diamond Head area, at **Kuhio Beach Park,** one of the best natural beaches in Waikiki and headquarters for the surfing and bikini crowd. It begins just past the Sheridan Moana Surfrider Hotel, at Uluniu Avenue. The beach has been considerably widened, and now it's better than ever. However, we should warn you that there is at least one 22-foot-deep hole in the midst of otherwise knee-high (for an adult) water, and there is no way such anomalies in the ocean floor can be corrected—fill them in one day and they'll be back the next. Parents of small children and nonswimmers should exercise caution here. In fact, the director of water safety for the City and County of Honolulu suggests that visitors always check with the lifeguard on duty at a beach before swimming.

Looking for a beach far from the maddening crowd (well, as far as you can get)? Take the bus going to Diamond Head on Kalakaua Avenue (on the makai side) to **Queen's Surf,** just across from Kapiolani Park, a lovely beach area frequented mostly by local families and, at the Diamond Head end, the island's gay population. There's a snack bar here, plus locker rooms, showers, and picnic tables. **Ala Moana Park** is a popular family beach, almost surfless, but sometimes polluted. Magic Island here tends to be cleaner. If you drive out to the marina behind the Hotel Ilikai, all the way to the left, you'll find a delightful beach between the Hilton Hawaiian Village and the marina. It's kind of an "in" spot for kamaainas, but tourists don't seem to know about it. There's also plenty of space to park here.

FITNESS There's no need to let up on your fitness program just because you're on vacation. If you like to do your daily routines on the beach, join the free exercise class every day except Sunday from 9 to 10:30am at the beach at Fort DeRussy.

GLIDER RIDES [SOARING] You can take a glider ride at Dillingham Airfield on the North Shore, using the long-established services of the **Original Glider Rides** (a service of Honolulu Soaring Club since 1970). You can get instruction in doing it yourself or go for a piloted joy ride in a sailplane ($70 for two passengers, $45 for one). Look ma, no engines! Phone "Mr. Bill" (tel. 677-3404) for information. Rates are subject to change. No reservations are required, and things glide along here seven days a week, 10:30am to 5:30pm. Bring your camera.

GOLF There are 14 public golf courses on Oahu, most with relatively low greens fees. The nearest one to Waikiki is the 18-hole **Ala Wai Golf Course** at 404 Kapahulu Ave. Reservations are taken by phone (tel. 296-4653) one week in advance starting at 6:30am. All reservations are usually given out by 7am. Huge lines of local people start to form before dawn to take advantage of any cancellations. Ala Wai is reputedly the busiest golf course in the world, with over 500 people playing daily. Visitor rates are $18 weekdays, $20 weekends. Cart rental is $11; club rental, $15. With a car, you can drive to the **Hawaii Kai Golf Course,** 8902 Kalanianaole Hwy., in about 20 minutes. It has an 18-hole par-3 course, an 18-hole championship course, and a driving range. Rates for the par-3 course are $36 with cart; for the championship, $80 with cart. There's a restaurant on the premises. Call 395-2358 for information and reservations.

If you're planning a drive out to the North Shore, you can take advantage of the little-known (to visitors) **Kahuku Municipal Golf Course,** which has the benefit of an ocean view and very low greens fees—for islanders. Out-of-state rates have recently been upped to $14 for 9 holes, $18 for 18 holes on weekdays, and $14 and $20 on weekends. The 2,725-yard course is seldom crowded except occasionally on weekends. Note that there is neither a pro shop nor a restaurant here. Tee times are required only on weekend mornings. For information, call 293-5842.

For a listing of golf courses elsewhere on Oahu, see "Golf and Tennis in Hawaii," available from the Hawaii Visitors Bureau.

HIKING If you'd like to discover what those mountains are actually like across the Ala Wai, the **Hawaiian Trail and Mountain Club** will take you on a hike along one of the numerous beautiful trails around Honolulu, where you'll feel far removed from both city and beach. You pack your own lunch and drinking water on these hikes, which usually start from the Iolani Palace grounds at 8am on Sunday and 9am on Saturday. The hiking fee is $1, plus a modest charge if you plan to carpool to the hiking site. Visitors are made welcome and usually make up about half the group. For a packet of valuable information about hiking and camping in Hawaii, as well as a schedule of upcoming hikes, send a legal-size stamped, self-addressed envelope plus $1.25 to P.O. Box 2238, Honolulu, HI 96804. If all you want is the schedule, just send the envelope (be sure to request the schedule!) and omit the $1.25. Or, you can check the schedule printed in the "Today" section of the *Honolulu Star-Bulletin*. For information, call 534-5515 or 488-1161. If you'd like to go hiking with the local branch of the **Sierra Club,** contact the Sierra Club, Hawaii Chapter, P.O. Box 2577, Honolulu, HI (tel. 808/538-6616).

For books, topographical and other maps, and information on camping, hiking, bicycling, and outdoor activities in Hawaii, contact **Hawaii Geographic Maps & Books,** P.O. Box 1698, Honolulu, HI 96806, to request their free brochures and lists. In addition, their *Information Packets* are informal, revised regularly, and designed to provide a variety of useful things not found in one place. The Hiking/Camping Information Packet is $7, as is the Adventure Packet: Both are $12, including postage. Another worthwhile thing to have is their impressive publication *Hawaii Parklands,* with 100 color photographs. It sells for $25 hardcover, $15 softcover, plus $3 postage and handling. Also very helpful to hikers are the books by Robert Smith: *Best of Hawaiian Hiking, Hiking Oahu, Hiking Maui, Hiking Kauai, Hiking the Big Island,* each $9 and available from Hawaii Geographic Books & Maps. Another excellent book is Craig Chisholm's *Hawaiian Hiking Trails,* $13 and also available from Hawaii Geographic Books & Maps, or from the publisher, Fernglen Press, 473 Sixth St., Lake Oswego, OR 97034.

Action Hawaii Adventures, P.O. Box 75548, Honolulu, HI 96815 (tel. 808/732-4453), offers unique island tours, including a mountain walk to the summit of Diamond Head. Expert guides accompany small groups of no more than 14 people and make learning safe, fun, and easy for everyone.

HULA DANCING You, too, can do the hula! Hula-dancing lessons are given everywhere—at the Ys, at the university, and at any number of private dance studios. Free classes are sometimes given at hotels and shopping centers, but since the times of these lessons change with the seasons, it's best to consult the local tourist papers. Lessons in Hawaiian dance are given at the **Bishop Museum Atheron Halau,** 1525 Bernice St. (tel. 847-3511), at 1pm Monday through Saturday and on the first Sunday of the month, free when you pay general museum admission of $6.95 for adults, $5.95 for those 6–17. Free hula classes are usually given Monday, Wednesday, and Friday at the **Royal Hawaiian Shopping Center,** Building C, third floor, at 10:30am. Call 922-0588 for further details.

ICE SKATING We realize that you probably didn't come to Hawaii to go ice skating, but if that's your pleasure, you'll love Honolulu's beautiful rink: the **Ice Palace.** Located in Stadium Mall, across from the rear of Aloha Stadium, this place has really caught on with the local folk. Admission is $5 for anyone over 6, free for children under 6; admission includes skate rental. The rink is open daily; call 487-9921 for public skating hours. Don't fret if you forget to pack warm hats, mittens, and gloves; there's a little shop here that will sell them to you.

MASSAGE After all this exertion, you may be in need of a massage. The **Honolulu School of Massage** at 1123 11th Ave. in Kaimuki (right behind Diamond Head) is a reputable, state-licensed organization that offers low-cost massages by apprentice massage therapists at a cost of $20 for half an hour, $35 for an hour. For a licensed massage therapist, costs are higher. And, oh yes, massage helps relieve jet lag, too. Call 733-0000 for an appointment. The school is accessible by bus no. 1, 3, or 14. Fees subject to change.

RUNNING Jogging is popular in Honolulu, as it is just about everywhere else. You can join those getting in shape for the **Honolulu Marathon** (it's held the first or second weekend in December) at a free Marathon Clinic, every Sunday at 7:30am at the bandstand in Kapiolani Park. If you're in town in mid-February, grab your sneakers and join some 34,000 other participants in the 8.2-mile **Great Aloha Run/Walk,** the largest running event in the islands, and the fifth-largest run in the United States. There's an entrance fee of $15–$20; proceeds go to charity. Call 735-6092 or write to Great Aloha Run/Walk, 710 Palekaua St., Honolulu, HI 96816.

SAILING With **Honolulu Sailing Company,** 47-335 Lulani St., Kaneohe, HI 96744 (tel. 808/239-3900, or toll free 800/829-0144), you can sail away aboard a sleek, modern yacht to the islands of Oahu, Maui, Lanai, and Molokai. This company runs day, overnight, and one-week cruises out of Honolulu Harbor, combining sailing and snorkeling, at rates of about $60 for a half day, $130 overnight. Nautical weddings and whale-watching cruises are specialties. Boats sleep 4–10 passengers. Comforts include hot and cold running water and private staterooms for couples. One-day sailing, snorkeling, and Zodiac raft trips on Oahu are also available for about $95 per person.

SNORKELING Once you start traveling around the island, you have a choice of literally dozens of beaches, each one beautiful. One of the nearest of these beaches, and an ideal one for snorkeling, is **Hanauma Bay** (you can rent snorkeling equipment at many places in Waikiki, and other snorkelers are always willing to help beginners). And you don't need your own car to get to Hanauma Bay; simply board the Hanauma Bay Shuttle, operated by TheBUS. It runs from Waikiki to Hanauma Bay every half hour from 8:45am to 1pm, and can be boarded at the Ala Moana Hotel, the Ilikai Hotel, or at any city bus stop. It returns every hour on the hour from noon to 4:30pm.

Note: At press time the beach was closed on Wednesday; check the local papers when you arrive.

Serious snorkelers and scuba divers who will be touring the neighboring islands may wish to write for a copy of the *Dive Hawaii Guide,* by Dive Hawaii, a nonprofit association, and the University of Hawaii Sea Grant Extension Service. More than 44 locations are mapped and described. Send $2 (includes postage and handling), or $3 outside the U.S., to UH/SGES, 1000 Pope Rd., MSB 226, Honolulu, HI 96822, Attn: Dive Hawaii Guide.

SUBMARINE DIVING Even if you don't scuba dive, there's still a great way to see the world beneath the waters. We refer to a dive on the **submarine *Atlantis,*** which descends to a depth of 100 feet in the waters off Waikiki, treating passengers to views of coral reef and brightly colored reef fish that normally only scuba divers can see. One of a growing fleet of such high-tech subs (there's another one in Kona on the Big Island, another on Maui, and several more in the Caribbean and Guam), the *Atlantis* is totally equipped for safety and comfort, is fully air-conditioned, and maintains normal atmospheric pressure—no chance of getting the bends. You will, however, get a thrill as you peer out the portholes and view the eerie world beneath the waves. The adventure begins at the Hilton Hawaiian Village where a catamaran takes you to the dive site, then back for an enjoyable sail along the Waikiki coast. Allow about two hours for the entire trip. Although the fee—$79 for adults, $48 for children—is high, this is such a special experience that we consider it a highly worthwhile splurge. For information, call 522-1710.

SURFING If you'd like to learn to surf, try the concessions at Kuhio Beach, or in front of the Sheraton Waikiki, Sheraton Moana Surfrider, or Hilton Hawaiian Village hotels, or inquire at the recreation desk of any large hotel. Lessons are about $20 per hour. You must be a strong swimmer. According to the experts, you'll need three months to become a real surfer, but if you're reasonably well coordinated, you should be able to learn enough to have some fun in a day or two. If you're not, don't torture yourself. Take a ride in an outrigger canoe instead. With six or seven others in the canoe, you paddle out to deep water, wait for a good wave, and then, just as a surfer does, ride its crest back to shore. It's a thrilling experience, slightly strenuous, but with little possibility of broken bones.

For experienced surfers, the best surfing area in these parts is known as **The Cliffs,** at the base of Diamond Head. In surfers' language, the waves here are high-performance, nonhollow walls (no tube rides), and are usually two to six feet high. They can be some of the most beautiful peaks in Hawaiian waters. Combine them with the views of Diamond Head and you've got a surfer's paradise. The Cliffs is immediately past the lighthouse on Diamond Head Road, just past Waikiki. There is parking on the road and a paved trail to the beach below. Showers are available. We'd consider this one for serious surfers only, but the watching is also great.

Surfing, by the way, was the favorite sport of Hawaiian royalty and originally had religious connotations. In the early part of this century, Jack London, among others, helped revive the sport, and today it's an absolute passion with every able-bodied islander, far surpassing the interest of the mainlander in, say, baseball or skiing. Of course, many mainlanders move to Hawaii for the lure of the surf. (A T-shirt we saw on our last trip proclaimed, WORK IS FOR THOSE WHO CAN'T SURF.) Radio weather reports always include a report on the latest surfing conditions. A special phone (tel. 836-1952) also gives the latest reports. And the proudest possession of any island teenager is, naturally, his or her surfboard.

TENNIS Tennis in Honolulu? Certainly. It's free at 26 public courts. Pick up the brochure called "Golf and Tennis in Hawaii" at the Hawaii Visitors Bureau for complete listings. The **Ilikai Hotel** has a lot of tennis action: six specially surfaced courts, ball machines, a full-time tennis pro, private lessons, daily clinics. Hours are 7am to 6pm daily, and the fee is $15 per hour singles, $30 doubles. The pro shop rents racquets and does overnight stringing. They'll even help you find suitable partners (tel. 949-3811).

8. EVENING ENTERTAINMENT

Honolulu has a rich cultural life: Classical music, opera, theater, and dance are abundant, and of excellent quality. And ticket prices are much lower than in most other artistic centers! Check the local papers when you arrive, and also call the **Mayor's Performance Hotline** (tel. 527-5666) for a recording that describes activities planned for the current month at Honolulu Hale (City Hall), Iolani Palace, Kapiolani Park Bandstand, and Tamarind Park on Bishop Street. The service also announces any last-minute cancellations.

PERFORMING ARTS

OPERA & CLASSICAL MUSIC

Classical-music lovers have no cause for complaint in Honolulu. Western concert artists of the stature of Emanuel Ax stop here en route to the Far East or on round-the-world tours; Japanese soloists and orchestras pay frequent visits. You might even catch opera companies and the like from China.

HONOLULU SYMPHONY, Ward Ave. and King St. Tel. 537-6191.

The symphony performs under the baton of music director Donald Johanos and famous guest conductors. Soloists include world-renowned virtuosos, and programs include choral works and appearances by nationally and internationally acclaimed ballet companies. Pops concerts and the Starlight Festival in the Waikiki Shell are among the most widely attended symphony events, as is the annual presentation of Handel's *Messiah*. The symphony recently received the first-place award by ASCAP for "adventuresome programming of contemporary music."

Admission: Tickets, $10–$40.

CHAMBER MUSIC HAWAII. Tel. 947-1975.

If you enjoy chamber music, you'll want to hear this excellent orchestra. Some 25 concerts a year are given at various locations, including the Honolulu Academy of Arts and Temple Emanu-El.

HAWAII OPERA THEATER. Tel. 521-6537.

Try to attend a performance of this company, which holds a yearly Opera Festival in February and March, featuring internationally acclaimed opera stars complemented by Hawaii's finest singers, a locally trained chorus, and the Honolulu Symphony. Last year's season featured Rossini's *The Barber of Seville,* Giordano's *Andrea Chenier,* and Massenet's *Manon.*

Admission: Tickets, $15–$40.

THEATER

Hawaiian theater is maturing and becoming more varied all the time. A number of professional and nonprofessional artists turn out some excellent productions.

The easiest way to find out what's playing when you're in town (and on neighbor islands, as well) is to call the **theater hotline** (tel. 988-3255) sponsored by the Hawaii State Theater Council. It's a 24-hour information line on all plays and musicals currently showing on Oahu, providing dates, places, and numbers to call for reservation information.

DIAMOND HEAD THEATER, 520 Makapuu Ave. Tel. 734-0274.

A year-round program of current Broadway shows, revivals, musicals, and classics are presented by this very popular group, which has been going strong since 1951 (it used to be known as the Honolulu Community Theater). Performances are held at the Diamond Head Theater, on the slopes of Diamond Head.

Admission: Tickets, $7–$35.

KUMU KAHUA, Tenney Theater at St. Andrew's Cathedral, 224 St. Emma St. Tel. 737-4161.

Want to see what local playwrights are doing? This is the place. This group performs only works by Hawaiian residents, or plays about Hawaii.

Admission: Tickets, $6 and $7.

JOHN F. KENNEDY THEATER, University of Hawaii at Manoa. Tel. 948-7655.

The beautiful 600-seat theater is the home of the university's Department of Theater and Dance, known throughout the world for its excellent programs in Asian as well as Western theater. Presentations may include Asian theater such as grand Kabuki, Noh, and Kyogen, or traditional Beijing Opera, performed in English by an all-student cast. Shakespeare, Western theater classics, contemporary plays, ethnic dance, classical ballet, and modern dance are also featured. Visiting troupes from around the world are presented occasionally.

Admission: Tickets, to $9.

MANOA VALLEY THEATER, 2833 E. Manoa Rd. Tel. 988-6131.

Now in its 24th season, this company (formerly the Hawaii Performing Arts Company) provides an intimate setting for a broad spectrum of theatrical offerings. The 150-seat theater lights up 42 weeks of the year for a variety of productions ranging from the Bard to Broadway, from classics to musical comedy. Prices depend on the production and the night of the week. Call for dates and availability of seats.

Admission: Tickets, $14–$20.

STARVING ARTISTS THEATRE COMPANY, 2445 Kaala St. Tel. 942-1942.

Artists-in-residence at the Mid-Pacific Institute, just mauka of the University of Hawaii, produce a full season of avant-garde and new plays, both local and international. They provide an excellent showcase for new artists and playwrights. Performances are usually held Thursday through Sunday.

Admission: Tickets, $12 adults, $8 students and seniors.

LOCAL CULTURAL ENTERTAINMENT

THEATER, SONG & DANCE There are quite a few opportunities to catch free Hawaiian entertainment. If you're in town on a Friday, don't miss the Tribute to King David Kalakaua at the **Hilton Hawaiian Village;** it's an imaginative re-creation of the period of Hawaiian monarchy in the late 19th century. Things get under way at 6:30pm with a march to the hotel's porte cochère, where the Hawaiian anthem is sung; from then on it's a torchlight ceremony, Hawaiian music, and hula dancing at 7, fireworks at 8, plus more entertainment until 10pm (tel. 949-4321 for details).

The same Hilton Hawaiian Village is also the place to catch dancers and musicians from the Polynesian Cultural Center who perform on the **Village Green** every Tuesday from 3 to 6pm. A different Polynesian culture is highlighted each month;

phone 847-8200 for information. Every evening between 5:30 and 9pm, the lovely poolside terrace at the **Sheraton Princess Kaiulani Hotel** is the scene of a free show featuring songs and dances of Polynesia. Have a drink or not, as you like (tel. 922-5811).

Just as you expected, virtually everyone in Hawaii does the hula. Island youngsters learn it just as mainland children take ballet or tap lessons. Social directors and hotel instructors patiently instruct the malihinis, and wherever you look there's a hula show under way. All of this is fun, and some of it is good dancing, but much of it is a bastardization of a noble and beautiful dance, Hawaii's most visible contribution to the arts.

Happily, there has been a great revival of interest in serious hula lately, and if you're lucky you may get to see outstanding dancing at some of the better nightclub shows (the Brothers Cazimero at the Monarch Room of the Royal Hawaiian Hotel, for one) or at concert presentations. True devotees of hula should visit the islands during the month of April. That's when the ✪ **Merrie Monarch Festival** is held in Hilo, on the Big Island of Hawaii, a week-long virtual Olympics of hula, with dancers from all the various hula halaus (schools) of the islands competing in both ancient and modern hulas. You probably won't be able to get tickets to the events themselves (they're usually sold out by the preceding January), but they are fully covered on television and are a true joy to watch. On a recent trip, we sat enthralled viewing the competition and the judging—as did just about everyone else on the islands.

One of the most delightful hula shows, in our opinion, is the **Young People's Hula Show,** presented every Sunday morning at 9:30am on the centerstage at the Ala Moana Shopping Center. The children, all students of Ka'ipolani Butterworth, ranging in age from about 3 to their teens, are talented nonprofessionals, bursting with charm and aloha. It's all free and more enjoyable than many an expensive nightclub show. (Their video, *Hawaii's Children in Dance,* could be a memorable gift.)

The **Kodak Hula Show,** a venerable Waikiki institution, showcases authentic music and dance by talented artists. Naturally, it's nirvana for photographers. There is special seating for the disabled. The show is held at the Waikiki Shell in Kapiolani Park, Tuesday through Thursday at 10am. Get here early for a good seat, because even with bleachers that seat 4,000 people, it's always crowded. (For free Hilo Hattie bus transportation, call 537-2926.)

Kuhio Mall presents a free hula show every night at 7pm and 8pm. Usually, there's a free show at the beach in front of the **Reef Hotel** every Sunday from 8pm to 9:30pm or 10pm. Lots of bright amateurs get into the act. Free concerts and cultural shows are given in the Great Hall of the **Hyatt Regency Waikiki,** often at noon or 5pm, but since the schedule varies greatly, you should check with the Hyatt Hostess Desk (tel. 922-9292) for exact times. The Pau Hana show, Friday at 5pm, featuring Aunty Malia Solomon, is a perennial favorite. Hawaiian music and dance performances are presented at the **Atherton Halau** of the Bishop Museum, Monday through Saturday at 1pm. There's free entertainment galore at the **Royal Hawaiian Shopping Center.** You can usually count on a minishow presented by the Polynesian Cultural Center, on Tuesday, Thursday, and Saturday between 10am and noon in the Fountain Courtyard. For exact times, and news of special programs, check the local papers.

Look for notices in the papers of concerts presented by **Dances We Dance,** an educational and performing organization that sponsors both ethnic and modern dance concerts throughout the state. On one trip we were lucky enough to catch a concert by the Ladies of Na Pualei O Likolehua, as part of a special season of Hawaiian dance. Performances are usually held in the state-of-the-art Mamiya Theatre at the St. Louis Center for the Arts, on the St. Louis–Chaminade campus, 3140 Waialae Ave. To see a noncommercial dance presentation by a respected hula halau like this one is a very special experience.

Probably the best ethnic dancing of the Pacific Islands is done by the dance group at the **Polynesian Cultural Center.** They often do free minishows at the Royal Hawaiian Shopping Center. Watch for outstanding programs of Japanese, Korean, and other Asian dances at the University of Hawaii.

HAWAII IMAX THEATRE For a look at Hawaii that most tourists never get, a visit to the Hawaii Imax Theatre, 325 Seaside Ave., just of Kalakaua (tel. 923-4629), is recommended. The gigantic screen is five stories tall and 70 feet wide, with wraparound stereo sound: The result is not a feeling of watching a film, but of being *in* it. *Hawaii: Born in Paradise,* the theater's première attraction, shows some extraordinary footage of active volcanoes, of life beneath Hawaiian waters, and of a heart-stopping climb up the gigantic sea cliffs of Molokai, the world's tallest, to rescue a dying plant species. By the time you read this, two more films will have been added to the agenda. Films are shown every hour on the hour, every day, from 8am to 10pm. The cost is $7.50 for adults, $5 for children 3–11. After the film, you emerge into a tasteful shopping gallery, the Gathering Place Museum Shop. Many items by local artists and craftspeople are featured, including fiber sculpture, basketry, jewelry, even traditional feather capes and quilts, some of it of museum quality.

CONCERTS Free concerts are generally held on Sunday at 1pm at the **Kapiolani Park Bandstand.** Entertainment includes Polynesian revues, ukulele clubs, visiting mainland troupes, jazz and rock musicians, and usually the famed Royal Hawaiian Band; call 926-4030 for more information. You can nearly always be sure to catch the Royal Hawaiian Band at its Friday noontime concerts at the **Iolani Palace bandstand.** These lunchtime concerts are very popular with the local people who work nearby; bring a lunch and have a listen. Also popular is the free concert at **Wilcox Park** (King Street next to Fort Street Mall) on the second and fourth Mondays of each month from noon to 1pm. On the fourth Thursday of each month, there's a free concert at 7pm in City Hall Courtyard. Or join the local crowd on Friday at noon for the **Mayor's Aloha Friday Music Break,** held at Tamarind Park, at the corner of Bishop and King Streets (tel. 527-5666).

LUAUS Luaus are fun affairs—everyone arrives dressed in aloha shirts and muumuus, a great ceremony is made of taking the pig out of the imu (camera buffs have been known to go wild with joy at this part), there's lively Polynesian entertainment, and the mai tais flow freely.

Honolulu offers a number of luaus, but one that's most consistently praised is the **Paradise Cove Luau** (tel. 973-LUAU, or toll free 800/657-7827 in the mainland U.S.) held in a Hawaiian theme park 27 miles from Waikiki, on a 12-acre beachfront site in the town of Ewa. (Nearby, Oahu's newest resort development, Ko Olina, is rising.) Guests can wander through a village of thatched huts, learn ancient Hawaiian games and crafts, enjoy the spectacular sunset over the ocean, help pull in the fish in the nets during the hukilau, and watch a program of ancient and modern hula at the imu ceremony. Then it's a buffet meal and a Polynesian show: The fire dancer alone is worth the price of admission. The round-trip bus fare from Waikiki is $6. Admission is $39.50 for adults, $32.50 for teenagers, $20 for children 6–12. The luau is held every night of the week.

(*Note:* At press time, Paradise Cove was undergoing a $5-million expansion program, planned for completion by the end of 1994.)

CLUB & MUSIC SCENE

NIGHTCLUBS, CABARET & COMEDY

Let's be perfectly honest: To see the top nightclub shows in Hawaii, you're going to break your budget—and then some. When a big name is entertaining, the local clubs usually impose a cover charge plus a minimum of two drinks, which can swiftly add up to more than you'd think. On top of that, many of them prefer to accommodate their dinner guests only—and dinner at these places is usually in the $50 or $60 bracket. Luckily, many of the clubs also have cocktail shows at about half the price, which usually include one drink and tax.

Here's the information on the top names and places. Check the local tourist papers when you're in town for exact details; a top star might just happen to be on the mainland when you're in the islands, but somebody new and unknown might be making a smashing debut.

A name to look for is Glenn Medeiros. He's a local boy who not only made good but is very good. Born on Kauai 21 years ago, he hit the Top 10 with his first record, *Nothing's Gonna Change My Love for You*, in 1987. Glenn has appeared on "The Tonight Show" and "Good Morning America." You'll be lucky to catch him; he may be touring Europe when you arrive here.

THE BROTHERS CAZIMERO, the Monarch Room in the Royal Hawaiian Hotel, 2259 Kalakaua Ave. Tel. 923-7311.

We'd give up almost anything to catch a show by the Caz. They are beloved champions of authentic Hawaiian music and dance, and many of their songs, and the dances of their company, featuring the incredible Leina'ala, are truly from the heart of Hawaii. No need to splurge for the dinner show unless you want to, since cocktail shows are presented Tuesday through Saturday at 8:30pm and again on Friday and Saturday at 10:30pm. Local people say this late show is the best one of all, a time when Robert and Roland "let their hair down" for a mostly local crowd. If the Brothers aren't in town, don't fret: The Monarch Room will have another top artist, perhaps songstress Emma Veary.

(*Note:* If you're in town on May 1, which is "Lei Day" in Hawaii, don't miss the Brothers Cazimero's annual concert at the Waikiki Shell. It's a fabulous production, and all of Honolulu comes dressed in their aloha finery. General admission is usually $15; reserved seats are around $20. Arrive early and bring a picnic supper.)

Admission: Cover charge, $25–$30 cocktail show, $59.50 dinner show.

CHARO!, in the Tropic Surf Club Showroom at the Hilton Hawaiian Village, 2005 Kalia Rd. Tel. 973-5828.

She sings, she dances, she tells naughty jokes, and she plays the flamenco guitar superbly. Of course she's international star Charo!, a nonstop bundle of Latin energy who puts on an entertaining show Monday through Saturday at 7pm.

Admission: Cover charge, cocktail show $26.50 adults, $18.50 children 5–12; dinner show $44.50 adults, $31 children 5–12.

FRANK DELIMA, in the Peacock Room, at the Queen Kapiolani Hotel, 150 Kapahulu Ave. Tel. 922-1941.

Although a lot of his material is local, Frank DeLima seems to be adored by both islanders and tourists alike. He's a musical comedian rather than a standup comic, and he uses the guys in his back-up group (who are also very funny) in his zany song parodies and skits. Frank is not smutty, just crazy, so you can feel perfectly comfortable bringing older children. Readers of *Honolulu* magazine have voted him "Best Local Celebrity/Entertainer." *Note:* Frank is highly visible these days—on TV, at benefit performances, at shopping-center promotions—so it's quite possible you may be able to see him for free. Watch for him. He's great! His show here is on Wednesday through Sunday at 9:30pm, with a second show on Friday and Saturday at 11:30pm.

Admission: $7 cover charge plus two-drink minimum, or $14.

AL HARRINGTON, Polynesian Palace at the Outrigger Reef Towers Hotel, 227 Lewers St. Tel. 923-3881.

The "South Pacific Man" can always be counted on for an excellent show; he's an island favorite. Cocktail shows are held Sunday through Friday at 5:45 and 8:45pm. Should you want to dine, there's a hot buffet before the early show.

Admission: Cover charge, cocktail show $29 adults, $20 children 8–15; dinner show $43 adults, $23 children 8–15.

JOHN HIROKAWA, in the Hilton Hawaiian Village Dome Showroom, 2005 Kalia Rd. Tel. 949-4321, ext. 25.

The "early show" at the Hilton, and one that's especially suited for families with children, features Hawaiian-born illusionist John Hirokawa, a very talented fellow. Kids love it. The fun and games begin at 6:30pm.

Admission: Cover charge, cocktail show $25 adults, $17.50 children; dinner show $44.50 adults, $31 children.

DON HO, at the Hula Hut, 286 Beachwalk. Tel. 923-8411.

Hawaii's best-known entertainer doesn't do as many solos as he used to, but he still does "Tiny Bubbles" and all the rest. Most of the time, he sings with his back-up group, The Aliis. The show is on Sunday through Friday at 9pm (dinner seating at 8pm, cocktail seating at 8:30pm).

Admission: Cover charge, cocktail show $24 adults, $16 children; dinner show $41.50 adults, $28.50 children.

DANNY KALEIKINI, in Hala Terrace of the Kahala Hilton Hotel, 5000 Kahala Ave. Tel. 734-2211.

Danny is undoubtedly one of the islands' top entertainers, a brilliant musician who dances, sings, plays a variety of instruments (including the nose flute), and watches over a talented company of Hawaiian entertainers. The show is deliberately low key and in excellent taste, suitable for a family evening. Showtime is 9pm, with seatings at 7 and 7:30pm Monday through Saturday.

Admission: Cover charge, cocktail show $25 adults, $15 children; dinner show $65.

PAU HANA SHOW, at the Hyatt Regency Waikiki, 2424 Kalakaua Ave. Tel. 923-1234.

On Friday at 5pm, when local people finish work, they like to head for this spot. So should you. Traditional Hawaiian music, dances, and songs are presented for the cost of a few drinks. You can also stand by the giant waterfall and just watch.

Admission: Free.

SHERATON'S SPECTACULAR POLYNESIAN REVUE, Ainahau Showroom, in the Princess Kaiulani Hotel, 120 Kaiulani Ave. Tel. 922-5811.

There are several good Polynesian shows on the beach, but if you're going to see just one, make it this stunning 1½-hour-long authentic Polynesian revue that pulls out all the stops (Fiji war chants, Samoan fire-knife dancers, Tahitian *aparimas,* and much more). You have a choice of a dinner show (consisting of an excellent prime rib buffet and one drink) or cocktail show.

Admission: Cover charge, dinner show $48 adults, $18 children; cocktail show $20.50 adults, $12 children.

SOCIETY OF SEVEN, Main Showroom, in the Outrigger Waikiki, 2335 Kalakaua Ave. Tel. 922-6408 or 923-0711.

For more than 20 years, the show put on by the seven talented entertainers who call themselves the Society of Seven has been an island favorite. These young men sing, act, play a variety of musical instruments, and even reprise Broadway musicals (we caught them once in their miniversion of *Phantom of the Opera*), and they know how to keep an audience cheering. Music, imitations, comedy routines, rock music, oldies, and island favorites are all part of the act. It's held at 8:30 and 10:30pm Monday through Saturday (on Wednesday at 8:30pm only). The cocktail show includes tax, tip, and either two standard drinks or one cocktail.

Admission: Cover charge, cocktail show $26 adults, $19.50 students 12–20, $16 children; dinner show $47.50 adults, $37 children under 11.

HONOLULU COMEDY CLUB, in the Ilikai Hotel, 1777 Ala Moana Blvd. Tel. 922-5998.

Comedy clubs are big everywhere these days, and Honolulu is no exception. This one features both local and mainland comedians in 90-minute performances held on Tuesday, Wednesday, and Thursday at 8:30pm, on Friday at 8 and 10pm, and on Saturday at 7, 9, and 11pm. Look for other Comedy Clubs at the Turtle Bay Hilton on Oahu, the Kauai Hilton, the Kona Surf Resort on the Big Island, and the Maui Marriott.

Admission: Cover charge, $12, which includes $4 admission to Annabelle's disco.

SUNSET DINNER CRUISE

Here's a nifty splurge that combines a cruise along the shoreline of Waikiki, a chance to catch a romantic sunset, a terrific buffet meal, a show, and dancing to live music! It all happens aboard the sleek new luxury vessel *Star of Honolulu,* the largest and most comfortable such ship afloat (its state-of-the-art ride maximizes smoothness and virtually eliminates the possibility of seasickness). The *Star of Honolulu* departs every day at 5:30pm from Kewalo Basin for the 2½-hour trip. While the upper decks provide fancier packages (at $90 and $180), the main deck's deal is just fine for us: $41.50 for adults, $20.50 for children, which includes the buffet, two free cocktails, the "Star of Honolulu Revue," and round-trip transportation from Waikiki. For reservations, call 808/536-3641, or toll free 800/334-6191 in the U.S.

DANCE CLUBS

The disco/rock scene is bigger, better, and noisier than ever in Honolulu. A recent look around revealed something like a dozen clubs packing them in, and more on the way (there's also a fairly high rate of turnover). Besides offering plenty of exercise, the local clubs are mostly inexpensive; usually, they have a modest cover charge or none at all, and just a few insist on a two-drink minimum and/or a fee. Live bands usually alternate with disco, and the action gets under way between 9 and 10pm in most clubs and only ends when everyone drops from exhaustion—anywhere between 2 and 4am.

In addition to the listings that follow, **Studebaker's,** in Restaurant Row (tel. 526-9888), is the best dancing spot outside Waikiki. Not only can you "bop till you drop," but you are given sustenance while doing so. See the listing under "Happy Hours" (below) for more details.

THE BLACK ORCHID, in Restaurant Row, 500 Ala Moana Blvd. Tel. 521-3111.

This is perhaps Honolulu's most sophisticated supper club. There's dancing from 10pm Tuesday through Saturday to groups like No Excuses, an up-tempo rock band; from 5:30 to 9pm, jazz singers like Azure McCall are usually on hand.

Admission: Cover charge, $10 Fri–Sat after 10pm.

BOBBY McGEE'S CONGLOMERATION, in the Colony East Hotel, 2885 Kalakaua Ave. Tel. 922-1282.

The staff of colorfully costumed characters here really attracts the guests. It's a lively spot, also known for good food. There's a live DJ who begins at 7pm every night, a great sound system, and dancing until 2am.

Admission: Cover charge, free Mon, $2–$5 Tues–Sun.

HOFBRAU WAIKIKI, in the International Market Place, 2330 Kalakaua Ave. Tel. 923-8982.

This restaurant-cum-dance hall has been on the Waikiki scene a long time. Between the oom-pah-pah band's sets, the waitresses, in authentic costumes, dance polkas with the customers. Food and drinks are inexpensive, and there is no minimum.

Admission: Free.

IRISH ROSE SALOON, in the Outrigger Towers Hotel, 227 Lewers St. Tel. 924-7711.

The 17th of every month is St. Patrick's Day at this jolly Irish pub, which boasts 200 kinds of beer. Everybody wears green, and Irish music is played. Dancing's every night (St. Paddy's day or not) from 9pm to 2am to a live band. There's also a free jukebox that plays old-time music, plus a giant TV for sports fans.

Admission: Free.

MAHARAJA RESTAURANT AND DISCO, at the Waikiki Trade Center, 2255 Kuhio Ave. Tel. 922-3030.

The first Maharajah Club outside Japan (which has 100), this $5-million extravaganza is reputed to have the best sound-and-light system in the islands. The theme is East Indian, the mood is opulent (mirrored ceilings, Italian marble), and the crowd is an international mix, which perhaps accounts for the stiff dress code—no jeans, T-shirts, or sneakers (no formal wear, either). They play all types of music, including Top-40 hits. A restaurant serves a wide range of both Japanese and Western dishes at moderate prices. Open daily from 8pm to 4am.

Admission: Cover charge, $5 Sun–Thurs, $8 Fri–Sat.

MONARCH ROOM, in the Royal Hawaiian Hotel, 2259 Kalakaua Ave. Tel. 923-7311.

Remember the Big Band days of the '30s and '40s, when people actually danced the fox-trot, the tango, and the waltz? Well, they still do, thanks to the Sunday-afternoon Tea Dances here. From 4:30 to 7:30pm, Del Courtney and the Royal Hawaiian Hotel Orchestra provide the sounds. You don't even need to order a drink; tea and coffee, as well as harder stuff, are available. Usually in recess from April through mid-June.

Admission: Cover charge, $6.

THE PINK CADILLAC, 478 Ena Rd. Tel. 942-5282.

In addition to its fancy name, the Pink Cadillac has progressive and new wave dancing from 9pm to 2am nightly. If all this dancing makes you hungry, try the Surf Café, located underneath the club, for drinks, music, burgers and things, open at 5pm with a nightly happy hour.

Admission: Cover charge, Tues and Thurs–Sun, $6 age 21 and over, $15 ages 18–20; Mon and Wed, free for 21 and over, $5 for 18–20; Tues and Thurs free for women.

THE POINT AFTER, in the Hawaiian Regent Hotel. Tel. 922-6611.

One of the most popular disco spots and perhaps the biggest singles scene in town, the Point After has European decor, twin dance floors, and high-tech video dancing that features popular rock tunes as well as "oldies but goodies." Between 9:30 and 10:30pm there's a male review.

Admission: Cover charge, $5 age 21 and over, $15 for 18–20; male review $13.

RUMOURS, at the Ramada Renaissance Ala Moana Hotel, 410 Atkinson Dr. Tel. 955-4811.

There's a fancy feeling and dress code to match at this completely redone spot, which has first-of-its-kind-in-Hawaii audio, video, and lighting gear. It features musical videos, a light show complete with special effects, and four of the islands' best DJs. During the Friday happy hour, they play music from the early '60s through the late '70s, which they call "The Big Chill."

Admission: Free Sun–Thurs and before 8pm Fri–Sat, $5 Fri–Sat after 8pm.

SCRUPLES, in the Waikiki Marketplace, 2310 Kuhio Ave. Tel. 923-9530.

One of the town's hottest nightspots, Scruples has DJs spinning Top-40 hits every night from 8pm to 4am.

Admission: Cover charge, $5.

SPATS DANCE CLUB, in the Hyatt Regency Waikiki, 2424 Kalakaua Ave. Tel. 923-1234.

Spats is a handsome and immensely popular room where you're likely to run into (or bump into) a big crowd on weekends. There are varied nightly entertainments and contests (singing contest, dancing contests, swimsuit contests, and such). Nightly drink specials are $1.50. The late-night Pasta Bar at the adjoining Spats Restaurant starts serving goodies at 10pm. Casual attire is suggested Sunday through Wednesday, "dapper attire" Thursday through Saturday.

Admission: Cover charge, $3 Sun–Thurs, $5 Fri–Sat.

WAVE WAIKIKI, 1877 Kalakaua Ave. Tel. 941-0424.

Hawaii's biggest, brassiest live rock-and-roll nightclub features a live band and light show every night, cocktails and dancing from 8pm to 4am. You must be 21 or over.

Admission: Cover charge, $5.

BAR SCENE

BARS WITH LIVE MUSIC

BEACH BAR, in the Sheraton Moana Surfrider, 2365 Kalakaua Ave. Tel. 922-3111.

The music at this bar begins at 7am and continues—with some interruptions—until 11pm at night. Name artists such as Winston Tan, Mahi Beamer, The Pandanus Club, Henry Kapono, and our personal favorite, Olomano, can be heard daily from 7 to 11am and 3 to 11pm. A neat place for a drink near the water's edge, the bar is tucked into one of Waikiki's classic oceanfront hotels, which has recently undergone a magnificent period restoration.

Admission: Free.

MAI TAI BAR, in the Royal Hawaiian Hotel, 2259 Kalakaua Ave. Tel. 923-7311.

Right on the sands of Waikiki, this is a glorious spot to hear Hawaiian music as the sun goes down. And who better to deliver it than Keith and Carmen Haugen, a highly admired local couple. They make their music from 5:30 to 8:30pm Tuesday through Saturday evenings, and there is no drink minimum.

Admission: Free.

SOUTH SEAS VILLAGE, 2112 Kalakaua Ave. Tel. 923-8484.

This one is a big favorite with the Honolulu theater crowd, who come to hear John Saclausa at the piano bar Monday through Friday from 7pm until 12:30am. John plays, people get up and sing, and everybody has a good time. Saturday night, it's karaoke.

Admission: Free.

COCKTAILS WITH A VIEW

HALA TERRACE, in the Kahala Hilton Hotel, 5000 Kahala Ave. Tel. 734-2211.

A romantic spot we favor greatly is this beachside rendezvous a short drive from Waikiki. You can sip your drinks on the patio and watch the surf roll in. At 8:30pm, a cover descends for the Danny Kaleikini dinner show.

Admission: Free before 8:30pm.

HANOHANO ROOM OF THE SHERATON-WAIKIKI, 2255 Kalakaua Ave. Tel. 922-4422.

For one of the most majestic views in town, try this glorious spot where the panorama stretches all the way from Diamond Head to Pearl Harbor. There's entertainment and piano music nightly, from 9:30pm on. Beers will cost you around $4; gin and tonic, $4.95. Cocktails served from 5 to 10:15pm. No drink minimum.

Admission: Free.

HOUSE WITHOUT A KEY, in the Halekulani Hotel, 2199 Kalia Rd. Tel. 923-2311.

If ever you've dreamed of picture-perfect Hawaii, treat yourself to sunset cocktails in the oceanside lounge of this classic Honolulu resort. Here, under a century-old kiawe tree, you can watch the waves splash up on the breakfront, see the sun sink into the ocean, and hear the music of a top island group, The Islanders (Sunday, Monday, Tuesday, and Thursday from 5 to 8:30pm) and the Hiram Olsen Trio (Wednesday, Friday, and Saturday from 5 to 8:30pm). Kanoe Miller, a former Miss Hawaii, does some beautiful dancing. Don't miss this one. A sunset cocktail pupu (appetizers) and light dinner menu is served from 5 to 9pm daily. Draft beers are $3.50; exotic drinks are higher.

Admission: Free.

PAPEETE BAR, in the Tahitian Lanai Restaurant at the Waikikian on the Beach Hotel, 1811 Ala Moana Blvd. Tel. 949-5311.

At some of the Waikiki hotels, the cocktail gardens overlook the lagoon—and one of our favorites of these is the Tahitian Lanai. In this delightfully "old Hawaii" hotel, a lively local crowd hangs out at the bar, known for its sing-alongs, from 5pm to 1am. During the afternoon happy hour, 2:30 to 6pm, beer and standard drinks are $2.50; later, $3.50.

TOP OF THE I, in the Ilikai Hotel, 1777 Ala Moana Blvd. Tel. 949-3811.

Waikiki is full of gorgeous rooms with a view, but for the most sensational of all, take the glass elevator on the outside of the Ilikai Hotel (it's exciting going up; don't miss it even if you're not a drinker or a dancer) to this spot at the top of the hotel. This is the place to see the million lights of the dazzling metropolis spread out before you. There's dancing and Hawaiian-style music.

Admission: Cover charge, $2.

TOP OF WAIKIKI, Waikiki Business Plaza Building, 2270 Kalakaua Ave. Tel. 923-3877.

At the center of Waikiki is a revolving restaurant that resembles a gigantic wedding cake. The top tier is the cocktail lounge, very glamorous by candlelight and starlight. Views of all of Waikiki are yours for the price of a drink. Beer begins at $3.25; a gin and tonic, $3.25.

Admission: Free.

HAPPY HOURS

Now we come to the more practical side of pub-crawling: how to drink at half the price and sometimes get enough free food for almost a meal at the same time. The trick here is to hit the bars during their happy hours (usually from 4 to 6pm, but sometimes greatly extended), when they serve free pupus or lower their prices, or both. Note that these hours and prices are apt to change often, but these places always offer a good deal of one sort or another.

CROW'S NEST, 2244 Kalakaua Ave. Tel. 923-2422.

There's a generously long happy hour (11am to 8pm) at this spot located above the Jolly Roger. Several readers have written to praise this place for being "the friendliest and cheapest bar in Waikiki." Entertainment is offered nightly from 8pm, along with plenty of free peanuts (their shells cover the floor). Beer is $1.50 and mai tais run $1.75; after 9pm they're $3.25 and $4.

Admission: Free.

MONTEREY BAY CANNERS LOUNGE, in the Outrigger Hotel, 2335 Kalakaua Ave. Tel. 922-5761.

There's nothing skimpy about the happy hour here. It runs from 7am to 7pm, and during all that time, mai tais are $1.75. As if that weren't enough, there's a second happy hour between 4 and 7pm, when well drinks and beer are $2.75. Oysters and clams on the half-shell are 85¢ each. And—you won't believe this—there's still a third happy hour, from 10:30pm to midnight. That's when well drinks are doubles at $3.25, beer is $3.25, and Irish coffee and chi chis are just $2.75.

Admission: Free.

RIGGER, in the Outrigger Hotel, 2325 Kalakaua Ave. Tel. 922-5544.

Here there's a big-screen TV for sports events and entertainment nightly beginning at 9pm. Popcorn is served free all day. The ever-popular mai tais are just $1.75 during the 6am to 6pm happy hour. From 6 to 10pm, Bloody Marys are $2.25.

ROSE AND CROWN, at King's Village, 131 Kaiulani Ave. Tel. 923-5833.

This jolly Old English pub offers brews from the mother country, of course, plus an assortment of beers and cocktails, sing-along piano (from 8pm to 1am Tuesday through Sunday), darts, all sorts of special nights. Plus happy hours that run from 11am to 7pm; during that time, beer is $1.50 and a gin and tonic costs $2.50; other times, they're $1 more. On Sunday, mai tais are $3.75, $4.25 at other times.

STUDEBAKER'S, in Restaurant Row, 500 Ala Moana. Tel. 526-9888.

$ The all-out winner for free food has to be this lively, deafeningly noisy, 1950s time warp complete with a bright-red Studebaker, lots of neon, and a DJ spinning platters. A free buffet is served along with your drinks weekdays from 4 to 8pm and on Saturday and Sunday from 6 to 9pm. There are always four hot main dishes—perhaps pepper steak, teriyaki chicken, or shrimp fettuccine, to name a few—plus four or five salads, brown breads, and raw veggies with dip. "Happy Hour" simply refers to the patrons' delight in the free buffet. (*Note:* No one under the age of 23 is allowed in after 4pm and IDs are checked.) Beer is $3 and $3.50; standard drinks, $3.50.

Admission: Cover charge, $1, plus one drink.

WAIKIKI BROILER, in the Waikiki Tower Hotel, 200 Lewers St. Tel. 923-8836.

All the way from 6am to 9pm the Waikiki Broiler serves up the mai tais and chi chis at low prices, $2.25 and $2.75. There's entertainment from 5 to 9pm.

Admission: Free.

CHAPTER 8

SAVVY SHOPPING IN HONOLULU

Muumuus and macadamia nuts, koa woods and calabashes, tapas and tiki figures—these are some of the exotic items you can shop for in the islands. Although Hawaii is not one of the great bargain-shopping areas of the world (no free-port prices or favorable money exchange for dollar-bearing Americans), it does offer a fascinating assortment of things Polynesian, Asian, and American for the inveterate browser and souvenir hunter. We'll skip the expensive items—jewelry, objets d'art, Asian brocades and silk, elegant resort wear—and stick to the good buys for the shopper who wants quality and low prices. Although many stores have upgraded their merchandise and are concentrating on higher-ticket items with which to entice affluent Japanese tourists, there are still plenty of good buys left.

1. WAIKIKI

Much of your island shopping can be done right in Waikiki: along Kalakaua Avenue and in the hotel gift shops, and at the International Market Place, Kuhio Mall, King's Village, Royal Hawaiian Shopping Center, the Atrium Shops at the Hyatt Regency Waikiki, and the Waikiki Shopping Plaza.

SHOPPING CENTERS

INTERNATIONAL MARKET PLACE, 2330 Kalakaua Ave. Tel. 923-9871.

The oldest and most colorful shopping area in Waikiki, this place is still fun, despite the fact that there are now so many booths and tourists that it sometimes reminds us of rush hour in the New York subway. And prices are apt to be a mite higher than they are in the department stores or at Ala Moana Center, although they might come down considerably if you do a bit of bargaining. And do note that comparison shopping pays off here; one booth might be selling T-shirts for $12 that one around the corner sells for $8 or $9. Informal, semi-open shops set around a giant banyan tree and interspersed among tropical plantings allow for al fresco browsing. Directly behind it, with an entrance on Kuhio Avenue, is Kuhio Mall, with more of the same. An entertaining scene, especially in the cool of evening.

Unfortunately, few of the shops here now carry genuine Hawaiian and Polynesian craft items, such as lauhala hats, carvings from native woods, or tapa cloth. What you will find are scads of places selling jewelry (everything from plastic to shell, ivory, coral, and lapis), candles, T-shirts, beach cover-ups, and resort wear. Many stands called **The Pearl Factory** sell pearls in the oyster. Shops and kiosks turn over with great rapidity, so our best advice is simply to roam wherever fancy leads you. If you like lovely Balinese clothing, check out a well-stocked shop called **Bali Designs,** which imports clothing for men and women direct from Indonesia. **Fingernail Fashions** offers original artwork, painted right on your nails. The **All Elvis Gift Shop** speaks for itself. Art lovers should pay a visit to **Arts of Paradise,** an attractive gallery featuring original art by artists residing in Hawaii. Frequent lecture and slide shows are presented.

The International Market Place is open daily from 9am to 11pm.

KUHIO MALL, 2301 Kuhio Ave. Tel. 922-2724.

Kuhio Mall is directly behind the International Market Place, and, at first glance, looks exactly like it. But there's something unique here. Up a flight of stairs, in delightful contrast to all the mass-produced goods sold everywhere, is an artisans' working gallery, called the **Craft Court,** where everything is made by hand. You deal directly with the craftspeople, who can often be seen making jewelry, throwing pots, sewing and painting on garments, and giving demonstrations of lauhala weaving and the like. One of our favorite booths here is called **Surf and Sand of Hawaii,** where Judy Vest specializes in hand-blown glass drops filled with surf and sand, for $15 as necklaces or Christmas baubles, $25 mounted on koa-wood boxes. At **Rags to Riches,** Sandra Akina does some fascinating jewelry of acrylic clay with shells, plus lovely hand-painted shirts. **Glen Okuma** is responsible for handsome baskets woven from the leaf of a coconut palm, using lost Hawaiian weaving techniques (from about $10; a coconut-weave hat is $25). **Hawaiian Flowers and Plants** has lots more than certified plants and cut flowers ready for the mainland. They also feature bamboo flutes and tapes of John Niemi playing the bamboo flute; tutu dolls from Maui and wood-carved nene birds, and, in their **Butterfly Emporium,** butterflies mounted, framed, and treated as works of art. Don't miss the Craft Court if you want to see what Hawaii's talented craftspeople are doing.

In addition to the artisans in Craft Court, Mark Martinez, the **Rainbow Letter Artist,** is the only artist in Hawaii who creates rainbow colored letters in the shape of local flora and fauna with a single stroke of his unique brushes. He works and sells his letter paintings on the ground level. **Pictures Plus,** also on the ground floor, features a display of posters and pictures by local artists at very affordable prices—and they can be shipped anywhere. Visitors can watch candle-making at **Island Candle and Young's Casuals** on the ground level. The candles, in unusual scents and shapes, including current cartoon characters, can be purchased at reasonable prices.

Free Polynesian shows are held nightly at 7 and 8pm, featuring Faye "Aloha" Dalire, a noted hula artist, whose halau (hula troupe) features many talented keikis. It's a charming show.

Kuhio Mall is open daily from 9am to 11pm.

ROYAL HAWAIIAN SHOPPING CENTER, 2201 Kalakaua Ave. Tel. 922-0588.

Across Kalakaua from the International Market Place is one of Waikiki's newer shopping centers, and in many respects its most sophisticated. "An oasis of green in Waikiki" is what the builders promised when ground was broken, and despite the outcry against the lavish use of concrete, it's pretty much what they've delivered. Occupying three city blocks along Kalakaua Avenue and fronting the entrance to the Royal Hawaiian and Sheraton Waikiki hotels, this stunning 6½-acre, 150-store complex is indeed graced with flowers and trees, ferns and shrubbery, and hundreds of trailing vines and Hawaiian plants. A high level of taste is evident in the shops, restaurants, and a huge variety of daily programs—Polynesian minishows, classes in coconut-frond weaving, ukulele playing, hula dancing, lei stringing, and Hawaiian quilting—as well as special events—enough to keep the visitor busy and happy for a

SAVVY SHOPPING IN WAIKIKI

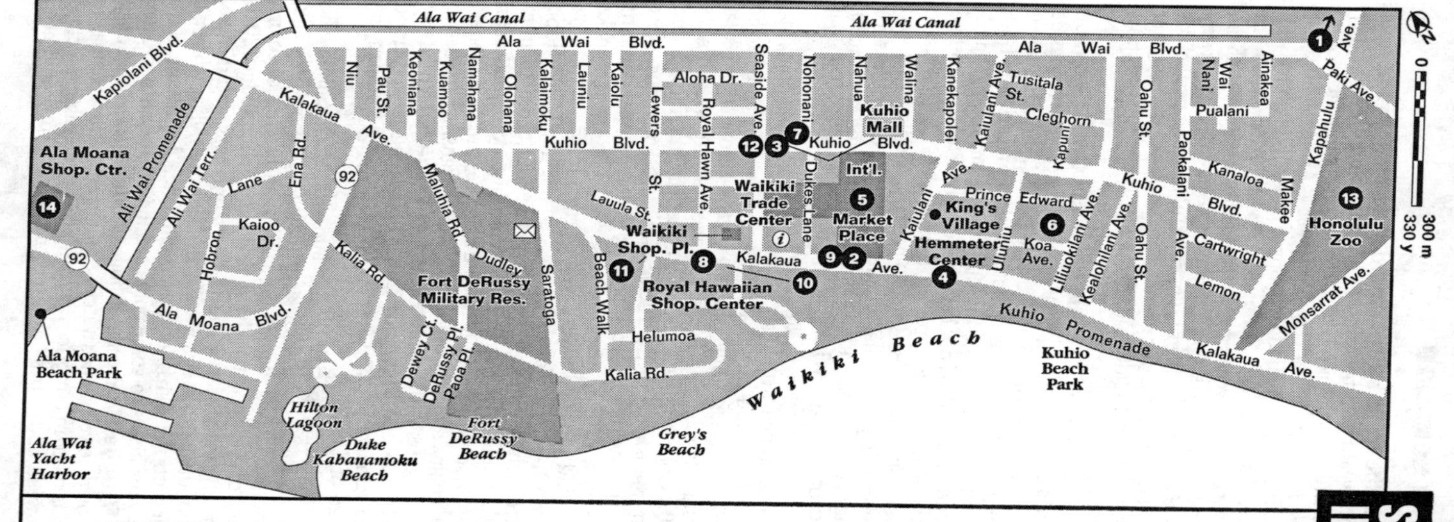

Ala Moana Center 14
Bailey's Antique Clothes & Thrift Shop 1
Casa d'Bella II 2
Craft Court 3
Hyatt Regency Waikiki Atrium shops 4
Hawaii Time 12
International Market Place 5

King's Village 6
Kuhio Mall 7
Kula Bay 8
Liberty House 9
Royal Hawaiian Shopping Center 10
Waikiki Shopping Plaza 11
The Zootique 13

Post Office ✉ Information ⓘ

long time. Unfortunately for us, the trend here is toward more and more upscale marketing: On the ground floor, wealthy visitors wait in line to get into the designer shops, such as Lancel, Chanel, and Louis Vuitton. On the second and third floors, **McInerny Galleria** features a series of pricey boutiques—Armani, Hermès, Valentino, and more of that ilk. However, the budget shopper can still do pretty well here at several discount stores such as the **Sale Studio at Andrade's** or **McInerny's Sale Studio,** where sportswear can be found for up to 75% off the original prices. Other lower-priced apparel shops include the ever-popular **Crazy Shirts** and **Sgt. Leisure,** the latter specializing in fun, colorful clothing perfect for the islands. **Allure** is a good spot to remember for exercise and swimwear—excellent selections and tops in value and quality. In addition, there are several unique spots where the merchandise is outstanding and prices are fair.

In this category, then, be sure to visit the ✪ **Little Hawaiian Craft Shop,** on the third floor, where a fantastic assortment of unusual finished jewelry sits alongside buckets and barrels of raw materials, the same kinds that were used by the ancient Hawaiians. This is a workshop for craftspeople using natural island materials in both traditional and contemporary styles. Replicas of museum pieces sit among hand-carved tikis and buckets of inexpensive shells. They have some wonderful hard-to-find sandalwood necklaces—fragrant, lovely, and well priced, from about $22. This is also a good source for Hawaiian quilting and cross-stitch—patterns, books, kits, and some finished pieces. Almost everything here is handmade in Hawaii. Great ideas for presents include kukui-nut rings at $6 (many kukui rings, pendants, and necklaces), coconut soap at $3, Hawaiian exotic wood keychains at $4.50 each, and coconut shell necklaces at $10.

The shop also includes an outstanding wood gallery that shows local woodworkers, such as Pai Pai, known for his wood-carved replicas of Hawaiian and Pacific images, and Salote, who works in stone. Only island woods—among them koa, mango, Norfolk pine, milo, macadamia, ohia lehus, and keawe—are used. Prices range from $3.50 to $3,000. Collectors will want to see the traditional and contemporary handcrafts from the islands of the Pacific—Fiji, the Solomons, New Guinea, Tonga, and Micronesia—with an ever-changing kaleidoscope of spirit figures, tapas, weavings, war clubs, drums, masks, and spears. The owners make frequent trips to these areas to find these treasures. Well worth a look.

The **Hawaiian Heirloom Jewelry Factory,** located on the third floor, deserves a stop. It conducts free factory tours every hour on the hour, from 10am to 4pm Monday through Friday. You'll learn something of the history of Hawaiian heirloom jewelry and see how these heavy gold handcrafted pieces are made today, each inscribed with the owner's name and accompanying floral designs. Also worth a stop for those who like Chinese crafts is the **China Market Place,** which has an excellent selection of cloisonné vases and handmade cloisonné animals, at very good prices. They also have tongue scrapers with a Chinese saying on an accompanying card, an amusing present for all of $1.25.

Ready to treat yourself to something special? Stop in and visit Marlo Shima who runs ✪ **Boutique Marlo,** on the second floor of Building A. Using only silk, cotton, and other natural fabrics, and dying them in the subtlest and softest of colors, Marlo creates women's clothing of great beauty. Although dresses go for about $80 to $200, you can find many modestly priced scarves, necklaces, fabric bags, and the like, with the same high standards of quality and beauty. We also like the stylish women's clothing at **C&C, Accessory** on the third floor, especially their handsome batik jackets for around $85. Treat your keikis to some cute clothing at **Sunshine Kids,** also on the third floor. **Van Brugge House** has a huge two-level store; the lower level sells pricey Australian opal jewelry and watches, plus pink and champagne diamonds, but the upper level is more in our price range. It's got a smashing selection of Australian-designed sportswear, and is truly a surfer's paradise—you could even get yourself a Surfarang (a surfer's boomerang) here. Check out the colorful wood carvings from Bali at **Coral Sea Imports.**

Between Buildings B and C is the **Royal Bridge,** with a scattering of carts and kiosks. We like the beautiful tote bags from India with bird designs offered by **Sun 'n' Sand.**

Although Asian storekeepers sell it in Honolulu, the ginseng available at **Ginseng King** is grown in Wisconsin. Stop in at their store, learn about the therapeutic effects of the centuries-old root, and perhaps buy a few tea bags (75¢ each), or a large bunch of the root itself ($50) to be used in making ginseng chicken soup.

If you've bought a lot, and are wondering how to get it all home, visit **GBC** on the second floor. They'll do professional packing, wrapping, and shipping, or else sell you the materials—corrugated boxes, mailing tubes, sealing tapes, etc.—that you'll need to do it yourself. United Parcel Service is available here, and there's a U.S. post office just next door.

Where can you eat here? We've already told you about **Spaghetti! Spaghetti!** in Chapter 6. There's also a lovely Chinese restaurant, **Beijing Garden; Naniwa-ya,** which has an old-fashioned Japanese-inn setting for popular Japanese food; and **Shilla Korean Restaurant** for authentic dishes. **Java Java** is an enjoyable espresso bar on the second level.

Free entertainment, lectures, and demonstrations go on all the time; check the local papers for details. The Royal Hawaiian Shopping Center is open from 9am to 10pm Monday through Saturday, until 9pm on Sunday.

ATRIUM SHOPS AT HYATT REGENCY WAIKIKI, 2424 Kalakaua Ave. Tel. 923-1234.

Towering 44 stories above Kalakaua Avenue between Kaiulani and Uluniu Avenues, the posh Hyatt Regency Waikiki houses a beautiful and elegant shopping complex. You may do more sightseeing than actual shopping here, but see it you must. The shops surround the central courtyard in three tiers; a spectacular waterfall splashes from the third tier into a crystal pool in the courtyard below. The center part of the courtyard is open at the top, a massive metal sculpture hovers above, and beyond that is the sky. At night the courtyard is lit by massive polished-brass lampposts. Combined with the brick-red ceramic-tile floor, it all creates an effect that is at once modern Hawaii and Hawaiian monarchy, each style complementing the other superbly. Sweeping staircases lead to the two upper tiers of shops, as do unobtrusive escalators.

As for the shops, they're a quality collection, and many, like **Gucci** and **Raku Leather,** are in line with the pricey atmosphere of this place. But there are several others for the budget-wise, like **Swim Inn, Nani Fashions II,** and **Crazy Shirts. The Royal Peddler** is known for gifts in depth, including handsome chess sets and nautical curios. **Hunting World** can outfit you for your next safari. **Cotton Cargo** has some great togs for women. Upscale resort clothes for women and a Mickey Mouse line for children can be found at **Annie's Fashions. Cal-Oahu** is a worthwhile source for really good shoes, plus lightweight luggage, hats, and bags. Mickey Mouse shirts and paraphernalia can be found at **Yokahama Okadaya.** Pick your favorite gems; there are plenty of sources to choose from: **The Coral Grotto, House of Opal, House of Jade,** and **Jewels of Hawaii** are all here. There's lots of fancy footwork to be seen at **Islander Thongs.** Check **Red Sail Sportswear** for very nice sweatshirts, T-shirts, jackets, and more. **Circle Gallery** offers outstanding art; note the special section on the Art of the Walt Disney Studios. There are now 70 shops on three floors.

A variety of free events takes place here every afternoon, from fashion shows to classes and demonstrations to special entertainment; check the local papers for exact details. The Atrium shops are open daily from 9am to 11pm.

KING'S VILLAGE, 131 Kaiulani Ave. Tel. 944-6855.

It's supposed to look like a 19th-century European town, with its cobblestone streets and old-fashioned architecture, but King's Village is very much a part of modern Honolulu. Behind the gates at the corner of Koa and Kaiulani Avenues, across the street from the Hyatt Regency Waikiki, is a cozy bazaar that contains a variety of shops, several restaurants, and an open market—all done up in a style that recalls the 19th-century monarchy period of Hawaiian history, when royal palaces were built in Honolulu, and Hawaiian kings and queens journeyed to London to be presented at the court of Queen Victoria.

The shops, however, are not so much European as the typical Honolulu-international mix, with lots of Asian and Polynesian crafts, plus plenty of Hawaiian resort wear and souvenirs. All are small and in good taste; King's Village is a commercial venture, certainly, but there's no commercial ugliness about it. We think you'll enjoy browsing here.

Prices at King's Village go from just a little to quite a lot. **Harriet's Ready Made and Fabrics,** for one, has held the line on inflation for many a year: Ready-to-wear garments begin at $24.50 for muumuus, $16.50 for aloha shirts. This is one of the few stores in Waikiki where you can buy fabric by the yard. And Harriet has some of the best prices on T-shirts anywhere—really nice all-cotton ones for just $9.50 (two for $18). Note the handsome dresses by Hans Jutte, from $60. A further example of the savings possible: Long beads went for $4.40 here that were $6 at a specialty store around the corner. In the area called Bishop Court, **Space Creations** has a wide variety of merchandise; we spotted leather goods, Balinese wood carvings, cuff links, and tie tacks made of shiny U.S. dimes for $24. You can take home a good wooden tiki for about $45, courtesy of **Hime,** an intriguing wood-carving shop, which has many lower-priced items as well, like a collection of whaling figurines. The **Royal Peddler** can always be depended upon for quality brass gifts with a nautical theme. They also have Waikiki's largest selection of Coca-Cola collectibles. And sometimes they have fairly zany items, like the "Hawaiian Snowman"—just a top hat in a bubble of water (he melted) for $4.

Do Re Mi is a shop that smells wonderful; it has all manner of potpourri and sachets, plus wooden toys and jumping jacks from Australia, as well as music boxes from Germany, Taiwan, and the U.S.

If you're a fan of European sports cars, don't miss **Euro Motor Emporium,** a "dream car" boutique, chock-full of sports-car accessories—at least you could get a cap to go with your Jaguar, Mercedes, or Ferrari.

There's a large branch of the ever-popular **Crazy Shirts** here: in addition to adorable shirts—we love the one of the exercising Kilbian cats reading "Feline Fitness Center Hawaii"—they have wonderful stuffed "hula cats" for $20.

Talk about antique jewelry! How would you like to wear jewels that are at least a million years old. Jewelry made from pyritized fossil ammonites and sterling silver begin at $34 for a pendant at the **Fossil Shop,** which also carries minerals, crystals, shells, and handmade boxes. A fossil fish, perhaps 55 million years old, sells here for a mere $35. For inexpensive jewelry, check **Christie's Hawaii,** on the top level, where we saw attractive chunky wooden necklaces, three for $10.

Leather Hawaii has some outstanding carryalls, including hand-painted canvas ones that are quite lovely. **Island Thongs** has more than just thongs—hats, visors, shoes. There are many whimsical candles, including pineapple candles starting at $8, at **Candle Odyssey.** All kinds of inexpensive fun watches, from Mickey Mouse character watches beginning at $25, make up the wares at **Hawaii Watch Shop.** The **Royal Selection** features beautiful china and crystal gifts. And **Cubby's Gifts** is just the place if you want to bring home stuffed animals for the kids; they have a huge selection.

King's Village has a number of fast-food outlets and restaurants, including **Sweet Memories** near the fountain up top. It offers goodies such as macadamia iced coffee, pies and cakes, cappuccino and espresso. And it's always good fun to stop by for a drink or a meal (steak-and-mushroom pie, ploughman's plate) at a new Olde English pub, the **Rose & Crown.** Happy hour features neat munchies and continues from 11am to 6:30pm, and there are sing-alongs at the piano every night. **Tanaka of Tokyo** and **Odoriki** are both popular for Japanese food. Free Polynesian shows are held every night at 7 and 8pm.

Open daily from 9am to 11pm.

WAIKIKI SHOPPING PLAZA, 2250 Kalakaua Ave. Tel. 923-1191.

The first impression one gets on seeing the enclosed Waikiki Shopping Plaza, at the corner of Kalakaua and Seaside, is that it more properly belongs in New York or San Francisco or some sophisticated European city. Shops like **Courrèges, Bally of Switzerland,** and **Hunting World** have little to do with the islands. But as you ascend the escalators to the four shopping floors, it gets better and more versatile, with more of an island flavor. The traffic-stopper here is the five-story fountain by island designer Bruce Hopper, a wondrous, half-million-dollar creation with lights that change colors, and fascinating Plexiglas spheres and bubbles that make the waters dance. There's a different point of interest at each level, creating new surprises as you ride the escalators.

If your Japanese isn't up to snuff, fully half the stores, their names, and merchandise descriptions will be unintelligible to you. Sticking to English, however, you can still browse around and find a few shops offering good bargains. On the first floor, as you enter from Kalakaua Avenue, is the enormous, two-level **Advantage Hawaii,** which offers good prices on a huge variety of souvenirs, food, aloha wear, and more. We recently spotted Aloha Teddy Bears on sale for $9. Check the racks at **Villa Roma,** a high-fashion shop for women (they often run clearances on sports items), and also ogle the pretties at their other shop, **Chocolates for Breakfast,** with delectable designer women's clothing and elegant evening wear. Stock up on some reading matter at **Waldenbooks,** which has a very large selection. Art lovers will enjoy the **Art Forum Gallery,** which also has branches in Tokyo, Osaka, and Los Angeles. **Swimsuit Warehouse** is known for wide selections and good bargains. The owner of the **Hawaii Cloisonné Factory** makes some nice jewelry, fashion artifacts not available anywhere else in the United States, and not expensive. Check out **Betty's,** on the fifth floor, for very inexpensive wooden necklaces and matching earring sets, among other gift items. This is a wholesale import-export place open to the public.

Eelskin, in case you hadn't noticed, is that leather from the sea that is extremely popular in Hawaii, and "wholesale outlets" abound: One of the best of these, **Ali Baba Imports,** is right here. Among the huge display of merchandise, we saw well-made eelskin wallets for about $18–$40, handbags for around $60. Note that Ali Baba has another store at the Waikiki Business Plaza, Suite 201, 2270 Kalakaua Ave., and a toll-free ordering number: 800/222-7785. You might also check and comparison-shop several other eelskin stores at the plaza, like **Leather from the Sea** and **Eelskin Elegance,** where we made some excellent purchases on our last trip.

While most of the shops at the Waikiki Shopping Plaza are not budget-oriented, the basement restaurants certainly are, with a bevy of fast-food counters offering varied ethnic foods. (See "Specialty Dining" in Chapter 6). Open daily from 9:30am to 9:30pm.

CLOTHING & GIFT SHOPS

CLOTHING

The manufacturers of Hawaiian clothing we like best include Malihini of Hawaii, Mamo Howell, Hawaiian Heritage, Bete, Sun Babies, Princess Kaiulani, Tori

Richards, Shan-Yin, Carol Bennett, and Kahala and Cook Street (better men's apparel); you'll find these brands all over town. Note, too, that most of the specialty shops will make up muumuus for mother, aloha shirts for dad, and children's versions of either in matching fabrics, and will also make clothes for your special size. (We should tell you that locals consider this very "touristy.") Many will make bikinis to order, or at least allow you to match the top of one to the bottom of another. Made-to-measure work usually takes just a day or two and in most cases costs no more than ready-made garments.

Prices for Hawaiian clothes are pretty standard everywhere: Better muumuus average $50–$60 (short), $70–$80 or more (long). To realize substantial savings on aloha wear, your best bets are two places outside Waikiki we'll tell you about later: Hilo Hattie's Fashion Center, and Muumuu Factory. For antique Hawaiian shirts, see "Vintage Aloha Shirts," below.

CASA D'BELLA II, 2352 Kalakaua Ave. Tel. 923-6426.

We like this store a lot. They carry some stylish designs from New York and California as well as local resort wear, and they have a good collection of fashion jewelry, too.

LIBERTY HOUSE, 2314 Kalakaua Ave. Tel. 941-2345.

The Waikiki branch of Hawaii's premier department store has an extremely attractive selection of clothing for men, women, and children, too, with a good collection of shoes and accessories for men, women, and juniors and an extensive selection of cosmetics and fragrances. Liberty House is not inexpensive, but it gives you an idea of the best of mainland and Hawaiian fashions.

VINTAGE ALOHA SHIRTS

You know, of course, that antique aloha shirts—those from the 1930s, 1940s, and 1950s—for some inexplicable reason, have become high fashion on the mainland. Why show-biz celebrities and socialites are willing to pay $100–$1,000 for rayon shirts that have been hanging in somebody's closet for 30 or 40 years is a mystery to us, but the demand is there.

BAILEY'S ANTIQUE CLOTHES & THRIFT SHOP, 758 Kapahulu Ave. Tel. 734-7628.

The shirts that make their way into places like this are snatched up quickly by folks like Robin Williams, Tom Selleck, and Steven Spielberg, to drop just a few names. Bailey's is a fascinating store, however (it also stocks other early island wear from various cultures), and it's well worth a look; if you can't afford one of the pricey items, choose one of their more than 1,000 shirts in the $5–$10 range, 1,200 shirts for $10–$20, or something like 300 shirts from the 1950s, which range from $20 to $125. Approximately 300 "silky" rayon shirts from the 1940s command prices of $100–$1,000. Have a look, too, at their nifty (albeit expensive) art deco and retro jewelry.

KULA BAY, in the Royal Hawaiian Hotel, 2259 Kalakaua Ave. Tel. 923-0042.

This store, which also has a branch at the Hilton Hawaiian Village (tel. 943-0771), has done some clever work taking authentic prints from shirts of the 1930s, 1940s, and early 1950s, having them painted on long-staple cotton in more muted colors, and turning out handsome, very well-tailored aloha shirts for about $50. For photos of the originals, and a history of the aloha shirt, read the book called *The Hawaiian Shirt*, by H. Thomas Steel (Abbeville Press), available at many local bookstores.

SOUVENIRS & GIFTS

ABC DISCOUNT STORES Scads of Honolulu tourists swear by the low prices at the ABC Discount Stores, and so do we! There are literally dozens of ABC stores in Waikiki, sometimes two to a block! You can usually expect to save 20%–25% here on small items, sometimes more. Hawaiian perfumes and boxes of chocolate-covered macadamia nuts are always a bargain here, and very welcome presents back home. In addition to gift items (many packaged ready for mailing), ABC has just about everything you need for a vacation at the beach, including bathing caps, sunglasses, straw beach mats for under $1, beach cover-ups, cosmetics, drugs, not to mention inexpensive luggage, groceries, deli, fresh produce, and liquor, and usually the lowest prices anywhere on Hawaiian scenic postcards. Most are open daily, from 7:30am to midnight. Truly indispensable resources for the Hawaii visitor.

OTHER SHOPS A number of budget stores that sell perfumes, cosmetics, and souvenirs can be found on Kalakaua in the area just Diamond Head of Uluniu Avenue, up toward the Queen Kapiolani Hotel. You can also count on good buys at **Holiday Mart,** which you'll read about ahead. **Woolworth's,** in the Bank of Hawaii Building on Kalakaua, now charges more for some standard souvenir items than ABC and some of the other shops, but their discount on jade, coral, opal, and 14-karat gold items is good. They will also mail your gifts and souvenirs home for you. **Long's Drugstore** in Ala Moana is another excellent source for small items; their values are consistently tops.

What to buy? Hawaiian perfumes make delightful small presents. Royal Hawaiian is the leading brand name for island fragrances—pikake, ginger, orchid, plumeria—all of them sweetly floral and worlds away from the sophistication of Paris. Gift packages complete with artificial orchids begin around $5; higher-priced perfumes have a real orchid right in the bottle.

As for jewelry, black coral, mined from the waters off Maui, is handsome in small tree shapes and in numerous other pins and pendants. An exquisite pink coral called angelskin has also been found off Maui waters. Blue coral is the "look" with jeans and casual tops. Crystals are popular here, as they are everywhere. You'll see all of these, in abundance, at jewelry stores all over the islands.

Several island manufacturers turn out attractive, inexpensive wooden jewelry. **Elena,** for one, does colorful wooden and composition fish, birds, and tropical flowers, in earrings, pins and necklaces, etc., beginning at $6 a pair for earrings. A firm called **"Oh My Gosh By Josh"** creates gecko and other delightful jewelry, with pins beginning under $10. And **Island Attitudes** has wonderful painted wooden jewelry with Polynesian themes. (The Hawaiian jewelry department at Liberty House—see above—usually has a good selection of these, often on sale.)

You can buy Hawaiian delicacies—such exotic tastes as guava jelly, coconut syrup, passion-fruit ambrosia, Kona coffee, macadamia nuts—at almost any grocery store, and should you want to send a package home, the best and most reasonably priced places are Long's Drugs, ABC Discount, and the **Waikiki A-1 Superette.** Pineapples ordered at Dole Pineapple's Cannery Square are also excellent value.

READERS RECOMMEND

Dole Pineapple Cannery, *Cannery Sq. (tel. 523-3653). "We ordered our pineapples to bring home at the Dole Pineapple Cannery Square. They delivered it right to our airline check-in place. These were the best pineapples we have ever had. Plus, they made wonderful gifts to bring back for office co-workers. We got 10 pineapples for around $20, and they were huge ones at that."*—Julie Clark, Olean, N.Y.

T-shirts, practically a uniform in Hawaii, make fun presents for almost everybody on your list; they're in every store, at every price. **Crazy Shirts,** which, like the ABC Discount Stores, seems to be on almost every block in Waikiki, can be counted on for witty designs, good fabrics, and prices of around $18 for Ts, around $40 for sweatshirts. For information on Crazy Shirts' factory outlet stores, see "Discount Shops and Factory Outlets" in "Shopping A to Z," in "Around Town," below.

Eelskin is another very big item for presents. Almost every eelskin store claims that it sells "wholesale." Reputedly the country's largest wholesaler, **Leather of the Sea,** in the Waikiki Shopping Plaza, 2250 Kalakaua Ave., fourth floor, has many good buys. Also in the same shopping center, **Ali Baba** and **Eelskin Elegance** offer good values. *Just bear in mind that eelskin has been known to demagnetize credit cards and bank cards, rendering them useless.*

2. ALA MOANA CENTER

Honolulu's fabulous modern shopping center (the largest open-air mall in the world), the Ala Moana Center, 1450 Ala Moana Blvd. (tel. 946-2811), just across Ala Moana Beach from Waikiki, is an example of island architecture at its best. Landscaped with trees, flowers, fountains, and a meandering stream down its Central Mall, which is graced with large works of sculpture, the Ala Moana Center is always packed with enough island families to make it worth seeing for that reason alone. But the stores are, of course, the main attraction—more than 150 of them, an international bazaar full of intriguing wares. We'll mention just a few, but shopping buffs will come back here many, many times.

One of Hawaii's biggest department stores, **Sears Roebuck,** is here, with the usual mainland amenities and the unusual Hawaiian specialties—like orchid plants (Sears will ship to the mainland and guarantees live delivery), and a tremendous selection of muumuus and island clothing at very reasonable prices. **J. C. Penney** is known for fashion and for excellent value in all departments, as is **Watumull's.** The flagship store of **Liberty House** is here, and most striking it is, its eaves decorated with Hawaiian tapas. Count on top-quality goods in all departments. Their specialty boutiques can be quite pricey.

We always enjoy browsing around in the large Japanese-owned department store ✪ **Shirokiya,** which has everything from state-of-the-art stereo to kids' T-shirts that glow in the dark, with a wonderful array of fashion, cosmetics, china, housewares, furniture, and fine arts in between. Check out the first-floor section on shiatsu foot massagers, chairs, etc. Give your feet a rest. Shirokiya's gourmet-food department, on the second floor, is worth a trip in itself. A vast array of wonderful sushi and other traditional Japanese fare is offered at dozens of booths and counters. There's plenty of food to take home. Or you can create a meal for yourself out of these offerings and then devour them on the spot, in the dining lanai. Most days from 3:30 to 8pm there's an evening buffet and sushi bar, priced according to what you eat.

Shirokiya is also a good place to find unusual and inexpensive gift items. Check the luggage accessories counter in particular: Handsome coasters with designs of Ukiyoe prints or antique kimonos make marvelous small presents for around $5. Fashion note: Shirokiya also carries socks, with a space for the big toes. You wear these *tabis* with your *zoris,* of course.

There are also dozens of small shops in the center, reflecting just about every interest and taste. One of our favorites is ✪ **Art Lines,** with a highly tasteful collection of jewelry, animal masks, carving, statuary, crystals, bells, Tiffany-type lamps, and the like, collected from all over the world—especially from Egypt, Morocco, India, Indonesia, Greece, and Africa. There's an exotic collection of sterling-silver earrings. Prices begin at $4.50 for a shark's tooth and could go as high as

$3,500 for a superb Buddha. This is Ala Moana's "bestseller" shop. Another of our favorites is **The Nature Store,** a restful oasis "dedicated to providing products and experiences which encourage the joyous observation, understanding, and appreciation of the world of nature." To that end, they feature everything from yoyos to telescopes, including a good selection of minerals and fossils, books on natural history, field guides, natural jewelry—lots of things that kids can enjoy, like an inflatable *Tyrannosaurus rex* for $19.95. Ask about their calendar of free events: You might be able to go birding in Kapiolani Park, or let the kids participate in a scavenger hunt in Ala Moana Park (for ages 5–9).

Summer's Place is also ecologically oriented and sells a good deal of "earth" merchandise, as well as interesting and unusual T-shirts, the best selection of rubber stamps and accessories on the island, licensed merchandise, and novelties. Sportswear bearing exclusive designs such as "Royal Hawaiian Polo Club" and "Island Logo Palm Tree" can be found at **Island Logo,** which also carries nylon bags and wallets, visors, hats, earrings, and other accessories.

Then there's **Paniolo Trading,** with clothes and accessories for the equestrian (*paniolo* means "cowboy" in Hawaiian). **Ethel's** has some stylish women's lines, including Liz Claiborne Petites. And **Benetton** brings the Italian sense of style here in vibrantly colored sportswear. **Banana Republic** is a must if you're going on safari, going on a trip, or just want to look stylish. These are not bargain stores, but everything is great quality for the price.

Quality is also the word at **Elephant Walk,** which has lovely hand-painted shirts, prints, Hawaiian dolls, jewelry, and wood chimes, among other treasures. The level of taste here is consistently high. Fashion is foremost at **Mosaic** and at **Villa Roma. Chocolates for Breakfast** has the sort of elegant clothing for women that never goes out of fashion. Bold, unusual designs grace the sportswear for women at **Défense d'Afficher,** whose shops originate in Paris. Only linen, cotton, and other natural fabrics are used to create the stylish fashions at **Alexia.**

Need something neat for the beach, the boat, or the bar? **Island Snow** is the place. Lots of good trinkets and small presents can be found at both **Ala Moana Gifts** and **Products of Hawaii.** At the latter, we saw wind chimes, prints, pot holders, candy, coffee, and many gift items, all at good prices.

Women going into ✪ **Headshots** looking like Plain Janes come out looking like high-fashion models. Headshots is a "contemporary photographic studio specializing in women and beauty." A $59 session includes complete makeup, hairstyling, the use of clothing, accessories, hats, flowers—whatever will turn Cinderella into the Princess. Or a sophisticated business look can be chosen. Men and kids, too, are welcome. Each client is given 10–12 contact proofs to keep; additional print orders are extra. And the results are extraordinary. If you've got a few hours to spare, photos taken here might turn out to be one of your most unusual souvenirs of Hawaii!

Prides of New Zealand seems a bit incongruous in hot Hawaii, selling woolen sweaters, sheepskin rugs, and sheepskin car seats, but the people here swear that sheepskin is cool. Stop in at **Musashiya** for wonderful patterns and fabrics, or pick up a surfboard at lively **Hawaiian Island Creations. Tahiti Imports** takes Tahitian prints of their own design and makes them into muumuus, aloha shirts, bikinis, and pareaus. They also sell their exquisite hand-printed fabrics by the yard.

The Sharper Image, the catalog store to end all catalog stores, is a fabulous playground for adults, so even if you have to push along the aisles with the crowds, don't miss it. Come in and try their exercise bikes, the self-massage table or massage chair (soothing after a hard day's shopping), and scads of other curiosities.

We often pick up gifts from the **Compleat Kitchen and More.** A company called What a Melon creates charming designs of Hawaiian flowers and fruits with a motto reading "Grown in Hawaii," and puts them on towels and more. We love their Manoa Lettuce Bag, with its pidgin commentary: "Mo bettah den da plastic from da supermarket." Agreed. We also like the handcrafted koa-wood paddles, chopsticks, and wine corks made at the Hilo Vocational Rehabilitation Center, $6.50, $10, and $12. Tutu Nene potholders, with Hawaiian quilt designs on one side and native Hawaiian animals on the other, would make nice gifts, as would the trays featuring designs from the menu covers of the Matson Line ships—pretty enough to hang as a wall decoration. **Island Shells** has lots of stunning jewelry, shell and wood chimes, shell roses, and the like, and prices are always fair. And their shell flower arrangements are beautiful. It's fun to go fly a kite in Honolulu, and the place to get your equipment is at **High Performance Kites,** right near the centerstage. Many of their kites come from one of our favorite places on Molokai, the Big Wind Kite Factory. Also near the centerstage, and in a sense the "heart" of the shopping center, is the ✪ **Honolulu Book Store,** with superb selections in every category, especially Hawaiiana, and newspapers that may—or may not—make you nostalgic for home, like the *Los Angeles Times, San Francisco Chronicle, New York Times,* and *Wall Street Journal.*

Need some decorating ideas? Striking posters, many with an Eastern motif, begin around $30 at the **Art Board.** Many fine prints and posters can be found at **Art Avenue. Otsuka Galleries** specializes in Asian art. **Iida's** is crammed with colorful Japanese giftware and decorations.

For nearly 30 years, **Irene's Hawaiian Gifts** has been a favorite with residents and visitors alike for unique island gifts. Their specialty is unusual carvings from native woods and collector's items like porcelain dolls, handcrafted Christmas ornaments, quilt kits, lauhala purses, hula implements, and koa-wood outrigger canoes with tapa sails, made locally and sold at good prices.

Feet getting to you? The **Slipper House** is a good place to replace whatever worn-out sandals you're trudging around in. They claim to have the widest selection of casual footwear in the state, with over 400 styles of made-in-Hawaii sandals, including hard-to-find golf slippers with cleats, for $23.25. They also have hard-to-find cotton *tabis* for $11.50, and a wide array of lightweight totes and carrying bags. Best known for traditional men's and boy's wear, beautifully made and well priced, **Reyn's** also features good-looking women's clothes, here and in many shops on Oahu and the neighbor islands. Check in at the big **Vim and Vigor Health Food Store** for excellent selections of honey, nut butters, whole grains, organic foods, superb home-baked goods that should not be missed, and other healthies. Stop in, too, at the **Crackseed Center,** if you want to know what Hawaiian youngsters clamor for (crackseeds, originally a Chinese confection, are a cross between seeds and candies—very sticky, very tasty).

Coffee-lovers should definitely pay a visit to **Gloria Jean's Coffee Bean,** where coffees from all over the world (not just Kona coffee) are featured. They're available by the cup and by the package. It's fun to stop at the little coffee bar for an espresso or the coffee of the day—perhaps a small Zimbabwe, or an iced decaf amaretto, for under $1. And there are many wonderful decaf coffees to take home, like Irish Creme, Chocolate Raspberry, or Vanilla Nut Creme. The aromas are irresistible. Chocaholics, too, will find the temptations at Ala Moana hard to resist, like the chocolates at **Ed and Don's** and **See's Candies.** And forget we ever told you about **Mrs. Field's Chocolate Chippery,** which turns out warm and moist cookies studded with chips, sold individually, or by the pound at around $8.

The newest addition to Ala Moana is **Palm Boulevard,** which is being called the Rodeo Drive of Honolulu. Budgeteers won't find much to buy here, but it's always fun to browse at the likes of Alion, Chanel, Polo/Ralph Lauren, Georg Jensen Silver, Gucci, Jaeger, and Adrienne Vittadini, to drop just a few names. Posh Neiman-Marcus will open here this year.

One of the most intriguing stores at Ala Moana is the **Foodland Supermarket.** It's like an international food fair, reflecting the cultures that make up Hawaii—and the rest of the world. You walk along seemingly endless aisles of exotic foods: fresh-frozen coconut milk, packages of weird-looking Japanese dried fish, health foods, tortillas, English biscuits, French cheese, you name it—if it's edible, this place has got it. The salad bar includes kimchee, lomi-lomi salmon, and fresh poi, so create your own lunch. You can, in addition, pick up some okolehao, Hawaii's potent ti-root drink, in the large liquor department. If life has become boring in that little kitchenette of yours, don't miss a visit here. There's also an inexpensive souvenir section.

For more bargains in souvenirs and small items at Ala Moana, it's trusty old **ABC Discount Stores, Long's,** and **Woolworth's.** Check out the weekly specials at the last named.

The best bargains at Ala Moana are available when the stores take to the sidewalks—the ground-floor level, that is—displaying racks and racks of clothing for very low prices.

Remember the center, too, for free entertainment during local holidays and at special ethnic celebrations; you may catch a Japanese or Philippine dance group, a Hawaiian show, or some of the island's top nightclub entertainers. For years now, the **Young People's Hula Show,** presented every Sunday at 9:30am on the centerstage, has been a Honolulu institution. Don't miss it. A more-or-less continuous program of local events and entertainment takes place on the centerstage.

Should you wish to make a contribution to various Hawaiian charities and educational organizations, you can do so easily. A kiosk on the street level called **Worthies** sells T-shirts of various attractive designs. They cost $10–$24, and proceeds go to benefit charities. A worthy idea.

Ala Moana Center has always been one of the best locales in town for inexpensive dining. And the 850-seat, glass-enclosed dining court called **Makai Market,** on the makai (ocean) side of the center, makes the possibilities for entertaining eating here better than ever. For a complete run-down of the possibilities here, see "Specialty Dining" in Chapter 6.

Most Ala Moana Center establishments stay open seven days a week: Monday through Friday from 9:30am to 9pm, on Saturday from 9:30am to 5:30pm (but restaurants at Makai Market close at 5pm), and on Sunday from 10am to 5pm.

From Kuhio Avenue in Waikiki, you can take TheBUS no. 8 and you'll be at Ala Moana (barring heavy traffic) in about 10 minutes. Parking areas are numerous—and they even have coconut palms coming through the concrete! If you should have any trouble finding a parking space, however, you can sometimes get valet service at peak shopping times and on holidays. Just drive up on the mall (or second) level, and around to the ocean side. Smack in the middle, midway between Sears and Liberty House, you'll find the service. The cost is $2, plus tip.

NEARBY SPECIAL SHOP There's a very special crafts shop located across the road and a block Ewa of Ala Moana Center, called ✪ **Creative Fibers,** 450 Piikoi St. (tel. 537-6374), just across Piikoi from Sears. It carries everything from needles and thread to glamorous batik jackets from Bali. Exotic cottons from Asia and Europe are stacked next to pareaus, for about $6 a yard. There are molas from Central America, Indian spreads, and other unusual fabrics, as well as kilim carpets and pillows from Turkey and Iran. You'll find beads, trinkets and jewelry, Turkish hand-weaves, silk scarves, and marvelous indigo cotton fabric designed by Escher of Holland and inspired by themes from Java. Kits for making fabric nursery-rhyme books are $6, and a delight. Closed Sunday.

3. AROUND TOWN

SHOPPING CENTERS

WARD WAREHOUSE, 1050 Ala Moana Blvd. Tel. 531-6411.

One of the most eye-catching of Honolulu's shopping centers is Ward Warehouse, located on Ward Avenue between Auahi Street and Ala Moana, across from Fisherman's Wharf. More than 65 shops and restaurants occupy the handsome two-story structures fashioned out of great rough-hewn planks, and there seems to be a higher-than-usual level of taste and selectivity here. It's a favorite shopping destination for local people and visitors alike.

A dazzling showplace for handcrafts is **Nohea Gallery,** a gallery and outlet for many local craftpeople: You'll see beautiful ceramics, leaded glass, fine furniture made of local hardwoods, flower pillows, jewelry, modern and traditional metal sculpture, and soft sculpture. Note the Old Hawaiian prints (from $12), and lovely notepapers, too. Fine-art posters, art reproductions, and original prints may also be found at **Frame Shack.** There are nicely matted small prints. They also have art-related T-shirts. If you're in town for a while and want to learn the fine art of making artificial flowers, stop in at **The Extra Dimension,** which sells beautiful flowers and gift items and represents the Miyuki Art Flower Studio of Hawaii. All the flowers are made of different fabrics and are quite handsome.

The most striking women's clothing at Ward Warehouse might well be found at **Mamo Howell.** Mamo Howell was a well-known island hula dancer and later became a Christian Dior model in Paris. She's turned her artistic flair to designing, and the results are stunning muumuus long and short; their inspiration comes mostly from Hawaiian-quilt motifs. Her designs are unmistakable once you've seen them—and you'll see them on the best-dressed women in town. Dresses are out of our price range (they go upward of $135), but quite affordable and also lovely are an array of small items using similar patterns, especially the quilted tote bags, lined with nylon, $35. Mamo creates charming children's clothing, too.

In the few years that it's been here, **Pomegranates in the Sun** has established a loyal following of fashion-conscious women. It features local artists and designers inspired by the Hawaiian atmosphere. There are many one-of-a-kind items. Prices are not generally low, but there are some affordable items: We saw delightful cotton sundresses at $55, long T-shirts for around $20, designer umbrellas from Australia at $30. Look for the smashing new Pomegrantes in the Sun in Haleiwa when you journey around the island.

There are tons of good buys—clothing, Balinese masks and carvings, paintings by Chinese artists, and more—at **Imports International.** Men can find good aloha shirts at $19; women can find many attractive items from Bali at delightfully low prices. If Bobbie or Diana are on hand, they'll help you coordinate an outfit. For discounts on the popular Bebe line of women's sportswear, check the **Bebe Discount Outlet,** where savings can be as much as 40%–75%.

Birkenstock Footprints deserves your attention: It's the place to get those clunky-looking, marvelous-feeling, naturally contoured sandals that give you a "barefoot on the beach" sensation even on hard surfaces. They're for men, women, and kids of all ages, and the average price is about $85 for adults, $56 for children.

You may want to pick up some Christmas ornaments from **Kris Kringle's Den,** or some gorgeous fans among the Chinese arts and crafts at **Heavenly Lotus.** They have charming inexpensive items—cinnabar necklaces at $10, Chinese cutout notepapers at $2.50, hand-painted T-shirts at $29—in addition to more costly treasures. Note the potpourris, sachets, and lacy and frilly things for bed and bath at **Private World.**

The **Executive Chef** is for the compulsive cook; we saw wineglasses, cookie molds, French copperware, and other kitchen joys, at good prices. One of their niftiest items is the Vacu-Vin, a wine resealing system for home use, at $20. You'll also find natural-sandstone coasters, Matson Line menu trays, and a delightful selection of Hawaiian gourmet items—papaya salsa, macadamia-nut mustard, passion-fruit butter, and Hawaiian teas like guava, papaya, and passion fruit.

Next door to the Executive Chef, the same management presents bath and travel accessories as well as unique personal-care items at **Bath and Butler.** We flipped for the line of kukui-nut-oil–based lotions, soaps, and bath gel made by Elizabeth's Fancy. Average price is $3.50. Try the Plumeria Lei moisture lotion; it captures the true fragrance of the islands. Check out their locally made backpacks, and their tote bags, too, in tropical and geometric prints.

Nora Estelle has terrific handbags and accessories, and a very large collection of Laurel Birch items, which we love—shirts, bags, cups, totes. Every kind of athletic shoe and then some is available at **Runners Route Plus,** and **Island Sunsport** is the place for swimwear for men and women. And the people at **L.A. Image** may change your life—they'll do your colors, suggest clothing, hairstyles, makeup—a complete makeover. And they have some clothing on hand, as well.

Candy fanatics will have to visit **Carousel Candyland,** like an old-fashioned candy store, with jellybeans in jars, rock candy, licorice drops, yummy chocolates made on the Big Island, and traditional Hawaiian treats such as crackseed and mocha crunch.

Conscientious Honolulu mommies shop **Child's Play** for creative play and learning materials, educational toys, and books. An excellent selection. They collect dollhouse miniatures in the gigantic dollhouse that is **My Favorite Things.** And moms-in-waiting, or those who've already delivered, find **In Bloom** just what they've been looking for: attractive maternity and baby clothes under one roof. As soon as baby gets older, they graduate to **In Bloom the Next Generation,** which has charming clothing, furniture, and gifts for children from age 2 up. Children of all ages, and men and women too, love the line of "Native clothing," all made from pure hand-woven cotton and hand-printed in original designs, at **The Native Company.**

Quality gift items—inlaid music boxes, scrimshaw, Italian porcelain antiques and collectibles—are easy to find at **Traditions.** Need a book or a tape, a newspaper or greeting card? **Waldenbooks** has a large branch here, and they'll order any book for you, at no extra charge.

End your excursion, perhaps, at the **Coffee Works,** a charming shop that purveys all manner of imported coffees, teas, and chocolates, as well as some very attractive vessels from which to sip them. Coffee makers, too. Happiness is a slice of carrot cake and a cup of café Vienna, at their coffee bar.

We've told you about the **Chowder House** for a quick seafood meal, the **Old Spaghetti Factory** for pasta in a fabulous setting, and **Restaurant Benkei** for some fabulous Japanese buffet meals. **Stuart Anderson's Cattle Company** is locally famous for well-priced prime ribs and chicken dinners, served in an upbeat setting with a great view of Kewalo Boat Basin. For light snacks, choose among the fast-food stands (seating in a central courtyard) at the **Food Express** (everything from burgers to saimin to health-food salads), or visit **Harpo's** for pizza. There are outside tables on the lower level.

Look for **The Art Cove** at Ward Warehouse. Since a different local artist is featured each day, you get a chance to meet and talk with the artist, perhaps buy some of his or her work at studio—not gallery—prices.

Ward Warehouse's Amphitheatre hosts a variety of events and entertainment, from tea dances to flower shows to Bon dances and then some. Shopping hours are 10am to 9pm Monday through Friday, until 5pm on Saturday, and from 11am to 4pm on Sunday. Restaurants stay open until late in the evening. From Waikiki, take TheBUS no. 8, marked WARD AVENUE, from Kuhio Avenue, or Kalia Road. It's about a 15-minute ride from Waikiki. And it's also located on the Waikiki Trolley route.

WARD CENTRE, 1200 Ala Moana Blvd. Tel. 531-6400.

Down the road a block from Ward Warehouse is Ward Centre, another sophisticated collection of boutiques and restaurants, all with a high level of charm and taste. The emphasis is on small, very expensive boutiques, so we usually find ourselves coming here to eat at some of our favorite restaurants—**Compadres,**

Crêpe Fever, Mocha Java, Keo's at Ward Centre, Andrew's, Il Fresco, Monterey Bay Canners, and **Ryan's Grill** (see Chapter 6, "Honolulu Dining," for details) and doing a lot of just looking, thanks.

Its fun to explore ✪ **Sedona,** "Your New Age Resource," a delightful store whose cactus in the window and crystals, jewelry, and such are reminiscent of that New Age town in Arizona. Check for news of the latest metaphysical happenings, perhaps pick up some Tinkerbells—"spherical meditation bells used to summon the nature spirits." Anytime after noon you can get a mini-phychic reading here.

Small women should definitely have a look at **Size Me Petite,** a shop with stylish collections for women 5′4″ and under.

Exquisite Treasures is a must for anyone who collects fine china. They have, for example, a complete line of Rosenthal china from Germany, not easily found in many other cities. And, of course, they ship.

Art lovers will want to spend time at **Art A La Carte,** a cooperative venture featuring the work of a dozen local artists who take turns "sitting" the gallery and often work right here. Unframed works begin at $25, matted cards at $10.

Of course, you'll want to stop by **Mary Catherine's** for "an extraordinary bakery experience"; this European-style bakery uses only fresh and natural ingredients, avoids additives and imitation flavors, and produces divine breads, cakes, and pastries on the order of chocolate decadence or Biarritz cake—that's a European delicacy made with cream cheese, coconut, and macadamia nuts. They also do some multigrain breads and wonderful scones, like the English raisin tea scones, the chocolate scones, and the very berry scones—with raspberries, strawberries, blackberries, and blueberries. If you just can't wait to sample the goodies, repair to the tables a few steps up, in the rear, where you can enjoy them—as many local businesspeople do—with an espresso or cappuccino. While your taste buds are thus activated, saunter over to **R. Field Wine Co.** at the opposite end of Ward Centre: In addition to fine wines, it stocks the likes of dried morels imported from France, smoked butterfish, Beluga caviar, and top-of-the-line pastas and cheeses flown in from Europe. Satisfying your sweet tooth, you can get the fabulous Crêpe Dentelle milk chocolate, Irish cream, strawberry, or cappuccino cordials, divine Kona coffee beans, or macadamia-nut popcorn among other goodies at **Honolulu Chocolate Company,** which also sells Valrhona—considered the world's finest chocolates. Watch out for the prices on this, however. We saw a chocolate bar for $5.75!

To reach Ward Centre, again take TheBUS no. 8 marked WARD AVENUE from Waikiki, a 15-minute ride.

KAHALA MALL, Waialae Kahala Shopping Complex. Tel. 732-7736.

Kahala Mall is an enclosed shopping center, with a main lobby like that of a hotel—carpeted and decorated with a beautiful fountain and plantings. Stretching out in various directions from the lobby are a bevy of interesting stores. Since the Kahala Mall has lately expanded from a popular neighborhood center into a "world-class shopping center," there's a great deal to see here. At some of the boutiques, it will be "just looking, thanks," but there are still many places of interest to the dollar-wise shopper.

Worth a special trip is ✪ **Following Sea,** a shop-gallery that represents the work of some 350 professional craft artists from 40 states, and sponsors outstanding monthly exhibitions. Everything is unique, and the inventory changes constantly. Prices range from a little to a lot, but there is a fine selection of ceramics, woodwork, and jewelry in the $30–$60 range. Their most popular items are hand-blown oil lamps, from $20. On a recent visit we saw koa, a native Hawaiian hardwood, beautifully crafted into notebook covers, chimes, jewel chests, and unique boxes, for $25–$300; plus exquisite leaded-glass boxes each with a beautiful seashell set into the top, for $53–$75. Following Sea is working with local craftspeople to develop new and unique items. Keep this place in mind for a gift for a special person—or for yourself.

Cotton Cargo bursts at the seams with lovely, pricey clothes—mostly from Mexico and India. Both custom-made and ready-to-wear couture clothing, plus accessories and jewelry, draw the cognoscenti to **Jeffrey Barr. Cielo** also excels in the couture look for fashion-conscious women; **Altillo** has the tops in European men's clothing. In a more familiar, popular-priced range, there's **The Gap, Benetton,** and the ubiquitous **Crazy Shirts. Alion** features the type of très chic clothing for milady that you see in *Vogue* and *Elle*.

One of our favorite shops, **Something Special,** is here, with its beautiful gifts, cards, English toiletries, Cane Haul Road and Raj T-shirts (delightful), Hawaiian-designed silk-screened Ts, toys, and all sorts of enchanting pretties. **B. Cool** has zany novelties, gifts, and cards. We like the selection of beautiful stationery, cards, desk accessories, bookmarks, and calendars at **The Paperie.** You can choose upbeat houseware gifts at **The Compleat Kitchen. Jennie's Garden** has a good selection of leis, cut flowers, arrangements, and quality houseplants.

Top off your shopping excursion with a snack or a meal at the **Yum Yum Tree,** a restaurant enormously popular with the neighborhood people for its well-priced food, deft service, and friendly atmosphere. Be sure to try a slice of their incredibly good pies—strawberry cheese and English toffee are among the choices; you'll want to take a whole pie home with you. Or enjoy a delicious northern Chinese meal at **Yen King,** one of the best such restaurants in these parts. **California Pizza Kitchen** is stylish with both table and counter seatings in a smart black-and-white room. Its pastas and pizzas—wood-fired with a variety of unusual toppings like Thai chicken or Cajun or vegetarian goat cheese—are light-years ahead of the ordinary. Other popular island restaurants represented here include **Bernard's New York Deli, Patti's Chinese Kitchen,** and **Randy's.**

To reach Kahala Mall, take Kapahulu to the Lunalillo Freeway East to the Waialae exit.

PEARLRIDGE SHOPPING CENTER, Aiea. Tel. 488-0981.

Out in Aiea, about a half-hour drive from Waikiki, is the Pearlridge Shopping Center, a multi-million-dollar complex that's a big favorite with the local people. Pearlridge boasts 170 stores, 16 theaters, two food courts, and three "phases." It's built on opposite sides of an 11-acre watercress farm. Shoppers travel between Phase I and Phase II in Hawaii's only monorail train. From your perch in the monorail, you'll enjoy a panoramic view of Pearl Harbor. Across the street, Pearlridge Phase III houses several more shops, theaters, and an office complex. Kids will enjoy Pearlridge and so will grownups; it's a good place to keep in mind for a rainy-day family excursion.

As at most of the shopping centers catering to the local trade, familiar names such as **Liberty House, Sears, J. C. Penney, Long's Drugs,** and **Woolworth's** dominate the scene. **Shirokiya** shows the Japanese influence, with many captivating art objects from Asia. For those who must have the very latest in fashions, Pearlridge is an embarrassment of riches. For women, **Contempo Casuals, Pepperkorn, Casual Corner,** and **Rosebuds** are just a few to tempt the shopper. For the latest in men's fashions, **Coda, Jeans West, Oak Tree, Visions USA,** and **Kramers** have it all. Other popular stores include **Taj Clubhouse, Benetton, Curious Porpoise,** and **Sam Goody.**

Point your kids in the direction of **Toys 'R Us** and they'll be happy: It's jammed with just about every imaginable kind of toy. **Fernandez Fun Factory's Flagship** in Pearlridge Phase II must surely be one of the world's fanciest "penny arcades," featuring the newest and most elaborate electronic games.

Hungry? Pearlridge has two food courts that "bring the world to you": **Zen's Korean Barb-B-Que, Elena's Filipino Foods, Panda Express, Tsuruya Noodle Shop,** and **Taco El Paso** suggest the possibilities. Free-standing restaurants include **Sizzler's Steakhouse, Denny's, Bravo, Bandito's, Monterey Bay Canners,** and **Anna Miller's Coffee Shop.**

Official store hours at Pearlridge are 10am to 9pm Monday through Saturday and 10am to 5pm on Sunday. You can easily squeeze your visit to Pearlridge into your trip to Pearl Harbor or Makaha. If you're driving to Pearl Harbor on Kam Highway, you see it on your right just after you reach Pearl Harbor's entrance to the U.S.S. *Arizona* Memorial. If you're driving out the H1 Freeway, take the Aiea exit. When driving out the Lunalillo Freeway from downtown, you'll see Pearlridge on the freeway directory signs. By bus, take TheBUS no. 20 from Waikiki to Pearlridge. *Note:* You can combine your visit to Pearlridge with one to the **Kam Super Swap Meet,** which is held at the Kam Drive-In, across from the shopping center, Wednesday and on weekends, beginning at 6am.

SHOPPING A TO Z

DISCOUNT SHOPS & FACTORY OUTLETS

BLAIR LTD, 404-A Ward Ave. Tel. 536-4907.

$ Visit this factory store for good buys in seconds of their fine monkeypod, koa, and other wood carvings. Blairs has been known for excellent quality for many years. Some of these factory-store items may have small flaws, but they can be repaired, and the savings are huge. (Many of our readers have been happy with their purchases here.)

CRAZY SHIRTS FACTORY OUTLET, in the Kokea Center, 1095 Dillingham Blvd. Tel. 841-5644.

$ You'll see Crazy Shirt stores all over the Hawaiian Islands—everybody loves their clever designs and sayings. They make great presents too, so if you want to buy a lot of them, you can save a bundle by going to their factory outlet stores, which offer factory seconds and display merchandise for 50% off retail prices; they frequently have special closeouts, which knock the prices down even further—to as much as 75%–85% off retail. Neat!

There's another outlet at the Costco Center (tel. 422-4552). Both stores are open everyday; phone for driving instructions.

HILO HATTIE FASHION CENTER, 700 Nimitz Hwy. Tel. 537-2926.

$ If garment factories appeal to you, here's one you can be bused to at no charge with extras thrown in. (They'll also take you to the Dole Pineapple Cannery.) This place offers something like 40,000 Hawaiian fashions to browse through, all for sale at factory prices, plus free refreshments, free hemming, and a lei greeting.

HOLIDAY MART, 801 Kaheka St. Tel. 946-1646.

$ A mecca for penny-pinchers, this huge discount store is in a residential neighborhood two blocks mauka of the Ala Moana Shopping Center. It's jammed with local people busy buying everything from groceries to books to toys to toasters, all at fat discounts. Buys are especially good if you watch for specials in Hawaiian wear for men, women, and keikis. While you're here, stock up on groceries and booze—the prices are excellent, much better than in the smaller stores at the beach. If it's time for lunch, you can join the crowd at the outside Chinese cafeteria deli, which has a good take-out department, as well as some 20 items on the steam table. Holiday Mart is open Monday through Saturday from 8am to midnight, until 10pm on Sunday.

LIBERTY HOUSE'S PENTHOUSE, 1 N. King St. Tel. 941-2345.

$ Downtown is where the local people do a lot of their shopping, and we'll let you in on a kamaaina secret known to very few tourists: Discounted merchandise from all the Liberty House stores around town is brought here, and the initial reduction is a whopping 50%. On top of that, the price is automatically dropped another 30% on the first Monday of each succeeding month. Most of the items consist of women's, children's and men's clothing and accessories. There are also terrific values on special-purchase items. On a recent shopping foray we found $100 handbags at $50, $150 dresses at $75, and $30 aloha shirts at $15. Enough said? At their clearinghouse, you can also get towels, sheets, pots and pans, and gift items at 50% off. This is one of those places where on some days you'll find nothing suitable, on other days you'll strike it rich!

The rest of Liberty House and the other Fort Street stores have merchandise similar to what you find in their Waikiki and Ala Moana branches, but perhaps a shade more citified, since they cater mostly to a local trade. It's fun to come here during the lunch hour, when local people are shopping, eating lunch on the many stone benches and seats that dot this fountained area, and watching their kids play in the sand. Traffic is closed off, creating one long window-shopping promenade. If you're hungry, stop at any of the restaurants or fast-food stands mentioned in Chapter 6.

MALIA: THE FACTORY OUTLET, 2200 Kam Hwy. (approached from Dillingham Blvd.). Tel. 847-3258.

Stunning savings—as much as 40%–70% off regular retail prices—make the 20-minute-or-so drive out to this store eminently worthwhile. Malia offers contemporary resort fashion—jackets, big shirts, cotton sweaters, skirts, and dresses. On a recent visit we walked away with a beautiful $64 silk sweater for $15 (they were selling two for $25). We've never seen muumuus here, but Malia does carry men's cotton aloha shirts in exclusive prints, $38 elsewhere, only $25–$28 here. Malia's selections change constantly and are better some days than others, but some typical examples would include $76 dresses for $56, $28 shorts for $15, $35 T-shirts for just $10. Great fun, good buys. Open Monday through Saturday from 9am to 5:30pm.

PRINCESS KAIULANI, 1222 Kaumaulii St. Tel. 847-4806.

This manufacturer was the first to start using pretty, small-figured, calico prints in pastel colors. Their dresses are ultra-feminine, with eyelet or lace or ruffles; the fabrics are top-quality. This attractive factory showroom offers its own products and others at about a 30% savings on most retail stores. Long muumuus, selling here in the $75–$80 range, would be well over $100 at most stores. Open to the public Monday through Saturday from 9am to 5pm.

THE ULTIMATE YOU, 1112 Auahi St. Tel. 523-3888.

Just opposite Ward Centre is a shop known to few tourists; but the "Bergdorf Goodman of the consignment shops," as it might be called, is very well known indeed to Hawaii's most fashion-conscious women. This is where they come for new and next-to-new high fashion at surprisingly low prices. Owner Kelsey Sears has contacts with socialites and celebrities in the islands, on the mainland, and in Europe; when they get slightly bored with their designer duds after a wearing or two (or when they've compulsively bought five-of-a-kind sweaters and never worn them), they send them to Sears, which resells them for anywhere from 50% to 90% off retail price. She insists that everything be in "pristine condition." Half the store consists of brand-new merchandise, much of it from European designers, that is also heavily discounted. Obviously, the stock here changes daily, so you never can tell what you'll find, but it's worth a look-see. Some examples: A $3,000 Gucci alligator handbag sold for $495; a $600 Yves St. Laurent skirt for $90; and $300 garments worn once or twice for $80 or $90. A $100 dress could go for as little as $49, a $75 silk blouse for as little as $25. "Every day mini-miracles happen here," Sears says. The Ultimate You is open Monday through Saturday from 10am to 6pm.

READERS RECOMMEND

Thrift Shops. *"The seven Goodwill stores on Oahu are great places to find good, 'gently used' muumuus from such stores as Liberty House, McInerny, Watumull, etc. They have a large selection, all dry-cleaned, for $7.95, sometimes less on sale. . . . I stopped in a Salvation Army store one day, and enjoyed it so much I went back. It was very clean and neat, and they had a big selection of muumuus, priced from $1.55 and up, about $10 for lovely Eastern brocades! I bought many, some just for the material, others to wear. One day, I got five long muumuus! They also have bathing suits for 98¢ and up, and monkeypod from 49¢. There are seven Salvation Army stores on the island. I also like the Thrift Shop at the University of Hawaii for books, Hawaiian clothes, jewelry, household items. It was open only Tuesday, Wednesday, and Thursday, so check before going (also closed during the month of August). The thrift shop at Central Union Church on Beretania, near Kalakaua, is one of the best. It's large, bright, clean, and well stocked with nice items at reasonable prices. Open on Wednesday from 9am to 3pm and on Saturday from 9am to noon. . . . I found another thrift shop, the Laniolu Good Samaritan Thrift Shop, 333 Lewers St., open Monday, Wednesday, and Friday from 9am to noon. It is in the Lutheran Senior Retirement Center, and profits go to the center."*—Mrs. Dorothy Astman, Northport, N.Y. [*Authors' Note:* Another excellent thrift shop is St. Andrew's Economy Shop at St. Andrew's Cathedral, downtown at Beretania and Queen Emma Streets (tel. 536-5939), open Monday, Wednesday, and Friday from 9:30am to 4pm, Saturday until 1pm. The Punahou Thrift Shop, run by the famed Punahou School, also offers good values, and is open Monday, Wednesday, and Friday from 9am to 2pm. Should you happen to be in town for the Punahou Carnival (usually held in mid- or late January, be sure to check their Flea Market, especially at the close of the event, for sometimes-extraordinary savings). The Iolani School thrift shop, at 563 Kamaku St., has great bargains. It's open on Wednesday from 10am to 3pm and on Monday and Saturday from 9am to noon. Hours can change at these shops, so be sure to phone before you go.]

Kamaka Hawaii, Inc., *550 South St. (tel. 531-3165). "We purchased a lovely ukulele from Kamaka Hawaii, Inc., where factory seconds are priced $185–$545, when available."*—William D. Devlin, San Francisco, Calif. [*Authors' Note:* Visitors are welcome to visit their small factory, where they hire predominantly disabled workers and train them as craftspeople.]

FASHIONS

NAKE'U AWAI, 1613 Houghtailing St. Tel. 841-1221.

This store is a bit out of the way—unless you combine it with a visit to the Bishop Museum—but it's worth a trip if you like unusual fabrics and designs. Joel Nake'u Awai is a young Hawaiian designer whose beautiful silk-screened fabrics are a blend of the traditional and the contemporary in Hawaiian art. After he designs and produces the textiles, he has them whipped up into long skirts, shirts, muumuus, bags, and sundresses. They're not cheap, but the prices are certainly competitive with those of the better department stores and specialty shops; and the designs are exclusive. We also saw some very good-looking T-shirts with Hawaiian designs and an interesting array of locally crafted items—lauhala fans, floppy-brimmed hats, gift cards, woven bags, and books of Hawaii—for $16 and up. Inquire about his fashion shows. If you can catch one of them you're in for a treat. They're as imaginative as the clothes and include appearances by guest luminaries. The shop is open only until 3:30pm Monday through Friday, until 2pm on Saturday.

FLEA MARKETS

ALOHA FLEA MARKET, Aloha Stadium. Tel. 486-1529.

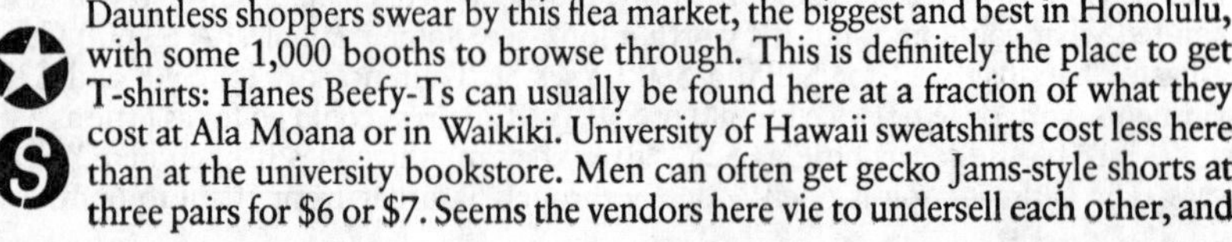

Dauntless shoppers swear by this flea market, the biggest and best in Honolulu, with some 1,000 booths to browse through. This is definitely the place to get T-shirts: Hanes Beefy-Ts can usually be found here at a fraction of what they cost at Ala Moana or in Waikiki. University of Hawaii sweatshirts cost less here than at the university bookstore. Men can often get gecko Jams-style shorts at three pairs for $6 or $7. Seems the vendors here vie to undersell each other, and the shoppers get the benefit. Aloha Flea Market is every Wednesday, Saturday, and Sunday (and daily for the three weeks before Christmas) from 6am to 3pm, and the really serious folks get there early. Take TheBUS no. 20 from Waikiki right to Aloha Stadium. Admission is 35¢ per person.

FOOD

If you're going to do any cooking in your kitchenette, you're going to be shocked when you do your first shopping for groceries. Food costs in Honolulu are substantially higher than in big cities on the mainland (almost one-third more, in some cases) and they are especially high in hotel shops. Hotel shops are a nice convenience, but if you're going to do any serious shopping, you're far better off taking your rented car and heading for the **supermarkets.**

The big Honolulu chains are Star, Times, Safeway, and Foodland (and Emjay's, a subsidiary of Foodland). There are several of each of these, with addresses, in the phonebook. Gem on Ward Avenue and Holiday Mart (801 Kaheka St., two blocks mauka of the Ala Moana Shopping Center), also offer low prices. In Waikiki, the best prices are found at Food Pantry, 2370 Kuhio Ave., an enormous supermarket located in central Waikiki, behind the International Market Place. Liquor prices are especially good here. There's another Food Pantry at 444 Hobron Lane, not far from the Ilikai Hotel. Prices are also good, although selection is limited, at the ABC Discount stores.

Natural foods are generally not inexpensive, so we were delighted to find "healthy food at prices that don't make you sick" at ✪ **Down to Earth Natural Foods,** 2525 S. King St. (tel. 947-7678), near University Avenue. *Honolulu* magazine has rated this friendly place as the best overall natural-food store in Honolulu. As big as a supermarket, Down to Earth has dozens of bins of grains and beans, a large refrigerator of organically grown fruits and vegetables, and a Natural Medicine Center that features, among other items, Chinese herbs, including ginseng and "dragon eggs." All products, including vitamin and mineral supplements, are totally vegetarian. Also on the premises is the Natural Deli for excellent vegetarian meals (see Chapter 6, "Honolulu Dining"). Open from 8am to 10pm every day.

Down to Earth is also associated with a stress-reduction center next door called the "Relaxation Station," which offers flotation tanks, massage, shiatsu, acupuncture—even brain-wave synchronization.

Just down the block, **Kokua Co-Op Natural Foods and Grocery,** 2357 S. Beretania St. (tel. 941-1922), offers a full line of natural foods and organic produce. They have fresh sandwiches, cold drinks, and a wide variety of snacks and gourmet vegetarian deli items. Open daily.

Terrific baked goods—freshly baked whole-grain breads (oatmeal, raisin, cinnamon, sprouted wheat), pies, and cakes—are the main reason for tracking down the popular **Vim and Vigor** store at Ala Moana Center. They also have good prices on an extensive selection of dried fruits, nut butters, fresh produce, and many other natural and organic items. Their snack bar is great, too.

If you'd like to shop for produce, fish, and meat with the locals, visit the **Ala Moana Farmer's Market** (a block from the Ala Moana–Ward intersection at Auahi Street), where the atmosphere is pungent and the prices low. It's a great place to get acquainted with local Hawaiian foods and taste sensations. The long, low building is lined with a number of stalls, some with ready-to-eat items. Here you can sample poi, raw fish, and other delicacies such as ogo, palu, and tako. In case you're not feeling all that adventurous, you can settle for a 12-ounce can of New Zealand corned beef or imu kalua pig, both cooked and ready for your own private luau. At **Haili's Hawaiian Foods,** in business since 1867, we saw one-day and two-day poi and even sour poi, all quite difficult to find.

It's also good fun—and good value—to attend one of the **People's Open Markets,** sponsored by the city of Honolulu. Farmers bring their produce to various spots on different days. The market closest to Waikiki takes place on Wednesday, from 9:45 to 10:45am, at Paki Playground; you'll find it on an outdoor basketball court behind the fire station on Kapahulu Avenue.

Get yourself downtown to **King's Bakery** at 1936 S. King St. (tel. 941-5211), which makes an incredibly delicious sweet bread; they will package and airmail this treat to the folks back home. A charge of $16 covers the shipping box, two loaves, and postage. Boxes of 6 and 12 are also available. You can sometimes find these breads sold at the airport, just before you reach the gate to board your plane.

GIFTS/NOVELTIES

MISSION HOUSES GIFT SHOP, Mission Houses Museum, 553 S. King St. Tel. 531-0481.

Here's an above-average selection of gift items, all of them reasonably priced. Some people find they can do almost all their gift shopping here. Consider, for example, mugs and drinking glasses ($6.50 and $6.75) and appliqué pillow kits ($14–$25) with Hawaiian quilt motifs. Or the tasteful T-shirts with Mission Houses or Hawaii quilt patterns or flowers ($16.95), the koa-wood bracelets ($16), Christmas ornaments made of lauhala and other local materials ($2–$10), temple bells ($9), and—hard-to-find—tapas that can be framed ($8). The shop also has an excellent selection of Hawaiiana, plus soaps, potpourris, and adorable finger puppets for children, at just $1.50. Open Monday through Saturday from 9am to 4pm and on Sunday from noon to 4pm; closed Monday holidays.

THE ZOOTIQUE, at the Honolulu Zoo, 151 Kapahulio Ave. Tel. 923-7472.

This gift shop of the Honolulu Zoo is filled with toys, books, kites, apparel, jewelry, and novelties with bird and animal themes. Our favorite items are the T-shirts made especially for the zoo with sayings like LION ON THE GRASS AT HONOLULU ZOO or SEE YOU LATER, ALLIGATOR, with accompanying drawings. Perhaps you'll walk away with some pop-up books, a stuffed animal or two, and some souvenirs sporting the zoo's logo. The Zootique is open from 8:30am to 4pm every day (except Christmas and New Year's), and all proceeds go to the Honolulu Zoo Hui, a nonprofit organization of friends of the zoo who raise funds for zoo improvements and educational programs.

READERS RECOMMEND

The Bishop Museum, *1525 Bernice St. (tel. 847-3511). "The Bishop Museum is always a 'must' on our list, but I want especially to recommend the museum bookstore and gift shop. It really is the only place to buy good books on Hawaii, beyond the picture books that have nice color pictures and price tags and little else, which one finds everywhere."*—John and Anne Duffield, Costa Mesa, Calif.

University of Hawaii Bookstore, *Manoa Campus (tel. 956-8252). "The University of Hawaii Bookstore is a delightful place to shop for take-home goodies: They have a wide variety of sweatshirts, jackets, caps, track bags, etc., all with the UH logo, plus lots of stationery, cards, etc."*—Brenda English, Fox Creek, Alberta, Canada.

The Hawaiian Kukui Nut Co., *P.O. Box 685, Waialua, Oahu, HI 96791 (tel. 808/637-5620, or toll free 800/367-6010). "I have been a psoriasis sufferer off and on for 30 years. I bought some Kukui Nut Oil from the Hawaiian Kukui Nut Co., and it has been great for my skin. It's $8 for four ounces. Mail orders are available. This oil is used to soften dry skin, ease tiny lines, soothe sunburn, rashes, and windburn. Early Hawaiians first discovered the plump, mellow nuts of their native kukui trees contained a pure, clear oil with amazing ability to protect their skin against the rigors of everyday life. For centuries, the Hawaiians kept* *this natural phenomenon a secret!*"—Judie Carbaugh, Sykesville, Md. [*Authors' Note:* Agreed. We, too, find kukui-nut oil extraordinary. It can be purchased at many shops in Waikiki and at the factory store in Waialua.]

JEWELRY & WATCHES

HAWAII TIME, 334 Seaside Ave., Suite 205. Tel. 922-7884.

Trust flight attendants to know the best places—they travel all over the world and love to bargain-hunt. One of them tipped us off that the prices here were "better than in Bangkok," and so they are. Everything from Mickey Mouse watches to top name brands is available at wholesale prices; most watches, for both men and women, go for $10–$100. If you need to have a watch repaired, try Patrick at Accurate Watch Repair, 1108 Fort Street Mall, Room 2C (tel. 521-3469).

KIMI'S FASHION, 96 N. King St. Tel. 599-7721.

If you're looking for freshwater pearls, this little Chinatown shop is *the* place. Owner Kimi Phung offers beautiful freshwater pearls at prices that are often lower than wholesale on the mainland; strands run $2–$70, and beautiful they are. People come from all over for Kimi's pearls, and once back home, they keep calling for reorders. She has a nice selection of handbags, as well.

LEIS

When local people need to buy leis, they usually head for Chinatown—and so should you. Although leis are sold all over town, especially at the airport and on the ocean side of Kalakaua Avenue, the best prices and finest quality can usually be found among the Chinatown lei sellers. There are several stores on Maunakea Street; some of our favorites are **Cindy's Lei Shoppe** at no. 1034, **Violet's** at no. 1165, **Jenny's Lei Stand** at no. 1151, and **Lin's** at no. 1107. A local friend advises us that **Aileen,** who has a little lei stand inside Aala's flower shop at 1104 Maunakea St., has done some extraordinary special-order work for her, always tries to give the fairest price possible, and feels it's rare that she is undersold. **Lita's Leis** is around the corner at 59 N. Beretania St., and **Aloha** is at the corner of Puuahi. Cindy and Lita both make beautiful haki-head leis that dry splendidly and can be worn for a long time. Cindy's carries the largest selection of flower leis in the state, and all six make up orchid, plumeria, double carnation, and other leis, at prices ranging from $5 to $10 and up, depending on the season and the availability of flowers. Should you want to send leis to your friends back home—a lovely but no longer inexpensive gift—expect to pay about $27 and up by Express Mail. (And they may not be very chipper when they arrive.) We also like the flowers—and the low prices—at **Chiyo's,** located inside and at the front of the Thrifty Drugstore at 3610 Waialae Ave. in the Waialae-Kahala area. You can shop by phone (tel. 734-6337 or 737-5055), and be assured that your order will be well and speedily taken care of. They'll bill you later.

If you'll see your friends within a day or two of your arrival, it's cheaper to carry flowers with you. Better still, give your friends the flower leis your Hawaiian friends will doubtless drape around your neck as they bid you aloha—if you can bear to part with them.

Buyers beware: The most expensive times to buy leis are May Day, the graduation season (end of May), and New Year's; that's when $5 vanda orchid leis can suddenly become $15–$18!

MISCELLANEOUS

LOCAL MOTION, 1714 Kapiolani Blvd., near Ala Moana Shopping Center. Tel. 955-SURF.

If you're really serious about surfing, or learning to surf, you should know about this place. Any surfer will tell you that in order to learn to surf safely and joyously you need good instruction and a well-constructed board. Many of those for rent at beach stands are outdated, hence the need for a source like Local Motion. Here you can rent a board for $20 for the first day and $15 for every day thereafter. By the week, it's $75. And they also sell snappy sports and leisure clothes. Local Motion is also at the Windward Mall in Kaneohe, at Koko Marina in Hawaii Kai, and at the Pearl Kai Shopping Center in Pearl City, as well as on Maui.

THE MILITARY SHOP OF HAWAII, 1921 Kalakaua Ave. Tel. 942-3414.
Once part of the Fort DeRussy Museum, this may well be the largest store of its kind in the country. Insignia, military patches from all the services, military models, camouflage clothing, and accessories are all for sale. And there's a large selection of military books as well. For those interested in such things, it's a fascinating spot. Open Monday through Saturday from 9am to 6pm; closed Christmas.

CHAPTER 9

TOURING OAHU

You haven't really seen Hawaii until you've left the urban sprawl of Waikiki and Honolulu and traveled to the other side of the mountains for a look at Windward Oahu. And what a look that is! There are jagged cliffs and coral beaches; Stone Age ruins and tropical suburbs; a vast military concentration; backwoods country towns sleeping in the sun; endless stretches of breadfruit, banana, papaya, hibiscus, lauhala, coconut palms—the glorious vegetation of the tropics so ubiquitous as to be completely taken for granted. And best of all, some of the most intriguing sightseeing attractions in the 50th state are here: Sea Life Park, the Byodo-In Temple, and the Polynesian Cultural Center.

Not one advertising billboard defaces the landscape; they're kapu in Hawaii. The only signs you will see are those of the Hawaii Visitors Bureau's red-and-yellow warrior pointing to the places of interest. There are dozens of spots for beachcombing and picnicking, so pack your bathing suit and lunch. If you get an early start, you can certainly make this trip in one day, but there's so much to see that two would be much more comfortable. We'll provide a basic itinerary around which you can plan your time.

TRANSPORTATION You can see a good part of the island by sticking to public transportation. TheBUS no. 55, "Circle Island," which leaves Ala Moana Center daily at 5 and 35 minutes after the hour from 6:05am on, will enable you to see many island points of interest: the big surf at Haleiwa, Sunset Beach, and the North Shore, the Polynesian Cultural Center, to name some. (The cost is $1.20, with no transfers; you'll have to pay 60¢ every time you reboard the bus.)

Many of our readers make the trip by public transportation and praise it highly, but we prefer to rent a car, since it's much more efficient time-wise and quite reasonable, especially for more than one person. *If you do drive, remember to lock your car doors and take your valuables with you when you get out to look at the sights. If you must lock things in your car trunk, do so before you arrive at your destination: You never know who may be watching.*

Alternatively, you could take one of the around-the-island sightseeing tours, such as those offered by **E Noa Tours** (tel. 941-6608) or **Akamai Tours** (tel. 971-4545).

MAPS The maps in this book are for the purpose of general orientation. When doing any extensive driving, we suggest you follow a more detailed road map. We have personally found the maps in *Drive Guide to Oahu,* free from any car-rental company, to be excellent.

1. WAIKIKI TO HEEIA

From Waikiki, drive Diamond Head on Kalakaua Avenue past Kapiolani Park to Diamond Head Road, which runs into Kahala Avenue past the sumptuous residential area of Black Point. Sculptor Kate Kelly's monument to aviatrix Amelia Earhart is just past the Diamond Head Lighthouse. On your right, a paved trail leads to the cliffs, where you can watch some fancy surfing. At the end of Kahala Avenue, where it hits the Waialae Golf Course, turn left onto Kealaolu Avenue; follow this road to Kalanianaole Highway (Hi. 72); the entrance will be on the right. Before you turn, you come to **Waialae Beach Park,** with modern facilities, covered pavilions, and wide, wide beaches, right next door to the prestigious Waialae Country Club. The swimming here is not too good, since there are many rocks in the water. Next door is the splendid Kahala Hilton Hotel; you might want to have a look at the lovely grounds.

Just before you reach Koko Head, you'll pass the entrance to Henry Kaiser's once-controversial **Hawaii Kai**—a 6,000-acre, $350-million housing development that's a small city in itself. You can drive in for your own tour of inspection. (A resident advises us that there's a beautiful view at the top of the hill past the Hawaii Kai Golf Course overlooking the ocean and the south end of Windward Oahu.) While you're in this area, you may want to stop in at **Waterfront Village,** a charming small shopping complex perched right out on the waters of Koko Marina, and tied in by walks and a shared parking lot with the much larger Hawaii Kai shopping center.

Koko Head and **Koko Crater,** now coming into view ahead, are reminders that Oahu, like all the Hawaiian Islands, is a volcanic mountain spewed out of the Pacific. During Oahu's last eruption (volcanologists say it was at least 10,000 years ago), these craters and the one that houses **Hanauma Bay** were born. One side of Koko Head has been washed away into the sea and the result is an idyllic beach, one of the most popular in the islands. Since the placid turquoise waters cover a cove in the purple coral reef, it's a perfect place for beginning and advanced snorkelers. (Rent snorkels in Waikiki or bring your own; none are available here.) Hanauma Bay is now a marine reserve, and so gentle have the fish become that parrot fish, bird wrasses, and others will eat bread from a swimmer's hand. There are dressing facilities, and camping, barbecue, and picnic areas. The beach is a very long walk from the parking area, but you can take a little bus from the parking lot to the beach for a small fee. *Be sure to lock your car and remove any valuables!* Needless to say, the islanders love this place, and the only problem is that you've almost always got to share it with quite a lot of them. The beach is now closed on Wednesday.

For the next few miles along Hi. 72, you drive along one of the most impressive stretches of rocky coastline in the islands. The black lava cliffs hurtle down to the sea to meet a surging purple Pacific, all set against a brilliant blue-green background of sky, trees, and flowers. Park the car at any of the designated areas or at the popular **Blow Hole,** where the water geysers up through an underwater vent. (The areas before the Blow Hole are just as pretty and much less crowded.) With the wind in your hair and the surf crashing below, you'll feel light-years away from civilization. Just beyond the Blow Hole is **Sandy Beach Park;** beyond that is **Makapuu Beach Park,** where people are actually surfing on those horrendous waves. These two beaches are strictly for the experts; beginners had better watch from the sand.

More important, this is the site of one of Hawaii's biggest sightseeing attractions—**Sea Life Park Hawaii,** where there's plenty of entertainment, education, and fun for the whole family. First, there's a show in the Hawaii Ocean Theater, a live training session in which porpoises and penguins show off their agility and brains. Shows alternate with those in the Whaler's Cove, which re-creates Hawaii's early whaling history in a narrated pageant. There's a ⅝-inch-scale replica of the whaling ship *Essex.* At the 300,000-gallon Hawaiian Reef Tank exhibit, you can descend three fathoms below the surface for a skindiver's-eye view of a typical offshore coral reef, full of brilliantly colored marine creatures, some 3,000 of them. Hammerhead sharks are just inches away—on the other side of the glass. You'll want to see the Kohole Kai Sea Lion Show and visit the sea lion feeding pool: You may feed the splashy animals fish, and try your luck at coaxing them to do a trick or two.

In addition, you'll want to visit the Bird Sanctuary, which shows species of marine

AN EXCURSION AROUND OAHU

- Bellows Beach Park 7
- Byodo-In Temple 10
- Diamond Head State Monument 1
- Dole Pineapple Pavilion 20
- Haiku Gardens 9
- Haleiwa Beach Park 17
- Ho'Omaluhia Botanical Garden 8
- Kahuku Sugar Mill 13
- Koko Head Regional Park 3
- Nuuanu Pali State Wayside 23
- Pineapple Variety Garden 18
- Polynesian Cultural Center 12
- Puu O Mahuka Heaiu 15
- Sacred Birthstones 19
- Sandy Beach Park 4
- Schofield Museum 21
- Sea Life Park 5
- Senator Fong's Plantation and Gardens 11
- Sunset Beach 14
- Tendai Mission of Hawaii 24
- Wahiaw Botanical Garden 22
- Waialae Beach Park 2
- Waimahalo Beach Park 6
- Waimea Falls Park 16

Airport

N 0 5 mi 8 km

PACIFIC OCEAN
Kauai Channel
Mokuleia Beach Park
Mokuleia
930
Waialua
Haleiwa
Waialua Bay
Haleiwa Beach Park
83
Waimea Bay
Waimea
Pupukea Beach Park
Sunset Beach
Kamehameha Hwy.
Kahuku
Laie
Hauula
Kaawa
Waimea Falls Park
Kawailoa Forest Reserve
Koolau Range
Ewa Forest Reserve
Leilehua Plateau
Wahiawa
Waianae Range
Makaha
93
Waianae
Maili
Nana Kuli
Farrington Hwy.
Makakilo City
Waipio Acres
Mililani Town
Honouliuli Forest Reserve
99
H2
Waipahu
Ewa
Ewa Beach
Pearl Harbor
Mamala Bay
Honolulu International Airport
HONOLULU
Pacific Palisades
Pearl City
Ewa Forest Reserve
H1
H3
Kaneohe Bay
Kahaluu
Ahuimanu
Heeia
Kaneohe Beach Park
Mokapu
Kailua Bay
Kailua
Kailua Beach Park
Bellows Field Beach Park
Kaneohe
63
Honolulu
Pali Hwy.
61
Watershed Forest Reserve
72
Waimanalo
Waimanalo Beach
Waimanalo Beach Park
Makapuu Beach Park
Koko Head Reg. Park
Sandy Beach
Lunalilo Frwy.
Kalanianaole Hwy.
Diamond Head State Mon.
Waialae Beach Park
Maunalua Bay
Hanauma Bay State Underwater Park
Kaiwi Channel

birds seldom seen by the public (the red-footed booby, masked booby, and albatross—also known as the goony bird—among others); visit the Penguin Habitat and the 1,500-gallon Touch Pool, where you can touch starfish, stingrays, and more. Stop in, too, at the Hawaiian Monk Seal Care Center and the Pacific Whaling Museum, which houses the largest collection of whaling artifacts—scrimshaw, harpoons, rope work—in the Pacific. You can pick up T-shirts, ceramic art, stuffed animals, marine jewelry, and the like at the Sea Life General Store.

Admission to the park is $14.95 for adults, $7.95 for juniors 6–12, free for children 5 and under. The park is open Saturday through Thursday from 9:30am to 5pm, on Friday until 10pm; on Friday, a Hawaiian show is included in regular park admission. For more information, call 259-7933 or the Waikiki office at 923-1531. Note that Sea Life Park provides a shuttle-bus service for a nominal fee. Public buses also make hourly runs to the park (call 531-1611 for information).

Continuing north on Hi. 72, you'll soon see **Rabbit Island,** where the water is turquoise. The inland view along this coast is also spectacular, thanks to the towering **Koolau Range;** its corrugated slopes (examples of erosion at work on volcanoes) provide a nice balance to the restless sea on your right.

Just past Sea Life Park, you'll find **Waimanalo Beach Park,** which many island families consider the best beach on Oahu: pleasant surf, grassy knolls, picnic tables, the works. You may want to come back here for a long stay. For now, drive on for a few more miles and, east off Hi. 72, you'll come upon what was long considered one of Oahu's most magnificent beaches by the few people lucky enough to enjoy it—the military. This is **Bellows Field Beach Park,** nestled against the mountains, a 46-acre strip of fine sand, lively but not dangerous surf, and wooded picnic groves of palm and pine. After long years, Bellows has been opened to the public, but on weekends only, from Friday noon to midnight Sunday; and on federal and state holidays. There are public bathhouses. (It's a favorite spot for tent and trailer camping; permits are available from the Recreation Department, City and County of Honolulu.) Bellows is a perfect place for a picnic lunch (bring your own, as there's nothing to buy), or a swim. The only danger (aside from an occasional Portuguese man-of-war) is that you may be tempted to spend the whole day and forget about your exploring. Keep going, for the best is yet to come.

At this point in the journey, make a brief side trip to **Kailua,** one of Honolulu's most pleasant suburbs. Stay on Hi. 72 until it intersects with Hi. 61, turn right (east) onto 61 and continue until you reach **Kailua,** a few miles down the road. The reason for this trip is the beach: **Kailua Beach Park,** and especially **Lanikai,** are absolutely beautiful, with gentle waves, white sand, and much smaller crowds than you see at Waikiki. We feel this is what Waikiki must have been like in the old, pretourist days.

If it's the weekend and you're in the mood for a hike, you should know about **Ho'omaluhia Botanical Garden** in Kaneohe, at the end of Luluku Road. Here, at the foot of the Koolau mountains, are pleasant hiking trails, a Hawaiian garden, a lake, and much more. At the center, you'll find a small art gallery and exhibit hall. There are escorted walks on Saturday from 10am to 12:30pm (3½ miles) and on Sunday from 1 to 3pm (2 miles). Groups under 20 can be accommodated, but both individuals and groups should phone in advance to make reservations for these hikes (tel. 235-6636). Wear proper footwear and take an umbrella since showers are common in any season. The garden is open daily from 9am to 4pm.

From Kaneohe, drive inland on Hi. 65 to Hi. 83, and go north. You might want to stop and stretch a bit at a lovely area called **Haiku Gardens,** just west of the Kahekili Highway. For years, Haiku Gardens Restaurant occupied this lovely kamaaina estate. Now it's a handsome Chart House Restaurant. The gardens are open to the public free, during daylight hours. A lily pond dominates all, and from it, trails lead off to, among other things, a lovely grove of golden bamboo from Java, Hawaiian grass huts, a palm grove, bird sanctuary, fragrant plantings of ginger and anthurium, and exotic fish ponds. To reach the gardens, turn left off the highway at Haiku Road and proceed mauka about a mile. It's open Tuesday through Sunday.

For devotees of Eastern culture, we know of no more rewarding spot in the islands than the **Byodo-In Temple** in the Valley of the Temples, which should be your next destination. It's about two miles from Haiku Road, and you can reach it by driving back to Kahekili Highway from Haiku Gardens and proceeding north. (If you haven't stopped at Haiku Gardens, continue on Kamehameha Highway to the intersection at Pineapple Hill, then turn left the way you came onto Kahekili Highway; you'll come to the Valley of the Temples in about half a mile.) An exact replica of the venerable Byodo-In, reputed to be the most beautiful temple in Uji, Japan, this temple was constructed at a cost of $2.6 million and dedicated on June 7, 1968, almost 100 years to the day after the first Japanese immigrants arrived in Hawaii. The temple sits in a magnificently landscaped classical Japanese garden fragrant with pine, plum, and bamboo. Inside, you can gaze at the intricately carved screens, and panels, and pay obeisance to the magnificent gold carving of Amida, the Buddha of the Western Paradise. Many of the Buddhist faithful in the islands come here, of course, but a visit is every bit as much an aesthetic as a spiritual experience. While you're meditating, turn the kids loose in the gardens, supply them with a package of fish food (thoughtfully sold in a tiny teahouse gift store), and let them feed the flashing carp in the two-acre reflecting lake. The shop also imports religious items and other Japanese gifts from Kyoto. Have a look. Admission is $2 for adults, $1 for children under 12.

On Saturday, Sunday, and Monday from 10am to 3:30pm, art lovers who have made an appointment in advance by calling 239-8146 can stop to see the exquisite **Hart, Tagami & Powell Gallery and Gardens,** just a few miles from the Valley of the Temples. This combination art gallery, aviary, and Japanese garden is the home and studio of two of Hawaii's leading painters, Hiroshi Tagami and Michael Powell. A visit here is a rare privilege, an extraordinary entry into a world of beauty. When you call for an appointment, ask for directions.

Just two miles past the Valley of the Temples, you'll come to one of Oahu's newer visitor's attractions: **Senator Fong's Plantation and Gardens.** Former U.S. Sen. Hiram Fong has opened his magnificient 725-acre estate to the public; visitors are taken on guided tours in open-air trams through five gardens named for the various presidents under whom Fong served in his 17 years in Congress. After the tour stop at the Visitors Center, perhaps have lunch or take a class in lei making. Check out the Banana Patch gift shop, too. Plan on an hour or so for this delightful excursion. Admission is $6.50 for adults, $3 for children 5–12. Open daily from 10am to 4pm; the last tram tour departs at 3pm (tel. 239-6775).

For a change of pace, get back on Hi. 83 and head south to **Heeia,** on Kaneohe Bay. This is a good place to stop, stretch your legs, and switch to another mode of transportation. Glass-bottom boats at **Heeia Kea Pier** take you on a narrated excursion at a charge of $7.50 for adults, $3.50 for children under 12. Cruises depart at approximately 10 and 11am, and 12:30, 1:30, and 2:30pm daily. Make advance reservations by calling 235-2888. Also, check to see if the water is clear that day; if not, there's not much point in going out. The Deli Snack and Gift Shop, right on the pier, offers local-style plate lunches (around $4), as well as the usual snacks.

ALTERNATE ROUTE TO HEEIA You can begin your around-the-island trip via the **Pali and Makiki Heights** and pick up the route at Kaneohe on Hi. 83. This route takes you to a major attraction that our recommended route omits—the view from the **Nuuanu Pali,** a glorious panorama from the top of a jagged cliff. It's a historic spot, too, because it was here that Kamehameha the Great vanquished the Oahuans in a fierce battle in 1795. Thousands of the defeated fell to their deaths on the rocks below. The only drawback to this route is that you miss the scenery in the Koko Head area, which we find more appealing.

To see the Pali, turn left off Nimitz Highway (Hi. 92) in downtown Honolulu onto

Nuuanu Avenue or Bishop Street. Follow it to Pali Highway (Hi. 61), which leads to the Pali.

Just before you reach the Pali, however, you might want to stop at one of the island's newer points of interest. Drive about a mile up the Pali and turn left at Jack Lane, to reach the beautiful **Tendai Mission of Hawaii** and its enormously impressive 25-foot statue of Senju Kannon, the Thousand-Armed Goddess of Mercy. The Tendai sect of Mahayana Buddhism ended 1,200 years of confining its worship halls to Japan when it opened the Hawaii mission in 1973. You're welcome to inspect the grounds and building any day during regular activity hours. (There are no specific times of opening or closing.) Occasionally, you'll see local groups using the facilities for flower-arranging, tea ceremonies, and handcraft exhibits.

Another spectacular view that we think you shouldn't miss is the one from **Makiki Heights,** which you can see on your way to Nuuanu Pali. In a way, we like it better than the Pali, since this is a top-of-the-world view, completely unobstructed. Here's how to get there: From Waikiki, take Kalakaua Avenue until it ends at South Beretania Street. Go past Makiki to Keeaumoku Street, turn right, cross H1, and turn right onto Wilder. After one block, turn left onto Makiki, which runs into Round Top Drive, then Tantalus Drive, and continues up, up, and up. The road, which is excellent all the way, goes through the Round Top Forest Reserve. Stop at **Puu Ualaka State Park** (open daily from 7am to 6:45pm) and have a look at the glorious view from Round Top. Back in the car, continue in the same direction you were going. When you reach H1 turn left and take it to the intersection with Hi. 61 (the Pali Highway), which leads to the Pali.

WHERE TO EAT

KANEOHE

Several shopping malls in Kaneohe offer a bonanza of inexpensive eateries. At the enclosed **Windward Mall,** for example, the standout restaurant is **Marie Callender's** (tel. 235-6655), a charming, airy spot, where $6.25 brings you a terrific pot-pie lunch. It's served in a ceramic casserole, has an all-vegetable crust, and is a meal in itself. Quiches, salads, and desserts are all fantastic here. **Thao Phya Thai** (tel. 235-3555) offers authentic Thai food, a garden atmosphere enlivened by Thai art, and a staff that radiates the Thai brand of warm aloha. We like to order their luscious vegetarian spring rolls as soon as we're seated, wrap them in lettuce, and dip them into a delicious sauce while we're making our menu decisions. Curries excel because they are made with fresh coconut milk. The same menu is in effect all day. *Aroy!*

If you head into the food court you'll find many more places to choose from. **Cinnabon,** for example, is a singular experience. Customers start lining up before opening time (10am) to buy incredible cinnamon rolls, each measuring about five inches wide by about three inches high, topped with a cream-cheese frosting! You can watch the team of bakers turn them out. People have been known to make a meal out of them, if not exactly a balanced one. They're $1.20 small, $1.90 large.

Pizza fans have **Harpo's,** and brag of their fresh veggies on hand-rolled dough, secret-recipe sausage, and hand-rolled homemade pastas. Two slices of their gourmet deep-dish-style pizzas, plus green salad and soda, will set you back $5.30 for pepperoni, $5.70 for vegetarian. If you've been to Ala Moana Center, you know that **Patti's Chinese Kitchen** is great. Now there's a Patti's here too, and it's inexpensive and filling.

Still hungry? The **Taco Shop** features tacos at $1.80 and enchiladas at $3.30; **Yunnie's Korean BBQ** offers barbecue chicken at $4.75, veggies and rice included. **Alejandro's** creates a variety of sandwiches from $3.75 to $4, all with lettuce, tomatoes, alfalfa sprouts, and macaroni salad. **Little Tokyo** displays a score of items in plastic replicas to help you decide, such as the fried mahimahi at $4.50. And don't forget the coffee shop on the second floor of **Liberty House,** where you can get vegetarian sandwiches at $3.55 and roast beef at $4.95, as well as hot plates, such as a health plate or honey-dipped chicken, each at $4.75. Windward Mall's opening and closing times vary with holidays, seasons, and days of the week.

READERS RECOMMEND

Smitty's, *across from Kaneohe Shopping Center (tel. 247-8533). "Don't forget Smitty's when you're in Kaneohe and you want to go to a really nice, comfortable, informal restaurant, but you don't want to spend much money. At Smitty's, most of your meals should be in the $4–$7 range at lunch, in the $5–$11 range at dinner. You'll sit there wondering how you can pay so little in such a nice restaurant. The menu has good variety for the whole family. And they sell pies to go. Smitty's is part of a very large Canadian chain. They're located across the street from the Kaneohe Bay Shopping Center."*—Mark Terry, Maui, Hawaii.

2. HEEIA TO LAIE

Outside Heeia, it's one awesome view after another as you drive north on Hi. 83 along the coast, weaving along past acres of tropical flowers and trees whose branches frequently arch across the whole width of the road. You can't miss spotting **Pineapple Hut** on the right, which has a good selection of carved wood, shells, macramé planters, and the like at reasonable prices.

You're now coming to the end of Kaneohe Bay, and the next HVB marker you'll see will point to an island that looks like its name, **Mokoli'i** (little lizard), also called Chinaman's Hat. On the other side of the road, covered by weeds, are the ruins of a century-old sugar mill. Cane grown here was once shipped by boat to "distant" Honolulu.

Just over two miles past the large garment factory building on your left, look for a fruit stand on the right. The only indication is a sign reading COLD COCONUT JUICE. Here you can purchase local fruits grown right in this area, at Waikane. In our opinion, they're the best.

In a short while you'll come to a rocky cliff that reminded the old Hawaiians of a crouching lion, hence its official name: **Crouching Lion.** The scenic **Crouching Lion Inn** is just in front. This area is fine for a picnic; **Kaaawa Beach Park** has good swimming, as does **Swanzy Beach State Park,** just south of Punaluu, and both are fully equipped with amenities. The next beach, at **Kahana Bay,** is safe for swimming inshore, but there are no dressing facilities, and the bottom is muddy.

As you approach **Hauula,** you'll see the HVB marker pointing to a side road leading to the 87-foot **Sacred Falls (Kaliuwaa).** Even though the trail is lined with impressive trees and flowers, our advice is to pass this one up; in order to see the falls and the mountain pool below, you have to hike for about an hour on a rather rough path. Over the past few years there have been a number of drownings, robberies, and accidents here; locals definitely consider this place bad news. Coming up now, the beach park at Hauula is well equipped with the usual bathing facilities, and the swimming is safe inshore. But keep going; you're about to reach the picturesque village of Laie, one of the high points of your Windward Oahu sojourn.

Laie is Salt Lake City with palm trees. No slouches at missionary work, the Mormons arrived in Hawaii not long after the first Protestants; more than 100 years ago they founded a large colony of Hawaiian and Samoan members of the Church of Jesus Christ of Latter-Day Saints, whose descendants still live here.

In 1919 the Mormons established a Hawaiian Temple, the first Mormon house of worship outside the mainland; in 1955 the Brigham Young University–Hawaii

Campus, a fully accredited liberal arts institution; and in 1963, the **Polynesian Cultural Center,** a loving re-creation of Polynesia in miniature. On beautifully landscaped grounds, seven authentic Polynesian villages—Tahitian, Marquesan, Samoan, Maori, Tongan, Fijian, and of course, Hawaiian—have been built, peopled with islanders who demonstrate the ancient crafts of making tapa (bark cloth), pounding taro roots into poi (a Hawaiian food staple), weaving baskets of lauhala, wood carving, and the like. All this is part of the church's effort to revitalize the ancient Polynesian cultures by giving them a dramatic showcase and, at the same time, to provide job opportunities for Polynesian young people who need to work their way through school.

A visit here is an absorbing excursion into a long-ago, faraway culture. You'll find such curiosities as a splendidly carved Maori war canoe, all 50 feet of it carved from a single log (it took 2 years to make—in ancient times, it would have taken 20); a native queen's house; Tongan grass huts lined with tapa; and Samoan sleeping quarters for a high chief. Most striking of all, perhaps, is the Maoris' sacred house of learning, with its carved and woven inside panels. (While you're in the Maori village, be sure to note the magnificent sculptures of Ken Coffey, including some striking images of Pele, done in milo, koa, and a variety of other tropical woods.) The *veddy* British accent of the Maori guides, dressed in island costumes, may come as a bit of a shock until you remember that they are New Zealanders, Commonwealth subjects. As you make your way around, either on foot or by canoe, you'll find that they and the other guides who explain their traditions with such deep feelings are the most impressive aspects of the cultural center. Perhaps the star of the village tours is a young man named Sielu, who gives a talk at the main square of the Samoan village, complete with demonstrations, such as how Samoans start a fire with one stick. He's like a highly informative stand-up comic—don't miss him!

Various events are scheduled throughout the day, like the Pageant of the Long Canoes, offered several times during the afternoon. It's a series of dances performed by young people from each of the villages on floating canoes. Especially enjoyable: the high-spirited performance of the Samoan group, decked out in brilliant yellow and blue.

The stellar evening entertainment is a spectacular production of Polynesian dancing and singing called *Mana! The Spirit of Our People*. It's just a trifle showbiz (colored waters, tricky lighting) and (to our thinking) a bit repetitious and overlong, but the performers—people brought from Polynesia to man the villages, or students at BYU Hawaii—are quite good, and some of them, such as the Fijian men in their traditional war dances, do probably the best ethnic dancing in the islands.

Polynesian Odyssey is shown at the cultural center's IMAX theater, on a screen seven stories high and 96 feet wide, with sky-rise seating and wraparound sound. Fantastic!

Best all-around value on tickets is the $50.50 Luau Package, which includes a tour of the villages, afternoon highlights, the movie, a traditional luau dinner, and tickets to the evening show. For $38.95, you can have it all except the movies, and have the Gateway Buffet (which includes sweet-and-sour ribs, island fish, and more instead of the luau meal). For the dinner-show package alone, prices are $35 for adults, $19.50 for children. And for everything *except* the dinner and show—that is, admission to the seven villages and all daytime activities—the charge is $25 for adults, $12.50 for children 5–11. *Note:* It is suggested that visitors arrive no later than 2pm to enjoy the full experience. If you're staying for the evening, you may want to plan this as a special excursion, rather than as part of an all-day, around-the-island trip.

Visitors can pick up tickets at the center's ticket office on the ground floor of the Royal Hawaiian Shopping Center, Building C. While you're there, check the schedule; there are often miniperformances on Tuesday, Thursday, and Saturday morning from 9:30 to 11:30am. You can also book round-trip motorcoach transportation at about $12 per adult, free for children under 5.

DINING AROUND OAHU

N 0 5 mi / 8 km

- Amorient Aquafarm 16
- Cinnamon's 16
- Crouching Lion Inn 14
- Gourmet World 8
- Harpo's 4
- Helemano Plantation 23
- Jameson's by the Sea 20
- Kemoo Farm 22
- Kiawe Q Hawaiian Barbecue 18
- Kua' Ai na 21
- Liberty House 10
- Little Tokyo 9
- Marie Callender's 1
- Patti's Chinese Kitchen 5
- Pikake Pavilion 17
- Rosie's Cantina 13
- Smitty's 11
- Taco Shop 6
- Texas Paniolo Café 12
- Thao Phya Thai 2
- Yunnie's Korea BBQ 7

Airport ✈

The Polynesian Cultural Center is open Monday through Saturday; closed Thanksgiving and Christmas. For further information, call the box office at 293-3333 or toll free 800/367-7060, or the Waikiki ticket office at 923-1861. If you're driving directly to Laie from Honolulu, take the Pali Highway (Hi. 61) and turn north on Kamehameha Highway (Hi. 83). Plan on at least an hour's drive.

While you're here, you'll also want to see the **Hawaiian Temple;** it stands back from the road on high ground, above a pond, an illuminated fountain, and at the head of a long avenue of royal palms. The best approach for a Taj Mahal–like vista is to leave the highway at Halelaa Boulevard. A complimentary Historical Laie Tour is available. You'll tour the Mormon Temple, Brigham Young University–Hawaii, and the Laie community on a re-created 1903 Hawaiian streetcar. By the way, not all the students here are Mormons; the school is open to others, provided they take the pledge not to smoke or drink, and "to live good Christian lives."

Laie-Maloo Beach used to be the scene of the Mormon hukilaus, once considered one of the island's top visitor attractions. The ocean at Laie-Maloo is safe for inshore swimming, although the beach is not a public park and has no dressing facilities.

You won't want to leave Laie without a drive out to **Laie Point** (the turnoff is just past the entrance to the cultural center), where you get a dramatic view of the rugged coastline. Walk out over the porous lava rock as far as you can go safely for the best view of all. Some old Hawaii hands swear it's the best view in the islands. Sunset devotees shouldn't miss this one.

READERS RECOMMEND

Polynesian Cultural Center. *"We highly recommend upgrading the Polynesian Cultural Center tour to an Ambassador tour. We paid extra for this, but we got a guided tour by one of the Brigham Young University students for the day, kukui-nut leis, special seating for the evening buffet, seating within the first five rows for the evening show, plus the intermission dessert of mango sherbet. We wished that we had had even a few more hours to spend here. The evening show is thrilling, the buffet food was some of the best we had during our whole vacation, and the student performers are all eager to please."*—Margaret A. Pyzik, Naperville, Ill.

"Please let your readers know that at the PCC it is best to follow the crowds. We thought we'd be smart and avoid the crowds, but it turned out that we missed almost every exhibition because we arrived at the wrong times."—Carol Robinson, Lubbock, Tex.

WHERE TO EAT

PUNALUU

A rustic, western appearance characterizes the **Texas Paniolo Café** (tel. 237-8521) inside and out. Located at 53-146 Kamehameha Hwy., it's housed in a wood-frame building with a front porch, and the interior walls resemble adobe. Country-western music wails from the jukebox during the day; at night, there's live entertainment. You'll just love the stuffed rattlesnake on the walls! And if you're braver than we are, you can also have rattlesnake chili at $8.75, a half-pound rattlesnake burger at $9.75, or a snake-and-three-egg omelet, with a shot of Cuervo Gold included for $11.50. If the rattlers are not available, however, there is plenty of other very tasty Tex-Mex food. Among the appetizers, we vote for the chili con queso—a crock of melted cheese, tomatoes, and green chiles with tostitos for dipping, $5.75. A bowl of beef chili with rice or beans is $5.95; a chiliburger or jalapeño burger with cheese is $7.25. Dessert offerings include such Texas treats as pecan pie. It's open Wednesday through Monday from 11am to 11pm and on Tuesday from 11am to 2pm.

READERS RECOMMEND

The Crouching Lion Inn, *51-666 Kamehameha Hwy. (tel. 237-8511). "The Crouching Lion Inn, just about five miles from the Polynesian Cultural Center, is one of the best restaurants in Windward Oahu. An imposing structure, the inn was the actual residence of a Norwegian contractor and his large family who emigrated to Hawaii in 1912; the original hand-wrought iron fixtures add a charming quality to both the inside dining room (in which a fire blazes nightly in an enormous stone fireplace) and the outer dining room overlooking the bay. Among the menu specialties, I highly recommend the Slavonic steak continental and the luscious chicken macadamia (boneless breast of chicken, dipped in a brandy-and-egg batter, deep-fried, laced with a sweet-and-sour sauce). Most main courses are $14.75–$17.95. Lunch is pleasant too, and at both lunch and dinner, every table receives a freshly baked loaf of bread, warm from the oven. And don't miss their 'mile high' coconut cream and other cream pies, each $3.50. Service is excellent, both pleasant and unobtrusive. I highly recommend the Crouching Lion as a first-class experience in leisurely dining in a beautiful setting, far removed from the hubbub of the city."*—Jane James, Pearl City, Hawaii.

3. LAIE TO HALEIWA

Highway 83 starts to run inland through sugar country at the village of Kahuku, the halfway point of your trip. The old **Kahuku Sugar Mill** has reopened, and while it no longer offers the excellent guided tour it once did, it's still worthwhile to make a stop here, especially for children to take a self-guided free minitour of the first room of the old mill. The awesome machinery is color-coded so you can tell the electrical system from the steam, water, or bagasse (fiber) system. Follow the arrows to view the process in order. You may take this tour any day between 10am and 6pm. Local vendors offer souvenir items on the grounds.

Back in the car, keep an eye out for the roadside stands; in summer, you can get home-grown watermelon here—the best on the island. And you can also get fabulous shrimp here in Kahuku at **Amorient Aquafarm,** where we always stop off for a luscious snack. Amorient Aquafarm is a 175-acre diversified shrimp and fish farm; they grow a variety of prawns and other seafood in one-acre ponds that are visible from the highway. Their stand, open every day from 10am to 5:30pm, offers freshly cooked shrimp tempura ($8 for a dozen pieces), shrimp cocktail ($5), or shrimp cooked tails ($12.50 per lb.). Feast at a roadside table or in your car.

The road reaches the shore again at Kuilima, where you might want to have a look at the sumptuous Turtle Bay Hilton and Country Club, one of the most beautiful resorts in the islands. The scenery is spectacular here, especially the view from the swimming pool, perched atop a cliff overlooking the ocean on two sides as the waves pound in. (If it's time for lunch, you might want to try the 11am-to-2:30pm "minideli" buffet in the scenic Bay View Lounge. There's a charge for parking here, but your parking ticket can be validated at lunch.)

Back to the car again for a drive down the coast a bit to **Sunset Beach,** with its huge breakers crashing in at your right. It's safe for summer swimming, but in winter it's a wild, windy stretch, exciting to walk along; better still, you may be lucky enough to see some spectacular surfing here, for this is Oahu's North Shore, currently *the* place for the surfing set. Traffic may be jammed for miles from here south to Haleiwa if there's an important surfing contest going on. If you're wondering whether you should try it yourself, be advised that the surfing areas range from pretty dangerous to very dangerous to one that's called "Banzai Pipeline." (Remember the wartime suicide cry of the Japanese?) **Waimea Bay,** just below Sunset, has the distinction of having Hawaii's biggest waves, sometimes crashing in as high as 30 feet. However, in the summer months Waimea Bay is tranquil, the waves are gentle, and swimming here is close to perfection. **Pupukea Beach Park,** for instance, has good swimming and outstanding snorkeling in the summer months.

While the surfers on Waimea Bay are tempting fate, you can survey a more primitive form of human sacrifice (and this time we're serious) by turning left onto Pupukea Road, one of the few paved roads here, opposite a fire station and next to a market. As soon as the road begins its ascent up the hill, take your first right and continue up to **Puu O Mahuka Heaiu.** Here, on a bluff overlooking Waimea Bay (another view-collector's spot), are the ruins of a temple where human sacrifice was practiced. When Captain Vancouver put in at Waimea Bay in 1792, three of his men were captured and offered to the bloodthirsty gods. Today all is tranquil here, and the faithful still come, offering bundles of ti leaves in homage. Sadly, the road leading up to this national historic landmark is littered with trash and abandoned automobiles.

For a refreshing change of pace, head back to nature now at **Waimea Falls Park,** off Hi. 83 a little south of Pupukea Road, opposite Waimea Bay Beach Park. There's a lot to do at this botanical Eden nestled in a lush, 1,800-acre historic Hawaiian valley. You can watch world-class cliff divers plunge 60 feet into the waterfall pool, or see the park's resident hula troupe, dressed in authentic costumes, perform beautiful ancient (*kahiko*) hula. At the Hawaiian Games Site, you can play the sports of old Hawaii, such as *ulu maika* (lawn bowling), *o'o ihe* (spear throwing), or *konane* (Hawaiian checkers). You can wander through more than 30 botanical gardens that showcase some of the world's most exotic and rare plants, or explore numerous trails that wind their way through the park. Hop onto the narrated minibus to the waterfall, then join knowledgeable park guides for walking tours through the gardens and historical sites. At the *kauhale kahiko* (ancient Hawaiian living site), step into old Hawaii and experience the way Hawaiians were thought to have once lived.

You can also enjoy a relaxed picnic in the grassy meadow or a sumptuous lunch at the **Pikake Pavilion,** a spacious open-air dining center overlooking the mouth of the valley. Grab a quick island snack or cold drink at one of several snack bars in the valley, or browse through **Charlie's Country Store** for island gifts and mementos.

Twice each month the park offers romantic evening strolls to the waterfall and back by the light of the full moon. A donation of $5 per family directly benefits the Waimea Arboretum Foundation, a nonprofit scientific and educational organization dedicated to protecting Hawaii's rare and endangered plants.

Waimea Falls Park is also one of Hawaii's most popular wedding locations; couples can exchange vows in a lush, secluded garden or next to a gorgeous waterfall. For more information on planning such a special event, contact the park's **Wedding Department** at 59-864 Kamehameha Hwy., Haleiwa, HI 96712.

Admission is $14.95 for adults, $7.95 for juniors ages 7–12, and free for children under 7. Waimea Falls Park is open daily, including holidays, from 10am to 5:30pm. For more information, call 638-8511 or 923-8448.

A few miles farther along Hi. 83, at **Haleiwa Beach Park** on Waialua Bay, you'll find the last swimming spot before you strike into the heart of Oahu. It's a fine family-type place—lawns, play areas, pergolas, dressing rooms, showers, fishing, camping, and a picnicking area.

YOUTH SCENE AT SUNSET BEACH AND HALEIWA If you're seriously interested—or even slightly—in the youth culture, you'll be welcome among the inhabitants of Sunset Beach and Haleiwa, an area that attracts a number of young people who want to live close to nature and the big surf. They're not putting on a show for sightseers or tourists, just quietly doing their thing—and an attractive thing it is. Haleiwa is like a very tiny version of Cape Cod's Provincetown, with its distinctively artsy atmosphere, small gift shops, art galleries, and boutiques. **Pomegranates in the Sun,** one of our favorite women's clothing shops from Ward Warehouse, has opened a store here at 66-145 Kamehameha Hwy., with a smashing collection of clothing by Hawaiian artists and designers inspired by the sun-drenched colors of

Hawaii. Hand-painted dresses and original designs, most of them made in the area, are offered by Inge Jausel at **Oogenesis Boutique** at 66-249 Kam Hwy. Japanese-inspired designs grace tops, pants ensembles, and simple dresses that can be worn belted or unbelted. Prices are reasonable. Under the "Inge Hawaii" label, these garments are now being sold in mainland stores. Inge's other store, **Rix,** 66-145 Kam Hwy., offers contemporary designs in fashion. **Deeni's Boutique,** at 66-079 Kam Hwy. in Haleiwa, specializes in swimwear, T-shirts, and sportswear, with some of the lowest prices and best selections in town. We always like to make a stop at the **North Shore Marketplace,** 66-250 Kam Hwy., especially to shop for jewelry, crystals, and a variety of arts and crafts at very good prices at Jungle Gems. "Stress bracelets" of various tension-relieving stones and gems are $20. Note, too, their collections of Venetian glass and African trading beads. A good place to do some gift shopping. Also in the same North Shore Marketplace complex is Kau'ala Tropical Farms, which offers free samples and fair prices on macadamia nuts. Coffee Gallery is a must for coffee fantatics, since they offer an enormous selection of Hawaiian and other coffees, roast their own beans, and sell them at very good prices. Organic coffee is available. You can also have a meal here on their outdoor terrace (see below).

Art lovers will want to browse the galleries in Haleiwa, especially places like the **Wyland Gallery,** 66-150 Kam Hwy., which specializes in the work of noted marine artist Wyland (everything from originals to posters), and also shows photographs, wood sculptures, and more. Have a look, too, at the **Fettig Art Studio,** 66-431 Kam Hwy., an important outlet for the local painters and potters. Hawaiiana is a specialty.

Hungry? You've come to the right town. Some of our favorite North Shore restaurants are here (see below). Wherever you eat, skip dessert and drive over to **Matsumoto's Grocery** at 66-087 Kam Hwy. in Haleiwa (across from the intersection of Emerson Street) for the ultimate shave-ice experience. Local people drive out from all over the island to line up here, while no fewer than four workers form an "assembly line" to shave and season the ice. We won't swear that you'll really love shave ice with ice cream and azuki beans on the bottom, but can you say you really know Hawaii unless you've tried it? Matsumoto's also sells nifty T-shirts, caps, and sweatshirts with their logo in pretty colors—great souvenirs. **Aoki's,** just down the road, is an alternative if the lines are just too long.

Since Sunset Beach is a spiritually attuned community, it abounds in centers for yoga, Zen, and other such disciplines; the people at any of the shops can give you information on any groups that may interest you. This area is a world apart from the urban crush of Honolulu, the tourist scene at Waikiki, and the rat race everywhere. Try to schedule your visit in time for the fantastic sunset, which turns the horizon to a brilliant blazing red.

WHERE TO EAT

HALEIWA

COFFEE GALLERY, in North Shore Marketplace, 66-250 Kam Hwy., Haleiwa. Tel. 637-5571.

Cuisine: AMERICAN/VEGETARIAN. **Reservations:** Not accepted.

$ Prices: Sandwiches $3.75–$5.95; main courses $7.95. AE, MC, V.

Open: Mon–Sat 6am–9pm, Sun 7am–9pm.

It's so pleasant to sit at the outdoor café here and have a very special cup of coffee or a light lunch or dinner at this informal place. Lunch features "bagelwiches," quiches, veggie burgers, salads, and chili and rice; dinner always offers a vegetarian specialty like tortillas, pesto, fettuccine, or lentil burgers, along with a house salad. Everything is fresh and baked right in back. To go along with the coffee, try a "death by chocolate brownie" ($1.15)—if you dare.

ROSIE'S CANTINA, in the Haleiwa Shopping Plaza, 66-165 Kam Hwy., Haleiwa. Tel. 637-3538.

Cuisine: MEXICAN. **Reservations:** Not required.

$ Prices: Appetizers $2.95–$3.75; main courses $10.75–$11.75. AE, MC, V.

Open: Sun–Thurs 7am–10pm, Fri–Sat 7–11pm.

This attractive, high-tech-looking spot is a favorite for tasty Mexican food. Rosie's serves all three meals, features delicious tortas (hamburger or chicken with fries or beans on thick bread), and offers spectacular savings at its Wednesday-night Taco Fiesta Buffets: from 5 to 7pm, it's all you can eat for $5 per person; the ante goes up to $7 per person between 7 and 9pm.

KIAWE Q HAWAIIAN BARBECUE, in the Haleiwa Shopping Plaza, 66-197 Kam Hwy., Haleiwa. Tel. 637-3502.

Cuisine: BARBECUE.

$ Prices: Main courses $2.95–$7.95. No credit cards.

Open: Daily 10am–9pm.

On the other side of the shopping plaza there's Kiawe Q, the home of Kiawe Q Hawaiian barbecue sauces and Hawaiian Passion Hot and Fire Chili Pepper sauces. You may want to take these sauces home with you, but first sample them here on a boneless barbecue chicken plate or sandwich, kiawe-wood smoked chicken, or kalbi-style beef. Take-out available.

JAMESON'S BY THE SEA, 62-540 Kam Hwy., Haleiwa. Tel. 637-4336.

Cuisine: SEAFOOD. **Reservations:** Recommended.

$ Prices: Appetizers $3.75–$9.50; main courses $15.95–$24.95. AE, DC, MC, V.

Open: Daily 11am–11pm.

This is a wonderfully picturesque spot for lunch or dinner. Savor the harbor view, the sunset, and great food and drink. Lunch is served downstairs in the Pub, and features hearty fish, seafood, and meat sandwiches; some excellent shrimp, crab, and seafood Louie salads; and a variety of interesting pupus. There are many well-priced daily lunch specials, including fresh fish. Dinner features seafood caught daily in local waters.

KUA' AINA SANDWICH, 66-214 Kam Hwy., Haleiwa. Tel. 637-6067.

Cuisine: SANDWICHES.

$ Prices: Sandwiches $4–$8. No credit cards.

Open: Daily 11am–8pm.

Where can you get the best sandwich on the North Shore, maybe on all of Oahu? We cast our vote for Kua' Aina, a sparkling sandwichery across the street from the courthouse in Haleiwa. It's tiny, neat as a pin, with wooden tables, framed pictures of local scenes, a few tables on the porch. And the atmosphere is casual, with people coming in off the beach. We haven't stopped raving yet about the sandwiches we had on our last visit: mahimahi with melted cheese, Ortega pepper, lettuce, and tomato at $4.95; tuna and avocado ("the tastiest combo in the Pacific") at $4; and a great baconburger at $4.45. Sandwiches are hearty enough to be a whole meal and are served on either a kaiser roll, honey wheat-berry bread, or earthy rye. A newspaper survey recently voted their hamburgers best on the island.

4. HALEIWA TO WAIKIKI

Follow Hi. 82 from Haleiwa and turn left onto Hi. 99 (Kamehameha Highway) as it climbs to **Leilehua Plateau.** Here the tall sugarcane gives way to seemingly endless miles of pineapple—dark green and golden against the red earth. It's the largest pineapple area in the world. Just as you're beginning to feel like the Ancient Mariner (you can't pick any), you'll find the **Dole Pineapple Pavilion,** just north of Wahiawa, where you can buy a whole "pine" or get half a dozen delicious spears, fresher than any you've ever tasted. The custom here is to sprinkle a little unrefined Hawaiian salt on the pineapple; it helps cut the acidity. You can also shop for Hawaiian souvenirs here and order fresh pineapple packs delivered to the airport for your flight back home. Dole does not conduct tours through the fields, but many operations are visible from the highway. In case you're curious, the variety of pineapple grown here is called sweet cayenne.

In the midst of these Wahiawa pineapple fields, one mile past the pineapple hut, is the Del Monte Corporation's **Pineapple Variety Garden,** near where the Kamehameha Highway becomes Hi. 80 for a short time. It's small, but it's well worth a brief stop to see a huge variety of species and pineapple plants from all over the world—Asia, Africa, South America, and various small islands. Just ignore the tremendous spiders that build their webs among the plants; they're nonaggressive and totally harmless—to people and pineapples.

Next stop is for the history-anthropology buffs: a Stone Age spot where the royal chieftains of Hawaii gave birth. Just before Wahiawa on Hi. 80, watch on the right for an HVB warrior marker pointing to a dirt road leading off to the right to a clump of eucalyptus trees in a pineapple field—the Sacred Birthstones-Kukaniloko. These large stones and the village that once surrounded the spot afforded prenatal care and birthing support to high chiefly women in childbirth—thus ensuring healthy mothers and children to continue the lineages of the high chiefs, the alii.

Just before you reach Wahiawa, still in the pineapple fields, you may want to stop and stretch your legs at a five-acre, working vegetable and flower farm called **Helemano Plantation,** which serves a tasty and inexpensive buffet lunch at $8.25 between 11am and 2:30pm. If it's past lunchtime, you can still browse at the gift shop, get some fresh produce at the country store, visit the bakery, or even join a lei-making class. Helemano Plantation provides many retarded people with training and vocational opportunities, and supports programs of Opportunities for the Retarded, Inc.

Now take Kamehameha Highway to Wahiawa, a town that serves as a center for personnel stationed at **Schofield Barracks** (where James Jones met his muse) and **Wheeler's Field.** It's also a huge pineapple depot. The bright spot here is **Kemoo Farm,** a famous name in these parts since 1921. The old restaurant building overlooking Lake Wilson now houses a good Mexican restaurant. Next door is the Kemoo Farms Visitor Center, where owner Dick Rodby has lined the walls and shelves with antiques, old photos, and historic memorabilia of the area, some of it for sale. Also for sale are Kemoo Farms' Happy Cakes (a very rich holiday fruitcake made with pineapples, coconuts, and macadamia nuts, a big favorite of Ronald Reagan's), homemade chocolates, macadamia-nut coffee, and other goodies. Visiting the Rodbys is a real treat, like seeing friends from home.

In this area you may also want to visit the **Schofield Museum,** with its military and historical documents (open daily from 9am to 4pm). Garden lovers will want to make a stop at the **Wahiawa Botanical Garden,** at 1396 California Ave. (three-quarters of a mile east of Kam Highway), 1,000 feet high, to wander through 27 lovely acres of rare trees, ferns, and shrubs, and a Hawaiian garden. Admission is free (open daily from 9am to 4pm).

You'll pass through more sugar fields as you drive along the now-four-lane Kamehameha Highway (99 once again) or the new Interstate H2. From here on, it's fast sailing home. At the intersection with Interstate H1, turn left and drive past Pearl Harbor (you might visit the U.S.S. *Arizona* Memorial if you have the time) and Honolulu International Airport. At Middle Street, turn right onto Hi. 92 (Nimitz Highway), which will take you past the harbor. Take Ala Moana and Kalakaua into Waikiki.

WHERE TO EAT

WAHIAWA

HELEMANO PLANTATION, 64-1510 Kam Hwy., Wahiawa. Tel. 622-3929.

Cuisine: CHINESE. **Reservations:** Not required.

$ Prices: Buffet or sandwich and salad bar $8.25. MC, V.

Open: Breakfast daily 7:30–11am; lunch daily 11am–2:30pm.

You can get a substantial, reasonably priced lunch in the big, gardenlike dining rooms of this spot, located on a five-acre complex amid pineapple fields on the outskirts of Wahiawa. Helemano Plantation is not only an agricultural farm, growing fruits, vegetables, and flowers; it's also a vocational and educational center for many of Hawaii's retarded citizens. They work as trainees in the many areas of Helemano: in the farm, the restaurant, the gift shop, country store, or in the bakeshop. Its Country Inn restaurant is known for its excellent Chinese cuisine and reasonable prices. At least five hot main courses are available each day, which might include roast duck, teriyaki beef, Chinese spareribs, beef with broccoli, spicy eggplant, and many more. A mini-lunch plate will cost you $3.95, and your choice of either a full all-you-can-eat Chinese buffet including fruit bar or a sandwich with all-you-can-eat salad bar is $8.25. You can also browse through the tempting display of freshly baked treats at the bakeshop, which includes island-style manapuas (steamed or baked buns stuffed with pork or chicken) as well as pineapple and coconut danish, and chocolate chip, peanut butter, and coconut-drop cookies. Stop by for the free hula show and take time to browse through their "Best of the Best" collection of handcrafted gifts and souvenirs made by the handicapped and disadvantaged from all over the world.

CHAPTER 10

KAUAI

One hundred ten miles to the west of Honolulu, yet seemingly light-years away, lies a tropical Switzerland. This is Kauai, the northernmost of the major Hawaiian islands, and one of the lushest tropical spots on earth. Kauai (pronounced correctly Kah-*wah*-ee, lazily Kah-*why*) is a small island, about 32 miles in diameter. Its central mountain receives an average of 500 inches of rainfall a year, making it one of the wettest spots on earth, which accounts for the lushness of the surrounding landscape.

Kauai is the oldest Hawaiian island both geologically and historically. In island lore, Kauai was the original home of Pele, the goddess of fire and volcanoes, before she moved southward. It was also the homeland of a race of pre-Polynesians whose origins are unknown. Some believe they were the survivors of the lost continent of Lemuria. In legend they're called Menehunes, South Sea leprechauns who stood about two feet tall, worked only in darkness, and accomplished formidable engineering feats between dusk and dawn.

The first Polynesian settlers chose Kauai, too, and landed at the mouth of the Wailua River somewhere between A.D. 500 and 900. They crossed the Pacific in double-hulled sailing vessels in a voyage of many months, probably from the Society Islands. Other Polynesians came later, but time stood still on Kauai and the rest of the Hawaiian Islands until 1778, when Captain Cook arrived at Waimea and the modern history of Hawaii began.

You can see all the important things in Kauai in three days—but the longer you stay, the luckier you are.

1. GETTING THERE & GETTING AROUND

GETTING THERE

BY PLANE About 15 minutes after your interisland plane takes off in Honolulu, it lands at the sleek new $36-million Richard A. Kawakami Terminal, the third-busiest airport in the state. Rent a car or hail a cab to get to Lihue town or other destinations.

INFORMATION

The headquarters of the **Hawaii Visitors Bureau** is at 3016 Umi St., Suite 207 (tel. 808/245-3971), on the second floor of Lihue Plaza. Information is available on just

WHAT'S SPECIAL ABOUT KAUAI

Natural Wonders

- ☐ Waimea Canyon, a 3,657-foot gorge dubbed the "Grand Canyon of the Pacific" by Mark Twain.
- ☐ Mount Waialeale, "the wettest spot on earth," receiving 480 inches of rain a year—best seen from a helicopter.
- ☐ Spouting Horn, a saltwater geyser where water spurts up through the lava rocks, sometimes to heights of 50 feet.

Beaches

- ☐ Superb swimming year round at Kalapaki Beach in Lihue and, on the southern and western shores, especially at Poipu Beach Park and Salt Pond Beach Park. In summer, along the north shore, at romantic Hanalei Bay (where *South Pacific* was filmed), Haena Beach Park, and Ke'e Beach.

Snorkeling

- ☐ At many spots around the island, especially good at Poipu Beach on the southern shore and Tunnels Beach on the north shore.

Museums and Historic Homes

- ☐ Kauai Museum, with changing art, heritage, and cultural exhibits of both Asia and Hawaii, as well as a permanent showcase of Hawaiiana.
- ☐ Grove Farm Homestead, a look back into the plantation days of 19th-century Hawaii.
- ☐ Hawaiian Art Museum and Bookstore, Kapaa and Kilaluea, with large selections of Hawaiian arts, crafts, books, music.
- ☐ Kilohana Plantation, a combination historical house, museum, restaurant, and shopping bazaar.
- ☐ Kokee Natural History Museum, a tiny museum devoted to the indigenous bird and plant life of the island.
- ☐ Wailoli Mission House in Hanalei, full of fascinating furniture, books, and mementos of 19th-century missionary days.

Botanical Gardens

- ☐ Moir's Gardens at Kiahuna Plantation, especially for their monstrous cactus plants, like something out of Middle Earth.
- ☐ National Tropical Botanical Gardens in Lawai, Kauai's best, a 286-acre tropical garden filled with more than 5,000 varieties of tropical plants on exquisite grounds; guided tours.
- ☐ Olu Pua Gardens in Kalakeho, a botanical showplace and historic house.

Hiking

- ☐ Some of the best in the islands, with magnificent trails on the Na Pali Coast and into Waimea Canyon.

Movie and TV Locations

- ☐ Some places on Kauai may seem familiar, if you've seen *Raiders of the Lost Ark, Indiana Jones and the Temple of Doom, The Thorn Birds, Blue Hawaii,* or *South Pacific*—to mention just a few.

about everything, including tips on where to play tennis and golf, deep-sea fishing charters, helicopter tours, boat tours, kayaking, and glider flights.

GETTING AROUND

BY RENTAL CAR For information on the major budget car-rental companies—offering excellent flat-rate packages on all the islands—see Chapter 2. If, however, you haven't done so, or prefer a time-plus-mileage deal, simply walk up to any of the car-rental agencies just across the road from the airport. We drove a car from

Sunshine of Hawaii (tel. 808/245-9541, or toll free 800/367-2977) on our last trip and were pleased with both the car and the courteous service. And it's especially nice that the cars are right at the airport. Rates begin at $22.95 daily for a compact two-door automatic with air conditioning, $139 weekly. For an automatic four-door with air conditioning, the price is $28.95 and $159.

BY BUS & TAXI While a car is definitely the best way to go, there is some public transportation. The **Kauai Bus,** a new company, operates a fleet of 15 buses that serve the entire island. For scheduling and destinations, phone 246-4622. The bus costs $1.

Should you need a cab for a short trip, **Kauai Cab** (tel. 246-9554) is a reliable outfit.

FAST FACTS KAUAI

Area Code The telephone area code is 808.

Babysitters Inquire at your hotel desk.

Business Hours See "Fast Facts: Hawaii," in Chapter 2.

Car Rentals See "Getting Around," above.

Climate See "When to Go," in Chapter 2.

Dentists Contact Dr. John R. Black, 4347 Rice St., Lihue (tel. 245-3582); or Dr. Mark Baird, 4-9768 Kuhio Hwy., Kapaa (tel. 822-9393).

Doctors Kauai Medical Group has clinics in Lihue (tel. 245-1500), Kapaa (tel. 822-3431), Koloa (tel. 742-1621), and Princeville (tel. 826-6300). Physicians are on call 24 hours (tel. 245-1831).

Emergencies Call 911.

Eyeglasses Try Jenkins Optical Service, 4491 Rice St., Lihue (tel. 245-7425).

Fax Services Phone Mart, Kukui Grove (tel. 245-9511), can assist you.

Holidays See "When to Go," in Chapter 2.

Hospitals Wilcox Memorial Hospital, 3420 Kuhio Hwy., Lihue (tel. 245-1100) has an emergency room open 24 hours.

Libraries Branches include Lihue Public Library, 4444 Hardy St., Lihue (tel. 245-3617); Kapaa Public Library (tel. 822-5041); and Koloa Public/School Library (tel. 742-1635).

Other Useful Numbers State Commission on Persons with Disabilities (tel. 245-4308; Voice/TDD); Helpline Kauai (tel. 245-3411); YWCA Sexual Assault Services (tel. 245-4144). On Call (tel. 246-1441) is a 24-hour free service offering news, sports, weather, community-service information, etc. See also the Aloha Pages of the Kauai telephone directory.

Photographic Needs The ABC Discount Store, in the Anchor Cove Shopping Center, and Long's offer the best prices.

Police Call 911 for emergencies, 245-9711 for all other matters.

Poison Control Center Call toll free 800/362-3585.

Post Office It's at 4441 Rice St., Lihue (tel. 245-4994).

Safety Exercise the same precautions you would elsewhere: Never leave valuables in your car, even in the trunk; leave personal valuables in hotel safes or in-room safes; don't flash cash conspicuously in public.

Taxis See "Getting Around," above.

Weather Information For current weather, call 245-6001; for a marine report, 245-3564; for a surf report, 335-3611.

2. WHERE TO STAY

Bed & Breakfast Hawaii, the largest reservation service in the islands, is headquartered right here in Kauai. Not only do they have a wide range of carefully inspected accommodations all over the state, but they also work with Dollar Rent A Car to provide lower prices on car rentals for their guests. For a free brochure, contact Bed & Breakfast Hawaii, P.O. Box 449, Kapaa, HI 96746 (tel. 808/822-7771, or toll free 800/733-1632; fax 808/822-2723). For $10, you receive a directory of homes and apartments with rooms for rent called *B&B Goes Hawaiian.*

IN & AROUND LIHUE

The town of Lihue and its adjacent Nawiliwili Harbor are the most centrally located places to stay in Kauai, since they're the starting points for your eastern and western tours of the island. Lihue is the county seat and the center of Kauai's government, commerce, and culture. It's also home to the gigantic new luxury resort, the Westin Kauai.

DOUBLES FOR $25

MOTEL LANI, 4240 Rice St. (P.O. Box 1836), Lihue, Kauai, HI 96766. Tel. 808/245-2965. 10 rms. TEL

$ Rates: $25–$35 single or double; from $35 triple. Each additional person $10 extra. No credit cards. **Parking:** Free.

The only budget accommodation in the center of town we think most visitors will find suitable. It's a pleasant place, patronized by both Hawaiians and tourists. Rooms are small but modern, with a small refrigerator. Rollaway cots are provided. Owner Janet Naumu requires a two-night deposit. Rates are subject to change without notice.

WORTH THE EXTRA BUCKS

ASTON KAHA LANI, 4460 Nehe Rd., Lihue, Kauai, HI 96766. Tel. 808/822-9331, or toll free 800/922-7866. Fax 808/922-8785. Telex 634479 ASTHI UW. 65 condominium apts.

$ Rates: Apr–Dec 21, $117–$145 one-bedroom apt;, $149–$177 two-bedroom apt; $230 three-bedroom apt. Dec 22–Mar, $147–$175 one-bedroom apt; $179–$207 two-bedroom apt; $260 three-bedroom apt. AE, CB, DC, MC, V. **Parking:** Free.

Located behind the Kauai Resort Hotel, adjacent to the beautiful Waolua Golf Course, on the beach at Wailua Bay, this condominium complex is great for those who want to swim in the ocean or pool, snorkel, golf, or play tennis (there is one court, lit for night play). Across the road is the Coco Palms Resort with its three fine restaurants, and just down the road Coconut Plantation beckons.

Kaha Lani means "Heavenly Place" in Hawaiian, and the resort is aptly named. Each unit is privately owned, so the decor is different in each. We've seen several units and found them all—well, heavenly. Each condo includes a full kitchen with dishwasher, a lanai, ceiling fans, and a clock radio. Room prices depend on whether the view is garden, ocean, or oceanfront. One-bedroom units can accommodate up to four people, the two-bedroom/two-bath apartments have room for six, and the three-bedroom/two-bath accommodations fit up to eight people. Some rooms are especially equipped for the disabled.

NAWILIWILI HARBOR

GARDEN ISLAND INN, 3445 Wilcox Rd., Lihue, Kauai, HI 96766. Tel. 808/245-7227, or toll free 800/648-0154. 16 rms, 5 suites. MINIBAR TV TEL

$ Rates: $45–$60 double; $55–$65 family room; $65–$85 suite. MC, V. **Parking:** Free.

One of Kauai's top budget choices is two miles from the center of town, at Nawiliwili Harbor, a stone's throw from all the activity of the spectacular Westin Kauai Lagoons Hotel. The Garden Island Inn is an older hotel that has been taken over by new owners, renovated from top to bottom, and spruced up with white paint and green trim. Owners Steven and Susan Layne have done a terrific job in transforming the three-story hotel, which is surrounded by lovely gardens and miniature waterfalls cascading into several koi pools. You can help yourself to bananas and the fruit on the orange and papaya trees, and be at beautiful Kalapaki Beach, one of our favorites in the islands, in about a minute.

Rooms are light and sunny, with rattan furniture and floral spreads, ceiling fans, tropical flowers, and original watercolors. Most have ocean views, and some include private lanais. Each room features a wet bar with refrigerator, cable color TV, microwave oven, and coffee maker complete with complimentary Kona coffee. Bedding is either a queen-size bed or two twin beds; bathrooms have showers but no tubs. The cheapest doubles are on the ground floor, and the more expensive doubles are on the second floor with private lanais. A suite with a living room, four beds, a microwave oven, and a large refrigerator could house a family of four. Another suite has a three-sided private lanai, a queen-size sofa bed in the living room and a queen-size bed in the bedroom, a microwave oven and a large refrigerator. Steve and Susan will lend guests golf clubs, snorkels, coolers, etc., at no charge.

THE EASTERN SHORE: COCONUT COAST

Nine miles out of Lihue, near where the Wailua River meets the ocean, begins Kauai's "Coconut Coast," stretching from here through the town of Kapaa. It's also known as Coconut Plantation. The area has beautiful scenery, lots of good, inexpensive restaurants, plus the Coconut Marketplace. The hotels here are more expensive than the ones in the Lihue area since they are situated directly on the ocean. Here on the windward side of the island the surf is rougher (and the weather apt to be rainier) than on the leeward side. If you have a car, it's no problem, since it's a short drive to the splendid beaches of leeward Poipu. If you don't have a car, however, and want to swim in the ocean, we recommend choosing a hotel in Poipu (see below).

DOUBLES FOR ABOUT $40 TO $75

HOTEL CORAL REEF, 1516 Kuhio Hwy., Kapaa, Kauai, HI 96746. Tel. 808/822-4481, or toll free 800/843-4659. 26 rms.

$ Rates (including continental breakfast): Apr–Dec 14, $41 double older wing, $67 double oceanfront wing; two-bedroom suite $59. Dec 15–Mar, $41 double older wing, $75 double oceanfront wing. Each additional person $10 extra; crib or rollaway, $10. DC, MC, V. **Parking:** Free.

This cute little hotel is right on the ocean and close to everything: public swimming beach, freshwater swimming pool, tennis court, library, launderette, and several great little budget restaurants. The hotel has a stretch of white, sandy beach, and there's good swimming and snorkeling in the deep water between the reefs. You could even make do without a car here.

There are two wings; the older wing offers plain but decent accommodations with private showers and rock-bottom prices. The newer, oceanfront wing, however, is a winner; the spacious rooms overlook the beach, which is just 50 yards away, and boast private lanais, small refrigerators, large glass sliding doors, louvered windows to catch the prevailing trade winds, and either double or twin beds. A complimentary continental breakfast is served every morning. There's an activities center and an activities director, barbecue grills, and snorkel rental. For reservations, contact Iron Mike & the Princess, Inc., at the above address.

KAPAA SANDS, 380 Papaloa Rd., Kapaa, Kauai, HI 96746. Tel. 808/882-4901, or toll free 800/222-4901. 17 rms. TV TEL

$ Rates: $75–$85 studio; $99–$101 two-bedroom apt. Minimum stay three days in summer, seven days in winter. MC, V. **Parking:** Free.

One of our favorite places to stay on Kauai is the comfortable and very attractive Kapaa Sands. It's just a few minutes' walk from Coconut Plantation, yet it's secluded and right on the beach. The pretty, two-story green buildings house studios and two-bedroom apartments; choose between garden with ocean view or oceanfront. All units have ceiling or floor fans. Studios have lanais and separate, fully equipped kitchens. The two-bedroom units are charming duplex apartments (two bedrooms and full bath upstairs, sofa bed and half-bath downstairs), each with two lanais.

KAPAA SHORE, 4-0900 Kuhio Hwy., Kapaa, Kauai, HI 96746. Tel. 808/822-3055. Fax 808/822-3055. 81 condominiums (40 for rent). A/C TV TEL

$ Rates: $65–$120 one-bedroom unit; $85–$140 two-bedroom unit. Weekly rates available. No credit cards. **Parking:** Free.

For a touch of luxury in Kapaa, this condominium complex may be just the ticket. It's right at the beach, and each apartment has a view of the ocean, garden, or pool. All are beautifully furnished, many in avocado-and-white decorative schemes, with fully equipped kitchens, and patio furniture to make dining on your lanai a treat. The one-bedroom units can accommodate up to four people, with a queen-size bed in the bedroom and a queen-size sofa in the living room. Six people can be cozy in the two-bedroom units, which are duplexes with vaulted ceilings, a queen-size bed in one of the bedrooms, two twins in the other, and a queen-size sleeper sofa in the living room. Facilities include a tennis court, 40-foot swimming pool, sunbathing decks, and barbecue area.

KAUAI SANDS HOTEL, 420 Papaloa Ave., Kapaa, Kauai, HI 96746 Tel. 808/822-4951, or toll free 800/367-7000 in U.S., 800/654-7020 in Canada. Fax 922-0052. 200 rms, 2 suites. A/C TV TEL

$ Rates: Apr to mid-Dec, $52–$60 single or double, $57–$67 single or double with kitchenette, $105 suite; with Budget Rent A Car, $79–$94 single or double, $105 single or double with kitchenette, $115 suite. Mid-Dec to Mar, $64–$74 single or double, $69–$79 single or double with kitchenette, $115 suite; with Budget Rent A Car, $106 single or double, $117 single or double with kitchenette, $125 suite. AE, MC, V.

This attractive and informal hotel is part of the hospitable locally owned and operated chain of Sand & Seaside Motels. It faces green lawns and a mile of white sand beach, beautiful but often rough for swimming; there are two swimming pools as well. Rooms are of good size, decorated in ocean hues of greens and blues. All have refrigerators, private lanais, and either two double beds or a king-size bed. Save money by patronizing the hotel's dining room, Al and Don's, which serves dinner main courses between $5.95 and $12, and features fresh catch of the day nightly.

Reservations: Sand & Seaside Hotel, Suite 714, 222 Kalakaua Ave., Honolulu, HI 96815; or call the hotel directly.

MOKIHANA OF KAUAI, 796 Kuhio Hwy., Kapaa, Kauai, HI 96746. Tel. 808/822-3971. 80 studio apts.

$ Rates: $59.95 single or double. MC, V. **Parking:** Free.

It's not easy to get an apartment at this attractive condominium complex in the busy winter months; that's when it's usually chock-full of owners. The best time for rentals is from late April through late September. Apartments are nicely furnished with limited kitchen facilities (refrigerator, hotplate, and electric frying pan), bath, and/or shower. The apartments are right on the oceanfront and two miles away from a championship golf course. Mokihana also boasts an 18-hole, par-36 putting green, shuffleboard, a large swimming pool, and a barbecue area. The original Bull Shed Restaurant, a superb steak house, is right on the waterfront. For information, contact Hawaii Kailani, 119 N. Commercial, Suite 1400, Bellingham, WA 98225 (tel. 206/676-1434).

ROYAL DRIVE COTTAGES, 147 Royal Dr., Kapaa, Kauai, HI 96747. Tel. 808/822-2321. 2 cottages.

$ Rates: $60 single; $75 double. Futon for a third person $10. 10% discount on stays of one week or longer. **Parking:** Free.

Up in the lush green hills of the Eden-like Wailua district, down a private road, you'll find Bob Levine's beautiful guest cottages. Bob refers to his little bit of paradise as a "cozy tropical hideaway," a most apt description. Each cottage has twin beds that make up as a king-size bed; a kitchen equipped with a small refrigerator, microwave oven, coffee maker, blender, and everything in the way of utensils for preparing and serving a meal; a private bath; ceiling fans; and views of the garden from every window. The first cottage has a huge screened lanai facing a part of the garden planted with palm trees, heliconia, ginger, and papaya trees. The second cottage is literally *in* the garden. It has a tiny porch with one chair; down the steps is an enormous kukui-nut tree with chairs under it; nearby is a fish pond filled with water hyacinths and inhabited by sparkling fish. The temptation to settle under the tree and never move is strong. Guests are invited to pick pomelos, papayas, and bananas in season. There are coolers, a big beachball, and a boogie board to tote to the beach. Bob's house is between the cottages and he is very available and happy to share his considerable knowledge of the islands and offer suggestions to help make your stay truly special.

DOUBLES FOR AROUND $90

ASTON KAUAI BEACHBOY HOTEL, 484 Kuhio Hwy., no. 100, Kapaa, Kauai, HI 96746. Tel. 808/822-3441, or toll free 800/922-7866. Fax 808/922-8785. Telex 634479 ASTHI UW. 243 rms. A/C TV TEL

$ Rates: Apr–Dec 21, $88–$118 double. Dec 22–Mar, $98–$128 single or double. Each additional person $10 extra. AE, CB, DC, MC, V. **Parking:** Free.

About a mile past the famed Coco Palms Resort, on the ocean side of the road, is a more moderately priced hotel that's also very pleasant. A branch of Honolulu's terrific Perry's Smorgy Restaurant, which serves three hearty and reasonably priced buffet meals a day, is on the premises. Rooms are nicely decorated, face either the garden or the sea, and each has its own private lanai, a small refrigerator, and a large dressing room. You can swim in the ocean—the hotel is located on the white sand beach at Coconut Plantation—or in the almost Olympic-size swimming pool. Coconut Marketplace, a Hawaiian-style shopping village, is just across the street.

BED & BREAKFASTS

KAY BARKER'S BED & BREAKFAST, P.O. Box 740, Kapaa, Kauai, HI 96746. Tel. 808/822-3073, or toll free 800/835-2845. 5 rms.

$ Rates (including breakfast): $25–$60 single; $45–$70 double. No credit cards. **Parking:** Free.

This very casual bed-and-breakfast inn is on the slopes of the Sleeping Giant mountain, a 10-minute drive from Hi. 56. The back deck runs the length of the house (80 ft.) and looks out over peaceful gardens and pastures. There is also a large living room and dining room, a separate TV room, a refrigerator for storing snacks, and a washer-dryer. Guests can also use ice chests, beach mats, and boogie boards.

The Lokelani Room, next to the kitchen, has a double bed and a private bath; it rents for $25 single, $45 double. The Plumeria Room (with a king-size bed or twin beds) and the Orchid Room (king-size bed) both have private bathrooms with showers and look out over the front garden; they rent for $40 single, $50 double. The Ginger Room, "the honeymooner's favorite," has its own entrance, wicker furniture, and a private bath with tub/shower, and overlooks the back garden and pasture lands of Mount Waialeale; rates are $50 single, $60 double. Hibiscus, a two-room cottage, is isolated in the back garden; it has large rooms, a king-size bed, a sitting room with wet bar, refrigerator, and microwave, and a private lanai from which to catch the great views, and it rents for $60 single, $70 double.

Gordon Barker, who runs the place, whips up good breakfasts (they might include fresh fruits and juices, banana-nut muffins, macadamia-nut pancakes, and beverages). Families with children are welcome. Smoking and "social drinking" are acceptable. If this place is full, he may be able to put you in touch with other B&Bs in the area.

FERN GROTTO INN, 4561 Kuamoo Rd., Wailua, Kauai, HI 96747. Tel. 808/822-2560. 3 rms.

$ Rates (including breakfast): $70–$90 single; $80–$100 double. MC. **Parking:** Free.

This plantation home in the midst of Wailua River State Park offers a serene atmosphere, gracious charms, and a practical location, just off Hi. 56, close to all the attractions of Coco Palms Resort, and a short walk to Wailua Beach. The three rooms—the Serena, Isabella, and Tara—are priced according to size. All are furnished with fine pieces and feature queen-size beds with designer sheets and comforters, goose-down pillows, and European down-feather beds; each has a private bathroom with quality amenities. Manager Sharon Knott serves a full tropical breakfast—fruits, croissants, bagels, muffins, cereals, Kona coffee, and herbal teas—on fine English china in the many-windowed Plantation Dining Room. Perfect for honeymooners and small wedding parties; the entire house may be rented.

THE SOUTHERN SHORE

In the other direction from Lihue, 12 miles south, stretches the idyllic Poipu Beach area, dry and sunny, where the surf crashes a Mediterranean blue-green on palm-fringed, white-sand beaches. Of course, this area is more expensive than Lihue, but you're right at the beach, in our opinion the best on Kauai.

DOUBLES FOR $20

KAHILI MOUNTAIN PARK, P.O. Box 298, Koloa, Kauai, HI 96756. Tel. 808/742-9921. 10 cabins, 15 cabinettes.

$ Rates: $20 cabinette for two; $35 cabin for two. Each additional person $4 extra. Minimum stay of two days required. No credit cards. **Parking:** Free.

If you are really into the great outdoors—but not enough to backpack it and sleep under the stars—try this camp, located seven miles from Poipu Beach, off Hi. 50 west, just beyond the seven-mile marker. Mount Kahili rises majestically behind the little cabins and cabinettes nestled near a small lake, where you can fish for bass and swim. The park is operated by the Seventh-Day Adventist church, and their school is on the premises.

The cabinettes are grouped in a circle around the bathroom-and-shower buildings. Each has one room, with a small dining lanai where there's a small refrigerator, a two-burner hotplate, and a sink. Cookware is furnished. Cabins, consisting of either one large room or two small ones, have a bathroom with a sink and toilet; there's a private shower outside each cabin. They also have a full-size refrigerator, as well as the two-burner stove and sink. All of the accommodations have screened windows with louvers. Linens are furnished. These facilities are very rustic, in a most beautiful setting. There is a laundry room on the premises. Prepayment in full is required for all reservations.

DOUBLES FOR $50 TO $70

CLASSIC VACATION COTTAGES, 2687 Onu Place (P.O. Box 901), Kalaheo, Kauai, HI 96741. Tel. 808/332-9201. Fax 808/742-7447. 3 cottages. TV.

$ Rates: $55 studio; $60 one-bedroom cottage; $60–$65 one-bedroom cottage with breakfast. Each additional person $10 extra. No credit cards. **Parking:** Free.

A stay in the tiny country town of Kalaheo is for those who prefer to be away from the tourist scene, yet close enough to enjoy its advantages. These three self-contained cottages on a hillside are set in a garden adjacent to the custom-built home of Richard and Wynnis Grow, in a residential neighborhood. The Grows have decorated them handsomely, with stained leaded windows, well-equipped kitchens, a living room and porch, and a double bed in the bedroom. The one-bedroom units have ocean or garden views for the same price, while the studio has a garden view. Each unit has its own barbecue; daily linen service is provided. Guests are welcome to use the hot tub, Jacuzzi, and outdoor barbecue. Snorkeling equipment and boogie boards are provided free, along with beach towels. The Kukuiolono Golf Course is a 5-minute drive away, and Poipu Beach about 10 minutes; tennis courts and a park for jogging are nearby.

GARDEN ISLE COTTAGES, 2666 Puuholu Rd., Koloa, Kauai, HI 96756. Tel. 808/742-6717. 13 studios and apts. TV

$ Rates: $51–$83 studio; $83–$104 one-bedroom apt; $146–$166 two-bedroom apt. No credit cards. **Parking:** Free.

An old Poipu favorite, this group of private cottages set in Hawaiian flower gardens offers true island ambience. The hospitable owners, Sharon and Robert Flynn (Bob is an artist), work hard at preserving the feeling of old Hawaii by using batiks, ethnic fabrics and furniture, and Bob's paintings and sculpture. There are three separate locations, all picturesque. Hale Melia, across the land from a small sunning beach and ocean lagoon, offers a small and large studio and a superb one-bedroom apartment with a very large living-dining room with an open-beamed lauhala ceiling, kitchen, and bath, surrounding an enclosed tropical-garden patio. Then there are the Sea Cliff Cottages, whose unique location—perched on a cliff over Koloa Landing, where the Waikamo Stream meets the ocean—gives them an idyllic ambience; you can watch the sun come up over the water from your lanai. There are four one-bedroom apartments for two people, plus another deluxe one-bedroom to which can be added a bedroom and bath, accommodating four. There are also two Sea Cliff studio apartments. Hale Waipahu, located on the highest point in Poipu at Poipu Crater, offers a 360° view of mountains, ocean, sunrises, and sunsets. Your own private "lap pool" overlooks the Poipu coast. There's a studio and a charming one-bedroom apartment with open-beamed ceilings, latticed dining lanai, full kitchen and bath. A smaller bedroom/bath suite is also available.

The office of Garden Isle Cottages is located in Robert Flynn's gallery and is open only from 9am to noon. Good restaurants are nearby, but remember that you'll need a car to get around here.

KOLOA LANDING COTTAGES, 2704B Hoonani Rd., Koloa, Kauai, HI 96756. Tel. 808/742-1470. 2 cottages, 2 studios, 1 house. TV TEL

$ Rates: $50 (plus $20 clean-out fee) studio single or double; $70 (plus $40 clean-out fee) two-bedroom/two-bath cottage for one or two, $85 for three or four; $100 (plus $60 clean-out fee) main house (two bedrooms, two baths) for one to four people, $10 each for up to two additional guests per day. No credit cards. **Parking:** Free.

Many people dream of moving to an island, having a lovely home of their own, and renting out a handful of cottages in their garden. Hans and Sylvia Zeevat (he is Dutch, she is Dutch-Indonesian), who came to Hawaii from Holland, have realized that dream on Kauai and the result is five wonderful, reasonably priced accommodations for those lucky enough to secure them. The Zeevats are exceptional hosts, and they delight in treating their guests like family: They ply them with fresh fruit from their own trees, and give them tips on where to snorkel and what to feed the fish. They have two cottages and two studios: Spacious and tastefully decorated, they have open-beamed ceilings, ceiling fans, cross-ventilation, well-equipped kitchens (blenders, dishwashers, microwave ovens, mixers, etc.), cable TVs, and—hard to find in Poipu—telephones with their own private numbers! Guests can have barbecues out in the garden; restaurants and good swimming beaches are a short walk or drive away. Each cottage has two bedrooms (queen-size beds), two baths, and a lovely living room. Studios accommodate one or two people, and one of them has no steps so it's very convenient for a disabled person. Since the Zeevats have moved to a nearby town, their own main house is also now available as a vacation rental. The two-bedroom/two-bath house has a large living room, dining area, and family room, a deck with private barbecue, and a carport. There's a full kitchen with microwave oven. Six could settle in comfortably here.

PRINCE KUHIO CONDOMINIUMS, 5160 Lawai Rd., Koloa, Kauai, HI 96756. Tel. 808/742-1409, or toll-free 800/722-1409. 48 rms. TV

$ Rates: Apr 15–Dec 15, $59 studio; $69–$79 one-bedroom apt; $95 two-bedroom penthouse. Dec 16–Apr 14, $74 studio; $89–$99 one-bedroom apt; $125–$140 two-bedroom penthouse. No credit cards. **Parking:** Free.

When people are traveling they need a friend, and Den and Dee Wilson, the amiable owners/managers here have such a talent for friendship that staying with them gives one the feeling of coming home. And it's a good place to come home to! The nicely furnished apartments overlook either Prince Kuhio Park and the ocean on one side or a lovely pool and a garden on the other; there's a beach known for good snorkeling right across the road, and there are good swimming beaches nearby (the one we like best is in front of the Hotel Sheraton). The famed Beach House Restaurant is a few steps away. A variety of studios for two and one-bedroom apartments for up to four are offered, all fully equipped for housekeeping with kitchen and comfortable living space and private lanai. Two handsome two-bedroom penthouses for four are also available. The central barbecue is a popular spot, and this is the kind of place where it's easy to make friends. For reservations contact Prince Kuhio Rentals, P.O. Box 1060, Koloa, Kauai, HI 96756, or call them at the above phone numbers.

POIPU PLANTATION, 1792 Pe'e Rd., Koloa, Kauai, HI 96756. Tel. 808/742-7038 or 742-6757, or toll free 800/733-1632. Fax 808/822-2723. 12 units. TV TEL

$ Rates: $70–$80 one-bedroom unit for two; $85 two-bedroom unit for two; $65–$75 bed-and-breakfast room. Each additional person $10 extra. No credit cards. **Parking:** Free.

Evie Warner and Al Davis, the very nice people who run the statewide Bed & Breakfast Hawaii (see above), have built some very attractive vacation-rental units behind their house on their own tropical acre of land, just up the road from Poipu

Beach Park, one of the best places to swim in this area. All the units are of good size, attractively furnished, and have tropical decor, ceiling fans, and excellent modern kitchens. Washers and dryers are outside.

The cheaper one-bedroom units are on the garden level, and the more expensive ones have ocean views. There are also several luxury duplexes with two bedrooms, two baths, even marble floors in the bathrooms. Evie and Al also run the Poipu Plantation Bed & Breakfast Inn right on the premises, offering three attractive rooms, each with private bath and TV; continental breakfast is included. The twin and queen rooms are $65, the king room is $75. There's a gazebo out in the garden, which is quite lovely, with its apple trees, blossoming plumerias, bougainvilleas, and gardenias. Evie and Al are friendly hosts and see to it that everybody is well cared for.

WORTH THE EXTRA BUCKS

KUHIO SHORES, 5050 Lawai Beach Rd., Koloa, Kauai, HI 96756. Tel. 808/742-7555, or toll free 800/367-8022. Fax 808/742-1599. 74 apts. TV TEL

$ Rates: $95–$135 one-bedroom apt; $135–$150 two-bedroom apt. Minimum stay four days. No credit cards. **Parking:** Free.

The big attraction at this large condominium complex is its location on the waterfront, just across from Prince Kuhio. One side of the building faces ocean waves, the other a more peaceful harbor; every room has a water view. The pleasantly furnished units have very large living rooms and fully equipped kitchens with dishwashers and garbage disposals, and the two-bedroom units have two bathrooms.

For information, write to R & R Realty & Rentals, RR 1, Box 70, Koloa, Kauai, HI 96756. Inquire about their other vacation rentals, too.

POIPU BEACH HOTEL, 2251 Poipu Rd., Koloa, Kauai, HI 96756. Tel. 808/742-1681, or toll free 800/426-4122. Fax 808/742-7124. 138 rms. A/C TV TEL

$ Rates: $100–$175 single or double; $250 two-bedroom suite. AE, DC, DISC, MC, V. **Parking:** Free.

Blessed with a perfect location right on the beach, this hotel, a Stouffer Resort, has long been one of our favorite places on Kauai. Rates have jumped quite a bit recently, but if you want an on-the-beach resort hotel, this is still a fine choice. The rooms are exactly the same, except for their locations and views: The cheaper rooms overlook the garden, while the more expensive rooms are ocean-view or beachfront. All are spacious and nicely furnished, with private lanais, a huge dressing area, and best of all, a compact little kitchenette unit that makes fixing breakfast or a quick meal a breeze. The three buildings surround the pool, whirlpool, and grassy area, and the dining room is right in the middle of it all. There are six tennis courts, with a pro shop next door. The neighboring property, the Stouffer Waiohai Beach Resort, is an exquisite resort hotel, all of whose guest services you can use, including the Waiohai Athletic Club (gym, Jacuzzi, sauna, and massage).

BED & BREAKFASTS

GLORIA'S SPOUTING HORN BED & BREAKFAST, 4464 Lawai Beach Rd., Koloa, Kauai, HI 96756. Tel. 808/742-6995. 5 rms.

$ Rates (including breakfast): $50–$120 single; $55–$125 double. Each additional person $20 extra; one-night stay $20 extra. 25% extra Dec 15–Jan 5. Add $5 to rates if payment is by credit card. MC, V.

If your idea of bliss is a hammock strung between two coconut palms overlooking the pounding surf, this is the place for you. Gloria's is located on an idyllic rocky coastline within sight and sound of the surf and the famed Spouting Horn saltwater geyser, and the hammock is right out there, behind the house. The house is charmingly furnished with American oak and English walnut antiques; there's a Baldwin piano, TV, and VCR in the living room; most guest rooms have queen-size beds, private lanais, and private baths. All but one of the rooms have a view of the ocean. One oceanfront accommodation catering to honeymooners is the Tea House; it overlooks a koi pond and features a private bath with Japanese-style soaking tub (for two!). Breakfast consists of a papaya boat filled with fresh, locally grown fruit, juices and beverages, and home-baked pastry or muffin. No children under 14, no pets, and smoking only on the lanai.

POIPU BED & BREAKFAST INN, 2720 Hoonani Rd., Koloa, Kauai, HI 96756. Tel. 808/742-1146, or toll free 800/552-0095. 8 rms and suites; 4 apts, cottages, and homes; 1 oceanfront condo.

$ Rates (including breakfast at B&B only); $90–$150 double. Rooms can be combined into two- or three-bedroom suites, from $155–$305: single occupancy $5 less; each additional person $15 extra; $10 more for stays of one night. Generous discounts for long stays. AE, CB, DC, DISC, MC, V.

We'd have to call this place one of the most beautiful bed-and-breakfast establishments in the islands. Dottie Cichon, an artist herself and a collector of art, has lovingly renovated and restored a 1933 plantation house, and filled it with carousel horses, pine antiques, ornate white Victorian wicker furniture, handcrafts, and tropical splashes of color everywhere. Rooms are luxury all the way: Each has its own private bath (with either a whirlpool tub and separate shower or a tub-shower combination), cable color TV and VCR, and clock radio. Some have wet bars and refrigerators. Continental breakfast—fruits, juices, muffins, pastries, beverages—is served in the morning out on the lanai or in the splendid "great room"; later on, the "great room" is the scene for afternoon tea and for evening popcorn-and-movie gatherings. (Incidentally, while most such places provide breakfast *and* bed, this is the only one we know that will provide breakfast *in* bed—if you ask.) Tennis and pool privileges at the nearby Kiahuna Tennis Club are included in the price of all rooms, and numerous beaches are just around the bend.

Four rooms are available in the new B&B annex, even closer to Poipu Beach. The beautiful cathedral-ceilinged great room and plantation-style white lattice breakfast lanai have a lovely ocean view overlooking a lush tropical garden. One of the loveliest of the rooms is fully handicapped accessible.

Although some are beyond our budget, Dottie also has a number of cottages for rent nearby and in Kalaheo; these range from a $65-a-night spacious one-bedroom unit with kitchenette to a super-luxury oceanfront two-bedroom/two-bath condominium at nearby Whaler's Cove, from $195. All are furnished in exquisite taste; some are as large as a complete home and could comfortably suit a family for a long stay.

Space does not permit us to detail all the offerings in Dottie's little "B&B empire," so contact her for further information.

VICTORIA PLACE, P.O. Box 930, Lawai, Kauai, HI 96765. Tel. 808/332-9300. 4 rms.

$ Rates (including breakfast): $55 Raindrop Room; $65 Calla Lily Room; $75 Shell Room; $95 Victoria's Other Secret. No credit cards. **Parking:** Free.

An eight-minute drive from the beautiful beaches of Poipu, Edee Seymour's place is a gem—a gem enhanced by the gracious hospitality and wonderful cooking of the host. It's back-to-back with the National Tropical Botanical Garden, which is no more than a stone's throw from the poolside breakfast lanai. Three of the guest rooms are located in one wing of the spacious, skylit home, opening directly through glass doors to the gardenlike pool area. The Raindrop Room is for single travelers only. The Shell Room has twin beds that can be put together to form a king-size bed, and it can become barrier-free with a portable wheelchair ramp; its private bathroom has a wheelchair-accessible shower. The Calla Lily Room has a queen-size bed, a gorgeous view of the pool, and, like the others, plenty of closet and bureau space, bookcases liberally filled, and teddy bears on the bed. The fourth room, Victoria's Other Secret, has its own entrance, a kitchen, a daybed and a California king-size bed on a loft above the main studio, a library of cookbooks, a double coffee maker, a huge walk-in closet, laundry facilities—everything! Breakfasts are special, maybe ginger and banana breads fresh from the oven, arrangements of tropical fruits presented on exquisite table settings with flowers everywhere. When you finish your breakfast feast, you can feast your eyes on Edee's glorious collection of shells and antiques. There's a library filled with almost as many books as the local library, and a TV room. Edee is happy to share her collection of restaurant menus and steer you to off-the-beaten-track fun. She can also help with car rentals, including hand-operated vehicles for the physically handicapped.

READERS RECOMMEND

Poipu Shores Condominium, *1775 Pe'e Rd., Koloa, HI 96756. (tel. 808/742-7700, or toll free 800/869-7959). "At the Poipu Shores Condominium, our town house at cliff's edge was wonderful. The waves crashed continually on the rocks below and we enjoyed watching the sea turtles and dolphins. The pool, also at the edge of the cliff, was perfect, and we were only a short five-minute walk from the public beach. Four of us shared this deluxe, two-bedroom/two-bath town house for $175 per night. It was huge and well equipped, with a deck that surrounded it on three sides. There is also a bar on the premises."*—Linda Lamb, Cole, S.C.

WESTERN KAUAI: KOKEE & WAIMEA

KOKEE

KOKEE LODGE, Kokee State Park, P.O. Box 819, Waimea, Kauai, HI 96796. Tel. 808/335-6061. 12 cabins.

$ Rates: $35 or $45 cabin. DC, DISC, MC, V. **Parking:** Free.

Forty-five miles from Lihue, in Kokee State Park (just beyond Waimea Canyon), you'll find Kokee Lodge, 3,600 feet up in bracing mountain air. The cabins are owned by the state but are operated by a private firm, and the prices are low—a practice we'd like to see imitated all over Hawaii. This is a place only for those who have enough time to really linger in Kauai (on a two- or three-day trip a stay would be impractical, since the time and cost of driving to the other sights of the island would outweigh the savings here). The cabins vary in size from one large room, which sleeps three, to two-bedroom units that will accommodate seven. The cabins are rustic, furnished with refrigerators, stoves, hot showers, basic eating and cooking utensils, blankets, linens, and pillows. You can buy a pile of wood and make a fire in the wood stove when the night air gets nippy in this cooler northern Kauai that seems a world away from beaches and coconut palms.

Daytime activities at Kokee include driving or hiking on gorgeous trails and swimming in hidden freshwater pools. You can hunt boar, wild goat, and game birds, fish for trout in the nearby mountain streams, or just laze in the sun.

Undoubtedly, you'll see the magnificent *moa* (chickens) of Kokee on the grounds of the lodge. These are jungle fowl, descendants of birds carried to Hawaii centuries ago by the Polynesians in their outrigger canoes. The brightly plumed chickens, protected by the state, survive only here, in the mountains of Kauai; those on the other islands were destroyed by mongeese, which, somehow, never got to Kauai.

Kokee Lodge Restaurant serves breakfast, lunch, and snacks daily from 8:30am to 5:30pm, dinners from 6 to 9pm only on Friday and Saturday. The restaurant provides take-out orders and snacks for outdoor picnics, and for those wishing to cook, there's a simple grocery store on the premises. Bring your own supplies, however, if you're planning on cooking anything fancy. There's also a cocktail lounge and a well-stocked gift shop. Management advises making early reservations, since holiday weekends are very popular here, and so is the trout-fishing season in August and September. Maximum stay is five days.

WAIMEA

A Bed-and-Breakfast

COOK'S LANDING BED & BATH, 9918 Waimea Rd. (P.O. Box 1113), Kauai HI 96796. Tel. 808/338-1451.

$ Rates (including breakfast): $60 single or double. Minimum stay two nights. No credit cards.

Those who would like to experience small-town life in Hawaii far from the tourist scene might enjoy this one. Just across the street from the post office in Waimea town, and at the base of Waimea Canyon, this is a tiny, private first-floor "mother-in-law's bed and bath" located in the home of Maggie and Eddie Taniguchi. A guest entrance at the back of the house leads to a bedroom and private bath, with double bed, ceiling fan, cable color TV, and clock radio. Guests can use the backyard covered patio with shared refrigerator/freezer and hibachi for barbecuing; they can also do light cooking in the kitchenette area of the room, which has a toaster, coffee maker, microwave oven, some cookware, and utensils. A black-sand beach is within walking distance, and very good beaches are a short drive away. No smoking allowed.

Worth the Extra Bucks

WAIMEA PLANTATION COTTAGES, 9600 Kaumualii Hwy., Waimea, HI 96796. Tel. 808/338-1625, or toll free 800/9-WAIMEA. 15 cottages. TV TEL

$ Rates: $95–$200 double. Minimum stay three nights (eight nights during holiday periods). MC, V.

About 45 minutes from Lihue Airport is a place where time literally seems to have stood still. The workers' cottages from the old Waimea Plantation have been restored or, in the case of the structures that were beyond restoration, rebuilt, adhering to the original 1919 blueprints. They're nestled in a grove of gigantic old coconi palms, just steps away from a black sand beach from which you can watch the sun set over Niihau. The cottages are furnished with updated versions of the furniture that was really in the house (although the workers surely did not have the luxury of private telephones and remote-control color TVs, blenders, coffee makers, rice cookers, toasters, ceiling fans, and state-of-the-art plumbing). Several of the units have four-poster beds, faithful reproductions of the ones that used to be here. There are multiple windows in each unit, from which to enjoy the views of the mountains, the waterfalls, and the abundant banyan and fruit trees on the grounds. Each cottage has a sign identifying the former occupant and his job. There's a large swimming pool and barbecue area, and a restaurant and sundry shop are in the works. At the time we visited, only the one- and two-bedroom cottages were completed; plans call for larger structures, such as the Manager's Estate and the Director's Cottage, which will accommodate up to nine guests. A nice choice for families—and for incurable Hawaiiana buffs!

READERS RECOMMEND

Camping in State and County Parks. *"We stayed at Polihale State Park and Kokee State Park. One needs permits to camp at any state park. On Kauai, the permits are issued at the state building in Lihue, or one can write to Division of State Parks, P.O. Box 1671, Lihue, HI 96761 (tel. 808/245-3444). Rangers checked our permits. To stay at county campgrounds, go to the county building in Lihue. If it's after 5pm, go to the police station. The county permits are*

$3 per person per night; the state permits are free, but the office is open only Monday through Friday from 8am to 4pm and identification must be presented for each adult."—Rebecca Kurtz, Anchorage, Alaska.

THE NORTH SHORE: PRINCEVILLE, HANALEI, HAENA

PRINCEVILLE & HANALEI

Think of Princeville, on the north shore of Kauai, and you think of luxury living, of championship golf and tennis amid a green sweep of mountains and valleys. You don't think of budget accommodations here, but we did find a few needles in the haystack; the lowest prices in Princeville are at a cute little B&B and at two condominium resorts run by Hawaiian Island Resorts. *Note:* If you want ocean swimming, choose this area only in summer. In winter, high surf and treacherous currents make the ocean dangerous.

Doubles for About $50

HALE HO'O MAHA, 4041 Ka'iana Place, Princeville, HI 96722. Tel. 808/826-1130. 2 rms (1 with bath). TV, TEL

$ Rates (including breakfast): $50–$65 single or double. MC, V. **Parking:** Free.

Toby and Kirby Guyer-Searles enjoy sharing their mountain home in its entirety with their guests. The single-story private residence, five minutes away from fine sand beaches, rivers, waterfalls, and riding stables, has windows all around with magnificent views of mountain, ocean, and golf course. A short walk leads to a natural swimming hole enclosed by lava rocks; waves break over one side and create a bubble-bath effect—private and lush. The home has two large bedrooms. The Pineapple Room has a seven-foot round bed, TV, private full bath, and private entrance off the lanai. The Mango Room has a queen-size bed, cable TV, and shared bath. Guests have full kitchen privileges and use of surf and boogie boards, beach mats, gas grill, washer-dryer, and cable TV. A continental breakfast is served on the lanai each morning. Smoking and social drinking are acceptable. Ask Kirby and Toby to show you the exquisite feather and satin leis they make. They sometimes take guests on trips to remote areas that require a four-wheel-drive.

Reservations: Write to Kirby Guyer-Searles, P.O. Box 422, Kilauea, Kauai, HI 96754.

HANALEI BAY INN, P.O. Box 122 (Hi. 50), Hanalei, Kauai, HI 96714. Tel. 808/826-9333. 4 studios, 1 cottage.

$ Rates: $59 studio single or double; $75 one-bedroom apt for up to four; $85 cottage for two, $95 for three. No credit cards. **Parking:** Free.

A good place to retreat from civilization for a bit, a block from the beach at Hanalei, this is an old-fashioned place. The four separate studios have simply equipped kitchenettes, and either twins or a queen-size bed. In back of the units is a spacious garden with banana, papaya, mango, and avocado trees; guests are welcome to step outside and pick their breakfast—in season. They'll lend you ice chests, head rests for the beach, and snorkeling equipment.

Doubles for About $80

HALE MOI, Ka Haku Rd., Princeville-Hanalei, Kauai, HI 96714. Tel. 808/826-9602, or toll free 800/657-7751. 40 apts. TV TEL

$ Rates: $80–$90 single or double; $100–$110 studio; $120–$130 1½-bedroom suite. AE, MC, V. **Parking:** Free.

Located across the way from the Pali Ke Kua, this complex overlooks a Robert Trent Jones golf course. The standard rooms have refrigerators and baths, the studios have full kitchens and baths, and the 1½-bedroom suites have full kitchens and two baths.

Reservations: Hawaiian Island Resorts, P.O. Box 212, Honolulu, HI 96810.

PALI KE KUA, Ka Haku Rd., Princeville-Hanalei, Kauai, HI 96714. Tel. 808/826-9066, or toll free 800/367-7042. Fax 808/743-0546. 98 apts. TV TEL

$ **Rates:** $80–$90 bedroom with bath; $120–$160 one-bedroom apt; $160–$185 two-bedroom apt. AE, MC, V. **Parking:** Free.

This two-story condominium complex overlooks the ocean from a point high on the cliffs. It's not advertised, but you can rent a bedroom and bath—they'll close off one of the bedrooms in the two-bedroom units. The one- and two-bedroom apartments are expensively furnished in modern decor and boast full kitchens with washer-dryers. Choose between mountain-view, ocean-view, and oceanfront; rates go up in that order.

Reservations: Hawaiian Island Resorts, P.O. Box 212, Honolulu, HI 96810.

Worth the Extra Bucks

THE CLIFFS AT PRINCEVILLE, P.O. Box 1005, Hanalei, HI 96714. Tel. 808/826-6219. Fax 808/526-2017. Telex 634135. 220 apts. A/C TV TEL

$ **Rates:** $100–$150 one-bedroom apt; $145–$195 one-bedroom plus loft. AE, CB, DC, DISC, JCB, MC, V. **Parking:** Free.

The largest condo complex in the area, The Cliffs is set amid graceful lawns and gardens and is perched atop cliffs overlooking the ocean far below. It offers as much peace, privacy, sports, or excitement as one would wish. Facilities include four tennis courts, a putting green, a large pool with Jacuzzi, and a recreation pavilion complete with a huge fireplace, wet bar, and an indoor whirlpool bath and sauna. All the suites are perfect little houses that have been decorated in excellent taste and are fully carpeted, beautifully and individually furnished in bamboo and oak, with oak doors, complete equipped kitchens, and cable TVs. These suites can be divided to provide the following possible combinations: a one-bedroom/two-bath unit for up to four, or a one-bedroom/two-bath unit with a loft for up to six. The Princeville Makai Golf Course, designed by Robert Trent Jones, is right at hand; the sandy beach at Hanalei is about a five-minute drive; and opportunities for horseback riding, surfing, windsurfing, scuba diving, and much more are all close by.

HANALEI BAY RESORT, 5380 Honoiki St. (P.O. Box 220), Hanalei, HI 96714. Tel. 808/826-6522, or toll free 800/827-4427. Fax 808/826-6680. 280 rms and suites. A/C TV TEL

$ **Rates:** $130–$210 double; $225–$260 two-bedroom suite; $340–$450 two-bedroom suite with kitchen. AE, DC, MC, V. **Parking:** Free.

This is the Hawaii of everyone's dreams: an oceanside resort surrounded by waterfalls and lush green mountains in a spectacular setting. Its lobby and outstanding Bali H'ai Restaurant are on the top level, and low-slung buildings wind down 20 acres to the white sands of Hanalei Beach below. The center pond in the porte-cochère drops into a waterfall that cascades into a free-form, sandy-bottom swimming pool with a natural sand "shoreline." There is also good ocean swimming, a longish walk or a short jitney ride away.

Buildings are named for flowers. Units are exquisitely furnished with antique replicas and handmade Hawaiian quilts, all designed to reflect the feeling of a Hawaiian plantation guesthouse. Hotel rooms include coffee makers; large suites have full electric kitchens. There are eight tennis courts (three lighted for night play), plus a full pro shop and teaching program; the 27-hole Princeville "Makai" course, at which guests get a discount, surrounds the property.

Bed-and-Breakfast in Hanalei

BED, BREAKFAST AND BEACH, at Hanalei Bay, P.O. Box 748, Hanalei, HI 96714. Tel. 808/826-6111. 3 rms, 1 efficiency apt.

$ Rates (including breakfast): $55–$75 single or double. Each additional person $15 extra. No credit cards.

Carolyn Barnes's stylish house is in a suburban neighborhood just 100 yards from Hanalei Bay, wonderful for summer swimming. The second-floor wraparound lanai is the perfect place for viewing sunsets over the ocean and sighting rainbows and waterfalls. The house is beautifully decorated with American oak antiques and Hawaiian memorabilia. Rooms, each with a queen-size bed, fan, and private bath, are romantically furnished with calico-print wallpapers and carefully selected linens and comforters. Honeymooners love this place! Also available is an apartment with a separate bedroom, private entrance, and an efficiency kitchen. A continental breakfast, island style, is served each morning on the lanai; it consists of a smoothie or juice, fresh island fruit, fresh-baked muffins, and coffee or tea. No smoking. Well-behaved children only; crib available.

HAENA

CAMP NAUE, YMCA OF KAUAI, P.O. Box 1786, Lihue, Kauai, HI 96766. Tel. 808/246-9090 or 246-4411. 42 bunks.

$ Rates: $12 bed; $10 tent space for one person. $7 each additional person. No credit cards.

Hikers, backpackers, campers, take note: If you're about to hike the Na Pali trail and need a place to relax and get a good night's sleep before or after, the YMCA of Kauai has a perfect solution for you. The camp is 1½ miles from the trailhead at Kalalau, right on the beach at Haena, in an idyllic setting under the ironwood and kumani trees. Two bunkhouses situated on the crest of the beach are divided into four separate areas, each with 10–12 bunk beds; the facilities are coed, but there are separate baths for men and women, and hot showers. Bring your own sleeping bag, as the camp does not provide linens or towels. There's a covered beachfront pavilion, a campfire area with picnic tables, and one of the island's best beaches—in summer—for swimming, snorkeling, and surfing (in winter, the ocean is very rough here). There is no refrigeration (the kitchen is for group use only), and if you need food supplies, it's best to stock up on them in Hanalei. You can also stop in at Jungle Bob's in Ching Young Village for backpacking supplies.

Camp Naue is usually filled with large groups, but often has space for walk-in visitors. They don't take reservations, but if you call their Lihue office at 246-9090 not more than two weeks in advance, they'll advise you of the likelihood of getting space here. On weekends, you can call the caretaker at the camp.

3. WHERE TO EAT

Dining on Kauai is always fun and can range from a bowl of saimin at a favorite local hangout, to spa cuisine at the top luxury resort—with many stops in between.

LIHUE & ENVIRONS

Lihue has some excellent budget restaurants frequented mostly by locals, and you'll be glad you joined them.

LIHUE

Meals for Less Than $10

DAIRY QUEEN KAUAI, 4302 Rice St. Tel. 245-2141.

Cuisine: AMERICAN/LOCAL. **Reservations:** Required for large groups only.
$ **Prices:** Appetizers $1.25–$2.50; main courses $4–$13.95. No credit cards.
Open: Daily 7am–10pm.

Locals, visitors, and condo dwellers have all discovered that the Dairy Queen hits the spot for an inexpensive local-style meal. The menu is the same all day and lists about 20 dishes for $4.30–$5.95; served with rice, mashed potatoes, or fries, and a choice of either soup or green salad, they include teriykai steak, char-broiled teri butterfish, pork chops with brown gravy, and beef stew. Dinner specials concentrate on seafood and steak: mahimahi, seafood platter, shrimp scampi, and prime rib, for $6.50–$13.95. Also available are burritos, tacos, chili, saimin, salads, and several sub sandwiches, including a vegetarian one. Kids will love the soda-fountain desserts. Breakfasts are among the most reasonable in town: omelets $3–$3.75 and local-style breakfasts like the Local Boy—two eggs, four pieces of Portuguese sausage, two scoops of rice, and coffee—all for $3.95.

EGGBERT'S: KAUAI'S FAMILY SPECIALTY RESTAURANT, 4483 Rice St. Tel. 245-6325.

Cuisine: AMERICAN. **Reservations:** Recommended.
$ **Prices:** Main courses $3.95–$6.75; breakfast $3.50–$8.75. AE, DC, MC, V.
Open: Mon–Sat 7am–3pm, Sun 7am–2pm.

This friendly little restaurant, in the Haleko Shops, is a popular breakfast place. And it's attractive, with wooden partitions, ferns, flowers, and ceiling fans. The day starts with a variety of terrific omelets and great banana hotcakes. Also excellent: five varieties of eggs Benedict. Their handmade hollandaise is quite special. Lounge service begins at 8am; their Bloody Marys are very popular, and drinks are reasonably priced. All breakfast items are served until 3pm, but lunch dishes are added on at 11am. You can have soups, salads, sandwiches, and burgers, for $3.65–$7.25. Dinner is sometimes on, sometimes off: Call to see if it's being served.

HAMURA SAIMIN STAND, 2956 Kress St. Tel. 245-3271.

Cuisine: LOCAL/JAPANESE.
$ **Prices:** Main courses $2–$4.80. No credit cards.
Open: Mon–Thurs 10am–2am, Fri–Sat 10am–4am, Sun 10am–midnight.

(S) Locals have sung the praises of this beloved Kauai institution and gobbled up its saimin for as long as anybody can remember. It's a very simple spot, a trifle weather-beaten on the outside; inside are two long rectangular counters with stools. Slide onto one, order anything on the small menu, and you're in for a great taste treat as well as one of the cheapest meals on Kauai. Our usual choice is the saimin special at $3.75—that's a large bowl of saimin topped with vegetables, eggs, and wontons—filling and delicious. Order a stick of tender barbecued chicken or beef, too (80¢), and finish up with their lilikoi chiffon pie at $1.05. All in all, quite a meal for $5.60.

KAUAI CHOP SUEY, in Pacific Ocean Plaza, 3051 Rice St., No. 107. Tel. 245-8790.

Cuisine: CANTONESE. **Reservations:** Not required.
$ **Prices:** Appetizers $3.50–$4.75; main courses $5.75–$8.75. No credit cards.
Open: Lunch Tues–Sat 11am–2pm; dinner Tues–Sun 4:30–9pm.

Despite the restaurant's unimaginative name, it serves superior food, all in the Cantonese style. There are about 75 items on the menu, at least 40 of them under $6. There's something for everyone: roast duck, egg foo yong, squid with vegetables, shrimp with broccoli, lemon chicken, stuffed tofu, sweet-and-sour pork, or char sui (an island favorite). And the soups—seaweed, scallop, abalone—are quite special. The place is large and comfortable, decorated in typical Chinese style. Large parties are seated at round tables with revolving lazy Susan centerpieces, the better to sample all the delicacies. The locals rave about this place.

KUN-JA, 4252 Rice St., at the corner of Hardy. Tel. 245-8792.

Cuisine: KOREAN. **Reservations:** Not required.

$ Prices: Main courses $4.75–$6.25. No credit cards.

Open: Mon–Sat 9:30am–8pm.

Simple, tidy, with just a few decorations, Kun-Ja is another local eatery where you can eat a delicious meal for around $6. Owner Kun-Ja Woo greets you with a smile, takes your order, and prepares your meal. She does all the usual Korean dishes, such as mun doo kook so (dumpling and noodle soup), kalbi (broiled short ribs), and pul koki (barbecued beef), plus a few specialties of her own, including a hot-and-spicy kimchee soup. Kun-Ja's Special is barbecued beef, chicken, and pork—a nice little meal in itself, since it's served with soup and several little dishes of mixed vegetables, sprouts, and rice. Should you want to have dinner here, remember that the restaurant closes early.

LIHUE BARBECUE INN, 2982 Kress St. Tel. 245-2921.

Cuisine: JAPANESE/CHINESE/AMERICAN. **Reservations:** Not required.

$ Prices: Main courses $6.95–$13.95; fixed-price lunch to $7.95. No credit cards.

Open: Breakfast/lunch Mon–Sat 7:30am–1:30pm; dinner Mon–Sat 4:30–8:30pm.

You'll know why the Barbecue Inn has been considered one of the best local restaurants in town for some 50 years when you have a look at the low prices on the menu, which lists more than 30 complete dinners, most under $10, including soup or fresh fruit cup, tossed green salad, vegetable, beverages, and dessert. Typical main courses are shrimp tempura, baked mahimahi, broiled teriyaki pork chops, corned beef brisket with cabbage, and chow mein chicken with spareribs. Fresh fish is served when available. Complete lunches are also a good deal—there are 40 choices, such as a seafood platter, Chinese chicken salad, a mahimahi sandwich, or teriyaki chicken, all for $6.25–$8.95. The menu changes daily, but whatever you have here will most likely be good—especially the freshly made pies (can you believe 95¢?) and the homemade bread. Try their frozen chi chis—among the best on the island. One of the most appealing inexpensive restaurants in Lihue, the Barbecue is mostly patronized by families.

RESTAURANT KIIBO, 2991 Umi St. Tel. 245-2650.

Cuisine: JAPANESE. **Reservations:** Recommended.

$ Prices: Main courses $7–$19. No credit cards.

Open: Lunch Mon–Fri 11am–1:30pm; dinner Mon–Sat 5:30–9pm. **Closed:** Hols.

The food is outstanding at this tiny, comfortable, nicely furnished restaurant. The pretty sushi bar up front gives way to a small dining room with 10 or so tables. Japanese lanterns supply the soft lighting, and Japanese folk art adorns the walls. Two of us had a lovely dinner here for under $25. Our meals included a flavorful miso soup, rice, tsukemono (pickled salad), and tea. We enjoyed our $9 chicken sukiyaki and $7.50 beef teriyaki to the accompaniment of soft Japanese music in the background. Other good choices include the tempura, which are sold à la carte at $1.50 each—a large platter of shrimp, vegetable, and seafood tempura should run about $11—and the donburi, huge bowls of rice topped with sukiyaki or teriyaki or something equally interesting, for $7–$9. A child's dinner is available at $6.25. Lunch offers similar dishes at lower prices. Chances are good that you'll be the only haoles at the Kiibo; it's a local favorite, off the usual tourist beat.

TIP TOP CAFE, 3173 Akahi St. Tel. 245-2343 or 245-2333.

Cuisine: CHINESE/AMERICAN. **Reservations:** Recommended.

$ Prices: Appetizers $1.50–$4; main courses $4–$6.95. No credit cards.

Open: Daily 6:45am–8:30pm.

Located just north of the Lihue Shopping Center, this air-conditioned family eatery is a local favorite. The prices are modest, and while the food is not of gourmet quality, it's dependable. We often have breakfast here (pancakes are served all day, and the macadamia-nut ones, $3, are delicious). Chinese plate lunches go for $4.75–$5.50, and lunch dishes, such as pork chops, are $4.50–$5. Dinners, such as teriyaki pork, breaded fish filet, and ground-round steaks with eggs, average $6.50, and that includes soup, salad or potato salad, rice or potatoes, and coffee. Either American- or Asian-style take-out lunches are available at $3.75. Pick up some homemade jams from the gift department. The Tip Top Bakery is famous for its macadamia-nut cookies and Portuguese sweet bread, baked fresh daily. Upstairs, the Tip Toe Inn offers modest motel rooms for $30 single, $39 double, $45 triple.

READERS RECOMMEND

Dani's Restaurant, *4201 Rice St., Lihue (tel. 245-4991). "Dani's Restaurant in Lihue was a delight. Not the usual tourist fare. Rice was served with breakfast steak and eggs for $4. Coffee always there. Friendly, folksy people."*—Jon and Andy McCormick, Port Allierni, British Columbia, Canada.

Meals for Less Than $15

COOK'S AT THE BEACH, in the Westin Kauai, at Kauai Lagoons. Tel. 245-5050.

Cuisine: INTERNATIONAL. **Reservations:** Not required.

$ **Prices:** Appetizers $6.50–$8.95; main courses $8.95–$19.50. AE, DC, MC, V.

Open: Daily 6:30am–10pm.

Dining at the fabulous Westin Kauai luxury resort need not be as expensive as you think. And since you're certainly going to want to see this amazing place, you might consider a meal at the very informal Cook's at the Beach, the closest thing to a family restaurant this jet-set resort has to offer. One side is completely open to the 26,000-square-foot swimming pool with its multiple waterfalls and immense marble animal statuary. For breakfast, the French toast made with Portuguese sweet bread is a popular choice. The lunch menu features an array of salads and sandwiches, plus a few dishes, for $6.95–$12.95. As the sun begins to set, you might want to try Hot Rock Cuisine, a new and healthful concept in dining in which you grill your own dish—maybe chicken fajitas or a seafood combination—on a pure natural rock heated to 500°. The dinner menu also features fresh pastas, sizzling platters, fresh island fish, and such local favorites as saimin, coconut shrimp, and fresh Pacific catch of the day. There's Hawaiian entertainment at poolside in the afternoon.

DUKE'S CANOE CLUB, at Kalapaki Beach. Tel. 246-9599.

Cuisine: SEAFOOD/STEAK. **Reservations:** Recommended.

$ **Prices:** Duke's Dinner House, main courses $14.95–$26.95. Duke's Kau Kau Grill, appetizers $4.95–$8.95; main courses $5.95–$9.95. AE, MC, V.

Open: Duke's Dinner House, dinner only, daily 5–10pm. Duke's Kau Kau Grill, dinner only, daily 4–11pm.

In front of the Westin Kauai, at Kalapaki Beach, Duke's is a mighty crowd-pleaser. It surrounds a waterfall, with tables interspersed among the rocks below, and overlooks the sands of Kalapaki Beach. Original mementos of the career of Duke Kahanamoku are everywhere, and huge outrigger canoes are on the ceiling. It's actually two restaurants in one: Upstairs is the more expensive Duke's Dinner House, featuring seafood, steaks, and ribs; and downstairs is Duke's Kau Kau Grill, a beachside café and lounge. Best prices for us budgeteers are downstairs: The menu includes local Hawaiian plates—barbecued chicken or ribs, fresh fish, teriyaki beef kebab, or stir-fry chicken cashew, all served with "two scoop" rice or fries and "one scoop" macaroni salad or baked beans, at $9.95. Burgers and sandwiches begin at $5.95. There are a few salads and neat pupus, such as saimin, sashimi, and calamari rings. Vegetarian dishes are also available.

Upstairs, the values are still good: several fresh fish dinners under $19, smoked ribs and chicken under $15, top sirloin at $14.95, and the spa-cuisine-style ginger chicken at $12.95. Most main courses include a tossed green salad, a basket of freshly baked banana–macadamia-nut muffins and dinner rolls, and steamed vegetable rice. Wherever you sit, don't miss the frozen mai tais (they're blended with passion-fruit sherbet) or desserts, like Kimo's original hula pie.

THE TERRACE, in the Kauai Lagoons Golf and Racquet Club, at the Westin Kauai. Tel. 245-5050.

Cuisine: SPA. **Reservations:** Not required.

$ Prices: Main courses $8.75–$11.50. AE, CB, DC, DISC, MC, JCB, V.

Open: Breakfast daily 6:30–11:30am; lunch daily 11:30am–2pm.

It's so pleasant to have a meal at the Terrace restaurant, in the Westin Kauai, an open-air spot serenely overlooking the swimming pool at the Spa and the Haupu mountains beyond. And you can feel virtuous while dining on light spa cuisine, all of it beautifully prepared, very tasty, and decently priced. Our favorite dishes here include the lemon-dill linguine with grilled chicken breast, the fresh mahimahi sandwich with Maui onions, and the warm prawns Kekaha salad. Every Friday between 11am and 2pm there's an authentic "Aloha Friday" menu with all the traditional dishes. The Terrace is very casual: Swim or tennis togs are acceptable.

Meals For Around $25

CAFE PORTOFINO, 3501 Rice St., Nawiliwili. Tel. 245-2121.

Cuisine: ITALIAN. **Reservations:** Recommended.

$ Prices: Appetizers $5.50–$7.75; main courses $12.50–$18.50. AE, MC, V.

Open: Lunch Mon–Fri 11am–2pm; dinner daily 5–10pm.

One of the more stylish spots in town, Café Portofino is the place for an elegant and not overly priced Italian meal. Windows all around the dining room and a big lanai overlooking Kalapaki Beach and Nawiliwili Harbor also afford a splendid view of the surrounding luxuriant mountains. The ambience is decidedly romantic: candles and flowers on the tables, opera music (Italian, of course!) on the stereo, sparkly glassware and silver, and abundant greenery hanging from the ceiling. We like the prosciutto and papaya (only in Hawaii) among the antipasti, the traditional Caesar among the salads, and, among the pastas, the lasagne made with seasonal vegetables. Rabbit in white wine, stuffed squid with spinach and cheese, and sweetbreads in a white cream sauce are some of the signature specialty items. Desserts vary daily, but always include freshly made gelati and sorbets.

KUKUI GROVE

Kauai's multi-million-dollar shopping center, Kukui Grove, just outside Lihue on Hi. 50 toward Poipu Beach, has several attractive budget eateries. In addition to the following restaurants, snacking possibilities include **Joni-Hana** for hot lunches and sushi to go; **Family Kitchen,** which feeds a local crowd with hearty breakfasts, $3.85 plate lunches, sandwiches, burgers, saimin, and sushi, in a pleasant self-serve, sit-down setting; **Yogurt Patio** for light food and sandwiches.

KUKUI NUT TREE INN, in Kukui Grove Shopping Center. Tel. 245-7005.

Cuisine: AMERICAN/LOCAL. **Reservations:** Not required.

$ Prices: Main courses $6.25–$9.95. AE, MC, V.

Open: Mon–Thurs 7:30am–9:30pm, Fri–Sat 7:30am–9pm, Sun 7:30am–4pm.

This family restaurant serves all three meals in a summerhouse atmosphere. Latticework arching over the booths and on the ceiling makes this family restaurant nicer than your average coffee shop and contributes to the summerhouse atmosphere.

The food is American with island touches, and prices are quite reasonable. The day starts with omelets and pancakes, plus local foods like taro cake or a Japanese breakfast—the traditional Asahi or the contemporary Fuji—each $6.25. Lunch features some 15 choices from $5.25 to $8.95, and that includes the likes of mahimahi tempura and teri combo, honey-stung fried chicken, and grilled beef liver with onions and bacon. Main courses are preceded by soup or fruit cocktail and are served with hot vegetables, garden greens, and rolls with butter. Especially popular are such salads as vegetarian chef, tofu, and Moloaa papaya with turkey salad, all served with unique locally made dressings. At dinner, the bill goes up about 70¢, but dessert is included. With prices like these, it's no wonder this place is always crowded. There are also special menus for keikis and kupunas (under 12 and over 65). Drinks are available.

SI CISCO'S MEXICAN CANTINA & RESTAURANT, in Kukui Grove Shopping Center. Tel. 245-8561.

Cuisine: MEXICAN. **Reservations:** Not required.

$ Prices: Appetizers $4.95–$7.95; main courses $8.95–$19.95. MC, V.

Open: Mon–Sat 11am–10pm, Sun 11:30am–5pm.

Probably the most popular specialty restaurant at Kukui Grove is Si Cisco's, in an attractive indoor-outdoor setting: many plants, stained-glass lanterns, ceiling fans, stucco walls, cozy booths. You can dine leisurely here on Mexican and American favorites. Combination plates run $8.95–$9.95. Don't pass up the margaritas; a 60-ounce pitcher is a mere $8.

STONES ESPRESSO CAFE, in Kukui Grove Shopping Center. Tel. 245-6564.

Cuisine: SNACKS.

$ Prices: Appetizers $1–$5; main courses $3–$5. AE, MC, V.

Open: Mon–Wed 9:30am–6pm, Thurs–Fri 9:30am–9pm, Sat 9:30am–5:30pm, Sun 10am–4pm.

Our favorite spot in the Kukui Grove Shopping Center is not a traditional restaurant at all—it's a café area in the midst of Stones Gallery and a lovely place for a sophisticated snack. Freshly roasted coffee is sold by the pound, and its fragrant aroma makes everything you eat here taste wonderful. In addition to a variety of coffees, espressos, cappuccinos, herbal teas, and coffee specialty drinks, you can get soups, bagels, dessert, quiche, and wonderful homemade cookies, scones, and muffins. Call for take-out orders.

KILOHANA PLANTATION

GAYLORD'S, Hi. 50, 1 mile southwest of Lihue. Tel. 245-9593.

Cuisine: CONTINENTAL. **Reservations:** Recommended for dinner.

$ Prices: Appetizers $3.95–$7.95; main courses $15.95–$24.95. AE, MC, V.

Open: Lunch daily Mon–Sat 11am–3:30pm; light supper 5–6:30pm; dinner daily 5–9pm; brunch Sun 10am–3pm.

One of the nicest restaurants to open on Kauai in many a tropical moon is Gaylord's, at Kilohana, the legendary plantation estate of the 1930s that has been lovingly restored and is open to the public. Gaylord's is a courtyard restaurant facing a manicured green lawn around which tables are arranged on three sides. The restaurant is done in whites, pinks, and greens, with soft-cushioned chairs and fresh flowers on every table. Dinner at Gaylord's *is* pricey, but at lunchtime you can have a first-class dining experience for a modest tab—and many agree that the food is better at lunchtime. We like both Gaylord's Papaya Runneth Over, island papaya stuffed with delicate bay shrimp (or salmon or chicken) salad, at $7.95; and the bay-shrimp-and-avocado sandwich on homemade bread, with a choice of soup or salad, fries or rice, at $7.95. Burgers run $6.95–$7.95. There is often a vegetarian selection of the day, which can't be beat for freshness, since many of the greens are grown right in

Kilohana's acres. Homemade desserts, such as Kilohana mud pie, French silk, and double-chocolate mousse, are special. The Sunday brunch menu offers cheese blintzes, eggs Benedict, croissant sandwiches, and the like for $9.95–$13.95. Special dinner selections for children under 10 are available every night for $9.95.

HANAMAULU

HANAMAULU RESTAURANT AND TEA HOUSE, Hi. 56. Tel. 245-2511.
Cuisine: JAPANESE/CHINESE. **Reservations:** Recommended.
$ Prices: Main courses $11–$17. MC, V.
Open: Lunch Tues–Fri 11am–1pm; dinner Tues–Sun 4:30–9pm.

This old-time favorite is known for its Japanese garden, beautifully landscaped with stone pagodas, pebbled paths, and a pond filled with carp. We suggest that you call a day in advance and reserve one of the charming *ozashiki,* or teahouse, rooms; you take off your shoes and sit on the floor at a long, low table, and the shoji screens are opened to face the lighted garden. (You may be able to get one of the rooms without reservations, but it's best to call ahead.) The food is excellent and inexpensive; the Chinese and Japanese plate lunches are a good value at $6.50. Special dinner platters are $12.50, and you can feast on a veritable Eastern banquet for about $15 per person. An excellent sushi bar and robatayaki are attractions here. The Miyaki family are cordial hosts.

THE EASTERN SHORE

This is the most populous part of the island and has many budget restaurants.

WAILUA & KAPAA

Meals for Less Than $15

ALOHA DINER, in Waipouli Complex, 4-971 Kuhio Hwy. Tel. 822-3851.
Cuisine: HAWAIIAN.
$ Prices: Main courses $3.50–$9.50. No credit cards.
Open: Breakfast/lunch Mon–Sat 10:30am–3pm; dinner Mon–Sat 5:30–9pm.

If you've developed a taste for real Hawaiian food, you can satisfy it here in plain surroundings. Best bets are the lunch specials for $5.75–$6.75, including kalua pig or laulau, lomi-lomi salmon, rice or poi; and the more elaborate dinner specials for $7.50–$9.50—including kalua pig or laulau, lomi-lomi salmon, chicken lau, poi or rice, and haupia (coconut pudding). Typical à la carte choices, at $3.50–$4.75, include beef stew, squid lau, and other favorites.

BUBBA'S, 1384 Kuhio Hwy. Tel. 823-0069.
Cuisine: SNACKS. **Reservations:** Not accepted.
$ Prices: $1.75–$3.25. No credit cards.
Open: Sun–Thurs 10:30am–10pm, Fri–Sat 10:30am–2am.

Bubba's calls itself an old-fashioned hamburger stand that "cheats tourists and drunks." Don't you believe it! The burgers, hot dogs, chicken burgers, fish and chips that you get here are really good and really cheap. You dine right on the sidewalk at polished wooden picnic tables with benches. The friendly proprietors know everyone who passes by, the food dispensed from their kitchen counter is plentiful and tasty, and the friendly spirit is contagious.

BULL SHED, 796 Kuhio Hwy. Tel. 822-3791.

Cuisine: AMERICAN. **Reservations:** Not accepted.
$ Prices: Main courses $10.95–$17.95 ($24.50 for steak and lobster). AE, MC, V.
Open: Dinner daily 5:30–10pm; cocktails from 3:30pm.

A favorite of steak and seafood lovers, the Bull Shed, just north of Coconut Plantation, behind the Mokihana of Kauai condos, is a Kauai tradition. The atmosphere is great: a large, airy, wooden-frame building overlooking the ocean, so close to it that waves wash up against the sea wall. If you're watching your budget or your waistline, you can make do with visits to the superb salad bar (salad bar alone is $6.95). Or splurge on some of the specialties, including prime rib, garlic tenderloin, yakitori, shrimp, and scallops, and a variety of Hawaiian fish. The price of the main courses includes steamed rice and a trip to the salad bar. The restaurant is apt to be crowded, so get there early; prime rib, the house favorite for which many people make a special trip, can run out early on.

CAPTAIN & THE COOK, 41-1380 Kuhio Hwy. Tel. 822-7128.

Cuisine: SNACKS. **Reservations:** Not accepted.
$ Prices: Pizza pies $9–$12; sandwiches $3.95–$4.95; main courses $6.95–$7.95. No credit cards.
Open: Mon–Sat 11am–9:30pm.

There are just two tables here, but lots of good things emerge from the kitchen for take-out: delicious pizza pies by the slice or the pie, broasted chicken (two pieces for $2.95), hearty sub sandwiches, and super stuffed baked potatoes topped with lots of goodies. Half a dozen pasta dishes are also tasty. They'll deliver to your hotel or condo free after 6pm.

COCO PALMS RESORT, Hi. 56. Tel. 822-4921.

Cuisine: BUFFETS. **Reservations:** Recommended.
$ Prices: Lunch buffet $11; Sun brunch $17.50. AE, CB, DC, DISC, JCB, MC, V.
Open: Lunch Mon–Sat 11am–2pm; brunch Sun 10am–2pm.

If you're in the mood for a treat, stop and have lunch at the glorious Coco Palms. Lunch is an extravagant buffet with several hot dishes—usually including chicken and roast beef—and many, many choices of vegetables, potatoes, salads, breads, yummy desserts, and fresh fruits. The lovely open dining room overlooks the palms and the lagoon, where their famous torch-lighting ceremony is held nightly at 7:30pm. Be sure to walk around the beautiful grounds and browse through their shops.

If you're making this trip on a Sunday, even better: Coco Palms' Sunday Champagne Brunch is one of the best on the island. It features a huge seafood buffet including such island favorites as fresh shrimp, sashimi, octopus, and lomi-lomi salmon; an omelet bar; eggs Benedict; and outrageous desserts.

JIMMY'S GRILL, 4-1354 Kuhio Hwy. Tel. 822-7000.

Cuisine: AMERICAN. **Reservations:** Not required.
$ Prices: Appetizers $5.20–$7.95; main courses $7.95–$16.95. MC, V.
Open: Daily 11am–11pm.

Ensconced in a large, two-story building with open-air and balcony dining upstairs, with good food, solid drinks, and an ongoing beach-party atmosphere, Jimmy's is a very popular restaurant in the heart of Kapaa. The downstairs bar, with its sandy floor and beachy decor, is a fun place to pop into just for a drink and some of their wonderful pupus—nachos, guacamole, sashimi, teri-beef, and amazing potato skins. If you want a bigger meal, climb the fire-engine-red staircase to the large dining room; the entire street side of the building is open, and a table here gives you a fine vantage point on busy Kapaa. The menu includes delicious salads, burgers, chicken, hot pastrami, and fresh-fish sandwiches for $6.25–$7.95. The specialties of the house—"World Famous" Slavonic steak, barbecued beef ribs, St. Louis–style pork ribs, spicy chicken, New York steak, fresh fish, and homemade pasta—are served up in generous portions. "Groovy Hour" is 4 to 6pm.

KING AND I, 4-901 Kuhio Hwy., in Waipouli Shopping Plaza. Tel. 822-1642.

Cuisine: THAI/VEGETARIAN. **Reservations:** Recommended.

$ Prices: Appetizers $5.25–$8.95; main courses $5.95–$8.50. AE, DC, MC, V.

Open: Dinner daily 4:30–9:30pm.

The King and I is a find. Featuring Thai cuisine, it's a small, family-run establishment, with crisp white tablecloths, nice paintings on the wall, greenery, orchids, Thai sculpture—a gentle atmosphere. The family grows all their own herbs and spices. The food is exceptionally good, and the prices are easy to take. Start with one of the appetizers, like the spring rolls or stuffed chicken wings, then have a soup (we like the Siam chicken-coconut soup) and a main dish, perhaps the garlic shrimp, the Siam eggplant with chicken, or one of the curries—like yellow curry with shrimp. (Watch out, though: Those curries can be hot, unless you tell your server you'd like them mild.) Vegetarians have a choice of 13 good dishes. Now for dessert: How about banana with coconut milk, followed by Thai iced coffee with milk? Super!

KOUNTRY KITCHEN, 1485 Kuhio Hwy. Tel. 822-3511.

Cuisine: AMERICAN/LOCAL. **Reservations:** Not required.

$ Prices: Appetizers $1.95–$3.75; main courses $6.95–$16.95. MC, V.

Open: Breakfast daily 6am–2pm; lunch daily 11am–2:30pm; dinner daily 5–8:30pm.

Kountry Kitchen is an old standby in Kapaa, a dressed-up diner with carpets, Tiffany-type lamps, gingham curtains at the windows. You can have complete dinners, such as fresh local fish, all-vegetable quiche, baked ham, country beef ribs, sesame shrimp, or broiled mahimahi, and your selection is accompanied by vegetable soup or salad, vegetables, rice or potatoes, and a loaf of home-baked bread. Beer and wine are available at dinner. The lunch menu offers sandwiches, super burgers, fried chicken, grilled mahimahi, chef's salad, and roast beef, from about $5.50 to $8. Don't be surprised if you see people lining up for breakfast: The crispy hash browns are a big favorite with all omelets and egg orders. The omelet bar is very popular, especially the build-your-own combination, since such unusual omelet ingredients as hamburger, tuna, raisins, and kimchee are all ready and waiting. Plan on spending $3.95–$7.50. And the coffee is great, too.

Note: The same management also runs Duane's Ono Charburgers in Anahola, a hamburger stand with a cult following all over the USA. You may see movie stars eating their "Gourmet Burgers."

MAKAI MEDITERRANEAN RESTAURANT, 1419 Kuhio Hwy. Tel. 822-3955.

Cuisine: MEDITERRANEAN. **Reservations:** Not required.

$ Prices: Appetizers $4.95–$6.95; main courses $8.95–$14.50. MC, V.

Open: Breakfast Mon–Sat 8am–11:30pm; lunch Mon–Sat 11:30am–2pm; dinner Mon–Sat 6–9:30pm.

Located on Kapaa's "restaurant row," Makai is a very pretty, tropical, laid-back, little place in a house across from the beach. Mediterranean-style cooking is their specialty, and although it is moderately priced, it is exquisitely prepared and presented. Can you imagine a ham, pineapple, and Monterey Jack cheese omelet for breakfast? You can have one here for around $6, among other breakfast delights, including homemade blueberry muffins, croissants, and eggs Benedict. Sandwiches, such as the fresh catch and tuna salad (made with fresh ahi), are excellent, as are the luncheon plates in the $5.25–$6.50 range. And there are pita sandwiches in the Greek manner, with marinated beef, chicken, lamb, and feta cheese. Favorite dinner dishes include ginger chicken pork médaillons with fresh baked pineapple, spit-roasted game hen, New York steak, and garlic prawns—all served with soup of the day or garden salad, and your choice of rice, pasta, or vegetable. Last time, we opted for mahimahi baked in phyllo served with an exquisite lemon-butter sauce. You can end your meal with a wonderful chocolate mousse or macadamia-nut–cream pie or, in season, key lime pie. And try the Greek wines, too.

NORBERTO'S EL CAFE, 1375 Kuhio Hwy. Tel. 822-3362.

Cuisine: MEXICAN/VEGETARIAN. **Reservations:** Not required.
$ Prices: Appetizers \$2.50–\$6.50; main courses \$7–\$12.95. AE, MC, V.
Open: Dinner daily 5:30–9pm.

Norberto's has been a local favorite since 1977. The attractive, two-level dining room is decorated in Mexican style, and the food is as tasty as ever. Norberto's always cooks with fresh ingredients, does not use lard or any other animal fats (so vegetarians can feel comfortable here), and offers excellent value. Don't worry about breaking the budget, as complete dinners are reasonably priced and include soup, vegetables, refried beans, and Spanish rice; there's plenty of chips and hot salsa on the table to go with your margaritas or beer. The steak or chicken fajitas are just about our favorites, but olés, too, for the rellenos Tampico and the nifty Mex-Mix Plate: That's a chicken chimichanga, a chicken taquito, and an enchilada with Spanish rice and beans, all for \$12.95. All dishes can be served vegetarian style if you ask. If you have any room left, top your meal off with a piece of rum cake or chocolate-cream pie, both homemade and delicious. A good family choice.

ONO-FAMILY RESTAURANT, 4-1292 Kuhio Hwy. Tel. 822-1710.

Cuisine: AMERICAN. **Reservations:** Not required.
$ Prices: Main courses \$3.65–\$13. AE, MC, V.
Open: Daily 7am–9pm.

Ono means "delicious" in Hawaiian, and this restaurant in the old Kapaa town lives up to its name. Pewter plates and fancy cookware hang on the wood-paneled walls, and European and Early American antiques and paintings add to the charm. This is a family-owned operation, and it shows in the care and attention that the owners lavish on their guests, especially senior citizens and children; many come back year after year because of that warm welcome. Omelets are featured at breakfast, and so are Canterbury eggs (grilled English muffins topped with turkey, ham, veggies, eggs, and cheese), at \$5.55, and quite a way to start the day. From 11am to 4pm, you can get "Special Delights" for \$4.55–\$7.95: their \$4.75 fish sandwich, with vegetables, sprouts, and cheddar cheese on grilled Branola bread, is a meal in itself; super burgers cost \$3.65–\$5.35; and, for the health conscious, there is a variety of buffalo burgers, which have 70% less fat and 50% less cholesterol than beef and taste just fine—they're \$5.25–\$6.75. Be sure to try their Portuguese bean soup; it's an island classic. A variety of fresh fish meals are served daily, along with chicken and beef dishes. The price of a main course includes Portuguese bean soup or tossed salad, rice pilaf or fries, fresh sauteéd vegetables, and molasses rye bread from the famous Jacques Bakery. There's a special menu for children.

PAPAYA'S NATURAL FOODS CAFE, 4-831 Kuhio Hwy., in Kauai Village, near Safeway. Tel. 823-0191.

Cuisine: NATURAL FOODS. **Reservations:** Not required.
$ Prices: Main courses \$5–\$9. MC, V.
Open: Daily 8am–8:30pm.

Lovers of natural foods need seek no further: They can find everything they need at this café adjacent to the huge Papaya's Natural Foods store. Chef Gordon, a former chef at the Pritikin Center in Santa Monica, California, shows off his talents in fresh fish and chicken dishes, pastas, thin-crust pizzas, delicious salads, focaccia sandwiches, and hearty, homemade soups. Organically grown fruits and vegetables, most of it from local farms, is used whenever possible. You might have a simple soup and salad meal for $2.75, a combination plate (a choice of any three salads) at $5.95, or a grilled fish plate at $8.50. Breakfast offers more healthful treats: whole-grain Belgian waffles with real maple syrup, strawberry- and banana-stuffed French toast, artichoke fritattas ($3–$4.25), to mention a few possibilities. There's outdoor seating under umbrellaed tables, and more seats inside. They'll happily pack a picnic lunch to go.

PARADISE HOT DOGS, 4-821 Kuhio Hwy., in Kauai Village. Tel. 822-1500.

Cuisine: SNACKS. **Reservations:** Not required.

$ Prices: Main courses $2.95–$6.50. No credit cards.

Open: Mon–Thurs 11am–8pm, Fri–Sat 11am–9pm, Sun 11am–5pm.

When is a hot dog more than a hot dog? When it's an old-fashioned German frank, the kind that chef Tyler Barnes made popular at his first restaurant in the Kiahuna Shopping Village in the Poipu area. Barnes also has a bigger restaurant here, with tables indoors and out. In addition to great franks, he also offers teri-chicken sandwiches ($5.25), nifty buffalo wings ($6.50), and very good Caesar salads ($3.80 and $5.25). Beer, wine, plus a vegetarian hot dog—char-boiled eggplant with miso sauce—as well.

PERRY'S SMORGY, in the Kauai Beach Boy Hotel, 4-484 Kuhio Hwy. Tel. 822-3111.

Cuisine: BUFFETS. **Reservations:** Not accepted.

$ Prices (including tax): Breakfast buffet $4.65; lunch buffet $6.20; dinner buffet $8.30; Sun brunch $7.95. AE, MC, V.

Open: Breakfast Mon–Sat 7–10:30am; lunch Mon–Sat 11am–2:30pm; dinner daily 5–9pm; brunch Sun 11am–2:30pm.

If you've been to Honolulu, you know the great value and dining to be had at the Perry's Smorgy restaurants. Perry's in Kauai has a glorious location overlooking the water. The dining room, which has both chairs and tables and booths, is enormous; the buffet tables are laden with goodies; and the price is always right. The breakfast bonanza features all you want of fresh fruits, juices, smoked ham and sausage, eggs, hotcakes, French toast, pastries, and wonderful Kona coffee. Lunch entitles you to unlimited fried chicken, mahimahi, beef stew, spaghetti, and garlic bread, plus plentiful helpings from the Orchid salad bar. Dinner includes a hand-carved round of beef, golden fried shrimp, mahimahi amandine, southern-style chicken, spaghetti, and garlic bread, plus the salad bar. Daily island specials—Hawaiian, Chinese, Japanese, American—are offered at lunch and dinner. All meals include beverage; lunch and dinner also include dessert. This is a super choice for families.

RESTAURANT KINTARO, 4-370 Kuhio Hwy., between Coco Palms and the Coconut Plantation. Tel. 822-3341.

Cuisine: JAPANESE. **Reservations:** Recommended.

$ Prices: Dinner $11.95–$26.95. AE, DC, JCB, MC, V.

Open: Dinner only, Mon–Sat 5:30–9:30pm.

Exquisite is the word for the dining experience at this sparkling bright restaurant, authentically Japanese down to the prettily wrapped chopsticks on the table. The rather bland exterior does not even suggest the harmonious Japanese scene inside: kites and kimonos on the walls, blond woods, shoji screens, a long sushi bar from which the chefs turn out tender marvels. Several complete dinners run $12.50–$14.95 and include a variety of delicious small dishes. First you are served chilled buckwheat noodles in a flavorful sauce, presented on a *zora,* a wooden box with bamboo top. Next, also served on traditional wooden platters, is miso soup, rice,

Japanese pickled vegetables, and your main course—it could be the delicious chicken yakitori (boneless broiled chicken, onion, bell pepper, and teriyaki sauce and salad) or salmon yaki. Or it could be a tasty tempura combination. Kintaro is justifiably proud of its teppan cuisine, including oysters, steak, lobster, and fresh island fish with scallops, for $13.95–$26.95. Be sure to have the green-tea ice cream for dessert. A pot of green tea accompanies your meal. There are various sushi and sashimi combinations for appetizers or for those who wish to eat at the sushi bar.

SIZZLER STEAK, SEAFOOD, SALAD RESTAURANT, in Wailua Shopping Plaza, 4361 Kuhio Hwy. Tel. 822-7404.

Cuisine: AMERICAN. **Reservations:** Not required.

$ Prices: Main courses $6–$16.50. AE, MC, V.

Open: Sun–Thurs 6am–10pm, Fri–Sat 6am–midnight.

Located across from the Kinipopo Shopping Village, Sizzler is one of the most popular budget restaurants in Kauai. It's a semi-self-service operation. You place your order at the counter and pay for it as soon as you come in, then you sit back at your table while your server brings you your food and serves you coffee. The best feature is the fresh soup, salad, and fruit-salad bar combined with the pasta and tostada bar, with luscious papayas and avocados grown a few trees away, delicious pastas, protein salads, breads, rolls, and sweets. You could easily make a complete meal of this alone: It's $7.50 for all you can eat (with a meal, it's $3.50 at lunch, $4 at dinner). However, most people opt for the meat and fish dishes; the steak, always excellent, is only $9. Fresh local game fish is featured every day. Breakfast is another bargain meal: $5 for eggs Benedict, $2.70 for French toast. And there are great drink specialties, too, including mai tais, chi chis, and daiquiris, for $1.80–$3.70. Bring a big appetite. Perfect for families.

WAILUA MARINA RESTAURANT, in Wailua River State Park. Tel. 822-4311.

Cuisine: SEAFOOD/STEAK. **Reservations:** Recommended.

$ Prices: Appetizers $1.50–$6.50; main courses $7.75–$24. AE, MC, V.

Open: Breakfast daily 9–11am; lunch daily 11am–2pm; dinner daily 5–9pm.

This has long been one of the most popular restaurants on Kauai, offering good food, good prices, and a very special setting. You can dine riverside and catch the breezes on the open lanai, or indoors in the huge dining room with its slanted ceilings and murals, stuffed fish, and turtle shells on the wall. How they manage to serve almost 20 dishes for $7.75–$15.50—including curry, prime rib of beef, stuffed prawns with crabmeat, and sirloin steak—is a mystery to us, especially since every meal includes delicious hot rolls with butter and a green salad with a choice of dressing (the bleu cheese is excellent), plus vegetables and a starch for that same low price. Our baked stuffed chicken cooked in plum sauce with a mini-lobster salad was quite good, and so was the house special of baked stuffed pork chops. Another 9 or 10 selections, including such seafood specialties as slipper-lobster tail and char-broiled mahimahi, range from $9.50 to $24. Homemade pies cost $1.75. Lunch offers more excellent bargains, like corned beef and cabbage at $4.95, a pineapple boat with fresh fruit at $4.95, and filet of mahimahi at $6.25. Most sandwiches are under $5. A find.

ZIPPY'S, 4-919 Kuhio Hwy., Waipouli. Tel. 822-9866.

Cuisine: AMERICAN/LOCAL. **Reservations:** Not required.

$ Prices: Plate lunches and dinners $5.50–$7.40. No credit cards.

Open: Daily 24 hours.

You know you can't go wrong at a Zippy's anywhere in Hawaii, and the one on Kuhio Highway (on the mountain side of the road) is no exception to the rule. Burgers start at $2.25; Zippy's special chili with rice (*ono*!) is $3.15 for a large bowl. A variety of plate lunches, such as beef teriyaki, breaded veal cutlet, and friend chicken, come with rice and salad. Best of all—Zippy's is always open!

READERS RECOMMEND

Fast Freddy's Diner, *4-1302 Kuhio Hwy. (tel. 822-0488). "Fast Freddy's near Kapaa is another 'local' place. They have a $2.20 breakfast special, which is good food for a great price."*—David and Bridget Badanes, Selden, N.Y.

Worth the Extra Bucks

A PACIFIC CAFE, in Kauai Village, Kuhio Hwy. Tel. 822-0013.
Cuisine: PACIFIC RIM. **Reservations:** Recommended.
$ Prices: Appetizers $4.75–$9.25; main courses $14.75–$24.50. DC, MC, V.
Open: Dinner Wed–Mon 5:30–10:30pm; brunch Sun 10:30am–2pm.

For a splurge meal worth every cent, indulge yourself with dinner at this restaurant that's created a stir in island food circles. A Pacific Café is the creation of executive chef/owner Jean-Marie Josselin, who's garnered awards for creative cooking in Paris, on the mainland, and here in Hawaii, where he was formerly executive chef at the Coco Palms Resort. Josselin has created a stylish restaurant that boasts Asian art and decor, native Hawaiian woods and plants, and an open kitchen with rôtisserie and a wood-burning grill and wok, so guests can watch the chefs create their magic. And magic it is—Josselin creates extraordinarily good ethnic dishes of the Pacific Rim, using a blend of Asian and European culinary techniques. The superb pottery on which you dine was created by Sophronia, Jean-Marie's wife.

Since the menu changes constantly to take advantage of the freshest local fish, game, and locally grown vegetables, there's no telling what you may encounter on a specific night, but here are some samples of his signature dishes. Appetizers include smoked chicken lumpia with a curried lime dip, or deep-fried sashimi with a wana sauce, or potato skins with smoked marlin and sour cream. For salads and soups, $4.25–$8.25, how about a sizzling squid salad with a sesame-lime dressing, or baked potato soup with smoked marlin, sour cream, and chives. It's easy to make a meal on two or three of the appetizers, soups, and salads. From the wood-burning grill come such main dishes as stir-fried Hawaiian lobster with Japanese eggplant and cashews, grilled rack of lamb with a plum-tamarind sauce, or grilled Hawaiian aku with a papaya black-bean relish. All main courses are served with vegetables and a choice of rices. Save room for dessert, preferably the platter of assorted miniature pastries baked fresh every day. Lunch is not available now, but is a possibility for the future.

COCONUT PLANTATION MARKETPLACE

It's hard to decide what's more fun, shopping or eating at the Coconut Marketplace. There's an international assortment of restaurants and snack bars here, and most are in the budget range.

Super Budget

See the people at **Big Mel's Deli & Picnic Basket** if you need a picnic lunch. They'll custom-make it for you, with meats, cheeses, salads, breads, and ice-cold drinks, and give you directions to secluded beaches as well. Picnic baskets for two are packed in unique local boxes and cost $12.95. They also have good sandwiches to eat right here, like po'boy subs, the "chicado" sandwich (chicken with avocado), tuna melts, and veggie sandwiches at $4.45.

Taco Dude is a bright spot for Mexican food. Pink chairs and white counters set the scene for such tasty items as burritos, tacos, quesadillas, and a taco salad, $1.75–$4.75. **Paradise Chicken-N-Ribs** gives you a choice of food off the broiler or from the fryer. Fried nuggets and strips are $4.25–$5.95; broiled chicken and baby back ribs are $4.95–$7.50.

The **Fish Hut** has tasty goodies galore: They feature fresh char-broiled fish—ahi, mahimahi, ono, and more—in sandwiches from $4.95, and as dinners from $6.95. And they also have Old English–style fish and chips, $4.95.

Café Espresso is a fun stop for banana-mac Belgian waffles, homemade soups, sandwiches, cappuccino, espresso, and more. And **Tradewinds,** a South Seas bar, is especially relaxing during the 4 to 6pm happy hour. At the rear of the marketplace is **Buzz's Steak and Lobster,** which often features an all-you-can-eat sandwich and salad bar at lunch, between 11am and 2:30pm, for $6.75.

Budget

JOLLY ROGER RESTAURANT, adjacent to Coconut Marketplace. Tel. 822-3451.

Cuisine: AMERICAN. **Reservations:** Not required.

$ Prices: Main courses $9.95–$12.95. AE, MC, V.

Open: Breakfast daily 6:30am–noon; lunch daily 11am–5pm; dinner daily 5–10pm.

Part of a family of island restaurants that offer consistently good food and service, this Jolly Roger is always busy, and with good reason. There's everything you ever wanted for breakfast, including the Mac-Waple, a golden-brown waffle smothered with spicy cinnamon apples and macadamia nuts, for about $3.95. Lunch features salads, sandwiches, burgers, and specialties like a stuffed quesadilla, fettuccine Alfredo, grilled mahimahi, or a Monte Cristo sandwich, for $6.25–$8.45. And for dinner, choose from the complete meals, such as smothered chicken, mahimahi, a delightful seafood combination platter, or chicken Polynesian with a fragrant sweet-and-sour sauce, all accompanied by soup or salad, hot vegetables, and a starch. Check the local tourist papers for discount coupons; you might be able to get the likes of two steak teriyaki dinners for $14.95. A prolonged happy hour goes from 11am to 7pm, and there's entertainment every night with cocktails served until 2am.

READERS RECOMMEND

Al & Don's Oceanfront Restaurant, *in the Kauai Sands Hotel (tel. 822-4221). "Your best dinner bargain near Coconut Plantation is Al & Don's Oceanfront Restaurant. The menu features a surprisingly extensive variety of dishes for a budget hotel, including fresh island fish, steak, ham steak Hawaiian, hibachi chicken, and cheese lasagne, for $7.50–$11.75, and the price includes soup or tossed salad, bread, french fries, whipped potatoes or rice, and dessert."*—Connie Tonken, Hartford, Conn.

THE NORTH SHORE: PRINCEVILLE-HANALEI

MEALS FOR LESS THAN $20

CHUCK'S STEAK HOUSE, at Princeville Center. Tel. 826-6211.

Cuisine: STEAK/SALAD. **Reservations:** Recommended for dinner and for parties of six or more at lunch.

$ Prices: Appetizers $3.35–$3.60; main courses $13.50–$26.95 ($36.95 for lobster). AE, CB, DC, MC, V.

Open: Lunch Mon–Fri 11:30am–2:30pm; dinner daily 6–10pm.

This is rightfully one of the most popular places at Princeville Center. An attractive porch, plants, ceiling fans, dark walls, secluded booths, paintings, and antiques everywhere set a cozy scene. Lunch is fun here, with daily specials for $5.60–$8.25, and an appealing salad bar ($6.25). Dinner features steaks and prime rib, seafood, and fresh-fish specials. All meals include salad bar, hot bread and butter, and steamed rice pilaf; the salad bar is available on its own for $8.50. For dessert, hesitate not: The mud pie is wonderful. Chuck's is also known for great tropical drinks and fine wines; cocktails are served Monday through Friday from 11:30am to 11pm and on Saturday and Sunday from 5 to 11pm.

HANALEI GOURMET, Old Hanalei School, Hanalei Center, 5-5161 Kuhio Hwy. Tel. 826-2524.

Cuisine: AMERICAN/DELI. **Reservations:** Not accepted.

$ Prices: Sandwiches and salads $3.95–$9.25; dinner specials $10–$15.95. MC, V.

Open: Mon–Thurs 8am–10:30pm, Fri–Sat 8am–midnight, Sun 8am–8pm.

Ever since it opened in the superbly restored Old Hanalei School, Hanalei Gourmet has been deservedly one of the most popular spots in Hanalei, with both locals and tourists. Half the operation is a bakery, cheese shop, and take-out deli, with a splendid wine cellar (almost 100 bottles). This is the place to get your picnic fixings if you're hiking the Na Pali coast or kayaking up a river. The other half of the operation is a cheery sit-down café that serves tropical drinks, breakfast, lunch, and dinner with a gourmet touch. Breakfast features their own muesli cereal, a croissant sandwich, bagel with lox and cream cheese, and a tangy huevos Santa Cruz, for $2.75 to $5.25. Lunch and dinner offer generous Italian sandwiches (the Oregon bay shrimp open-face, on Russian black bread, with bay shrimp and melted Jack cheese, is one of the best, at $7.25); imaginative salads and antipasti; varied pupu plates of meats, cheeses, and smoked fish; and bountiful "Shrimp Boils"—that's unpeeled shrimp boiled in seasoned broth and served with melted garlic butter, from $8.75. Dinner specials on the chalkboard might include ahi fettuccine Alfredo or spinach lasagne. Desserts, fresh from the bakery, are on the delicious and decadent side. There's live entertainment in the evenings, Tuesday through Saturday, when local performers join ranks, on occasion, with jazz stars from Honolulu and the mainland. A lively spot.

HANALEI SHELL HOUSE, 5-5156 Kuhio Hwy. Tel. 826-7977.

Cuisine: AMERICAN. **Reservations:** Recommended at dinner.

$ Prices: Appetizers $2.95–$7.95; main courses $7.95–$19.95. AE, MC, V.

Open: Daily 8am–10:30pm.

This small restaurant on the main street in Hanalei has long been popular with the locals. It's been in the same family for years, and now the younger generation—Steve and Linda—has taken over and spruced it up so that it looks quite good, with wooden tables, ceiling fans, and plenty of greens. They serve breakfast from 8 to 11am, with several specials, including Mexican quesadillas. Lunch features half-pound burgers ($4.75–$5.75), omelets, and quesadillas. The dinner menu always includes fresh, locally caught fish, sautéed or broiled, market-priced; blackened fish Cajun style was $17.95. Exotic tropical cocktails are available all day, seven days a week, from 8am to 11pm, and the bar up front is always lively. Dinner is served later here than at any other place in the area (until 11pm).

ZELO'S CAFE, at Princeville Center. Tel. 826-9700.

Cuisine: AMERICAN. **Reservations:** Not accepted.

$ Prices: Appetizers $3.25–$5.25; main courses $5.25–$16.95. MC, V.

Open: Mon–Thurs 8am–10pm, Fri–Sat 8am–midnight, Sun 9am–4pm.

Where can you find a goodly percentage of the employees of the Princeville Center come lunch or snack time? One of two places: either in Zelo's Café, a pretty tile-and-woody spot with a counter and tables out on a small lanai—or in their offices enjoying Zelo's take-out goodies. We're not surprised: Zelo's Café serves tasty food at modest prices. At both lunch and dinner, for example, you can have dishes like a super spinach lasagne at $8.50 or a Cajun chicken salad with pan-blackened boneless breast of chicken over crisp salad greens for $8.95, or a tempeh salad sandwich for the vegetarians in the crowd for $6.50. More salads, plus burgers, are served up at both meals, and delicious pastas and fresh fish, market-priced, at dinner.

Ching Young Village Shopping Center

There are several budget eateries at this shopping center. **Foong Wong** is a large, simple restaurant, rather sparsely decorated, but with good, if somewhat bland, Cantonese food. Plate lunches run about $4.65–$6.15, and such dishes as Szechuan beef, curry chicken, and eggplant with garlic sauce are all under $8. The **Village Snack and Bakery Shop** has plate lunches, such as fried chicken and teriyaki beef, for $5.95, and is also a popular spot for breakfast, which runs $2.75–$5.50. The best treats here are the home-baked pies: guava, lilikoi, chiffon, lemon-cream cheese, at $1.50 a slice. Box lunches are $5.75, with a salad and drink.

Or you can get your pizzas on a homemade whole-wheat crust with sesame seeds at **Pizza Hanalei,** which really works at making a good pie; they use fresh vegetable toppings and herbs picked from their own garden. It's $1.90 for a slice, $6.90 for a small pie, or try their unusual pizzaritto: That's cheese, vegetables, meats, and spices rolled up into a pizza shell and eaten like a burrito, $3.95.

Also at Hanalei, on Saturday and Sunday from 11am to 4pm, you'll find Roger Kennedy and his ✪ **Tropical Taco,** a green truck next to the Hanalei River at the parking lot of the Dolphin Restaurant, where he dishes up gourmet-quality, all-organic burritos, tacos, and the like, all including beans, meat, lettuce, salsa, cheese, and sour cream (vegetarian combos, too), a complete lunch for around $3–$5. The menu is on a surfboard hooked to the front of the "Taco Wagon." Take your food over to the shady riverbank just a few steps away and enjoy your picnic Mexicana.

THE SOUTHERN & WESTERN ROUTE

You should have no problem dining on your trip around the southern and western end of the island, for there are several excellent choices. Not all, however, are in the budget category.

OLD KOLOA TOWN

Meals for Less Than $15

KOLOA BROILER, Koloa Rd. Tel. 742-9122.

Cuisine: AMERICAN. **Reservations:** Not required.

$ Prices: Appetizers $3.25–$3.75; main courses $6.75–$10.95. AE, DC, MC, V.

Open: Daily 11am–10pm.

✪ If you don't like the way your food is done at this restaurant in the heart of Old Koloa Town, a few miles from Poipu Beach, you have no one but yourself to blame. This cute little place is one of those broil-it-yourself affairs—and that way, they really manage to keep the prices down. You can choose from top sirloin, marinated beef kebab, mahimahi, barbecued chicken, and beef burger; fresh fish is sometimes available at market price. The price of all main courses includes salad bar, baked beans, rice, and sourdough bread. Lunch offers the same choices, but the burger is $4.75. The only dessert on the menu is macadamia-nut ice cream, so you may want to walk over to the Koloa Ice House (see below) for mud pie. The Koloa Broiler is a lively, fun kind of place, simply decorated (try to get a seat out on the lanai), with a bar, a list of exotic drinks, and lots of local people enjoying their meals.

KOLOA ICE HOUSE AND DELI, 5482 Koloa Rd. Tel. 742-6063.

Cuisine: DELI/VEGETARIAN. **Reservations:** Not accepted.

$ Prices: Main courses $4–$5. No credit cards.

Open: Daily 9:30am–9:30pm.

Two blocks from the Koloa Broiler and across the street from the U.S. Post Office, this green wooden historic building has just a few tables and booths inside, but it's also fun to sit at any of the eight tables in the garden lanai. You can get a good variety of deli and veggie sandwiches here, as well as mahimahi sandwiches, quiches, nachos, bagels and cream cheese, burritos, homemade soup, and veggie burgers. On our last visit, we tried the mahimahi burger and the tofu veggie burger on an onion roll, each $4.35 and real fillers, stuffed with heaps of lettuce, sprouts, tomatoes, and onions, with a pickle on the side. They're famous for their Volcano Mud Pie—a cookie-crust ice-cream pie at $4—and a number of other sweet treats. They also have real old-fashioned shave ice—made in one of the last original machines in Hawaii. Everything here is available for take-out.

PANCHO & LEFTY'S CANTINA & RESTAURANTE, Koloa Rd., Old Koloa Town. Tel. 742-7377.

Cuisine: MEXICAN. **Reservations:** Not required.

$ Prices: Appetizers $4.95–$6.95; main courses $5.25–$14.95. AE, MC, V.

Open: Breakfast daily 7am–noon; lunch/dinner daily 11am–10pm.

Everything about Pancho & Lefty's bespeaks sunny Mexico: parrots in the windows, a fountain of greenery, baskets, wooden tables, sombreros on the walls—even the salt-and-pepper shakers are in the shape of red peppers! The restaurant, which got started in Maui a few years ago, has been so successful that it's opened branches here and on the Big Island, and the food is the same—spicy, delicious, inexpensive. You can start the day with a Mexican breakfast—Lefty's Mexican omelet with chorizo and jalapeño, or huevos rancheros or a breakfast burrito, $6.95–$7.95, as well as the more usual American offerings. The menu is the same at lunch and dinner: You can't go wrong with the huge seafood salad in a taco shell ($9.95), the steak or chicken fajitas to which you add your own amounts of guacamole, salsa, and sour cream ($11.95–$12.95), or with specialty items like the enchiladas rancheros or pechuga pollo relleno (chicken breast stuffed with Jack cheese and chiles, batter-fried and topped with enchilada sauce). Begin your meal with a tropical drink from the lively bar, end with an ice-cream pie for dessert, and top it all off with a Café Siesta—maybe a Mexican coffee (tequila and Kahlúa) or a non-Mexican, but altogether satisfying, Irish coffee.

TAQUERIA NORTENOS, 2827-A Poipu Rd., Koloa. Tel. 742-7222.

Cuisine: MEXICAN. **Reservations:** Not required.

$ Prices: Appetizers $1.35–$2.35; main courses $1.90–$5.05. No credit cards.

Open: Thurs–Tues 11am–11pm, Wed 11am–5:30pm.

Next to the Kukuila Store in Koloa is a tiny taco bar that packs a mighty wallop. Owner Ed Sills, former chef at the prestigious Plantation Garden Restaurant, and his wife, Morgan, have been running their own place for several years now, turning out excellent food and keeping the prices low. You should be able to get a good meal here for under $6. They often do regional specialties, such as posole (pork-and-hominy stew) and enchiladas of various sorts. When you want some good Mexican munchies, pop in for tacos ($2–$2.40), burritos ($2.65–$3.40), tostadas ($2.65–$3.40), or nachos ($2.35). Pick up your food at the counter and eat in the tiny dining room or take it out. Call them in advance and they'll pack you a nice picnic for the beach.

POIPU

Meals for Less Than $15

BRENNECKE'S BEACH BROILER, 2100 Hoone Rd., Poipu. Tel. 742-7588.

Cuisine: AMERICAN. **Reservations:** Recommended.

$ Prices: Appetizers $3.95–$12.95; main courses $6.50–$21.95. AE, DC, MC, V.

Open: Lunch daily noon–4pm; dinner daily 4–10:30pm.

Located on the second (and top) floor of the building across from Poipu Beach Park, the Beach Broiler likes to proclaim that it's "Right on the beach . . . right on the price." All true. Decorated with window boxes blooming with bright flowers and the names of island fish spelled out in big white letters on the wall above the kitchen, this is a most attractive place. A variety of original tropical drinks—with or without liquor—might get the meal off to a good start.

The menu offers plenty of possibilities, so choose anything from a sandwich, salad, or pupus at lunch, to the same plus main courses at dinner. The Beach burger, fresh fish, and French dip-au-jus sandwiches served with nachos are excellent, $6.95–$8.95. On the low side of the dinner menu, summer chicken, skewered with vegetables, is $13.95; durum-wheat pasta, cooked al dente with butter and vegetables in the lightest of cream sauces, is $11.95; the same pasta with fresh clams is $14.95. And fresh island fish, kiawe-broiled and served with pasta primavera, is $9.95. All main courses include a choice of delicious clam chowder or a light salad, garlic bread, and pasta primavera. Several keiki dinners go for $3.95–$8.95.

During the Sunshine Happy Hour, 2 to 4pm, most drinks are reduced in price, and mai tais are $3; late lunches and appetizers are also available. Browse in their minideli for some island foods that you might want to bring back to your apartment, plus beach and gift items.

CANTINA FLAMINGO, 2301 Nalo Rd. Tel. 742-9505.

Cuisine: MEXICAN. **Reservations:** Not accepted.
$ Prices: Appetizers $4.95–$6.95; main courses $8.25–$14.50. No credit cards.
Open: Daily 3:30–9:30pm.

The flamingos are made of neon, but the food is authentic Mexican and absolutely terrific—and there's nothing on the menu for more than $14.50. No wonder this place is always packed! But don't despair; a short wait (they don't accept reservations) gives you a seat at a bountiful Mexican table. There's an airy feeling to this attractive restaurant, with its open-beamed ceiling, plants, sombreros, a wall of brick, even two large aquariums in which Black African Belly piranhas survey the scene. Of course, you'll want to start your meal with margaritas—they come in nine different fresh-fruit flavors—but the plain is just fine with us. Proceed to such appetizers as the cheesy quesadillas or the sopa de albóndigas, a tomato-vegetable-based broth with spicy baked meatballs. You can't go wrong with any of the main dishes: We can personally tell you that the seafood fajitas (a cantina specialty), the arroz con pollo, and the flautas Kauai (stuffed with chicken, shrimp, broccoli, and cheese, then puffed fried) were all super. Deep-fried ice cream is nifty, too, especially since it's made with Lappert's macadamia-nut ice cream. A meal at Cantina Flamingo is an experience you'll want to repeat—as soon as possible. Nachos are free during Mexican Munchie Time, from 3:30 to 5pm. To reach the restaurant, take your first left past Brennecke's Beach.

KEOKI'S PARADISE, 2360 Kiahuna Plantation Dr., Poipu. Tel. 742-7534.

Cuisine: SEAFOOD/STEAK/MEXICAN. **Reservations:** Recommended.
$ Prices: Appetizers $2.95–$8.95; main courses $4.50–$29.95. AE, MC, V.
Open: Dinner daily 5:30–10pm; lounge menu daily 4:30pm–midnight.

We think you'll agree that this restaurant, at the entrance to the Kiahuna Shopping Village, is aptly named. Open and airy, it overlooks a gemlike lagoon. Soda-fountain chairs at the bar are painted cheerful reds; the bar, with its own roof, looks like a little Polynesian *palapa*. All dinners are accompanied by tossed green salad with house dressing, a basket of freshly baked muffins and French rolls, and steamed herb rice. There are plenty of selections in the $9.95–$13.95 range, like filet of mahimahi, top sirloin, New York–steak sandwiches, Polynesian chicken, Koloa pork ribs, and low-cholesterol "spa cuisine" ginger chicken. Seafood selections and prime rib are higher. It's fun to start with the Fisherman's Chowder (*ono!*) at $2.95, and sample the side dish of onions and mushrooms, at $3.95. In a Mexican mood? A variety of appetizers and main courses, from guacamole to steak fajitas cost $4.95–$9.95 in the lounge. Keoki's Paradise claims that its Hula Pie is "what the sailors swam to shore for." The idyllic setting and the friendly ambience here are sure to make you want to linger . . . and linger. The restaurant is run by the same talented management that runs Duke's Canoe Club and Sharkey's in Kauai, and, on Maui, Kimo's, Leilani's, Kapalua Bar and Grill, and Chico's.

PARADISE HOT DOGS, in Kiahuna Shopping Village, Poipu Rd. Tel. 742-7667.

Cuisine: SNACKS.

$ Prices: Main dishes, $2.95–$5.50. No credit cards.

Open: Mon–Sat 10am–9pm, Sun 11am–6pm.

The lowly hot dog is elevated to special status at the Kiahuna Shopping Village. Thanks to chef Tyler Barnes, visitors to this little counter-with-tables place can now get the only old-fashioned German franks on Kauai. Barnes, who gets the veal-and-pork franks (low in fats, nitrates, and salt) from a German sausage factory on the West Coast, steams them in a beer-and-water mixture in the traditional way. He calls this one "The Plain Paradise" ($2.95). But he also does more elaborate things, like topping his foot-long dogs with pineapple and teriyaki sauce, or with Swiss-cheese fondue in white wine, or with mango chutney and grated coconut. For nonmeat-eaters, there's char-broiled mahimahi filet dog (The Sea Dog), and char-broiled eggplant with miso sauce (The Rising Sun). Take your dog, fries, homemade chili, and whatever, sit down at one of the two or three outdoor tables out front or in the little garden area off to the side, and rest your feet before you continue your shopping. Call for take-out orders.

PIZZA BELLA, in Kiahuna Shopping Village, Poipu Rd. Tel. 742-9571.

Cuisine: ITALIAN. **Reservations:** Not required.

$ Prices: Appetizers $2.95–$3.95; main courses $6.25–$10.75. MC, V.

Open: Daily 11:30am–10pm.

This is much more than your average "pizza parlor." It has an attractive layout—black-and-white tile floors, white wicker chairs, greenery, ceiling fans, even a few outside tables. Here you can dine on 10-inch, California-style gourmet pizzas—topped with homemade sauce and four cheeses; or with barbecued chicken and cilantro; or perhaps with a melange of seafood for $8.95–$10.75. Less modern tastes might go for the old-fashioned pies, the hot and cold sandwiches, and several pastas, including a veggie lasagne. There's wine, beer, and a nice atmosphere. Keep Pizza Bella in mind for lunch or a light dinner if you're staying in the Poipu area; they also deliver.

Worth the Extra Bucks

BEACH HOUSE RESTAURANT, 5022 Lawai Beach Rd. (Spouting Horn Rd.). Tel. 742-7575.

Cuisine: SEAFOOD/STEAK. **Reservations:** Recommended.

$ Prices: Appetizers $4.50–$8.50; main courses $16.75–$29.50. AE, MC, V.

Open: Dinner only, daily 5:30–10:30pm (bar open from 4:30pm).

Nestled right on the sand, this is an idyllic spot, perhaps the best around for viewing the sunset, the surfers, maybe an occasional whale or two in winter, or just waves crashing on the beach beneath the stars. Decorated in elegant, understated, modern lines and adorned with many flowers, the restaurant has 22 fabulous window tables; these are on a first-come, first-served basis, with a reservation. Wherever you sit, though, you'll enjoy gracious service and excellent food. Fresh fish and seafood are the specialties of the house, and when they say "fresh" they really mean it: The restaurant is often the first stop for local fishermen docking at Kukuliulu Harbor. Broiled ahi and sautéed opakapaka are excellent, king crab legs is a house specialty, and there are many combinations of fish, seafood, and steak. Dinners are accompanied by salad, rice or fries, and home-baked muffins. Start your meal with exotic pupus and end with any of the blended ice-cream and liqueur drinks. There's a good list of French and California wines, and several pleasing house wines sold by the glass. In short, this is a place to relax, celebrate, and throw cares and calories to the winds.

HANAPEPE

GREEN GARDEN, Hwy. 50. Tel. 335-5422.

Cuisine: AMERICAN. **Reservations:** Recommended for dinner.

$ Prices: Main courses $6–$20. AE, MC, V.

Open: Breakfast/lunch daily 7am–2pm; dinner Wed–Mon 5–9pm.

The Green Garden is a Kauai tradition, a more than 40-year-old restaurant run by Sumika Hamabata and her family. You'll feel as if you're sitting in the middle of a greenhouse, with orchids on the tables, plants everywhere, an entire screened wall facing a garden, bamboo chairs, and white walls.

For a real treat, do as the locals do: Call them at least half an hour in advance and order a family-style meal, with a variety of Chinese and local dishes. Or you can make a lunch on one of their sandwich specials, like the fresh fish on toast for about $5 and under. Lunch selections, for $5.50–$6, include sweet-and-sour spareribs, a seafood special, and Korean-style boneless barbecued chicken. Dinner is a complete meal, featuring similar main courses, all accompanied by homemade soup or fruit cup, tossed salad, a starch, vegetables and rolls, and beverage. Fresh fish of the day is a mere $11, and kiawe broiler specials, such as filet mignon at $13, are also well priced.

Be sure to save room for Sue's homemade pies—macadamia nut, lilikoi, chocolate cream—absolute marvels, and only $1.50. Note that if a tour bus happens to disgorge its hungry passengers here, things can get a bit hectic. Better to come on the late side of the lunch hour.

KALAHEO

BRICK OVEN PIZZA, 2-2555 Kaumualii Hwy. Tel. 332-8561.

Cuisine: PIZZA/SANDWICHES. **Reservations:** Not accepted.

$ Prices: Appetizers 60¢–$5.95; main courses $2.35–$10.95. MC, V.

Open: Tues–Sun 11am–10:30pm.

On the main road in Kalaheo is this family-run, family-style restaurant that's been making delicious "pizza with the homemade touch" for many years now. It's a cozy restaurant with red-and-white gingham tablecloths in true pizzeria fashion. Children are treated especially nicely here. Hearth-baked pies with delicious crust, either whole wheat or white brushed with garlic butter, start at $7.35 for a 10-inch plain cheese pie, and go all the way up to $22.85 for a 15-inch pizza with almost everything. In addition to pizza, there are hot sandwiches, including a vegetarian one, and a yummy seafood-style pizza bread. Green salads are available, and so are wine and beer. Call ahead for pizza to go.

WAIMEA

INTERNATIONAL MUSEUM CAFE, at the town square in Waimea. Tel. 338-0403.

Cuisine: VEGETARIAN/ECLECTIC. **Reservations:** Not accepted.

$ Prices: Appetizers $2–$3.50; main courses $6.95–$9.95.

Open: Daily 11am–5pm; Sun 10am–8pm.

Eclectic is the word for this place—part museum, part café, and quite unlike any other restaurant anywhere. Rebecca and Jerry Beisler, the owners of this wonderland, have collected decorative arts from "A to Z—Afghanistan to

Zaire." There are ceremonial kimonos, Chinese jades, a magnificent headdress encrusted with turquoises, a lama's hat, an authentic shaman's garb, and pottery everywhere. Behind the bar is a delightful collection of vintage Ritz Cracker and Coca-Cola and Animal Cracker memorabilia. In such a setting, Rebecca produces food that's a delight for those eating light and healthy. She obtains all the produce from the local farmer's market, and, depending on what's fresh, offers homemade soups, salads, sandwiches, and many imaginative vegetarian dishes. There is fresh fish and a chicken dish every day too. For breakfast there are omelettes, soufflés, sometimes huevos rancheros. Sunday is the day Rebecca "cooks up a country"; she chooses a country and prepares soup, entrée, salad, and dessert accordingly; you partake of whatever you want. The price is anywhere from $5.95 to $18.95. Always on hand are old-fashioned fountain desserts and daily dessert specials, an intriguing list of tropical drinks, and wines from California, Europe, and Maui. (Incidentally, this is the only bar in Waimea where you can buy a drink without ordering food.) Since the café is so close to Waimea Canyon, it's an ideal place to pick up a picnic basket, which Rebecca creates to order. Just tell her what you want, and it will be ready and waiting—and terrific. Picking it up is half the fun.

WRANGLER'S, 9582 Kaumualii Hwy. Tel. 338-1218.

Cuisine: MEXICAN/AMERICAN. **Reservations:** Not necessary.

$ Prices: Appetizers $1.50–$6.75; main courses $7.95–$17.95.

Open: Mon–Thurs 11am–9pm, Fri–Sat 11am–10pm.

There aren't too many places to eat in Waimea, so it's good to know about this one for a meal when you're coming down from Waimea Canyon. Located in a restored historical plantation building on the main street, Wrangler's is decorated with a blend of the old and the new: ceiling fans, a blaring stereo, and memorabilia of Waimea's plantation days—an old carousel horse, an old saddle and tack, a two-person buggy. Eat indoors at black booths with white tablecloths, or outdoors on the porch at wooden tables with big rattan chairs. The menu is a mix—there are lots of Mexican dishes (faux crab taco or burrito, shrimp Mexicano, etc., served with soup or salad); broiler items like chicken teriyaki, kal bi ribs, and sizzling steak; a variety of seafood dishes, including catch of the day; plus sandwiches, salads, and burgers. Good value here and an unusual atmosphere.

KOKEE

KOKEE LODGE, in Kokee State Park. Tel. 335-6061.

Cuisine: INTERNATIONAL. **Reservations:** Recommended.

$ Prices: Main courses $13.95–$16.95. DC, DISC, MC, V.

Open: Breakfast daily 8:30–11:30am; lunch daily 11:30am–3:30pm; dinner Fri–Sat 6–9pm.

If you're going to Waimea Canyon—and, of course, you should—it's nice to know that you can tie your visit in with a meal at Kokee Lodge in Kokee State Park. The kitchen is presided over by Sherrie Orr, who adds her unique natural-food specialties to the menu. The rustic dining room affords views of both mountain and meadow and is quite pleasant. At lunch you can get a variety of salads, sandwiches (some of the selections guava-smoked on the premises, $2.95–$9.95), Portuguese bean soup (the local soul food), or a modestly priced daily special. After you've watched the sun go down over the canyon, it's fun to relax here with a drink and dine on the likes of boneless Cornish game hen, kal bi ribs, teriyaki steak, filet of Pacific ono, or vegetarian fettuccine. Any time of the day, try their delicious homemade hot cornbread, served with Kauai honey, at $2.75. Desserts—like lilikoi chiffon, chocolate temptation, and Alakai Swamp pie—are always delicious. They serve Lappert's coffee (the best), a variety of teas, and cocktails, beer, and wine, as well.

CHAPTER 11

WHAT TO SEE & DO ON KAUAI

There are plenty of opportunities on Kauai for hiking, fishing, camping, golf, water sports, and such for those who have the time to stay and enjoy them. Check with the **Hawaii Visitors Bureau,** 3016 Umi St., Suite 207, on the second floor of Lihue Plaza (tel. 808/245-3971), or write to them at P.O. Box 507, Lihue, HI 96766. Information on hiking, camping, fishing, and hunting is available at the Department of Land & Natural Resources, in the state building in Lihue, 3060 Eiwa St. (tel. 808/245-4444). For State Forest Reserve trail information, write to the District Forester, Division of Forestry and Wildlife, P.O. Box 1671, Lihue, HI 96766; for state park information, write to the Park Superintendent, Division of State Parks, P.O. Box 1671, Lihue, HI 96766.

SUGGESTED ITINERARIES

Count on at least three days to see Kauai. After Lihue, the first two should be devoted to separate all-day trips, which between them circle the island; to skip either would be unthinkable.

IF YOU HAVE ONE DAY We recommend a trip to the eastern and northern parts of the island, all the way to Hanalei, Hanea, and the Na Pali cliffs. Begin this trip seeing the sights of Lihue.

IF YOU HAVE TWO DAYS Spend the first day as above. The second day we would go to the southern and western parts of the island, whose high points are Poipu Beach, Waimea Canyon, and the magnificent end-of-the-road climax, Kalalau Lookout.

IF YOU HAVE THREE DAYS After seeing the main sights, spend the third day on side excursions, swimming, and going back to all the idyllic little spots you discovered on the first two trips.

IF YOU HAVE FIVE DAYS OR MORE If you're lucky enough to have this much time in Kauai, break up your round-the-island trips, spending more time at each attraction, giving yourself half a day for swimming, golf, hiking, kayaking. Be sure to see the wonders of the Westin Kauai at Kauai Lagoons, take time for a river trip to the Fern Grotto, browse through the Kauai Museum, hike the Na Pali Coast, tour the National Tropical Botanical Garden, or watch whales on a Pacific Safari cruise.

1. ADVENTURE TOURS

On **Kauai Mountain Tours,** P.O. Box 3069, Lihue, Kauai, HI 96766 (tel. 808/245-7224), a knowledgeable guide will take you on a one-of-a-kind trip into the Na Pali Kona Forest Reserve in an air-conditioned four-wheel-drive vehicle that traverses the winding mountain roads around the back of Waimea Canyon. It's around $80 for a seven-hour tour, with lunch and a light continental breakfast included; a half-day tour (no meals) is $40.

Crane Tours, c/o Bill Crane, 15101 Magnolia Blvd., H10, Sherman Oaks, CA 91403 (tel. 818/724-2213, or Ron Jones at 714/773-5570), offers both kayaking trips and moderately strenuous trips for experienced backpackers to the Na Pali Coast and Waimea Canyon. The cost is approximately $775–$850. This company is known for excellent values, terrific meals, and thoughtful service. They also offer a variety of excursions to the Big Island.

Rick Haviland and his excellent crew at **Outfitters Kauai,** Poipu Plaza, 2827-A Poipu Rd. (P.O. Box 1149), Poipu Beach, Koloa, HI 96756 (tel. 808/742-9667), are known for a variety of enjoyable and well-run trips, via kayak or bicycle. In addition to simple half-day kayaking trips for beginners ($48) and one-day sea-kayaking adventures along Kauai's southeast coast in the shadow of 2,000-foot cliffs ($105 for a full-day excursion), this outfit also offers an escorted Kayak Experience along the Na Pali cliffs, either as a one-day trip from Haena to Polihale, or a two-day (or more) expedition featuring camping at Kalakau and Milolii—some of the most breathtakingly beautiful spots in the islands. Two-person kayaks may also be rented for self-guided tours to jungle rivers. Each boat comes with racks/straps to secure it to your car, maps, and information to help you select the ideal river. Cost is $35 or $65 for one- or two-person kayaks.

Outfitters Kauai also offers adventure for the cyclist. For personal tours, they rent mountain bikes of high quality, which are well maintained and well suited for off-road riding through Kauai's backcountry. They provide helmets, water bottles, spare tubes with pumps, and extensive trail information based on years of riding and exploring on Kauai. Car racks are available to carry bikes to other locations. Bikes rent for $28 a day, $84 for four days, $140 for a week.

New and very exciting are Outfitters Kauai's Kokee Mountain Bike Tours. Participants ride the cool high forest backroads above Waimea Canyon in an ecosystem that supports plants, trees, and birds, many of which are found only here. A skilled guide discusses the legends and natural history of Kokee. The cost is $58. Outfitters Kauai are the only licensed operators of a guided mountain-bike tour in the state parks of Hawaii.

Kayak Kauai–Na Pali Outfitters, 1340 Kuhio Hwy. (tel. 808/822-9179), or on the main street in Hanalei (P.O. Box 508), Hanalei, HI 96714 (tel. 808/926-9844), offers summer (May to September) sea-kayak journeys for thrillseekers along 14 miles of Kauai's dramatic Na Pali coastline that involve some of the most challenging wilderness paddling to be found in Hawaii. Five-day packages cost $782 per person. The same company offers guided one-day kayak trips around the Na Pali cliffs, including lunch on an isolated beach ($115), and a three-hour Hanalei Wildlife

IMPRESSIONS

Kauai—Nowhere in the entire national park system is there scenic beauty like this.

—STEWART UDALL, 1963

Refuge and Bay Snorkel Tour and/or Kapaa Reef Paddle & Snorkel Tour ($45). During the winter months there are sea-kayak trips to Kipu Kai, "the Little Na Pali," on Kauai's south shore: paddling, snorkeling, and whale-watching ($90). Hiking and camping trips are also available. Guided one-day hikes cost $75; several-day camping expeditions, $150 per day. They'll guide or tell you how to get to barrier reefs, wildlife refuges, canyon trails, rain forests, and waterfalls.

2. LIHUE

Once a sleepy plantation village, Lihue is beginning to look startingly modern, with shopping centers, supermarkets, megaresorts, and the like.

ATTRACTIONS

THE WESTIN KAUAI, Kalapaki Beach, Lihue, Kauai, HI 96766, at Kauai Lagoons. Tel. 245-5050.

Seldom does a resort become a sightseeing attraction in itself, but the $380-million Westin Kauai breaks just about every preconception of what a resort is. Everybody on Kauai has an opinion about it: Some think it's too grandiose for a small Hawaiian island and would look better in, say, Las Vegas; others think it's just what the jet set ordered. Certainly you should see it, and plan several hours or even a day to take in its many wonders, natural and artificial.

The megaresort to end all megaresorts, the Westin Kauai is built on an 800-acre spread of land at Kalapaki Beach called Kauai Lagoons, a network of artificial lagoons and inland waterways that connects the hotel buildings to such features as 15 restaurants, two golf courses designed by Jack Nicklaus, seven tennis courts and a stadium, a European health spa, and six islands, which serve as habitats for exotic wildlife.

Best of all, you needn't stay here to play here. You can come to dine, to shop, to see the massive reproductions of Asian art treasures, to stroll around the 21-acre reflecting pool with its white-marble statuary reminiscent of Versailles, or to have a drink by the side of the largest swimming pool in Hawaii with its own fountains and waterfalls. Or work out or be pampered at the spa (call 246-5062 for information and appointments before you come and to find out which facilities are open to nonhotel guests). For more details on the spa, see "Educational/Alternative Travel" in Chapter 2.

Here's how you go about your visit. Park your car and make your way to the visitor center. Then you can explore on your own, or hop either a 35-passenger Venetian mahogany launch ($14 for adults, $4 for children) or a canopied outrigger canoe ($18 for adults, $7 for children) to visit the wildlife islands and see all of the resort as well. You'll even pass by the on-the-water wedding chapel, which surely must be the world's most romantic setting in which to tie the knot: The bride arrives in a horse-drawn white carriage, the groom in a black limousine. Rides in carriages pulled by magnificent Clydesdales, Belgians, and Percherons are also available ($15 for adults, $7 for children) to explore the grounds.

If you're feeling hungry, or thirsty, you've come to the right place: There are restaurants and lounges galore, offering everything from ultimate luxury to casual elegance. Best bets for budget watchers are **Cook's at the Beach,** the **Terrace,** and **Duke's Canoe Club** (see "Where to Eat" in Chapter 10). But if you're feeling very splurgy indeed, then you have some delightful options. For lovers of Japanese food, **Tempura Gardens** is an experience: Kyoto-style cuisine is served in a setting

KAUAI SIGHTS & ATTRACTIONS

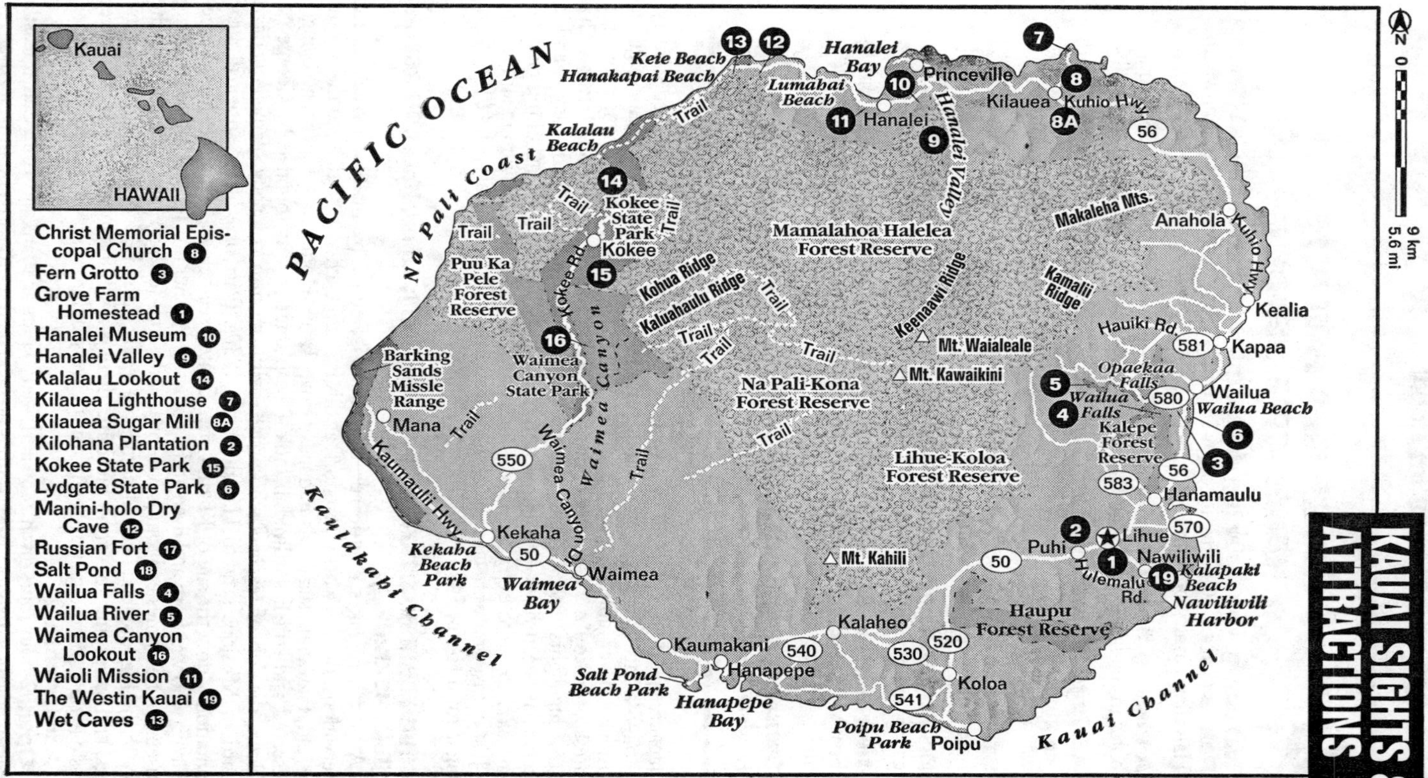

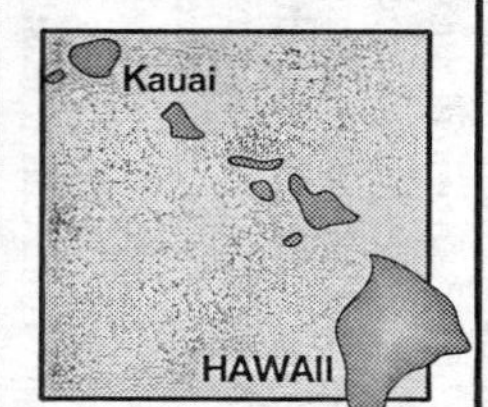

- Christ Memorial Episcopal Church 8
- Fern Grotto 3
- Grove Farm Homestead 1
- Hanalei Museum 10
- Hanalei Valley 9
- Kalalau Lookout 14
- Kilauea Lighthouse 7
- Kilauea Sugar Mill 8A
- Kilohana Plantation 2
- Kokee State Park 15
- Lydgate State Park 6
- Manini-holo Dry Cave 12
- Russian Fort 17
- Salt Pond 18
- Wailua Falls 4
- Wailua River 5
- Waimea Canyon Lookout 16
- Waioli Mission 11
- The Westin Kauai 19
- Wet Caves 13

N 0 9 km 5.6 mi

PACIFIC OCEAN
Na Pali Coast
Kaulakahi Channel
Kauai Channel
Kele Beach
Hanakapai Beach
Hanalei Bay
Princeville
Lumahai Beach
Hanalei
Hanalei Valley
Kilauea
Kuhio Hwy.
56
Kalalau Beach
Trail
Kokee State Park
Kokee
Kokee Rd.
Puu Ka Pele Forest Reserve
Mamalahoa Halelea Forest Reserve
Makaleha Mts.
Anahola
Kohua Ridge
Kaluahaulu Ridge
Keenaawi Ridge
Kamalii Ridge
Kealia
Hauiki Rd.
581
Kapaa
Mt. Waialeale
Mt. Kawaikini
Barking Sands Missle Range
Waimea Canyon State Park
Waimea Canyon
Na Pali-Kona Forest Reserve
Opaekaa Falls
Wailua
580
Wailua Beach
Wailua Falls
Kalepe Forest Reserve
Mana
550
Waimea Canyon Dr.
Lihue-Koloa Forest Reserve
583
Hanamaulu
Kaumaulii Hwy.
Kekaha
50
Waimea
Kekaha Beach Park
Waimea Bay
Mt. Kahili
Puhi
Lihue
570
Nawiliwili
Hulemalu Rd.
Kalapaki Beach
Nawiliwili Harbor
Haupu Forest Reserve
Kalaheo
520
540
530
Kaumakani
Hanapepe
Koloa
Salt Pond Beach Park
Hanapepe Bay
541
Poipu Beach Park
Poipu

FROMMER'S FAVORITE KAUAI EXPERIENCES

Watching the evening torchlighting ceremony at Coco Palms Hotel On the site of an ancient coconut grove and lagoon, where Hawaiian royalty once lived.

A visit to Spouting Horn Park See the geysers shoot up through holes in the lava rock as the sea pounds relentlessly against the black rocks.

A trip to Waimea Canyon Visit the "Grand Canyon of the Pacific" to see one of the most spectacular views in all Hawaii, with a stop for lunch on the way down at Kokee Lodge, in the bracing mountain air.

Swimming and snorkeling at Poipu Beach One of the island's best—great for family fun.

Driving the northern route, Hi. 56 Travel all the way to Hanalei to catch one of Hawaii's most spectacular sunsets.

Touring the Westin Kauai at Kauai Lagoons By foot and by boat you'll see its incredible grounds, wildlife habitats, magnificent artworks, and a 21-acre reflecting pool.

Swimming at Kalapaki Beach In front of the Westin Kauai, it has gentle, rolling surf.

of Japanese gardens, complete with waterfall, koi-fish pools, and sculptured statuary. Although a meal here will cost you at least $30, rest assured that Japanese guests consider it a veritable bargain, since the same meal in Japan would run into three figures! **Sharkey's Fish Market** specializes in Hawaiian seafood. **Inn on the Cliffs** highlights Pacific Rim cuisine, fresh local seafood, and pasta—and a spectacular ocean view. And, lest we forget, Kalapaki Beach, the heart of this glorious complex, is open to everybody and is one of the nicest places to swim in all Hawaii.

Just in case you were curious, paying guests at the Westin Kauai spend $195–$395 a night for a room, $400 to $1,700 for a suite.

GROVE FARM HOMESTEAD, P.O. Box 1631, Lihue, Kauai, HI 96766. Tel. 245-3202.

A visit here takes a little advance planning, either by mail or by calling for reservations. But it's worth the effort, as this is a trip backward in time, to the days of the old Hawaiian sugar plantations. Grove Farm Homestead has been lovingly preserved and still has a lived-in look. The plantation was founded by George N. Wilcox, the son of teachers who arrived with the fifth company of the American Board of Missions sent to Hawaii in the 1830s. (Part of Wilcox's original sugar plantation is now the site of Kukui Grove Center; see below.) His niece, Miss Mabel Wilcox, who was born and lived at the homestead all her life, left her estate as a living museum. The homestead tour is leisurely, with stops for light refreshments along the way in the big kitchen. The old homes are lovely, furnished with antiques, Oriental rugs, and handsome koa-wood furniture; there is an abundance of books, and sheet music is open on the piano. You'll visit the very different servants' quarters, too.

Admission: $3.

Open: 2-hour tours given Mon and Wed–Thurs at 10am and 1pm. Call at least a week in advance, or write (reservations are accepted up to three months in advance).

KILOHANA PLANTATION, Hi. 50. Tel. 245-7818.

Gaylord Parke Wilcox, the nephew of the founder of Grove Farm Plantation, built his dream house back in 1935 and called it Kilohana, which, in Hawaiian, means "not to be surpassed." The Wilcox family lived at the estate for 35 years, during which time it was the setting for much of the cultural and social life of upper-class Kauai. Restored to look just as it did in the 1930s, with many of its actual furnishings and artifacts, it's now a combination historical house-museum and shopping bazaar, with boutiques taking over the old children's nursery, the family bedrooms, the library, the cloakrooms, and the restored guest cottages on the estate grounds. None of the shops is inexpensive, but all offer quality in accordance with Kilohana's standard of excellence.

Before you begin your shopping, stop in to have a look at the foyer of the main house, where you'll see two enormous monkeypod calabashes—reputedly the largest in the state of Hawaii. In the olden days, Hawaiian kings stored their feather quilts in such calabashes: Later, missionary women used them as "trunks" for patchwork quilts. These, however, are replicas, made for the movie *Hawaii.* Then, visit the Kilohana Information Center, which also houses **Island Memories.** It boasts museum-quality replicas and one-of-a-kind island crafts. You'll find a few authentic Hawaiian quilts, quilting kits, artifacts from New Guinea, Balinese masks, aloha chimes with lovely tones, and stylish art deco posters of the 1930s, re-creating old advertisements. They're $35, unframed. **Kilohana Galleries** is noted for its collection of work by Hawaiian artists. Check out its Artisan's Room, too, for fine crafts—and its Hawaiian Collection Room for rare Niihau-shell leis, wood carvings, and a good sampling of scrimshaw. **Hemmeter Collection** carries art from the East, including cloisonné, porcelain, and bronze figurines, vases, and statues. Fine jewelry is offered at **Kilohana Jewelry Box.** Lush tropical-print clothing for women can be found at **Noa Noa.**

On the estate grounds, **Stones at Kilohana,** in the A. S. Wilcox 1910 Guest Cottage, specializes in arts and crafts from all over the Pacific—including Tonga, Samoa, New Guinea, and Fiji. You'll see traditional handwork, wood bowls, hand-screened aloha shirts, ritual and ceremonial items, Hawaiian photographs by such artists as Boone Morrison, Pegge Hopper prints, jewelry, pottery, and sculpture. This is a companion shop to Stones at Kukui Grove (see below).

In addition to browsing and shopping at Kilohana, you can take a 20-minute, horse-drawn carriage ride ($7), an hour's ride through sugarcane fields ($20), a guided tour, or a walk through the extensive manicured lawns and gardens. When you get hungry, you can have an excellent meal at the charming courtyard restaurant, Gaylord's (see "Where to Eat" in Chapter 10).

The Kilohana Plantation is located on Hi. 50, two miles southwest of Lihue, headed toward Poipu. It's on the other side of the road and very close to the Kukui Grove Shopping Center. Open daily from 9am.

KAUAI MUSEUM, 4428 Rice St. Tel. 245-6931.

A visit to this museum, adjacent to the shopping center and across from the post office, is well worth your while. Stop in first at the Wilcox Building to examine the changing art, heritage, and cultural exhibits of both Asia and Hawaii. The Museum Shop here is one of our favorites, with its fine collections of South Pacific handcrafts, tapas, baskets, rare Niihau shell leis, Hawaiian books, prints, koa calabashes, and other wooden ware. The Rice Building, entered through a covered paved walkway and courtyard, contains the permanent exhibit, "The Story of Kauai," an ecological and geological history complete with photographs, dioramas, and an exciting video. Be sure to see the Plantation Gallery, a permanent showcase for a collection of splendid Hawaiian quilts, plus koa furniture, china, etc.

Admission: $3 adults; free for children under 18 accompanied by an adult.
Open: Mon–Fri 9am–4:30pm, Sat 9am–1pm.

LIHUE PUBLIC LIBRARY, 4344 Hardy St. Tel. 245-3617.

The latest audiovisual aids, including closed-circuit television, are available in this handsome contemporary building, located a few blocks away from Kauai Museum. Note Jerome Wallace's impressive abstract batik mural measuring 10 feet high and 27 feet long. Ask about their free programs, which include films, art shows, story hours, and ethnic programs.

Admission: Free.

Open: Hours vary with season but are usually Mon–Sat 8am–4:30pm, plus some evening hours.

SPORTS & RECREATION

THE BEACH To get to the town beach, follow Hi. 50 a mile toward the sea from Lihue up until its junction with Hi. 51. You'll come to the deep-water port of **Nawiliwili** (where the wiliwili trees once grew), Kauai's largest harbor and the site of a bulk-sugar plant that looks out on Kalapaki Beach across the bay. Although it adjoins the grounds of the luxurious Westin Kauai, this is the town beach, and you're welcome to use it. The surf, similar to that at Waikiki, is fairly gentle, with enough long rollers to make surfing or outrigger canoe rides great fun. There's easy access to the sand from the Anchor Cove Shopping Center.

FITNESS CENTERS Physical fitness buffs don't have to miss their daily workouts while on Kauai. Next door to the Kukui Grove Center, at 4370 Kukui Grove St. (tel. 245-7877), is the **Kauai Athletic Club,** where guests may indulge in aerobic classes, weightlifting, racquetball, lap swimming, etc., to their heart's content, at fees of $12 per day. It's a beautiful, classy club, and the instructors are excellent. Massage is available. It has reciprocal privileges with many health clubs, maybe yours. There's a full deli for healthy snacks, protein drinks, sandwiches, and soups. Open Monday through Friday from 7am to 10pm and on Saturday and Sunday from 8am to 6pm.

Note: The spa at the Westin Kauai (see above) also has many excellent facilities and services.

SHOPPING

KUKUI GROVE CENTER, Hi. 50. Tel. 245-7784.

Pint-sized Lihue now has the largest of all neighbor-island shopping malls, the $25-million Kukui Grove Center. Since it's just four miles from the airport on Hi. 50 (headed toward Poipu), it makes a logical first stop in town to stock up on food and vacation needs.

Star Market has everything from boogie boards to gourmet take-out foods. At **Sears,** you can shop for the whole family, rent a car, survey a good selection of Hawaiian wear and island souvenirs. Such other trusty island familiars as **Long's, Woolworth's, Liberty House, Waldenbooks,** and **J. C. Penney** are here. One of our favorite stops is **Stones Gallery,** which shows a large selection of indigenous arts and crafts of Hawaii, plus tasteful graphics, ceramics, jewelry, and other fine crafts, most by local artisans. This might be the place for you to buy a print by Pegge Hopper (her portraits of Hawaiian women are very popular in the islands; prices start at $15 and run into the hundreds), or a hand-painted T-shirt for $25, or a variety of posters that begin at $10, unframed. Gaze at the magnificent art-to-wear creations, maybe pick up an original design T-shirt by Kauai artists, for $15–$25. Note, too, the woven baskets, the tapa cloth, and the photos of Old Hawaii by Boone Morrison. In the center of the store is **Stones Espresso Café,** with wonderful teas and coffees to take home or sip in the store along with light meals and heavenly pastries (see Chapter 10).

Indo-Pacific Trading Company specializes in Indonesian furniture, both antique and new. Sure, these pieces are too big for your suitcase, but they'll ship anywhere. Have a look. (There's another store of the same name in Old Koloa Town, which specializes in more-portable Indonesian crafts; see below.) In addition to attractive kitchenware for the condo crowd, the **Deli & Bread Connection** has some terrific food to take home and eat: deli sandwiches, cheeses, pâtés, wines, coffee and teas, plus bread and rolls fresh from its own bakery (which smells wonderful!). Try the fresh cinnamon rolls and the macadamia-nut rolls baked daily. They also have delicious hot soups.

Of the clothing boutiques, we especially like the tasteful collection at **Alexandra-Christian. Sally's Creations** has created some coral fashion rings and earrings, averaging about $10. **Kauai Beach Co.** has a colorful selection of screen-printed Kauai T-shirts, sweatshirts, and coverups for adults and kids, too. Basic items galore can be found at **E-Z Discount.** And **General Nutrition Centers** runs many specials and is a good place to replenish your vitamin supply—as well as get some fruit or vegetable juice.

The **Kukui Nut Tree Inn** for family-style meals and **Si Cisco's Mexican Restaurant** for spicy south-of-the-border fare are the big restaurant draws here, but there are also several good snack shops (see "Where to Eat" in Chapter 10).

Free entertainment is often presented on the mall stage; check the local papers for details. The Kukui Grove Center is open Monday through Thursday and on Saturday from 9:30am to 5:30pm, on Friday from 9:30am to 9pm, and on Sunday from 10am to 4pm.

HILO HATTIE'S FASHION CENTER, 3252 Kuhio Hwy. Tel. 245-3404.

This is always a good budget stop for resort fashions. Call ahead and they'll take you to their factory outlet, where you can buy men's aloha shirts and women's short muumuus from $16, plus souvenirs, and macadamia-nut candies. There are always great specials here.

EVENING ENTERTAINMENT

Watch the papers for news of free shows put on at the **Kukui Grove Center**—these shows by local entertainers are sometimes every bit as good as those at the high-priced clubs. The shows often take place on Friday nights or Saturday mornings, right in the mall.

THE WESTIN KAUAI, at Kauai Lagoons. Tel. 245-5050.

It won't cost you a thing to catch the **torch-lighting ceremony** at the Westin Kauai's Kalapaki Beach. The ceremony is held every evening at dusk. As a double-hulled canoe is paddled to shore, Hawaiian dances and chants are performed and tales of old Hawaii are told. The torches are lit, and then the evening's festivities begin.

Also at the Westin Kauai, The Cliffs has a jazzy trio for dancing under the stars.

Admission: Torch-lighting ceremony, free.

KAUAI COMEDY CLUB, 4331 Kava Beach Dr., at Kauai Hilton. Tel. 245-1955.

If it's a Wednesday, Thursday, or Friday, you can catch mainland comics doing their acts at the Kauai Hilton. Showtime is 8:30pm. Dinner-show packages begin at 6:30pm: Dinner is an Italian buffet on Wednesday, a Chinese buffet on Thursday, and a Kauai Clambake on Friday.

Admission: $12 show only, $25 "Gobble and Giggle" package.

CLUB JETTY, at Nawiliwili Harbor. Tel. 245-4970.

Down the road from the Westin Kauai at Nawiliwili Harbor, where the luxury cruise liners dock, is Club Jetty, out there on the wharf for many years. A new management has taken over, remodeled the old place, and turned it into a happy mingling grounds for tourists and locals. Doors open at 8pm for pupus, disco, and live music. There are often contests, comedy shows, and the like, and nobody thinks of leaving until about 4am. Happy hour, when there's a $1 discount on all drinks, runs from 8 to 10pm. Thursday is $1 night, when domestic beers and well drinks go for that price.

Admission: Free before 10pm, $4 after 10pm.

HAP'S HIDEAWAY, 2975 Ewalu St. Tel. 245-3473.

Looking for the cheapest drinks on Kauai? Hap's claims to have them, starting with 12-ounce draft beef for $1.25. Haps shows live sports events via satellite on four color monitors. They also have more than 750 songs on the jukebox including Top-40 and country-and-western music, a happy hour that stretches from 1pm to 2am, a Montana accent, and not even a trace of Polynesian atmosphere.

Admission: Free.

SI CISCO'S CANTINA, at the Kukui Grove Center. Tel. 245-8561.

This is a popular bar and lounge where you can admire the artwork, listen to local entertainers, and sip huge pitcherfuls of margaritas for $8. Open daily from 11am to 11pm or midnight.

Admission: Free.

3. EXCURSION ALONG THE EASTERN & NORTHERN SHORES

Now you're ready for one of the big trips, an excursion by automobile along the glorious eastern and northern shores of Kauai. Hawaii 56, which starts at Kuhio Highway in Lihue town, takes you the entire length of the tour. The distance is about 40 miles each way, and it will take you a full day.

KAPAIA & HANAMAULA

After you've gone a few miles out of town at Kapaia, you'll find a turnoff to the left to **Wailua Falls,** about four miles inland. Watch for the white fence on the right of the road and listen for the sound of rushing water; soon you'll see the HVB marker. After you've seen the falls, don't be tempted to drive farther; turn around here and drive back.

Look now, on the left as you're driving to Wailua on the Kuhio Highway (Hi. 56), for a quaint store called **Kapaia Stitchery** (tel. 245-2281), especially appealing in that many things in it are made by hand. Owner Julie Yukimura makes dresses, muumuus, pareaus, and aloha shirts, which she sells at low prices. Or you may select your own fabrics (Hawaiian print fabrics start at about $6 a yard for cotton) and have clothing custom made. Julie also asks local craftspeople, especially senior citizens, to make things up for her. Most exciting of these are the patchwork coverlets made of Hawaiian fabrics by four local grandmothers: Prices are about $85–$90 and would be at least twice as much anywhere else. Much-sought-after traditional Hawaiian quilts ($2,000–$4,000) are also in good supply. Hawaiian quilting cushions can be made to order ($90 for an excellent piece of work). And do-it-yourselfers can find Hawaiian-quilt pillow kits and hand-painted needlepoint designs of local flowers and themes. Small children on your gift list will be enchanted with the soft-sculpture fairy-tale dolls; some are reversible, such as Cinderella and the fairy godmother, which turns into the wicked stepmother; some depict Hansel and Gretel's house or Goldilocks and the Three Bears; all are around $22–$28. There's always something new and interesting here; it's worth a stop.

READERS RECOMMEND

Scuba Diving and Sailboarding. *"Our teenagers loved their 30-foot scuba dive with Fathom Five Divers (tel. 742-6991). This is a dive for those wondering if they want to go deeper and need to take more lessons to certify. They were very helpful people, patient and kind. The $65 each includes 1½ hours of instruction, diving, and all equipment and transportation. . . . Kalapaki Beach rental provides instruction and equipment for $55 for three hours of sailboard lessons. Two lessons and you can become certified in this sport."*—Mr. and Mrs. Steven Benner, Nevada, Mo.

WAILUA

Continuing on Hi. 56, you'll soon come to the mouth of the **Wailua River** and one of the most historic areas in Hawaii. Here, where the Polynesians first landed, were once seven *heiaus,* or temple sites, by the sacred (*wailua*) waters. Just before you get there, you'll come to **Lydgate Park,** on the right, a grassy picnic area directly on the water, in which are the remains of an ancient "City of Refuge." You'll get a better idea of what a City of Refuge actually looked like when you see the restored one at Kona on the Big Island. But the concept here was precisely the same. In the days when the Hawaiians still carried on their polytheistic nature worship, life was bound by a rigid system of *kapus,* or taboos, violations that were punishable by death. But if an offender, or a prisoner of war, could run or swim to a City of Refuge, he could be purified and was then allowed to go free. Not too much of the City of Refuge remains, but if you wade out into the river you may discover some ancient carvings on the rocks, once part of the heiau. More practically, **Lydgate Park Beach** is one of the best beaches on Kauai for children. Two natural "pools," created by rocks, make it safe for them to swim and play in the ocean. The snorkeling is lovely, there are stripies and butterfly fish feeding on the rock, the water is clean and clear, and the sand is white. There are rest rooms, showers, and barbecue pits near the beach. Recently, alas, there have been reports of vandalism here.

The Wailua, one of the two navigable rivers in Hawaii, is also the place where you can rent a tour boat for an idyllic three-mile trip to the fantastically beautiful **Fern Grotto**—an enormous fern-fronted cave under a gentle cascade of water, unapproachable any other way. Personally, we'd love to take this trip in our own private craft and, instead of being "entertained," spend the time contemplating the rare tropical trees and flowers that line the bank and pondering about the old Kauai alii whose bones still lie undiscovered in the secret burial caves of the cliffs above. But the tour boats are well run, the captains are entertaining, and the musicians' singing of the "Hawaiian Wedding Song" in the natural amphitheater of the Fern Grotto is a unique experience.

The cost of the 1½-hour boat trip is $10 ($5 for children 4–12), and both **Waialeale Boat Tours** (tel. 822-4908) and **Smith Motor Boat Service** (tel. 822-3467) make the cruises. You should call in advance to make a reservation.

You may want to make a little excursion to visit **Smith's Tropical Paradise,** a 22½-acre botanical garden that features a Japanese garden, a replica of Easter Island, huge tiki heads, a tropical fruit garden, and a small Polynesian village. Adults pay $5; children, $2.50. Open 8:30am to 4pm. This is also the site of an excellent luau and Polynesian show; you can see the show alone for $10.50, or enjoy the whole shebang for about $45. For reservations, call 822-4654 or 822-9599.

At this point on Hi. 56, a side road called the **King's Highway** (named after the kings who had to be carried uphill in a litter, lest their sacred feet touch the ground) leads to the restored heiau, **Holo-Holo-Ku.** It's so serene here now that it's hard to imagine that this was once a site for human sacrifice to calm the ancient gods.

Now you move on from Hawaiiana to observe some of the history of the Japanese settlers in Hawaii, recorded in a quaint cemetery just up the wooden stairs to the right of the heiau. If you continue driving along the King's Highway, you'll pass a rice field and soon, **Poliahu Heiau,** now a park that affords you a splendid view of the Wailua River. Next is **Opaekaa Falls,** plunging down from a high cliff (the name, quaintly, means rolling shrimp).

At the top of the falls, nestled in a lush green valley is the **Kamokila Hawaiian Village,** where an ancient settlement has been restored. A guided tour here ($5 for adults, $1.50 for children) is an excellent way to gain an experience of premissionary Hawaii. Knowledgeable guides will show you the Oracle Tower (where villagers left gifts for the gods), the warriors' houses, the men's and women's eating houses, the medicine house (landscaped with Hawaiian medicinal plants), the chief's house, living house, sleeping house, and birthing house (in which are actual ancient Hawaiian birthing stones found in the area). You'll see craft and salt-making demonstrations, watch a demonstration of Hawaiian games, and then be invited to participate in them. A visitor is sure to come away with quite a respectable knowledge of the traditional ways of the Hawaiian people. Kamokila Hawaiian Village (tel. 822-1192) is open Monday through Saturday from 9am to 4pm.

At some point, you're going to want to visit **Coco Palms,** perhaps for its splendid evening torch-lighting ceremony. Have a look at some of the attractive shops here; they are more reasonably priced than you might expect. The **Chapel in the Palms,** scene of many a Hawaiian wedding, was originally built by Columbia Pictures for the movie *Sadie Thompson,* starring Rita Hayworth, which was filmed here on the grounds.

On the ocean side of the road, at 4-370 Kuhio Hwy., is **Restaurant Kintaro,** where shoppers should make a stop even if they're not planning to eat. In an annex to the restaurant is **D. S. Collection,** a gallery-shop showing paintings, ceramics, glass, and other works by local artists, as well as some handsome imports from Japan: ivory, celadon, kokeshi dolls. Many good gift ideas here, and prices begin modestly.

COCONUT MARKETPLACE Back on the highway now, continue toward the Coconut Plantation hotels and there, near the Islander on the Beach and the Kauai Beach Boy, you'll find Coconut Marketplace. It's a handsome setup, with concrete planked walkways, country decor, flowers and shrubs everywhere, and enough diverting shops (more than 70 at last count) to keep you busy for an hour or two.

We have a few special favorites, like ✪ **Waves of One Sea,** with such international gifts as lacquered boxes from Thailand, Fukagawa porcelains from Japan, Russian stone carvings, and Lomonosov porcelain. There is an outstanding collection of Hawaiian koa-wood boxes, and of hand-carved reproductions of priceless primitive art. Handmade jewelry of peacock and pheasant feathers begins at $20 for earrings; chokers start at $50. Note the handmade collector's dolls, from $19, and the charming Margaret Leach storyboard prints.

Plantation Stitchery specializes in needlepoints and patterns, and has a few dresses, too. **Tahiti Imports** sells beautiful clothing and hand-screened fabrics at very reasonable prices. **Ye Olde Ship Store** is the place for maritime art, antiques, and a fabulous collection of scrimshaw, the largest on Kauai. All the work is done on antique fossilized ivory, which is becoming rarer all the time, and some distinctive pieces have high-investment potential. If you're looking for something simpler, you might pick up some antique brass ship keys (ca. 1875–1925) from Hawaiian and other Pacific ships, which would make inexpensive and unusual little gifts—under $5.

Be sure to visit the exquisite **Kahn Gallery,** where a consistently high level of taste is evident in the selection of original artwork and limited-edition graphics by Hawaiian artists. Roy Tabora, George Sumner, Jan Parker, David Lee and Betty Hay Freeland are among their stars. Posters of the work of these artists, among those of other artists, can be found at **Island Images,** on the other side of the Marketplace. Small paintings to carry home and limited-edition prints could start low, although most are in the several-hundred-dollar range. There's another Kahn Gallery at the new Anchor Cove shopping center in Nawiliwili.

Isle Style lives up to its name with above-average crafts, accessories, jewelry (like titanium bracelets and earrings), stained-glass mirrors, hand-painted T-shirts by local artists, copper or stuffed geckos, and genuine shell jewelry boxes. **The Dragon Fly** has a unique look for Hawaiian clothing—beautiful pastel shades of 100% cotton, hand-embroidered, women's casual clothing. Prices range from $25 and styles include sundresses, jumpsuits, and baby wear in the same soft colors.

Elephant Walk can always be counted on for beautiful gift items: wind chimes, oil lamps, dolls, shell flowers, and the like. You can get scrimshaw, 14-karat-gold charms, and Niihau-shell necklaces, which begin at $35 (and go way up!) at **Kauai Gold;** nuts, candies, and beautiful inexpensive flower leis at **Nutcracker Sweet. Crazy Shirts** has T-shirts with great designs—the gecko Ts are taking Kauai by storm.

The Whalers' General Store is one of those very useful sundry shops, with everything from macadamia-nut brittle to liquor, sandals, shell souvenirs, and drugstore items. Many kinds of coffees are for sale at **Café Espresso,** including chocolate-macadamia nut and decaffeinated Hawaiian Kona. While you're here, have a cappuccino or espresso, or a homemade banana-macadamia Belgian waffle.

If you'd like to fly a kite on Kauai beach, the people at **High as a Kite** have some beauties for you, which begin at $7 and go up to around $300 (some can be used for decorative art). Kyle, the "Kite dude," teaches people how to fly them. Huggable plush animals, made on Kauai, are store exclusives. Men's aloha shirts by Reyn Spooner cannot be beat; they have the best patterns. This local outpost of **Reyn's** has women's shirts, muumuus, and other sportswear. We saw some elegant muumuus for kids, as well as many other lovelies, at **Happy Kauaian,** which also has special selections for queen sizes and petites, and sells fabrics, too. **Coco Resorts Shop** has great things for the whole family. And **Just You and Me, Kid** specializes in tasteful things for the kids: Hawaiian toys, games, souvenirs, dolls, and books, plus a good selection of Hawaiian T-shirts and aloha wear.

The kids will get a kick out of playing with the heavy equipment from the defunct **Kilauea Sugar Mill** that has been transformed into sculptural fountains they can control. When they tire of that, they may enjoy running to the top of the high wooden tower to see the beautiful view. And they'll be delighted with the children's hula show presented by the local hula schools every Thursday, Friday, and Saturday at 4pm. Be sure to check the calendar of events posted at each entrance for additional free daily activities.

Hungry? No problem. The marketplace abounds in snack bars and restaurants offering inexpensive meals (see "Where to Eat" in Chapter 10). And if you want to catch a first-run movie, **Plantation Cinema I and II** are right here. The marketplace is open daily from 9am to 9pm, with free entertainment every day.

READERS RECOMMEND

A note of caution. *"Our camera bag with camera equipment was stolen from our car, even though it was locked, while we watched the free Polynesian show at the Marketplace at Coconut Plantation, which is held on Thursday, Friday, and Saturday afternoon between 4 and 5pm. Local police advise that all equipment—even in car trunks—can be a target for theft, since most people enjoy the show and thieves know they won't be returning to their car at that time."*—Karolyn Fairbanks, Oroville, Calif.

KAPAA & KEALIA

From Hi. 56, back on the northern drive, you'll soon see a remarkable formation on the left as you enter Kapaa, the **Sleeping Giant**—the subject of another Menehune tall tale. The old fellow, so the story goes, was a kind of Gulliver whom the South Sea Lilliputians inadvertently killed.

On the opposite side of the road, opposite Foodland, look for a little store shaped like a Samoan house and called **Marta's Boat,** 770 Kuhio Hwy. (tel. 822-3926). Marta Curry, who has five young children of her own, understands the needs of mothers and children and has a stock of items both pretty and practical, much of it handmade. Her specialty is 100% cotton (or silk or rayon; she does not carry blends) aloha clothing for children. Cotton T-shirts and infant sets hand-painted by local artists are especially lovely. She also has a good selection of educational toys, many of which are good for the long plane ride home. Moms should have a look at the inviting adult clothing racks. Next door is an old Kauai favorite, a natural-foods store run by her husband, Ambrose Curry, where you might pick up a cooling bottled fruit drink or a snack, or stock up on supplies.

READERS RECOMMEND

The Sleeping Giant. *"During our stay on Kauai we met some really nice people who took us to the top of Sleeping Giant. Take a jug of water, a camera, and a snack and leave early in the morning. The site at the top is beautiful. You hike past waterfalls, through large pine forests that make you think of the North Woods. This is an easy hike; we were a party of all ages, 6–65. Go to the intersection at Coco Palms and ask for directions. Even some of the locals don't know about this."*—The Quid Family, Schaumburg, Ill.

KAUAI VILLAGE SHOPPING CENTER A stop at the new Kauai Village Shopping Center, 4-831 Kuhio Hwy. (tel. 822-9272), is well worth your time: There's a Hawaiian museum and gift shop here, the largest natural-foods store in the islands, an excellent shop featuring hand-painted clothing, and one of the famous Wyland Galleries.

The **Kauai Village Museum & Gift Shop** is in the clock tower building of Kauai Village, a short stroll from the big Pay-N-Save store. It is a special project of Aloha International, a nonprofit group founded by Dr. Serge Kahili King, dedicated to "Peace Through Aloha." The museum/store is a major part of the fund-raising program for a world peace center being built on Kauai. Wednesday-night meetings by the leaders of Aloha International are held here, as are classes and workshops on Hawaiian culture. The museum and its minitheater, showing videos, are free to the public. The gift shop is a delight, with many made-in-Hawaii arts and crafts, especially native-wood products; volcanic glass, native olivine, and kukui-nut jewelry; books on Hawaiian shamanism and Hawaiiana; Hawaiian music, videos, maps; fine arts cards, prints, and posters; potted native trees and plants; and novel gift items. Children's Hawaiian story and activity books, toys, and games are also featured as part of the attempt to preserve and pass on the essence of Hawaiian culture. Prices are reasonable, and all profits go to foster these worthy goals. (If you would like more information on Aloha International, write to them at P.O. Box 665, Kilauea, HI 96754.)

If you're into health foods, then a stop at **Papaya's Natural Foods,** in Kauai Village (tel. 823-0191), is a must. This is the largest health-food store on Kauai, and one of the nicest in the islands. Their stock is extensive, they carry the best products (doctors send their patients here for vitamins and supplements), and they have a good selection of organic, locally grown produce. They also have a great deli counter and a wonderful little café (see "Where to Eat" in Chapter 10) where you can have everything from a soup-and-salad lunch for under $3, to a full meal.

Jacqueline Sibthorpe, the artist behind **Art to Wear Silks,** located directly under the clock tower at Kauai Village (tel. 822-7511), is right on the premises, creating her magnificent hand-painted clothing before your eyes. She paints on cotton and silk in tropical colors, and while her clothes are not inexpensive, they are unique works of art. Check out the creations here and at her other store, Art to Wear Kauai, 1435 Kuhio Hwy., across from Kapaa Beach Park (tel. 822-1125). We saw long hand-painted T-shirts for $45, children's T-shirts at $12.95, muumuus from Bali made of hand-batiked fabrics for around $70, and most exciting of all, her signature silk "cocoons," $230. There's a neat collection of jewelry, too.

Wyland, the unique artist whose studies of marine life are seen all over Hawaii (and on various controversial "whaling walls" in Oahu and Maui), has a new gallery here at Kauai Village (tel. 822-9855). Always worth a look.

IN KAPAA The **Hee-Fat Marketplace,** at 4-1354 Kuhio Hwy., in the heart of Kapaa, has a number of small shops; the one that's taking off mightily right now is called **Hot Rocket Clothing** (tel. 822-7848). Owner Jay Schneider stocks exclusive T-shirts (most are $15) and sweatshirts (most are $45) that are hand painted and silk-screened here. Some of the more striking designs include "Marilyn Monroe," "Andy," and "Hot Gecko, Hawaii." Lots of hip clothing for men and women, jewelry, accessories, and more.

Paul Wroblewski has assembled quite a collection of antiques at **The Only Show in Town,** 4-1495 Kuhio Hwy. (tel. 822-1442), in a beautifully restored old house on the mauka side of Kapaa's main street. There is a veritable museum of old bottles, and Paul is very knowledgeable on the subject. There's also a huge collection of vintage political buttons and American trade memorabilia, particularly Coca-Cola items. We loved the costume jewelry from the '20s through the '40s—lots of rhinestones, lots of glitz. Vintage aloha shirts, "silkies" and cotton, abound, and the back room is filled with "gently used" old clothes. A theater friend of ours on Kauai tells us he makes a beeline for this shop when dressing a period show. These folks also serve soft drinks and small snacks up at the front of the shop. We could get lost here for hours!

Some of the most beautiful fish in Polynesian waters live in the rocks and reefs around Kauai. The friendly, professional staff at **Sea Sage,** a dive shop at 4-1378 Kuhio Hwy. (tel. 822-3841), in Kapaa, can make the introductions for you, via various snorkeling and scuba-diving excursions. They'll rent you snorkeling equipment at $8 for 24 hours, and they run a "snorkel picnic" for $45. A half-day introduction to scuba-diving is $75, including all equipment. There are many other excursions for more experienced snorkelers and scuba-divers, and a full line of snorkeling and scuba equipment is for sale or rent. Reservations should be made in advance: Call them for details.

MOVING NORTH Continuing on, now, turn half a mile up the hill just before the bridge over Kealia Stream and you'll come to **St. Catherine's Catholic Church,** which boasts murals by leading Hawaiian artists: Jean Charlot, Juliette May Fraser, and Tseng Yu Ho.

Beyond Kealia, watch for the turnoff to **Anahola Beach** for a glimpse of one of those golden, jewellike beaches that ring the island.

EAST KAUAI EVENING ENTERTAINMENT

COCO PALMS RESORT, Wailua. Tel. 822-4921.

You must see the Coco Palms at night. Five miles out of town on Wailua Bay, it's on the site of an ancient coconut grove and lagoon, where Hawaiian royalty once lived. Flaming torches cast eerie shadows on the water, and there's much blowing of conch shells and other ritualistic goings-on, with an effect that reassures the visiting movie stars here that they've never left the set.

From 5 to 8:30 or 9pm, Friday through Monday and Wednesday, you can combine this with a few drinks in the Lagoon Terrace Lounge, where you'll hear singer/guitarist Rich Hanapi play Hawaiian music, traditional and contemporary. Or you might want to spring for the Torch-lighting Buffet meal at $18.95, and watch the venerable Larry Rivera Polynesian Show.

Admission: Torch-lighting ceremony, free; Larry Rivera Polynesian show, $5 cover with dinner, $10 for show only.

SHERATON COCONUT BEACH HOTEL, Coconut Plantation. Tel. 822-3455 (ext. 651 for luau reservations).

This hotel is a leader in entertainment on the island. You can usually find a trio like Boogie Plus Two playing music to dance and listen to, on Friday and Saturday from 8 to 11pm, at its Cook's Landing Lounge. Sunday through Thursday from 8 to 11pm, one-man band Cameron Rafael performs contemporary and Hawaiian dance music. Sheraton's luau is on every night except Monday at 6:30pm, and it's an island favorite.

Admission: Lounge, free; luau, $47 adults, $28 children 2–12, $21.50 for the show only (no food).

KAUAI RESORT, 3-5920 Kuhio Hwy. Tel. 245-3939, ext. 45.

Brothers Kimo and Robbie, favorite island singers of "Na Kaholokula" and the hulas of Puamohala are featured on Tuesday and Saturday nights at 7:30pm in the Pacific Room. On Monday, Wednesday, and Friday at 7pm, Leilani's Polynesian Revue showcases a charming group of youngsters. You can come just for the show or you can have the prime rib buffet dinner, served between 6 and 8:30pm, which includes the cost of the show.

Admission: $10 show only, $16.50 show and dinner.

JOLLY ROGER, Coconut Plantation. Tel. 822-3451.

Probably the longest happy hour—let's call it a "happy day"—takes place here daily from 11am to 7pm. Standard drinks are available at special prices. Karaoke begins every night at 8pm. No cover charge.

KILAUEA

Just in case you didn't know, Kilauea is the "Undisputed Guava Capital of the World." To make you aware of that fact—and to tell you everything about guava you ever wanted to know but were afraid to ask—**Guava Kai Plantation** (tel. 828-1925) has opened its doors to the public. (As you're driving on Hi. 56, you'll notice its sign off to the left. It's open daily from 9am to 5pm. Some 480 acres of guava orchards are under commercial cultivation here; you can see the orchards and the processing plant, visit the gift shop, and get free samples of guava juice and the fruit itself. You might also want to stop into their restaurant to have a sandwich and sample the likes of guava muffins, guava-glazed cinnamon rolls, guava sherbet, and guava chiffon cake. After this sweet interlude, get back on the road and on to the lighthouse.

The first church you'll see as you drive into Kilauea town, **Christ Memorial Episcopal Church,** has only-in-Hawaii architecture. It's made of lava rock. Its windows, executed in England, are of the finest design and construction. On the other side of the road you'll soon see **St. Sylvester's Catholic Church** in Kilauea—something new in church architecture. This octagonal "church-in-the-round," constructed of lava and wood, has a beautiful, open feeling. You'll recognize the work of Jean Charlot again, this time in the fresco paintings of the stations of the cross.

Now follow the road for two more miles to **Kilauea Lighthouse** (turn right into Kilauea to Lighthouse Road, which becomes Kilauea Point National Wildlife Refuge). Kilauea Lighthouse, high on a bluff that drops sharply to the sea on three sides, affords a magnificent view of the northern coastline of the island. Birds drift effortlessly in the wind like paper kites sent up by schoolchildren; below, the turquoise sea smashes against the black lava cliffs. The historic lighthouse was built in 1913, has an 8-foot-high clam-shaped lens, but is no longer operative (a small light, 30 feet north of the old structure, is the present Kilauea light). The old U.S. Coast Guard Lighthouse Station has been taken over by the U.S. Fish and Wildlife Service. Birdlovers will have a field day here, as the area is frequented by such unique Pacific sea birds as the red-footed booby, the wedge-tailed shearwater, the white-tailed and red-tailed tropic bird, and the Laysan albatross. Whales, spinner dolphins, and Pacific sea-green turtles are also seen in the area. Docents at the visitor center next door to the lighthouse can answer questions and point out current wildlife activity. Check out the bookstore with its books on Hawaiian natural history. The Kilauea Point Refuge is open daily from 10am to 4pm.

On the way to Kilauea Lighthouse, the **Kong Lung Center** makes a good stop for shopping, stretching, and having a snack. The buildings are turn-of-the-century plantation, and the atmosphere is charming. The Kong Lung Company (tel. 828-1822) is Kauai's oldest plantation general store (1881) and it's very special, stocked with beautiful antiques, tasteful craft items (we spotted handsome African baskets and made-on-Kauai ceramics on our last visit), home accessories, and imaginative gift items. It has perhaps the best collection of muumuus on Kauai, plus batiks and clothing from all over the Pacific. Also in this little enclave is an excellent gardenlike Italian restaurant called **Casa di Amici** (tel. 828-1388), where you can have a very pleasant lunch: Italian sub sandwiches that are a meal in themselves for $5–$7, salads in the same price range, and fabulous rich desserts. (Lunch is served Monday through Friday from 11:30am to 2:30pm; dinner is daily from 5 to 9:30pm.)

Continue past **Kalihiwai Bay,** whose sleepy little village was twice destroyed by tidal waves, in 1946 and 1957, a reminder that the much-celebrated mildness of Hawaii is a sometime thing.

HANALEI

ATTRACTIONS

The glorious views continue. Keep watching for the lookout at **Hanalei Valley,** where you'll be treated to one of the special sights of the islands. The floor of Hanalei Valley, which you see below, is almost Asian, with neatly terraced taro patches and the silvery Hanalei River snaking through the dark greens of the mountains. (A sunset visit here is spectacular; plan it for a later trip if you have time.) You may want to drive through the luxury resort development of **Princeville, at Hanalei** and perhaps have lunch here at **Chuck's Steak House** or **Zelo's Café.**

Back on the road, you'll soon come to **Hanalei Beach,** one of the most imposing beaches in the islands, but swimming is safe only in summer months and only at the old boat pier at the river mouth. In winter, beware of high surf and undertow. To get to the beach, turn right at St. William's Catholic Church (another Jean Charlot mural is inside). There's a public pavilion, dressing rooms, and picnic facilities; your fellow bathers will include many local families.

In Hanalei Valley itself, history buffs will want to note the old **Waioli Mission.** The original church, built in 1841, is now used as a community center. More interesting, we think, is the old **Mission House,** restored in 1921 and full of fascinating furniture, books, and mementos of 19th-century Hawaii. On Tuesday, Thursday, and Saturday between 9am and 3pm, you can take a guided tour here, for which there is no admission charge, although donations are welcomed. Plan on 30–40 minutes for this excellent tour. For groups of 10–20 people, however, advance reservations are required and can be made by calling Barnes Riznik (tel. 245-3202) or writing to P.O. Box 1631, Lihue, Kauai, HI 96766.

SHOPPING

We loved the funky old Ching Young General Store that had sat in the middle of Hanalei town forever, so we looked upon its demise and the construction of the **Ching Young Village Shopping Center** with mixed emotions. The old-time aura is gone, certainly, but this is a pleasant and practical place with a few shops that are worth your time. The most tasteful of these, for us, is ✪ **On the Road to**

Hanalei (tel. 826-7360), which shows arts and crafts from Bali, China, Thailand, Guatemala, and many other places, as well as Hawaii. We saw beautiful tie-dyed pareaus, for $25–$35, tie-dyed shawls at $75, and books by Hawaiian artists. Textiles and wall hangings from all over the world are featured, including precious ikats from Bali. The gallery section of the store shows original masks from Africa and Indonesia, baskets and tapa cloth from the South Pacific. There's also a good collection of jewelry by local artists.

Spinning Dolphin (tel. 826-7461) creates custom T-shirts, silk-screened while you watch. **Jen's Jewelry and Gift Shop** (tel. 826-2588) features Asian carvings, fans, and the like. **Jungle Bob's** (tel. 826-6664) can set you up for outdoor adventures; they have backpacking supplies, sportswear, and a good selection of books on Hawaii, as well. Take time to walk around the corner and up the flight of stairs to **Artisans Guild of Kauai,** where some of Kauai's finest craftspeople show their work.

If you need some fresh produce, vitamins, or natural sandwiches, stop in at **Hanalei Health & Natural Foods** (tel. 826-6990). **Hanalei Florist** can provide you with fresh flowers. Other practical resources at Ching Young Village include a **Big Save Market;** a Chinese restaurant, **Foong Wong** (tel. 826-6996); and several fast-food operations.

Stacey and Cavan Crane "fly" luscious tie-dye and batik dresses from the front porch of **Earth Bones,** 5-1383 Kuhio Hwy. (across from Ching Young Village), all the better to entice you into their colorful shop, chockablock with pretty things. Silver earrings depicting dolphins, whales, geckos, and such are priced at $12–$24. There are unusual T-shirts with designs by Escher, some lovely hair ornaments, all wound with silk and dripping with tassels, at two for $9. One-of-a-kind tank-style batik dresses are $44. A great selection of scarves, pareaus, and skirts are all hand-dyed.

Now visit Hanalei's newest attraction: the **Old Hanalei School** (tel. 826-7677). Built in 1926, this actually was an old school; it's on the National Register of Historic Places as architecturally significant, and its design became a standard throughout Hawaii for school buildings. Carol and Gaylord Wilcox, of the prominent Kauai family who also restored Kilohana Plantation, saved the old building, moved it four blocks from its original site, and have lovingly restored it, keeping its significant architectural details intact throughout.

Among the several shops here, **Tropical Tantrum** (tel. 822-7301), is a winner, with hand-painted women's clothing by artists Lauri Johns and Parker Price, a brother-and-sister team from Texas. They also show works by other island artists; prices start at around $60. **Island Images** (tel. 826-6677) shows first-rate prints and posters, and **Hanalei Surf** (tel. 826-9000) is for the big-waves set.

Stop in at **The Hanalei Gourmet** (tel. 826-2524) here to pick up some cheese, wines, delicious deli and bakery items, or to get a picnic basket. You can also have a tasty meal here (see "Where to Eat" in Chapter 10) and join the local crowd for evenings of live music Tuesday through Saturday.

One of our favorite shops in this area is called **Ola's** (tel. 826-6937), and it's right on the main road next door to the Dolphin Restaurant in Hanalei. This is a serenely tasteful environment, a showcase for American crafts—in wood, glass, ceramic, metal, fiber, and mixed media. We love the whimsical hand-blown glass paperweights by John Simpson of Massachusetts, from $45; the wooden bowls by Jack Straka of the Big Island, from $70; and the hand-painted pewter pins by the Tin Woodsman, from $13. There are many boxes from all over the country. And many delights for children, too—toys, books, whimsy. A wonderful spot.

LUMAHAI BEACH

Lumahai Beach is next, and you'll recognize it immediately from pictures appearing in dozens of books, postcards, and magazines. It's probably the most widely photographed beach on the island, and deserves its fame: golden sand, a long tongue of black-lava rock stretching to the sea, a background of unearthly blue-green mountain. If the surf is not high, swimming will be safe here. It's a little difficult to find the entrance to the trail down to the beach (not indicated by any signs), but once you do, it's easy to get down. If the surf is up, admire the view and move on.

HAENA

Beyond Lumahai beach stretches the Haena region, where the shoreline gets dreamier by the mile. You can swim anywhere along here, but be very careful of surf and undertow in the winter months. Many people consider **Haena Beach Park** one of the best beaches on the island (although we personally prefer to swim at Ke'e, described below), and you won't go wrong swimming, camping, or picnicking here. Haena is what you always imagined the South Seas would be like—golden curving beaches, coconut palms, lush foliage, and jagged cliffs tumbling down to the sea. Is it any surprise that this spot was chosen as Bali Ha'i for the movie *South Pacific*?

On this drive through the Haena region, watch on the left side of the road for the **Manimi-holo Dry Cave,** which was supposedly dug by the Menehunes to capture an evil spirit that had stolen some fish. This is the area from which the Menehunes were also said to have left Hawaii. A short distance from here, up a small rise, is the first of two **Wet Caves,** the **Waikapalae;** about 200 yards farther is the second, the **Waikanaloa.** For once, the Menehunes were not responsible—the caves were reputedly dug by Pele in a search for fire. Finding fresh water instead, she left in disgust. It's reported that you can swim in these pools (the old Hawaiians used to jump off the ledges into them), but we think you'll do better to wait for the end of the road a few hundred yards ahead and an out-of-this-world beach, ✪ **Ke'e.** This is one of those gentle, perfect beaches that's almost impossible to tear yourself away from. As you loll on the sand under the towering mountains, listening to the Pacific, which has quieted down to a ripple beside you, it's not hard to picture this spot when it was the site of a most sacred temple of Laka, the goddess of the hula. Nearby are the remains of a heiau that guarded the sacred hula halau, to which novitiates came from all over the islands to study the dances, meles, and religious traditions of their people. From the cliffs above, specially trained men would throw burning torches into the sea (possibly in connection with temple rites). To your left are the cliffs of the **Na Pali Coast** (see below) and the end of your auto trip.

PRINCEVILLE/HANALEI EVENING ENTERTAINMENT

Although most clubs levy no cover charge, that may change if there is a featured artist. And be sure to check local papers and/or call for information before you attend any of these: Performers and times change frequently.

CHARO'S, Haena. Tel. 826-6422.

Fortune is fickle. We're told that the really "in" crowd in Kauai now hangs out at this beautiful restaurant and bar on the beach near the Colony Resort in Haena. Haena is about a 15-minute drive from Hanalei, along many winding roads and narrow, one-vehicle-only bridges, so we suggest a "designated driver" if you're coming out here to eat, drink, and make merry. No cover charge.

HANALEI GOURMET, in the Old Hanalei School Building, Hanalei Center. Tel. 826-2524.

This casual café is always jumping! There's usually entertainment Wednesday through Sunday; easy listening and jazz fusion on Saturday, rock and roll on Friday, contemporary music the other nights. No cover charge.

HAPPY TALK LOUNGE, in the Hanalei Bay Resort at Princeville. Tel. 826-6522.

There's something going on here virtually every night of the week. On Saturday at 6pm, it might be contemporary Hawaiian music by the Kauai Boys. Cousins Tommy Tokioka and Abe Cummings perform contemporary and Hawaiian music on Tuesday, Thursday, and Friday evenings from 6 to 9pm. Jazz buffs have a special treat on Wednesday, Friday, and Sunday from 5:30 to 9pm, when they can hear Michele and Miachaelle performing jazz standards with Richard Simon on acoustic bass; on Sunday afternoon from 3 to 7pm they can bring their own instruments and join in on the liveliest jam session on Kauai! No cover charge.

TAHITI NUI, Hi. 56, Hanalei. Tel. 826-6277.

Tahiti Nui has been the place for local color for many years. Done up with pareau fabric, Tahitian wood carvings on the walls, bamboo, and a thatched ceiling, the atmosphere is super-friendly. There's entertainment in the lounge every night, and on Sunday and Monday you'll hear country-and-western music. But the best entertainment here is impromptu; local entertainers often come in and sing, and owner Auntie Louise Marston, a bubbly Tahitian, can usually be persuaded to sing and do the hula. Louise also serves dinner, with a limited menu ($11–$19) including chicken curry with fresh papaya or pineapple, smoked ribs, or catch of the day, served with rice, bread, and salad. There's a delightful luau on Wednesday and Friday nights; reservations are a must—this show is so popular that people even call from the mainland for reservations!

Admission: Luau, $35 adults, $17.50 children 6–11, free for children under 5.

4. SEEING THE NA PALI COAST

If you'd like to see the spectacularly beautiful Na Pali Coast, southwest of Haena, you have three travel alternatives: by foot, by boat, and by helicopter. For the first, you can get some excellent information in the book called *Hiking Kauai* by Robert Smith, available in local bookstores. Of the many boat trips offered, two are quite special. **Captain Zodiac Raft Expeditions,** P.O. Box 456, Hanalei, Kauai, HI 96714 (tel. 808/826-9371, or toll free 800/422-7824), takes small groups out in boats similar to those used for shooting the rapids on the Colorado River. The trip is usually smooth and gentle, but can be as wet and wild as the Colorado River on occasion; a licensed Coast Guard captain is in command. A full day's expedition costs $105–$115 (depending on season), and includes a landing at a remote beach, a picnic lunch, snorkeling, and a hike back to an ancient Hawaiian fishing village. Morning and afternoon excursions are $75–$85.

If "easy adventure" is more your style, take one of the cruises offered by the **Na Pali Coast Cruise Line,** 4402 Wailo Rd., Kauai, HI 96705 (tel. 804/335-5078). The 130-foot-long *Na Pali Queen* carries about 50–100 people along the Na Pali Coast in comfort and style, provides time for swimming and snorkeling from the aft swimming platform, and serves one meal, either lunch or dinner. Small groups can take off for rafting trips into the sea caves in summer months only. Cost is $95 for a six-hour trip.

Helicopter trips are perhaps the most exciting way of all to see Kauai and to experience the grandeur of its remote and isolated areas. These are not inexpensive (figure roughly $2 a minute), with prices starting around $100 and going up to $200 per person for trips over Waimea Canyon and the Na Pali Coast, into the wilderness areas of Kauai, often swooping down the canyon walls to make stops at pristine beaches. Early-morning and sunset flights can be the most beautiful of all. A number of companies are now offering tours, and competition can be fierce. **Will Squyres** (tel. 245-7541) is a veteran helicopter tour operator with thousands of flying miles under his belt; his tours are highly thought of. **Jack Harter** (tel. 245-3774) was the first of the Kauai helicopter pilots and still rates very highly. **Papillon Helicopters** (tel. 826-6591) is the largest in the state; **Kauai Helicopters** (tel. 245-7403), **Island Helicopters Kauai** (tel. 245-8588), and **South Seas Helicopters** (tel. 245-7781) are all highly reputable. **Ohana Helicopters** (tel. 245-3996), one of the newer companies, is doing a nice job, as are **Bruce Needham Helicopters** (tel. 335-3115) and **Safari Helicopters** (tel. 246-0136). **Air Kauai** (tel. 246-4666) flies right inside the canyons and craters. **Niihau Helicopters** (tel. 335-3500) is the only one with a license to fly over Niihau, the "forbidden island"; its inflight narration concerns that island's history. Photographers are advised to bring plenty of film and a wide-angle lens if possible.

READERS RECOMMEND

Raft Riders *(tel. 828-1166). "Our best excursion in Kauai was a raft ride up the Na Pali coast. We urge readers to go on this excursion with Raft Riders. . . . Raft Riders is owned and operated by Captain Mark. The groups are smaller and Captain Mark gives you really personalized service and will gladly accommodate any request within reason. He charges the same price ($65) as his larger competitors. Open only in summer."*—Sally and Ben Marzouk, Great Neck, N.Y.

Captain Andy's Sunset Cruise *(tel. 822-7833). "Captain Andy's Sunset Cruise was lovely; the cruise lasts two hours, and during the last half hour, you are served pupus and soft drinks as you watch the sun sink. The catamaran holds about 40 passengers, $35 each (children under 12, $25). Our teenagers sat at the very front of the boat and got their faces full of salt water and loved it. Captain Andy also does half-day sails for snorkeling and whale and dolphin watching."*—Mr. and Mrs. Steven Benner, Nevada, Mo.

5. EXCURSION ALONG THE SOUTHERN & WESTERN SHORES

This tour is about as long as the eastern and northern one and requires another full day. Since the high point is Waimea Canyon, you might check with the forest ranger on duty before leaving (tel. 335-5871) to find out if there's fog over the canyon; if so, it might be preferable to save this trip for another day, if you have one. You may want a sweater, for the slightly cooler (but still pleasant) 4,000-foot altitude of the Kokee region. Most of this drive is along Hi. 50.

Starting from Lihue, you'll pass through the town of Puhi and then you'll see a mountain formation called Queen Victoria's Profile on your left. Continue driving until you see Hi. 52 on your left, which leads you through a spectacular arch of towering eucalyptus trees (popularly called the Tree Tunnel) and into the little town of Koloa.

KOLOA

Hawaii's first sugar-plantation town, Koloa was established in 1835 and continued through most of the 19th century as a busy seaport and home to a thriving sugar mill. The old plantation town has been restored, and now **Old Koloa Town** is an attractive collection of shops and restaurants, plus a few historic sites, such as the

Koloa Hotel, a five-room inn built in 1898 for traveling salesmen from Honolulu, and its authentically restored *ofuro,* or Japanese bathhouse. Note the huge monkeypod tree planted in 1925; it stretches halfway across the road.

SHOPPING AT OLD KOLOA TOWN The shops at Old Koloa Town, most of which are open daily from 10am until 9pm, are worth browsing through. Perhaps the most appealing is the **Indo-Pacific Trading Company,** 3432 Poipu Rd. (tel. 742-7655), with an eclectic collection of fine arts and gifts, much of it from Hawaii, mainland Asia, the South Pacific, and the Indonesian Archipelago. Owners Bob and Sutji Gunter make frequent trips to find their treasures; we spotted aboriginal sand paintings from Australia at $88, hand-carved wooden flowers from Bali for just a few dollars, batik pareaus at $30, and great men's shirts from $40. Note the artifacts from Papua New Guinea. At a smaller shop in the complex, called **Nona-Koloa,** they carry jewelry, clothing, batik, and lace, which they've collected from India, Tahiti, and Thailand.

Island Images Fine Arts Prints is an outpost of the distinguished Kahn Gallery at Coconut Marketplace and Anchor Cove. Most prints start around $30, but limited-edition graphic prints and serigraphs by some of Hawaii's leading artists—names like George Sumner, Roy Tabora, and Pegge Hopper—begin at $300. **Ralston Fine Art Gallery** handles originals by Hawaiian artists, such as Dane Clark, Frederick Kenknight, and Christian Riese Lassen.

Looking for a bathing suit? You'll do well at **Swim Inn** or **Snazzy Rags** or **Surf Sports.** We found great black tote bags with Kauai prints for $30 at **Sgt. Leisure Resort Patrol.** And **Tots, Tees, 'N' Toes** dispenses just what you'd expect—things for kids and teenagers, cute hand-screened T-shirts for babies, and plenty of sandals for men and women. Across from the office of Pacific Safari, from which you can book boat tours (see below), is a little shop called **"Pacific Safari presents Ted Andrews, Sculptor."** Andrews's work is exciting and very reasonably priced, from $12 for brass butterflies and $20 for brass kites on teak bases, on up to several hundred dollars for major pieces. About the only place in Old Koloa Town that hasn't been restored to the nines is **Sueoka's,** an old mom-and-pop–type grocery and sundries shop. Lappert's coffee and macadamia nuts are sold at good prices. Just behind and attached to Sueoka's is a snack bar where you can get sandwiches and local-style plate lunches for about $3–$4.

Some of the most enjoyable shopping on Kauai takes place here in Koloa, at the Koloa Ball Park, every Monday at noon—and other days at other island locales. It's called the **Sunshine Market,** similar to the greenmarkets and farmer's markets in other states and cities. Local vegetable and fruit growers truck in their produce fresh from their farms, and so do local flower growers and other vendors: The result is a shopping bonanza for anybody who likes to eat! Come early, because everything is snatched up in about an hour, as prices are incredibly low. Island papayas, bananas, lettuces, tomatoes, sprouts, you-name-it, are sold at a fraction of supermarket prices. There are usually a few trucks selling coconuts; the vendors will husk and crack them for you right there; you can drink the milk and take the rest of the coconut home, or eat it all.

In addition to the Monday at noon market at Koloa Ball Park, there's one on Wednesday at 3pm at the Kapaa Ball Park, on Thursday from 4 to 6pm at the First United Church of Christ in Hanapepe, on Friday at 3pm at the Vidinha Stadium in Lihue, and on Saturday from 10am to noon at the Puu Lani Produce and fruit stand in Kilauea. For more information on Sunshine Markets, call 826-9288.

POIPU

With its glorious dry climate, golden sandy beaches, and breathtakingly beautiful surf, Poipu is one of the choice areas of Kauai. From Koloa, Poipu Road leads you right into the heart of the area.

ATTRACTIONS

Your first stop here might be at a place rich in both Hawaiian history and horticultural splendor, **Moir Gardens at Kiahuna Plantation.** As for the history, it was supposedly on this site that Laka, goddess of the hula and sister of Pele, goddess of the volcanoes, trained her initiates. The gardens are spectacular; many of the monstrous cactus plants look like something out of Middle Earth. There's no charge to walk around the gardens, and there are sometimes tours leaving from the registration desk of the resort. You can walk from here onto the beautiful grounds of the Sheraton Kauai Hotel. To reach the gardens, drive roughly 14 miles from Lihue on Hi. 50; then take Hi. 52 to the Gardens at Kiahuna Plantation.

Poipu Beach, which you'll reach soon after turning left past Plantation Gardens, is one of the best swimming beaches on the island. Youngsters can swim in a shallow little pool; there's rolling surf farther out, and a picnic area and pavilion here, too. But please be warned: It's very, very easy to cut your feet on the rocks and coral here; we've seen it happen innumerable times. Please wear foot coverings to be safe. Another word of advice: Don't spend the *entire* day here, as there's plenty to see coming up ahead.

READERS RECOMMEND

Snorkeling and Shopping at Poipu Beach. *"The best snorkeling we've ever seen—including the Caribbean—was in the little bay directly in front of the Poipu Beach Hotel. The water is a little wavy here, but if you go out in the morning, it is manageable. The fish are absolutely unbelievable. . . . There is a little market of jewelry vendors by the Spouting Horn near Poipu Beach almost every day. We picked up some gorgeous coral and shell necklaces of good quality at three for $5!"*—Susan and Terry Young, Crystal Lake, Ill.

WHALE WATCHING Kauai waters host not only swimmers and surfers and snorkelers, but also hundreds of humpback whales which migrate here every winter (December through March) from Alaskan and Arctic waters, seeking warm climes in which to mate and breed. How do you get to see these nonpaying guests? Easy! You take one of the whale-watching cruises that have become so popular in Kauai and Maui in recent years. One of the best is run by **Pacific Safari,** which takes no more than 26 passengers at a time aboard their ocean-certified 36-foot yacht with glass panels providing panoramic views of the underwater world. The two-hour whale-sighting cruise costs $42 per person. Underwater hydrophones are linked to a 10-speaker stereo sound system, so it's quite possible that you'll get to hear the whales singing! Bring those cameras, of course, plus comfortable clothes, and motion-sickness preventives for those who may need them. The same company also offers a Sunset Safari, Appetizer Cruise, a Snorkel Safari, a Jungle River Safari, and more. Most cruises depart from Kukuiula Harbor in this area. Pacific Safari's reservation office is in Old Koloa Town, or you may call them at 742-7033.

SHOPPING If you're not surfeited by shopping yet, by all means, drive in to see the **Kiahuna Shopping Village** (right off Poipu Road, opposite Kiahuna Plantation), a tasteful selection of island stores, none of them cheap, but all high in quality. Children from a local hula halau are featured performers in a free show presented here on Thursday at 5:30pm. This shopping center is open Monday through Saturday from 9am to 9pm and on Sunday from 9am to 6pm.

One of our favorite shops here is **Tideline Gallery.** They have the largest collection of volcanic-glass jewelry on Kauai; handsome earrings start at $22, and necklaces go for $22–$115. Note, too, their Hawaiian koa-wood jewelry, done by a local Hawaiian family, from $18 for koa earrings to $198 for a seven-strand necklace. Batik paintings, marine sculptures, and rare coral jewelry are all special here.

Elephant Walk has kaleidoscopes, African wood musical instruments, hand-painted clothing, exquisite koa-wood furniture by Martin and MacArthur. We love the Made in Paradise Magic Island Girls—hula dancer dolls at $39. Note the line of jewelry made of niobium, a rare metal of intense hues, by Holly Yash. Earrings, bracelets, necklaces, go for $16–$195. For a modestly priced gift, get a shirt holder shell for just $8. Fine art by such painters as Hisashi Otsuka, Caroline Young, and Anthony Casay complement a collection of marine antiquities and artifacts at the **Ship Store Gallery.** And don't miss Beryl Cook's whimsical works at **Paradise Posters & Prints.** A dozen local artists are responsible for all the hand-painted lovelies at **South Pacific Collection**—dresses, jackets, T-shirts, accessories, jewelry—even hand-painted shoes. Great tote bags go for $43. **Skids** is a shop featuring classy sandals for every season. You'll find those Hawaiian golf thongs here, as well as Aqua Socks at $35—essential for walking on sharp coral reefs. They also have hand-painted shirts, nice totes, and tops. **Tropical Shirts** has just that—myriad original silk-screened T-shirts, some with tropical flowers. Most are hand-screened and embroidered on Kauai.

Feeling hungry? **Keoki's Paradise,** one of our favorite Kauai restaurants, is right here; so is **Pizza Bella,** for a light Italian meal, and **Paradise Hot Dogs** (see "Where to Eat" in Chapter 10). You can also satisfy the hungries with frozen yogurt from **Zack's** or a delicious scoop of ice cream from **Shipwreck Ice Cream.**

Koloa Gallery is a pint-sized shop at the Beach House Restaurant, 5022 Spouting Horn Rd., where one could literally spend hours browsing and admiring the treasures therein. There are Niihau-shell baubles galore, some beautiful jade and lapis pieces, and whimsical wooden painted jewelry. We fell in love with a sterling-silver gecko pendant, done in paintstaking detail right down to each tiny toe, at $39. All this plus essentials like postcards and greeting cards, too.

EVENING ENTERTAINMENT

This side of Kauai is perhaps a bit quieter after the sun sets—but there's still plenty going on.

POIPU BEACH HOTEL, 2249 Poipu Rd. Tel. 742-1681.

Undoubtedly the liveliest place in the area. The Poipu Beach Café offers dancing and entertainment nightly—and that might include reggae, rock, or contemporary music. Sporting events are shown on the big-screen TV.

Admission: Cover varies with artists, up to $3.

STOUFFER WAIOHAI BEACH RESORT, 2249 Poipu Rd. Tel. 742-9511.

Right on the oceanfront, the Terrace Bar here is one of the most romantic spots in Kauai. Live Hawaiian entertainment, featuring different artists, is presented every night, from 7:30 to 10pm, and there's room for dancing. There's also room for a nighttime walk on the beach. Have a drink at the bar, enjoy the view, and perhaps decide to come back here for a meal the next night (their salad bar is one of the best around and their Sunday champagne brunch is renowned far and wide). No cover charge.

SHERATON KAUAI, 2440 Hoonani Rd. Tel. 742-1661.

There's entertainment nightly at the Drum Lounge overlooking the ocean, and dancing to groups like the Top-40 Seattle Band. If you're in Kauai on a Wednesday, you'll enjoy the Sheraton's "Legends of Polynesia" show, featuring all the traditional hoopla, including an amazing fire dance. Cocktails start at 6pm, dinner at 6:45, the show at 8pm. Reservations required.

Admission: No cover charge at the Drum Lounge; luau, $42 adults, $24 children.

PLANTATION GARDENS RESTAURANT, at Kiahuna Plantation. Tel. 742-1695.

The setting for drinks is pure tropical magic in this restaurant, once the gracious home of a plantation manager. No cover charge.

CANTINA FLAMINGO, 2301 Nalo Rd. Tel. 742-9505.

Don't forget to drop by the Flamingo Cantina around the Mexican Munchie hour, 3:30 to 5pm, when the nachos are free. No cover charge.

BRENNECKE'S BEACH BROILER, 2100 Hoone Rd. Tel. 742-7588.

There's always a lively group hanging out in the bar/lounge of this restaurant. No cover charge.

SAMPAN HARBOR, LAWAI & KALAHEO

Trace your way back now to the fork in the road and this time take the other branch, the one on the right. Continuing past Kuhio Park (on the site of the birthplace of Prince Kuhio), you come to Kukuiula Small Boat Harbor, more familiarly known as **Sampan Harbor.** Be sure to walk out on the wharf for an absolutely gorgeous view; about a mile ahead to the right is **Spouting Horn,** where the water spurts up through several holes in the lava rock, and to your left the blue-green Pacific crashes upon the black rocks. When you can tear yourself away, have a look at the vendors selling jewelry outside the parking lot; quality is high and the prices are consistently among the lowest in the islands. A great place to take care of a lot of gift shopping.

Which eelskin wholesale house is the most wholesale? Hard to say, because such outfits abound in the islands (especially in Honolulu). Certainly, one of the biggest and best is **Lee Sand's Wholesale Eelskin Warehouse** at the Hawaiian Trading Post, which you can find right outside Lawai, on Koloa Road, where Hi. 50 meets Hi. 530. Sands, who claims to be the original importer of eelskin from Asia, sells to major eelskin distributors throughout the country and to such prestigious stores as Bloomingdale's in New York, where you can be certain the prices are much higher than what you find here. We saw lovely handbags from about $60. It is said that eelskin is 150% stronger than leather and becomes softer and more supple with use. (It's the kind of bag you just can't wear out.) As if eelskin weren't exotic enough, this warehouse also sells accessories made of lizard, sea snake (snakeskin sneakers were $67), and (ugh!) chicken feet. Novelty items like wooden postcards and jewelry are also sold here.

Just outside Lee Sand's is a cute little hut called **Mustard's Last Stand,** where you're free to add not only mustard, but also guacamole, sauerkraut, salsa, chili, fresh mushrooms, and three kinds of cheese to any hot dogs, sausages, or hamburgers you buy there. They also have Lappert's ice cream. If you've got the kids in tow, they may want to take time out from touring for a game of miniature golf at **Geckoland,** a course with a Kauai theme. Open daily from 9am to 7pm.

You'll have to make reservations and pay $15 to tour the **National Tropical Botanical Garden** in Lawai, but nature lovers and photographers will find it eminently worthwhile. The 186-acre garden adjoins 100 acres of Allerton Gardens, a private estate. Tours lasting 2½–3 hours covering the National Tropical Botanical Garden and the entire Allerton Estate are given daily at 9am and 1pm. To reserve an escorted tour, which is limited to 12 people, and for driving directions, phone the visitor center (tel. 332-7361) or write to Reservations Secretary, P.O. Box 340, Lawai, Kauai, HI 96765. Whether or not you take a tour, you might want to stop by the Museum and Gift Shop, with its living botanical displays, walking tour of the visitor-center plants, and native Hawaiian and tropical plants, open daily from 7:30am to 4pm. Tea and coffee are always available at the gift shop.

Just outside Kalaheo, watch for enchanting **Kukui-O-Lono Park.** The entrance is through a majestic stone gate, just south of Kalaheo. The name means light of the god Lono; at one time kukui-oil torches here provided a beacon for fishermen at sea. Now the place is a public nine-hole golf course (greens fees are very reasonable) and a small park, where you can see a Stone Age Hawaiian exhibit and a charming Japanese garden. There are birds everywhere.

READERS RECOMMEND

Olu Pua Gardens. *"We stopped to visit the very beautiful Olu Pua Gardens, a botanical showplace in Kalaheo. But there's more here than just magnificent plants, trees, and flowers: The guesthouse served as a stopping-off place for U.S. presidents and dignitaries en route to and from the Far Pacific. The drafts for the peace treaty ending the war with Japan were crafted there before being carried on to Tokyo. The charming guide told us that Olu Pua is now up for sale, and they are hoping someone interested in preserving the grounds as is will buy it. Up to now it's not on any historical preservation list, but it certainly should be."*—Helen Schwarz Robbins, Little Rock, Ark. [*Author's Note:* Olu Pua is open Monday through Friday for guided tours only, at 9:30 and 11:30am and 1:30pm. It's located just past the town of Kalaheo, en route to Waimea Canyon.]

HANAPEPE

Another of the wondrous scenic views of Hawaii awaits you as you approach the town of Hanapepe. Stop at the overlook for a glorious vista of **Hanapepe Valley** below, where rice shoots, guava trees, and taro patches cover the fertile floor. Waimea Canyon is off in the distance to the left. Hanapepe, where you ought to stop for lunch at the **Green Garden** (see "Where to Eat" in Chapter 10), is quaint, with old wooden, balconied Chinese shops and an air not unlike that of an Old West town. Just past the Green Garden is a shrine, hallowed among those devoted to great ice cream. This is the factory-outlet store for **Lappert's Ice Cream.** Lappert's has created a bit of a sensation since it was introduced in Kauai a few years ago by Walter Lappert, who hails from Austria. It's found in all the best restaurants, and its flavors—passion fruit, mango, coconut–macadamia-nut fudge, Kauai Pie, fresh-fruit sherbet, praline, pecan 'n' cream, and Kona coffee, just to hint at the possibilities—are without peer. Sugar-free and fat-free flavors are also available. There are two reasons for getting your ice cream here: One, they have the best selection of flavors on the island; and two, since this is the factory outlet, they always have a scoop-of-the-day special for just 75¢ (as opposed to their regular price of $1.95 for a single scoop, $2.95 for a double). Even those who normally don't care much about ice cream become converts after the first swallow.

Art gallery, bookshop, coffee shop, gift shop—the **Hanapepe Bookstore and Espresso Bar,** at 3830 Hanapepe Rd., is all these, as well as one of the most imaginative shops on Kauai. It started life long ago as a drugstore, and the counter from that store is now the coffee bar, where you can sip the best espresso on the island, as well as feast on the likes of multigrain waffles (before 11am), vegetable pot pies, tofu veggie burgers, fresh-baked croissants, prune tea cake, scones, espresso muffins, and the Death by Chocolate cake, whose name speaks for itself. There's a fine collection of Hawaiian reading material for such a small shop: plenty of Kristin Zambucka and Herb Kane, Hawaiian stories for children, many books on Hawaiian crafts and language. Locally made gift items include Hawaiian potpourri, carved wooden candelabra, silver and wooden jewelry, and pillow covers and bib aprons made in the patterns of Hawaiian quilts. There's also a super selection of greeting cards, including most of the magnificent Kim Taylor Reece photographic cards. New Age–type background music sets the mood for browsing.

Just past Hanapepe, turn left at the HANAPEPE REFUSE TRANSFER STATION sign. Go three-tenths of a mile and turn right at the HVB marker, and you'll find yourself at **Salt Pond.** It looks like a marsh dotted with strange covered walls, and it's here that salt is mined and dried (some of the drying beds in operation date back to the 17th century) as the Hawaiians have been doing it for centuries. You may be lucky and arrive while they are working; members of a local *hui* collect the crystals during the summer months. Then you can head for **Salt Pond Pavilion,** a great swimming and picnicking beach, with safe, calm water. This beach is a good place to recoup your strength for the next big series of sensations coming up at Waimea Canyon.

WAIMEA

But first you arrive at the town of Waimea, which, like Wailua, is steeped in history. A favorite deep-water harbor in the olden days, it was the center of government before the coming of whites, and the place where Captain Cook decided to come ashore in 1778. Whalers and trading ships put in here for provisions on their long voyages in the Pacific. It was also here that the first missionaries landed on Kauai, in 1820. And it was on this site that an employee of the Russian Fur Company, Dr. Anton Scheffer, built a fort and equipped himself with a Hawaiian retinue, promising Chief Kaumuali help in defeating Kamehameha. The latter got wind of the scheme and gave Kaumuali orders to get his foreign ally out of Hawaii—which he did, pronto. But the **ruins of the old fort,** a stone wall mostly hidden by weeds, are still here; an HVB marker points the way on your left, before you come to the Waimea River. The fort may one day be restored—already rest rooms and parking facilities have been built, and some of the old stonework is now visible. Until then, however, there's not much else to see here; the interest is mostly historical.

After you've passed the **Captain Cook Monument** and just before the police station, look for the turnoff to the **Menehune Ditch.** Follow the river about 1¼ miles, past some Japanese shops, a Buddhist temple, taro patches, rice paddies, and tiny houses; when you come to a narrow bridge swinging across the river, stop and look for a stone wall protruding above the road for a few feet on the left side. This is all that remains visible of the Menehune Ditch, a remarkable engineering accomplishment that brought water to the neighboring fields several miles down from the mountain. The curious stonecutting here has convinced anthropologists that some pre-Polynesian race created the aqueduct. Who else but the Menehunes? It is said that they did the whole thing in one night and were rewarded by the pleased citizens of Waimea with a fantastic feast of shrimp, their favorite food. They later made so much noise celebrating that they woke the birds on Oahu, 100 miles away. While you're busy creating some legends of your own, you might see some Hawaiian Huck Finns, placidly floating down the river on rafts made of logs tied together, little bothered by either Menehunes or tourists.

The main highway now continues beyond **Kekaha** to the arid countryside around **Mana,** and beyond that to some enormous sand dunes known as the **Barking Sands.** The Kauaians swear they say "woof" when you slide down them, but that's pretty hard to prove. The U.S. Navy has now closed the area, so take the shorter drive to the canyon; you turn off the highway just past Waimea to Hi. 550. (A possible side trip at this point could be to **Polihale State Park;** just continue on Hi. 50, past Mana. Polihale Beach is surely one of the most spectacular beaches in Hawaii, with awesome cliffs and sparkling white sand, but swimming here is treacherous. For sunbathing, walking, and a picnic, though, it's fine.)

WAIMEA CANYON

Now the road starts going up, through forests of eucalyptus, silver oak, and koa; soon you'll see the white ohia trees with their red blossoms of lehua (you'll see lehua again when you visit Volcanoes National Park in Hawaii). On you go, to the first lookout, Waimea Canyon Lookout. Park your car and prepare yourself for one of the most spectacular views in all Hawaii. You're standing now at the top of a 3,657-foot gorge, about a mile wide and 10 miles long. Millions of years ago this was the scene of a tremendous geologic fault, a great crack in the dome of the island; erosion, streams, and ocean waves cut the cliffs into jagged shapes whose colors change with the sun and the clouds—blue and green in the morning, melting into vermilion, copper, and gold as the sun moves across it and finally sets. The gorge is comparable to, though smaller than, the Grand Canyon, and sometimes outdoes it in colorfulness.

Now the road continues another eight miles, and you're at **Kokee State Park,** very different from anything else you've seen on Kauai. You're in the midst of bracing mountain country now, with wonderful hiking trails, freshwater streams for trout fishing (rainbow-trout season is each August and September) and swimming, wild fruit to pick in season, and wild pigs and goats to hunt. The forest ranger here will give you details on trails. You can relax for a few minutes at the **Kokee Museum,** right next to the **Kokee Lodge Restaurant** and **Kokee Cabins** (see Chapter 10), where you could spend a long, blissful holiday.

From here, it's just four miles for a spectacular climax to this trip, the view from the **Kalalau Lookout.** Driving the winding road for these last few miles, you will pass the Kokee tracking station, now world famous for its part in the success of the *Apollo II* mission to the moon. It was from this site that a laser beam was flashed to reflectors that Neil Armstrong had set up on the lunar surface. At Kalalau, the thick tropical forest suddenly drops 4,000 feet down to the breathtakingly blue sea beyond, where it melts imperceptibly into the horizon. Below, on the knifelike ridges, are the remnants of irrigation ditches, tar patches, and signs of careful cultivation that have been long since abandoned to the elements. Read Jack London's story, "Koolau the Leper" (in *A Hawaiian Reader*), for a fictional rendering of the indomitable Koolau, who hid in the ridges here and single-handedly held off the Hawaii National Guard in its attempt to get him to the leper colony at Molokai. His heroic wife crossed the dizzyingly narrow ridges hundreds of times in five years to bring food to her husband and son until they both died of the fearful disease and left her to return to her people alone.

This marks the end of your trip. Depending on whether you want an early or late view of Waimea Canyon, you might schedule some of the other sights for the return trip. Another possibility is to drive directly to the canyon in the morning, to avoid having your views obstructed by clouds, which sometimes form in the afternoon. Then plan your other events—perhaps lunch at the Green Garden, a swim at Poipu Beach—for the return trip in the afternoon.

CHAPTER 12

THE BIG ISLAND

Ever hear of a tropical island with black beaches, snowcapped mountains, cedar forests, and one of the largest cattle ranches in the world? This is Hawaii, the orchid capital of America, about 200 miles southeast of Honolulu and twice as large as all the other Hawaiian Islands combined (4,030 square miles). Hawaii is also the residence of Pele, the ancient goddess of volcanoes, who stages some spectacular eruptions every couple of years. Islanders most often refer to Hawaii as the Big Island, but it's also called the Orchid Island or the Volcano Island; all the names are appropriate, and all reflect the fascination many have with this astonishing continent in miniature. To know the 50th state, you must know the island of Hawaii.

You'll know why this is called the Orchid Island as soon as you arrive at Hilo's General Lyman Field. Rain may be helping those orchids to grow, but don't despair, it's just a "Hawaiian blessing" and it probably won't last long. Nobody in Hilo lets a little drizzle interfere with life. (In winter an occasional rainstorm will hit this part of the island harder than any other.)

Hilo, the only real city on the island and the second largest in the state, is the takeoff point for the imposing Hawaii Volcanoes National Park and the lava-scarred Puna area. Located on the east coast, Hilo has been experiencing a slump of late, but it still has its own gentle charm.

Most residents of Hilo are convinced that this is the world's greatest little city, and they wouldn't consider living anywhere else. The fact that they live between the devil and the deep-blue sea bothers them not a bit. Huge mountains dominate the skyline: Mauna Kea is an extinct volcano, but Mauna Loa is still very much alive.

If you've read James Michener's *Hawaii,* you'll remember that the Alii Nui Noelani went to Hilo in 1832 to confront Pele and implore her to halt the fiery lava that came close to destroying the town. Pele has toyed with the idea more than a few times since, as recently as 1935, 1942, and 1984, but she has always spared the city—even without the intervention of priestesses. The citizens are convinced she always will.

The citizens are just as nonchalant about tidal waves—at least they were until 1960. On the May morning when seismic waves hurtled across the Pacific headed for Hawaii, the citizens of Hilo had mere hours to evacuate; instead, some of them actually went down to the bridge to watch the show. This time the gods were not so kind. Sixty-one people were swept into the waves, and a big chunk of waterfront area was wiped out. For several years after, one could see the devastation along the ocean side of Kamehameha Avenue; now there is grass and palm trees. Past Pauahi Street, however, look to your right and see the surprisingly modern architecture of the county and state office buildings. Despite much opposition, they were built to inspire confidence in the devastated bayside area, and so far there hasn't been further tsunami activity.

WHAT'S SPECIAL ABOUT THE BIG ISLAND

Natural Wonders

- ☐ Active volcanoes, especially Kilauea in Hawaii Volcanoes National Park, which has been spewing red-hot lava for the last nine years.
- ☐ Mauna Kea, one of the world's great volcanoes, rising 13,796 feet above sea level.
- ☐ Rainbow Falls in Hilo, where rainbows form in the morning mist.

Sports and Recreation

- ☐ Hiking a diversity of trails, ranging from fern forests to black sand beaches, over lava fields, through desert scrubs, and along dramatic coastlines.
- ☐ Scuba diving and snorkeling on the Kona Coast with its fascinating natural rock and coral formations.

Museums

- ☐ Lyman House Memorial Museum Complex in Hilo, especially for a look at how the missionaries lived; many cultural and natural history exhibits as well.
- ☐ Puuopelu, a historic home at Parker Ranch in Waimea, with a superb collection of impressionist works.
- ☐ Kamuela Museum, in Waimea, a small museum full of curiosities including ancient and royal Hawaiian artifacts.
- ☐ Hulihee Palace, in Kailua-Kona, museum of Hawaiiana, once a vacation home for Hawaiian royalty.

Beaches

- ☐ The black sand beach at Punalu'u, on the southern coast.
- ☐ Hapuna Beach and Samuel Spencer Beach Park, on the west coast, fine for swimming.

Arts and Crafts

- ☐ Volcano Art Center, at Hawaii Volcanoes National Park, for superb work by Big Island artists.
- ☐ Galleries islandwide, especially at Holualoa, above Kailua-Kona, an artists' colony.

Historic Sites

- ☐ Pu'uhonua o Honaunau National Historical Park, the remains, partially restored, of a place of sanctuary built over 400 years ago.
- ☐ Petrogylphs along the Kohala coasts—stick figures drawn by the ancient Hawaiians.

This knowledge impresses itself strongly on the mind of the visitor, making Hilo far more than a make-believe world for tourists. It forms a curious backdrop to the beauty and gentleness of this city arching around a crescent bay (Hilo's name means new moon). Once a whaling port of the Pacific, Hilo is still a seaport, from which raw sugar (note the bulk-sugar plant on the waterfront) and cattle are shipped to the other islands and the mainland. Flowers are big business, too; 132 inches of rainfall a year (most of it at night—but there are plenty of misty mornings, too) make the orchids and anthuriums grow like crabgrass on a suburban lawn. Nearly a quarter of a million tropical blossoms are sent from Hilo all over the world.

The **Kona Coast,** in the west, is to the Big Island what Waikiki is to Oahu: the resort area. The little town of Kailua-Kona is the tourist center. Unlike Waikiki, though, it still has a small-town charm. Once the playground of the Hawaiian alii, Kona lures deep-sea fishermen (its marlin grounds are the best in the Pacific), families, and anyone looking for relaxed, tropical beauty.

SEEING THE ISLAND ON A BUDGET

Like all the neighbor islands, the Big Island is more expensive for the budget tourist than Oahu; nevertheless, you should be able to stay fairly close to your $75-a-day budget. Your car rental—unless it's split up three or four ways—is your biggest expense here, for driving distances are great, especially from one side of the island to the other (about 100 miles).

The island is large enough to have two airports, one on the east coast outside the small city of Hilo, the other at Kailua-Kona on the west coast. Which city should you choose as your first stop? We've done it both ways, and our considered opinion is that it doesn't make a particle of difference. Let your itinerary and the airline schedules—the ease with which you can make connections to the next island on your agenda—be the determining factor.

From either Hilo or Kailua-Kona, you can drive the 100 miles across the island and see all the sights. We prefer to visit each side of the island separately, but you can make one side your base if you don't mind long drives. (Please limit your driving to daytime hours for safety!) Read up on the sights, hotels, restaurants, and nightlife in each area, and you'll know just where you want to stay and for how long.

1. GETTING THERE & GETTING AROUND

GETTING THERE

BY PLANE Both Hawaiian and Aloha Airlines will take you from Honolulu to Hilo on the east or to Kailua-Kona on the west in roughly half an hour. You can also fly directly to or from Kona from the West Coast. Pick up your car at **General Lyman Field** in Hilo or at **Keahole Airport** in Kona, or take a cab, as there is no public transportation to take you to your hotel in either area. At Keahole, you can save money over regular cab fares by calling SpeediShuttle, which can take you from the airport to Kailua-Kona town, for example, for only $7, while a taxi would cost $16–$18, plus baggage charge. There are courtesy phones located at the Aloha and Hawaiian baggage-claim areas, or phone 329-5433 in advance. They offer transportation to any location on the Big Island, as well as economical guided tours.

GETTING AROUND

BY BUS Within both the Hilo and Kona areas, **Dial-A-Ride Transportation Service** is available weekdays from 7am to 3pm. This service, which includes accommodations for disabled and nonambulatory persons, provides "curb to curb" transportation service other than the fixed route and schedule service; it must be requested one day in advance. For information and reservations, call 961-3148 in Hilo, 323-2085 in Kona.

The **Mass Transportation Agency (MTA)** provides islandwide public transportation bus service with buses operating Monday through Saturday, and fares ranging from 75¢ to $6 per ride. Bus routes connect Hilo with Kailua-Kona, Waimea, Honokaa, Pahoa, and Hawaii Volcanoes National Park, among others. Call MTA at 935-8241. Bus schedules are sometimes available at the **State Visitor Information**

booths in the airport, and usually at the **Hawaii Visitors Bureau** in the Hilo Plaza Building, 180 Kinoole St., Suite 105, (tel. 961-5797). Mrs. Lei Branco is the helpful woman to contact.

In Hilo For all practical purposes, you're going to need a car in Hilo, even though there is a city bus system. It's limited; however, the **Hele-On** bus does make two trips a day around town, one early in the morning, one in midafternoon. You can ask for the bus schedule at your hotel or call the MTA (tel. 935-8241).

For a charming ride back into Hilo's past, you can hop aboard a **Sampan Bus.** These nostalgic old vehicles, recently revived, operate every half hour between 8am and 6pm Monday through Friday, and can be boarded at the Hilo Lagoon Center, the Hilo Hawaiian Hotel, Long's Drugs, J. C. Penney, and the Lyman House Museum, among other stops, at a cost of 50¢. Check at your hotel desk or the HVB for a complete list of stops.

BY RENTAL CAR Most agencies on the Big Island offer a flat rate with unlimited mileage—you buy the gas. You have your choice of the trusty and popular inter-island outfits like **Alamo, Avis, Dollar,** and **Budget,** whose main offices are all in Honolulu (see "Getting Around," in Chapter 4, for details), or local agencies like **Sunshine of Hawaii Rent-A-Car Systems** (tel. 935-1108 in Hilo or 329-2926 in Kona, or toll free 800/367-2977), which offers two-door automatic compacts with air conditioning at $22.95 daily, four-door automatic compacts with air conditioning for $28.95. Rates are slightly lower in summer. Advance reservations are a good idea at any time and a must in peak seasons; other times, you may be able to get your best deal by careful on-the-spot shopping.

One of your biggest expenses if you're driving from Hilo to Kona or vice versa will be the drop off charge; it's usually a hefty $45 from Hilo to Kona or $30 from Kona to Hilo. The cheapest way to avoid it is to take the county bus which crosses the island for a cost of $6 (see details, above), then rent a car in Kona if necessary. The only drawback is that you will miss the sightseeing en route.

READERS RECOMMEND

Car Rentals. *"Your advice was to call around. We did, and found that Avis had the best rates for one week on a special. We originally were to have a Geo Metro, unlimited mileage for one week, at a $99 rate! When we went to pick up our car, we had a coupon for an upgrade: Avis was out of the upgrade for a Geo Metro, so we poor souls ended up with a double upgrade: an Oldsmobile 98! The service was excellent, and the car was in tip-top condition. The price was right. Call around!"*—Catherine and Mike Praisewater, Albuquerque, N.M.

FAST FACTS THE BIG ISLAND

Area Code The telephone area code is 808.

Babysitters Inquire at your hotel desk.

Car Rentals See "Getting Around," above.

Climate See "When to Go," in Chapter 2.

Dentists Contact Hilo Dental Associates, 475 Kinoole St., Hilo (tel. 935-1149); Dr. Frank Sayre/Dr. Daniel Walker, Frame 10 Center, Kailua-Kona (tel. 329-8067/8180); or Dr. Craig Kimura, Kamuela Office Center (tel. 885-3300).

Doctors Contact the Hilo Medical Group, 1292 Waianuenue Ave., Hilo (tel. 961-6631); Kaiser Permanente, 75-184 Hualalalai Rd., Kona (tel. 329-3866); or Waimea Medical Associates, Kamuela (tel. 885-7351).

Emergencies Ambulance, fire, and rescue 961-6022.

Holidays See "When to Go," in Chapter 2.

Hospitals Major facilities are Hilo Hospital, 1190 Waianuenue Ave. (tel. 969-4111), and Kona Hospital, Keealekekua (tel. 329-9111).

Libraries Branches include the Hilo Public Library (tel. 935-5407), the Kona Public Library (tel. 329-2196), and the Kamuela Public Library (tel. 885-4651).

Other Useful Numbers To learn about services for the disabled, call the Commission on Persons with Disabilities (tel. 933-4747). Big Island Crisis & Help Line in Hilo (tel. 969-9111) and Kona (tel. 329-9111), and Sexual Assault Crisis Line (tel. 935-0677), can assist you. On Call (tel. 935-1666), a 24-hour free service available from any pushbutton phone, offers the latest news, sports, local and worldwide weather, community services, horoscopes, soap-opera updates, and more. Complete listings are given in the Aloha Pages of the Hawaii (Big Island) telephone book.

Photographic Needs Long's Drug Store, with branches at 555 Kilauea Ave., Hilo (tel. 935-6474), and 75-5595 Palani Rd., Kailua-Kona (tel. 329-8477), carries camera supplies.

Police In Hilo, call 935-3311; in Kona, 329-3311; in Kamuela, 885-7334.

Poison Control Center Call toll free 800/362-3585.

Post Office: In Hilo, the Post Office is at 1299 Kekuanaoa Ave. (tel. 935-2821); in Kona, there is a branch at 74-5577 Palani Rd. (tel. 329-1927); in Kamuela, the Post Office is on Lindsey Rd., off Hi. 19 (tel. 885-4026).

Safety Exercise the same precautions you would elsewhere: Never leave valuables in your car, even in the trunk; leave personal valuables in hotel safes or in-room safes; don't flash cash conspicuously in public.

Taxis Call A-1 Bob's Taxi in Hilo (tel. 959-4800), or Kona Airport Taxi (tel. 329-7779).

Weather Information For conditions on Hilo, call 935-8555; on the Big Island, 961-5582. For marine forecasts, call 935-9883.

2. WHERE TO STAY

The Big Island is rich in **bed-and-breakfast** accommodations, and more are cropping up all the time. We'll tell you about many of these as we cover specific locations, but first you should know about ✪ **Hawaii's Best Bed & Breakfasts,** run by Barbara Campbell, who was formerly director of sales and marketing at the prestigious Kona Village Resort. Barbara's standards are uncompromising: She handles only upscale B&B lodgings, each home selected for its distinctive personality, attention to details, and the warm hospitality of its hosts. Selections range from the most traditional host-home rooms to splendid private country cottages, some on the grounds of fabulous estates. Her service covers all the major islands. Daily rates run \$65–\$150 double, and weekly rates are available at some properties. Call or write for a brochure describing these hidden gems. P.O. Box 563, Kamuela, HI 96743 (tel. 808/885-4550, or toll free 800/262-9912 for reservations).

Then there's **My Island,** P.O. Box 100, Volcano, HI 96785, created by Gordon Morse and his wife, Joann: they offer rentals in 28 houses, plus an all-island reservation system. Call the Morses (the whole family is in the business) on their hotline—808/967-7110 or 808/967-7216—any time between 6am and 10pm Hawaiian time (fax 808/967-7110). They urge people to move around the Big Island, experiencing the different climates and atmospheres of the various districts, from Hilo to Puna to Volcano, from Kailua to Waimea to Honokaa, and then some. Accommodations range from "nice mom-and-pop houses" to a splendid plantation-manager's estate with a pool and solarium set amid acres of jungle. Prices range from $30 to $45 single, $45 to $85 double, depending on location and what Morse calls "the jazziness of the place."

Volcano Reservations, P.O. Box 998, Volcano Village, HI 96785 (tel. 808/967-7786, or toll free 800/937-7786), is run by Brian and Lisha Crawford, whose charming Chalet Kilauea at Volcano is listed below. They have accommodations all over the island, ranging from budget to luxury, including B&Bs, vacation homes, cottages, and condos, in a wide price range.

Bed & Breakfast Hawaii, P.O. Box 449, Kapaa, Kauai, HI 96746 (tel. 808/822-7771, or toll free 800/733-1632; fax 808/822-2723), is an all-island reservation system. Rates start at $45 single, $50 double. Send them $10 for a copy of their directory of homes and apartments called *B&B Goes Hawaiian.*

HILO

DOUBLES FOR $36 TO $45

ARNOTT'S LODGE, 98 Apapane Rd., Hilo, HI 96720. Tel. 808/969-7097. Fax 808/961-9638. 30 bunk beds in 10 dormitory rooms, 11 rms, 5 suites.

$ Rates: $15 bunk; $26 single; $36 double; $80 two-bedroom suite for up to five people. Each additional person $5. Seventh day free on weekly rate paid in advance. No credit cards. **Parking:** Free.

Ⓢ Here's your best budget buy in Hilo. Popular with everyone from European student backpackers to families and small groups, Arnott's Lodge is a converted three-story apartment building nestled in a lush tropical area, just a few minutes' walk to ocean beach parks and a short drive to the center of Hilo. Some of the rooms are hostel style with shared baths, but there are also singles, doubles, and suites. The suites are especially good for families or small groups; they have a living room with convertible sofa, two bedrooms (one with a double bed, one with a single), a kitchen with a small refrigerator, and a private bath. All rooms have ceiling fans. Everything at Arnott's is simple, clean, casual—and very cozy. A resident manager is on hand to help plan activities and assist with bicycle rentals. The Guest Pavilion is available 24 hours a day for "eating and drinking, partying, relaxing, gathering, late-night conversation." Simple cooking facilities are available, and you can also pick up a $3.50 spaghetti dinner here every night. There's a TV lounge and laundry facilities.

HILO HOTEL, 142 Kinoole St., Hilo, HI 96720. Tel. 808/961-3733. Fax 808/935-7836. 21 rms, 6 apts. A/C TV TEL

$ Rates (including continental breakfast): $39–$45 single or double; $115 two-bedroom apt. Room-and-car package, $62–$68 single or double; $142 apt. AE, DC, MC, V. **Parking:** Free.

Worlds away from the pleasantly hokey tourist world of Banyan Drive is the Hilo Hotel, a businessperson's hotel in the center of town. The outside is very pleasant, with lava-rock walls, a large swimming pool, spacious gardens, and the excellent Fuji Restaurant for Japanese food and drinks, where the locals like to gather. The hotel rooms are clean and adequate, and each one has a refrigerator. The higher-priced rooms also include a TV. Complimentary continental breakfast is served every morning from 7 to 10am. The hotel is very proud of its newer Niolopa Wing, which offers extraordinary value for a family; there are six very large (800–900 sq. ft.) two-bedroom apartments, fully furnished, equipped with TV, all the utilities, and three telephones per unit, for up to four guests.

HILO ACCOMMODATIONS & DINING

Hilo Bay
Amauulu Rd.
Wailuku River
Kaiulani St.
Wainaku
Wailuku
Keawe St.
Mamo
Bayfront Hwy.
Kamehameha
Waianuenue
Laimana
Haili St.
Alae
Alamuku
Punahele
Amakihi
Ponahawai St.
Komohana
Kapiolani St.
Ululani St.
Kinoole St.
Hualalai
Wailoa
Kilauea Ave.
Aala
Pauahi
Apuni
Lanihuli
Mohouli St.
Kohola
Banyan Dr.
Kalanianaole Ave.
Hilo International Airport
Waiakea Sq.
Kanoelehua Ave.
Kalanikoa
Piilani St.
Hualani St.
Mililani St.
Manono St.
Hinano St.
Laukapu St.
Kekuanaoa St.
To Volcanoes National Park

ACCOMMODATIONS:
- Arnott's Lodge 9
- Dolphin Bay Hotel 1
- Hale Kai-Bjornen Bed & Breakfast 2
- Hilo Hotel 3
- Hilo Seaside Hotel 4
- Maureen's Bed & Breakfast 5
- Our Place-Papaikou's B & B 6
- Uncle Billy's Hilo Bay Hotel 7
- Waiakea Villas Hotel 8
- Wild Ginger Inn 10

DINING:
- Bears' Coffee 1
- Cafe 100 2
- Dick's Coffee House 3
- Dohies 22
- Don's Grill 4
- Fiascos 5
- Harrington's 6
- Hukilau Restaurant 7
- Jimmy's Drive Inn 8
- Karrot's Kitchen 11
- K.K. Tei Restaurant 9
- Kay's 10
- Lehua's Bay City Bar & Grill 12
- Nihon Restaurant & Cultural Center 13
- Pescatore 21
- Restaurant Fuji 14
- Restaurant Osaka 15
- Restaurant Satsuki 16
- Reuben's Mexican Food 17
- Royal Siam Thai Restaurant 20
- The Seaside 18
- Ting-Hao Mandarin Restaurant 19

WILD GINGER INN, 100 Puueo St., Hilo, HI 96720. Tel. 808/935-5566, or toll free 800/822-1887. 30 rms.

$ Rates (including continental breakfast): $45 single or double. No credit cards. **Parking:** Free.

Here's something unique—a 30-room bed-and-breakfast inn! Robert and Sandra Woodword, an attractive California couple who used to live on a yacht in Sausalito, moved to Hilo a few years ago, took over a 1940s plantation-style hotel, and are gradually converting it into a charming, old-fashioned inn. The setting is very pretty, a short walk from town, and the rooms look out on a large lawn and a garden lush with wild torch ginger, bamboo, and a private stream. Rooms are small and plain but comfortable enough, and all have private bath with shower but no tub. They have ceiling fans instead of air conditioning; TV and phones are available in the spacious lobbies, lit at night with Mexican *luminarias*. The lobby is also the scene of a plentiful serve-yourself breakfast, with scrumptious muffins from Karrot's (a local Hilo bakery), granola, papayas, limes from their own trees, and Kona coffee. A coin-operated laundry is available. Improvements are being made here continuously: The future is bright.

DOUBLES FOR $49 TO $69

DOLPHIN BAY HOTEL, 333 Iliahi St., Hilo, HI 96720. Tel. 808/935-1466. 18 units. TV

$ Rates: $39–$49 single; $49–$59 double; $69 one-bedroom apt; $79 two-bedroom apt. Each additional person $8. Discounted weekly rates available. MC, V. **Parking:** Free.

Every now and then you come across a little hotel where you know you could comfortably settle down for a long, long time. Such a place is the Dolphin Bay Hotel, in a quiet residential neighborhood just a four-block walk from town. The hotel buildings are scattered throughout a lush tropical garden resplendent with papayas, breadfruits, bananas, and the like; you are invited to step right outside your room and pick your breakfast! The accommodations are modern, quite large, and nicely furnished, with full kitchens and large tub/shower combinations in the bathrooms. The standard studios sleep one or two comfortably. The superior studios, usually with a twin and a queen-size bed (plus a built-in Roman-style tub!), are larger and can easily sleep three. There's also a marvelous honeymoon room with an open-beamed ceiling and a large lanai for $57; and some really spacious one- and two-bedroom apartments, perfect for families. Since the hotel is near Hilo Bay, a cooling breeze keeps the units comfortable all year. Manager John Alexander dispenses the warmth and hospitality that have made this one of our best island finds over the years. He and his staff will map out tours, arrange trips, and advise on the best restaurants. Write or phone in advance, since the guests who come back each year—many from Canada and the Midwest—keep this place hopping. Lots of readers' hurrahs for this one continue to come in every year, even though there is no pool. Certified orchids are available right on the grounds at the Iliahi Nursery.

HILO SEASIDE HOTEL, 126 Banyan Dr., Hilo, HI 96720. Tel. 808/935-0821. Fax 808/969-9195. 135 rms. A/C TV TEL

$ Rates: Single or double, $54–$59 standard; $59–$65 superior; $66–$72 deluxe; $76–$92 with kitchenette. Cars available for $15 more per day. Each additional person $12. Children 12 and under stay free in parent's room when using existing bedding. Rate increase expected. AE, DC, MC, V. **Parking:** Free.

The Hilo Seaside Hotel (formerly the Hilo Hukilau Hotel) near Hilo Bay has long been a pleasant place to stay. The local branch of the kamaaina-owned Sand & Seaside Hotels (there are others in Kona, Kauai, and Maui) has attractive rooms (most with air conditioning) with lanais—rooms that overlook either the freshwater swimming pool, a fish pond, or lush tropical gardens. The hotel has been attractively renovated, and the lobby is decorated with contemporary tiles and Oriental hardwood floors. Wood fenceposts, Polynesian murals, and tikis permit you to forget the mainland. The popular Hukilau Restaurant and Cocktail Lounge is a longtime favorite for well-priced meals.

Reservations: Sand & Seaside Hotels, 2222 Kalakaua Ave., Suite 714, Honolulu, HI 96815 (tel. toll free 800/367-7000 in the mainland U.S., 800/654-7020 in Canada; fax 808/922-0052).

UNCLE BILLY'S HILO BAY HOTEL, 87 Banyan Dr., Hilo, HI 96720. Tel. 808/935-0861, or toll free 800/367-5102. Fax 808/935-7903. 135 rms. A/C TV TEL

$ Rates: Single or double, $69 standard; $74 superior; $79 deluxe; $89 oceanfront; $79 with kitchenette. Add $15 for room-car-breakfast package. AE, DC, DISC, MC, V. **Parking:** Free.

Uncle Billy's, owned and operated by a Hawaiian family, is a happy place. It's run on "Hawaiian time" and the pace is leisurely; you can feel that pleasant Polynesian paralysis setting in the moment you step into the South Seas lobby decorated with fish nets and tapa-covered walls. All rooms have a private lanai. The higher-priced rooms are huge: Two double beds look lost in the room. Most rooms face a tropical garden that leads to a path to the swimming pool, next to the ocean on Hilo Bay. Uncle Billy's Fish & Steak Restaurant, right in the hotel, is a fun place for food and entertainment (see "Big Island Evening Entertainment," in Chapter 13).

WAIAKEA VILLAS HOTEL, 400 Hualani St., Hilo, HI 96720. Tel. 808/961-2841. Fax 808/961-6797. 141 units. A/C TV

$ Rates: $60–$75 standard studio, $70–$85 studio with kitchenette, $80–$95 large deluxe studio with kitchenette; $100–$115 one-bedroom suite; $135–$145 honeymoon suite. Phone $5 extra; crib, $9; each additional person, $10. Children under 12 stay free in parent's room (without extra bed). AE, DC, MC, V. **Parking:** Free.

Close to the airport, shopping centers, golf courses, sports complexes, and scenic routes, the Waiakea Villas Hotel is set amid 14½ acres of meandering waterways and lagoons in a giant tropical garden. Rooms, in handsome Polynesian-style buildings, are very large, and furnished in the island style: Private lanais all overlook either garden or waterways. Each room has either a king-size bed or two double beds. Each room (except the standard) has a kitchenette (refrigerator, stove, burners, but no small appliances). There's a swimming pool and tennis court on the grounds, as well as two restaurants: John Michaleas for American food and Miyo for authentic Japanese cooking.

BED & BREAKFASTS

HALE KAI-BJORNEN BED & BREAKFAST, 111 Honolii Pali, Hilo, HI 96720 Tel. 808/935-6330. 4 rms (none with bath). 1 cottage. TV TEL

$ Rates (including breakfast): $80–$90 double; $95 one-bedroom guest cottage with kitchen. Minimum stay three days. **Parking:** Free.

★ You'll be warmly welcomed and made to feel right at home at Evonne Bjornen's bed-and-breakfast. And what a home it is, a superb double-decker house with an entire wall of glass overlooking Hilo Bay and the island's best surfing spot, Honalii Surfing Beach. Guests have use of the magnificent living room looking out over the waterfront, and just beyond it, a pool with Jacuzzi and comfy lounge chairs. Downstairs are three bedrooms plus a family room, all beautifully furnished, with either a king- or queen-size bed. Mrs. Bjornen is a friendly woman who truly enjoys having guests in her home. Her husband, Paul Tallett, is a native Hawaiian, a well-known fisherman and hunter, ready to entertain you with songs on the ukulele and tell you about his island and the old tales of Hawaii. Mrs. Bjornen likes to whip up fabulous breakfasts, and often puts her telescope out on the porch so that guests can watch the volcano when it's in action! Staying here is like being on a lovely retreat—you may forget to go out and explore Hilo.

MAUREEN'S BED AND BREAKFAST, 1896 Kalanianaole St., Hilo, HI 96720. Tel. 808/935-9018. 6 rms (none with bath).

$ Rates (including breakfast): $35 single; $60 double. No credit cards.

Owner Maureen Small has restored a classic redwood house built in 1935 and lovingly decorated it with oak, mahogany, and koa-wood antiques. The living room is out of another era: a 30-foot vaulted ceiling, with double staircases leading to a wraparound balcony. Rooms have semiprivate baths. The two upstairs rooms, with views of the mountains, are very large and have California (extra-large) king-size beds. The two downstairs rooms (one large, one small) have double beds and a garden view. Two single rooms also share a bath. The grounds are manicured Japanese gardens with koi ponds. James Kealoha Beach Park is just across the street (it has a sandy bottom, brackish water, and is okay for doing laps), and Richardson Ocean Beach Park (good for snorkeling) is a mile down the road. In addition to the usual fresh-fruit-and-main-course breakfast, Maureen likes to serve fresh fish whenever her fishing friends are lucky.

OUR PLACE–PAPAIKOU'S B&B, P.O. Box 469, Papaikou, HI 96781. Tel. 808/964-5250, or toll free 800/245-5250. 4 rms (1 with bath).

$ Rates (including breakfast): $50 double; $55 Early American/Oriental loft or tree-house room; $65 master bedroom. Each additional person $5. No credit cards. **Parking:** Free.

Four miles north of Hilo, on Hi. 19, Our Place–Papaikou's B&B is a charming place to stay close to Hilo town. Sharon Miller, a former Rolfer, and Ouida Taherne, M.D., both gave up busy lifestyles in California and Mississippi to move to Hilo and set up a guesthouse here. They've found a lovely cedar-paneled home overlooking a stream, set amid lush tropical vegetation. The "Great Room," splendid with its cathedral ceiling, has a library, fireplace, grand piano, and cable TV/VCR—all of which guests are invited to enjoy. Four rooms share a common lanai that looks out over Kupuu Stream. There are two doubles, a master bedroom with a private bath, and a loft. Miller and Taherne are excellent cooks (they do complete breakfasts) and are friendly, helpful hosts—and their prices are right.

THE NORTHERN ROUTE

HONOKAA

Doubles for $35 to $55

HOTEL HONOKAA CLUB, Honokaa, HI 96727. Tel. 808/775-0678. 14 rms.

$ Rates: $32 single, $39–$41 single with TV; $35 double, $42–$44 double with TV. MC, V. **Parking:** Free.

Forty miles north of Hilo on the northern, or Hamakaua coast, route, and not far from the cattle country of the Parker Ranch, is the venerable Hotel Honokaa Club, which has been serving local businesspeople and hunters for more than 50 years. Undemanding types will find the rooms acceptable. The hotel's inexpensive restaurant (dinner only) and bar are very popular with the local people.

WAIPIO WAYSIDE, P.O. Box 840, Honokaa, HI 96727. Tel. 808/775-0275, or toll free 800/833-8849. 5 rms (2 with bath).

$ Rates (including breakfast): $50–$80 single; $55–$85 double. DC, MC, V. **Parking:** Free.

Two miles from the center of Honokaa, on the ocean side, is Waipio Wayside, one of the most charming new B&Bs to open in this area. Jacqueline Horne, from California's Silicon Valley, settled in these peaceful parts, and renovated a 1938 sugar plantation home. It's now decorated to recall the charms of old Hawaii. Bordered by a white picket fence and set on 1½ acres of tropical fruit and vegetable gardens, the house overlooks sugarcane fields and the ocean far below. The outside deck with its double hammocks and the gazebo for sunset watching are popular spots; so, too, are the kitchen, where Jackie, a gourmet cook, often whips up special treats (she serves a full breakfast) and the living room with its 31-inch TV/VCR, where she might schedule a Japanese film festival complete with popcorn. The rooms are beautifully decorated with antique furniture, Chinese rugs, and silk drapes hand-painted by a local artist. Two rooms at the front of the house, the Moon Room with a full-size bed and the Plantation Room with twin beds, share a bath. At the back of the house is the Chinese Room, with its antique Chinese reclining barber's chairs; it overlooks the deck and gazebo, and has a half-bath. The Library Room upstairs is very special, with blond-wood paneling, an ocean view, skylights over the bed and shower, and something like 300 books on the shelves. The Bird's Eye Room at the back of the house is special, too—a spacious private bedroom suite with its own bath, blond-wood paneling, and a patchwork quilt on the bed. Double doors open onto the deck and a view of gardens, sugarcane fields, and ocean beyond. A great spot for a peaceful retreat.

KUKUIHAELE

Doubles for $60 to $70

HAMAKUA HIDEAWAY, P.O. Box 5104, Kukuihaele, HI 96727. Tel. 808/775-7425. 2 units.

$ Rates: $60 for two people for two or more days, $75 for one night only. Discounted weekly and monthly rates available. No credit cards. **Parking:** Free.

Searching for the perfect romantic hideaway? Search no more. We've found it seven miles north of Honokaa, at Hamakua Hideaway, a charming home perched high on a cliff and affording magnificent views of breathtaking Waipio Valley and the dazzling ocean below. Kristan and Jim Hunt, a friendly couple who built the home themselves, have also created two separate guest accommodations, one connecting to the main house, the other down the way a bit, out on the cliff. The Tree House Suite, which connects to the main house, is nestled into a mango tree; has sunshine and windows on all sides, a private bath, and a kitchen; and is beautifully furnished. The Cliff House, nestled above a 50-foot waterfall, is more like a little house, with its own wood stove, a loft with a futon above, complete kitchen, and a private bath with sunken tub. Both units have glorious views and as much privacy as one would wish. The Hunts' three tow-headed little boys add to the overall charm. Hamakua is mid-island, about an hour from either Hilo or Kona Coast locations.

WAIPIO RIDGE VACATION RENTAL, P.O. Box 5039, Kukuihaele, HI 96726. Tel. 808/775-0603. 1 cottage.

$ Rates: $70 double for only one night, $60 double for more than one night, $380 double per week. Each additional person $15 extra. No credit cards. **Parking:** Free.

A thousand feet above the floor of Waipio Valley, Roger Lasko's little cottage commands a spectacular view; from this distance, the surf breaking below gently lulls one to sleep. The modestly furnished cottage contains a large living room, a bedroom, a well-equipped kitchen, a dining area, and bath. Lasko's friendly dog, Bingo, is in residence. Lasko, a woodshop instructor in the Honokaa school system, lives next door; his phone is available for use.

WAIPIO VALLEY

A Super-Budget Choice

WAIPIO HOTEL, Waipio Valley. Tel. 808/775-0368 in Waipio or 808/935-7466 in Hilo; or write to Tom Araki, 25 Malama Place, Hilo, HI 96720. 5 rms (none with bath).

$ Rates: $15 single. No credit cards.

Remote and scarcely populated Waipio Valley, which can be reached only by a four-wheel-drive vehicle or by hiking down the steep cliffs, actually has two places where you might spend a night or two. It's like living in the jungle, with all its lush beauty—but also with the possibility of jungle rains. Tom Araki's Waipio Hotel has all of five rooms and one bath, and has absolutely no truck with such modern amenities as hot water, telephones, restaurants, or even electricity. A friend of ours, a very successful businesswoman in Honolulu, swears she'd rather spend her vacation here, at Tom Araki's $15-a-night hotel, than anywhere else. You no longer have to bring your own sleeping bag: Linens and blankets are furnished.

Worth the Extra Bucks

WAIPIO TREEHOUSE and THE HALE, Waipio Valley. Tel. 808/775-7160; or write to Linda Beech, P.O. Box 5086, Honokaa, HI 96727. 2 houses.

$ Rates: $150 for two. Children under 12 stay free with parents; children over 12, $25 extra. AE, MC, V.

Waipio Valley also offers a possible haven for incurable romantics who don't mind splurging a bit for a home in the trees. The Treehouse, 30 feet up in a 60-foot monkeypod tree, faces a 1,000-foot waterfall, sleeps three, and even has a kitchen. A skylight offers moonlit views through the leaves. You can swim under the waterfall or in the ocean, about a 1½-mile walk from here. Hot furo (deep hot tub) baths are available in an adjoining building. Fresh fruits can be picked on nearby paths. It could be paradise. For those who want more room to stretch out in, there's the Hale on the ground level. This is a private cottage with a living room, a loft, a full kitchen, and views of not one, but two waterfalls. Four to six people can be accommodated (there's a king-size bed, a queen-size bed, and a double futon). A massage therapist is on hand to help guests unwind totally. When you call to make reservations, they'll help you arrange transportation down into the valley: a four-wheel-drive is required.

KAMUELA

Doubles for $54 to $95

KAMUELA INN, Kawaihae Rd. (P.O. Box 1994), Kamuela, HI 96743. Tel. 808/885-4243. Fax 808/885-8857. 19 rms, 12 suites.

$ Rates (including continental breakfast): $54, $67, $72, or $79 single or double; $83–$93 kitchenette suite; $165 deluxe suite. AE, DC, DISC, MC, V. **Parking:** Free.

From Honokaa, it's 15 miles on Hi. 19 to Kamuela or Waimea, heart of the Parker Ranch cattle kingdom. A good place to stay in this deliciously cool mountain town is the Kamuela Inn, an old standby that has been attractively renovated. Rooms in the older building are all nicely furnished, and kitchenettes are well equipped with all utensils, even including rice cookers. Two penthouse suites rented together are a nice arrangement for a large family or two couples traveling together: The front suite, which sleeps two on a queen-size bed, has an expansive mountain view, a full bath,

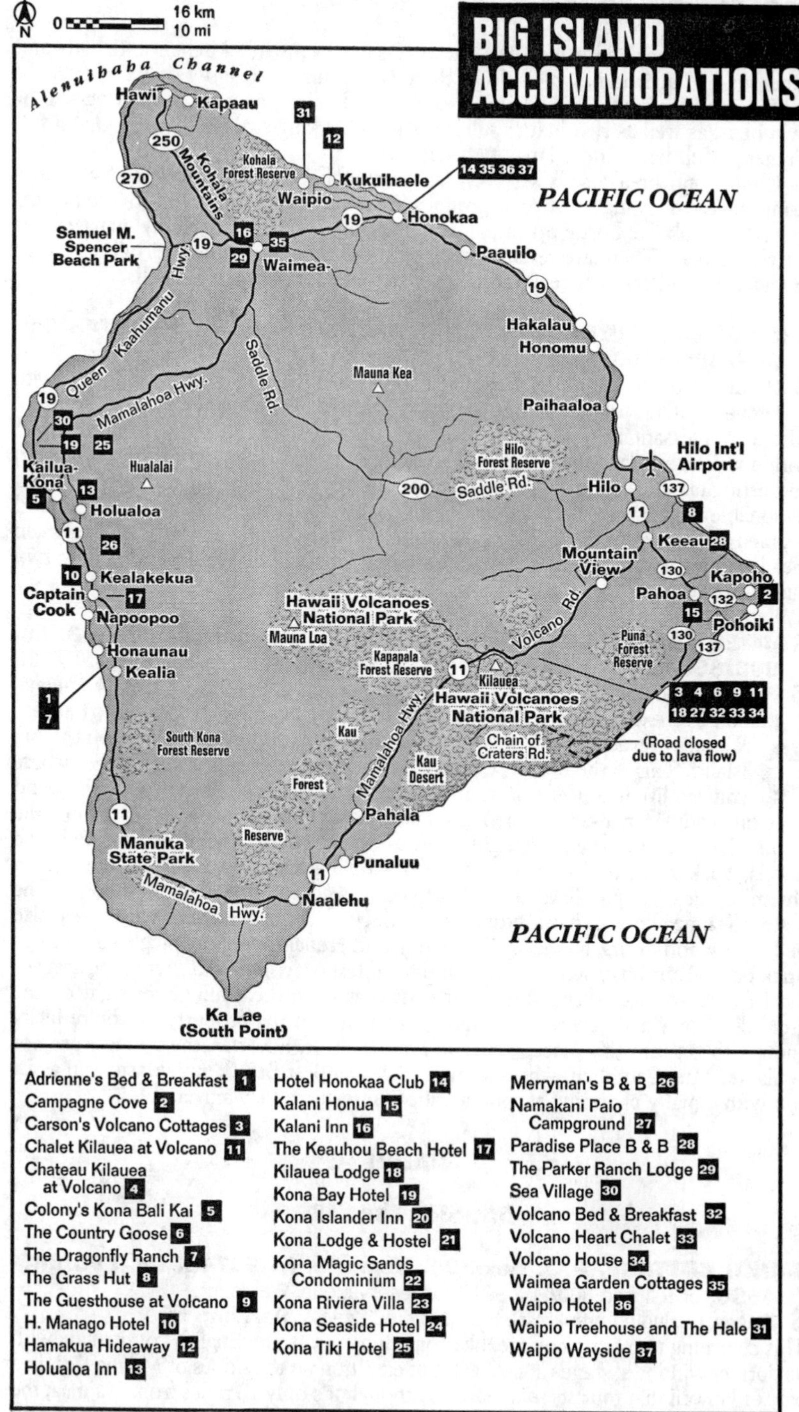

BIG ISLAND ACCOMMODATIONS
16 km
10 mi
N
Alenuihaha Channel
PACIFIC OCEAN
Hawi
Kapaau
250
270
Kohala Mountains
Kohala Forest Reserve
Waipio
Kukuihaele
Honokaa
19
Samuel M. Spencer Beach Park
Waimea-
Paauilo
Hakalau
Honomu
Paihaaloa
Mauna Kea
Saddle Rd.
Queen Kaahumanu Hwy.
Mamalahoa Hwy.
Kailua-Kona
Hualalai
Holualoa
Kealakekua
Captain Cook
Napoopoo
Honaunau
Kealia
Hilo Forest Reserve
Hilo Int'l Airport
Hilo
200
137
Keeau
Mountain View
Kapoho
Pahoa
132
130
Pohoiki
Volcano Rd.
Hawaii Volcanoes National Park
Mauna Loa
Kapapala Forest Reserve
Puna Forest Reserve
Kilauea
South Kona Forest Reserve
Kau Forest Reserve
Chain of Craters Rd.
(Road closed due to lava flow)
Kau Desert
Pahala
Punaluu
Manuka State Park
Naalehu
Ka Lae (South Point)
Adrienne's Bed & Breakfast 1
Campagne Cove 2
Carson's Volcano Cottages 3
Chalet Kilauea at Volcano 11
Chateau Kilauea at Volcano 4
Colony's Kona Bali Kai 5
The Country Goose 6
The Dragonfly Ranch 7
The Grass Hut 8
The Guesthouse at Volcano 9
H. Manago Hotel 10
Hamakua Hideaway 12
Holualoa Inn 13
Hotel Honokaa Club 14
Kalani Honua 15
Kalani Inn 16
The Keauhou Beach Hotel 17
Kilauea Lodge 18
Kona Bay Hotel 19
Kona Islander Inn 20
Kona Lodge & Hostel 21
Kona Magic Sands Condominium 22
Kona Riviera Villa 23
Kona Seaside Hotel 24
Kona Tiki Hotel 25
Merryman's B & B 26
Namakani Paio Campground 27
Paradise Place B & B 28
The Parker Ranch Lodge 29
Sea Village 30
Volcano Bed & Breakfast 32
Volcano Heart Chalet 33
Volcano House 34
Waimea Garden Cottages 35
Waipio Hotel 36
Waipio Treehouse and The Hale 31
Waipio Wayside 37

and a private lanai with wet bar; the rear suite has a full kitchen and bath and generous-size bedroom, which sleeps three with a king-size and a single bed.

The recently completed Mauna Kea Wing offers rooms with either king-size or twin beds, as well as two luxury suites, each with a king-size bed, two singles, a full kitchen, a full bath, and a lanai with hot tub.

Continental breakfast is served in a cheery coffee lounge with broad windows admitting the morning sun. Scenic grounds (there's a bottlebrush tree with red flowers that really look like bottle brushes) just outside the hotel and a friendly management are pluses here. There are restaurants nearby and good swimming 12 miles away at Hapuna Beach Park. For reservations, contact manager Earnest Russell.

THE PARKER RANCH LODGE, P.O. Box 458, Kamuela, HI 96743. Tel. 808/885-4100. Fax 808/885-6711. 20 units. TV TEL

$ Rates (including tax): $74.25 single or double, $85.15 single or double with kitchen. Additional person $10 extra. AE, MC, V. **Parking:** Free.

Also very pleasant in this area is the Parker Ranch Lodge, a modern motor hotel within walking distance of the Parker Ranch Center and all its sightseeing, shopping, and eating facilities. Horseback riding and golf are nearby, some excellent beaches a reasonable drive away. Each room boasts quality furnishings, attractive decor, and beamed ceiling. From this cool, 2,500-foot elevation you have a view of rolling green meadowlands and mountains. Singles have one king-size bed and doubles have two queen-size beds.

WAIMEA GARDEN COTTAGES, P.O. Box 563, Kamuela, HI 96743. Tel. 808/885-4550, or toll free 800/262-9912 for reservations. 2 cottages. TV TEL

$ Rates (including breakfast): Cottage $95 per night, $600 per week. Additional person $15 extra. No credit cards. Minimum stay three nights. **Parking:** Free.

Waimea Garden Cottages has to be one of our very favorite places on the Big Island. This is the perfect country retreat: two elegant private cottages where you can live in graceful surroundings, do your own cooking if you wish, spend your time riding or hiking in the mountains, or swimming at Hapuna Beach or the Mauna Kea Beach Hotel, just eight miles down the road. (The hosts provide beach towels, back rests, and coolers for the beach.) Barbara and Charlie Campbell, a charming local couple, have created the cottages adjacent to their own home. The newest Waimea cottage has a sitting room, gracious bedroom alcove with queen-size bed, hardwood floors, fireplace, TV, stereo, and French doors opening to a spacious brick patio. Your hosts welcome you with breakfast provisions and a tempting array of local fruits. You can even gather your own eggs from the family hens right on the grounds. The Waiakea Stream meanders right behind the property. If you're lucky enough to get into this place, you're in for a treat. If, however, the cottages are not available, Mrs. Campbell, who also runs Hawaii's Best Bed & Breakfasts, can assist you with equally charming accommodations elsewhere in Waimea.

WAIKII

Doubles for $95

WAIKII COTTAGE, P.O. Box 520, Kamuela, HI 96743. Tel. 808/885-4550, or toll free 800/262-9912 for reservations. 2 apts.

$ Rates (including breakfast): $95. No credit cards. **Parking:** Free.

This charming two-story cottage, like something out of the English countryside with its dormer windows, stands at a 4,700-foot elevation on the slopes of Mauna Kea, in a part of Hawaii that tourists seldom see. Although it's only 12 miles from Waimea, the cottage, on the Saddle Road that crosses between Mauna Loa and Mauna Kea, has a very different, very rural feeling, set apart from the rest of the world. The owners, whose home is nearby, raise cattle; they have also created a locally renowned English-style garden, abloom with roses and hollyhocks in the summer months, which guests are invited to tour. Each floor of the cottage is beautifully decorated, furnished with tasteful antiques and quilts (there's a fireplace in the upstairs unit), and offers every luxury. Mornings and evenings are brisk, so bring some warm clothes.

For this B&B, special arrangements have been made with a car-rental company that allows travel on the Saddle Road, usually forbidden to tourists.

THE SOUTHERN ROUTE

Driving the southern route (Hi. 11) between Hilo and Kona, there are a number of delightful places to spend a night or two. First, we'll tell you about two bed-and-breakfast choices in Keaau, about a 15-minute drive out of Hilo, and en route to Hawaii Volcanoes National Park; then we'll look at a cluster of guesthouses in the Volcano area itself. Finally, we'll stop at the most famous hotel in the area, perched right on the brink of Kilauea Crater, explore some nearby campgrounds, visit a house at the beach at Kapoho, and stop off at an international conference and retreat center which also takes travelers.

KEAAU

Doubles for About $50

THE GRASS HUT B&B, 6245 29th St. (HCR 6245), Keaau, HI 96749. Tel. 808/966-8956. 2 suites. TV

$ Rates (including breakfast): $50 suite for two. Additional adult $10 extra; additional child, $5. No credit cards.

Located six miles south of Keaau in Paradise Park, the Grass Hut is a home away from home. Owners Bob and Linda Kurtz make their guests feel at home in the relaxed family atmosphere—children are welcome and a crib can be furnished. There's no specific check-in or check-out time. The two suites (one incorporating an old lava flow) feature a kitchenette, bath, and TV. Continental breakfast is served in a tropical garden. The best part about staying here is Bob and Linda, who cannot do enough to help their guests. No phone call is too much trouble, no favor is too great; everyone feels as if they are staying with family or old friends when they experience a night at the Grass Hut.

PARADISE PLACE B&B, HCR 9558, Keaau, HI 96749-9318. Tel. 808/966-4600. 2 rms. TV

$ Rates (including breakfast): $50 single; $55 double. $5 surcharge for one-night stay; seventh night free. No credit cards.

Another popular B&B in Paradise Park, six miles south of Keaau, is Paradise Place, owned by Laura Richman and Steve Peyton. It's in a seven-acre rural setting, just half a mile from the ocean. The view from the two rooms takes in the steaming volcano in the distance and the tropical garden right outside the door. Each room has its own private entrance, bath, kitchenette with full refrigerator, washer and dryer, patio, and hammock.

READERS RECOMMEND

Paradise Place B&B. *"This was the life! Large bedroom, TV, VCR, a large bathroom with everything you need and don't need—iron, shampoos, conditioners, razors, hand lotions, sun-*

burn ointments, etc.—a wonderful kitchen with a dynamic view of Pu'uo'o, the smoking volcanic vent. The kitchen also had a microwave, toaster oven, a fully-stocked refrigerator, telephone, gorgeous paintings. The den was wonderful! Beautiful Hawaiian memorabilia, stereo, a second TV, beautiful wicker furniture. The backyard had a picnic table, swing, and a barbecue grill which we used for all of our meals. We went to the ocean a couple of times in the early morning. Each time we saw a whale and dolphins frolicking just 50 feet from shore. This was truly paradise. Steven and Laura checked on us to make sure we were comfortable and if we had enough food in the cabinets and the refrigerator. They lent us maps, snorkeling gear, ice chest, packs, and lawn chairs to use when we went out exploring and snorkeling. They gave us wonderful tips on where to go and the fastest way to get there. We had the most fantastic time with the best hospitality for an economical price. We enjoyed Steve and Laura's company very much."—Catherine and Mike Praisewater, Albuquerque, N.M.

VOLCANO AREA

The Volcano area is perfect for the guesthouse lifestyle. Country cottages are places where you can bring the kids, relax, drive off to the volcano or to the black sand beaches farther south, or just savor the simple charms of country life. But do bear in mind that the weather is highly changeable here, and in the mountains, rains come and go.

Doubles for $50 to $60

CARSON'S VOLCANO COTTAGE, 501 Sixth St., Mauna Loa Estates (P.O. Box 503), Volcano, HI 96785. Tel. 808/967-7683, or toll free 800/845-LAVA. 4 rms, 1 suite.

$ Rates (including breakfast): $50 single; $60 double; $120 suite. Additional person $15. Vacation-home rentals, from $65 for two. MC, V. **Parking:** Free.

Hosts Tom and Brenda Carson love meeting new people and try to provide them with a welcome and peaceful environment. They have a private, cozy cottage that sleeps five, and a three-room cottage; all rooms have private baths and private entrances, and two have kitchenettes. Rooms are furnished in Victorian Polynesian, Asian, country, or southwestern style, with many unique pieces, homey touches, and fresh flowers indoors and out. The Carsons leave a fruit boat, muffins, Kona coffee, tea, and cocoa for the guests to prepare at their leisure. And there's a hot tub nestled among giant Hawaiian tree ferns. Vacation homes are affordable, and some sleep up to six.

THE COUNTRY GOOSE, Ruby Ave. (P.O. Box 597), Volcano, HI 96785. Tel. 808/967-7759. 1 rm, 2 vacation houses.

$ Rates: $60 double (including full breakfast); $85 two-bedroom/two-bath house for two; $95 three-bedroom/two-bath house. Each additional person $20. No credit cards. **Parking:** Free.

Joan Earley's house is decorated with all kinds of country geese—wood, ceramic, cloth—sent to her by guests who've enjoyed her hospitality and her delicious breakfasts. She likes nothing better than to whip up some buttermilk pancakes or quiches, or Hawaiian French toast made from Portuguese sweet bread, or Belgian waffles with fresh strawberries for her guests. The full breakfast comes with the bedroom and sitting room, with its own private entrance and private bath. It has a king-size bed and a double futon on a frame, a TV, and a VCR. It can accommodate up to four people. Around the corner are her two vacation houses. The two-bedroom cedar house can accommodate up to six people, and the three-bedroom up to 12—so they're both very popular for small groups or family reunions.

THE GUESTHOUSE AT VOLCANO, 11-3733 Ala Ohia St. (P.O. Box 6), Volcano, HI 96785. Tel. 808/967-7775, or toll free 800/736-7140. Fax 808/967-8295. 1 one-bedroom cottage.

$ Rates: $60 for two people. Additional person $10 extra. Minimum stay two days; seventh day free. No credit cards. **Parking:** Free.

Bonnie Goodell is in charge at the Guesthouse at Volcano, a perfect place for a family to settle into. It consists of a living room downstairs with a double hideaway bed, a complete kitchen, and a nice bedroom upstairs with two twins and a queen-size foldout bed. The apartment is fully furnished, including phone, black-and-white TV, books, magazines, games, electric heater, bikes for children, and even wool socks! The big outside porch has kids' toys and a big sink area for "cookouts, muddy boots, berries, etc." If Bonnie is booked, she will probably be able to help you find another similar place.

VOLCANO BED & BREAKFAST, 19-3950 Keonelehua St. (P.O. Box 22), Volcano, HI 96785. Tel. 808/967-7779. Fax 808/967-7619. 3 rms (none with bath). TV

$ **Rates** (including full breakfast): $45–$50 single; $50–$55 double. Additional person $15 extra. MC, V. **Parking:** Free.

This cozy little country house set in a pretty landscaped area is run by Jim and Sandy Pedersen. The entire house is turned over to the pleasure of their guests, who are free to enjoy the downstairs area, with its sun room, reading room, fireplace, piano, and cable TV—it would make an ideal spot for a small family reunion. There are two nicely decorated sleeping rooms with double beds upstairs, and one room done in bright yellow downstairs; baths are semiprivate. Breakfast features Sandy's French toast and homemade jams and jellies. The Pedersens describe themselves as "friendly, gracious Christian hosts with inside information about where to go and what to see."

VOLCANO HEART CHALET. Tel. 808/967-8644 or 967-8563 (eves). 3 rms.

$ **Rates:** $50 single or double per night, $300 single or double per week. Minimum stay two nights. No credit cards. **Parking:** Free.

Although they reside in Maui most of the time, JoLoyce and John Kaia make their Volcano area home available to guests. The two-story cedar house, surrounded by trees, consists of three bedrooms (all with private locks), containing either queen-size or twin beds, warm comforters for cool nights, and either private or shared baths. All guests can use the glass-enclosed porch for cooking and eating and the carpeted lounging and exercise room. Guests are provided with coffee, tea, cocoa, and fresh pastry. Adults only; no smoking.

Reservations: P.O. Box 404, Hana, Maui, HI 96713.

Doubles for $75 to $95

CHALET KILAUEA AT VOLCANO, off Hi. 11 at the corner of Wright/Lasskapu Rd. (P.O. Box 998), Volcano Village, HI 96785. Tel. 808/967-7786, or toll free 800/937-7786. 3 rms, 1 suite, 3 vacation homes.

$ **Rates:** $65 single; $75 double; $95 suite; from $65 vacation home. Additional person $15 extra. AE, MC, V. **Parking:** Free.

After traveling around the world for nine years, Brian and Lisha Crawford settled down in Volcano Village, just a mile from Hawaii Volcanoes National Park, and opened a bed-and-breakfast. They had plenty of art and unique furniture from their travels with which to decorate. The three rooms in the main house include: the Continental Lace room, with a queen-size bed, lace curtains, ballet slippers on the wall, straw hat on the hat rack, and daybed for reading; the Oriental Jade room, done in rose, black, and jade colors, complete with king-size bed and antique Chinese screens; and the Out of Africa room, with treasures from Africa—masks, baskets, artwork. That's not all: Outside is a two-story "tree-house suite" with a master bedroom upstairs complete with wraparound windows overlooking tree ferns, and a mini-kitchen and dayroom downstairs. The hot tub on the lanai is available, a fire is lit every night, and breakfast consists of two gourmet courses.

Chalet Kilauea's vacation homes are spacious and graced with charming decor. All offer a full kitchen and tasty breakfast foods. The Ohia Holiday Cottage at $65, the

Hapuu Forest Cabin at $85, and the Hoku Hawaiian House at $100 are the ultimate in Volcano comfort.

HYDRANGEA COTTAGE, P.O. Box 563, Kamuela, HI 96743. Tel. toll free 800/262-9912. 1 cottage.

$ Rates: $95 double. Minimum stay two days. No credit cards. **Parking:** Free.

Return visitors agree that Hydrangea Cottage, on a beautiful three-acre estate, is a rare jewel in this high-country mountain village. The cottage guest book overflows with praise from past guests with compliments on everything from the serene setting, luxurious furnishings, and beautiful fragrance of the redwood interior to the host's gracious hospitality and exquisite attention to every detail (including antique robes provided for guest use). The owner, who lives on Oahu, escapes as often as possible to her Big Island retreat, a spacious executive home located adjacent to the cottage. When the owner/hostess is not in residence, guests are left in the capable hands of her caretaker, Grace, who lives nearby. The cottage, with views of tall hapuu ferns and ohia trees from every window, has a separate bedroom with a queen-size bed, bath with full tub, a wood stove in a cozy living room, washer/dryer, and a full kitchen that has been stocked with breakfast provisions. The hostess's spacious home is also available for executive or family retreats on request. No smoking; no children.

KILAUEA LODGE, Old Volcano Rd. (P.O. Box 116), Volcano Village, HI 96785. Tel. 808/967-7366. Fax 808/967-7367. 10 rms, 1 suite, 1 cottage.

$ Rates (including full breakfast): $85–$125 single or double. Additional person $15 extra. MC, V. **Parking:** Free.

Perhaps the most beautiful rooms in this area are at Kilauea Lodge, one mile Hilo-side of Hawaii Volcanoes National Park, in Volcano Village. When you see the lodge—set on 10 acres of greenery, bordered by magnificent ferns and towering pine trees—you'll know why everybody on the Big Island is excited about it. This former YMCA mountain retreat has now become a restaurant offering excellent meals (sorely needed in this area) and an inn offering exquisite rooms. Lorna and Albert Jeyte (she comes from Honolulu, he hails from Germany) are in charge here: He performs the magic in the kitchen; she's created the magic in the guest rooms. You'd never believe this used to be a YMCA dorm! Architects have opened up the top of the building to create a skylight, flooding the rooms with natural light. Hawaiian quilt patterns (some of the quilts are antiques) set the mostly soft pastel color schemes for the woodwork. Furniture is made of light oak, even down to the oak tissue box. Each room is decorated differently—most are in the country style; one is strikingly Japanese—some have toasty electric blankets, and working fireplaces. The one-bedroom cottage has a queen-size bed in the bedroom and a queen-size sofa in the living room; it can sleep up to four.

VOLCANO HOUSE, P.O. Box 53, Hawaii Volcanoes National Park, HI 96718. Tel. 808/967-7321. Fax 808/967-4829. 50 rms.

$ Rates: In Ohia Wing, $79 single or double. In the main building, $105 single or double without crater view, $131 single or double with crater view. Additional person $10 extra. AE, DC, MC, V. **Parking:** Free.

The famed and venerable Volcano House is right on the brink of Kilauea Crater, where the ancient *kahunas* (priests) once gathered to make sacrifices to Pele. This hotel has changed hands several times in recent years, but the new management has things well in hand. All the guest rooms have been renovated and refurbished with koa furniture, including koa rockers in the rooms in the main building, and cheerful Hawaiian comforters. The least-expensive rooms are in the Ohia Wing, a separate building away from the main building. Better and more expensive rooms, in the main building, vary depending on their view of the crater. Even if you don't stay at Volcano House, at least come by to soak up the atmosphere or have a meal. Enjoying a breakfast here in the early-morning mountain air, seated at a table near the window where you can gaze right into the volcano as you savor your ono French toast and ohelo-berry preserves, is one of the special treats of Hawaii.

A Campground

Any former Boy Scouts or Girl Scouts in the crowd? You might try one of the 10 cabins at **Namakani Paio Campground,** in Hawaii Volcanoes National Park, three miles beyond Volcano House, at approximately 4,000 feet elevation. For those "who desire true outdoor living," the cabins, furnished with a double bed and two single bunk beds, have a Polynesian design and frame construction. Each cabin has its own lanai but shares a bathhouse. The cost is $31 for four people, including a linen bag (sheets, pillows, towel, soap, one blanket) for each bed. Extra blankets or sleeping bags are recommended; it gets cold at this elevation. Contact Volcano House (the concessionaires) at Hawaii Volcanoes National Park, HI 96718 (tel. 808/967-7321).

KAPOHO BEACH

Doubles for $70

CHAMPAGNE COVE, Kapoho Beach. Tel. 808/959-4487. 2 three-bedroom apts. TV

$ Rates: $70 for one or two readers of this book (mention when making reservations); $75 for one or two other guests. Extra charge for additional guests. Minimum stay one week, with some exceptions. No credit cards. **Parking:** Free.

Drs. Keith and Norma Godfrey, retired chiropractors from Alaska, live in Hilo, but they rent this vacation hideaway, built on a lava bed where the ocean meets the volcanic flows at Kapoho Beach in the Puna area. It's a stark setting, but the house is warm, cozy, and beautifully decorated. Each of the two stories is a complete apartment with a superb kitchen, all modern appliances, a living room, and three attractive bedrooms. The rates make this an extraordinary bargain. What a place for a family reunion! You can swim in a heated pool right in front of the house, or walk a short distance to a black sand beach and a warm tide pool in the ocean (good for snorkeling). The house is a half-hour drive from Hilo.

Reservations: Drs. Keith and Norma Godfrey, 1714 Lei Lehua St., Hilo, HI 96720.

KEHENA

Doubles for $62

KALANI HONUA INTERCULTURAL CONFERENCE AND RETREAT CENTER, RR2, Box 4500, Pahoa, HI 96778. Tel. 808/965-7828, or toll free 800/800-6886 for registration only. 30 rms, 3 cottages.

$ Rates: $52 single without bath, $65 single with bath; $62 double without bath, $75 double with bath; $28 each triple or quad with shared bath; $85 cottage.

Although most guests come to Kalani Honua for conferences and retreats, there's no reason why other travelers cannot enjoy its lovely facilities close to the black sand beach at Kehena. Photographers, especially, enjoy the dawn-facing lava cliffs overlooking the sea, adjacent to the facility. Kalani Honua is situated five minutes from the former town of Kalapana, buried under a flood of molten lava in 1990.

Spacious grounds house rustic conference facilities, a dining hall with lanai seating, café, giftshop, sauna, 25-meter pool, and Jacuzzi (the pool area is clothing-optional after 7pm); massage is available. Nearby are natural warm springs and steam caves, and the beach at Kehena is famed for the dolphins, which frequently play with swimmers. Winter months bring humpback whales, which also come quite close to shore.

Rooms, in four cedar lodges and private cottages, are simply decorated and comfortable. Tent space (you bring the tent and linens) costs $15 per person. Meals are mostly vegetarian and skillfully prepared by a caring staff. Write or phone to receive a current list of workshops in yoga, holistic health, or the arts at Kalanai Honua.

KAILUA-KONA

DOUBLES FOR $26

H. MANAGO HOTEL, Hi. 11 (P.O. Box 145), Captain Cook, HI 96704. Tel. 808/323-2642. 64 rms.

$ **Rates:** Older building, $23 single without bath; $26 double without bath; $28 triple without bath. Newer wing, $35–$38 single with bath; $38–$41 double with bath; $41–$44 triple with bath. Japanese room with private furo, $49 single; $52 double. MC, V. **Parking:** Free.

Thirteen miles south of Kailua, on Hi. 11—and 1,400 feet high in coffee country—is the H. Manago Hotel, where you'll find some of the most reasonable accommodations in the Kona area. But staying here means more than getting a clean, comfortable room for rock-bottom prices; it's also a way to get to know nontourist Hawaii. The Manago Hotel is part of the history of the Kona coast, a favorite with island people since 1917, when two young Japanese immigrants, Kinzo and Osame Manago, started serving meals in their own house and gave the salesmen and truck drivers who wanted to stay overnight a futon to sleep on. The dining room and hotel grew over the years, and now a third generation of family management has taken over. The older rooms, with community bath, are strictly for nonfussy types. Rooms in the newer wing, with private baths and lanais, are modern and comfortable, and are nicely decorated with lovely brass-trimmed oak furniture, and fern-patterned quilted spreads in soft colors. The gardens that they overlook, incidentally, are tended by 94-year-old Osame Manago, who grows rare orchids and anthuriums in one garden, and fresh vegetables, which are served in the restaurant, in the other. She also creates the hand-knotted patchwork quilts found in many of the newer rooms. A deluxe Japanese-style room, with futons and its own furo (deep hot tub), is dedicated to Kinzo and Osame. It's delightfully quiet and cool here throughout the year. The hotel restaurant is a favorite with local people for its home-style Japanese and American cooking: breakfast starts at $4; lunch and dinner, about $6–$10.75 (a typical meal is beef or fish with three kinds of vegetables, and beverage). They're known for their pork chops. And incidentally, the three-story frame building looks down the foot of the mountain to Kealakekua Bay, where Captain Cook met his end. Owner Dwight Manago advises reserving about three weeks ahead in season, two weeks other times.

DOUBLES FOR $50 TO $75

ADRIENNE'S BED & BREAKFAST, Honaunau, HI 96704. Tel. 808/328-9726, or toll free 800/328-9726. Fax 808/328-9787. 3 rms, 1 suite. TV.

$ **Rates** (including breakfast): $50–$60 single or double; $70 suite. Additional adult $15 extra; additional child, $10. AE, MC, V. **Parking:** Free.

Adrienne and Reginald Ritz-Batty are a hospitable couple who really like people, so if you book a room at Adrienne's Bed & Breakfast, in Honaunau, (about a half-hour drive from Kailua town) you'll be treated like a friend. Not only will they share their knowledge of the Big Island with you, but they'll invite you to join them in the living room in the evenings to choose a film from the more than 1,000 movies in their collection to watch on their VCR—or the one in your room. Of course, Adrienne will have blueberry–macadamia-nut muffins, homemade Hawaiian coconut bread, cheese, and cinnamon-raisin breads, made daily, which you can enjoy along with Kona coffee, fresh fruits (papayas, white pineapples, tangerines, avocados) from their gardens, and she'll serve them to you out on the lanai, with its unobstructed view of the ocean. You're also invited to soak in the hot tub on the lanai or just laze in the hammock. The rooms are all nicely decorated; one room has a king-size bed plus a queen-size sofa bed, which makes it a good bet for a family. All rooms have private baths, color cable TVs with VCRs, and small refrigerators.

Reservations: RR1 BE, Captain Cook, HI 96704.

THE DRAGONFLY RANCH, 11 miles from Kailua-Kona, near the City of Refuge (P.O. Box 675), Honaunau, HI 96726. Tel. 808/328-2159, or toll free 800/487-2159. 2 rms, 3 suites.

$ Rates (including breakfast): $70 double per night, $350 per week; Redwood Cottage or the Writer's Studio, $100 for one night, $250 for three nights, $500 per week; Outdoor Waterbed Honeymoon Suite $140 for one night, $350 for three nights, $700 per week. MC, V. **Parking:** Free.

Barbara Moore-Link and David Link, the lovely couple who run the Dragonfly Ranch (a flower farm) in Honaunau, offer their place for families and small groups for weddings, reunions, workshops, and private retreats. They also have extraordinary accommodations for travelers and honeymooners, and you'll be happy if you luck into one of these unusual spaces. Our favorite is the Outdoor Waterbed Honeymoon Suite, in a jungle setting with private bathroom, outdoor shower with an old-fashioned sitz bath, and a kitchenette. The king-size bed has a marvelous view of Honaunau Bay, while the adjoining redwood room (viewing the "pink garden") has a queen-size sofa bed. This suite accommodates four people, but is ideally suited for two as a romantic getaway. The self-contained Redwood Cottage in the meadow is super-cozy, with a hammock out on the deck, a double bed, kitchenette, toilet, and outdoor shower; extra guests can squeeze in on the futons. The Writer's Studio is a spacious 20- by 22-foot apartment with its own kitchen, private bathroom, outdoor shower, king-size bed, and additional futons. For music lovers, David has a vast selection of music, a piano, a professional recording studio—and he also gives music lessons. All units have stereo cassette players and, upon request, guests are provided with cable TV, VCR, and videotapes. For breakfast, there are baked goods (such as whole-wheat croissants) and fresh home-grown fruits. Guests are welcome to harvest their own bananas and papayas, as well as the more exotic star fruit, soursop, or chocolate zapote in season. And Barbara offers the use of a massage chair, dream pillows, aroma therapy, and flower essences.

The Dragonfly Ranch, itself a refuge, is just a two-minute drive from the ancient Place of Sanctuary (Pu'uhonua o Honaunau National Park), with some of the world's finest diving and snorkeling. An assortment of snorkeling gear is available for guests' use. If you're lucky, the dolphins might choose to swim with you. Barbara and David provide tips on secret, secluded beaches within a 20-minute drive of the ranch, and can even teach beginners to snorkel. The Dragonfly is 19 miles south of Kailua-Kona, and great for total escape. As one guest put it: "peacefulness personified."

KONA ISLANDER INN, 75-5776 Kuakini Hwy., Kailua-Kona, HI 96740. Tel. 808/329-3181, or toll free 800/922-7866 in the U.S., 800/445-6633 in Canada. Fax 808/922-8785. Telex 634479 ASTHIUW. 144 rms. A/C TV TEL

$ Rates: Apr–Dec 21, $74–$89 single or double. Dec 22–Mar, $89–$99 single or double. Additional person $10 extra. AE, DC, JCB, MC, V. **Parking:** Free.

One of the older hotels in Kailua, and in the process of being refurbished as we went to press, this plantation-style complex boasts one of the most central locations in town, plus a pool set in a glorious garden and a barbecue pit out by the pool. All the rooms are identical, but the price is determined by location: garden, poolside, or with ocean view. Rooms are decorated in earth tones, with rich orange carpets; all have either a queen-size bed or two twin beds, shower (no tub), and a private lanai furnished with a table and two director's chairs. There's a refrigerator in every unit, and the kitchenette package of hotplate and utensils is available for $10 more.

KONA MAGIC SANDS CONDOMINIUM, 77-6452 Alii Dr., Kailua-Kona, HI 96740. Tel. 808/329-9177. Fax 808/329-5480. 37 studio apts. TV

$ **Rates:** $65–$75 studio apt for two. Additional person $10 extra. Minimum stay three days. AE, MC, V. **Parking:** Free.

Each and every apartment at the Kona Magic Sands Condominium overlooks the pounding ocean and the glorious sunsets of Kona. This is one of the older condos in the area, not as luxurious as some, but it's very beachy and cozy—the kind of place where it feels good to kick off your sandals and take life easy. The good-size studio apartments, furnished for two guests, have full kitchens; instead of a separate bedroom, they have a sleeping alcove off the living room, with a double, queen, or sofa bed. There are palm trees outside your window, a freshwater pool for swimming, and the convenience of having Jameson's by the Sea, a top restaurant, right downstairs. A few of the extra-large apartments have lanais overlooking the beach.

Reservations: Kona Vacation Resort, P.O. Box 1071, Kailua-Kona, HI 96745 (tel. toll free 800/367-5168 in the mainland U.S., 800/800-KONA in Canada).

KONA RIVIERA VILLA, 75-6124 Alii Dr., Kailua-Kona, HI 96740. Tel. 808/329-1996. 10 1-bedroom apts. TV TEL

$ **Rates:** $65 garden, $70–$90 ocean-view, $90–$100 oceanfront. Additional person $10 extra. No credit cards. Minimum stay three nights. **Parking:** Free.

The Kona Riviera Villa is the kind of place we like best: charming, intimate, low-key, and affordable. It's an older condominium complex, set just far enough back from the water to bring in the cooling breezes—and not too much ocean noise. A freshwater swimming pool and patio with barbecue grill overlook the ocean, too rough here for swimming, but fine for snorkelers and surfers. Each apartment is comfortably furnished and nicely decorated. All units have one bedroom, and some of the living rooms have sofa beds, so that up to four people can be accommodated. Kitchens are electric, equipped with dishwashers and garbage disposals. This is a congenial place, so much so that many of the same guests come back year after year, and rates are very modest for this luxury area. Make reservations well in advance.

KONA SEASIDE HOTEL, 75-5646 Palani Rd., Kailua-Kona, HI 96740. Tel. 808/329-2455. Fax 808/329-6157. 225 rms, 14 kitchenette rms. A/C TV TEL

$ **Rates:** $49 standard; $54 pool; $59 tower; $64 deluxe; $89 kitchenette. Dec 15–Mar, add $10 to all rates. Cars available for $15 more per day. Additional person $12 extra. Children 12 and under stay free with parents when using existing bedding. Rate increase expected. AE, DC, MC, V. **Parking:** Free.

A good choice smack in the center of Kailua is the Kona Seaside Hotel and Kona Seaside Pool Wing, at the intersection of Kuakini Highway (Hi. 11) and Palani Road (Hi. 19)—just a parking lot away from the shopping and restaurant excitement of Alii Drive. Size is the byword—large rooms, spacious lanais, and an extra-large pool. Blue is the theme of the well-appointed rooms.

The rooms in the Kona Seaside Pool Wing (formerly the Hukilau Hotel), most of them overlooking another large lovely pool, are smartly furnished and have twin- or king-size beds; from many you can see the harbor across the road. Or you may just want to laze on the sun deck, which looks out on Alii Drive and the harbor, and watch the world go by below you. The pool wing leads directly into Stan's Restaurant, which serves three reasonably priced meals every day and has a popular cocktail lounge.

Reservations: Sand & Seaside Hotels, 2222 Kalakaua Ave., Suite 714, Honolulu, HI 96815 (tel. toll free 800/367-7000 in the U.S., 800/654-7020 in Canada; fax 808/922-0052).

KONA TIKI HOTEL, Alii Dr. (P.O. Box 1567), Kailua-Kona, HI 96740. Tel. 808/329-1425. 15 rms.

$ Rates: $55 single or double, $60 single or double with kitchenette. Additional person $5 extra (maximum of three people per room). Minimum stay three days. No credit cards. **Parking:** Free.

In a garden setting overlooking the ocean, away from the bustle of the center of town and very close to the Kona Hilton, is the petite Kona Tiki Hotel, a longtime budget stop in Kona. All the rooms have private oceanfront lanais looking out on the blue-green pounding surf (and it really does pound—noisily—against the sea wall). The ocean is great for fishing and snorkeling; there's a freshwater pool for gentler swimming. All rooms include queen-size beds, ceiling fans, and a small refrigerator in every room. They have recently been redone in blue-and-green color schemes, with light furniture and new kitchenette units and refrigerators. Friendliness abounds at the Kona Tiki; it's the kind of small, family-owned hotel where guests usually get to know one another. Kona coffee and doughnuts are available in the morning. You can drive to the center of town in 3 minutes or walk in 15 minutes. Reserve a month in advance usually, two months in advance in busy seasons. Specify first and second choices on rooms with or without kitchenette (very few kitchenettes are available).

MERRYMAN'S BED & BREAKFAST, P.O. Box 474, Kealekekua, HI 86750. Tel. 808/323-2276, or toll free 800/545-4390. 4 rms. TV

$ Rates (including breakfast): $55 single without bath, $70 single with bath; $65 double with shared bath, $80 double with private bath. MC, V. **Parking:** Free.

Don and Penny Merryman's pretty home 1,500 feet up on a hill in Kealekekua, about a half-hour drive from Kailua town, has plenty of charm: rooms filled with handsome antiques (the Victorian room has a four-poster bed), views of Kealekekua Bay far below or a lovely garden, and two large lanais (one with a refrigerator and microwave), where guests can relax and have breakfast. Don and Penny, a young couple from Alaska, are gracious hosts, and they usually put out something special for their guests: maybe quiche, or bagels and cream cheese, plus fruit, teas, and Kona coffee, of course—it's grown right down on the slopes of the mountain. Each room has its own TV and refrigerator.

PAPA CHANG'S HALE OHANA, 73-1026 Ahikawa St., Kailua-Kona, HI 96740. Tel. 808/325-5118, or toll free 800/435-4253. 8 rms.

$ Rates (including breakfast): $65 per day, $400 per week, with one double bed; $85 per day, $500 per week, with two double beds. Minimum stay two days; for stays of one day, if available, add $15 to the rates. MC, V. **Parking:** Free.

A cross between a modern hotel and a homey B&B, Art Chang's place is one-of-a-kind. Chang, a retired airline maintenance supervisor, built it himself, not far from Keahole Airport (it attracts many airline people) and about a 20-minute drive into Kailua town, in a cool suburban area 1,000 feet above sea level. It was the dream of Chang and his late wife, Myrtle, to create a place where people on vacation could enjoy roomy areas. There's an enormous deck on each floor of the two-story polehouse, an equally enormous common room on each floor, with a television set, a dining room and kitchen, and a fully equipped laundry room. Guests have the run of all of them. Breakfast, which is put out in the common rooms, consists of fruit from the gardens—papayas, pineapple, bananas, grapefruit, limes—plus toast, crackers, coffee. There's a good-sized pool out back. Larger rooms with two double beds boast 440 square feet of space, and each includes a small refrigerator and microwave oven, a double vanity, and a bidet. Smaller rooms, 300 square feet, are similarly equipped. Telephones and TVs are available on request. The grounds are beautifully landscaped with manilla palms and fruit trees, and from the decks where visitors like to relax, there's a fine view of the coastline and of Maui, off in the distance.

UNCLE BILLY'S KONA BAY HOTEL, 75-5739 Alii Dr., Kailua-Kona, HI 96740. Tel. 808/935-7903. Fax 808/935-7903. 145 rms. A/C TV TEL

$ Rates: Apr–Dec 15, $72 single or double; $79 double with car and breakfast. Dec 16–Mar add $10 to all rates. Children under 18 stay free in parent's room. Additional person $10 extra. AE, DC, DISC, MC, V. **Parking:** Free.

Uncle Billy's Kona Bay Hotel, right in the center of town, is run by the same family that manages Uncle Billy's Hilo Bay Hotel. This newer hotel is landscaped with bridges and ponds, and a Polynesian longhouse restaurant surrounds a large circular swimming pool. The thatched roof over the registration desk and the koa-wood tables in the lobby create a warm Hawaiian feeling. The hotel's restaurant, Banana Bay, is popular for its $4.95 breakfast and $8.95 dinner buffets. The rooms, smartly decorated in gray, blue, and mauve, are of a comfortable size. Each room has a good-size lanai and a refrigerator; many have two double beds. Some rooms have an ocean view.

Reservations: Kona Bay Hotel, 87 Banyan Dr., Hilo, HI 96720. (tel. toll free 800/367-5102).

WORTH THE EXTRA BUCKS

COLONY'S KONA BALI KAI, 76-6246 Alii Dr., Kailua-Kona, HI 96740. Tel. 808/329-9381, or toll free 800/367-6040. Fax 808/526-2017. 155 apts. A/C TV TEL

$ Rates: Apr–Dec 22, $90–$145 one-bedroom apt; $160 two-bedroom apt. Dec 23–Mar, add $30 to all rates. Children under 17 stay free in parents' room using existing bedding. AE, CB, DC, DISC, JCB, MC, V. **Parking:** Free.

The oceanfront Kona Bali Kai is another lovely condominium resort. The rooms are exquisitely and individually furnished, with every convenience—full kitchens, washer-dryers in oceanside units, daily maid service (unusual in most condominiums), and lanais from which those in the main building can watch the spectacular surf and tireless surfers (other buildings afford partial views of mighty Mount Hualalai or lush gardens). The surf is too strong here for casual swimmers, but there's a good swimming beach a mile away, and right at home is a sunning beach amid the coral-reef tidal pools, a swimming pool, Jacuzzi, and sauna. There are barbecue grills on the beach, and a Pupu Pantry in the lobby area for essentials, groceries, and sandwiches. Arrangements can be made at the activities desk in the lobby for golf (three miles south), tennis (two miles north), or for a variety of adventures nearby. One-bedroom apartments can sleep up to four people, and the spectacular two-bedroom/two-bath apartments can comfortably sleep up to six.

HOLUALOA INN, P.O. Box 222, Holualoa, HI 96725. Tel. 808/324-1121. 6 rms.

$ Rates (including full breakfast): $100–$200 single or double. 15% discount on stays of one week or longer. Minimum stay two days; maximum stay two weeks. AE, MC, V. **Parking:** Free.

Grander than most B&Bs and smaller than most hotels, the Holualoa Inn is in a class by itself: It's an exquisite small inn set high up in the mountains in the farming community/art colony of Holualoa, about a 15-minute drive from the ocean at Kailua-Kona, which provides its magnificent views. The three-level mansion set in a 40-acre estate was originally built as a mountain hideaway for *Honolulu Advertiser* president Thurston Twigg-Smith. Now his nephew Desmond Twigg-Smith has taken it over and superbly decorated its guest bedrooms, which he rents out on a B&B basis to those lucky enough to find this serenely beautiful spot. The house is built of cedar wood, its floors of eucalyptus, its windows of spun glass. The handsome living room has a fireplace, reading areas, even a billiard table. The formal dining room is the scene of morning breakfasts of fresh fruits, juices, pancakes, sausages, pastries, and homemade muffins. And the rooms are enchanting, each one done differently: one with an Asian theme, another in Balinese style, a third in Polynesian decor, a fourth with a Hawaiian-hibiscus motif. Two new rooms, under construction at the time of this writing, will have king-size beds and their own Jacuzzis. In addition to the use of the living and dining rooms upstairs, guests also have a common room on the lower level, where they can store food in the refrigerator. There's a large swimming pool outside, a tower from which to watch the sunset, and everywhere, the singing of birds.

KAILUA PLANTATION HOUSE, 75-5948 Alii Dr., Kailua-Kona, HI 96740. Tel. 808/329-3727. 5 rms. A/C TV TEL

$ Rates (including breakfast): $120, $125, $145, $150, or $175 double. MC, V. **Parking:** Free.

This is Kona's only oceanfront bed-and-breakfast inn, elegant to the max. Exquisite rooms, each furnished differently and romantically (some with four-poster beds, one with a skylight above the platform whirlpool bath for two) are ideal for honeymooners. All have small refrigerators, hot-beverage equipment, and their own private lanais. There's an outdoor dipping pool and spa. Breakfast can be taken in the elegantly furnished living room or out on the oceanfront lanai, with a view of the waters pounding the black boulders and surfers riding the waves. Hostess Lisa Berger is helpful with tips and information.

SEA VILLAGE, 75-6002 Alii Dr., Kailua-Kona, HI 96740. Tel. 808/329-1000. 131 apts.

$ Rates: Apr 16–Dec 15, $90–$106 one-bedroom apt; $114–$132 two-bedroom apt. Dec 16–Apr 15, $106–$126 one-bedroom apt; $130–$150 two-bedroom apt. Minimum stay three nights. 10% discount on monthly rates available in summer. AE, DISC, MC, V. **Parking:** Free.

Condominiums are very big in Kona these days, and surely one of the nicest is the Sea Village, an idyllic spot overlooking the ocean just outside town. This is a large resort complex, with a tennis court, swimming pool, and Jacuzzi on the premises, as well as snorkeling off the rocks in front of the hotel for strong swimmers. Living quarters are outstanding: The apartments are beautifully furnished, ultraspacious and luxurious, with huge living rooms, one or two bedrooms, and shiny modern kitchens fitted with every appliance including dishwashers, washer-dryers, and refrigerators with automatic ice makers. Bathrooms are lovely, and there is ample closet and storage space, weekly chamber service, and private lanais. Views are of the garden or the ocean; the oceanfront apartments are the most expensive. Rates here are higher than our usual budget ones, but if you come during off-season, you might be able to manage it, keeping in mind that the one-bedroom apartments sleep four and the two-bedrooms sleep six.

Reservations: Paradise Management Corp., Kukui Plaza C-207, 50 S. Beretania St., Honolulu, HI 96813. (tel. toll free 800/367-5205; fax 808/533-4621).

WHITE SANDS VILLAGE, 77-6469 Alii Dr., Kailua-Kona, HI 96740. Tel. 808/329-6402, or toll free 800/345-2823. Fax 808/326-2401. 108 condominium units. A/C TV TEL

$ Rates: $85–$150 per day two-bedroom unit. April–Dec 15, $510–$700 per week; Dec 16–Mar, $700–$1,050 per week. AE, MC, V. **Parking:** Free.

The thing we like best about this place is that it's just across from Magic Sands Beach, one of the few remaining beaches in the area. It's a large condo complex, with many recreational facilities, including a pool, sauna, Jacuzzi, tennis courts, and barbecue area. Each of the two-bedroom units, large enough to sleep four, is individually owned, so furnishings and appointments vary.

As is usual with complexes of this type, several realtors handle apartments here; one with a good number of units is Jean Metz, of Triad Management Realtors, in the North Kona Shopping Center, 75-5629-P Kuahini Hwy., Kailua-Kona, HI 96740; you can reach her at the numbers listed above. Triad also handles many other vacation rentals—approximately 125 condominiums and houses—so see what she has to offer.

READERS RECOMMEND

Keauhou Beach Hotel, *78-6740 Alii Dr., Kailua-Kona, HI 96740. "The Keauhou Beach Hotel at Keauhou-Kona was exceptional! It was lovely in every way. It had such a Hawaiian atmosphere, with its oceanside bar, torchlit gardens, pool with waterfall, and restaurant over the lagoon. Their weekend seafood buffet was exceptional. They even upgraded our partial-ocean-view rooms to full ocean-view at no extra charge ($101 for partial ocean-view). I highly recommend this place."*—Martha Farwell, Illinois City, Ill.

3. WHERE TO EAT

Big Island restaurants offer a marvelous variety of foods, in every price range, and to suit every taste. Hilo is especially good for the budget traveler, since its restaurants cater mostly to locals rather than tourists. Dine with them and you'll save a bundle.

HILO

MEALS FOR LESS THAN $12

BEARS' COFFEE, 110 Keawe St. Tel. 935-0708.

Cuisine: GOURMET DELI/VEGETARIAN/DESSERTS. **Reservations:** Not accepted.

$ Prices: $2.50–$7. No credit cards.

Open: Mon–Fri 7am–5pm, Sat 8am–4pm.

Bears' Coffee, a stylish little place (marble-top tables indoors and out, hand-stenciled walls) that adjoins the Most Irresistible Shop in Hilo, is proving to be irresistible—so much so that its original menu of a variety of coffees and pastries keeps expanding: Now they start the day with breakfast items like "souffléd eggs" (steamed light and fluffy on the espresso machine) and "egg busters" (eggs, cheese, and ham on English muffin), and offer deli and vegetarian sandwiches ($3.60–$3.95), salads, designer bagels (create your own toppings), hot and cold soups, in addition to the original coffee and pastry menu. What fun to indulge in coffee and espresso drinks like caffè latte or Mexican chocolate, and desserts like carrot cake, lemon–poppy-seed coffee cake, or raspberry cheesecake, plus their luscious chocolate brownies. You can also buy fresh-roasted coffee beans by the pound to take home. House coffee is 95¢ per cup, and pastries run $2.50–$3. They pack neat picnic lunches to go—call two hours ahead. Bearvo!

CAFE 100, 969 Kilauea Ave. Tel. 935-8683.

Cuisine: LOCAL. **Reservations:** Not accepted.

$ Prices: $1–$4.75.

Open: Mon–Thurs 5:45am–8:30pm, Fri–Sat 6:45am–9:30pm.

Whenever we used to drive by Café 100, we'd notice long lines of island people at the windows of this popular drive-in. We joined them one day and found out why: It's hard to spend more than $5 for a full hot lunch. Fried chicken, beef stew, breaded mahimahi, and teriyaki steak are all served with rice and potato-macaroni salad. Hiloans swear by the local favorite, which is reputed to have been invented here: LocoMoco, a hearty meal of a hamburger patty and fried egg on rice, topped with brown gravy; it's $1.50. They even have LocoMoco T-shirts! Chili, burgers, and sandwiches of all kinds start at $1. Try their specialties: yummy mahimahi sandwiches and Goody Goody sherbet. Café 100 is good to remember when you're in a hurry and the traveler's checks are running low

DICK'S COFFEE HOUSE, 1235-1 Kilauea Ave., in the Hilo Shopping Center. Tel. 935-2769.

Cuisine: AMERICAN.

$ Prices: Main courses $3.95–$7.25. MC, V.

Open: Breakfast daily 7–11am; lunch Mon–Sat 11am–4pm; dinner Mon–Sat 4–10pm.

Dick's, a lively local place with sporting pennants on the walls, is one of the most popular coffee shops in town. On the à la carte dinner menu, you could choose chicken cutlet, grilled fish filet, teriyaki steak Oriental, or grilled pork chops, most in the $4.60–$5.35 range, with New York–cut steak at $7.25; your main course comes with soup or salad, starch, rolls, and butter. Lunch features burgers from $3.20, gourmet sandwiches like pastrami on French bread or a steak sandwich for under $4—and homemade pies and cream pies for dessert for around $1.15! Daily lunch specials go for $2.50–$2.75, and there are also weekday lunch and dinner specials under $4. Breakfast is inexpensive, too: You could have a complete breakfast of grilled mahimahi, with toast, and hash browns or rice, for $2.80. A local friend raves about the fried chicken and the rhubarb pie, but advises that you come early, as only one pie is baked each day.

DON'S GRILL, 485 Hinano St. Tel. 935-9099.

Cuisine: AMERICAN. **Reservations:** Not required.

$ Prices: Complete meals $6.95–$10.95. MC, V.

Open: Mon–Fri 10:30am–9pm, Sat–Sun 10am–9pm.

Don's Grill, near the Waiakea Villas Hotel, has everything a good family restaurant should have: It's large, comfortable, and inexpensive, and the food is fresh and good. Owner Don Hoota has won a large local following for this place. Tuck into one of the booths and treat yourself to a complete dinner—honest!—for just $6.95 to $9.95 (only the seafood platter and New York steak, at $10.95, are higher); along with your main course of rôtisseried chicken (the house specialty), or barbecued ribs, or filet of fish, you get a choice of soup or salad, a starch, hot vegetables, rolls, and a beverage. They also have good sandwiches, burgers, plus local favorites like LocoMoco, saimin, and homemade chili; it's hard to go wrong.

DOTTY'S COFFEE SHOP AND RESTAURANT, Puainako town center. Tel. 959-6477.

Cuisine: AMERICAN. **Reservations:** Not required.

$ Prices: Main courses $5.25–$9.75. MC, V.

Open: Breakfast daily 7–11am; lunch daily 11am–2pm; dinner daily 5pm–closing.

If you love fresh fish *and* modest prices, this is a place to know about. Every evening, Dotty Frasco and her family do a fish-of-the-day special for under $10—and that might be ahi or mahimahi or ono—nicely grilled in garlic butter and white wine. What a deal! Everything else at Dotty's spiffy little coffee shop (green booths, nice photos on the wall) is a good deal too, since this is real home-cooking, with everything made from scratch ("We don't have a can opener," says Dotty). People come from all over just for her roast chicken and roast turkey, which she uses in her turkey plate. Popular dishes include grilled pork chops, liver and bacon, sautéed shrimp, calamari, and shrimp scampi. Lunches, moderately priced, feature salads, sandwiches, and burgers. Dotty's pies are homemade, and at $1.60, we wouldn't think of resisting.

JIMMY'S DRIVE INN, 362 Kinoole St. Tel. 935-5571.

Cuisine: JAPANESE/AMERICAN. **Reservations:** Not required.

$ Prices: Main courses $5.50–$8.10. MC, V.

Open: Mon–Sat 8am–9:30pm.

Jimmy's Drive Inn is a popular place offering some of the best prices in town. The "drive inn" is misleading; you don't eat in your car but at clean chrome tables or at the counter. There are daily Japanese dinner specials like chicken-katsu, beef stew, fish tempura, grilled salmon steak, and captain's platter, which go for $5.50–$8.10—quite a bargain considering that they're accompanied by rice, vegetables, and coffee or iced tea. On the regular menu are about half a dozen complete dinners and complete seafood dinners, most priced between $5 and $6.10; and these include such main courses as barbecued steak, liver and bacon, ahi, butterfish, and shrimp tempura, all accompanied by soup or salad, fries or rice, vegetable, bread, dessert, and beverage.

KARROT'S KITCHEN, 197 Keawe St. Tel. 935-6191.

Cuisine: THAI/HEALTH FOODS. **Reservations:** Not accepted.

$ Prices: Main courses $4.50–$6.30. MC, V.

Open: Mon–Fri 7am–8pm, Sat 8am–2pm.

This very attractive, modernistic restaurant, with its sleek black counter and about five tables, sits up front at the Spencer Health & Fitness Center. It's the kind of place you like to patronize when you want a quick and nutritious meal. Best choices here are the several Thai specialties—mixed vegetables, gado gado, pad Thai, cashew chicken, Thai shrimp with garlic. It's also fun to stop by here for breakfast, especially for their blueberry-filled pancakes with whipped cream, at $2.95. They bake wonderful muffins here, so grab a few for your picnic basket.

KAY'S, 684 Kilauea Ave. Tel. 969-1776.

Cuisine: KOREAN. **Reservations:** Not required.

$ Prices: Appetizers $1–$1.50; main courses $5.95–$8.25.

Open: Breakfast/lunch Tues–Fri 6am–2pm, Sat–Sun 5am–2pm; dinner Tues–Sun 5–8:30pm.

One of our favorite Hilo eateries is Kay's, which serves just about the best barbecued chicken we've ever tasted, anywhere. Local friends put us on to this large, Korean-style family restaurant, full of local color: screaming babies, people reading the newspapers, Formica tables, orange-leather booths. But never mind. The atmosphere is friendly, the staff is charming, and the food is ridiculously inexpensive, and so good that you'll want to come back more than once. The house specialty is the Korean crispy fried chicken, which we found a bit heavy; instead, go with the barbecued chicken—it's boned, flattened, marinated in a very light shoyu sauce in the Korean manner, and simply delicious. All dinners include hot rice, miso soup, vegetable of the day, and four kinds of kimchee. You can order your meal either small or large (we found small to be adequate). One choice—Korean barbecued beef, ka bi, barbecued chicken, fried fish, shoyu pork, etc.—is $5.95 small, $6.25 for a full order; two choices are $6.25 and $7.25; three choices, $7.25 and $8.25. Don't be misled by the sign reading KAY'S LUNCH CENTER; Kay now serves dinner too, thank heaven.

KEN'S HOUSE OF PANCAKES, 1730 Kamehameha Ave., at the intersection of Hi. 19 and Hi. 11. Tel. 935-8711.

Cuisine: AMERICAN/LOCAL. **Reservations:** Not accepted.

$ Prices: Breakfast dishes $3.85–$5.95; dinner main courses $5.65–$8.45. AE, DC, DISC, MC, V.

Open: Daily 24 hours.

The only place in town open 24 hours a day, Ken's is known for serving its entire menu around the clock. That means that at whatever time of day you're hungry for, say, macadamia nut or fresh banana pancakes, eggs Benedict, or eggs with Scottish bangers or Portuguese sausage, Ken's will dish them up and at very reasonable prices. New management has taken over this popular Hilo landmark, and they've added local Hawaiian specialties at lunch and dinner. Good burgers, sandwiches, salads, home-

BIG ISLAND DINING

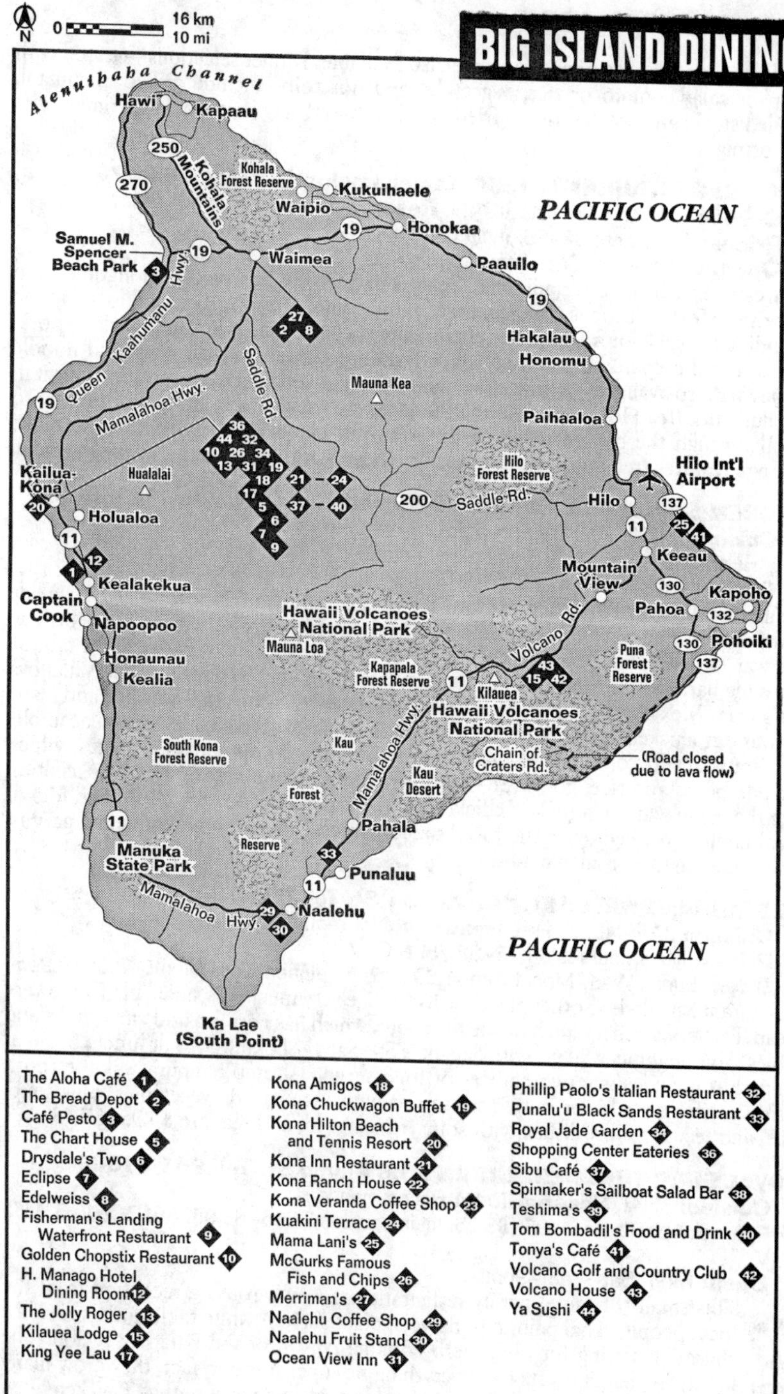
0 16 km 10 mi
N
Alenuihaha Channel
PACIFIC OCEAN
Hawi
Kapaau
250
270
Kohala Mountains
Kohala Forest Reserve
Kukuihaele
Waipio
19
Honokaa
Samuel M. Spencer Beach Park
Waimea
Paauilo
Queen Kaahumanu Hwy
Saddle Rd.
Hakalau
Honomu
Mauna Kea
Mamalahoa Hwy.
Paihaaloa
Hilo Forest Reserve
Hilo Int'l Airport
Kailua-Kona
Hualalai
200
Saddle Rd.
Hilo
137
Holualoa
11
Keeau
Kealakekua
Mountain View
130
Kapoho
Captain Cook
Hawaii Volcanoes National Park
Pahoa
132
Napoopoo
Mauna Loa
Volcano Rd.
Pohoiki
Honaunau
Puna Forest Reserve
Kapapala Forest Reserve
Kealia
Kilauea
Hawaii Volcanoes National Park
South Kona Forest Reserve
Kau
Chain of Craters Rd.
(Road closed due to lava flow)
Kau Desert
Forest
Mamalahoa Hwy.
Pahala
Reserve
Manuka State Park
Punaluu
Mamalahoa Hwy.
Naalehu
PACIFIC OCEAN
Ka Lae (South Point)
The Aloha Café 1
The Bread Depot 2
Café Pesto 3
The Chart House 5
Drysdale's Two 6
Eclipse 7
Edelweiss 8
Fisherman's Landing Waterfront Restaurant 9
Golden Chopstix Restaurant 10
H. Manago Hotel Dining Room 12
The Jolly Roger 13
Kilauea Lodge 15
King Yee Lau 17
Kona Amigos 18
Kona Chuckwagon Buffet 19
Kona Hilton Beach and Tennis Resort 20
Kona Inn Restaurant 21
Kona Ranch House 22
Kona Veranda Coffee Shop 23
Kuakini Terrace 24
Mama Lani's 25
McGurks Famous Fish and Chips 26
Merriman's 27
Naalehu Coffee Shop 29
Naalehu Fruit Stand 30
Ocean View Inn 31
Phillip Paolo's Italian Restaurant 32
Punalu'u Black Sands Restaurant 33
Royal Jade Garden 34
Shopping Center Eateries 36
Sibu Café 37
Spinnaker's Sailboat Salad Bar 38
Teshima's 39
Tom Bombadil's Food and Drink 40
Tonya's Café 41
Volcano Golf and Country Club 42
Volcano House 43
Ya Sushi 44

made pies, and fountain specialties are also available. Dinner selections—served with soup or salad, potato or rice, vegetable, and hot roll—include grilled mahimahi, broiled steak, and southern-style fried chicken. Everything is available anytime of the day or night.

K.K. TEI RESTAURANT, 1550 Kamehameha Hwy. Tel. 961-3791.

Cuisine: JAPANESE/AMERICAN. **Reservations:** Recommended.

$ Prices: Appetizers $2–$6; main courses $8–$15. AE, MC, V.

Open: Lunch Mon–Sat 11am–2pm; dinner Mon–Sat 5–9pm.

You can relax in a very traditional Japanese setting at this place, a longtime Hilo favorite. Most selections are Japanese, with some American specialties. Plan on spending $5–$11 for a complete lunch. Dinner choices include beef, chicken, pork, and seafood prepared in a variety of styles. Soups, salads, sandwiches, and noodle dishes are also available. If there are at least seven of you, call for reservations to sit in the authentic Tea House overlooking the Japanese rock garden and pond. Be sure to stroll through the garden to enjoy the beautiful plants and flowers. The Karaoke Lounge features free pupus from opening at 11am until closing at 2 in the morning.

REUBEN'S MEXICAN FOOD, 336 Kamehameha Ave. Tel. 961-2552.

Cuisine: MEXICAN. **Reservations:** Not required.

$ Prices: Appetizers $2.75; main courses $6–$8. MC, V.

Open: Mon–Sat 11am–9pm.

Reuben's Mexican Food, across from the waterfront, is a real local hangout. Aside from its shocking-pink color scheme and Mexican murals on the wall, it has little in the way of decor, but it's large (there's plenty of breathing room between the tables), has a big bar, and the food is good. Reuben's is run by chef Reuben and Sue Villanova (he's from Mexico, she's from Hilo). Our appetizer of nachos ($3) was hot and tasty; so was our chicken flautas (a flour tortilla with chicken, shredded lettuce, guacamole, and sour cream) combination plate for $7.50. Some 34 combination plates, which include beans and rice, go for $6–$8. There are a few interesting house specialties, like the gallina adovada (baked chicken), and a crab salad, $5–$8. You'll find lots of local families here enjoying the food, the low prices, and the memorable margaritas. The same menu is available all day.

RESTAURANT SATSUKI, 168 Keawe St. Tel. 935-7880.

Cuisine: JAPANESE. **Reservations:** Not required.

$ Prices: Main courses $4.75–$8.75. MC, V.

Open: Lunch Wed–Mon 11am–1:30 or 2pm; dinner Wed–Mon 5–8:30 or 9pm.

Restaurant Satsuki is another place the locals like very much: It's small, plain, and very clean. Partitions and a screen divide the room, which has Formica and vinyl chairs and tables. You might as well go with Satsuki's Special Teishoku ($5.75 at lunch, $6.50 at dinner); it includes any two choices of fried shrimp, shrimp tempura, yakitori, pork teriyaki, beef teriyaki, or butterfish, served with various side vegetables, plus soup, rice, and tea. Donburi dishes with soup, tsukemono, and tea, are $4.95–$7.45.

ROYAL SIAM THAI RESTAURANT, 68 Mamo St. Tel. 961-6100.

Cuisine: THAI. **Reservations:** Recommended.

$ Prices: Appetizers $4.95–$5.95; main courses $4.95–$8.95. AE, DC, JCB, MC, V.

Open: Mon–Sat 11am–9pm.

This small (11-table) family restaurant has won a rousing reception from the local people. Thai paintings, flowers, planters, and white tablecloths provide a charming setting for the superb cooking typical of the Bangkok region. The family in charge insists that everything be super-fresh; in fact, they grow many of the vegetables and spices in their own gardens to ensure that. Chicken sateh with peanut sauce and spring rolls are terrific appetizers, and among the main courses, you can't go wrong with the cashew chicken, Thai noodles with chicken, or Thai garlic shrimp. They do all the traditional curries—yellow, green, red—with chicken, beef, or vegetables; if you're lucky and they have fresh salmon, order your curry made with that. Vegetarians have a full menu of their own. *Warning:* Ask that your food be prepared mild, unless you *really* like it hot! Try the local coconut ice cream or the unusual tapioca pudding made with taro. Lunch is an especially good buy, since specials begin at just $4.95.

TING-HAO MANDARIN RESTAURANT, Puainako town center. Tel. 959-6288.

Cuisine: CHINESE. **Reservations:** Recommended.
$ Prices: Appetizers $3–$5.50; main courses $5–$9. MC, V.
Open: Lunch Mon–Sat 10:30am–2:30pm; dinner daily 4:30–9pm.

What brings the Mercedes and other fancy cars to the modest Puainako town center? Although not many tourists know of it, the Chinese population has discovered the Ting-Hao Mandarin Restaurant, and they come to enjoy the wizardry of master chef Ting Cheng, whose repertoire includes some 200 banquet dishes. He cooks Peking, Mandarin, Szechuan, and Cantonese style, so there is quite a variety on the menu. Everything we've tried—and we've dined here many times—has been special. And they never use MSG! Corn eggdrop soup is unusual and subtly flavored; potstickers, those tasty dumplings that are both steamed and fried (on one side), are a great beginning to your meal. Outstanding main courses in the Mandarin style include shredded pork with fungus and golden egg, shredded pork with garlic sauce (watch out, it's hot!), and the eggplant with garlic sauce, each $5. Unusual and delicious, too, are the Kung Pao ika (cuttlefish) with spicy paprikas, $7; the Kung Pao shrimp with spicy paprikas, $8; the minced chicken with lettuce, $9; and the chicken with cashew nuts, $6. Most main dishes are inexpensive and hearty enough to fill you up for many hours. In fact, we find the portions here so generous that we usually wind up taking containers back to our kitchenette apartment for the next day's lunch. At lunch, there are four daily specials, served with spareribs or an eggroll, for $4.25. Vegetarians can enjoy a number of good dishes. Ting-Hao is a large, very clean restaurant, simply decorated, with fans and prints on the wall. Service is helpful and friendly; there's a warm, family feeling here. Puainako town center is past the airport, and not far from Prince Kuhio Plaza; the restaurant is near the big Sack 'n' Save store.

MEALS FOR LESS THAN $20

FIASCOS, 200 Kanoelehua Ave., at Waiakea Square. Tel. 935-7666.

Cuisine: AMERICAN. **Reservations:** Recommended on weekends.
$ Prices: Appetizers $2.95–$5.50; main courses $5.95–$16.95. AE, DISC, MC, V.
Open: Sun–Thurs 7am–10pm, Fri–Sat 7am–11pm.

This is one of Hilo's most popular and enjoyable restaurants. It's done up attractively, with lots of plants and wood, and the atmosphere is lively and upbeat. The food (notwithstanding the rather precious menu descriptions depicting the journeys of one mythical Hans Fiasco) is consistently good, and there are enough possibilities to appeal to a variety of tastes and budgets. Appetizers include potato skins, nachos, "yummy drummies" (batter-fried chicken drumettes with hot barbecue sauce), and a fantastic baked Brie, topped with macadamia nuts and served with fresh fruit and hot sourdough bread. Many Hilo folks swear by their salad bar; it's a bountiful table of fruits and vegetables, served with homemade dressings, $5.95 alone, $6.95 with soup, $2.95 with any meal. If you come here on a weekday between 11:30am and 2pm, you can have a choice of four soups and salad bar for $5.95. There's a fresh fish sandwich every day. Hot dishes, served at both lunch and dinner, include many items for $5.50–$10.95, like stir-fry chicken, herb chicken, and country-fried steak. And there are good pastas too, including pasta Alfredo at $6.95.

Desserts? Their strawberry crêpe filled with ice cream or their chocolate–macadamia-nut mousse could be a meal in itself. Breakfast includes international favorites and health-conscious specialties as well. Upstairs at Fiascos, a 1950s and 1960s dance club swings into action on Thursday, Friday, and Saturday nights from 8:30pm to 2am. Fiascos is good fun and good food for the price.

HARRINGTON'S, 135 Kalanianaole St. Tel. 961-4966.
Cuisine: STEAK/SEAFOOD. **Reservations:** Recommended.
$ Prices: Appetizers $2.75–$7.95; main courses $12.25–$18.95. MC, V.
Open: Dinner only, daily 5:30–10pm.

Overlooking the Ice Pond at Reed's Bay, near Banyan Drive, is Harrington's, one of Hilo's most upbeat restaurants. There's an atmosphere of casual elegance in the open-air dining room and lounge, a lively mood, and delicious food. Plan on this one for a splurge meal, since most main dishes—like mahimahi forestière, New York steak, chicken marsala, sautéed scallops, and the like—are in the $12–$18 range (they are accompanied by rolls, choice of salads and a starch). There is a way, however, to eat here inexpensively, if lightly. Ask to be seated in the lounge rather than the main dining room, and along with your beer or drink you can order from the appetizer and side-dish menu, which means that items like deep-fried calamari strips, mushrooms tempura, etc., ranging from $3.25 to $7.95, will be served cut up, pupu style. You could even have a stuffed potato for $2.25 and a house salad (Caesar or pasta or tossed greens) for $2.95. Be sure to make reservations if you do sit in the dining room, since this is a very, very popular scene.

HUKILAU RESTAURANT, in the Hilo Seaside Hotel, 126 Banyan Dr. Tel. 935-4222.
Cuisine: AMERICAN/SEAFOOD. **Reservations:** Not required.
$ Prices: Main courses $7.95–$17.95. MC, V.
Open: Breakfast daily 7–10:30am; lunch Mon–Sat 10:30am–11pm; dinner daily 4–8:30pm.

This popular oldtimer, the Hukilau Restaurant continues to be a Hilo favorite. Best buys here are at lunchtime: A daily lunch special at $4.35 includes a main dish, salad bar, rice or potato. And at least half a dozen à la carte dishes (including filet of mahimahi steak, calf's liver, and a Reuben sandwich) are also $4.35. At dinner, choose from either the seafood menu or the regular menu. Seafood dinners offer choices such as salmon steak, fresh fried oysters, rainbow trout, and fresh fish of the day, accompanied by soup of the day and salad bar. Favorites on the regular dinner menu include the prime rib roast, teriyaki steak, and steak and lobster, again with soup and the salad bar. Breakfast is fun here too, especially when you have pineapple hotcakes or French toast with macadamia nuts. The dining room is pleasant, and the staff has plenty of aloha.

LEHUA'S BAY CITY BAR & GRILL, 90 Kamehameha Ave. Tel. 935-8055.
Cuisine: PACIFIC. **Reservations:** Recommended for parties of six or more.
$ Prices: Appetizers $2–$7; main courses $7–$20. MC, V.
Open: Lunch Mon–Sat 11am–5pm; dinner Mon–Sat 5–10pm.

This is the kind of sophisticated bistro that you'd expect to find in, say, San Francisco, rather than downtown in sleepy little Hilo. But there it is, attractively decorated in subdued shades of gray, with plants in the center of the room, mobiles hanging from the ceiling, a stage, a dance floor, and a big bar up front, from which flow some of the best margaritas in town. Owners Mark Himmel and Larry Johnson describe their reasonably priced cuisine as "East meets West with an island flair"—and that's just what it is. Almost everything is homemade; only the freshest ingredients are used, seasonings and sauces are imaginative, and since many dishes are marinated and char-broiled, it's possible to eat food that's light as well as delicious. There are some wonderful appetizers at dinner, like char-broiled prawns marinated in lime juice and served with a dill-cucumber sauce, the chicken yakitori on skewers, and the summer rolls—char-broiled chicken wrapped in lettuce and mint leaves, in the Thai style. Homemade soups are a good bet, as are the salads and burgers; a char-broiled chicken burger is a house specialty at $6.75. All main courses are accompanied by delicious char-broiled garlic toast, a garden salad (the creamy garlic dressing is very good), a hot vegetable and a choice of fries, baked potato, or rice. They include barbecued ribs, char-broiled chicken, mixed grill, catch of the day, and porterhouse steak. Spinach lasagne, and the sauté medley of fresh vegetables will keep the vegetarians in the crowd contented.

Lunch offers similar dishes at lower prices, including soup-and-sandwich specials of the day, burgers, a very popular chicken with papaya salad, and the hearty Bay City saimin; it's the classic noodle dish, but topped with char-broiled chicken, shrimp, and fresh vegetables, $6.95. Desserts are homemade and super: Save some room for either the White Russian mousse or the chocolate banana cake, $2.95 and $3.50. On Friday and Saturday nights, Lehua's turns into the place for live entertainment, which continues late, usually until about 2am.

NIHON RESTAURANT & CULTURAL CENTER, 123 Lihiwai St. Tel. 969-1133.

Cuisine: JAPANESE. **Reservations:** Recommended.

$ **Prices:** Sushi $2.50–$14.95; main courses $6–$17. CB, DC, MC, V.

Open: Lunch Mon–Sat 11am–1:30pm; dinner Mon–Sat 5–8pm.

For a true taste of Japan, the place to go is the Nihon Cultural Center, overlooking Hilo Bay and lovely Liliuokalani Gardens. The Nihon Restaurant houses an art gallery, a traditional tearoom, an auditorium for cultural events, and at the heart of it all, a restaurant where traditional Japanese chefs ply their art. Of course there is a sushi bar—the menu describes these dainty morsels of fish and rice as "health foods"—and a dining room for regular Japanese meals. Tempura and tonkatsu lunches are $8.95 and $7.95; sashimi is market-priced. Lunch specials, for $8.25, include a choice of two items and accompaniments; dinners include the traditional sukiyaki. Complete combination dinners feature tempura, sashimi, and beef teriyaki. Traditional Japanese soup, pickled vegetables, and rice accompany the meals. Of course there's saké or Japanese beer to wash down your meal, and homemade green-tea ice cream for dessert. The sushi bar is open at the same time as the dining room.

PESCATORE, 235 Keawe St., at the corner of Haili. Tel. 969-9090.

Cuisine: ITALIAN. **Reservations:** Recommended, especially at dinner.

$ **Prices:** Appetizers $4.95–$9.95; main courses $13.95–$21.95. DC, MC, V.

Open: Lunch daily 11am–2pm; dinner Sun–Thurs 5:30–9pm, Fri–Sat 5:30–10pm.

Gourmet Italian cuisine is a rarity anywhere on the Big Island, so it's nice to find this little place right here in Hilo. Attractively decorated with green tablecloths, red chairs, and shuttered windows with lace curtains, it's a homey and inviting spot. And the food is inviting too, all of it done with great style. Among the antipasti, the carpaccio al pesce—fresh raw ahi—gets kudos, as does the char-broiled polenta in a red wine sauce, with shrimp, mussels, and calamari. There are specialty pasta, meat, and fish dishes to choose from every night (they do wonderful fish preparations), but good regular menu choices include the agnello marinata (char-broiled lamb chops), the pollo piccata (sautéed chicken breast in a lemon-caper sauce), and a lusty cioppino (the Italian version of a bouillabaisse). Desserts are wondrous, especially that double-chocolate–truffle cake made with espresso syrup—and the amaretto bread pudding, too.

RESTAURANT FUJI, in the Hilo Hotel, 142 Kinoole St. Tel. 961-3733.

Cuisine: JAPANESE. **Reservations:** Not accepted.

$ Prices: $6.50–$13.85. AE, DC, MC, V.
Open: Lunch Tues–Sun 11am–2pm; dinner Tues–Sun 5–9pm.

For a traditional, authentic Japanese meal—and for an excellent bargain as well—count on Restaurant Fuji. This is one of those gracious, relaxed places where you can really get comfortable; you can sit at the tempura bar (where you watch your dishes simmer and sizzle), at the comfortably spaced tables in the dining room, or at tables with hibachi grills overlooking the pool. At lunchtime recently, we sampled the very good butterfish ($12.50), with green salad, soup, vegetables, rice, and tea. Dinner features many reasonably priced dishes, like the tasty yosenabe teishoku at $10.90, and a melange of seafood, chicken, and vegetable tempura at $10.80.

THE SEASIDE, 1790 Kalanianaole Ave. Tel. 935-8825.
Cuisine: SEAFOOD. **Reservations:** Required.
$ Prices: Main courses $10.50–$17.95. MC, V.
Open: Dinner only, Tues–Sun 5:30–8:30pm.

Want to eat the freshest fish in Hilo? Then head for the Seaside, a few miles out of Hilo town in the Kaukaha area, where the mullet or aholehole or rainbow trout on your plate will be taken out of the pond when you call to make your reservation! The Seaside, highly respected by Hilo people for years and virtually unknown to tourists, is actually a fish farm; the Japanese family in charge have been cultivating fish here for more than 50 years, in the same way that mullet was historically fattened in special fish ponds for the alii of old Hawaii. They catch fingerlings from the Waiola River, keep them in pens for six months, then release them into the pond for five years. Rainbow trout thrive in Hawaii's warm waters, and take less time to mature—just a year. The 30-acre pond, leased from the state, is set on 50 acres of land in a rural area. Susuma Nakagowa, a former research entomologist with the U.S. Department of Agriculture, took over the fish farm from his parents; now, he and his wife and son, Colin, the restaurant manager, are in charge.

If you come before dinner while it's still light, somebody will show you around and explain the operation to you. (The place is a favorite stop for school groups and those interested in aquaculture.) Then on to the simple dining room where you can have your fish prepared in the traditional way, steamed in ti leaves, with onion slices and lemon juice, or fried. The menu is quite simple: For dinner, there's mullet or trout at $12.50; a combination of any fish with chicken, $13.50; chicken only, $10.50; a combination of one steamed fish and one fried fish (perhaps the best choice for first-timers), $17.95. Bottled wine is available. And for dessert—homemade apple pie. This place is not fancy, but the fish is the freshest, and coming here is a real experience in nontourist, old-time Hawaii. Be sure to call first, as they serve only when they have fish available. A nice adventure for the kids, too.

BETWEEN HILO & KONA ON THE NORTHERN ROUTE

In Chapter 13 we'll describe the drive from Hilo to the resort center of Kona, a trip you should take. Here are some suggestions for meals as you drive the northern route, along the Hamakua Coast (Hi. 19). First stop: Waimea.

WAIMEA

Meals for Less Than $12

THE BREAD DEPOT, in Opelo Plaza, Waimea. Tel. 885-6354.
Cuisine: BAKED GOODS/SOUPS/SANDWICHES.
$ Prices: Appetizers $2.50–$4.50; main course $4.50–$5.35. CB, DC, MC, V.

Open: Mon–Fri 6am–5:30pm.

There's something about eating in a bakery that's, well, warm and homey and smells delicious. Maybe that's why the Bread Depot is such a big hit with everybody in Waimea. Chef Georges Amtablian is both baker and cook, and his cinnamon buns and sourdough French bread, which he sells to local restaurants, are famous in these parts. Doors open at 6am, and soon folks are lining up for those giant cinnamon buns or a variety of healthful muffins, apple turnovers, and delicious ham-and-cheese brioches. At lunchtime (11:30am to 3pm), you can choose a sandwich on a fresh-baked roll for $4.50 or go for one of the delicious soups. Georges, a stickler for fresh and natural ingredients, prepares a special soup every day: Boston clam chowder, cream of potato with leek, and old-fashioned chicken-noodle soup are among the possibilities. Or try one of his daily specials: It could be boneless chicken leg stuffed with wild rice, with soup and salad; chicken enchiladas; tuna casserole; or quiche—each around $5. This French chef knows his stuff! If you're en route to one of the nearby beaches, you can pick up a nice picnic lunch here, too.

CAFE PESTO, in the Kawaihae Shopping Center, Kawaihae. Tel. 882-1071.

Cuisine: ITALIAN/PIZZA/PASTA. **Reservations:** Not required.

$ **Prices:** Appetizers $2.95–$6.95; small pizzas $6.95–$10.95; pastas $5.95–$10.95. MC, V.

Open: Sun–Thurs 11am–9pm, Fri–Sat 11am–10pm.

If you're driving on Hi. 19 to Kona after leaving Waimea, it's no trouble at all to stop off first at the harbor town of Kawaihae, where you'll find the highly praised Café Pesto. So popular has this gourmet pizza-pasta restaurant become that it's regularly patronized by folks staying at the plush resorts of the Kohala coast, as well as by food fans from all over the island. Two noted Big Island chefs, Jim Williams and David Palmer have put their considerable talents into creating a "pizza-pasta-provocative menu"—which translates into exotic pizzas and pastas, gourmet hot sandwiches, and some satisfyingly rich desserts. It's all served in a sophisticated black-and-white café atmosphere with a single rose on every table. Fine Italian wines and cold beers are available, and paintings by local artists change every month. Have someone in your party order one of the pastas, someone else one of the pizzas; that way, you get a chance to sample. Of the pastas, the ceviche pasta salad with cilantro pesto is delicious, with its Tahitian lime-marinated scallops and shrimps; the Thai curry pasta salad, with shrimp, sun-dried tomatoes, red onions, and spinach, is another taste treat. As for those pizza pies, they begin with a base of handmade and baked-to-order crust (a blend of white, rye, and wheat flours, plus olive oil and honey); they're topped with gourmet cheeses, fresh herbs, sun-dried tomatoes, and the like. The house special, and our favorite, is the pizza Oriental al pesto—fresh basil pesto, roasted garlic, sun-dried tomatoes, and Japanese eggplant. Scampi al pesto is also quite special. Soups and desserts also have the gourmet touch. Call ahead and they'll have your orders ready for take-out if you wish.

Meals for Less Than $25

THE BARON, Kinohou St. Tel. 885-5888.

Cuisine: PACIFIC RIM/CONTINENTAL. **Reservations:** Recommended.

$ **Prices:** Appetizers $6.50–$9.50; main courses $16–$20. MC, V.

Open: Lunch daily 11am–2pm; dinner daily 5–11pm; brunch Sun 10am–4pm.

A new gourmet restaurant has the local residents cheering. First it's beautiful, like a garden indoors and out, built around a gigantic East Indian banyan tree whose root system is above ground. One wall looks like a tropical greenhouse. Two famous Big Island chefs, Heinz-Dieter Hennig and Brend Bree have combined their considerable talents to create a sophisticated cuisine that offers the best of Pacific Rim and continental styles. Soups, for example, include both a Pacific seafood bisque and a liver-dumpling soup; appetizers feature an Oriental vegetable lumpia plus frogs' legs provençal and oysters Rockefeller. For your main course, you might choose stuffed red snapper prepared in the Japanese manner, beef à la Stroganoff, Chinese lemon chicken, or sauerbraten. Light dishes, pastas, and vegetarian dishes are available every night. The dessert tray is bountiful and quite irresistible. Deli selections are available in the mornings, and there's a luncheon buffet at $9.95. If you're driving across the island on a Sunday, treat yourself to their elaborate Sunday brunch buffet for $12.95.

EDELWEISS, Kawaihae Rd. Tel. 885-6800.

Cuisine: GERMAN. **Reservations:** Not accepted.

$ Prices: Appetizers $4.75–$5.75; complete dinners $14.50–$19.50. MC, V.

Open: Lunch Tues–Sat 11:30am–1:30pm; dinner Tues–Sat 5–9pm.

Another famous gourmet restaurant in Waimea is Edelweiss, a homey place with a European country feeling, seating only about 50 guests. So renowned has master chef-owner Hans Peter Hager's reputation become that there's usually a wait of an hour or so at dinnertime. But it's usually not too crowded at lunchtime; just be sure you get there before 1:30pm or you won't be seated. Hans Peter's cuisine does not disappoint. The luncheon specialty of bratwurst and sauerkraut is $4.95; also popular is the Puu Haloa ranch burger at $5.75, or in a more continental mood, the sautéed chicken breast with champignons and Monterey Jack cheese, $6.50. Complete dinners are served with soup of the day, salad, and beverage, and include such dishes as roast duck bigarade braised with a light orange sauce, wienerschnitzel, roast pork with sauerkraut, a wonderful roast rack of lamb for two, and the Edelweiss specialty—sautéed veal, lamb, beef, and bacon with pfifferling (European wild mushrooms)—very tasty, indeed. Since Hans Peter is also a master pastry chef, you'd be well advised to save room for dessert, especially if the incredible Grand Marnier parfait is available that day. Black Forest cake, chocolate mousse, fresh peach pie, and Edelweiss tart with raspberry sauce are also heavenly.

MERRIMAN'S, in Opelo Plaza, Hi. 19. Tel. 885-6822.

Cuisine: ISLAND REGIONAL. **Reservations:** Recommended.

$ Prices: Appetizers $3.75–$6.75; main courses $12.50–$24.50. AE, MC, V.

Open: Lunch Mon–Fri 11:30am–1pm; dinner daily 5:30–9pm.

Ask local people about the best restaurants in Waimea and the first name you're likely to hear is Merriman's. In fact, ask anybody on the Big Island and you'll get the same answer. Merriman's is rated four stars by just about everybody, and Peter Merriman, the 37-year-old owner, is rapidly gaining a reputation as one of the most innovative young chefs in the country. Stop by for a meal and see why. Merriman uses only the freshest and finest local products—10 different kinds of mangoes, for example, each with a subtly different flavor, or white pineapples, or shellfish he may have gone diving for himself—to produce an imaginative, contemporary, and highly sophisticated cuisine. The setting is lovely: a Hawaiian art deco room done in soft peach/green colors, with comfortable upholstered chairs, and many plants and flowers that create a light, airy feeling in the daytime. In the evening the atmosphere is more intimate, with flickering candles on the tables highlighting the original paintings on the walls and the island memorabilia of the 1920s, '30s, and '40s.

With such a creative chef as Merriman, the menu changes frequently—but you can be sure that whatever you eat will be outstanding. On the low side of the menu, you might go for the stir-fried vegetables with spicy curry at $12.50, or the chicken and green-papaya curry at $14.50. Among the memorable signature dishes, around $20 or market-priced, are the wok-charred ahi (seared on the outside, sashimi inside), the Kalva ranch lamb, and the Kahuku shrimp and clams, stir-fried with mint and chiles. A salad of fresh Waimea greens, a vegetable, and starch accompany all dishes. To begin your meal, try shrimp summer rolls, or goat cheese baked in phyllo dough, or a Caesar salad that's just a bit different—with sashimi.

Lunch is very reasonable and still of the same high gourmet quality. We could happily make an entire meal of the bouillabaisse, its fresh fish and shellfish piping hot in a saffron broth, $8.25. Or try the salade niçoise, again with the distinctive Merriman difference—made with artichokes, potatoes, and grilled fish on a bed of tossed greens, $6.75. Desserts, like the fabulous lilikoi mousse, are great at both meals. And the wine list is priced invitingly.

BETWEEN HILO & KONA ON THE SOUTHERN ROUTE

There are several interesting choices for meals on this trip which we've listed below. One interesting stop is about halfway between Hilo and Kona, when you come upon an oasis in the laval flows. This is the beautiful town of Naalehu, the southernmost community in the United States. As you drive through town, keep your eyes peeled for the **Naalehu Fruit Stand,** next door to the library. Locals swear by this one! You get your food at the counter, then take it to eat at tables outside. Try one of their unique pizza sandwiches on homemade Italian bread, $6 for a whole sandwich. They also have the more usual kinds of pizzas, homemade pies, fruit breads, giant cookies, health foods, and deli sandwiches.

KEAAU

Meals for Less Than $10

TONYA'S CAFÉ, across from the post office and Keaau town center. Tel. 966-8091.

Cuisine: INTERNATIONAL VEGETARIAN. **Reservations:** Not accepted.
$ Prices: Appetizers $2–$5.50; main courses $3.50–$5.75. No credit cards.
Open: Mon–Fri 11am–7pm.

Ⓢ Natural-food types should look in on Tonya's Café, across from the shopping center and next door to Keaau Natural Foods. Tonya Miller spent 15 years cooking vegetarian foods "all over California," and now she's on the Big Island, offering international vegetarian cuisine, with many dishes of Thai, Italian, Mexican, and especially Jamaican inspiration (she learned many of her recipes in Jamaica). For about $5.75, you can get a complete meal with a hot dish, soup or salad, and bread. A large organic salad is $3.50; a bowl of soup, $3.50. There are also vegetable juices, fruit smoothies, homemade corn muffins, and some wonderful peanut butter macadamia cookies. This is a tidy little place, very small, with just a few tables inside and out: Eat here, or take food out.

IN & AROUND HAWAII VOLCANOES NATIONAL PARK

Meals for Less Than $15

NAALEHU COFFEE SHOP, Naalehu. Tel. 929-7238.

Cuisine: AMERICAN. **Reservations:** Not required.
$ Prices: Appetizers $2.95–$12.95; main courses $4.95–$12.95. No credit cards.
Open: Daily 7:30am–8pm.

Here, in the southernmost town in the United States, the venerable Naalehu Coffee Shop has been doing business since 1949. Owners Roy and Arda Toguchi serve local dishes, fresh fish from South Point Kau, gold oranges, local bananas, and other local produce. The Hawaiian fishburger is a house specialty; other good sandwiches include the Farmer John Baked Ham and the oven-baked turkey sandwich, accompanied by relishes and salad, $4.95–$6.95. Lunch and dinner main courses are served with salad, vegetable, bread, and rice or potatoes. After your meal, check out the art gallery and Menehune Treasure Chest and browse among the local handcrafts. If you approach from Hilo, make your third left when you pass the school; from Kona, turn right when you pass the theater.

PUNALU'U BLACK SANDS RESTAURANT, Punalu'u. Tel. 928-8528.

Cuisine: AMERICAN. **Reservations:** Recommended.

$ Prices: Appetizers $5–$9; main courses $11.95–$25. buffet lunch $10.95 adults, $7.25 children. MC, V.

Open: Lunch daily 10:30am–4:30pm (buffet served to 2pm); dinner daily 5:30–8:30pm.

It's about an hour's drive from Hawaii Volcanoes National Park to Punalu'u, home of the famous Black Sands Beach—and of the Punalu'u Black Sands Restaurant. Here, in a dramatic indoor-outdoor setting, you can enjoy a truly lavish buffet lunch, including fresh tropical fruits on ice, island greens, fresh and pickled vegetables, a tropical Waldorf salad, fruit and vegetable molds, as well as a choice of three hot main dishes (meat, fish, poultry), plus steamed rice and butter rolls. Delicious Punalu'u sweet bread comes from their own country bakery, as do a variety of desserts. Tea (hot, minted, or fruit) and coffee round out the meal. Salads and sandwiches are available on the à la carte menu. If you're in the area at night, come by for another delicious meal: Fresh fish of the day is featured, along with broiler specialties like teriyaki chicken, pork chops, veal, and steak. The à la carte luncheon menu is served daily.

VOLCANO GOLF AND COUNTRY CLUB, Volcano. Tel. 967-8828.

Cuisine: AMERICAN. **Reservations:** Not required.

$ Prices: Appetizers $1.75–$2.75; main courses $5–$7. AE, MC, V.

Open: Continental breakfast Mon–Fri 7–10am; full breakfast Sat–Sun and hols 7–10am; lunch daily 11am–3pm, late lunch to 5pm.

Two miles south of the Hawaii Volcanoes National Park entrance, watch for the sign that reads GOLF COURSE, directly across from the Kilauea Military Camp. It will lead you to the Volcano Golf and Country Club, where many local people take visitors to avoid the Volcano House crowds. The clubhouse, open to the public, has a rustic modern dining room with glass windows, huge ceiling, and wood-burning fireplace. From the windows, you can gaze at Mauna Loa and often sight the rare Hawaiian nene goose. Complete lunches, including soup or salad, vegetable, rice or fries, offer such dishes as mahimahi, honey-stung chicken, chili, and pastas, and run $4.25–$7.50. Excellent burgers cost $5.50.

Meals for Less Than $20

KILAUEA LODGE, Volcano. Tel. 967-7366.

Cuisine: AMERICAN/CONTINENTAL. **Reservations:** Recommended.

$ Prices: Appetizers $4.25–$6.50; main courses $12.50–$21.50. MC, V.

Open: Dinner only, daily 5:30–9pm.

One mile Hilo-side of Hawaii Volcanoes National Park is Kilauea Lodge, a current "hot" place for dining in the area. The huge room is dominated by the "Fireplace of Friendship," its rocks donated by civic and youth organizations from 32 countries around the Pacific during the years when this was a mountain retreat of the YMCA. The place is still warm and friendly, the dining room is spacious and attractive, and chef Albert Jeyte is known for excellent continental dinners with a touch of local flavor, everything made from the freshest of ingredients. Main courses come with tiny loaves of freshly baked bread and homemade soups. There are at least four specials every day—perhaps ahi, roast duck, lamb provençal, or Hasenpfeffer (that's rabbit in wine sauce); venison and game are often on the menu. Regular dishes include seafood, beef, chicken, fresh fish of the day, plus a few vegetarian dishes, like eggplant suprême and fettuccine primavera. For dessert try the macadamia-nut or ohelo-berry pie—quite special.

VOLCANO HOUSE, in Hawaii Volcanoes National Park. Tel. 967-7321.

Cuisine: AMERICAN. **Reservations:** Recommended for dinner.

$ Prices: Appetizers $3–$9.50; main courses $14.95–$26.50; buffet breakfast $7.50; buffet lunch $11. AE, DC, MC, V.

Open: Breakfast daily 7–10:30am; lunch daily 11am–1:30pm; dinner daily 5:30–8pm.

The traditional lunch stop here has long been Volcano House, noted for its lovely buffet—a tempting array of salads, fruits, and main dishes, served with beverage and dessert, in a spectacular setting overlooking Halemaumau Crater. The dining room at Volcano House, named Ka Ohelo, in honor of the sister of Madame Pele, the fire goddess, has seating on two levels to provide views for up to 260 people. However, since lunch is a very busy time, what with all the tour buses disgorging hungry passengers, we prefer to come here for a superb and quiet breakfast served late (until 10am). Just remember to offer some of the ohelo-berry preserves to Madame Pele first, as a sign of respect. (Ohelo is sacred to Pele; you can also sample it in ohelo-berry pie, served at Volcano House's snack shop.) The dinner menu includes scampi, prime rib, New York steak, sautéed mahimahi, and Cornish game hen; main dishes are served with a dinner salad, rice or potatoes, and vegetables, plus homemade sweet breads and rolls.

KONA RESTAURANTS

There are three distinct areas on the Kona coast for dining: first, the Kailua-Kona area, home of the busiest tourist scene; second, Keauhou-Kona, just south of Kailua-Kona, and also a tourist area; and third, Up Mauka, in the coffee-growing country in the mountains, where most of the local folks live.

IN KAILUA-KONA

Meals for Less Than $12

THE JOLLY ROGER, Waterfront Row, 75-776 Alii Dr. Tel. 329-1355.

Cuisine: AMERICAN. **Reservations:** Not accepted.

$ Prices: Appetizers $3.45–$6.25; main courses $8.25–$11.95. AE, MC, V.

Open: Daily 6:30am–10pm.

Honolulu has its Restaurant Row, and Kailua-Kona has its Waterfront Row, a handsome on-the-ocean, multiple-level dining-shopping complex with a boardwalk and plenty of space from which to watch the pounding surf. One of the more reasonable dining establishments here is the Jolly Roger. The on-the-water location is superb and the food is the kind you remember from the popular Jolly Rogers in Waikiki: good American fare with reasonable full-course meals, including teriyaki steak, barbecued beef ribs, fish-fry platter, and chicken Polynesian. (Watch the local papers for two-for-one dinner offers for about $18.) Jolly Roger also has lots of sandwiches and salads at lunch, plus hearty breakfasts, which many people consider their best meal. Eggs Benedict, delicious Mac-Waples (waffles with cinnamon apples and macadamia nuts), and steak and eggs go for about $3.95–$6.75. Jolly Roger serves food continuously every day from 6:30am to 10pm, with contemporary music groups playing from 9:30pm to 1:30am. Nice for a drink at sunset, too.

KONA CHUCKWAGON BUFFET, 74-5565 Luhia St., at Kaiwi Sq. Tel. 329-2818.

Cuisine: AMERICAN. **Reservations:** Not required.

$ Prices: Breakfast buffet $5.50; lunch buffet $6.95; dinner buffet $9.95. No credit cards.

Open: Daily 7am–9pm.

For those who like hearty buffet meals, the Kona Chuckwagon Buffet is a good bet. At dinner and lunch, there are at least three meats on the table (perhaps ham, prime rib, barbecued beef ribs, or fried chicken), plus chili, potatoes, vegetables, rices, and a soup and salad bar with a selection of 20 items. (Kaiwi Square is the first street as you enter Kailua from the airport.)

KONA RANCH HOUSE, Hi. 11, at the corner of Kuakini and Palani.

Cuisine: AMERICAN. **Reservations:** Not required.

$ Prices: Paniolo Room, complete meal $7.95–$10.95; Plantation Lanai, complete meal $10.95–$22.95. AE, CB, DC, MC, V.

Open: Breakfast/lunch 7am–2pm; dinner daily 5–9pm.

Take your choice of food and mood at the Kona Ranch House, really two restaurants in one. For a splurge, choose the lovely Plantation Lanai, so pretty in wicker and green: Dinner features steaks and seafood ranging from $10.95 to $22.95. For a meal that's right within our budget, choose the adjoining Paniolo Room or "family-style" room, open for dinner from 5 to 9pm. There are several light dinners at just $7.95—thinly sliced roast pork, broiled or sautéed fish filets, broiled teriyaki chicken breast, and thinly sliced roast beef—which are served with a choice of soup or salad or starch. Heartier appetites can enjoy dishes like grilled liver and onions, paniolo stew, ratatouille, or vegetarian spaghetti with garlic bread, served with soup or salad and a choice of starch, for $7.95–$10.95. Feeling really famished? Indulge in the Ranch House barbecue platter—a broiled half-chicken, barbecued beef ribs, pork spareribs, pork chops, combo chicken and ribs, or barbecued sliced beef. With them come soup or salad, corn on the cob, rice, fries, onion rings, baked beans, or mashed potatoes, all for $14.95. Children's menus, burgers, tasty tropical drinks, luscious homemade desserts—Kona Ranch House has all of this, and reasonably priced lunches and breakfasts, too.

McGURK'S FAMOUS FISH AND CHIPS, in the Kailua Bay Shopping Plaza, 75-5699 Alii Dr. Tel. 329-8956.

Cuisine: SEAFOOD/SANDWICHES. **Reservations:** Not required.

$ Prices: Main courses $5.95–$9.85. No credit cards.

Open: Mon–Fri 11am–8pm, Sat–Sun noon–7pm.

McGurk's Famous Fish and Chips is a good choice for a quick lunch or dinner. Located near Hulihee Palace, and decorated in white and blue with nautical accents, McGurk's has both indoor and outdoor tables. You might take out fish-and-chips (three pieces at $7.50), shrimp-and-chips (three pieces at $4.95), or sandwiches ($2.95–$3.95); or stay and have a fresh mahimahi sandwich ($4.95), dinner and chef salads ($2.85–$5.95), or a scallop and chips plate with macadamia-nut coleslaw ($6.95), while enjoying a splendid ocean view. Local friends report that they make the best hamburger in Kona!

OCEAN VIEW INN, Alii Dr. Tel. 329-9988.

Cuisine: AMERICAN/CHINESE/VEGETARIAN. **Reservations:** Not accepted.

$ Prices: Main courses $2.75–$8.95.

Open: Breakfast Tues–Sun 6:30–10am; lunch Tues–Sun 11am–2:45pm; dinner Tues–Sun 5:15–9pm.

Every time we dine at the Ocean View Inn, we realize why it has survived and thrived for so many years while other newer, flashier establishments come and go. This business has been owned by the same family for over half a century. It's a big, comfy place, nothing fancy; the view across the road is ocean all the way, the tables are filled with local residents, and the waitresses are old-timers who know their trade. American and Chinese meals are inexpensive and generous. And there is a wide variety of Chinese vegetarian dishes that are surprisingly delicious. Vegetarians bored with yet another salad bar had best make tracks for this place. Dishes based on vegetarian beef (textured vegetable protein) and tofu run $2.95–$4.75; the sweet-and-sour crisp vegetarian wontons rank with the tastiest

Chinese food anywhere. Complete dinners ($6.50–$12.50) offer good value: They include soup or fruit cup, rice or mashed potato or fries, green salad, tea, and coffee. At a recent meal we dined on broiled ahi (the fish of the day), and for the same $8.25 could have had broiled ono, breaded mahimahi, or butterfish. There are at least 24 other choices between $5.50 and $8.95, including corned beef and cabbage, fried chicken, and roast pork with apple sauce. And there are over 80 Chinese dishes beginning at $2.75. Lunch is also a good buy, with many hot plates to choose from, like shoyu chicken or teriyaki steak, for $4.95–$6.50. These are served with rice or potato, salad, and beverage. Breakfast has everything from ham and eggs and French toast to beef stew, saimin, and poi. The bar is open from 6:30am to 9pm.

QUINN'S ALMOST BY THE SEA, 75-5655A Palani Rd. Tel. 329-3822.

Cuisine: SEAFOOD/STEAK/VEGETARIAN. **Reservations:** Not accepted.
$ **Prices:** Appetizers $2.75–$7.50; main courses $4.50–$18.95. MC, V.
Open: Daily 11am–2am.

There's an informal, relaxed feeling about this place. A lively young crowd hangs out in the garden dining lanai, whose two open walls and one of lava rock give an outdoor feeling. Blue-canvas director's chairs and laminated wooden tables continue the same mood. There's food here for just about every taste, and all of it is good: fresh seafood and fish, caught and delivered from the pier across the street; juicy steaks; selections for vegetarians; lots of salads with homemade dressings. Entrées come with salad, vegetables, and potato or rice. Lunch is served all day, which means that you can come by at any time for their great fresh fish sandwich or perhaps the fish lo-cal plate. French dip, burgers, and roast beef sandwiches are priced about $5.50–$7.25. Lots of cheer inside at the bar. Local residents consider Quinn's a favorite.

SIBU CAFE, in Banyan Court, 75-5695 Alii Dr. Tel. 329-1112.

Cuisine: INDONESIAN. **Reservations:** Not accepted.
$ **Prices:** Appetizers $3–$4; main courses $9.50–$11.50. No credit cards.
Open: Daily 11:30am–9pm.

The exotic Sibu Café is a semiopen place where you can sample the mood and food of Indonesia. Balinese decorations, tables topped with sarongs covered with glass, and revolving fans overhead set the scene for wonderfully flavorful food. Every year, readers write to tell us that this was their favorite place! The house specialty is satay: skewers of marinated meats or vegetables broiled over an open flame. Far Eastern dishes like Balinese chicken, spicy pork, ginger beef, Indian curries, and vegetarian stir-fries are also delicious, and everything is accompanied by either brown or fried rice plus a marinated cucumber-and-onion salad. Combination plates are excellent, as is their special peanut sauce. Prices go up a few dollars at dinnertime. Daily Indonesian and international specials are also available, spiced to taste, and there are always several vegetarian dishes.

READERS RECOMMEND

Golden Chopstix Restaurant, *in Kaahumanu Plaza, Kaiwi St. (tel. 329-4527). "There was one restaurant in particular that we returned to several times. It is the Golden Chopstix Restaurant in Kailua-Kona, in the industrial area. They serve huge portions, are reasonably priced, and the biggest bonus of all is that they don't saturate their food with MSG, so we didn't experience any of the usual after effects. Superb food with an out-of-this-world special sauce. Aloha!"*—Sandy and Dave Heinrich, Forks, Wash.

Meals for Less Than $18

ECLIPSE, 75-5711 Kuakini Hwy. Tel. 329-4686.

Cuisine: CONTINENTAL. **Reservations:** Recommended.

$ **Prices:** Appetizers $5.95–$7.50; main courses $6.95–$9.95. AE, MC, V.
Open: Lunch Mon–Fri 11am–2pm; dinner daily 5–9pm; disco Wed–Sun 10pm–2am; ballroom dancing Sun 7:30–10pm.

Established over a decade ago, The Eclipse is one of the "in" spots for Kona's business-lunch crowd because of its good food and fast and efficient service—qualities that we tourists enjoy, too. The lunch menu is quite extensive, featuring everything from crêpes to dieters' salads. We recommend the Greek salad, a meal in itself for $5.95. For dinner, you might try the eggplant or prawns as an appetizer, and then move on to a pasta, a poultry dish, or a steak-and-seafood combination for a main course. Fresh catch of the day or lobster is available at market price. The chef offers daily specials with island fish and local produce. This fern-filled restaurant is a quiet retreat most of the time, but as one of Kona's few late dancing spots, the Eclipse is transformed into a foot-stomping disco after 10pm. It's also the only place in the area that offers ballroom dancing. Dress for lunch is business/resort attire; at dinner people wear everything from muumuus to suits.

FISHERMAN'S LANDING WATERFRONT RESTAURANT, in the Kona Shopping Village, 75-5739 Alii Dr. Tel. 326-2555.

Cuisine: SEAFOOD. **Reservations:** Recommended, especially for dinner.
$ **Prices:** Appetizers $3.95–$7.95; main courses $10.95–$22.95. AE, DC, MC, V.
Open: Lunch daily 11:30am–2:30pm; dinner daily 5–10pm.

The Fisherman's Landing Waterfront Restaurant is a seafood restaurant in a spectacular setting. Splashing fountains, pools, and nautical decorations all set the stage for the grand show put on by the pounding surf smashing up on the beach. It's most reasonable to come here at lunchtime, when broiler items like teriyaki beef, chicken Hawaiian, and a variety of salads go for about $6–$9. If you're willing to splurge, enjoy their superb fresh fish, Far Eastern and wok specialties, and meat selections like veal Oscar and New Orleans blackened steak at dinner. The fish is broiled over kiawe coals and served with a choice of three butter sauces; it can also be sautéed or blackened to your order. All main courses are accompanied by soup or salad (their Oriental salad is superb) and freshly baked bread from the restaurant's own ovens. Don't miss their stuffed mushrooms among the pupus—a real treat. Save room for dessert too, like the lava macadamia-nut ice-cream pie. There's music every night, Hawaiian and contemporary. The cocktail lounge is open from 11am to closing.

KONA AMIGOS, 75-5669 Alii Dr., Tel. 326-2840.

Cuisine: MEXICAN. **Reservations:** Recommended.
$ **Prices:** Appetizers $5.25–$7.75; main courses $8.50–$12.95. AE, DC, DISC, MC, V.
Open: Daily 11am–10pm (bar service to midnight).

This second-story restaurant, perched above the crowds on Alii Drive, is within prime viewing distance of the hub of activity on the Kailua Pier. Attractively decorated with a south-of-the-border theme, it's a great place to catch a Kona sunset or watch the passersby. They even have bargain "Sunset Specials" on drinks from 4 to 6pm: margaritas or draft beer for $1.50. Hungry? Try their appetizers. We recommend the fried calamari, the nachos, or the shrimp cocktail. At lunchtime, the menu features an array of burgers and salads in addition to the usual Mexican standbys. Dinner selections include burritos, chimichangas, combination plates, and even fresh fish and steaks prepared with a Mexican flair. Service is friendly, but can be slow. Kona Amigos can be crowded during the height of the tourist season, so be sure to reserve to avoid long waits for dinner.

KONA INN RESTAURANT, in the Kona Inn Shopping Village, 75-5744 Alii Dr. Tel. 329-4455.

Cuisine: AMERICAN/SEAFOOD. **Reservations:** Recommended at dinner.

$ Prices: Appetizers $2.95–$8.95; main courses $3.95–$9.95 on the Café Grill menu, $12.95–$18.95 and up on the regular dinner menu.

Open: Café Grill menu daily 11:30am–midnight; dinner menu daily 5:30–10pm.

The lovely Kona Inn Restaurant is a splurge for us at dinner, but it's such a special spot, with a spectacular view of the bay and some tables perched right at water's edge, that it's worth your while to have lunch here or choose from the Café Grill menu anytime. You can have Hawaiian chicken for $6.95, calamari for $5.95, pasta and chicken salad for $7.95, and a host of good sandwiches for $3.95–$9.95. Having a cocktail out on the oceanfront lanai is lovely, too.

SU'S THAI KITCHEN, 74-5588A Pawai Place. Tel. 326-7708.

Cuisine: THAI. **Reservations:** Not required.

$ Prices: Appetizers $4.95–$8.95; main courses $7.95–$17.95. MC, V.

Open: Lunch Mon–Fri 11am–2:30pm; dinner daily 5–9pm.

Tucked away in the industrial area not far from town, this cute little indoor-outdoor restaurant with a pleasant garden draws fans from near and far: Everybody loves the exotic, authentic Thai dishes. Two people could have an exotic dinner here for under $25! Not only can you go with all the old stand-bys like Pad Thai or a variety of curries and coconut milk–based soups, but you can also try some rather unusual offerings: a whole fish in a sweet chili sauce, crab claws in a pot, or stir-fried chicken with macadamia nuts. Vegetarians have a dozen dishes of their own. Lunch specials are a good deal: Every dish is $5.95. Ask to be seated out on the lanai.

TOM BOMBADIL'S FOOD AND DRINK, 75-5864 Walua Rd., off Alii Dr. Tel. 329-1292 or 329-2173.

Cuisine: AMERICAN. **Reservations:** Not required.

$ Prices: Appetizers $1.95–$8.95; main courses $8.75–$15.95. MC, V.

Open: Daily 11am–10pm.

There's an outpost of Middle Earth right on Alii Drive, across from the Kona Hilton Hotel, known as Tom Bombadil's Food and Drink. And while murals and decor and names on the menu are mythic (Aragorn pizza, Misty Mountain sandwiches, Elven King salads), the food is downright substantial and filling. Tom Bombadil's is known for its broasted chicken (the unique taste is a result of its being deep-fried under pressure), about $6.55 for a two-piece dinner; for pizzas (from $3.30 for a small); and for hot or cold sandwiches (like roast beef dip or turkey, bacon, and avocado), direct from Goldberry's Pantry. Sandwiches range from $5.75 up to $9.25 for the huge submarine. There are also tasty appetizers such as batter-fried zucchini and an appetizer platter that two or three hungry hobbits could share, plus salads, pastas, and flame-broiled specialties, which include fresh fish of the day, chicken teriyaki, hamburgers, and New York steak. You can enjoy ocean-view dining from the covered lanai, relax in the cozy pub area with a drink, or view live satellite coverage of sporting events on their cocktail patio. All food is available for take-out; you can call in your order first.

YA SUSHI, at Waterfront Row, 75-5770 Alii Dr. Tel. 326-5453.

Cuisine: JAPANESE. **Reservations:** Recommended for large groups.

$ Prices: $4.50 average for two pieces; combo dishes $8.50–$16.50. MC, V.

Open: Lunch Mon–Fri 11:30am–2:30pm; dinner daily 5:30–9:30pm.

This intimate sushi bar, hidden among the larger restaurants at Waterfront Row, is "the real McCoy" of sushi bars. Experienced chefs from Japan prepare just-caught fish before your very eyes as you watch from the ringside counter seats. The menu offers the usual fresh array of sushi, plus a variety of rolled sushi. For the more daring and more advanced sushi fanatics, try the cuttlefish, uni (sea urchin roe), or octopus. You know a sushi bar is good by the clientele; visitors from Japan frequently dine here. Although the items on the menu are inexpensive, your bill can quickly climb as you keep ordering. For the real bargain, we recommend the combo dishes, which provide plenty to eat.

Worth the Extra Bucks

THE CANOEHOUSE, at the Mauna Lani Bay Hotel, Kohala Coast. Tel. 885-6622.

Cuisine: PACIFIC RIM. **Reservations:** Recommended.

$ **Prices:** Appetizers \$10–\$14.50; main courses \$26–\$32. AE, DC, DISC, MC, V.

Open: Dinner only, daily 6–10pm.

Well worth the half-hour drive from Kailua town, this is one of the most enjoyable restaurants in all Hawaii. The al fresco setting, overlooking the moonlit beach, is extraordinary, and so is chef Alan Wong's menu, full of taste surprises from the countries of the Pacific Basin. Wong uses only the freshest of ingredients and employs light and healthful low-fat methods of food preparation. There are so many wonderful things on the menu that it's hard to choose—but crab summer rolls with vegetables and herbs and curried chicken lumpia with a coconut ginger dip make great starters. Seared peppered ahi, opakapaka with a ginger-scallion crust on a miso vinaigrette, grilled tenderloin beef medallions in a coconut-chili sauce with shiitake mushrooms, and grilled chicken marinated in macadamia-nut oil begin to suggest the possibilities for main courses. Dessert is unforgettable: a quintet of regional specialties that include banana lumpia, ginger crème brûlée, pomelo cheesecake, macadamia fudge cake, and tropical fruit sorbet. Two of you can share, with great pleasure. There's music for dancing every night.

THE CHART HOUSE, at Waterfront Row, 75-5770 Alii Dr. Tel. 329-2451.

Cuisine: STEAK/SEAFOOD. **Reservations:** Recommended.

$ **Prices:** Appetizers \$4.95–\$9.25; main courses \$12.75–\$35. AE, DC, DISC, MC, V.

Open: Dinner only daily 5–10pm.

If you've ever dined at a Chart House restaurant (there are very popular ones on Maui and Oahu), you know you can expect nothing but the best from these restaurants in the way of food, service, and ambience. This Chart House is no exception. It's architecturally striking, with huge sails hanging from the tall ceilings, an upstairs open-air lounge, koa-wood booths, beautiful fabrics and decor within. Note the photographs of legendary Hawaiian athletes on the walls. The Chart House is a bit above our usual price range, but stick to their fabulous soup-and-salad bar, and you have a meal for \$12.75. Or stay on the low side of the menu with items like teriyaki chicken at \$15.95, broiled smoked chicken at \$16.25, or baked scallops at \$17.25. All these come with either unlimited salad bar or New England clam chowder and freshly baked squaw or sourdough bread. Daily seafood and fresh fish selections run about \$18–\$23. As for desserts, we wouldn't dream of passing up their mud pie, even at \$4.25. An alternative is to come here simply for pupus and a drink in the outdoor cocktail lounge, and watch the sunset as you munch on the likes of garlic jalapeño cheese bread, New England clam chowder, or baked Brie with roasted almonds (\$4.95–\$9.25).

PALM CAFE, at the Coconut Grove Market Place, 75-5819 Alii Dr. Tel. 329-7765.

Cuisine: ASIAN/FRENCH. **Reservations:** Recommended.

$ **Prices:** Appetizers \$5–\$9.50; main courses \$14–\$23.50. AE, MC, V.

Open: Dinner only, daily 5–10pm.

Everything about this new restaurant is special—from the great location overlooking Alii Drive and the waterfront (sunset-watchers, take note), the spacious cool interior with upholstered wicker chairs, and the arrangement of bonsai on every table, to the unique cuisine prepared by chef/owner Daniel Thiebaut, who describes his style as

"French by way of Japan." Sauces are flavorful but not heavy; only the freshest natural ingredients are used; garnishes are edible. Fish preparations shine, especially the Coho salmon with a Maui onion confit, shiitake in a bok choy cabbage pocket, and red wine sauce; or the pepper Hawaiian snapper with tomato fondue and Thai salsa. Roast loin of veal is teamed with spiny lobster, all in a black-bean sauce with a chile and yellow sweet-pepper coulis. Signature appetizers include the seared yellowfin tuna on a bed of spicy leek and jicama stir-fry, and the ravioli stuffed with Chinese greens, with balsamic vinegar and ginger beurre blanc. There are specials and vegetarian dishes every night. Desserts are strictly for sybarites, like the chocolate croquant: two crunchy wafers filled with chocolate mousse and topped with a Tahitian vanilla ginger sauce. Once a month, visiting chefs prepare some outstanding meals here: If you catch one of these, you're in for a special treat.

KONA "UP MAUKA"

Meals for Less Than $6

MRS. SHIRLEY, Hi. 11, Captain Cook. Tel. 323-2080.

Cuisine: AMERICAN/LOCAL. **Reservations:** Not accepted.
$ **Prices:** Plate lunches $2.80–$6; dinner specials $5.95. No credit cards.
Open: Daily 7am–8pm.

Friends of ours who live in this area never eat dinner at home on Sunday anymore; it doesn't pay to cook when Mrs. Shirley is dishing up her oven-roasted turkey dinner, complete with stuffing, mashed potatoes, cranberry jelly, green salad, and hot roll—for only $5.95! And that's not the only reason for giving thanks: This friendly, local-style restaurant has specials every day, which could be Filipino, Hawaiian, Chinese, Japanese, or American. On Friday it's likely to be pot roast, baked ham, or baked pork. There's always stew, chili, teriyaki and Korean chicken, seafood platters, burgers ($2.50–$2.90). Everything is homemade, including the desserts—bread pudding and pies, mochi and cheesecake ($1–$2). Mrs. Shirley also offers some hearty bento box lunches and can do vegetarian or fruit-box lunches on request.

Meals for Less Than $14

THE ALOHA CAFE, Hi. 11, Kainaliu. Tel. 322-3383.

Cuisine: NATURAL FOODS. **Reservations:** Not required.
$ **Prices:** Main courses $4.95–$14.95. MC, V.
Open: Breakfast Mon–Sat 8–11:30am; lunch Mon–Sat 11:30am–4pm; dinner Mon–Sat 4–8pm; brunch Sun 9am–2pm.

On your way to City of Refuge at Honaunau (see Chapter 13, "What to See and Do on the Big Island"), try the Aloha Café. Located in the lobby of the Aloha Theater in Kainaliu, it has wonderful, healthful food and an unusual atmosphere. The artistically decorated counter-service café is in the lobby of the theater, but it's even more fun to sit out on the terraced lanai that borders the building, especially all the way down near the meadow. The menu features homemade vegetarian burritos, tostadas, nachos, and quesadillas, generous sandwiches (veggie, tofu/avocado, fresh fish), and char-broiled burgers. These items run about $5.25–$6.95. Dinner adds filet mignon at $14.95, fresh fish (market-priced), and several vegetarian specials. Wines and beers are available. If you get here in time for breakfast, you'll be treated to three-egg omelets, pancakes, and whole-wheat French toast, $5.50–$6.50. Even if you don't have a meal here, stop in for some of the homemade fresh baked goods. The day we were there it was raspberry linzer tortes. Ono! Their baked goods, sandwiches, and burritos are also served at the World Square Theater in Kailua, and you don't have to pay admission to the theater to get the food. The Aloha Café, by the way, seems to be local headquarters for transplanted mainlanders to hang out, so it's always a fun stop. Their adjoining health-food and gift store can provide picnic ingredients—cheese, organic fruits (we recently tried organic lichees!), and vegetables. They also offer a large selection of gifts and cards, specializing in children's gifts and books. The store is open Monday through Saturday from 8am to 8pm and on Sunday from 9am to 5pm.

DRYSDALE'S TWO, in the Keauhou Shopping Village. Tel. 322-0070.

Cuisine: AMERICAN. **Reservations:** Not accepted.

$ Prices: Appetizers $3–$7.95; main courses $8.75–$13.70. AE, MC, V.

Open: Daily 11am–midnight.

Drysdale's Two, in the graceful Keauhou Shopping Village, is a popular gathering spot, especially with sports fans who will be sitting in the huge, pennant-bedecked bar area, watching their favorite teams on the TV. There are several attractive dining areas here too, as well as very good food on a popular-priced menu that is served all day long. Possibilities include such specialties as barbecued pork back ribs, breast of chicken teriyaki, and a vegetable stir-fry, excellent hamburgers, including low-fat buffalo burgers (honest!), for $4.90–$6.85; and hearty meat sandwiches, croissant sandwiches, homemade chili, and a good variety of salads, including a fresh Hawaiian fruit salad with sherbet at $7.95. Just about any taste can be accommodated here. Fabulous tropical drinks and ice-cream/liquor drinks are great for sipping out on the lanai; Peggy's Peanut Butter Ice Cream Pie is a must for dessert, at $3.75.

H. MANAGO HOTEL DINING ROOM, in the H. Manago Hotel, Captain Cook, Tel. 323-2642.

Cuisine: AMERICAN. **Reservations:** Not required.

$ Prices: Main courses $6–$10.75. MC, V.

Open: Breakfast Tues–Sun 7–9am; lunch Tues–Sun 11am–2pm; dinner Tues–Thurs 5–7:30pm, Fri–Sun 5–7pm.

This old-fashioned family-style restaurant is the place to catch a slice of local life. It has enjoyed a good reputation for years among the local people, although very few tourists make their way here. Everything is served family style: big plates of rice, salad (the macaroni salad is especially good), vegetables, and whatever the cook has made that night are brought out and served to everyone at the table, along with such main dishes as pork chops, liver, ahi, opelo, ono, mahimahi, or steak. The menu is limited and the food is not fancy, but this is a good chance to experience the nontourist life of the Kona Coast. Very pleasant.

KUAKINI TERRACE, at the Keauhou Beach Hotel, 76-6740 Alii Dr. Tel. 322-3441.

Cuisine: BUFFETS/CHINESE/SEAFOOD. **Reservations:** Recommended.

$ Prices: Chinese buffet $12.95 adults, $6.95 children; seafood buffet, $19.95 adults, $9.95 children; Sun champagne brunch $16.95 adults, $8.95 children. AE, MC, V.

Open: Breakfast daily 6:30–11am; lunch daily 11am–5pm; dinner daily 5–9pm.

Keauhou is one of the loveliest areas of the Kona Coast, with its historic sites, glorious views of the bay and mountains, and grand resort hotels. It's well worth a short drive out here to enjoy the fabulous buffets for which the Kuakini Terrace has become known. Set in an open-air atmosphere, the restaurant affords views of the hotel's lush and beautifully landscaped grounds, as well as an enticing view of Kahaluu Bay. The buffet table is also enticing: Monday through Thursday evening it's a super Chinese feast, the tables laden with many unusual Far Eastern salads, greens, hot dishes like Chinese roast duck, steamed clams with black beans, sweet-and-sour shrimp, Chinese barbecued spareribs; there's a complete dim sum table, and a table of luscious desserts, as well. Considering the setting, the charm, and the quality of the food, this is definitely one of the best buys in town. Also very popular is their seafood buffet, served Friday through Sunday. Sunday champagne brunch is another winner, with a wide selection of local favorites.

TESHIMA'S, Hi. 11, Honalo. Tel. 322-9140.
Cuisine: JAPANESE. **Reservations:** Not required.
$ Prices: Main courses $6–$9.50. No credit cards.
Open: Breakfast/lunch daily 6:30am–2pm; dinner daily 5–10pm.

For a change of ambience from the tourist world of Kailua, drive out on Hi. 11 (one block mauka from the main street of Kailua), a few miles south to Teshima's, at Honalo in coffee-growing country, a very popular place for over 45 years with the local Japanese, Hawaiians, Filipinos, and haoles. You might spot Sen. Dan Inouye there—he always comes in for a meal when he's in Kona. Say hello to Mrs. Teshima—she's a great lady. On one visit she proudly showed us the report that Teshima's had won first prize—the Gold Plate Award—for the best Japanese cuisine on the Big Island, from the *Gourmet Guide of Hawaii*. You can have a complete Teishoku lunch of miso soup, sashimi, sukiyaki, plus various side dishes, served on an attractive black-lacquered tray, for $6–$7.25. At dinner, vegetable tempura and shrimp tempura run $7.50 and $9.50, and there are plenty of dishes like sashimi, beef, pork, or chicken tofu, for $6.50–$9.50, all served with miso soup, tsukemono, rice, and tea. Sashimi is market-priced.

SPECIALTY DINING

Shopping Center Eateries

Kona Coast Shopping Center The lively Kona Coast Shopping Center, near the intersection of Hi. 11 and Hi. 19, offers you a chance to mingle with the local folk at some inexpensive restaurants. The branch of the **Sizzler** national chain is always busy, for they offer consistently good value in steaks, seafood, and salad bars. There's always a special on fresh fish of the day, plus prices like $8.60 for sirloin steak, $10 for steak and hibachi chicken or prime rib. Open 6am to 10pm Sunday through Thursday, till midnight on Friday and Saturday. The answer to a hungry family's prayer, **Bianelli's,** a new gourmet pizza shop, has been drawing kudos from the local crowd. You can have traditional hand-tossed New York–style pizza or deep-dish Chicago-style pizza with the usual toppings. Most pies run about $8.95 small; some gourmet specialties like Greek, Mexican, Gourmet Vegetarian, or Gourmet Garlic (if you dare) pies start at $11.95. Among the pasta dishes, the $7.65 lasagne, either traditional or vegetarian, made with eggplant, is a knockout. **Kim's Place** is a small Korean take-out shop, where traditional dishes like kal bi, bulgogi, Korean chicken, and the like, are all around $4—and all very good. **Betty's Chinese Kitchen,** small but sparkling, offers Chinese food in serve-yourself cafeteria style; most dishes are $3.90 for two portions, $4.65 for three, $5.30 for four. Betty also has an interesting selection of dim sum—pork manapua, brown sugar manapua, eggrolls, and Chinese doughnuts, for 35¢–85¢ each. You can't go wrong with the hearty sandwiches on cracked-wheat bread sold at the health-food store, **Kona Healthways.** It's around $3.95, hearty and delicious.

Lanihau Center Across the road is a newer shopping plaza, Lanihau Center, which also has several restaurants and fast-food places. **Royal Jade Garden** is a cheerful, attractive Chinese restaurant, with large round tables, fans, and paintings on the walls, and a good menu with many reasonably priced main courses. Pork and beef dishes run $4.95–$5.95 and there are almost two dozen seafood dishes—spicy shrimp, deep-fried oysters, abalone with black mushrooms—that go for $6.75–$15.95. You could have some baked goods or a sandwich at **Buns in the Sun,** pick up some **Kentucky Fried Chicken** here, or snack on natural, fat-free (and quite delicious!) frozen yogurt at **Penguin's Place,** the first local branch of the popular West Coast chain.

Kopiko Plaza Just below Lanihau Center, across from Hilo Hattie's, is Kopiko Plaza and **Kona Mix Plate,** which local friends swear by. The food is good and cheap, and the service is fast. Sautéed mahimahi and broiled mahimahi, each $4.60, are as good as dishes you'd pay more than twice as much for elsewhere. Take-out or eat in, at just a few bare-bones tables.

Fast Food at the Food Arcade at Waterfront Row

Having a meal at the fast-food restaurants at Waterfront Row is no hardship at all; there's a nice variety of places and numerous oceanfront tables to which you can take your food. Our favorite here is ✪ **Spinnaker's Salad Bar and Café Salsa.** It is actually a sailboat, complete with mast, upon which is set a very attractive buffet that includes not only plenty of fresh, green vegetables, but also dishes like tabbouleh, brown rice with steamed veggies, Caesar's daily pasta and rice dish (the house specialty), pesto, homemade breads (herb cheese, garlic parmesan, sourdough squaw bread). The nice thing about this place is that you pay for your salad by the pound ($4), so you determine how much you wish to eat and spend. They have recently added a full Mexican menu, with everything made from scratch. Try the Mucho Macho Burrito (everything they've got wrapped in a tortilla and smothered in sauce and melted cheese) at $4.95. They also have fabulous Häagen-Dazs ice cream concoctions, like a volcano sundae and a mocha double-nut fudge mud pie.

Other fast-food possibilities at Waterfront Row include **The Coffee Pub of Kona,** where you might treat yourself to a dessert and an espresso; and **Hot Diggity Dog,** which bakes its own buns and tops them with gourmet hot dogs and sausages, including turkey franks.

Two Bakeries Plus

Although it's not really a restaurant, **Suzanne's Bake Shop,** at 75-5702 Alii Dr., a few doors from Mokuaikaua Church, serves as a breakfast place and snack shop for many people. The doors are open at 4:30am every morning, and that's when fragrant and flavorful muffins, doughnuts, danish, iron bars and iron cookies, and other goodies start coming out of the ovens. Pastries are 70¢–$1.95 each, and the caramel-macadamia-nut danish is a special treat. Sandwiches, Kona coffee, cold sodas, and ready-made cakes are also available. A few chairs and tables outside afford a view of the passing parade and the ocean across the street. Open daily.

If you're in the industrial area, it might be fun to drive over to 74-5467 Kaiwi St. and check out **The French Bakery,** which supplies many top restaurants in the area and also sells directly to the public. Although the name and the pastry chef are French, it's actually an international bakery, with quite an array of interesting goodies, including French bread, whole-wheat croissants, blueberry brioches, rum balls, German three-seed muffins, and a selection of sandwiches, too. For something different, try the Tongan bread (some of the employees come from Tonga), and fill it with either chicken or spinach or a sausage/bacon combo, $2.95 and quite good. There's a table for coffee and your selection.

CHAPTER 13

WHAT TO SEE & DO ON THE BIG ISLAND

- **BIG ISLAND CALENDAR OF EVENTS**
1. **ADVENTURE TOURS**
2. **HILO & ENVIRONS**
- **FROMMER'S FAVORITE BIG ISLAND EXPERIENCES**
3. **HAWAII VOLCANOES NATIONAL PARK**
4. **THE PUNA REGION**
5. **FROM HILO TO THE KONA COAST**
6. **THE KONA COAST**
7. **BIG ISLAND EVENING ENTERTAINMENT**

There's so much to see on the Big Island—active volcanoes, verdant tropical valleys, ancient historical sites, black-sand beaches, snowcapped mountains, lush rain forests, and funky old plantation towns where "Old Hawaii" still lives—that ideally you should spend a week or more exploring and enjoying this continent in miniature. However, even if you have only a few days there's much you can accomplish. You'll want to spend at least one or two nights in picturesque Hilo or perhaps in Volcano Village (where there are numerous guesthouses), then maybe a night or two on the dry and sunny Kona Coast. You could also arrive at Hilo, drive immediately to Hawaii Volcanoes National Park (about an hour's drive), spend a few hours there, then continue right across the island on the southern route to Kona, where you can relax in the sun for as long as you want. Or fly into Kona and reverse the trip, from west to east. The following itinerary will give you basic information with which you can do your own improvising.

SUGGESTED ITINERARIES

IF YOU HAVE ONE DAY Spend the day at Hawaii Volcanoes National Park, the premier sight of the Big Island.

IF YOU HAVE TWO DAYS Spend your first day as above. On the second day, explore Hilo and visit the Puna area.

IF YOU HAVE THREE DAYS Use your first two days as suggested above. Spend the third day driving across the island from Hilo to Kailua-Kona on the Hamakaua Coast (northern route), stopping off at the cowboy mountain town of Waimea, perhaps touring the Parker Ranch there.

IF YOU HAVE FOUR DAYS Spend the first three days as recommended above. On the fourth day, tour the Kailua-Kona area and upcountry Kona Coast, driving to Pu'uhonua o Honaunau National Historical Park, an ancient "Place of Refuge."

IF YOU HAVE FIVE DAYS After spending your first four days as suggested above, use the fifth day for an exciting excursion: Go diving in a submarine off the Kona coast; or descend 1,000 feet in a four-wheel-drive vehicle into remote, Eden-like Waipio Valley, site of an ancient Hawaiian settlement; or take a safari to the top of snowcapped Mauna Kea (13,796 ft.) to see an unforgettable sunset and night sky. Or just go swimming at lovely Hapuna Beach.

BIG ISLAND CALENDAR OF EVENTS

MARCH

- ☐ **Skiing Events.** Open, International, and Ski Club races on Mauna Kea; first week in March. Pele's Cup, the world's highest cross-country race atop Mauna Loa; second week in March, weather permitting (no snow, no skiing). For information, telephone 808/737-4394.

APRIL

✪ ***MERRIE MONARCH FESTIVAL.*** *Competitions, workshops, performances, and more hula than you can shake a hip at. The statewide olympics of hula.*

Where: *Wailoa Center.* ***When:*** *April 15, 16, 17.* ***How:*** *Around January 1, 1993, send ticket order to Merrie Monarch Festival, Dorothy Thompson, Director, Waiakea Villas, Building 8, Room 289, 400 Hulani St., Hilo, HI 96720 (tel. 808/935-9168). Send a cashier's check or postal money order only. (Note: If orders are received too far in advance, they will be returned with a request to resubmit closer to January 1.) Prices for 1993 were unavailable at press time; for 1992 they were $15 for open seating, $20 for reserved seating.*

MAY

- ☐ **Lei Day.** There's lei-making in most of the hotel lobbies. May 1.
- ☐ **Big Island Spring Art Festival.** A major event for local artists and a wonderful chance to see the best of island arts. Wailoa Center, Hilo. For information, telephone 808/933-4360. Month of May.
- ☐ **Golden Goddess Fishing Tournament.** A ladies-only two-day tournament in Kailua-Kona. End of May. For information, telephone 808/322-3832.

JUNE

- ☐ **Kamehameha Day Celebrations.** Complete with entertainment, crafts, demonstrations, food booths, and a Royal Court Procession. Coconut Island, Hilo. Free. Sponsored by Malia Puka O Ka Lani Church; for information, telephone 808/935-9338. June 11.
- ☐ **Hawaii State Horticultural Show.** Held yearly at Edith Kanakaole Multi-Purpose Stadium, Hilo. Displays of anthuriums and plants by members of the Hawaii Anthurium Industry. For information, telephone 808/965-9522.

JULY

☐ **Independence Day Celebrations.** Rodeos in Waimea and Naalehu, rough-water swimming in Hapuna, and an anniversary celebration for Pu'uhonua o Honaunau in Kona, showing off old Hawaiian crafts in a cultural festival. July 4.

AUGUST

✪ ***HAWAIIAN INTERNATIONAL BILLFISH TOURNAMENT.*** *This is the world's leading international Marlin fishing tournament, and each year it draws fishers and fans from everywhere.*

Where: *Kailua-Kona pier.* ***When:*** *August 14–29, parade August 22.* ***How:*** *Book rooms well in advance—the place will be mobbed. For information, telephone 808/836-0974.*

SEPTEMBER/OCTOBER

☐ **Aloha Week Festivals.** The opening ceremony is at Halemaumau, with dance performances and offerings to Pele. Mid-September to late October.

OCTOBER

✪ ***GATORADE IRONMAN WORLD TRIATHLON CHAMPIONSHIPS.*** *Only world-class athletes need apply. This internationally acclaimed event includes a 2.4 mile swim, a 112-mile bicycle ride, and a 26.2 mile run, with no resting between events.*

Where: *Kailua-Kona.* ***When:*** *Usually in the first week in October.* ***How:*** *Make reservations at least six months in advance. Every available room on the Big Island will be taken.*

1. ADVENTURE TOURS

EYE OF THE WHALE, MARINE/WILDERNESS ADVENTURES, P.O. Box 1269, Kapaau, HI 96755. Tel. 808/889-0227, or toll free 800/657-7730.

With a goal of promoting understanding of Hawaii's delicate ecosystem through firsthand experience, Beth and Mark Goodoni lead 7- to 10-day hiking/sailing adventures for groups of no more than 10 people. Days are spent outdoors, hiking through mountain valleys and jungles or sailing the Big Island's Kona coast. Nights are spent either on boats (for sailing trips) or in scenic inns and B&Bs. There is no backpacking or camping. Beth, a marine biologist and seasoned naturalist, introduces participants to the natural history of Hawaii, emphasizing the origin and identification of tropical flora, the development and exploration of coral-reef ecosystems, and the biology and observation of marine mammals. On the boat, she's the crew; husband Mark is the licensed USCG captain. Cost is $125–$150 per day, including meals, accommodations, transportation, and inter-island fares. A highlight of the trip is a private luau, where guests learn to dig the imu, string their own leis, and dance the old-time hulas.

CRANE TOURS, c/o Bill Crane, 15101 Magnolia Blvd., H10 Sherman Oaks, CA 91403. Tel. 818/742-2213, or Ron Jones, 714/773-5570.

Crane Tours offers two summer trips to the Big Island: "The Volcanoes of Pele" and "Green Sands Beach, City of Refuge, and South Point." The cost is $650–$700. The company, known for excellent value and service, also offers many excursions to the island of Kauai.

KAYAK KAUAI—NA PALI OUTFITTERS, P.O. Box 508, Hanalei, Kauai, HI 96714. Tel. 808/926-9844.

Five days of kayaking tours on the Big Island every February, either from Kailua-Kona to Kawaihae or South Point to Milolii. The cost is $750 per person, including meals.

2. HILO & ENVIRONS

The best way to see Hilo and environs is on a driving tour. Below are two tours. It's possible to do both in one day if you're pressed for time.

DRIVING TOUR 1

Start: Hilo Tropical Gardens.
Finish: Reed's Bay Park.
Time: Two to four hours, depending on how long you spend at major stops.
Best Time: Early mornings, to see as much as possible.
Worst Time: Late afternoon.

Our first tour of Hilo begins with a visit to:

1. **Hilo Tropical Gardens.** Follow Hi. 12 to the eastern strip of town; you'll find the gardens at 1477 Kalanianaole Ave., about two miles from the airport. Paved walkways (accessible to the disabled) lead you through a tiny jungle of tropical flowers, shrubs and trees, splendid orchids, native Hawaiian plants and herbs, past water lily pools, waterfalls, even a Japanese pond with a footbridge and statuary. After you've seen the gardens and used up a little bit of film, stop in at their gift shop for Hawaiian handcrafts, wood products, and, of course, flowers. Anything can be shipped home. Admission is $1. There's a free hula show on Saturday at 10am. Open daily from 9am to 4:30pm. Call 935-4957 for driving directions.

   Make your way back to town, now, toward Hilo Bay, where you'll soon spot the:
2. **Wailoa Center,** whose building resembles a volcano. Located just behind the state office building, it features free exhibits ranging from cultural to natural history, and a permanent exhibit on tsunamis (tidal waves). Services and admission are free. The entrance is on Piopio Street, between the state office building and Kamehameha Avenue. Open Monday, Tuesday, Thursday, and Friday from 8am to 4:30pm, on Wednesday from noon to 8:30pm, and on Saturday from 9am to 3pm. From here it's not far to the:
3. **Suisan Fish Market,** where the freshest fish in town can be found. Weekdays at 8am the fishermen's catch is lined up and auctioned off to restaurants and grocery stores around the island. The public is invited. Don't miss the opportunity not only to experience this fast-paced auction, but to see the magnificent bounty of Hawaii's waters: huge marlin, tunas weighing over 200 pounds, prehistoric-looking broadbill swordfish, and many other species. Coming up soon is the:
4. **Nihon Japanese Culture Center,** which, in addition to serving authentic and

FROMMER'S FAVORITE BIG ISLAND EXPERIENCES

A Visit to Hawaii Volcanoes National Park Start with breakfast at historic Volcano House, and end with a stop at the Volcano Art Center.

A Submarine Dive in the *Atlantis* Dive 80–100 feet below the surface into the clear waters of Kona Bay to explore the world of the coral reef.

A Walk into the Tropical Rain Forest and Wild Jungle at Hawaii Tropical Botanical Gardens Travel seven miles north of Hilo to 17 acres of waterfalls, meandering streams, and more than 1,600 plant species, some bordering a wild stretch of ocean.

Doing Anything in the Picturesque Mountain Town of Waimea Shop the boutiques and galleries, sightsee, stroll, as long as it's not raining.

Taking the Waipio Valley Shuttle down into One of Hawaii's Few Remaining Shangri-las See almost-deserted Waipio Valley, where there's a black sand beach, an ancient fish pond, and the dramatic Hiilawe Falls.

Snorkeling at Kaahaluu Beach Park on the Kona Shore Snorkel in a pretty lagoon bordered by salt-and-pepper sand, thanks to an ancient lava flow. This is the best snorkeling on the Big Island.

excellent Japanese cuisine (see "Where to Eat," in Chapter 12), has an art gallery, a tearoom, and music, dancing, films, and other entertainment. Check to see if anything special is going on. Coming up on your right is:

5. **Liliuokalani Gardens** with its lovely Japanese bridges, ponds, plants, and stone lanterns. It's believed to be the largest such formal Japanese garden and park outside Japan. Look for the authentic Japanese tea ceremony house. On your left is:
6. **Coconut Island,** a favorite picnic spot for the local people. If you continue around the park, you'll find yourself on Banyan Drive, which takes you past many of the resort hotels in the city. The magnificent trees are labeled in honor of the celebrities who planted them: James A. Farley was one, Amelia Earhart another; Cecil B. De Mille has a tree, as does Mrs. De Mille. Continuing in the same direction you'll come to:
7. **Reed's Bay Park,** a cool picnic spot on the bay.

DRIVING TOUR 2

Start: Nani Maui Gardens.
Finish: Lyman House Memorial Museum Complex.
Time: Two to four hours, depending on stops.
Best Time: Early morning, so that you can see Rainbow Falls at its best.
Worst Time: Late afternoon.

To see one of our favorite gardens, drive about three miles south on Hi. 11 (the road to the volcano) from Hilo Airport, then turn left onto Makalika Street just after Hi. 11

divides. Drive seven-tenths of a mile (look for the familiar Hawaiian warrior sign for the turnoff), and you'll soon find:

1. **Nani Maui Gardens,** a wonderland of 20 acres of the fruits and flowers of many lands; their orchid garden, with thousands of varieties, is the largest in Hawaii. A ginger/helicona garden, an anthurium garden, a tropical water-lily and carp pond, an enclosed nursery, and an artifical waterfall and stream are also featured. You can tour the gardens by foot, on a tram ($3 per person), or by renting a golf cart, which seats four people, at $8. Lunch, available from 10:30am to 2:30pm, features a buffet and sandwiches. The gift shop is a good source for souvenir items, art posters by local artists, and USDA certified plants and flowers to ship back home. You can stay in the gardens as long as you like, to picnic or just relax. Open daily from 8am to 5pm, with an admission charge of $5. Call 959-3541 for information. Drive back up Hi. 11 and pick up Hi. 19. About seven miles north of Hilo on the four-mile scenic route at Onomea Bay, near Hi. 19, is the:
2. **Hawaii Tropical Botanical Garden,** a spectacular garden in a valley on the ocean—acclaimed as one of the most beautiful areas in Hawaii. Nature trails meander through a true tropical rain forest, cross streams and pass by spectacular waterfalls, and provide ocean vistas along the rugged coast. The garden displays a vast variety of palms, bromeliads, gingers, exotic ornamentals, and rare plants collected from all parts of the tropical world, more than 1,800 different species. For serious students of nature and lovers of natural beauty—not to mention photographers—it's a paradise. Admission is $12 (children under 16, free), which is tax-deductible because the garden is a nonprofit foundation. It's open every day (except New Year's Day, Thanksgiving, and Christmas Days), rain or shine (they furnish umbrellas), from 8:30am to 4pm. Call 946-5233 for exact driving directions. No food is sold and there are no picnicking facilities.

   On Hi. 11 just outside the city is the:
3. **Panaewa Rain Forest Zoo.** Turn right on the Stainback Highway and watch for signs on the right for the zoo. This is by no means the big time as zoos go; it's a small place, but with its own special Hawaiian charm. You'll see denizens of the South American rain forest, the rare Hawaiian nene (goose), the Hawaiian pueo (owl), many brightly plumaged birds, lions wading through a jungle stream, and peacocks roaming the grounds; cutest of all are the monkeys, especially the capuchins, which seem to enjoy the funny humans walking about. Free admission. Open every day from 9am to 4:15pm.

   Now it's time for some Kamehameha lore, since the Big Island is where that doughty old warrior was born and where he first started dreaming his dreams of glory and conquest.

   Continue driving on Kamehameha Avenue, turn left onto Waianuenue Street, and drive three blocks to the modern county library on the right side. See the two stones out in front? The bigger one is the:
4. **Naha Stone,** Kamehameha's Excalibur. According to Naha legend, only a chief of the royal blood could even budge the gigantic boulder; any warrior strong enough to turn it over would have the strength to conquer and unify all the islands of Hawaii. Kamehameha did the deed, but since the stone weighs at least a ton, no one has bothered, as yet, to repeat it. Off Waianuenue Avenue at Rainbow Drive is:
5. **Rainbow Falls.** The best time to see this sight is early in the morning: Try to come between 9:15 and 10am, when the sun gets up high enough over the mango trees so that you might see rainbows forming in the mist. It's pretty at any time, however, and so are the beautiful yellow flowers growing near the parking lot. Continue along Waianuenue about two miles to Peepee Street to the:
6. **Boiling Pots,** deep pools that appear to be boiling as turbulent water flows over the lava bed of the river. From the parking lot you can walk over to the edge and observe the show below. Both Rainbow Falls and the Boiling Pots are part of the

HAWAII SIGHTS & ATTRACTIONS

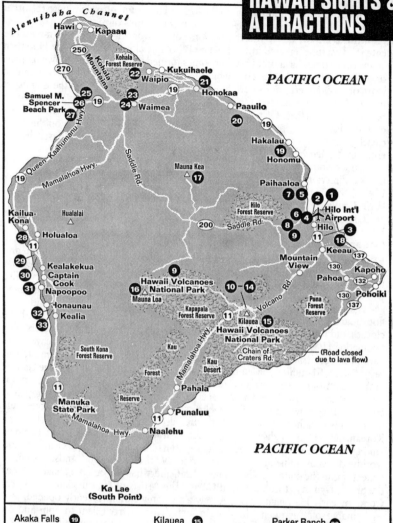

Alenuihaha Channel
PACIFIC OCEAN
Hawi
Kapaau
Kohala Mountains
Kohala Forest Reserve
Waipio
Kukuihaele
Honokaa
Samuel M. Spencer Beach Park
Waimea
Paauilo
Queen Kaahumanu Hwy.
Saddle Rd.
Hakalau
Honomu
Mauna Kea
Mamalahoa Hwy.
Paihaaloa
Hilo Int'l Airport
Hilo
Hilo Forest Reserve
Saddle Rd.
Kailua-Kona
Hualalai
Holualoa
Keeau
Mountain View
Kealakekua
Captain Cook
Napoopoo
Hawaii Volcanoes National Park
Mauna Loa
Kapoho
Pahoa
Pohoiki
Volcano Rd.
Puna Forest Reserve
Honaunau
Kealia
Kapapala Forest Reserve
Kilauea
Hawaii Volcanoes National Park
Chain of Craters Rd.
(Road closed due to lava flow)
South Kona Forest Reserve
Kau Forest Reserve
Kau Desert
Mamalahoa Hwy.
Pahala
Manuka State Park
Punaluu
Mamalahoa Hwy.
Naalehu
PACIFIC OCEAN
Ka Lae (South Point)

- Akaka Falls 19
- Boiling Pots 8
- Captain Cook Monument 31
- Hapuna Beach 27
- Hawaiian Holiday Macadamia Nut Plant 21
- Hawaii Tropical Botanical Garden 5
- Hawaii Volcanoes National Park 9
- Hilo Tropical Gardens 1
- Hulihee Palace 28
- Kaumana Cave 9
- Kahaluu Beach Park 29
- Kalopa State Recreation Area 20
- Kilauea 15
- Kilauea Military Rest Camp 12
- Liliuokalani Gardens 2
- Lyman House Memorial Museum Complex 4
- Mauna Kea 17
- Mauna Loa 16
- Mauna Loa Macadamia Nut Mill 18
- Mokuaikaua Church 30
- Naha Stone 6
- Nani Mau Gardens 3
- The Painted Church 33
- Parker Ranch 23
- Pu'uhonua O Honaunau National Historic Park 32
- Puukohola Heiau National Historic Site 25
- Rainbow Falls 7
- Thurston Lava Tube 14
- Samuel Spencer Park 26
- Volcano Arts Center 10
- Volcano House 11
- Waimea Center 24
- Waipio Valley 22

Wailuku River State Park. Return to the fork at Hi. 20 and turn right onto the other branch of the fork, Kaumana Drive. About three miles out is:

7. **Kaumana Cave,** where you can see some of the work of Pele at close range. The cave is a lava tube, created in 1881, when Pele came closer to wiping out Hilo than at any other time. Lava tubes are sometimes formed when lava flows down a ravine or gully; the top and sides cool while the center keeps racing along. Millions of years of volcanic eruptions have left hollow tubes like this all over the islands; in many of them are hidden the bones of the alii, which were always buried in remote, secret places. Of the two tubes here, only the one on the right—whose entrance is an exquisite fern grotto—is safe for exploration. The one on the left is treacherous, and who knows—perhaps the bones of Kamehameha, never discovered, are buried here.

   Retrace your steps to Kamehameha Avenue, and turn onto Haili Street in a mauka direction (away from the bay and uphill); cross Keawe, Kinoole, and Ululani Streets, and on the left-hand side you'll see:

8. **Haili Church.** Its architecture is pure New England, but its fame stems from its great Hawaiian choir. Continuing up Haili Street from the Haili Church, cross Kapiolani Street, and on the right-hand side you'll find the:

9. **Lyman House Memorial Museum Complex,** at 276 Haili St. The original Lyman House is another of those old mission homes that the grandchildren and great-grandchildren turned into a museum; this one, originally built in 1839, has been fully restored and furnished as a home of the late 19th century. The white-frame building, Hilo's oldest structure, contains hand-molded New England glass windows, doors made of native koa wood, and the original wide koa floorboards. As you tour the rooms, you'll see how the missionary family lived: the clothes, old four-poster beds, and white marble-top table stands and dressers. The fascinating Hawaiian artifacts and worldwide curios that used to be displayed here have now been transferred to the recently built Lyman Museum building. In this very modern $1-million museum addition, you begin at the Island Heritage Gallery on the first floor, where a raised relief map shows routes taken by all the groups that came to Hawaii. Then you can see the artifacts of each group and study their cultures; the Hawaiian exhibit includes a full-size grass house, Stone Age implements, feather leis, etc. There are also Chinese, Japanese, Portuguese, Korean, and Filipino displays. The second floor also has fascinating exhibits, among them the Earth Heritage Gallery with its display of volcanic eruptions and worldwide gem mineral collections, one of the finest and most extensive collections in the country. The Chinese Art Gallery has pieces dating back as far as the Shang Dynasty, 13th century B.C., and the Artists of Hawaii Gallery features works by early Hawaiian artists. A new astronomy exhibit recently opened.

   Lyman House is open Monday through Saturday from 9am to 5pm and on Sunday from 1 to 4pm. Admission is $4.50 for adults, $2.50 for children 6–17.

SHOPPING

Shopping is concentrated in three areas here: at the Kaiko'o Hilo Mall, just behind the county and state buildings; downtown, where stores and boutiques are housed in quaint wooden buildings; and out on Hi. 11, at the newer megabucks Prince Kuhio Plaza Shopping Center.

KAIKO'O HILO MALL

Kaiko'o Hilo Mall, with its supermarket, specialty shops, and drugstores, is of most interest to local people, but we always do very well at the **J. C. Penney's** here, where values and selections are excellent in every department. It's a good place to shop for muumuus, and luggage too. And we always like to have a look at **Book Gallery 2,** especially to browse through their wide selection of island cookbooks: They carry all the local cookbooks of church groups, women's groups, and the like. They have a good selection of Hawaiiana, books for the keikis back home, and some unique Petroglyph Press paperbacks, printed right here in Hilo.

DOWNTOWN

If you're in Hilo on a Saturday morning and you don't mind getting up early, go downtown to the bus terminal at the corner of Mamo Street and Kamehameha Highway at about 6am. This is the scene for Hilo's biggest **Farmer's Market,** where people come from all over to pick up produce, lots of flowers, some fish, and some arts and crafts, at low, low prices. They sell out quickly, so it's best to be there early. A Farmer's Market is also held on Wednesday morning, but Saturday is the big event.

ABUNDANT LIFE NATURAL FOODS STORE, 292 Kamehameha Ave. Tel. 935-7411.

Almost 17 years old, this is Hilo's most complete natural-foods store. Along with the top major brands of supplements, quality skin-care products, groceries, and the like, Abundant Life carries a unique selection of local and imported items. Their deli section is great for a healthy and hearty meal on the run, and their produce section features locally grown fruits and vegetables—strawberry-papayas, apple-bananas, mangoes, tangerines, avocados, and more. Organic, raw, unsalted macadamia nuts and honey from the Big Island are also treats.

THE CRYSTAL GROTTO, 290 Kamehameha Ave. Tel. 935-2284.

Wendy Gilliam creates a wonderful atmosphere in her shop: There's New Age music to listen to and an eyeful of unique gift items—handcrafted custom jewelry, crystals, Hawaiiana, Native American arts and crafts, posters, books, and more—to look at. She has hard-to-find items like kukui-nut oil, and an extensive selection of beads for craftspeople. Check here for news of New Age and holistic workshops. Tapes and videos are available. A most inviting place, hard to tear yourself away from.

GAMELAN GALLERY, 272 Keawe St. Tel. 969-7655.

One of Hilo's most distinctive shops, this is a showcase for the handcrafts of Indonesia, many of them personally collected by Marc Platt, whose wife, Eva, is in charge of the shop. And while you may not be able to afford the bronze masks or the wood sculpture or the rare textiles, there are quite a few very affordable items—batik T-shirts at $20 and $30, shirts and shorts made from used batik sarongs, hand-woven Ikat bags from $10, for example. Traditional shadow puppets, baskets made from rattan and straw grass, and lacquered boxes are among the many treasures here.

OLD TOWN PRINTERS & STATIONERS, 201 Kinoole St. Tel. 935-8927.

Across the street from the Hawaii Visitors Bureau is the retail store of the Petroglyph Press, which has been publishing books on Hawaiiana since 1962. Drop in to browse through their publications, notes, and postcards, including many with Hawaiian designs. In addition, walk a few blocks to their other store, Basically Books (see below).

BASICALLY BOOKS, 46 Waianuenue Ave. Tel. 961-0144.

Basically Books specializes in Hawaii and the Pacific, with videotapes and a complete selection of maps of Hawaii including USGS topographic maps, NOAA nautical charts, and road and street maps. They also have a good selection of travel books, posters, and attractive souvenirs, as well as a selection of maps for destinations worldwide.

BIG ISLAND GALLERY, 95 Waianuenue Ave., at Keawe St. Tel. 969-3313.

There's an artistic touch to a handful of downtown shops, all of them on or close to Keawe Street. This one features contemporary works by Big Island artists and craftspeople: painting, metal and wood sculpture, feather work, jewelry, pottery, and more. Unique to the Big Island is molten lava art: You can get these lava bowls while they're hot! Note the unique sculptures of Calvin Hashimoto. Antique kimonos are sometimes available.

SIG ZANE DESIGNS, 1222 Kamehameha Ave. Tel. 935-7077.

Sig Zane Designs is known for its distinctive designs in Hawaiian sportswear. You'll see them sold at many places in Hawaii, but this is the source: muumuus, T-shirts, aloha shirts, pareaus, handsome quilted designer jackets, jewelry, accessories, all bearing Sig's signature touch. Everything is 100% cotton. Prices are not low, but this is top of the line.

THE MOST IRRESISTIBLE SHOP IN HILO, 110 Keawe St. Tel. 935-9644.

Housed with several other boutiques in the renovated and quite attractive 1922 Pacific Building is one of our favorite shops. It's always worth a look-see, since owner Sally Mermel is forever coming up with something new and exciting for her flocks of loyal customers. Examples: one-of-a-kind jewelry by local artisans (earrings made of Hawaiian woods, dolphin rings); Hawaiian quilt-design mugs in a variety of pastel colors; lovely pareaus from Tahiti, Hawaii, Indonesia, and Italy, some of them exclusive here; koa-wood cutting boards and rice paddles; island perfumes; T-shirts with designs of whales, sharks, volcanoes, and turtles—and lots more, the best selection in Hilo. Hawaiian jams, jellies, and fruit butters make great small take-home presents: try the lilikoi butter made in Volcano—delicious. Speaking of which, adjoining the shop is Bears' Coffee (see Chapter 12), with wonderful coffees, light foods, and desserts, all with a bear theme—Bear Claws, Teddy Bear Pie—and more.

CUNNINGHAM GALLERY, 116 Keawe St. Tel. 935-7223.

Here you'll find prints and paintings by local artists, such as Pegge Hopper, John Thomas, Robert Nelson, Tom Rassacher, and Kim Taylor Reese. Attractive koa-wood–frame mirrors start at around $75. Cards by Guy Buffet, Herb Kane, Jane Chao, and others begin at just $1.25.

FUTON CONNECTION, 104 Keawe St. Tel. 935-8066.

A lot of the items here are too big for you to carry home, but do have a look at their crystals and jewelry, their lovely Japanese rice-paper shades ($25, and they can be mailed), cotton kimonos, colorful wall fans, and lots more.

PRINCE KUHIO SHOPPING PLAZA

This mall will remind you of Kaahumanu Center on Maui or Kukui Grove on Kauai; it's vast, it cost millions to build (in this case, $47.5 million), and it boasts the traditional big department stores like **Liberty House, Sears,** and **Woolworth's,** plus a handful of charming little boutiques. **The Most Irresistible Shop in Hilo,** mentioned above, has another branch here with the same tasteful merchandise. **Imagination Loves Toys** is an educational toy center, with all kinds of creative playthings. The main store of the **Book Gallery** is here, with its excellent selection of Hawaiiana, self-help books of all kinds, local cookbooks, and children's books. The **Hilo Hattie Fashion Center** is well worth a visit. The company is the largest manufacturer of aloha wear in the state; the store carries gifts, candies, and jewelry in addition to clothing, all at less-than-usual prices. Everybody gets a complimentary shell lei and refreshments too. (In fact, you can even get free transportation here by calling 961-3077.) **Contempo Casuals** is known for trendy sportswear, beach clothing, disco wear, and creative costume jewelry at reasonable prices. **Tee's 'n' Togs** has lots of cute tops that can be imprinted with your choice of design, or personalized, and **Casual Corner** has nice contemporary women's fashions. **The Candy Store** is great fun, full of hard-to-find local delicacies like dried abalone and a large variety of preserved seeds, sweet-and-sour apricots, shredded mango seeds, and such. There are lots of imported and local cookies, like macadamia-nut snowball cookies too.

There are some pleasant places to eat here, like **Francesca's** and **Boomer's,** with the mood of a 1950s diner, but keep in mind that you're about a two-minute drive from the Puainako town center, home to **Dotty's Coffee Shop** and the **Ting-Hao Mandarin Restaurant,** one of the best Chinese restaurants in town (see "Where to Eat," in Chapter 12).

READERS RECOMMEND

Tips on Buying Flowers. *"John Alexander, the delightful host at the Dolphin Bay in Hilo, gave us a helpful hint that we want to pass on. He told us to buy our flowers at an inexpensive place, such as a grocery store or small florist, obtain a carton, and pack them carefully with shredded, wet newspapers, covered with plastic, to keep them moist. We did this, and carried them on the plane with us. I am writing this over a week later and they are still in good shape. I have four dozen anthuriums and six birds of paradise to give to my friends, and all for just a little over $15."*—Mrs. Dean James, Celina, Ohio.

"A United Airlines employee at Kahului gave me this helpful tip. If your plane stops in Hilo en route home, buy flowers at the airport—fresher and cheaper. I bought a beautiful orchid, carnation, and plumeria lei, and orchid plants were $1–$2 less than at other flower stands elsewhere. The saleswomen were extremely helpful and cordial."—Elizabeth C. Greer, El Cerrito, Calif.

SPORTS & RECREATION

Your ramblings have worn you out, your budget hotel doesn't have a pool, and you want a swim. Where do you go? We'd start out on Kalanianaole Avenue, drive three miles to **Onekahakaha Beach Park** or a mile farther to **James Kealoha Park,** where the swimming in the rocky bay is okay if not memorable. But it's pleasant to drive through this Keaukaha area, the most beautiful part of Hilo, to see the exquisite private homes, some with their own tranquil Oriental fish ponds. Picnic and swimming spots continue until the end of the paved road. Watch for the signs pointing to **Richardson's Ocean Park,** the home of an outdoor marine recreation and interpretive center. You can swim, snorkel, fish, and surf in waters that front the center; tour a coastal trail which features coastal plants and brackish water ponds; and picnic on the lawn areas. The center contains marine-life displays that interpret nearby ocean and coastal environments. Open Monday through Saturday from 8:30am to 4:30pm. Free admission. Call 935-3830 for details.

If you favor pool swimming, join the local people at the Olympic-size **Sparky Kawamoto Swim Stadium** at Kuawa and Kalanikoa Streets, near the civic auditorium (tel. 935-8907). Admission is free. Open Monday through Friday, from 11am to 1pm for adults, from 1 to 4pm and 6 to 8pm for everybody; on Saturday and Sunday, from 10am to noon for adults and 1 to 4pm for everybody.

3. HAWAII VOLCANOES NATIONAL PARK

You mustn't leave the Big Island without paying homage to the goddess Pele. Not to visit her residence at Halemaumau, the firepit crater of Kilauea (this is the smaller volcano nestled along the southeastern slope of Mauna Loa), would be unthinkable. If Pele is entertaining, you're in for one of the world's great natural spectacles; if not, just a look at a volcano and damage it has done in the past will be a big experience.

It's more exciting than ever to visit the volcano, because for several years there has been a great deal of activity in Mauna Ulu, Pauahi Crater, and others. These new eruptions on the flanks of Kilauea have been big enough to spurt enormous fountains of fire 1,800 feet up above the crater's rim. In 1984 both Kilauea and Mauna Loa were active at the same time, the first time this had happened since 1868. Lava flows came dangerously close to the city of Hilo. As of this writing eight years later, Pele is still acting up. Call 967-7977 anytime for recorded information on eruptions, or try the park rangers at 967-7311 before you start, for news of the latest eruptions and viewing conditions. But whether or not anything is happening, the volcano trip is a must. Try to plan this for a morning trip, as clouds often appear in the afternoons.

EN ROUTE TO THE PARK

Take Hi. 11 out of Hilo for about 30 miles until you reach Hawaii Volcanoes National Park. Be sure to take a warm sweater and a raincoat; the air gets refreshingly cool 4,000 feet up at Kilauea Crater. The weather can change quickly and dramatically, as sunshine gives way to mist and fog.

There are several possible stops en route for flower fanciers. The first, at the 14-mile marker in the tiny town of Mountain View, is the **Hawaiian Flower Garden Nursery,** which specializes in anthuriums at very low prices. (While you're on the main street of Mountain View, look for the Mountain View Bakery and see if they have some of their "stone cookies.") The next stop—at the 20-mile marker—could be at **Hirano Store,** which, at the time of our last visit, had an excellent view of the ongoing eruption of the volcano at ground level. At the 22-mile marker is **Akatsuku Orchid Gardens,** a lovely botanical-type garden with many varieties of orchids; you'll receive one free as a gift. Just before you get to the park, it's fun to stop in at tiny **Volcano Village and Volcano Store** (on Hi. 11, make a right at Haunani Road directly to the store). Half the porch is the home of a snack bar and small restaurant called Volcano Diner; the other half is the place where local people go to scoop up reasonably priced flowers: Just to give you an example, we saw Birds of Paradise for 50¢ a blossom, a dozen calla lilies for $2.50, king protea for $4 and less. Prices of flowers vary every day. The store will pack and ship anywhere in the United States. Poke around inside a bit—it's great for local color. On our last trip, we discovered lilikoi butter (seven ounces for $4.85), a fabulous preserve made from passion fruit. The bulletin board out front often has leads on cottages to rent and news of local events.

SEEING & TOURING THE PARK

Once you reach the park (entrance $5 per car, good for seven days; free for those over 62), signs will direct you to the **Kilauea Visitor Center,** which should be your first stop. Check with the very helpful park rangers here for directions on the current eruption—if any. Be advised that if an eruption is going on, extreme caution must be exercised on the hiking trails, as there may be earth cracks anywhere, hundreds of feet deep, and a fall could be deadly. Those with heart and respiratory problems should beware of noxious fumes, children must be kept under control, and all visitors should protect themselves from the intense rays of the sun. Most visitors, however, simply drive to the important points on Crater Rim Drive (more about that ahead), which is much safer. If you can afford it, there is, of course, nothing to compare to the spectacular helicopter flights directly over the lava flows.

First, though, explore the visitor center a bit. You can get information here on self-guided walks, the Kipuka Puaulu Walk, which is a one-mile loop, and the Halemaumau Trail, a 6½-mile round-trip hike. Trail guides for both are available at the visitor center. And try not to miss the terrific color films of the latest eruptions, shown every hour on the hour from 9am until 4pm. Until recently, there was a display case here consisting of letters from people who had taken rocks from the volcano—despite being warned never to do so—and had spells of bad luck, and sent the rocks back. Many of the letters ask forgiveness of Madame Pele. For example: "My friends are no longer in my life, I am divorced, I've lost my business, my property is being foreclosed. Pele is angry about something. . . . I took the rock. . . . Pele is a very busy woman and surely she would not miss a handful of stones from the firepit. Right? Wrong!" More letters and more rocks continue to make their way back to Hawaii.

VOLCANO ARTS CENTER & VOLCANO HOUSE

Now that you know not to break any Hawaiian kapus by taking lava rocks back home, walk a few doors from park headquarters to the **Volcano Art Center,** P.O. Box 104, Hawaii Volcanoes National Park, HI 96718 (tel. 967-7511). Here, in the 1877 original Volcano House Hotel, a nonprofit group shows the work of some 200 artists and craftspeople, most of them from the Big Island. Fine arts reflective of Hawaii, bowls and sculptures of native Hawaiian woods, and posters are for sale, as well as small distinctive gift items. Note the Jack Straka native-wood bowls, the Chiu Leong raku pottery, the Dietrich Varez block prints, and the "Trashface Jewelry" of wearable art made from found and recycled objects by Ira Ono, considered collector's items. There are concerts and special events as well as excellent arts programs for long-term visitors. During the month of December, Christmas is celebrated with a blazing fire, hot apple cider, holiday music, and Santa Claus too. Always a worthwhile stop.

Note: If Ira Ono's "Trashface Jewelry" excites you, as it does us, call the artist and make an appointment to visit his studio to see more (tel. 967-7621). His "Spirit Fans"—personal collages composed of one's mementoes—are outstanding. Ono, a well-known performance artist, is a most engaging fellow. (And if you're staying in Volcano, and it rains—well, here's a way to make the best of a rainy day.)

Just across the road from the Volcano Art Center is **Volcano House** (see Chapter 12). Situated on the rim of the crater, it's a magical spot. Eruption movies are shown in the lobby every evening. It's cozy just to sit here for a few minutes in front of the fireplace, where the fire, so it is said, has been burning continuously for over 100 years. Burning ohia logs fill the air with a wonderful aroma.

Some simple nature trails begin right in back of Volcano House, and we urge you to take at least one. The upland air is fragrant, the vegetation glorious, the views

---

IMPRESSIONS

I have seen Vesuvius since, but it was a mere toy, a child's volcano, a soup-kettle, compared to this [Kilauea].

—MARK TWAIN, 1872

spectacular. The silvery trees that look something like gnarled birches are ohia, and their red-pompom blossoms are lehua, the flower of the Big Island, sacred to Pele. (It's rumored that if you pick one, it will rain before you arrive home.) That's the big bald dome of **Mauna Loa** towering 10,000 feet above you into the heavens; you're on **Kilauea,** which rises on its southeastern slopes. Pele hangs out in Halemaumau, the firepit of this enormous, 2½-mile-long crater.

There may be trouble in this paradise, however, according to conservationists and local people who are launching a mighty protest to stop the industrialization of the Big Island. Geothermal drilling is already getting under way on the slopes of Kilauea Volcano, in the midst of a Hawaiian rain forest. Planned for the near future are geothermal wells, power lines crisscrossing the island, a metals-smelting plant, a "spaceport," and an underseas cable, all of which could produce huge quantities of toxic waste and severely harm the environment. Native Hawaiians also consider the drilling a desecration of their religion and their respect for the goddess Pele and her sacred places. If you'd like to get more information, perhaps help them in their cause, contact the Pele Defense Fund, P.O. Box 404, Volcano, HI 96785 (tel. 808/935-1633).

AROUND CRATER RIM DRIVE

To see the important views, take Crater Rim Drive, the 11-mile circle road, in either direction around the rim of Kilauea Crater. The rangers' map is easy to follow. Begin your trip around this wonderland of rain forests and volcanic desert at the **Sulfur Banks,** just west of park headquarters. The banks have that familiar rotten-egg odor. Farther along the road you'll see eerie wisps of steam coming out of some fissures, but don't be alarmed—they've been puffing along for centuries. You can stop to enjoy a hot blast from the steam jets, a natural underground "sauna."

Just beyond the Kilauea Military Rest Camp is a road that swings off to the right and across the highway that brought you here; if you follow this side path, you'll come upon an interesting clump of tree molds, formed in the same freakish way as the ones at Puna. The 100-acre **bird park** (Kipuka Pualu) is here too, a sweet spot for a picnic or a nature ramble through many rare trees; but you'll have to be sharp to spot the birds chirping away above your head.

Driving back to the rim of the crater road, turn right and continue the journey into the weird world ahead. You'll get your first view of Halemaumau, that awesome firepit 3,000 feet wide and 300–400 feet deep, from the lookout at the **Thomas A. Jaggar Museum.** Stop inside, too, to learn something about the history and development of volcanoes, and to see the murals by artist Herb Kane on the legends of Pele. The museum is named in honor of Thomas A. Jaggar, the first person to understand the necessity of having trained observers on site before and after volcanic eruptions.

Continue along the well-marked Crater Rim Road now to **Halemaumau Overlook** itself, the home of Pele. When Pele decides to act up, everyone from here to the Philippines seems to descend on the area; whole families sit bundled in their cars all night long watching the awesome fireworks. Nobody can say when Pele will blow her top again. It is still local custom to appease her, but now that human sacrifice is out of fashion, she is reputed to accept bottles of gin! For a more intimate glimpse of Halemaumau, the three-mile (one-way) hike through a hushed forest to the eerie heart of the volcano is recommended. The walk, a tough one, starts at Volcano House; be sure to get the descriptive pamphlet at park headquarters to guide you.

The drive now takes you to the area hit by the 1959 eruption of Kilauea Iki (Little Kilauea; all the volcanoes have little siblings here). A boardwalk has been set up over the cinder ash here; and a walk along this **Devastation Trail** will take you past the twisted ghosts of white trees felled by the lava. At the end of the trail you can look down into the **Kilauea Iki Crater.** (This walk takes about 15 minutes, so to conserve energy you might send one member of your party back to the parking lot to bring the car around to the lookout area at the end of the walk.) A favorite four-mile hike around the crater's edge begins here.

The forest takes over at **Thurston Lava Tube,** a few miles farther, and a magnificent prehistoric fern forest it is. The lava tube shaded by this little grotto is another of those volcanic curiosities, even more spectacular than the one you saw in Hilo.

Now, if you have some more time to spend—at least two to three hours—and are feeling adventurous, continue around Crater Rim Drive until you come to the **Chain of Craters Road.** It's a dramatic drive, the road descending 2,700 feet in 24 miles, all the way to the point where, if the current eruption is still going on, the lava flows enter the sea. They create steam clouds that are visibly white during the day and orange or red at night. You'll pass a jungle of ferns, an ohia forest, historic lava flows, and sea arches, as you go all the way down to the sea. Somewhere near the **Kamoamoa Campgrounds** you'll find the mobile visitors center, built after the Wahaulua Visitors Center burned last year in a fire sparked by a lava flow from Kilauea. This area may still be active by the time you read this, so there is no telling exactly where the visitors center will be. Recent eruptions have created a new black sand beach here. *Note:* Since a lava flow has covered part of Chain of Craters Road, blocking the park's eastern boundary, there is no longer any way to continue on Hi. 130, which once led to Kalapana and the black sand beach at Kaimu, destroyed by recent lava flows. You will have to return to park headquarters the same way you came, via the Chain of Craters Road. Note also that there is no food or gasoline available along this route, but both are available in Volcano Village, one mile Hilo-side of Hawaii Volcanoes National Park.

HUNTING & CAMPING IN THE VOLCANO AREA

If you're brave enough to tackle Mauna Loa (the largest mountain in the world, more than 32,000 feet from sea floor to summit—18,000 of them below sea level), make your requests for information and permits for overnight trips to the Superintendent, Hawaii Volcanoes National Park, HI 96718. The area is under the jurisdiction of the federal government and is administered by the National Park Service, U.S. Department of the Interior. There is an overnight camping area at the **Namakani Paio Campground,** two miles from Volcano House. Ten cabins, nicely furnished, with beds and cooking utensils, each sleep four people, at about $31 per night (for more details, see "Where to Stay," in Chapter 12).

In addition, Hawaii Volcanoes National Park manages three drive-in campgrounds on a first-come, first-served basis at no charge: These are the above-mentioned Namakani Paio on Hi. 11, 2½ miles west of park headquarters, with eating shelters, fireplaces, water, and rest rooms; **Kipuka Nene,** on Hilina Pali Road, 11½ miles south of park headquarters, with eating shelters, fireplaces, water, and pit toilets; and **Kamoamoa,** in the coastal area, with eating shelters, fireplaces, pit toilets, and water at a nearby area. Wood is not provided at any site. You cannot reserve sites in these campgrounds in advance. There is no camping fee, and no permits are required. However, your stay is limited to no more than seven days in any one campground.

Backpackers who wish to camp in the volcano area must register at the Kilauea Visitor Center before beginning their trip (shelters and cabins are managed on a first-come, first-served basis at no charge). They may use the two Mauna Loa Trail Cabins (one at Red Hill at an elevation of 10,000 feet, 10 miles from the end of the Mauna Loa Strip Road, and another on the southwest side of Mokuaweoweo, the summit caldera, at an elevation of 13,250 feet, each with bunks but no mattresses), or the Pepeiao Cabin, another patrol cabin on the Ka'u Desert Trail at Kipuka Pepeiao.

Oddly enough, Mauna Loa's sister, **Mauna Kea,** belongs to the state, and is administered by the State Department of Land and Natural Resources, which is responsible for the maintenance of the camping facilities on the mountain. This is great hunting country, and many of the sportsmen use bow and arrow. Mammal game consists of wild pigs and sheep; the birds are pheasant, chukar partridge, and quail. For the details on seasons and licenses, write to the Division of Forestry and Wildlife, P.O. Box 4849, Hilo, HI 96720.

Slightly higher up the mountain, in the saddle at 6,500 feet, **Pohakuloa** is the base camp for recreational activities in the Mauna Kea area. It has seven housekeeping cabins that sleep up to six each, and rates are from $10 for one person to $30 for six people. These are completely furnished and equipped with bedding, dishes, an electric range, and a refrigerator. Also available are two immense barracks, each containing four units, each with eight beds—just great for a huge family or a U.N. convention. Prices range from $8 for one to $2 per person for 64 people. One huge mess hall with a restaurant-size kitchen is shared by both buildings. You can contact the Department of Land and Natural Resources, Division of State Parks, 75 Aupuni St. (P.O. Box 936), Hilo, HI 96721 (tel. 808/933-4200).

For additional information on camping around the Big Island, details on current conditions of parks, fees, etc., contact the County Department of Parks and Recreation, 25 Aupuni St., Hilo, HI 96720. Summers and holidays should be booked far in advance.

4. THE PUNA REGION

Although everybody goes to Kilauea, many tourists miss one of the most fascinating places nearby—the Puna region east of the volcano. Here you can gain an understanding of what a volcanic eruption means, not as a geologic curiosity, but rather in terms of the farms, stores, orchards, graveyards, and cucumber patches that got in its way. From Hilo, make the volcano trip your first priority; if you have a little extra time, visit the fascinating Puna region too.

FROM HILO TO KEAAU

This outing begins on Volcano Highway (Hi. 11), which branches off from Kamehameha Avenue southward past the airport. About six miles out of Hilo, you'll come to a possible stop, the **Mauna Loa Macadamia Nut Mill and Orchard,** the world's leading grower, processor, and marketer of macadamia nuts. Luther Burbank called macadamias "the perfect nut." This major island crop tastes better than peanuts. On the drive from the highway to the visitor center (past roads with names like Butter Candy Trail and Macadamia Road), you'll see hundreds of thousands of macadamia trees. From an observation gallery you can see the processing and packing operation, and observe colorful displays about history and horticulture. You can also take a mini–nature walk through a macadamia-nut grove with papaya, monkeypod, and banana trees. Open daily from 9am to 5pm.

You may want to turn left off Volcano Highway and drive through town until you find Hi. 130 and **Keaau,** an old, rather run-down plantation town that is now home to many artists and craftspeople. Just mauka of the Keaau Police Station is **Puna Tropical Buds** (in the historic Plantation Store), a good stop if you're planning to send flowers to anybody back home. You can buy a dozen anthuriums here and, with packaging and mailing, the cost is a mere $23, several dollars less than what you'd pay at shops in Kona. They also sell inter-island airline tickets at substantial discounts when available. And once you're back home, send the nice people here $31 and they'll ship you, pronto, a gorgeous tropical bouquet. (Write to Jonna & Scotty, P.O. Box 1593, Keaau, HI 96749; tel. 966-8116.)

On the same street, across from the shopping center, is **Keaau Natural Foods,** one of the best-stocked health-food stores on the Big Island, with lots of organic produce, a nice selection of deli items (dips, tabbouleh, vegetarian sandwiches, carrot juice, etc.) to munch on. You can also stock up on guilt-free temptations like Russian tea cake and date bars, made only with unbleached flour and little or no sugar. Also in stock: incense, candles, hammocks, sandals, T-shirts, and the like.

PAHOA

Back on Hi. 130 now, you'll find Pahoa about 10 miles farther south. Here you'll enter the area that bore the brunt of the 1955 eruption of Kilauea. This had been peaceful farm country for 100 years, dotted with papaya orchards, sugarcane fields, coffee farms, pasture lands. Then a rift in the mountain opened, and the lava fountains began to spout erratic caldrons that might turn a farm into ashes, but leave a gravestone or an old building untouched. You'll see cinder cones along the road and tiny craters still steaming. The most spectacular—and chilling—scenery comes later.

Downtown Pahoa is a funky little town you may want to explore a bit, especially if you're interested in art. Stop in at the **Pahoa Arts and Crafts Guild** on the boardwalk, a co-op gallery/shop run by local artists. Oils, watercolors, prints, metals, baskets, and jewelry are all represented, and prices are fair. Another favorite on the boardwalk is the **Lépad Art Gallery,** which offers limited-edition photographs, art, and art displays, plus a wide range of oils, watercolors, drawings, sculpture, ceramics, and collectibles by local and national artists. Most works are in the $30–$50 category, with some as high as $2,000, as low as $1. You can get natural deli foods at **Pahoa Natural Groceries.** And keep your eyes open for the local vendors who can sometimes be found downtown, selling anthuriums, puka products, papayas, and the like—all at very reasonable prices. Look for the one who sometimes sells six papayas for $1. Don't be lazy: Get out of your car and stock up! Nowhere can you beat these prices.

Hungry? The **Paradise West Café** is your best choice, famous for its homemade soups, fresh fish, and veggie specials, all at reasonable prices. If it's morning (7am to noon), stop in at the **Paradise West Coffee Shop,** where the favorites are three-egg omelets, a popular fresh fish Benedict, and tofu scramble.

FROM PAHOA TO KAIMU

Continue along Hi. 130, and prepare yourself for a chilling sight: a look at the lava flow that destroyed the idyllic garden community of Kalapana in May 1990. Flows from the Pu'u o'o vent of Kilauea, which began erupting in 1983, finally reached the sea seven years later, after destroying in its terrible path at least 123 houses, a church, local stores, and the idyllic Harry K. Brown Park. Also in its path was the Star of the Sea Painted Church, one of the two "painted churches" on the island, known for its colorful, indoor murals painted in 1931. The church was removed before the lava flow could consume it, and was to be relocated somewhere in this area (check local sources for its exact whereabouts).

Also destroyed by lava was the black sand beach at Kaimu and the junction connecting Hi. 130 and Hi. 137. Consequently, you'll have to retrace your path up Hi. 130 and look for the sign indicating the turnoff to **Opihikao.** The ride down to Opihikao is like going through an enchanted forest: Huge ohia trees form a canopy across the top of the road, papaya farms dot the landscape, and a cornucopia of flowers grows wild along the roadside.

At the junction of Opihikao Road and Hi. 137, turn right; between the 17- and 18-mile markers on Hi. 137 you'll see a banner that reads KALANI HONUA. **Kalani Honua** is a unique conference and retreat center, on 20 secluded acres, hosting classes, workshops, performances, and special events year round. They also offer lodging, accommodations, and meals (see Chapter 12). You may wish to stop and browse in the gift shop, which features clothing and craft items including colorful tropical pareos. Dinner is served daily at 6:30pm. The cuisine is mostly gourmet vegetarian (quite delicious), and reservations are suggested (tel. 965-7828).

Four miles from Kalani Honua the road has been blocked by a lava flow. Again, the only thing to do is to retrace your steps on Hi. 137, this time bypassing Opihikao Road and continuing on Hi. 137 toward Kapoho. This fantastic 15-mile trip is one of the most exotic coastlines in Hawaii. From the red roller coaster of a road, you'll see where the tropical jungle alternates with black rivers of lava that laid waste miles of earth before they reached their violent end in the steaming Pacific. The sea pounds relentlessly on the black lava rocks, eventually grinding them into more black sand; on the land the jungle creeps back slowly reclaiming the land for itself and breaking it down into what will once again be red earth. This is how the islands of Hawaii—and many of the earth's surfaces—were formed, and no textbook description will ever leave such a vivid picture in your mind.

Continuing toward Kapoho on Hi. 137, you'll find two good spots for picnicking, fishing, or hiking (no swimming): **MacKenzie State Park** near Opihikao and **Isaac Hale Park** at Pohoiki. Continue on Hi. 137 until you reach Kapoho, a Hawaiian Pompeii that was buried under spectacular lava flows in 1960. The day-by-day fight to keep the village from being overwhelmed by the lava flow and pumice cinders from the new cinder cone (which now overlooks the remains of Kapoho) was one of the most dramatic episodes in recent Hawaiian history. A cinder cone on the concrete floor is all that remains of Nakamura's Store, and nearby, a desolate lighthouse stands inland from the new coastline created by the lava flow. Come back from Kapoho on Hi. 132 and stop, perhaps at the **Geothermal Visitors Center** in Pohoiki. Free tours are held from 7am to 5:30pm every day. Nearby is **Lava Tree State Park.** An old lava flow encircled the trees here, and they were eventually burned out, but the lava trunk molds remain, surrealistic witness to the whims of Pele.

You'll note that we've now described a triangle almost back to Pahoa; from here it's Hi. 130 back to Keaau, and then home to Hilo.

5. FROM HILO TO THE KONA COAST

THE THREE ROUTES There are three possible routes across the Big Island from Hilo to the Kona coast.

(1) The Southern Route. If you're continuing on from the volcano, simply follow the excellent Hi. 11 another 90 miles. You'll pass through the Ka'u Lava Desert (where an explosion of Kilauea in 1790 routed an army of Kamehameha's chief enemy, Keoua); you might stop off at Punalu'u to see the black sand beach. You'll hit the pretty little village of Naalehu before encountering miles of lava flows, until you get to the other side of Mauna Loa and the welcoming Kona coast.

(2) The Northern Route: The Hamakua Coast. If you're starting from Hilo, however, and have already been to the volcano, it's impractical to take the 126-mile southern route, when you can reach Kona directly in 96 miles, and sample in-between terrain so varied that Hawaii seems more like a small continent than a large island. We're referring to the drive along the majestic Hamakua coast, through the rolling pasture lands of the Parker Ranch, and then around Mauna Kea and Hualalai Volcano to Kona.

(3) The Saddle Road. An alternative route for the first 50 miles of this trip crosses over the saddle between Mauna Loa and Mauna Kea, giving you wild, unforgettable views of both—but also a not-so-comfortable ride. Car-rental companies prohibit driving on this Saddle Road—Hi. 200 out of Hilo—mostly because help is so far away. Should your car break down, the towing charge is enormous, not to mention your being stranded in the wilderness!

The drive in the opposite direction, from Kona to Hilo, is described briefly at the end of this section.

READERS RECOMMEND

For Stargazers. "*A unique adventure is offered by the University of Hawaii Institute for Astronomy. You must rent a four-wheel-drive vehicle in Hilo (the institute can provide you with a current list), which permits you to drive the Saddle Road up to Humuula Ranger Station. Turning north (toward Mauna Kea) you can drive on a steep but paved road to the visitor center for an orientation to the observatories at the summit. On weekends (telephone to be sure), the university offers a free tour at the 13,700-foot summit area of the UH observatory—and frequently at night they allow visitors during observing sessions. The summit can be cold, below freezing, in fact; you can usually find enough snow for a snowball toss! The atmosphere is rarefied; this trip is not for those with emphysema or anybody who is a heavy smoker. The university makes no charges; you must rent your own vehicle.*"—Willis H. Moore, Honolulu, Hawaii. [*Authors' Note:* Contact the Hawaii Institute for Astronomy, 2680 Woodlawn Dr., Honolulu, (tel. 808/956-8312).]

HAMAKUA COAST DRIVE

HILO TO HONOKAA

The drive we prefer—and the one that we'll explore in depth—starts from Hilo on Hi. 19, paralleling Kamehameha Avenue along the waterfront and heading for the northern shore of the island and the Hamakua coast. This is sugar-plantation country, miles of cane stretching inland to the valleys (the produce eventually goes to the bulk-sugar plant in Hilo and then to the mainland); the coastline is a jagged edge curving around the sea, broken up by gorges and streams tumbling down from the snowcapped heights of Mauna Kea. The views from the modern and speedy Hi. 19 are good, but if you really want to soak up the scenery, get off now and then on the old road that winds through the gullies and goes to the sea.

Ten miles out of Hilo, at Honomu, the HVB marker indicates the way to **Akaka Falls.** Four miles inland on a country road, you'll find not only the falls—perhaps the most beautiful in the islands, plunging dizzily 420 feet into a mountain pool—but also a breathtakingly beautiful bit of tropical forest turned into a park which is lush and fragrant with wild ginger, ancient ferns, and glorious tropical trees and flowers. It's a rhapsodic spot, very difficult to leave. Console yourself, then, with a bit of snacking and shopping in Honomu. At **Ishigo's General Store** you can pick up a hot cup of Kona coffee, as well as some scrumptious pastries at the bakery adjoining it. A few steps down the road is the **Akaka Falls Flea Market,** fun and inexpensive.

The little town of **Laupahoehoe**—you can drive down to it from the highway—is a "leaf of lava" jutting into the Pacific, its local park another idyllic spot for a picnic. But it's also a grim reminder of the savagery of nature that's always possible in Hawaii; it was in a school building here that 20 children and their teachers were swept away into the sea by the 1946 tidal wave.

If you have time for a little hiking and nature study, watch for the signs leading to **Kalopa,** a 100-acre Native Forest State Park containing trees, shrubs, and ferns indigenous to pre-Polynesian Hawaii, with trails through the ohia rain forest and many spectacular views—a nice spot for a picnic. Cabins are available for rental here through the County Department of Parks and Recreation.

Thirty miles past Akaka Falls is **Honokaa,** second-largest city of the Big Island and the site of the **Hawaiian Holiday Macadamia Nut Plant.** You can view the plant and visit the retail store, which features a mind-boggling array of 200 macadamia-nut products. A macadamia-nut festival is held here in late August. Follow the warrior signs to the MACADAMIA NUT CAPITAL OF THE WORLD, open daily from 9am to 6pm for self-guided tours. On your way down the hill to the factory, you might want to stop in at **Kamaaina Woods** on Lehua Street, a factory and gift shop that turns out distinctive carvings in koa, milo, and other local woods. Koa bowls are their specialty. A glass panel separates the visitors from the artisans who are busy transforming raw koa logs into finished products. Handcrafted items begin under $5. (There is another Kamaaina Woods in Waimea, in Opelo Plaza.) Open weekdays and most Saturdays from 9am to 5pm.

WAIPIO VALLEY

Honokaa is best known as the takeoff point to pastoral Waipio Valley. This side trip from your cross-island route takes you eight miles from Honokaa, branching off to the right on Hi. 240. The best way to explore this spectacular valley (where 7,000 full-blooded Hawaiians lived less than 100 years ago; today there are fewer than 10, plus a few hippie families) is by the **Waipio Valley Shuttle,** a 1½-hour four-wheel-drive–vehicle tour starting and ending at the Waipio Valley Lookout. The tour takes you down into the valley, through taro fields, a $200,000 Ti House, the Lalakea fish pond, a black sand beach, and the dramatic Hiilawe Falls (the water drops 1,200 feet here when it's running). Cost of the shuttle trip is $26 for adults, $13 for children under 11. Trips leave daily on the hour from 8am to 4pm. Make reservations by calling 775-7121 in Kukuihaele.

It costs more—$35—than the four-wheel-drive trip, but an excursion into Waipio Valley on a mule-driven wagon would surely be memorable. ✪ **Waipio Valley Wagon Tours** runs a three-hour tour each morning at 9:30am and again at 12:30pm to explore the sights of the valley; mule power takes you across Waipio's streams and rivers. The tour includes a stop at a swimming hole in the river and at the largest black sand beach in Hawaii. Reserve at least 24 hours in advance (tel. 775-9518).

Whether or not you go down into Waipio Valley, you should make a stop at **Waipio Valley Lookout** for one of the most spectacular views in the islands. From the steep pali, the waves below look like bits of foamy lace. In winter, you can often see whales frolicking offshore. There are picnic tables and rest rooms; it could be an ideal spot to break your trip. And by all means, pay a visit to ✪ **Waipio Valley Artworks,** snuggled in the sleepy town of Kukuihaele, which overlooks the valley (turn at the sign that reads KUKUIHAELE 1 MILE). Waipio Valley Artworks showcases the works of island artists exclusively, with some incredible wood products (they have the largest selection of bowls and other practical wood items on the island), as well as ceramics, basketry, hand-painted silk scarves, and original art and prints. Prices begin at $3.75 and go up, with a large selection of items to choose from under $35.

WAIMEA & PARKER RANCH

On the next leg of your trip you'll begin to see why Hawaii is so often called a continent in miniature. West of Honokaa, winding inland on Hi. 19, the sugar plantations of the tropics give way to mountain forests of cedar and eucalyptus as you climb up the slopes of Mauna Kea toward a vast prairie of rangelands and the plateau of Kamuela (also known as Waimea) and the 225,000-acre **Parker Ranch,** one of the largest cattle ranches in the United States under single ownership.

King Kamehameha started the whole thing, quite inadvertently, when he accepted a few longhorn cattle as a gift from the English explorer Capt. George Vancouver. The cattle multiplied and ran wild until John Parker, a young seaman from Newton, Massachusetts, tamed them and started his ranch. The Parker family still owns it today, and many of the current generation of paniolos are descendants of the original Hawaiian cowboys. The Parker Ranch is the biggest, but certainly not the only one—ranching is a way of life on the Big Island.

The Parker Ranch is headquartered in **Waimea,** a bright little mountain town that is one of the fastest-growing shopping areas on the Big Island, with delightful boutiques, galleries, and upscale restaurants opening all the time.

There are two visitor facilities at Parker Ranch that are well worth your time. The first is the **Parker Ranch Visitor Center,** where you'll see a video presentation of ranch history providing an insight into daily operations on the ranch, as well as the Duke Kahanamoku Memorial Room with trophies, memorabilia, and Olympic medals of Hawaii's most famous athlete. It's open Monday through Saturday from 9am to 4pm; admission is $5 for adults, $3.75 for children. The second is the **Historic Parker Ranch Homes** and their beautiful gardens. Mana, the 1847 home of the ranch founder, is built entirely of koa wood and is open for touring. Puuopelu, home of the current ranch owner, actor Richard Smart, houses a splendid art collection, with the works of many impressionist masters as well as objets d'art personally collected from around the world by Richard Smart. It's open Tuesday through Saturday from 10am to 5pm, and admission is $7.50 for adults, $5 for children. Better yet, buy a combined admission at $10 adults, $7.50 children, and see both.

A visit to **Hale Kea** gives you a chance to step back a bit into Hawaii's past, as well as to browse, shop, enjoy the views, and maybe have a meal as well. Originally built in 1897, the splendid estate house is set on 11 acres of rolling hills and gardens; it was once the home of Parker Ranch managers, and later became a country place for Laurance Rockefeller (developer of the Mauna Kea Beach Hotel). Its indoor rooms, completely restored with antiques and period pieces, is the scene of **Hartwell's at Hale Kea,** where you could have a pleasant lunch for around $10 (poached fish salad, croissant clubhouse, papaya salad, etc.). Dinner and Sunday brunch are also served.

The cottages and guest quarters of the estate now house a number of upscale shops. Of these, we especially like **Robin Bunton's Waimea Gallery,** full of beautiful works—sculpture, paintings, wall hangings, woodblock prints, Oriental furnishings, Japanese kimonos, superb jewelry. **Tutu Nene** is the original source of the stuffed nene birds that one sees around the islands. Some of the proceeds go to help the nene, the rare Hawaiian goose, make a comeback. Prices begin around $10. The **Vintage Country Shoppe** features charming old-fashioned clothing for women and children. **China Clipper** has everything from Hawaiian quilts to shell objects to sweatshirts, and more. **Noa Noa** has a store here, with wild tropical prints on its hand-painted clothing. When you've done shopping, stroll up to the gazebo to savor the view—you might find a wedding party here, as it's a popular spot for festive occasions.

Another stop in this area could well be the **Kamuela Museum** (tel. 885-4724), the largest private museum in Hawaii, founded and owned by Albert K. Solomon, Sr., and Harriet M. Solomon, great-great-granddaughter of John Palmer Parker, the founder of Parker Ranch. You'll see ancient and royal Hawaiian artifacts (many of which were formerly in Iolani Palace in Honolulu) alongside European and Asian objets d'art, plus cultural objects brought to the islands by various ethnic groups in the 19th century. The museum, a charmer, is at the junction of Hi. 19 and Hi. 250; open daily, including holidays, from 8am to 4pm; $2.50 admission for adults, $1 for children under 12.

Waimea is also something of a cultural center for the Big Island and during your visit, you may be lucky enough to catch performances by such groups as the Peking Acrobats, the Honolulu Symphony, or the Morca Dance Theatre at the 500-seat **Kahilu Theatre and Town Hall,** just across from the Parker Ranch Visitor Center. For ticket information, call 885-6017.

Shopping in Waimea

PARKER SQUARE One of our favorite shopping complexes in town, Parker Square has a group of tasteful boutiques. The most exciting is ✪ **Gallery of Great Things,** which shows an extraordinary collection of works by local and Pacific island artists; we coveted the stunning appliquéed quilts from Tahiti and the handcrafted silver jewelry from Bali. Prices can go way up, but many things are surprisingly affordable: We saw koa-wood rice paddles at $7, koa-wood hair sticks at $9, Tutu Nene potholders at $10, and feather necklaces at $45. The **Waimea General Store** is a tasteful bazaar with a highly sophisticated potpourri of merchandise: distinctive handcrafts, kitchen gadgets, toys and games, handmade baby quilts, men's clothing, ceramics. There's an excellent collection of Hawaiian books. **Bentley's** is an exquisite store, like a French country home, with furniture, hand-painted wicker baskets, dried flower wreaths, and much more. **Gifts in Mind** has a fine array of clothing plus.

Almost directly across from Parker Square, you'll find the **Waimea Coffee Company,** with an array of sandwiches, soups, quiches, and various coffees. And they sell coffee-making supplies and espresso machines as well.

PARKER RANCH SHOPPING CENTER This mall is given over mostly to local shopping, but there are a few interesting shops for the visitor. At the **Parker Ranch Store,** adjacent to the visitor center, you can buy many Parker Ranch logo items, including sweatshirts and jogging outfits. At **Topstick Fiber Arts Espresso Galleries,** everything—quilts, clothing, pillows—is handmade, usually by an island artisan. They have one of the best selections of pillow quilts on the island. **Reyn's** well-known island shops for men and women has an outpost here too. You'll find quality women's fashions (dresses, tops, bags, accessories) at **Lady L.** And **Blue Sky Art & Apparel** has lovely clothes in rainbow colors. **Big Island Natural Foods** has the usual healthy selections.

WAIMEA CENTER The newest shopping mall in town seems to be of interest mostly to local folks, but **Capricorn** is an excellent bookstore, and **Princess Kaiulani Fashions** offers great muumuus. Should you need to have packages wrapped and mailed home, a visit to **Postmark** is in order. For meals on the run, there's **Subway** for hero sandwiches, and **TCBY**—The Country's Best Yogurt—for low-cal shakes, parfaits, fruit sundaes, crêpes, and Belgian waffles.

C & S CYCLE AND SURF. Tel. 885-5005.

This store, madly popular with the local people, has just about everything needed for the active life, including skateboards, boogie boards, and skate, surf, and bike clothing and accessories. There are often free giveaways: Who knows? You could win a boogie board or a water-balloon slingshot or even a mountain bike! Look for owner D'Armand Cook's shop at the first traffic light in Waimea.

SIDE TRIP FROM WAIMEA TO HAWI

From the cool green oasis of Waimea you can make another side excursion, 22 miles to the little town of Hawi, on the northernmost tip of the Big Island. The drive is along Hi. 250, winding uphill through the slopes of the Kohala Mountains, and the sights are unforgettable—the Pacific on your left, looking like a blue-velvet lake lost in misty horizons; the shimmering, unearthly peaks of Mauna Kea, Mauna Loa, and Hualalei, their slopes a jumble of wildflowers, twisted fences of tree branches, and giant cactus. Your destination, **Hawi,** is an end-of-the-world spot, recommended for those who like to be far away from the nagging complexities of civilization.

Hawi's riches—and those of its neighboring **Kohala district**—are in its memories. The great Kamehameha was born in this area, and if you travel east a few miles to **Kapaau,** you'll see a statue of the local hero that looks amazingly like the one you saw in Honolulu. Actually, this one is the original; it was made in Florence, lost at sea, and then found after another just like it had been fashioned for the capital.

The trip to this North Kohala area is thrilling, but remember that you've got to come down the road again (Hi. 270), which links up to Hi. 19 and the Kona coast, adding a total of 44 miles to your cross-island trip.

READERS RECOMMEND

Pololu Valley Look Out. *"We took a nice side trip to Pololu Valley Lookout on the northern tip in the Kohala district. After viewing the beautiful valley we stopped about three miles back down the road from the lookout on Hi. 27 at Keokea Park, which had a lovely view, picnic tables, outdoor showers, and a little sea pool. There is a sign off Hi. 27; you can drive in from the road about one mile."* —Mr. and Mrs. Donald Plumlee, Santa Clara, Calif.

WAIMEA TO KONA VIA THE KOHALA COAST

From Waimea, you could zip right along the coastal road, Hi. 19, and be in Kailua-Kona within an hour. However, it's fun to stop off along the way to have a look at some of the fabled Kohala coast resorts that dot these shores, and maybe have a meal or a swim. Anae'hoomalu Bay, a splendid crescent-shaped white sand beach with public facilities and picnic tables, is actually the beach fronting the glorious Royal Waikoloan Hotel. And very close to that is the megaresort that everyone in Hawaii seems to be talking about and wants to see: the ✪ **Hyatt Regency Waikoloa.** You should see it and plan an hour or two to enjoy it: If you can't squeeze the time in on your cross-island trip, then come back once you've settled in Kona. Guests of the $360-million fantasy resort pay anywhere from $235 to $2,700 a day for their accommodations, but you can enjoy many of the resort's facilities as a visitor. For something organized, call the Hyatt (tel. 885-1234, ext. 2715) and reserve a space on one of their guided tours: an art tour, a garden and wildlife tour, a petroglyph tour, a facilities tour, and a back-of-the-house tour. What we like to do is simply hop one of the canal boats or space-age tubular trams that continually circle the property, and stop where fancy leads us. There are lush tropical gardens and a wildlife collection; a mile-long museum walkway filled with superb examples of Pacific and Asian art; a shopping arcade with upscale boutiques; enormous swimming pools with slides, waterfalls, grottoes (one even has a "riverpool," and its currents float guests from level to level); and a million-gallon saltwater lagoon, teeming with tropical fish, which is the home of six tame bottle-nose dolphins. Definitely get off the boat here, for here's your chance to play—or watch other folks play—with these highly intelligent and loving mammals. By winning a daily lottery, guests and visitors alike can get to swim with the dolphins (call the hotel the day before to participate in the lottery). Conservation issues are emphasized in this 30-minute learning session. And up to 20 children a day can join a "Dolphin Discovery" program to meet the friendly mammals. A portion of the encounter fees goes to the Waikoloa Marine Life Fund. Even if you don't get to take part in a session, it's fun to have a drink or a bite at **Hang Ten,** the snack bar overlooking Dolphin Pond, and watch. You're also welcome to watch the daily training sessions at 12:30pm. Kids will adore this one.

Feeling hungry? Nothing could be better than lunch (11am to 5pm) at the outdoor-indoor **Orchid Café,** near the main swimming pool, which features cuisine naturelle. Lunch need not cost you more than $12–$16, and the food is remarkable—among the best of its kind we've had anywhere. Just to give you an idea, at a recent meal we started with a spicy tortilla soup and an exquisitely delicate, chilled guava-papaya soup topped with macadamia-nut cream; went on to main courses of a grilled tuna-steak sandwich with mustard mayonnaise and a smoked-salmon pasta salad; then topped off our meal with a fabulous Mandarin key lime pie with papaya sauce—and each dish was better than the last. We can hardly wait to eat there again. When you're feeling flush, come back and have a fabulous dinner at **Donatoni's,** a formal dining room decorated with masterpiece paintings, which serves perhaps the best northern Italian cuisine on the Big Island. A number of other restaurants, lounges, and entertainments are available here, including a traditional luau called **Legends of Polynesia;** it's held every Monday, Wednesday, and Friday at 6pm; you can see the show and have a cocktail for $29 (dinner show is $55).

If you can tear yourself away from the Hyatt, and you still feel like seeing more playgrounds of the rich and famous, look for the entrance to the ✪ **Mauna Lani Bay Hotel,** five miles north on Hi. 19; to our way of thinking, it's one of the most purely beautiful resorts anywhere, especially in its landscaping and gardens and the massive indoor waterfall in the Grand Atrium. Golfers rave about the Francis Ii Brown golf course here, an 18-hole championship course carved out of barren lava. The hotel has won numerous awards for excellence, including the coveted Five-Diamond Award from AAA. If time permits (or if not, come back later once you're snugly ensconced in Kona), have a splurge meal at one of the most enchanting of its seven restaurants, the **Canoe House,** which features Pacific Rim cuisine by a master chef in an al fresco oceanfront setting—incomparable! (Call 885-6622 for reservations.)

In the same Mauna Lani Resort which houses the Mauna Lani Bay Hotel is the newer **Ritz-Carlton Mauna Lani,** another exquisite gem nestled between the ocean and the lava desert. You're welcome to take a look around and admire the glamorous setting and the lovely beach.

You can then continue along the coastal road, Queen Kaahumanu Highway (Hi. 19), until you reach Kailua-Kona.

ALTERNATE ROUTE TO KONA

Alternatively, you can leave Waimea on Hi. 19 and drive about 12 miles to the deep-water port of **Kawaihae,** where you descend through prairie land, grazing cows, and ocean vistas all about you, until you're suddenly in sultry tropics.

On the road above the harbor is **Puukohola Heiau National Historic Site,** a well-preserved heiau and historical park that figures prominently in the history of the islands. Here Kaahumanu, the sweetheart-queen of the great Kamehameha, began after his death the breakdown of the dread kapu (taboo) system by the startling act of eating in public with men (previously, such an act would have been punished by death). But the place is better remembered for a bloody deed. Remember Keoua, Kamehameha's biggest rival, the one who lost an army at K'au? Kamehameha had decided to dedicate this heiau to the war god Kukailimoku, and invited Keoua to a peace parley in the new temple. Instead of offering peace, however, he had Keoua speared as he approached the land and sacrificed him to the god. Then Kamehameha was free to unify Hawaii and the other islands.

After digesting this gory bit of history, you deserve a change of pace. A mile and a half back, on a right fork just past Samuel Spencer Park, is the landmark ✪ **Mauna Kea Beach Hotel,** the original world-class resort on the Kohala coast. The architecture and landscaping are elegantly imaginative, the rooms nestling along the brow of a hill overlooking the crystal waters off Mauna Kea Beach below. You can wander a little about the public areas of this seaside caravansary; perhaps you'll bump into a celebrity or two en route to the golf course. Note the magnificent plantings, the authentic Hawaiian quilts, and the splendid art collection, which ranges from Asian bronzes and a gigantic 7th-century Indian Buddha to primitive masks and wood carvings from New Guinea. The beach is open to the public (but only 10 parking spaces are provided!), and you can also join the leisure class at lunch: A lovely, splurge buffet runs around $22. (Considering that there are hot dishes like stuffed Cornish hen and beef Wellington among the dazzling array of fresh fruits, salads, cheeses, hors d'oeuvres, home-baked breads, and scrumptious desserts, it's worth the money.) The Sunday buffet brunch is reported to be even more spectacular!

Nearby are two public beaches where you might want to stop for a picnic: **Samuel Spencer Park** (popular with campers and sometimes a bit unkempt) and, about three miles farther south, the more spacious **Hapuna Beach** (watch for signs warning about dangerous tides and rip currents). Continue on Hi. 19 through the lava desert, which on clear days will afford glorious views of all the volcanoes of Hawaii and perhaps of Haleakala on Maui, too. Lava flows from Mauna Loa and Hualalai mark the eerie landscape, punctuating the miles until you emerge at last into the verdant world of the Kona coast.

(*Note:* We're sorry to have to issue this caveat, but we've been told that rowdies sometimes hide in the bushes near these beaches, wait for tourists to dutifully put their valuables in the trunks of their cars, and then proceed to pick the locks while the tourists are out on the beach. If you're going to put anything in your trunk, do so a few miles before you reach your destination.)

SOUTHERN ROUTE FROM KONA TO HILO

If you've arrived at Kona first, you could drive across the island to Hilo on Hi. 11, through the K'au Desert and miles and miles of lava flows, desolate enough to be reminiscent of Doré's engravings. But before the landscape turns bleak, there's plenty of magnificent scenery. If you make the trip in November or December, you'll see unbelievably beautiful poinsettias.

For a swim, try **Hookena Beach Park,** 22 miles from Kailua. It's a long drive down the road to an almost-deserted, lovely sandy beach. **Manuka State Park,** farther on, with its arboretum of extraordinary plants and trees, is a good spot to stretch your legs and perhaps have a picnic lunch. The approach to the little village of **Waiohinu** is marvelously scenic, and the village itself, once a small farming center, is one of the quaintest on the Big Island. Have a look at the monkeypod tree planted by Mark Twain, and a few miles farther on you can make a side trip (about a mile and a half off the highway) to the black sand beach at **Punaluu.**

Another favorite jaunt is the 12-mile drive off the highway outside Naalehu down to **Ka Lae** (South Point). Local people fish here on this wild shore of cliffs and surf, the southernmost point in the United States.

Now you approach the desolate K'au region where Pele obligingly destroyed an army of Keoua, Kamehameha's archenemy, in 1790; the footprints of the victims can be seen under glass. The landscape is moonlike, and not only metaphorically; space scientists are studying the lava fields of the Big Island because they believe it's similar to conditions on the moon. The lava flows lead you to Kilauea, Hawaii Volcanoes National Park, and on to Hilo.

READERS RECOMMEND

Scenic Drives. *"It is interesting to drive up the 13-mile road on the slope of Mauna Loa for the view. From there the trail leads to the summit. On this ride in the morning at 7am, I saw plenty of wild pigs and wild goats. Before Waiohini, it is worthwhile to drive 9 miles down to the left to the South Point (Ka Lae), the southernmost point of the U.S. There is a lighthouse and steep cliffs. The fishermen have to tow the fish over the cliffs from their boats."*—Prof. Dr. W. K. Brauers, Berchem-Antwerp, Belgium.

6. THE KONA COAST

A man we know in Kona, a refugee from the Bronx, swears he will never go back home: "I've found my bit of paradise right here, and I'm staying!" A lot of other people have waxed ecstatic about Kona, the vacation resort of Hawaiian royalty ever since the word got out that the sun shines here about 344 days a year. (Kona winds, that nasty stuff they get in Honolulu, should properly be called southerly winds, say the Konaites.) It's such a deliciously lazy spot that you may be very content to do nothing at all. Of course, looking at the surf as it smashes along the black-lava coast, noting the brilliant varieties of bougainvillea, the plumeria, and the jasmine tumbling about everywhere, and lazing on the beach can keep you pretty busy. But we suggest that you take a day off from these labors and have a look at the sights. Kona is an important historic center; within the space of a few miles, Captain Cook met his end, the New England missionaries got their start, and Kamehameha enjoyed his golden age.

KAILUA-KONA This tiny village is the resort center, modern enough to be comfortable, but still unspoiled. Ami Gay, the very helpful woman at the Hawaii Visitors Bureau office, in the Kona Plaza Shopping Arcade, can help you with all sorts of practical information. There's a U.S. Post Office in the General Store at the Kona Shopping Village, across the street.

DRIVING TOUR — Kallua-Kona to Pu'uhonua o Honaunau National Historical Park

Start: King Kamehameha's Kona Beach Resort.
Finish: Kahaluu Beach Park.
Time: Two to four hours.
Best Time: Begin early, so you can spend as long as you like.
Worst Time: Late in the day.

Your sightseeing tour begins with a stop at:

1. **King Kamehameha's Kona Beach Resort.** There's only one street, Alii Drive, running down the length of Kailua town, so you won't get lost. The hotel is in the northern end of town, at the site of the monarch's heiau, which has been restored. There are tasteful museum-caliber displays throughout the lobby highlighting Hawaiian history and various free activities: Ethnobotanical, historical, and "hula experience" tours are held several times a week (inquire at the hotel for a schedule). Just about 150 years ago, Kamehameha ruled the Hawaiian Islands from a grass-roofed palace on this very site. (Lahaina became the next capital; Honolulu did not become the capital until 1820.) The old king died here in 1819, only a year before the first missionaries arrived from Boston, bringing with them the purposeful Protestant ethic that would effectively end the Polynesian era in Hawaii. The missionaries were responsible for the:
2. **Mokuaikaua Church,** standing on the mauka side of Alii Drive, a handsome coral-and-stone structure that's the oldest Christian church in Hawaii, built in 1838. Note the sanctuary inside; its architecture is New England, but it's made of two Hawaiian woods, koa and ohia. Across from it, on the ocean side of the street, is:
3. **Hulihee Palace.** Until 1916 this was a vacation home for Hawaiian royalty. Now it's a museum, full of Hawaiian furniture and effects, as well as more primitive curiosities like Kamehameha's exercise stone (it weighs about 180 pounds, so maybe that story about the Naha Stone isn't so crazy after all). Check out the charming little gift shop; it has an especially nice selection of native woods (handsome koa-wood dinner plates are $35), plus books and jewelry. Profits go to the Daughters of Hawaii. The museum is open daily from 9am to 4pm; closed federal holidays. Admission is $4 for adults, $1 for students 12–18, 50¢ for children under 12.

The shore road extends for about six more miles, but we're going to leave it temporarily, taking a left at Hualalai Street and heading out of town on Hi. 11 (the mauka road) to explore:

4. Kona "Up Mauka." Upcountry Kona is far removed from the tourist scene at Kailua-Kona. It is, for one thing, the place where Kona coffee, that dark, rich brew you've seen all over the islands, is grown. Hawaii is the only state in the union that has a commercial coffee crop. There are no big plantations, only small farms where everybody in the family pitches in to bring in the crop. Watch the road for the shiny green leaves of the coffee bushes with little clusters of red berries at harvest time. There are small cattle ranches here too, although they're not visible from the road. You'll see the local folk at places like the H. Manago Hotel in Captain Cook.

The drive is a beautiful one, winding through the cool mountain slopes, with fruit trees and showers of blossoms all around. A possible stop for garden lovers is an unusual new bonsai center, located about 6 miles south of Kailua town. Between the 115- and 116-mile markers of Hi. 11, turn up at the junction of Hi. 180 (Mamaloa Highway) and follow the three Hawaii Visitors Bureau markers to the:

5. Fuku-Bonsai Center. Nine themed gardens and an indoor educational center explore the worlds of Japanese bonsai, Chinese penjing, and Hawaiian and indoor bonsais. The gardens, beautiful as they are, are still in their early stages and will not be completed for many years. While you're waiting, you may want to pick up some bonsais to send back home: A certified nursery is on the grounds.

Now, for those in the mood for a little offbeat shopping, continue along the road until you come to:

6. Kainaliu Village and Kealakekua. In Kainaliu, Kimura's is a favorite old-timer. Some say Mrs. Kimura has the best collection of fabrics in the islands. Hawaiian and Japanese prints are specialties, and prices are reasonable. A favorite newcomer here is Crystal Star Gallery, local New Age headquarters. There are quartz crystals, jewelry, pendants, paintings, carvings, books, all at good prices and nicely presented. Look for the Aloha Café in Kainaliu now, and perhaps stop in for a tempting pastry or snack (see "Where to Eat," in Chapter 12). Next door is the Aloha Village Store, with cards, baskets, toys, and gourmet items, plus healthy snacks and vitamins. Across from it is Blue Ginger Gallery, a showcase for about 50 local artists. You'll find an enticing collection of stained glass, ceramics, jewelry, hand-painted silks, and more, plus many crafts from Bali. Paradise Found Boutique is the place for unique clothing, like raw silk outfits designed here and made in China, a line of batik designer clothes, beautifully cut lacework garments from Indonesia, as well as sought-after antique aloha shirts. There are gift items by local artisans as well as Asian imports, too. They have another shop down in Kailua town.

A popular shop in Kealakekua is the Grass Shack, a real grass shack that has been here almost forever. The inside is laden with tasteful and authentic Hawaiian and South Pacific handcrafts. The nice people here will give you a native flower and some coffee beans for planting as you leave; within three to four weeks (the time it takes for the seed to germinate) you'll be on your way to having your own potted coffee plant.

The Kealakekua Arts Center is worth a stop to see artisans at work doing sculpture, raku pottery, stained glass, painting, batiking, and the like. There's a florist here and antiques for sale. And there's also the charming Gallery Café, with a pleasant atmosphere, indoor or outdoor seating, and a small menu that features soups, salads, sandwiches, and pastas. Best choice is the lasagne, vegetarian or meat, for $5.95 or $6.95. They pack delicious picnic baskets which you might want to remember for your hiking and/or snorkeling trip to Kealakekua Bay (see the reader's recommendation, below).

If it's Thursday or Saturday between 8am and 3pm, stop in at Kona Scenic Flea Market in Kealakekua, just off Hi. 11 on Haleki Street. Vendors sell everything from apples to antiques, from crafts to clothing, and a great time is had by all.

After about 12 miles from the beginning, the road winds gently down the slopes of the mountain (watch for the HVB marker), past Royal Kona Coffee Mill (the only remaining mill still in operation) and Museum, through the lush tropical village of Napoopoo on to Kealakekua Bay. Visitors are welcome at the mill. Now, pause for a bit of history and a look at the:

7. Captain Cook Monument, visible across the bay, erected at a spot near where he was killed in 1779. It was here that Cook and his men pulled into the Kona coast a year after their first landing on Kauai, were again treated as gods, and then wore out their welcome. When their ship was damaged in a storm and they returned to Kealakekua a second time, the men got into a fight with the natives, and Cook was killed trying to break it up. You can't see the monument up close unless you approach it from the water or hike down a dirt trail (for hiking directions, see the reader's recommendation, below). There's a "Captain Cook Cruise" that leaves Kailua wharf daily (tel. 329-6411); it gives you a good look at the monument and lets you swim and snorkel in the bay. It's a good way to combine a suntan and a history lesson for $39.95 for adults, $19.95 for children 2–12. The cost includes a continental breakfast and a barbecue lunch.

There are two plaques you can see on the Napoopoo shore: One commemorates the first Christian funeral in the islands; the other is in honor of the remarkable young Hawaiian boy, Opukahaia, who swam out to a ship in 1808, got a job as a cabin boy, converted to Christianity, and convinced the missionaries that they were needed here in the pagan, ignorant Sandwich Islands. Right near the shrines are a few jewelry stands that offer good buys in clothing and necklaces of local seeds and kukui-nut leis.

Continuing along the shore road now to Honaunau, you'll pass Keei Battlefield, a lava-scarred stretch where Kamehameha started winning wars. In the tiny fishing village of Keei, there's a beach with good swimming. But the best is yet to come: The highpoint of this little excursion is a visit to:

8. Pu'uhonua o Honaunau National Historical Park. This ancient, partially restored Pu'uhonua still has about it the air of sanctuary for which it was built over 400 years ago. In the days when many chieftains ruled in the islands, each territory had a spot designated as a place of refuge to which kapu breakers, war refugees, and defeated warriors could escape; here they could be cleansed of their offenses and return, purified, to their tribes. (There is another such place on the island of Kauai, near Lydgate Park, but this one is far better preserved.) The heiau, Hale-o-Keawe, the temple of the purifying priests, has been reconstructed (it was in such temples that the bones of the high chiefs of Kona—which had mana, or spiritual power—were kept), and so have the tall ki'i carved for the god Lono. After you've driven into the park and left your car in the parking lot (an improvement over the old days when the only way to get here was to run, or, if one came from the north, to swim, since the feet of commoners were not fit to tread on the Royal Grounds) on the north side of the place of refuge, we suggest you take in one of the orientation talks given daily at 10, 10:30, and 11am, and at 2:30, 3, and 3:30pm, in the spacious amphitheater staffed by the National Park Service, which administers this facility. Besides explaining the concept of refuge, the park ranger also talks about the plants and trees of the area. Then you're free to have a swim (but sunbathing is not allowed), a picnic, go snorkeling or fishing—or just absorb the peace on your own. Or you can tour the area by yourself with a self-guiding leaflet. "Cultural demonstrators" are usually on hand, carving woods, weaving, and performing other ancient Hawaiian tasks. Canoes, fishnets, and traps are on display, and often are being used outside the huts.

Entrance fee is $1 per person, to a maximum of $3 per vehicle (children under 17 and seniors over 61 enter free).

There's one more curious sight in Honaunau, which you reach by turning north on a side road as you go back up the highway. This is:

9. The Painted Church, the name that everyone gives to St. Benedict's Church. The Catholic missionaries created biblical murals that gave a feeling of spaciousness to the tiny church, presumably so that the congregation would have more of a feeling of the outdoors—to which pagan nature worship had accustomed them. Between Pu'uhonua o Honaunau and the Painted Church, you might want to make a stop at:

10. Wakefield Gardens and Restaurant (tel. 328-9930). You can take a free, self-guided tour through this five-acre botanical garden and macadamia-nut orchard, with some 1,000 varieties of plants and flowers. The gift shop sells those little macs very reasonably ($5 buys 2½ pounds in the shell), and also features small wood items made by local artisans. They also have a very pleasant restaurant offering mostly vegetarian fare, daily specials at $5.95, and homemade soups, salads, and sandwiches. Homemade desserts—on the order of Mystery Macadamia Nut Pie, Hawaiian Spice Delight, and Lime Cream Pie—are a prize-winning specialty. And they have the best macadamia-nut brittle anywhere! They're on Hi. 160, open daily from 11am to 3pm.

Back on Hi. 11 and headed toward Kailua now, you may want to make a stop three miles south of Captain Cook at the:

11. Kona Plantation Coffee Company. The meadow below is a good place to let kids run loose. Attractions include a 5,000-foot lava tube to walk through, ornamental pheasants strolling the grounds, and lauhala weaving exhibits. Upstairs, you can watch coffee and macadamia nuts being roasted and scoop up a few free samples. The company has the largest selection of Kona coffees in the area, and they sell and ship them at very good prices: Eight ounces of Pure Kona Chocolate Macadamia Nut Coffee sells for about $8. There's also a café for light foods and picnic lunches, and a gift shop, all tastefully arranged—and prices here are lower than in Kailua.

Now continue for about 11 miles until you come to a turnoff to the left that brings you back to the shore at Keauhou Bay. Before you descend, though, you might want to stop off to have a look at the handsome:

12. Keauhou Shopping Village. Here you could have a drink or a meal with the local sports fans gathered around the large-screen TVs at Drysdale's Two (see "Where to Eat," in Chapter 12), or an espresso or cappuccino at Henri's Fine Candies and Coffee. There are some attractive small shops here, like Alapaki, with top-quality gifts made in Hawaii—handcrafted native woods, hand-carved coral sculptures, feather hatbands and leis, and much more; the Keauhou Village Book Shop, where, in addition to a vast array of books, we found wonderful old postcards reading ALOHA FROM WAIKIKI, 1935. There's also Possible Dreams, with prints, gift items, silk flowers, kaleidoscopes, and an enchanting collection of circus animals, starting at $15.95, from Carousel Memories; Small World has a large selection of both clothing and toys for children. At The Showcase Gallery you can find works by leading island painters and craftspeople, perhaps originals by Phan Barker and Leah Neimoth, posters by Robert Lyn Nelson. A collection of beautiful jewelry ranges from about $20 to $150.

Drive down to the shore now to visit our next destination, the grounds and public areas of the fabulous:

13. Kona Surf Resort. The Asian and Polynesian art objects scattered about, the glorious use of natural materials, the 14½ acres and 30,000 plants on the property make it a sightseeing stop in its own right. Complimentary garden tours are given on Monday, Wednesday, and Friday at 9am, but you're welcome to come on your own and have a look.

A possible shopping stop in this area might be Liberty House Clearance Center at the Keauhou Bay Hotel. No telling what you'll find at a place like this on any particular day, but we've seen $40 jeans for $10, $50 bathing suits for as low as $7, $50 leather bags for $25. Items are from various Liberty House shops on the island; it's worth a look.

Continuing back to Kailua now, the old vies with the new for attention everywhere. To your left is a modern small-boat harbor; to your right, faintly visible on the mountain slopes, are the remains of a rocky royal slide, down which the alii of Hawaii once scooted into the water. Coming into sight soon is:

14. Kahaluu Beach Park, and your sightseeing labors are over. Now you can concentrate on the important business of Kona, sunworshiping. Kahaluu Beach Park is a fine place for swimming, snorkeling, and picnicking. Snorkelers claim it's the best place on the Big Island. There's a pretty lagoon, the swimming is safe, and the sand, once a fine white, is now salt-and-pepper, thanks to an ancient lava flow that came pounding across it. Even prettier is White Sands Beach (sometimes called Disappearing Beach, since the high surf occasionally removes and then returns the sand), a gorgeous, if tiny, spot. Palm trees arch across the sand, the surf is a Mediterranean blue, and the brilliant reds, yellows, and purples of tropical blossoms are everywhere. It can be dangerous, though, when the surf is rough.

Back in Kailua, you can swim in front of the luxurious King Kamehameha's Kona Beach Resort; the beach here is a public one, something that old King Kam would probably have approved of. The water is very gentle, safe for kids.

READERS RECOMMEND

Hiking and Snorkeling at Kealakekua Bay. *"The Captain Cook Monument at Kealakekua Bay is a fabulous snorkeling spot. Seeing dolphins and whales is not uncommon. The bay is an undersea marine reserve, and the fish are very tame. Buy some fish food for them at the snorkel and dive shops—it really attracts them. Here are the directions for hiking to the monument. Turn off Hi. 11 onto Napoopoo Road and go down about 200 yards to the dirt road on the right. Park your car there, being careful not to block the gate. Walk down the road, staying toward the left. As the coast becomes visible, the trail veers to the left. Eventually you'll come to the water and the monument. The hike down takes 30–45 minutes. On the return, it's all uphill and mostly unshaded. Wear walking shoes (not sandals) and take water and food. Picnic lunches are available at the Galley Restaurant. Horseback rides and picnics are available to the monument with King's Trail Rides (tel. 323-2388) for a cost of $95."*—Barbara Moore-Link Honaunau, Hawaii.

Whale Watching. *"If you want to go whale watching on a small boat, with somebody who* really *knows about humpback whales, then you should sail with Capt. Dan McSweeney in Kona (tel. 322-0028). The boat only holds 32 passengers, so you don't have a problem walking around the boat taking pictures. What makes it so much fun is listening to Dan McSweeney talk about his stories researching the humpbacks, and hearing about the lives of humpbacks. It was like being on a Jacques Cousteau expedition. McSweeney even had hydrophones so we could hear the whales singing. We were fortunate to see breaching whales. The cost was $37 per person for three hours, including snacks and drinks. It was great."*—Catherine and Mike Praisewater, Albuquerque, N.M.

MORE ATTRACTIONS

Before you leave the Kailua-Kona area, drive out to Keahole Airport, especially if you have children with you, to visit the **Astronaut Ellison S. Onizuka Space Center** (tel. 329-3441), a living memorial to Hawaii's first astronaut. Interactive and audiovisual exhibits provide a lively educational experience of America's manned space program: Especially exciting for kids is the "Manned Manuevering Unit" in which the visitor is strapped into an MMU and manipulates the hand controls to rendezvous with an object in space. Open daily from 8:30am to 4:30pm; admission is $2 for adults, 50¢ for children 18 and under.

UNDERWATER ADVENTURES

A definitely "thrill-of-a-lifetime" experience is a dive aboard the submarine ***Atlantis,*** which takes passengers 80–100 feet down into the clear waters of Kona Bay to explore an exotic world usually seen only by scuba divers or research scientists. You'll feel as if you're in a Jacques Cousteau documentary, gazing out of the portholes as schools of brightly colored tropical fish—butterfly fish and saddle wrasses, moray eels and often a barracuda or two, all denizens of the coral reefs—surround the sub: It's something like an aquarium in reverse, with you inside the glass. Divers are sent down to feed the fish, so there's always something to see. (Bring cameras with high-speed film, 400 ASA, as flashbulbs will not work through the portholes.)

The 65-foot submarine, one of a growing fleet of such high-tech recreational subs (they also operate in Waikiki, from the Hilton Hawaiian Village; and in Maui, from the Pioneer Inn in Lahaina), is superbly equipped for safety and comfort; it is air-conditioned and maintains normal atmospheric pressure. Everyone from youngsters (over 4) to septuagenarians enjoy it. Although the cost of the dive—$79 for adults, $48 for children—is high, this is a unique adventure, well worth a splurge. There are six dives daily, departing from the office of Atlantis Submarines in King Kamehameha's Kona Beach Resort; a launch takes you out to the boarding site in the bay. For reservations, phone 329-6626 in Kona, or toll free 800/548-6262 from the mainland.

To see the wonders of the coral reefs *without* diving, there's a new option available in Kona: a cruise aboard the 4-passenger ***Nautilus II,*** a semi-submersible craft whose keel sits 6½ feet below the surface of the water. Thus you can enjoy shallow-water viewing (5–30 feet down) of turtles, dolphin, eagle rays, octopus, and the like, while sitting in the hull. And since part of the boat is always above the surface of the water, you can go topside at any time out into the open air. The boat is air-conditioned, and accessible to people of any age. One-hour trips depart daily between 9:30am and 3:30pm from the Kailua Pier (the office is underneath the Café Calypso, just across from the pier). The cost is $29.95 for adults, $19.95 for those under 12. For reservations, phone 326-2003, or toll free 800/821-2210 from the mainland.

READERS RECOMMEND

Glass-Bottom Boat Tour. *"We found a great glass-bottom boat tour in Kona: Captain Bob's Original Kona Reef Tours (tel. 987-8588), charging $14.95 for adults and $7.50 for children. It was very informative and interesting, and didn't have any distractions, such as hula lessons or a refreshment stand—big pluses, as far as we're concerned!"*—Jan Bell, St. Charles, Mo.

OTHER ADVENTURES & SPORTS

If you can afford a fee of about $95–$100 for a roughly seven-hour trip, you can have a great adventure with **Paradise Safaris,** P.O. Box A-D, Kailua-Kona, HI 96745 (tel. 322-2366), an outfit that takes small groups in four-wheel-drive vans almost 14,000 feet up to the top of Mauna Kea to experience extraordinary sunsets (visibility is 100 miles) and have a look at the night sky through their large portable telescope. A stop is made at the Onizuka Center for International Astronomy, which honors

Ellison S. Onizuka. They pick up at West Hawaii hotels and, thankfully, even provide warm parkas and hot drinks against the chilly mountain air. Be sure you're in good physical condition and can handle high altitudes for this one (not recommended for scuba divers). Call 322-2366, or write in advance to Paradise Safaris.

DEEP-SEA FISHING Deep-sea fishers consider Kona their favorite place in the world. Most fishing charters are beyond our budget, but whether you go out fishing or not, you can view the catch of Kona's fisherfolk. The morning weigh-in of the giants is from noon to 1pm, the afternoon one from 4 to 5pm, at the pier in front of King Kamehameha's Kona Beach Resort.

READERS RECOMMEND

The Party Boat *(tel. 329-2177). "We highly recommend combining deep-sea fishing and snorkeling on* The Party Boat *out of Kona. For $40, we cruised the coast on this catamaran for 5½ hours. We snorkeled for 2½ hours, all gear provided, and were served breakfast and lunch. There was also 2½ hours of fishing. The boat had bathrooms and a bar. The crew even grilled the barracuda we caught for lunch. We girls had a much better deal than our fellows, who sat on another fishing boat 4½ hours for $75 and never caught a thing! They even had to bring their own food. Check this out."*—Martha Farwell, Illinois City, Ill.

GOLF Golf? That's easy too. The place to play is at the beautiful **Keauhou Kona Course,** six miles south of Kona; make arrangements at your hotel.

HIKING Those who would like to hike through the Big Island's beautiful trails are advised not to hike on their own outside the national parks, but to consult local hiking clubs and try to join one of their excursions. If no group hikes are scheduled, they can advise you on where you can hike safely. The offices of the Hawaii Visitors Bureau can give you information on local clubs, or, write to the local office of the Sierra Club, P.O. Box 1137, Hilo, HI 96721.

Another good possibility is to join one of the day-long or half-day hikes led by psychologist and longtime Hawaii resident Dr. Hugh Montgomery, of **Hawaiian Walkways,** P.O. Box 2193, Kamuela, HI 96743 (tel. 808/885-7759, or toll free 800/457-7759 in the mainland U.S. and Canada). One walk is along an ancient Hawaiian shoreline trail; another is a valley walk in the Kohala Mountains, following the jungle stream of a rain forest and seeing the ancient petroglyphs at Puako; and a third is a hike down Mauna Kea, beginning at 13,000 feet, near Lake Waiau, one of the highest lakes in the world. All-day hikes, which include lunch, cost $80; half-day hikes are $45.

RAFTING EXPEDITIONS Here's a chance for an extraordinary adventure—a four-hour raft excursion to remote sea grottos, caves, and ancient ruins on a shallow-draft, 23-foot Captain Zodiac inflatable craft. Well known for its expeditions along the Na Pali coast on Kauai, Captain Zodiac is now in Kona. Two tours a day sail out of Honokohau Harbor, with pickups at Keauhou Bay, sailing the Kona coast and stopping for spectacular snorkeling (instruction provided for first-timers) in the crystalline waters of Kealakekua Bay. Groups are small, the crew members are all knowledgeable naturalists, and a good time is had by all. Dolphins often accompany the rafts, and whales are usually visible in the winter months. Cost of the trip, including a light tropical lunch, is $57 for adults, $47 for children 2–12. Because the trip can get a mite bumpy, pregnant women or people with back problems are not accepted as passengers. For information and reservations, contact Captain Zodiac, P.O. Box 5612, Kailua-Kona, HI 96745 (tel. 808/329-3199, or toll free 800/247-1848).

SNORKELING A number of our readers have written over the years to recommend an idyllic snorkeling adventure aboard the *Kamanu*, a 36-foot catamaran run by **Kamanu Charters** (tel. 329-2021, or toll free 800/348-3091 for reservations). The great thing about this trip is that it's just as simple for nonswimmers as it is for Red Cross lifeguards, since those who wish to may enter the water in an inner tube. Capt. Jay Lambert, the owner/operator of the tours, claims that snorkeling is even easier than swimming, requiring little exertion or water knowledge. And everybody likes to hand-feed the many varieties of small tropical-reef fish abounding in the crystalline waters where the boat drops anchor. Those who only want to sail without getting wet are welcome, too. You receive free transportation by van to the boat, then sail to an isolated reef; equipment, professional instruction, and even a glass of guava juice or beer and wine and fresh local fruit are provided, all at $40 for adults, $22 for children 12 and under (free for toddlers under 2). Prescription masks, to improve vision, are free; and underwater cameras are available. Jay also runs exclusive sunset/cocktail sails.

READERS RECOMMEND

A Snorkeling Cruise. *"Allow yourself enough time when planning your vacation to be able to see and do everything you want, and some extra time for just relaxing and enjoying the Hawaiian way of life. We did the Big Island in five days and moved on to Kauai for four more days. It just wasn't enough time! We managed to see everything, but didn't have the time to stop and really enjoy the beauty of the areas. . . . The highlight of our trip was the snorkeling cruise on the* Fairwinds *(tel. 322-2788) in Kona. The crew was great and took us to Kealakekua Bay. I'm ready to go back just to snorkel and relax on the beaches, which I got to do only once!"*—Sandy and Dave Heinrich, Forks, Wash.

TENNIS If it's tennis you're after, try the free public court at the Kailua Playground near the Kona Sunset Hotel, or the four courts at the Old Airport Tennis Court. Courts are also available at nominal cost at King Kamehameha's Kona Beach Resort, the Keauhou Beach Hotel, the Kona Hilton Beach and Tennis Resort, and the Kona Surf Hotel.

SHOPPING IN KAILUA-KONA

The shopping scene has blossomed like everything else in this bubbling resort town. At last count, there were something like 100 stores and shops, some in quaint arcades, some in small centers and hotels, others just there, all on or just off Alii Drive.

KONA SQUARE A good place to begin might be the Kona Square Mall, across from King Kamehameha's Kona Beach Resort. ✪ **Island Silversmiths,** a longtime favorite, has a sign on the door that reads, WE ONLY LOOK EXPENSIVE, and they're right. We saw coral rings here for $6 that were $15 in hotel gift shops nearby. They're known for their sterling-silver charms: The most popular is the Humuhumunukunukuapua's (oh well, just ask for Hawaii's state fish), $34. Also nice is their Cleopatra silver perfume ring at $25.

ALONG ALII DRIVE Right across the road is another neat jewelry store called **Goldfish Jewelry.** WE CATCH YOUR EYE is their motto. Their specialty is 14-karat-gold charms—pineapple, marlin, reef fish, whale's tails, and the like. Prices start at $10, average $40–$50.

Whatever else you do, don't miss the ✪ **Kona Arts & Crafts Gallery,** across from the sea wall at 75-5699-0 Alii Dr. It's one of the few places that deals solely in genuine Hawaiian crafts: Their wood carvings, for example, are made only of native woods such as milo, ohia, and koa. Prices vary for the works of fine art here, but there are many small treasures: Hawaiian sand-art petroglyphs from $7.95, banana-bark art, notecards by local artists, bookmarks made from the flowers of Hawaii, opihi and sea urchin jewelry, limu art (limu is an edible seaweed). Note their chime collection:

They bear the imprints of native ferns grown on volcanic soil, pressed and fired at the temperature of red-hot lava, and they have a worldwide reputation; they're priced from $14.95. The shop also carries genuine hula instruments (made of gourds with seeds), and much more. Owners Fred and Sally Nannestad are knowledgeable about their collection and take time to explain the intricacies of these native arts. It's a very worthwhile stop.

If you haven't brought the right walking shoes with you (doesn't it always happen), pay a visit to **Sandal Stop** in Seaside Mall. Their motto is BEST SELECTION/BEST PRICE—and they sincerely try to live up to it. Sandals by Birkenstock, S.A.S, Timberland, Clarks of England, Island Slipper, and much more.

KONA INN SHOPPING VILLAGE Cross the street now to the ocean side where you'll find the biggest cluster of shops in town at the rambling Kona Inn Shopping Village. With more than 40 shops and restaurants and a waterfront location, it's always pleasant for browsing about. Shops come and go here, but you'll certainly find much to attract you. Women will come away with a different look from **Noa Noa.** Joan Simon's wild tropical designs on natural fabrics are stunning, and prices are not unreasonable. They also carry a selection of Indonesian artifacts which range from baskets at $39, on up to collectors' items such as masks at $100–$350, as well as Ikat textiles, which make splendid wall hangings, starting around $175. Imagination runs wild at **Alleygecko's,** which boasts colorful gifts from all over the world. Balinese wooden "guardian" figures hang from the ceiling; there is all manner of stuffed geckos, an enormous collection of brightly colored magnets, Japanese prints, Indonesian shirts, and lots more. Don't miss. Hawaiian clothing for kids is well priced at **Kona Children's Wear,** whose selections go from infants through young teens. Light cottons for women, and darling dresses for little girls, too, are featured at **Dragonfly Hawaii.** Like to sew? Check out **Fare Tahiti,** a fabric shop with Hawaiian and Tahitian prints, mostly cottons, from $7.50 per yard. Note, too, their hand-decorated pareaus, made on Maui, air-brushed in rainbow colors, at $26.50. They also sell men's tapa shirts, women's short and long dresses, and needlepoint and cross-stitch charts and kits.

Tropical Touch is a delight, crammed full of colorful merchandise, most of it from Bali. There are wonderful cloth flowers, bags, pillows, carvings, and more. **Crystal Visions of Hawaii** is charming, with crystals, jewelry, mystical gifts and cards, and even a "Visionary Art Gallery." We found stylish modern and vintage fashions and jewelry for women at **Flamingo's.** Need a hat to keep the sun off your head? **Big Island Hat Company** has plenty to choose from, including custom-blocked Panamas. They also have handcrafted Hawaiian feather-lei hatbands. **Island Life Tee Shirt Company** sports some exclusive Kona designs on their T-shirts, which are silk-screened by owner Roberta Fair. (The same shirts are also available at **Island Salsa,** in World Square and at **At the Beach** in Alii Sunset Plaza, about $18.)

Hula Heaven is one of those places collectors of vintage aloha shirts seek out, and it's one of the best in the islands. Do people actually wear these shirts? We know that celebrities love them, but with prices going from $100 to $1,000 for silk and rayon shirts of the 1940s and 1950s, our guess is that most of them wind up framed on somebody's walls. Also fun: the vintage aloha items that collectors snap up, like "nodders" (hula dolls with nodding heads) for $45–$75, and menu covers from the Royal Hawaiian Hotel and cruise ships of the Matson Line of the 1930s and 1940s, for about $25–$125. They also feature reproductions of most vintage items, at more affordable prices.

KONA PLAZA SHOPPING ARCADE Running out of things to read? Help is at hand at **Middle Earth Book Shoppe,** across Alii Drive and one flight up in the Kona Plaza Shopping Arcade, stocked with a good selection of maps and charts as well as books. We also like **Marlin Casuals** in this same arcade; it always offers very tasteful resort wear at competitive prices. **Paradise Found,** next to Suzanne's Bakery, specializes in resort wear that is elegant and casual at the same time; prices are good. Note their hand-painted items on raw silk.

WATERFRONT ROW There aren't many shops at Waterfront Row, but for those who love fine Hawaiian crafts, a visit to **Alapaki** is in order. Everything here is made in Hawaii, from traditional music instruments, calabashes, and poi bowls, up to modern interpretations of traditional handcrafts. (They have a larger store at the Keauhou Shopping Village; see our "Driving Tour," above.) It's a good place for special, one-of-a-kind gifts.

KONA COAST SHOPPING CENTER Near the intersection of Hi. 11 and Hi. 190 is the Kona Coast Shopping Center. **KTA,** a big supermarket, is a good place to stock up on food for your kitchenette. It also might pay to join the local folks at places like **Pay'n'Save,** a huge drugstore with very low prices for film and other items, and **Kona Health Ways,** with a large selection of herbs, roots, teas, spices, and some fresh produce.

LANIHAU CENTER On the other side of the highway at 75-5595 Palani Rd. is the newer Lanihau Center. It's mostly of interest to local people, but you can shop for produce, baked goods, national brands, beers, and wines at low prices at the cavernous **Food4Less** supermarket, which is open 24 hours a day, seven days a week; browse through the fashion racks and get a free shell lei and cup of Kona coffee at the **Hilo Hattie Fashion Center;** explore **Long's Drugs** and **Waldenbooks.**

If candy is your passion, be sure to drop in at **Kailua Candy Company** in Kona Square. It will be hard to resist buying some of these handmade and hand-packed candies, made with real butter, no preservatives, and a great deal of pride by the family that operates the business. They have received national recognition from *Chocolatier* and *Bon Appétit* magazines. Prices average around $15 a pound. If you'd like to be taken on a tour of the kitchen, drive out to the industrial area, a few blocks from Alii Drive; take your first right after the intersection of Hi. 11 and Hi. 190; look for the "Hawaiian Warrior" marker. Tours are held Monday through Friday between 9am and 3pm. Free samples of chocolates and dry-roasted macadamia nuts are offered at both places. And as long as you're in the industrial area, you might as well stop in at a local favorite, **Pot Beli Delli,** to pick up some of their New York–style deli sandwiches (about $4–$6) and you'll be all set for a picnic down the road at the old airport beach. Call 329-9454 for special or large orders by 10am for a noontime pickup.

7. BIG ISLAND EVENING ENTERTAINMENT

HILO

Nightlife is quieter than it used to be in Hilo, what with the closing or conversion into condominium apartments of several major hotels. However, there's still enough to keep you busy making the rounds of some of the favorite places.

For an inexpensive, family-style evening in Hilo, try **Uncle Billy's Restaurant** at the Hilo Bay Hotel. The hotel and restaurant are owned and operated by Uncle Billy and his Hawaiian family, and each night from 6:30 to 8:30pm there's a free hula show, a totally nonslick warm-hearted revue. Dinners feature fish just caught in Hilo waters, at $9.45–$14.95; sandwiches are available for light eaters. Watch the local papers for news of entertainment at the posh **Hawaii Naniloa Hotel,** 93 Banyan

Dr.; name performers from Honolulu sometimes play the Crown Room. At their Karaoke Bar, which stays open from 11am until late at night, music to sing along to starts about 7pm.

If it's just drinks and music you're after, there are several good spots around Hilo. **Harrington's,** 135 Kalanianaole St. has a scenic location overlooking the Ice Pond at Reed's Bay. You can enjoy live entertainment in the lounge Monday through Saturday nights, and have reasonably priced appetizers and drinks in a wonderfully romantic setting. They open at 4:30pm for the sunset cocktail hour. The upstairs room of **Hans Fiasco's,** 200 Kanoelehua Ave., becomes a dance club on Thursday, Friday, and Saturday, from 8:30pm to 2am. Music of the 1950s and 1960s is featured. Sophisticated **Lehua Bay City Bar and Grill,** 90 Kamehameha Ave., has newer and bigger digs now, and more space for live music and dancing, nightly from 9pm. One of the town's "in" spots.

KK Tei's Lounge, 1550 Kamehameha Ave., features karaoke sing-alongs, from 11am until closing Monday through Saturday nights. There's a vast selection of both Japanese and American songs.

The plush Hilo Hawaiian Hotel (71 Banyan Dr.) has a **Menehuneland Lounge** with the little people scrambling all over the walls. Local friends rave about the authentic Hawaiian music presented Monday through Friday from 5 to 9pm by Alberta and Alvina Kalima, who also have their own hula halau which performs on Wednesday. The Bobo Brown Trio performs contemporary music for dancing and listening every Friday and Saturday from 8pm to 1am. No cover, no minimum, and some of the best prices for beer and house wine in town. In the historic downtown area, at 60 Keawe St., there's elegant **Roussels,** a French-Créole restaurant in a converted old bank. You can have cocktails there or after-dinner drinks nightly, perhaps treat yourself to some dark French-roast coffee, brewed right at your table, along with a traditional dessert like New Orleans bread pudding with a sweet whisky sauce; on weekends, there's usually jazz music and dancing, no cover or minimum, in the lounge. There's no entertainment and scarcely any atmosphere at the **Hilo Seaside Hotel bar** (126 Banyan Way), but always a local crowd full of fun, a big TV screen, and drinks at some of the lowest prices in town. When the bars close down, you can get some nourishment over at **Ken's House of Pancakes,** 1730 Kamehameha Ave. (see "Where to Eat," in Chapter 12), where they serve not only pancakes and omelets, but everything on the menu around the clock.

KAILUA-KONA

There's plenty of nighttime entertainment in these parts, much of it centered around the big hotels. The **Keauhou Beach Hotel** is the place for fans of Hawaiian music, which can be heard every night from 5 to 11pm in the Makai Bar. Much beloved here is Uncle George Naope, who sings and plays on Monday, Tuesday, Thursday, Friday, and Saturday. Ho'lua is another respected group that plays here. Sunday from 4 to 8pm the Jazz Club meets in the Makai Bar. And Kapio and Kalehua, a Hawaiian duet, entertain every Friday, Saturday, and Sunday from 5 to 9pm in the Kuakini Terrace, while the seafood buffet (see Chapter 12) is being served.

In the mood for a luau? Kona's only **beachfront luau,** and one of the best in town, is held every Sunday, Tuesday, and Thursday at King Kamehameha's Kona Beach Resort. The traditional rituals and feasting are followed by the Ports of Polynesia Revue, featuring traditional Pacific island dances. Cost is $42 for adults, $15 for children 6–12. But you needn't pay anything to come and see the torchlighting ceremony. Just take yourself to the beach at 6pm and watch the beautiful ceremony, as torches are lit on land and sea in the shadow of an ancient heiau. Then you might proceed to the Billfish Bar, situated around the lovely pool, where there is a variety of musical entertainment every night from 5:30 to 10:30pm.

One of the most popular lounges in town is **Don Drysdale's Club 53** in the

Kona Inn Shopping Village, on Kailua Bay, overlooking the waterfront. Exotic drinks—like Frozen Babbon, Fuzzy Willie, and Hawaiian Sunset—are unique, and the pupus—shrimp scampi, deep-fried spicy buffalo wings, and potato skins—are really special. There are burgers and sandwiches too, to go along with the drinks.

Have you heard about karaoke? It's been the rage in Japan for years, and now it's here, on Wednesday, Thursday, and Friday from 8 to 11pm, at the **Windjammer Lounge** of the Kona Hilton. Karaoke means "empty orchestra," an orchestra minus the singer. Here, a laser-disc video machine provides the words, and guests—which could mean you—take turns at providing the singing. It's lots of fun, with inexpensive drinks, and a $2.25 beer special.

The terrace overlooking the ocean at **Fisherman's Landing** is a wonderfully romantic spot, great for sunset watching or star gazing. Hawaiian and contemporary music every evening, from 6:30pm on. The cocktail lounges at **Jolly Roger, Kona Inn, The Chart House,** and Phillip Paolo's are all seaside, offering super scenery along with the libations. At **Phillip Paolo's,** jazz and blues takes centerstage on Friday and Saturday at 9pm.

Keep the **Kona Surf Resort** in mind, especially on Tuesday and Friday nights, when you can watch a free Polynesian Paradise Revue from 5:30 to 7pm on the Nalu Terrace, on the cliffs overlooking Keauhou Bay. Have a tropical drink and enjoy the show. For some sophisticated entertainment, catch the **Kona Comedy Club** (an offshoot of the popular Honolulu Comedy Club) on Tuesday nights at 8pm; tickets are $12.

If you're in a disco mood, go to romantic **Eclipse,** 75-5711 Kuakini Hwy., across from Foodland—candles, wooden beams, mirrors, and the disco sound. Sunday night it's big-band music. Dinner from 5pm, dancing from 10pm Tuesday through Sunday. The **Windjammer Lounge** of the Kona Hilton has become another rock music venue: Silk & Steel, Kona's "top rock ensemble," gives out oldies, contemporary, Hawaiian, and country-western music on Saturday, Sunday, and Monday.

The Windjammer Lounge, by the way, is one of the most scenic spots around, where you can listen to the sound of the surf smashing up against the rocks as you sit out on the patio and watch the Pacific perform. Walking around the big hotels like the Hilton, examining the gardens and lagoons by moonlight and floodlight, is a show in itself.

CHAPTER 14

MAUI

Even though she lives two blocks away from highly celebrated Waikiki Beach, a woman we know in Honolulu regularly spends her vacations on Maui. The reason? To go to the beach! In addition, however, to possessing some of the world's most marvelous beaches, this second-largest island in the Hawaiian archipelago boasts one of the great natural wonders of the planet: Haleakala, the world's largest dormant volcano. Add to all this a string of gorgeous little jungle valleys where the modern world seems incredibly remote, a picturesque whaling town kicking its heels after a long sleep in the South Seas sun, and a wonderfully hospitable local citizenry intent on convincing you that Maui *no ka oi*—Maui is the greatest! You just might end up agreeing.

INTRODUCING MAUI

The second-largest island in the Hawaiian chain, Maui is about 70 miles southeast of Oahu, and can be reached via plane in about 20 minutes. Geologically, the island is the result of the work of two volcanoes, Puu Kukui in the west and Haleakala in the east, which formed separate land masses as they grew and eventually created the valley in between which is now Central Maui—hence its nickname, the Valley Isle. But according to the legends of the ancient Hawaiians, their own special god, Maui, pulled up both ends of the island from the sea bottom with his fishhook. (There's an imposing statue of Maui doing just that on the grounds of the Stouffer Wailea Beach Resort.) The island is 729 square miles, 25 miles from north to south and 38.4 miles from east to west. Roads are excellent and it's very easy to explore.

Maui has been going through the throes of enormous expansion. But while new hotels and condominium apartments are being built at a formidable rate, the island still manages to retain a graceful, unhurried feeling. The laws here are stricter, and nowhere on Maui has there been such wanton destruction of natural beauty as there has been in Waikiki.

You'll find accommodations and restaurants in all price ranges, but generally Maui is more expensive than Waikiki. Again, your biggest expense will be car rentals or guided tours, your only alternative on an island with very limited public transportation.

IMPRESSIONS

It [Haleakala] was a scene of vast bleakness and desolation, stern, forbidding, fascinating . . . a place of fire and earthquake, a workshop of nature still cluttered with the raw beginnings of world-making. . . . It was all unreal and unbelievable.

—JACK LONDON, 1911

WHAT'S SPECIAL ABOUT MAUI

Natural Wonders

- ☐ Haleakala Crater, 10,023 feet high, the world's largest dormant volcano with a crater big enough to swallow a city.
- ☐ Hana, one of the most unspoiled places in all Hawaii, reached by a 50-mile road around the base of Haleakala, with 617 hairpin turns, 56 one-lane bridges, dozens of sparkling waterfalls, plus bamboo groves and gardens.

Sports and Recreation

- ☐ Superb sandy swimming beaches all over the island, from Kapalua Beach in the west to Kamaole Beach Parks and Big Beach in the south to Hana Beach Park in the east.
- ☐ Snorkeling spots in West Maui, Kapalua and Kaanapali Beaches; in East Maui, Wailea Beach; the offshore island of Molokini, reachable by boat only.
- ☐ Hookipa County Beach Park in Paia, Windsurfing Capital of the World, scene of many a competition; winter waves can be as high as 15 feet.
- ☐ A chance to ride 10,000 feet down Haleakala Volcano on a guided bike tour; all you need is a cool head—and good brakes.
- ☐ Alaskan humpback whales, wintering in Maui to mate and bear their young, visible from many coastal locations and on whale-watching cruises.
- ☐ Fourth of July Rodeo in Makawao, erstwhile cowboy town.

Museums

- ☐ Alexander & Baldwin Sugar Museum in Puunene, especially for its working model of sugar-factory machinery.
- ☐ Bailey House Museum in Wailuku, with fascinating exhibits from Stone Age Hawaii to missionary days.
- ☐ Whalers Village Museum, at Whalers Village Shopping Complex at Kaanapali Beach, with photos, artifacts, and an absorbing collection of whaling memorabilia.

Historic Lahaina

- ☐ Baldwin Home, a missionary house museum, one of the projects of the Lahaina Restoration Foundation.
- ☐ The *Carthaginian*, an authentic replica of a 19th-century sailing vessel, also run by the Lahaina Restoration Foundation.

Antiques

- ☐ Good antique hunting on North Market Street in Wailuku.

Local Foods and Wines

- ☐ Maui onions, the sweetest in the world (sometimes called Kula onions).
- ☐ Maui potato chips, available in local stores—the best.
- ☐ Maui champagne grapes, grown on the slopes of Haleakala by Tedeschi Vineyards.

Mountain Flowers

- ☐ Proteas, grown on farms along the lower slopes of Haleakala.
- ☐ Silverswords, rare botanical specimens which blossom only once, and only on lava rocks at the highest altitudes; found on the higher slopes of Haleakala.

Shopping

- ☐ Lahaina, with numerous shopping complexes and hundreds of exciting individual stores.
- ☐ Whaler's Shopping Village at Kaanapali Beach.
- ☐ Kaahumanu Shopping Center and Maui Mall in Kahului.
- ☐ Artistic boutiques and galleries in Paia and Makawao.

1. GETTING THERE & GETTING AROUND

GETTING THERE

BY PLANE Your plane will probably land at the very modern and airy **Kahului Airport.** The terminal is located in the seven-mile-wide valley that binds together the two great volcanic masses of Maui, the West Maui Mountains and Haleakala on the east. You're just a few miles here from modern Kahului and graceful old Wailuku, neighboring towns competing peacefully for the title of largest city. There is shuttle service from the airport to Kihei and Kaanapali. If you need assistance, stop by the state information kiosk at the airport.

If you're going to be staying in West Maui, you can save some driving time by flying directly to the new **Kapalua–West Maui Airport** via either Hawaiian or Princeville Airlines.

ORIENTATION

Maui is small enough so that you can logically make your headquarters at one hotel and take off each day for various sightseeing and beach excursions: to Haleakala, to the historic old whaling town of Lahaina, and to remote, romantic Hana.

The **Wailuku-Kahului** area, closest to the main airport, is centrally located for sightseeing excursions but lacks a really good beach. The best beach area close to Kahului is **Kihei** (about a 15-minute drive) and this also enjoys a central location. The liveliest and most beautiful area, to our taste, is the **Lahaina-Kaanapali-Napili** region, about 40 miles from Kahului, generally more expensive than the Kihei area, which has a far greater number of condo accommodations. All of these places work as a base; the only place on the island that is inconvenient as a base if you want to move around is **Hana** in East Maui, a three-hour drive from the airport; you might want to plan an overnight stay there as the drive each way is a long one, although most people do it on a one-day trip.

TOURIST INFORMATION The **Maui Visitors Bureau** is a short drive from the airport, at 2500 Alamaha St., Kahului (tel. 808/871-8691), directly en route to Lahaina or Kihei.

GETTING AROUND

Maui has no major public transportation system, save for a few shuttles from resort areas to selected shopping centers.

TRAVEL ARRANGEMENTS FOR THE DISABLED Maui definitely need not be off-limits to the physically handicapped—even those who want to partake of the island's exhilarating outdoor activities. Jan and David McKown, the young couple who run **Over the Rainbow Tours,** 186 Mehani Circle, Kihei, Maui, HI 96753 (tel. 808/879-5521), can help out in a number of areas, from airline flights, airport arrangements, wheelchair vans, accommodations in hotels or condos or private homes, and personal care service to arranging helicopter or kayak trips, snorkeling, or even scuba diving. After entertaining David's brother, a quadriplegic, on Maui, they realized that they had a great deal of resources and information they could share with others—which they do, with a great deal of care and aloha. They can act as a full-service travel, tour, and activity agency for the disabled. Write or call for a brochure and information.

BY RENTAL CAR As in all the neighbor islands, the major low-cost, all-island car-rental companies—like **Dollar, Alamo, National, Budget, Tropical**—are all represented on Maui. The best place to make your reservations with these companies is in Honolulu (see "Getting Around," in Chapter 4, for details).

Some of the local agencies can also offer you good deals, at either flat rates or time plus mileage. **Sunshine of Hawaii** (tel. 871-6222 in Kahului, 661-5646 in Lahaina, or toll free 800/678-6000) is an excellent company. Rates begin at $33.95 daily, $199 weekly, for a two-door automatic compact with air conditioning; at $39.95 daily, $219.95 weekly, for a four-door automatic compact with air conditioning. (Rates are subject to change.) They're right at the airport.

Word of Mouth Rent-A-Used-Car, 607 Haleakala Hwy., Maui, HI 96732 (tel. 808/877-2436, or toll free 800/533-5929), can set you up in a subcompact for $85 a week, or $95 a week with air conditioning; a five-passenger Nissan Sentra would be $100 per week. No daily rates. Most of their cars are '86 and '87 models.

Atlas Rent A Car, P.O. Box 126, Puunene, Maui, HI 96784 (tel. 808/871-2860, or toll free 800/367-5238 in the U.S. and Canada), offers a late-model compact from $12.65 per day with "absolutely no hidden charges." All sizes of cars are available. They rent the Suzuki Samurai four-wheel-drive for as little as $29.95 per day. They will provide prompt and courteous airport service.

In the Lahaina-Kaanapali area, you can get a good deal on flat rates from **Rainbow,** 741 Wainee St., Lahaina (tel. 661-8734), which charges $22.50–$29.50 per day for Toyota Tercel compacts.

MAUI

Area Code The telephone area code is 808.

Babysitters Inquire at your hotel desk.

Business Hours See "Fast Facts: Hawaii," in Chapter 2.

Car Rentals See "Getting Around," above.

Climate See "When to Go," in Chapter 2.

Dentists Emergency dental care is available from Maui Dental Center, 162 Alamaha St., Kahului (tel. 871-6283).

Doctors Doctors on Call will make hotel visits (tel. 667-7676). Maui Physicians also makes hotel calls (tel. 669-9600). West Maui Healthcare Center, Whalers Village, Suite H-7, has a 24-hour phone number: 667-9721.

Emergencies Call 911 for police, fire, and ambulance.

Eyeglasses International Optical, Maui Mall Shopping Center, in Kahului, (tel. 871-0784), will fix glasses while you wait. At Lahaina Optical, 888 Wainee St., Lahaina (tel. 661-8926), most glasses can be made in one hour.

Fax Services Contact Phone Mart Kahului (tel. 877-7345), Kaahumanu Shopping Center, 275 Kaahumanu Ave.

Holidays See "When to Go," in Chapter 2.

Hospitals Major hospitals are Maui Memorial Hospital, 221 Mahalani,

IMPRESSIONS

We are an island community gone mad, behaving like a limitless continent on a world that has already turned into a crowded, strained island.
—Hawaiian Historian Gavan Daws, 1974, at Visitors Center, Haleakala National Park.

Wailuku (tel. 244-9056); Hana Medical Center, Hana Highway, Hana (tel. 248-8924); and Kula Hospital, 204 Kula Hwy., Kula (tel. 878-1221).

Libraries Branches include Kahului Public Library, 20 School St. (tel. 877-5048); Kihei Public Library, 131 S. Kihei Rd. (tel. 879-1141); Lahaina Public Library, 860 Wharf St. (tel. 661-0566); Makawao Public Library, 1159 Makawao Ave. (tel. 572-8094); and Wailuku Public Library, 251 High St. (tel. 244-3945).

Newspapers The *Maui News* is the most important daily paper.

Other Useful Numbers Help is available from the State Commission on Persons with Disabilities (tel. 244-4441; voice/TDD); Sexual Assault Crisis Center (tel. 242-4357); and Suicide and Crisis Center (tel. 244-7404). On Call (tel. 246-1441), a 24-hour free service available from any pushbutton phone, offers the latest news, local and worldwide weather, community services, sports, horoscopes, soap opera updates, and more. See also the Aloha Pages of the Maui telephone book.

Photographic Needs ABC Discount Stores and Long's Drug Store offers the best prices.

Poison Control Center Call toll free 800/362-3585.

Post Office In Kihei, it's at 1254 S. Kihei Rd. (tel. 879-2403); in Kahului, 138 S. Puunene Ave. (tel. 871-4710); in Lahaina, 1870 Honoapiilani Hwy. (tel. 667-6611).

Safety Exercise the same precautions you would elsewhere: Never leave valuables in your car, even in the trunk; leave personal valuables in hotel safes or in-room safes; don't flash cash conspicuously in public.

Taxis Alii Taxi offers islandwide 24-hour service (tel. 661-3688, 661-0133, or 667-2605).

Weather Reports For current weather, call 877-5111 from 4:30 to 8:30pm; for Haleakala weather, 572-7749; for surf and wave conditions, 877-3477.

2. WHERE TO STAY

Although most of the new condominium apartments are in the luxury category, some are fine for us. But even with these additions to the hotel scene, a room on Maui is probably going to be more expensive than one in Waikiki. Meals go from budget to luxury, but there are plenty of opportunities to do your own cooking.

BED & BREAKFAST Those of you looking for bed-and-breakfast homes should know about **B&B Maui Style,** P.O. Box 98, Puunene, HI 96784 (tel. 808/879-7865, or toll free 800/848-5567). Although headquartered in the Kihei area, where many of its accommodations are located, B&B Maui Style has discoveries all over the island, in Lahaina, Iao Valley, and upcountry in Kula, Haiku, and Olinda. They delight in being "matchmakers," finding just the right accommodation, the right host, and the right price for their clients. On their roster are rooms in private houses, which run from $45 to $60 for a single or double, and vacation rentals in condos, cottages, studios, and homes, which go for $65–$100. A very popular car-and-condo package starts at $84. And they also have some secluded, romantic hideaways at higher prices, and even magnificent properties suitable for retreats or executive conferences. The staff is available for advice and assistance once you're on Maui. They now also have accommodations on the Big Island and Kauai.

READERS RECOMMEND

Renting condos reasonably. *"If you check want ads in large metropolitan newspapers, you may find condos for rent a lot cheaper than by going through a travel agency. We've done this many times, in many different areas, and we have always been pleased with the results. For example, on Maui we stayed at Napili Shores and saved over $30 a night by making the arrangements ourselves, after calling a listing we saw in the* San Francisco Chronicle."—Deborah Shulman, Santa Cruz, Calif.

Camping on Maui. *"Camping is still inexpensive. On Maui, for Baldwin Park (a county park), you pay $3 per adult and 50¢ per child. State parks are free. For county park permits: War Memorial Gym (next to Baldwin High School), Kaahumanu Avenue, Wailuku, Maui, HI 96793. Office hours are Monday through Friday from 8am to 4pm. For state park permits: State Office Building, 54 High St., Wailuku, Maui, HI 96793."*—Frank Bogard, Pasadena, Calif.

KAHULUI

Kahului has a string of four hotels within minutes of the main airport and across the road from three very attractive shopping centers dotted with inexpensive restaurants. The ocean, here, however, is rocky and can be fairly rough. With the development of a very good beach area in Kihei, just 15 minutes away, these hotels have become largely the place for local business travelers and for very large tour groups, rather than individual tourists, since Kahului does offer a central location for touring all of Maui.

EDY AND RAY ROBERTS B&B, 433 Nihoa St., Kahului, Maui, HI 96732. Tel. 808/244-4667. 2 rms (neither with bath), 1 cottage.

$ Rates (including breakfast): $50 for one person, $55 for two. No credit cards. Minimum stay two nights for rooms, one week for cottage. **Parking:** Free.

Mr. and Mrs. Robert's home is located just a few minutes away from Kahului airport and thus enjoys a good, central location for touring Maui. One of the two rooms has twin beds, the other a queen-size bed; they share a common bath. Guests can relax in the quiet surroundings of the pool, ureka palms, and coconut trees. Continental breakfast is served out on the patio each morning. Adults only, and no smokers. Reservations should be made at least a month in advance.

MAUI SEASIDE HOTEL, 100 W. Kaahumanu Ave., Kahului, Maui, HI 96732. Tel. 808/877-3311, or toll free 800/367-7000 from the mainland U.S., 800/654-7020 from Canada, 800/451-6754 inter-island. 190 rms, 10 kitchenette units, 6 suites. A/C TV TEL

$ Rates: Apr–Dec 14, $64–$78 single or double; $83 kitchenette unit; $88 junior suite. Dec 15–Mar, add $10 per room per night. Each additional person $12 extra. Children 12 and under stay free with parent using existing beds. Add $15 per night for rental car. AE, MC, V. **Parking:** Free.

Your best bet in Kahului is the Maui Seaside, which encompasses the old Maui Hukilau Hotel (known as its pool wing). The entire complex has recently been renovated and is very attractive; there is also a new sand beach. Rooms are large, light, and tastefully furnished, with two double beds. The standard rooms face the garden, while the deluxe rooms are beside the pool. The superior tower rooms are the most expensive and include a refrigerator by request.

You can save money by dining at Vi's, which offers a long menu of seafood, American, Mexican, Italian, and Asian dishes—most for $6.50–$10.50.

Reservations: Contact Sands and Seaside Resorts, 2222 Kalakaua Ave., Suite 714, Honolulu, HI 96815 (tel. toll free 800/367-7000).

WAILUKU

DOUBLES FOR $35 TO $43

BANANA BUNGALOW HOTEL AND INTERNATIONAL HOSTEL, 310 N. Market St., Wailuku, Maui, HI 96783. Tel. 808/244-5090, or toll free 800/846-7835. 27 rms (none with bath).

$ Rates: $29 single; $35 double; $13 per person in shared community rooms. MC, V. **Parking:** Free.

(S) A low-cost accommodation with a casual atmosphere, well suited for international backpackers, budget travelers, and windsurfers. An older building that once housed the Valley Isle Lodge and the Happy Valley Inn has been completely renovated, painted inside and out, and done up smartly. Single rooms have a double bed, double rooms have either a queen-size bed or twins, and community rooms house three or four people in either twin beds or new cedar bunks. Bathrooms are shared. There's a reading lounge with cable TV and guest refrigerators, a guest pay phone, an activities desk, and a laundry room. What makes this place especially nice is that managers Mark and Jana Folger and owner Keith Schwebel (who traveled around the world and managed youth hotels in California before beginning this venture) aim to create a community feeling here. They've set up picnic tables, hammocks, and a barbecue grill in the garden and encourage guests to cook breakfast and dinner together on a share-the-cost basis. Two or three times a week they plan group trips, the most popular of which is an all-day excursion and 12-mile hike into Haleakala Crater, including lunch—for all of $15! Guests can also rent cars at only $10 a day on stays of three or more days. There's a volleyball court, a Ping-Pong table, and a windsurfer storage shed—as well as ample parking on their side street.

NORTHSHORE INN, 2080 Vineyard St., Wailuku, Maui, HI 96793. Tel. 808/242-8999. 78 beds (no rms with bath).

$ Rates: $33 single; $43 double or twin; $16.50 per person in community rooms. AE, MC, V. **Parking:** Free.

(S) Here's good news for the active budget crowd—travelers, hikers, scuba divers, windsurfers, bikers, etc. This hotel right in the heart of historic Wailuku town offers some of the most reasonable rates on Maui. After traveling around the world, owner Katie Moore looked for a way to settle on Maui and create an inexpensive, comfortable, friendly lodging. She discovered the old Wailuku Grand Hotel and has completely renovated and remodeled the old building, so that it's now quite pleasant. There's a common room with TV, VCR, coffeepot, and games; a full kitchen where guests may cook; and a storage room for bicycles, surfboards, and other equipment.

The six double rooms are small but cozy, with white stucco walls, roll-up blinds, a small refrigerator, and either double or twin beds. There are 12 community rooms, with three double-decker beds each, and a refrigerator. There are no private bathrooms, but there are six shared bathrooms, all with showers. The Northshore Inn attracts a lively international crowd and appears to be always full. It's convenient to many inexpensive restaurants, and good beaches are about a 15-minute drive away.

KIHEI-WAILEA

The closest beach area to Kahului (about 15 minutes away) is the Kihei-Wailea section of Maui—a windswept stretch of sea and sand, with miles and miles of unspoiled ocean beach, the waves lapping at your feet, air warm and dry, and the mighty volcano of Haleakala and its changing cloud colors to gaze at from the shore. It's blessed with the least rain and best weather on all of Maui. Full-scale tourist development began here not so long ago, and the area has blossomed mightily since then, with scores of condominiums, plus new restaurants and small shopping centers opening to keep pace. There are splendid luxury resorts in Wailea and Makena: the Maui Inter-Continental Wailea, the Stouffer Wailea Beach Hotel, the Four Seasons, the Hyatt Regency Wailea, the Maui Prince, and the Makena Surf, with more coming up. Beaches here can be rather windy in the afternoon (swim in the morning and save sightseeing for later). Despite its beauty, the Kihei-Wailea region remains less glamorous and exciting, at least for us, than the Lahaina-Kaanapali region (see below), but if you like a quiet vacation, you'll do well at any of the places described below.

DOUBLES FOR $50 TO $65

KAMAOLE BEACH ROYALE RESORT, 2385 S. Kihei Rd., Kihei, Maui, HI 96753. Tel. 808/879-3131, or toll free 800/421-3661. Fax 808/879-9163. 63 condo units (44 for rental). TV TEL

$ **Rates:** Apr 14–Dec 15, $65 one-bedroom apt for two; $75–$80 two-bedroom/two-bath apt for two; $85 three-bedroom/two-bath apartment with double lanai for two. Dec 16–Apr 13, $90 one-bedroom apt for two; $100–$105 two-bedroom/two-bath apt for two; $110 three-bedroom/two-bath apt with double lanai for two. Each additional person $10 extra. Minimum stay five days. No credit cards. **Parking:** Free.

This attractive condominium complex boasts tastefully furnished apartments, each with its own private lanai, ceiling fans, all-electric kitchen with dishwasher and washer-dryer. There's a roof garden for sunbathing and a swimming pool in a tropical garden. The complex is across the road and just a short walk from one of the lovely Kamaole beaches, with excellent swimming. Reserve well in advance as this is a popular place.

KAUHALE MAKAI RESORT, 978 S. Kihei Rd., Kihei, Maui, HI 96753. Tel. 808/879-8888, or toll free 800/367-5634. 168 condo units. A/C TV TEL

$ **Rates:** Apr 16–Dec 14. $60 studio for one or two; $70 one-bedroom apt; $85–$100 two-bedroom apt. Dec 15–Apr 15, $75 studio for one or two; $95 one-bedroom apt; $120–$130 two-bedroom apt. No credit cards. **Parking:** Free.

(S) We've always shied away from high-rise condominiums, but after we visited Kauhale Makai (Village by the Sea) we were convinced that, in this case at least, bigger also means better. Accommodations are in two five-story buildings, and some have been superbly decorated by their owners. All have full kitchen, laundry, central air conditioning, and color TV. The two buildings, right on the ocean, are separated by a well-tended lawn on which there is a pool and putting green, Jacuzzi, and barbecues. Also available are sauna and shuffleboard, tennis courts and golf. An in-house convenience shop makes housekeeping easy in case you've forgotten something at the supermarket in Kihei, or in Kahului, 15 minutes away.

Reservations: As with most condominiums, several rental agents handle units here, but the one offering the most reasonably priced units is Village Rentals, Azeka's Place (P.O. Box 1471), Kihei, Maui, HI 96753 (tel. toll free 800/367-5634).

KEALIA CONDOMINIUM RESORT, 191 N. Kihei Rd., Kihei, Maui, HI 96753. Tel. 808/879-0952, or toll free 800/367-5222. 30 condo units. A/C TV TEL

$ Rates: May–Nov, $55 studio; $75 one-bedroom apt for two. Dec–Apr, $75 studio; $90 one-bedroom apt. Each additional person $10 extra. Minimum stay four nights. No credit cards. **Parking:** Free.

Its beachfront location and sensible prices are pluses for this high-rise condominium with nicely furnished studios and apartments. All have cable TVs, full kitchens, washer-dryers, and lanais with ocean views. There's an attractive swimming pool and sunning area on the grounds, as well as the glorious beach.

KIHEI AKAHI, 2531 S. Kihei Rd., Kihei, Maui, HI 96753. Tel. 808/879-1881, or toll free 800/367-5242 on the U.S. mainland, 800/663-2101 in British Columbia and Alberta, Canada. Fax 808/879-7825. 70 studios and apts. TV TEL

$ Rates: Apr–Dec 14, $60 studio; $75 one-bedroom apt; $100 two-bedroom/two-bath apt. Dec 15–Mar 31, $80 studio; $95 one-bedroom apt; $100 two-bedroom/two-bath apt. Rates apply to stays of four (minimum) to six nights; less on longer stays. Inquire about possible car-rental packages with Alamo Rent A Car. No credit cards. **Parking:** Free.

Located across from a beautiful swimming beach, Kihei Akahi has the lowest rates of any of the many properties managed by Condominium Rentals Hawaii, a large real-estate agency. Facilities include two swimming pools, barbecue grills, and a tennis court. Nicely furnished units have fully equipped kitchens, including washer-dryers, and private lanais.

Reservations: For reservations and information, contact Condominium Rentals Hawaii, 2439 S. Kihei Rd., Suite 205A, Kihei, Maui, HI 96753.

KIHEI ALII KAI, 2387 S. Kihei Rd., c/o Leisure Properties, P.O. Box 985, Kihei, Maui, HI 96753. Tel. 808/879-6770, or toll free 800/888-MAUI on the U.S. mainland. Fax 808/874-0840. 127 condo units (46 for rental). TV TEL

$ Rates: Apr 15–Dec 14, $65 one-bedroom apt for two; $80 two-bedroom apt for four; $90 two-bedroom/two-bath apt for four; $110 three-bedroom/two-bath apt for six. Dec 15–Apr 14, $90 one-bedroom apt for two; $105 two-bedroom apt for four; $115 two-bedroom/two-bath apt for four; $130 three-bedroom/two-bath apt for six. Each additional person $7 extra. Minimum stay three nights. MC, V. **Parking:** Free.

Although you'll have to walk a few steps and cross the road to get to beautiful Kamaole Beach, that effort will save you considerable dollars. It's much cheaper to stay here than at most beachfront condos. This is a well-kept and nicely run property. Each individually decorated apartment has its own private lanai and a full kitchen and washer-dryer. There are two tennis courts, a pool with spa, sauna, barbecue, and eating area.

KIHEI KAI, 61 N. Kihei Rd., Kihei, Maui, HI 96753. Tel. 808/879-2357, or toll free 800/735-2357. 24 one-bedroom apts. A/C TV

$ Rates: Apr 16–Dec 15, $60–$75 apt for two. Dec 16–Apr 15, $75–$90 apt for two. Minimum stay four days in summer, seven days in winter. Each additional person $5 extra (maximum of four per apt). No credit cards. **Parking:** Free.

This one is a surprise: From the road, all one sees is a parking lot. But the front of this complex is sandy beach! These are very pleasant, breezy units, well suited for families. And the low price for on-the-beach accommodations has to make this one of the best bargains in Maui! All units are nicely furnished, and most have a view of the ocean from their private 16-foot lanais; rates depend on view and location. Self-service laundry facility, swimming pool, and barbecue area, too.

LEINAALA OCEANFRONT CONDOMINIUMS, 998 S. Kihei Rd., Kihei,

Maui, HI 96753. Tel. 808/879-2235, or toll free 800/334-3305. 24 apts. A/C TV

$ Rates: Apr 15–Dec 14, $65 studio for two; $75 one-bedroom apt for two; $100 two-bedroom apt for four. Dec 15–Apr 14, $85 one-bedroom apt for two; $110 two-bedroom apt for four. Each additional person $10 extra. Minimum stay four nights. Monthly rates available. No credit cards. **Parking:** Free.

Tennis buffs will be in heaven here, because this cozy little complex of apartments is sandwiched on both sides between public courts. After your game, you can cool off in the freshwater swimming pool, or snorkel or windsurf in the ocean right out front. The best swimming beaches in Kihei are about a mile away. The one- and two-bedroom apartments are nicely and individually furnished, with fully equipped kitchens. Each of them is oceanfront, with glorious ocean and sunset views, and the place is very quiet.

LIHI KAI COTTAGES, 2121 Iliili Rd., Kihei, Maui, HI 96753. Tel. 808/879-2335, or toll free 800/LIHIKAI. 9 cottages. TV

$ Rates: $59 one-bedroom cottage for two persons, for stays of three to six nights (cheaper on longer stays). Each additional person $10 extra. Minimum stay three days. No credit cards. **Parking:** Free.

This has been a staple in the Kihei area for many years. The complex of one-bedroom cottages is set in a garden and looks out over a protected bay and small-boat landing. Although the furnishings here are showing their age and may seem a bit spartan compared to the newer, lusher condominiums elsewhere, the rooms are acceptable, each with wall-to-wall carpeting, kitchen, and a private lanai with floral landscaping. Kalama Park, a lovely, uncrowded swimming beach, is right at hand. Managers Jack and Mary Cooper and their daughter, Annie, truly go out of their way to help their guests. They ask that you book reservations as far in advance as possible, especially during the high season, because so many guests keep coming back year after year.

NANI KAI HALE, 73 N. Kihei Rd., Kihei, Maui, HI 96753. Tel. 808/879-9120, or toll free 800/367-6032 on the mainland U.S., 800/367-3705 in British Columbia and Alberta, Canada. Fax 808/875-0630. 46 condo units. TV TEL

$ Rates: Apr 16–Dec 14, $50 double; $65 studio; $80–$90 one-bedroom apt for two; $125–$130 two-bedroom apt for four. Rates apply to stays of three to six days, cheaper on longer stays. Dec 15–Apr 15, $65 double; $85 studio; $110–$125 one-bedroom apt for two; $140–$150 two-bedroom apt for four. Each additional person $10 extra; children under 5 stay free in parents' unit. MC, V. **Parking:** Free.

Right at the entrance to the Kihei area, this old-timer is blessed with a beachfront location. There's a barbecue and picnic area, and a congenial group around the pool or out on the sandy beach. Swimming is excellent, but snorkeling is limited. These are condominium apartments, so decor varies with the individual owners, but all are attractively furnished and have either queen-size or twin beds, sofa beds in the living rooms, well-equipped kitchens, and private lanais. Most of the one- and two-bedroom apartments have two baths.

NONALANI, 455 S. Kihei Rd., Kihei, Maui, HI 96753. Tel. 808/879-2497, or toll free 800/733-2688. 8 cottages.

$ Rates: Apr 16–Nov, $65 cottage for two. Dec–Apr 15, $75 cottage for two. Minimum stay four nights in summer, seven nights in winter. Weekly and monthly rates available. No credit cards. **Parking:** Free.

Each of the eight cottages that comprise Nonalani stands alone in a grassy tree-filled area, within sight of the ocean. There is a beach for swimming and walking 20 yards away. Each cottage has a living room, full bedroom (with a queen-size bed), kitchen, and an open lanai with dining table. Since there are two beds in the living room, a family of four could be comfortable here. For reservations, contact Dave and Nona Kong at the above address.

PUNAHOA BEACH APARTMENTS, 2142 Iliili Rd., Kihei, Maui, HI 96753. Tel. 808/879-2720. 15 units. TV TEL

$ Rates: Apr 15–Dec 14, $59 studio; $78–$80 one-bedroom apt; $83–$107 two-bedroom apt. Dec 15–Apr 14, $77 studio; $104–$106 one-bedroom apt; $112–$136 two-bedroom apt. Minimum stay five days. No credit cards. **Parking:** Free.

You'll be in good hands if you choose to stay at this little place. Each of the units has a private lanai, ocean views, a fully equipped kitchen, and smart, modern furnishings. It's surrounded by gardens, and it's right on the ocean. Sandy beaches, with good swimming and surfing, are adjacent; children love it around the rocks because of the fish. Punahoa gets booked way ahead with repeat visitors in winter, but accommodations are easier to come by in summer.

SHORES OF MAUI, 2075 S. Kihei Rd., Kihei, Maui, HI 96753-8799. Tel. 808/879-9140, or toll free 800/367-8002. Fax 808/879-6221. 50 condo units. A/C TV TEL

$ Rates: Apr 15–Dec 19, $65 one-bedroom apt for two; $90 two-bedroom apt for four. Dec 20–Apr 14, $90 one-bedroom apt for two; $115 two-bedroom apt for four. Each additional person $8 extra. Minimum stay three days. MC, V. **Parking:** Free.

All units are oceanfront at this attractive, two-level condo complex across the street from the beach. Snorkeling is good, and there's a sandy swimming beach just a block away. You can relax in the good-size swimming pool, soak in the spa, play a little tennis, enjoy a barbecue here. Apartments are nicely and individually decorated, all with dishwasher and washer-dryer. The two-bedroom units also have two baths.

SUNSEEKER RESORT, 551 S. Kihei Rd. (P.O. Box 276), Kihei, Maui, HI 96753. Tel. 808/879-1261. Fax 808/874-3877. 8 units. TV TEL

$ Rates: $55 studio with kitchen; $65 one-bedroom apt; $80–$90 two-bedroom apt. Each additional person $6 extra. Minimum stay three days for studios and one-bedroom apts, seven days for two-bedroom apts. No credit cards. **Parking:** Free.

Two former readers of this book, Milt and Eileen Preston, started traveling to the islands some years back and then decided to settle there. They've had their own place across the road from Kihei Beach for quite a while now, and will give you a warm welcome. All units have king-size beds, cheerful color schemes, original artwork, upholstered furniture on the lanais, cross-ventilation, and a full kitchen with microwave oven. Picture windows face the ocean. Hawaiian pitched roofs add a Polynesian touch. The two-bedroom apartments have two baths and a huge fenced, private Polynesian garden in back. The Prestons will provide you with free barbecue equipment. The Sunseeker Resort is near the beach at the spot where the 1792 arrival of Capt. George Vancouver is commemorated by an HVB marker and a Thunderbird totem carved by the Nootka people on Vancouver Island.

DOUBLES FOR $75 TO $95

ASTON MAUI LU RESORT, 575 S. Kihei Rd., Kihei, Maui, HI 96753. Tel. 808/879-5881, or toll free 800/922-7866 on the U.S. mainland, 800/445-6633 in Canada, 800/342-1551 inter-island. Fax 808/922-8785. Telex 634479 ASTHIUW. 170 rms. A/C TV TEL

$ Rates: Apr–Dec 21, $80–$115 double. Dec 22–Mar, $90–$125 double. Each additional person $10 extra. AE, DC, MC, V. **Parking:** Free.

The traditional big hotel in this area, this is a collection of low-rise, Polynesian-style buildings on 40 acres of tropical grounds, complete with a large Maui-shaped swimming pool, sandy beach, tennis courts, and a spirit of *ohana* or "family" reminiscent of an older, more gracious Hawaii. The rates here are much lower than at the fancier new resorts in Wailea, and good value, especially when you consider that they have many handy conveniences, including refrigerator and coffee maker. Furnishings are attractive. The Long House Restaurant serves excellent dinners.

Reservations: Aston Hotels and Resorts, 2255 Kuhio Ave., Honolulu, HI 96815; or call the above toll-free numbers.

HALE KAMAOLE, 2737 S. Kihei Rd., Kihei, Maui, HI 96753. Tel. 808/879-2698, or toll free 800/367-5242 in the U.S., 800/663-2101 in Canada. Fax 808/879-7825. 188 apts. TV TEL

$ Rates: Apr–Oct, $75 one-bedroom apt; $100 two-bedroom/two-bath apt. Nov–Dec 14, $85 one-bedroom apt; $110 two-bedroom/two-bath apt. Dec 15–Apr, $105 one-bedroom apt; $135 two-bedroom/two-bath apt. Rates apply to stays of four (minimum) to six nights; cheaper on longer stays. Each additional person $12 extra. No credit cards. **Parking:** Free.

This low-rise apartment complex is across the street from a fine swimming beach. No studios, only lovely one-bedroom units and split-level two-bedroom/two-bath apartments. All units are nicely furnished and have complete kitchens. Facilities include a tennis court, two pools, and barbecue grills.

Reservations: For reservations or information, contact Condominium Rentals Hawaii, 2439 S. Kihei Rd., Suite 205-A, Kihei, Maui, HI 96753; or call the toll-free numbers above.

KOA RESORT, 811 S. Kihei Rd., Kihei, Maui, HI 96753. Tel. 808/879-1161, or toll free 800/877-1314 on the U.S. mainland and Canada. 54 rms. A/C TV TEL

$ Rates: Apr–Nov, $80 one-bedroom apt for up to four; $95 two-bedroom apt for up to four, $105 for up to six; $130 three-bedroom/two-bath apt for up to eight, $150 with three baths. Dec–Mar, $100 one-bedroom apt for up to four; $115 two-bedroom apt for up to four, $125 for up to six; $150 three-bedroom/two-bath apt for up to eight, $175 with three baths. Each additional person $10 extra. Minimum stay five nights; 15% discount for monthly stays. No credit cards. **Parking:** Free.

It's so cozy and comfortable, you could easily spend a long time living here—and many people do. The five two-story wooden buildings are across the road from the ocean and surrounded by over 5½ acres of green gardens and lawns. There are two tennis courts, an 18-hole putting green, an oversize pool spanned by a bridge, a Jacuzzi, barbecues, and shuffleboard courts. Apartments are spacious and comfortable, with nice furnishings, cable TV, fully equipped kitchens, and large lanais. Rates are decent for Maui. The best buy is the one-bedroom/one-bath unit for four people.

KAMAOLE NALU RESORT, 2450 S. Kihei Rd., Kihei, Maui, HI 96753-8694. Tel. 808/879-1006, or toll free 800/767-1497. Fax 808/879-8693. 36 two-bedroom apts. TV TEL

$ Rates: Apr 15–Dec 15, $95 ocean-view apt for two, $105 oceanfront. Dec 16–Apr 14, $130 ocean-view apt for two, $140 oceanfront. Each additional person $12 extra. Special rates of $90 oceanfront, $80 ocean-view, may be offered June–Sept. Rates subject to change. Minimum stay three nights. No credit cards. **Parking:** Free.

Nestled between two lovely beach parks, Kamaole 1 and Kamaole 2, this one is for those who love the water. There's also a swimming pool and a barbecue grill. Apartments are all individually and nicely furnished, and good buys, considering that each has a living room, a fully equipped kitchen with dishwasher and laundry facilities, two baths, and a private lanai. A nice place for a family to spread out in.

LUANA KAI RESORT, 940 S. Kihei Rd., Kihei, Maui, HI 96753. Tel. 808/879-1268, or toll free 800/669-1127. Fax 808/879-1455. 113 condo units. TV TEL

$ Rates: Apr–Dec 19, $77–$87 one-bedroom apt; $97–$117 two-bedroom apt; $147 three-bedroom apt. Dec 20–Mar, $102–$112 one-bedroom apt; $122–$142 two-bedroom apt; $183 three-bedroom apt. AE, DC, MC, V. **Parking:** Free.

Gracefully situated on eight acres of beautifully landscaped grounds, this is one of the nicest condos in the Kihei area. Step from your room—well, almost—to the ocean or swimming pool, heated whirlpool, saunas, tennis courts, putting green, barbecue area; everything is close at hand. Best of all, there's a peaceful feeling here. Inside, carved wooden doors lead to one-, two-, and three-bedroom apartments luxuriously furnished in light woods, all with full electric kitchens, lanais, and every comfort for vacation living.

MANA KAI MAUI CONDOMINIUM HOTEL, 2960 S. Kihei Rd., Kihei, Maui, HI 96753. Tel. 808/879-1561, or toll free 800/525-2025 on the mainland U.S. and in Canada. Fax 808/874-5042. 66 hotel rms, 66 condo apts. TV TEL

$ Rates (including car with unlimited mileage): Apr 17–Dec 16, $90 double (including breakfast); $155 one-bedroom apt; $175 two-bedroom apt for four. Dec 17–Apr 16, $95 double (including breakfast); $175 one-bedroom apt; $195 two-bedroom apt for four. Each additional person $10 extra. AE, CB, DC, MC, V. **Parking:** Free.

A unique resort in this area—or any other, for that matter—Mana Kai Maui offers a combination of condominium apartments and regular hotel rooms in a lively, upbeat setting. Situated on a mile-long, beautiful crescent of beach (it's known as one of the best snorkeling beaches around), with a pool, an open-air restaurant, and all sorts of activities going on, it offers a lot under one roof. The hotel rooms have the lowest rates; these are small bedrooms with either a king-size bed or twins, and an attractive bathroom with a large vanity sink. Apartments include full kitchen with refrigerator, range, dishwasher, and dishes.

MENEHUNE SHORES, 760 S. Kihei Rd. (P.O. Box 556), Kihei, Maui, HI 96753. Tel. 808/879-5828, or toll free 800/558-9117 in the U.S. and Canada. Fax 808/879-5218. 70 condo units.

$ Rates: Apr 16–Dec 15, $80 one-bedroom apt for two; $94.50 one-bedroom/two-bath apt for two; $107.50 two-bedroom/two-bath apt for four; $127.50 three-bedroom/two-bath apt for four, $147.50 for six. Dec 16–Apr 15, $95 one-bedroom for two; $117.50 one-bedroom/two-bath apt for two; $127.50 two-bedroom/two-bath apt for four; $137.50 three-bedroom/two-bath apt for four, $157.50 for six. Each additional person $5.60 extra. Minimum stay five days. No credit cards. **Parking:** Free.

For family accommodations, try this big, beautiful condominium complex on the beach at Kihei. You could almost stay here and not want to leave the grounds—there's the ocean, a heated swimming pool, and the "Royal Fishpond," a protected stone-and-reef formation built by the ancient Hawaiians, right on the premises, as well as a restaurant. There's even a whale-watching platform in the roof garden. All apartments face the ocean, are individually decorated, and have a full electric kitchen, with refrigerator/freezer and washer-dryer. The two- and three-bedroom apartments have two bathrooms each.

WAILEA OCEANFRONT HOTEL, 2980 S. Kihei Rd., Kihei, Maui, HI 96753. Tel. 808/879-7744, or toll free 800/367-5004 in the U.S. and Canada, 800/272-5275 inter-island. Fax 808/533-0472. Telex 723-8582. 88 rms. A/C TV TEL

$ Rates (including car rental): Apr–Dec 17, $85–$100 double; $160 one-bedroom family unit. Dec 18–Mar, $95–$110 double; $170 one-bedroom family unit. AE, MC, V.

An on-the-beach location and some of the more moderate prices in the Wailea area are pluses for this hotel, located at the entrance to the Wailea Beach Resort. Two championship golf courses and 14 tennis courts are within walking distance of the hotel, and right out front is a beautiful crescent of sandy beach, perfect for swimming and snorkeling. No need for a pool here. Corelli's on the Beach, a sophisticated spot for gourmet Italian dining, is right on the premises. Rooms are comfortable, nicely furnished, each with its own refrigerator. Most of the rooms are in the standard category, which means they have either double or twin beds and a garden view.

Reservations: Contact Hawaiian Pacific Resorts, 1150 S. King St., Honolulu, HI 96814; or call the toll-free numbers above.

BED & BREAKFAST

BED, BREAKFAST, BOOKS & BEACH, 3270 Kehala Dr., Kihei, Maui, HI 96753. Tel. 808/879-0097. 2 rms. TEL

$ Rates (including breakfast): $70 mountain room; $80 ocean room. $5 less for stays of three to six nights, $10 less for a week or more. MC, V. **Parking:** Free.

A mile from the ocean in Maui Meadows, the home of spiritual psychotherapists Natalie and John Tyler is filled with classical music, fine art, and books. Guests can enjoy breakfast ("natural high-energy gourmet") on a screened porch with views of mountains and the songs of birds, plus sunsets over the ocean with cool drinks and pupus on the deck. A variety of options ranges from champagne breakfasts in bed for honeymooners to daily meditations to gourmet dinners and trips to "secret and isolated places." No smoking. Shared baths.

MAALAEA BAY

Down by the small-boat harbor at Maalaea Bay, a few miles from Kihei, is a wonderful beach area, and perched here, at Maalaea Village, is a small group of condominiums.

DOUBLES FOR $65

HONO KAI RESORT, RR 1, Box 389, Maalaea Village, Maui, HI 96793. Tel. 808/244-7012, or toll free 800/367-6084. 40 condo units. TV TEL

$ Rates: Summer, $65 one-bedroom apt with garden view, $80 oceanfront. Winter, $75 one-bedroom apt with garden view, $90 oceanfront. Minimum stay five days. Inquire about summer specials. No credit cards. **Parking:** Free.

Hono Kai is one of the most reasonably priced condominiums in the area, and would make an ideal place for a family vacation. You can swim in front of your door or at the public beach 50 yards away—or try your luck with surf at the harbor, which, according to some of the locals, is "the fastest surf in the world."

All units are on the ocean side of the street, and all are pleasantly furnished. Shoji doors separate the living room and bedroom. There are full kitchens, including dishwashers, and cable TV with HBO on request, even use of boogie boards and surfboards free. There's a swimming pool, washers and dryers on every floor, and two good restaurants—Buzz's Steak House and The Waterfront—nearby. We've had several good reports from our readers about this place and about rental agent Jeanne McJannet, who also represents two adjoining properties, Makani A Kai and Kanai A Nalu, as part of Maalaea Bay Rentals.

LAHAINA

The area surrounding the historic old whaling town of Lahaina, on Maui's west coast about 30 miles from Kahului, might be a good place to move on to after a day or two in the Kahului or Kihei area; or it could serve as a base for your entire stay in Maui.

A NEARBY CAMPGROUND

CAMP PECUSA, 800 Olowalu Village Rd., Lahaina, Maui, HI 96761. Tel. 808/661-4304.

$ Rates: $3 per night.

Here's a chance to live on the beach, laze in a hammock on the shore, and sleep in your own tent under the stars. Camp Pecusa is an Episcopal Church Camp located on a secluded beach in Olowalu, 6½ miles southeast of Lahaina, 100 yards off the highway and behind a sugarcane field. From the campgrounds you have great views of Kahoolawe Island, Haleakala, and the West Maui Mountains, and from November through May, of humpback whales swimming just offshore. This is basic, no-frills camping. Campsites are scattered under sea grape and monkeypod trees, with fire pits and picnic tables. A central shower and portable toilets (kept very clean) are furnished. The parking area for the campsite is lighted at night, and security is furnished by the managers, Linda and Norm Nelson, who live on the property. Snorkeling from the beach is excellent; there is a coral reef and surge channels extend several hundred yards offshore. You must furnish all your own equipment, as there is none for rent.

For an information sheet on Camp Pecusa, send a stamped, self-addressed envelope to the address above.

DOUBLES FOR $30

PIONEER INN, 658 Wharf St., Lahaina, Maui, HI 96761-1295. Tel. 808/661-3636, or toll free 800/457-5457. Fax 808/667-5708. 48 rms. A/C TEL

$ Rates: Original wing, $30–$35 single or double without bath, $35–$42 single or double with bath. Mauka building, $70–$80 single or double with bath. Each additional person $10 extra, $5 per child under 5. AE, CB, DC, JCB, MC, V. **Parking:** Free on-street or for a fee at nearby garages.

This island landmark is in the heart of it all, out on the wharf overlooking the harbor, and a historic sight in its own right. For years, kamaainas, tourists, movie stars, sailors, and beachcombers sat out on the big lanai in front, wondering what was happening back in civilization. Well, Lahaina is very civilized now, but the old hotel is still there, quaint and colorful, and the old rooms, clean but not at all fancy, have the lowest prices in Lahaina. Rooms in the newer mauka building are much nicer, with air conditioning, private bath, and lanai. Most rooms have a queen-size bed plus a twin. Fun for adventurous types. And the food is good. The Harpooner's Lanai serves breakfast and lunch (and more potent stuff all day), and at night you can broil your own steak on the patio.

DOUBLES FOR $75 TO $105

LAHAINA HOTEL, 127 Lahainaluna Rd., Lahaina, Maui, HI 96761. Tel. 808/661-0577, or toll-free 800/669-3444. Fax 808/667-9480. 13 rms. A/C TEL

$ **Rates** (including breakfast): $89–$99 standard single or double; $129 large single or double (with queen- or king-size bed). AE, MC, V. **Parking:** $7 per day.

Anyone who remembers the shabby old Lahainaluna Hotel will be stunned to see the magical transformation it has undergone, emerging as the Lahaina Hotel, an intimate inn with all the grace and charm of turn-of-the-century Lahaina. The hotel was re-created from the ground up (the electrical wiring and plumbing were completely replaced), at a cost of $3 million, by Rick Ralston, of Crazy Shirts fame. Ralston, one of Hawaii's most avid preservationists, saw to it that every detail of the period restoration was complete, from the turn-of-the-century wood, brass, full-size iron beds, Oriental rugs, and wood wardrobe closets to the marble mantel clocks, leaded-glass lampshades, and even the lace runners on the dressers. All the antiques are from his personal collection. Modern conveniences include new private baths, ceiling "fly fans," and luxurious decorator fabrics and wall coverings. Guests are served a continental breakfast to enjoy either in bed or in the wicker rocking chairs on their balconies, which overlook busy Lahainaluna Street in the midst of Lahaina town. All rooms are one flight up, on the second floor; downstairs is a small, graceful lobby and, adjoining it, David Paul's Lahaina Grill, an upscale restaurant serving New American cuisine. If you can afford the tab, a stay here is clearly a special experience. Inquire about their special wedding packages.

LAHAINA ROADS CONDOMINIUMS, 1403 Front St., Lahaina, Maui, HI 96761. Tel. 808/661-3166, or toll free 800/624-8203. 12 condo units. TV

$ **Rates:** Apr 16–Dec 15, $75 one-bedroom apt for two; $105 two-bedroom apt for four; $150 penthouse apt for four. Dec 16–Apr 15, $95 one-bedroom apt for two; $124 two-bedroom apt for four; $200 penthouse apt for four. Each additional person $10 extra. Minimum stay three days. MC, V. **Parking:** Free.

If you'd like to settle into your own little apartment right in Lahaina, this could be your place. The five-story elevator building at the Kaanapali end of Front Street sits in a cool and breezy spot right on a good snorkeling beach; you can look down at the ocean—and watch some spectacular sunsets—from your own lanai. A swimming beach is half a mile up the road, but there's a freshwater pool right at home. The attractively fully furnished apartments are soundproof, with wall-to-wall carpeting, fully equipped kitchens with washer and dryer, and large living rooms with convertible couches; local calls are free from your own telephone. Penthouse apartments have two baths. Cleaning service on request. A free shuttle to downtown Lahaina and Kaanapali is within three blocks.

LAHAINA SHORES BEACH RESORT, 475 Front St., Lahaina, Maui, HI 96761. Tel. 808/661-4835, or toll free 800/628-6699. Fax 808/661-0147. Condo units. A/C TV TEL

$ **Rates:** Apr 21–Dec 15, $95–$115 studio for two; $120–$140 one-bedroom apt for three; $160–$180 penthouse apt for four. Dec 16–Apr 20, $105–$135 studio for two; $145–$170 one-bedroom apt for three; $190–$225 penthouse apt for four. Cribs and rollaways $10 extra. Car/condo and special seasonal packages available. AE, MC, V. **Parking:** Free.

Considering that you can swim right in front of the hotel, this beachfront resort might be worth stretching your budget for a bit. All the units have complete electric kitchens, wall-to-wall carpeting, and lanais offering ocean or mountain views. The cheaper units face the mountains while the more expensive ones have ocean views or are oceanfront. The seven-story building, a charming example of Victorian architecture, is very much in keeping with the rest of old Lahaina—a welcome contrast to the burgeoning concrete high-rises flourishing all over the rest of the island. A swimming pool with adjacent heated therapeutic Jacuzzi sits on the ocean side, just off the huge, airy lobby. You can swim in Lahaina Harbor, right in front of the hotel, and play tennis across the street.

Reservations: Write to 50 Nohea Kai Dr., Lahaina, HI 96761; or call the toll-free number above.

MAUI ISLANDER, 660 Wainee St., Lahaina, Maui, HI 96761. Tel. 808/667-9766, or toll free 800/367-5226. Fax 808/661-3733. 372 rms. A/C TV TEL

$ Rates: $83 double; $95 studio for up to three; $107 one-bedroom suite for up to four. AE, DC, MC, V. **Parking:** Free.

Without a car, almost any vacation on Maui is difficult. But lack of wheels will not be a hindrance to anyone who chooses to stay at this hotel, which affords peace and privacy (its units are spread out over nine acres on tropical grounds), while providing proximity to everything you could want in the area; it's a three-block walk to a sandy beach, a two-block stroll to the activities of Lahaina Harbor, a block away from the shops and restaurants of Front Street, two blocks to the supermarket, and a short free bus ride to the resort life at Kaanapali Beach. You can be picked up at the airport and taken to the Maui Islander at nominal cost. And the hotel-condo itself is lovely, its units simply but nicely decorated in island style with light woods, tile bathroom, tidy kitchen (hotel rooms have refrigerators only). Right at home is a swimming pool, a barbecue and picnic area, and a tennis court lit for night play. Good value in this pricey area.

PLANTATION INN, 174 Lahainaluna Rd., Lahaina, Maui, HI 96761. Tel. 808/667-9225, or toll free 800/433-6815. Fax 808/667-9293. 14 rms, 4 suites. A/C TV TEL

$ Rates: $99–$145 double; $175 suite. Honeymoon and dive packages available. AE, DISC, MC, V. **Parking:** Free.

Just a block from the bustling waterfront and main street of Lahaina is this small, quiet, European-style country inn whose owners have come up with some terrific innovations in the art of making guests happy. Each of the soundproofed rooms is exquisitely decorated with antiques, stained glass, hardwood floors, brass and poster beds, ceiling fans, and floral wallpaper and bedspread. The TV (VCR on request) is tucked away in a graceful armoire; there are silk flower bouquets in every room; wall prints are charming. Some suites have cooking facilities. Guests have the use of a 12-foot-deep tiled pool with spa and sun deck out back, plus a club house for private meetings or dining. Guests receive a 50% discount or breakfast (worth over $10) at Gerard's, one of Maui's best French restaurants, which occupies the front parlor and veranda of the Plantation Inn. The inn books cars as a courtesy to their guests, with rates starting as low as $18 a day or $95 a week for a subcompact. The inn also provides snorkeling equipment, golf clubs, coolers, beach mats, just about anything you need for a neat and nifty vacation.

PUAMANA, 721 Wainee St., P.O. Box 515, Lahaina, Maui, HI 96767. Tel. 808/667-2251, or toll free 800/628-6731 in the U.S. and Canada. 40 condo units. A/C TV TEL

$ Rates: Apr 16–Dec 14, $105 one-bedroom garden-view apt for up to four, $150 center garden, $170 oceanfront; $155, $200, or $240 two-bedroom house for up to six; $315 three-bedroom oceanfront house for up to six. Dec 15–Apr 15, $130 one-bedroom garden-view apt, $150 center garden, $180 oceanfront; $175, $250, or $280 two-bedroom house for up to six; $350 three-bedroom oceanfront house for up to six. Minimum stay three nights. AE, DISC, MC, V. **Parking:** Free.

Not a commercial resort, a hotel, or a typical condo development, Puamana is the first planned residential development on Maui, a colony of privately owned town houses set on 28 acres of tropical gardens right on the beach. The place is secluded, private, and very peaceful, yet it's a short drive from all the shopping and restaurant excitement of downtown Lahaina. Puamana was a private estate in the 1920s, part of a large sugar plantation; the plantation manager's home is now the clubhouse, with a patio overlooking the ocean (the ideal place for sunset watching), a library, card rooms, sauna, and office. There are three swimming pools (one, for adults only, right on the beach), a Laykold tennis court, paddle tennis and badminton, and table tennis, too. The town houses, built back in the 1960s, are all individually furnished, all comfortable, with complete kitchens, sofa beds in the living rooms; they can sleep four to six.

KAANAPALI TO KAPALUA

A few miles outside Lahaina, on Maui's exquisite west coast, you approach the Kaanapali-Napili-Kapalua region, one of Hawaii's most desirable vacation areas, blessed with miles of gorgeous beach and stunningly blue skies, with several world-famous championship golf courses thrown in for good measure. The road curves around a series of graceful bays, perhaps the most beautiful of which is Napili Bay, a gorgeous little stretch of sea and sand where not very long ago the breadfruit, papaya, and lichee trees ran helter-skelter to the sea. For us, this area is the end of the rainbow, and we don't mean the one likely to be arching across the sugarcane fields as you approach. The road reaches its end at the magnificent Kapalua Resort, one of Hawaii's most naturally beautiful playgrounds.

DOUBLES FOR $65 TO $90

COCONUT INN, 181 Hui Rd. F, Napili, Maui, HI 96761. Tel. 808/669-5712, or toll free 800/367-8006. Fax 808/669-4485. 40 units. TV TEL

$ Rates (including continental breakfast): Apr–Dec 24, $75 studio for two; $85 one-bedroom apt for two; $95 deluxe one-bedroom apt with loft, for up to four. Dec 25–Mar, $85 studio for two; $95 one-bedroom apt for two; $105 deluxe one-bedroom apt with loft, for up to four. Inquire about their well-priced room/car and honeymoon packages. MC, V. **Parking:** Free.

Not a hotel, not a condo, but a country inn in the European manner is what this place calls itself. Just five minutes away from Kapalua, and sharing the glorious views and scenery of that lush resort, the Coconut Inn overlooks Napili Bay from its hillside retreat. The two-story inn is situated mauka—several blocks up the hill on the mountain side of the road. It's a 10-minute walk or 5-minute drive to the ocean—which gives it more of a country than a beachy feeling. Prices are reasonable for this area.

Units are nicely decorated in the island style, not large, but comfortable enough, and with fully equipped kitchen and bath with both tub and shower. All have twin or king-size beds. The studios can accommodate two people, while the one-bedroom and loft units both fit four. The two buildings are set in a small garden that shelters a pool, a hot tub, and a special "quiet area" surrounding a small pond and brook. You're welcome to cut flowers from the garden to brighten your room, or herbs from the garden to enrich your cooking. And as if all this weren't enough, the continental breakfast includes freshly baked banana bread, bran muffins, island fruit, and brewed Kona coffee (there's a choice of coconut, chocolate, or regular).

HALE KAI, 3691 Lower Honoapiilani Rd., Lahaina, Maui, HI 96761. Tel. 808/669-6333, or toll free 800/446-7307. 40 condo units. TV TEL

$ Rates: From $90 one-bedroom apt for two; from $120 two-bedroom apt for four; $120–$140 three-bedroom apt for six. Third person free; each additional person $8 extra. Minimum stay three nights (two weeks at Christmas). No credit cards. **Parking:** Free.

These graceful apartments look out on flowering gardens, a park, and a good-size pool that fronts on the ocean beach. Each apartment is decorated differently and each has a different view: Some guests come back year after year for the ocean view, others for the quiet parkside units. Rooms on the upper levels have handsome cathedral ceilings. All are furnished nicely with electric kitchens and private lanais.

HALE MAUI APARTMENT HOTEL, 3711 Lower Honoapiilani Rd. (P.O. Box 516), Lahaina, Maui, HI 96767. Tel. 808/669-6312. 12 suites. TV

$ Rates: Apr 15–Dec 15, $60–$85 one-bedroom suite for two. Dec 16–Apr 14, $75–$85 one-bedroom suite for two. Each additional person $8 extra. No credit cards. **Parking:** Free.

Hans and Eva Zimmerman have been in charge at this small hotel right on the ocean for almost 25 years now. The suites, each holding up to five guests, have been newly refurbished, and all have private lanais, radios, and good kitchens. There's a nice barbecue area out back. There's no pool, but steps from the lawn lead right into the water.

HONOKAWAI PALMS, 3666 Lower Honoapiilani Rd., Lahaina, Maui, HI 96761. Tel. 808/667-2712, or toll free 800/669-MAUI. Fax 808/661-5875. 30 apts. TV TEL

$ Rates: $65 one-bedroom ocean-view apt for two (third and fourth person $6 each); $65 two-bedroom garden apt for two (third through sixth person $6 each). Minimum stay four nights; 10% discount on stays of seven or more nights. No credit cards. **Parking:** Free.

This is one of the older apartment complexes in this area, not as luxuriously furnished as some of the newer condos, but good value for the money and just across the road from a small beach park. Apartments are spacious and comfortably furnished. The more desirable one-bedroom apartments have ocean view and lanai. There's a large pool to dunk in, a barbecue area, and ample electric kitchens to make cooking easy. The management is friendly and helpful. Coffee is served mornings at the pool.

Reservations: Write to 72 Wainee St., Suite 213, Lahaina, HI 96761; or call the toll-free number above.

HOYOCHI NIKKO, 3901 Lower Honoapiilani Rd., Lahaina, Maui, HI 96761. Tel. 808/669-8343. 18 condo units. TV

$ Rates: $90 standard one-bedroom apt for two; $100 large one-bedroom apt for two. Each additional person (up to two only) $10 extra. Minimum stay seven days; discounts available in summer. No credit cards. **Parking:** Free.

You get the feeling of gracious retreat here at the "Resort of the Sunbeam," from the Asian architecture of the complex to the spacious oceanfront lawn and garden where you could easily laze away peaceful days. You can walk down the lawn stairs to the ocean and swim and snorkel inside the reef area, or swim in a freshwater pool in the garden. The units range in size from standard to large to "special." All have private lanais with full ocean views, "long boy" twin beds (a few queen-size), cable color TVs, and fully equipped kitchens with washer-dryers. There's a grill for barbecues, and sometimes mai-tai parties are held out in the garden. Despite the Japanese name, most of the guests here are North American, and many of them return each year.

THE KAHILI, 5500 Honoapiilani Rd., Lahaina, Maui, HI 96761. Tel. 808/669-5635, or toll free 800/786-7867 or 800/SUNSETS. Fax 808/669-2561. 30 condo units. TV

$ Rates: Apr–Dec 20, $79 studio for two; $110 one-bedroom/two-bath apt for up to four. Dec 21–Mar, $99 studio for two; $130 one-bedroom/two-bath apt for up to four. Children under 18 stay free with parents using existing beds. Rollaway bed $16 extra; crib, $5. AE, MC, V. **Parking:** Free.

Kapalua is one of Hawaii's poshest resort areas, but at its gateway, adjacent to the world-famous Kapalua Bay Golf Course, is this moderately priced complex. Guest rooms, attractively furnished in tropical prints, all have complete kitchens and in-room washer-dryers. Napili Bay and Kapalua Bay, with their excellent swimming beaches, are just a short walk away, making this one cozy for serious swimmers and snorkelers as well as golfers. It's just across the road from the ocean, heading up towards the mountains. On the premises are a pool, Jacuzzi, and barbecue, and there are 10 tennis courts nearby.

KALEIALOHA, 3785 Lower Honoapiilani Rd., Lahaina, Maui, HI 96761. Tel. 808/669-8197, or toll free 800/222-8688. Fax 808/669-2502. 67 apts. TV TEL

$ Rates: $75 studio for two; $85–$95 one-bedroom ocean-view apt for two. Each additional person (over age 2) $7.50 extra. MC, V. **Parking:** Free.

This lovely condo resort offers large, pleasantly furnished studios and one-bedroom apartments. The studios have two *punees* (couches), and one-bedrooms have a queen-size bed and a double sofa bed in the living room that opens up to sleep two more. The well-equipped kitchens boast dishwashers and washer-dryers. The cheaper rooms have a mountain view, while the more expensive rooms face the ocean. Phones are available at $1 a day. As for swimming, you can relax around a pool sheltered from the parking area out front by an interior courtyard, or try the ocean out back; swimming isn't bad within the protective outer reef.

MAHINA SURF, 4057 Lower Honoapiilani Rd., Lahaina, Maui, HI 96761. Tel. 808/669-6068, or toll free 800/367-6086. 56 units. TV TEL

$ Rates: Apr 15–Dec 14, $85 one-bedroom apt; $100–$105 two-bedroom apt. Each additional person (including children) $8 extra. Minimum stay three nights. Discounts on weekly and monthly rates. Inquire about excellent deals on car rentals. MC, V. **Parking:** Free.

This a fine place to settle in for real at-home living. The units are not only charming and attractively furnished, but well priced for the area. Sizes of the apartments vary, but all are little "homes"; the cutest are those two-bedroom apartments with a loft area upstairs that serves as a second bedroom—these are big enough to sleep six. The one-bedroom apartment can accommodate up to four people. Mahina Surf is situated on a rocky strip of oceanfront, and snorkeling is fine, but there is no sandy beach. There is, however, a big pool as compensation.

MAUIAN HOTEL, 5441 Honoapiilani Rd., Lahaina, Maui, HI 96761. Tel. 808/669-6205, or toll free 800/367-5034. Fax 808/669-0109. 44 apts.

$ Rates: Apr 15–Dec 14, $66–$100 studio apt for two. Dec 15–Apr 14, $104–$124 studio apt for two. Rates flexible based on occupancy (call for details). Third person $9 extra; fourth person, $6. MC, V. **Parking:** Free.

The swimming here at Napili Bay, from a gentle, reef-protected beach, is among the best in the islands. These attractive studio apartments are big enough for four, each with private lanai, electric kitchen (including microwave oven), one queen-size and one trundle bed (that opens into two), and all the conveniences of home. For those capable of tearing themselves away from the idyllic beach, there's shuffleboard, a TV room, and a freshwater swimming pool. Facilities include a big laundry and ironing area. There's a weekly Aloha Party.

MAUI PARK, 3626 Lower Honoapiilani Rd., Lahaina, Maui, HI 96761. Tel. 808/669-6622, or toll free 800/922-7866 on the U.S. mainland, 800/445-6633 in Canada, 800/342-1551 inter-island. Fax 808/922-8785. 228 units. A/C TV TEL

$ Rates: Apr–Dec 21, $87 studio for two; $109 one-bedroom apt for four; $153 two-bedroom apt for six. Dec 22–Mar, $98 studio for two; $118 one-bedroom apt for four; $164 two-bedroom apt for six. AE, CB, DC, JCB, MC, V. **Parking:** Free.

This economy hotel, just across the road from Honokawai Beach Park, is proving very popular. The Maui Park, under the management of Aston Hotels & Resorts, consists of six separate buildings surrounding a nearly Olympic-size swimming pool and sunning area. It features apartment-size studios and larger units attractively furnished, with full kitchens, cable TVs, clock radios, large closets, and daily cleaning service. The three-story buildings do not have elevators, but three rooms are accessible to the disabled. There's 24-hour service at the desk, and a grocery and sundry store right at hand, which makes cooking at home very easy.

MAUI SANDS, 3600 Honoapiilani Rd. (c/o Maui Resort Management, Suite H-2) Lahaina, Maui, HI 96761. Tel. 808/669-9110, or toll free 800/367-5037 on the U.S. mainland and Canada. Fax 808/669-8790. 76 condo apts. A/C TV TEL

$ **Rates:** $80 standard one-bedroom apartment for up to three, $105 garden, $135 oceanfront; $100 standard two-bedroom apt for up to five, $130 garden, $160 oceanfront. Each additional person $9 extra. Minimum stay varies from 2 to 10 nights (at Christmas). Ask about weekly rates and discounts on long stays and special "Off-Season" rates. MC, V. **Parking:** Free.

These apartments are ideal for families with lots of kids or for two couples traveling together. Imagine an enormous living room (about the size of two average hotel rooms put together), beautifully decorated, with two small but comfortable bedrooms, twin beds in one, a queen-size in the other; a full electric kitchen; tropical ceiling fans; a view of gardens or ocean from your private lanai; and enough space for six people to stretch out. You can get it all here at this attractive spot just past the Kaanapali gold coast area for about half the price of the luxury resorts. The apartments close to the road are for heavy sleepers.

Since the Maui Sands was built when it was feasible to buy large lots of land, there is plenty of it to spare; the grounds are abloom with lovely trees and plants. Facilities include a big laundry, a comfortable swimming pool and sunning area, and a narrow sliver of beach (it's been washed away by storms but, hopefully, will return). At sunset, it's pure enchantment as you watch the sun sink right between the islands of Molokai and Lanai off in the distance. The condo complex is completely refurbished, including new furniture. Managers Kay and Adel Kunisawa are cordial hosts. Readers continue to praise this one. In fact, one of our readers, the Rev. Bob Waliszewski, wrote us about Maui Sands: "I called Maui Sands on their toll-free number because their rates were among the best in the Kaanapali area. And I thought I'd ask them if they had a discount rate for clergy. As it turned out, they gave me a 20% discount. Other clergy would, I'm sure, be glad to know this."

The same Maui Resort Management is in charge at some of the select units at Papakea, right next door, and these little homes are even more luxurious. Creature comforts include two pools, two Swedish saunas, two tennis courts, shuffleboard, barbecues, putting green, and picnic areas. Of course, it's all on the beach. Studio rooms for two start at $134. Discounts available on weekly stays. Call the same toll-free number—800/367-5037—any time between 8am and 5pm to make reservations.

NAPILI SUNSET, 46 Hui Dr., Lahaina, Maui, HI 96761. Tel. 808/669-8083, or toll free 800/447-9229 in the U.S., 800/223-4611 in Canada. Fax 808/669-2730. 25 condo units. TV TEL

$ **Rates:** $85 garden-view studio for two; $159 beachfront one-bedroom apt for two; $249 two-bedroom beachfront apt for four. Each additional person $12 extra. MC, V. **Parking:** Free.

Here's a homey setting on a beautiful sandy beach where the swimming is super. All the one- and two-bedroom apartments are beachfront in two low-rise buildings; the less-expensive studios are in a building about 100 yards away. The units are of good size, attractively furnished, with fully equipped kitchens including microwaves, and ceiling fans—and local calls are free on your own phone. There's a swimming pool, a laundry room, and a grocery and general store next door, so it's easy to pick up food and then bring it back to the on-the-beach barbecues to fix dinner. The resort excitement of Kapalua—with its golf course, tennis courts, shops, and restaurants—is just a short walk away.

NOELANI, 4095 Lower Honoapiilani Rd., Lahaina, Maui, HI 96761. Tel. 808/669-8374, or toll free 800/367-6030 in the U.S. and Canada. Fax 808/669-7904. 40 condo apts. TV TEL

$ Rates: $77 studio; $97 one-bedroom apt; $130 two-bedroom apt; $155 three-bedroom apt. Each additional person $7.50 extra. Minimum stay three days. Weekly and monthly rates available, as well as car/condo packages. AE, MC, V. **Parking:** Free.

Located in the Kahana area, these oceanfront condominiums are beautifully furnished, and the view from your oceanfront lanai—of Molokai and Lanai, blue seas, and tropical gardens—is even more beautiful. There are two freshwater swimming pools at seaside (heated for evening swimming), good snorkeling is right in front, and a wide sandy beach is adjacent to the property. Managers John and Donna Lorenz host mai-tai parties in an oceanfront cabaña several times a month so that guests can get to know one another. And there's a concierge service, with orientation continental breakfasts at poolside. Readers have praised the warm, homey atmosphere here. Rooms are furnished in tropical decor, and have microwave ovens and in-room videos. Studios have dressing room, bath, and kitchen. One-, two-, and three-bedroom units have their own washer-dryer and dishwasher. There is also a launderette for those staying in one of the studios.

POHAILANI MAUI, 4435 Lower Honoapiilani Rd., Lahaina, Maui, HI 96761. Tel. 808/669-6994. Fax 808/669-4046. 114 condo apts.

$ Rates: $65 studio with ocean view or two-bedroom apt with garden view. Each additional person $5 extra. Minimum stay three nights. MC, V. **Parking:** Free.

This complex offers some of the most reasonable rates in West Maui. There are 29 units at water's edge, plus another 85 two-bedroom duplex apartments on the mountainside. Two tennis courts, two pools, and other facilities are spread out over eight acres—not to mention a stretch of sandy beach, perfect for gentle ocean swimming. Each of the seaside units is spacious, attractively furnished in studio style (with such touches as big, old-fashioned ceiling fans), and boasts a large kitchenette plus a lanai that's perfectly enormous. TVs can be rented.

DOUBLES FOR $95 TO $119

HONOKEANA COVE RESORT CONDOMINIUMS, 5255 Lower Honoapiilani Rd., Lahaina, Maui, HI 96761. Tel. 808/669-6441, or toll free 800/237-4948 (call collect from Canada). 38 condo units. TV TEL

$ Rates: $95–$105 one-bedroom apt for two; $135 two-bedroom apt for four; $155 three-bedroom apt for six; $150 two-bedroom town house for four. Each additional person $10–$15 extra. No credit cards. **Parking:** Free.

If snorkeling is your passion, you're going to be very happy at this lovely resort condominium directly on a private, rocky cove where the snorkeling is tops. Swimmers need walk only about five minutes to a gentle sandy beach. Each apartment is close to the water and the pool oceanside; the grounds are also ideal for whale-spotting. We were told that a whale once gave birth at the entrance to the cove! When you're not busy watching whales, snorkeling, or admiring the grounds with its beautiful trees—we spotted a 160-year-old kamani nut (or false almond) tree—you can be enjoying the view from your lanai and the comforts of your apartment, each individually owned and decorated. All have fully equipped kitchens with dishwashers. Outdoor barbecues are provided. The management is cordial, arranging a pupu party every Friday to bring the guests together.

NAPILI SURF BEACH RESORT, 50 Napili Place, Lahaina, Maui, HI 96761. Tel. 808/669-8002, or toll free 800/541-0638 on the U.S. mainland and Canada. TV TEL

$ **Rates:** $99–$110 studio for two; $150 one-bedroom apt for two. Each additional person $15 extra. No credit cards. **Parking:** Free.

This complex, with its soundproof luxury units perched on the tip of Napili Bay, on a particularly lovely curve of beach, is one of the nicest places to stay in the area. Each of the units is well equipped for easy housekeeping, handsomely furnished, and with private lanais that overlook the garden or ocean. Even the lowest-priced accommodations, in the Puamala building, are cozy and small, but superneat and functionally designed, with full kitchens, dishwashers, radios with digital clocks, the works. There may be discounts on these units in the summer months. Every Friday evening guests get together out on the lawn for an aloha party, when there may be special entertainment, or just some friends and guests who like to sit around with a guitar and sing the old songs. In such a gracious setting, the coconut palms swaying in the evening wind and the sea lapping gently at your feet, it's hard to remember what you were planning to worry about.

PAKI MAUI, 3615 Lower Honoapiilani Hwy., Lahaina, Maui, HI 96761. Tel. 808/669-8325, or toll free 800/535-0085 on the U.S. mainland and Canada. Fax 808/669-7987. 19 units. TV TEL

$ **Rates** (including continental breakfast): $119–$139 studio for two; $119–$159 one-bedroom for up to four; $149–$219 two-bedroom for up to six. Each additional person $15 extra. AE, MC, V. **Parking:** Free.

This lovely condominium suite resort is right on the oceanfront. The grounds are lush, with a waterfall, a swimming pool, and a pond with koi fish in the center of the property. Rooms are individually furnished with a great deal of charm, and all boast fully equipped kitchens and private lanais with splendid views of Molokai and Lanai out there across the waters. Free continental breakfasts, and a sunset manager's cocktail reception every day.

Reservations: Write Hawaii Condofree Resorts, 2155 Kalakaua Ave., Suite 706, Honolulu, HI 96815; or call the toll-free number above.

POLYNESIAN SHORES, 3975 Lower Honoapiilani Rd., Lahaina, Maui, HI 96761. Tel. 808/669-6065, or toll free 800/433-6284 on the U.S. mainland, 800/488-2179 in Canada. Fax 808/669-0909. 52 apts. TV TEL

$ **Rates:** $105 one-bedroom apt for two; $125 two-bedroom/two-bath loft apt for two, $145 for four; $155 three-bedroom/three-bath apt for four. Minimum stay three nights. MC, V. **Parking:** Free.

It's ocean all the way at this one, the kind of small, relaxed place where everybody feels right at home—so much so that many of the same people come back year after year. Every apartment has an ocean view from its own private lanai, there's a deck on the oceanfront with barbecue facilities, and it's a great place to watch for whales. Snorkeling is good right out front; swimming is better at a nearby sandy beach, about a five-minute walk away. The grounds are so lush that guests can pick bananas right off the trees. Once a week there's a pupu party on the Tiki Deck. Apartments are nicely furnished, with separate living rooms and private baths with tub and shower.

READERS RECOMMEND

Napili Bay, *33 Hui Dr., Lahaina, Maui, HI 96761 (tel. 808/669-6044). "We highly recommend the Napili Bay, close to Kaanapali Beach and Lahaina. These are studio apartments with one queen-size bed and two singles and kitchen; they are reasonably priced.*

We had clean, fresh linens each day, including beach towels; the rooms are not air-conditioned, but have adjustable shutters so you can feel the incredibly refreshing trade winds and hear the ocean at night. It cost us $50 for groceries for two people for a week, and we ate well. Efficiencies are great! The owners were like grandparents to us, extremely friendly and accommodating."—Francine Schept, White Plains, N.Y.

WORTH THE EXTRA BUCKS

KAANAPALI BEACH HOTEL, 2525 Kaanapali Hwy., Lahaina, Maui, HI 96761-1987. Tel. 808/661-0011, or toll free 800/657-7700. Fax 808/667-5616. Telex 405184. 430 rms. A/C TV TEL

$ Rates: $135 single or double standard, $175 superior. Each additional person $20 extra. AE, MC, V. **Parking:** Free.

The luxury resorts of Kaanapali are well beyond our budget, but just in case you're wondering which of the hotels has the lowest prices, it's this one. Even standard rooms here are large and well decorated, and have refrigerators and private lanais facing into a garden. The Kaanapali Beach Hotel has a spacious, open feeling with its huge garden, a whale of a swimming pool (yes, it's in the shape of a whale), a beautiful ocean beach right next to the rock formation (which makes it good for snorkeling) on which the neighboring Sheraton Maui sits, and all the comforts of the luxury life. It's easy to save money dining here, since the coffee shop serves three low-priced buffet meals a day. Certainly worth a splurge—if your pocketbook is up to it. The Kaanapali Beach aims to be "the most Hawaiian of the hotels," and its gracious staff and unusually sensitive management live up to that ideal. All the Hawaiian activities here—from learning Hawaiian games to *real* hula lessons—reflect the beliefs of the old Hawaiians and the responsibility to live in harmony with one's surroundings. The hotel's Hawaiian education program for its employees is widely admired in Hawaii's hotel industry.

READERS RECOMMEND

Kahana Village, *4531 Honoapiilani Rd., Lahaina, Maui, HI 96761 (tel. toll free 800/824-3065). "We have stayed at Kahana Village five times. The units are very spacious and well appointed. When two couples share a two-bedroom unit, or if three couples share a three-bedroom unit, the rate is quite reasonable in today's world. Kahana Village also attracts families and, unless you are terribly fond of children, should be avoided during school holiday periods."*—Bob Harrison and Hal Goodstein, Provincetown, Mass. [*Authors' Note:* Kahana Village is a beautiful oceanfront resort located on a sandy beach. Off-season rates for two-bedroom apartments are $140 ocean-view, $170 oceanfront; three-bedroom apartments are $185 ocean-view, $210 oceanfront.]

Papakea Beach Resort, *Kaanapali Beach, Lahaina, Maui, HI 96761 (tel. toll free 800/367-5637). "We had a one-bedroom unit with a huge sleeping loft (really a two-bedroom). Papakea is a vision of loveliness everywhere you look. The grounds are meticulously tended and filled with beautiful plantings. Other bonuses were two putting greens, two pools, two Jacuzzis, 'swimmercize' classes each morning, tennis clinics, and a rum-punch party by the pool with entertainment on Friday. This is a quiet, family-oriented resort, yet very close to the abundant restaurants, supermarkets, and shops of Kaanapali."*—Frances S. Kielt, West Hartford, Conn. [*Author's Note:* Current rates would be about $134 for a studio room in summer.]

MOUNTAINSIDE BED & BREAKFASTS

If you like mountains better than beach, charming private homes better than impersonal hotels or condos, and refreshingly old-fashioned prices best of all, we've got some good news for you. We've discovered 14 delightful "up-country" guest-houses and vacation rentals—six in Kula, two in Makawao on the slopes of Haleakala volcano (ideal locations if you want to drive to the summit to catch the sunrise), and six off the Hana road, in the tiny town of Haiku. You can't go wrong at any of these, although each has a slightly different style and personality.

IN KULA

AHINAHINA FARM BED AND BREAKFAST, 210 Ahinahina Place, Kula, Maui, HI 96790. Tel. 808/878-6096, or toll free 800/241-MAUI. 1 studio, 1 cottage. TV

$ **Rates** (including breakfast): $75 studio for two with a three-night minimum ($85 for one or two nights), $10 for each additional person; $90 cottage for two with a three-night minimum ($110 for one or two nights), $15 for each additional person. No children under 12. No credit cards. **Parking:** Free.

Here's a chance to stay on a working upcountry citrus farm, at a 2,150-foot elevation in the wind-shadow of Mount Haleakala—a location that means sunny days, cool nights, and upcountry peace and quiet. Mike Endres grows Bearrs Seedless lime commercially; his wife, Annette, tends an orchid greenhouse and kitchen garden: Both are warm-hearted people who delight in sharing their lovely home and cottage with guests. They provide special assistance and information for hikers and walkers; honeymooners are given special attention and amenities. A cozy studio apartment attached to their home, but with its own private entrance and parking, has an efficiency kitchen, a queen-size bed with thick comforters, color TV, and a spacious covered deck. It's best suited for two, but a child or extra guest might sleep on a futon. A free-standing two-bedroom cottage, with its own private drive and parking, is also a delight, also beautifully decorated with a living room, dining area, a queen-size bed in one bedroom, twin beds in the other, and a fully equipped kitchen with dishwasher and washer-dryer. From its large covered deck you have a view of ducks marching about in a neighbor's pond—she is the only licensed breeder of endangered duck species on Maui. Smoking is not allowed. Breakfast includes fresh fruit, home-baked muffins and breads (like Annette's mango bread), cereals, and coffee and tea. Guests are also welcome to pick from the pineapples, bananas, and grapefruits growing on the grounds. Views abound: sunset over Maalea Bay, sunrise and moonrise over the mountains. From both Ahinahina Farm and its next-door neighbor, Elaine's Upcountry Guest Rooms, you're a 20- to 40-minute drive to good swimming beaches.

BLOOM COTTAGE, 229 Kula Hwy. (R.R.2, Box 229), Kula, Maui, HI 96790. Tel. 808/878-1425. 1 cottage. TV TEL

$ **Rates** (including breakfast): Aug–Sept and Apr–May, $95 per night. Oct–Mar and June–July, $105. Minimum stay two nights. Each additional person $10 extra. No credit cards. **Parking:** Free.

Wonderfully private and romantic, with sweeping views of pasturelands going down to the sea, Bloom Cottage stands by itself behind a pretty house owned by Lynne and Herb Horner, a busy young couple who work for the *Maui News* and the Maui Oil Company, respectively. The charming 700-square-foot cottage is tastefully decorated in English country style, and has a four-poster queen-size bed in the sleeping area plus a single bed in the second bedroom, plus a double foldout futon, which would be so nice by the living room fireplace (yes, they have them up here in the mountains). The fully equipped kitchen includes a microwave oven, and Lynne and Herb stock the refrigerator with coffees, teas, yogurt, fruit juices, and muffins. Guests can pick a wide variety of culinary herbs that grow in the garden. No smoking in the cottage; no pets; not suitable for small children.

ELAINE'S UPCOUNTRY GUEST ROOMS, 2112 Naalae Rd., Kula, Maui, HI 96790. Tel. 808/878-6623. 3 rms, 1 cottage.

$ **Rates** (including breakfast): $50 double (third person $7.50), two-night minimum stay; $85 cottage for four (fifth and sixth adults $10 each, $7 for each child), three-night minimum stay. No credit cards. **Parking:** Free.

We'd call Elaine and Murray Gildersleeve's splendid home in Kula probably the best value for the money. The Gildersleeves are a retired couple from Alaska: Murray devotes a lot of attention to his pineapple farm right on the premises and Elaine looks after the guests. Their Hawaiian pole house is designer-elegant, with three guest bedrooms on the ground floor sharing their own kitchen and living room. Guests are welcome to use the refrigerator and to cook breakfast or whatever meals they like—a rare privilege in a guesthouse. The three bedrooms are beautifully furnished, and have private baths and either two twin beds or a king- or queen-size bed (third person sleeps on a futon). Rooms have a splendid view of the West Maui mountains and Haleakala.

Next to the main house is a delightful cottage made to order for a family. With a queen-size bed in the bedroom, twin beds in the loft, and two window seats in the living room that can also be used as extra beds—six people can sleep comfortably. There's a complete kitchen, windows on three sides, bougainvillea growing outside, and a charming decor within. The Gildersleeves ask that guests do not smoke or drink.

HALEMANU, 221 Kawehi Place, Kula, Maui, HI 96720. Tel. 808/878-2729. 1 rm.

$ Rates (including breakfast): $70 single or double. Minimum stay two nights. No credit cards. **Parking:** Free.

Halemanu ("House of the Birds") is a spectacular country home filled with fine arts and artifacts 2,500 feet up on the slopes of Haleakala, seemingly light-years away from the rest of civilization. Maui-raised owner Carol Austin, who delights in sharing her home, her intimate knowledge of the area, and often her time with visitors, provides a charming guest room with a queen-size bed and private bath, entered from a large deck with a nonpareil 180° view of the countryside below. Staying with Carol is like staying with a friend and becoming part of the family, although guests have as much privacy as they wish. They have the use of the entire house, including the kitchen and the loft area with its TV, VCR, movie collection, typewriter, and fax. Carol, now a columnist for the *Maui News,* is a former caterer and gourmet cook, so there's no telling what she may be inspired to serve for breakfast. Since she's single, she often takes people snorkeling or hiking, or sometimes asks them to join her for a pasta dinner.

KULA VIEW BED & BREAKFAST, 140 Holopuni Rd. (P.O. Box 322), Kula, Maui, HI 96790. Tel. 808/878-6736. 1 suite. TV TEL

$ Rates (including breakfast): $75 single or double. No credit cards. **Parking:** Free.

Susan Kauai, who comes from an old-time kamaaina family and knows Maui better than most people, is in charge here. Her luxuriously furnished suite is located on the upper level of her home with a private entrance and its own deck. There's a queen-size bed, a reading area, a wicker breakfast nook, a mini-refrigerator, and a private shower. Telephone and television are available on request. Susan is a gracious host who helps guests plan their holidays, fills their room with fresh flowers from her garden, and serves breakfasts in the room—Kona coffee or tea, lush island fruits, and home-baked breads and muffins. She has blankets and warm clothing on hand for those sunrise trips to Haleakala, whose summit is not far away.

RUSTY AND FRANK KUNZ, 513 Lower Kimo Dr., Kula, Maui, HI 96790. Tel. 808/878-2137. 1 apt, 1 house. TV

$ Rates (including breakfast): $65 two-bedroom apt; $100 owner's home for up to four people. Each additional person $10 extra. No credit cards. **Parking:** $1 per night.

This lovely modern home is at an elevation of 3,000 feet, set on eight acres of lawns and pastures, 20 miles from the summit of Haleakala Crater. The views are of the

West Maui mountains, a carnation farm, and Kihei beach way below in the distance. Rusty and Frank Kunz divide their time between this home and one on Oahu. On Maui, they always have a two-bedroom vacation apartment available for rental—it's an excellent bargain and has its own private entrance, a deck (perfect for sunset watching), a fireplace, a kitchenette (refrigerator, toaster-oven, two-burner hotplate, sink), and a private bath. Children are welcome.

From November to June, when they're not on Maui, the Kunzes will, on occasion, rent their own quarters, a handsome home with a large fireplace that goes through from the living room to the master bedroom, full kitchen, and private bath. It's big enough for either one or two couples. Inquire also about their reasonable vacation rentals in Lanikai on the island of Oahu, a block from the beach.

Reservations: Contact Rusty and Frank Kunz, 1332 Mokolea Dr., Kailua, HI 91734; or phone the number above on Maui, or 808/263-4546 on Oahu.

OFF HANA ROAD

BAMBOO MOUNTAIN SANCTUARY, 911 Kapakalua Rd., Haiku, Maui, HI 96708. Tel. 808/572-5106. 5 rms (3 with bath).

$ **Rates** (including breakfast): $55 single; $75 double; seventh day free. No credit cards.

Once it was the old Maui Zendo, a Japanese monastery. Now this mountainside plantation house is a bed-and-breakfast establishment, but it still has an air of retreat about it. It's on the same grounds as Akahai Farm, one of the islands' primary New Age retreat and conference centers. If you're attending a workshop at Akahai Farms, you may want to stay here for a few days before or after. Or just come to the place itself, enjoy the peace and quiet, the wonderful grounds, with hiking trails, a natural swimming hole in the gulch, waterfalls, a hot tub. Built over 50 years ago, with huge octagonal windows that overlook the ocean, the house has five bedrooms, each with a queen-size or double futon on a frame, Japanese artwork on the walls. Some have private baths; all share the shower. There's a very large communal area and a deck where breakfast—including papayas from their own trees and bananas from their own banana plantation—is served. Hosts Rick and Lauren Smith make everyone feel like part of the family.

HAIKULEANA, 69 Haiku Rd., Haiku, Maui, HI 96708-8974. Tel. 808/575-2890. 3 rms.

$ **Rates** (including breakfast): $65 single; $80 double. No credit cards. **Parking:** Free.

This charming old house is set amid 1½ acres of garden with fruit trees and flowers. It was built around 1850 for a doctor from Scotland, but has been refurbished and tastefully decorated in country style with some antiques, tropical period pieces, and comforters on the beds. The house still has its original, 12-foot, open-beam ceilings. Owner Dr. Frederick Fox, Jr., has three nicely decorated guest rooms, two with queen-size beds, one with twin beds, each with its own private bath. Television is available. A full breakfast is served, with Hawaiian seasonal fruits and freshly baked breads. Not suitable for children under 6 or for pets; smoking is not allowed indoors. Haikuleana is 15 minutes from the airport and shopping centers, centrally located en route to Hana and Haleakala, and just two miles from Hookipa Beach, famous for windsurfing as well as close to secluded coves for snorkeling and scuba diving.

HALFWAY TO HANA HOUSE, 100 Waipio Rd. (P.O. Box 675), Haiku, Maui, HI 96708. Tel. 808/572-1176. 1 studio.

$ **Rates** (including breakfast): $55 single; $65 double. Minimum stay two nights. No credit cards. **Parking:** Free.

A 20-minute drive from Paia town on the Hana road, Gail Pickholz's cozy private studio has a spectacular location with a 180° wraparound ocean view. The studio has a double bed, a mini-kitchen and bath, and a breakfast patio that looks through a green valley to the ocean with bamboo groves, a citrus orchard, tropical flowers, and vegetable and herb gardens. Freshwater pools and waterfalls are half a mile away. Gail, who has lived on Maui for 24 years, delights in graceful touches like chocolate-covered macadamia nuts on the pillow and dazzling arrangements of tropical fruit at breakfast. She's helpful with restaurant and adventure tips, and may even invite you to go snorkeling with her on a Sunday morning.

HUELO POINT FLOWER FARM B&B, P.O. Box 1195, Paia, Maui, HI 96779. Tel. 808/572-1850. 1 cottage.

$ Rates: $75 single; $85 double. No credit cards. **Parking:** Free.

This is surely one of the most spectacular—and romantic—B&Bs in Hawaii, a great favorite with honeymoon couples. The glass-walled gazebo sits atop a 300-foot cliff overlooking Waipio Bay: From the patio where you have breakfast, you can often watch whales and dolphins at play. Closeby are waterfalls and natural pools for swimming, and right on the property is a dramatic natural swimming pool with a waterfall, plus an oceanfront hot tub. The gazebo has a queen-size mattress, two wicker chairs, a dining table and chairs, a CD player with stereo, and a private half-bath with a sheltered outside shower; cooking facilities are limited to a hotplate, small refrigerator, microwave, toaster oven, and basic dishes. Guy and Doug, the hosts, live in a spectacular executive house on the property (also available for rental by the week at $1,850) and grow tropical flowers and organic fruits and vegetables on their two-acre retreat; guests are welcome to pick whatever they like. Although this is an isolated, jungle valley, you can drive to restaurants and shops in Paia or Makawao in 20 minutes, to the airport in 35.

PILIALOHA, 205 Kaupakalua Rd., Haiku, Maui, HI 96798. Tel. 808/572-1440. Fax 808/572-4612. 1 cottage. TV TEL

$ Rates (including breakfast): $75 for two. Each additional person $10 extra. Seventh day free on weekly stay. No credit cards. **Parking:** Free.

A dollhouse of a bed-and-breakfast cottage sits in these cool upcountry lands, next door to the home of Bill and Machiko Heyde, a young couple who aim to treat their guests as friends (*pilialoha* means "friendship" in Hawaiian). Lovingly decorated, and with a little garden out front, it's a cozy retreat, ideal for two, but able to sleep up to six, what with its queen-size bed in the bedroom, a twin bed in an adjoining room, a queen-size sofa bed in the living room, and futons in the closet. There's a full kitchen in which to cook your own meals, and Machiko puts out teas and coffees, fresh tropical fruits, and home-baked pastries, breads, and muffins every morning. The cable TV has its own VCR. There's a washer-dryer, ironing board and iron, plus beach chairs, mats, snorkeling equipment to borrow—everything you need for easy vacation living.

TEA HOUSE COTTAGE BED AND BREAKFAST, P.O. Box 335, Haiku, Maui, HI 86708. Tel. 808/572-5610. 1 rm (without bath).

$ Rates (including breakfast): $55 single; $65 double. No credit cards. **Parking:** Free.

You park your car and follow a tree-lined path to the front door. The cottage sits in the midst of a tropical jungle filled with flowering plants, bananas, and palm trees. The picturesque screened lanai leads to a charming living room and bedroom filled with antiques and Oriental rugs. No electrical poles mar the landscape; an alternative-energy system provides utilities and phone. You swim in natural pools half a mile away, stroll along moonlit paths, listen to the sound of the surf pounding the cliffs. Does this sound like the ultimate retreat from civilization? It is, and it's located in Haiku, a mile off the Hana Highway (18 miles east of Kahului), going toward the ocean. Ann DeWeese, an artist whose studio is on the premises, is the proprietor and she makes the cottage available to guests who can appreciate the simple life. She provides fresh fruits, home-baked breads, and very good coffee and teas for breakfast. Sorry, there's no indoor bath; it's outside and requires a flashlight to get to at night. Other than that, this could be heaven. Smoking is permitted outdoors only.

MAKAWAO & OLINDA

Makawao is Maui's own little cowboy town, fast turning into a mecca for city dwellers in search of the rural life. Beyond it, Olinda is even more peaceful, a true end-of-the-road retreat.

HALEAKALA BED & BREAKFAST, 41 Manienie Rd., Makawao, Maui, HI 96758. Tel. 808/572-7988. 4 rms (2 with bath). TV TEL

$ Rates (including breakfast): $50 cedar cottage; $65 queen room; $75 master bedroom; $85-family-size room. No credit cards. **Parking:** Free.

This huge, beautiful home is on two acres, on the slopes of Haleakala in the Makawao area. Owner Mara Marin, a local environmental activist, calls her place a "hometel," since guests have use of the entire house and like it so much they often extend their stays. Guests have their own living room with a TV and a deck from which to watch the magnificent Maui sunsets and sip wine under the stars. Full kitchen and dining room privileges are available. The queen room is petite and cozy; the master bedroom comes complete with king-size bed, a huge walk-in closet, and lovely views of the mountain. The family-size room is 400 square feet, light and airy, with its own entrance. The octagonal cedar cottage is a cozy charmer, totally private—but guests must use the bathroom indoors. Breakfast includes juice, coffee, and giant muffins, or sometimes a treat like Mara's homemade haupia (Hawaiian coconut pudding). The front door looks up directly to the 10,000-foot summit of Mount Haleakala.

MCKAY COUNTRY COTTAGE, 536 Olinda Rd., Makawao, Maui, HI 96768. Tel. 808/572-1453. 1 cottage. TV TEL

$ Rates (including breakfast): $95 cottage for two. Each additional person $15 extra. Minimum stay two days. No credit cards. **Parking:** Free.

Five miles up the hill from Makawao, on a country road that winds through a forest of 150-foot-tall blue-gum eucalyptus trees, lies the village of Olinda; and it's here, at the top of Olinda Road, at a 4,000-foot elevation, that lucky travelers will find one of the nicest cottages and B&Bs on Maui. McKay Country Cottage sits amid a 12-acre protea farm with its own driveway, a short distance from the home of Shaun and Stewart McKay. Shaun, a member of the noted Baldwin family, among Maui's missionary founders, and Stewart, a painter and decorator from Scotland, are very special hosts, indeed; their warmth and graciousness are evident everywhere on the property. They've furnished the cottage handsomely with original art by Maui artists, protea from their garden, lace curtains, a king-size bed in the bedroom, a queen-size pullout sofa in the living room (it sleeps four adults, and futons are available for the kids), a full kitchen, and a working fireplace with enough wood for cool mountain nights. What fun to sit on the cushioned window seats, or out on the deck, and gaze at central Maui and famed Hookipa windsurfing beach far below! First-day breakfast supplies are left in the refrigerator for you.

READERS RECOMMEND

Poli Poli Springs State Park. *"Your readers may be interested in hearing about the cabin at Poli Poli Springs State Park, on the slopes of Haleakala at 6,472 feet. The cabin is in a heavily wooded camping area—there are even redwoods—and the view, of central and western Maui, as well as Molokai and Lanai, is outstanding. The park is crisscrossed with miles of hiking trails, some of which lead to Haleakala Crater. The cabin has three bedrooms and will sleep up to 10. There is some furniture, a wood heating stove, a gas cooking range, complete* *cooking utensils, and bedding. There is no electricity. For information and reservations, write or call the State Department of Land and Natural Resources, Division of State Parks, 54 S. High St., Wailuku, Maui, HI 96793 (tel. 808/243-5354)."*—Roberta Rosen, Long Beach, Calif. [*Authors' Note:* Charges are $14 for two people for the entire cabin. A campground for tent camping is also available, free of charge; reservations are required.]

HANA

Since Hana is one of the more remote, untouched areas on all Maui (in all Hawaii, in fact), you might well want to spend a few days here just relaxing far away from civilization. Happily, the number of reasonably priced accommodations is growing.

RENTAL AGENCIES

Manager Stan Collins of **Hana Bay Vacation Rentals,** P.O. Box 318, Hana, Maui, HI 96713 (tel. 808/248-7727, or toll free 800/657-7970), rents a dozen properties scattered throughout the Hana area, with a wide variety of locations, including on the beach, in and out of town, plus some in very secluded and private places. They offer apartments, cabins, and homes, with either one, two, or three bedrooms, with ocean and mountain views. All are fully equipped with the essentials for comfortable vacation living. They can accommodate as few as 1, as many as 15 in a group, at prices ranging from $65 to $200 per night for two people, plus $10–$25 for each additional person. Each cabin and home is private, and all have full kitchens, telephones, and cable TVs. A half-million-dollar home sleeps six, at rates of $200 per night, three-day minimum. Stan can also arrange car rentals in Hana if you decide to fly direct; he will have you picked up at the airport.

Sina Fournier is the rental agent for **Hana Kai Holidays,** P.O. Box 536, Hana, Maui, HI 96713 (tel. 808/248-7742, or toll free 800/548-0478), and she has a number of options for Hana vacationers, starting at just $45 a night for a studio with private bath and ocean view, to oceanfront and other cottages ranging in price from $60 a night, all the way up to $225 for a large house with swimming pool and spa. Accommodations also include condominium apartments at the Hana Kai–Maui Resort (see below), which begin at $110 per night. Contact Sina Fournier or her son, Duke Walls, and they will try to find the right setup for you. Many accommodations are within walking distance of the beach: Some of the houses are directly on Hana Bay.

READERS RECOMMEND

Kaia Ranch & Co., *Ulaino Rd. (P.O. Box 404), Hana, Maui, HI 96713 (tel. 808/248-7725). "Kaia Ranch was a delightful 'real old Hana' experience—very clean and well kept."*—Mark Bendich, Washington, D.C. [*Authors' Note:* Kaia Ranch is a 27-acre tropical flower farm with one guest cottage in a picnic pavilion, nicely furnished with a queen-size bed, kitchen, and private bath, which rents for $50 a night single or double, with a two-night minimum stay ($75 on a one-night stay). Hosts are John and JoLoyce Kaiai, a friendly couple. No electricity, just old-fashioned kerosene lamps, plenty of dogs, cats, and horses on the property. Hosts do not smoke or drink. Adults only. A big breakfast is served every morning. The hosts can arrange a scenic helicopter tour that will drop you right at the ranch.]

DOUBLES FOR $20

WAIANAPANAPA STATE PARK. 12 cabins.

$ Rates: $10 per person in a two-room cabin; tent camping free. Maximum stay in cabins five nights. No credit cards. **Parking:** Free.

Ⓢ The most inexpensive accommodations in Hana are available courtesy of the Division of State Parks. These are the housekeeping cabins in this state park, a few trails away from a black sand beach. Local families like to come here to escape from civilization. The attractive bungalows are snuggled among the pandanus trees, some overlooking the ocean, and are supplied with bedding, towels, cooking utensils, dishes, electricity, and plenty of hot water. The only drawback may be mosquitoes; a reader who spent a hot August week here advised taking insect spray and repellent. Each two-room cabin has its own lanai and accommodates six people. Tent campers can use the campground free of charge, but reservations are required.

Reservations: Contact the Department of Land and Natural Resources, Division of State Parks, 54 S. High St., Wailuku, Maui, HI 96793 (tel. 808/243-5354), six months to a year in advance as this idyllic spot continues to grow in popularity.

DOUBLES FOR $55

ALOHA COTTAGES, 73 Keawa Place (P.O. Box 205), Hana, Maui, HI 96713. Tel. 808/248-8420. 5 cottages.

$ Rates: $55–$85 cottage for two. Each additional person $10–$20 extra. No credit cards. **Parking:** Free.

Located conveniently close to Hana Bay and the stores are these pleasant redwood cottages managed by Mrs. F. Nakamura. Each cottage has either two or three bedrooms (queen-size or twin beds), a living room, complete kitchen, and one or two bathrooms. And each has a view of Hana Bay or Kukui Head. These older, plain cottages are clean, well ventilated, and comfortably furnished. All necessities are provided, including daily cleaning service. Three cottages have TVs.

DOUBLES FOR $80 TO $110

HANA KAI–MAUI RESORT CONDOMINIUMS, 1533 Uakea Rd. (P.O. Box 38), Hana, Maui, HI 96713. Tel. 808/248-8426, or toll free 800/346-2772. Fax 808/248-7482. 11 apts.

$ Rates: $110 studio for two (third person $10); $125 one-bedroom apt for two (third to fifth persons $10 each). Children under 11 stay free with their parents. AE, MC, V. **Parking:** Free.

For deluxe studio and one-bedroom apartments where you can prepare your own meals (almost a necessity in Hana, where there are very few eating places), this resort is a fine choice. The condo units are located by the ocean on lush, tropical grounds. Studios include a bath with tub/shower combination, dressing vanity, well-equipped kitchen, and private lanai—a spacious open room where you can enjoy the ocean just a few feet away. Pluses include a large patio area a few steps away from the ocean, with gas barbecues, Ping-Pong, shuffleboard, horseshoes, and snorkeling equipment. The beach is better for surfers than for swimmers, but good swimming beaches are within an easy drive.

HANA PLANTATION HOUSES, P.O. Box 489, Hana, Maui, HI 96713. Tel. 808/248-7248, or toll free 800/657-7723. Fax 808/248-8240. 6 studios and houses.

$ Rates: From $80 for a tiny studio for one or two to $195 for a five-bedroom/three bath beach house. CB, DC, MC, V. **Parking:** Free.

Blair Shurtleff and Tom Nunn aim to provide their guests with "a vacation that will leave you feeling rejuvenated and thoroughly relaxed." We're sure they succeed, for just contemplating the lovely custom homes they've created for visitors is relaxing in itself. The main compound, on five superbly landscaped acres abloom with ginger, helicona, banana, and papaya (which guests are welcome to pick), includes a plantation-style home that accommodates up to four guests at $140, a Japanese-style studio for two at $80, and a Japanese/Balinese-style two-bedroom cottage for four at $110.

A few miles away, near Hana Bay and picturesque beaches, is a two-story plantation house with two accommodations (upstairs, for four people, $140; downstairs, for two people, $100), and a superb solar-powered beach house for four, for $160 (with annex for two, $195). Amenities are plentiful. There are Jacuzzis indoors and out. Each house has its own kitchen and even its own coffee grinder, with Hana Plantation House's own labeled coffee beans. Hosts Blair and Tom are always on hand to advise guests on activities and to help them meet the people of Hana. A three-minute walk from the main compound is a secluded, natural spring- and ocean-fed pool, surrounded by lush, tropical plants. The ocean is a few steps away, and beautiful Hamoa Beach is less than a mile away. Waterfalls and jungle trails abound.

3. WHERE TO EAT

KAHULUI

In and around the big shopping centers across the way from the hotels—the Kahului Shopping Center, the Maui Mall, and the Kaahumanu Shopping Center—are several places that are fine for a modest meal.

MAUI MALL

Meals for Less Than $10

SIR WILFRED'S ESPRESSO CAFFE, Maui Mall, 355 Kamehameha Ave. Tel. 877-3711.

Cuisine: GOURMET DELI/VEGETARIAN.

$ **Prices:** Main courses $2.95–$6.95. AE, DC, MC, V.

Open: Mon–Thurs 9am–6pm, Fri 9am–9pm, Sat 9am–5:30pm, Sun 11am–5pm.

The front area of Sir Wilfred's Coffee, Tea, Tobacco is the Espresso Caffè, which serves breakfasts and light lunches, soups, home-baked croissants, and fine wines by the glass at good prices. Decorated with island woods and featuring paintings by local artists, it's a very attractive and inviting spot. Prices are low, and the quality of the food, atmosphere, and service is high. Try their breakfast special of "fluffy eggs" (which manage to be just that, with no fats or oils being used), served on a whole-wheat croissant. The talented chef also makes a flavorful pesto pasta salad, Wailea pea salad (peas, celery, nuts, bacon, and sour cream), and unusual Boboli pizza. Cappuccino flavors include chocolate, coconut, almond, mint, and orange. Look for their pastry and coffee bar at the Cannery in Lahaina.

SIZZLER STEAK, SEAFOOD, SALAD RESTAURANT, Maui Mall, 355 Kamehameha Ave. Tel. 871-1120.

Cuisine: AMERICAN. **Reservations:** Not accepted.

$ **Prices:** Soup/salad/fruit bar $8; main courses $6–$17. AE, MC, V.

Open: Sun–Thurs 6am–10pm, Fri–Sat 6am–midnight.

When you've seen one Sizzler, you've seen them all. And as far as we're concerned, the more there are in the islands, the better. This one is a beauty, with handsome decor and a large area for lanai dining. The menu has as much seafood and salad as it has steak, so take your choice. On Maui, seafood is an especially good choice; where else can one get the fresh catch of the day—mahi, ahi, swordfish, ulua—for $6–$6.60? Add the soup, salad, fresh fruit, pastas and tostada bar for $3.50 more ($4 at dinner) and you've got quite a meal. Lunches run from a fish sandwich at $4 to a steak lunch at $5.40. There are special menus for seniors and children, and great steaks for $8–$8.70, for sirloin. Cocktails are available. The weekend Breakfast Bar at $8 is another great value.

KAAHUMANU SHOPPING CENTER

Here's a tip for lovers of sushi. Visit the bento (take-out) section at **Shirokiya's,** the Japanese department store at Kaahumanu Mall, order an assortment of sushi for about $4.50–$6.75 and have yourself a picnic. The food is scrumptious (other Japanese dishes are also available), and the price is about half of what it would cost to have sushi in a restaurant.

Meals for Less Than $12

KOHO GRILL AND BAR, at Kaahumanu Shopping Center. Tel. 877-5588.

Cuisine: AMERICAN. **Reservations:** Not required.

$ **Prices:** Appetizers $3.25–$5.75; main courses $8.65–$12.95. MC, V.

Open: Sat–Thurs 8am–10pm, Fri 8am–11pm.

This one's a big local favorite, especially at lunch and before and after the movies. We like it anytime: It's attractively decorated in island style, with paintings by local artists on the walls, the menu is varied, the service excellent, the atmosphere friendly, and the prices certainly right. Burgers are great at lunchtime, and so are the sandwiches, the plate lunches ($4.95–$5.65), and such international offerings as quiche, fajitas, tacos, and a blackened lemon chicken. Dinner offers pastas, stir-fries, more Cajun dishes, and steak and seafood offerings on the order of char-broiled fresh island catch of the day, pescado Veracruz, or top sirloin. Most main courses are served with salad or soup and a side dish. Come before 11am and treat yourself to one of their terrific omelets. Happy hour, 3 to 6pm, is very popular, and so is the Sports Bar with its large-screen TV.

The newer Koho's, at the Napili Shopping Center in Napili, is also proving to be a crowd pleaser; same menu, and casual and upbeat atmosphere.

MAUI BEACH HOTEL. Tel. 877-0051.

Cuisine: ASIAN BUFFET. **Reservations:** Not required.

$ **Prices:** Buffet lunch, $11 (including tax and tip) for all you can eat. AE, DC, MC, V.

Open: Lunch only, daily 11am–2pm.

If you like buffet meals as much as we do, then you should know about the Rainbow buffet lunch served in the pretty main dining room and pool terrace. Locals like it because it includes many Asian dishes not usually seen on buffet meals: We ourselves are partial to the tsukemono (pickled-vegetable salad) and kamaboku (fish cakes). Also there for the taking—and still more taking—are those delicious Kula onions, Maui potato chips, lots of greens, rice, hot breads, three hot main courses daily (fish, chicken, and a beef item, plus a noodle dish), soup, and cakes baked daily by the hotel's own bakery shop.

MING YUEN, 162 Alamaha St. Tel. 871-7787.

Cuisine: CHINESE. **Reservations:** Recommended.

$ **Prices:** Appetizers $3.75–$5.95; main courses $5.95–$8.50. MC, V.

Open: Lunch Mon–Sat 11:30am–5pm; dinner daily 5–9pm.

Attractive, moderately priced Chinese restaurants are hard to find on Maui, so praise be for Ming Yuen in the Kahului Light Industrial Park, off Hi. 380. The food here just gets better all the time, and the service, by many longtime employees, provides a "family feeling." The specials here are authentic Cantonese and the spicier Szechuan cuisine. We always like to start off with crispy wonton and Chinese spring rolls, $3.75 and $3.95. The menu offers a very wide choice—Mongolian beef, lemon chicken, moo shu pork (a personal favorite), and scallops with black-bean sauce. If you prefer something spicier, choose the hot Szechuan eggplant, one of their excellent vegetarian dishes. The desserts here are a little different; we like the Mandarin or chocolate mousse. Should you happen to be on Maui during Chinese New Year in February, don't miss their 10-course banquet, complete with firecrackers. Fabulous! Even if it's not New Year's, all you need is a party of eight people and you can enjoy a splendid banquet anytime, starting at about $13 a person.

SPECIALTY DINING

Lunch/Brunch

CLASS ACT, Maui Community College, 310 Kaahumanu Ave. Tel. 242-1210.

Cuisine: AMERICAN. **Reservations:** Recommended.

$ **Prices:** Five-course lunch $8. No credit cards.

Open: Lunch only, Wed and Fri 11am–12:30pm. **Closed:** Mid-May to mid-Sept.

The benefits of higher education can definitely be enjoyed at Class Act. Students in the college's food-service program get a chance to practice their skills; you get a chance to have a five-course gourmet meal for a mere $8. What a deal! The decor is pleasant enough, with new furniture and drapes, and the food can be excellent. For appetizers, you might be served fried scallops with spicy tartar sauce, or calamari sauté; then there's soup or salad and a choice of two selections, one of which is termed "traditional" and the other "nutritious"—low-fat, low-cholesterol, and all those good things. Sample dishes include broiled butterfly lamb, Cajun Cornish game hen, mahimahi with shoyu sesame butter. Then comes dessert and beverage. Yes, there's a catch. Lunch is the only meal served. On Wednesday, half of the students cook and the other half serve; on Friday, they switch. High marks for this one!

Maui Community College also serves a cafeteria lunch from 11am to 12:30pm Monday through Thursday; plate lunch, including soup, is $4; salad and sandwich bar, 30¢ per ounce.

MAUI BAGEL, 201 Dairy Rd. Tel. 871-4825.

Cuisine: BAGELS/DELI/SANDWICHES.

$ **Prices:** Bagels and sandwiches $1–$5. No credit cards.

Open: Mon–Sat 6:30am–5:30pm.

Maui Bagel is an idea whose time has come. It's the only bagel bakery on Maui (there aren't so many bagel bakeries elsewhere in the islands, come to think of it), and it's been doing a thriving business ever since it opened five years ago. Since Maui Bagel is near the airport and on your route to Hana or Haleakala, it's a good first—or last—stop on the island, as well as a good spot to get a picnic lunch for your sightseeing trips. It's a cute little place, with blue-and-white café curtains and a warm, friendly atmosphere.

In addition to seven varieties of bagels, warm from the oven, as well as delicious French, rye, and wheat bread baked daily, and challah on Friday, they also have yummy bakery items (brownies, macaroons, streudel, etc.), plus very good deli selections. So lunch might include a curried chicken salad or lox and bagel, as well as vegetarian items like pesto garlic calzone, focaccia, black-bean enchilada, or a tofu sub. There's an excellent selection of salads, meats, and cheese by the pound. Call ahead for take-out.

WAILUKU

If you'd like to sample "local" food, there's no better place than Wailuku, which is a bit off the tourist track (it's the commercial and professional center of the island and the seat of Maui County). Prices are geared for the locals, which means that they're refreshingly low.

If you're in the mood for local color—and flavor—visit **Takamiya Market** on

North Market Street. This old-time grocery store has a huge selection of prepared foods to go, like sushi or smoked salmon belly or mahi tempura or whatever, all at small prices. Our local spies tell us they are "outrageous." While you're there, throw in a piece or two of their equally outrageous "lemon booze cake" or "pistachio booze cake" for very good measure.

MEALS FOR LESS THAN $12

CHUMS, 1900 Main St. Tel. 244-1000.

Cuisine: LOCAL. **Reservations:** Not accepted.

$ Prices: Main courses $4.50–$7.25. MC, V.

Open: Breakfast Mon–Sat 6:30–11am, Sun 7–11am; lunch/dinner Mon–Sat 11am–10:30pm, Sun 11am–10pm.

Local-style food served in hearty portions at old-fashioned prices, and in gracious surroundings—that's the combination that made Chums a favorite right from the start. The pretty dining room has koa-wood booths, many plants, and old, classic posters on the walls—great place for "chums" to hang out. And the food is delicious, from the homemade oxtail soup with grated ginger, two scoops of rice and Chinese parsley, practically a meal in itself ($5.75); to the burgers and sandwiches ($4.50–$5.50); to the island-style plate meals—mahimahi, hamburger steak, roast pork and the like—all served with vegetables and macaroni salad plus a choice of rice or potatoes, for $4.95–$6.95. Breakfast favorites include more island favorites, like fried rice with an egg or Loco Moco—that's a hamburger patty, an egg, rice, and gravy, at $3.25.

MAUI BOY RESTAURANT, 2102 Vineyard St. Tel. 244-7243.

Cuisine: LOCAL. **Reservations:** Not required.

$ Prices: Main courses $5.25–$7.25. MC, V.

Open: Breakfast daily 7–11am; lunch/dinner daily 11am–9pm.

Ramshackle outside, but coffeehouse cute inside, Maui Boy is a find. At lunchtime it's mobbed with local professionals and with county office workers. Breakfast is popular too, and filling: three-egg omelets ($3.50–$5.25) come with a choice of rice or hash browns, plus two dollar-size hotcakes. And we love their French toast, made from Portuguese sweet bread with strawberry or blueberry filling, $3.50. A savvy local friend considers Maui Boy to have the best teriyaki on Maui; we tried their teri ono special at a recent lunch, and were not disappointed: a generous serving of fish, potatoes, and macaroni salad, all for $6.95, and delicious. Plate lunches—including roast beef, chicken katsu, teri chicken, Korean shortribs, and mahimahi—all come with rice or whipped potatoes, vegetables *and* potato macaroni salad, guaranteeing your carbohydrate fix for the day.

SAENG'S THAI CUISINE, 2119 Vineyard St. Tel. 244-1568.

Cuisine: THAI. **Reservations:** Not required.

$ Prices: Appetizers $4.95–$7.25; main courses $5.50–$9.95. MC, V.

Open: Lunch Mon–Sat 11am–2:30pm; dinner daily 5–9:30pm.

Another very popular local spot, this is a gardenlike restaurant (one row of tables looks like a gazebo), with tiled floors and lush greenery. Hawaii provides aromatic herbs throughout the year, just as Thailand does, and these are used to advantage in the cooking here. Specialties of the house include kai yang (grilled Cornish hen, marinated with lemongrass and kaffir lime leaves), shrimp asparagus, and cashew-nut chicken delight, each $7.25. Vegetarians are well taken care of, with a choice of 16 dishes, including a fairly mild garlic mixed vegetables and a sweet-basil tofu which, if you choose, can be very hot. A typical Thai tapioca pudding as well as an untypical coffee or macadamia-nut mud pie tops off a refreshing meal.

SAM SATO'S, 318 N. Market St. Tel. 244-7124.

Cuisine: LOCAL. **Reservations:** Not accepted.

$ Prices: Plate lunches $3.90–$5. No credit cards.

Open: Mon–Wed and Fri–Sat 8am–2pm.

This is your totally local, down-home Wailuku restaurant. It has a big lunchroom and no decor to speak of, but it's always filled with local families and office workers happily gobbling up chow fun, wonton soup, plate lunches, or sandwiches. Try their wonton special—it's hearty, delicious, and a complete meal at $3.55. This is the place where you should sample those filled pastries called manju, as Sam Sato's is reputed to have the best on Maui.

SIAM THAI, 123 N. Market St. Tel. 244-3817.

Cuisine: THAI. **Reservations:** Not required.

$ Prices: Appetizers $4.25–$7.25; main courses $5.95–$12.95. AE, CB, DC, MC, V.

Open: Lunch Mon–Fri 11am–2:30pm; dinner daily 5–9:30pm.

A big favorite among the residents of East Maui, this restaurant serves inexpensive, delicious Thai food. It's a pretty place too, typically Asian in decor, with travel posters, plants, a reclining Buddha near a small aquarium. You won't go wrong with the Evil Prince dishes (take your choice of beef, chicken, pork, or vegetables); the meat is sautéed in hot spices with fresh sweet basil and served on a bed of chopped cabbage. Even those who hate eggplant are converted by the eggplant tofu dish; it's sautéed with fresh basil and hot sauce, and available either hot, medium, or mild. Then there's Tofu Delight, tofu and other vegetables sautéed in a special sauce and served over steamed bean sprouts. Thai ginger shrimp sautéed with string beans and ginger, served on cabbage, is another winner.

TOKYO TEI, 1063 E. Lower Main St. Tel. 242-9630.

Cuisine: JAPANESE. **Reservations:** Recommended.

$ Prices: Appetizers $2.75; main courses $5–$11.75. MC, V.

Open: Lunch Mon–Sat 11am–1:30pm; dinner Mon–Sat 5–8:30pm, Sun 5–8pm.

A local favorite: The atmosphere is simple and pleasant, the quality of the food high, and the prices easy to take. Lunch and dinner include rice, miso soup, and pickled vegetables along with such main courses as teriyaki pork, beef sukiyaki, and sashimi. You'll know why the restaurant is famous for its tempura dishes once you bite into the shrimp tempura—four large, flavorful shrimp, served with rice and soup, along with the traditional Japanese accompaniments. And their teishoko combination plates, $8–$9, are very popular. This is a nice place for families, as children are treated graciously here.

IN & AROUND PAIA

Paia is one of our favorite little towns—full of seekers from everywhere who've found the natural lifestyle they were looking for in these Hawaiian uplands. Since the area is only a 15-minute drive from Kahului, at the beginning of the road to Hana and just past the cutoff to Hi. 37 (the Haleakala Highway), a visit to the restaurants here can be worked into almost any itinerary.

MEALS FOR LESS THAN $20

THE WUNDERBAR, 89 Hana Hwy. Tel. 579-8808.

Cuisine: GERMAN/SWISS/EUROPEAN/AMERICAN. **Reservations:** Recommended.

$ Prices: Appetizers $5.50–$9; main courses $12–$16. MC, V.

Open: Breakfast daily 7:30–11:30am; lunch daily 11:30am–2pm; pupus and salads daily 2:30–6pm; dinner daily 6–10pm (bar open till 1am).

There's a warm, *gemütlich* feeling about the new Wunderbar Restaurant and Bar.

The place is attractive, with a handsome, huge wooden bar, tables made of monkeypod woods, a little garden patio out back. The chef, who has cooked in seven different European countries, brings traditional style plus an island flair to such dishes as wienerschnitzel, beef Stroganoff, Hungarian goulash, and schweinebraten, the house special: a roast loin of pork with old-fashioned German-style braised red cabbage and parsley potatoes. The house pasta special is something a little different: seafood stewed in plum tomatoes, with garlic, white wine, and fresh dill. Start your meal with half an order of that, perhaps, or with one of the regular soups or appetizers, like the potato-leek soup or the calamari rings with aioli, or a Greek salad. Fresh fish and seafood are prepared in a variety of styles. By all means, plan your meal with dessert in mind—it would be a shame to miss the likes of homemade Black Forest cherry cake, the ice-cream soufflé Grand Marnier or the apfelkuechle, baked apple slices in cinnamon sugar, topped with vanilla sauce or ice cream.

WORTH THE EXTRA BUCKS

HALIIMAILE GENERAL STORE, 900 Haliimaile Rd., Haliimaile. Tel. 572-2666.

Cuisine: AMERICAN. **Reservations:** Recommended for dinner.
$ Prices: Appetizers $4–$11; main courses $12–$24. MC, V.
Open: Lunch Tues–Sat 11am–3pm; dinner Tues–Sun 6–9:30pm; brunch Sun 10am–3pm.

Folks who live in East Maui and are accustomed to driving long distances for a gourmet meal can't believe their luck, now that this place is firmly established right in their area, in the midst of 1,000 acres of pineapple fields. Owners Beverly and Joe Gannon (Bev also runs a highly successful catering business called Fresh Approach) have created a charming place with super-high ceilings, walls covered with shelves of lovely pottery and china, and chairs painted a sparkly blue green. It's bright and busy, with the feeling of a sophisticated San Francisco restaurant.

The best time to check out the gourmet touch is at lunch (the restaurant is not far from the roads to either Haleakala or Hana, so it can fit into one of our excursions), when you can get imaginative sandwiches like fresh grilled ahi on an onion roll with homemade tartar sauce for $9, or the smoked-turkey sandwich with cranberry mayonnaise on black bread for $7. There are daily specials, such as turkey melt and corn tortilla enchiladas.

Dinner is a bit pricier, but values are still good, and the food is extraordinary. Our favorite appetizers include the fresh ahi sashimi with Cajun spices and the Brie-and-grape quesadilla, served hot with a surprising sweet pea guacamole. Main courses are equally imaginative: soused shrimp and scallops, flamed with cognac, a lemon-rosemary fettuccine, Louisiana Créole and rack of lamb Hunan style, among a long list; all main courses are served with fresh vegetables, starch, and delicious sourdough bread. The pastry chef here is a master, so be sure to save room for dessert.

SPECIALTY DINING

Picnic Fare

PIC-NICS, Baldwin Ave. Tel. 579-8021.

Cuisine: SANDWICHES/BOX LUNCHES. **Reservations:** Not accepted.
$ Prices: Sandwiches $4.15–$4.95; box lunches $7.95–$15.95. No credit cards.
Open: Daily 7:30am–7pm.

If you need a picnic lunch for your trip to Haleakala or Hana, this is the place to stock up in Paia (you'll recognize it by a bright orange-and-yellow awning). Pic-nics, a cheerful, clean Formica-tables-and-benches place, is known all over the area for its sandwiches: especially the spinach-nut burgers, served on whole-wheat sesame buns, and piled high with lettuce, tomato, sprouts, and dressing; they're $4.35

and terrific. They also serve a filet of mahimahi for just $4.95. Everything is delicious, since they use, as much as possible, freshly grown local produce and organically raised island beef. The very popular excursion lunches include sandwiches, Maui potato chips, salads, seasonal fruits, beverages, great muffins, and homemade cookies and desserts, plus many other basket stuffers, and begin at $7.95. No need to call ahead—your order will be prepared quickly. Pic-nics also features cappuccino, freshly baked breakfast pastries, scrambled eggs, and muffins for breakfast while you're waiting for your order.

Vegetarian

THE VEGAN RESTAURANT, 115 Baldwin Ave. Tel. 579-9144.

Cuisine: GOURMET VEGETARIAN. **Reservations:** Not accepted.

$ **Prices:** Main courses $4.95–$7.95. No credit cards.

Open: Dinner only, Tues–Sun 4:30–8:30pm.

A "vegan," according to the people here, is "one who abstains from supporting businesses or consuming products derived from the abuse of animals in any form." If this coincides with your own beliefs, by all means, stop in at this casual little place which is very popular with locals. It is run by Gentle World, a nonprofit educational center dedicated to pure vegetarian nutrition. Not only does it offer very good food, but it also publishes and sells books on the order of *The Cookbook for People Who Love Animals,* and *Pregnancy, Children, and the Vegan Diet.* The staff, all volunteers, turn out some delicious dishes, like vegan burgers, bean-burrito sandwiches, curried vegetables with basmati rice, and delicious smoothies like the Banini—a banana/tahini combination. We like their desserts too, especially the vanilla cake with cashew frosting and fruit topping and the strawberry shortcake.

KULA & MAKAWAO

Since there is no food to be had in Haleakala National Park, you might want to eat on your way to or from the crater. We've often found that being at the 10,000-foot altitude of Haleakala can build up quite an appetite.

MEALS FOR LESS THAN $15

CASANOVA ITALIAN RESTAURANT AND DELI, 1188 Makawao Ave., Makawao. Tel. 572-0220.

Cuisine: ITALIAN. **Reservations:** Recommended at dinner.

$ **Prices:** Restaurant, appetizers $3.50–$8.50; main courses $6.95–$20; pizzas under $10. Deli, most dishes around $5. MC, V.

Open: Deli, daily 8:30am–7:30pm. Restaurant, lunch daily 11am–2am; dinner daily 5–9pm.

An enjoyable place to eat is in nearby Makawao, a few miles off your route to Haleakala, but worth making a little detour for; turn right at Pukalani. Casanova looks as if it belongs more in Rome or Milan, Bologna or Naples, than it does in cowboy-town Makawao. These cities are, in fact, the homes of the four young partners, all professionals in other fields, whose restaurant has created quite a stir: People come from all over Maui for their fresh pastas and divine pastries; Casanova supplies them to some of the best hotels and restaurants on the island. There are two parts to the operation. One is the original deli, which serves breakfast, lunch, snacks, and classic Italian dishes in the $5 range. They have sandwiches with an international flair, such as Paris (Brie with artichoke hearts) and Parma (prosciutto and tomatoes), plus sensational pastries in the $2–$3 range: lemon-brandy cheesecake and chocolate cheesecake are worthy of bravos, and people drive miles for their tiramisu.

KULA LODGE, Hi. 377, Kula. Tel. 878-2517.

Cuisine: AMERICAN. **Reservations:** Recommended at dinner.

$ **Prices:** Appetizers \$3.50–\$7; main courses \$8–\$18.95. MC, V.
Open: Breakfast daily 6:30–11:30am; lunch daily 11:30am–5pm; dinner daily 5:30–9:30pm (Early Bird dinner 5:30–6:30pm).

The most scenic spot for a meal in this area is on the slopes of Haleakala in the delightful mountain town of Kula. This charming country inn has a real fireplace and a nonpareil view. Go ahead, feast at breakfast on their eggs Benedict, served with cottage fries and a rich hollandaise; it's \$7.25 and delicious. Lunch offers sandwiches and burgers, soups, salads, and such main courses as teriyaki chicken, sautéed mahimahi, and shrimp curry for \$5.25–\$6.95. Prices escalate for gourmet dinners, which feature Caesar salad, escargots, and dishes like pepper steak Madagascar, fresh fish of the day, sesame chicken, and shrimp scampi.

The front part of the main restaurant, done in Hawaiian woods and with works by local artists on the walls, is divided into a café and bar on one side and a huge dance floor and stage area on the other; the fine-dining area is in back. Our personal favorite is the café area, Jl Caffè dominated by a huge, wood-fired pizza oven from Italy, from which emerge delicious crispy-crusted pizzas with a decidedly imaginative flair, like the Genova (pesto sauce, prawns, and fresh tomato) or the Romana (goat cheese, roasted peppers, thyme, and garlic). They're all delicious, and so are the antipasti, and an incredible salad of chicory with Gorgonzola cheese, walnuts, and fresh pears, at \$5.50. The wine list is moderately priced. There's live jazz on Tuesday night. On Wednesday and Thursday nights there's disco and dancing, and live entertainment on weekends, featuring some of Hawaii's major performers, and an occasional jazz great from the mainland, too. The \$5 cover is waived for diners.

POLLI'S CANTINA, 1202 Makawao Ave., at the corner of Olinda Rd., Makawao. Tel. 572-7808.
Cuisine: MEXICAN. **Reservations:** Not accepted.
$ **Prices:** Appetizers \$3–\$6.50; main courses \$6.50–\$15. AE, DC, MC, V.
Open: Daily 11:30am–midnight; brunch Sun 10:30am–2pm.

This old standby is a cute little place that specializes in "cold beer and hot food." The decor is Mexican, the clientele is local, the music is lively, and the food is very tasty. Taco salad is \$6; cheese enchiladas, \$7.50 for two; a bowl of chili, \$4.50. Many vegetarian dishes are available too. We love their desserts, especially the buñuelos: Mexican pastries topped with vanilla ice cream, drizzled hot pure maple syrup, and cinnamon, \$3.50. *Muy bueno!* Polli's has live entertainment Thursday through Saturday evenings. Happy hour is from 2:30 to 5pm.

READERS RECOMMEND

Kitada's, *in Makawao (tel. 572-7241). "Makawao has our all-time-great cheap eats. At Kitada's, a place where the locals eat, you can get a clean, simple booth, a friendly proprietor, and really good Japanese-style food such as a \$3 steak teriyaki lunch plate, including rice and a cucumberlike salad. Sandwiches are around \$2. Two of us ate well one lunchtime for a total of \$6."*—Loisellin Datta, Bethesda, Md.

SPECIALTY DINING

Breakfast/Lunch

BULLOCK'S OF HAWAII, 3494 Haleakala Hwy., Pukalani. Tel. 572-7220.
Cuisine: AMERICAN.
$ **Prices:** Breakfast \$2.75–\$6.75; burgers \$2.75–\$3.95. (Prices subject to change.)
Open: Daily 7:30am–3pm.

At Bullock's, about halfway between Kahului and the park entrance, you can get an inexpensive snack, delicious hamburgers, cheeseburgers, and "moonburgers" (a meal in themselves). Try the shakes, a combination of nectars, juices, and ice cream; we loved the guava, but they also have pineapple, mocha, and coffee, each $2.95. Breakfasts include hash browns, toast, rice, and upcountry jumbo eggs delivered fresh daily. Steak and eggs is also offered.

GRANDMA'S COFFEE HOUSE, Hi. 37, Keokea. Tel. 878-2140.

Cuisine: AMERICAN. **Reservations:** Not accepted.

$ **Prices:** Main dishes $1.50–$5.65. No credit cards.

Open: Mon–Sat 7am–5pm.

This makes a nice stop if you're driving to Tedeschi Vineyards after you come down from the volcano (see Chapter 15). It's a green building right next to the gas station in the tiny town of Keokea. Alfred Franco, a young man whose family has been growing and roasting coffee on Maui since 1918 (you can buy a pound to take home), opened this little mom-and-pop café about five years ago. It's always busy, filled with neighborhood people who come for his wife's freshly baked breads, coffee cakes, cinnamon rolls, and such. Sit down, have a sandwich, a bowl of chili or saimin, a salad or a bread pudding or a pineapple coconut square, and some fragrant coffee—perhaps cappuccino or café au lait. Photos on the wall, café curtains, and antique bottles make for a cozy scene.

KIHEI

This area has a number of good eating spots for budget-watchers, most in shopping centers or malls.

KAI NANI VILLAGE

Meals for Less Than $20

THE GREEK BISTRO, in Kai Nani Village, 2511 S. Kihei Rd. Tel. 879-9330.

Cuisine: GREEK. **Reservations:** Not accepted.

$ **Prices:** Appetizers $2.25–$5.95; main courses $9.95–$14.95. AE, MC, V.

Open: Lunch daily 11am–5pm; dinner daily 5–9:30pm.

In the rear courtyard of Kai Nani Village, this cute little place has about 18 tables, some of them outside (the bar is inside), so it's fun to sit under the blue-and-white striped umbrellas, listen to the Greek music, sip some wine, and pretend you're near the Mediterranean. Dinner offers "homemade Greek food" on the order of moussaka, lamb shish kebab, spakopita, and pastitsio (Greek lasagne); it also offers such "bistro specialties" as a chicken-and-mushroom pasta, Mediterranean chicken, and the house specialty, fresh fish Greek style. Everything is very nicely done. The lunch menu is similar, but smaller. A lamb gyro sandwich (spiced roast of lamb) served in pita bread makes a tasty dish at either meal for $5.95 small, $7.95 large. For dessert, go with the homemade baklava, $2.95. Lots of readers' letters praise this one.

KIHEI PRIME RIB HOUSE, in Kai Nani Village, 2511 S. Kihei Rd. Tel. 879-1954.

Cuisine: AMERICAN. **Reservations:** Recommended after 6:30pm.

$ **Prices:** Main courses $17.95–$32.95; Early Bird specials $10.95–$12.95. CB, DC, MC, V.

Open: Dinner only, daily 5–10pm.

This has long been an island favorite. It's a bit high for our budget, but arrive early—between 5 and 6pm—and enjoy their Early Bird specials: prime rib dinner, Polynesian chicken, or fresh island fish—ahi is the best—for $10.95–$12.95. Their salad bar, included with all dinners, uses only locally grown fruits and vegetables, and can be enjoyed alone at $10.95. All main courses include salad bar. Ocean-view dining and the work of internationally known artists on the walls add to the warmth and charm.

KEALIA BEACH PLAZA

MARGARITA'S BEACH CANTINA, in Kealia Beach Plaza, 101 N. Kihei Rd. Tel. 879-5275.

Cuisine: MEXICAN. **Reservations:** Not required.

$ Prices: Appetizers $2.50–$7.95; main courses $7.95–$16.95. AE, DC, MC, V.

Open: Daily 11:30am–midnight.

Here's one restaurant that really lives up to its name: It's practically *on* the beach, with a huge dining lanai with umbrellaed tables that jut right out over the water. The inside is pleasant too, with tall, beamed ceilings, wooden tables, straw chairs, tile floors, plants, and piñatas. The lanai is quite a spot for sunset watching, whale watching, people watching, or just sitting in perfect contentment as you sip your margaritas and munch on delicious Mexican food with an island flair. Everything is made from scratch each day. Margarita's Munchies (appetizers) are first-rate, including buffalo wings, south-of-the-border nachos, and sombrero caliente. Combination plates are well priced at $7.95–$10.95, and steak, lobster, fresh fish, and steak specials are featured, at higher prices.

SPECIALTY DINING

Lunch/Brunch/Buffet

THE NEW YORK DELI, in Dolphin Plaza, 2395 S. Kihei Rd. Tel. 879-1115.

Cuisine: DELI.

$ Prices: Sandwiches $4.95–$5.95. No credit cards.

Open: Daily 9am–8pm.

Just across the courtyard from Pizza Fresh (see below) is the New York Deli, which should be a must for any homesick New Yorkers—they even have a picture of former mayor Ed Koch on the wall. The wonderful bagels air-expressed from the homeland, the hot pastrami and corned-beef-on-rye sandwiches ($4.95), the hot and cold heros, and the pasta and potato salads, sold by the pound, will all soothe the pangs of Manhattan separation anxiety. This is a tiny but sparkly place, with brick floors, red-checkered cloths on all of three tables. Have an espresso or cappuccino and a slice of their New York cheesecake, or pick up your lunch and take off for the beach (you won't miss New York a bit).

PIZZA FRESH, in Dolphin Plaza, 2395 S. Kihei Rd. Tel. 879-1525.

Cuisine: PIZZA.

$ Prices: Appetizers $3.95–$4.95; pizzas $6.95–$26.95. No credit cards.

Open: Daily 3–9pm.

Doug and Georgann Malone, the couple who run Pizza Fresh, came to Maui with a reputation to live up to; their pies had been voted "Best Pizza in Dallas." They may also be the best pizza on Maui. Their motto "We make it, you bake it" means that this is something to take back to your condo rather than eat there. We sampled their Garden Lite pizza—a whole-wheat vegetarian special with a variety of veggies, light on the cheeses and with a thin crust—quite delicious. Other possibilities include Hawaiian-style (Canadian bacon, pineapple, mushrooms, etc.) and the traditional pies. On Tuesday all pizzas are half price. Free delivery in the Kihei, Wailea, and Makena areas. Call-in orders for pickup or delivery are appreciated.

There's another Pizza Fresh in Makawao, at 1043 Makawao Ave., and a newer one in Napili.

PERRY'S SMORGY RESTAURANT, in Kukui Mall, across from Kalama Beach Park, 1819 S. Kihei Rd. Tel. 874-7616.

Cuisine: SMORGASBORD. **Reservations:** Not accepted.

$ **Prices:** Breakfast buffet $4.95; lunch buffet $5.95; dinner buffet and Sun brunch $8.95. (Prices subject to change). AE, MC, V.

Open: Breakfast Mon–Sat 7–10:30am; lunch daily 11am–2:30pm; dinner daily 5–9pm; brunch Sun 11am–2:30pm.

Perry's Smorgy has long been one of Honolulu's best budget restaurants; now it's one of Maui's best buys as well. The dining room is large and handsome with windows on two sides and pleasant seating areas. Island specialties—Hawaiian, Chinese, Japanese, and American—are available at lunch and dinner. Help yourself to all you want of hot dishes like mahimahi, beef and vegetable stews, chicken, spaghetti; at dinner the hand-carved round of beef steals the show, along with golden fried shrimp and sliced turkey. There are huge fruit and salad bars at both meals as well. The dessert table offers cakes, pies, puddings, even an ice-cream sundae bar with a choice of toppings. At breakfast, it's scrambled eggs and French toast, pancakes, sausages and carved ham, plus doughnuts and muffins and a fresh fruit bar too, with Hawaiian papaya and pineapple. A perfect family choice.

SAND WITCH, at Sugar Beach, 145 N. Kihei Rd. Tel. 879-3262.

Cuisine: SANDWICHES/SNACKS/SALADS.

$ **Prices:** Appetizers $3.95–$5.95; main courses $2.95–$6.95. AE, MC, V.

Open: Daily 11am–11pm.

In addition to turning out great tropical drinks, this cozy beach bar cooks up a variety of hot dogs, pupus, burritos, burgers, and "Sheer Witchery" sandwiches to go with them. Piled high with meats, cheeses, onions, tomatoes grown on Maui, sprouts, and romaine lettuce, they are a meal in themselves. Eat indoors or proceed directly to the beach.

SUBWAY SALADS AND SANDWICHES, in Kukui Mall, 1819 S. Kihei Rd. Tel. 879-9955.

Cuisine: SUBS.

$ **Prices:** Six-inch subs $2.90–$4.70; foot-long subs $4.20–$6.60. No credit cards.

Open: Daily 9am–late.

If you like to eat sandwiches at any and all hours of the day, you should also know about this branch of the popular Subway chain. At a Subway, you can get hot and cold subs—seafood and crab, roast beef, vegetarian, meatball, steak, and sirloin, to name a few—served on super-fresh breads and rolls; you know they're fresh because you can watch them being baked right up front. Free fixings include cheese, onions, lettuce, tomatoes, pickles, peppers, and olives. A dining room has comfortable seating, but it's most fun to take your subs out to the beach. There are half a dozen other Subways on Maui.

WAILEA

Wailea, just beyond the Kihei area, is Maui's newest resort area and perhaps its most spectacular. The grand hotels here—like the Four Seasons, Stouffer Wailea Beach Resort, Maui Inter-Continental Wailea, and the new Grand Hyatt Wailea—are all top of the line and very pricey; so, too, are their restaurants. But here's a way to get in on the fun for the price of a Sunday brunch.

WORTH THE EXTRA BUCKS

CARELLI'S ON THE BEACH, in the Wailea Oceanfront Hotel, 2890 S. Kihei Rd. Tel. 875-0001.

Cuisine: ITALIAN. **Reservations:** Not accepted.
$ Prices: Appetizers $8–$14; main courses $12–$26. MC, V.
Open: Dinner daily 5:30–10pm; limited late menu daily 10–11:30pm.

Don't be surprised if you find Harry Hamlin or Joni Mitchell or some other such luminary dining at Carelli's—it's the hottest spot in the Kihei-Wailea area. The reasons are not hard to find: a magnificent, on-the-beach location, a sophisticated European ambience, and a superb Italian fine-dining menu. Start with the antipasti—the staff will put together any combination from the seafood bar: The ahi carpaccio, "Italian sashimi" is a favorite. Salads have a sophisticated touch: The Caesar is prepared with Dungeness crab and avocado. Pizza of the day emerges from the Neapolitan wood-burning oven (the day we were there, it was prosciutto with pears and Gorgonzola cheese). Then on to pastas and such house specialties as grilled lamb, cioppino, grilled breast of chicken, and fish of the day, always done with a different and imaginative sauce. Desserts vary daily too, and can be quite special: We like the chocolate–peanut-butter gelato and the banana moon torte. There's a $15 minimum at the tables, so if you just want to eat lightly, be seated at Rocco's Mangia Bar, where there is no minimum. And from here you also have a better view of those wonderful stern portraits of Italian family elders that watch over the entranceway.

RAFFLES, in the Stouffer Wailea Beach Resort, 3550 Wailea Alanui. Tel. 879-4900.

Cuisine: CONTINENTAL. **Reservations:** Required.
$ Prices: Appetizers $5–$12.50; main courses $22–$32; Sun champagne brunch $26 adults, $14 children under 12. AE, DC, DISC, JCB, MC, V.
Open: Dinner daily 6:30–11pm; brunch Sun 9am–2pm.

When we get rich, we're going to have all our meals here. Definitely! Until that happy day, however, it's fun to play rich by having a "Big Splurge" Sunday champagne brunch in this lovely dining room, 10-time winner of the coveted *Travel Holiday* Award. It's considered to be the most elaborate Sunday champagne brunch on Maui, which is perhaps a bit of an understatement. Consider just a few of the delights on the table: omelets made to order; gravlax marinated in dill sauce; lox and bagels; sushi; rack of lamb; prime roast beef; homemade breads and rolls; crab salad in avocado; several pastas; green salads of arugula, radicchio, and spinach; and the world's most incredible pancake dish, pancakes Romanoff—thin pancakes layered with fresh raspberry purée, topped with meringue, with strawberry sauce for ladling! And a staggering dessert table as well. You can come for this feast as early as 9am and stay until 2pm, if you like, or any portion in between. Of course, the glasses of champagne and the cups of steaming coffee are bottomless. You can enjoy the same meal in the Palm Terrace restaurant in a more open setting with a view to the gardens and ocean: The buffet tables are in between the two.

Note: True Sunday brunch devotees might also want to try the splendid offering at the Maui Prince Hotel's Prince Court Restaurant, with a fabulous array of gourmet foods, including 28 different desserts! It's on from 10am to 1pm and costs $24 (not including champagne).

LAHAINA

Lahaina is undoubtedly Maui's most enjoyable dining area. It's got everything, from French country bistros to barbecue houses to glamorous oceanside watering spots—and everywhere, the casual mood reflects its easy, relaxed approach to living.

MEALS FOR LESS THAN $10

SUNRISE CAFE, 693A Front St., at the corner of Market St. Tel. 661-3326.

Cuisine: AMERICAN. **Reservations:** Not accepted.

$ Prices: Sandwiches $3.95; main courses $6.95. No credit cards.
Open: Daily 5:30am–10:30pm.

Home-cooking, low prices and a very casual atmosphere have made this little place, just across the road from the library (and next door to Lappert's), very popular very quickly. Shaped like a half circle, with some tables inside and others out on the busy street, this is a mom-and-daughter operation: Mom Song Cajudoi is the expert chef, and her daughter, Melanie, is the charming waitress. Every day Song prepares some specials, mostly vegetarian, like a lasagne or tofu Caesar salad. If you're not feeling too hungry, you could have just a bowl of homemade soup with French bread for $2.95, or a croissant sandwich for $3.50; or quiches, or some luscious pastries from the Bakery, Lahaina's best. Freshly squeezed carrot juice and healthy drinks like spirulina protein are also available for disciplined souls.

THAI CHEF, in the Lahaina Shopping Center. Tel. 667-2814.
Cuisine: THAI. **Reservations:** Not required.
$ Prices: Appetizers $2.50–$11.95; main courses $5.50–$13.95. AE, DC, MC, V.
Open: Lunch Mon–Fri 11am–2:30pm; dinner daily 5–10pm.

The local people praise this cute little restaurant offering Thai specialties in a pleasant setting, with Thai decorations on the walls, lacy curtains, and white tablecloths under glass. Tell the waiter if you want your food mild, medium, or hot, so he can help you choose from among salads, soups (we like the chicken soup simmered in coconut milk with ginger at $8.50), a variety of curries, noodles, and such specialty dishes as stuffed chicken wings or sautéed seafood with bean sauce. Vegetarians have a complete menu of their own: appetizers, soups, noodles, and main dishes. Prices are reasonable. No liquor is served, so BYOB.

READERS RECOMMEND

Denny's, *in Lahaina Square (tel. 667-7898). "The overall price increase was more obvious on Maui than elsewhere, but we found the Denny's in Lahaina Square to be a treat. The decor is like no other Denny's seen by us across the country: lovely fans in motion, live plants on each table and in the rest room, along with attractive, framed prints and a decorated, vaulted ceiling. And I found a delicious pineapple boat served with a choice of bread or crackers. What an unexpected treat."*—Elizabeth Greer, El Cerrito, Calif. [*Authors' Note:* Denny's is open 24 hours daily. There's another excellent Denny's in Kihei, at the Kamaole Shopping Center.]

MEALS FOR LESS THAN $25

AVALON, 844 Front St. Tel. 667-5559.
Cuisine: PACIFIC RIM. **Reservations:** Recommended at dinner.
$ Prices: Appetizers $5.95–$14.95; main courses $12.95–$26.95. AE, DC, DISC, MC, V.
Open: Daily noon–midnight.

In Arthurian legend, Avalon was another name for Paradise, the place where heroes went to reap their eternal reward. You can reap some culinary rewards right here and now by going to the restaurant of the same name in the courtyard of the Mariners Alley shopping mall. Quite simply, it's the best restaurant to open in Lahaina in many a year. The creation of a transplanted Southern Californian, chef Mark Ellman, Avalon provides an exuberant and imaginative dining experience without a drop of pretension. The dining room is prettily decorated with old posters and antique Hawaiian shirts on the wall, oversize Fiestaware and flowered cloths on the tables. If you're watching the budget, come just for lunch (under $12), or order one of the exotic vegetarian dishes on the dinner menu. Better still, throw caution to the wind and indulge yourself this once. This is the kind of restaurant people write home about.

Avalon presents contemporary Hawaiian regional cuisine, with inspirations from Southeast Asia, using many fresh, local ingredients. Many ingredients are grown in a nearby farmyard. The chef will not use MSG, not even salt, and does all his seasoning with herbs. All sauces are made to order, and all dishes may be ordered mild, medium, or spicy. If you're on a special diet, they will do their best. Now then, what to order? While you're sipping something pleasant to start, perhaps the KGB Cooler (Absolut Citron with freshly squeezed lemonade over ice) or a glass of champagne with crushed fresh raspberries, discuss the daily specials with the waiter. Chef Mark is always trying something new, so you can never tell what heavenly treats may be in store (at a recent meal, for example, we started with homemade shrimp ravioli with shiitake mushrooms and sun-dried tomatoes in a Szechuan cream sauce). Always on the menu are such treats, among the appetizers, as summer rolls, Maui onion rings with a homemade tamarind catsup, and shrimp Thai style.

Among the main courses, fresh fish of the day, fresh sea scallops, and large Asian prawns can be ordered with a variety of sauces. Vegetarians will love the Gado Gado salad, a classic Balinese dish of steamed vegetables on brown rice, with peanut sauce and condiments.

Still with us? How can we describe the caramel Miranda, the only dessert offered? Imagine a plate of fresh raspberries and strawberries, framed on one side by an incredibly delicious, thick, warm caramel sauce, on the other side by a giant scoop of Häagen-Dazs macadamia-nut brittle ice cream. Unforgettable! Depending on the season and the availability of exotic fruits, it might include, instead, coquitos (full-grown minicoconuts from Chile), or Kula blackberries and huckleberries. If you don't get to have dinner here, at least come by afterward for coffee and dessert (about $5).

CHILI'S GRILL & BAR, in Lahaina Center, 900 Front St. Tel. 661-3665.

Cuisine: AMERICAN/SOUTHWESTERN. **Reservations:** Not accepted.

$ Prices: Appetizers $2.45–$7.25; main courses $5.45–$17.95. AE, MC, V.

Open: Daily 11am–11pm.

A family restaurant with a dinner-house atmosphere, Chili's is done in southwestern motif, with lots of painted wood, tile floors and table tops, cactus plants, exposed wood ceilings and booths. Cocktails are served in a casual and fun atmosphere; lanai seating is available. The menu is eclectic, with everything from gourmet burgers, baby back ribs, quesadillas, and fajitas to a grilled tuna or shrimp Caesar salad. Among the starters, we like the "Awesome Blossom"—that's whole onion sliced to blossom, and then battered and deep-fried; and for dessert, the frozen Oreo yogurt pie is something a bit different. Kids have their own menu—grilled cheese, hot dogs, chicken, and burgers, served with fries, for $3.95.

CHRIS' SMOKEHOUSE BBQ, Honoapiilani Hwy. and Hinau St. Tel. 667-2111.

Cuisine: BARBECUE. **Reservations:** Not required.

$ Prices: Appetizers $2.25–$6; main courses $6–$17. MC, V.

Open: Daily 11am–10pm.

Stacks of kiawe wood and Hawaiian ranch decor set an upcountry mood, but here we are in tropical Lahaina. The baby back pork ribs and kiawe chicken are good and tasty—they're smoked over kiawe wood and broiled over kiawe charcoal to give them a very special flavor. There are five complete dinners on the menu at $10.95—and that means that along with your rack of baby back pork ribs, hot links, half a smoked kiawe chicken, char-broiled boneless breast of chicken, or beef ribs, you also get freshly baked cornbread with honey-macadamia-nut butter, coleslaw, and a choice of ranch-style baked beans, homemade steak fries, or steamed rice. Higher-priced dinner main courses include various combination plates, New York strip steak, and charcoal-broiled fresh fish.

Come at lunchtime and you can sample Chris's tasty smoked meats in open-face sandwiches with barbecue sauce at $4.95–$6.95, served with coleslaw or steak fries. You're given a plain, white paper placemat and crayons for doodling while you're having a drink and waiting for your meal. Amusing and creative examples of customers' artwork are displayed throughout the restaurant. Happy hour is on every day from 3 to 5pm.

COMPADRES MEXICAN BAR & GRILL, at the Lahaina Cannery, 1221 Honoapiilani Hwy. Tel. 661-7189.

Cuisine: MEXICAN. **Reservations:** Not required.

$ **Prices:** Appetizers $5.95–$12.95; main courses $7.45–$19.95. AE, DC, MC, V.

Open: Mon–Sat 10am–11pm, Sun 10am–10pm (bar open to 1am).

The first neighbor island location of Honolulu's popular Compadres Restaurant is a smash hit in Lahaina. And rightfully so, for the same formula—a combination of terrific food, respectable prices, wonderful setting, and an upbeat, fun atmosphere—that made the original Compadres one of Honolulu's "Top 20 Restaurants" is very much in evidence here. The setting is both casual and exotic, with a fountain, an aviary, a garden of greenery, pastel-colored terra-cotta pots, and an array of Mexican artifacts enhancing the indoor-outdoor dining setting. The chefs take their inspiration from the cooking of northern Mexico, Arizona, and California, and strive for food that is wholesome as well as flavorful. They use only the freshest of ingredients, make everything from scratch, and never use lard, so that many dishes are suitable for vegetarians. For the calorie-conscious, they've come up with a number of "Compadres 400" selections, dishes of 400 or fewer calories.

House specialties include chicken, shrimp, and beef fajitas, seafood tacos, mahimahi a la Vera Cruz, arroz con pollo, camarones al mojo de ajo (large gulf shrimp sautéed in fresh lime, white wine, garlic, and butter), and an array of fresh fish preparations. We love the nachos and the queso fundido among the appetizers, the taco split and mud pie among the desserts—not to mention those super margaritas!

Weekend breakfasts, served from 10am to 2pm, feature traditional favorites and are great fun.

COUNTRY KITCHEN, in the Lahaina Square Shopping Center, 900 Front St. Tel. 661-3330.

Cuisine: FRENCH. **Reservations:** Recommended for dinner.

$ **Prices:** Complete lunches $6.95; complete dinners $15.95. No credit cards.

Open: Lunch Mon–Fri 11:30am–2pm; dinner Mon–Sat 5:30–10pm.

When was the last time you had a delicious French dinner, complete from soup and salad to main course to beverage and dessert, for $15.95? Believe it or not, such a meal is now available in pricey Lahaina, thanks to Jacqueline and Bob Webb, formerly of La Bretagne. They've decorated this little place simply, with flowered wallpaper and café curtains. Everything is home-cooked, and while prime ribs, fresh fish with a chef's sauce of the day, prawns, and two pasta dishes are always on the dinner menu, other choices might include chicken breast on Monday, roast pork on Tuesday, osso buco on Wednesday, leg of lamb on Thursday, roast duckling on Friday, couscous on Saturday. For dessert, try the baked pear or apple pudding. No liquor is served, so BYOB.

Lunch also offers good values: You can order main courses such as prime ribs or fresh fish à la carte; or go with the complete meal at $6.95, with a choice of selections such as burgundy beef, vegetable lasagne, mahimai, and roast pork with sauerkraut or red cabbage.

HARD ROCK CAFE, at Lahaina Center, 900 Front St. Tel. 667-7400.

Cuisine: AMERICAN. **Reservations:** Not accepted.

$ **Prices:** Appetizers $2.75–$6.25; main courses $10.95–$13.95. AE, DISC, MC, V.

Open: Daily 11am–10pm.

If ever a restaurant was suited to the Lahaina night scene, this is certainly it. Like Lahaina itself, it's big, noisy, brash—and very endearing. Like its companion restaurants around the world, this Hard Rock is decorated with rock music memorabilia and 1950s artifacts; here they mingle with surfboards and ukuleles on the walls. Nonstop piped-in rock music makes it unlikely that you can indulge in much conversation with the waiter, but the choices are easy. Everything is made from scratch, using the freshest of ingredients, and "absolutely no preservatives or additives." We'll have to agree with the menu that "If you've been to the Hard Rock and haven't had our lime chicken or watermelon ribs, then you haven't been to the Hard Rock!" In addition to that lime barbecued chicken ($10.95) and those watermelon ribs ($12.50), other good choices might include fresh fish of the day (market-priced), grilled and served with a baked potato and green salad; a variety of burgers and sandwiches including grilled ahi; a top-notch grilled tostada salad; and, of course, a batch of Maui onion rings. Desserts are out of the '50s, too; root beer float, hot fudge sundaes, and our favorite, the fresh strawberries on homemade angelfood cake, topped with pure whipped cream.

You're likely to see lines at the door of Hard Rock, but don't be put off; they are usually for the HRC logo shop, which dispenses insanely popular T-shirts, baseball caps, cigarette lighters, and the like; the restaurant is so large that you're usually seated in a very short time.

KIMO'S, 845 Front St. Tel. 661-4811.

Cuisine: STEAK/SEAFOOD. **Reservations:** Recommended.

$ **Prices:** Appetizers $2.50–$9.95; main courses $7.95–$25.95. AE, MC, V.

Open: Lunch (downstairs bar) daily 11:30am–2:30pm; dinner (upstairs restaurant) daily 5–10:30pm.

Call Kimo's your quintessential Lahaina-style restaurant. It's been there forever right out on the waterfront, serves good fresh fish and steaks, and is a perfect place to nurse a drink, discuss the meaning of life, and/or watch a sunset from the upstairs oceanfront dining room. By sticking carefully to the low side of the menu, you can dine quite reasonably: A cheeseburger is $6.95; New York steak sandwich, Polynesian chicken, and kushiyaki (marinated chicken breast and sirloin brochette) are all $9.95. Health nuts are kept well in mind with the "spa-cuisine style" marinated chicken breast, low in calories, salt, and cholesterol; it's called ginger chicken and is $9.95. And everything you order comes with tossed green salad with house dressing, a basket of freshly baked carrot muffins and French rolls, and steamed herb rice. There's limited service downstairs during the day: The bar menu features lunch with fish, meat, and veggie sandwiches as well as a Cobb salad, for $5.95–$9.95; pupus are served at the bar between 3 and 5pm.

KOBE JAPANESE STEAK HOUSE, 136 Dickenson St. Tel. 667-5555.

Cuisine: JAPANESE. **Reservations:** Recommended.

$ **Prices:** Sushi $7.25–$16.50; main courses $12.90–$27.90. AE, JCB, MC, V.

Open: Dinner only, daily 5:30–9pm.

What a surprise this place is! Just one block behind traditional Baldwin House is what could pass for an authentic Japanese country inn, magnificently decorated with traditional Japanese arts and artifacts, and serving delicious food in a most entertaining setting. You could eat at the enormous sushi bar (sushi assortments run $7.25–$16.50), but we prefer to take our seats at one of the communal tables, and, along with other diners, spur the master chef on as he whips up our meal at the center grill, teppanyaki-hibachi style. In such a setting, people dining alone, friends dining together, even families with children can all feel comfortable. Every meal begins with grilled teppan shrimp pupus, followed by shabu-shabu soup. Then the chef takes whatever you've chosen—steak, chicken, shrimp—and sautés it with fresh vegetables and flavorful sauces. For dessert, wonderful green-tea ice cream and green tea itself, hearty because it's roasted with rice. Teriyaki chicken is $13.90; hibachi steak, $19.50; teppan shrimp, $18.90; and a steak-and-shrimp teriyaki combo is $21.90. Other steak, fish, and lobster choices go higher. We like to start the meal with warm sake; Japanese beer goes well with this food, and regular drinks and cocktails are also available. Special children's menus are available.

Cocktail service begins at 5pm and continues to 2am. Plenty of free parking.

LAHAINA COOLERS RESTAURANT & BAR, 180 Dickenson St. Tel. 661-7082.

Cuisine: NEW AMERICAN. **Reservations:** Not required.

$ Prices: Appetizers $3.50–$7; main courses $8–$13. AE, DC, MC, V.

Open: Breakfast daily 7–11am; lunch/dinner daily 11:30am–midnight.

Located two blocks from busy Front Street, Lahaina Coolers is exactly the kind of place Lahaina needed—a place where you can get creative, upbeat food at almost any time of the day, in a relaxing setting and at a reasonable price. No wonder it became so popular so quickly! The restaurant looks like somebody's summer porch, with open windows on three sides (windsurfing sails provide shade), blue-and-white tiled floor, white chairs, whirling fans overhead, lots of potted plants—a very summery ambience. You can order anything on the lunch and dinner menus from noon to midnight—and there's a wealth of choices. For a snack or a starter, the spinach and feta cheese quesadilla and the tempura calamari rings are both great. Among the salads, you can't go wrong with the sesame chicken with water chestnuts and papaya, the Greek salad, or the mandarin chicken ($6.75–$7.75). Or maybe you'll want to try a tropic pizza: Evil Jungle pizza, Thai-style chicken in a spicy peanut sauce, is a whimsical takeoff on the popular Thai dish ($10.50). There are burgers from the grill, as well as grilled chicken breast, Moroccan chicken, spinach enchilada, veggie stir-fry, and New York steak. And they have some neat pastas too.

Perhaps you'd better come here with a little group so you can sample a lot. But don't miss dessert: The chocolate taco filled with tropical fruit and berry "salsa" is worth a postcard home. The breakfast menu includes a variety of omelets and specialty egg dishes. The lively bar is popular, especially during the 4 to 6pm and 10pm to closing happy hours "8 days a week," when drinks and pupus are less. And don't miss their mango daiquiri!

LONGHI'S, 888 Front St. Tel. 667-2288.

Cuisine: ITALIAN. **Reservations:** Not accepted.

$ Prices: Appetizers $4–$7; main courses $12–$25. AE, DISC, MC, V.

Open: Daily 7:30am–10:30pm.

Everybody seems to like this across-from-the-ocean café, where Italian-accented specialties are fresh and hearty, the mood convivial (lots of plants, koa tables, a lively bar, and friendly service), and the desserts—and sunsets—super-special. Sit upstairs or downstairs—the rooms are similar, but there's an even better ocean view upstairs. Manager Peter Longhi goes to great lengths (like to New York and Italy) to bring in the finest and freshest cheeses, produce, and Italian cold cuts, makes his own pastas, bakes his own breads and pastries, and maintains a high standard throughout. Our main problem here is that the menu is always verbal, and so long that you feel you need to take notes; it's also difficult to figure out just how much your meal is going to cost. It's easy for the bill to escalate, since main courses are served alone, and side dishes can add up (salads from $5, fresh vegetables for $4.50–$8, etc.), so our recommendation is either go all out and consider this a big splurge, or tell the servers how much you want to spend and let them plan the menu for you. (You can also ask for a menu with prices before being seated.) The last time we dined at Longhi's, linguine with a delicious pesto sauce was $16; eggplant parmigiana was $12. It was $20 for shrimps, scallops, and pasta scampi, and $23 for fresh Maui fish.

It's wise to eat lightly and save your strength, in fact, because Longhi's other-worldly desserts have become something of a legend around town; there have been 1,000 different ones in the restaurant's 15-year history. You never know what they'll come up with, but you might sample, as five of us once did, an incredible strawberry shortcake, a superb macadamia-nut pie (better than any pecan pie we had ever tasted), an unusual chocolate-cake pie (chocolate cake between pie crusts with custard between the layers), a mouth-watering mango-topped cheesecake, and a cooling strawberry mousse. All desserts are priced at $5, and they are huge, so be sure to bring a friend to help you. There's an extensive wine list, including selections that you can order by the glass; Longhi's has won many awards from wine societies. The breakfast menu includes frittatas, omelets, homemade coffee cake, and strudel. On Friday and Saturday nights various bands provide music for dancing, from 10:30pm until 1:30am. Complimentary valet parking from 5pm.

MARIE CALLENDER'S, at the Lahaina Cannery, 1221 Honoapiilani Hwy. Tel. 667-7437.

Cuisine: AMERICAN. **Reservations:** Not required.

$ Prices: Appetizers $5–$7; main courses $7–$17. AE, MC, V.

Open: Daily 7am–10pm.

This restaurant is as American as apple—or chicken pot—pie. Both are served with gusto at this charming place, which has just about everything the cost-conscious diner could desire: a gracious, pink-and-pretty setting, comfortable seating that invites relaxing with friends, a wide variety of dishes, and wholesome American cooking—all at very realistic prices. As for that chicken pot pie, it's as good as we've tasted, with a flaky crust, lots of chicken chunks and vegetables, and makes a satisfying meal, with soup or salad, at $8.95.

Salads are also a specialty: Chicken Cobb, chicken curry, and chef's salad are all delicious, as are the fresh pasta dishes, the quiches, omelets, and a variety of burgers and sandwiches. After 4pm, dinner main courses like chicken teriyaki, fajitas, and meatloaf are added to the menu, and are served with salad or soup, pasta or rice or fries, plus cornbread with honey butter. Now for dessert: Marie Callender's is known for its home-baked pies, so have a slice here—of fresh peach or sour-cream blueberry, rhubarb or butterscotch or macadamia-nut cream ($2.50–$3.25), and see if you can resist taking a whole pie back to your hotel with you. Breakfast is very good too; we recommend the banana–macadamia-nut waffles.

MOOSE McGILLYCUDDY'S PUB/CAFE, 844 Front St. Tel. 667-7758.

Cuisine: AMERICAN. **Reservations:** Not accepted.

$ Prices: Appetizers $4.25–$8.95; main courses $6.95–$17.95. AE, MC, V.

Open: Breakfast daily 7–11am; lunch daily 11am–5pm; dinner daily 4:30–10pm.

Like the Moose in Waikiki, this pub/café offers the same brand of good food, good drinks, and good fun here in Lahaina. It's one flight up, with a big bar, a lively atmosphere, and some tables set out on the lanai overlooking busy Front Street. The Moose is known as a "bargain" in pricey Lahaina; main courses include teriyaki chicken, stuffed mahimahi, porter-house steak, and prime rib, and come with soup or salad, baked potato or rice or fries, and hot garlic bread. Early Bird dinners, served from 4:30 to 5:30pm, feature prime rib, mahimahi amandine, and half a char-broiled chicken for only $7.95, plus steak and lobster at $14.95. Then there are other favorites like the giant taco salad at $6.95, Mexican specialties like chimichanga or giant burrito at $7.95, a variety of burgers like the University Burger ("highly ranked bacon and intelligent Cheddar") for $4.25–$7.50. Margaritas and daiquiris are the big drink selections here, along with coffee drinks, Hawaiian exotics, and way-out house specialties.

The Moose's breakfast specials are considered the best deals in Lahaina: the Early Bird, served from 7:30 to 9am, $3 for two eggs, bacon, toast, and orange juice; and the Beggar's Banquet, $3.60 for three eggs any style, with potatoes or rice and Texas toast.

OLD LAHAINA CAFE, 505 Front St. Tel. 661-3303.

Cuisine: SEAFOOD/AMERICAN. **Reservations:** Not accepted.

$ Prices: Appetizers $4.95–$6.95; main courses $9.95–$16.95. AE, MC, V.

Open: Breakfast daily 7:30–11:30am; lunch daily noon–3pm; dinner daily 5:30–10pm.

What could be nicer than a beachside breakfast or lunch or a sunset dinner in this charming café overlooking the grounds of the Old Lahaina Luau? This is sophisticated cuisine, using fresh local ingredients and featuring just-caught fish with a variety of preparations—maybe kiawe broiled with shoyu lime chile, or poached with passion-fruit cream—dreamed up by veteran chef Michael Ducheneau, who trained at the Culinary Institute of America. There are also vegetarian selections, broiled chicken and steak, and a luau dinner as well. The lunch menu—which can also be ordered in the evening—features hot and cold sandwiches (including kalua pig!) and some hearty salads, like the Upcountry Maui with grilled ahi. Breakfast offers many bargains, beginning at $3.95 for a generous continental breakfast. What with the view, and the sounds of the luau entertainment below, this is just the place to sit and linger over a fabulous tropical drink. Most Hawaiian!

READERS RECOMMEND

The Chart House, *1450 Front St. (tel. 661-0937). "This place is not to be missed! It was simply wonderful—service excellent, food delicious, atmosphere tops!"*—Sue Tamny, Hersham, Penna. [*Authors' Note:* We agree. It's a great place, specializing in steak and seafood, and serving dinner daily from 5pm. Dinner should run about $25 or more. There's another Chart House in Kahului (tel. 877-2476).]

"We figured out how to beat the system at the Chart House, which serves a terrific dinner, but never takes reservations. Put your name down on their list and then go shopping in Lahaina; they'll let you know when to be back."—Bob Harrison and Hal Goodstein, Provincetown, Mass.

David Paul's Grill, *127 Lahainaluna Rd. (tel. 667-5117). "Attached to the Lahainaluna Hotel is David Paul's Grill. This is a delightful venue for a big-splurge meal. Wicker furnishings, black-and-white tiled floors, excellent service and food served with more imagination and panache than most other restaurants in Hawaii. I dined on oysters with a chili sauce followed by soft-shell crab on angel-hair pasta with basil sauce."*—Mrs. Jane Beecham, Victoria, Australia.

SPECIALTY DINING

Dining Complexes

WHARF CINEMA CENTER Not only does the Wharf Cinema Center, a shopping complex at 658 Front St., have some of the most tasteful boutiques in the area, it also has a good supply of quick-service restaurants.

For breakfast or lunch al fresco, try **Lani's Pancake Cottage.** The indoor area with its counters and booths is pleasant enough, but several restaurants, Lani's among them, share a large terrace with umbrellaed tables. Breakfast is available until closing, so any time is fine for banana or strawberry pancakes ($3.95 and $4.50) or the omelet to end all omelets: the Chef's Mess Omelet, made of five eggs and filled with the likes of Ortega chili and cheese, bell peppers, Swiss cheese, etc.—$14 for two of you, $16 for three. Their tuna melt sandwich—grilled tuna and cheese with a small green salad—makes a good lunch at $4.75, and so do such main courses as a chile relleno burger, a bowl of chili, or honey-dipped fried chicken, for $5–$7.95. Beer and wine are available. Open 6:30am to 2:30pm only.

Chicago-style pizzas and pastas are the fare at **Pizza Patio,** which also shares the umbrellaed tables outside. We like their special house pizzas, like the Canuck (Canadian bacon, tomatoes, and shrimp), $11.95 small, $19.95 medium. Pasta dishes

($7.95–$9.95) are also good, as are their Italian calzones and homemade lasagne, meat or vegetarian, at $10.

Subways, one of our favorite sandwich shops, has a branch here (see "Specialty Dining," in Kihei, above). And for an Asian plate lunch, you'll do well at **Song's Kitchen,** in the rear of the Wharf. All is tidy and clean, and lunches run $3.85–$5.95.

Tucked away in a cozy corner on the first floor of the Wharf is a Mexican restaurant the local people like a lot: **Pancho and Lefty's,** with a bar up front, booths and tables in the back. They always run a daily lunch special, guaranteed to be big and filling—like their chiles rellenos, made with south-of-the-border chili spiked with tequila and orange juice! Main dishes run about $7.95–$15.95, and their frozen margaritas are among the best around.

Up in the front area of the Wharf, the **Blue Lagoon Tropical Bar & Grill** is just the place to relax, indoors in the dining room or outdoors on the gardenlike lanai with a tropical drink (the Lahaina Sunrise was invented here), and maybe a char-broiled chicken sandwich or mahimahi Cajun style, the house specialty of hibachi chicken, or a steak-and-shrimp combo plate. Sandwiches run $5.95–$7.95, main courses are $11.95–$15.95, and there are daily lunch and dinner specials. They have some neat desserts too.

Should you be in the mood for a slight splurge, you can't do better than a teppanyaki-hibachi–style meal at the famed **Benihana of Tokyo,** which maintains stylish digs upstairs. An Asian treat. And if all you want is a brownie or a muffin or a divine macroon to nibble on, and perhaps a cup of coffee to go with it, try the delicious homemade goodies (courtesy of the Bakery) at **Whaler's Book Shoppe and Coffee House,** a combination bookstore and European café, where you can sip and sit in un-Lahaina-like peace.

LAHAINA CENTER In addition to the **Hard Rock Café** and **Chili's** (see above), the handsome Lahaina Center at 900 Front St. offers just what the hungry tourist longs for—a couple of places where you can get good, quick meals at rock-bottom prices. The take-out–oriented menu at **Arakawa's Chinese Food** reflects Mandarin, Szechuan, and Hunan styles of cookery. Every day there's a special at $4.45; regular menu choices are $2.55 small, $4 large. Outdoor seating is available. **Maui Munchies** offers wholesome food at relaxing prices—Italian dishes, sandwiches on a French roll (chicken, jalapeño sausage, strip steak, tuna), plate lunch and dinner specials, for $4.95–$6.50. Homemade hash browns and breakfast sandwiches are served all day. For $2 you can have all the **Ben & Jerry's** ice cream or frozen yogurt you can handle.

LAHAINA CANNERY Lahaina Cannery is at 1221 Honoapiilani Hwy. on the Kaanapali side of town. **Compadres** and **Marie Callender's** (see above) are the big sit-down restaurants here. But don't ignore the restaurants in the food court: **Athens,** for one, turns out tasty traditional Greek specialties at modest prices. Then, of course, there are the standard fast-food outlets like **Yami Yogurt, Hamburger King, McConnel's Ice Cream,** and **Orange Julius.** But be imaginative and stop in for some flavored coffees and cappuccinos.

LAHAINA SQUARE Lahaina Square Shopping Center, 840 Waimee St., caters to the local people, not to the tourist trade, which means it's a good place for hungry budgeteers to note. In addition to **Thai Chef** (see above) and a good sandwich place, **Amilio's Delicatessen** (see below), there is a familiar **Jack in the Box,** as well as a **Baskin-Robbins** and a large **Denny's.**

Natural Foods

WESTSIDE NATURAL FOODS, 136 Dickenson St. Tel. 667-2855.
Cuisine: VEGETARIAN.

$ Prices: Appetizers from $1.50; main courses $4.95. No credit cards.
Open: Mon–Sat 7:30am–9pm, Sun 9am–7pm.

There's no natural-foods restaurant in Lahaina at the moment, but this local health-food store has salads, sandwiches, soup of the day, smoothies, and hot food to eat informally at outdoor tables or to go. Main courses include lasagne, chili, and enchiladas. The shopping is good here too: You can get unsprayed pineapples and starfruits grown in Lahaina.

Picnic/Take-Out Fare

AMILIO'S DELICATESSEN, at Lahaina Square Shopping Center, 840 Waimee St. Tel. 661-8551.
Cuisine: DELI.
$ Prices: Sandwiches $3.35–$4.50. No credit cards.
Open: Mon–Fri 8am–8pm, Sat–Sun 8am–4pm.

This deli makes good sandwiches, some with an Italian flair, to take out or eat here; the price range goes from $3.35 for tuna or cheese to $4.50 for Amilio's special of many meats and cheeses. There's apt to be a special offer, like one sandwich at $1 when you buy another deli sandwich at full price. There's a choice of good breads, deli meats, and cheese if you wish to make your own sandwiches. Local-style plate lunches are good buys at $3.95.

THE BAKERY, 991 Lihmahina Place. Tel. 667-9062.
Cuisine: BREADS/PASTRIES/SANDWICHES.
$ Prices: Pastries from 85¢; breads from $1.25; sandwiches $2.50–$4.50. No credit cards.
Open: Mon–Sat 6am–4pm, Sun 6am–noon.

Next to the train depot (the Lahaina-Kaanapali Railroad "Sugar-Cane Train") is a "Maui secret." Many of the fine restaurants in town get their bread and pastries here. The Bakery is a popular spot, crowded with locals who come early in the morning for the best croissants around, and brioches and pain au lait, hot from the oven. Chocolate-cream-cheese croissants and coconut macaroons are memorable. Herb bread ($1.25) is their specialty. They also offer gourmet-quality deli items and sandwiches to go (on the order of cheese broccoli or smoked pork loin and cheese). It's worth stopping by just to inhale the aromas! Local friends advise that their prices on California wines, Maui champagne, and imported champagne too, are so good that they should be kept a secret!

MR. SUB, 129 Lahainaluna Rd., near Front St. Tel. 667-5683.
Cuisine: SANDWICHES/SALADS.
$ Prices: Sandwiches $2.75–$5.50. No credit cards.
Open: Mon–Fri 7am–5pm, Sat 7am–4pm.

Long one of Honolulu's most popular submarine shops, Mr. Sub is repeating its quality act in Lahaina, with wonderfully fresh ingredients, seven varieties of breads and rolls, great salads, quick service, and low prices. You can eat right in their air-conditioned shop, but the best bet is to choose from the 31 combination sandwiches (or create your own combination) and head for your picnic. Special picnic packages, with coolers for the beach, include a sandwich, chips, fruit, and a drink, and run about $5–$7. Call them the day before, and everything will be ready for pickup by 7am.

KAANAPALI BEACH

The strip of luxury hotels along Kaanapali Beach boasts a goodly share of luxury restaurants, but very few where the budget diner can relax. Some worthy exceptions:

MEALS FOR LESS THAN $10

KAANAPALI BEACH HOTEL KOFFEE SHOP, 2525 Kaanapali Pkwy. Tel. 661-0011.

Cuisine: BUFFETS. **Reservations:** Not required.

$ **Prices:** Breakfast buffet $5.95; lunch buffet $5.95; afternoon deli buffet $4.95; dinner buffet $9.95.

Open: Breakfast daily 6–10:45am; lunch daily 11am–2pm; afternoon deli buffet daily 2–4pm; dinner buffet daily 4–9pm.

The Kaanapali Beach Hotel, one of the most Hawaiian of Maui's hotels, is always doing something nice for the visitor, and what could be nicer than this—quality food served buffet style all day long, and at very low prices. Plan to catch the dinner buffet and work it in with the free Sunset Hula Show, held nightly at 6:30pm. Both lunch and dinner buffets feature a choice of six main courses (including fish, chicken, beef, pork), a salad-soup-and-fruit bar, rice, vegetables, desserts, and beverages; in addition, the dinner buffet offers prime ribs. During the afternoon deli buffet, you help yourself to soup, salad, and desserts, and fix your own sandwiches. Breakfast features fresh pineapple and papaya, eggs, pancakes, French toast, sausage, ham, muffins, and more.

MEALS FOR LESS THAN $15

COOK'S AT THE BEACH, in the Westin Maui Resort, 2365 Kaanapali Pkwy. Tel. 667-2525.

Cuisine: AMERICAN. **Reservations:** Not accepted.

$ **Prices:** Appetizers $4–$8.75; main courses $7.50–$14.75; breakfast brunch $13.75; prime rib buffet $21.75. AE, CB, DC, DISC, MC, V.

Open: Breakfast daily 6:30–11am; lunch daily 11:30am–2pm; dinner buffet daily 6–9pm; brunch Sun 9am–2pm.

It's worth the price of admission just to see the spectacular grounds of this hotel, with its waterfalls and islands and tropical lagoons, but it's also reasonable for the whole family to eat poolside at Cook's at the Beach, which even has a kid's menu, served "from 11:30am until bedtime," for $3.50–$4.75. But the real knockout here is the prime rib buffet, a fabulous spread featuring unlimited roast beef carved to order, plus fresh local seafood, salads, and desserts, for $21.75. While you're feasting, enjoy a free hula show Tuesday through Saturday at 7pm. True seafood lovers should opt for the seafood buffet at the Villa at the same hotel, a restaurant set on a tropical lagoon. The $21.75 meal features freshly cut sashimi, lomi-lomi salmon, steamed Alaskan snow crab legs, and catch of the day.

READERS RECOMMEND

The Swan Court, *in the Hyatt Regency Hotel, Kaanapali (tel. 661-1234, ext. 4420 until 5pm, ext. 4455 after 5pm). "The Swan Court is by far the most delightful place for 'the big splurge.' The restaurant is open to a pond/garden setting with black and white swans gliding by; service is very attentive and food is excellent. Most main courses are in the $20–$35 range, and there is a huge dessert buffet at dinner. Breakfast is also served here, buffet style, as well as from menu selections. The Swan Court accepts reservations; however, hotel guests have first priority on reservations between 7 and 9pm, so it's easier for 'outsiders' to get reservations between 6 and 7 or after 9pm."*—Bob Harrison and Hal Goodstein, Provincetown, Mass.

WHALER'S VILLAGE

There's a salty but slick flavor to the handsome complex of shops and museums at Maui's Whaler's Village, and you can be sure that old-time seamen never had food as good as you'll find in the village's restaurants.

MEALS FOR LESS THAN $15

CHICO'S CANTINA & CAFE, in Whaler's Village. Tel. 667-2777.

Cuisine: MEXICAN. **Reservations:** Recommended.

$ Prices: Appetizers $4–$6; main courses $6.95–$11.95. AE, MC, V.

Open: Lunch daily 11:30am–2:30pm; dinner daily 5:30–10:30pm.

The atmosphere is tropical (white adobe walls, colorful Mexican hangings, heavy wooden furniture) and the menu is half-Mexican, half-American. On the Mexican side, there are combination plates for $9.50–$10.95; fajitas, enchiladas, burritos, and all the rest; and such specialties as carnitas, carne asada, pollo asada, and mahimahi done in the style of Vera Cruz, each $10.95. American favorites feature mango fettuccine and smoked chicken, London broil, and Cajun shrimp, plus chicken and ribs barbecues, sandwiches, salads, burgers—in short, a menu to please many tastes. If you come by during their popular happy hour from 3 to 6pm, you can enjoy $1 margaritas, and a draft beer and a generous portion of nachos for only $2.90! There's Mexican music during lunch and dinner, then rock 'n' roll late night and during happy hour. A fun spot.

MEALS FOR LESS THAN $20

EL CRABCATCHER, in Whaler's Village. Tel. 661-4423.

Cuisine: SEAFOOD. **Reservations:** Recommended.

$ Prices: Poolside Café, appetizers $2.95–$8.95; main courses $10.95–$12.95; Oceanfront Terrace, appetizers $3.95–$10.95; main courses $12.95–$21.95. AE, CB, DC, MC, V.

Open: Poolside Café, daily 3–10pm. Oceanfront Terrace, lunch daily 11:30am–3:30pm; dinner daily 5:30–10pm.

The only restaurant we know of with its own pool right on a glorious beach, El Crabcatcher is a fabulous sunset choice. If you're watching the budget, arrive at the Poolside Café between 5:30 and 6:30pm for the Sunset Specials: that's when you get fresh fish, New York steak, Cajun mahimahi, or steamed clams for a mere $9.95, including soup and salad. Later on these same selections are only $10.95–$12.95, and there are also yummy pupus—including the house specialty of crab-stuffed mushrooms and Maui onions—plus sandwiches, salads, and desserts. You can also keep an eye on the budget in the Oceanfront Terrace by having one of the light suppers—including sautéed shrimp and char-broiled breast of chicken—from $13.95–$14.95. Regular dinner dishes, served with vegetables and a basket of breads, run $16.95 (seafood brochette) to $21.95 (fresh crab-stuffed fish). Naughty hula pie is the dessert of choice. There's Hawaiian music daily from 5:30 to 7:30pm, contemporary and popular music Tuesday through Saturday from 9:30pm to 12:30am.

THE RUSTY HARPOON, in Whaler's Village. Tel. 661-3123.

Cuisine: CONTEMPORARY AMERICAN. **Reservations:** Recommended for parties of six or more.

$ Prices: Appetizers $1.25–$9.25; main courses $14.75–$22.95. AE, DC, MC, V.

Open: Breakfast daily 8–11am; lunch daily 11am–5pm; dinner daily 5–10pm.

This Whaler's Village standby for many years boasts a handsome interior (green colors, beautiful woods, a view of the ocean as well as the kitchen from every table), and a new menu concept: "nouvelle California–Maui cuisine." And it's still known for excellent value for the dollar. Come for the Early Bird specials, nightly between 5 and 6pm, and for $10–$11 you can have dishes like pasta primavera, salsa chicken, prime rib, or fresh fish of the day, including fresh vegetables and rice pilaf or pasta. Regular dinner main courses, accompanied by fresh vegetable and rice pilaf or pasta, include chicken piccata, stir-fry beef, shrimp scampi, fettuccine primavera, and crab Alfredo. Rusty's still has its famous half-pound burgers at $7.50–$8.50, and there are some super salads—shrimp Louie, chicken walnut, fresh fruit, three-salad taster—for

$8.75–$9.25. Appetizers have an international flavor, from fried mozzarella to kalbi ribs to nachos. Rusty's uses only fresh local produce and makes its own pastas and wonderful fresh island desserts. Of course those famous fresh-fruit daiquiris (how about banana or pineapple?) are still there and still make Rusty's the "Daiquiri Capital of the World." There's a full bar, a lively crowd, lots of fun. And, oh yes, that sunset over the ocean is terrific!

KAHANA

MEALS FOR LESS THAN $20

KAHANA KEYES RESTAURANT, 4327 Lower Honoapiilani Rd., at the Valley Isle Resort. Tel. 669-8071.

Cuisine: AMERICAN. **Reservations:** Recommended.

$ Prices: Appetizers $3.50–$5.95; main courses $9.95–$17.95. AE, MC, V.

Open: Dinner only, daily 5–10pm.

Located three miles north of the Kaanapali Beach Resort, this has long been a favorite in the Kahana area. People like it because it has one of the best salad bars in the area (reputed to be Maui's largest), plus a variety of Early Bird dinners (from 5 to 7pm) from $9.95 for prime rib, as well as all-night specials which include steak and lobster at $13.95. The regular menu features steak and seafood, ($11.95–$17.95), plus broiler items ($10.95–$14.95). Salad bar alone is just $8.50. Every night local bands play contemporary Hawaiian music plus Top 40s and oldies, with dancing until 1:30am.

POWERHOUSE BAR Y GRILL, 4405 Honoapiilani Hwy., at Kahana Gateway. Tel. 669-6950.

Cuisine: MEXICAN. **Reservations:** Recommended.

$ Prices: Appetizers $4.25–$9.50; main courses $9.75–$17.95. AE, DISC, MC, V.

Open: Dinner only, daily 5–9:30pm (bar daily 10:30am–1am).

Is Powerhouse the best Mexican restaurant on Maui? Our local friends rave about it, and we can see why. The atmosphere is convivial, and the whole place, painted firehouse red—just like the original Powerhouse in Crested Butte, Colorado—evokes a feeling of good cheer. The high spirits begin up at the huge bar, which boasts super margaritas, at least 20 different tequilas, and the largest and best selection of Mexican beers on Maui—with some 502 beer glasses! The food is also cause for cheer. Everything is made from scratch: They fry their own chips and make their own salsa. These are the dishes of Mexico City and Guadalajara and Vera Cruz, even including the hard-to-find Mexican delicacy cabrito (baby goat). Our favorites are the combination plates of two mesquite-roasted items—steak, goat, shrimp, chicken breast, quail, or fresh fish. And you won't go wrong with the tampiqueña steak or the chicken flautas, or the fajitas both sizzling and mesquite. Dessert is *simpático* too, especially the amaretto cheesecake.

ROY'S KAHANA BAR AND GRILL, 4405 Honoapiilani Hwy., at Kahana Gateway. Tel. 669-6999.

Cuisine: EAST-WEST. **Reservations:** Recommended.

$ Prices: Appetizers $5.75–$7.50; main courses $11.95–$26.50. AE, DC, JCB, MC, V.

Open: Dinner only, daily 5:30–9:30pm.

Honolulu's most highly praised restaurant is now on Maui, and the mood and food are every bit as good—which means wonderful. *Wunderkind* chef Roy Yamaguchi blends the best of European and Asian cooking styles and techniques and uses the freshest of local ingredients to produce a new and exciting Hawaiian cuisine. And the setting is upbeat and exciting too—a large, room with an open kitchen, wraparound picture windows giving onto views of rolling meadows, paintings by local artists on the walls, gorgeous flower arrangements everywhere.

Roy's innovations are apparent in such beginners as Asian-style spinach-and-spicy-shrimp salad in a warm sesame vinaigrette or island-style potstickers in a lobster Thai-peanut sauce; in such main courses as the mesquite-smoked Peking duck or the grilled chicken linguine with feta cheese and Mediterranean-style vegetables. Every night there's a long list of specials, including four or five imaginative fish presentations. And prices are surprisingly modest for food of this caliber. You could make a light meal of one of the individual pizzas—maybe Szechuan-style shrimp pizza—for $6.95, or splurge with the Mongolian leg of lamb and blackened ahi for $26.50. Desserts change every night and are always memorable—consider the macadamia-nut tart or the mascarpone cheesecake, for starters. No wonder this is Maui's "hottest" new dinery.

READERS RECOMMEND

Dollies, *4310 Honoapiilani Hwy. (tel. 669-0266). "My husband and I both highly recommend Dollies, a pub and café which serves a good selection of sandwiches, salads, pizza, and more. The pizza is made on the premises and is absolutely delicious. The fettuccine Alfredo kept my 5-year-old niece quiet for an extended length of time. Their selection of beers is quite unmatched—even though the English beer is served quite a bit too cold!"*—Carole A. Greenwood, Angus, Ontario.

KAPALUA

MEALS FOR LESS THAN $25

THE MARKET CAFE, at Kapalua Shops, 115 Bay Dr. Tel. 669-4888.

Cuisine: ITALIAN. **Reservations:** Recommended.

$ **Prices:** Appetizers $4.95–$8.95; main courses $7.95–$11.95. AE, DC, MC, V.

Open: Breakfast Mon–Sat 8–11am, Sun 8am–1pm; lunch daily 11am–3pm; happy hour 3–6pm.

You'd hardly expect to find any moderately priced eating places in the posh pastures of Kapalua Bay Resort, but now there are two! The Market Café is half restaurant, half gourmet deli, a fun choice for a variety of deli sandwiches ($6.95–$9.95), burgers, and Italian-style main selections. Breakfast offers such sophisticated choices as eggs Benedict or béarnaise, lox and bagels with cream cheese, and pancakes cooked with fresh fruit.

PLANTATION HOUSE RESTAURANT, in the Plantation Golf Course Clubhouse, 2000 Plantation Club Dr. Tel. 669-6299.

Cuisine: ISLAND REGIONAL. **Reservations:** Recommended.

$ **Prices:** Appetizers $6.95–$8.95; main courses $14.95–$21.95.

Open: Breakfast daily 8–11am; lunch daily 11am–4pm; dinner daily 5:30–10pm.

There's a traditional, "old Hawaii" feeling about this handsome restaurant, reminiscent of the way things were back in the '40s—simple, comfortable, elegant. It sits high on a hill, affording extraordinary 360° views from various parts of the dining room—of the mountains, the ocean, the golf course, and the most spectacular sunsets on Maui. Whitewashed mahogany, tables made of teak, upholstered chairs with pineapple carved back, original artworks gracing the walls, and a double-sided fireplace dominating the room create the feeling of a warm and cozy lodge. Dinnertime appetizers are great fun, especially the crab cakes with a green-peppercorn–lime mayonnaise and Hawaiian-style sashimi. House specialties among the entrées include fresh local fish in a variety of presentations (we like it char-broiled and served with a shiitake-soy sauce), wok-fried jumbo prawns, breast of fresh duck, and mixed grill. Lunch is very reasonable, with such dishes as chicken breast, steak, and wok-fried vegetables, going for $6.25–$9.95, all accompanied by a choice of soup or salad, and fresh vegetables or sticky rice. Good sandwiches, salads, burgers, and pizzas too. As for desserts, fudge brownies with ice cream and chocolate sauce and the pot de crème au chocolate are delightful decadence personified.

THE POOL TERRACE, 1 Bay Dr., at Kapalua Bay Hotel and Villas. Tel. 669-5656.

Cuisine: AMERICAN. **Reservations:** Recommended.

$ Prices: Appetizers $5.25–$9.25; main courses $12.95–$17.95. AE, DC, JCB, MC, V.

Open: Daily 11am–9:30pm (cocktails till 11pm).

Sit either indoors or outdoors at this lovely spot, overlooking sweeping lawns and the sparkling ocean below. Burgers and sandwiches start at $8.25, a Thai Pan chicken salad makes a meal for $9.50, and pizzas run $11.75–$12.50. Kids enjoy their own menu—hot dogs, spaghetti and such. Lower-priced main courses include Jamaican jerk chicken, cashew chicken, and linguine. And desserts and coffee drinks are tempting, even if you don't have a full meal.

HANA

Outside of the famed—and very expensive—Hotel Hana-Maui, there are very few public restaurants in Hana. The hotel restaurant is wonderful, but very pricey.

SPECIALTY DINING

Breakfast/Lunch/Snacks

HANA RANCH RESTAURANT, Tel. 248-8255.

Cuisine: AMERICAN. **Reservations:** Recommended.

$ Prices: Appetizers $2.50–$5.50; main courses $18–$37. AE, DC, MC, V.

Open: Buffet lunch 11:30am–3pm; take-out counter 6:30am–4pm.

The Hana Ranch Restaurant is a bit away from the Hotel Hana-Maui, but still in the same Hana Ranch complex. It's a medium-priced choice, with an indoor dining room that features a nice buffet lunch for $9.95. A take-out counter serves up burgers, sandwiches, and hot dogs.

TUTU'S, at Hana Bay. Tel. 248-8224.

Cuisine: LOCAL. **Reservations:** Not accepted.

$ Prices: Plate lunches $5.25–$5.50. No credit cards.

Open: Daily 9:30am–4pm.

This longtime favorite is the best place for a reasonable lunch (or breakfast). Tutu's specializes in local-style plate lunches, plus very good fresh-fruit salads, green salads, sandwiches, ice cream, and such.

CHAPTER 15

WHAT TO SEE & DO ON MAUI

Ideally, it would be nice to have a week or more to spend in Maui. But if you have only a few days, you can still get to see and experience much of Maui's magic. *Note:* Excellent maps are in the *Maui Drive Guide*, free from your car-rental company.

SUGGESTED ITINERARIES

IF YOU HAVE ONE DAY Spend your day seeing mighty Haleakala Crater. On the way to or from Haleakala, explore the windsurfing mecca of Paia and the funky little cowboy town of Makawao, getting magnificent vistas of upcountry Maui all the way.

IF YOU HAVE TWO DAYS Spend your first day as suggested above. On your second day visit Lahaina, the old capital of the Hawaiian Islands, and enjoy its vibrant street life—shops, restaurants, galleries—and then drive north to the Kaanapali stretch of glamorous hotels and beaches, all the way to Kapalua.

IF YOU HAVE THREE DAYS Use the first two days as recommended above. On the third day, make the drive around the base of Haleakala to isolated and exquisitely beautiful Hana.

IF YOU HAVE FIVE DAYS OR MORE To the above itineraries, add a trip to Wailuku to go antique hunting; stop in Kihei for a swim at one of its excellent beaches; then drive on to see the magnificent pleasure palaces of Wailea and Makena, and maybe have a swim there too. If you can, plan to stay overnight at Hana. As time permits, break up your sightseeing with swimming, riding, tennis, hiking, snorkeling trips—Maui offers endless opportunities for the outdoor life.

HIKING ON MAUI

So you want to get off the beaten path, away from the tourist routine, and explore the backcountry, the mountains, the jungles, and waterfalls and rain forests, perhaps even trek into the crater of mighty Haleakala, on foot? The best way we know to do all this is to team up with an amazing gentleman named ✪ **Ken Schmitt,** a professional nature guide and much more. Schmitt has lived on Maui for 14 years, three of them in the open—sleeping under the stars, living on wild fruits and vegetables on the jungle paths. He is a scholar, an explorer, and an expert in the natural history and geology of Maui, and in the ancient legends and wisdom of Hawaii. He leads very small groups, or individuals, on a variety of 50 different hikes, which range from easy walks to arduous treks, and cost anywhere from $60 per person for a half-day tropical-valley hike to $100 for an excursion into Haleakala (children under 16 are charged $40–$65). Personalized trips concentrating on special interests can be arranged. We've had ecstatic reports on these hikes.

We asked Ken what he might suggest for our budget-conscious readers: "Take one or two of my day hikes to find out everything necessary to enjoy camping or backpacking on Maui. Then you can live for free, fishing and eating wild fruit, taro, and sweet potatoes. Of course, not everyone wants to live this way, but it can be done, and I will show you how. Each of my excursions is a workshop in natural history and environmental knowledge. In one day I can teach people as much as they could learn in weeks of research, including the following: locating safe and beautiful places to camp; selecting an itinerary appropriate to current weather conditions and personal interests and abilities; finding trailheads and following the trails; what fruit is in season and where to find it in the wilderness; where to rent equipment and what is needed; possible hazards in the environment and how to cope with them; how to get around without a car; where to buy inexpensive groceries, including farms that sell their own fresh fruit and vegetables. The emphasis of my programs is on enhancing our connection with our natural environment and teaching the skills that we need to feel comfortable in Hawaii."

Sounds great to us. You can contact Ken Schmitt in advance at **Hike Maui,** P.O. Box 330969, Kahului, HI 96733 (tel. 808/879-5270).

READERS RECOMMEND

Hiking on Maui. "*Maui has some 150-odd miles of coastline with some superb beaches. But if you're bored with sun and sand, try something different—say, a hike into Maui's backcountry, and enjoy some of the pristine beauty seldom seen by the average tourist. Pick up the book* Hiking Maui, *by Robert Smith (Wilderness Press); it's splendid reading. It also covers a large variety of hikes, complete with maps, difficulty ratings, where to obtain permission if needed, with a sensitive, no-nonsense approach to hiking. Our favorites: the Iao Stream (no. 16) or, for the more history minded, the King's Highway (no. 15) in La Perouse Bay.*"—J. A. Drouin, Edmonton, Alberta, Canada.

1. KAHULUI-WAILUKU & KIHEI-WAILEA

KAHULUI AREA

SIGHTS & ATTRACTIONS

Kahului is too new to have any historic sights, but it's considered a good example by city planners of what a model city should be. Kahului boasts the only deep-water harbor on Maui, a bulk-sugar-loading plant, the cannery of the Maui Pineapple Company, and the Hawaiian Commercial and Sugar Company, the driving force behind the town's development (most of the homes belong to plantation workers). Out near the airport, at the **Kanaha Pond Wildfowl Sanctuary,** you can see where migratory birds from the U.S. Northwest take their winter vacations. Birds can be viewed from the observation hut at the intersection of Hi. 36 and Hi. 396.

SAVVY SHOPPING

You can spend a pleasant hour or so browsing through Kahului's shopping centers.

KAAHUMANU SHOPPING CENTER A better name for Maui's biggest shopping complex, located at 275 Kaahumanu Ave., might be Ala Moana No. 2. Like its Honolulu counterpart, it has **Sears** at one end, Liberty House at the other, and that fascinating Japanese department store, Shirokiya, in between.

Most of the 50-odd stores here are geared to local residents, but there are a few places catering to gift buyers. Our favorite of these is **Maui's Best,** which features locally made crafts: handmade jewelry, potpourri oils and creams, koa-wood boxes, Christmas tree ornaments, great hand-painted T-shirts—all reasonably priced. They also have coffees, teas, and delicious Island Princess candies. Texas customers swear the macadamia-nut popcorn and macadamia-nut brittle is even better than the kind at Neiman-Marcus!

Check out the Penthouse at **Liberty House.** Like its Honolulu counterpart, it features closeout merchandise—clothing, shoes, linens, towels, and the like—from various Liberty House stores. You never know what great bargains you might find here.

The Coffee Store is always fun, with a large roaster and sacks of coffee up front, every kind of coffee and coffee accessories to buy, and a neat little coffee bar and café area, with tables and bakery selections in back: café mocha, cappuccino, filled croissants, bagels, quiches, and lasagne, for $2–$4.50. Among the attractive gift items here, huge Hawaiian quilted pot holders at $13.

You can get island prints by the yard, well priced, at **Sew Special,** which also has some wall hangings that would make neat gifts. Kids and hobbyists will enjoy **Kay-Bee Toys,** a very large shop with good values. **Hopaco,** a well-known stationery shop, has some interesting games. You might find some sake cups to take home with you, or charming Hakata dolls, at **Shirokiya,** which also has those wonderful sushi take-out lunches we told you about in the preceding chapter. In case you haven't sampled crackseeds yet, **Camellia Imports** is the place.

MAUI MALL It's also fun to visit the Maui Mall, located at 52 Kaahumanu Ave., a

FROMMER'S FAVORITE MAUI EXPERIENCES

Getting up Before the Sun Drive to Haleakala Crater to catch first light as the sun rises over Haleakala. Have hot coffee and a mango muffin at Sunrise Market and Protea Farm on the way down.

Sailing from Lahaina to Lanai Sail one of the sleek, multihulled yachts of Trilogy Excursions from Lahaina to Lanai, where you can go swimming and snorkeling.

Antique Hunting and Browsing Wander through the stores in Wailuku; then check out the books, crystals, jewelry, and the like at Miracles Unlimited.

Enjoying a Multimedia Spectacle Fly over an active volcano on the Big Island, scuba dive below the surface of the ocean on Maui, or swoop down into Kauai's Waimea Canyon—all vicariously at the Hawaii Experience Dome Theater in Lahaina.

Swimming and Snorkeling at Fleming Beach in West Maui Enjoy a perfect crescent of white sand and gentle surf—an ideal spot for the whole family.

Poking Through Paia's Shops and Arts-and-Crafts Galleries Have lunch at the Wunderbar, a local hangout, then watch windsurfers at nearby Hookipa Beach.

busy scene with its frequent sidewalk sales and free entertainment; check the local papers for announcements.

Look for the kiosk called **Crystal Dreams,** which has lots more than crystals. We spotted some chimes made of crystal, brass, and copper that start at about $8.75 and go up to about $50, and lots of lovely jewelry, including beige shell nerite leis, very rare, mostly from the South China Seas, for about $300.

Toys 'n' Joys is a fun store for the kids. **Allison's Place** features youngish sportswear. **JR's Music Shop** has some very good selections. **Long's Drugs** offers some of the best values for souvenirs and sundry items. And you can stock up on groceries at **Star Super Market,** where the locals shop; if you're going to be cooking in your kitchenette apartment, it pays to stop here after getting off the plane before driving on to the more expensive resort areas. You can pick up a T-shirt that reads JUST MAUIED at the **T-Shirt Factory.**

Roy's Photo Center probably has the most complete supply of camera accessories and films on Maui. **Sir Wilfred's Coffee, Tea, Tobacco Shop** has more than its name implies; in addition to a great selection of pipes, cigars, tobacco, and coffee beans, it also has gourmet gifts and gadgets, plus an espresso bar, a full bar, and a delightful menu of light foods at Sir Wilfred's Espresso Caffè. They always have tasteful handmade ceramic mugs, from about $8. Stop in at **Waldenbooks** if you've run out of reading material, and at **Maui Natural Foods** for anything and everything in the health-food line; it's the most complete store of its kind in the area.

DAIRY CENTER Our favorite store at Dairy Center, 395 Dairy Rd., is **Baby's Choice,** which features lovely children's clothing and maternity wear, including fashionable swim wear for mothers-to-be.

SWAP MEET Flea-market fans will have a good time here. Every Saturday morning from 6:30am to noon, vendors gather next to the post office on Puunene Street to sell everything from vegetables and flowers to new and used clothing, jewelry, beautiful baskets and sculptures, exotic items from all over the world. Always worth a stop. Check with your hotel desk to make sure it's on.

KAHULUI EVENING ENTERTAINMENT

Nightlife is limited in this area. Your best bet is in the big hotels. Check the shopping centers for free Polynesian shows, presented several times a week. Maui Mall, for one, sometimes presents top revues from Honolulu clubs—free.

EAST WEST DINING ROOM, 170 Kaahumanu Ave., in Maui Palms Hotel. Tel. 877-0071.

On Friday and Saturday from 8pm to midnight, you can dance to Top-40s rock and contemporary music here.

Admission: Free.

RED DRAGON ROOM, 170 Kaahumanu Ave., in Maui Beach Hotel. Tel. 877-0051.

The mood is more mod than Hawaiian; a DJ keeps the crowd happy on Friday and Saturday from 10pm to 2am.

Admission: Free.

LUIGI'S PASTA AND PIZZERIA, at Maui Mall, 355 Kamehameha Ave. Tel. 877-3761.

This busy family eatery is always a popular place at night. There's women's disco

MAUI SIGHTS & ATTRACTIONS

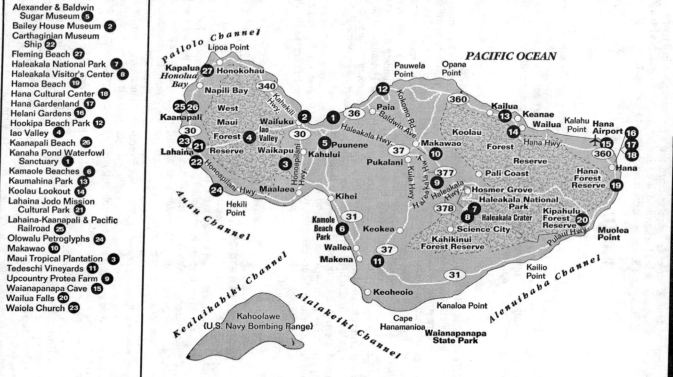

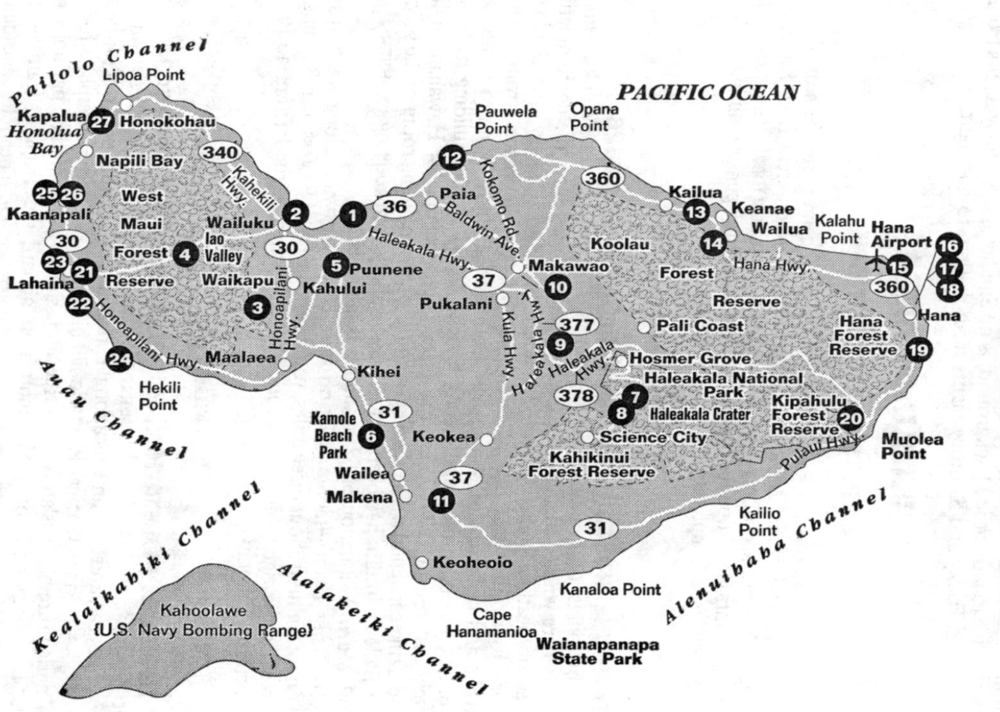

- Alexander & Baldwin Sugar Museum 5
- Bailey House Museum 2
- Carthaginian Museum Ship 22
- Fleming Beach 27
- Haleakala National Park 7
- Haleakala Visitor's Center 8
- Hamoa Beach 19
- Hana Cultural Center 18
- Hana Gardenland 17
- Helani Gardens 16
- Hookipa Beach Park 12
- Iao Valley 4
- Kaanapali Beach 26
- Kanaha Pond Waterfowl Sanctuary 1
- Kamaole Beaches 6
- Kaumahina Park 13
- Koolau Lookout 14
- Lahaina Jodo Mission Cultural Park 21
- Lahaina-Kaanapali & Pacific Railroad 25
- Olowalu Petroglyphs 24
- Makawao 10
- Maui Tropical Plantation 3
- Tedeschi Vineyards 11
- Upcountry Protea Farm 9
- Waianapanapa Cave 15
- Wailua Falls 20
- Waiola Church 23

dancing on Wednesday from 10pm to 1am, and on Thursday night disco dancing from 10pm to 1am. Karaoke (a Japanese craze that's becoming big in Hawaii—singing along live to a recorded background) is on Sunday and Monday nights from 9 to 11:30pm and Friday and Saturday nights from 9:30pm to midnight.

WAILUKU AREA

SIGHTS & ATTRACTIONS

Historic old Wailuku, the commercial and professional center and the seat of Maui County (which also includes Molokai and Lanai), is quite different from Kahului—even though it's right next door. It's a bit ramshackle, strictly local. It's great fun for browsing and antique shopping (see below), and for inexpensive dining at local "greasy spoons" (see Chapter 14).

Wailuku

BAILEY HOUSE MUSEUM, 2375-A Main St. Tel. 244-3326.

These buildings, on beautiful shaded grounds, once housed the Wailuku Female Seminary (where young females could be kept safely "away from the contaminating influences of heathen society") and the home of Edward Bailey, the seminary instructor. Today they are full of fascinating bits of Hawaiiana, from ancient petroglyphs and necklaces of human hair worn by the alii of Maui to missionary patchwork quilts and furnishings. Dating back to 1833–50, the building itself was completely restored in 1974–75, and is an excellent example of Hawaiian quality work and Yankee ingenuity. The smaller building, once the dining room of the school and later Bailey's studio, has been restored as a gallery with rotating exhibits.

Admission: A donation of $2 for adults is appreciated.

Open: Daily 10am–4:30pm. **Directions:** Drive westward along Kaahumanu Avenue out of Kahului about three miles; you'll pass the Maui Professional Building at High Street on the right, and then, about a block farther, to the left on Iao Road, you'll reach the museum.

Waikapu

MAUI TROPICAL PLANTATION, Hi. 30, Waikapu. Tel. 244-7643.

Not far from Wailuku, in the sugar-plantation village of Waikapu, you can sightsee, shop, eat, and have an educational experience—all under one roof (or better yet, one sky)—at Maui Tropical Plantation. This showplace and marketplace for the tropical agriculture of the islands offers free admission to its agricultural pavilions and exhibits, but charges $8 for a 45-minute tour aboard the Tropical Tram, which traverses some 50 acres planted in bananas, papayas, coffee, pineapple, macadamia nuts, sugarcane, and other crops. What we like best about this place is the Tropical Market, where a huge variety of made-on-Maui products, plantation-grown fresh fruit, and gift items are available. And a mailing service makes it easy to send gifts back home. Mailing service is also available at their Tropical Nursery, where you can get orchids, hibiscus, or anthuriums.

There are dining and entertainment possibilities here as well. The Tropical Restaurant offers a buffet luncheon and à la carte service for light meals. A Hawaiian Country Barbecue, complete with square dancing and a quick tram ride through the fields, takes place every Monday, Wednesday, and Friday at 5pm, featuring Buddy Fo and his Hawaiian Country Band. Dinner is an all-you-can-eat Hawaiian tropical feast. Cost is $48.90 for adults, $20.80 for children. Inquire about transportation available from Lahaina/Kaanapali and Kihei/Wailea for the Hawaiian Country Barbecue.

Admission: Plantation, free; Tropical Express tour, $8 adults, $3 children.

Open: Daily 9am–5pm. The Tropical Express tour leaves every 45 minutes, 9:15am–4pm.

Iao Valley

Drive down Hi. 30 in the direction of Iao Valley, and about two miles from Wailuku, on the right, you'll note a sign reading BLACK GORGE PRESIDENT KENNEDY PROFILE. The jagged mountain cliff ahead of you, which does bear a resemblance to JFK's profile, has been there for centuries, but not until relatively recently, of course, did people begin to notice its timely significance.

In another mile you'll come to Iao Valley, a wildly beautiful gorge dominated by the **Iao Needle,** 2,250 feet of green-covered lava rock reaching straight up into the sky. In this dramatic setting, Kamehameha won the battle that was to give him the island of Maui; the local warriors, accustomed to spears and javelins, were no match for Kamehameha's forces supplied with cannon by two English sailors. The carnage was so intense that the waters of Iao Stream were dammed up by the bodies of the conquered, giving the stream its present name: Kepaniwai, damming of the waters. Now all is tranquil here, save for the shouts of happy keikis wading through the pools at **Kepaniwai Park,** where present-day Mauians love to go for a picnic or a swim. Beautifully landscaped gardens with Asian pagodas, swimming, and wading pools provide a palatial playground in this crisp mountain valley.

Puunene

THE ALEXANDER & BALDWIN SUGAR MUSEUM, 3957 Hansen Rd., Puunene. Tel. 871-8058.

This former residence of superintendents of the mill (still in operation next door) has been transformed into a tasteful museum with artifacts dating back to 1878, absorbing photo murals, and authentic scale models, which include a working model of sugar-factory machinery. Educational for the kids, entertaining for grownups too. Be sure to visit the museum shop, with unique items relating to the sugar industry and plantation life, including contributions of the various ethnic groups who came to the islands to work the plantations.

Admission: $3 adults, $1.50 students 6–17, free for children under 6.

Open: Mon–Fri 9:30am–4:30pm. **Directions:** From Kahului, take Hi. 350 to Hi. 311 toward Kihei.

SAVVY SHOPPING

Shopping in Wailuku is offbeat. Shops are unpretentious, not a bit touristy. Antiques lovers will be in heaven at **Antique Row,** a cluster of shops and galleries on North Market Street offering one-of-a-kind items from around the globe as well as from times gone by. Start at **Traders of the Lost Art** where you might find owner Tye Hartall, unless he happens to be on one of his yearly journeys to New Guinea to collect ancestral carvings and primitive ritual art. His shop is reminiscent of a New Guinea spirit house, complete with split drums, crocodile tables, and a host of spirit masks and figures. An appointment may be necessary: Call 242-7753.

One of our favorite stops here is ✪ **Hula Moon,** 13 Market St., where several merchants have set up shop under one roof. Here you'll find bottles, paintings, Asian and African art, antique jewelry and colored glass, toys, dolls, china, antique aloha shirts, and more. Although some of the merchandise is new, most of it is old, like the sheet music, photographs, fans, books, part of a fascinating collection of Hawaiiana at Makani, Ltd.

Memory Lane, at 158 N. Market St., is where Joe Ransberger shows the unusual and one-of-a-kind items he's collected from all over the world. Joe specializes in American artists—originals, lithos, stone engravings, woodblock prints—and also has a good collection of Hawaiiana too. He has those "silky" aloha shirts, starting at about $15 and going as high as $350. **Alii Antiques,** 1608 N. Market St., is known for its fine collection of Asian art from the Ming and Ch'ing Dynasties, as well as items from Europe and the mainland. A recent browse turned up antique guns from the Civil War, Persian rugs, paintings by local artists.

More antique and offbeat emporiums are in store for this neighborhood, so if antiques are your thing, be sure to save some time for exploring this area.

MIRACLES UNLIMITED, 81 Central Ave. Tel. 242-7799.

This is where you go if you're into matters spiritual and esoteric. The quaint little white shop "under the rainbow" houses a nice collection of metaphysical books, tapes, crystals, cards, and such, and some very beautiful crystal-jewelry creations. They also show art-to-wear clothing by local craftspeople (from $30).

From here it's just a few doors away to **Alaya Unlimited,** 52 Central Ave., where you can get their free "Island Calendar of Events" to find out who's lecturing or giving a meditation workshop. (You can also call Suzie O at 244-7400 for this information, and to find out when the next "Ohana Luncheon," featuring noted New Age speakers, will be held.)

DOWN TO EARTH NATURAL FOODS, 1910 Vineyard St. Tel. 242-6821.

Now, if you need to stock up on certified organic produce, natural groceries, vitamins, herbs, and body-care products, this is the place to go. They also have homemade vegetarian food you can take with you.

ELAINE GIMA, 21 Market St. Tel. 242-1839.

Elaine Gima is undoubtedly Maui's—perhaps Hawaii's—foremost silk artist, and her extraordinary hand-painted garments have won major crafts awards. Now she's opened her own shop in Wailuku, and while her pricier creations may not be within reach, there are, surprisingly, many affordable things here: T-shirts, solid cotton and rayon knits, silk shells from $45, blouses, men's cotton aloha shirts from $45. Any of her men's silk ties with Hawaiian motifs or her fanciful scarves would make fine presents, at $20. Well worth a visit.

KIHEI-WAILEA AREA

If you're staying in Kahului, Kihei is a good nearby beach, about a 20-minute drive, via Hi. 350, and then Hi. 311 right to Kihei.

SIGHTS & ATTRACTIONS

Just past the end of Kihei, the road takes you into one of the most beautiful planned destination resorts in the islands. Should you like to see how the other half lives, by all means, visit some of the splendid, multi-million-dollar resorts here; they are examples of island indoor-outdoor architecture at its best. You definitely must make a stop at the **Grand Hyatt Wailea Resort,** the "Taj Mahal" of the Hyatts, newly opened to the tune of $800 million. Explore the spectacular grounds, note the Ferdinand Botero sculpture garden, stop in for a reasonably priced meal at Café Kula (spa cuisine with a special menu for children) or at the charming Bistro Molokini. Spa Grande at the Hyatt is equal to the best in Europe, and, surprisingly, many of their treatments are quite affordable. Then you'll want to visit the **Maui Inter-Continental Wailea Resort,** newly redone to make it more Hawaiian in feeling and more gracious than ever: Its Hula Moons Restaurant, decorated with artwork and poetry of Don Blanding, is a delight. **Stouffer Wailea Beach Resort,** an AAA Five-Diamond winner for more than nine years, has beautiful grounds, splendid artworks, the cute little Maui Onion for an inexpensive meal, Raffles and the Palm Court for superb

Sunday brunches. **Four Seasons Resort Wailea** is exquisite, like a never-ending flower garden indoors and out. Its Pacific Grill is a wonderful choice for a medium-priced meal. Stop by, have a drink or a meal at any of these places, stroll the beach (all beaches are public in Hawaii), and enjoy a taste of *la dolce vita,* Hawaii style.

Drive a little farther and you can explore the **Makena Resort Maui Prince Hotel,** very modern and elegantly understated. Two waterfalls run down into the central courtyard and lead to the Japanese rock garden. You may want to stop in at the Café Kiowai on the garden level for an exotic dessert and a cup of coffee. Better yet, come back on a Sunday morning for one of the most elaborate and exquisite Sunday brunches in Maui ($24).

SAVVY SHOPPING

While there's nothing remarkable about shopping in the Kihei-Wailea area, shopping malls are going up at a great rate, so you could easily spend an hour or two browsing, before—or after—the beach.

AZEKA PLACE Look for Azeka Place, a lively shopping center at 1280 S. Kihei Rd. (on the ocean side of the road), and browse a bit. **Rainbow Connection** is a tasteful boutique which, in addition to its many condo decorative items, has a unique jewelry collection: We admired the handmade, hand-painted porcelain jewelry, the earrings and necklaces made of Hawaiian volcanic glass, the brass shell items, and jewelry and hand-carved wooden mirrors from Bali. Browse through a good selection of books at **Silversword Bookstore;** pick up some beachware at **Leilani** or **Tropical Traders.**

You may want to stop in at **Vagabond,** where you can not only rent a surfboard, but also stock up on bags, tank shirts, and all kinds of necessities for the beachcomber's lifestyle. **Wow! Swimwear** has something for "everybody." **Maui Dive Shop** can outfit you for scuba or snorkeling and take you on a tour. **O'Rourke's Tourist Trap** is a good place to get any necessities you forgot to pack, as well as postcards, monkeypod souvenirs, and the like. Look to **Liberty House** for its usual excellent selections. There are plenty of bathing suits and beach fashions at **Maui Clothing Company.** And **Little Polynesians** is great for kids' stuff.

International House of Pancakes and **Luigi's Pasta & Pizzeria** are old favorites here.

WAILEA SHOPPING VILLAGE This place at the Wailea Resort is always worth a stop. Many artistic and cultural events are held here, free, and the shops are of high quality. Yes, there sometimes is a herd of elephants at **Elephant Walk.** Last time we were there, the cute creatures were made of clay and priced from about $42 up. **Maui's Best,** which we told you about (above) at Kaahumanu Center in Kahului, has a location here, with a more extensive clothing collection (beautiful, but expensive). Other tasteful shops here include **Alexia Natural Fashions** (natural-fabric clothing from Greece, for women), and **Sea and Shell,** which has nicer-than-usual island gifts, with a good selection of wind chimes. Stop by on a Tuesday at 1:30pm and catch a free Polynesian show.

MARKETS If you're in Kihei on a Wednesday, Friday, or Saturday morning, visit the **Kihei Open Air Marketplace,** an enjoyable flea market held at 1945 S. Kihei Rd., next to McDonald's, from 8am to 3pm. You can find everything here from T-shirts to works by local artisans, all at great prices. We saw some beautiful hand-painted blouses here for $17; the next day, we spotted them in a gift shop for $25!

Pick up some Molokai watermelon, Hana sweet corn, or other locally grown produce at the **Maui Farmer's Market,** on Tuesday and Friday from 2 to 5:30pm on the grounds of the Suda store. Cheeses, juices, and freshly baked breads are also available. (The farmer's market moves to Honokawai, in West Maui, on Monday and Thursday from 7:30am to 1:30pm.)

SPORTS & RECREATION

SWIMMING Ready to call it a day and relax on the beach? This area has some of Maui's best swimming spots. ✪ **Kamaole Beaches I, II, and III** are fine, but the beach is public everywhere, and you can swim wherever you like. Look for the public-access sign pointing to **Ulua/Mokapu Beaches** near the Stouffer Wailea Beach Resort, park your car (there's a small paved area), and head for a lovely stretch of sand and ocean, with public rest rooms and showers. Past Wailea you come to **Makena** and **Big Beach,** one of the prettiest beaches on Maui and a great favorite with the locals. Swimming and bodysurfing are excellent here.

WHALE WATCHING From mid-December until the end of April, some 800 celebrities arrive at Maui, and everybody wants to see them. It's estimated that approximately 800 North Pacific humpback whales migrate 3,000 miles from their home in Alaska to mate and bear their young in the warm waters of Hawaii. You can probably spot a few whales from the beach or your lanai, but it's also fun to take one of the **whale-watching excursion boats** that leave daily from Maui harbors.

All the cruises are good, but we like to support the ones run by the **Pacific Whale Foundation.** When you travel with them, you're in the company of expert research scientists, and proceeds benefit the foundation's research and conservation efforts to save the endangered humpback whale. Cruises depart daily from Maalaea and Lahaina harbors, last 2½ hours, guarantee whales (or go again for free), and cost $27.50 for adults, $15 for children 3–12. Be sure to bring your camera for some spectacular shots.

Call the **Whale Hotline** (tel. 879-8811, or toll free 800-942-5311 from the mainland).

READERS RECOMMEND

Snorkeling at La Perouse Bay. *"We have our own snorkeling equipment and enjoy seeking the less-crowded spots. If you drive on the road that goes past Kihei and Wailea, south of Wailea the road continues to Makena. At the end of the road is a massive lava flow that forms La Perouse Bay, which is now an official sanctuary for over 90 species of exotic reef fish. We were the only ones snorkeling there. A word of caution: It's quite rocky, so be sure to wear something on your feet."*—Mr. and Mrs. Dennis W. Randall, Seattle, Wash.

EVENING ENTERTAINMENT

Luaus

There are several luaus to choose from in this area, but check local listings when you arrive; prices, days, and entertainers change frequently.

Maui's Merriest Luau (tel. 879-1922 for reservations) takes place on Tuesday and Thursday evenings at 5pm at the oceanfront Luau Gardens at the Maui Inter-Continental Wailea Resort. A lavish buffet meal precedes the colorful Polynesian Revue featuring Paradyse and Ka Poe O Hawaii. Adults pay $45; children $22.

If you can't make the luau, do the next best thing: Attend the ✪ **Aloha Mele Luncheon** (tel. 879-1922 for reservations), held every Friday between 10:30am and 2pm at the same hotel. One of Maui's most-loved performers, Jesse Nakooka (who has hosted his own luau in the past), presents a two-hour celebration of aloha, filled with songs, stories, and hulas. Guests can choose either a continental selection, a sumptuous salad, or a typical Hawaiian plate with luau foods. Cost is $16.50 per person. On Friday evenings, the same Maui Inter-Continental Wailea Resort presents live Hawaiian entertainment poolside at the Hula Terrace from 5 to 8pm. Complimentary pupus come along with the cost of your drinks.

If it's a Monday or Thursday, it must be the luau at the **Stouffer Wailea Beach Resort** (tel. 874-4900 for reservations), a traditional Hawaiian party held in a beachfront garden setting and featuring "Memories of the Pacific." Luau time is 6pm. Adults pay $42; children under 12, $26.

Dancing and Listening

INU INU LOUNGE, in the Maui Inter-Continental Wailea, 3700 Wailea Alaniu. Tel. 879-1922.

The *Maui News* has called this "one of Maui's best places for dancing and listening to music." And so it is. On Sunday and Monday nights, disco starts at 9pm. You can have cocktails at sunset time, then dance to live music Tuesday through Saturday nights from 8pm to about 1:30am.

Admission: Free, except Fri–Sat and special hols.

Free Polynesian Show

MAUI PRINCE HOTEL, 5400 Makena Alaniu. Tel. 847-1111.

Remember this one for Friday nights from 6:30 to 8pm. That's when musicians Tarvin Makia and Alla Villaren sing Hawaiian songs and three hula dancers perform. The show is held in the central courtyard of the hotel.

Admission: Free.

2. HALEAKALA, HOUSE OF THE SUN

Any schoolchild on Maui can tell you the story of the demigod Maui, the good-natured Polynesian Prometheus who gave human beings fire, lifted the Hawaiian Islands out of the sea on his fishhook, and trapped the sun in its lair until it agreed to move more slowly around the earth—so that his mother could have more time to dry her tapa before night came! And where did this last, most splendid achievement take place? Why, right at Haleakala, 10,023 feet up in the sky, just about the closest any Stone Age person—or god—ever got to the sun.

With or without benefit of legends, Haleakala is an awesome place. It's the world's largest dormant volcano (its last eruption occurred two centuries ago), whose 33-mile-long, 24-mile-wide, 10,000-foot-high dimensions make Vesuvius seem like a mud puddle. Even more spectacular is the size of the volcano's crater: 7½ miles long, 2½ miles wide, big enough to swallow a modern metropolis or two within its moonlike desert. Haleakala is one of the great scenic wonders of Hawaii.

EXCURSION TO THE SUMMIT

Plan on at least three hours for the Haleakala excursion (37 miles from the airport each way) and bring a warm sweater or jacket with you (it gets surprisingly cold and windy almost two miles up). Note that anyone with a cardiac condition is advised not to make this trip because of the stress of the high altitude. We feel it's best to get an early start on this trip, since there's less likelihood of clouds early in the day. You might call the park headquarters (tel. 572-7749) to check on cloud, road, and weather conditions before you start out.

There's no place to eat once you enter **Haleakala National Park,** but you might pack a picnic lunch and stop at **Hosmer's Grove** on the lower slopes. You can get sandwiches at **Subway,** in the Pukalani Terrace Shopping Center, in Pukalani, about halfway between Kahului and the park. You might also stop off at the **Pukalani**

Superette, a real upcountry store, where you can get mangoes for about half of what they cost in town, plus delicious homemade sushi and lumpia, and local Japanese and Filipino delicacies.

The drive starts in Kahului on Hi. 32; head eastward to the Haleakala Highway (Hi. 36), and turn right. Shortly after Hi. 36 swings left, it's intersected on the right by Hi. 37, which takes you to Hi. 377, the Upper Kula Road, where you head up into a cool forest of flowers, cactus, and eucalyptus.

Now watch for the turnoff to Hi. 378 to the left, Haleakala Crater Road, a serpentine two-lane highway curving through the clouds. You'll see cattle and horses on the pasturelands of Haleakala Ranch as you climb the slopes of the volcano. At 6,700 feet, you reach the entrance to Haleakala National Park. You'll then see Hosmer's Grove on the left, a scenic place to picnic (or camp) among rare trees and plants. Temperate tree seedlings from around the world have been planted here, along a half-mile trail of native shrubs and trees that are home for a variety of birds; you may see a pueo (short-eared owl) or a ring-necked pheasant. Stop at **park headquarters** a mile ahead at 7,030 feet, where the friendly and knowledgeable rangers will give you maps, instructions, directions for hiking the trails, and camping permits. Admission to the park is $3 per car and $1 per bicycle. Senior citizens admitted free. The choicest way to see Haleakala is to go into the crater on foot or horseback, but you must check with the rangers before you do.

Now you're ready for the ascent on this South Seas Everest, to the **Haleakala Observatory Visitors Center,** almost two miles up, on the edge of the crater. Inside the octagonal observatory, you learn that the early Hawaiians used the crater as a highway across eastern Maui, camping in its caves and building rock shelters. The last eruption in the crater was prehistoric, although there was an eruption on the flanks of Haleakala just 200 years ago, and very likely the volcano will erupt again; it is *dormant,* not extinct. But the most thrilling show is what lies beyond the glass: a dark kaleidoscope of clouds and colors and light played against what might well be the deserts of the moon. On a clear day you can see over 100 miles to the horizon, your field of vision encompassing 30,000 square miles of the Pacific; from this altitude, the volcano's vast cones look like so many sand dunes. Their rustlike colors change as the day grows old. At sunrise the crater is in shadow; it seems to give birth to the sun. From midday to sunset the play of sun and shadow is more subtle, and sunset, according to some, is the most muted and lovely of all. One of the easiest ways to get a spirited debate going among Mauians is to ask whether sunset or sunrise is more superlative at Haleakala; suffice it to say that both are considered among the great natural sights of the world.

The summit of Haleakala is half a mile beyond, at **Red Hill,** atop a cinder cone 10,023 feet high. Nearby, there's a satellite-tracking station and a **Science City** complex (the clear air here in mid-Pacific permits research that could be done nowhere else), which you reach via the Skyline Drive.

On the way down from Haleakala, you should stop for some different—and spectacular—views of the crater at Kalahaku and Leleiwi lookouts. At **Kalahaku Lookout,** you view the vast crater on one side; on the other you'll spot western Maui and your first silverswords (unless you've seen some on the Big Island). The silversword is a botanical rarity, a plant that will grow only on lava rock, at the highest altitudes. These curious, oversize cousins of the sunflower have swordlike leaves, and when they're ready to blossom (between June and October) they shoot up a stalk the size of a man. The whole thing turns into a tower of pink and lavender flowers, blooms once, and dies, scattering its seeds into the cinders to begin the phenomenon all over again. At the next lookout, **Leleiwi Lookout,** you may, with great luck, get to see the rather spooky specter of the Brocken; the sun must be strong at your back with misty clouds overhead in order for you to see your own shadow in the rainbow-mist of the crater. It doesn't happen often, but when it does, it's unforgettable; a ranger told us that he has seen it many times, and with as many as seven rainbows!

Coming down from the heights of Haleakala, it's pleasant to stop on the lower slopes at **Sunrise Market and Protea Farm,** near the beginning of Crater Road. You can have a free sample of Maui pineapple, buy some sandwiches, homemade fudge, or local fruits, and get a cup of coffee and a muffin (maybe mango or banana or walnut) to go with it. If you like, take your picnic lunch out to the tables surrounding the protea fields outside. Sunrise Market has just about the best prices around on pineapples to carry home, plus a variety of gift items. As for the protea farm part of the operation, this is a good chance to walk around and see protea growing in their natural habitat (several protea farms dot these Maui uplands; protea are becoming a big commercial crop). Their protea gift shop displays fresh protea bouquets, as well as dried arrangements, and crafts, which can be shipped home.

READERS RECOMMEND

Seeing Haleakala. *"We thoroughly enjoyed Haleakala. It is fantastic. However, for those who want to stop at the various lookouts, particularly the area near the silversword plants, be sure to have some insect repellent. We were pestered by some of the meanest flies we have ever seen. They love faces and bare legs."*—Don and Nancy Gossard, Bellevue, Wash. [*Authors' Note:* In the tropics, mosquitoes come (and thankfully, go), depending on seasons and changing climatic conditions. Our advice: Always have your insect repellent handy in country areas.]

"It's becoming very popular to get up early to catch sunrise on Haleakala. The total experience of leaving the hotel at about 3am, driving up the mountain in pitch blackness, meeting other people with the same crazy idea, then slowly waiting for the sun to rise over the crater is absolutely breathtaking. At that hour, however, a sweater, jacket, and blanket may suffice for only some. It was cold! Bring breakfast/lunch and enjoy amid other sun/nature worshipers or on your own."—Francine Schept, White Plains, N.Y.

"On the early-morning drive to Haleakala Crater for sunrise it took me an hour and 10 minutes from Kahului, and I am a cautious driver. It was freezing at the visitors center—about 45° in late August—so I would suggest gloves, especially for photographers; my 'shutter finger' was stiff from the cold! First light—30–40 minutes before sunrise—is as lovely as the sunrise and should not be missed. On the way down, I was the only person to stop at Leleiwi Lookout, sharing it with a park ranger for two hours; I think the view from the lookout is superior to the one at the visitors center."—Martha F. Battenfeld, Brighton, Mass.

CAMPING

Strong hikers, take note: You can spend a magnificent two or three days in Haleakala for spectacularly low prices. At Haleakala National Park there are three primitive cabins, each sleeping 12, for overnight lodging. The cabins have wood-burning stoves and cooking and eating utensils. All you need bring is food, water, a sleeping bag, and matches! The three form a sort of triangle in the crater, and you can go from one to the other on your explorations. **Kapalaoa Cabin** is at the middle of the southern end of the crater, **Paliku Cabin** is northeast of Kapalaoa at the eastern tip, and **Holua Cabin** is northwest of Paliku across at the western tip of the crater. Write to the Superintendent, Haleakala National Park, P.O. Box 369, Makawao, Maui, HI 96768, to make reservations for use of the cabins. Give the details of your proposed trip, the number in your party, dates of the stay, and names of the specific cabins you wish to use each night. The price is minimal: $9 per person per night, $6.50 for children 12 and under, with a minimum of $15 per night, plus a $15 key deposit, plus the $3 entrance fee to the national park. There is an additional charge of $3 per person per night for firewood. Cabins may be occupied for no more than three consecutive nights, with a maximum of two nights' stay in any one cabin. So popular are these cabins that assignments for each month are chosen by lottery 60 days prior to the beginning of the month. In other words, if you want a reservation sometime in the month of July, be sure your request is received before May 1.

We should note that these cabins—and these trails—are for experienced hikers in good physical condition: The Park Service warns that "wilderness travel is arduous; the elevation and exertion required to return from the crater floor place excessive physical demands upon the body. Pits, cliffs, caves, and associated sharp rocks are dangerous."

RIDING & BIKING

If you'd like to ride down into the crater, get in touch with the people at **Pony Express Tours,** P.O. Box 535, Kula, Maui, HI 96790 (tel. 808/667-2200), who offer half-day rides down to the crater floor and back up, lunch included, at $110 per person. A full-day ride explores the crater floor extensively, and costs $123 per person. Gentler one- and two-hour rides are also offered at Haleakala Ranch, on the beautiful lower slopes of the mountain, for $30 and $50. For all trips, you must wear long pants and closed-toe shoes. All levels of riding experience are accommodated, with well-trained horses and experienced guides. You must be at least 10 years of age and weigh no more than 230 pounds. Pony Express Tours can also be reached through any of the Activity Desks in Lahaina and Kaanapali.

Did you know that you can coast downhill on a bicycle, all the way from the 10,000-foot summit of Haleakala to sea level below? You must be a skilled rider and in good physical condition, and it helps if your nerves are in good shape. Several outfits offer these tours: Our local correspondent, who lived to tell the tale, claims that **Cruiser Bob's Haleakala Downhill** (tel. 667-7717 for reservations) offers the best experience. They have both sunrise and day trips. Riders of all ages are welcomed, but there is a five-foot-minimum height requirement. The price is approximately $100 and may vary slightly from season to season. A neat family adventure.

Cruiser Bob also offers complete Maui nonmotoring travel packages, which include two-day Hana Coaster camping trips. Call toll free 800/654-7717 for details.

READERS RECOMMEND

Biking Down Haleakala. *"I went biking down Haleakala in late November, the rainy season, and felt it was more a survival trip than a fun thing to do. Check on the weather first before booking. It rained the whole way down and the leader tried to make it fun, even though everyone was very cold and soaked to the bone."*—Jim and Deb Phillips, Hastings, Neb.

MAKAWAO

On your way back down from Haleakala, it's easy to visit Makawao, Maui's very own cowboy town, the scene every Fourth of July of the famed Makawao Rodeo. Turn right at Pukalani and continue for just a few miles and you'll find yourself on the main street, whose clapboard storefronts make it look like something out of the Old West.

WHERE TO EAT

This is a good place to stop off for a snack: Local people swear by the fried doughnuts on a stick at **Komoda's General Store**—as well as by their great macadamia-nut cookies and cream puffs. **Kitada's Kau Kau Korner** is known for the best saimin upcountry; many of the local people come here for home-cooked meals. **Casanova Italian Restaurant and Deli** (see "Where to Eat," in Chapter 14) is right here on Makawao Avenue. The **Courtyard Deli** is a charming little place at 3620 Baldwin Ave., with just a few marble-top tables, at which you might enjoy an imaginative sandwich or salad (several vegetarian choices) or a coffee from the espresso bar, accompanied by wonderful, ever-changing desserts—like maple-bread pudding with vanilla sauce. You could pick up some sandwiches or California sushi at the **Rodeo General Store,** or have dinner at the **Makawao Steak House** at 3612 Baldwin Ave., which has long been popular in these parts.

SAVVY SHOPPING

As a sophisticated, upscale group moves into Makawao and other upcountry towns, the local shops are changing too, with blacksmith shops and barbershops and pool halls giving way to trendy boutiques and art galleries. Baldwin Avenue offers many enjoyable examples. Examine the fashionable women's clothing, leather goods, and jewelry collection at **Maui Moorea and Legends;** check out the hand-painted handbags, hats, and silk-screened T-shirts by noted island artists at **Gecko Trading Company;** browse through Hawaiian crafts, vintage aloha shirts, plus more antiques and collectibles at **Coconut Classics.** Stop in to see the handsome clothing, gift items, and jewelry at **Collections,** and the attractive women's wear at **Holiday & Co.**

The restored Makawao Theater Building is worth a stop for three reasons. The first is **Viewpoints Gallery** in the rear, Maui's only fine-arts cooperative, showing the works of 30 Maui artists in a variety of media. In the front of the building is **Goodies,** which sells snazzy dresses, jewelry, crystals, pretty T-shirts, and lots more; and across from that is **Upcountry Legends,** which also has clothing, jewelry, and the like, as well as locally made Hawaiian quilt pillows and other lovely handcrafts. The **Courtyard Deli** (see above) makes a fourth reason.

If you've got the kids with you, they can sit and read while you shop at **Maui Child.** The **Rabbit Hole** is a charming children's bookstore. Across from Casanova's you'll find **Miracle Bookery, Too,** an encore of the popular New Age bookstore in Wailuku. And if you're into health foods, **Down to Earth** is the place to stock up.

Art lovers should also make a stop at **Hui No'eau Visual Arts Center** at 2841 Baldwin Ave. You may be able to see a class in progress and visit the current exhibition of fine art. Open Tuesday through Sunday.

EVENING ENTERTAINMENT

CASANOVA ITALIAN RESTAURANT, 1188 Makawao Ave. Tel. 572-4978.

Maui's cowboy town, Makawao, suddenly became an entertainment venue when Casanova opened a few years ago. Now they consistently bring in big talents—performers like jazz greats Mose Allison and Jon Hendricks, rock-and-roll artists Mick Taylor and Billy Preston, zydeco musician C. J. Chenier and his Red Hot Louisiana Band, to name just a few. On Wednesday and Thursday it's disco dancing with a live DJ from 10pm to 1am. And there's music to dine by most nights.

Admission: Usually $12–$20 for name entertainment, $5 on disco nights.

A STOP AT PAIA

Unless you're planning to stop at Paia on the way to Hana (see "Road to Hana," below), we recommend that you do so now. Instead of taking the road back to Pukalani, just take Baldwin Avenue a few miles into Paia, where you can shop for gifts and antiques and hobnob with the local people before heading back home.

UNUSUAL SIDE TRIP

An unusual side trip you might want to take on your way back from an early trip to Haleakala is to the **Tedeschi Vineyards,** on Hi. 37 in beautiful upcountry Maui at the Ulupalakua Ranch. It's about 10 miles—via winding mountain roads—from the town of Kula. Hawaii's only winery, Tedeschi cultivates 22 acres of grapes on the slopes of Haleakala to produce two champagnes, a blush, and a red table wine in the beaujolais nouveau tradition. It also produces a pleasant light, dry pineapple wine. You're welcome to take a free guided tour daily, from 9:30am to 2:30pm, to observe various phases of the bottling operation. After the tour, stop in at the tasting room in one of the early 18th-century buildings, sample the wines, perhaps purchase some. If you've brought your picnic lunch, there are tables outside the tasting room, amid beautiful scenery and spectacular views.

3. ROAD TO HANA

Some 10,000 feet down from the moon canyons of Haleakala, curving around the base of the old volcano, is a world light-years away, a place of such tropical lushness and splendor that it conjures up the word "primeval." This is remote Hana and the curving road leading to it—a road carved under the fringe of the lava cliffs, plunging down on one side to the sea, emerging on the other from overhanging jungle watered by the thousand streams of Haleakala.

In all of Hana, there are just a few dozen modestly priced accommodations. (The town's chief industry is the exquisite Hana Kai–Maui Resort, which caters to wealthy travelers only.) If you can reserve one of these (see "Where to Stay," in Chapter 14), it would be worth your while to stay overnight; otherwise, you'll have to do Hana in a one-day trip. Count on two to three hours each way, more if you want to savor the magnificent scenery. And be sure to check with the Highway Department about road conditions before you take off. If the weather has been wet, you could get stuck in landslides or mud. If it's raining heavily, forget the Hana trip altogether. Parts of the road are easily washed away, and it may take hours for you to be rescued (which happened one year to friends of ours). There's always tomorrow, or the next visit to Maui.

Even though extensive highway repaving has made it much easier to drive the Hana road, it is still rugged and winding. There are plenty who love it as well as some who think that, despite the glory of the scenery, it's just not worth the effort. A picnic lunch is essential, unless you want to eat at the expensive Hana-Maui or one of the little snack shops on the road or in Hana. Besides, you'll be traveling through the kind of country for which picnics surely were originally invented.

Hana glories in its remoteness. Rumor has it that a road is not being built because the local people like to keep Hana the way it is—difficult to get to. The current road was not completed until 1927, and by that time the Hasegawa General Store had already been in business 15 years and a hotel was already operating there. Hana's lush isolation attracted the late aviator and environmentalist Charles Lindbergh, who spent his vacations in Hana and is now buried there (the Lindbergh family has requested that his gravesite be kept private).

Because of its remoteness, Hana has been slow in accepting change. Throughout its history it has assimilated new cultures, new religions, and new institutions, but Hana has not become part of them; rather, they have become a part of Hana.

READERS RECOMMEND

Hana Cassette Guide (tel. 572-0550). *"On Maui we found a service that I would recommend highly to anybody planning to take the road to Hana.* Hana Cassette Guide *is available for $20 from Craig at the Shell Service Station on County Road 380, before Hi. 36. Craig is a local photographer who narrates the tape himself, and he's a joy to listen to. He is well versed in local lore, legends, and facts about the 54 bridges, the uncountable waterfalls, and the scenic views. We took the tape player out of the car whenever we stopped and the people around were interested in hearing the comments. Also included is a picture book of the* *wildflowers and a souvenir map. We consider this our 'Best Buy' on our trip to Maui."*—Dennis N. Benson, Uniontown, Ohio. [*Author's Note:* Craig also has a cassette tour of Haleakala, which we sampled on our last visit and found excellent. Scott Golladay of Best of Maui Cassette Tours, 333 Dairy Rd., Kahului (tel. 871-1555), also offers entertaining tours to Hana and Haleakala. Included in the cost of $25 is a free T-shirt, either I SURVIVED MAUI'S HANA HIGHWAY or HALEAKALA HOUSE OF THE SUN. They go out of their way to help visitors, and provide discount coupons for picnic lunches. Look for the bright-yellow awning on the left, just before the Union 76 station, on the way to the airport.]

Akamai Tours, *532 Keolani Place (tel. 871-9551). "We found we saved $5 each by dealing direct with Akamai Tours in Kahului for our trip to Hana. We saved $15 by driving to their office, then another $5 for arranging our trip direct with them rather than through an agent. We agree that it was much better to take this tour than to drive ourselves, and all the passengers felt the same way. Also, our driver took us all the way through to Hana and back to Kahului without turning back, while our rental car would have had to return the same way. It was his interesting facts about the flora and fauna that made the trip really worthwhile. We saw peacocks, bird's nests, etc., some of which we would have missed had it not been for him."*—Elizabeth Lundh, North Vancouver, British Columbia, Canada.

A Reader's Warning. *"I'd like to pass on some information I learned the hard way. I mentioned to a clerk in a market that I was planning to drive to Hana the next day. He said, 'If it's raining when you get halfway, turn back, or you can get stuck out there.' I assumed he was being overly cautious. It sprinkled off and on as we drove to Hana, but it's a long trip and we didn't want to waste our day. The sun was shining as we visited the Seven Sacred Pools, and water rushed from the very top pool to the ocean. On our way back, cloudy but no rain, we were stopped in a line of about 30 cars, trapped by a landslide on a narrow, cliff-hugging road. Rescue crews had been called, but it took two hours with men, shovels, and a bulldozer to clear the road so we could get by. It could have been a tragedy, and we learned to take seriously what the Hawaiians say. They know best!"*—Mrs. Donald B. Newton, Saratoga, Calif.

FIRST STOP: PAIA

Start eastward on Hi. 32 in Kahului or Wailuku and switch (right) to Hi. 36. You may want to stop at **Pic-nics** on Baldwin Avenue in Paia to pick up a picnic lunch (see "Where to Eat," Chapter 14).

SAVVY SHOPPING

Take some time now, or on the return trip, to browse in some of the antiques, decorator, and gift shops that have sprung up in this unspoiled, upcountry community. The nice thing about shopping in Paia is that it's a local, not a tourist, area. Rents are not as high as in Lahaina or Kihei, so shopkeepers can afford to sell lovely things at good prices.

Be sure to visit the ✪ **Maui Crafts Guild,** at 43 Hana Hwy., a cooperative gallery showing outstanding work by local craftspeople. The two-story gallery carries a variety of crafts, ranging from bamboo (directly from the bamboo groves of Maui) to wooden bowls and boxes, jewelry, quilting designs, ceramics, woodblock, and lithographic prints to hand-painted clothing designs on silk and cotton. Prices are practically wholesale: artist/members, who run the business themselves and wait on visitors, take only a 10% markup. Prices can go way up for some of the furniture, wall sculptures, and stained glass, but there are many items at small prices too: We recently spotted printed tablecloths at $22, Raku pottery at $22, and lauhala ornaments at $9. Look for some of the handsome ceramic ware by Dot's Pots.

One of the nicest of the local shops is **Tropical Emporium,** at 104 Hana Hwy., where Veronica Popejoy specializes in natural fabrics (cottons, silks, rayons), and will coordinate a "look" for you that will work back home too. Another popular shop in this little cluster (they're all on either side of, or across the road from, the Wunderbar Restaurant on Hana Highway) is **Jaggers,** 100 Hana Hwy., where you'll find a neat collection of men's shirts and ladies' fashions, lots of accessories to choose from, and a friendly staff.

Nuage Bleu has high-style women's wear and accessories, as well as a line of aroma-therapy oils. We like the adorable kiddy clothes—especially the slippers with animal faces for $10—at **Just You and Me, Kid.** Posters, pottery, and locally woven baskets of natural fibers are among the varied wares at **Paia Gallery and Gifts. Summerhouse,** 83 Hana Hwy., is an old favorite here. Their specialties are casual island wear in natural fibers, Asian imports, and a swimsuit collection extraordinaire.

Around the corner from these shops at 12 Baldwin Ave. is **The Clothes Addict,** a spot that has been sought out by such customers as Billy Joel, Cindy Lauper, and Ringo Starr for its collection of vintage rayon and silk aloha shirts. This is one of the major sources for these shirts in Hawaii: The collection, from the '30s, '40s, and '50s, comes from Canada, the mainland, and Japan. If you can't afford the prices ($50–$500), just browse and have a look at some of their other fashionable sportswear. Then cross the street and check **Studio 27** at 27 Baldwin Ave., where Wes and Sue Redpath show some wonderful women's clothing, designed by Sue in Maui and made up in Bali; you might luck onto a fantastic sale here as we recently did. Note, too, the Kii Lii petroglyph earrings made of pewter, $18, an unusual remembrance of Hawaii. **Yoki's Boutique,** at 21 Baldwin Ave., has exotic clothing, jewelry, fashion items, and sensual lingerie. And **North Shore Silks and Body Shop** shows outstanding hand-painted women's clothing, plus lingerie, massage oils, and lotion; they will custom-scent anything you want. We noted a large decorative fan from Bali, hand-screened and hand-painted, a real find at $25.

SIGHTS & ATTRACTIONS

Before you get back on the road to Hana, you might want to make a short detour in Paia to **Hookipa County Beach Park,** otherwise known as the "Windsurfing Capital of the World." Windsurfing, or sailboarding, as it is also known, is an enormously popular sport, and nowhere are conditions better for it than right here on the northern shore of Maui. It's fun to watch the windsurfers anytime, and if there happens to be a competition going on (make local inquiries), you're in for a special treat. The park is right on the road. Get out your cameras—the views are incredible.

BACK ON THE ROAD

Now it's back on the road to Hana. The highway runs straight and easy, through cane fields, until you get to Pauwela. Here's where the road becomes an Amalfi Drive of the Pacific; the view is spectacular, but keep your eye on the curves. The variety of vegetation is enough to drive a botanist—or photographer—wild. Waterfalls, pools, green gulches beckon at every turn. You'll be tempted to stop and explore a hundred times, but keep going, at least until you get to **Kaumahina Park,** where you might consider picnicking high on the cliff, looking down at the black sand beach of Honomanu Bay below, watching the local folk fish and swim.

Believe it or not, from here on the scenery gets even better. From the road, you can look down on the wet taro patches and the peaceful villages of **Keanae** and **Wailua,** to which a short side trip, to see the old Catholic church built of lava rock and cemented with coral, is eminently worthwhile. It seems that this coral was strewn ashore after an unusual storm in the 1860s, providing the villagers with the necessary material to construct their church. To commemorate this miracle, they constructed the **Miracle of Fatima Shrine,** which you will see on the Wailua Bay Road, at the 18-mile marker (turn left at the road sign).

In a little while, you get another vista of Keanae from **Koolau Lookout.** In the other direction you look through a gap in the cliff over into Haleakala. A little farther on is **Puaa Kaa Park,** another made-in-heaven picnic spot. The flowers are gorgeous here, and so are the two natural pools, each with its own waterfall. You might have a swim here before you continue.

On you go, past grazing lands and tiny villages, to **Waianapanapa Cave,** another possible side excursion. This lava tube filled with water is the place where a jealous Stone Age Othello was said to have slain his Desdemona. Every April the water is supposed to turn blood-red in remembrance. Near the cave is a black sand beach (not always safe for swimming), another great place for a picnic.

Just before reaching Hana, you arrive at **Helani Gardens,** a 17-acre tropical botanical garden, through which you may take a self-guided tour. They also have rest rooms and a picnic area. Admission is $2 for adults, $1 for children 6–16.

Another wonderful garden awaits you when you enter Hana. ✪ **Hana Gardenland,** at the corner of Kalo and Hana Road, has five acres of splendid botanical gardens, plus a gallery, plants, gifts, and Hawaiian crafts for sale. By the time you read this, there might be a delightful café in operation, with fresh salads, sandwiches, smoothies, many kinds of coffees, and herbal teas. Rest rooms available. Admission free. (*Note:* The same people who run Hana Plantation Houses, described in Chapter 14, are the new owners, bringing their imagination and flair to this place.)

HANA

Not a little history was made at Hana. The Big Three—Captain Cook, the Protestant missionaries, and vacationing Hawaiian royalty—were all here. You can even follow the road to a historic Stone Age delivery room near the cinder cone of **Kauiki Head,** where Kamehameha's favorite wife, Kaahaumana, was born (there's a plaque near the lighthouse). Or you can just walk around the town for a while and soak up the atmosphere. A must on your list of sights should be the **Hasagawa General Store** where, it is reported, you can get anything and everything your heart desires (just like at Alice's Restaurant) in one place. (The old Hasagawa's burned down, but a new store has been constructed at the Old Hana Theater, on Hana Road, opposite the Chevron Station.) A song was written about this place some years ago, and its spirit has not changed in spite of all the hullabaloo. As for practical matters, the store has everything from soup to nuts and bolts, from gasoline and muumuus, but because of the scarcity of restaurants in Hana, the food department—plenty of local fruit, some vegetables, mostly sausage meats, and some staples—will be of most interest to you. And you may not be able to resist—as we couldn't—the bumper stickers that read: FIGHT SMOG—BUY HORSES, HASAGAWA GENERAL STORE or WE VISITED HASAGAWA GENERAL STORE—FAR FROM WAIKIKI.

A visit to the ✪ **Hana Cultural Center** (tel. 248-8622), in the middle of town, will fill you in on a bit of the history and background of this quaint town. Opened in 1983, the cultural center got most of its collection from local residents, and it's full of wonderful old photographs, Hawaiian quilts (note the unusual Hawaiian-flag quilt dating from the 1920s), plenty of memorabilia from the '30s and '40s, as well as artifacts and tools, and rare shells. Admission is free, but donations are welcome; the center is open daily from 10am to 4pm.

Hana's best beach, **Hamoa,** is at the Hotel Hana-Maui, but you can also swim at the public beach on Hana Bay, at the black sand beach at Waianapanapa State Park, and at the red sand beach (ask locals how to get there). Most visitors drive about 10 miles past Hana on to Kipahulu, an unspoiled extension of Haleakala National Park and **Ohe'o Gulch** (formerly, but incorrectly, known as the Seven Sacred Pools), a gorgeous little spot for a swim. Here the pools drop into one another and then into the sea. But it's a roller-coaster ride on a rough, narrow road filled with potholes, and again, unless you enjoy this kind of driving, it may not be worth your nerves.

En route to Ohe'o Gulch, you'll pass **Wailua Gulch** and a splendid double fall cascading down the slopes of Haleakala. Nearby is a memorial to Helio, one of the island's first Catholics, a formidable proselytizer and converter. A tribute to his work stands nearby—the *Virgin of the Roadside,* a marble statue made in Italy and draped every day with the fragrant flower leis of the Hawaiians.

The good road runs out a little farther on at Kipahulu, so it's back along the northern route, retracing your way past jungle and sea to home base.

READERS RECOMMEND

Staying in Hana. *"Our four nights at Waianapanapa Park were at our No. 1 idyllic spot. Hana was having a week-long Aloha Week festival. We went to a real Hawaiian luau with great performers for $6; the previous night the ladies of the village gave a real hula show at the village soccer field—free. October is a great time to go to Hana, as there are very few guests. Try the red sand beach for snorkeling at Hana Park, near the old frame schoolhouse, now a library, and follow the trail down a meadow, around a cliff, to a secluded beach behind a natural lava breakwall. Caution: Young couples still swim in the buff here!"*—Richard Welse, Westfield Center, Ohio.

"When hiking to the red sand beach in Hana, wear strong shoes, as the track is very narrow, with a steep cliff face on one side in some parts. We found the snorkeling equal to the best on the island. Since it is a nudist beach, though, one often sees more than fish underwater!"—Mrs. Jane Beecham, Victoria, Australia.

4. LAHAINA, KAANAPALI & KAPALUA

If Haleakala and Hana are nature's showplaces on Maui, Lahaina is humanity's. It was there that some of the most dramatic and colorful history of Hawaii was made: 100 years ago Lahaina was the whaling capital of the Pacific, the cultural center of the Hawaiian Islands (and for a time its capital), and the scene of an often-violent power struggle between missionaries and sailors for—quite literally—the bodies and souls of the Hawaiians.

Your trip to Lahaina and the western Maui coast happily combines history with some of the most beautiful scenery in the islands. Take your bathing suit and skip the picnic lunch, since there are plenty of places en route where you can eat. Since there's no paved road completely circling the western tip of Maui, we'll take the road as far as Honokahua, and return by driving back along the same road to Kahului—a route that is more interesting and comfortable than the drive on the unpaved portion between Honokahua and Waihee on the northern shore.

The trip begins on Hi. 32, which you follow through Wailuku to Hi. 30 (High Street), where you turn left. At Maalaea the road swings right at the sea and continues along the base of the West Maui Mountains, along a wild stretch of cliffs pounded by strong seas, until it reaches Lahaina, 22 miles from Kahului. During the winter months, whale sightings are frequent along this stretch of ocean.

LAHAINA

Lahaina today is a comfortable plantation town, with pretty little cottages, a cannery, a sugar mill, and acres of cane and pineapple stretching to the base of the misty western Maui hills. Thanks to its having been declared a National Historic Landmark property, it still retains its late 19th- and early 20th-century architectural charm. New buildings must fit in with this architectural scheme, so there's no danger that it will ever look like Waikiki.

SIGHTS & ATTRACTIONS

STROLLING AROUND TOWN For some years, Lahaina has been in the process of a restoration that will cover the 150 or so years during which Hawaii rose from the Stone Age to statehood—from the reign of King Kamehameha I to the annexation of Hawaii by the United States. Re-created will be the days when Lahaina was the capital of the Hawaiian monarchy (before the king, in 1843, moved the palace to Honolulu, where there was a better harbor); the coming of the missionaries; the whaling period, and the beginning of the sugar industry. The restoration is being lovingly and authentically carried out by the **Lahaina Restoration Foundation,** a devoted group of local citizens and county and state interests. You may visit their office in the Master's Reading Room at the corner of Front Street and Dickenson Street (tel. 661-3262), open Monday through Friday from 9am to 4pm, for further information.

As you tour Lahaina, you'll notice various signs reading LAHAINA HISTORIC SITE: those with a square at the bottom indicate buildings that are either original or restored; those with a circle indicate structures that no longer exist. A booklet called *Lahaina Historical Guide,* free at many Lahaina locations, provides useful maps and descriptions.

Begin your exploration out on the old pier in the center of town, where you can gaze at the famed **Lahaina Roads;** from the 1820s to the 1860s this was the favorite Pacific anchorage of the American whaling fleet. Over on your left are the soft greens of Lanai, to the north the peaks of Molokai, on the south the gentle slopes of Kahoolawe. During the winter and early spring, you may get to see some nonpaying tourists sporting about in the water; these are the sperm whales that migrate from their Aleutian homes to spawn in the warmer waters off Lahaina.

For the whalers, this place was practical as well as beautiful: They were safe here in a protected harbor, they could come or go on any wind, and there was plenty of fresh water at the local spring, plenty of island fruits, fowl, and potatoes. And there were also Hawaiian women, who, in the old hospitable way of the South Seas, made the sailors feel welcome by swimming out to the ships and staying a while. To the missionaries, this was the abomination of abominations, and it was on this score that violent battles were fought. More than once, sailors ran through the streets setting houses on fire, rioting, beating up anyone who got in their way, even cannonading the mission house. You can see the evidence of those days at **Hale Paaho,** the old stone prison (on Prison Street, off Main), where sailors were frequent guests while the forays lasted.

Across the street from the waterfront you'll see the **Pioneer Inn,** which may look oddly familiar—it has been the set for many a South Seas movie saga. Back in 1901 (it has since been tastefully renovated and enlarged) it was quite the place, the scene of arrival and departure parties for the elegant passengers of the Inter-Island Steamship Company, whose vessels sailed out of Lahaina. And since it was too difficult to make the hot trek to central Maui immediately, arriving passengers usually spent the night here. Walk in and have a look around: Note the lovely stained-glass window one flight up from the entrance to the Harpooner's Lanai and the grandfather clock at the foot. The lanai itself is a wonderful place to waste a few years of your life while soaking up the atmosphere.

Across Wharf Street from the hotel, a little to the north of the lighthouse, is the site of a palace used by Kamehameha in 1801, when he was busy collecting taxes on Maui and the adjoining islands. And across from that, where the Lahaina Branch Library now stands, is another spot dear to the lovers of the Hawaiian monarchy, the **royal taro patch** where Kamehameha III betook his sacred person to demonstrate the dignity of labor.

The huge banyan tree just south of the Pioneer Inn covers two-thirds of an acre; it's the favorite hotel for the town's noisy mynah bird population. In the front of the tree is the **Court House,** a post office, and police station, the post office part of which has been functioning since 1859. Between the Court House and the Pioneer Inn, you'll see the first completed project of the Lahaina Restoration, the **Fort Wall.** It's built on the site of the original fort, but since rebuilding the whole fort would have destroyed the famed banyan tree, the authorities decided to reconstruct the wall instead, as a ruin—a ruin that never existed.

Now that you've seen how the whalers lived, let's see how their arch opponents, the missionaries, fared. Walk one block mauka of the waterfront to Front Street and the **Baldwin Home**—so typical, with its upstairs and downstairs verandas, of New England in Polynesia. The old house, built in the late 1830s with walls of coral and stone, served as a home for the Rev. Dwight Baldwin, a physician and community leader as well as a missionary (and incidentally, the founder of a dynasty; the Baldwins are still an important family on Maui). Thanks to the Lahaina Restoration Foundation, the house has been faithfully restored; you can examine Dr. Baldwin's medical kit (the instruments look like something out of a Frankenstein film), kitchen utensils, china closets, old photographs and books, the family's furniture and mementos—all the little touches of missionary life 100 and more years ago. Open daily. Admission is $5 for families, $2 for adults, and free for children accompanied by their parents for a personally guided tour.

After you've seen Baldwin House, stop next door to visit the **Master's Reading Room,** a former seamen's library and chapel that now houses the office of the Lahaina Restoration Foundation. The unique coral-block-and-fieldstone construction has been preserved exactly as originally built in 1847.

Next stop might be the **Wo Hing Temple,** on Front Street, near Mariner's Alley. The restored 1912 fraternal hall is now a museum, with a display on the history of the Chinese in Lahaina. Stop in at the **Cook House Theater,** adjacent, which shows movies of Hawaii taken by Thomas Edison in 1898 and 1903. Open daily from 9am to 9pm; admission donation requested.

The Restoration Foundation also operates the floating museum ship ***Carthaginian,*** moored opposite the Pioneer Inn. Its "World of the Whale" exhibit features a series of colorful multimedia displays on whaling, whales, and the sea life of Hawaii. Maui's own humpback whale, which comes to these waters each winter to mate and calve, gets special treatment through videotape presentations made on the spot by the National Geographic Society, the New York Zoological Society, and others. The ship is a replica of a 19th-century brig and is open daily from 9am to 4:30pm. Admission is $5 for families, $3 for adults, $2 for seniors, free for children with their parents.

Head now for Wainee Street (to the right of Lahainaluna Road); here, where the recently built **Waiola Church** now stands, is the site of Wainee, the first mission church in Lahaina, to which the Reverend Baldwin came as pastor in 1835. The old cemetery is fascinating. Buried among the graves of the missionary families are some of the most important members of the Kamehameha dynasty, including no fewer than two wives of Old King Kam: Queen Keoupuolani, his highest-born wife, and Queen Kalakaua.

On the grounds of Lahainaluna High School stands **Hale Pai,** the original printing house of Lahainaluna Seminary, which the missionaries built in 1813. From the hand press here came the school books and religious texts that spread the Word. The coral-and-lava structure has been turned into a charming museum by the Restoration Foundation. Open Monday through Saturday from 10am to 4pm.

For those interested in Asian culture, it would be unthinkable to leave Lahaina without a visit to the **Lahaina Jodo Mission Cultural Park.** In a beautiful spot perched above the water is a 3½-ton statue of Amitabha Buddha, erected to commemorate the centennial anniversary of Japanese immigration in Hawaii. It's the largest Buddha outside Japan. You can meditate here as long as you wish, strike the huge temple bell, and perhaps leave a small donation in the offertory (there is no admission charge). *Note:* It's easy to miss this place. As you drive along Front Street, look for the big sign that reads JESUS COMING SOON. Then turn makai on Ala Moana Street and you'll find the Buddha.

JUST OUTSIDE TOWN Opposite Wahikuli State Park is the **Lahaina Civic Center,** an auditorium and gym, with a dramatic mosaic by one of Maui's most famous artists, Tadashi Sato.

Five miles east of Lahaina, on the highway headed toward Kahului, are the well-preserved **Olowalu Petroglyphs.** Two to three hundred years old, these rock carvings depicted the occupations—fishing, canoe-paddling, weaving, etc.—of the early Hawaiians. Unfortunately, they are rather difficult to get to.

On the other side of Lahaina, on the road leading toward Kaanapali, is another historical spot, the **Royal Coconut Grove of Mala.** Mala, one of the wives of Kamehameha, brought the trees from Oahu over a century ago. They are now being replaced by local citizens as part of the restoration.

CULTURAL ENTERTAINMENT

Check the local papers for news of frequent entertainment at the malls and shopping centers. On one visit to the **Wharf Cinema Center,** for example, we saw a full Polynesian revue, including Samoan knife dances done by women on the center stage. And **The Cannery** presents a vast amount of free entertainment, so be sure to see if anything is going on while you're there. You may be lucky enough to catch someone of the caliber of noted island funny man Frank DeLima, as we did on a recent visit. Fabulous!

HAWAII EXPERIENCE DOME THEATER, 824 Front St. Tel. 661-8314.

If there's one entertainment experience in Lahaina not to be missed, it has to be the 45-minute movie *Hawaii: Islands of the Gods,* at the Hawaii Experience Dome Theater. To call it a movie is really an injustice, for the traditional boundaries between viewer and film are broken down here as the floor of the planetariumlike theater seems to give way under you, and off you go, soaring into space. Soon you're flying over a burning volcano on the Big Island or swooping down into Kauai's Waimea Canyon, bicycling at breakneck speed down the slopes of mighty Haleakala, or scuba diving far below the surface of the ocean to the breeding grounds of the humpback whale off the coast of Maui. It's all courtesy of state-of-the-art technology. The screen is 60 feet around and more than 25 feet from the center, and your vision is a full 180°, which makes you feel you're part of the picture. The Dome Theater was created here by the Dankworths, who originated the concept in Alaska. "Hawaii is like Alaska," says Jim Dankworth, "in that it has so many extraordinary areas that are largely inaccessible to the average visitor. We wanted to capture that—to show the natural beauty, the history, the culture of the islands in a way that has never been done before." They have succeeded to an astonishing degree. For its price, this has to be the best bargain on Maui. We can hardly wait to see it again.

Admission: $5.95.

Open: Daily, hourly 10am–10pm.

READERS RECOMMEND

Tom Barefoot's Cashback Tours, *834 Front St. (tel. 661-8889). "Your readers may want to know about Tom Barefoot's Cashback Tours. You can book any and all of your activities through them and get an immediate 10% cash back at time of purchase."*—Pat McCallum, Bethesda, MD.

Information Tourist Booth, *in front of the Wharf Cinema Center, 658 Front St. "Ask anyone at the Information Tourist Booth for specialized personal tourist trips. They are always coming up with new things to show tourists. One day they took us to a windsurfing competition at Hookipa Beach; another time they arranged for three of us to hike into the interior with a native Hawaiian guide."*—Rue Drew, New York, N.Y.

SAILING TO LANAI

If sailing, snorkeling, swimming, whale watching, and rustic sightseeing—or any combination of the above—appeal to you, splurge once and spend a perfect day sailing to the island of Lanai aboard one of the sleek, multihulled yachts of ✪ **Trilogy Excursions** (tel. 661-4743, or toll free 800/874-2666 from the mainland). Jim and Randy of "The Sailing Coon Family" pioneered these trips back in 1973, and they are recognized today as the best on the Maui docks. The all-day excursion begins at 6:45am; watching the morning light brighten as you sail out of Lahaina Harbor is magical. Hot coffee and Mom Coon's home-baked cinnamon buns are served on board, and within about 1½ hours you're at Lanai. Then it's superb snorkeling (lessons for beginners) at the Hulupo'e Bay Marine Preserve, swimming on a crystal beach, an excellent lunch of barbecued chicken prepared over kiawe wood by the captain and served in a comfortable dining lanai overlooking the water. Another highlight of the trip is the tour around Lanai in an air-conditioned van; the native guides are delightful and will fill you in on island lore. (Should you want to stop off here at the venerable Hotel Lanai for the night, you can arrange to do so in advance and pick up another Trilogy boat the next day.)

Then it's back to Lahaina, and, with luck, a sighting of whales in season, maybe dolphins. Whales and dolphins cannot be guaranteed, but a thoroughly enjoyable day—and a return to Lahaina around 4:30pm—certainly can be. Bring the kids and the cameras.

The Trilogy Excursion costs $139 for adults, $69.50 for children 3–12, plus tax. Reservations are essential, as space is limited.

READERS RECOMMEND

Watching the Weather. *"Beware of heading off on a snorkeling cruise if the sea is up at all. I had the most miserable six hours either being sick or feeling sick, along with about another 10 hapless souls on a trip to Molokini and Lanai. We had nine-foot swells and even when the boat was moored, snorkeling was difficult with the rough seas. Make sure of the weather forecast before you go!!!"*—Mrs. Jane Beecham, Victoria, Australia.

SAVVY SHOPPING

We must confess: The thing we love to do most in Lahaina is shop. While the reconstruction of the historical sights is proceeding slowly, Lahaina (and Whaler's Village at Kaanapali Beach, see below) is fast emerging as one of the best shopping areas in the islands, second only to Honolulu. On each one of our visits there are new and exciting shops, boutiques, galleries to visit. Perhaps it's the influence of the young people and other newcomers moving into the area; they keep everything constantly stimulating and alive.

First, let's get your car parked. Finding a spot on the street is not easy, although it's often possible on Front Street, on the ocean side. There are 800 parking spaces at the new Lahaina Center, a good walk to the center of town. Also try the Lahaina Shopping Center, the area behind the Wharf Shopping Center, at the corner of Front and Prison Streets, and at the corner of Front and Shaw Streets. If none of that works, however, drive to one of the commercial parking lots, such as the one behind Baldwin House, at the corner of Luakini and Dickenson Streets: Charges are reasonable. Across from the parking lot is a place where you can get fresh island produce to take home, and in front of that is a stand selling ice-cold coconut juice.

Cool and refreshed now, let's start our wanderings.

Malls and Shopping Centers

LAHAINA MARKETPLACE, Front St. just south of Lahainaluna Rd.

Walk all the way to the back of the Lahaina Marketplace and you'll find ✪ **Donna's Designs,** three little booths where Donna Sorenson does some fanciful hand-painted T-shirts and coverups (100% cotton, machine washable), and sells them for the lowest prices around: $10–$36. Bags are $38. Donna points out—

and we agree—that since shops directly on Front Street come and go at a rapid rate because of the high rentals, you're apt to get better bargains if you go slightly "off Front Street."

Kula Bay Tropical Clothing has come up with a novel idea. Realizing that most men don't want to spend several hundred dollars on an antique aloha shirt, they've taken the prints from vintage shirts of the '30s, '40s, and early '50s, had them printed in more muted colors, put them on long-staple cotton (instead of rayon or silk), accessorized them with coconut or mother-of-pearl buttons, and come up with a winning collection. Shirts are $45–$60. There's also a good array of classic design clothing in this "gentlemen's shop." Also in Honolulu and Kauai.

LAHAINA CENTER, 900 Front St.

Maui's enormous new shopping center is at the Kaanapali end of town, between the ocean and Wainee Street. Everything about this place is big, including the biggest Hilo Hattie's Fashion Center in the neighbor islands, large Liberty House and Woolworth stores, and—especially welcome in a town where parking spaces are scarcer than gold nuggets—an 800-car parking lot! Since it's also the home of the Hard Rock Café and Chili's, this is now one of the most popular locations in town.

Art lovers must definitely make a pilgrimage to see the stunning ✪ **Madaline Michaels Gallery,** which specializes in three-dimensional media and showcases the work of Mexican sculptor Sergio Bustamente exclusively in Hawaii. The bright colors and dreamlike essence of Bustamente's creations make his work unforgettable. Also outstanding: the life-size and lifelike sculpture of Jack Dowd, the whimsical animals created by Todd Warner, and the menehune magic of Steve Smeltzer, among others. A must-see. Innovative works by yet-to-be-discovered island artists are on view at **Studio Blue;** come in and discover some treasures for yourself. Paintings, sculpture, pottery, jewelry are in a more-affordable-than-usual range for work of this caliber.

For artistry in women's and children's clothing, visit **Dragon Fly Hawaii.** Designed in California, these garments are decorated with a combination of appliqué, embroidery, and cutwork, done by hand in China. The result: enchantingly pretty creations.

Other top-of-the-line women's boutiques include **Bebe Beach,** offering playwear for the international set, and **Fashion Link,** focusing on unique hand-painted clothing, mostly by Maui artists. Popular-priced sportswear stores include **Local Motion,** which sells mostly 100% cotton clothing along with their surfboards, and **Splash! Hawaii** for an extensive collection of women's swimwear, including a made-in-Hawaii line called "Out of the Blue." **Wet Seal** provides rock music, video screens, and high-tech decor as a background for its youthful women's fashions.

Got the kids with you? Take them to **Maui Kids & Company,** where they'll love the aloha wear and swimwear as well as the great selection of toys and accessories. Soft, stuffed geckos "dressed" in island fabrics and an assortment of Hawaiian dolls in traditional costumes make neat gifts. **Youth's International Wear** is another good spot, with major name brands in children's and young people's clothing.

For budget buys in aloha wear and island gifts, it's hard to beat **Hilo Hattie's Fashion Center.** Selections are enormous, prices are right, and the nice people here even give you free pineapple-orange juice and a shell lei when you walk in. If you're waiting for someone who's shopping, you can relax in the lounge, watching island videos or reading the local papers.

Other popular shops here include **Watch-N-See,** which features the largest collection of Swatch Watches in Hawaii, as well as sunglasses; a very large **ABC** store; and a surprisingly upscale **Woolworth's.** Of course you already know about **Liberty House,** Hawaii's premier department store, with its usual quality selection of nationally recognized brands as well as lovely made-in-Hawaii merchandise.

WHARF CINEMA CENTER, 658 Front St.

Central to the Lahaina shopping scene, this stunning three-story arcade is built around a giant tree, with a fountain and a stage on the lower level, a glass elevator, a triplex theater complex, a number of attractive eating places, and dozens of shops reflecting quality and taste, some more so than others. Shops stay open late, so a visit here can be a good evening's activity. (The free Lahaina Express trolley, a double-decker British bus, makes its last run to Kaanapali at 10pm; it runs daily from Kaanapali every 35 minutes, beginning at 9:30am.)

Here you'll find places like **Seegerpeople,** which offers three-dimensional photo sculptures—of you, your family, your kids, your group. Photo sessions last an hour, it takes another hour for proofs, and then (in about four weeks) you have a sculptural collage unlike any other. Prices begin at $40 for one person, one pose; each additional pose is $25. Have a look around and admire.

We've always liked the fashions—in good taste and well priced—at **Luana's Originals.** Much of the clothing—for both men and women—is made on Maui. Luana shows distinctive prints by Island Silks, and has a good selection of totes and beach bags (there's another Luana's at 869 Front St.). Look for the GREENPEACE HAWAII signs; they'll lead you right to **Earth and Company,** which sponsors Greenpeace Hawaii, and sell "gifts of environmental consciousness"—artwork, posters, jewelry, T-shirts, and more—at moderate prices.

Everything at ✪ **Tropical Artware** is handmade—by 25 local artists and by craftspeople from around the world. This is one of the best sources for hard-to-find dichroic glass jewelry; metallic vapors positioned into glass create a range of subtly changing colors. Dichroic glass rings begin in the $20s; earcuffs and earrings start as low as $12. They're also known for their whimsical animal carvings, a large selection of Balinese silver at the best prices on the island, and custom-fit toe rings! **Sweet Nothings** is an attractive lingerie boutique, and **Monograms Plus** offers embroidered monograms on just about anything and everything. **Gigi's Fashion Boutique** boasts classic design clothing from the '20s, '30s, and '40s.

Have you always wanted a genuine Panama hat? The **Maui Mad Hatter** has them, plus scads of other chapeaux—every known type of hat weave, including Maui lauhala, for men, women, and children. Proprietor Shell Hansen, who's been here for over 20 years now, claims, "If you've got the head, I've got the hat." Most hats run $3–$40 and up; prices are very competitive and value is excellent. Other Hawaiian handmade items available include ukuleles, and feather and silk leis. (*Note:* If you'd like to see how hats are made, you can arrange to visit Hansen's Wailuku warehouse: Call 661-8125 for information.) Children can be nicely outfitted with island clothes at **Little Polynesians.**

We never miss a visit to the **Whaler's Book Shoppe,** a combination bookstore and European café, where you can sip and sit on their peaceful patio. We often find stunning local books of art and photography and Hawaiiana here that are not readily available elsewhere: Especially lovely is a book called *Maui on My Mind,* a beautiful book for $34.95.

LAHAINA CANNERY, 1221 Honoapiilani Hwy.

Once it was a pineapple cannery. Now the heavy equipment and the factory workers are gone, and in their place are a supermarket, a drugstore, scads of boutiques and restaurants, and plenty of tourists. One of Lahaina's newer shopping centers, and its first enclosed, air-conditioned one, the Cannery is a very pleasant place to shop. It's sunny but cool, with lots of light and space. It's a boon to people staying out this way, since the **Safeway Supermarket** stays open around the clock, and **Long's Drugs** fills a variety of needs. There is ample parking, as well as free shuttle service from the Honokawai and Kaanapali areas. There's often free entertainment, like a Polynesian revue featuring dancers from the Maui Marriott's luau, which we caught recently.

As for the smaller shops, there are many branches of popular island stores like **Sir Wilfred's Coffee, Tea, Tobacco,** which has great selections of their own coffee beans (unique flavors like Kona Hula Pie and Kona Banana Nut, regular and decaf) and of gift items as well; we're especially partial to their collection of Laurel Birch bags, cups, jewelry, T-shirts, umbrellas, and the like. Then there's men's and women's clothiers **Reyns,** where you must check out their Artwear collections of T-shirts; they'd make wonderful gifts. Other favorites include **Alexia Natural Fashion** for stylish women's clothing in raw silk, linen, and cotton; **Blue Ginger Designs,** where everything is made of hand-blocked batik fabrics; and **Super Whale,** which always has wonderful children's clothing. **Plantation Clothiers** is also a winner for children's clothing, mostly of the handmade and hand-painted variety, and there are equally lovely (and pricey) items for mom too. We like the fanciful women's clothing at **Arabesque,** and the array of high-flyers at **Kite Factory. Lahaina Scrimshaw** (see Whaler's Village in Kaanapali) has an impressive collection here too. For collectors of maps and old prints, **Lahaina Printsellers** is a must stop.

Maui on My Mind is one of the more tasteful shops around, with a variety of wearable crafts and handmade jewelry. They even have T-shirts with prints by some of Maui's favorite artists; we like Robert Lyn Nelson's underwater scenes, at $16.

Rocky Mountain Chocolate Factory will dip frozen bananas in chocolate for you, and will mail their famous fudge, chocolate-covered macadamias, and what-not anywhere.

While you're thinking of food, you can check out the variety of fast-food outlets here, sit down and have a bite at one of the tables in the big central courtyard. For a more serious meal, try **Marie Callender's,** an outpost of the Oahu favorite known for its wonderful pot pies, or **Compadres,** for Mexican food, drinks, and fun.

Attention chocoholics and/or potato-chip junkies, or any combination of the above: Before you leave the Cannery, stop in at **Long's Drugs** and treat yourself to Maui's latest gourmet munchie craze: **Chocolate Chips of Maui.** Believe it or not, these are original Maui potato chips, dipped by hand in either rich dark chocolate or milk chocolate, packed in an elegant box, and signed by the dipper. They can be gobbled as is or, if you can wait, frozen and served with ice cream or sherbet or brandied whipped cream! A four-ounce box is $4.

READERS RECOMMEND

Take Home Maui, *Dickenson St., near Front St. "This place handles shipping fruit, but has a great sandwich deli with exotic fruits. Very inexpensive and only four outdoor tables."*—Robin Ritchee, Lahaina, Hawaii.

Pearl Factories. *"Be careful with any of the pearl factories dotted all over Front Street. While picking your own oyster and getting your own cultured pearl out of it is fun for $6 (the bait), having the pearl mounted on gold is very overpriced (the hook). Check the price on the whole package (which is not posted anywhere) before doing anything, or just insist on doing the pearl part only."*—K.L., New York, N.Y.

Special Shops

SOUTH SEAS TRADING POST, 851 Front St. Tel. 661-3168.

There aren't too many places like the South Seas Trading Post left in Lahaina, places where the owners still search out and find authentic South Seas and Asian treasures. Although there are many collector's items here—primitive art from New Guinea, bronzes and Buddhas from Thailand, precious jades from China—most of the items are surprisingly affordable: Consider, for example, one-of-a-kind jewelry designs using antique pieces ($25–$75), freshwater pearl necklaces with precious gemstones (from $18), 100-year-old porcelain spoons from China (at $10), Christmas ornaments in the shape of Hawaiian tutus ($3.50)—and much more.

THE WHALER LTD., 866 Front St. Tel. 661-4592.

The Whaler is just about the only honest-and-true nautical shop in the old whaling port of Lahaina. They have lanterns that run on oil, brass lamps and hooks in various shapes, scrimshaw and ivory carvings, carvings of whales and whalers, and a fine collection of American crafts, especially paper weights and perfume bottles. Note their collection of etched, sandblasted, and sculptured Art Glass, each piece with a nautical or island theme—whales, fish, flowers.

THE ENDANGERED SPECIES STORE, 707 Front St. Tel. 661-0208.

Should you wish a T-shirt that reads PROTECT THE DOLPHINS or PRESERVE HAWAII'S RAIN FOREST or some such, this is the place. This imaginative shop devoted to protecting the environment also has framed posters by such marine artists as Christian Reese Lassen and Robert Lynn Nelson, all very handsome.

LAHAINA HAT COMPANY, 709 Front St. Tel. 661-8618.

If you can't find a hat here, you're not really trying! The collection is enormous, and all are reasonably priced. They carry a good selection of tote bags too.

NOA NOA, at the Banyan Inn, 704 Front St. Tel. 661-0223.

Wild and wonderful tropical prints on all natural fabrics make the selections here outstanding and not overpriced. Women's clothing, as well as some Balinese artifacts and accessories are available.

TEMPLE OF ART, 156 Lahainaluna Rd. Tel. 661-6224.

There's no way you can miss this one—the huge copper pyramid out front is in direct proportion to the Great Pyramid of Giza. The gallery specializes in Hawaiian art, and has some rare and unusual jewelry as well, but we spotted some masks from just $15. The owner's name is—honest!—Angel Gabriel.

Swap Meet

Handmade Hawaiian dresses, baskets, hand-painted clothing and T-shirts, and handcrafted jewelry are just some of the items for sale at the Sunday-afternoon **Lahaina Crafts Fair.** It's held either once, twice, or three times a month at the Lahaina Civic Center, next to the main post office in Lahaina. Check with your hotel desk to see when it's scheduled.

READERS RECOMMEND

Salvation Army Thrift Shop, *off Front St. "Best bet for shopping in Lahaina: The Salvation Army Thrift Shop off Front Street, near the Lahaina Shores Hotel, had very reasonable used and new clothing selling a few blocks away for five times the amount. The best sales appear to be on Saturday."*—Michael and Arlene Gladstone, Merrick, N.Y.

EVENING ENTERTAINMENT

Lahaina at night is the place for the drinking set, with no shortage of swinging bars. And for families, check the local papers to see what entertainment is being presented at the malls.

Luaus

Should you be in the mood for a luau, we can't think of a nicer one than the ✪ **Old Lahaina Luau,** right out on the beach behind the shopping arcade at 505 Front St. (tel. 667-1998). This is a smaller and more personal, old-time luau than many of the slick hotel presentations; *Maui Magazine* called it "the best on the island." And the setting, on the grounds of Kamehameha's royal compound, is picture perfect: You dine as the sun sets over the water, then watch the traditional hulas of Hawaii by starlight. There is an open bar. The luau is held Monday through Saturday evenings at

5:30pm at a cost of $46 for adults, $23 for children 12 and under. Call for reservations.

Drinking, Dancing, and Listening

In addition to the places listed below, keep in mind the following: The **Whales Tale Restaurant,** 666 Front St., always attracts a lively crowd for good food and moderately priced drinks. There's live music from 3 to 10pm. Another big drinking scene takes place at the **Old Whaler's Grog Shop and Harpooner's Lanai** of the Pioneer Inn on Front Street. The **Hard Rock Café** at Lahaina Center, 900 Front St., has one of the biggest bars in town and one of the jolliest crowds. **Compadres Bar & Grill** at the Lahaina Cannery is the spot for Mexican munchies and great margaritas. Looking for a late, late happy hour? You'll find it at the **Kobe Japanese Steak House,** 136 Dickenson St., from 10pm to 2am. **Lahaina Coolers,** 180 Dickenson St., offers two popular happy hours, one from 4 to 6pm, the other from 10pm to midnight, every day.

BLACKIE'S BAR, at the corner of Kapunakea St. and Hi. 30. Tel. 667-7679.

The entrance to Blackie's Bar is lined with pictures of shipwrecks and boats damaged at sea. Hence the logical conclusion in the bar's motto: PROMOTE SAFE BOATING—STAY ASHORE AND DRINK AT BLACKIE'S BAR. While the cold, cold beer, the drinks and Mexican munchies, burgers, and homemade meatloaf sandwiches are very good, what brings the crowds here is Blackie Gadarian himself, an outspoken local character and a patron of very good jazz. Blackie brings in local musicians as well as celebrity performers four nights a week, on Monday, Wednesday, Friday, and Sunday, from 5:30 to 8:30pm. You'll recognize Blackie's by the second-story gazebo, topped with an orange roof, just above Blackie's Boat Yard.

Admission: "No cover charge, but you must drink, drink, drink."

MOOSE MCGILLICUDDY'S PUB & CAFE, 844 Front St. Tel. 667-7758.

The young crowd comes here to listen to rock and roll. There's a 4-to-8pm happy hour every day, special prices on Tijuana Tuesdays, Ladies' Night on Thursday, videos every night, and on Thursday, Friday, and Saturday, live bands from 9:30pm until closing.

Admission: $3 Thurs–Sat after 9pm.

Art Night

Lahaina boasts numerous galleries, and the best time to visit them is on Friday night. Friday evening, from 7 to 9pm, is "Art Night" in Lahaina; galleries present special appearances by artists and offer free entertainment and refreshments. Great fun! Check the local papers for what's happening where. Among the numerous galleries involved are **South Seas Trading Post, Dolphin Galleries, Wyland Gallery, Center Art Galleries–Hawaii,** and the **Lahaina Arts Society.**

ON TO KAANAPALI

If you want to continue your sightseeing out in the Kaanapali resort area now, there are two ways to go, in addition to driving your own car. The first is free: It's the **Lahaina Express,** a quaint green trolley that provides shuttle service between Banyan Tree Square and the hotels in the Kaanapali Resort every 35 minutes from 9:30am on. The last trolley leaves the Wharf Cinema Center in Lahaina at 10pm (for information, phone the Wharf Shops at 661-8748).

It's more fun, however (and also more expensive: $11 round-trip, $7.50 one way, half fare for children), to hop the old-timey **Lahaina-Kaanapali & Pacific Railroad,** a reconstructed, turn-of-the-century sugarcane train, for the 12-mile round-trip between Lahaina and Kaanapali. You'll be entertained with songs and stories en route by a singing conductor, and kids will get a kick out of the hoot of the locomotive's whistle. The railroad terminal is on Honoapiilani Highway, one block north of Papalaua Street; there is free transportation via a double-decker bus from the harbor and Front Street. Before or after the trip, you might want to check out the stand at the station that sells fresh coconuts, chilled for eating and drinking, plus fresh-trimmed sugarcane. And don't miss **Sugar Cane Gifts** (tel. 661-3325) right at the railroad depot. They have some of the most handsome T-shirts and sweatshirts we've seen on Maui, as well as a variety of other gift items. Manager Shellie Fletcher is willing to accept mail orders as well.

While you're in the industrial area near the sugarcane train, have a look around, too, at some of the outlet stores. These include **Coral and Gifts, Posters Maui, Lahaina Printsellers, J. R.'s Music Shop,** and the **Lobster and Roses** sportswear outlet. Merchandise varies from day to day, but value can be excellent.

SIGHTS & ATTRACTIONS

Now for some sightseeing, shopping, and swimming at the glamorous hotels of the Kaanapali Beach Resort (signs from the road lead you directly down to the hotel). Your first stop should be at the splendid ✪ **Hyatt Regency Maui,** where you can have a look at the $80-million, 20-acre complex, lush with waterfalls, gardens, tropical birds, an acre-long swimming pool with its own bar in a lava cavern, an atrium lobby surrounding a 70-foot-tall banyan tree, and an elegant shopping arcade that rivals Rodeo Drive. A walk here is like touring a park and botanical garden and an indoor-outdoor museum of priceless Asian art. This aesthetic and architectural tour de force offers gorgeous vistas wherever you look. You might want to pause and have a drink at the Weeping Banyan Bar beside a lagoon—and please don't throw crumbs at the penguins! Note, too, the unusual ceilings in the shops—there is one in stained glass—and perhaps pick up a trinket at a place like Elephant Walk, where prices go way up for safari exotica, but are relatively down-to-earth for elephant-hair jewelry.

By all means, pay a visit to the **Maui Marriott Resort,** on Kaanapali Drive next to the Hyatt Regency. This is an example of modern hotel architecture and landscaping at its best, especially beautiful at night, when lights, flowers, and tropical moon over the ocean create dazzling effects.

Your next stop should definitely be the **Westin Maui Resort,** a sensational $165-million remake of the old Maui Surf Hotel. It's a toss-up as to whether this or the Hyatt Regency Maui (both Christopher Hemmeter creations) is the more sumptuous—you decide. This gorgeous pleasure palace by the sea has $2½ million worth of artwork gracing the public areas and gardens, a spectacular, multilevel swimming pool complex fed by waterfalls and bridges (twice as big as the giant pool at the Hyatt Regency), and swans gliding just a few feet from the registration desk. Art tours are held on Tuesday and Thursday at 9am and last an hour; wildlife tours are held on Sunday, Monday, Wednesday, and Friday at 10am—a great chance to photograph the flamingos, swans, and macaws. You'll need reservations (tel. 667-2525).

As you continue driving, you may want to stop at the **Sheraton Maui Hotel,** which sits atop **Black Rock,** the perch from which the souls of the dead Hawaiians were said to leap into the spirit world beyond. The majestic hotel, not in the least bit haunted, is worth having a look at, especially for the 360° view from the top, a sweeping panorama of ocean, islands, and mountains. The tasteful Polynesian formal lobby is on the top floor; you've got to take the elevators down to everything else, including Kaanapali Beach.

SAVVY SHOPPING

WHALER'S VILLAGE The main shopping attraction out here is Whaler's Village, recently done over and now bigger and better than ever. The one- and two-story buildings are of uniform design and materials, authentic reproductions of the type of buildings that the New England missionaries constructed in Lahaina between 1830 and 1890. First, pay a visit to the **Whalers Village Museum** (on the third floor of Building G), study its absorbing collection of whaling memorabilia, and perhaps see the whaling film shown every half hour in the museum's theater. After you've boned up on history and soaked in some gorgeous views, you can concentrate on the serious business of shopping—and there's plenty to concentrate on.

The ✪ **Endangered Species Store** is the kind of place the whole family will like. Kids will find minerals and fossils for collecting, and books on the environment; adults will like the posters by Christian Reese Lassen and Robert Lynn Nelson, the Maui tote bags and animal prints, and the EXTINCTION IS FOREVER T-shirts. And everyone will like the pool and parrot up front: Toss a coin, make a wish; proceeds go to further environmental causes.

If you're ready to invest in some really fine jewelry, then pay a visit to the **Dolphin Gallery.** Everything is exclusive here, of the highest quality, and fairly priced: We love their selection of "spinner rings," gray Tahitian pearls, and the blue stone called tanzanite.

"One-of-a-kind," "rare," "unusual"—these are words to describe the very special offerings at ✪ **Sea & Shell.** Many of the employees do watercolors or create belts and hair jewelry; owners Michael and Madaline Abrams do all the beautiful mountings and mirrors, and offer unique jewelry by island artisans, like the Kroma Glass line. Wonderful "bird bags" in the shapes of swans, flamingoes, and toucans are a conversation piece anywhere. There's more of the same at Madaline and Michael's Collectibles at 713 Front St. in Lahaina.

The ✪ **Ka Honu Gift Gallery** is a delight, with lots of Hawaiian handmade works: dolls, ceramics, bowls of milo and koa wood, and Christmas ornaments like Santa on a surfboard, at $10.95. They have a large collection of Niihau shell necklaces. And don't miss **Nohea Gallery,** which shows dazzling works—ceramics, jewelry, sculpture, flower pillows, and the like—by local craftspeople. **Maui on My Mind** has its share of fine crafts too—handcrafted baskets, pottery, and jewelry. They carry Guy Buffet T-shirts, Robert Lynn Nelson posters, beautiful koa-wood jewelry boxes, eyeglass cases with leaf prints on raw silk, delightful at $14.

If money were no object, we'd simply buy out all the fabulous designs by local Hawaiian artists at **Silks Kaanapali Ltd.** In addition to hand-painted and unusually designed clothing, the shop carries striking bags and other accessories, starting around $30. **Maui Water Wear** has a great selection of swimsuits.

You can have a great time at **The Sharper Image**—at no cost. Work out on the exercise bikes, then massage your back as you experience a Japanese shiatsu massage table or a luxury recliner. Oh yes, you could buy something here too, like an airplane lamp—it taxis for takeoff—at $89.95. Scrimshaw collectors should head straight for **Lahaina Scrimshaw,** where there's an impressive selection of quality scrimshaw (done on nonendangered fossil walrus ivory), as well as a prize antiques collection, including some particularly fine Buddhas from Thailand. Do-it-yourself scrimshaw kits go for $8.95–$21.

Lahaina Printsellers has some fascinating antique maps and prints that would look great on those walls back home. **Esprit, Canoe, Cotton Cargo,** and **Waldenbooks,** island regulars, are all represented here.

Whalers Village is open from 9:30am to 10pm daily, and can be reached by foot on the beachwalk or on Kaanapali Resort's free trolley. If you drive, you will, unfortunately, have to pay for parking.

SPORTS & RECREATION

One of the nicest things about the Hawaiian Islands is that all beaches—even those at the fanciest hotels—are open to the public. As you stroll by the beachfront hotels (the

Sheraton Maui, the Royal Lahaina, the Kaanapali Beach, the Marriott, the Westin Maui, the Hyatt Regency), you can stop by for a snack or a drink and treat yourself to a swim. **Kaanapali Beach** is wider in some places than others (storms occasionally carry away some of the sand), and we prefer the areas in front of the Westin Maui, the Royal Lahaina, and Sheraton Maui; the latter is known for fabulous snorkeling at **Black Rock,** right in front of the hotel. Unfortunately, there is very little public parking in this area, and hotel parking lots may be crowded. You may want to swim behind Whaler's Village, which has a good beach, but you'll have to pay for parking in their indoor lot.

READERS RECOMMEND

Black Rock Cove. *"While Maui has many scenic beaches, there aren't many easily accessible from hardtop roads that are consistently suitable for novice snorkelers. In calm conditions, several of the west-coast beaches are acceptable. But when swells or windy conditions exist, your choices rapidly dwindle. One very notable exception is Black Rock Cove at Kaanapali. This sheltered cove has clear water and scores of colorful, small fish. If you are staying outside this immediate area, just park in the Whaler's Village lot, walk to the beach, and head north about a quarter of a mile; the cove is just below the Sheraton Maui Hotel."*—Dale Knutsen, Ridgecrest, Calif.

Snorkeling near Kaanapali Airport. *"The best snorkeling we found was at the southern edge of the Kaanapali Airport. The water was clear and safe for children, the coral plentiful and well below the surface, and the variety of fish amazing. Even beginning snorkelers will enjoy this beach, which is reached by turning in at the last Kaanapali sign going north, then walking about 50 yards down to the beach."*—Nick Howell, Camp Springs, Md.

Aquatic Charters of Maui *(tel. 879-0976). "One of our most pleasant experiences was taking a private charter boat to Molokini for snorkeling. The cost was the same as for the large boats, and the individualized attention from the owners was terrific. We heartily recommend the Aquatic Charters of Maui with Jim and Robyn Friend."*—Lindsay and Jay Johnson, Columbus, Ohio.

Rainbow Ranch, *near Kaanapali Beach (tel. 669-4991). "We took advantage of riding at the Rainbow Ranch, near Kaanapali Beach. A variety of riding tours is available at all levels of experience for reasonable prices. Good-quality horses and great guides."*—Patti Connor, Arlington, Mass.

EVENING ENTERTAINMENT

Fun and games await you at the big beach hotels at Kaanapali. One of the greatest shows in town takes place every night at the **Sheraton Maui,** and it costs absolutely nothing to be in the audience. As the sun begins to set over the water, torches are lit all the way to the point. A native Hawaiian boy stands atop Black Rock (that eerie perch from which the souls of the dead were supposed to depart to the other world), throws his leis into the water, and then looks down some 20 feet or so to the waiting ocean below. The crowd—on the beach, lining the lobby floors—holds it breath. He plunges in, surfaces, and the evening festivities are under way.

If you need something to steady your nerves after viewing the diving spectacle described above, make your way to the nautically decorated "On the Rocks" Bar. The ship models, volcanic rock floor-to-ceiling columns, and the tables with compass designs are all unusual and handsome, but somehow we never notice anything except the view; from the crest of this black-lava cliff overlooking the sea it's a spectacular one, a must for us collectors of Hawaiian sunsets.

Luaus and Dinner Shows

Choosing among all the luau and dinner shows in the Kaanapali area can be difficult: All of them are good, but none is inexpensive (most run $40).

The **Royal Lahaina Luau,** at the Royal Lahaina Resort (tel. 661-3611 for reservations), is considered one of the best; it's presented nightly, September through May at 5:30pm, June through August at 6pm. It costs $44.25 for adults, $20.80 for children 12 and under.

Drums of the Pacific at the Hyatt Regency Maui (tel. 667-4420 for reservations) offers a spectacular production of Pacific dancing (Samoan slap dances, Tahitian drum dances and shimmies, spear and knife dances, fire dances, etc.), along with a traditional Luau Buffet and an imu ceremony. Festivities are held in an outdoor amphitheater beneath the stars. The dinner show is $44 for adults, $36 for children 6–12, but you can see the same show and enjoy a cocktail for just $26.

Another top choice is the **Marriott Luau,** at the Maui Marriott on Kaanapali Beach (tel. 667-1200 for reservations), held at the hotel's beautiful oceanfront luau gardens Tuesday through Sunday at 5pm. Admission is $43.50 for adults, $20 for children.

The ✪ **Aloha Friday Luau** takes place just once a week—on Friday night—at the Kaanapali Beach Hotel (tel. 661-0011), and it may well be "Maui's Most Hawaiian Luau." It is preceded by an afternoon arts-and-crafts fair, with Hawaiian games and entertainment, free, from 1 to 6pm. Luau cost is $37.50 for adults, $18.75 for children 5–12.

Karaoke Sing-along

LOBBY BAR, at the Maui Marriott. Tel. 667-1200.

In case you've not yet experienced karaoke, here's your chance. On Thursday, Friday, and Saturday nights from 8 to 11pm, and on Friday and Saturday from 8 to 11:30pm, there's a show in which you could be the star. Just walk up to the mike, choose from more than 5,000 popular tunes (words on the video screen), and sing along. Drink specials and pupus too. No cover, no minimum.

Contemporary and Hawaiian Music

EL CRABCATCHER, at Whaler's Village. Tel. 661-4423.

This oh-so-pleasant restaurant facing the beach is the place to have drinks or dinner and hear contemporary Hawaiian music daily from 5:30 to 7:30pm. Contemporary music is also played Tuesday through Saturday from 9:30pm to 12:30am.

Dancing

MAKAI BAR, at the Maui Marriott. Tel. 667-1200.

There's contemporary live music and dancing here every night—plus spectacular sunsets.

A Comedy Club

LOBBY BAR, at the Maui Marriott. Tel. 667-1200 for reservations.

The Honolulu Comedy Club is one of the top nightclub attractions in Waikiki; on Sunday night it moves to Maui. You never know who the talent will be, but be assured they are among the nation's hottest standup comedians; you've probably seen them on TV with Johnny Carson or Jay Leno or David Letterman or Arsenio Hall.

Admission: $12. No one under 21 admitted.

TO KAPALUA & NEARBY BEACHES

As you drive north from Kaanapali on Honoapiilani Highway through Kahana and Napili and finally to Kapalua, you're seeing some of the most beautiful countryside in West Maui. Some of the best beaches are here too, as well as the Kapalua Bay Resort, a particularly lovely spot perched on a promontory and surrounded by blue sea.

Although you could conceivably swim at Honokawai Beach Park, it's not particularly desirable, so we suggest you drive farther along until you come to some better beaches. One is **Napili Bay,** which has a small sign showing the public right-of-way; look for it—and park—when you see the sign for the Napili Surf Beach Resort. Our favorite, still farther north on this road, is old **Fleming Beach** (also known as **Kapalua Beach**), a perfect crescent of white sand, gentle surf, the ideal spot for the whole family to swim, play, and snorkel. There's a public right-of-way sign past the Napili Kai Beach Club, which leads to a small parking lot for this very popular beach. If it's full, we'll let you in on a secret: The parking lot at the Shops at Kapalua, adjacent to the plush Kapalua Bay Hotel, usually has plenty of space and you can walk from it, through the hotel, and down through the lovely grounds to the ocean. The Kapalua Bay Hotel itself is exquisite, and well worth a look.

Note: Despite any information you may receive locally, nude sunbathing is definitely against the law in the state of Hawaii.

FREE SHOWS

Cooks at the Beach, at the Westin Maui Resort (tel. 667-2525), is a charming indoor-outdoor café that hosts a free hula show Tuesday through Saturday at 7pm.

One of Maui's best entertainments is free. It's the presentation of ✪ **Hula Kahiko O Hawaii** at the Shops at Kapalua, at the Kapalua Bay Resort, every Thursday morning at 10am. Unlike most hulas done in commercial shows, these are the authentic ancient dances of Hawaii, presented by a local hula halau (school), with Kumu Hula Cliff Ahue relating enchanting stories of Hawaii's history and ancient religion. It's all done in the spirit of Tutu Inez Ashdown, a great lady who originated these programs and is Maui County's historian emeritus. Local friends call this one of the best-kept secrets on the island!

READERS RECOMMEND

Touring Napili Bay. *"We found the prettiest part of Maui to be that short section of Hi. 30 that goes past the Napili Bay area: towering cliffs, crashing waves, lush valleys. Few tourists seem to drive up here because they know the road ends. We packed a picnic dinner and ate it in total isolation on a cliff overlooking the water. It was one of the best moments of our honeymoon."*—Sue and Terry Young, Crystal Lake, Ill.

SAVVY SHOPPING

THE SHOPS AT KAPALUA We always stop to visit the Shops at Kapalua, at the Kapalua Bay Resort, one of the most serenely tasteful of island marketplaces. Most of the shops here are way beyond our budget, but there are many affordable items at places like **Kapalua Kids,** which can outfit teens as well as children, and at the **Kapalua Shop,** where you can pick up T-shirts, bags, and many accessories with the distinctive trademark logo: the Kapalua butterfly. **By the Bay** is a gift gallery with many delightful items from around the world.

Like its other shop in Lahaina, the **South Seas Trading Post** showcases arts, handcrafts, and jewelry from Bali, New Guinea, and Asian and South Pacific shores, much of it of museum quality. But there are some charming low-priced items too. We especially like the jewelry created from 350- to 600-year-old shards of Ming Dynasty Chinese porcelain: These are set in sterling-silver rings, pendants, and earrings, and start at just $25.

Have a sandwich and an espresso, now, at the European-style **Market Café,** which also purveys cookbooks, cheeses, wines, and deli items. Or walk through the lobby of the adjoining Kapalua Bay Hotel and have lunch at the lovely **Pool Terrace.** Best of all, wander out to the **Bay Club.** Here you can have a fancier lunch, a drink, or simply a walk outside to see the breathtaking views, with blue sea at every vista. Beautiful Kapalua Beach is right below you. Let the peace and beauty of the beaches stay in your memory as you turn around and go back the way you came—the road continuing around the island is a poor one, and usually off-limits to drivers of rented cars.

READERS RECOMMEND

The Road to Kahakuloa. *"The road past Nakalele Point to Kahakuloa marked 'impassable' on most tourist maps is definitely just that! The trip is 14 miles, not 5 as stated in most brochures, and a total disaster. We ventured a couple of miles on the road ourselves and had to turn around when the road became too narrow for our car. However, a couple we were traveling with covered the entire 14 miles, and it took them several hours, which they say were harrowing at best. The scenery is not any more spectacular than you can find on other island roads and the driving is so nerve-racking it is unlikely you will be able to spare any time to view the scenery anyway. The road to Hana is described as treacherous in some brochures, but it is no comparison to this road—save yourself some time and nerves and just don't bother with this route."*—Mr. and Mrs. Wes Alton, Edmonton, Alberta, Canada.

Honolua Bay. *"The best snorkeling beach on Maui (we discovered it ourselves and it was later pointed out to us by islanders) is Honolua Bay on the north end of the island near the end of Hi. 30. Overnight camping permits should be obtained from the Maui Pineapple Company in Lahaina, but we did not have one and had no problems."*—Sandra Johnson, Santa Paula, Calif.

CHAPTER 16
MOLOKAI

What's the most Hawaiian of the Hawaiian Islands? If you're thinking in terms of the Hawaii of 50 years ago—the Hawaii before high-rises and shopping centers, before billboards and commercialism, it might well be the little island of Molokai. The closest of the neighbor islands—only 20 minutes by plane from Oahu—261-square-mile Molokai is the least developed and most sparsely populated of the major Hawaiian Islands. Its resident population (about 6,000) has the highest percentage of people with native Hawaiian ancestry anywhere in the islands (with the exception, of course, of privately owned Niihau). The environment is rural and the lifestyle traditional. Imagine a place with no buildings over three stories high, no elevators, no traffic lights (let alone freeways!), no movie theaters, no fast-food or supermarket chains. Instead, think of great natural beauty, vast uncrowded spaces, and ideal conditions for golfing, hunting, riding, windsurfing, big-game fishing, boating (swimming is not ideal here, since the beaches can be beautiful but the water rough), and leading the lazy life in an unspoiled setting. If that's the kind of relaxed Hawaii you're thinking about, then you should definitely visit Molokai.

Molokai sometimes gets overflow visitors from better-known tourist destinations, people who didn't even know what or where Molokai was. Yet once they start to unwind here, they find they like it, and come back again. Kamaainas have been in the know about Molokai for a long time: It's a favorite weekend spot for family holidays.

In the past, Molokai was known mostly as a pineapple plantation island and as a treatment center for Hansen's disease (leprosy) at Kalaupapa. It was here that Father Damien did his magnificent work among the lepers. But somehow the tidal wave of progress that has swept the islands since statehood left Molokai behind; it appears, at first glance, like a midwestern town in the Depression '30s. Yet there's a down-homeness and a realness here that most people find appealing, and a genuine friendliness among the locals. Artists and craftspeople, seeking a last refuge from overpriced civilization, have settled here. In some parts of the island there is a sense of tranquility that's almost palpable. And Molokai is changing. Although the pineapple industry has been phased out and many of the local people are experiencing hard economic times, luxury facilities for visitors are on the rise. Before Molokai changes too much, come see what rural Hawaii is still like. A visit to Molokai can be a rewarding experience, especially since you won't have to break the bank to do it; prices here are still somewhat lower than elsewhere in the state.

Molokai, now "The Friendly Isle," was once known as "The Lonely Isle." The power of Molokai's kahuna priests was feared throughout the other islands. Warring island kings kept a respectable distance from Molokai until, in 1790, Kamehameha the Great came to negotiate for the hand of the queen, Keoupuolani. Five years later he returned with an army to conquer Molokai on his drive for Oahu and dominion over all of Hawaii.

As far as mass tourism goes, the friendliness in Molokai's current name hasn't really been tested yet. You might easily be the only mainland visitor on the 15- or

20-minute flight from Oahu or Maui, and your fellow passengers will likely be island people visiting relatives or plantation people arriving on business.

Today Molokai presents a tranquil scene, an island mostly given to rural pursuits. The only town really worthy of the name is Kaunakakai, on the southern shore, almost in the center of the island, and it has only one street. A thickly forested backcountry populated with axis deer, pheasant, turkey, and other wild game makes life exciting for the hunter. For those of you who just like to look and sightsee, there is magnificent Halawa Valley, on the southeastern coast, about 25 miles from Kaunakakai, with its healing pool at the foot of Moaula Falls; the less-rugged Palaau Park, about 10 miles north of Kaunakakai, with its Phallic Rock and Kalaupapa Lookout; and Kalaupapa itself, an isolated peninsula, once an exile colony for the victims of leprosy, which today you can visit on a guided tour. But more about that later.

You won't have to rough it on Molokai. The few hotel facilities are excellent, the roads for the most part are quite good, and you'll be able to get whatever comforts and supplies you need—from rental cars to color movie film. The drinking water is as pure as you'll find anywhere in the world, and the restaurants, especially those in the three major hotels on the island, serve very good meals.

One word of advice: Go directly to your hotel from the airport and get comfortable and adjusted to Molokai before visiting its nearby principal town, Kaunakakai. This sleepy village, made famous by the song "Cock-eyed Major," is best appreciated once you're in the Molokai mood. Especially after Waikiki.

To get a little head start on your sightseeing, you might note that, between the airport and town, on the ocean side of the road is Kapuaiwa, one of the last surviving royal coconut groves in the Hawaiian Islands, planted in the latter part of the 19th century. It was planted in honor of Kamehameha V and given his pet name. Opposite the grove is Church Row, a lineup of tiny rustic churches.

DESTINATION MOLOKAI Molokai is serious about putting out the welcome mat for visitors and, to that end, it has set up the Destination Molokai Association to promote tourism. If you phone their toll-free number, they'll send you a comprehensive brochure listing hotels, resort condominiums, tour companies, auto-rental companies, restaurants, visitor activities, and airlines serving the island, as well as individual brochures put out by these firms. From Canada and the continental United States, as well as Alaska, Puerto Rico, and the Virgin Islands, call toll free 800/367-ISLE. If you're already in the islands, call 553-5288 on Molokai. Their office is under the mango tree at the Pau Hana Inn.

Destination Molokai has put out a 15-minute travel video covering Molokai's scenic and historic attractions, as well as its visitor accommodations and services. If you'd like a copy of *Destination Molokai,* available in both VHS and Beta formats, send a check for $9.95 (includes shipping and handling) to Vacations on Video, 1309 E. Northern, Phoenix, AZ 85020 (make the check out to International Travel Promotions, Inc.).

1. GETTING THERE & GETTING AROUND

GETTING THERE

BY PLANE

Molokai is 20 air minutes from Honolulu, 15 minutes from Maui. It is easily reached via **Hawaiian Airlines,** which runs 50-seat DH-7 aircraft into Hoolehua Airport on a frequent schedule. Two commuter airlines, which run small planes (anywhere from 9- to 18-seaters), also fly to Molokai: These are **Air Molokai** and **Aloha Island Air.** Flying low on these small planes can be quite thrilling, as we discovered on a recent Air Molokai flight. Molokai lies between the islands of Oahu and Maui (it can easily be seen from western Maui) and is, in fact, part of Maui County. Route it on your way to or from either Maui or Honolulu. A one-day trip is quite feasible.

READERS RECOMMEND

Flying via Kalaupapa. *"If possible, when flying from Maui to Molokai, take an Aloha Island Airlines Twin Otter flight via Kalaupapa. One flies on a level with the 3,000-foot-high cliffs on the northern shore of Molokai, and what a spectacular sight that is! In using this form of inter-island transport, we got for free what most people would pay $75–$100 for on a helicopter tour! This flight was the highlight of our trip."*—Mrs. Jane Beecham, Victoria, Australia.

BY SHIP

A more leisurely—and scenic—way to get to Molokai is to take the inter-island ferry, ***The Maui Princess,*** a 118-foot luxury vessel that plies the routes between Maui and Molokai every day. It's about a 1¼-hour trip. One-way fare is $25 for adults, $12.50 for children. The tour is narrated, there are plentiful opportunities for taking pictures, and if it's between December and May, you may spot a few humpback whales taking the same trip you are. For reservations, call 533-6899 on Oahu, 661-8397 on Maui, 553-5736 on Molokai. From the mainland, call toll free 800/833-5800.

READERS RECOMMEND

Agriculture Inspection. *"If you're leaving Molokai to go back to the mainland, there is no agriculture inspector there. Consequently, you must check all your luggage to Honolulu, pick it up there and take it to the agriculture inspectors, then to your airline back to the mainland. This is a real chore as both Aloha Island Air and Hawaiian Airlines are miles from the main terminal and a porter costs $4 and a taxi about the same, to say nothing of the walk you have to put in! In other words, if you're doing Molokai, don't do it last before you return."*—Howard S. Walker, Sequim, Wash.

GETTING AROUND

BY RENTAL CAR

You're going to need a car if you want to explore Molokai on your own, and it won't be difficult to get one, since Molokai now has local outlets of four major all-island rental companies: Budget Rent A Car, Dollar Rent A Car, Tropical Rent-A-Car, and Avis. (See Chapter 2 for details on all-island rentals.) They're all located at the airport. Rates vary according to the season and business, but some typical rates on our last visit follow—all rates quoted include unlimited mileage. **Budget Rent A Car** (toll free 800/527-0700) charges $22 for economy automatics with air conditioning. **Dollar Rent A Car** (tel. toll free 800/367-7006) offers two-door, standard compacts for $38 and compact automatics for the same rate. They also rent Jeeps. At **Avis** (tel. toll free 800/331-1212), rates are about $20.55 a day for a four-door compact with air conditioning. **Tropical Rent-A-Car** (tel. toll free 800/678-6000) charges $33.95 for an economy car (without air conditioning), $39.95 for a subcompact automatic with air conditioning, $32 for a four-door compact automatic with air conditioning. Remember that these rates are always subject to fluctuation, so it's wise to shop around.

BY TAXI & TOUR SERVICE

Need a taxi? Up until a few years ago, there was no such animal on Molokai, but now there are several, all owned by lifelong Molokai residents. **T.E.E.M. Cab Molokai** (tel. 553-3433), which is owned and operated by David and Cookie Robbins, offers islandwide cab service, including airport and harbor pickup and hotel transfers, 24 hours a day seven days a week. Personalized taxi tours from 2½ hours to a full day in length are also offered. Additional services: providing tour guides for visitors with their own rented car and sightseeing consultation. Discounts are available for seniors and students. Call for information and reservations.

Kukui Tours & Limousines (tel. 553-5133), run by Vandale K. Dudoit, Jr., and Joyce Dudoit, prides itself on its personal service and attention. Their air-conditioned limos provide half-day and full-day tours of the island, plus airport–hotel shuttle service.

Thadd R. Camara's **Molokai Limousine Taxi Service** (tel. 553-3979; call collect from other Hawaiian islands) calls itself Molokai's "first VIP limousine taxi service." All standard taxi services are available, including airport and harbor pickup and hotel transfers, on a 24-hour basis. They also provide several half-day and full-day sightseeing tours in their luxury stretch Lincoln Town Car limo.

Operated by Alex and Pat Puaa, **Molokai Off Road Tours & Taxi** (tel. 553-3369) offers mountain and coastline tours at $75 each ($65 each for three or more people). They also have the lowest-priced airport-to-hotel shuttle service.

FAST FACTS Molokai is part of Maui County. For details, see "Fast Facts: Maui," in Chapter 14. For local emergencies on Molokai, call 553-5355 for **police,** 553-5401 for **fire,** 553-5911 for an **ambulance,** and 553-5331 for **Molokai General Hospital.**

2. WHERE TO STAY

Molokai now has a grand total of eight hotels and condos plus a few bed-and-breakfasts—and that's more than twice what it had a few years ago! Since there are so few, we'll give you the details on all of them; they're not all budget, but they all offer good quality for the money.

KAUNAKAKAI

Kaunakakai is Molokai's most central area, and the following hotels are just a mile or so down the road from the town's center, Ala Malama Street.

DOUBLES FOR $45

PAU HANA INN, Kamehameha Hwy. (P.O. Box 546), Kaunakakai, Molokai, HI 96748. Tel. 808/553-5342, or toll free 800/922-7866. Telex 634479 ASTHI UW. 42 units.

$ Rates: $45–$90 single or double; $90 studio; $125 suite. Each additional person $10 extra. AE, CB, DC, MC, V. **Parking:** Free.

The drive from Hoolehua Airport to the town of Kaunakakai takes about 10 minutes, across what seems to be typical western grazing land. About a quarter of a mile from the town, following Hi. 45 along the beach, you'll see the Pau Hana Inn, the best choice in town for budgeteers, the most local and the most laid-back. Pau Hana is a relaxed, cottage-type hotel with some units in the garden, others facing the ocean or pool. All rooms and public areas have been refurbished recently. The lowest rates are for small, plain, but clean budget rooms, with two twin beds and shower, in the longhouse. The more expensive rooms, by the pool or the ocean, accommodate up to four people with two double or queen-size beds. The superior rooms with kitchenettes and deluxe oceanfront suites sleep up to four people. The one-bedroom units have kitchenette, sitting room, a queen-size bed and a couch, also for four. A swimming pool compensates for the rather poor ocean beach. The oceanfront Banyan Tree Terrace Restaurant is open for three reasonably priced meals a day. On weekends, it's the local hot spot for dancing. Pau Hana Inn is now affiliated with Aston Hotels & Resorts in Honolulu, which also operates Hotel Molokai (see below).

DOUBLES FOR $59 TO $85

HOTEL MOLOKAI, Kamehameha Hwy. (P.O. Box 546), Kaunakakai, Molokai, HI 96748. Tel. 808/553-5347, or toll free 800/922-7866. Fax 808/922-8785. Telex 634479 ASTHI UW. 51 rms.

$ Rates: $59–$125 single or double. Each additional person $10 extra. AE, CB, DC, MC, V. **Parking:** Free.

The Hotel Molokai is a modern Polynesian village that maintains the aura of the gracious past. The separate, three-unit cottages have lovely rustic bedrooms with baths and all the modern-day comforts, including wall-to-wall carpeting and very comfortable basket swings out on the furnished lanais. There's a swimming pool (the waterfront here is a shallow lagoon behind the reef, popular for snorkeling but not good for swimming), a comfortable open lobby, and the Holo Holo Kai Restaurant, where the "family" (staff) entertains their guests at dinner. Although this is an oceanfront hotel, the waves break a quarter mile out, leaving the lagoon tranquil and still, with only a lapping sound to lull you to sleep. (*Note:* Light sleepers may want to ask for a room away from the restaurant area.) The cheapest rooms are standard, superior rooms are on the garden floor, and deluxe rooms on the upper floor have a lanai or face the ocean. Only deluxe rooms can accommodate one or two extra people.

MOLOKAI SHORES, Kamehameha Hwy. (P.O. Box 1037), Kaunakakai, Molokai, HI 96748. Tel. 808/553-5954. 102 apts. TV

$ Rates: Apr–Dec 19, $85 one-bedroom apt; $115 two-bedroom apt. Dec 20–Mar, $95 one-bedroom apt; $125 two-bedroom apt. Each additional person $10 extra. Discounted weekly rates available. DC, MC, V. **Parking:** Free.

Molokai Shores is located just a mile from Kaunakakai, between the Pau Hana Inn and the Hotel Molokai. The three-story, oceanfront apartment building has very pleasant units, all with ocean views, well-equipped kitchens, and private lanais overlooking tropical lawns. The one-bedroom units accommodate up to four people; the two-bedroom units, which have two baths, accommodate up to six. Picnic tables, barbecue units, and a putting green make outdoor life pleasant, and there's a pool for swimming (the beach is not particularly good here).

Reservations: Hawaiian Island resorts, P.O. Box 212, Honolulu, HI 96810 (tel. toll free 800/367-7042).

EASTERN SHORE

The eastern shore of Molokai is a newer area for tourist development and it's quite lovely, a good base of operations for ocean swimming and excursions to Halawa Valley.

DOUBLES FOR $50 TO $66

KAMALO BED & BREAKFAST, Star Rte., Box 128, Kaunakakai, Molokai, HI 96748. Tel. 808/558-8236. 1 cottage.

$ Rates (including breakfast): $60 double. Minimum stay three days. No credit cards. **Parking:** Free.

On the eastern end of Molokai, this private B&B country cottage faces a large lawn surrounded by five acres of flowers and trees. The cottage, which is fully equipped with cooking and dining facilities, has two couches that convert to twin beds at night, a stall shower, and a pleasant deck for lounging and watching the birds. Breakfast items are provided. Maximum occupancy is two adults (no children). Snorkeling/swimming beaches are about an 8- to 10-mile drive.

SWENSON'S VACATION COTTAGE, P.O. Box 280, Kualapuu, Molokai, HI 96757. Tel. 808/567-9268. Fax 808/567-8721. 1 cottage. TV TEL

$ Rates: $50 double. Minimum stay two nights. No credit cards. **Parking:** Free.

Just past the 16-mile marker at Pukoo is a perfect retreat for those who really want to get away from it all. Diane and Larry Swenson, whose house fronts a sandy swimming beach, rent a fully equipped beachfront cottage with living room, kitchen, bedroom, and bath. You're welcome to pick bananas, papayas, and mangos in season from the trees, and since the house sits in a coconut grove, the ground is usually covered with coconuts, which the owners will husk for you. Within walking distance is Pukoo Lagoon, and from your window, views of Maui, Lanai, and the ocean.

WAVECREST RESORT, Star Rte., Box 155, Kaunakakai, Molokai, HI 96748. Tel. 808/558-8101, or toll free 800/367-2980. 126 units. TV

$ Rates: $66–$76 ocean-view apt ($91–$101 with car); $78–$86 oceanfront apt ($101–$111 with car). Each additional person $5 extra. AE, MC, V. **Parking:** Free.

Nestled against the eastern Molokai mountains, Wavecrest Resort has tennis courts, a swimming pool, and all the amenities necessary for at-home resort living. There's not much of a beach, but it's okay for fishing. The apartments are all smartly furnished with fully equipped electric kitchens. From your private lanai, you can see Maui across the water.

DOUBLES FOR $85

HONOMUNI HOUSE, Star Rte., Box 306, Kaunakakai, Molokai, HI 96748. Tel. 808/558-8383. 1 cottage. TV

$ Rates: $85 double per night, $510 per week. Each additional adult $10 extra; each additional child, $5. No credit cards. **Parking:** Free.

It's an easy walk to the beach from Honomuni House, a country cottage that can accommodate up to four adults. There's a private enclosed sleeping area, a large living/dining area with color TV and a sofa bed, a nicely equipped kitchen, a full bath plus a hot-water shower outdoors, and a covered lanai. Hosts Jan and Keaho, who are educators in marine biology and Pacific studies, are available to answer questions and they invite guests to enjoy the papayas and other tropical fruits fresh from their garden.

KALUAKOI RESORT

Molokai's loveliest resort area is on the western shore, about 15 miles from the airport, next to the glorious, 3-mile stretch of almost-deserted Kepuhi Beach. Kaluakoi Resort, a 6,700-acre development, includes the luxurious Kaluakoi Hotel & Golf Club, along with three very pleasant condominium colonies.

DOUBLES FOR $85 TO $105

COLONY'S KALUAKOI HOTEL & GOLF CLUB, P.O. Box 1977, Maunaloa, Molokai, HI 96770. Tel. 808/552-2555, or toll free 800/777-1700. Fax 808/552-2821. 174 rms. TV TEL

$ Rates: $100–$125 double; $135–$140 studio; $155–$175 suite for four; $240

one-bedroom ocean-view cottage for four. Each additional person $15 extra. AE, CB, DC, DISC, JCB, MC, V.

This is the grandest of Molokai hotels. The rooms, which are in two-story buildings overlooking ocean or golf course, are beautifully appointed (some have high-beamed ceilings) with wood, rattan furnishings, and vibrant Polynesian colors. All rooms have refrigerators. Besides the beautiful ocean (often not safe for swimming), there's a handsome free-form swimming pool, bar service at poolside, the championship 18-hole Kaluakoi Golf Course (a golfing friend tells us that at night deer come out to drink at the water hazards), four lighted tennis courts and a tennis pro, and all sorts of shops and services. Ohia Lodge provides excellent meals. As we sipped a cool drink by the pool recently, one of the guests smiled at us and said: "I think I'll never leave." We could understand that feeling; it's like being at one of the beach hotels at Kaanapali on Maui, but with nothing else around.

In addition to regular rates, the hotel also offers all-inclusive Colony Club rates, which cover room, transfers to and from the airport, all meals (run of the menu, no limitations), unlimited bar drinks in the lounge, 18 holes of golf per day, unlimited tennis, unlimited snorkeling, bicycles, nightly movies, and more. Rates begin at $378 per night double.

KALUAKOI VILLAS, Kaluakoi Resort, P.O. Box 200, Maunaloa, Molokai, HI 96770. Tel. 808/552-2727, or toll free 800/525-1470. Fax 808/552-2201. 103 units. TV

$ Rates: $105–$135 studio; $135–$165 suite; $185 golf/ocean villa. AE, MC, V. **Parking:** Free.

Kaluakoi Villas is new, very luxurious, and very lovely. All its units have private lanais affording some degree of ocean view, and are richly decorated in the island mode with rattan furnishings. They boast a refrigerator, a countertop range, cooking utensils, china, and glassware: The golf and ocean villas have a full range and a dishwasher. All the activities of Kaluakoi Resort—the restaurants, day-and-night tennis courts, and 18-hole championship golf course—are available to guests. On the property are a free-form swimming pool and Jacuzzi. Golf and tennis packages are available.

KE NANI KAI, P.O: Box, 146, Maunaloa, Molokai, HI 96770. Tel. 808/552-2761, or toll free 800/888-2791. Fax 808/552-0045. 120 apts. TV TEL

$ Rates: $105–$115 one-bedroom apt for up to four; $125–$135 two-bedroom apt for up to six. Crib $8 extra. Minimum stay two nights. AE, MC, V. **Parking:** Free.

There's an air of tranquility about Ke Nani Kai that makes you feel like you could stay for weeks and simply unwind, never missing civilization a bit. Located at the entrance to the Kaluakoi Hotel (actually, between the 8th and 17th fairways of the golf course), this is a superb condominium resort, with some 55 units available to the general public. The apartments, each with a view of garden or ocean, are handsomely furnished, with very large living rooms, bedrooms with sliding doors, lanais affording splendid views, superbly equipped kitchens, VCRs, and washers and dryers in every unit. On the grounds are an enormous swimming pool (with a shower in the shape of a tiki god), two tennis courts, a whirlpool spa; the beach is just a short walk away. Hanging flowers cover the trellises of the units. This is the most popular condo in the area for families because of the large pool and the large dining/barbecue facilities.

PANIOLO HALE, P.O. Box 190, Maunaloa, Molokai, HI 96770. Tel. 808/552-2731, or toll free 800/367-2984 (call collect from Canada and Hawaii). Fax 808/552-2280. 77 apts. TV TEL

$ Rates: $85–$125 studio for two; $105–$145 one-bedroom apt for up to four; $125 two-bedroom apt for up to four. Fifth and sixth persons in two-bedroom apt $10 each. Minimum stay three nights. AE, MC, V. **Parking:** Free.

Next door to the Kaluakoi Hotel, on Kepuhi Beach, Paniolo Hale is adjacent to the golf course; in fact, one must cross the fairway to get to the beach. Wild deer and turkeys are frequently seen on the grounds. There is a swimming pool and a paddle-tennis court, and guests receive a reduced rate when golfing at Kaluakoi. The Kaluakoi Hotel also offers its four lighted tennis courts to Paniolo Hale guests for a nominal fee. This is a luxury condominium complex. The best buys are the one-bedroom units, which have two baths and sleep up to four; the two-bedroom units, also with two baths, sleep up to six. Hot tubs are available on the lanais of all two-bedroom units for an additional charge. There are also ocean-view units. All the apartments have full kitchens, VCRs, and attractive island furnishings, and each unit has its own screened lanai (a touch of old Hawaii), which you walk right onto from your room, without going through a door. The nearest restaurant is at the Kaluakoi Hotel, about a block away along the sea wall, and the nearest grocery store is seven miles away. We continue to receive good reports on this one. Inquire about air/room/car packages or golf specials.

3. WHERE TO EAT

Molokai has only a smattering of restaurants, but you can eat well here.

KAUNAKAKAI

Let's start out on Ala Malama, the main street of Kaunakakai, where you can mingle with the locals for some down-home good food, at old-fashioned low prices.

MEALS FOR LESS THAN $10

KANEMITSU BAKERY AND COFFEE SHOP, Ala Malama St. Tel. 553-5855.

Cuisine: LOCAL.

$ Prices: Plate lunches $3.90–$4.80. No credit cards.

Open: Wed–Mon 5:30am–8pm.

When was the last time you had a hot dog for $1, a hamburger for $1.40, and club sandwiches that go up to $3.30? These are the kinds of prices that have made this place a local standby for years. There are reasonable breakfasts too, and a prime rib dinner every Friday night for all of $9.95. Kanemitsu is primarily a bakery, and a famous one, known for its flavorful Molokai French bread (a great gift item, by the way, for friends in Honolulu). They also bake excellent cheese and onion breads, and all breads and pastries are baked without preservatives. This humble bakery actually turns out up to 1,500 loaves a day.

OUTPOST NATURAL FOODS, 70 Makaena St. Tel. 553-3377.

Cuisine: NATURAL FOODS.

$ Prices: Appetizers $2–$4.50; main courses $4.25–$4.95. No credit cards.

Open: Mon–Fri 10am–3pm.

Outpost Natural Foods, at the west end of town (behind Kalama's Service Station), is a natural-foods store and juice bar/restaurant with picnic tables outside that's quite pleasant for a light and healthful meal. In addition to freshly squeezed Molokai orange juice, carrot juice, and the like, they offer vegetarian sandwiches for around $3 (the whole-grain bread is baked fresh in Hawaii, the organic lettuce and greens are grown on Molokai), salads, burritos, and a special hot lunch every day. The hot lunch has to be one of the best buys in town, since it always includes a main course, such as a pasta or tofu dish or stir-fry veggies, plus salad, for $4.50. Everything is available for take-out. Very popular here is the self-serve machine, which dispenses a luscious all-fruit ice cream.

OVIEDO'S LUNCH COUNTER, Ala Malama St. Tel. 553-5014.

Cuisine: FILIPINO.

$ Prices: Lunch or dinner plates $6.75. No credit cards.

Open: Daily 10am–7pm.

To sample Filipino food, sit down for lunch or get a take-out plate at Oviedo's, a simple, home-style restaurant on the main street in Kaunakakai. Oviedo's features such Filipino specialties as pork adobo (adobo is a kind of stew), tripe stew, and roast pork.

RABANG'S RESTAURANT, Ala Malama St. Tel. 553-5841.

Cuisine: FILIPINO.

$ Prices: Main dishes around $6. No credit cards.

Open: Daily 10am–9pm.

Take-out Filipino food is also available at Kaunakakai Market on Ala Malama, next door to Molokai Fish and Dive. Here, in addition to groceries, meat, vegetables, and liquor, one can get a good rice and adobo dish, a different one every weekday, for about $6, served "from 10am until food *pau*," according to the owner, Mrs. Rabang. Roast pork is served every Friday. She also suggests that you try the Filipino dessert called *halohalo*—ask her to explain what it is. (If you've been to Molokai before, you might remember the Rabang's former little restaurant up in Kualapuu.)

MEALS FOR LESS THAN $20

BANYAN TREE TERRACE, at the Pau Hana Inn. Tel. 553-5342.

Cuisine: AMERICAN. **Reservations:** Recommended at dinner.

$ Prices: Appetizers $4–$7.95; main courses $9.75–$16.95. MC, V.

Open: Breakfast daily 6:30–10:30am; lunch daily 11:30am–2pm; dinner daily 6–9pm.

Whether you're seated indoors in a big rustic dining room with a tremendous fireplace or outdoors under the enormous, spreading Bengalese banyan tree out on the beach (the scene of nighttime entertainment), you're going to find a meal here very pleasant. The banyan, also known as an East Indian fig tree, has been standing sentinel over the ocean here for almost 100 years. Dinner is well priced, with such main dishes as fresh catch of the day, shrimp tempura, barbecued beef short ribs, seafood platter, and top sirloin. Specialty of the house is prime rib, a 10-ounce cut for $13.95. The price includes soup and salad bar, hot vegetables, a choice of starch, and Molokai French bread. Lunch features daily specials at $4.95; with soup and salad bar, $6.85. And they have homemade pizza on Thursday.

HOLO HOLO KAI, at the Hotel Molokai. Tel. 553-5347.

Cuisine: AMERICAN. **Reservations:** Recommended at dinner.

$ Prices: Appetizers $3.25–$7.50; main courses $8.95–$16.95. DC, MC, V.

Open: Breakfast daily 7–11am; lunch daily 11:30am–2pm; dinner daily 6–10pm.

Hotel Molokai's dining room enjoys an excellent location right on the edge of the ocean and open to its charms. And the food is very good, too. Dinner is well priced, since all main dishes—such as teri chicken, barbecued ribs, shrimp scampi, prime rib, New York steak, and mahimahi—are accompanied by rice, the vegetable of the day, freshly baked bread, and an unlimited salad bar. People rave about their hearty beef stew, a local favorite. Lunch features salads, sandwiches, and burgers, plus hot main dishes like beef stew, french dip, and mahimahi, for $3.75–$6.75. Local musicians entertain at dinner.

Here's a special tip for those of you who are going to be in Molokai for only one day. Take an early-morning flight out from Honolulu or Maui, and go directly from the airport to the Hotel Molokai. Treat yourself to one of their famous breakfast specialties—Holo Holo Kai French toast (which is Molokai bread in a banana-egg batter, with a choice of meats) or our personal favorite, papaya hotcakes, topped with crushed macadamia nuts, plus a choice of breakfast meats. Both these treats are under $5. Now, after your coffee, you're set for a day of exploring Molokai.

MAUNALOA & KALUAKOI RESORT

Maunaloa, the sleepy little plantation town on the western shore, boasts one of the island's most enjoyable budget eateries and its most glamorous luxury restaurant.

MEALS FOR LESS THAN $12

JO JO'S CAFE, Maunaloa. Tel. 552-2803.

Cuisine: AMERICAN. **Reservations:** Not accepted.

$ **Prices:** Appetizers $4; main courses $7–$10. No credit cards.

Open: Lunch Mon–Tues and Thurs–Sat noon–2:45pm; dinner Mon–Tues and Thurs–Sat 5–7:45pm.

For a real budget meal in this area, dine with the islanders at homey Jo Jo's Café, not far from the Kaluakoi Resort; it's in Maunaloa, in the tavern section of the old Pooh's Restaurant. The menu is the same all day, and prices are low for the likes of chopped steak, Korean ribs, teriyaki plates, and such. All main courses are served with vegetables and a scoop of rice. Jo Jo's specialty is fish; they serve several different fish dishes every day, either frozen or fresh, whenever it's available, so you may be lucky enough to get ahi, mahimahi, ono, aku, or opakapaka, very reasonably priced at $4.75–$6.95. Bring your own bottle from the Maunaloa General Store across the way. Hamburgers, surfburgers, hot dogs, saimin, and salad are available too. For dessert, try one of their fresh island homemade toppings on an ice-cream sundae, or have a piece of pie—all for $1.50–$2. Management suggests you come early for dinner, since they take no reservations, and sometimes it's SRO. Funky and fun.

WORTH THE EXTRA BUCKS

OHIA LODGE, at the Kaluakoi Hotel & Golf Club, Kaluakoi Resort. Tel. 552-2555.

Cuisine: AMERICAN/ASIAN. **Reservations:** Recommended.

$ **Prices:** Appetizers $2.75–$9.75; main courses $12.95–$21.50. AE, CB, DC, DISC, JCB, MC, V.

Open: Breakfast daily 6:30–10:30am; lunch daily noon–2pm; dinner daily 6–9pm.

Many of the local people feel that the glamorous Ohia Lodge, a South Seas spot overlooking the water, is the best dining room on Molokai. There's music for dancing here every night. The most reasonable items on the menu are the pasta choices, from pasta Alfredo at $12.95 to a seafood jamboree of shrimp, scallops, and island fish at $16.95. There are also steak, lamb, and fresh fish dishes. We like the Indonesian chicken at $15.75, and the lemon chicken at $14.75. Main courses come with rice pilaf and fresh sautéed vegetables. Appetizers include spring rolls, Cajun catch, and chicken satay. Lunch is fun too, with a variety of light meals, good salads (chicken salad in papaya boat, sesame chicken, tropical fruit salad, etc.), sandwiches (vegetarian to flame-broiled steak), and lovely desserts: We like the cappuccino crunch pie at $3.75. Molokai Country Breakfasts are hearty ways to start the morning.

KUALAPUU

You'll probably be driving through the little town of Kualapuu at some point in your stay on Molokai, perhaps to visit the Kalaupapa Lookout, or the Mule Barn, or the Meyer Sugar Mill. Here's where you should eat.

MEALS FOR LESS THAN $10

KUALAPUU COOK HOUSE, Tel. 567-6185.

Cuisine: AMERICAN. **Reservations:** Not required.

$ Prices: Main courses $4.95–$7.25. No credit cards.

Open: Mon–Fri 7am–8pm, Sat 7am–4pm.

Look for Kualupuu Cook House, a welcome addition to restaurant-poor Molokai, as you head up Kalae Road and then take a left turn onto Farrington Road. It actually was a cook house, back in the days of the Del Monte Plantation. Now owner Nanette Yamashita has turned it into a quality eating place, with seating either indoors or on an outdoor patio. Fresh foods are featured at very reasonable prices, like $4.30 for a complete breakfast—eggs, meat, rice, and pancakes or French toast. At lunch and dinner, nothing on the regular à la carte menu is over $7.25; local favorites are served, as well as gourmet burgers, made from hamburger ground fresh every day. A daily plate special gives you a full meal for $5–$7, including main course, salad, rice, and beverage. And for dessert, you must have one of Nanette's homemade pies and cakes. She bakes daily, and always makes pumpkin, custard, and apple pies. Her cream and chiffon pies are made from fresh local fruits in season. Honey-butter cake is another popular specialty.

EN ROUTE TO HALAWA VALLEY

MEALS FOR LESS THAN $7

NEIGHBORHOOD STORE 'N COUNTER. Tel. 558-8933.

Cuisine: LOCAL.

$ Prices: Plate lunches $5–$6.75. No credit cards.

Open: Daily 9am–5pm.

If you're driving the long 25 miles out to Halawa Valley, you'll want to know about the Neighborhood Store 'n Counter at the 16-mile marker going east. They have local-style plate lunches, burgers, ice cream, and sodas. You can take your food and eat outside under the trees.

4. WHAT TO SEE & DO

Sightseeing on Molokai requires a bit more determination than it does on the other islands. A visit to the island's most spectacular scenic spot, Halawa Valley, involves some rugged driving and an hour's hike. To reach Kalaupapa, the major point of interest on the island, you have to fly, hike, or ride a mule down a steep *pali.* But if you're willing to put up with a few obstacles, you might find sightseeing on Molokai among the most rewarding adventures of your trip to Hawaii. Sightseeing tours and local guides are especially helpful on this island. For things to do, consult the *Molokai News* or the *Molokai Dispatch,* both free at local stores.

SUGGESTED ITINERARIES

IF YOU HAVE ONE DAY Make the trip to Kalaupapa Settlement—either by plane or by muleback.

IF YOU HAVE TWO DAYS Spend your first day at the settlement. On the second day, drive to Halawa Valley and swim at the base of Moaula Falls. Or take a hike with Discover Molokai Guided Nature Tours (see below).

IF YOU HAVE THREE DAYS Use your first two days as suggested above. For your third day, book a safari at the Molokai Ranch Wildlife Park in the morning, and spend the afternoon in the plantation town of Maunaloa shopping for arts and crafts.

IF YOU HAVE FIVE DAYS OR MORE After spending three days as suggested above, if you have more time take the Molokai Wagon Ride, or visit Palaau State Park, Purdy's Nut Farm, and the Meyer Sugar Mill.

SPECIAL EVENTS

Molokai is usually a relatively quiet place, but there are two events that draw the crowds from all over the islands. The first is the famous **Molokai-to-Oahu Canoe Race,** the most important event in the sport of outrigger canoeing. Participants paddle from Molokai to Fort DeRussy Beach in Honolulu in traditional Hawaiian canoes, going over some very rough water. The women's race takes place in September, the men's race in October.

An expression of the island's commitment to the preservation of authentic Hawaiian culture, the annual **Molokai Ka Hula Piko**—A Celebration of the Birth of Hula on Molokai—is now in its third season. Local hula halaus (schools) are joined by leading vocal and instrumental groups. There are also makahiki games, demonstrations of traditional Hawaiian crafts, and food booths selling Molokai specialties. According to legend, Molokai was the birthplace of the hula and it was here, at Ka'ana, that the goddess Laka learned to dance from her sister Kapo, and then spread the art of hula throughout the Hawaiian islands. For information on exact dates, usually in May, call Destination Molokai (tel. toll free 800/367-4753 in the U.S. and Canada).

THE TOP ATTRACTIONS

HALAWA VALLEY & MOAULA FALLS

For a beautiful day on Molokai, get up early, have your hotel pack you a picnic box lunch (or put one together from the supermarkets in town), hop into your car, and head for Halawa Valley. The trip is just about 25 miles from Kaunakakai along Kamehameha IV Highway, but it will probably take you two hours to get there, since the last part of the driving is rough going. This is Molokai's southeastern coast, dotted with ancient heiaus, old fish ponds (some of which are used for scientific studies), and many coastal churches built by Father Damien and others. You won't be able to see the heiaus unless you get permission to go on private property, but you can stop in at **St. Joseph's Catholic Church** in Kamalo. The church, with a lovely statue of Father Damien beside it, was designed and built by Father Damien, who was a skilled carpenter. A little farther is Father Damien's **Our Lady of Sorrows Church,** where you'll see a statue of Damien in a pavilion near the church. As you drive by the Kamalo mountains, watch for rainbows and double rainbows—they're not uncommon here. When you get to Mapulehu at mile 15, you may want to make a stop at the **Mapulehu Glass House,** an enormous greenhouse which is the largest glass house in Hawaii. This is a flower farm, and beautiful blossoms are available to take with you or ship home. Visitors are taken right into the greenhouse. They're two driveways east of the 15-mile marker, on the mountain side of the highway, and are open only Monday through Friday from 7am to noon, or by appointment (tel. 558-8160). At mile 15½, look on the right for a sign to the **Mapulehu Mango Grove,** the largest mango patch in Hawaii, with over 2,000 mango trees of many varieties, and a coconut grove. You can stop to pick up some tropical fruits here, as well as mango and other fruit juices at a little stand fronting the ocean. (Snorkeling tours and equipment are also available.) You'll begin seeing sandy beach again in the Pukoo area. There are many secluded little beach coves along this coast, but they're unmarked and difficult to find, so it's best to ask local people for directions. From the beach here, you can see Maui, only nine miles across the water.

About 20 miles out, past Pauwalu, the broad country road begins to narrow, and soon you're on a one-lane road where the sharp turns force the car to practically creep along while the scenery becomes more beautiful every minute. Then you begin to climb up through the ranchlands of **Puu O Hoku Ranch,** from which a narrow road takes you into the Halawa Valley. We hope you do make it into the valley, because this is a veritable tropical paradise, a remote Shangri-la that one may find difficult to believe still exists. Once a populous area, it was swept by a tidal wave in 1946 and largely deserted. You can explore the valley (a few people still live here), have a swim in the bay, or make a roughly two-hour hike to the valley's most spectacular point, **Moaula Falls.** (You'll probably need mosquito repellent.) The rewards are a picnic or a swim at the base of a waterfall that plunges relentlessly down from dizzying heights. The water is cold and delicious, but according to Molokai legend, it's only safe to swim here if the ti leaf that you throw in floats. If it sinks, you'll have to make your own decision. Remember to make this trip in the morning, since, after a hike back to your car, you'll have to drive another two hours or so back to your hotel.

READERS RECOMMEND

Moaula Falls. *"To get to Moaula Falls, go up the dirt road in front of the small green church on the left side of the river as you face the falls. The small parking lot across from the church is the best place to leave your car. As you go up the road, past several houses, stay on the main road until it ends and a trail begins. Go up the trail about 100 yards to a row of rocks across the trail. Turn to the right here and follow the trail down to the stream. You have to cross both forks of the stream here. When you get to the other side, find a trail that goes up the hill perpendicular to the stream. (When you cross a mud flat, you'll see an orange mark on a tree. Here, go right through some heavy grass. When you leave the grass, look behind you as you go up the trail. If you see some more orange marks, you know you're on the trail.) Shortly you come upon a major trail that has been blocked off to the right. Turn left and now follow the white plastic pipe and white arrows marking the trail to the falls for a spectacular hike and view of the falls and the pool below."*—Mr. and Mrs. Wayne Ditmer, Mott, N. Dak.

KALAUPAPA SETTLEMENT

Many people who have never been to Hawaii have heard about Father Damien of Belgium and what he did for the destitute lepers on Molokai over a century ago. Volunteering for the post, he set up a church on the isolated peninsula where victims of the dread disease were unceremoniously dumped and left to die. Damien ministered to their physical and spiritual needs and made Kalaupapa liveable for them for 16 years, until he himself succumbed to the disease. In 1989, on the 100th anniversary of his death, a Damien Centennial Year was declared by both the state of Hawaii and the government of Belgium. Representatives of the Roman Catholic church (Father Damien is a candidate for canonization), government officials, and the faithful from throughout the world gathered on Molokai to honor him. He performed his labors here at Kalaupapa, where a center for the treatment of leprosy—now called Hansen's disease—is still operating. Fewer than 100 patients and former patients are still at Kalaupapa, and to visit their island home is a moving experience. It is not, however, a trip we advise everyone to make. It's not for those who get nervous just thinking about diseases (although leprosy has been arrested by modern drugs and is presumably not contagious), and it's definitely not for the idly curious. The residents of Kalaupapa do not wish to be regarded as a tourist attraction. Getting to their beautifully but tragically isolated home takes a bit of doing, and the emotions the trip

MOLOKAI SIGHTS & ATTRACTIONS

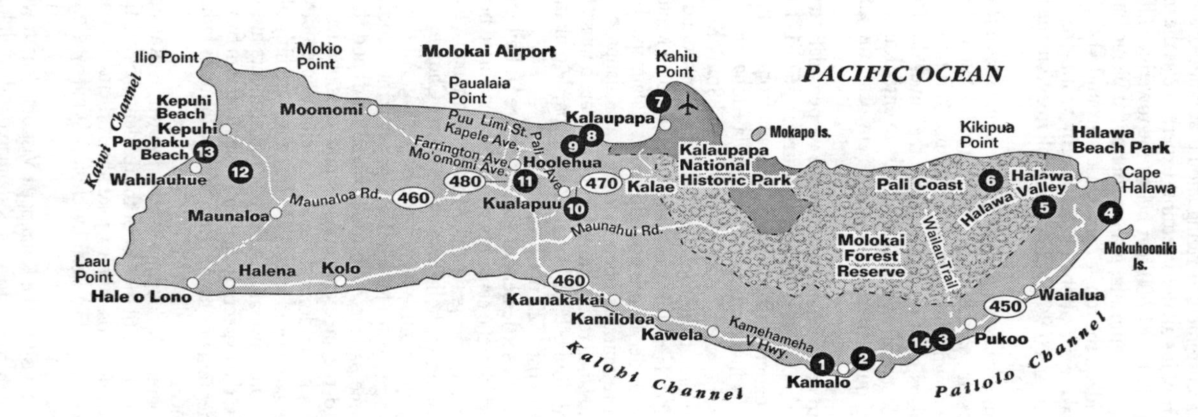

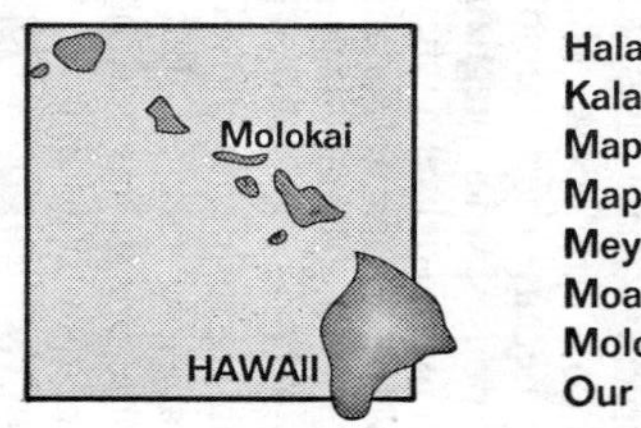

- Halawa Valley 6
- Kalaupapa Settlement 7
- Mapulehu Glass House 3
- Mapulehu Mango Grove 14
- Meyer Sugar Mill 10
- Moaula Falls 5
- Molokai Ranch Wildlife Park 12
- Our Lady of Sorrows Church 2
- Palaau State Park 9
- Papohaku Beach 13
- Phallic Rock 8
- Purdy's All Natural Macadamia Nut Farm 11
- Puu O Hoku Ranch 4
- St. Joseph's Catholic Church 1

Airport

can raise have been overwhelming to more than one visitor. We can promise only one thing: It is a special kind of experience, one not easily forgotten.

There are a couple of ways to get to Kalaupapa. The one that's the most exciting is the famous mule trip run by **Rare Adventures / Molokai Mule Ride.** Mule riders should be between 16 and 70 years of age and weigh no more than 225 pounds. We might add that only those who are accustomed to riding should attempt this one, although many nonriders do take the trip. It's an unforgettable experience as the mule descends a spectacular, steep switchback trail 1,600 feet below the towering cliffs at Kalae into Kalaupapa. You are met at the peninsula, given a tour and a picnic lunch, and then returned to the trail for the ride to the top at 2pm. Cost is around $120. Call the stables at 567-6088. You can make reservations in advance by writing to Rare Adventures, Ltd., P.O. Box 200, Kualapuu, HI 96757, or calling toll free from the U.S. mainland, 800/843-5978.

It's more economical, of course, to hike down the trail; it's a scenic 3⅛-mile cliff walk that should take about 1½ hours. It's safe for most hikers; the hike up the *pali*, however, is arduous, and if you hike down, you must also hike up. You must be at Kalae Stables by 8:30am, since all hikers must go down before the mules do. **Rare Adventures "Molokai Hike-In"** costs $30 and includes a pass to enter Kalaupapa Peninsula, a picnic lunch, and the ground tour of the settlement. Call the above numbers in advance.

There is, of course, an easier way to get to Kalaupapa, the one we personally favor, and that's by air. Call Richard Marks's **Damien Molokai Tours** at 567-6171 (the only tour service operated by former patients, who know Kalaupapa from the inside out), and they will arrange for you to fly in from upper Molokai via Aloha Island Air for $42 round-trip (best time to call is between 7 and 9am and 5 and 8pm). Keep in mind that you cannot walk past the gate at the top of the cliff trail or around the peninsula without a permit, according to Health Department rules (Damien Molokai Tours will handle all permits). Minors under 16 are not allowed at Kalaupapa. Bring some lunch, as there are no stores or restaurants open to visitors at Kalaupapa. You may bring cameras and binoculars. Advance reservations for the tour are a must: Call 567-6171, or write Damien Molokai Tours, P.O. Box 1, Kalaupapa, Molokai, HI 96742. The full, four-hour grand tour costs $22 per person.

What you'll see on the tour—the early settlement of Kalawo where St. Philomena Church, built by Father Damien, still stands; the cemetery where he was buried before his remains were returned to Belgium; the grave of Mother Marianne (also a candidate for canonization by the Roman Catholic church); Siloama Church; and a glorious view of Molokai's towering mountains—is just the beginning. All the tour guides are ex-patients, people who can give you a look at Kalaupapa off the record. It's a magnificent sight—a testimony to the patients who took barren lands and turned them into Eden, and a testimony to the medical pioneers and missionaries who preserved so many lives. Kalaupapa is a paradoxical place; it seems domestic, with many cozy little houses where people garden and watch TV, but it is incredibly silent, partly because there are no children. Only a small minority of the residents live with their spouses; when pregnancy occurs, the expectant mother is usually flown from the island for the delivery, where she either remains to raise her child without its father or chooses to return to Kalaupapa alone.

Under legislation passed by Congress, Kalaupapa—now known as Kalaupapa National Historic Park—will be left as it is until the last of the residents has died. The remaining residents, most in their 50s and 60s, like to joke about themselves as an "endangered species." But all of them now live here by choice. What was once a veritable prison has now become a sanctuary.

The newest addition to the tour is a visit to the Kalaupapa Visitors Center, which has an excellent bookshop dealing with the history of Kalaupapa and Molokai. If you're lucky, your tour might include Richard Marks's own collection of Kalaupapa memorabilia, including antique bottles and clocks.

Note: On a recent visit to Kalaupapa, flying direct from Honolulu, we met two women who were making the exact same trip that we were; however, because they had booked the entire trip as a "tour" via a well-known tour operator, their cost was almost double ours. Make your own air arrangements and contact Damien Tours as we suggested: No need to waste your money.

READERS RECOMMEND

Discover Molokai Guided Nature Trips. *"Both of us are appreciative of two residents and their willingness to share this island with visitors. Ken and Gayle Gibson are transplants from the mainland who have made Molokai their home. Ken has begun an informal, friendly service which includes guided nature walks and farm visits. We had the wonderful opportunity of going on many hikes with them—to a quiet beach (we were the only ones there!), and the Halawa Valley Waterfalls Hike. Ken's knowledge of the history of the Polynesians and the vegetation, and his friendliness and eagerness to share this island's rich history, added another dimension to our trip. His tours are highly personalized, for only two to four people. Prices range from $50 to $75 per person. Gayle provided delectable sandwiches and home-grown vegetables for our lunches."*—Tom and Debbie Farynowski, Columbus, Ohio. [*Authors' Note:* Ken Gibson can be reached at Discover Molokai, P.O. Box 123, Moanaloa, Molokai, HI 96770 (tel. 808/552-2975 collect). His standard tours include an Old Hawaii excursion (ancient religious sites, a sacrificial temple from the 1300s, a walk to the top of Halawa Falls), a Waikolu Lookout Forest Trip (via four-wheel-drive vehicle to the Enchanted Forest Trail to hear rare birds singing and view the isolated north-shore sea cliffs and remote valleys), the Kalaupapa Trail Hike and Father Damien Tour (a hike down the *pali* onto Kalaupapa Peninsula, a tour of the settlement, and an optional plane trip out), and the Secret Beach Hike-Snorkel (a hike or Jeep ride to a magnificent secluded beach, then a snorkel to see a shipwreck). All trips include Molokai history, Hawaiian lifestyle information, geology, and plantlife. Hikes are moderate (easy walks can be arranged) and suitable for all ages. Ken also offers custom tours for individuals and small groups, which might include kayaking, outrigger canoes, Hawaiian fishing, and overnight excursions. Recommended!]

MORE ATTRACTIONS

A TRIP THROUGH PALAAU PARK TO KUALAPUU

Even if you don't get to Kalaupapa itself, you should pay a visit to the Kalaupapa Overlook in Palaau Park. It's an easy trip on very good roads, about 10 miles from Kaunakakai on Hi. 460. After you make your right on Hi. 470 and begin to climb to Upper Molokai, the air becomes fragrant with eucalyptus and pine. Park your car at **Palaau State Park,** a well-maintained and popular camping and picnicking spot for local residents. A short walk through towering cypress and pine and suddenly you're high, high up, looking down immense cliffs to the Kalaupapa Peninsula below. From the overlook, you can see the world's tallest sea cliffs, 3,300 feet high at Umilehi Point. A series of six informative plaques tell the Kalaupapa story, but official descriptions seem superfluous. Just standing here, gazing down at the peninsula below, you are caught up in some of the tremendous sorrow of those who lived their lives of exile at Kalaupapa.

There is another trail, this one a bit longer (and steeply uphill some of the way) that leads to the **Phallic Rock.** According to legend, barren women who made offerings to the rock and spent the night here would then become capable of bearing children. Supposedly, an unfaithful husband of one of the minor goddesses was transformed into this rock and his mana still remains here.

While you're pondering this story (wrongdoers were often turned into stone in Hawaiian mythology), get back into your car and drive down the hill. Two miles below the overlook, on Hi. 470, you may want to pay a visit to the **R. W. Meyer Sugar Mill** (tel. 567-6436), an authentic restoration of an 1878 sugar mill now in operating condition after almost a century of neglect. The only surviving 19th-century sugar mill in Hawaii, it is listed on the National Register of Historic Places. Local volunteer labor spent several years on its restoration. The original machinery, including the mule-drive cane crusher, is still in operating condition. Photos and memorabilia of the mill's original owner, and of his Hawaiian-born wife, Kalama Waha, provide a glimpse into early Molokai history. The mill is open Monday through Saturday from 10am to noon and on Sunday from 10am to 2pm, for guided and self-guided tours. Admission is $2.50 for adults, $1 for students.

Continue down the road now to the little town of Kualapuu, where, now that the Del Monte pineapple plantation has been phased out, diversified agriculture is a growing industry (Molokai is now the state's leading producer of watermelon). Here you'll also find the pleasant little **Kualapuu Cook House Restaurant** (see "Where to Eat," above, in this chapter). Turn left on Puupeelua Avenue and you'll be back on the airport road.

If you're in the mood for traveling, continue west on Hi. 460 past the airport; you'll be on Maunaloa Road, which goes 10 miles to the old Dole pineapple village at Maunaloa, about 1,300 feet high, with its unusual little crafts shops (see "Shopping," below).

PURDY'S NUT FARM

We don't know of any other macadamia farm in Hawaii where either the owner or his mother will greet you personally and take you on a tour of the orchards. But Purdy's All Natural Macadamia Nut Farm is different. Tuddie Purdy and his mother guide you through the only working macadamia-nut grove on the island, and not only do they tell you all you ever wanted to know about macadamia nuts, but they also show you a variety of Hawaiian fruits and flowers. Most fun of all, you get to crack some macadamia nuts and try them raw. Then you'll be given some fruit and macadamia-blossom honey to taste, plus samples of their Ono Toasted Macadamia Nuts, which are remarkably light, surprisingly non-oily, and absolutely delicious. You can buy them on the spot (they'll also give you the recipe), as well as raw macadamia nuts out of the shell, and the honey. The farm is located on 1½ acres in Hoolehua Hawaiian Homesteads and is open Monday through Saturday from 9am to 1pm, on Sunday from 10am to 1pm, or by appointment (tel. 567-6601 daytime, 567-6495 in the evening). It's not far from the airport, but it's best to ask them for driving directions. If you're in Molokai for a one-day trip, this could be a fun way to start the day. Admission is free.

FROMMER'S FAVORITE MOLOKAI EXPERIENCES

Touring Molokai Ranch Wildlife Park Feed the giraffes that gather around to see the funny people on Pilipo Solitario's safaris.

Taking the Molokai Wagon Ride Admire a 13th-century heiau, then party on the beach with Hawaiian music, traditional Hawaiian net throwing, and lots of fun and games.

Driving to Maunaloa Town Visit Jonathan Socher's Big Wind Kite Factory and his Plantation Gallery, and see the work of local artists and craftspeople in one of the most laid-back shopping scenes in the islands.

Flying into Kalaupapa Peninsula Tour the settlement for the treatment of Hansen's disease with ex-patient Richard Marks of Damien Tours, the "mayor of Kalaupapa."

MOLOKAI RANCH WILDLIFE PARK

Yes, you can go on a safari of sorts on Molokai, a camera safari, to see more than 1,000 African and Asian animals that live on the grounds of this 1,000-acre natural wildlife preserve. The dry terrain of western Molokai happens to be quite similar to that of the Kalahari Desert of Botswana, in Africa. The animals, which include giraffe, zebra (there's a rare, white stripeless one with blue eyes), Barbary sheep, Indian black buck, eland, oryx, greater kudu, sika and axis deer, East African crowned crane, rhea, and wild turkey, thrive here. Safari Chief Pilipo Solitario, known as "the man who talks to animals," leads visitors on a 90-minute tour in an air-conditioned van, stopping often for photos and allowing the animals, which appear out of the thickets and ravines when they hear his horn, to feed out of his hand. After the tour of the park, visitors adjourn to the picnic and petting area where they can feed the curious and friendly giraffes that gather around to see the funny people. Cost of the tour is $30 for adults, $20 for children under 12; arrangements can be made at the Kaluakoi Hotel Travel Desk, or by calling 552-2555 or 552-2767. Readers really like this one.

WAGON RIDES

This Molokai adventure is very popular. Your horse-drawn (or horse- and mule-drawn) wagon stops first at the Ili Ili O Pae Heiau, one of Hawaii's largest and best-preserved temples, built in the 13th century, where a guide explains the historical background; then it's back down the trail to the Mapulehu Mango Grove, the largest mango grove in the world. Then it's on to the beach for a Molokai-style barbecue and a fabulous party, complete with Hawaiian music, traditional Hawaiian net throwing, fishing, coconut husking, and many surprises. Guests are invited to try their hand at all the activities. Cost is $35 for adults, $17.50 for children 5–12, free for those under 5. Guided horseback rides are also available. For reservations, call Larry Helm at **Molokai Wagon Ride** (tel. 567-6773 from 6 to 8am and after 6pm, or 558-8380, the wagon-ride site, from 9:30am to 12:30pm, daily.

SPORTS & RECREATION

SAILING, SNORKELING & FISHING

Satan's Doll, a 42-foot sloop, takes passengers on two-hour sunset sails ($30), half-day sailing and whale-watching trips ($40), and sailings to Lanai for a full day of swimming, snorkeling, sailing lessons, and whale watching ($75). There's a minimum of four passengers per trip. Contact Molokai Charters, P.O. Box 1207, Kaunakakai, Molokai, HI 96748 (tel. 808/443-5852).

Those interested in sport fishing should contact **Capt. Joe Reich** at P.O. Box 835, Kaunakakai, Molokai, HI 96748 (tel. 808/558-8377).

GOLF

Golfing is pleasantly inexpensive at Molokai's newest course, the recently reconstructed **Ironwood Hills Golf Club,** on Kalae Highway (tel. 567-6000). For example, seniors get to play 18 holes for just $8; other visitors, $12. All this and power golf carts, too. For information on Molokai's most spectacular course, the championship, 6,618-yard **Kaluakoi Golf Course** at Maunaloa, phone 552-2739.

SCENIC BIPLANE RIDES

This might well be Hawaii's ultimate flying experience! **John Luke,** P.O. Box 1977, Kaunakakai, Molokai, HI 96748 (tel. 808/567-6100 or 558-8446), a veteran pilot with 37 years in the air, takes people out for scenic flights in an open-cockpit biplane that was used as a primary trainer during World War II by the U.S. Army Air Force.

Passengers sit in front, the pilot in back: You don helmet and goggles and experience what flight was like in the early days. Luke claims that Molokai is the best of all the Hawaiian islands to flight-see; on the north shore alone, there are thousands of waterfalls after a rain. Flights are not inexpensive: They begin at $90 for a short "open-cockpit flight experience" over Mo'Omomi Beach, and go up to $280 for the spectacular trip to the south shore, the Halawa Valley, and the north shore. But it could be the thrill of a lifetime!

THE BEACH

Papohaku Beach, on Molokai's western shore, part of Kaluakoi Resort, is the largest white-sand beach in the Hawaiian Islands, almost three miles long. It's the ideal spot for a beach picnic, but not—alas—for ocean swimming, since the water here is usually quite rough in winter, and there may be undertows and rip tides in summer. There's access at Papohaku Beach Park, which has picnic grounds, barbecues, showers, a pavilion with rest rooms and changing area, plus parking. Camping is also available.

SHOPPING

Molokai is perhaps the only place in the islands that is *not* heaven for shopping buffs. There is so little available here that many locals go off-island (they'll fly to Honolulu on one of the little commuter planes) to do their shopping—even their grocery shopping! The local supermarkets, grocery shops, and liquor stores on Ala Malama, the main street of Kaunakakai, a general store here and there in the country, and a handful of craft shops just about do it.

KAUNAKAKAI

MOLOKAI DRUGS, Ala Malama St. Tel. 553-5790.

For the best selection of books on the island, try Molokai Drugs, on Ala Malama. They have a particularly good selection of Hawaiiana, and also sell local crafts and gift items in addition to the usual drugs and sundries.

MOLOKAI FISH AND DIVE, Ala Malama St. Tel. 553-5926.

To learn where the fish are biting, and to get fishing, diving, snorkeling, and camping gear, plus boogie boards and golf balls, this is the place to go. But they're more than just a sporting-goods store; they have the largest collection of Molokai souvenirs on the island, including a huge selection of T-shirts, designed and printed for them and sold exclusively here. Next door is their boutique for island fashions, called Molokai Island Creations.

MOLOKAI ISLAND CREATIONS, Ala Malama St. Tel. 553-5926.

This friendly boutique has Hawaiian-made swimwear, muumuus, and children's clothing at surprisingly affordable prices, plus a unique collection of jewelry, including sea opal, coral, and sterling silver. They also have a good selection of books on Hawaii, cards, and much more. There's plenty to catch your eye here.

MOLOKAI WINES 'N' SPIRITS UNLIMITED. Tel. 553-5009.

You can shop late, until 10:30pm every day, at Molokai Wines.

OUTPOST NATURAL FOODS, 70 Makaena St. Tel. 553-3377.

To stock up on organic local produce—papayas, bananas, avocados, sprouts, etc.—try Outpost Natural Foods (next door to the Civic Center), which sells the usual health-food fare plus other items at the lowest possible prices. They also have an excellent lunch bar (see "Where to Eat," above, in this chapter). Pick up a fruit smoothie, a sandwich, a burrito, or some Molokai Taro Chips, a local delicacy.

IMAMURA'S, Ala Malama St. Tel. 553-5615.

Like an old-fashioned general store, Imamura's has a little bit of everything, and is lots of fun to poke around in.

THE MOLOKAI GIFT SHOP, in the Hotel Molokai, Kaunakakai. Tel. 553-5801.

Hotel shopping is limited on Molokai, but do stop in at the Molokai Gift Shop, where proprietor Maria Watanabe offers clothing, T-shirts, books, sundries, and crafts by Molokai artists. We've found some nice things here, and prices are usually lower than on the other islands.

MAUNALOA

Our favorite Molokai shopping is out in Maunaloa (not far from the Kaluakoi Resort). Once a thriving plantation town, Maunaloa has been declining since Dole closed shop in 1975; however, young artisans are seeking it out and showing their wares here. We should tell you at the start that this is the most laid-back "shopping area" we've ever come across, with only one street, and with shops staying open more or less as inspiration moves the owners, who often seem to be out fishing or surfing or visiting Honolulu.

BIG WIND KITE FACTORY. Tel. 552-2364.

Owner Jonathan Socher is always on hand and happy to greet visitors. He and his wife, Daphne, not only create beautiful, high-flying kites (which are sold in many island shops), but they even offer free flying lessons with modern 100-m.p.h. "aerobatic kites." It's also fun to take a tour of their minifactory, where they demonstrate the techniques of kite making. Their most popular items are pineapple windsox and minikites at $14.95, and rainbow-spinning windsox at $15–$35. Their Hula Girl Kite—"She Dances in the Sky"—is also very popular at $35. They now make their own two-string rainbow stunt kites, from $35. Last year the Sochers were invited to participate in Bali's International Kite Festival and now have a spectacular collection of Indonesian and Malaysian kites on display.

PLANTATION GALLERY. Tel. 552-2364.

Jonathan Socher's Plantation Gallery, which shows the work of several island artisans, is adjacent to the kite factory. One is the Tao Woodcarver (Bill Decker), who creates beautiful hand-carved bowls and boxes of rare Hawaiian woods; large items, like desks and sculpture, are available on commission. Unless the surf is up, you'll probably find Butch Tabanao and his deerhorn jewelry, hair combs (from $12), and cribbage boards (around $40) made from the axis deer of Molokai. There's raku pottery sculpture by Katie Leong from $20, and Hawaiian pillowcase quilts by Ginger La Voie at $25. Several local artists do hand-painted shirts at $25, long-sleeved tops at $42. On our last visit, Jonathan proudly showed us his new collection of personally chosen imports from Bali and Southeast Asia: He calls this the "Bali Hale Gift Shop." It's full of delightful surprises, such as colorful wooden bird mobiles and birds of paradise stalks, at $25 and $35; batik pillow covers; pareaus; wonderful Balinese masks called "guardians" or "crib angels"; magnificent batik quilts for $400; and colorful wooden bird and fish earrings at $7.50, and you get another pair free. Note, too, the collection of books, cards, and prints by leading island artists. The gallery/shop is decorated with orchid plants and an aquarium, and there's a garden outside. For lovers of the unusual, this is a must stop.

QUILTING LESSONS

If you're interested in quilting, get in touch with **Ginger Lavoie**—Fiber Artist of Molokai, Star Route, Box 359, Kaunakakai, Molokai, HI 96748 (tel. 808/558-8227), one of the finest quilters in the islands. She gives classes every Wednesday morning at the Hotel Molokai and Friday morning at the Kaluakoi Resort. Complimentary lessons are offered with the purchase of one of her kits. She also has available for sale original quilt designs, fully basted quilts, and easy kits, as well as silk-screened T-shirts.

EVENING ENTERTAINMENT

Nightlife on Molokai, as we travelers know it, is almost all in the major hotels, and it's largely impromptu. It all depends on when local people feel like doing things (people here are not apt to let work interfere with their lives!). But check the local papers; there may be a hula show or even a luau at the Pau Hana Inn when you're in town. And there's music to dance by every night at the Ohia Lodge at the Kaluakoi Hotel.

APPENDIX

A. HAWAIIAN VOCABULARY

There are just 12 letters in the Hawaiian alphabet: five vowels—*a, e, i, o, u*—and seven consonants—*h, k, l, m, n, p, w*. Every syllable ends in a vowel, every vowel is pronounced, and the accent is almost always on the next-to-the-last syllable, as it is in Spanish. Consonants receive their English sounds, but vowels get the Latin pronunciation: *a* as in farm, *e* as in they, *i* as in machine, *o* as in cold, and *u* as in tutor. Note, also, that when a *w* comes before the final vowel in a word, it is given the "v" sound, as in Hawaii. Purists say Ha-VYE-ee for Hawaii, but most people call it Ha-WYE-ee.

The following glossary will give you an idea of what the Hawaiian language sounds like. No one, of course, expects you to go around spouting phrases like "Holo ehia keia?" to ask what time it is, but a familiarity with the most important words is what distinguishes the kamaainas from the malihinis.

WORDS

ENGLISH	HAWAIIAN	PRONUNCIATION
Rough lava	**Aa**	AH-ah
Eat	**Ai**	EYE
Friends as in "Aloha, aikane"	**Aikane**	eye-KAH-nay
Smart	**Akamai**	ah-kah-MY
Road, as in Ala Moana (Ocean Road)	**Ala**	AL-lah
Noblemen, the old royalty of Hawaii	**Alii**	ah-LEE-ee
Welcome, farwell, love	**Aloha**	ah-LOW-hah
No	**Aole**	Ah-OH-lay
Alas! woe!	**Auwe**	OW-way
In the direction of Ewa, a town on Oahu ("Drive Ewa five blocks.")	**Ewa**	EH-vah
The pandanus tree, the leaves of which are used for weaving	**Hala**	HAH-lah
Pineapple	**Halakahiki**	hah-lah-kah-HEE-kee
School (as in hula halau)	**Halau**	HAH-lau
House	**Hale**	HAH-lay
To work	**Hana**	HAH-nah
Caucasian, white	**Haole**	HOW-lay
White man	**Haolekane**	how-lay-KAY-nay
White woman	**Haolewahine**	how-lay-wah-HEE-nay
A small part, a half	**Hapa**	HAH-pah

ENGLISH	HAWAIIAN	PRONUNCIATION
Pregnant (originally "to carry")	**Hapai**	Hah-PIE
Happiness	**Hauoli**	how-OH-lee
Ancient temple	**Heiau**	hey-EE-au
To go, to walk	**Hle**	HEY-lay
To sleep	**Haimoe**	hee-ah-MOW-ay
Ashamed	**Hilahila**	hee-lah-HEE-lah
To run	**Holo**	HO-low
To have fun, to relax	**Holoholo**	ho-low-HO-low
Formal dress with train	**Holoku**	ho-low-KOO
A cross between a holoku and a muumuu (long and without a train)	**Holomuu**	ho-low-MOO
To kiss, as in "Honikaua wikiwiki!" (Kiss me quick!)	**Honi**	HO-nee
To flatter	**Hoomalimali**	ho-oh-mah-lee-MAH-lee
Angry	**Huhu**	HOO-hoo
A club, an assembly	**Hui**	HOO-ee
A fishing festival	**Hukilau**	hoo-KEE-lau
A dance, to dance	**Hula**	HOO-lah
Underground oven lined with hot rocks, used for cooking the luau pig	**Imu**	EE-moo
Sweetheart	**Ipo**	EE-po
The	**Ka**	KAH
Ancient (as in hula kahiko)	**Kahiko**	kah-HEE-ko
Sea	**Kai**	KYE
Money	**Kala**	KAH-lah
To bake underground	**Kalua**	kah-loo-AH
Old-timer	**Kamaaina**	Kah-mah-EYE-nah
Man	**Kane**	KAH-nay
Tapa, a bark cloth	**Kapa**	KAH-pah
Crooked	**Kapakahi**	kah-pah-KAH-hee
Forbidden, keep out	**Kapu**	kah-POO
Food	**Kaukau**	kow-KOW
Child	**Keiki**	Kay-KEE
Help, cooperation	**Kokua**	ko-KOO-ah
South	**Kona**	KO-nah
Sun, light, day	**La**	LAH
Porch	**Lanai**	Lah-NYE
Heaven, sky	**Lani**	Lah-NEE
Leaf of the hala or pandanus tree	**Lauhala**	lau-HAH-lah
Garland	**Lei**	LAY
Stupid	**Lolo**	low-LOW
Massage	**Lomilomi**	low-mee-LOW-mee
Feast	**Luau**	LOO-au
Thank you	**Mahalo**	mah-HAH-low

ENGLISH	HAWAIIAN	PRONUNCIATION
Good, fine	**Ma'i ka'i**	mah-ee-KAH-ee
Toward the sea	**Makai**	mah-KEY
Stranger, newcomer	**Malihini**	mah-lee-HEE-nee
Free	**Manawahi**	mah-nah-WAH-hee
Toward the mountains	**Mauka**	MAU-kah
Song, chant	**Mele**	MAY-lay
A mysterious race who inhabited the island before the Polynesians (mythology claims they were pygmies)	**Menehune**	may-nay-HOO-nay
Loose dress (Hawaiian version of missionaries' "Mother Hubbards")	**Muumuu**	moo-oo-MOO-oo
Lovely	**Nani**	NAN-nee
Coconut	**Niu**	nee-OO
Big, as in "mahalo nui" ("big thanks")	**Nui**	NOO-ee
Sweet taste, delicious	**Ono**	OH-no
Belly	**Opu**	OH-poo
Stubborn	**Paakiki**	pah-ah-KEE-kee
Precipice	**Pali**	PAH-lee
Hawaiian cowboy	**Panilolo**	pah-nee-OH-low
Finished	**Pau**	POW
Trouble	**Pilikia**	pee-lee-KEE-ah
Crushed taro root	**Poi**	POY
Hole	**Puka**	POO-kah
Couch	**Punee**	poo-NAY-ay
Hors d'oeuvre	**Pupu**	POO-poo
Crazy	**Pupule**	poo-POO-lay
Rain	**Ua**	OO-ah
Speech, mouth	**Waha**	wah-HAH
Female, woman, girl	**Wahine**	wah-HEE-nay
Fresh water	**Wai**	WHY
To hurry	**Wikiwiki**	wee-kee-wee-kee

PHRASES

ENGLISH	HAWAIIAN	PRONUNCIATION
Be careful	**Malama pono**	mah-LAH-mah PO-no
Bottoms up	**Okole maluna**	oh-KO-lay mah-LOO-nah
Come and eat	**Hele mai ai**	hey-lay-MY-eye
Come here	**Hele mai**	HEY-lay MY
Come in and sit down	**Komo mai e noho iho**	ko-MO my ay NO-ho EE-ho
For love	**No ke aloha**	no kay ah-LOW-hah
Go away	**Hele aku oe**	HEY-lay AH-koo OH-ay
Good evening	**Aloha ahiahi**	ah-LOW-hah AH-hee-AH-hee

ENGLISH	HAWAIIAN	PRONUNCIATION
Good morning	**Aloha kakahiaka**	ah-LOW-hah kah-kah-hee-AH-kah
Greatest love to you	**Aloha nui oe**	ah-LOW-hah NOO-ee OH-ay
Happy Birthday	**Hauoli la hanau**	hah-OO-oh-lee lah hoh-NAH-oo
Happy New Year	**Hauoli Makahiki Hou**	hah-OO-oh-lee man-kah-HEE-kee HO-oo
Here's to your happiness	**Hauoli Maoli oe**	hah-OO-oh-lee mah-OH-lee OH-ay
How are you?	**Pehea oe?**	pay-HAY-ah OH-ay
I am fine	**Ma'i ka'i**	mah-EE kah-EE
I am sorry	**Ua kaumaha au**	OO-ah cow-mah-HAH OW
I have enough	**Ua lawa au**	OO-ah LAH-wah OW
I love you	**Aloha wauia oe**	ah-LOW-hah vow-EE-ah OH-ay
It isn't so	**Aole pela**	ah-OH-lay PAY-lah
Let's go	**E hele kaua**	au-HEY-lay COW-ah
Many thanks	**Mahalo nui loa**	mah-HAH-low NOO-ee LOW-ah
Merry Christmas	**Mele Kalikimaka**	may-LAY-kah-lee-kee-MAH-kah
Much love	**Aloha nui loa**	ah-LOW-hah NOO-ee LOW-ah
No trouble	**Aole pilikia**	ah-OH-lay pee-lee-KEE-ah
What is your name?	**Owai kau inoa?**	OH-why KAH-oo ee-NO-ah

PIDGIN

Despite the efforts of educators to stamp it out, pidgin, that code language of the islands, continues its not-so-underground existence. The Chinese developed it in their first contacts with English-speaking people, but you'll hear it spoken today by all the racial groups, from haoles to Hawaiians. Beachboys, cab drivers, university students, a few who don't know better and a lot who do, all occasionally descend into pidgin. Although its subtleties are unintelligible to the newcomer (that's part of the idea), you'll be able to pick up a few words: *wasamala, wasetime, lesgo, da kine.*

You'll hear all kinds of theories about the indestructibility of pidgin. Some sociological types feel it's a subtle form of rebellion by the dispossessed Hawaiian, not unlike the jargon of mainland African Americans. The psychological types call it more of an adolescent code, a desire for teenagers to have their own language. Others say it's just plain bad English. Take your choice, whatever *da kine* reason, pidgin is "in" in Hawaii.

Note: After you've been in the islands a bit, get yourself a copy of Peppo's *Pidgin to Da Max*. It's one of Hawaii's most popular humor-cartoon books (over 130,000 copies in print), available in any bookstore, and an absolute hoot! We reprint the "Word of Caution to the Non-local: If you don't already speak pidgin, you might need some help from local friends to understand this book. Remember: *Pidgin to Da Max* is not a tourist guide to pidgin. So don't try to speak after reading this book. You'll just get into trouble." We agree. Don't try to speak pidgin. Just read the book—maybe on the plane trip back home—and try to keep yourself from rolling in the aisles. It's

$4.95, published by Bess Press, Honolulu. There is, in fact, a whole series of Peppo's Pidgin books now, another one of which is *Fax to Da Max,* which lists "Everything You Never Knew You Wanted to Know About Hawaii," plus lots of "useless fax," too. Another howler.

B. GLOSSARY OF ISLAND FOODS

Chinese, Japanese, Korean, Filipino, and Portuguese influences are all reflected on island menus—as well as American and Hawaiian, of course. Here are some helpful definitions:

Adobo Filipino dish made with pork or chicken.
Bento Japanese box lunch.
Chicken luau Chicken cooked with coconut milk and taro or spinach leaves.
Crackseed Chinese confection that's a cross between preserved fruit and candy. Kids go crazy for these sticky sweets.
Guava Slightly tart tree fruit made into jams and juice. They grow wild on the mountainsides, and are under cultivation on Kauai, at Guava Kai Plantation.
Haupia Coconut pudding, the traditional luau dessert.
Kona coffee The best! Grown on the Big Island in many small family plantations.
Kimchee Korea's contribution, pickled cabbage with red-hot peppers.
Laulau Ti leaves stuffed with pork, salt fish, bananas, sweet potatoes, and taro shoots, then steamed.
Lilikoi Passion fruit (named after the passion of Christ). A tart fruit that's turned into wonderful juice or sherbet.
Pipikaula Jerked beef.
Macadamia nuts Delicious nuts grown on plantations on the Big Island. Chocolate-covered macadamias are one of the most delicious gifts you can bring the folks back home.
Malasadas Deep-fried Portuguese doughnuts, served hot and sugared. They have no holes.
Manapuas Steamed dumplings filled with pork, meat, or bean paste. The Chinese call them dim sum.
Maui onions Mild, sweet onions, sometimes known as Kula onions.
Papayas Grown on the Big Island, available everywhere: one of the favorite breakfast fruits in the islands. Highly nutritious and rich in vitamin C.
Poi Staple starch of the Hawaiian diet, made from cooked and mashed taro root. Very digestible and nutritious. To the ancient Hawaiians, the poi bowl had an almost spiritual significance.
Poha Wild berry, used in jams.
Portuguese bean soup Savory soup made from Portuguese sausages, beans, and vegetables, a veritable meal in a bowl.
Portuguese sweet bread Very soft bread made with eggs, wonderful in French toast.
Saimin Most popular soup in the islands, a thin noodle broth topped with bits of fish, shrimp, chicken, or pork, and vegetables.
Sashimi Raw fish, a favorite Japanese delicacy.
Sushi Vinegared rice topped with either raw fish or other toppings, and then rolled in seaweed, another great Japanese delicacy.

INDEX

GENERAL INFORMATION

DESTINATIONS

KEY TO ABBREVIATIONS: *B* = Budget; *B&B* = Bed-and-Breakfast; *M* = Moderate; *$* = special value; * = an authors' personal favorite

FROMMER GUIDES

	Retail Price	Code
Alaska 1990–91	$14.95	C001
Arizona 1993–94	$18.00	C101
Australia 1992–93	$18.00	C002
Austria/Hungary 1991–92	$14.95	C003
Belgium/Holland/Luxembourg 1993–94	$18.00	C106
Bermuda/Bahamas 1992–93	$17.00	C005
Brazil 1991–92	$14.95	C006
California 1992	$18.00	C007
Canada 1992–93	$18.00	C009
Caribbean 1993	$18.00	C102
The Carolinas/Georgia 1992–93	$17.00	C034
Colorado 1993–94	$16.00	C100
Cruises 1993–94	$19.00	C107
DE/MD/PA & NJ Shore 1992–93	$19.00	C012
Egypt 1990–91	$14.95	C013
England 1993	$18.00	C109
Florida 1993	$18.00	C104
France 1992–93	$20.00	C017
Germany 1993	$19.00	C108
Italy 1992	$19.00	C019
Jamaica/Barbados 1993–94	$15.00	C105
Japan 1992–93	$19.00	C020
Morocco 1992–93	$18.00	C021
Nepal 1992–93	$18.00	C038
New England 1992	$17.00	C023
New Mexico 1991–92	$13.95	C024
New York State 1992–93	$19.00	C025
Northwest 1991–92	$16.95	C026
Portugal 1992–93	$16.00	C027
Puerto Rico 1993–94	$15.00	C103
Puerto Vallarta/Manzanillo/Guadalajara 1992–93	$14.00	C028
Scandinavia 1991–92	$18.95	C029
Scotland 1992–93	$16.00	C040
Skiing Europe 1989–90	$14.95	C030
South Pacific 1992–93	$20.00	C031
Switzerland/Liechtenstein 1992–93	$19.00	C032
Thailand 1992–93	$20.00	C033
USA 1991–92	$16.95	C035
Virgin Islands 1992–93	$13.00	C036
Virginia 1992–93	$14.00	C037
Yucatán 1992–93	$18.00	C110

FROMMER $-A-DAY GUIDES

	Retail Price	Code
Australia on $45 a Day 1993–94	$18.00	D102
Costa Rica/Guatemala/Belize on $35 a Day 1991–92	$15.95	D004
Eastern Europe on $25 a Day 1991–92	$16.95	D005
England on $60 a Day 1993	$18.00	D107
Europe on $45 a Day 1993	$19.00	D106
Greece on $45 a Day 1993–94	$19.00	D100
Hawaii on $75 a Day 1993	$19.00	D104
India on $40 a Day 1992–93	$20.00	D010
Ireland on $40 a Day 1992–93	$17.00	D011
Israel on $45 a Day 1993–94	$18.00	D101
Mexico on $50 a Day 1993	$19.00	D105
New York on $70 a Day 1992–93	$16.00	D016
New Zealand on $45 a Day 1993–94	$18.00	D103
Scotland/Wales on $50 a Day 1992–93	$18.00	D019
South America on $40 a Day 1991–92	$15.95	D020
Spain on $50 a Day 1991–92	$15.95	D021
Turkey on $40 a Day 1992	$22.00	D023
Washington, D.C. on $40 a Day 1992	$17.00	D024

FROMMER CITY $-A-DAY GUIDES

	Retail Price	Code		Retail Price	Code
Berlin on $40 a Day 1992–93	$12.00	D002	Madrid on $50 a Day 1992–93	$13.00	D014
Copenhagen on $50 a Day 1992–93	$12.00	D003	Paris on $45 a Day 1992–93	$12.00	D018
London on $45 a Day 1992–93	$12.00	D013	Stockholm on $50 a Day 1992–93	$13.00	D022

FROMMER TOURING GUIDES

Amsterdam	$10.95	T001	New York	$10.95	T008
Australia	$10.95	T002	Paris	$ 8.95	T009
Barcelona	$14.00	T015	Rome	$10.95	T010
Brazil	$10.95	T003	Scotland	$ 9.95	T011
Egypt	$ 8.95	T004	Sicily	$14.95	T017
Florence	$ 8.95	T005	Thailand	$12.95	T012
Hong Kong/Singapore/ Macau	$10.95	T006	Tokyo	$15.00	T016
Kenya	$13.95	T018	Turkey	$10.95	T013
London	$12.95	T007	Venice	$ 8.95	T014

FROMMER'S FAMILY GUIDES

California with Kids	$16.95	F001	San Francisco with Kids	$17.00	F004
Los Angeles with Kids	$17.00	F002	Washington, D.C. with Kids	$17.00	F005
New York City with Kids	$18.00	F003			

FROMMER CITY GUIDES

Amsterdam/Holland 1991–92	$ 8.95	S001	Miami 1991–92	$ 8.95	S021
Athens 1991–92	$ 8.95	S002	Minneapolis/St. Paul 1991–92	$ 8.95	S022
Atlanta 1991–92	$ 8.95	S003	Montréal/Québec City 1991–92	$ 8.95	S023
Atlantic City/Cape May 1991–92	$ 8.95	S004	New Orleans 1993–94	$13.00	S103
Bangkok 1992–93	$13.00	S005	New York 1992	$12.00	S025
Barcelona/Majorca/ Minorca/Ibiza 1992	$12.00	S006	Orlando 1993	$13.00	S101
Belgium 1989–90	$ 5.95	S007	Paris 1993–94	$13.00	S109
Berlin 1991–92	$10.00	S008	Philadelphia 1991–92	$ 8.95	S028
Boston 1991–92	$ 8.95	S009	Rio 1991–92	$ 8.95	S029
Cancún/Cozumel/ Yucatán 1991–92	$ 8.95	S010	Rome 1991–92	$ 8.95	S030
Chicago 1991–92	$ 9.95	S011	Salt Lake City 1991–92	$ 8.95	S031
Denver/Boulder/ Colorado Springs 1990–91	$ 7.95	S012	San Diego 1993–94	$13.00	S107
Dublin/Ireland 1991–92	$ 8.95	S013	San Francisco 1993	$13.00	S104
Hawaii 1992	$12.00	S014	Santa Fe/Taos/ Albuquerque 1993–94	$13.00	S108
Hong Kong 1992–93	$12.00	S015	Seattle/Portland 1992–93	$12.00	S035
Honolulu/Oahu 1993	$13.00	S106	St. Louis/Kansas City 1991–92	$ 9.95	S036
Las Vegas 1991–92	$ 8.95	S016	Sydney 1991–92	$ 8.95	S037
Lisbon/Madrid/Costa del Sol 1991–92	$ 8.95	S017	Tampa/St. Petersburg 1993–94	$13.00	S105
London 1993	$13.00	S100	Tokyo 1992–93	$13.00	S039
Los Angeles 1991–92	$ 8.95	S019	Toronto 1991–92	$ 8.95	S040
Mexico City/Acapulco 1991–92	$ 8.95	S020	Vancouver/Victoria 1990–91	$ 7.95	S041
			Washington, D.C. 1993	$13.00	S102

Other Titles Available at Membership Prices—

SPECIAL EDITIONS

	Retail Price	Code		Retail Price	Code
Bed & Breakfast North America	$14.95	P002	Marilyn Wood's Wonderful Weekends (within 250-mile radius of New York City)	$11.95	P017
Caribbean Hideaways	$16.00	P005	New World of Travel 1991 by Arthur Frommer	$16.95	P018
Honeymoon Destinations	$14.95	P006	Where to Stay USA	$13.95	P015

GAULT MILLAU'S "BEST OF" GUIDES

Chicago	$15.95	G002	New England	$15.95	G010
Florida	$17.00	G003	New Orleans	$16.95	G011
France	$16.95	G004	New York	$16.95	G012
Germany	$18.00	G018	Paris	$16.95	G013
Hawaii	$16.95	G006	San Francisco	$16.95	G014
Hong Kong	$16.95	G007	Thailand	$17.95	G019
London	$16.95	G009	Toronto	$17.00	G020
Los Angeles	$16.95	G005	Washington, D.C.	$16.95	G017

THE REAL GUIDES

Amsterdam	$13.00	R100	Morocco	$14.00	R111
Barcelona	$13.00	R101	Nepal	$14.00	R018
Berlin	$11.95	R002	New York	$13.00	R019
Brazil	$13.95	R003	Able to Travel (avail April '93)	$20.00	R112
California & the West Coast	$17.00	R102	Paris	$13.00	R020
Canada	$15.00	R103	Peru	$12.95	R021
Czechoslovakia	$14.00	R104	Poland	$13.95	R022
Egypt	$19.00	R105	Portugal	$15.00	R023
Florida	$14.00	R006	Prague	$15.00	R113
France	$18.00	R106	San Francisco & the Bay Area	$11.95	R024
Germany	$18.00	R107	Scandinavia	$14.95	R025
Greece	$18.00	R108	Spain	$16.00	R026
Guatemala/Belize	$14.00	R109	Thailand	$17.00	R114
Holland/Belgium/Luxembourg	$16.00	R031	Tunisia	$17.00	R115
Hong Kong/Macau	$11.95	R011	Turkey	$13.95	R116
Hungary	$12.95	R012	U.S.A.	$18.00	R117
Ireland	$17.00	R110	Venice	$11.95	R028
Italy	$13.95	R014	Women Travel	$12.95	R029
Kenya	$12.95	R015	Yugoslavia	$12.95	R030
Mexico	$11.95	R016			